# THE OXFORD HANDBOOK OF

POSTCOLONIAL BIBLICAL CRITICISM

THE OXFORD HANDBOOK OF
POSTCOLONIAL BIBLICAL CRITICISM

Edited by
R. S. SUGIRTHARAJAH

OXFORD
UNIVERSITY PRESS

OXFORD
UNIVERSITY PRESS

Oxford University Press is a department of the University of Oxford. It furthers the University's objective of excellence in research, scholarship, and education by publishing worldwide. Oxford is a registered trade mark of Oxford University Press in the UK and certain other countries.

Published in the United States of America by Oxford University Press
198 Madison Avenue, New York, NY 10016, United States of America.

© Oxford University Press 2023

All rights reserved. No part of this publication may be reproduced, stored in a retrieval system, or transmitted, in any form or by any means, without the prior permission in writing of Oxford University Press, or as expressly permitted by law, by license, or under terms agreed with the appropriate reproduction rights organization. Inquiries concerning reproduction outside the scope of the above should be sent to the Rights Department, Oxford University Press, at the address above.

You must not circulate this work in any other form
and you must impose this same condition on any acquirer.

Library of Congress Cataloging-in-Publication Data
Names: Sugirtharajah, R. S. (Rasiah S.), editor.
Title: The Oxford handbook of postcolonial biblical criticism / edited by R.S. Sugirtharajah.
Description: New York, NY, United States of America : Oxford University Press, [2023] |
Series: Oxford handbooks series | Includes bibliographical references and index. |
Identifiers: LCCN 2022053494 (print) | LCCN 2022053495 (ebook) |
ISBN 9780190888459 (hardback) | ISBN 9780190888480 (epub) | ISBN 9780190888466 (online)
Subjects: LCSH: Bible—Postcolonial criticism.
Classification: LCC BS521.86 .O94 2023 (print) | LCC BS521.86 (ebook) |
DDC 220.6—dc23/eng/20230105
LC record available at https://lccn.loc.gov/2022053494
LC ebook record available at https://lccn.loc.gov/2022053495

DOI: 10.1093/oxfordhb/9780190888459.001.0001

Printed by Marquis Book Printing, Canada

Contents

Acknowledgments ix
Contributors xi

Introduction: The Bible, Empires and Postcolonial Criticism 1
R. S. Sugirtharajah

PART I: BIBLICAL EMPIRES IN THE HEBREW SCRIPTURES, INTER-TESTAMENTAL WRITINGS, THE NEW TESTAMENT, AND THE CHRISTIAN APOCRYPHA

1. The Egyptian Empire in the Bible 25
   D. N. Premnath

2. The Neo-Assyrian Empire through a Postcolonial Lens 49
   Safwat Marzouk

3. The Babylonian Empire in the Bible 70
   Hemchand Gossai

4. Anointed Saviors or Oppressive Enslavers?: Achaemenid Administration and Judean Subjects 88
   Daniel L. Smith-Christopher

5. Jewish Negotiations of Hellenistic Power 118
   Warren Carter

6. The Roman Empire in the Synoptic Gospels 140
   Judith A. Diehl

7. John's Writings and Empire: Views of Empire Studies and Postcolonial Criticism 162
   Jin Young Choi

8. The Roman Empire in Paul's Letters 190
   TAT-SIONG BENNY LIEW

9. The Roman Empire in the Book of Revelation 213
   JACQUELINE M. HIDALGO

10. The Apocryphal Acts of Thomas and Empire 239
    CLARA A. B. JOSEPH

PART II: MODERN EUROPEAN AND ASIAN EMPIRES

11. Scriptural Battlefields: The Old Testament, Legal Culture, and the Polemics of the Spanish New World Empire, 1492–1821 261
    JORGE CAÑIZARES-ESGUERRA AND ADRIAN MASTERS

12. The Bible and the Dutch Empire 296
    JANNEKE STEGEMAN

13. The Bible and the British Empire 329
    RALPH BROADBENT

14. White Woman's Burden and the Bible during the British Occupation of Singapore 353
    CHIN MING STEPHEN LIM

15. The Bible in the German Empire 370
    JOERG RIEGER

16. The Bible and American Empire 397
    JUDITH H. NEWMAN

17. The Colonizing Other: The Japanese Challenge for Postcolonial Biblical Criticism 427
    EMILY ANDERSON

18. The Bible in the Korean Resistance against the Japanese Empire (1910–1945) 448
    JINA KANG

PART III: EMPIRES AND TRANSLATIONS

19. Competing Narratives on Bible Translation in India: Missionary
    Linguistics, Postcolonial Criticism, and Translation Studies   471
    HEPHZIBAH ISRAEL

20. Bible Translation in the Colonial Project in Africa and Its Impact
    on African Languages and Cultures   495
    DORA R. MBUWAYESANGO

21. Cross-Textual Interpretation as Postcolonial Strategy in Bible
    Translation in Asia   510
    ARCHIE C. C. LEE

PART IV: POSTCOLONIAL SOCIAL AND ETHICAL CONCERNS

22. Postcolonial Biblical Criticism and Queer Studies   533
    JEREMY PUNT

23. Race, Scriptures, and the Postcolonial World   558
    VINCENT L. WIMBUSH

24. Ecology and Postcolonial Biblical Criticism   577
    ELLEN F. DAVIS

25. Bible, Empire, Liberalism, and Racial Capitalism   598
    STEED VERNYL DAVIDSON

PART V: POSTCOLONIAL BIBLICAL CRITICISM AND COGNATE DISCIPLINES

26. Postcolonial Biblical Criticism and Feminist Studies   623
    SUSANNE SCHOLZ

27. Postcolonial Liberation: Decolonizing Biblical Studies in the South
    African Postcolony   647
    GERALD O. WEST

28. Materialist/Marxist Interpretations and Postcolonial Biblical
    Criticism   677
    NIALL MCKAY

PART VI: POSTCOLONIALISM, BIBLICAL STUDIES, AND THEORETICAL ORIENTATIONS

29. The Rise of Postcolonial Criticism in Biblical Studies and Its Current Status 703
    RAJ NADELLA

30. Empire, Postcolonial Criticism, and Biblical Studies 735
    SHARON JACOB

Index 751

Acknowledgments

This handbook was planned in what now feels like a completely different time, long before anyone had heard of Covid-19. Needless to say, the pandemic turned our lives upside down and has caused much anxiety and uncertainty. Given these difficulties, it is a minor miracle that the volume has come into existence.

I was immensely fortunate to have the help and support of so many people who made this compendium possible. Robert Repino, Senior Editor at Oxford University Press, invited me to edit this volume. He did not simply stop with commissioning this project; he also took an active part in seeing through various stages of the production of the book. Robert is a perfect editor: persistent, attentive, and committed to things that matter most. I am grateful to him for his immeasurable patience, gentleness, and generosity all through these years.

This volume would not have come to be without the contributors. All the authors assembled here are leading figures in their field. Their expertly written pieces set the standard for the genre of handbooks and, more pertinently, make a stirring case for postcolonial thinking. A scholarly collection like this also depends heavily on the peer reviewers. I am grateful to these anonymous readers for their perceptive comments made in solidarity, which enriched the chapters. Incidentally, none of the peers whom I approached declined my invitation. This is probably some kind of record in the world of peer reviewing.

I am enormously fortunate to be able to rely on Ralph Broadbent for various issues ranging from the content of the volume to sorting out my computer queries.

I owe huge thanks to the fabulous production teams who made possible the entry of the volume into both the digital and physical universe, namely Arulmozhi Kulothugan of SPi Global and Afrose Anwar and Jaishree Srijan of Newgen KnowledgeWorks for their extraordinary magic in handling the manuscripts. A special thanks goes to Jaishree for expertly superintending the volume through the last critical stages of production.

As ever, I owe the biggest debt of gratitude to my wife Sharada, who has all these years given me much wisdom, hope, and assurance.

R. S. Sugirtharajah
Bournville, Birmingham UK
February 1, 2023

Contributors

Emily Anderson, Project Curator at Japanese American National Museum, Los Angeles

Ralph Broadbent, Independent Scholar

Jorge Cañizares-Esguerra, Alice Drysdale Sheffield Professor of History, The University of Texas at Austin

Warren Carter, LaDonna Kramer Meinders Professor of New Testament at Phillips Seminary

Jin Young Choi, Professor of New Testament and Christian Origins and the Baptist Missionary Training School Professorial Chair in Biblical Studies, Colgate Rochester Crozer Divinity School

Steed Vernyl Davidson, Vice President for Academic Affairs, Dean of the Faculty, and Professor of Hebrew Bible/Old Testament, McCormick Theological Seminary

Ellen F. Davis, Amos Ragan Kearns Distinguished Professor of Bible and Practical Theology, Duke University

Judith A. Diehl, Retired, Denver Seminary

Hemchand Gossai, Associate Dean, Humanities and Social Sciences, Northern Virginia Community College

Jacqueline M. Hidalgo, Professor of Latina/o/x Studies and Religion, Williams College

Hephzibah Israel, Senior Lecturer in Translation Studies, University of Edinburgh

Sharon Jacob, Visiting Professor of New Testament & Postcolonial Studies, Claremont School of Theology

Clara A. B. Joseph, Professor, University of Calgary

Jina Kang, Assistant Professor of Hebrew Bible/Old Testament at McCormick Theological Seminary

Archie C. C. Lee, Honorary Senior Research Fellow, Institute of Chinese Studies, The Chinese University of Hong Kong and University Distinguished Professor of Humanities and Social Science, Shandong University

Tat-siong Benny Liew, Class of 1956 Professor in New Testament Studies, College of the Holy Cross

Chin Ming Stephen Lim, Lecturer in Biblical Studies, Hong Kong Sheng Kong Hui Ming Hua Theological College; Adjunct Lecturer in Theology with the School of Theology, Charles Sturt University, Australia

Safwat Marzouk, Associate Professor of Old Testament, Union Presbyterian Seminary

Adrian Masters, Project Leader, GloVib, University of Trier

Dora R. Mbuwayesango, Professor and Dean of Students, Hood Theological Seminary

Niall McKay, Public and Contextual Theology Research Fellow with Charles Sturt University, Australia and a Research Associate with Stellenbosch University, South Africa

Raj Nadella, Samuel A. Cartledge Associate Professor of New Testament, Columbia Theological Seminary

Judith H. Newman, Professor of Hebrew Bible and Early Judaism, University of Toronto

D. N. Premnath, Retired, Independent Scholar

Jeremy Punt, Professor, Stellenbosch University

Joerg Rieger, Distinguished Professor of Theology, Cal Turner Chair in Wesleyan Studies, Director of the Wendland-Cook Program in Religion and Justice, Vanderbilt University

Susanne Scholz, Professor of Old Testament, Southern Methodist University

Daniel L. Smith-Christopher, Professor of Biblical Studies, Loyola Marymount University

Janneke Stegeman, Independent Researcher

R. S. Sugirtharajah, Professor Emeritus, University of Birmingham

Gerald O. West, Professor Emeritus, University of KwaZulu-Natal, South Africa

Vincent L. Wimbush, Institute for Signifying Scriptures

INTRODUCTION

The Bible, Empires, and Postcolonial Criticism

R. S. SUGIRTHARAJAH

This volume is coming out at a time when so many people are agitated and confused by the current contentious debates about "culture wars," "Black Lives Matter," "deplatforming," and "statues must fall." These debates about historical injustices are not simply about the present but also about the legacy of the past, particularly the colonial past. Behind these cultural commotions are issues of empire, enslavement, race, and sexism, and especially questions of how and whose history is to be celebrated and remembered. Western empires and their residual effects are still impinging on every domain of the contemporary world. Together, these issues and debates constitute the staple ingredients of postcolonial criticism.

Though it has its origins in English studies departments, postcolonialism has given interpretative sustenance and vigor to disciplines varying from medieval to medical studies. This volume focuses mainly on postcolonial criticism and its application in the field of biblical studies, which is both complex and controversial.

Biblical books, as with any other historical and literary documents, include conflicting statements about empire. Just as the Bible contains more passages on violence and warmongering than on peace and reconciliation, it also contains more on colonial impulses and tendencies than anti-colonial inclinations.

Postcolonialism is, of course, a notoriously difficult concept to define. Each discipline provides its own definition. One of the salient characteristics of postcolonialism is that its meaning is not fixed permanently. It is essentially an evolving rather than a neatly defined theory. It has gathered new energy and force and has shed old connotations. The central function of postcolonial criticism is to be a contestatory force, more of a moral stance than a theory or a dogma. It has raised and sometimes even imposed moral questions regarding the prevailing critical mood of the time, and has compelled many scholars to abandon the traditional historical mindset and embrace ethical exegesis.

Its function is intercessory and intervening, allowing silenced and written-out passages and personalities to have a visibility and a voice. Postcolonial criticism is essentially a redemptive exegesis, absolving biblical interpretations from their earlier imperial associations. What postcolonialism has demonstrated is that hermeneutics is not just about texts and textures. It is about history, politics, culture, and, above all, peoples and their lives.

Since its emergence in the late twentieth century, postcolonial biblical criticism has challenged received wisdom, especially the colonial impulses embedded in biblical texts and their interpretations, in visual representations of biblical narratives, and in the colonial nature of institutions. Years of postcolonial biblical criticism have helped disturb and complicate triumphalist and haughty understandings and assumptions made about biblical concepts such as the Kingdom of God, the Cosmic Christ, and the single male Messiah figure. Postcolonialism also introduced a new element of critical inquiry to investigate the presence of empires in biblical texts. Until then, biblical interpreters often focused on the intentions and functions of the biblical writers, prophets, and kings in terms of individuals and their interests. As a result, the plunder and conquest by various biblical empires under which they functioned disappeared. Scholars essentially tried to hide and forget the concept of empire. One of the feats of postcolonial criticism has been to contest the slanted view of the righteousness and goodness of the empire.

What the empire does, through its missionaries, civil servants, and travel writers, is to insist on and demand a single definitive story. Ambiguities and complexities are ironed out and a sense of certainty and absolute truth is introduced. Hitherto biblical scholars have been reading the Bible as a single story. The trouble with a single reading is that it nullifies other stories, spins out clichés, and creates the impression that the Christian revelatory story is final while other stories are patchy and partial. Postcolonialism, to its credit, has constantly resisted the idea of a single story and encouraged the need to hear and heed multiple voices, varying from ethnic to gender to sexual orientations.

But postcolonialism is not simply about excavating forgotten personalities and texts from obscurity. It also demonstrates how scholars from the former colonies read the mainstream texts, thereby exposing the limitations of reading the biblical world from the confines of a white, straight, male, Eurocentric perspective. It is telling stories that make a person feel uncertain and uncomfortable. Postcolonialism, at its best, should challenge our convictions and certitudes and prod us into examining our default hermeneutical settings. It should challenge Western biblical interpreters to be more conscious of their discipline's past dubious role in the building of empire. Moreover, the field urges these elite interpreters to take an anti-colonial stance. The usefulness of the theory lies in illuminating the discipline's historical role in the empire and urging biblical exegetes to acknowledge imperial tendencies and traces in their works, as well as actively seeking reparation. In short, postcolonial biblical criticism is about which stories get told, who is telling them, against whom they are told, whom to believe, whose interpretations have value and weight, and essentially who is in charge.

Evolving Phases, Newer Appearances

Much has changed within the field since the inception of postcolonial criticism. One such change is the discernible shift in the credibility and the character of the Bible. A document that was associated with radical political causes of the 1960s and 1970s has also become the source for neoliberal values. Christian scriptures that served as an effective tool for pressuring those in power have now become a tool for those in power to pressurize the weak and the vulnerable. A text that spoke of liberation, freedom, and the Jubilee values of redistribution and reparation is now more often made to talk about capitalism, the free-market economy and the creation of private wealth. While the radical Bible advances the notion of communal freedom and common ownership, the right-wing Bible espouses the cause of individual liberty and the privatization of property and public institutions.[1]

The Bible was then seen as a pluralistic book having intertextual connections with various scriptures, enjoying theological kinship and a mutual spiritual worldview. It is now regarded as a stand-alone book subscribing to a single theological message.

Before postcolonialism, biblical criticism was largely related to the biblical past and little else. Biblical criticism provided solutions to problems that only professional scholars faced, and those scholars introduced these issues as if they were universal and relevant to all. Historical criticism and its intellectual descendants, such as redaction, narrative, and canonical criticism, were about the texts and about the historical past or philological clarifications. Western biblical interpreters in particular were concerned about syntax or dating the books or making aesthetic judgments about the book's prose and poetry, and showed little awareness of the politics embedded in the texts. It was postcolonial biblical criticism that forced biblical scholarship to look at current concerns such as race and gender in the light of the legacy of empire and to rethink the structures of power. Basically, historical criticism shuts out the world in order to focus on the text; postcolonialism drags in the world in order to assess its ideological content.

Another distinctive development has been the greater awareness of the nature of empires. They are not static; they mutate and morph into new incarnations. The old territorial empire has new avatars in the form of digital empires. John Naughton, a cultural commentator, put it in apocalyptical terms: the four horsemen of the Internet—Google, Facebook, Apple, and Amazon.[2] Old territorial empires had boundaries and clearly defined power structures but the new empires in the forms of Silicon Valley tech companies penetrate every domain of our lives. What oil and natural resources were for earlier empires, data has become for digital empires, and there is an intense struggle to control it.

Imperial motives have varied, and, more importantly, the mission statements of the dominant nations, too, have changed to justify their rapacious activities. At the height of modern colonialism, British colonialists, and for that matter most of the Western imperialists, saw their task in noble terms as bringing civilization and Christianity to "savage" nations. Then, in the twenty-first century, American involvement in Iraq and Afghanistan was supposedly a decent act championing democratic values and human rights, especially the upliftment of women. Now there is a new imperial power rising in the East in the form of China, which sees itself as a benevolent partner in fostering global prosperity. Unlike the championing of anti-colonial national struggle of the Third World people in the Mao era, the present Chinese government portrays itself as the global emancipator of the economically oppressed, minus the left-leaning rhetoric. China's Maritime Silk Road and its Belt and Road Initiative, which is operative in nearly sixty countries are attempts to transform the global economy. In other words, empires old or new would like to project themselves as rescuers and liberators rather than abusers or evil doers.

Another noticeable change in the field is the wider recognition that people have resisted colonialism since its inception, and their resistance was not merely the result of Enlightenment-induced Western values. The colonized have been active agents, offering sometimes fierce opposition since its commencement. The colonial canard that the enslaved have never done anything is not true. From the Bandanese resistance in 1621 to the Haitian revolution (1791–1804), the Kandyan Wars (1803), the Demerara revolt (1823), the Indian insurrection (1857), and the Morant Bay uprising (1865), the colonized and the enslaved have been there at the forefront of rebellion in all phases of the imperial process. The historian Caroline Elkins notes that in the nineteenth century there were "over 250 separate armed conflicts in the British empire, with at least one in any given year."[3] These resisters worked on the universal ethical agenda that stressed freedom and emancipation for all. These anti-colonial activities are not simply seen as isolated actions of the colonized in the far-flung places of empires. Priyamvada Gopal, in her illuminating book *Insurgent Empire*, has chronicled the energetic association between anti-colonial "liberation struggles in the colonies" and the "emergence of metropolitan dissent on colonial questions."[4] These metropole dissidents who were profoundly shaped and influenced by such protests in the colonies challenged the empire from within. Gopal laments that this fact has gone mostly unnoticed in postcolonial studies. Such a negligence is due to deficient remembrances of empire.

The constituency of the struggle has also changed. The great moral and political crusades and ideological struggles have ceded ground to modern right-wing causes, which are championed by religious fundamentalists or far-right white supremacists. They represent narrow religious and ideological interests over perceptions of race, gender, and the common good. Along with this, the nature of the victim has dramatically changed. The new claimants of victimhood are not the marginalized minorities but establishment figures who claim that society's structures are stacked against them. When Donald Trump thunders through his Twitter feed that there is "Presidential Harassment" and that he is somehow the victim of the white supremacist protests in Charlottesville, and when the English nationalist Brexiteers complain that they are being dispossessed and unfairly discriminated against in their own country, they project and parade themselves as the new smeared and subjugated. The most perilous thing the privileged majority feel is that they are in decline and deserve better treatment. The strategy of the privileged has been to flip all of it over and claim powerlessness and disempowerment. The identity politics that gave voices to blacks, dalits, feminists, tribals, burakumins, gays and lesbians, which were once seen as positive and progressive forces, have now come to be seen, especially by societal elites, as burdensome and divisive in pitting community against community. For them, race, gender, and caste are not genuine grievances but rather signs of abuse and tyranny.

Another change has to do with the notion of a saintly and noble subaltern. That has given way to a more nuanced understanding that the oppressed, while robustly resisting hegemonic powers that can themselves wield power in alarming ways.

An additional and appalling change is the rigorous attempt at a revisionist history of colonialism. An egregious example of this is the recent report by the Commission on Race and Ethnic Disparities, a UK government-commissioned report on the present status of race relations. Tony Sewell, who wrote the Introduction, spins a novel way of looking at enslavement. He notes that the slave period was not only about "profit and suffering," but also about how "culturally African people transformed themselves into a re-modeled African/Britain." The idea that the enslaved themselves benefitted from the system that oppressed them is being recycled and magnifies the same arguments used by the owners of the enslaved people.[5]

Finally, and alarmingly, one of the strongly expressed and clear messages of postcolonial theory, memorably popularized by the Kenyan author Ngũgĩ wa Thiong'o, "decolonizing the mind,"[6] is now being marshaled by religious fundamentalists and the advocates of far-right causes. A pernicious example is that of Indian far-right Hindu groups who claim that all knowledge production about India is a Western form of colonialism and control. Their message is that Indians should decolonize their minds of such defamation and degradation of India and claim assertively all that is Hindu.[7] One of the tragedies of contemporary times is that right-wing and religious nationalist organizations are co-opting the words and concepts of resistance that were part of the liberation movements, and in the process are ruining their emancipatory meanings.

In sum, postcolonialism emerged at a time when the world was beginning to lean toward secular, progressive, and liberal worldviews. Now it is confronted with a world that is increasingly fundamentalistic, nativistic, and nationalistic.

Biblical Scholarship and its Collusion with Colonialism

A theological critique of empire and its links with biblical scholarship is yet to be written. In the nineteenth century, other disciplines in the humanities, such as history, anthropology, and English literature, acted as handmaidens of British imperialism and attempted to justify the empire and rationalize the acts of conquests. Biblical scholars were willing partners in the colonial cause. Impelled by the Enlightenment-driven linear view of history, and aligned with the biblical notion of eschatology, which judged certain people and nations to be damned as backward and obsolete, they provided moral justification for colonialism. While historical, anthropological, and English studies have reappraised their involvement in the colonial project, biblical scholarship still remains reluctant.

There is an amnesiac streak among Western biblical scholars when it comes to empire, a long-standing and established institutionalized hermeneutical illiteracy and thoughtlessness in regard to the issue of empire and imperialism. There is a manifestly a misremembering going on among Western biblical scholars. While anthropologists and historians emphasized cultural differences, economic conditions, and physical appearances of the "Native," biblical scholars used biblical religion as a yardstick to evaluate the "other." They created a simple "true-false dichotomy" and also set distinctive, scriptural, and conceptual boundaries that marked them out as different from each other. An egregious example was the work of G. Ernest Wright. In his characteristic evangelical tone, he confidently declared that the religions which surrounded Israel were "most dangerous and disintegrative," and that "the faith of Israel,"[8] even in its earliest and basic forms, was "so utterly different from that of the contemporary" religions, and as such this distinction could not be simply explained by evolutionary process or environmental influences.[9] It was such thinking that helped to create a "Christian mentality," a simplistic notion of belief and unbelief, of true and false religion—a contrast that still persists. Western biblical scholarship was largely responsible for dividing and placing people in two broad and opposing categories: elect and damned, polished and primitive, and sophisticated colonizers and naive enslaved. While studying cultures and texts, biblical scholars were looking for pure truth, pure religion, and pure theology, predetermined by their Christendom mindset.

Biblical scholars were answerable for putting forward the idea most orthodox Christians believe: that biblical religion, with its emphasis on belief in a single God, a robust written scriptural tradition, a savior figure, and a universally applicable faith, is the true religion, and the other religions are degenerate and in need of revival and, in some cases, replacement. The European empires were about greed and power. They needed theological and moral validation for what they were doing. Some biblical scholars willingly abetted in this.

ENTANGLEMENT OF THE EMPIRE AND THE BIBLE

Although in popular perception the Bible is seen as a book for the common people, in reality it has been enlisted by empires, the elite, and the establishment. The Bible is not only a book of imperialism; it is also a book *for* imperialism. It is not only a book of empires; it is also a book that sustained both ancient and modern empires. It also wielded one of the characteristics of the empire: that of annexing other peoples' textual resources and possessions.

There are a number of biblical projects associated with empire and imperialism. One is the formulation of the biblical canon. The canonization process is a complicated one and is not the central concern of this volume. Suffice to say that it was a process that lasted the first four centuries of Christianity and even beyond. Empires and emperors played a vital role in producing an agreed-upon version of the core Christian story amid the disparate Gospel retellings. The immediate reason for the settlement of the canon was prompted by the needs of empire rather than the wants of the nascent Christian communities.

Emperor Constantine, the ruler of the Roman Empire, who was concerned about the unity of the church and the unity of the state, perceived the Bible as a unifying force. Hence he desired fifty Bibles to be placed in the various churches throughout the empire.[10] The imperial command to superintend the production of the Bible was entrusted to Eusebius, a confidante of the emperor. In coming up with a selection of books that would become the standardized Bible, Eusebius opted for the list produced by Athanasius, which met the requirements of the empire of the day and the needs of the church. This list resolved the dispute between the Eastern and Western churches regarding the status of the letter to the Hebrews and the Book of Revelation. It is possible to conjecture that the last seven books—the letter to the Hebrews, James, 2 and 3 John, 2 Peter, Jude, and Revelation—were added to the list not on the basis of their theological contents or their historical importance. Instead, their addition was prompted by the coexistence of competing churches and also to meet the needs of the state. In other words, the New Testament canon was settled for practical purposes and for political convenience and expediency. The list of books accepted as normative symbolized both the unity of the church and the unity of the state. The Athanasian canonical list that won the day was a document of political accommodation and compromise.[11] The canonical process had little to do with a Holy Spirit–inspired act, as Christian apologists would like to claim, but was essentially a political act made by human beings. Such a selection process led to the view that the writings which were not accepted by the established church were inferior and unworthy.

The imperial aims of a single God for one nation coincided with the church's ambition of proclaiming one God, one faith, one baptism, one church, and one book. It was Emperor Constantine's intervention that resulted in the closure of the New Testament canon. The emperor was very keen that these copies of the Bible should to be produced in fine parchment, and he was willing to meet the expenses, including the transportation of the books to churches. Among these extravagantly illustrated codexes, some of the progressive social, economic, and political programs integral to and envisioned in the Bible, such as Jubilee laws, Mary's Magnificat, and the Nazareth Manifesto, would have been out of place.

The apotheosis of the royal sponsorship of the Bible was the commissioning of the King James Version (KJV). Just as in the case of Emperor Constantine, James I, too, wanted to settle religious tension in his kingdom and reinforce his position as one ruler of the twin thrones of Scotland and England, modeled on the biblical spirit of "one king and one temple." He not only initiated a new translation and but also directed what words should be used or not used. His main motive was to cancel the popular Geneva Version, which in its margins contained anti-monarchical and seditious comments and even encouraged disobedience to kings. Any mention of tyrant or tyranny was embargoed. The translators of the KJV removed the word "tyrant," which occurred nearly 400 times in the Geneva Bible. A translation that was produced to encourage freedom to subjects ended up prescribing obedience and subservience. The text was envisioned to strengthen the authority of the state rather than the sovereignty of God. Another example of the KJV's strengthening the cause of the state is evident in the occurrence of the word "nation," which was employed four times more than the Vulgate's use of the Latin equivalent, *natio*. The hope was that the whole church and the state should be "bound unto" new translation and "none other."[12] Eventually, the King James Bible came to be seen as the Bible of the establishment. It was the same James who, seven years after the publication of the Bible that carried his name, granted the royal approval for the Company of Adventurers of London Trading to the Ports of Africa, a joint stock company, a company among other things involved in the trade of enslaved Africans.

The imperial involvement in Bible production continued as recently as the nineteenth century, when the Russian ruler Alexander I initiated a modern Russian version. He, too, faced personal and political crisis, especially after the fall of St. Petersburg to the forces of Napoleon. Faced with uncertainty, Alexander urged the St. Petersburg Bible Society (now the Russian Bible Society), to translate and publish a new Russian version of the Bible. As with the King James Version, it also had "imperial blessings and proscriptions." The Russian conservative elements were so strong that the resultant version had a short-lived existence and remained in storage.[13]

The Christian New Testament was an earlier example of textual annexation of other peoples' scriptural resources. Currently fashionable and contentious terms such as "cultural appropriation" and "cultural imperialism" are not as recent or original or cutting edge as their modern advocates assert. Cultural appropriation is at the core of the New Testament. Israel's unique name, its histories, its patriarchs and promises, its election, its alliances with God, its covenant, and its theologies were taken over by the writers of the New Testament books. The Christian reading of a sin-focused interpretation of the Hebrew Bible, appealing to Jesus as improving the teaching of Hebrew prophets and sages, and the shaping of them to fit in with Christian eschatological thinking, were salient markers of the Christian appropriation of the cultural resources of the other. The Gentiles, who did not have any link with Abraham, had now become Abraham's offspring and heirs. Likewise, the Gentile Christians who did not experience the agonizing ordeal of deportation were now described as "elect exiles of the Dispersion in Pontus, Galatia, Cappadocia, Asia, and Bithynia" (1 Peter 1:1) Like all colonialists who appropriate other peoples' lands and cultural heritages, these early Christian interpreters denied the "continued validity" of the Hebrew scriptures and insisted, as Susannah Heschel observed, that their version of the reading was the "exclusive truth."[14]

Another example of the Bible's close association with empire is the proliferation of Gospel harmonies. The majority of the Gospel harmonies were produced in the sixteenth century when European powers were emerging as empires. Harvey McArthur, who studied the production of Gospel harmonies, concluded that there was a paucity of harmonies in the previous centuries compared to their dramatic proliferation in the sixteenth century.[15] While ecclesiastical authorities tried to control unwieldy and awkward Gospel narratives and make them into a smooth and suitable text, the same century saw Spain and Portugal embarking on a mission to conquer and tame wild and unruly peoples and render them rational and acceptable. More vitally, contrary to popular perception, the Roman Catholic harmonies outnumbered those produced by the Protestants. The Protestants caught up in the nineteenth century when Gospel harmonies proliferated in England when it emerged as a colonial power.

It was at the height of the British Empire that the "Lives of Jesus"—a historical genre—flourished in England. These Victorian Lives of Jesus, perceptively documented by Daniel Pals, were different the from the ones that emerged in Germany at that time. The German enterprise was undertaken "entirely with the help of library and lexicon," and it "engaged in comparative, critical analysis,"[16] whereas the works of English theologians were largely a mixture of theology, confession, and oriental romanticism. This Jesus seemed to be at home with Galilean pastures and rocky Judean hills. Jesus appeared as a wonder worker and spoke to his contemporaries as a teacher. He saw his task as fulfilling a noble cause of redeeming humankind and establishing the Kingdom of God on earth. In essence, he was the "savior of mankind." This Jesus consoled and consolidated the faith of the English and protected them from the deeply technical and German philological studies of the scripture. What Pals failed to note was that the British missionaries working in the colonies produced their own versions of the Lives of Jesus, not to reassure the populace as the British lives did, but to encourage the cause of the British Empire in India.

An example of such lives can be seen in the works of Bernard Lucas, a missionary educator who was on the staff of the United Theological College, Bangalore. In these writings Lucas essentially replaced the Kingdom of God with the empire of Christ. The "empire of Christ" is a euphemistic reference to the British Empire. The Raj was imagined as the universal empire of Truth, and Jesus as an indisputable sovereign, and before him all nations "bow in lowly obeisance."[17] Evangelization, for Lucas, was the "building of an empire into which are incorporated all the kingdoms of the world."[18] Lucas's Jesus did not destroy the distinctive elements of other faiths that have nourished and sustained Indians for a long time, but took over the vital elements of them and interweaved them with the Gospel. His ambitious hope was that this spiritual amalgam would lead India "into a union of loyal devotion to the eternal and universal Christ."[19] Unlike the British Lives of Jesus, Lucas's words of Jesus's were not calming and comforting, but were "imperial."[20] Any resistance or patriotic tendencies among Indians, which Lucas called *swadeshism*, were seen as a "treason" against the empire. If the "Lives" of Jesus written in England were reassuring for the faith of British Christians, the "Lives" produced in the empire convinced Indians that their true identity as Indian Christian patriots was as an integral part of the British Empire. The portrayal of Jesus that emerged in the colonies was that of an empire-builder and a provider of "imperial ideas and imperial resources."[21] The same Lucas portrayed Paul as an imperial ideal and imagined Britishers as the heirs to the "same imperial ideal."[22] It is worth noting that it was in the Reagan era, by which time America had muscled its way in as the new empire, that Jesus studies flourished in the US under the aegis of the male- and white-dominated Jesus Seminar.

In sum, the Bible and empires are inseparable. They owe their existence to each other, and may also provide enough strength and substance to ensure their mutual continuing survival and longevity.

Contours of the Volume

Postcolonial biblical criticism is an assorted entity. It has always been contested from within and without, and has a variety of manifestations. On surveying the literature, one can discern the existence of three categories of approach to the Bible and empire: the Bible as an anti-imperial text, as an ambivalent tract, and as a doubtful resource.

The first of these, the anti-imperial text, views the Bible as offering an opposition to imperialism in spite of the atrocities of the empires recorded in it. Biblical narratives are portrayed as a depository of God's resistance and as offering a subversive message and an alternative to dominant imperial institutions. An example of this is the Pauline paradigm of local assemblies of Christ, which are projected as a suitable substitute for imperial organizations.[23] Those who hold on to this position make revolutionary assertions and subtle political claims but package them in conventional Christian propagandist terms. They paint a beneficial picture of empire, but concede that biblical empires are awkward and oppressive. Such readings encourage modern empires to intervene as a moral duty and as a divine imperative. The second approach, the ambivalent tract, perceives the Bible as a complex and arguable document that needs a nuanced reading. But a simple reductive reading of the Bible as pro- or anti-empire is not sustainable. The third category, a doubtful resource, questions the efficacy and usefulness of the Bible given its overwhelmingly imperial disposition and tones. Their question: Is the Christian scripture worth salvaging? This volume offers a home to these multiple and diverse voices.

This volume contains six sections. It opens with biblical empires. From the days of the Mesopotamian empire to modern imperialism, the majority of humanity has at some point or another been under the control of a domineering authority. The essays assembled under the first heading, "Biblical Empires in the Hebrew Scriptures, Intertestamental Writings, the New Testament, and the Christian Apocrypha," focus on the nature and scope of biblical empires such as the Assyrian, Egyptian, Babylonian, Grecian (Hellenistic), and Roman; how they pervaded every area of life in the ancient world; and how biblical writers responded, negotiated, and worked out different strategies as a way of responding to the imperial presence. There are certain common themes that run through these chapters. They refer to a significant number of biblical verses related to the biblical empires and how they were employed to characterize the "other" and serve as a benchmark either as an example or to shame Israel.

D. N. Premnath opens the account with an expertly written essay that highlights the complex and multidimensional aspect of interaction between the Egyptian Empire and the Israelites in the field of political governance, economy, religion, literary compositions, and iconography. He concedes that it is not easy to identify the nature and the extent of these exchanges, but he is of the conviction that there remain "enough vestiges" to indicate the Egyptian influences. Safwat Marzouk follows this with his definition of who the Assyrians were and with the basic aspects of their empire as expressed through religion and military tactics, as well as the impact of Assyrian rule on those whom it invaded. The essay ends with a reflection on the decolonization envisioned by the books of Nahum and Jonah, which replace earthly empires with a divine one, offering the possibility of forgiveness if human empires repent and change their repressive ways. Hemchand Gossai shows in his detailed essay how, like other biblical empires, the depiction of the Babylonian Empire shifts between positive and negative images. He devotes much space to the Babylonian captivity of the Judeans, which played a significant role in elucidating the nature and the experience of exile, homecoming, despair, and betrayal, which are ongoing and have universal resonances. On looking at the Persian Empire, Dan Smith-Christopher takes note of the current political implications of studying the Achaemenid Empire and records how biblical scholarship has been unashamedly pro- Hellenistic or pro-Roman. Looking at a few selected Hebraic texts from a postcolonial point of view, Smith-Christopher convincingly demonstrates that the attitude of these texts toward Persians was anything but positive. Warren Carter investigates the often overlooked aspects of the negotiations that went on between Jewish writings such as the Old Testament Pseudepigrapha, the Apocrypha, and the Dead Sea Scrolls and the Hellenistic imperial power that began at the time of Alexander (323 BCE) through the emergence of the Roman hegemon (63 CE). He draws attention to some substantial exchanges and some of the overlooked complexities, such as the invisibility of the agency of the colonized and the mutual dependency of the rulers and the ruled.

Adolf Deissmann commented, before postcolonialism appeared in the hermeneutical firmament, that the New Testament was "a book of the imperial age."[24] The essays in the second part of this section amplify his claim and demonstrate how various New Testament writings responded to the Roman Empire—some as an anti-imperial narrative offering a countercultural message, and others as a complicated and compromised document. Judith A. Diehl endorses the former view and traces subversive language and symbols concealed in the Synoptic Gospels, though these are regarded as religious texts. Her conviction is that, in the end, God's eternal empire will finally prevail, which might for some sound like Christian triumphalism. The next two essayists take a different view and challenge the counter-imperial rhetoric. In her scrupulous investigation of the scholars of empire studies, a field distinctly different from that of postcolonial approaches, Jin Young Choi challenges their views that the Johannine writings offer a counter-imperial rhetoric. This, in her view, reinscribed Christian exceptionalism.

Navigating through a vast amount of scholarly literature, she demonstrates how postcolonial criticism pays more attention to colonizing tendencies in the Johannine text, which produced a socially stratified order and peripheralized the other.

Tat-siong Benny Liew calls for a much more nuanced assessment of Paul and contends that to portray him as either pro- or anti–Roman Empire will be "unrealistic and reductionistic" because it fails to take into account the complexities of the Roman Empire, Paul's personality, his rhetoric, and his interpretative strategies.

Jacqueline M. Hidalgo shows in her thoughtful essay on the Book of Revelation specifically how much of the "fantastic imagery" of the text has to do with teasing and responding to the Roman imperial power. She also charts the contemporary debate about Rome and how scholars have examined it from the rhetoric of gender and power and used it as a template to wrestle with their own views of empire, both ancient and modern. As many contributors of this volume have argued, she, too, reiterates that the ethics of interpretation should be the focus of postcolonial scholarship. The last chapter in this section is on the Christian Apocrypha, especially the Acts of Thomas. This slim text has an added attraction to Clara Joseph, because there is a living community of Christians in India who claim their heritage through St. Thomas. Often dubbed as inauthentic, the text clearly states the ubiquitous presence of empire, this time not Roman but Christian. Joseph's contention is that modern-day scholarship on the Acts of Thomas is "overdetermined" by Western colonial assumptions, and her plea is that this apocryphal text deserves a re-examination, and she herself has done the task skillfully here.

The second section, "Modern European and Asian Empires," shifts our attention to the role of the Bible in the expansion of modern empires such as the Spanish, Portuguese, Dutch, British, German, and United States. As with the case of the previous section, the essays here highlight the biblical passages these empire-builders mobilized to strengthen their claim on the colonies and draw attention to their hermeneutical presuppositions of the imperial project.

This section opens with a detailed essay on the Spanish Empire. Jorge Cañizares-Esguerra and Adrian Masters demonstrate how crucial the Old Testament was for the imperial project of Spain, supplying biblical passages that legitimized the conquest, taxation, and mining rights. Ironically, as the authors point out, it was the same book that provided textual ammunition to patriots, Indians, women, and nuns to challenge their oppressors. It was the pliability of the Bible that supported both monarchical and republican causes. The authors end with an acknowledgment that their essay is only a textual trailer and that the Old Testament's versatility as a master text for imperialism needs further investigation and re-evaluation. They gravely observe that without further examination, the history of Europe will remain both flawed and shallow.

Janneke Stegeman charts the hermeneutical history of how the newly independent Dutch nation freed itself from Catholic Spanish rulers and soon became a colonial power itself. Like its former masters, the Dutch themselves drew heavily from the biblical narratives and reconfiguring the nation as the modern-day Israel, drawing on the supersessionist biblical texts as a scriptural warrant for colonial adventure. She concludes with a lament that, despite decolonization, "genuine" Dutchness is still tethered to Christianity and whiteness.

Ralph Broadbent's essay is about the British Empire. In the first part, he succinctly surveys the historiography of the British Empire and the theoretical presuppositions of postcolonialism. In the second, he uncovers how British biblical scholars who were by birth or education part of the ruling class provided scriptural sanction for Britain's imperial exploitation. His essay reveals that it is a complex hierarchical ideology involving the monarchy, the aristocracy, the poor, the women, and the oriental "Other" who were portrayed as savages and child-like. He ends by posing a provocative and a blunt question: In spite of the valiant efforts to use the Bible to uplift the plight of the poor, colonized, and women, do the Christian scriptures, which are inherently hierarchal and replete with colonial intentions, have any relevant message for the post-imperial age?

Stephen Lim's chapter looks at the Bible's complicity in British-occupied Singapore. This time the empire-builders were not men but women who took upon themselves the civilizing mission as the white woman's burden. Lim forensically analyses articles that appeared in a periodical run by the Ladies Bible and Tract Society, which published biblical expositions supporting the interests of the British Empire. These articles provided biblical warrant for morally dubious activities, ranging from opium trade ("make friends with the mammon") to producing docile colonial subjects, especially young Chinese women ("in the event of bad government, . . . not to be impatient, or to take the matter into their own hands"). His essay also scrutinizes how the indigenous Biblewomen who were trained by the white women missionaries uncritically internalized and routinely replicated Western Christian exceptionalism and found scriptural resources in order to both denigrate and discredit their Chineseness. Lim laments that the relative freedom and autonomy that the white women had in running their own affairs in the colonies was not extended to the colonized Other. In other words, a male imperialism was exchanged for a female one.

Joerg Rieger's essay sketches the history of how German intellectual production was shaped by the "colonial fantasies" of the German Empire—an empire that lasted merely three decades. These scholarly outputs spawned a variety of biblical engagements which varied from Schleiermacher's liberal theology to practical missionary efforts to the famous history of religions school. Rieger's observation is that despite the prevalence of "colonial spirit" at that time, all these attempts by German theologians exemplified some kind of openness about the "other," sometimes positively and at times negatively. He is intrigued by the paucity of German scholars who are engaged with German colonialism. Rieger's question could be equally leveled at most of the Western biblical scholars who are also reluctant to investigate the Bible's role in strengthening various European countries and their imperial intentions. Judith Newman, in her competent reading of American history, uncovers how the scriptural discourse of the Anglo-American settlers justified the occupancy of the lands of Native Americans and holding in bondage African Americans. Her chapter also includes a fascinating account of the differing ways the mapping of the land was undertaken by settlers, Native Americans, and Mormons. Her chapter also contains a sensitive reading of the story of Ham, which was racialized to uphold the "slavocracy" of the Southern plantation owners, and a counter-reading of the same narrative by African Americans as a way of regaining their identity and integrity.

This section also includes two essays on an Asian empire: imperial Japan. These chapters illustrate how Japanese Christians employed the Bible to support or subvert the country's occupation of Korea, and how Koreans, who themselves were at the receiving end of Japanese occupation, used the Bible to endorse or energize opposition to the Japanese presence. Emily Anderson describes very vividly how Japanese Christians— a minority in their country with their own fraught history—deliberated and coped with integrating "ostensibly a foreign religion" and their place and position as imperial subjects in an emerging empire. What she has touched upon in this chapter is only one of few examples of non-Western Christians who compromised with and confronted the imperial power, drawing on the same Christian scriptures for their complicitous stance and dissent. Jina Kang's essay narrates expertly the Korean experience and how the Bible became an inventive tool both in being supportive of and resistant to Japanese imperialism. As such, Kang contends that hermeneutics becomes a complex and messy process faced with the aspirations of Korean nationalists, Japanese Christian missionaries, and the local Marxist literary critics. Her contention is that in the hostile world of early twentieth-century Korea, the Bible was an effective tool to reflect upon and engage with the imperialistic intentions of the Japanese.

Before moving to the next section, an observation and a question. It is plainly clear that empires are inherently paradoxical. Every noble cause is matched with monstrous acts. If the British are remembered for the 1919 Jallianwala Bagh massacre of innocent Indians, the Dutch are equally guilty of killing innocent Englishmen in Ambon in 1623. The intriguing question is whether one empire was better than the other. A character in Amitav Ghosh's novel *The Glass Palace* provides a tendentious answer: "There are no good masters and bad masters. In a way the better the master, worse is the condition of the slave, because it makes him forget what he is."[25]

Bible translation played a critical role in strengthening the imperialistic intentions of Western empires. Section three, "Empires and Translations," contains essays on India (Hephzibah Israel), China (Archie Lee), and various African cultures (Dora R. Mbuwayesango). What emerges from these perspicuous essays is that translation is not an innocent or serene activity, as it is perceived in the popular imagination. In many cases it is a violent act, violating local languages, cultures, and biblical texts, as Mbuwayesango and Lee have forensically demonstrated in their essays. In certain cases, hardened Christian doctrinal points of view took priority over faithfulness to biblical texts, and the colonial mindset perceived indigenous languages as worthless in conveying God's word, and, even worse, as a threat to the Gospel, and thus needed to be cleansed. Israel's essay makes a powerful case for Bible translations that should go beyond narrow linguistic choices and look for potential ideological and theological insights embedded in the texts. Lee proposes a cross-textual approach that would take into account both Asian and biblical texts. Mbuwayesango urges African biblical scholars to scrutinize African versions and how they match against biblical languages and African indigenous cultures and languages. The lingering question is whether the sole aim of Bible translation is conversion, or whether it should move out of its missiological context in which it has been entrenched since its inception?

Section four, "Postcolonial Social and Ethical Concerns," deals with how race, environmental, and queer discourses have adopted postcolonial biblical insights to meet their existential needs. Ellen F. Davis, in addition to nation-state colonialism, draws attention to "geophysical imperialism." She proposes an eco-agrarian approach to ancient Israel's scriptures. The multifaceted interdependency of arable land, animals, and human communities represented and inscribed in the pages of Israel's scriptures enables us to comprehend the various understandings of God and humanity. She is convinced that such an approach will be "exegetically accurate and theologically rich." Jeremy Punt, after methodically identifying mutual and shared thematic and methodological interests between postcolonialism and queer studies, lists his own items for future investigation. Vincent Wimbush, in his distinctive style, demonstrates how postcolonialism, the Bible, and race are intriguingly entangled, and his plea is that their survival depends on moving beyond the traditional attachment to texts and paying more attention to lives, social relations, and power dynamics. Steed Davidson's chapter argues that race and capitalism were part of liberal imperialism's agenda to make the world a better place in the mold of Western values and Christian vision. This civilizing mission was further strengthened by the justification provided by the Bible. The main thrust of the chapter is about how resistance to empire and to the Bible came from the often marginalized Rastafarians, who themselves had a complicated and controversial history. It was they who provided alternative sources that had a destabilizing effect on both on the empire and the Bible.

Section five, "Postcolonial Biblical Criticism and Cognate Disciplines," contains chapters that deal with the transformative nature of postcolonialism and how its theoretical maneuverings impinge on related fields such as feminism, liberation hermeneutics, and Marxism. Susanne Scholz, Gerald West, and Niall McKay highlight mutual goals and hopes and divergences of these current intellectual and liberative discourses as they intervene and interrogate the accepted knowledges and destabilize their compliances. Susanne Scholz's mastery of feminist postcolonial biblical interpretation is faultless. Her essay assembles a stellar cast of feminist biblical theoreticians and is filled with practical textual examples. It also investigates the often discounted and prejudicial history of gendered interpretation. She concludes with an appeal, arguing that postcolonial biblical criticism should stand in solidarity with other progressive forces which work for justice and peace. West passionately restates his career-long call for decolonizing African biblical interpretation, which should instead draw deeply from the legacy of South African black theology and address contemporary social issues. McKay's essay is a reiteration of his staunch conviction that there are several benefits of Marxist theory to the postcolonial cause. These include an analysis of the social and political factors and the ideological forces behind both biblical texts and their interpreters, as well as the uncovering of the capitalist assumptions in modern critical approaches such as the historical-critical and social-scientific methods. He ends with a collegial counseling, which all these essayists would readily endorse: that postcolonial criticism should not lose its liberative intent and potential.

The last section, "Postcolonialism, Biblical Studies, and Theoretical Orientations," contains essays on the emergence of postcolonial biblical criticism, and its history, methods, theories, and prominent practitioners. The first essay, by Raj Nadella, provides a competent account of the origins of postcolonial biblical criticism, its evolution over the years, its earlier practitioners, and its interdisciplinary nature. He concludes with an earnest request that postcolonialism should shed its overly obscure and opaque theoretical language and engage with the public in a transparent language. Sharon Jacob's contribution traces the complicated history of the Bible and the ancient, colonial, and postcolonial empires. She demonstrates deftly how this relationship has been constantly changed, transformed, and modified. She also sketches the efforts of biblical scholars who kept a "steady and unwavering gaze" on biblical empires. Although historical criticism noted the incidental presence of empire, it was these scholars who made empire a significant part of their scholarly work. Her observation that the relationship between the Bible and empires did not develop in an abstract way is highly pertinent.

As a way of summing up, I end with the remarks of two philosophers—one a German and the other a Martinican. Walter Benjamin observed that "there is no document of civilization which is not at the same time a document of barbarism."[26] Frantz Fanon, in his celebrated *Wretched of the Earth*, wrote: "Everything that is affirmed can, at the same instant, be denied with the same force."[27] Although these sayings do not directly refer to the Bible, their observations are a perfect fit for the Bible. The chapters assembled here are a telling witness to the enslaving and emancipatory tendencies in the Bible. The other message that comes through these chapters is that every scriptural claim made by colonizers to justify their dominance could be repudiated and repurposed by the subjugated people by delving into the same Bible in ways contrary to the intentions of the text and the colonizers.

Concerns and Conclusions

Biblical scholars' approach to the Bible has been largely historical and contextual. Their hermeneutical activities are generally restricted to speaking to fellow hermeneuts and about themselves. For them the challenge comes from each other's works. Biblical scholars generally avoided intervening in matters or debates outside their discipline. Edward Said called for critical practice that he labeled a "program of interference."[28] What this interference involved was a committed and politicized breaching of disciplinary borders. It is stepping outside the discipline itself. It is not the familiar crossing of interdisciplinary borders but more radical than that. It is, if need be, "breaking out of disciplinary ghettos"—ghettos to which biblical scholars have been accustomed and confined to. The benefits of specialization can be tempting. It comfortably keeps scholars in their soothing and settled places.

Western biblical scholars who praise the prophets for their daring courage to speak truth to power are often reluctant to do the same thing to their governments. My biggest challenge has been to find an American biblical scholar to write an entry on how the Bible influenced the shaping of American history from the days of the Puritans to its emergence as a modern empire. Incidentally, there is not a single book on the topic yet.

The reluctance among mainstream European or American scholars to embrace postcolonialism could be traced to its combative style of subverting and disturbing hegemonic discourse or holding power to account. A confrontational style is not the natural instinct of biblical scholars. Biblical scholarship has been in the business of providing the comfort of a simple faith rather than offering a challenge. Their style tends to be cautious and offering assurance to readers rather than championing political or social causes. There are a many such examples. When historical criticism dented the cherished beliefs of Christians, English biblical scholars sought to limit the damage by mobilizing the very method to soothe the fears of the faithful. The Oxford and Cambridge scholars, especially the Cambridge Three—Lightfoot, Westcott, and Hort—adopted what Daniel Pals called a "cautious and reassuring style of criticism."[29]

The trend continues in the current quest for the historical Jesus. One of the prominent members of the Jesus Seminar, Marcus Borg, persistently made it clear that the quest for the historical Jesus, involving a study of various historical developments to understand the pre-Easter Jesus, did not exhaust the relevance of the risen Jesus. He envisaged his task as projecting a post-Easter Jesus who was no "longer a person of flesh and blood, limited in time and space" as "the historical Jesus had been," but one whom the faithful could experience "anywhere and everywhere."[30] He spins a soft message, a kind of comforting narrative that churchgoers would prefer to hear.

Biblical scholars could cleverly work out an exegesis without coming within striking distance of seeming to have a political opinion. But they are not always shy about taking ideological positions when their own nations are perceived to be under threat. A recent fascinating collection of essays on the First World War and biblical scholarship has shown that, with the exception of a few, the majority of biblical scholars from the United Kingdom and Germany utilized their scholarship to support their respective nations in their war effort to achieve national goals and ideals. Their patriotism was more evident when some of them enlisted in the armed forces or offered their services to the government rather than raising theological questions about the rights and wrongs of war. More importantly, they "brought their own disciplinary expertise" and their status as public intellectuals to "bear on the matter of war,"[31] published articles in newspapers, and lectured to the public. Hermann Gunkel even wrote a jingoistic doggerel that portrayed the British as Judas. Scholars who always venerated objectivity and showed diligent detachment during peacetime did not shy away from reading into the texts a championing of nationalistic causes.

The default position of the majority of white Western biblical scholars has been to embrace the achievements of empire while only mildly condemning its atrocities. They were convinced by their belief that history was on their side. Despite their Christian calling, biblical scholars failed to notice the atrocities and pillaging of their own colonial governments. Colonialism was seen as part of God's plan for the less privileged peoples of the world, effected through a temporary and passing phase of Western rule. They failed to challenge racism and the enslavement it spawned. This position is exemplified by Max Warren, who perceived empire not as an "unmixed evil" but "acclaimed as truly good."[32] For him, a Caesar is not "an enemy but a beloved enemy,"[33] and therefore there is a reluctance to offer any evaluation of empire, which should be left to the end-time judgment. The following statement from Stephen Neil, an Anglican who worked in India during the peak of British rule in India, is a representative example of this approach: "The history of the Christian mission in the colonial period must in the end be left to the judgement of God, who alone knows all the facts, and who alone can exercise a perfectly objective and merciful judgement."[34]

Are the days of empire over then? There is a tendency to evaluate the modern European empires as if they have come to an end. While colonialism is formally over, neocolonial relations pervade the current global order, from the balance of power in international institutions and trade negotiations to interference in the affairs of former colonies. Empire has not totally disappeared. It has transformed into new forms of exploitation. The United Kingdom may no longer engage in the slave trade, for example, but it still exploits cheap labor from former Eastern European and South Asian countries. The East India Company might have gone, but Britain's powerful corporations, replicating its model, bring goods and resources from former colonies.

The United States has repositioned its imperial portfolio and become what Daniel Immerwahr calls a "pointillist empire," where its widely strewn military bases enable it to imagine itself as world's guardian and guarantor.[35]

The tired argument that at least the British built the railways is no longer credible or maintainable anymore. As Priya Satia memorably put it, no historian would say that "yes, Hitler was horrible to the Jews, but, on the other hand, he built the autobahn!"[36]

Is there a sell-by date for postcolonialism? Most of the critical theories come with an expiry date. Just as with the liberation hermeneutic, the constant question that is being asked is whether postcolonial criticism will go out of fashion.

Provided that there is an ill-conceived capitalistic urge for growth and there are humans and their labor, along with anything that could be extracted from the earth and turned into a commodity, such as oil, copper, metal, mercury, or lithium, there will be colonialism. Insofar as there are righteous people who imagine that they have a divine calling to eradicate evil, there will be scope for postcolonial criticism. The belief that there is "a stronger race, a higher-grade race, a more worldly-wise race," as Winston Churchill said in defending the expropriation of Native Americans and Aboriginal Australians,[37] or as the former president of the United States, Donald Trump, thundered at the US assembly, "[I]f the righteous many do not confront the wicked few, then evil will triumph,"[38] there will be plenty of possibilities for postcolonial critics to act. There are colonial wars still going on, such as the recent invasion of Ukraine by Russia. To these potential conditions, one could add the scriptures, which provide sanctions and invest people with a special elected status and permit them to conquer and convert other peoples' lands and souls. While this goes on, there will be a great deal of work for postcolonial criticism.

Finally, we can be certain of two things. As long as empire-builders continue to solicit support from their scriptures for their imperial exploitations, there will be biblical scholars, especially those who have faced the heavy hand of colonialism, who will continue to correct and challenge, using readings contrary to the intentions of the text. Postcolonial criticism has the potential analytical mechanisms to grasp and guide the contemporary neocolonial condition of the world. Empire and its residual effects continue to have an impact on every dominion of the contemporary world.

There is a danger, too, in that we fight not the struggles of the present but those of the past. Like the narrator in Anna Burns's Booker Prize–winning novel *Milkman*, one of the enticements is to forgo everything and retreat into the "safety of the scroll and papyrus of earlier centuries."[39] This is one of the temptations of being a postcolonial critic. The future requires us to look at current concerns and refashion the structures of race, power, and technology into a more liberated relationship. Another persistent question is this: How do we defy being imprisoned in the imagination of others or constrained by the colonializers account of ourselves? In doing so, how do we avoid the being a collaborator in the West's agenda, or falling into a blatant nativism?

For too long, we, especially those from the former colonies, have been living with the West's imagination of ourselves, or, as Amitava Kumar, in his *Immigrant, Montana*, put it colorfully, as "a prisoner in the museum of someone's imagination."[40] The time has come, as a character in Madeline Thien's novel *Do Not Say We Have Nothing* says, for us to "take responsibility for our minds,"[41] a message at the core of postcolonial thinking.

Notes

1. For examples of how the Bible has been mobilized for right-wing causes, see Tony Keddie, *Republican Jesus: How the Right Has Rewritten the Gospels* (Oakland: University of California Press, 2020).
2. John Naughton, "Can you see Emperor Zuckerberg's New Clothes," *The Observer: The New Review*, April 17, 2016, 25.
3. Caroline Elkins, *Legacy of Violence: A History of the British Empire* (London: Bodley Head, 2022), 9.
4. Priyamvada Gopal, *Insurgent Empire: Anticolonial Resistance and British Dissent* (London: Verso, 2019), 7.
5. Foreword, Introduction, and Full recommendations. To see the full version go to Foreword, introduction, and full recommendations - GOV.UK (www.gov.uk).
6. Ngũgĩ wa Thiong'o, *Decolonizing the Mind: The Politics of Language in African Literature* (London: James Currey, 1986).
7. See P. R. Ramesh, "Decolonizing the Mind," *Open*, May 20, 2022.
8. G. Ernest Wright, *The Old Testament against its Environment*. Studies in Biblical Theology No. 2 (London: SCM Press, 1950), 13.
9. Wright, *The Old Testament*, 7.

10. David L. Duncan, *Constantine's Bible: Politics and the Making of the New Testament* (Minneapolis: Fortress Press, 2006), 121.
11. Roy W. Hoover, "How the Books of the New Testament were Chosen," *Bible Review* 9, no. 2 (1993): 44–47.
12. David Norton, *The King James Bible: A Short History from Tyndale to Today* (Cambridge: Cambridge University Press, 2011), 84.
13. Stephen K. Batalden, *Russian Bible Wars: Modern Scriptural Translation and Cultural Authority* (Cambridge: Cambridge University Press, 2013).
14. Susannah Heschel, "Theology as a Vision for Colonialism: From Supersessionism to Dejudaization of German Protestantism," in *Germany's Colonial Past*, edited by Eric Ames, Marcia Klotz, and Lora Wildenthal (Lincoln: University of Nebraska Press, 2005), 148.
15. Harvey K. McArthur, *The Quest through the Centuries: The Search for the Historical Jesus* (Philadelphia: Fortress Press, 1966), 86.
16. Daniel L. Pals, *The Victorian "Lives" of Jesus* (San Antonio: Trinity University Press, 1982), 71.
17. Bernard Lucas, *Christ for India. Being a Presentation of the Christian Message to the Religious Thought of India* (London: Macmillan, 1910), 181.
18. Bernard Lucas, *The Empire of Christ. Being a Study of the Missionary Enterprise in the Light of Modern Religious Thought* (London: Macmillan, 1907), 20.
19. Lucas, *The Empire of Christ*, 34.
20. Lucas, *Christ for India*, 204.
21. Lucas, *The Empire of Christ*, 140.
22. Lucas, *The Empire of Christ*, 151.
23. Richard Horsley, ed., *In the Shadow of Empire: Reclaiming the Bible as a History of Faithful Resistance* (Louisville: Westminster John Knox Press, 2008), 180.
24. Adolf Deissmann, *Light from the Ancient East: The New Testament Illustrated by Recently Discovered Texts of the Graeco-Roman World* (London: Hodder and Stoughton, 1910), 344.
25. Amitava Ghosh, *The Glass Palace* (New Delhi: Harper Collins, 2000), 438.
26. I owe this quote to Emma Smith, *Portable Magic: A History of Books and Their Readers* (London: Allen Lane, 2022), 17.
27. Frantz Fanon, *The Wretched of the Earth* (London: Penguin Books, 1967), 233.
28. Edward W. Said, *Reflections on Exile and other Essays* (Cambridge, MA: Harvard University Press, 2000), 146.
29. Pals, *The Victorian "Lives" of Jesus*, 148.
30. Marcus J. Borg, *Meeting Jesus Again for the First Time: The Historical Jesus and the Heart of Contemporary Faith* (San Francisco: Harper, 1994), 16.
31. Andrew Mein, "Biblical Scholarship at War, 1914–1918," in *The First World War and the Mobilization of Biblical Scholarship*, edited by Andrew Mein, Nathan MacDonald, and Matthew A Collins (London: T&T Clark, 2020), 6.
32. M. A. C. Warren, *Caesar: The Beloved Enemy: Three Studies in the Relation of Church and State*, The Reinecker Lectures at the Virginia Theological Seminary (London: SCM Press Ltd, 1955), 32.
33. Warren, *Caeser*, 94.
34. Stephen Neill, *Colonialism and Christian Missions* (London: Lutterworth Press, 1966), 424.
35. Daniel Immerwahr, *How to Hide an Empire: A Short History of the Greater United States* (London: Bodley Head, 2019).

36. Priya Satia, *Time's Monster: History, Conscience and Britain's Empire* (London: Allen Lane, 2020), 277.
37. Satia, *Times Monster*, 134.
38. Julain Borger, "Trump Stuns UN with threat to 'totally destroy' North Korea," *The Guardian* September 20, 2017, 1.
39. Anna Burns, *Milkman* (London: Faber and Faber, 2018), 113.
40. Amitava Kumar, *Immigrant, Montana* (London: Faber and Faber, 2017).
41. Madeline Thein, *Do Not Say We Have Nothing* (London: Granta, 2016), 135.

PART I

BIBLICAL EMPIRES IN THE HEBREW SCRIPTURES, INTER-TESTAMENTAL WRITINGS, THE NEW TESTAMENT, AND THE CHRISTIAN APOCRYPHA

CHAPTER 1

THE EGYPTIAN EMPIRE IN THE BIBLE

D. N. PREMNATH

Egypt as an Ideological Construct

Some broad statistical information may be of help in setting up the context for this discussion. The words "Egypt" (referring to the land) and "Egyptians" (referring to the people) occur about 740 times in the Hebrew Bible.[1] A significant portion of these occurrences appear in the Pentateuch. The largest group of references to Egypt in the Hebrew Bible (about 135) has to do with the Exodus.[2] Despite the preponderance of the references to Egypt, specific information concerning the various aspects of the Egyptian Empire or society is minimal. Most of them appear in the Joseph saga. Some toponyms, such as "land of Rameses" (Gen 47:11; Ex 12:37) and "Ōn" (Gen 41:45, 50), are mentioned. References to "the Nile" appear only in the pharaoh's dreams.[3] Other than references to some customs such as divination (Gen 44:5, 15), embalming (Gen 50:2–3), segregated eating practices (Gen 43:32), and adoption practices (Gen 40:12), not many instances of ethnographical data are mentioned.[4] Susanne Binder has drawn attention to Egyptian parallels from the New Kingdom period to details of the special honor conferred upon Joseph by the pharaoh in Genesis 41:41–43. The induction into a high office symbolized by the gift of a signet ring, linen, a gold chain, and a chariot ride are rooted in Egyptian tradition.[5] Despite the examples discussed so far, the nature of the references to Egypt in the Pentateuch, for the most part, lends support to F. V. Greifenhagen's contention that Egypt serves as an ideological map. He uses the notion of cognitive or mental maps from human geography.[6] Mental maps have a selective or tangential connection to the reality they seek to present. They are products of selective perception and representation, "which actually excludes, augments, distorts and schematizes."[7] Here Greifenhagen is drawing upon the works of Roger Downs and David Stea.[8] Cognitive maps reveal more about the concerns and situations of those who are producing the maps than the actual realities the maps seek to represent. The cognitive maps' main purpose is to construct and maintain identities that thereby provide a framework for preserving memories.⁹ References to Egypt in the Pentateuch similarly reveal less about the actual reality of Egypt and more about the ideological agenda of the producers of the text.

Greifenhagen's hypothesis is that the Pentateuch is primarily concerned about presenting the origins of biblical Israel. In this presentation, issues of identity are central. "Construction of identity proceeds via comparison with an 'other.' In the Pentateuch, it is Egypt that predominantly plays the role of the 'other' over against Israel."¹⁰ Scholars have long recognized the positive and negative aspects of the rhetoric about Egypt, especially in the Pentateuch. References to Egypt as "both a house of bondage and a place of refuge, a powerful ally and dangerous foe" contribute to this ambivalence.¹¹ Greifenhagen provides a detailed and insightful analysis of this dynamic. It is beyond the purview of this study to summarize various aspects of the ideological map in the Pentateuch or provide a full analysis of the topic in terms of the context, text, and redactional thrust of the final form of the Pentateuch. At the risk of simplifying, key points germane to the current study will be highlighted.

The ambivalent attitude toward Egypt raises some key questions: How does one explain the presence of opposing perspectives? What contexts can one postulate for divergent perspectives as well the overall agenda of producers of the text? In addressing these issues, particular attention will be given to Greifenhagen's analysis along with insights from a postcolonial perspective. For Greifenhagen, the broad master narrative of the Pentateuch as far as Israel's identity is that "biblical Israel has its roots in Mesopotamia."¹² Before the Israelites possess the Promised Land, there is the sojourn in Egypt. The nature of the sojourn, which is associated with disease, slavery, and, more importantly, loss of its identity, makes Egypt a dangerous, inhospitable place.¹³ This is the basis of the overwhelmingly negative portrayal of Egypt in the Pentateuch. Egypt plays the role of the "Other." The "us versus them" rhetoric is very well captured in Exodus 1:9–10: "He [the king] said to his people, 'Look, the Israelites are more numerous and more powerful than we. Come, let us deal shrewdly with them, or they will increase and, in the event of war join our enemies and fight against us and escape from the land." Through the king's speech, the narrator underscores the ethnic divide between Israel and Egypt.¹⁴ In another sense, the negative portrayal of Egypt has to do with Israel's experience of the socioeconomic and political aspects of life in Egypt in particular and Late Bronze Canaanite structures in general. One has to see the new Israel's identity not only in relation to the Exodus but also in relation to the formation of premonarchic Israel. The departure from Egypt signifies a rejection of its oppressive socioeconomic and political structures. The Moses movement preserves a vision of freedom, which indicts the existing oppressive structures. The vision for the new community in the premonarchic period has to be the opposite of the realities that they were part of and which they had to reject.

Even though the negative portrayal of Egypt is dominant in the Pentateuch, there is also "an alternative perspective in which Egypt is viewed positively as a place of refuge, of plenty and of enrichment, an alluring and attractive place."¹⁵ This is evident in the ancestral narratives. In the Abraham/Sarah cycle of narratives, Egypt is a place of plenty and survival. There is fear, deception, and danger but there is also enrichment.¹⁶ Egypt rarely figures in the Jacob/Rachel narratives. Most of the references to Egypt in Genesis appear in the Joseph cycle. Egypt is presented in a positive light as a place where Israel can multiply, gain landholdings, and prosper. The significance of Egypt is highlighted through the accounts of Joseph's rise to power (Gen 39–41), the move of Jacob and his sons to Egypt (Gen 45–47), Joseph's rule in Egypt (Gen 47:13–26), and the account of Jacob's death and burial (Gen 50:15–26). In the last section, there is an undermining of Egypt when Jacob insists that he should not be buried in Egypt. His wishes are fulfilled when his body is embalmed and taken back to Canaan for burial. It is striking that in the account of Joseph's rise to power, the Egyptianizing of Joseph is presented without any condemnation.[17] The Joseph tradition also has a softer take on Joseph's two sons who are born to an Egyptian wife. While the lineage of Ishmael has been rejected earlier (Gen 17:20–21), the problem of Joseph's sons is resolved by Jacob embracing them as "mine" (Gen 48:5). In the ancestral narratives, a fundamental concern is the safeguarding of the Mesopotamian lineage. Egypt, though a necessary diversion, poses a threat to the Mesopotamian lineage.[18] Egypt is a place from which one has to depart eventually.[19]

The positive and negative aspects of Egypt carry over into the book of Exodus, especially as the book opens. Egypt is a positive place for the Israelites because they greatly increased in number. Another positive aspect is the portrayal of Moses, which has parallels to the Joseph narratives. Joseph is an Israelite who assimilates into Egypt and ascends to a position of power in the pharaoh's court. Moses, a Hebrew by birth, becomes Egyptianized by being adopted by the pharaoh's daughter.[20] By virtue of their connections to Egypt, they are both "Israelite-Egyptian hybrid heroes."[21] In terms of the master narrative that Greifenhagen posits, the pro-Egyptian perspectives implicit in the stories of Joseph and Moses create a tension. A postcolonial perspective on hybridity may offer insights into this tension.

One particular aspect of postcolonial criticism is pertinent to the present study—that is, postcolonial criticism as a reading strategy. Some of the pioneers on postcolonialism, such as Edward Said and Gayatri Spivak, view it as a reading strategy; while others, such as Homi Bhabha, see it as a state or condition.[22] R. S. Sugirtharajah has done pioneering work on incorporating postcolonial criticism into biblical studies. He characterizes postcolonialism primarily as a contesting discourse fueled by resistance to oppressive, dominant thoughts and attitudes.[23] The purpose is to expose and challenge the link between ideas and power. Earlier versions of resistance discourse in postcolonialism were predicated on binary opposites: us–them, East–West, center–periphery, and colonizer–colonized. Sugirtharajah points out that there might be another alternative to the uncritical admiration of native values and outright rejection of all that is Western. In this connection, he brings out an important development in postcolonial thought—to find potential points of contact between the colonizer and the colonized while challenging colonialism. The alternative is "to integrate and forge a new perspective by critically and profitably syncretizing ingredients from both vernacular and metropolitan centres."[24] In the following discussion, it will be shown that the ambivalent attitude to Egypt prevalent in the Pentateuch is really an attempt to integrate and forge a new perspective. One such attempt is the portrayal of Joseph and Moses as Israelite-Egyptian hybrids.

The concept of hybridity merits some clarification because of its peculiar history. The metaphor has its origin in literary studies, where literature scholars first adopted the term "hybrid" to describe the mixing of textual elements such as genres, characterization, dialects, and perspectives. Mikhail Bakhtin introduced the concept of hybrid/hybridization to signify "the fusion of *two* utterances into one."[25] The result is what he calls *heteroglossia*, which "is *another's speech in another's language*, serving to express authorial intentions but in a refracted way."[26] He argued that such hybrid speech is a special type of the double-voicedness that is intended to serve two speakers at the same time—the direct intention of the character who is speaking and the refracted intention of the author. The double-voicedness of the hybrids is not meant to resolve because "the internally persuasive social languages stand in a dialogic and potentially subversive relationship to the narrator's discourse."[27] Postcolonial scholars co-opted the metaphor to the context of colonization, where hybridity became the result of political, linguistic, and cultural codependence of the colonizer and the colonized in a contact zone.[28] Lynda Walsh elaborates: "Hybrids formed whenever the colonizer uttered his/her language in the contact zone and whenever the colonized spoke or wrote in the colonial language."[29] With the adaptation of the term "hybridity" and its meaning, labels such as *métissage*, *mestizaje*, creolization, heterogeneity, syncretism, mediation, and double-consciousness began to emerge in literary as well as postcolonial studies.[30] At the same time, questions regarding the limitations of the concept also began to surface. Before taking stock of the limitations, listing a few positive aspects of the concept would be in order. Hybridity helped to break the impasse of either/or logic and to reveal that what may appear as either/or may, in fact, be both/and.[31] By allowing the colonizer and the colonized to share a contact zone, hybridity shifts the balance of power even if it is partial.[32] The inequality is not fully rectified but nonetheless it is addressed.

One of the criticisms is that hybridity might be an oversimplification of reality. It may be time to think of hybridity and hybridization as part of a larger process of "cultural polygenesis" and thus provide a way to stress the multiple origins of cultural identity.[33] In other words, it is important to understand how individual identities or cultures emerge out of multiple sources and how, in the process, identities and cultures transform one another.[34] The most serious objection to hybridity is that it is "only meaningful if it signified against 'pure' blood, culture, tradition, or nationality—all of which were imaginary."[35] Circling back to Greifenhagen's contention about the presence of a master narrative in the Pentateuch, is there such a thing as a master narrative pure and simple? Couldn't the master narrative itself be a product of cultural polygenesis? Limitations aside, the trajectory of Egypt as an ideological construct is clearly present in the Hebrew Bible.

Egyptian Activity in the Hebrew Bible

This section addresses references to Egyptian activity, some of which may be explicit but a few may be of a circumstantial nature. For the following discussion, it would be helpful to have a frame of reference for the history of the Egyptian Empire. One of the major challenges to the study of the Egyptian Empire is the lack of a comprehensive history. Egyptologists often cite an earlier attempt by Manetho, an Egyptian priest of the third century BCE, to write a comprehensive account. Unfortunately, Manetho's work has not survived in its entirety, but references to excerpts can be found in the work of later historians. One such reference point is the work of Flavius Josephus in the first century CE.[36]

In the modern era, scholars primarily trained in Semitic languages focus on studies of Egyptian culture and history. Methodologically, this has had some implications. The understanding of the Egyptian language was guided by the use of grammatical and morphological features of Semitic languages.[37] Any information gained with reference to ancient Egypt was often used to corroborate or illuminate the biblical accounts. This tendency, as one might expect, has had rewards as well as pitfalls. By the latter half of the twentieth century, however, Egyptology had evolved as a discipline in and of itself.[38] John Currid points to a curious tendency among present biblical scholars who are not convinced about the historical and cultural connections between Egypt and the Hebrew Bible.[39] Randall C. Bailey wonders if there is a connection between the lack of interest in Egypt and a tendency in cartography to represent Egypt as part of the ancient Near East/West Asia rather than Africa.[40] Whether this tendency is intentional or not, one has to be sensitive to the de-Africanization of Egypt and its ramifications for interpreting the Bible in African and African American contexts.[41]

For the purpose of situating the references to Egyptian activity in the Levant, the following chronological sequence of dynastic periods may be of help:[42] 3050–2656 BCE: Dynasties 1–2; 2686–2181 BCE: Dynasties 3–6 (Old Kingdom); 2181–2040 BCE: Dynasties 7–11 (First Intermediate Period); 2040–1782 BCE: Dynasties 12–13 (Middle Kingdom); 1782–1570 BCE: Dynasties 14–17 (Second Intermediate Period); 1570–1069 BCE: Dynasties 18–20 (New Kingdom); 1069–656 BCE: Dynasties 21–25 (Third Intermediate Period); and 656–332 BCE: Dynasties 26–31 (Late Period). In this sequence, it may be helpful to think of three phases marked by centralized regimes and creative cultural impact in the form of Old, Middle, and New Kingdoms. These highpoints were interspersed with periods of stagnation, decline, and transition often referred to as the First, Second, and Third Intermediate Periods.[43] The chronological sequence from the emergence of Israel in the late second millennium BCE to the destruction of Jerusalem in 587/585 BCE would be contemporaneous with the Egyptian Third Intermediate Period and the early part of the Late Period.[44] With the advent of knowledge concerning Egypt in the nineteenth century, there was interest in showing how the stories of Joseph, the Exodus, and Moses contain historical information validating the reliability of the biblical narratives.[45] Given the strides in scholarly approaches to the biblical narratives in past centuries, particularly with reference to the later redaction of the Pentateuch, it would be problematic to use them for historical reconstruction without a critical and interdisciplinary appraisal. Nonetheless, how does one explain the presence of Egyptian motifs and traditions in the Hebrew Bible, particularly the ancestral narratives in Genesis 12–50?

In studying Egyptian history, the Second Intermediate Period offers some intriguing information. A key development in this period was the occupation of the northeast Delta region by the Hyksos, a Semitic-speaking people.[46] The Hyksos domination seems to have been established through a gradual immigration, motivated by keen economic interests, rather than by a single sweeping invasion.[47] It is very likely that there were military confrontations when there was resistance. James K. Hoffmeier points to the presence of Semitic-speaking peoples in the region with whom the Hyksos shared a commonality as a possible reason for not needing to conquer them through military subjugation.[48] The Nile Valley had been an attractive settlement option for the Semites from western Asia long before the Hyksos occupation. With the support of epigraphic and archaeological data, Hoffmeier makes a case for the movement of people from the Levant to Egypt in times of drought and famine dating back to the end of the Old Kingdom and continuing through the Second Intermediate Period.[49] There has been a longstanding debate concerning the historicity as well as specific dates of ancestral narratives in Genesis. While these issues are outside the purview of this essay, it is intriguing to note that the circumstances prompting the migration of the ancestors to Egypt seem to fit the era between the end of the Middle Kingdom through the Second Intermediate Period.

The beginning of the Late Bronze Age saw the rise of the Egyptian Empire in the Levant. This coincides with the end of the Hyksos rule in Egypt.[50] It has been suggested that Thutmose I of the 18th Dynasty was the first pharaoh to become active in Syria-Palestine.[51] The main incentive for the pharaoh was to have control over the small feudal states in the Syria-Palestine region and thereby control the key trade routes—the Via Maris, which ran along the coastal strip, and the King's Highway through the Transjordanian plateau connecting Syria in the north and Arabia to the south. The Egyptian strategy was to achieve control by establishing a network of vassals with garrisons.[52] One such garrison town was Beth-Shean (Tel el-Hosn) in northern Israel, located between the Jordan Valley and the eastern end of the Jezreel Valley.[53] The excavators found rich material culture relating to the 19th and 20th dynasties in the form of Egyptian pottery, royal scarabs, cylinder seals, jewelry, clay figurines, dedicatory inscriptions, monuments, statues, and clay coffins.[54] Importantly, Egyptian sources from the 19th Dynasty also make a mention of Beth-Shean in the topographic lists of Sety I.[55] Much of the population who lived in Beth-Shean seem to have been Egyptian officials and military personnel. There is also indication that a Canaanite portion of the population worked alongside the Egyptians.[56]

Contacts between Egypt and Israel in the David-Solomonic era are mostly anecdotal. There are some curious episodes involving Egypt and Egyptians in the deuteronomistic history. From David's reign, we read about the rescue of an Egyptian from starvation in I Samuel 30:11–17 who later joins David's forces. In 2 Samuel 23:2–22 (also found in I Chr 11:23–24), the valor of Benaiah ben Jehoiada in fighting a spear-wielding Egyptian with his staff and killing him is recounted. 1 Kings 11:14–22 presents the story of Hadad, the Edomite heir who sought asylum in Egypt when David and Joab carried out a massacre in Edom. The pharaoh raised Hadad and married him off to his queen's sister. Upon hearing the news of David's death, Hadad returned to Edom to rebel against Solomon. Some of the details in the story—namely the gift of a house, food allowance, and land for cultivation provided to Hadad—have been attested as common practices from Egyptian sources.[57] A similar asylum story is associated with Jeroboam I when he fled to Egypt to escape Solomon's plot to kill him (1 Kgs 11:40). The biblical account mentions King Shishak of Egypt who is identified as Sheshonq I of the 22nd Dynasty.[58]

Biblical narratives pertaining to Solomon seem to indicate contacts with Egypt and other territories. According to 1 Kings 3:1, Solomon was married to the daughter of an Egyptian pharaoh. Curiously, both the pharaoh and his daughter are unnamed. However, this very brief reference is important for a couple of reasons. While providing an alternative to costly warfare, the diplomatic marriage of Solomon to the pharaoh's daughter in fact secured Egypt as an ally of Israel. In addition, it is conceivable that the officials in the entourage of the Egyptian princess formed the core of a pro-Egyptian faction in Judah that had a lasting sphere of influence in the Judean court until the Exile.[59] Whether one sees the pro-Egyptian faction as a legacy of Solomon's diplomatic foreign alliance or a later dynamic of the sixth-century BCE Judean court remains an open question. In 1 Kings 9:16, we learn that Solomon received Gezer as a wedding gift from the pharaoh. Many questions abound as to the motive behind the gift as well as the timing. Abraham Malamat proposed that Solomon's marriage to the daughter of the pharaoh—most likely Siamun of the 21st Dynasty—took place early in Solomon's reign around 967/966 BCE.[60] Malamat also argues that the pharaoh did not set out to conquer Gezer only to give it away later as a gift. His original intent was to campaign against Jerusalem; but when the pharaoh realized that Solomon had consolidated his power internally, he opted for a diplomatic course by offering Gezer as a gift.[61] What did the pharaoh get in return for this concession? Malamat suggests a couple of possibilities.[62] One, the pharaoh might have sought the help of Solomon in neutralizing the potential threat in Philistia. Another possibility was to reap some benefit from Solomon's international trade. This raises questions about the import of horses from "Egypt" and Que referred to in I Kings 10:28–29 (with parallels in 2 Chr 1:16–17 and 9:28). Egypt (*Miṣrāim*) as a possible source of horse trade has been challenged and, consequently, the text has been emended to *Muṣri*, which would then locate both places in the north.[63] Yutaka Ikeda had argued that Solomon's horse trade was carried out with the help of the king of Hamath. In support of this, Ikeda interprets the reference to "the store-cities of Hamath" (2 Chr 8:3–4) to mean a strategic base that served not only as a relay station in the trade between Anatolia and Israel but also as a place where horses were reared and kept until they were ready for use.[64] Interestingly, 2 Chronicles 8:6 mentions "towns for his chariots and towns for his cavalry." Malamat points out that Solomon's undertaking of the Red Sea trade (1 Kgs 9:26–29; 10:11–12, 22), as well as his horse trading with Muṣri and Que, was to obtain the items straight from the sources thereby bypassing the Egyptian role.[65] This would explain Siamun's concession of Gezer to gain a share in Solomon's commercial ventures.

The advent of the 22nd Dynasty in Egypt with the rule of Sheshonq I brought a shift in Egyptian foreign policy by way of an aggressive approach to gain control over Upper and Lower Egypt as well as Nubia.[66] Sheshonq also had designs to reestablish Egyptian hegemony over Palestine. Two biblical accounts lend support to this. Toward the second half of his reign, Solomon placed Jeroboam I in charge of the corvée operation in the north. Jeroboam was able to build his power base by taking advantage of the resentment and oppression of the northern tribes. Following his unsuccessful rebellion against Solomon, Jeroboam fled to Egypt and sought asylum with Sheshonq. From Jeroboam's perspective, seeking Sheshonq's help bolstered his chances of success. From Sheshonq's perspective, supporting Jeroboam would destabilize Solomon's rule by creating unrest in the north.[67] This, in turn, would prepare the ground for the Egyptian campaign into Palestine during Rehoboam's reign.

Sheshonq's campaign into Palestine is documented not only in the Bible (1 Kgs 14:25; 2 Chr 12:2) but also in the pharaoh's victory relief at Karnak temple. Additionally, a fragment of a large Egyptian stele bearing the name of Sheshonq was found at Megiddo. The biblical accounts make the point that Sheshonq came up against Jerusalem. However, in the list of place names found at the Karnak temple inscription, there is no mention of Jerusalem. Instead, it contains many place names in the northern kingdom along with sites in the Negev region.[68] In piecing together the epigraphic and archaeological data, Bernd Schipper makes the important point that the aim of Sheshonq's campaign was to gain control over trade routes along the coastal plain and southern Negev as well as strategic cities along the routes.[69]

The ascendance of the Assyrian Empire in the ninth and eighth centuries BCE signaled a shift in the international power politics of the Fertile Crescent. The westward expansion of the Assyrians in the ninth century primarily focused on northern Syria and the Palestine region. Judah was not involved in the anti-Assyrian coalitions of the ninth century. The Egyptians were not interested in getting involved in this conflict to keep the buffer zone (Judah) conflict-free.[70] However, this scenario changed in the eighth century when the Assyrians began to penetrate toward the south. None of the Egyptian rulers of this time was powerful enough to undertake a military confrontation with Assyria.

The last king of northern Israel, Hoshea, who had been a vassal of Assyria, sought Egypt's help. 2 Kings 17:4 reports in a cryptic fashion that "the king of Assyria found treachery in Hoshea; for he had sent messengers to King So of Egypt." The Hebrew word *Sô'* is taken as an abbreviation for the Egyptian name Osorkon,[71] presumably Osorkon IV of the Bubastis-Tanis Territories.[72] In the last quarter of the eighth century BCE, the Cushite kings of the 25th Dynasty began to unite and strengthen Egypt. The control over smaller local powers led them to initiate an aggressive foreign policy toward Syria-Palestine.[73]

Some of the eighth-century prophetic oracles from the Hebrew Bible give voice to concerns about reliance on foreign powers. Specific references include: "Ephraim has become like a dove, silly and without sense; they call upon Egypt, they go to Assyria (Hosea 7:11)." "They make a treaty with Assyria but oil is carried to Egypt (Hosea 12:1c)." These oracles refer to to Hoshea initially paying tribute to Assyria but later changing his allegiance to seek help from Egypt. Hosea's cryptic reference also captures how local agricultural specialties such as wine and olive oil were exported in exchange for strategic military items and support. Oracles from Isaiah (30:1–5 and 31:1–3) are critical of the emissaries sent to Egypt to secure support for the anti-Assyrian coalition. This may be a reference to the coalition headed by Hezekiah of Judah comprising Byblos, Sidon, Ashkelon, Ekron, Ammon, Edom, and Moab.[74] The wording of the Isaianic passages implies the presence of a pro-Egyptian group in Judah seeking military support from Egypt. Additionally, Isaiah 18:1–2 presents a description of the Cushite land and its messengers who were sent to the Judean court. The passages also mention the delegation from Assyria headed by Rabshakeh who chides Judah for its reliance on Egypt (Isa 36:6; 2 Kgs 18:21). However, there is no corroboration from the biblical and Assyrian sources that the Egyptians actually sent troops to protect Jerusalem in 701 BCE.

With the steady decline of the Assyrian Empire beginning with 640 BCE, the Egyptians began asserting their influence in the southern Levant. Bernd Schipper cites epigraphic sources in support of Egyptian hegemony and its organization of the territories under its control; these include the Serapeum Stele from the reign of Psammetichus I; the Statue of the Messenger Pediese; and the Hebrew-Egyptian ostraca from Meṣad Hashavyahu, Arad, and Tell el-Qudeirat.[75] The Egyptian intervention in Judean politics is recounted in 2 Kings 23. On his way to meet the king of Assyria, Pharaoh Necho II is encountered by his vassal Josiah. The biblical account simply says: "King Josiah went to meet him; but when Pharaoh Necho met him at Megiddo, he killed him" (2 Kgs 23:29b). When the people of Jerusalem installed Jehoahaz as Josiah's successor, Necho prevented him from ruling and imprisoned him in Riblah in the land of Hamath and imposed a special tax on Judah (2 Kgs 23:33). Then Necho appointed Eliakim, another son of Josiah, to be the king of Judah and changed his name to Jehoiakim (2 Kgs 23:34). The biblical account also includes information about the devastating effect of the pharaoh's demands in gold and silver that had to be raised from the people of Judah through taxation (2 Kgs 23:35). Although the Egyptian hegemony lasted for a relatively short period, it had given rise to a pro-Egyptian party within Judah, which fled to Egypt when the Babylonians began establishing their control in Judah (Jer 43:8–44: 30).

Egyptian Influence

This section briefly outlines the ways in which Egyptian influence had an impact on various aspects of Israelite society. The following areas will be touched upon: political administration, economic exchange, religious ideas, literary aspects, and iconography.

Political Administration

With regard to political administration, two areas in particular have been studied to discern an Egyptian influence: civil administrative structures and taxation systems.

However, scholars have been cautious in positing an explicit borrowing of the Egyptian models and structures. The starting point for this discussion is a list of officials mentioned in connection with the reigns of David and Solomon. Constraints of space limit this discussion to salient points only. There are two lists of officials from the time of David (2 Sam 8:15–18 with a parallel account in 1 Chr 18:14–17 and 2 Sam 20:23–26) and one list from Solomon (1 Kgs 4:1–6). The earlier list from David references two titles: the *sôpher* (scribe or royal secretary) and the *mazkîr* (royal herald). The scribal office is seen as analogous to the Egyptian scribal title *sš š'.t* (referring to the royal letter-writer of the pharaoh).[76] The Egyptian parallel to *mazkîr* is seen in the Egyptian office of *wḥm. w* (royal herald).[77] The second list from David adds the new office of *'al hammas* (Overseer of Corvée [forced labor]). Three more new offices are introduced in Solomon's list: *'al hanniṣṣābîm* (Overseer of Prefects/Governors); *rē'eh hammelek* (royal counselor along the lines of a *consigliere*); and *'al habbayit* (Overseer of the Royal Estate). With respect to the Hebrew royal counselor, Tryggve Mettinger suggests that the Egyptian *rḫ. nśw.t* ("King's acquaintance") might be a parallel.[78] The Canaanite variation of this title, *ruḫi šarri*, appears in the Amarna letters.[79]

The office of the Overseer of Prefects/Governors appears only in 1 Kings 4:5. The detailed list of the Prefects in verses 7–19 gives an insight into the administrative division of the territory under Solomon. Whether or not Solomon retained the traditional tribal boundaries had been a subject of debate. W. F. Albright, defending Albrecht Alt's analysis, argued that the reorganization of the territory by Solomon followed "the old tribal divisions as closely as the new conditions established by David's conquests and the shifting of trade centres allowed, so we may safely assume that David organized his fiscal system on a tribal basis."[80] G. Ernest Wright took the opposite point of view and stated that, as a result of the radical change brought about by David and Solomon in the political, religious, and economic life of Israel, the tribal system was at an end. In its place were "administrative provinces, ruled by *niṣṣābîm* (prefects) who were appointed by and were responsible solely to the royal administration in Jerusalem."[81] Mettinger takes a middle position that "a shift from the tribal system can be noted only in some special cases."[82] The realigning of the traditional tribal boundaries by Solomon was geared toward weakening the traditional tribal alliances and creating new allegiances that could serve as a basis for political administration, military conscription, and, most importantly, ensuring a steady flow of provisions to the royal household. Rather than seeing specific offices and titles as having been influenced by the Egyptian prototypes, D. B. Redford draws attention to the effective taxation system, which was put in place by Solomon.[83] Redford points to the parallels in the detailed description of the annual levy system by Sheshonq I. On the stele found in Herakleopolis, mention is made of how Sheshonq restored the daily ox offering in the temple of Arsaphes and decreed a levy on the towns and villages of Herakleopolis.[84]

The Egyptian administrative system had a well-developed structure of taxation as may be seen in the varied vocabulary for tax and taxation.[85] The beneficiaries of the proceeds of the annual levy were temples, garrison posts, and foreign settlements under royal authority; workers in quarries or construction sites; and royal residences and harems.[86]

The parallels between Sheshonq's and Solomon's provisioning systems include division of the territory into twelve districts, each district furnishing provisions for one month of the year; and use of the levy to stock garrison posts (1 Kgs 5:8–9).[87]

Scholars have been either dismissive or cautious about acknowledging the direct influence of the Egyptian prototypes on Israelite structures and practices. One of the arguments put forward is that the prototypes might have come through Canaanite adaptations. However, two things offer support for the influence of the Egyptian prototypes. One factor is Egypt's longstanding presence and involvement in the Levant and its legacy thereof; the presence of Egyptian garrisons in Beth-Shean is a case in point. Second, the use of hieratic numerals as symbols in Israel offers strong evidence for the Egyptian prototypes in Israelite administration. The hieratic numerals were an outgrowth of the hieroglyphic symbols for numbers. It was a system of measurement based on multiples of ten rounded off to the higher power. Aharoni draws attention to the use of hieratic numerals in ostraca and shekel weights in Samaria, Arad, Lachish, Wadi Muraba'at, and Meṣad Hashavyahu.[88] In this connection it is worth noting one of the earlier attempts at recognizing the use of hieratic numerals in the Gezer Calendar by J. B. Segal. He argued that the symbol used after the word *yrḥ* in lines 1, 2, and 6 and after *qṣr* in line 5 of the Gezer inscription is the symbol for the Egyptian numeral 2.[89] Segal also points to the archaeological evidence in support of the Egyptian influence in Gezer.[90]

The representation of the system of weights also reflects Egyptian influence. For instance, of the dome-shaped weights found at Ophel, the single big group was the 8-shekel weight.[91] The average mass of the 8- shekel weight was approximately equivalent to the mass of one Egyptian *deben*. The formula of *8 shekels = 1 deben* would have been a useful equation in foreign exchange with Egyptians.[92] Accordingly, the hieratic numerals for 4-, 8-, 16-, and 24-shekel weights actually corresponded to 5, 10, 20, and 30 in Egyptian parlance. The discrepancy has been explained based on the Egyptian *qebet* value to which they correspond. Each Egyptian *deben* consisted of 10 *qebet*.[93] This can be further corroborated by the reference to "four shekels of silver" in the Meṣad Hashavyahu ostracon, which is followed by the two signs found on the stone weights worth the value of five.[94]

Economic Exchange

Some aspects of the discussion under political administration apply here as well. The nature and function of the taxation setup and system of weights interface with the political apparatus and economic exchange. In both Egypt and Israel, the state was at the heart of economic and political developments. By way of introducing an institutional economic perspective on the highland kingdoms of the southern Levant, Daniel Master identifies three overlapping contexts of exchange: the monarchy, the market, and the trade route.[95] The same personnel or objects could exist in all three contexts but the rationale and rules of participation may vary.[96] Within each context, the goal of the participants was to maximize the opportunities to get richer.[97]

The power of the monarchy was mediated through its governing structures symbolized particularly by the palace and the temple. The power of the palace was based on its role as an economic and political institution, particularly in its control of strategic resources such as metals, and its oversight of taxation and corvée Through diplomatic and economic connections, the ruling elite created a hierarchical order and maintained it by "carefully calibrated rhetoric, trade, gift exchanges, royal marriages, and warfare."[98] While the temple was a key organization in Egypt and Mesopotamia, in ancient Israel and Judah the "temple economy was neither extensive nor exclusive."[99] However, it definitely had an economic role in collecting the surplus for the monarchy. As the prescription in Deuteronomy 16:16 indicates, three times a year all the males should appear in the place the Lord chooses and that they should not come empty-handed. Deuteronomy 14:28 reminds every Israelite about the obligation of the tithe of their produce. This was an effective way of funneling the surplus into the royal coffers.[100]

Markets are as much a process as physical locations. As they were primarily places of exchange, it is hard to find archaeological traces of markets.[101] It is conceivable that there were permanent markets or trading centers under the aegis of palaces or temples. Hence, it makes sense to think in terms of a system of tiered markets in which some catered to the needs of local consumers and others provided space for traders of the caravans.[102] This brings into focus the part played by trade routes in ancient trade and commerce. In the Levant, two longstanding exchange systems played a critical role in transporting goods: ships that brought goods from Phoenicia across the Mediterranean; and the camel caravans that brought goods from the Arabian Peninsula across the desert.[103] For the monarchy, the control and protection of the flow of goods from the East and the West was a priority. Consequently, tolls and taxes from the caravan trade constituted a significant source of revenue for the monarchy. The revenue was used for ensuring the status of the monarch, beautification of the capital, fortification of defense systems, maintaining the standing army and chariots, hiring mercenary forces, giving gifts to important neighbors, patrolling the travel routes, and securing assistance from superpowers such as Egypt.[104] In a fundamental sense, the trade routes linked the palace and the trading caravans. These routes opened alternative vistas to the domestic markets for acquiring riches. Hence, kingdoms of antiquity maintained and monopolized interregional and international trade. Mention has already been made of the Egyptian incursion into the southern Levant in the tenth century BCE for the purpose of controlling the trading routes and important cities. Although the biblical accounts credit Solomon with several trading ventures, it was not until the first half of the eighth century BCE that Israel and Judah were able to control the area from Hamath to the Sea of ʿArabah (2 Kgs 14:25).

The economic environment in Egypt was associated with major achievements such as pyramids, palaces, temples, conquests, and conspicuous wealth.[105] All of these required a basic skill: securing and administering resources. The interesting feature about this is that while the basic purpose was to generate maximum benefit for the elite, in the process the benefit was spread in a small way to a wider population.[106] This was accomplished through taxation that brought in resources by way of grain, which was then redistributed to the population engaged in state labor. The state-administered, redistributive aspect of the Egyptian economy has been well documented for various periods.[107] David Warburton points to a unique aspect of the Egyptian economy: "Given the propensity for building tombs and temples, the economy had an outlet for projects which guaranteed that the government could invest in activities for which there was 'infinitely elastic demand.'"[108] With the penchant for temples, tombs, and all the storage items therein, there was no risk of saturating the demand of the market. The demand for royal tombs was infinite as they kept expanding or building new ones. The more goods were moved into the tombs, the better it was for the economy.[109] One cannot overlook the burden on the poor peasants who produced the surplus and provided the labor. However, the reduction of agricultural underemployment is noteworthy.[110] As Warburton says, "The Egyptian state increased employment by taxation and investment."[111] Warburton clarifies that the study of the Egyptian economy requires an unconventional approach because it is based on the grain standard and not the gold standard assumed by many of the modern economic approaches.[112] In contrast, the Israelite economy might offer another scenario. That Solomon's economic policies pushed the kingdom to the brink of disaster does not reflect a favorable influence from the Egyptian model. This ad hoc conclusion needs a future study in depth.

Religious Ideas

Space constraints permit only offering some key highlights concerning various features of the Egyptian religious sphere. Most aspects of Egyptian religion are tied to nature and observation of the universe. Prominent were "the love of sunlight, the solar cycle and the comfort brought by the regular rhythms of nature."[113] In a particular way, the agricultural cycle tied to the ebb and flow of the Nile was influential. Images drawn from natural phenomena were often used to explain incomprehensible cosmic phenomena. For instance, the movement of the sun was explained as a celestial boat ride or the flight of a scarab beetle.[114] Egyptians thought of life after death as a mirror image of life on earth with same material requirements and desires.[115]

Given the preoccupation with nature, it is not surprising that there was an interest in the origin of creation. Biblical treatments of the origins in Genesis have often held up the Mesopotamian template, particularly from *Enuma Elish*, as the standard. James Atwell argues for an Egyptian background for the first creation story (Gen 1:1–2:4a).[116] He highlights features such as how the rising of the sun coaxes the natural order to come to life; how the flowers open, birds fly, and fish dart in the river; and how humans go to work as darkness is driven out.[117] Atwell also sees a parallel to the *rûaḥ 'ĕlōhîm* (Spirit/wind of God) in the description of Amun as breath or wind, the dynamic principle of existence.[118] Psalm 104 offers a further source for reflecting on the creation motif. The specific parallels between Psalm 104 and Akenhaten's *Hymn to Aten* have long been recognized. James K. Hoffmeier identifies some key theological themes in the short and great versions of the Aten hymns: Aten as the living, life-giving deity; Aten as the universal creator of heaven and earth, all lands, rivers, seas, people, animals, and vegetation; the manifestation of Aten's power daily in the movement of the sun; Aten alone is God; and Aten as transcendent yet accessible in the way he nourishes and sustains creation in all its forms.[119] In a broad sense, the wisdom tradition's fascination with the creation theme is given a local manifestation through mythology and cultic celebration as reflected in Psalm 104, which helps in understanding the inspiration and motivation behind the Genesis narrative.[120]

A related idea to the Egyptian theme of creation is the concept of *Maat/Maet* representing the vision of order in the universe and its relationship to the natural world.[121] *Maat* is presented as both a concept and a goddess. In the creation account from *The Coffin Texts* from the Middle Kingdom, *Atum* is the primary spirit, *Shu* is life, and *Tefnut* is the world order. *Tefnut* is later identified with *Maat*.[122] The creation process is repeated every morning when the sun comes up. According to another Egyptian cosmogony, *Re*, the sun god, overcomes the power of chaos on the primeval hill and institutes *Maat*, the world order, which is absolute and eternal.[123] The concept of *Maat* seems to have been the core of the Egyptian understanding of justice. The basic understanding was that the order in natural phenomena, which was established at the time of creation, is manifested in society as justice. The original meaning of the term *Maat* has a sense of straightness or evenness.[124] In this connection, it is worth noting some symbolic representations of the goddess *Maat*.[125] She is regularly pictured standing on the front part of the hull of the sun-ship accompanying *Re* on his course across the sky. Additionally, a small figurine of *Maat* was lifted up by the priest at the close of the temple service.[126] This act reiterated the fact that the order and justice once established at the time of creation has been established once again. Apart from being an assurance to the worshippers, this act was also an assurance to the gods that the order would be intact. In the Egyptian conception, this is the response the gods expected rather than material offerings. In an ethical sense, *Maat* was the task that humans set for themselves. There have been attempts to interpret the Hebrew term ṣedāqā (righteousness) with similar import.[127] One could see here a connection to the Israelite wisdom thinking. The principle of retributive justice is based on the correlation between cause and effect, the moral choices one makes, and the consequences one faces.

The custom of anointing the Hebrew rulers might have an Egyptian origin. While anointing was not part of the coronation ceremonies of rulers in Egypt, it was part of the ritual of appointing officials and vassals.[128] Roland de Vaux made the argument long ago that the installation of the vassals in Syria-Palestine by Egyptian rulers was symbolically represented through anointing.[129] Citing the reference in *Amarna Letter 51*, Ronald Williams suggests that the Israelites adopted this practice with the meaning that the royal ruler was a vassal of Yahweh, just as officials in Syria-Palestine were vassals of the Egyptian emperor.[130] Stephen Thompson, on the basis of some epigraphic material, concludes that there is no evidence for the practice of anointing in Egypt and that the reference in the *Amarna Letter* 51 might be a practice already in vogue in Syria-Palestine and not necessarily introduced by the Egyptians.[131]

Literary Aspects

In this section, the following categories will be briefly highlighted: loan words and phrases, genres, and literary connections. Building on the earlier works of German scholars in the late nineteenth and early twentieth centuries,[132] Thomas Lambdin compiled a catalogue of Egyptian loan words in Hebrew.[133] Words with clear connections to the Egyptian language are distributed in the realm of manufacturing, garment, scribal implements, measures, traded goods, precious stones, and societal classes.[134] The influence of Egyptian idioms is seen in phrases such as "eternal home," "wall of bronze," "broken of arm," "way of the living," "tree of life," and "putting face between knees."[135]

The international character of the wisdom genre has been widely recognized. The basic approach to life's mysteries, the human predicament, and the universe in which humans live have prompted societies from time immemorial to evolve a code of conduct to cope with life and its mysteries. One finds these perspectives on life in any society, whether it is called "wisdom" or referred to by some other name. While Israelite wisdom has its own particularities, scholars have found parallels between Egyptian teachings and biblical wisdom both in idiom and context. Formulae such as "If (you are a . . .)," "better is . . . than"; the format of the conversation between father and son; and motifs such as typical fool, ideal person, and ear as a receptacle of instruction are found in both literatures.[136] The collection of sayings in Proverbs 22:17–23:14 bears a remarkable resemblance to the *Wisdom of Amenemope*. The emphasis on ethical behavior and personal piety is a common thread in both.[137] In more recent years, Nili Shupak has shown how the image of the evil woman and the good woman from the Egyptian *Instruction of Ptahhotep, the Instruction of Any, Ankhsheshonqy*, and *Hardjedef B:IV* provide some examples of influence on the figures of the foreign/strange woman and the wife of one's youth in Proverbs 1–9.[138]

Another genre having discernible Egyptian influence is love poetry. Michael Fox's work on the Song of Songs drew attention to the Egyptian influence particularly in the use of the dialogic structure of love poetry, praise of the beloved, and creating a world through the words of the characters.[139] In view of the late date generally assigned to the Song of Songs, explaining direct Egyptian influence becomes problematic. Hence, Hagedorn proposes the Ptolemaic period as a possible contender in which the author(s) of the Song of Songs could have been familiar with both Egyptian and Greek poetry.[140]

The literary corpus in terms of hymnology is illustrated in the parallels to the *Hymn of Aten* in Psalm 104 as mentioned earlier. Redford points to some Egyptian compositions in the 19th and 20th Dynasties that are similar to the biblical Penitential psalms. Many of the Egyptian compositions are preserved on stelae with a formulaic structure consisting of an appeal to a god, description of the illness, confession of sin, and a vow to testify to the god's saving power.[141]

Iconography

The Egyptian influence was mediated not only through literary compositions but also through iconography. The Canaanites, the Phoenicians, and the Israelites to a lesser extent made use of the rich iconography of Egypt. Of particular interest are "solar images associated with kingship, including the winged solar disk, the winged cobra, the eye of Horus and the falcon."[142] Among the cultic objects found at Beth-Shean, an Egyptian garrison town, were faience amulets depicting Egyptian deities, cobra figurines, goose/duck heads, and vessels with animal-shaped spouts. This demonstrates the influence of Egyptian iconography on locally produced objects.[143]

The foregoing exploration is an attempt to provide a window into the complex and multi-dimensional aspects of the interaction between Egypt and Israel. For several millennia, Egypt was a strong presence in the political, economic, and cultural landscape of western Asia. As a result, it was inevitable that there was exchange of ideas, practices, and traditions. Although it is difficult to pinpoint the links and specify the nature and extent of Egyptian influences, enough vestiges remain to bear witness to the exchange.

Notes

1. C. B. Copher, "Egypt and Ethiopia in the Old Testament," *Journal of African Civilizations* 6, no. 2 (1984): 163.
2. Copher, "Egypt and Ethiopia in the Old Testament," 164.
3. F. V. Greifenhagen, *Egypt on the Pentateuch's Ideological Map: Constructing Biblical Israel's Identity*, ed. D. J. A. Clines and Philip Davies, JSOT Supplement Series 361 (London: Sheffield Academic Press, 2002), 44.
4. Greifenhagen, *Egypt on the Pentateuch's Ideological Map*, 38.
5. Susanne Binder, "Joseph's Rewarding and Investiture (Genesis 41:41–43) and the Gold of Honour in New Kingdom Egypt," in *Egypt, Canaan and Israel: History, Imperialism and Literature*, ed. Shay Bar, Dan'el Kahn, and J. J. Shirley, proceedings of a Conference at the University of Haifa, May 3–7, 2009 (Leiden: Brill, 2011), 44–64.
6. Greifenhagen, *Egypt on the Pentateuch's Ideological Map*, 7.
7. Greifenhagen, *Egypt on the Pentateuch's Ideological Map*, 7.
8. Roger M. Downs and David Stea, eds., *Image and Environment: Cognitive Mapping and Spatial Behavior* (Chicago: Aldine, 1973); Roger M. Downs and David Stea, eds., *Maps in Minds: Reflections on Cognitive Mapping* (New York: Harper & Row, 1977).
9. Greifenhagen, *Egypt on the Pentateuch's Ideological Map*, 7–8.
10. Greifenhagen, *Egypt on the Pentateuch's Ideological Map*, 22.
11. Carolyn Higginbotham, "Egypt and the Bible," in *The New Interpreter's Dictionary of the Bible*, ed. Katherine Sakenfeld, vol. 2 (Nashville, TN: Abingdon, 2006–2009), 224.
12. Greifenhagen, *Egypt on the Pentateuch's Ideological Map*, 10.
13. Greifenhagen, *Egypt on the Pentateuch's Ideological Map*, 260.
14. Greifenhagen, *Egypt on the Pentateuch's Ideological Map*, 52.
15. Greifenhagen, *Egypt on the Pentateuch's Ideological Map*, 261.

16. Greifenhagen, *Egypt on the Pentateuch's Ideological Map*, 29.
17. Greifenhagen, *Egypt on the Pentateuch's Ideological Map*, 37.
18. Greifenhagen, *Egypt on the Pentateuch's Ideological Map*, 33.
19. Greifenhagen, *Egypt on the Pentateuch's Ideological Map*, 53.
20. James Nohrnberg, "Moses," in *Images of Man and God: Old Testament Short Stories in Literary Focus*, ed. B. O. Long, Bible and Literature 1 (Sheffield: Almond Press, 1981), 37–39.
21. Greifenhagen, *Egypt on the Pentateuch's Ideological Map*, 265.
22. R. S. Sugirtharajah, "A Postcolonial Exploration of Collusion and Construction in Biblical Interpretation," in *The Postcolonial Bible*, ed. R. S. Sugirtharajah (Sheffield: Sheffield Academic Press, 1998), 93, 91–116.
23. Sugirtharajah, "A Postcolonial Exploration," 93.
24. Sugirtharajah, "A Postcolonial Exploration," 94.
25. Mikhail M. Bakhtin, *Dialogic Imagination: Four Essays*, ed. Michael Holquist and trans. Caryl Emerson and Michael Holquist (Austin: University of Texas Press, 1981), 361.
26. Bakhtin, *Dialogic Imagination*, 324.
27. Lynda Walsh, "Accountability: Towards a Definition of Hybridity for Scholars of Transnational Rhetorics," *Rhetorica: A Journal of the History of Rhetoric* 30, no. 4:(2012): 394.
28. Mary L. Pratt, "Arts of the Contact Zone," *Profession* (1991): 34.
29. Walsh, "Accountability," 395.
30. Walsh, "Accountability," 396.
31. Cyrus R. K. Patell, "Comparative American Studies: Hybridity and Beyond," *America Literary History* 11, no. 1(1999): 177.
32. Patell, "Comparative American Studies," 177.
33. Patell, "Comparative American Studies," 178.
34. Patell, "Comparative American Studies," 179.
35. Walsh, "Accountability," 396.
36. Donald B. Redford, *Egypt, Canaan, and Israel in Ancient Times* (Princeton, NJ: Princeton University Press, 1992), 98.
37. Higginbotham, "Egypt and the Bible," 225.
38. Higginbotham, "Egypt and the Bible," 225.
39. John Currid, *Ancient Egypt and the Old Testament* (Grand Rapids, MI: Baker Books, 1997), 8–9.
40. Randall C. Bailey, "Beyond Identification: The Use of Africans in Old Testament Poetry and Narrative," in *Stony the Road We Trod: African American Biblical Interpretation*, ed. Cain H. Felder (Minneapolis: Fortress Press, 1991), 165. The present author is indebted to Tewoldemedhin Habtu's essay for raising this issue: Habtu, "The Images of Egypt in the Old Testament: Reflections on African Hermeneutics," in *Interpreting the Old Testament in Africa: Papers from the International Symposium on Africa and the Old Testament in Nairobi, October 1999*, ed. Mary Getui (Bern, Switzerland: Peter Lang, 2012), 56–57.
41. Bailey, "Beyond Identification."
42. Douglas J. Brewer and Emily Teeter, *Egypt and the Egyptians*, 2nd ed. (Cambridge, UK: Cambridge University Press, 2007), 30–59.
43. William Y. Adams, "The First Colonial Empire," in *Expanding Empires: Cultural Interaction and Exchange in World Societies from Ancient to Early Modern Times*, ed. Wendy F. Kasinec and Michael A. Polushin, The World Beat Series No. 2 (Wilmington, DE: Scholarly Resource Books, 2002), 14.

44. Bernd U. Schipper, "Egypt and Israel: The Ways of Cultural Contacts in the Late Bronze Age and Iron Age (20th–26th Dynasty)," *Journal of Ancient Egyptian Interconnections* 4, no. 3 (2012): 31.
45. Schipper, "Egypt and Israel," 30.
46. Redford, *Egypt, Canaan, and Israel*, 98; also Brewer and Teeter, *Egypt and the Egyptians*, 44–45.
47. Brewer and Teeter, *Egypt and the Egyptians*, 45.
48. James K. Hoffmeier, *Israel in Egypt: The Evidence for the Authenticity of the Exodus Tradition* (Oxford: Oxford University Press, 1997), 65.
49. Hoffmeier, *Israel in Egypt*, 54–68.
50. James Weinstein, "The Egyptian Empire in Palestine: A Reassessment," *BASOR* 241 (1981): 1.
51. Weinstein, "Egyptian Empire in Palestine," 31.
52. Weinstein, "Egyptian Empire in Palestine," 31.
53. Amihai Mazar, "The Egyptian Garrison Town at Beth-Shean," in *Egypt, Canaan and Israel: History, Imperialism and Literature*, proceedings of a Conference at the University of Haifa, May 3–7, 2009, ed. Shay Bar, Dan'el Kahn, and J. J. Shirley (Leiden: Brill, 2011), 156.
54. Mazar, "Egyptian Garrison Town," 159–180.
55. Mazar, "Egyptian Garrison Town," 158.
56. Mazar, "Egyptian Garrison Town," 180.
57. Kenneth A. Kitchen, "Egypt and Israel during the First Millennium BC," in *Congress Volume: Jerusalem, 1986*, ed. John Emerton, Supplements to Vetus Testamentum 40 (Leiden: E. J. Brill, 1988), 109; also K. A. Kitchen, *The Third Intermediate Period in Egypt (1100–650 B.C.)* (Warminster, UK: Aris & Phillips, 1973), 273–274.
58. Ronald Williams, "Egypt and Israel," in *The Legacy of Egypt*, ed. J. R. Harris, 2nd ed. (Oxford: Clarendon Press, 1971), 260.
59. M. Görg, "Weisheit als Provokation: Religionsgeschichtliche und theologische Aspeckte der jahwistischen Sündenfallerzählung," *Wissenschaft und Weisheit* 49 (1986): 85. Cited by Paul S. Ash, *David, Solomon and Egypt: A Reassessment*, JSOT Supple. Series 297 (Sheffield: Sheffield Academic Press, 1999), 18.
60. Abraham Malamat, "A Political Look at the Kingdom of David and Solomon and Its Relations with Egypt," in *Studies in the Period of David and Solomon and Other Essays*, ed. Tomoo Ishida, papers read at the International Symposium for Biblical Studies, Tokyo, December 5–7, 1979 (Winona Lake, IN: Eisenbrauns, 1982), 198.
61. Malamat, "A Political Look," 199.
62. Malamat, "Political Look," 201.
63. Brian Peckham, "Israel and Phoenicia," in *Magnalia Dei: The Mighty Acts of God: Essays on the Bible and Archaeology in Memory of G. E. Wright*, ed. F. M. Cross, W. E. Lemke, and P. D. Miller Jr. (Garden City, NY: Doubleday, 1976), 242, n. 59; also John Gray, *I & II Kings* (Philadelphia: Westminster Press, 1970), 264, 269, 215–238.
64. Yutaka Ikeda, "Solomon's Trade in Horses and Chariots in International Setting," in *Studies in the Period of David and Solomon and Other Essays*, ed. T. Ishida, papers read at the International Symposium for Biblical Studies, Tokyo, December 5–7, 1979 (Winona Lake, IN: Eisenbrauns, 1982), 237–238.
65. Malamat, "Political Look," 201.
66. Malamat, "Political Look," 203.
67. Malamat, "Political Look," 203.

68. Schipper, "Egypt and Israel: The Ways of Cultural Contacts," 35–36.
69. Schipper, "Egypt and Israel: The Ways of Cultural Contacts," 36.
70. Schipper, "Egypt and Israel: The Ways of Cultural Contacts," 36.
71. Schipper, "Egypt and Israel: The Ways of Cultural Contacts," 37.
72. Kitchen, *Third Intermediate Period*, 355.
73. Schipper, "Egypt and Israel: The Ways of Cultural Contacts," 37.
74. Schipper, "Egypt and Israel: The Ways of Cultural Contacts," 38.
75. Schipper, "Egypt and Israel: The Ways of Cultural Contacts," 38.
76. Tryggve Mettinger, *Solomonic State Officials: A Study of the Civil Government Officials of the Israelite Monarchy*, Coniectanea Biblical Old Testament Series 5 (Lund, Sweden: CWK Gleerup, 1971), 48.
77. Mettinger, *Solomonic State Officials*, 61.
78. Mettinger, *Solomonic State Officials*, 67.
79. Mettinger, *Solomonic State Officials*, 67.
80. William F. Albright, "The Administrative Divisions of Israel and Judah," *Journal of the Palestine Oriental Society* 5 (1925): 20. A. Alt, "Israels Gaue unter Salomo," *Kleine Schriftenzur Geschichte des Volkes Israel* II (Munich: Beck, 1913), 76–89.
81. G. Ernest Wright, "The Provinces of Solomon (I Kings 4:7–19)," *Eretz Israel* 8 (1967): 67.
82. Mettinger, *Solomonic State Officials*, 126.
83. D. B. Redford, "Studies in Relations between Palestine and Egypt during the First Millennium B.C.," in *Studies on the Ancient Palestinian World*, ed. J. W. Wevers and D. B. Redford (Toronto: Toronto University Press, 1972), 144, 141–156.
84. Redford, "Studies in Relations between Palestine and Egypt," 153.
85. Redford, "Studies in Relations between Palestine and Egypt," 144–145.
86. Redford, "Studies in Relations between Palestine and Egypt," 146.
87. Redford, "Studies in Relations between Palestine and Egypt," 154–155.
88. Y. Aharoni, "The Use of Hieratic Numerals in Hebrew Ostraca and the Shekel Weights," *BASOR* 184 (1966): 13–19; also Y. Aharoni, "Three Hebrew Ostraca from Arad," *BASOR* 197 (1970): 16–42.
89. J. B. Segal, "YRḤ in the Gezer Calendar," *Journal of Semitic Studies* 7 (1962): 217.
90. Segal, "YRḤ in the Gezer Calendar," 218. Also see Robert McCalister, *The Excavation of Gezer 1902–1905 and 1907–1909* (London: Palestine Exploration Fund, 1912), 307–331.
91. R. B. Y. Scott, "The Scale Weights from Ophel, 1963–64," *Palestine Exploration Quarterly* 97 (1965): 135.
92. Scott, "Scale Weights from Ophel," 135.
93. Aharoni, "Use of Hieratic Numerals," 18.
94. Scott, "Scale Weights from Ophel," 137.
95. Daniel Master, "Economy and Exchange in the Iron Age Kingdoms of the Southern Levant," *BASOR* 372 (November 2014): 83.
96. Master, "Economy and Exchange," 83.
97. Master, "Economy and Exchange," 83.
98. Alexander Joffe, "The Rise of Secondary States in the Iron Age Levant," *Journal of the Economic and Social History of the Orient* 45/4 (2002): 427.
99. Master, "Economy and Exchange," 85.
100. W. Eugene Claburn, "Fiscal Basis of Josiah's Reforms," *JBL* 92, no. 1 (1973): 11–22.
101. Master, "Economy and Exchange," 87.
102. Master, "Economy and Exchange," 89.

103. Master, "Economy and Exchange," 89.
104. John S. Holladay Jr., "Hezekiah's Tribute, Long-Distance Trade, and the Wealth of Nations ca. 1000–600 BC: New Perspective," in *Confronting the Past: Archaeological and Historical Essays on Ancient Israel in Honor of William G. Dever*, ed. William Dever, Seymour Gitin, and J. Edward Wright (Winona Lake, IN: Eisenbrauns, 2006), 327, 309–331.
105. Barry J. Kemp, *Ancient Egypt: Anatomy of a Civilization* (1989; reprint, London and New York: Routledge, 1993), 111.
106. Kemp, *Ancient Egypt*, 111.
107. Kemp, *Ancient Egypt*, 111–136; 232–260.
108. David Warburton, "Economic Thinking in Egyptology," *Studien zur Altägyptischen Kultur* 26 (1998): 145.
109. Warburton, "Economic Thinking in Egyptology," 145.
110. Warburton, "Economic Thinking in Egyptology," 145.
111. Warburton, "Economic Thinking in Egyptology," 149.
112. Warburton, "Economic Thinking in Egyptology," 145.
113. Brewer and Teeter, *Egypt and Egyptians*, 98.
114. Brewer and Teeter, *Egypt and Egyptians*, 98.
115. Brewer and Teeter, *Egypt and Egyptians*, 98.
116. James E. Atwell, "An Egyptian Source for Genesis," *Journal of Theological Studies*, 51, no. 2 (October 2000): 441–477.
117. Atwell, "An Egyptian Source for Genesis," 449–450.
118. Atwell, "An Egyptian Source for Genesis," 455.
119. James K. Hoffmeier, *Akhenaten and the Origins of Monotheism* (Oxford: Oxford University Press, 2015), 229.
120. Hoffmeier, *Akhenaten and the Origins of Monotheism*, 461.
121. Hoffmeier, *Akhenaten and the Origins of Monotheism*, 458.
122. Raymond O. Faulkner, *Ancient Egyptian Coffin Texts, Vol. I* (Warminster: Aris & Phillips, 1973), 83–85. For a more detailed treatment of this see D. N. Premnath, "The Concepts of Ṛta and Maat: A Study in Comparison," *Biblical Interpretation* 2, no. 3 (1994): 325–339.
123. Claas J. Bleeker, *Egyptian Festivals: Enactments of Religious Renewals* (Leiden: E. J. Brill, 1967), 39; also Premnath, "Concepts of Ṛta and Maat," 331.
124. S. Morenz, *Egyptian Religion*, trans. Ann E. Keep (Ithaca: Cornell University Press, 1973), 113.
125. Premnath, "Concepts of Ṛta and Maat," 332.
126. Robert T. Clark, *Myth and Symbol in Ancient Egypt* (London: Thames and Hudson, 1959), 27.
127. H. H. Schmid, *Gerechtigkeit als Weltordnung. Hintergrund und Geschichte der alttestamentlichen Gerechtigkeitsbegriffes* (Tübingen: Mohr/Siebeck, 1968).
128. Redford, *Egypt, Canaan, and Israel*, 368.
129. Roland de Vaux, *Ancient Israel: Its Life and Institutions*, trans. John McHugh (New York: McGraw-Hill, 1961), 103–105.
130. Williams, "Egypt and Israel," 275.
131. Stephen E. Thompson, "The Anointing of Officials in Egypt," *Journal of Near Eastern Studies* 53, no. 1 (1994): 15–25.
132. Adolf Erman, "Das Verhältnis des Ägyptischen zu den semitischen Sprachen," *Zeitschrift der deutschen morgenländischenGesellschaft* 46 (1892): 93–129. Wilhelm Gesenius,

Otto Weber, W. Max Müller, Frants Buhl, and Heinrich Zimmern, *Hebräisches und aramäisches Handwörterbuch über das Alte Testament*, 17th ed. (Berlin: Springer, 1915).

133. Thomas O. Lambdin, "Egyptian Loan Words in the Old Testament," *Journal of the American Oriental Society* 73, no. 3 (July–September, 1953): 145–155.
134. Lambdin, "Egyptian Loan Words," 145–155; also Redford, *Egypt, Canaan, and Israel*, 385.
135. Williams, "Egypt and Israel," 265–267.
136. Redford, *Egypt, Canaan, and Israel*, 392.
137. Williams, "Egypt and Israel," 277–278.
138. Nili Shupak, "Female Imagery in Proverbs 1–9 in the Light of Egyptian Sources," *Vetus Testamentum* 61, no. 2 (2011): 310–323.
139. Michael Fox, *The Song of Songs and the Ancient Egyptian Love Songs* (Madison: University of Wisconsin Press, 1985).
140. Anselm C. Hagedorn, "What Kind of Love Is It? Egyptian, Hebrew or Greek?" *Die Welt des Orients* 46, no. 1 (2016): 90–106.
141. Redford, *Egypt, Canaan, and Israel*, 389.
142. Higginbotham, "Egypt and the Bible," 225.
143. Mazar, "Egyptian Garrison Town at Beth-Shean," 179–180.

Bibliography

Adams, William Y. "The First Colonial Empire." In *Expanding Empires: Cultural Interaction and Exchange in World Societies from Ancient to Early Modern Times*, edited by Wendy F. Kasinec and Michael A. Polushin, 13–29. The World Beat Series No. 2. Wilmington, DE: Scholarly Resource Books, 2002.

Aharoni, Yohanan. "The Use of Hieratic Numerals in Hebrew Ostraca and the Shekel Weights." *BASOR* 184 (1966): 13–19.

Aharoni, Yohanan. "Three Hebrew Ostraca from Arad." *BASOR* 197 (1970): 16–42.

Albright, William F. "The Administrative Divisions of Israel and Judah." *Journal of the Palestine Oriental Society* 5 (1925): 17–54.

Alt, Albrecht. *Kleine Schriften zur Geschichte des Volkes Israel* II. Munich: Beck, 1913.

Ash, Paul S. *David, Solomon and Egypt: A Reassessment*. JSOT Supple. 297. Sheffield: Sheffield Academic Press, 1999.

Atwell, James E. "An Egyptian Source for Genesis." *Journal of Theological Studies* 51, no. 2 (October 2000): 441–477.

Bailey, Randall C. "Beyond Identification: The Use of Africans in Old Testament Poetry and Narrative." In *Stony the Road We Trod: African American Biblical Interpretation*, edited by Cain H. Felder, 165–184. Minneapolis: Fortress Press, 1991.

Bakhtin, Mikhail M. *Dialogic Imagination: Four Essays*. Ed. Michael Holquist and trans. Caryl Emerson and Michael Holquist. Austin: University of Texas Press, 1981.

Binder, Susanne. "Joseph's Rewarding and Investiture (Genesis 41:41–43) and the Gold of Honour in New Kingdom Egypt." In *Egypt, Canaan and Israel: History, Imperialism and Literature*, edited by Shay Bar, Dan'el Kahn, and J. J. Shirley, 44–64. Proceedings of a Conference at the University of Haifa, May 3–7, 2009. Leiden: Brill, 2011.

Bleeker, Claas J. *Egyptian Festivals: Enactments of Religious Renewals*. Leiden: E. J. Brill, 1967.

Brewer, Douglas J., and Emily Teeter. *Egypt and the Egyptians*. 2nd ed. Cambridge, UK: Cambridge University Press, 2007.

Claburn, W. Eugene. "Fiscal Basis of Josiah's Reforms." *JBL* 92, no. 1 (1973): 11–22.
Clark, Robert T. *Myth and Symbol in Ancient Egypt*. London: Thames and Hudson, 1959.
Copher, C. B. "Egypt and Ethiopia in the Old Testament." *Journal of African Civilizations* 6, no. 2 (1984): 163–178.
Currid, John. *Ancient Egypt and the Old Testament*. Grand Rapids, MI: Baker Books, 1997.
Downs, Roger M., and David Stea. Eds. *Image and Environment: Cognitive Mapping and Spatial Behavior*. Chicago: Aldine, 1973.
Downs, Roger M., and David Stea. Eds. *Maps in Minds: Reflections on Cognitive Mapping*. New York: Harper & Row, 1977.
Erman, Adolf. "Das Verhältnis des Ägyptischen zu den semitischen Sprachen." *Zeitschrift der deutschen Morgenländischen Gesellschaft* 46 (1892): 93–129.
Faulkner, Raymond O. *Ancient Egyptian Coffin Texts*. Vol. 1. Warminster: Aris & Phillips, 1973.
Fox, Michael. *The Song of Songs and the Ancient Egyptian Love Songs*. Madison: University of Wisconsin Press, 1985.
Gesenius, Wilhelm, Otto Weber, W. Max Müller, Frants Buhl, and Heinrich Zimmern. *Hebräisches und aramäisches Handwörterbuch über das Alte Testament*. 17th ed. Berlin: Springer, 1915.
Görg, Manfred. "Weisheit als Provokation: Religionsgeschichtliche und theologische Aspeckte der jahwistischen Sündenfallerzählung." *Wissenschaft und Weisheit* 49 (1986): 81–98.
Gray, John. *I & II Kings*. Philadelphia: Westminster Press, 1970.
Greifenhagen, F. V. *Egypt on the Pentateuch's Ideological Map: Constructing Biblical Israel's Identity*, edited by D. J. A. Clines and Philip Davies. JSOT Supplement Series 361. London: Sheffield Academic Press, 2002.
Habtu, Tewoldemedhin. "The Images of Egypt in the Old Testament: Reflections on African Hermeneutics." In *Interpreting the Old Testament in Africa: Papers from the International Symposium on Africa and the Old Testament in Nairobi, 1999*, edited by Mary Getui, 56–57. Bern, Switzerland: Peter Lang, 2012.
Hagedorn, Anselm C. "What Kind of Love Is It? Egyptian, Hebrew or Greek?" *Die Welt des Orients* 46, no. 1 (2016): 90–106.
Higginbotham, Carolyn. "Egypt and the Bible." In *The New Interpreter's Dictionary of the Bible*, edited by Katherine Sakenfeld, 224–226. Vol. 2. Nashville, TN: Abingdon, 2006–2009.
Hoffmeier, James K. *Israel in Egypt. The Evidence for the Authenticity of the Exodus Tradition*. Oxford: Oxford University Press, 1997.
Hoffmeier, James K. *Akhenaten and the Origins of Monotheism*. Oxford: Oxford University Press, 2015.
Holladay, John S., Jr. "Hezekiah's Tribute, Long-Distance Trade, and the Wealth of Nations ca. 1000–600 BC: New Perspective." In *Confronting the Past: Archaeological and Historical Essays on Ancient Israel in Honor of William G. Dever*, edited by William Dever, Seymour Gitin, and J. Edward Wright, 309–331. Winona Lake, IN: Eisenbrauns, 2006.
Ikeda, Yutaka. "Solomon's Trade in Horses and Chariots in International Setting." In *Studies in the Period of David and Solomon and Other Essays*, edited by T. Ishida, 215–238. Papers read at the International Symposium for Biblical Studies, Tokyo, December 5–7, 1979. Winona Lake, IN: Eisenbrauns, 1982.
Joffe, Alexander. "The Rise of Secondary States in the Iron Age Levant." *Journal of the Economic and Social History of the Orient* 45, no. 4 (2002): 425–467.
Kemp, Barry J. *Ancient Egypt: Anatomy of a Civilization*. Reprint ed. London and New York: Routledge, 1993.

Kitchen, Kenneth A. *The Third Intermediate Period in Egypt (1100–650 B.C.)*. Warminster: Aris & Phillips, 1973.

Kitchen, Kenneth A. "Egypt and Israel during the First Millennium BC." In *Congress Volume: Jerusalem, 1986*, edited by John Emerton, 107–123. Supplements to Vetus Testamentum 40. Leiden: E. J. Brill, 1988.

Lambdin, Thomas O. "Egyptian Loan Words in the Old Testament." *Journal of the American Oriental Society* 73, no. 3 (July–September, 1953): 145–155.

Malamat, Abraham. "A Political Look at the Kingdom of David and Solomon and Its Relations with Egypt." In *Studies in the Period of David and Solomon and Other Essays*, edited by Tomoo Ishida, 189–204. Papers read at the International Symposium for Biblical Studies, Tokyo, 5–7 December 1979. Winona Lake, IN: Eisenbrauns, 1982.

Master, Daniel. "Economy and Exchange in the Iron Age Kingdoms of the Southern Levant." *BASOR* 372 (2014): 81–97.

Mazar, Amihai. "The Egyptian Garrison Town at Beth-Shean." In *Egypt, Canaan and Israel: History, Imperialism and Literature*, edited by Shay Bar, Dan'el Kahn, and J. J. Shirley, 155–189. Proceedings of a Conference at the University of Haifa, May 3–7, 2009. Leiden: Brill, 2011.

McCalister, Robert. *The Excavation of Gezer 1902–1905 and 1907–1909*. London: Palestine Exploration Fund, 1912.

Mettinger, Tryggve. *Solomonic State Officials: A Study of the Civil Government Officials of the Israelite Monarchy*. Coniectanea Biblical Old Testament Series 5. Lund, Sweden: CWK Gleerup, 1971.

Morenz, Sigfried. *Egyptian Religion*. Trans. Ann E. Keep. Ithaca: Cornell University Press, 1973.

Nohrnberg, James. "Moses." In *Images of Man and God: Old Testament Short Stories in Literary Focus*, ed. B. O. Long, 35–57. Bible and Literature 1. Sheffield: Almond Press, 1981.

Patell, Cyrus R. K. "Comparative American Studies: Hybridity and Beyond." *America Literary History* 11, no. 1(1999): 166–186.

Peckham, Brian. "Israel and Phoenicia." In *Magnalia Dei: The Mighty Acts of God. Essays on the Bible and Archaeology in Memory of G. E. Wright*, edited by F. M. Cross, W. E. Lemke, and P. D. Miller Jr., 224–248. Garden City, NY: Doubleday, 1976.

Pratt, Mary Louise. "Arts of the Contact Zone." *Profession* (1991): 33–40.

Premnath, D. N. "The Concepts of Ṛta and Maat: A Study in Comparison." *Biblical Interpretation* 2, no. 3 (1994): 325–339.

Redford, Donald B. "Studies in Relations between Palestine and Egypt during the First Millennium B.C." In *Studies on the Ancient Palestinian World*, edited by J. W. Wevers and D. B. Redford, 141–156. Toronto: Toronto University Press, 1972.

Redford, Donald B. *Egypt, Canaan, and Israel in Ancient Times*. Princeton, NJ: Princeton University Press, 1992.

Schipper, Bernd U. "Egypt and Israel: The Ways of Cultural Contacts in the Late Bronze Age and Iron Age (20th–26th Dynasty)." *Journal of Ancient Egyptian Interconnections* 4, no. 3 (2012): 30–47.

Schmid, Hans H. *Gerechtigkeit als Weltordnung. Hintergrund und Geschichte der alttestamentlichen Gerechtigkeitsbegriffes*. Tübingen: Mohr/Siebeck, 1968.

Scott, Robert B. Y. "The Scale Weights from Ophel, 1963–64." *Palestine Exploration Quarterly* 97 (1965): 128–139.

Segal, Judah B. "YRḤ in the Gezer Calendar." *Journal of Semitic Studies* 7 (1962): 212–221.

Shupak, Nili. "Female Imagery in Proverbs 1–9 in the Light of Egyptian Sources." *Vetus Testamentum* 61, no. 2 (2011): 310–323.

Sugirtharajah, R. S. *The Postcolonial Bible*. Sheffield: Sheffield Academic Press, 1998.
Thompson, Stephen E. "The Anointing of Officials in Egypt." *Journal of Near Eastern Studies* 53, no. 1 (1994): 15–25.
Vaux, Roland de. *Ancient Israel: Its Life and Institutions*. Trans. John McHugh. New York: McGraw-Hill, 1961.
Walsh, Lynda. "Accountability: Towards a Definition of Hybridity for Scholars of Transnational Rhetorics." *Rhetorica: A Journal of the History of Rhetoric* 30, no. 4 (2012): 392–431.
Warburton, David. "Economic Thinking in Egyptology." *Studien zur Altägyptischen Kultur* 26 (1998): 143–170.
Weinstein, James. "The Egyptian Empire in Palestine: A Reassessment." *BASOR* 241 (1981): 1–28.
Williams, Ronald. "Egypt and Israel." In *The Legacy of Egypt*, edited by J. R. Harris, 257–290. 2nd ed. Oxford: Clarendon Press, 1971.
Wright, G. Ernest. "The Provinces of Solomon (I Kings 4: 7–19)." *Eretz Israel* 8 (1967): 58–68.

CHAPTER 2

THE NEO-ASSYRIAN EMPIRE THROUGH A POSTCOLONIAL LENS

SAFWAT MARZOUK

WHO WERE THE ASSYRIANS?

BEFORE exploring the tenets of the worldview of the Assyrian empire, brief remarks on the history of the Assyrians are necessary. One way of telling the history of the Assyrians focuses on how they began to form themselves as a political entity. Around 2000 BCE, after the fall of the kingdom of Ur, on the banks of the Tigris in modern-day Northern Iraq, Aššur became an independent city-state. In the following centuries the city maintained its cultural independence even though it was periodically under the rule of the surrounding kingdoms—until the decline of the Mittani kingdom in the fourteenth century BCE, when Aššur began to form its own independent kingdom that was able to navigate its relations with other powerful kingdoms such as Babylon and Egypt.[1] The era known as the Middle Assyrian Period (1353–935 BCE) witnessed an Assyrian expansion into the territories formerly controlled by the Mittani kingdom. The Assyrian empire started to expand westward as a result of the disintegration of the Hittite empire (ca. 1600–1200 BCE) and southward as Assyria held a tighter grip over its southern neighbor Babylon (during the reign of the Assyrian king Tukuli-Ninurta, ca. 1244–1208 BCE). The fertile lands of Nineveh and Arbela were included along with Aššur to form the heartland of the empire. This period of imperial expansion was put to an end with the appearance of the Arameans sometime in the eleventh century BCE; the Arameans cost the Assyrians a loss in their territories in the northwestern parts of Mesopotamia.

After a century of decline, the Assyrians started to regain control and to expand their territories during the reign of Aššur-dan II (934–912) by pushing back against the

Arameans. Restoring control over the area, called Al-Jazira (the island), located between the Tigris and Euphrates rivers, was essential for the resurgence of the Assyrian empire because it supplied food for them and because it enabled them to control west-east and north-south trade routes.[2] During the reign of Aššurnaṣirpal II, who was named the founder of the Neo-Assyrian empire,[3] the Assyrian empire, whose capital became the city of Kalhu (Nimrud), expanded its control to the Taurus mountains in the north and Mediterranean trade routes in the west.[4] Shalmaneser III (ca. 858–824) tried to assert Assyrian sovereignty in the west by leading four campaigns against a coalition of Syrian city-states and Israel (during the reign of Ahab). While Assyrian records show that Israel paid a tribute to Assyria during the reign of the Israelite king Jehu, and although the Assyrians plundered many of the cities of Aram-Damascus, the campaigns of Shalmaneser against Damascus during the reign of Hazael did not succeed in subduing their western neighbor. The Assyrian empire suffered an extended setback also because of the revolt in the Urartu kingdom, which led to a period known as the "period of local autonomy" (827–745 BCE).[5]

With the rise of Tiglath-Pileser III (745–727) to the throne, the Neo-Assyrian empire was set on its way to the peak of its expansion. During his campaigns against the Urartu kingdom and the Syrian kingdoms, Tiglath-Pileser conducted two policies: stripping these provinces of their independence and "bidirectional deportations that displaced thousands all over the empire."[6] In one of his campaigns to the west (734–732 BCE), Tiglath-Pileser intended to deal with a revolt led by Rezin/Radyān of Damascus, the Assyrian king who besieged Damascus, annexed parts of Israel, received tribute from Judah, and marched through Philistia all the way to the Egyptian border in order to cut any assistance to the Levantine states. Shalmaneser V (727–722 BCE) continued the Assyrian policies toward Israel; he besieged and conquered Samaria for three years, when Hoshea, the Israelite king, refused to pay the tribute seeking Egyptian military aid against Assyria. The reign of Sargon II (722–705) witnessed struggles in some areas (e.g., Babylon, Hamath), an expansion of the empire in other areas (e.g., Ekron, Gaza), a defeat of an Egyptian army, and subjugation of Judah. Sennacherib (705–681 BCE), who made Nineveh the capital of the Assyrian empire, spent the initial years of his reign repressing revolts in the southern parts of the empire (in Babylon, Elam, and Arabia) and western parts of the empire (in Phoenicia and Judah). After a conflict over the throne, Esarhaddon (680–669 BCE) continued the expansion of the Assyrian empire by conquering parts of Egypt during 675–671 BCE. Esarhaddon made his people and his vassal states swear their allegiance to his son Aššurbanipal (668–626 BCE), who continued his father's attempts to subdue Egypt. The last decades of the history of the Neo-Assyrian empire witnessed a decline in power due to internal conflicts and due to the growing number of revolts across the empire. The Babylonians and Medes joined in alliance and were able to capture Nineveh, the capital of Assyria, after a three-month siege (ca. 612 BCE).[7] The Assyrians, who once constructed an empire, continued to live after the fall of Nineveh under the rule of other empires (e.g., Babylon, Persia, etc.).

The Worldview of the Assyrian Empire

Mario Liverani has extensively studied the Assyrian empire. His monograph *Assyria: The Imperial Mission* lays out the imperial ideology of the Assyrian empire.[8] In the following paragraphs I will offer a summary of some of the basic aspects about the Assyrian empire. These aspects will include the role religion played, the military tactics of the Assyrian empire, and the impact of the expansion of the empire on the peoples they have invaded and subjugated.

Empire and Religion

The Royal Inscriptions of the Neo-Assyrian kings give us a glimpse into the theological worldview that informed the propaganda of the Assyrian empire.[9] The military activities of the Assyrian empire were conducted because a god commanded the king to expand the empire or because there was a threat to the sovereignty of the empire so that the king had to pray to the gods who assured the king of his victory. The inscription of Aššurnaṣirpal II begins with a claim that it was the deity who made him great and who commanded him to rule and to subdue the lands: "When Aššur, my great god, who called me by name and made my sovereignty supreme over the kings of the four quarters, had made my great name supreme, he placed his merciless weapon in my lordly hands and sternly commanded me to rule, subdue, and direct the lands and mighty highlands. With the support of Aššur my lord, I kept marching along difficult routes (and) over rugged mountains with the mass of my troops and there was no opponent."[10] The mission of Shalmaneser III was commanded by the god to "exercise dominion over and to subdue all the lands unsubmissive to Aššur."[11] Esarhaddon claims that "the god Aššur, the father of the gods, gave me (the power) to pull down and repopulate and to enlarge Assyrian territory."[12] In some cases, the Assyrian Royal Inscriptions ground the warfare of the empire in the notion of self-defense. Sennacherib describes the Chaldean and Elamite coalition that sought to fight him in the following way: "[They] banded their forces together. Like a spring invasion of a swarm of locusts, they were advancing toward me as a group to do battle. The dust of their feet covered the wide heavens like a heavy cloud in the deep of winter. . . . But I prayed to Aššur, Sîn, Šamaš, Bêl, Nabû, Nergal, Ištar of Nineveh, and Ištar of Arbela, the gods who support me, for victory over my strong enemy and they immediately heeded my prayers and came to my aid."[13]

Another key aspect of the Neo-Assyrian propaganda is the role the god Aššur played in accomplishing the defeat of the enemies on behalf of the king. The Royal Inscription of the king Shalmaneser III reads: "The fear of the splendor of Aššur, my lord, overwhelmed them."[14] When the enemy resists the Assyrian empire and if they trust in their own power, the same inscription mentioned previously goes on to say: "Aḫuni, [the man] of Bīt Adini trusted in the massed might of his troops, and he became hostile against me in order to make war and battle. With the support of Aššur and the great gods, my lords, I fought with him. I decisively defeated him. I confined him to his city."[15] When the victory takes place, the king offers praise and worship to the gods: "At that time, I praised the majesty of the great gods; I proclaimed the valor of Aššur and Šamaš." Praising the gods is followed by self-aggrandizing claims in behalf of the king: "I made a large royal statue of myself [and] I wrote on it my heroic deeds [and] my victorious achievements."[16]

The gods command the king to expand the empire; they listen to the prayers of the king when he needs their support; and the king offers praise to the deities after the victory is achieved through their encouragement, support, and overwhelming weapons. The king is portrayed as the divine agent who maintains order, justice, and peace by eliminating any forces that disrupt the order that the deities willed. Beate Pongratz-Lesiten notes: "Establishing and maintaining order and eliminating disruptive forces was ... the primary task of the king, whose duty it was to harmonize the condition of the world with the ideal primeval order created by the gods. This task situated the king at the threshold between history and the mythological and emblematic, helping to explain the recurrent use of the king as hunter, as warrior, as caretaker of the cult, and as a shepherd of his people."[17] In the context of ancient Assyria, the political and the religious, the military and the cultic, and historical and the mythological dimensions and worldviews were intertwined and shaped one another.

Expanding the Territories and the Portrayal of Self and Other

The Assyrian kings expanded the empire at the command of the deity. Liverani observed a tension in the Assyrian perspective about borders. He notes that the word *miṣru* can refer to a border or frontier; the former is a static boundary, while the latter refers to a dynamic border. Liverani explains this tension in this way: "The internal borders of the cosmos, the just kingdom protected by the god, are and must be stable and immovable, while it is only the external frontier of the cosmos's periphery that must be advanced as far as possible."[18] The Royal Inscriptions reflect the expansive nature of the Assyrian empire by way of using expressions such as: "I departed from Nineveh," "I crossed the Tigris River," "I traversed Mount X," and "I crossed the Euphrates."[19] Liverani notes three recurring motifs in Assyrian royal inscriptions that convey the boasting of the Assyrian kings, but they also underline the expansionist "mission." These motifs include: "boasting of opening new pathways, boasting of reaching previously unknown regions and people, and boasting for subjugating kingdoms or regions that had never been conquered before."[20] Assyrian Royal Inscriptions describe the kings in ways that reflect the idealization of the imperial ideology and that celebrate the expansion of the empire. The titles include: "king of the four corners of the earth," "king of the Lower and Upper Sea," "strong king," "opener of remote regions in the mountains," "subduer of the insubmissive," and "conqueror of enemy regions." Aššurbanipal speaks of his expanding empire even into the desert: "[My troops] passed through remote paths, ascended high mountains, penetrated deep forests, between large trees and bushes, through a road of scrubs, right into a desert, a place of thirst and hunger, where there are no birds of the sky or asses or gazelles. For a distance of 100 double-hours from Nineveh ... I continued my pursuit."[21]

The success of the military campaigns was communicated to the Assyrian god, who commissioned the expedition, as well as to the Assyrian public. At the same time the expansion of the territories of the empire was conveyed to the conquered territories by placing steles that marked the boundaries of the territories of the empire and they were also meant to promote the Assyrian hegemony and the power of its king.[22] Steles and other images were placed even beyond the territories of the empire in order to embody the universality of the Assyrian empire and to celebrate the success of the Assyrian god and its king in extending the empire's borders. Sargon II's inscription reads: "In that time, I have a stele (*narû*) made and I had the images (*ṣalmu*) of the great gods my lords inscribed upon it. I erected a colossal image of my kingship before them for my life. I wrote upon it [the names of] all the lands that, from sunrise to sunset, trusting in the help of Aššur, Nabû, and Marduk, I submitted to the yoke of my lordship."[23]

Assyrian kings claimed universal dominion. In some instances, some kings claimed the title "king of the four quarters of the earth," while others used the directions of "west, north, south, and east" in order to map out the expansion of their sovereignty. "From sea to sea" and "from sunrise to sunset" were also ways that the Assyrian kings used to speak of the scope of their reign. The dominion of the heartland of Assyrian extended to the parts of the world that they have considered to be the periphery. The portrayal of the peoples who live in the periphery as rebellious peoples because they do not bring tribute or pay homage to the Assyrian kings justified the Assyrian mission to subdue them and bring them under the sovereignty of the Assyrian empire. The periphery is defined as those who "do not eat grain like humans do, do not build houses like humans do, do not build cities like humans do."[24] People in the periphery are constructed as the other to those who live in the center. While the center is a civilized ordered city, the periphery, especially the mountainous areas, is the place where people do not build cities or conduct burials. They have the "instincts of dogs, or wolves"; they are "unclassifiable as people."[25]

Mattias Karlsson offers an intriguing study titled "Alterity in Ancient Assyrian Propaganda." Royal tiles or epithets, textual narrative, and royal iconography are combined to investigate how the Other is constructed by the Assyrian discourse and image. Karlsson concludes: "The Other appears in four different positions. Firstly, he appears as passive and inferior (governance-related) being dominated, shepherded, supported, and administered. This kind of subaltern is often spoken of, particularly as dominated. Secondly, there is the passive and inferior (campaign-related) Other, being attacked, conquered, tamed, seized, and slayed. He is often talked of, in particular with regard to the acts of conquered and slayed. Thirdly, another type of Other is active and inferior (campaign-related). This subaltern responds to the Assyrian king's requests by fighting, fleeing, fearing, paying (tribute), and submitting.... Fourthly, the Other is active and superior, in his capacity of a successor who is called upon in royal inscriptions to preserve and respect the works of his predecessors, thus acting from a position of strength. This kind of Other fails to heed this call and is desecrating in relation to his predecessors' monuments. He could also be a royal predecessor defamed by his successor."[26] The dominant image of the Other is that of being "conquered," "dominated," "slain," and "desecrating."

Treaties or Conquest

As the Assyrian empire expanded, its enemies had two possible choices: opposition, which meant war against the giant military machinery of the empire; or surrender, which meant being subjugated politically and economically to the imperial sovereign. Liverani notes that "normally, and with few exceptions, kingdoms decided to surrender, while chiefdoms tried to resist. In the face of Assyria's evident military superiority, surrender was surely the more rational choice, and it was the only way to avoid graver misfortunes such as destructions, massacre, and deportation; grievous economic losses (in the form of tribute or plunder) were unavoidable irrespective of a polity's chosen strategy."[27] A treaty would entail: (1) a king, who represents the whole nation and swears allegiance to the Assyrian god Aššur and king; and (2) the vassal state that pays a tribute to the Assyrian empire. One of the implications of the treaty is that vassal states were prohibited from entering into other pacts that sought alliances rebelling against the Assyrian empire, nor could they aid enemies against Assyria. The Assyrian god is the guarantor of the oaths, and any transgression of the treaty is considered a "sin" against the god.[28] States that rebelled against the Assyrian empire would suffer from terrible consequences, which could include: natural disasters such as famines caused by the gods, whom these states disrespected by their loyalty oaths; or siege and warfare, which were seen as justifiable responses against these rebellious states.

Terror

Terror was one of the tactics that the Assyrian empire used in order to assert its sovereignty. As an exercise of terror, the Assyrian kings would pile up the bodies or body parts of the defeated troops: "I felled with the sword 300 of their fighting men. I made a pile of heads in front of the city"; "I filled the wide plain with the corpses [lit., defeat) of his warriors"; "Like Adad, I rained down upon them a devastating flood. I piled them in diches [and] filed the extensive plain with the corpses of their warriors."[29] Assyrian kings boast about their military successes and the impact of these expansions on the surrounding nations. Sometimes these nations bring their tribute to the Assyrian king because of reports of the majestic power of the king, and sometimes it is because of the terror that grew in their hearts because they heard of the fearsome power of the Assyrians. Tiglath-Pileser III explains how his victories in the Levant made the Arab chiefs bring tribute and pay homage: "The people of the cities Massa, Teima, Saba, Ḫayapa, Badanu, and Ḫatte, and those of Idiba'ilu, who are on the border of the western lands, whom none had known about, and whose country is remote, they heard about the fame of my majesty and my heroic deeds, and they beseeched my lordship. As one, they brought before me gold, silver, camels, and all types of aromatics as their payment, and they kissed my feet."[30]

The kings of the far islands in the seas west and east of Assyria brought tribute to the king of Assyria when they heard of the power and splendor of the Assyrian gods and the Assyrian king. The kings of these distant lands, whose lands were not known to any of the ancestors of the king Sargon II, brought tributes to the king when they heard of the exploits of the king in Chaldea and in Syria. The king describes the fear that overtook these kings when he says, "their hearts despaired, terror overcame them."[31] The conquest of another nation begins with the overwhelming fear that the Assyrian god bestows on the Assyrian king. The assaulted kingdom is besieged, and they suffer from famines and plagues to the point of eating their own children; they also get punished militarily.[32] The punishment is inscribed on their body and textualized in the Royal Inscriptions. One Royal Inscription describes the defeat of a rebellious state in the following words: "I flayed as many nobles as had rebelled against me and draped their skins over the pile [the pile was erected in front of the newly appointed ruler of this nation]. Some I spared within the pile, some I erected on stakes around the pile. I flayed many right through the land and draped their skins over the walls. I slashed the flesh of the royal eunuchs who were guilty. I brought Aḫi-yababa [someone who was captured from the rebellious city] to Nineveh, flayed him, and draped his skin over the wall of Nineveh."[33] The intention behind the bodily punishment, which is inscribed in the royal texts, is to function as spectacle of the power of the king, the powerlessness of the rebellious peoples, and the spread of control by war of terror over those who encountered the slain bodies or those who read the inscribed texts.[34]

Economic and Environmental Impact of the Empire

The periphery may seem rebellious, yet they possessed material goods that were not available in the center of Assyrian empire. Liverani notes, "The Mesopotamian division between center and periphery is in origin a function of the acquisition of raw materials, even if it is subsequently displaced by an imperialist interpretation expressed in political-military terms."[35] As the troops of the king advance, they receive the tribute from their vassal states. The tribute could include: "silver, gold, oxen, sheep, [and] wine." In another context the tribute includes: "silver, gold, oxen, sheep, wine, [and] his daughter with her rich dowry."[36] Needless to say, these tributes deprive the vassal states of the means to prosper economically and they contribute to the accumulation of wealth in the Assyrian homeland. The Assyrian empire took pleasure in collecting goods such as trees, plants, and animals as part of exotic tributes and in order to manifest how they subjugate their enemies, and they used them for purposes of building temples and palaces and expanding their gardens. Royal women were also taken or received as part of tributes or gifts. The Assyrian practice of "multidirectional deportation" or "cross-deportation" was intended to "destroy the ethno-political unity of the conquered territories, to supplant local identities with the multi-ethnicity of empire, and to do this while maintaining the productive capacity of the affected provinces." But Liverani is quick to note that "the economic burden imposed on them [the provinces] was sure to bring about an unavoidable demographic and productive decline. Indeed, Assyria was primarily interested in ensuring that the old royal houses and the old ruling classes were unable to cultivate projects of recovery or revenge. There is an evident differentiation in the destination of deportees depending on their rank and labor specialization. Common people (farmers, mostly) were employed as an agricultural labor force or in construction projects; specialists were instead concentrated in the capital."[37] Moving populations from one province to the other or to Assyria contributed to the economic prosperity of the empire and the weakening of those whom the Assyrians had controlled.

The impact of the empire did not just reach the individual communities; the military activities and imperial ambitions of Assyria also altered the very landscape and the presumed natural order of things. In the description of the eighth campaign of Sargon II there is a reference to the natural challenges that the Assyrian king encountered as he conquered new territories. The mountains themselves were a challenge, but so were the trees that were on the mountains: "Among the mountains, high mountains, imposing peaks, difficult slopes, where there is no path for chariots and infantry, through which the powerful cascades whose rumbling can be heard from a mile away like thunder, did I cut their way, [mountains] covered with all kinds of trees, thick as reeds, and the best fruit trees and vines, terrifying to anyone who desires to cross them, which no king had ever traversed, the interior of which no prince among my predecessors had ever seen. I felled their large trunks, I hacked through their difficult slopes with bronze pickaxes, and a narrow path, a means of passage, through which the soldiers had to pass in single file, I constructed through them [the mountains] for the transit of my army. I carried my chariot on shoulders of soldiers], while I went on horseback at the head of my troops and the horsemen of my retinue passed through the crossing in single file."[38] The purpose of a statement like this is for the king to boast about his accomplishments. But in an indirect way, these words show that the expansion of the empire had its negative impact on the natural world as it influenced the communities that were conquered.

The Empire Writes Back

The following section will discuss three examples from the Hebrew Bible that engage with the Assyrian empire.[39] These examples include the portrayal of Assyria in the book of Isaiah, the debate about the Assyrian background for the book of Deuteronomy, and finally the views of Nahum and Jonah on the city of Nineveh.

The Assyrian Empire in the Book of Isaiah

Assyria figures prominently in the literature that is preserved in Isaiah 1–39. Most of these oracles come from Isaiah of Jerusalem himself who was active in the eighth century BCE during the expansion of the Assyrian empire westward. Three major events took place during the lifetime of Isaiah of Jerusalem that reflect the complexity of theology and politics in the shadow of the empire. The small kingdoms of Israel and Judah were entangled with the Neo-Assyrian empire in the events of the so-called Syro-Ephramite war in 735–734 BCE, the capture of Samaria in 722 BCE, and the assault on Jerusalem in 701 BCE. The prophet Isaiah engaged with these events from a theological perceptive that reflects an awareness of the Assyrian imperial propaganda.

In the period 738–734 BCE, the kingdom of Judah, where Isaiah was active as a prophet, was caught in a political and militant conflict between Assyria, on the one hand, and a coalition led by Aram and including Israel, on the other hand, that rebelled against the Assyrian empire and sought to force Judah into joining them. The prophet Isaiah warned King Ahaz of Judah not to fear the assault of the Israelite-Aramean coalition and not to seek military aid from Assyria. Instead, the prophet urged the king to trust that YHWH is sovereign and that YHWH will deliver Judah from this conflict. But because Ahaz did not put his trust in YHWH and instead paid the tribute to the Assyrians, the prophet in Isaiah 8:7–8 declares to the people of Judah that YHWH will use the Assyrians as a tool for judgment: "Therefore, the Lord is bringing up against it the mighty flood waters of the River, the king of Assyria and all his glory; it will rise above all its channels and overflow all its banks; it will sweep on into Judah as a flood, and, pouring over, it will reach up to the neck; and its outspread wings will fill the breadth of your land, O Immanuel." Peter Machinist has argued that this text is reflecting an awareness on the prophet's part of the Assyrian propaganda. In these two verses Isaiah compares the Assyrian military activity to that of the flood; a similar description is used in the Assyrian Royal Inscriptions.[40]

Machinist discusses at least six common motifs in the Neo-Assyrian inscriptions that are also reflected in the traditions of Isaiah of Jerusalem. The image of Assyria that is constructed in the book of Isaiah is that of "an overwhelming military machine, destroying all resistance in its path, devastating the lands of its enemies, hauling away huge numbers of spoils and captives to its capital or elsewhere in its realm, and rearranging by this devastation and deportation the political physiognomy of the entire region."[41] The prophet Isaiah subverted the imperial propaganda for his own theological and literary purposes. Thus, a text like Isaiah can be considered a resistance script. Through inversion of the Assyrian rhetoric, the prophet simultaneously critiques the Judean royal circles for their lack of trust in their God, YHWH, and subverts the Assyrian military might under the sovereignty of the God of Judah. Isaiah 10:5–19, according to Machinist, reverses one of the central claims of the Assyrian propaganda, namely, that the expansion of the empire was taking place because the Assyrian God Assur had commanded it and made it possible. Furthermore, quite often the Assyrian kings explained their military devastations against the small nations as a punishment because their vassal states did not honor their treaties; instead they rebelled, relying on their own power. Isaiah deconstructs these claims by asserting that the ultimate power is not in the hands or, rather, the wings of the god of the empire (Aššur), but rather in the hands of the God of the underdog, Judah. Furthermore, "the Assyrian become in Isaiah what the 'enemy' was in his own inscriptions, who 'trusted in his own strength' and 'did not fear the oath of the gods.'"[42]

As a small nation, Judah was caught between the severity of the tribute that was demanded of it under the hegemony of the Assyrian empire and the potential of freedom that lies in rebelling against the empire. During the reign of King Hezekiah, and more specifically around 705 BCE, Judah rebelled against the Assyrians and sought help from its southern neighbor, Egypt. Assyria's response was devastating. In 701 BCE, the Assyrian king Sennacherib led a military campaign to extinguish the hopes of the Judeans to be freed from the yoke of the empire. Assyrian sources such as Sennacherib's Royal Inscriptions and reliefs from the Assyrian king's palace capture in word and image the destruction that the Assyrian army left behind in the Shephelah region. The Assyrians did not conquer Jerusalem. Yet King Hezekiah of Judah was forced to pay a heavy tribute. A biblical report of the heavy tribute can be found in 2 Kings 18:13–16, which narrates how Hezekiah used all of the silver that was in the temple and the palace and even had to peel gold off the doors and doorposts of the temple in order to pay the tribute.[43]

The Bible, however, contains another tradition that offers a theological reflection on these disastrous developments that surrounded the campaign of Sennacherib. Shawn Zelig Aster suggests that the texts of 2 Kings 18:17–19:37 and its parallel texts of Isaiah 36–37 offer a theological response to the Assyrian imperial propaganda.[44] These texts engage with the empire and its military might from a theological perspective with an interest in the question about the power of YHWH and his ability to save Jerusalem from the expanding mighty empire of Assyria. As mentioned above, the Assyrian imperial worldview entailed the support of the god Aššur for the military and economic expansions of the empire. No wonder, then, that the biblical representation of the speech of Rab-Shakeh, the Assyrian general of the campaign against Judah, focused on the fact that non-Assyrian gods were unable to deliver their respective nations from the Assyrian military destructive machinery (Isa 37:10–13). Aster writes, "Isa 36–37 interprets the conflict between Judah and Assyria as an ideological one. Assyrian claims of empire, which vaunt the worldwide dominion of Assur and the invincibility of the Assyrian king, are taken as implied attacks on the worldwide dominion and omnipotence of YHWH. There is no reason to assume that Assyrians actually mentioned YHWH in their propaganda, but the prophet interprets Assyrian claims of empire as implicit attacks on YHWH."[45] Referencing the common motif that appears in the Royal Inscriptions of the Assyrian kings, namely, that the kings go up to the peaks of the mountains on their chariots cutting down trees as an expression of their outstanding might, Isaiah 37:21–32 underscores the point that behind the military threats there is a theological question: Who is in control, YHWH or the Assyrian empire? The prayer of King Hezekiah in Isaiah 37:20 answers this question by affirming that when YHWH saves Jerusalem all the nations of the earth will know that it is YHWH who is, indeed, the ruler of the universe and not the Assyrians.

Deuteronomy and the Assyrian Treaties

One of the often-discussed topics that relate to the book of Deuteronomy is its relationship with the Assyrian treaties, known as the Vassal Treaties or the Succession Treaties, more specifically the Vassal Treaties of Esarhaddon (VTE) or the Succession Treaties of Esarhaddon (STE). In these treaties the Assyrian king Esarhaddon sought to ensure a peaceful transition of power to his son Aššurbanipal by making the Assyrians and the vassal states swear allegiance to his son's throne. Given that this type of treaty contains blessings and curses, which is similar to the blessings and curses found in the book of Deuteronomy in chapters 13 and 28, scholars for over fifty years now have been suggesting that the book of Deuteronomy is subverting the Assyrian imperial ideology by transferring the allegiance of the people of Judah from the Assyrians to YHWH.

Scholarly suggestions have ranged from arguing that Deuteronomy is "translating" a specific type of the Assyrian treaties to arguing that Deuteronomy is "alluding" to a world view embedded in these treaties. In speaking of direct connections between Deuteronomy and the Assyrian Vassal Treaties, scholars differ whether the author(s) of Deuteronomy relied on one specific treaty or were engaged with a literary genre in its broad manifestation. For example, Weinfeld suggests that parts of Deuteronomy were "literally transcribed from a Mesopotamian treaty" and that the scribes responsible for this literary production "transposed an entire and consecutive series of maledictions."[46] Other scholars, however, are more specific in their proposals. That is, some scholars suggest a specific treaty as the target that Deuteronomy mimics. It has been suggested that Deuteronomy 13 mimics the VTE. Bernard Levinson argued that the author(s) of Deuteronomy 13 was familiar with the Succession Treaty of the VTE. He goes on to suggest that, as part of their creative literary reworking of the VTE, "Those authors transformed the Neo-Assyrian formula requiring exclusive loyalty to the 'word of Esarhaddon' (*abutu ša Aššur-aḫu-iddina*) into one that demanded fidelity to the word (רבדה) of Israel's overlord, Yahweh, as proclaimed by Moses."[47] In his study of Deuteronomy 28, Rintje Frankena suggests that the author of the text likely had access to a written form of a treaty from the time of Ashurbanipal.[48] In this case, the author of this text might have been part of a ceremony for vassal states who were present at the coronation of Ashurbanipal over Assyria during the reign of Manasseh of Judah (ca. 672 BCE). Hans Ulrich Steymans argues that Deuteronomy 28 shows close affinities with the VTE.[49] These literary connections encompass direct translation, free transmission, and adaptation. The sections in Deuteronomy that reflect connections with the VTE, for Steymans, come from the period from 672 BCE to the reform of Josiah in 622 BCE. The discovery of a copy of the VTE in Tell Dayinat has provided a support to the possibility that the author(s) of Deuteronomy 13 and 28 were familiar with the style, content, and language of these treaties. Steymans provides various examples of linguistic and thematic connections between the VTE and Deuteronomy 28.[50]

> May all the grea[t go]ds of heaven and earth who inhabit the universe and mentioned by name in this tablet, strike you, look at you in anger and *curse* (*arratu*) you grimly with a painful *curse* (*arāru*). (VTE § 56).

> *Cursed* (ארור) shall you be when you come in, and cursed shall you be when you go out. The LORD will send upon you disaster, panic, and frustration in everything you attempt to do, until you are destroyed and perish quickly, on account of the evil of your deeds, because you have forsaken me (Deut 28:19–20).

> May all the gods that are [mentioned by name] in th[is] treaty tablet make the ground as narrow as a brick for you. May they make your ground like iron (so that) nothing can sprout from it. Just as rain does not fall from a brazen heaven so may rain and dew not come upon your fields and your meadows; instead of dew may burning coals rain on your land. (VTE § 63)

> The sky over your head shall be bronze, and the earth under you iron. The LORD will change the rain of your land into powder, and only dust shall come down upon you from the sky until you are destroyed. (Deut 28:23–24)

These and additional examples that Steymans discusses in his work lead him and others to date the beginning of the composition of Deuteronomy to the seventh century as a theological response to the Assyrian empire.

There is another scholarly voice that questions the dependence of Deuteronomy on the VTE. Some scholars suggest that Deuteronomy is not dependent on one single treaty but rather that it is in conversation with a broad ancient Near Eastern scribal culture (Mesopotamian or North West Semitic) that has produced a genre of treaties, some of which we have access to and others that we do not have access to. In her monograph *Israel and the Assyrians*, Carly Crouch argues that Deuteronomy does not contain any distinctive features that would signal to its readers an attempt to subvert the Assyrian imperial power. Crouch writes: "In the absence of the consistent and frequent use of distinctively Assyrian words, phrases, or ideas, which might have succeeded in signaling to Deuteronomy's audience a desire to be interpreted as an adaptation of Assyrian source material, these texts will have been understood and interpreted as a new work: one recognized as using existing native ideas and language to articulate its particular agenda, but an essentially new work. No more, no less."[51] In order to support this argument, Crouch begins with a theoretical discussion of what makes a "subversion" or an "allusion" work. Two conditions can be highlighted in this regard: (1) The new work must have distinctive features that would signal the earlier work or tradition that is being subverted; and (2) The audience of the new work must be familiar with the work that is sought to be subverted. After comparing Deuteronomy 13 and 28 with their counterparts from the VTE, Crouch concludes that these connections are too broad to sustain the argument that these passages were alluding to the VTE let alone translating them. She posits, "although some conceptual similarities exist between Deuteronomy and VTE, these similarities are not specific, distinctive, or frequent enough to act as an effective signal. They are, rather, the kind of similarities that arise when members of different societies use similar language to express similar norms in similar circumstances. Deuteronomy, therefore, should not be read as a subversive adaptation of VTE."[52] Furthermore, the themes of loyalty, blessings, and curses are quite common in ancient Near Eastern scribal traditions, so one can suggest there is subversion of a specific Assyrian loyalty oath. In addition, the majority of phrases, themes, and concepts that are present in Deuteronomy 13 and 28 are known elsewhere in the Hebrew Bible so that a Judahite audience would not have immediately assumed an Assyrian reference was being made by these texts. Finally, Crouch notes that "outside of Deut 13 and 28, there are no distinctively Assyrian elements in the laws that might signal a specific concern with Assyria or Assyrians. Rather, the rest of the core of the book is focused on issues internal to the community and the population of the southern Levant."[53] As the debate over the relationship between the book of Deuteronomy and the VTE continues among scholars, I would like to offer two remarks from a postcolonial perspective.[54]

Two Reflections on the Notion of Subversion

Scholarly discussions on the relationship between the biblical traditions embedded in Isaiah or Deuteronomy and the Assyrian imperial discourse have focused on the notion of subversion. From a postcolonial perspective this conversation can be taken further in two directions. First, postcolonial criticism has reflected extensively on another phenomenon, namely, mimicry, which can be fruitful in unpacking the ways the subaltern has responded, consciously or subconsciously, to the rhetoric and mission of the empire. Mimicry, simply defined, is the colonial attempt to make the colonized like the colonizer but not quite. But mimicry is not only about the colonizer; it also describes how the colonized undermines the colonial mission because, through repetition and difference, the colonized exposes the underlying anxiety and instability that mark the identity of the colonizer. Integrating the results of the linguistic or historical analyses of biblical texts and Assyrian literature with how postcolonial critics discuss the notion of mimicry will push the discussion beyond the subversive function of mimicry. Not all mimicry is subversive. Mimicry can help in drawing a more complex picture of how the colonized who are in power benefit from the imperial discourse and how the colonized who are the bottom of their colonial society struggle under the discourse that is imposed on them. Some manifestations of mimicry are explicit and even excessive. To the contrary, mimicry can also help in explaining the absence of clear markers of Assyrian discourse in Deuteronomy, as was pointed out by Carly Crouch, because for mimicry to function as a discourse of resistance it must be marked by a "repetition of partial presence" of the colonizer.[55] Partial presence is a significant trope in the notion of mimicry because it shows that difference still exists even in the midst of mimicry, and thus it points to the potential failure of the colonizer's mission and the ability of the colonized to resist the authority of the colonizer.[56]

Second, the biblical texts that were written by the powerless have fallen into the hands of the powerful and have been used to justify imperial expansions by European states and the United States. The texts that were written in order to undermine the Assyrian empire by way of mimicking its discourse left no marks to suggest they were meant to be subversive texts. These texts have become part of the fabric of the American Christian imagination without paying attention to the power differential between the powerless (ancient Israel) and the powerful (the United States). This is ironic to say the least. In 2003, when the United States waged a war against Iraq, the home of ancient Assyria, journalistic reports came out showing how George W. Bush embraced the book of Isaiah, which contains oracles against Assyria and Babylon. The irony here is that the texts that were written by the powerless to subvert the Assyrian imperial discourse have become the text of the empire (the United States) that invaded the powerless descendants of the Assyrians. This instance has important implications for postcolonial studies. Postcolonial analyses offer the world a gift because it is interested in power analyses. In addition, when postcolonial criticism is engaged with texts in their historical context as well as with readers and their contexts, postcolonial criticism seeks to empower the powerless by way of critiquing those who are in power and abuse the texts for their own political gain.[57]

During the war on Iraq, not only were texts relating to Assyria and its capital Nineveh employed to justify the war but also the biblical story of the book of Jonah played a significant role for Iraqi Christians who were affected by the war. Mitri Raheb mentions an important incident during the war on Iraq in 1991: "Peter Arnett, the C.N.N. correspondent in Baghdad, showed some pictures of Iraq on television on that same day, Sunday. Among other things that he showed was a church in Nineveh. A bomb had damaged the roof, dropped into the nave, and destroyed some church furniture and books. What remained was open to view. Some nuns and Iraqi Christians stood in the background; the priest was celebrating the Mass at the altar. I found it interesting that the book of the prophet Jonah was being read in that church on that same Sunday. . . . That this book of the prophet was an important one to read during those days—by those Iraqi Christians."[58] In other words, the ancient texts are simply old artifacts to gaze at, analyze, and study from a distance. They are animated in the world by those who abuse them to justify imperialism and violence, by those who are oppressed to find comfort in times of violence and stress, and by those who wish to resist the empire and work toward peace and justice.[59]

The Empire: Judgment or Transformation

The Book of the Twelve in the Hebrew Bible contains two books that are concerned with the fate of Nineveh. While the book of Nahum proclaims a message of divine judgment over Nineveh, in the book of Jonah the Ninevites understand the message of the prophet to be a call to repentance, which in turn saved them from the impending divine judgment.[60] These two books combined offer a rich path for postcolonial criticism to explore in relation to the violence of the empire. Both books show the complexity of and the telos of resisting the empire. If studied from a postcolonial perspective, both books invite the reader to explore important themes that relate to the possibility of the repentance and transformation of the empire. Is there a place in the process of decolonization for the empire to be called to change its ways of violence and oppression? Another theme is discussed in these two books that can enrich postcolonial studies in general and postcolonial reflection with regard to the Assyrian empire in particular: What does justice look like in the midst of repentance and reconciliation? How can the empire be transformed, while held accountable for its violence? Decolonization can take place by way of repentance or by way of divine judgment, and even in the event of reconciliation reparation is essential to reach a just reconciliation.

These two possibilities, judgment and forgiveness, can be traced in the Assyrian literature in the context of how the Assyrians treated the nations that broke their treaties. Liverani discusses these two possibilities in his monograph *Assyria the Imperial Mission*. A text from the time of Aššurbanipal describes the disasters that have come upon some Arab tribes because they have broken their treaty with the Assyrian gods and kings. "Uaite' with his troops, who did not respect my treaty, and who fled from before the weapons of Aššur my lord, the hero Erra (the plague god) rampaged against them. Famine spread among them: they ate the flesh of their children in hunger. Like a cruel destiny, the gods decreed the fulfillment of the curses down in their treaties." Later in the text, words are put in the mouths of the tribes who realize that these disasters have come upon them because they have broken the treaties: "The people of Arabia consulted one another, saying: 'for what reason has such cruelty fallen upon Arabia?' and (answering): 'It is because we did not respect the oath sworn to Aššur, and because we sinned against the benevolence of king Ashurbanipal.'"[61] Breaking political treaties was considered a sin against the Assyrian deities. A text from the time of King Esarhaddon puts words in the mouth of a vassal king who transgressed against Assyria, saying: "I committed a great sin against Aššur, and I did not listen to the words of the king my lord, ... the oath of the great gods, which I transgressed, and the word of your kingship, which I despised have caught up with me. May the anger of your heart be appeased. Have mercy on me and remove my punishment."[62] Here the rebellious king seeks to be acquitted from the sin and punishment. The Assyrian king Sargon II is an example of an Assyrian king who pardoned his enemies: "I had mercy on them, I hearkened to their prayers, I heard their supplication, and I said to them: *aḫulap!*"[63] In a similar way, it is reported that Aššurbanipal had mercy on Nikû (Necho) of Egypt, sparing his life and restoring him to his throne in Sais. While still paying a tribute, Nikû received favors from the Assyrian king. In another text, Aššurbanipal speaks of himself in the following way: "I, Ashurbanipal, who has a big heart, who does not hold a grudge, who forgives sins, had mercy on Tammaritu and permitted him and the offspring of his father's house to stay in my palace."[64] Thus, Assyrian literature shows a complex image of the Assyrian empire that exercised both punishment and forgiveness toward its vassal states. Contrary to the propaganda of the Assyrian empire, which gave the king the prerogative to forgive or punish, the books of Nahum and Jonah make the point that it is YHWH, the God of the peripheral Israel, who holds this power.

The book of Nahum contains an extended oracle against Nineveh, the capital of the Assyrian empire. Although the exact date of the book cannot be pinpointed with certainty, scholars believe that the book to have likely emerged within the period from the capture of Thebes by the Assyrians (663 BCE) to the capture of Nineveh by the Babylonians (612 BCE) or soon after. The book begins with a poem that celebrates YHWH as a divine warrior (Nah 1:2–8). This poem is believed to have developed independently and was integrated in the book through editorial work. The poem does not mention Assyria or Nineveh, but placing it at the beginning of the book gives a cosmological perspective on the judgment that is soon to be pronounced against Nineveh and Assyria. The poem intends to assert that the historical defeat of Assyria and the destruction of Nineveh by the Babylonians in 612 BCE is essentially the result of the work of YHWH, the God of Judah: "The Theophonic hymn accentuates the theological orientation of Nahum by emphasizing the invincibility of YHWH against his enemies."[65] The remaining parts of the book of Nahum pronounce judgment and destruction against Assyria's military machinery. No matter how large the number of its troops, Nineveh has no hope (1:12; 3:15–17). No swords or chariots or walls will protect the city (2:1–10). The empire with its mighty army that conquered and took gold and silver as booty, the city that received many emissaries with tributes, will now be plundered and all that is within it will be taken away (2:8). The empire that brought fear and terror upon all of its enemies will now experience the horror that it perpetuated for decades (2:10).

In his subversive discourse, the prophet Nahum undermines the Assyrian propaganda in similar ways to what we have seen in Isaiah. Peter Machinist points out connections between Isaiah and Nahum in their response to the Assyrian empire: (1) As noted in the preceding discussion, the Assyrian kings used the metaphor of the flood in order to animate the destructiveness of their campaigns. Nahum 1:8 describes the agents whom the divine warrior, YHWH, uses in order to defeat his enemies: "even in a rushing flood. He will make a full end of his adversaries, and will pursue his enemies into darkness."[66] (2) Nahum also speaks of the liberating act of YHWH in terms of breaking the bar and the yoke that represent the Assyrian hegemony (Nah 1:13, 3). Using the image of the lion in order to embody the fierce power of the Assyrian empire does not stand a chance before the judgment of YHWH, who turns the wild beasts into prey of the sword (Nah 2:11–13).[67] The main point of the book of Nahum is that the Assyrian empire, which has terrorized its neighbors, will eventually fall and its destruction is caused by the power of YHWH. In this way the book of Nahum seeks to decolonize the oppressed Judeans from the hegemony of the Assyrians by way of asserting the sovereignty of YHWH, the God of Judah. The destruction of the empire and its yoke, as well as the reversal of fortune, is one way of putting an end to the terror and oppression of the empire.

There is yet another response to the Assyrian empire that seeks to decolonize the oppressed, not by way of destroying the capital of the empire but by way of calling the empire to be transformed and to relent in its ways of violence. In judgment or in repentance, the program of decolonization is underway, because liberation from the empire is dependent on the sovereignty of God who brings about justice or who forgives the repenting empire. The book of Jonah is also concerned with the fate of Nineveh. Dating the book of Jonah is futile, and therefore determining its relationship to the book of Nahum is difficult to assess. Because both texts are part of the Book of the Twelve and because they now stand together in the Bible, I follow the view that these two texts should be kept in dialogue, creating a tension around divine justice and mercy. For our purposes here, postcolonial criticism can engage with the empire through the message of Jonah and the response of the Ninevites calling the empire to put an end to its use of violence, realizing that the God of the oppressed is at work bringing justice and liberation by breaking the cycle of violence. Decolonization is a complex process that is surrounded with many tensions and obscurities as is the relation between Nahum and Jonah as well as the overall meaning of the book of Jonah itself.

God sends the prophet Jonah to Nineveh with a very short message: "Forty days more, and Nineveh shall be overthrown!" The meaning of the message of Jonah is ambiguous because the Hebrew word *hfk* means to "be overthrown" or "to be overturned." As the text betrays its author, the prophetic message betrays the prophet who utters it. The Ninevites determine the meaning of the message through their response. They believe the word that was sent to them. They fast and put on sackcloth as a sign of remorse and penitence. The transformation begins with the people and not the king; but once the king hears of it, he commands what has already been done. The king is stripped of his power before he takes off his garment. The king leaves his throne, puts on sackcloth, and sits in ashes; all of this is a posture of repentance. He urges everyone to "cry mightily to God. All shall turn from their evil ways and from the violence that is in their hands. Who knows? God may relent and change his mind; he may turn from his fierce anger, so that we do not perish" (Jonah 3:9). As a result, God also "repents" and decides not to bring the evil that God had planned to bring upon them. Although God relented here about the punishment of the Ninevites, the whole book of Jonah ends in an ambiguous way: "Then the LORD said, 'You are concerned about the bush, for which you did not labor and which you did not grow; it came into being in a night and perished in a night. And should I not be concerned about Nineveh, that great city, in which there are more than a hundred and twenty thousand persons who do not know their right hand from their left, and also many animals?'" (Jonah 4:10–11). There is no interrogative at the beginning of verse 11; therefore, it could read: "I will not have concern about Nineveh." This adds to the ambiguity of the meaning of the book of Jonah: Has God forgiven Nineveh? Has Nineveh been transformed? The ambiguity of the meaning of Jonah and the difficulty of determining how Jonah's message relates to Nahum's message underlines the theological tension that surrounds how God relates to the empire that has filled the earth of violence.

It is my contention, however, that both Nahum and Jonah seek to decolonize the oppressed from the hegemony of the empire by asserting divine sovereignty to bring about justice upon the empire and by asserting divine freedom to forgive if the empire repents and if it changes its ways of violence.[68] Keeping both books in dialogue provides a rich language for the process of decolonization that seeks the liberation of the oppressed and that seeks the transformation of those commited to colonial and imperial violence. The recognition of the violence of the empire as sin and the call for repentance and transformation connects well with Robert Heaney's articulation of a postcolonial theology. Heaney addresses Christian communities that perpetuate colonialism and supremacy, asserting that the Spirit calls to "*penance*. Penance involves acts of reparation. Penance demonstrates that the church has heard, often through the prophetic voice of those who have experienced coloniality, the voice of God's judgment and grace."[69] One hopes that decolonization, either by judgment or repentance, would lead to the actualization of the prophetic vision of Isaiah who hoped, "On that day Israel will be the third with Egypt and Assyria, a blessing in the midst of the earth, whom the LORD of hosts has blessed, saying, "Blessed be Egypt my people, and Assyria the work of my hands, and Israel my heritage" (Isa 19:24–25).

NOTES

1. Karen Radner, *Ancient Assyria: A Very Short Introduction* (Oxford: Oxford University Press, 2015), 2–3.
2. K. Lawson Younger Jr., "Assyria's Expansion West of the Euphrates (ca. 870–701 BCE)," in *Archaeology and History of Eighth-Century Judah*, ed. Zev I. Farber and Jacob L. Wright (Atlanta: SBL Press, 2018), 17.
3. H. W. F. Saggs, *The Might That Was Assyria* (London: Sidgwick & Jackson, 1984), 72.
4. Christopher B. Hays with Peter Machinist, "Assyria and the Assyrians," in *The World around the Old Testament: The People and Places of the Ancient Near East*, ed. Bill T. Arnold and Brent A. Strawn (Grand Rapids: Baker Academic, 2016), 45.
5. John Anthony Brinkman, *A Political History of Post-Kassite Babylonia, 1158–722 B.C.* (AnOr 43; Rome: Pontifical Biblical Institute), 218–219.
6. Younger, "Assyria's Expansion," 25.
7. Christopher B. Hays, "Who Were the Assyrians?" *BAR* 45:3 (2019): 51–56, 66.
8. Mario Liverani, *Assyria: The Imperial Mission*, trans. Andrea Trameri and Jonathan Valk (Winona Lake, IN: Eisenbrauns, 2017).
9. Albert Kirk Grayson, *The Royal Inscriptions of Mesopotamia: Assyrian Periods* (Toronto: University of Toronto Press, 1987); and The *Royal Inscriptions of the Neo-Assyrian Period*, vols. 1–5 (Winona Lake, IN: Eisenbrauns, 2011–2018). Hereafter abbreviated as RIMA and RINAP.
10. RIMA 2, no. 101.1: i 40–43; cited in Liverani, *Assyria*, 15.
11. RIMA 3, no. 102.1:11–13; cited in Liverani, *Assyria*, 16.
12. RINAP 4, no. 1: Ii 30–39; cited in Liverani, *Assyria*, 20–21.
13. RINAP 3/1, no. 22: v 43–62; cited in Liverani, *Assyria*, 121.
14. K. Lawson Younger Jr., "Neo-Assyrian Inscriptions, Shalmaneser III, Kurkh Monolith" *COS* 2.113A, 261.
15. Younger, "Shalmaneser III," *COS* 2.113A, 261. A longer description goes on like this: "They prepared for war. They marched against me to do battle. With the exalted power of the divine standard which goes before me (and) with the fierce weapons which Aššur, my lord, gave, I fought with them. I decisively defeated them" (*COS* 2.113A, 262).

16. Younger, "Shalmaneser III," *COS* 2.113A, 262.
17. Beate Pongrats-Leisten, *Religion and Ideology in Assyria*, Studies in Ancient Near Eastern Records, 6 (Berlin: De Gruyter, 2015), 145.
18. Liverani, *Assyria*, 52.
19. See the examples in *COS* 2.113A, 261–262.
20. Liverani, *Assyria*, 41.
21. Liverani, *Assyria*, 47.
22. Liverani, *Assyria*, 92.
23. Liverani, *Assyria*, 97.
24. Liverani, *Assyria*, 60.
25. Liverani, *Assyria*, 60.
26. Mattias Karlsson, *Alterity in Ancient Assyrian Propaganda*, The Neo-Assyrian Text Corpus Project, State Archives Assyria Studies, vol. 26 (Winona Lake, IN: Eisenbrauns, 2017), 119–120.
27. Liverani, *Assyria*, 132.
28. Liverani, *Assyria*, 135.
29. *COS* 2.113A, 262.
30. Liverani, *Assyria*, 49.
31. Liverani, *Assyria*, 49.
32. Liverani, *Assyria*, 136–137.
33. Liverani, *Assyira*, 144.
34. Michel Foucault, *Discipline and Punish: The Birth of the Prison*, trans. Alan Sheridan (New York: Vintage Books, 1977).
35. Liverani, *Assyria*, 61.
36. *COS* 2.113A, 262.
37. Liverani, *Assyria*, 192–193.
38. Liverani, *Assyria*, 46.
39. I am borrowing this expression from Bill Ashcroft, Gareth Griffiths, and Helen Tiffin, *The Empire Writes Back* (London: Routledge, 1989).
40. Peter Machinist, "Assyria and Its Image in the First Isaiah," *JAOS* 103 (1983): 719–737, esp. 727.
41. Machinist, "Assyria," 722.
42. Machinist, "Assyria," 734.
43. See the discussion in Hays with Machinist, "Assyria and the Assyrians," 91–95, who discuss the conflicting narratives of what happened in 701 and scholarly construction of the relationship between Judah and Assyria during the time of Hezekiah.
44. Shawn Zelig Aster, "The Shock of Assyrian Imperial Ideology and the Responses of Biblical Authors in the Late Eighth Century," in *Archaeology and History of Eighth-Century Judah*, ed. Zev I. Farber and Jacob L. Wright (Atlanta: SBL Press, 2018), 475–488. For a full treatment of the topic see Shawn Zelig Aster, *Reflections of Empire in Isaiah 1–39: Responses to Assyrian Ideology*, Ancient Near East Monographs, 19 (Atlanta: SBL Press, 2017).
45. Aster, "Shock of Assyrian Imperial Ideology," 484.
46. M. Weinfeld, "Traces of Assyrian Treaty Formulae in Deuteronomy," *Bib* 46 (1965): 417–427.
47. B. M. Levinson, "Esarhaddon's Succession Treaty as the Source for the Canon Formula in Deuteronomy 13:1," *JAOS* 130 (2010): 337–348, 337.
48. Rintje Frankena, "The Vassal-Treaties of Esarhaddon and the Dating of Deuteronomy," *OTS* 14 (1965): 122–154.

49. H. U. Steymans, *Deuteronomium 28 und die Adê zur Thronfolgeregelung Asarhaddons: Segen und Fluch im Alten Orient und in Israel* (OBO 145. Gottingen: Vandenhoeck & Ruprecht, 1995).
50. Hans Ulrich Steymans, "Deuteronomy 28 and Tell Tayinat," *Verbum et Ecclesia* 34(2), Art. #870, 13 pages. http://dx.doi.org/10.4102/ve.v34i2.870.
51. Carly L. Crouch, *Israel and the Assyrians: Deuteronomy, the Succession Treaty of Esarhaddon, and the Nature of Subversion*, Ancient Near East Monographs, 8 (Atlanta: SBL Press, 2014).
52. Crouch, *Israel and the Assyrians*, 180.
53. Crouch, *Israel and the Assyrians*, 183.
54. See Hans Ulrich Steymans review of Carly Crouch's work in *Review of Biblical Literature* (02/2016); and Jeremy M. Hutton and C. L. Crouch, "Deuteronomy as a Translation of Assyrian Treaties: An 'Optimal Translation' Approach," *Hebrew Bible and Ancient Israel* 7.2 (2018): 201–252.
55. Homi Bhabha, *The Location of Culture* (London: Routledge, 1994, 2006), 126.
56. For the colonized, mimicry is not a telos in itself and it does not mean assimilation into the identity of the colonizer. "Only by stressing the way in which the text transforms the societies and institutions within which it functions (its 'transformative work') can such a mimicry be avoided and replaced by a theory and practice which embraces difference and absence as material signs of power rather than negation, of freedom not subjugation, of creativity not limitation." Aschcroft, Griffiths, and Tiffin, *Empire Writes Back*, 166.
57. Assyria, which was seen by the prophet Isaiah to be an agent of judgment, itself was brought under the divine judgment (Isa 10:13–14). From this observation R. S. Sugirtharajah warns contemporary leaders who abuse these biblical texts for their political advancement: "The Hebrew scriptures seem to suggest that empires, because of their military strength and the power that comes with it, are more than likely to behave arrogantly. Discrimination, oppression, inhumanity, cruelty and all forms of barbarity are not less barbarous because they are carried out by nations chosen as God's instrument. Presidents and prime ministers who seek biblical support for the messianic role of empires do well to realize that the same Bible has another harrowing message. Empires are an unreliable way of solving the world's problems, and those who take the sword will inevitably die by it." R. S. Sugirtharajah, *The Bible and Empire: Postcolonial Explorations* (Cambridge: Cambridge University Press, 2005), 191.
58. Mitri Raheb, *I Am a Palestinian Christian*, trans. Ruth Gritsch (Minneapolis: Fortress Press, 1995), 94.
59. One of the ways orientalism manifests itself in Western academies that study ancient communities of the ancient Near East is that these communities are usually treated as ancient and "dead" communities. Scholars who are leaning toward a historical approach shy away from asking the question about the connection between contemporary communities that live in the spaces they study and the ancient communities that inhibited these spaces. It is important to consider the continuity and the discontinuity between ancient and contemporary communities. It is no surprise that a prominent Assyriologist, A. Leo Oppenheim, titled his book *Ancient Mesopotamia: A Portrait of a Dead Civilization* (Chicago: University of Chicago Press, 1964). Contemporary Assyrian communities, however, in Iraq or the diaspora emphasize their relationship with the ancient Assyrians. Thus a decolonial approach that listens to the communities that are being studied should take this narrative into consideration and should pay attention to the contemporary suffering

of the Assyrian community that has been a target of genocide. John Joseph, *The Modern Assyrians of the Middle East: Encounters with Western Christian Missions, Archaeologists, and Colonial Powers* (Leiden: Brill, 2000); Hannibal Travis, ed., *The Assyrian Genocide: Cultural and Political Legacies* (London: Routledge, 2018).

60. Two important observations are in order: 1. Many scholars have suggested that the book of Jonah is not concerned with the Assyrian empire per se. The book has its own theological framework that deals with God's relationship with non-Israelites or as for others it deals with true and false prophecy. The fact that the story chose Nineveh for its focus calls the reader to consider the possibility that a conversation between Nahum (who is concerned with the fate of the capital of the Assyrian empire) and Jonah was intended. And the fact that the story chose to connect the tradition with a prophet from the Assyrian period might be telling (2 Kings 14:25; ca. 785 BCE). Ancient and modern readers continue to wonder about the relationship between Nahum and Jonah: Beate Ego, "The Repentance of Nineveh in the Story of Jonah and Nahum's Prophecy of the City's Destruction—A Coherent Reading of the Book of the Twelve as Reflected in the Aggada," in *Thematic Threads in the Book of the Twelve*, ed. Paul L. Redditt and Aaron Schart, BZAW 325 (Berlin: Walter de Gruyter, 2003), 155–164; Charles Conroy, "Jonah and Nahum in the Book of the Twelve: Who Has the Last Word?" *Proceedings of the Irish Biblical Association* 32 (2009): 1–23. 2. As I emphasize the notion of repentance and forgiveness in the story of Jonah, this is not meant to finalize the meaning of the book. The book has many facets to it, but that it can have multiple meanings does not take away the notion of forgiveness and repentance as an important theme in the book. Furthermore, my point in this section is far from animating Jonah as a pre-Christian Jew nor do I intend to use Jonah in order to defame Nahum. I think both voices are important theologically for postcolonial criticism. For the complexity of the meaning of the book of Jonah see Thomas Bolin, *Freedom Beyond Forgiveness: The Book of Jonah Re-Examined*, JSOTSS 236 (Sheffield: Sheffield Academic Press, 1997); and Yvonne Sherwood, *A Biblical Text and Its Afterlives: The Survival of Jonah in Western Culture* (Cambridge: Cambridge University Press, 2000).

61. Liverani, *Assyria*, 136–137.

62. RINAP 4, no. 33:I 22–24, Liverani, *Assyria*, 136. "With entreaty, prayer, expressions of humility, and kneeling against the wall of the city, he was bitterly crying: 'woe,' beseeching my lordship with open hands, and saying 'aḫulap' again and again to the heroic Aššur my lord and to the praise of my heroism." Liverani, *Assyria*, 146.

63. The etymology of the word *aḫulap* is uncertain, but Liverani reports that it might mean something along the lines of: forgiveness, salvation, cessation of punishment. Liverani, *Assyria*, 146.

64. Liverani, *Assyria*, 147.

65. James Nogalski, *The Book of the Twelve: Micah—Malachi*, Smyth & Helwys Bible Commentary (Macon, GA: Smyth & Helwys, 2011), 602.

66. See the reference to the rivers and the canals later in the book in Nahum 2:7, 9 [Heb. 2:6, 8 in Engl.].

67. Machinist, "Assyria," 735–736.

68. Janet Gains, *Forgiveness in a Wounded World: Jonah's Dilemma*, ed. Dennis Olson, SBL, Studies in Biblical Literature (Atlanta: Society of Biblical Literature, 2003).

69. Robert S. Heaney, *Post-Colonial Theology: Finding God and Each Other amidst Hate* (Eugene, OR: Cascade Books, 2019), 148.

CHAPTER 3

THE BABYLONIAN EMPIRE IN THE BIBLE

HEMCHAND GOSSAI

INTRODUCTION

This essay will approach the topic of the Babylonian Empire in the Bible broadly in terms of themes rather than focusing on each occurrence of the topic in biblical references. In this regard, several representative texts will be explored. Babylon and the Babylonian Empire have been characterized generally in negative terms, though in certain instances they are also identified positively. One of the important factors to reckon with in exploring the Babylonian Empire in the Bible centers on the multiple manifestations in which Babylon appears and how the topic is developed in the Bible. Within the limited scope here, one would note that, in Revelation 17–18, Babylon is characterized as a "whore" and the "whore of Babylon." In Genesis 11 the Tower of Babel episode extends the complexity and multifaceted representations of Babylon, while Daniel 3–4 recounts the interaction between Daniel and the Babylonian king. However, the most dominant role of the Babylonian Empire in the Bible is the Babylonian exile, with the repeated reference to Nebuchadnezzar as "God's servant." Psalm 137 captures the brutality of the exiles' experience and the longing for what once were their circumstances. Catherine Keller, in exploring the role of Empire and postcolonialism, argues:

> Empire indicates an organizational illness of history, clearly but not necessarily terminal.... Let us say that empire is a recurrent condition, an extraordinarily adaptive one that grows rapidly in each new manifestation, vicariously consuming the space it occupies.... [Y]et within imperial space allergy may turn into attraction; traditions may collude and mingle, birthing all manner of strange religio-cultural hybrids.[1]

The spectrum has to be understood contextually. The relevance of the Babylonian Empire and its influence on and role in Israel should not be predicated only on the interpreter's ideology or an ingrained theological orientation. While there are certainly hermeneutical trajectories one might pursue, the reality is that the Babylonian imperial influence is grounded in universal themes that are shaped by the particularities of contexts, experiences, social groups, and so on. Themes such as mercy, imperial power, exile, homecoming, despair, and betrayal, among others, have ongoing universal pertinence and applicability.

As important as historical foundations and *Sitz im Leben* may be in interpretation, we read the texts from where we are, defined in part by who we are. Interpreters reading alongside each other, but coming from different circumstances, will invariably explore texts differently, and that certainly enriches and widens the scope of the hermeneutical discourse. The conclusions may be different even as the lenses are different. The fluidity of such possibilities is a matter of challenging not only the status quo and established currency but also the acknowledged realization that each of us brings particular, contextual, and unique experiences to the text. Whatever hermeneutical principles are applied as ancient texts and themes are explored, there must also be an awareness of the voice of the text.

Across the centuries, the Babylonian Empire and its imperial machinations have been cited to cast derisive characterizations and allusions to contemporary empires. "Babylon is used in U.S. culture and commentary both to valorize and disparage empire's drive to unity, and also, in another vein to celebrate and denigrate the heterogeneity that might disrupt that unity."[2] Babylon would come to represent, figuratively, all that stands over and against God's Kingdom. Invariably Babylon has become the foil for some religious and political institutions that see themselves as the "New Israel" and Babylon as the classic archetype of the evil empire. For example, Babylon's propensity for extravagance in its architectural splendor, coupled with the brutal imperialism that the early Christian community assigned to Rome, which had displayed similar qualities, earned Rome the title of Babylon (Rev 14:8; 18:1–24).

The military and political reach of the Babylonian Empire has left, and continues to leave, its mark on society. The devastating presence of the Babylonian imperial force allows the reality of the exile and other defining moments of Babylonian influence in the Bible to endure as both historical reminiscences and consequential factors.

Exile, Despair, and Homecoming

Israel, God, and the Babylonian Empire intersect at multiple points, including the diverse reasons that precipitated the Babylonian exile. The ubiquitous presence of the Babylonian exile and its ripple effects in the Bible and society will be the principal focus of this discussion.

Reading texts in isolation might very well lead one to conclude that it was one incident or issue that was the generating factor that brought about the Babylonian exile. Collectively, however, we witness the range of interconnected issues that set in motion the exilic experience. It seems, as Halpern has argued, "the cause of the exile was cumulative, that the punishment meted out to peccant kings and their followers did not altogether expunge the guilt from the land."[3] The point is that collective actions of the people cannot be reduced or collapsed to only a single issue such as the profanity of the Temple or the corruption of Temple worship, as significant as these are. The extent of the Babylonian exile is such that it is inconceivable that it reflects the actions of one individual, one leader, or for that matter even one isolated community. By any measure, the exile seems to incorporate a level of punishment that spans time and space. With such a backdrop, the healing and restoration that will be necessary will not eventuate in one moment either: "The guilt of the nation has accrued over time."[4]

> [T]herefore thus says the Lord, the God of Israel, I am bringing upon Jerusalem and Judah such evil that the ears of everyone who hears of it will tingle. I will stretch over Jerusalem the measuring line for Samaria, and the plummet for the house of Ahab; I will wipe Jerusalem as one wipes a dish, wiping it and turning it upside down. I will cast off the remnant of my heritage, and give them into the hand of their enemies; they shall become a prey and a spoil to all their enemies, because they have done what is evil in my sight and have provoked me to anger, since the day their ancestors came out of Egypt, even to this day." (II Kings 21:10–15)

Perhaps it is the description in II Kings 21:15 that gives rise to the argument that the sins have been cumulative. The punishment is widespread and devastating with language of finality in the phrases "wipe Jerusalem. . . and turning it upside down" and Jerusalem becoming "a prey and spoil" for the enemy. Thus the description goes on to say "because they have done what is evil in my sight and have provoked me to anger, since *the day their ancestors came out of Egypt*, even to this day." The pain and degree of punishment would be reflected in the agonizing laments of the exiles.

The kings of both Babylon and Judah have enmeshed themselves in power struggles that further precipitated the suffering of the people, and such power struggles led inexorably to the exile. The actions of the kings and their penchant for power along with the Judean kings' ill-advised appeasement would shape the exilic experience. The fact is that, given the nature of their existence, the powerless masses did not have any consequential impact. This, of course, reflects one of the inherent mechanisms of a stratified society. For example, the alliances between Nebuchadnezzar and Jehoiachin might in the short term appear to have mutual benefits for both, but such an alliance came at a considerable cost: "Babylonian favor toward Jehoiachin, albeit that it exalts him above other captive kings, has its limits, namely, that of him remaining a modestly pensioned client in perpetual detention in Babylon."[5] Thus, while the kings enter into alliances that appear to have personal benefits, the exiles are left to negotiate a new identity in a foreign land. "Testing might be a social marker for those in transition, adapting and attempting to locate self-worth and sense of belonging and loyalty to prove something valid or contrarily a bias, seeking fairness especially from a minority's point of view."[6]

> Why have you forgotten us completely?
> Why have you forsaken us these many days?
> Restore us to yourself, O, Lord that we may be restored; renew our days as of old—

Unless you have utterly rejected us,
And are angry with us beyond measure? (Lam 5:20–22)

Even with the divine promise of homecoming for the exiles in Babylon, there is no particular prospect of emancipation, and so the prescient question is: Why leave a place in the captor's land, where more than likely roots are established, and return to a place that for many is no longer home?[7]

Frederick Niedner has noted, "The brutality of exile finds expressions in the Hebrew word for it גלה which means literally 'to go naked.' The expression derives from the Assyrian practice of stripping captives before driving them on forced marches to other regions."[8] The exiles will be stripped bare, and if not literally in this instance, certainly in other ways, as they seek to forge, survive, and live out a new identity. Judah's belief in its own military powers was in part responsible for the consequence of being utterly subordinated and taken into exile. Whatever militaristic inclination or impulse Judah might have had, ultimately force would not be the quality that would define it. Instead, as an exiled community without a time line for leaving the land of captivity, the people have been given a new ethic for living. The choice between שלום and military powers appears pointed and clear cut.[9]

> By the rivers of Babylon—
> there we sat down and there we wept
> when we remembered Zion.
> On the willows there
> we hung up our harps.
> For there our captors
> asked us for songs,
> and our tormentors asked for mirth, saying,
> "Sing us one of the songs of Zion!"
> How could we sing the Lord's song
> in a foreign land?
> If I forget you, O Jerusalem,
> let my right hand wither!
> Let my tongue cling to the roof of my mouth,
> if I do not remember you,
> if I do not set Jerusalem
> above my highest joy.
> Remember, O Lord, against the Edomites
> the day of Jerusalem's fall,
> how they said, "Tear it down! Tear it down!
> Down to its foundations!"
> O daughter Babylon, you devastator!
> Happy shall they be who pay you back
> what you have done to us!
> Happy shall they be who take your little ones
> and dash them against the rock! (Psalm 137)

"The spirit of revenge is overpowering, especially in the chilling final verse."[10]

It is important to note that Psalm 137, with its brutal imagery in verse 9, is placed firmly in the canonical context of psalms of praise and thanksgiving.

> Yet why would Psalm 137, accentuated by laments and curses, be placed in the midst of these thanksgiving and praise psalms. This is a bold but unconventional move that proposes to give thanks and praise through laments laden with honest feelings of enmity. Thanks and praise arise not only from the positive elements in life. Rather, the true mark of these practices in finding courage and strength to praise and give thanks when there is nothing worthwhile or praiseworthy.[11]

Psalm 137 begins with weeping, and this is punctuated by the memory of what once was. Jerusalem is on the minds and hearts of the exiles, and the sharpness of their memory, precisely because of its importance, brings a particular kind of melancholia. In this state of stark honesty and heartbrokenness, the exiles believe that they cannot sing songs of home—not because they are incapable but because memory coupled with taunts by their captors make it impossible to be joyful. While their tormentors ask for joy, the exiles are in a state of despair. Despite the divine promise of a homecoming in time, in the present exilic reality, joy has retreated in the distance. Fear and anger, despair and longing all make for an expression of violence that is shocking. Yet, in this context it is an appeal to God.

Revenge and pain are born out of the depth of suffering and a sense of betrayal and abandonment in the exilic experience. As much as any other text of Lamentation, Psalm 137 provides a backdrop of what exile is like in Babylon. The qualities of life, the range of emotions, the grasp of a lost existence, the evaporating of hopes and aspirations, and the loss of belonging and home have all left an indelible mark on the exiles. "It is not difficult to imagine why the Psalmist would utter such devastating words. The events of 587 entailed not only a collective experience of the destruction of the Temple and the city, but also the painful loss of children."[12] Yet, this psalm is not only about unrestrained violent revenge but also about how, in the midst of extraordinary and life-transforming despair, the exiles' memory will not allow them to neglect or forget the history of their relationship with God and Jerusalem. Thus, the canonical placement of Psalm 137 alongside psalms of praise and lament is not in any way misplaced. Rather, this is an appeal to God in the midst of the suffering brought about by God and sanctioned by God. One of the protracted and persistent themes in Psalm 137 is the idea of how to balance the need for cultural assimilation while ensuring that one's religious and national identity is maintained. Further, it addresses how to ensure that the voice of the exiles is not muted or silenced, so they are able to complain and appeal to God with searing cries and not resort to violent acts.

> Taken literally, the Hebrew of Lam. 2:18a reads: "their heart cried," and serves as a reminder that the suffering and despair of the exiles come from their hearts, hidden from the world, but known to God. These tears will continue, and the belief is that

God might still respond. For the audience then, and now, the idea of crying from the heart, or "heartbroken" is acutely understood with a sense that what comes from the heart comes from the core of who one is, stripped of all pretense, and only God ultimately knows. The exploration of this theme is predicated on the suffering of the exiles in Babylon and God's punishment.... What cannot be lost in the reading and interpretation is that the suffering in the Exile was brought about by God's action, and a promise that says, I will return, and I will bring you home, and then the total silence and seeming impotence that ensues. Can the representation of divine speech ever regain plausibility?[13]

The exiles know that the Babylonian exile will not last forever, and as much as the temptation to seek revenge is present, it is the memory of the exiles and their appeal to God that contextualizes the climactic verse. One of the definable elements borne out of the Babylonian influence is the painful reality of loss of life as captives and exiles.

A further theme in Psalm 137 surrounds the influence of Babylon on Israel. The psalm accentuates the devastating violence of Edom against Israel, its blood relative. Perhaps foremost is the unconscionable action of Edom in its betrayal of the Judeans by turning them over to the Babylonians. The psalm stands as a sharp recollection of those who have caused them pain and provides a juxtaposition of both covenantal kin and enemy. Psalm 137 underlines the unbridled freedom to question and challenge God, knowing that in so doing they will not nullify the covenant relationship. Thus, we have the terrifying vision of smashing heads of Babylonian children, and perhaps this also indirectly indicts God on allowing the devastating violence against the Jewish children. The point here that should not be subsumed is: "Trauma can lead to transformation, but it could also lead to absolute disintegration if we are left to our own persecutory fears and anxiety."[14] We know that trauma does not leave one untouched and there are certainly intended and unintended consequences.

> Could "there" for an exile or prisoner become what his or her "here" was in a life taken away? ... Can one be forced to sing in a fabricated "here" not only for the captors, but also sing songs in tribute to God, the silent God, the God who sent them into exile? Under these circumstances can that place ever become "here"? Even if it were possible to go home again, unlikely as that was ... there was no home. One may certainly point to the construction of the second Temple and the rebuilding of the city and the reinstituting of the religious laws ... but as important and even momentous as these were, the construction of meaning and trust are much more intense and difficult to undergo. Yet, such construction of meaning and trust are foundational.[15]

My Servant

There is an inescapable interface between divine and imperial power regarding the Babylonian Empire in the Bible. The path defining God and Israel is not one-dimensional; the journey includes God and the world and Israel and the nations. What is needed is a soul-searching reckoning of the Babylonian Empire and its imperial impulses. Can one speak about Israel—about the canonical process and about the canon itself—without seriously and fully embracing the complex role of Babylon and the expansive shadow of the Babylonian Empire. As John Rose terms it, it is about "Jerusalem's creative collision with Babylon."[16] As the relational interface between God and Babylon evolves, it becomes clear that King Nebuchadnezzar estimates himself to be God's counterpart in terms of power. He cultivates his "divine" quality while seeking to subvert that of YHWH, all the while designated as *my servant* by God. However, in functioning at the behest of YHWH, a postcolonial reading would view such divine bidding as subversive by definition.

> Sit in silence, and go into darkness,
> daughter Chaldea!
> For you shall no more be called
> the mistress of kingdoms.
> I was angry with my people,
> I profaned my heritage;
> I gave them into your hand,
> you showed them no mercy;
> on the aged you made your yoke
> exceedingly heavy.
> You said, "I shall be mistress forever,"
> so that you did not lay these things to heart
> or remember their end. (Isaiah 47:5–7)

The issues that led to the exile are clearly, sharply, and succinctly delineated in this Isaiah text. There is a finely honed introspective moment that clarifies who controls and defines the contours of power. Even though Nebuchadnezzar is the servant and architect of the destruction of Jerusalem and the execution of the exile, his role is at the behest of God and ultimately subversive. What is transparent is that despite Nebuchadnezzar's relentless quest to usurp the role and power of God, it will not happen. Nebuchadnezzar's role as God's servant will be predicated on fulfilling YHWH's expectation, including mercy to the exiles.

> Such to you are those with whom you have labored,
> who have trafficked with you from your youth;
> they all wander about in their own paths;
> there is no one to save you. (Isa 47:15)

Thus, when the Babylonian king does not follow through on showing mercy, the king and Babylon will be punished. As Isa 47:15 indicates, Babylon will not be able to save itself from its imperial trajectory. Despite the numerous reminders of the distinction between divine and imperial power, Nebuchadnezzar's overt malevolence is regularly on display. It is evident that Nebuchadnezzar acts in a manner where he is the principal beneficiary. Thus, for example, after Daniel and his friends are sentenced to death, "The king answered the Chaldeans; this is a public decree: if you do not tell me both the dream and its interpretation, you shall be torn limb from limb, and your houses shall be laid in ruins" (Dan 2:5). Yet, at the end of the episode, Nebuchadnezzar appears to express his gratitude. This, however, does not last for any particular length of time as once again, in Daniel 3, the king demands public adoration and worship, and with their refusal, Daniel and his friends are sentenced to death in a fiery furnace.

> Belteshazzar answered, "My lord, may the dream be for those who hate you, and its interpretation for your enemies! The tree that you saw, which grew great and strong, so that its top reached to heaven and was visible to the end of the whole earth, whose foliage was beautiful and its fruit abundant, and which provided food for all, under which animals of the field lived, and in whose branches the birds of the air had nests—it is you, O king! You have grown great and strong. Your greatness has increased and reaches to heaven, and your sovereignty to the ends of the earth. . . . [T]his is the interpretation, O king, and it is a decree of the Most High that has come upon my lord the king: You shall be driven away from human society, and your dwelling shall be with the wild animals. You shall be made to eat grass like oxen, you shall be bathed with the dew of heaven, and seven times shall pass over you, until you have learned that the Most High has sovereignty over the kingdom of mortals, and gives it to whom he will. As it was commanded to leave the stump and roots of the tree, your kingdom shall be re-established for you from the time that you learn that Heaven is sovereign. Therefore, O king, may my counsel be acceptable to you: atone for your sins with righteousness, and your iniquities with mercy to the oppressed, so that your prosperity may be prolonged." (Dan 4:19–27)

The Daniel narrative memorializes a reminder that the role of Nebuchadnezzar and the Babylonian Empire did not disappear and fade into the shadows after the exile. Rather, there continues in Daniel the ongoing juxtaposition of divine and imperial power, and the counter challenge by Daniel and his friends to Nebuchadnezzar who sought to supplant the role of YHWH. It is no surprise that the principal issue in the dream and its interpretation is that of power and the immanent loss of imperial power. Moreover, we see in these Daniel episodes the ongoing and perpetual manifestations of the Babylonian presence. The quest by the Babylonian king essentially remains the same: imperial power over and against divine power. In this Daniel episode, there is an indication by Nebuchadnezzar that there will be punishment of those who would not show the expected obeisance to him as divine.

> Rather than focusing on the homeland and that community, Daniel and his friends were willing to join the ranks of their new community; but they refused Babylonian religious identity as represented by the king's rations for priests. Thus Daniel and his three friends understood eating the rations as conversion or religious syncretism.

But by rejecting the king's ration, they maintained adherence to their religious and ethical convictions.[17]

One cannot underestimate the degree to which Nebuchadnezzar sought to enhance his own sense of self and tyrannical power. As God's servant, he frames mercy through a discernible sense of force and brutality. He seeks divine status through force and entitlement, and when this is not acknowledged with the respective honor and adoration, those who refuse to acquiesce to such deference are punished, invariably with the threat of death. This sense of instability and lack of constancy, coupled with capriciousness, can be identified throughout the Hebrew Bible. "It is striking that King Nebuchadnezzar is not very consistent in his beliefs. He is not the typical servant of the LORD we know from the other books of the Hebrew Bible. He remains the fickle tyrant with his good and bad days."[18]

First, God designates King Nebuchadnezzar as "my servant"; shocking by any measure not least being the fact that Nebuchadnezzar was the principal architect of both the annexation and the captivity of Judah. The "plucking up and breaking down; the destroying and overthrowing" attest to the degree to which God will go in identifying with a suitable imperial destroyer. The imperial roles here are inextricably intertwined. God employs the enemy as his servant, not for the first time in Hebrew scripture, but here Nebuchadnezzar will "ravish" the people.[19]

I am going to send for all the tribes of the north, says the Lord, even for King Nebuchadnezzar of Babylon, my servant, and I will bring them against this land and its inhabitants, and against all these nations around; I will utterly destroy them, and make them an object of horror and of hissing, and an everlasting disgrace. (Jer 25:9)

Now I have given all these lands into the hand of King Nebuchadnezzar of Babylon, my servant, and I have given him even the wild animals of the field to serve him. (Jer 27:6)

[A]nd say to them, Thus says the Lord of hosts, the God of Israel: I am going to send and take my servant King Nebuchadnezzar of Babylon, and he will set his throne above these stones that I have buried, and he will spread his royal canopy over them. (Jer 43:10)

These three instances in Jeremiah (25:9; 27:6; 43:10) where Nebuchadnezzar is referred to as God's servant certainly makes this designation decidedly disquieting. These texts seem to suggest a transferring of divine power and loyalty, as well as the apparent abandonment of Judah; in so doing there is an apparent fracturing of the relationship between God and the Jews. The breadth of power attributed to the Babylonian king is evidenced as he is granted power over all of creation. While the emphasis in these texts is typically on the exile of the Jews, it is clear that Nebuchadnezzar has an all-encompassing spectrum of power over creation. The nations are commanded to obey or face the consequences.

For thus says the Lord of hosts, the God of Israel: I have put an iron yoke on the neck of all these nations so that they may serve King Nebuchadnezzar of Babylon, and they shall indeed serve him; I have even given him the wild animals. (Jer 28:14)

Smelik has noted that "Nebuchadnezzar is the master of all the nations of the earth, including Judah, because the LORD has appointed him to rule over the world."[20] As we see in Jeremiah 29:21, the idea of being God's servant is wide-ranging in scope. "Thus says the Lord of hosts, the God of Israel, concerning Ahab son of Kolaiah and Zedekiah son of Maaseiah, who are prophesying a lie to you in my name: I am going to deliver them into the hand of King Nebuchadnezzar of Babylon, and he shall kill them before your eyes." In this precise pronouncement, God consigns to Nebuchadnezzar two false prophets to be executed. Nebuchadnezzar as God's servant is also God's executioner. The *imperial hand* that is required to be merciful will also be the *imperial hand* that executes on God's behalf.

Besides the positive influence and expectation of mercy and righteousness on the part of the Babylonian king, there is also the likelihood of unintended negative consequences. For example, the actions of the false prophets about whom Jeremiah speaks are so egregious that the term used by the prophet to describe their punishment is קלה. The significance of the term in this context lies in its rare usage as a form of punishment. It hints at the fact that this punishment is akin to the death penalty. The term is applied expressly for those who have been entrusted to speak the prophetic truth. But even as the citizens were heading into exile, the false prophets have chosen audaciously to proclaim a false sense of security and peace when there was no peace. "They [the false prophets] proclaimed the end of Babylonian hegemony over Judah. Therefore, fear of their spreading a spirit of rebellion appears to be Nebuchadnezzar's most likely motive for ordering their execution: consonant with Jeremiah's interpretation of history, Nebuchadnezzar acts here as a mere instrument of God's plan."[21] Moreover, these false prophets were actively undermining the punitive measures and the capacity for good and survival that YHWH spoke through the prophet Jeremiah. The devastation of their actions is such that קלה stands over against the typical Hebrew term used for burning. "Jer 29:22 uses the root קלה ('to burn, roast') to refer to the execution of the condemned prophets, rather than שרף which is the verb that normally refers to the burning of the individual in the Bible."[22]

Such a dramatic and pointed expression of the divine punishment underscores the blatant disregard of the divine message by the false prophets as they lead the people intentionally into a false sense of security and hope. In particular, misappropriating the notion of peace as the impetus for security is singularly egregious given the significance and hopeful quality of peace. False prophets preaching false hope will be executed using the language of being roasted to death. There is undoubtedly an influence of Israel on Babylon and the manner in which punishment might be meted out and the gruesome nature of the punishment.

An inherent challenge in the relationship between the kings of Babylon and YHWH is the nonnegotiable expectation by YHWH that there must be mercy by the Babylonian kings. In whatever context or circumstance, mercy is foundational, and given the Jeremiah 28:14 text outlining the breadth of control, all of creation must be granted mercy. The imperial Babylonian leadership however did not seem to share such a perspective, nor were they particularly committed in ensuring justice for an exiled people.

> Israel, when it is theologically intentional, and will not entertain the notion that "might makes right." Positively, this claim asserts that political power inherently and intrinsically has in its very fabric the reality of mercy, the practice of humaneness, or as Daniel dares to say to Nebuchadnezzar the care of the oppressed.[23]

The intersection of Babylon as servant and Babylon as oppressive imperial power is incontestably stated. There is no conversation between YHWH and Nebuchadnezzar or between Jeremiah and Nebuchadnezzar. No power, howsoever defined by various successes, is not above or beyond divine mercy, given the inseparable weaving of Israelite and Babylonian identities. Literally and as a figurative representation of imperial power in a distinct and discernible demonstration, the Empire is not beyond mercy and redemption. Even though Nebuchadnezzar might not feel compelled to show mercy to the exiles, both king and Empire will be held accountable, and this would be one of the foundational factors for indictment and punishment. The Empire is not free to live and function on its own accord or to function only by *its* particular code of ethics. Despite being in exile, the people will remain God's covenant people. Babylon's imperial power will not last forever, as there will be an inevitable collapse. Certainly, one of the cautionary admonitions generated is not to dilute or abandon the moral fabric of a society for the sake of imperial military power.

Ultimately however, it would be a mistake to dismiss Nebuchadnezzar as a foil to simply emphasize the power of God. There is an important subversive place for the Empire in the divine imagination. Counter to Nebuchadnezzar's role as captor, homecoming for the exiles will be orchestrated by another unlikely servant of God—God's anointed, Cyrus, the Persian king.

> [T]he wrath of the gods did not lead to a Babylonian defeat, but to the appointment of a righteous, although foreign, ruler by a merciful God. Cyrus' victory did not cause the downfall of the city of Babylon. Instead, his actions resulted in the liberation of Babylon's inhabitants from a wicked tyrant and in an end to their misery."[24]

In the displacement of Nabonidus as king over Babylon, Cyrus was placed as king over Persia. God's choice of Cyrus demonstrates the importance of liberation and freedom over political ideology, nationality, or religious identity. Cyrus, like Nebuchadnezzar, is called "God's servant," but for markedly different reasons. What we do know is that the title "my servant" does not necessarily mean that the individual is righteous or virtuous but rather that in prescribed circumstances the person acts at God's behest.

> King Nebuchadnezzar, however, is just the opposite of King Cyrus. He is responsible for the destruction of the Temple of Jerusalem and for the deportation of part of the population. . . . Nebuchadnezzar would be the last person to be honoured by God

with the title נרי, this epithet is thrice bestowed on him—at least in the Hebrew text of Jeremiah.[25]

"My servant" could be a designation for a national leader who is anointed, such as David or Solomon; an outsider, such as Cyrus or Nebuchadnezzar; or one who might be seen as a family patriarch. Divine servanthood may therefore be attributed to anyone—and the spectrum spans the individual to the nation. The difference in the characteristic nature of Nebuchadnezzar and Cyrus further underlines the complexity of the moniker "my servant." YHWH's servant may function to bring about bondage or freedom, mercy or punishment.

Welfare of the Other

"Thus says the Lord, the God of Israel, to whom you sent me to present your plea before him: If you will only remain in this land, then I will build you up and not pull you down; I will plant you, and not pluck you up; for I am sorry for the disaster that I have brought upon you. Do not be afraid of the king of Babylon, as you have been; do not be afraid of him, says the Lord, for I am with you, to save you and to rescue you from his hand. I will grant you mercy, and he will have mercy on you and restore you to your native soil. But if you continue to say, 'We will not stay in this land,' thus disobeying the voice of the Lord your God and saying, 'No, we will go to the land of Egypt, where we shall not see war, or hear the sound of the trumpet, or be hungry for bread, and there we will stay,' then hear the word of the Lord, O remnant of Judah. Thus says the Lord of hosts, the God of Israel: If you are determined to enter Egypt and go to settle there, then the sword that you fear shall overtake you there, in the land of Egypt; and the famine that you dread shall follow close after you into Egypt; and there you shall die. All the people who have determined to go to Egypt to settle there shall die by the sword, by famine, and by pestilence; they shall have no remnant or survivor from the disaster that I am bringing upon them." (Jer 42:9–17)

In this text the prophet outlines the complex reasons why YHWH sent the people into exile while simultaneously expressing the palpable sorrow that is inherent in such a decision. In the midst of such a consequential decision there is divine regret. On the one hand, there is the intransigence and arrogance of Judah's successive kings, but on the other there is the promissory mercy that is expressed. However, while there is divine sorrow and the promise of mercy, important and essential as these are, they are not enough for the nullification of the exile decision. As if to underline the decision that exile in Babylon is not negotiable, the people are also given a dire warning with commensurate dire consequences. Given the circumstances and the reality of captivity, the exiles might have entertained the idea of escaping into Egypt instead of living out their exile in Babylon. However, yielding to such a temptation is preempted by God. Not only will such an action be viewed as blatant disregard and disobedience of a divine mandate, it will also inevitably lead to a Babylonian reprisal against what will be perceived as overt defiance of the Babylonian power. In normal times, the Lord would have crushed the Babylonian enemy, but in this time of woe, the Babylonian king has become a servant to the Lord instead of the foe. "Therefore the people of Judah should obey their oppressor, King Nebuchadnezzar, and therefore the exile in Babylon should accept their difficult life without protest or despair."[26] Shrouded in the language of punishment is a veiled sense of protection of the exiles.

In the Babylonian exile, the Jews are called upon to redefine their identity, and they are told that their very identity will be inextricably interwoven with that of the Babylonians. This will not be the people's choice, but rather a divine and prophetic mandate. This exile becomes, among many things, an occasion for a sharp redefining of how imperial power, which posits itself as invincible, will potentially be reshaped in the face of a newly construed peace ethic.

> Take wives and have sons and daughters; take wives for your sons, and give your daughters in marriage, that they may bear sons and daughters; multiply there, and do not decrease. But seek the welfare of the city where I have sent you into exile, and pray to the Lord on its behalf, for in its welfare you will find your welfare. (Jer 29:6–7)

The outline in Jeremiah 29 sets the platform for this potential transformation, and perhaps the Babylonian Empire will ultimately show mercy and, as a template for all nations, will come to demonstrate the nature of divine power. As one sees in Jeremiah 29, the manner in which relationships between citizens and exiles, migrants and refugees, and others are forged and nurtured may differ significantly from established norms. This is *shalom* versus *war*, where one's existence is integrally tied to the very existence, sustenance, and care of the other. "The impossibility for the descendants of the deportees to resettle in the traditional homeland was therefore the norm rather than the exception. It meant that they had no realistic option but to seek the welfare of the cities to which they were sent (Jer 29:7) if they were to prosper or even survive."[27] It is clear that Jeremiah's idea of being in exile and what such a reality will mean is distinctly different from those of others. This is notably seen in the interface with Hananiah, whose message on the surface appears positive and more humane. Yet, it might be Jeremiah's vision of the future, predicated painfully on the present exile, that would seek to bring about a reconstruction of an equitable relationship between the common people and the elite, both of whom will face the exile together. Jeremiah's vision is a painful one, but it contains a vision of the future. O'Connor insightfully notes:

> Blaming becomes a strategy for survival. . . . As a theology of human responsibility for the politics of the world, blaming is a prophetic survival tactic for the nation. . . . Jeremiah's accusations are a balm in Gilead, a healing ointment for the wounds of the people. It is difficult to see Jeremiah's blaming as a healing vision today, except for one important point. Jeremiah's theology of blame insists on the human capacity to

shape the course of events. It reminds us of our vocation to live in fidelity, justice and right relationship with others with the cosmos and with God.[28]

It might be that on the surface blaming is negative and inflammatory, but it must be noted that this blaming is generated by God and Jeremiah's vision of a new future. This is part of the essential vision as the exiles begin a new journey of שׁלום.

Compassion begets compassion. While in exile, the Jews are expected to be shown compassion and mercy. What the Babylonian Empire has exemplified with clarity is the fact that compassion, mercy, and justice are not narrowly construed and located in an exclusive geography. As the king of Babylon functions as God's servant, he must simultaneously reflect the divine qualities. In Jeremiah 29, there is a sense of how YHWH uses the Babylonian establishment to shape an ethic of compassion and community on the part of the Jews. In this respect, YHWH, Nebuchadnezzar, Judah, and Babylon have identities that intersect at significant points.

The Babylonian Empire and its leadership acknowledge and execute legitimately the necessary and essential changes. While there might be a variety of ways in which the transformation will eventuate, there are two qualities in particular that are essential, namely righteousness and mercy for the oppressed. Ultimately the story about the Babylonian captivity not only regards what the exiles need to do to survive in terms of the relationship to their captors but also shows an understanding of Babylon and the role it has to play in executing the mercy of God.

The Babylonian king might have believed that he was beyond admonition and censure and thus that his power was limitless in the present. In reality, neither his rule nor his power was infinite. This is not to suggest that YHWH does not care about the immediate reality but rather that YHWH has a particular vision of the future. What we do know is that ultimately it is YHWH who will prevail over the imperial king Nebuchadnezzar. The evidence is that neither Israel and the exiles nor Nebuchadnezzar and the Babylonian Empire will remain unchanged or persist beyond change. Thus, a notable example is Daniel's interpretation of the dream sequence in Daniel 4 and Nebuchadnezzar's quest to determine the meaning. When Daniel's interpretation is given to the king, it is couched in language that specifies the dire prospects of the king's future, together with the counsel and wisdom to care and to show mercy and righteousness for the oppressed. That is to say, the possibility for change and redemption is embodied in the dream.

Two ideas converge at this point. First, it is possible that mercy and righteousness are both within the parameters of an imperial government, and that these realities are not mutually exclusive. Second, there is the pronounced notion that those with power who choose to rule with force, but without a sense of justice, mercy, and righteousness, may for a while feel the quality of permanence in their potency, but such self-assurance will not last. Ultimately empires collapse under such an unsustainable burden of unfiltered power, as in fact the Babylonian Empire did. As Brueggemann writes:

> Again the inclination of God and the disposition of Babylon are intimately related to each other. It is not doubted that the Babylonian empire could be a place of mercy.

The exiles can be a place of compassion, but that can only be because God hears prayers and attends to the needs of the exiles. The Empire is a place where God's inclination for mercy can indeed be effected in a concrete, public way. Babylon can enact what God grants.[29]

What we note in the YHWH/Babylon interaction is the increased flexing of imperial force as a quest to control and establish unbridled power. "Jews and the God of the Jews must come to terms with the definitional role of Babylon. It was exactly the experience and metaphor of *Babylonian exile* that made the question of mercy so acute."[30] It is an irrefutable reality that, for all Jews after the exile, Babylon and the Babylonian exile will leave an indelible mark on their identity. But this mark is also very much in evidence in the relationship with YHWH, who orchestrated both the exile and the deliverance. Babylon thus would be a place of mercy in the context of captivity, and the identity of the exiles will be redefined. It comes to shape one's identity and an understanding of all relationships and belonging thereafter. Brueggemann, citing Jacob Neusner (*Understanding Seeking Faith* [Atlanta: scholars Press, 1986], 137–141) has observed that it is exactly this exilic experience that has become a "paradigm for the self-understanding of all Judaism, a paradigm only loosely connected with the historical realities."[31]

FUTURE CONSIDERATIONS

It is conceivable that the Babylonian Empire and its defining role in the exile/migration of the Jews have given shape to a biblical template for how one lives as a migrant. We know that historically migration happens for a variety of reasons, and the biblical memory constitutes forced migration. Could the experience of Babylonian captivity aid in defining the manner in which refugees and others might be welcomed in a community? This remains a lingering existential question. Equally aligned is the notion of how a community or nation welcomes the exiled and migrants who seek refuge. Such a template for refugee status has had extraordinary implications and served as an impetus for centuries as refugees and migrants from a variety of geographical contexts and a spectrum of particularities, including religion, ethnicity, nationality, caste, political affiliations, economics, and, perhaps most notably war, have sought a haven. "Attention to the social, economic, and traumatic factors in circumstances and contexts of subordination, disaster, warfare, or political oppression (either individually or group) has led in recent years . . . to increased attention to Posttraumatic Stress Disorder."[32] While a development of forced migration and the ensuing trauma generated by such migration is beyond the scope of this essay, it is an area that is being addressed by scholars.

In particular we might reflect on those persons whose lives were defined by an exilic experience in which they were made voiceless through the actions of those with human power and the punitive actions of God. Many may be called the "in-between generation," as the exiles in Babylon might have been classified. Their lives had to be acculturated to the extent that they embraced the mores of Babylon while seeking the welfare of their captors. Given the duration of the Babylonian exile, many of the in-between generation would only know Babylon as their home. It is a common hallmark for exiles and refugees that for a while they may have a longing for "home," but invariably "home" may very well be the idea of belonging and not necessarily a geographical location. "The basic social construction of reality is how does one live and even advance in the diaspora—individually or collectively? How does one survive in the wilderness, individually or collectively?"[33]

The experience of the Babylonian exiles and the overarching shadow of the Babylonian Empire on Israel are factors that undoubtedly have influenced and shaped the manner in which a society is defined through neighborliness. With a morphing or conflation of Babylon and Babel, one of the realities that might have influenced Judah is the theme that diversity is to be embraced as a strength and, perhaps, that the idea of neighborliness and care for the other will challenge the narrowly construed rebuilding of Jerusalem and the reconstituting of a community of faith. The exilic experience established the inextricable connection between one's welfare and that of the other, particularly when the other's identity is that of oppressor and enemy. Such a principle is not guided by nationality, religion, ethnicity, status, station in life, or similar influences. The exile in Babylon underlines the philosophical and practical approach to governing and the politics of government. Along the lines of the Tower of Babel story, Leon Kass, for example, advocates for war and conflict as a manner in which unity is brought about.[34] As an often unexpected and perhaps unintended consequence, such an impulse for war and conflict might in fact have the opposite effect. As Erin Runions writes, "Somewhat counter intuitively, in this view, multiplicity and conflict push humans to seek out *unified* truths and virtues."[35]

Notes

1. Catherine Keller, "The Love of Postcolonialism: Theology in the Interstices of Empire," *Postcolonial Theologies: Divinity and Empire*, edited by Michael Nausner and Mayra Rivera (St. Louis, MO: Chalice, 2004), 221–222.
2. Erin Runions, "Empire's Allure: Babylon and the Exception to Law in Two Conservative Discourses," *Journal of the American Academy of Religion* 77, no. 3 (September 2009): 681.
3. Baruch Halpern, "Why Manasseh Is Blamed for the Babylonian Exile: The Evolution of a Biblical Tradition," *Vetus Testamentum* 48, no. 4 (October 1998): 482
4. Ibid., 484.
5. Donald F. Murray, "Of All the Years the Hopes—or Fears? Jehoiachin in Babylon," *Journal of Biblical Literature* 120, no. 2 (2001): 263.
6. John Ahn, "Made in Babylon: Daniel I," in *T&T Clark Handbook to Asian American Biblical Hermeneutics*, edited by Uriah Kim and Seung Ai Yang (London: T&T Clark, 2019), 318.
7. See Hemchand Gossai, "Jeremiah's Welfare Ethic and the Challenge to Imperial Militarism," in *Post Colonial Commentary and the Old Testamen* (London: Bloomsbury Academic Press, 2019), 259.

8. Frederick A. Niedner Jr., "Rachel's Lament," *Word and World* 22, no. 4 (2002): 408.
9. See Gossai, "Jeremiah's Welfare," 264.
10. David W. Stowe, "Babylon Revisited: Psalm 137 as American Protest Song," *Black Music Research Journal* 32, no. 1 (Spring 2012): 97.
11. John Ahn, "Psalm 137: Complex Communal Laments," *Journal of Biblical Literature* 127, no. 2 (2008): 275–276.
12. Ibid., 287.
13. Hemchand Gossai, "Reading Lamentations after the Shoah," in *Reading Lamentations Intertextually*, LHBOT Series, edited by Brittany Melton and Heath Thomas (London: Bloomsbury Academic Press, 2019), n.p.
14. Victor Jeleniewski Seidler, "'Their Hearts Melted and Became as Water,' Lamentations: Ethics after the Shoah," *EuroJ* 44, no. 2 (2011): 706.
15. Gossai, "Reading Lamentations," n.p.
16. John Rose, "Jerusalem's Creative Collision with Babylon," *Holy Land Studies* 11, no. 2 (2012): 217.
17. Ahn, "Made in Babylon," 324.
18. Klaas A. D. Smelik, "My Servant Nebuchadnezzar: The Use of Epithet, 'My Servant' for the Babylonian King Nebuchadnezzar in the Book of Jeremiah," *Vetus Testamentum* 64 (2014): 128.
19. Gossai, "Jeremiah's Welfare," 263.
20. Smelik, "My Servant Nebuchadnezzar," 123.
21. Beaulieu, "Babylonian Background," 279.
22. Ibid., 289.
23. Brueggemann, "At the Mercy of Babylon," 15.
24. Smelik, "My Servant Nebuchadnezzar," 114.
25. Ibid., 117.
26. Ibid., 134.
27. Joseph Blenkinsopp, "A Case of Benign Imperial Neglect and Its Consequences," *Biblical Interpretation* 8, nos. 1–2 (2000): 135.
28. Kathleen M. O'Connor, "Surviving Disaster in the Book of Jeremiah," *Word and World* 22, no. 4 (2002): 372.
29. Brueggemann, "At the Mercy of Babylon," 11.
30. Ibid., 16.
31. Ibid.
32. Daniel Smith-Christopher, *A Biblical Theology of Exile: Overtures to Biblical Theology* (Minneapolis: Fortress Press, 2002), 89.
33. Ahn, "Made in Babylon," 319.
34. Leon Kass, *The Beginning of Wisdom: Reading Genesis* (Chicago: University of Chicago Press, 2003).
35. Runions, "Empire's Allure," 694.

Bibliography

Ahn, John. "Made in Babylon: Daniel I." In *T&T Clark Handbook to Asian American Biblical Hermeneutics*, edited by Uriah Kim and Seung Ai Yang, 217–328. London: T&T Clark, 2019.

Ahn, John. "Psalm 137: Complex Communal Laments." *Journal of Biblical Literature* 127, no. 2 (2008): 267–289.

Beaulieu, Paul-Alain. "The Babylonian Background of the Motif of the Fiery Furnace in Daniel 3." *Journal of Biblical Literature* 128, no. 2 (2009): 273–290.

Blenkinsopp, Joseph. "A Case of Benign Imperial Neglect and Its Consequences." *Biblical Interpretation* 8, nos. 1–2 (2000): 129–136.

Brueggemann, Walter. "At the Mercy of Babylon: A Subversive Rereading of the Empire." *Journal of Biblical Literature* 110, no. 1 (1991): 3–22.

Freedman, David Noel. "The Structure of Psalm 137." In *Near Eastern Studies in Honor of William Foxwell Albright*, edited by Hans Goedicke, 207–223. Baltimore/London: Johns Hopkins University Press, 1971.

Gossai, Hemchand. "Jeremiah's Welfare Ethic and the Challenge to Imperial Militarism." In *Post Colonial Commentary and the Old Testament*, 258–274. London: Bloomsbury Academic Press, 2019.

Gossai, Hemchand. "Reading Lamentations after the Shoah." In *Reading Lamentations Intertextually*, LHBOT Series, edited by Brittany Melton and Heath Thomas, n.p. London: Bloomsbury Academic Press, 2019.

Halpern, Baruch. "Why Manasseh Is Blamed for the Babylonian Exile: The Evolution of a Biblical Tradition." *Vetus Testamentum* 48, no. 4 (October 1998): 473–514.

Kass, Leon. *The Beginning of Wisdom: Reading Genesis*. Chicago: University of Chicago Press, 2003.

Keller, Catherine. "The Love of Postcolonialism: Theology in the Interstices of Empire." *Postcolonial Theologies: Divinity and Empire*, edited by Michael Nausner and Mayra Rivera, 221–242. St. Louis, MO: Chalice, 2004.

Murray, Donald F. "Of All the Years the Hopes—or Fears? Jehoiachin in Babylon." *Journal of Biblical Literature* 120, no. 2 (2001): 245–265.

Niedner, Frederick A., Jr. "Rachel's Lament." *Word and World* 22, no. 4 (2002): 406–414.

O'Connor, Kathleen M. "Surviving Disaster in the Book of Jeremiah." *Word and World* 22, no. 4 (2002): 369–377.

Rose, John. "Jerusalem's Creative Collision with Babylon." *Holy Land Studies* 11, no. 2 (2012): 217–222.

Runions, Erin. "Empire's Allure: Babylon and the Exception to Law in Two Conservative Discourses." *Journal of the American Academy of Religion* 77, no. 3 (September 2009): 680–711.

Seidler, Victor Jeleniewski. "'Their Hearts Melted and Became as Water.' Lamentations: Ethics after the Shoah." *EuroJ* 44, no. 2 (2011): 91–105.

Smelik, Klaas A. D. "My Servant Nebuchadnezzar: The Use of Epithet, 'My Servant' for the Babylonian King Nebuchadnezzar in the Book of Jeremiah." *Vetus Testamentum* 64 (2014): 109–134.

Smith-Christopher, Daniel. *A Biblical Theology of Exile*. Overtures to Biblical Theology. Minneapolis: Fortress Press, 2002.

Stowe, David W. "Babylon Revisited: Psalm 137 as American Protest Song." *Black Music Research Journal* 32, no. 1 (Spring 2012): 95–112.

VanTer Toorn, Karel. "In the Lion's Den: The Babylonian Background of a Biblical Motif." *Catholic Biblical Quarterly* 60, no. 4 (October 1998): 626–641.

CHAPTER 4

ANOINTED SAVIORS OR OPPRESSIVE ENSLAVERS?

Achaemenid Administration and Judean Subjects

DANIEL L. SMITH-CHRISTOPHER

INTRODUCTION

My friend, Archbishop Donald Tamihere from Aotearoa/New Zealand, like many Māori men, still carries some of the aches and pains of playing rugby as a younger man. He once explained to me the Aotearoa/New Zealand popular reference to a "hospital pass." A rugby term, it refers to a high, looping pass that hangs in the air long enough for all the players on the opposing team to clearly see where it is going—and therefore have plenty of time to converge on the unfortunate player likely to catch it! As a biblical scholar himself, the archbishop will no doubt approve of my use of the term in this context, because any essay attempting to deal with "attitudes to Persian rule," whether referring to the Bible or classical sources in dialogue with Achaemenid ancient sources, is the parade example of a historiographic "hospital pass." In Ancient Near Eastern studies, this is a no man's land caught up in twentieth- and twenty-first-century political passions, not to mention sixth- to third-century BCE political passions, as well as the controversies surrounding a limited range of ancient evidence. In sum, it is a perfect storm for postcolonial analysis. It isn't difficult to provide evidence for proceeding with caution.

The Passions of Achaemenid History

In 2008 an article appeared in the British tabloid the *Daily Telegraph* titled "Cyrus Cylinder's Ancient Bill of Rights 'Is Just Propaganda.'" Written by Harry De Quetteville, it described the display of a museum-quality facsimile of the ancient "Cyrus Cylinder" as a part of a celebration of "human rights" in the Security Council rooms of the United Nations.[1] The display, it seems, incited a debate among historians. The Cyrus Cylinder, a sixth-century BCE cuneiform "building inscription" written to celebrate Cyrus's rebuilding of the largest ancient Babylonian sanctuary after his conquest of Babylon, was written to clarify that Cyrus was chosen as the legitimate ruler by none other than the city's patron, the (Babylonian) god Marduk. The cuneiform inscription, excavated from the ruins of Babylon in 1879, had become the unlikely focus of debate, again.

The subtitle in the *Telegraph* article clarified: "A 2500 year old Persian treasure dubbed the world's 'first bill of human rights' has been branded a piece of shameless 'propaganda' by German historians." The "German historian" in question, Josef Wiesehöfer, derided it as "a propaganda inscription." Further comments were cited from Tom Holland, the author of the popular book on ancient history *Persian Fire*: "It's nonsense, absolute nonsense.... The ancient Persians were not some early form of Swedish Social Democrats." According to De Quetteville, Holland added that the UN's adoption of the cylinder stemmed in part from a desire to claim some Eastern roots "when it is so Western in its philosophical underpinnings."[2] Yet, De Quetteville, writes, "For all the criticisms of the Cyrus cylinder, it is unlikely to change perceptions of it in Iran, where Cyrus and the cylinder are regarded with intense national pride. 'It is a source of great pride,' said Mr Holland, 'but like many things said about Persia in Iran, it has to be taken with a big pinch of salt.'"[3]

In the original inscription, the founder of the Achaemenid Empire, Cyrus the Great, proclaimed that Marduk, the Babylonian heavenly patron, had "taken him by the hand" and invited him to be the new ruler of Babylon: "Without battle and fighting he (Marduk) let him (Cyrus) enter his city Babylon. He saved Babylon from its oppression."[4] Cyrus thus claims legitimacy as the new ruler, piously proclaiming his respect for the old traditions, and the inscription speaks of Cyrus having "benefited all," which is why the people "knelt before him, kissed his feet, rejoiced at his kingship, their faces shone."[5]

Two years after the events reported in the *Daily Telegraph*, the visit of the Cyrus Cylinder to Tehran was celebrated by then president Mahmoud Ahmadinejad. Golnaz Esfandiari reported (in the online publication of Radio Free Europe) that "[d]uring the event, the Iranian president put a keffiyeh, which is part of the uniform of the pro-government Basij militia, around the neck of a man dressed as Cyrus the Great." Esfandiari then wrote about the furious controversies among Iranians, some of whom wrote of their disbelief that someone of the ideological orientation of Ahmadinejad would have stated that the Cyrus Cylinder represents respect for human beings' greatness and basic rights.

> ... The cylinder ... emphasizes that everyone is entitled to freedom of thought and choice and also underscores the necessity to fight oppression.[6]

In October 2013, the ancient Persians were in the popular press once again. As Lori Katchadourian also notes in the opening chapter of her fine work on the archaeology of empires,[7] the widely respected magazine the *Economist* utilized a photo of one of the relief carvings from ancient Achaemenid building ruins to illustrate a cover story on Western problems in dealing with modern Iran. Showing an ancient lion biting the torso of a gazelle, the headline on the cover accompanied the grisly scene with bold letters, "Can Iran Be Stopped?" (the fierce lion appearing to represent a hostile Iran).

What is of interest here is that discussions of the Cyrus Cylinder are also virtually ubiquitous in modern biblical commentary literature dealing with those biblical passages that are most often cited as significant indicators of Judean attitudes toward Persian rule, as we will soon see. Furthermore, the striking reliefs from the royal buildings and monuments of the Achaemenids (starting especially with projects initiated by Darius 1, ca. 522 BCE, and his successors), as well as iconography visible on seals and other decorations, have also become a primary source for debating Persian political ideologies in biblical analysis,[8] as well as proposals with regard to biblical reactions to exiles directly encountering Persian iconography.[9]

Uses of Achaemenid period antiquities in the modern media, however, are only the most public displays of an ongoing debate among historians about the Achaemenids and their empire in recent literature. An excellent summary is provided by T. C. McCaskie,[10] who became intrigued with the debates going on, as it were, down the halls of ancient history departments in academia (he identifies as primarily an Africa scholar). McCaskie writes about the work on ancient Persia, especially since the 1980s, as composed "in conscious opposition to venerable ancient Greek readings of the history and culture of Persia,"[11] and notes that the European scholars of the nineteenth century had almost universally described the Achaemenid Persians as "oriental despots ... decadent, and ruled over by women and eunuchs."[12] In the 1980s, however, Heleen Sancisi-Weerdenburg (University of Groningen), working with the French ancient historian Pierre Briant (University of Toulouse), started the "Achaemenid History Workshops" that produced a number of widely cited academic volumes of historical analysis—again routinely cited in biblical analysis as well. In addition to Amelie Kuhrt, whose 2007 magisterial, 800+ page collection of classical sources on Persian history is now becoming a standard reference work, these recent moves toward a more "Persian"-focused approach to historiography have taken up the challenge of criticizing generations of scholarly bias against the Persians that was informed largely by an allegedly uncritical adoption of the attitudes of the ancient Greek writers that McCaskie summarized, particularly from Herodotus and Xenophon. A similar summary of the academic tradition of anti-Persian, pro-Greek readings of ancient history is provided in Llewellyn-Jones and Robson's "Introduction" to their 2010 edition of Ctesias's *History of Persia*, where they argue for a careful, but certainly less dismissively critical, approach to citing Ctesias as a historical source.[13] In general, McCaskie observes that Greek history was written in Western academia as "our Greeks," and thus, as McCaskie observes further, attitudes toward "those Persians" continue to influence even contemporary Western relations with modern Iran, as well as ancient sources:

> The new Achaemenid history is snared within the coils of its ancient Greek narrative sources. It can argue for a change of optic, a few from Persepolis rather than Athens. It cannot in a truly meaningful sense overcome the Greek sources as evidence. Instead it has to confront them on their own terrain, which has always privileged the cultural and the literary over the historical. They are ideologically charged standard-bearers of Western self-knowing.[14]

The reason that these debates must be acknowledged before any analysis of "Judean attitudes" to Persia is precisely because the ancient textual and architectural sources that have been debated by classicists and historians (and, clearly, the occasional journalist covering Iranian affairs), are the *same ancient sources* appealed to in biblical commentary literature as well. While it has clearly been argued that *historical* attitudes (of ancient Greek authors, for example) have influenced *contemporary* political perspectives, that interesting argument is not addressed here directly—although biblical scholars clearly read the work of classics historians as well.

Biblical Attitudes toward Persian Rule

Social and political attitudes and ideas in the Hebrew Bible/Old Testament are typically initiated in the commentary literature in the context of the discussions surrounding certain "key" biblical texts—one might even call them "trigger texts" for questions about Persian rule. The first three are well established debates, but the fourth one is relatively recent:

- The naming of Cyrus as YHWH's chosen, indeed *anointed* "messiah" in Isaiah 45:1.
- The reference to life under Persian rule as "slavery" and "distress" toward the end of Ezra's famous prayer appearing in Nehemiah 9 (esp. vv. 36–37).
- Attitudes discernible in the "Diaspora Stories" of Daniel and Esther.
- Attitudes toward Persian Rule in the Elephantine documents, esp. Ahiqar.

There are certainly other texts that generate similar heat on the issue of Judean attitudes to Persian rule, but our chosen texts are particularly noteworthy in that they appear, at first glance, to represent the most starkly polarized differences of attitude, but are also texts that are routinely cited in discussions of the others. Let us briefly comment on the first three sets of texts.

The Anointing of Cyrus in Isaiah 45:1

A proclamation of Cyrus as an "anointed Messiah" famously appears in Isaiah 45:1:

> Thus says the LORD to his anointed, to Cyrus. (NRSV)

The commentary literature is typically rather emotive in response to this passage. Westermann, for example, calls Isaiah 45:1 "astonishing" and "shocking."[15] Reimer refers to a "theopolitical surprise,"[16] while Brueggemann states that this verse is "among the most remarkable in the Bible,"[17] and furthermore, that it is a "breathtaking affirmation," and he asks whether the prophet believes that Cyrus was, in fact, a "bearer of Davidic promises?"[18] Shalom Paul writes that this phrase "most likely came as an utter shock to exiled Judeans."[19] Notably, it is universally held to be important to read this striking proclamation in its immediate context in Isaiah 44:28–45:5, but especially 45:5:

> I am the LORD, and there is no other; besides me there is no god. I arm you, though you do not know me ...

Such a passage is thought to minimize any mistake of presuming that Cyrus "knew what he was doing" in reference to the Hebrew God's intentions. There are differences, however, with regard to what such a "wider context" actually tells us. Westermann (often cited by later commentators) argued that the passage suggests that no "permanent relationship" (with God) is implied, and that Cyrus is employed only in relation to Israel, and certainly no "conversion" of Cyrus should be understood.[20] God, Westermann suggests, can even use evil people. Shalom Paul, for example, notes that many more terms of kingship in the Israelite tradition are cited in the immediate context—shepherd, and foundation—but also agrees with Westermann in stating that the passage as a whole shows that YHWH's power will be seen in what God can do with Cyrus.[21] Similarly, Sweeney believes that God's use of Cyrus establishes YHWH's power and prominence.[22] Brueggemann concurs, stating that "everything is settled on Yahweh's terms."[23] Finally, citing 44:28, Goldingay and Payne add that Cyrus is "merely Yahweh's underling and agent."[24] Thus, one could read the statement of Cyrus as God's anointed as even a subversive statement denying ultimate power to the Persians. If this is a kind of resistance, it is certainly subtle. Furthermore, others have read this quite differently.

For example, a more controversial reading is Fried's proposal in her widely noted 2002 article arguing that the writer of Deutero-Isaiah was, quite simply, a "collaborator," and she compared the writer to other examples that we have from ancient history: "Why did Udjahorresnet give Cambyses and Darius the title Pharaoh? Why did the Marduk priesthood allow Cambyses to participate in the Akitu festival? They were collaborators."[25]

When she asks why Deutero-Isaiah "handed over to Cyrus" the royal Judean title of Yahweh's anointed as well as the "entire royal Judean court theology associated with it," Fried concludes that the motivation was

> to facilitate local acceptance of the foreign ruler . . . self interest was no doubt one reason for his actions, but not his sole motivation. Like his counterparts in Egypt and Babylon, Deutero-Isaiah was convinced that Cyrus was in actuality the genuine Judean king, i.e. YHWH's anointed, his Messiah, because Cyrus was able to do what a legitimate king must do: he brought back the status quo ante. He rebuilt the temple, ordered the temple vessels replaced in it, and permitted the Jews to return to worship their God in Zion restored.[26]

In fact, Westermann also cites the Cyrus Cylinder,[27] which he stated has "astonishingly close parallels" to Deutero-Isaiah's apparent praise of Cyrus as the one chosen by the deity, but as we have previously noted, Westermann insists that this is only God's temporary use of Cyrus, and not some kind of generalized endorsement of Persian rule. Reimer specifically objects to Fried's notion of Cyrus being proclaimed Messiah, apparently appropriating the Royal covenant, as a kind of collaborationist move. Reimer argues that Deutero-Isaiah praises only YHWH, not Cyrus,[28] and then proceeds to cite the very *Daily Telegraph* article with which we began this essay, pointing out that in that article, Amelie Kuhrt objected to the idea that the Cyrus Cylinder is about human rights. Cyrus is "no different than Assyria before him."[29] Finally, Paul notes that it was a Rabbinic tradition to argue that it was the *prophet who was anointed*, to speak *to* Cyrus about God's intentions, and not any authorization of Cyrus directly.[30]

In other words, interpretation of Deutero-Isaiah 45:1 is heavily informed by debates about the meaning of ancient inscriptions like the Cyrus Cylinder, and whether the Cylinder was merely a piece of ancient propaganda, and thus implying that modern readers of the Bible, much less the writers of Deutero-Isaiah, should not be so gullible as to believe that Cyrus had genuine interest in his Hebrew subjects and their religion. Sweeney believes that Cyrus's apparent "largesse" was simply part of his preparations for his planned invasion of Egypt.[31]

Whether Deutero-Isaiah writes of Cyrus, and by implication the Persians, in a positive way as a pious conqueror—or whether he/she writes that God can use even an "Oriental despot"—seems to be an open debate with regard to a passage like Isaiah 45:1, and its' surrounding contexts. Is there any further light from a consideration of the next two passages?

"Slaves in Our Own Land"

Toward the end of Nehemiah 9, Ezra the Priest is finishing a long prayer that is normally considered a parade example of the "Penitential Prayer" genre of biblical poetry of prayer. The relevant verses, Nehemiah 9:36–37, appear as follows:

> [36] Here we are, slaves to this day—slaves in the land that you gave to our ancestors to enjoy its fruit and its good gifts. [37] Its rich yield goes to the kings whom you have set over us because of our sins; they have power also over our bodies and over our livestock at their pleasure, and we are in great distress.

Myers, for example, was already voicing an opinion that has become a rather typical summary judgment on the prayer as a whole in Nehemiah 9, when he stated that the negative comments are really part of a confession of guilt: "This prayer psalm is a marvelous expression of God's continued faithfulness to his covenant despite the nation's equally continued apostasy."[32] However, Myers was writing before the clearer identification of the prayer genre we now know as the "Penitential Prayer" in historiography of Second Temple Judaism. In two excellent summary volumes, Werline, Boda, and Falk have defined the Penitential Prayer tradition as an important post-exilic genre,[33] while acknowledging that the application of the form can vary in specific settings.[34] Among the most significant common elements of the "Penitential Prayer" genre in the three central biblical examples (Daniel 9, Ezra 9, and Nehemiah 9), we note the following three motifs:

(A) **Importance of the Ethics of Moses**

Daniel 9:5; Ezra 9:10–11; Nehemiah 9:13–14

(B) **Statement of Shame associated with Sins of Ancestors**

Daniel 9:8; Ezra 9:6–7; Nehemiah 9:16–17

The key here is that our passage of concern in Nehemiah 9:36–37 is also part of a standard motif:

(C) **Exile, Slavery, or Present Circumstances were noted in previous warnings:**

> Ezra 9: 7–9: *... and for our iniquities we, our kings, and our priests have been handed over to the kings of the lands, to the sword, to captivity, to plundering, and to utter shame, as is now the case.*
> Daniel 9:12: He has confirmed his words, which he spoke against us and against our rulers, by bringing upon us a calamity so great that what has been done against Jerusalem has never before been done under the whole heaven. 9:13: Just as it is written in the law of Moses, *all this calamity has come upon us ...*

Is the significance of the *critical tone* in Nehemiah 9, and its description of the grave present circumstances, to be somehow reduced by noting that this text represents a common "motif"—as if to propose that it is merely "part of the standard form" and thus does not really communicate the attitude of the writer (beyond, one presumes, being a faithful repeater of classic styles no matter what the context)? So, for example, Van Wijk-Bos argued that since the prayer began with a reference to Egyptian oppression (vv. 9–15), a comparison is made toward the end (e.g., "we are slaves...").[35]

However, some redactional arguments clearly result in removing the passage from the Persian period entirely (and proposing a later Hellenistic period), *based on a negative understanding of the prayer*—referring to oppression in comparison with Egypt, for example. But on what historical basis? Surely one does not use this particular prayer "form" in cases where the negative sense of living in conditions that indicate God's judgment does *not* apply. That is to say, why assign it to the Persian period *at all* if the times were not in any way oppressive? Are all assignments of negative attitudes toward Persian rulers a "hidden transcript" that really intends to critique Hellenistic rulers by safely naming previous Persian rulers so as not to offend Hellenistic ones? Yet reactions to these final verses in Nehemiah 9 in the commentary literature remain decidedly mixed, and scholars clearly struggle to make sense of the tone of the passage in the face of what they presume to be the overall *positive* attitude toward Persian rule in the Hebrew Bible.

Rudolph, for example, had also expressed some surprise about the political "attitude" that is evident in these words in Ezra's prayer in Nehemiah 9. In comments that attempt to summarize what appears to be a "divided loyalty" in Ezra (which include a few thoughts that might be taken as, at the very least, a bit indelicate), Rudolph stated:

> [I]t must remain doubtful whether Ezra really wanted to serve, with equal devotion, the two spheres of life in which he stood, Judaism and the Persian people. It would not be the only occasion when a Jew is loyal—on the outside—and yet gives up nothing of his Jewish hopes and longings in his heart (see Moses Mendelssohn).[36]

Clearly noting the attitude of resistance, Myers also proposed that this "shift" (in attitude) may indicate editing:

> The last verse may reflect a period different from that of the time of Ezra, when the Persian king endeavored to assist the Jews... the whole prayer ends with an acknowledgment of the wrongs committed by the people and emphasizes the consequent hardships being endured by them. Through it all runs the implied hope that Yahweh has taken note and will grant them relief. Inasmuch as there is no direct connection between the prayer and the surrounding events—it is not ascribed to any person or persons by MT—it may have been added later.[37]

Fensham, too, noted that a clear sense of "covenant" is implied in the prayer: "Sins would be punished... at the same time the people of God were never abandoned by him, because of his covenant and covenant love,"[38] but then he, too, cites both Rudolph and Myers that this could not be Ezra, because Ezra "*would not have referred in this way* [my emphasis] to the Persian kings, because they had assisted the Jews." But Fensham hedges his bets:

> We must keep in mind, however, that the Jews were subjects of the Persian kings. They had to pay taxes to them. If Nehemiah could call Artaxerxes "this man" (Neh 1:11) in his prayer, it is quite acceptable to maintain that Ezra could have used the terminology of vv. 36–37."[39]

Noting the rather sudden end of the prayer, Clines states that:

> the abruptness is really a mark of the delicacy of the author's spirituality (cf. the very similar stance of Ezra's prayer, Ezr. 9:6–15). It may be that any more explicit appeal was precluded as politically dangerous, but the desire for national independence is already quite clear in the prayer as it stands.[40]

But Clines also takes note that the prayer certainly must be said to contain a resentment: ". . . at the apparently arbitrary rule of their masters."[41] Williamson also suggests that vss. 36–37 show signs of the influence of communal lament forms,[42] but argues that the prayer as a whole does not fit a single *gattung*. However, Williamson is among a number of scholars who believe that the prayer as a whole is from a separate source and only edited into this collection at a later time: "[I]t has uncharacteristically little to do with its immediate context, but it was of considerable importance for the final editor's purpose."[43] But at the same time, the covenant promises of God noted in the prayer (which, as we have now seen, is part of the Penitential Prayer form in any case) provides the basis for a strong contrast between God's promises and the present circumstances. Williamson further notes that the use of terms like "oppression" and "adversaries" echoes v. 27, and thus serves a purpose in the prayer:

> The gift of the land with the attendant enjoyment of all its produce, for instance, has been noted as the leading topic of the prayer so far. . . . The author has therefore only to hold up to God the present situation of life in the land under a foreign power which creams off its benefits (vv. 36–37) for the irony of the contrast between divinely determined history and current short-fall to make its inherent request most pointedly apparent.[44]

Blenkinsopp also strongly argued that this prayer does not go back to the time of Ezra-Nehemiah (mid-fifth century BCE), but then argued even more forcefully that it is the political attitude of the prayer that makes the assignment to fifth-century figures Ezra or Nehemiah highly problematic:

> The outright claim to independent possession of the land, which is one of the dominant themes of the prayer, and allusion to the oppressive and arbitrary nature of foreign rule, create further difficulties for this hypothesis. For while Ezra-Nehemiah

never loses sight of the basic unacceptability of foreign domination, allusions to it are carefully nuanced (Ezra 9:8; Neh 1:11) and are outweighed, if only for prudential reasons, by emphasis on the benevolent and providential aspects of Persian rule.[45]

This tendency to argue against the historical context of the prayer in the fifth century, and certainly not to the Persian-appointed officials Ezra or Nehemiah, is most strongly argued by the recent work of Kyung-jin Min. Min proposes that the earliest material in Ezra-Nehemiah reveals that the "author's tendency is to accept the political status quo and to view the Persian kings as vehicles of God's grace,"[46] and therefore the earliest writers of Ezra and Nehemiah "certainly supported" the Persians:

> There is nothing here that would be objectionable to a support of the Persian policy. Indeed, it is important to note that, immediately following the prayer, relief is sought through a public commitment, by the whole people, to the laws codified in the covenant—a procedure which, as we have seen, would certainly have met with Persian approval.[47]

Clearly, there has been a tendency in the commentary literature to read Ezra-Nehemiah, especially in the "original materials" (that contain Nehemiah describing his service to the Persian ruler, and the correspondence that allowed the rebuilding of the Temple) as expressing a supportive, even grateful, attitude toward Persian rule. The strikingly negative evaluation of Persian rule in Nehemiah 9:36–37 is routinely assigned to a later date, when attitudes toward Persian rule presumably changed for the worse (or even applied to later Hellenistic regimes). What is not at issue here is whether the prayer in Nehemiah 9 is early or late—Williamson's arguments in particular with regard to the awkward lack of connection to surrounding materialssurely suggests that it is somewhat instrusive here. What *is* at issue, however, is the fact that the negative *attitude* toward Persian rule is almost routinely seen as further indication of a late date—as if the "attitude" *necessarily* reflects ("surely") a later time, and this is arguably also a primary driver of shifting the date of the passage to a later time, perhaps when the alleged benevolence of Cyrus has been forgotten under more negative conditions of later Achaemenid rulers, or even Hellenistic rulers.

Once again, the background of Ezra-Nehemiah typically includes discussions of "the Cyrus Cylinder"[48] to assist in establishing what may have been a positive "attitude" toward early Persian rule, even in the face of strikingly negative language in Nehemiah 9, which then suggests that Nehemiah 9 must be from a later time—or someone other than Ezra and Nehemiah.

However, it must be said that this is hardly the only indication of Persian rulers as potentially despotic. Even though it is seen to "support" the returning exilic group, the threats of the Achaemenid ruler against those who would oppose Ezra give one pause:

> **Ezra 6:11:** Furthermore I decree that if anyone alters this edict, a beam shall be pulled out of the house of the perpetrator, who then shall be impaled on it. The house shall be made a dunghill ...

Is this, too, to be assigned a Hellenistic date? Or is it to be thought "permissible violence" because it supports "our" Ezra? Grabbe, for one, believes this threat to be a Judean's invention.[49] Either way, such chilling language seems to be thought perfectly appropriate to assign to a Persian ruler. As in the interpretation of the prayer in Nehemiah 9, I consider the burden of proof to rest on the side of those who want to argue that such negative tones applied to Persian rulers are somehow anachronistic and entirely misplaced.

Diaspora Stories (esp. Daniel 1–6)

Finally, we need only make a few observations with regard to the stories of Daniel and Esther. Setting to one side the contentious issues of the dating of the stories of Daniel 1–6 (late Persian? Ptolemaic? Seleucid?), there has been an interesting ongoing discussion on the "attitude" toward the authorities—perhaps Hellenistic rulers described as "Persian," although I would argue that it is still possible that the stories come from oral traditions from the late Persian period.[50] It is widely noted that the name of the ruler here is intended to be Darius *the Persian*, who established himself the emperor of Achaemenid Persia after putting down a series of revolts immediately following the death of Cambyses, the son of Cyrus, ca. 522–520 BCE. Darius, in short, was not a "Mede." In any case, we begin by drawing attention to the following elements of Daniel 6, namely the appointment of Daniel by the king as an advisor over "the whole kingdom," which sets up the Persian ruler's horror that he seems to have inadvertently signed a decree that would condemn his Jewish associate to death. After Daniel is spared from death of mauling, the story famously concludes:

> [26] I make a decree, that in all my royal dominion people should tremble and fear before the God of Daniel: For he is the living God, enduring forever. His kingdom shall never be destroyed, and his dominion has no end.

Similarly, in Esther, the following passages are also cited to establish positive ideas about the Persians: Esther 2:17–18; 5:2–3; 7:2–3; 9:12–14, among others. And, in an echo to the standard ending of the Daniel stories, the final verse of Esther reads:

> [3] For Mordecai the Jew was next in rank to King Ahasuerus, and he was powerful among the Jews and popular with his many kindred, for he sought the good of his people and interceded for the welfare of all his descendants.

It is interesting that we can identify quite a spectrum of opinion in the scholarship dealing with the "attitude" toward Persian rule in the book of Daniel, moving from more positive to more negative (A–C) *as a direct function of the influence of postcolonial analysis:*

A: *Positive Attitudes in Daniel*

Paying particularly close attention to the "attitude" presumably revealed in passages in Daniel and Esther such as those we just considered—concern for their Jewish advisor or even the queen—Humphreys famously argued in his widely cited 1973 article, "Lifestyle for the Diaspora," that these stories revealed that:

> One could, as a Jew, overcome adversity . . . it is within these foreign courts that the heroes move, and the possibility of a life, rewarding and creative, in this setting is affirmed. The heroes are successful and high ranking courtiers at the end of each tale. Such a life is not without pitfalls and dangers, but one can meet these and still remain a loyal Jew and devotee of his deity[51]

There has been a strong tradition of agreement with Humphrey's sanguine evaluation of these tales as proposing a positive Jewish life in diaspora. Citing Humphreys, Goldingay's 1989 commentary on Daniel refers to the "romance" and "romantic themes" of the Court Stories[52] and the enjoyment of "beating pagans at their own game, with friendliness of the court official."[53] Collins was a bit more hesitant in his important 1993 commentary, but nonetheless states that the Court Tales are not written from a perspective on persecution. For chapter 6, the "Lion's Den" story, Collins argues that "the gentile monarch is singularly well disposed to Daniel and the conspiracy against the Jewish hero is inspired by envy at his successful career at court."[54] He concedes that there may be a stronger case for a more negative attitude in the "Fiery Furnace" episode in chapter 3, but "even there, however, the Gentile king is not attempting to suppress the Jewish cult (or any other) . . . the story has a happy ending in which the youths are miraculously preserved and the king freely gives praise to their God. All of this is different from the situation reflected in Daniel 7–12."[55] The stories, in short, suggest "[a] basically optimistic view of the world."[56]

This argument persists in more recent commentary literature on the Daniel texts. Henze, for example, writes about the "surprising" element of the portrayal of Daniel, specifically

> his ability to have an amicable relationship with the monarchs at whose courts he serves. Daniel never subjects Nebuchadnezzar, Belshazzar or Darius to severe criticism. To the contrary, the encounter between the Jewish sage and his heathen sovereigns occurs in an atmosphere which is best characterized as cordial and mutually supportive. This is most surprising in the case of Nebuchadnezzar, the destroyer of the Jerusalem Temple and architect of the Babylonian Exile (Dan 1:1–2), who is criticized fiercely by other voices in the Hebrew Bible. In the book of Daniel, by contrast, the atmosphere of harmony is propelled to an extreme and borders on the absurd.[57]

Henze is hardly alone. Lucas writes: "They show a generally positive attitude to gentile courtiers or royal advisors, trained in the language and literature Chaldeans."[58] More recently, Tawny Holm's major 2013 study is notable for the number of times she refers to the Daniel court tales as "entertaining" stories,[59] "popular and humorous,"[60] and "popular" stories[61] that "display their entertainment function in the optimistic outcome of each episode about Daniel or the three friends."[62] Holm further writes of "the repetition of optimistic outcomes for Daniel or his friends," which eventually "emphasizes that righteous Jews during the Babylonian exile led rewarding, successful lives," and thus Holm argues that the more nationalist attitudes that are "antagonistic to foreign rule" occur only in the Apocalyptic visions. [63] Similarly, Seow's 2003 commentary states that Daniel 1–6 portrays a variety of circumstances that "the faithful may encounter as a people living under foreign domination," but that it is in the visions of 7–12 that we change to "an environment of terrible oppression by an arrogant and blasphemous tyrant."[64]

B: *Growing Ambiguity on the Daniel Stories?*

Arguably under the influence of postcolonial analysis, however, some recent commentators have become a bit more cautious. I would argue that among the first significant *challenges* to the Court Tales as exhibiting *positive* attitudes toward foreign rule was Dana Fewell's important 1991 work, *Circle of Sovereignty*,[65] and I gratefully drew on her more critical views when I took it further to propose Daniel tales as "Resistance Literature" in my own commentary on Daniel—and I also note that both Polaski and Newsom have raised concerns in response. Polaski, for example, believes that the writers of the Daniel tales would have had a "comfortable, if not uniformly secure, relationship to state power,"[66] and thus:

> Daniel, the scribes' hero, is even more clever (and less revolutionary) than Smith-Christopher asserts. He resists the empire but is fully at home in its ways of power: he knows the value of an inscription, performs the duty of an ideal bureaucrat, and is quick to assure Darius that all is well, giving him information on which to base one more edict. If Daniel is a subversive, then he is a subversive whose actions in fact buttress the authority of the empire.[67]

In Carol Newsom's recent commentary, she entitles a section "Danielic Court Tales: Accommodationist or Resistance Literature?" and therein contrasts the early and influential essay of Humphreys with Smith-Christopher's emphasis on Daniel as resistance literature.[68] Her compromise, however, is to cite the language of "hybridity" and conclude that it is a bit of both. Similarly, Seow proposes a balanced view by stating that "[t]he sacerdotal language of Nebuchadnezzar's obeisance before Daniel shocks the reader into the realization that the powerless may yet represent the eternal and indestructible rule of God."[69]

C: *Postcolonial Influences on Negative Readings of Court Tales*

Under the *explicit* influence of postcolonial analysis, questions are focused on the conditions of empire, and the related cultural subordination and attacks on minority identity. From this perspective, it is clear that the Daniel Tales can be read as far more critical of their foreign context. For example, there are clear themes in much of the Court Tale literature—not only Daniel—suggesting Judeans being "singled out" for their minority identities. Is all this to be dismissed as merely dramatic license in telling a good story in the late Persian or even Hellenistic period?:

> Then Haman said to King Ahasuerus, "There is a certain people scattered and separated among the peoples in all the provinces of your kingdom; their laws are different from those of every other people, and they do not keep the king's laws, so that it is not appropriate for the king to tolerate them."
>
> (Esther 3:8)

> The men said, "We shall not find any ground for complaint against this Daniel unless we find it in connection with the law of his God."
>
> (Daniel 6:5, cf. Tobit, where he is persecuted for his charitable practices in obedience to Hebrew tradition, so Tobit 1:19–20)

Why are these elements part of the story? They certainly were not prominent, for example, in Ahiqar (despite his likely Aramean background), which many consider our earliest example of a "court tale" that may well have influenced Hebrew writing. However, what is the social context of such court tales? As many have proposed, even widely agreed fictional stories like Daniel, Esther, and Joseph seem to insist on the general memory of diaspora existence that is hardly one of comfort, ease, and success. However, some have even proposed that a few details may not be entirely fictional. In Daniel, especially 3 and 6, we have the more startling examples of horrific punishments presumed to be fictional drama. But Beaulieu is not ready to dismiss all of this as merely dramatic story-telling:

> [W]e have three instances in Mesopotamia where the manner of execution by burning is specified, and all three cases involve being thrown into an oven or a furnace. However, these sources have not been discussed in previous commentaries on Daniel 3.[70]

Beaulieu goes further, suggesting that such elements of the Court Tales, including denunciations of the Jewish courtiers, "very probably originates in actual conflicts that erupted during the reign of Nabonidus."[71] Finally, Muller has proposed that "a closer look at the description of the foreign courts quickly reveals that accurate information about life at the court was not the dominant concern of the biblical author. Instead, we find numerous gross exaggerations in the often fanciful description of the court: for his banquet the king invites 'a thousand nobles' (Dan 5:1) . . . the king's rage, finally, is both excessive and cruel (Dan 1:10; 2:5.12)." So why is Muller's view important for our consideration here? Precisely because he denies that such tales describe actual conditions! He writes:

> [A] text with such exaggerations is not likely to stem from circles who had an intimate knowledge of the Babylonian court. To the contrary, the extravagant descriptions are

wishful projections of the disenfranchised, reflecting the social misery of those who seek comfort in such fantasies. Hardly the product of the well-to-do Jews in exile, the legends originally circulated "among the poorest of the Babylonian Jewry."[72]

We are beginning to be far more alive to a truncated reading of, for example, Daniel 6: "The king said to Daniel, 'May your God, whom you faithfully serve, deliver you!'" (v. 16b), that too quickly neglects the first half of that verse: "Then the king gave the command, and Daniel was brought and thrown into the den of lions" (16a). That Darius felt bad as he tossed his beloved Jewish advisor to the lions is the very definition of cold comfort, but this is hardly atypical of the book. Daniel is a book that contains threats of beheadings (1:10), being "torn limb from limb," and "destruction of your houses" (2:5); being thrown into a "furnace of blazing fire" (3:6); exile (4:25); humiliation and desecration of sacred Jewish relics (5:3), not to mention regicide (5:30); before we even arrive at mauling by lions in chapter 6. Esther, in addition, can hardly be matched by even Joshua for the level of bloodshed celebrated in the final chapters—even if it is celebrated as a response to the grave threat to the Jewish people themselves, who are accused of being: "a certain people scattered and separated among the peoples" (3:8). Tobit, too, remembers the grave dangers in burying Jewish victims of Assyrian aggression (1:18).

Whether all this is intended to be commentary on Hellenistic rulers (if one argues for a late date for the Daniel and Esther traditions) or genuine memories of "attitudes toward our rulers" in the Persian period (oral traditions from late Persian period) that were characterized by unsettling memories of danger and suffering, it will hardly do to suggest that these writings entirely misrepresent a proposed good life in Achaemenid Persia (citing Isaiah 45:1, or permission to rebuild the Temple in Ezra 1–5) simply to make a point about later Hellenistic rulers. Furthermore, if we are going to practice, wholesale, the application of a kind of political "allegorical method" whereby Persian period rulers are merely "stand-ins" for evil Ptolemaic or Seleucid rulers, then where might this stop? Are the Egyptian "oppressors of the slaves" in Exodus merely "stand-ins" for later Hellenistic rulers as well? Why not the Babylonians and/or the Persians?

The Tale of Ahiqar in Modern Debate

Before leaving a brief survey of these famous "trigger texts," it is important to note that a more recent debate about "attitudes toward Persian rulers" has also now been taken up by those concerned with the Aramaic documents from the Judean military colony based on the island of Elephantine in the fifth century (the texts are typically dated ca. 410–400 BCE, thus roughly during the reign of Darius II[73]). What is important about this debate, however, is that it is not possible to argue that these materials are "really" speaking of the Hellenistic period. Becking summarizes the context helpfully:

> On the island, as well as in the nearby Syene at the banks of the Nile, a Persian garrison was established in order to control the Persian interests in the trade going

up and down the Nile from the Delta region into sub-Saharan Africa. All this is documented in the many Aramaic and Demotic inscriptions that were excavated on the island in the beginning of the twentieth century.[74]

Among the recovered Aramaic texts—many of which tell an interesting story about conflict between the Jewish community and antagonistic locals—including the destruction of their Temple—are two somewhat surprising texts. One is an Aramaic translation of the "Behistun" inscription that justified the rise of Darius. It would seem that Darius clearly needed to justify his rule, since he was not a descendent of Cyrus and Cambyses. But we also have the earliest extant version of the story of Ahiqar, believed to be originally a Mesopotamian story. Ahiqar, of course, turns up later in the book of Tobit as a claimed Jewish ancestor (Tob 1:21–22, etc.).

However, what is the "attitude" toward rulers in Ahiqar? Van der Toorn states that the Elephantine Judeans' "encounter with Ahiqar introduced them to a 'skillful scribe' whose unfailing loyalty to his foreign masters had saved him from disgrace,"[75] and it thus represents a "Court Tale" with similarities to Daniel, Esther, and Joseph. But here again we must ask: Is Van der Toorn's suggestion that the story is about "loyalty to . . . foreign masters" justified?

In this story, Ahiqar is falsely accused by an ungrateful relative, condemned to death by the Assyrian monarch, but secretly spared by a sympathetic official (the similarity to Herodotus's tale of the birth of Cyrus is not to be missed here). However, Ahiqar's status is revived when it is revealed that he is still alive—and just in time to save the Assyrian monarch with his wise counsel so that the Assyrian monarch is not humiliated by Pharaoh. Is this a tale advising unquestioned allegiance to your Imperial overlord?

Wigand is sure that it is. Her 2018 essay states this rather starkly: "The story conveys no critical tones, but an unconditional loyalty to the king."[76] Accepting the general argument that the Ahiqar material was, among other things, also a school text,[77] Wigand writes:

> For the schoolchildren on Elephantine, who were instructed to behave as civil servants on the basis of texts such as the Bisutun inscription, a fictional-narrative text such as the Ahiqar composition could be " . . . eine Bebilderung für die Fügung unter das persische system" ("an illustration of submission to the Persian system").[78]

Notably, Oshima takes the view that Daniel is more negative toward foreign rulers, but then argues that Ahiqar is different:

> In contrast to the Book of Daniel, the Ahiqar text contains no polemic against the Mesopotamian religion. The biblical Daniel, however, uses every opportunity to deny and discredit the authority of the Mesopotamian gods and institutions, both the palace and the temples. . . . By contrast, just as other Assyrian thinkers did, the author of the Ahiqar text accepts the Assyrian king as the highest authority of the human world.[79]

Olyan's studies of Ahiqar, however, propose more ambiguities about kingship than Wigand's confident argument that Ahiqar and Behistun are lessons in loyalty. Olyan points out the ambiguities in Ahiqar when the two "goods" of loyalty to a ruler and loyalty to a friend appear to be in conflict, as they most certainly are in the story:

> The dynamic of loyalty and betrayal is also evidenced implicitly in the choice of an innocent friend over a king, a central issue in the narrative of the encounter. When faithfulness to the king competes with fidelity toward a blameless friend, the narrative suggests that loyalty to the friend takes precedence, thereby contradicting the absolute claim of Ahiqar (Saying #87) regarding obedience to a king.[80]

Becking has also noted this same ambiguity:

> The narrator quite frankly reports about the subversive actions of Aḥiqar and Nabusumiskun when hiding each other from the royal wrath and misleading the king by presenting a dead body as if that were the body of the disloyal sage. This intertwining of themes indicates the subtle space for maneuvering that scribes and advisers needed at the court and that the scribes in Elephantine needed in their negotiations with the Persian power and their ethnic loyalty.[81]

Finally, going even further, Seth Bledsoe and Katherine Southwood both propose a reading of Ahiqar (and Behistun) that is even *more* skeptical about "loyalty to the king." From an explicitly postcolonial perspective, they raise serious questions about what lessons are to be derived from the sayings and the story of Ahiqar. Bledsoe acknowledges the typical reading which proposes that Ahiqar and a copy of the text of the Darius-era Behistun inscription suggest that both are "state-sanctioned" documents, perhaps "strongly influenced by a propagandist imperial agenda,"[82] and that Behistun and Ahiqar document a "reaffirmation of loyalty of Aramaic Judeans to the Persian Empire."[83] But Bledsoe is not entirely convinced, pointing out that such a view "pays attention only to the praise of the king,"[84] when the story and the "wise sayings" (esp. sayings 79–92) that accompany the story characterize the king in the story, and kings in general in the sayings, with "a noticeable fickleness, much like the characterization of kings in the biblical narratives of Esther or Daniel, where the monarchs are quickly and easily persuaded by their advisers into handing out severe punishments."[85] Furthermore, Bledsoe writes, in the story itself, "we may be able to detect a hint of dissatisfaction, or at the very least, disillusionment with the office of the king in terms of upholding justice."[86] Bledsoe suggests that not only is there much in these texts that speak "against reading this text as a proponent of unflinching loyalty," but, "at the very least, the text calls attention to the problematic aspects of life under foreign rule."[87]

Southwood goes further. Invoking James Scott's work on what the subordinated levels of society really think about their leadership when they are allowed to speak privately ("private" transcripts) as opposed to required words of praise in public (hence "public" transcripts), Southwood believes that the Ahiqar story and sayings must be read with considerable nuance, and that they are neither so clearly accommodationist or "loyal" as they are often argued to be. She agrees that the subject of kingship—and its legitimacy—seems to be a topic of concern in these documents:

> One striking aspect of the Elephantine evidence is the theme of kingship and power that emerges not only in Ahiqar, but also in the Behistun inscription (TAD C. col. 2.1), which Becking suggests was commissioned by Persian authorities to promote supporting Persian ideologies in scribal education.[88]

The central characters in the Ahiqar story, of course, disobey the king. And thus, "by disobeying the king they are resisting his power and dominance. But they do so in such a way that betrays clearly the underground understanding between them of what counts as justice."[89] Thus, while only apparently "loyal" (as the characters in the story must be), they must plot their own course of action without the knowledge or permission of the monarch, and be very careful about what he may find out. The sayings advise caution before power at every step. This is not the same as endorsing power as legitimate—only as threatening and powerful. As Southwood concludes:

> [W]ithout an option openly to speak truth to power, audiences at Elephantine must use subtlety and restraint to navigate the complexities of life as subordinates: for "a bird is a word—and he who sends it forth is a person of no intelligence..."
>
> (TAD C col. 6:82).[90]

We know that the Ahiqar tradition was appropriated into Jewish tradition officially in the book of Tobit, interceding with the Assyrian ruler on Tobit's behalf—but by Tobit 14, Marincic is surely right when he argues that the characters of Tobias and Tobit were actually written using the Ahiqar tradition as a "foil" against which to assert even more righteous characters. The writer of Tobit "obviously wanted Ahiqar and Nadan to remain present as negative models for Tobit and Tobias, who, as their names suggest (Tob meaning 'good'), receive their authentication on an exemplary rather than historical level."[91]

Thus, it is interesting that Ahiqar is invoked in a book like Tobit that also emphasizes the dangers of the foreign monarch, and specifically the dangers of living Jewish values under foreign rule (cf. Dan 3, Dan 6; Est), and the lethal potential for being "found out" (Tob 1:18–22).

In sum, it would appear that even in the case of Ahiqar scholarship, postcolonial perspectives tend toward a much more nuanced reading of "Court Stories," proposing that these materials do not successfully serve as endorsements of foreign rule, and at best serve to warn Jews of the dangers of foreign rule, while at worst they warn Jews to be faithful, and perhaps be prepared for the need to face, if not always escape, lethal threats. I would propose that Ahiqar advises, at best, to watch your tongue before serious threats, and at worst, know where the best escape routes may be and where one can hide. This is hardly a lesson in loyalty.

Greek and Persian "Sources" and Their Interpretation

Scanning Kuhrt's "Corpus of Sources" for the Achaemenid period, it doesn't take long to establish why Western scholarship, following the Greeks, traditionally saw Persia in the negative ways that it did—sometimes grudgingly admired, but ultimately using condemning language. To wit (heavily citing Herodotus):

In the famous description of Astyages dreams about the future rise of Cyrus, Astyages impaled dream interpreters who helped Cyrus escape (Herodotus 1, 127–128; 130[92]). Cambyses famous brutal cruelty in Egypt is rehearsed by Herodotus (III, 14–15[93]), as well as his cruelty against family, courtiers, and officials (H III. 32[94]); compare also to Ctesias (Persica = FGrH 688 F13; 11–15[95]); descriptions of the enslavement of the people of Cyprus (Herodotus V, 108–116.1[96]); descriptions of the gluttony of the Persian royal banquets featuring "thousand animals butchered each day for the king" (Heracleides of Cumae, Persica[97]); stories of brutality to advisors who overstep their boundaries, such as Pythius asking for one of his four sons to be spared a military campaign, and in response Xerxes murders the son in anger (Herodotus VII, 28–29; 38–39[98]); descriptions of taxation of the satrapies, including the provision that Babylon must annually supply 500 boys for castration (Herodatus III, 89–97[99]); the fact that supplying the Persian kind on military campaigns would impoverish local villages along the way (Herodatus VII, 118–119[100]); and finally, the shock of Alexander and his men finding so much gold and silver in the Persian capitals (Plutarch, *Life of Alexander*, 36.1–2[101]).

I have largely avoided Ctesias here, in recognition of the fact that his *Persica* has been famously dismissed ("seraglio and eunuch perfumes, mixed with the foul stench of blood," "reckless with the truth," "absurd fantasies," "gossip," "trivialized history,"—see summary of classical views by scholars in Llewellyn-Jones and Robson[102]). However, it is interesting that Llewellyn-Jones and Robson argue, in their recent edition of Ctesias, that he needs to be read as "court intrigue" and they agree with some recent historians who suggest that "the reader has no cause to disbelieve the historicity of his accounts of tortures, rivalries, and conflicts among the Achaemenid royal family and their courtiers."[103]

Interestingly, Llewellyn-Jones and Robson cite the Davidic Succession Narratives in 1–2 Samuel, as well as Esther, to argue that Ctesias needs to be read for what it is, not for what it is not: "it is clear that, on all levels, Ctesias is deliberately blending historical fact and novella-style storytelling in order to create a rich, fluid, and gripping historical drama."[104]

In sum, just as it would be problematic to dismiss entirely the "attitude" and "mood" of the narratives of Daniel and Esther along with quite reasonable doubts about historicity of the detailed stories themselves, recent scholarship is calling for reading Ctesias as "story-teller" who may not be simply concocting stories out of thin air—he is intending to represent something real—with added drama. Finally, consider similar debates about interpreting Persian building decorations.

The Apadana: Monumental Evidence?

Finally, we can briefly consider debates surrounding Persian iconography on the palace of Persepolis—the "Apadana." Foreigners are portrayed in procession bearing agricultural produce and other items, but how are these foreigners portrayed—in defeat? In humiliation? Possibly in celebration? The modern discussions focus on what is usually called the "B" sides of the Northwest- and Southern-facing central staircases on the exterior.

Brent Strawn[105] has recently followed a suggestion by John Wright that these carvings may relate to nations bearing gifts in Isaiah 60–62, but the ongoing discussion is precisely about the *agency* of the foreign peoples bearing gifts to present to Darius 1, the presumed Persian monarch. It is interesting that classical scholars sometimes appear to risk being influenced by later Roman practices of victorious processions. Ostenberg, for example, writes with regard to Rome:

> The defeated were frequently ordered to bestow gifts, as were allies. Others brought gifts in gratitude, signaling submissive loyalty. Still, even if gifts might be spoils in all but name, nomenclature mattered. While spoils always implied pure conquest, gifts signaled some degree of voluntary acting and loyalty, both for the donor and the recipient. Thus, the ways in which spoils and gifts were staged in the triumphal procession are bound to reveal Roman manifestations of herself and her relations to the surrounding world.[106]

This nicely summarizes the importance of a close look at Persepolis. Are the nations pictured with more agency, even if it is Persian propaganda, on the walls of Persepolis? Margaret Root writes:

> The entire Apadana relief system presents a complex synthesis of the actual and the ideal. . . . The peoples shown offering encomia here correspond to the peoples listed in imperial inscriptions tabulating the extent of the empire under Darius. . . . These, then, are the conquered peoples whom we should expect (on the basis of comparisons with Near Eastern tradition) to see prostrate in submission at the feet of the King. Instead, we see the leading delegate of each group about to be brought forward by the hand, gracefully and with dignity, up into the presence of the king. This hand-holding image stems not from the age-old Near Eastern repertoire of tribute scenes, but rather from the equally venerable repertoire of apotheosis scenes, where a suppliant is led forward by the hand or wrist into the presence of a deity—and where the aspect of submission is moral or spiritual, not military.[107]

Thus, Root refers to the imagery as an "ecumenical pageant."[108] Briant, however, is a bit more cautious about this imagery and its message. The art of Persepolis, he states, reflects textual descriptions of empire:

> Every available text indicates that in this way the Great Kings periodically reaffirmed their dominion over the peoples they controlled. They recalled their obligations to them and constrained them to exhibit publically their subjugation by the offering of gifts. In this way, they also staked out the extent of their immediate power over territories and subjects.[109]

Like Nehemiah 9, Isaiah 45:1, and the Diaspora Stories, the Apadana friezes are clearly ambiguous about the agency of the tributaries with their gifts, whether they are there to symbolize forced control (so Briant) or awe-inspiring invitations to meet a deity (so Root) or "voluntary actions."[110]

When enumerating the various peoples at Persepolis[111] and all the gifts brought by the various peoples (Susa Foundation Charter[112]), is this a kind of "staging of Empire" (Herodotus VII, 61–80; 83–7.1; 89–94.1; 95) with the descriptions of the various nationalities and their weapons, animals, and equipment, or is this some kind of recognition of, some would argue an affirmation of, diversity by the Achaemenid rulers within their empire? Are we to read these declarations as the megalomaniacal claims of "Oriental despotic" rulers, or pious statements of quasi-"human rights" recognized by Achaemenid rulers awestruck with the responsibilities laid upon them by Ahura-Mazda?

Summary

Contemporary biblical scholars must read all such ancient texts, biblical or otherwise, with a reasonable sense of what is possible. The Bible certainly contains protest literature—complaints about rulers and their oppression, as well as praises of rulers—when one considers the deeply divided opinions about David himself as God's chosen shepherd.

It cannot be dismissed that "Ezra" is complaining about Persian treatment in Nehemiah 9 based only on praise of Cyrus as "anointed" elsewhere in the text. In the "post-James Scott" era of postcolonial analysis, biblical texts simply can no longer be read as inevitably positive if resistance or even opposition is not absolutely clear and forthright. What is called for is a nuanced argument about resistance *and* collaboration. In Scott's work, for example, we are warned against accepting "at face value" the public statements (the "public transcripts") of those who live under centralized and potentially despotic rule. What they actually believe, and what they say at home among trusted friends ("private transcripts"), indicates that low-level "resistance" may be going on when we too quickly accepted the public pronouncements at face value—especially *when there are hints of other views present*,[113] and in the Bible, there most certainly are such hints, and in quite public contexts.

Not only are we well aware of agitation against Persian rule in Egypt and elsewhere that may have tempted Judean support (summarized by Perdue, Carter, and Baker[114]), it is furthermore clear that both Haggai and especially Zechariah indicate Judean political agitation against Persian rule in support of home rule—and Zerubbabel's name, which was obviously originally present, has somehow been removed from the "crowning" narrative of Zechariah 6:11, perhaps indicating Persian threats against a usurper Davidic descendent like Zerubbabel (the "branch") being set up.[115] Despite such indications of "private transcripts" under Persian rule, biblical scholars remain ambivalent. Consider Gerstenberger's recent observations in his 2012 study on the Persian period:

> [W]e are not able to know how ancient people felt when they were asked about their Persian rulers. Some biblical texts, for instance, share the euphoria of those who celebrated the Persian conquest as deliverance. Others intimate that it was precisely under Persian aegis that the gap between rich and poor was wider than otherwise. The financial need of the empire was so immense that taxes were collected mercilessly and as thoroughly as possible, and many sank into social misery (See Neh. 5:1–4). It is hardly surprising that a lament against the rulers who drive their subordinates hard for "great gain" could become popular in Judah ... the relationship to the Empire was ambivalent, yet to a large extent there was a positive attitude to the emperor.[116]

The problem, of course, is that it is so easy to overlook one reality that remains crystal clear across the centuries—so obvious that it is rarely named—namely, that the Persians ran an empire, not a democratic people's commune: "In its foreign rule, the Achaemenids were not the tolerant and benign rulers their propaganda depicted."[117] That being the case, although it is the purpose of this article to raise questions about the way this issue has been processed, I will indicate my own bias on the matter by leaving the last word to Bruce Lincoln's 2007 study of the Achaemenid self-image in text and image:

> Three basic constructs thus characterize Achaemenian ideology, each one profoundly religious and brilliantly suited to represent the empire's most aggressive tendencies and its most audacious ambitions as righteous, sacred, and holy. It is as an ensemble, however, where the three are exceptionally potent, and this ensemble recurs—with contextual and dialectal variations, to be sure—in the discourse of most successful empires as a condition of their possibility. The three components, as we have repeatedly observed, are (1) a starkly dualistic ethics in which the opposition good/evil is aligned with that of self/other and correlated discriminatory binaries, (2) a theology of election that secures the ruler's legitimacy by constituting him as God's chosen agent, (3) and a sense of soteriological mission that represents *imperial aggression as salvific action taken on behalf of divine principles, thereby recoding the empire's victims as its beneficiaries* [my emphasis][118]

Let us no more fall victim to Persian propaganda about righteousness than we do Pilate's cynical theatrics in washing his hands just before Roman authority executed yet another Jew.

Notes

1. Harry De Quetteville, "Cyrus Cylinder's Ancient Bill of Rights 'Is Just Propaganda,'" *Daily Telegraph*, July 16, 2008.
2. De Quetteville, "Cyrus Cylinder's Ancient Bill of Rights."
3. De Quetteville, "Cyrus Cylinder's Ancient Bill of Rights."
4. Amelie Kuhrt, *The Persian Empire: A Corpus of Sources from the Achaemenid Period* (London: Routledge, 2007), 70–72.
5. Kuhrt, *The Persian Empire*, 71.
6. Golnaz Esfandiari, "Historic Cyrus Cylinder Called 'A Strange in Its Own Home,'" (Radio Free Europe, September 14, 2010), www.rferl.org/a/Historic_Cyrus_Cylinder_Called_A_Stranger_In_Its_Own_Home/2157345.html.
7. Lori Khatchadourian, *Imperial Matter: Ancient Persia and the Archaeology of Empires* (Berkeley: University of California Press, 2016), xxiv.
8. Brent Strawn, "'A World under Control': Isaiah 60 and the Apadana Reliefs from Persepolis," in *Approaching Yehud: New Approaches to the Study of the Persian Period* (Atlanta: SBL Press, 2007), 85–116/
9. Othmar Keel and Christoph Uehlinger, Gods, Goddesses, and Images of God in Ancient Israel (Minneapolis: Fortress Press, 1996); Christoph Uehlinger, "Virtual Vision vs. Actual Show: Strategies of Visualization in the Book of Ezekiel," *Die Welt des Orients* 45 (2015): 62–84.
10. T. C. McCaskie, "'As on a Darkling Plain': Practitioners, Publics, Propagandists, and Ancient Historiography," *Comparative Studies in Society and History* 54 (2012): 145–173.
11. McCaskie, "'As on a Darkling Plain,'" 145.
12. McCaskie, "'As on a Darkling Plain,'" 150.
13. Lloyd Llewellyn-Jones and James Robson, *Ctesias' History of Persia: Tales of the Orient* (London: Routledge, 2010), 24–27.
14. McCaskie, "'As on a Darkling Plain,'" 171.
15. Claus Westermann, *Isaiah 40–66: A Commentary* (Grand Rapids, MI: Eerdmans), 1969), 158.
16. David Reimer, "Isaiah and Politics," in *Interpreting Isaiah: Issues and Approaches*, edited by D. G. Firth and H. G. M. Williamson (Downers Grove: Intervarsity Academic, 2009), 96.
17. Walter Brueggemann, *Isaiah 40–66* (Philadelphia: Westminster/John Knox Press, 1998), 75.
18. Brueggemann, *Isaiah 40–66*, 75.
19. Shalom Paul, *Isaiah 40–66* (Grand Rapids, MI: Eerdmans, 2012), 252.
20. Westermann, *Isaiah 40–66*, 160–161.
21. Paul, *Isaiah 40–66*, 251–253.
22. Marvin Sweeney, *Isaiah 40–66* (Grand Rapids: Eerdmans, 2016), 128.
23. Brueggemann, *Isaiah 40–66*, 77.
24. John Goldingay and David Payne, *Isaiah 40–66*, Vol. 1 (London: T&T Clark, 2007), 14.

25. Lisbeth S. Fried, "Cyrus the Messiah? The Historical Background to Isaiah 45:1," *Harvard Theological Review* 95 (2002): 386.
26. Fried, "Cyrus the Messiah?," 390, 392–393.
27. Westermann, *Isaiah 40–66*, 158.
28. Reimer, "Isaiah and Politics," 100.
29. Kuhrt, cited in Reimer, "Isaiah and Politics," 100.
30. B. Megillah 12a, cited in Paul, *Isaiah 40–66*, 252–253.
31. Sweeney, *Isaiah 40–66*, 128–129.
32. Jacob Myers, *Ezra-Nehemiah* (Garden City, NY: Doubleday, 1965), 167.
33. Mark Boda, Daniel Falk, and Rodney Werline, eds., Seeking the Favor of God, 2 vols., (Atlanta: Society of Biblical Literature, 2006–2007).
34. Rodney Werline, "Reflections on Pentitential Prayer: Definition and Form," in Boda, Falk, and Werline, *Seeking the Favor of God*, Volume 2: *The Development of Penitential Prayer in Second Temple Judaism*, 209–225.
35. Johanna W. H. Van Wijk-Bos, *Ezra, Nehemiah, and Esther* (Philadelphia: Westminster John Knox Press, 1998), 82.
36. Wilhelm Rudolph, *Esra und Nehemia* (Tubingen: Mohr/Siebeck, 1949), 171. My translation.
37. Myers, *Ezra-Nehemiah*, 170.
38. F. Charles Fensham, *The Books of Ezra and Nehemiah* (Grand Rapids, MI: Eerdmans, 1982), 233.
39. Fensham, *The Books of Ezra and Nehemiah*, 234.
40. D. J. Clines, *Ezra, Nehemiah, Esther* (Grand Rapids, MI: Eerdmans, 1984), 198.
41. Clines, *Ezra, Nehemiah, Esther*, 199.
42. H. G. M. Williamson, *Ezra, Nehemiah* (Nashville: Thomas Nelson, 1985), 306–307.
43. Williamson, *Ezra, Nehemiah*, 309.
44. Williamson, *Ezra, Nehemiah*, 317.
45. J. Blenkinsopp, *Ezra-Nehemiah* (London: SCM, 1988), 301.
46. Kyung-jin Min, *The Levitical Authorship of Ezra-Nehemiah* (London: T&T Clark, 2004), 38.
47. Min, *The Levitical Authorship*, 112–113.
48. E.g., Williamson, *Ezra, Nehemiah*, 8; Blenkinsopp, *Ezra-Nehemiah*, 74, etc.
49. Lester Grabbe, *Ezra-Nehemiah* (London: Routledge, 1998), 24.
50. Daniel Smith-Christopher, "Daniel, and the Additions to Daniel," in *The New Interpreter's Bible*, Vol. VII (Nashville: Abingdon Press, 1996), 19–194; Lorenzo DiTommaso, *The Book of Daniel and the Apocryphal Daniel Literature* (Leiden: Brill, 2005). DiTommaso is among those ready to accept a late Persian period origin for the earliest of these stories, but not the present forms.
51. W. L. Humphreys, "A Life-Style for the Diaspora: A Study of the Tales of Daniel," *Journal of Biblical Literature* 92 (1973): 221, 223.
52. John Goldingay, *Daniel* (Nashville: Thomas Nelson, 1989), 6–7.
53. Goldingay, *Daniel*, 7.
54. John Collins, *Daniel: A Commentary on the Book of Daniel* (Minneapolis: Fortress Press, 1994), 33.
55. Collins, *Daniel*, 33.
56. Collins, *Daniel*, 44.
57. Matthias Henze, "The Narrative Frame of Daniel: A Literary Assessment," *Journal for the Study of Judaism in the Persian, Hellenistic, and Roman Period* 32 (2001): 12.

58. E. C. Lucas, "Daniel: Resolving the Enigma," *Vetus Testamentum* 50 (2000): 77.
59. Tawny L. Holm, *Of Courtiers and Kings: The Biblical Daniel Narratives and Ancient Story-Collections* (Winona Lake, IN: Eisenbrauns, 2013), 5, 118.
60. Holm, 15, *Of Courtiers and Kings*, 192.
61. Holm, *Of Courtiers and Kings*, 192.
62. Holm, *Of Courtiers and Kings*, 206.
63. Holm, *Of Courtiers and Kings*, 208, cf. Henze, "The Narrative Frame of Daniel," 6.
64. C. L. Seow, *Daniel* (Louisville, KY: Westminster John Knox Press, 2003), 10.
65. Danna Nolan Fewell, *Circle of Sovereignty: A Story of Stories in Daniel 1–6* (Sheffield, UK: Almond Press, 1988).
66. Donald C. Polaski, "Mene, Mene, Tekel, Parsin: Writing and Resistance in Daniel 5 and 6," *Journal of Biblical Literature* 123, no. 4 (2004): 649.
67. Polaski, "Mene, Mene, Tekel, Parsin," 668.
68. That is to say, all of Daniel, not only the visions, see Carol Newsom, *Daniel: A Commentary* (Lousiville, KY: Westminster John Knox Press, 2014), 12.
69. C. L. Seow, "The Rule of God in the Book of Daniel," in David and Zion: Biblical Studies in Honor of J. J. M. Roberts, edited by B. Batto and K. L. Roberts (Winona Lake, IN: Eisenbrauns, 2005), 225.
70. Paul-Alain Beaulieu, "The Babylonian Background of the Motif of the Fiery Furnace in Daniel 3," *Journal of Biblical Literature* 128, no. 2 (2009): 282.
71. Beaulieu, "The Babylonian Background," 286.
72. H. P. Müller, "Märchen, Legende und Enderwartung: Zum Verständnis des Buches Daniel," *Vetus Testamentum* 26, no. 3 (1976): 341.
73. Takayoshi Oshima, "How 'Mesopotamian' Was Ahiqar the Wise? A Search for Ahiqar in Cuneiform Texts," in *Wandering Aramaeans: Aramaeans outside Syria: Textual and Archaeological Perspectives*, edited by A. Berlejung, A. M. Maeir, and A. Schule (Wiesbaden: Harrassowitz Verlag, 2017), 147.
74. Bob Becking, "Love and Friendship in Elephantine," in *With the Loyal You Show Yourself Loyal: Essays on Relationships in the Hebrew Bible in Honor of Saul M. Olyan*, edited by T. M. Lemos, J. D. Rosenblum, K. B. Stern, and D. Scoggins-Ballentine (Atlanta: The Society of Biblical Literature, 2021), 81.
75. Karel Van der Toorn, *Becoming Diaspora Jews: Behind the Story of Elephantine* (New Haven, CT: Yale University Press, 2019), 25.
76. Ann-Firstin Wigand, "Politische Loyalität und religiöse Legitimierung," *Die Welt des Orients* 48 (2018): 132.
77. Cf. W. Schniedewind, *A Social History of Hebrew: Its Origins through the Rabbinic Period* (New Haven, CT: Yale University Press, 2013), 143.
78. Wigand, "Politische Loyalität," 146.
79. Oshima, "How 'Mesopotamian' was Ahiqar," 161.
80. Olyan, "The Literary Dynamic of Loyalty," 267.
81. Bob Becking, "Love and Friendship in Elephantine," in *With the Loyal You Show Yourself Loyal: Essays on Relationships in the Hebrew Bible in Honor of Saul M. Olyan*, edited by T. M. Lemos, J. D. Rosenblum, K. B. Stern, and D. Scoggins-Ballentine (Atlanta: Society of Biblical Literature, 2021), 85–86.
82. Seth A. Bledsoe, "Conflicting Loyalties: King and Context in the Aramaic Book of Ahiqar," in *Political Memory in and after the Persian Empire*, edited by J. Silverman and C. Waerzeggers (Atlanta: SBL Press, 2015), 240.

83. Bledsoe, "Conflicting Loyalties," 241.
84. Bledsoe, "Conflicting Loyalties," 253.
85. Bledsoe, "Conflicting Loyalties," 254, cf. 252–257.
86. Bledose, "Conflicting Loyalties," 255.
87. Bledsoe, "Conflicting Loyalties," 259–260, 264.
88. Katherine Southwood, "Performing Deference in Ahiqar: The Significance of a Politics of Resistance in the Narrative and Proverbs of Ahiqar," *Zeitschrift für die alttestamentliche Wissenschaft* 133 (2021): 47.
89. Southwood, "Performing Deference in Ahiqar," 49.
90. Southwood, "Performing Deference in Ahiqar," 54.
91. Marko Marincic, "The Grand Vizier, the Prophet, and the Satirist: Transformations of the Oriental Ahiqar Romance in Ancient Prose Fictions," in *The Ancient Novel and Beyond*, edited by S. Panayotakis (Leiden: Brill, 2003), 56.
92. Kuhrt, *The Persian Empire*, 57.
93. Kuhrt, *The Persian Empire*, 113.
94. Kuhrt, *The Persian Empire*, 131–132.
95. Kuhrt, *The Persian Empire*, 163–164.
96. Kuhrt, *The Persian Empire*, 219–220.
97. Kuhrt, *The Persian Empire*, 610.
98. Kuhrt, *The Persian Empire*, 645–646.
99. Kuhrt, *The Persian Empire*, 63–674.
100. Kuhrt, *The Persian Empire*, 712.
101. Kuhrt, *The Persian Empire*, 679.
102. Llewellyn-Jones and Robson, *Ctesias' History of Persia*, 22–24.
103. Llewellyn-Jones and Robson, *Ctesias' History of Persia*, 30.
104. Llewellyn-Jones and Robson, *Ctesias' History of Persia*, 76.
105. Brent Strawn, "'A World under Control': Isaiah 60 and the Apadana Reliefs from Persepolis," in *Approaching Yehud: New Approaches to the Study of the Persian Period*, edited by Jon Berquist (Atlanta: Society of Biblical Literature, 2007), 85–116.
106. Ida Ostenberg, *Staging the World: Spoils, Captives, and Representations in the Roman Triumphal Procession* (Oxford: Oxford University Press, 2009), 266.
107. Margaret Cool Root, "The Parthenon Frieze and the Apadana Reliefs at Persepolis: Reassessing a Programmatic Relationship," *American Journal of Archaeology* 89 (1985): 112.
108. Root, "The Parthenon Frieze," 119, cf. also Silverman, *Persepolis and Jerusalem*, 70.
109. Pierre Briant, *From Cyrus to Alexander: A History of the Persian Empire* (Winona Lake, IN: Eisenbrauns, 2002, 2002), 193.
110. Strawn, "'A World under Control,'" 115–116.
111. Kuhrt, *The Persian Empire*, 483–487.
112. Kuhrt, *The Persian Empire*, 492–497.
113. The classic works by James Scott are: *The Weapons of the Weak: Everyday Forms of Peasant Resistance* (New Haven, CT: Yale University Press, 1987) and *Domination and the Art of Resistance: Hidden Transcripts* (New Haven, CT: Yale University Press. 1992).
114. Leo Perdue, Warren Carter, and Coleman Baker, *Israel and Empire: A Postcolonial History of Israel and Early Judaism* (London: Bloomsbury/T&T Clark, 2015), 121–122.
115. Perdue, Carter, and Baker, *Israel and Empire*, 126–128.
116. Erhard S. Gerstenberger, *Israel in the Persian Period: The Fifth and Fourth Centuries B.C.E*, translated by Siegfried S. Schatzmann (Leiden: E.J. Brill, 2012), 58.

117. Perdue, Carter, and Baker, *Israel and Empire*, 108.
118. Bruce Lincoln, *Religion, Empire, and Torture: The Case of Achaemenian Persia, with a Postscript on Abu Ghraib* (Chicago: University of Chicago Press, 2007), 95.

Bibliography

Almagor, Eran. "The Political and the Divine in Achaemenid Royal Inscriptions." In *Ancient Historiography on War and Empire*, edited by T. Howe, S. Muller, and R. Stoneman, 26–54. Oxford: Oxbow Books, 2017.

Beaulieu, Paul-Alain. "The Babylonian Background of the Motif of the Fiery Furnace in Daniel 3." *Journal of Biblical Literature* 128 (2009): 273–290.

Becking, Bob. "Love and Friendship in Elephantine." In *With the Loyal You Show Yourself Loyal: Essays on Relationships in the Hebrew Bible in Honor of Saul M. Olyan*, edited by T. M. Lemos, J. D. Rosenblum, K. B. Stern, and D. Scoggins-Ballentine, 81–96. Atlanta: Society of Biblical Literature, 2021.

Bledsoe, Seth A. "Conflicting Loyalties: King and Context in the Aramaic Book of Ahiqar." In *Political Memory in and after the Persian Empire*, edited by J. Silverman and C. Waerzeggers, 39–68. Atlanta: SBL Press, 2015.

Blenkinsopp, J. *Ezra-Nehemiah*. Old Testament Library. London: SCM, 1988.

Boda, Mark, Daniel Falk, and Rodney Werline, eds. *Seeking the Favor of God*, Volume 1: *The Origins of Penitential Prayer in Second Temple Judaism*. SBLEJL 21. Atlanta: Society of Biblical Literature, 2006.

Boda, Mark, Daniel Falk, and Rodney Werline, eds. *Seeking the Favor of God*, Volume 2: *The Development of Penitential Prayer in Second Temple Judaism*. SBLEJL 22. Atlanta: Society of Biblical Literature: E.J. Brill, 2007.

Briant, Pierre. *From Cyrus to Alexander: A History of the Persian Empire*. Winona Lake, IN: Eisenbrauns, 2002.

Brueggemann, Walter. *Isaiah 40–66*. Westminster Bible Companion. Philadelphia: Westminster John Knox Press, 1998.

Calmeyer, Peter. "Textual Sources for the Interpretation of Achaemenian Palace Decorations." *Iran* 18 (1980): 55–63.

Childs, Brevard. *Isaiah*. Old Testament Library. Lousiville, KY: Westminster John Knox Press, 2001.

Clines, D. J. *Ezra, Nehemiah, Esther*. The New Century Bible Commentary. Grand Rapids, MI: Eerdmans, 1984.

Collins, John J. *Daniel: A Commentary on the Book of Daniel*. Hermeneia: A Critical & Historical Commentary on the Bible. Minneapolis, MN: Fortress Press, 1994.

De Quetteville, Harry. "Cyrus Cylinder's Ancient Bill of Rights 'Is Just Propaganda.'" *Telegraph*, July 16, 2008. www.telegraph.co.uk/news/worldnews/europe/germany/2420263/Cyrus-cylinders-ancient-bill-of-rights-is-just-propaganda.html.

Esfandiari, Golnaz. "Historic Cyrus Cylinder Called 'A Stranger in Its Own Home.'" Radio Free Europe, September 14, 2010. www.rferl.org/a/Historic_Cyrus_Cylinder_Called_A_Stranger_In_Its_Own_Home/2157345.html.Copyright (c)2010 RFE/RL, Inc. Reprinted with the permission of Radio Free Europe/Radio Liberty, 1201 Connecticut Ave NW, Ste 400, Washington DC 20036.

Fensham, F. Charles. *The Books of Ezra and Nehemiah*. New International Commentary on the Old Testament. Grand Rapids, MI: Eerdmanns, 1982.

Fewell, Danna Nolan. *Circle of Sovereignty: A Story of Stories in Daniel 1–6*. Sheffield, UK: Almond Press, 1988.

Firth, David G., and H. G. M. Williamson, eds. 2009. *Interpreting Isaiah: Issues and Approaches*. Downers Grove, IL: Intervarsity Press.

Fried, Lisbeth S. "Cyrus the Messiah? The Historical Background to Isaiah 45:1." *Harvard Theological Review* 95 (2002): 373–393.

Friesen, Ivan. *Isaiah*. The Believers Bible Commentary. Harrisonburg, Virginia: Herald Press, 2013.

Gerstenberger, Erhard S. *Israel in the Persian Period: The Fifth and Fourth Centuries B.C.E.* Translated by Siegfried S. Schatzmann. Leiden: E.J. Brill, 2012.

Goldingay, John. *Daniel*. Word Biblical Commentary. Nashville: Thomas Nelson, 1989.

Goldingay, John, and David Payne. *Isaiah 40–66*, Vol. 1. International Critical Commentary. London: T&T Clark, 2007.

Grabbe, Lester. *Ezra-Nehemiah*. Old Testament Readings. London: Routledge, 1998.

Hanson, Paul. *Isaiah 40–66*. The Interpretation Commentary. Philadelphia: John Knox Press, 1995.

Henze, Matthias. "The Narrative Frame of Daniel: A Literary Assessment." *Journal for the Study of Judaism in the Persian, Hellenistic, and Roman Period* 32 (2001): 5–24.

Holland, Tom. *Persian Fire*. New York: Doubleday, 2006.

Holm, Tawny L. *Of Courtiers and Kings: The Biblical Daniel Narratives and Ancient Story-Collections*. Winona Lake, IN: Eisenbrauns, 2013.

Humphreys, W. L. "A Life-Style for Diaspora: A Study of the Tales of Esther and Daniel." *Journal of Biblical Literature* 92 (1973): 211–233.

Keel, Othmar, and Christoph Uehlinger. *Gods, Goddesses, and Images of God in Ancient Israel*. Minneapolis: Fortress Press, 1996.

Khatchadourian, Lori. 2016. *Imperial Matter: Ancient Persia and the Archaeology of Empires*. Berkeley: University of California Press.

Kuhrt, Amelie. *The Persian Empire: A Corpus of Sources from the Achaemenid Period*. London: Routledge, 2007a.

Kuhrt, Amelie. "The Problem of Achaemenid 'Religious Policy.'" In *Die Welt der Gotterbilder*, edited by Hermann Spiekermann and Brigitte Groneberg, 117–142. Beihefte zur Zeitschrift für die alttestamentliche Wissenschaft, Band 376. Berlin: Walter de Gruyter, 2007b.

Lincoln, Bruce. *Religion, Empire, and Torture: The Case of Achaemenian Persia, with a Postscript on Abu Ghraib*. Chicago: University of Chicago Press, 2007.

Llewellyn-Jones, Lloyd, and James Robson. *Ctesias' History of Persia: Tales of the Orient*. Routledge Classical Translations. London: Routledge, 2010.

Lucas, E. C. "Daniel: Resolving the Enigma." *Vetus Testamentum* 50 (2000): 66–80.

Marincic, Marko. "The Grand Vizier, the Prophet, and the Satirist: Transformations of the Oriental Ahiqar Romance in Ancient Prose Fictions." In *The Ancient Novel and Beyond*, edited by S. Panayotakis, 53–70. Leiden: Brill, 2003.

McCaskie, T. C. "'As on a Darkling Plain': Practitioners, Publics, Propagandists, and Ancient Historiography." *Comparative Studies in Society and History* 54 (2012): 145–173.

Min, Kyung-jin, *The Levitical Authorship of Ezra-Nehemiah*. JSOT Supplement Series, no. 409. London: T&T Clark, 2004.

Morgan, Janett. *Greek Perspectives on the Achaemenid Empire: Persia through the Looking Glass.* Edinburgh: Edinburgh University Press, 2016.

Müller, H.-P. "Märchen, Legende und Enderwartung: Zum Verständnis des Buches Daniel." *Vetus Testamentum* 26 (1976): 338–350.

Myers, Jacob. *Ezra-Nehemiah.* The Anchor Bible. Garden City, NY: Doubleday, 1965.

Nagy, Gergory. "The Idea of an Archetype in Texts Stemming from the Empire founded by Cyrus the Great." In *The Archaeology of Greece and Rome: Studies in Honour of Anthony Snodgrass*, edited by J. Bintliff and K. Rutter, 337–357. Edinburgh: Edinburgh University Press, 2016.

Newsom, Carol. *Daniel: A Commentary.* Louisville, KY: Westminster John Knox Press, 2014.

Olyan, Saul M. "The Literary Dynamic of Loyalty and Betrayal in the Aramaic Ahiqar Narrative." *Journal of Near Eastern Studies* 79 (2020): 261–269.

Oshima, Takayoshi. "How 'Mesopotamian' Was Ahiqar the Wise? A Search for Ahiqar in Cuneiform Texts." In *Wandering Aramaeans: Aramaeans outside Syria: Textual and Archaeological Perspectives*, edited by A. Berlejung, A. M. Maeir, and A. Schule, 141–167. Wiesbaden: Harrassowitz Verlag, 2017.

Ostenberg, Ida. *Staging the World: Spoils, Captives, and Representations in the Roman Triumphal Procession.* Oxford: Oxford University Press, 2009.

Oswalt, John. *Isaiah 40–66.* New International Commentary on the Old Testament. Grand Rapids, MI: Eerdmans, 1998.

Paul, Shalom. *Isaiah 40–66.* Eerdmans Critical Commentary. Grand Rapids, MI: Eerdmans, 2012.

Perdue, Leo, Warren Carter, and Coleman Baker. *Israel and Empire: A Postcolonial History of Israel and Early Judaism.* London: Bloomsbury/T&T Clark, 2015.

Polaski, Donald C. "Mene, Mene, Tekel, Parsin: Writing and Resistance in Daniel 5 and 6." *Journal of Biblical Literature* 123 (2004): 649–669.

Reimer, David. "Isaiah and Politics." In *Interpreting Isaiah: Issues and Approaches*, edited by D. G. Firth and H. G. M. Williamson, 84–103. Downers Grove, IL: Intervarsity Academic, 2009.

Roberts, J. J. M. "God's Imperial Reign According to the Psalter." *Horizons in Biblical Theology* 23 (2001): 211–221.

Root, Margaret Cool. "The Parthenon Frieze and the Apadana Reliefs at Persepolis: Reassessing a Programmatic Relationship." *American Journal of Archaeology* 89 (1985): 103–120.

Rudolph, Wilhelm. *Esra und Nehemia.* Handbuch zum Alten Testament 20. Tubingen, Germany: Mohr/Siebeck, 1949.

Schniedewind, W. *A Social History of Hebrew: Its Origins through the Rabbinic Period.* New Haven, CT: Yale University Press, 2013.

Scott, James. *The Weapons of the Weak: Everyday Forms of Peasant Resistance.* New Haven, CT: Yale University Press, 1987.

Scott, James. *Domination and the Art of Resistance: Hidden Transcripts.* New Haven, CT: Yale University Press, 1992.

Seow, C. L. *Daniel.* Westminster Bible Companion. Louisville, KY: Westminster John Knox Press, 2003a.

Seow, C. L. "From Mountain to Mountain: The Reign of God in Daniel 2." In *A God So Near: Essays on Old Testament Theology in Honor of Patrick D. Miller*, edited by B.A. Strawn and N.R. Bowen, 355–374. University Park: Pennsylvanian State University Press, 2003b.

Seow, C. L. "The Rule of God in the Book of Daniel." In *David and Zion: Biblical Studies in Honor of J. J. M. Roberts*, edited by B. Batto and K. L. Roberts, 219–246. Winona Lake, IN: Eisenbrauns, 2005.

Silverman, Jason. *Persepolis and Jerusalem: Iranian Influence on the Apocalyptic Hermeneutic.* LHB/OTS 558. London: T&T Clark, 2012.

Smith-Christopher, Daniel, "Daniel, and the Additions to Daniel." In *The New Interpreter's Bible*, Vol. VII, 19–194. Nashville: Abingdon Press, 1996.

Southwood, Katherine. "Performing Deference in Ahiqar: The Significance of a Politics of Resistance in the Narrative and Proverbs of Ahiqar." *Zeitschrift für die alttestamentliche Wissenschaft* 133 (2021): 42–55.

Strawn, Brent. "'A World under Control': Isaiah 60 and the Apadana Reliefs from Persepolis." In *Approaching Yehud: New Approaches to the Study of the Persian Period*, edited by Jon Berquist, 85–116. Semeia Studies 50. Atlanta: Society of Biblical Literature, 2007.

Sweeney, Marvin. *Isaiah 40–66.* Forms of Old Testament Literature. Grand Rapids, MI: Eerdmans, 2016.

Uehlinger, Christoph. "Virtual Vision vs. Actual Show: Strategies of Visualization in the Book of Ezekiel." *Die Welt des Orients* 45 (2015): 62–84.

Van der Toorn, Karel. *Becoming Diaspora Jews: Behind the Story of Elephantine.* New Haven, CT: Yale University Press, 2019.

Werline, Rodney. "Reflections on Penitential Prayer: Definition and Form." In *Seeking the Favor of God*, Volume 2: *The Development of Penitential Prayer in Second Temple Judaism*, edited by Mark Boda, Daniel Falk, and Rodney Werline, 209–225. SBLEJL 22. Atlanta: Society of Biblical Literature, 2007.

Westermann, Claus. *Isaiah 40–66: A Commentary.* Grand Rapids, MI: Eerdmans, 1969.

Wigand, Ann-Firstin. "Politische Loyalität und religiöse Legitimierung." *Die Welt des Orients* 48 (2018): 128–150.

Williamson, H. G. M. *Ezra, Nehemiah.* Word Biblical Commentary 16. Nashville: Thomas Nelson, 1985.

Van Wijk-Bos, Johanna W. H. *Ezra, Nehemiah, and Esther.* The Westminster Bible Companion. Philadelphia: Westminster John Knox Press, 1998.

CHAPTER 5

JEWISH NEGOTIATIONS OF HELLENISTIC POWER

WARREN CARTER

How did Jewish writings negotiate Hellenistic imperial and cultural power beginning in the time of Alexander and continuing through the Ptolemaic and Seleucid empires until the assertion of Roman hegemony over Judaea/Israel (323 BCE–63 BCE)?[1] This time period was marked by a process of cultural fluidity and fusion stimulated by the spread of Greek language, ideas, and political imperial power that interpenetrated local cultures, both in Judaea/Israel and among diasporic Jewish communities.[2] Numerous Jewish writings emerged in this period, including writings found in collections that we know as the Old Testament Pseudepigrapha, The Apocrypha, and the Dead Sea Scrolls, along with "canonical" texts such as Ecclesiastes/Qohelet and Daniel. While space permits discussion of only a small sample of texts, it will be sufficient to identify at least some aspects of the multivalent assertion and negotiation of Hellenistic power. The discussion will largely but not exclusively concentrate on those aspects whose provenance, when it can be established, is Israel/Judaea.

When the Macedonian Alexander died (323 BCE), he had defeated the world's superpower Persia and conquered territory from Greece in the east to India in the west and Egypt to the south. Whatever constructions of masculinity and kingly political rule one employs to determine whether Alexander was "great" or not, there is no doubting his legacy.[3] And whatever his motivations, which have been much discussed and disputed, the repercussions of his actions continued for centuries. One successor, Ptolemy, established the Ptolemaic Dynasty in Egypt, while another, Seleucus, established the Seleucid Dynasty in Syria. These Hellenistic dynasties divided and disputed the defeated Persian Empire, including wars over Judaea controlled by the Ptolemies in the third century BCE and by the Seleucids in the second century BCE. Ptolemy 1 (d. ca. 283 BCE), for instance, is said to have captured Judaea and Jerusalem and to have taken "a great many captives" to Egypt, subsequently numbered at 120,000 (Josephus, *Ant* 12.3–11). These Hellenistic dynasties continued economic extractions and sociocultural-political control until both fell to the Romans in the first century BCE.

Beyond military conquests and political regimes, Alexander's actions released cultural forces that spread across the ancient world. These cultural forces fused with local cultures in numerous ways and to varying degrees, setting up interdependencies between colonizers and colonized. Armies depended on local peoples for food supplies, gaining and repairing equipment, securing transportation and local knowledge, and adding recruits. Military victories were coded with messages and strategies of superior political power, gods, and culture. Alliances with local elites expanded administrative personnel and skills. Greek language, culture, and political authority spread through intermarriages and trade interactions; religious syncretism; the establishment of cities as administrative, commercial, and cultural-educational centers that dominated surrounding territory; and the collection of taxes and tributes.

The argument in this essay is that, beyond binaries of engagement and resistance, a postcolonial reading illumines multivalent and complex dynamics that comprise shifting Jewish negotiations of the Greek empires: the Ptolemies of Egypt, the Seleucids of Syria, and, subsequently, the (imitative) Hasmoneans themselves in Judaea/Israel. These dynamics include inequalities in the assertions of power; the often-invisible colonized and their agencies and voices; and strategies marked by ambivalence, mimicry, consensual-conflictive hybridity, native fractures, and the mutual dependence of colonizer and colonized. The following discussion will highlight how a few exemplars from the large number and diverse genres of Jewish writings from this period negotiate this spread of Hellenistic/Ptolemaic/Seleucid power.

SOME PREVIOUS DISCUSSIONS

Initial scholarly emphases examined the question of the spread of power with a binary of largely fixed and oppositional entities, perhaps reflecting the negative use of the terms *Hellenismos* to describe a threatening manifestation of Greek political-cultural power and religion in 2 Macc 4:13 and *Ioudaismos* to signify the religion of Jewish people under attack (2 Macc 2:21). Victor Tcherikover understood the writings as apologetic in providing a defense of Judaism's customs and beliefs for Jewish readers and thereby strengthening practice and identity.[4]

More recently, focusing on Jewish perceptions of Greeks, and rejecting apologetic approaches and assumptions of dissonance, Erich Gruen recognizes that Judaism and Hellenism were not competing or incompatible systems, nor were they accurately conceived as fixed binaries. Rather, Judaism was not static and was always being refashioned in relation to its particular circumstances. Gruen argues for less antithetical or antagonistic interactions with Hellenistic culture—as familiar more than foreign or threatening—though some interactions were not without tensions.[5]

John Barclay similarly rejects defensive, apologetic, and dissonance-emphasizing approaches. He argues that Hellenistic Jews were "cultural negotiators" who did not understand Hellenistic culture as a foreign entity but moved comfortably within the culture while both "using" and "refusing" aspects of it for a range of purposes.[6] In so doing, Jews made choices, neither receiving Hellenistic culture uncritically nor rejecting it completely. Barclay recognizes the impact of power on Jewish "choices" in negotiating the dominant culture, including the use of hidden transcripts to subvert or mock the dominant culture, to assert Jewish traditions, and thereby to fashion new versions of Judaism while maintaining common, defining core practices. That is, even when the political-cultural dominance of Hellenistic power seemed unassailable, and open and direct attack was not an option, it could be contested in ways that were not militarily violent and that expressed creative dissent.

John Collins agrees with Gruen and Barclay that Jewish writings took Hellenistic culture for granted and affirmed common values with it.[7] He recalls that throughout the Hellenistic period Greeks generally recognized and tolerated Jewish distinctiveness—though, of course, differences could result in conflict. Collins argues that interactions were not always peaceable and that the consciousness of being different meant the assertion of a separate identity and distinctive practices. These distinctive practices, Collins argues, centered on worship. Greek language, philosophy, and even political allegiance provided no threat, but "Jewish identity was a matter of religious observance." What they "refused" (using Barclay's language) about Hellenism was religious, especially polytheism/monotheism, the worship of idols, and profanation of food laws. For Collins, "the most striking thing about the Jewish encounter with Hellenism . . . was the persistence of Jewish separatism in matters of worship and cult. There was a limit to Hellenization, which is best expressed in the distinction between cult and culture."[8] Collins's argument is helpful even if some aspects of it are questionable, such as its propensity to a unified Jewish identity rather than a recognition of emergent identities that involve not only geographic and ethnic identifications but also political, religious, and cultural factors.[9]

These recognitions of the familiar more than the foreign, of using and refusing, of cultural welcome and cultic distinctiveness helpfully identify important dynamics of imperialized situations. Yet they cannot embrace all the complexities and multivalence of colonizer-colonized interactions. What might a postcolonial discussion contribute to these discussions?[10]

Postcolonial Approaches

A postcolonial analysis faces some difficulties since conventional disciplinary practices have often focused on rulers, battles, settlers, and one-way traffic in cultural influence. These practices have given relatively little attention to matters of priority for postcolonial studies: the multivalent dynamics of imperial power, the perspectives of native inhabitants, the impact on peasants and land, poverty among nonelites, and reciprocal interactions between colonizers and colonized. Of course any approach is challenged by the scarcity and nature of the sources.[11] Most sources are "top-down," originating from elite and/or educated powerful males and expressing their perspectives. It is hard enough to hear the subaltern speak even when there are nonelite sources, as Gayatri Spivak has emphasized, let alone when such sources are rare.[12]

In a helpful article, Roger Bagnall wonders whether the terms "colonial" or "postcolonial" are commensurate with the Ptolemaic and Seleucid empires.[13] After testing several definitions, Bagnall argues that the impositions and inequalities of imperial power are at the heart of any postcolonial investigation. Such impositions and inequalities are certainly in play for these Greek empires, though engagement with Frantz Fanon, Homi Bhabha, and other postcolonial theorists recognizes that "imposition" must also embrace reciprocity, hybridity, ambivalence, mimicry, and fractures.

Fernando Segovia's postcolonial "optic" or "way of looking" investigates the complexities or intersectionalities of imperial-colonial experiences (including dynamics of power, gender, class, race/ethnicity, sexual orientations, etc.) along with the visions of societal interactions and humanity operative in these situations.[14] This optic foregrounds the exercise of power in imperial-colonial contexts, including its inequalities; a focus on the often-invisible colonized and their agencies and voices; and situations marked by ambivalence, mimicry, consensual-conflictive hybridity, and the accommodative and disruptive. A postcolonial optic opens up an imaginative vista to identify likely dynamics not always explicit in the surviving historical data.

Three key terms from postcolonial theory name significant interactions one might expect to find as colonized Jews negotiated Hellenistic colonizers. *Ambivalence* denotes the ambiguity or instability of the imperial-colonized situation, especially the dynamic of how the colonizer was dominant yet dependent on the colonized as well as the colonized's attraction toward and resistance of imperializing power.[15] Fanon captures this latter ambivalence in remarking that "the colonized subject is a persecuted man who is forever dreaming of becoming the persecutor."[16] *Mimicry* is a central part of this conflictual-complicit dynamic, as the imperializer disrupts local culture and the subordinated element repeats and appropriates the imperializer's language, culture, structures, and so on, thereby confounding the "simple" dynamic of imperial "power over."[17] Mimicry, though, is never an exact representation; it is, in Bhabha's famous phrase, "almost the same but not quite,"[18] that is, an imperfect copy. Mimicry has the potential for parody, menace, and instability; it often leads to mockery, which thereby challenges and decenters imperial authority. For Bhabha, hybridity is pervasive since the imperial-colonial interaction is reciprocal. The mixing or hybridity of languages and cultures identifies a crucial interdependence of, or reciprocity between, colonizer and colonized, constituting what Bhabha calls an "in-between" or third space marked by contest and hybridity, constructed and deconstructed identities, negotiated traditions, and cultural differences.[19]

Fanon identifies a fourth dynamic of considerable significance for the Hellenistic period. The phenomenon of horizontal violence denotes fractures and conflicts among the colonized over interpretations of native traditions, practices, identities, strategies, and access to and competition for imperial favors as vertical power is exerted on them.[20] Fanon identifies in these horizontal struggles three dynamics. Subjugated peoples are hemmed in and contained by imperial controls and restriction. They mimic the competitiveness and violent domination of their oppressors, yearning for and at times benefiting from the power they simultaneously and angrily resist. In addition, subjugated peoples employ horizontal violence as a means of avoiding direct confrontation with the oppressor, substituting attacks on each other rather than directly confronting an oppressive force. Horizontal violence and fractures thus attest to the restricting pressure of overwhelming imperial power, its imitation, and its engagement by avoidance and attacks on substitute groups.[21]

Sample Texts and Dynamics

One dynamic in colonized Judaea/Israel under the Ptolemies and Seleucids involves native elite contests for wealth, power, and imperial favor. Josephus's fictionalized account of the third-century BCE elite male Joseph, son of Tobias, who, employing military violence, doubled the Ptolemaic king's tax revenue while increasing his own wealth and power, attests to predictable colonizer-colonized interactions (*Ant* 12.158–236). The colonized situation is one of competition and violence among native elite factions, especially the Tobiad and Oniad Jerusalem priestly aristocracies, as they seek the favor of competing Ptolemaics and Seleucid colonizers. While Joseph outbids his peers, much distress and impoverishment result for colonized poor farmers whose production is claimed through taxation and socioeconomic violence. Colonizers depend on and profit from native struggles and strategies.

Another key dynamic featured military violence.[22] Lester Grabbe observes that following Alexander's death and the power struggles that resulted in Ptolemaic dominance of Israel/Judaea, "Palestine was fought in and over" at least nine times.[23] A postcolonial optic alerts us to disruptions of trade and barter, the material damage for peasant farmers and households from looted crops and animals, resultant hunger and lack, physical attacks, rape of native peoples and property, enslavements, and the humiliating indignities of being a subordinate. Even as a colonizer asserts power, it depends on the subjugated's production and labor. From such indignities often emerge ambivalent expressions of consent and conflict, counterpractices and counternarratives that contest and negate the dominant version of reality, fantasize about revenge on the oppressor, and imagine different worlds.[24]

Some of these dynamics are evident in the fictional work of 3 Maccabees, which was written well after the Ptolemaic period though it was set within a construction of that era.[25] The narrative presents King Ptolemy IV Philopator (reigned 222–204BCE) as one who exercises absolute power. Having been rebuffed from entering the Jerusalem temple (3 Macc 1:8–2:24), the king angrily seeks revenge by attempting to kill Jews in Alexandria. God protects them the Jews, and when Ptolemy's efforts fail he becomes a supporter of the Jews. Historically, the unlikely scene contravenes Ptolemaic respect for local temples. Theologically, the narrative plays out a Deuteronomically informed vision of God's active protection for faithful Jews in the Diaspora. Narratively, the ruler Ptolemy removes and then restores Jewish identity and practices at a whim. The Jews' precarious situation, dependent on the colonizer's fickle favor, contextualizes yet qualifies the fantasy of revenge and celebration of Jewish freedom (6:30–7:23). And while the text constructs Ptolemaic power as violent and dangerous, any attempts to differentiate colonized and colonizer falter when the king sanctions horizontal violence in permitting Jews to kill those who did not remain faithful through the ordeal (7:12–15). Those who are subordinated mimic and violently enact the intolerance of difference exhibited by Ptolemy. And as much as the work positions cultic practice as the boundary of hybridity (so Collins), it does so in a narrative written in Greek that employs rhetorical techniques such as *pathos* (arousing emotion) and prosopopoeia (constructing speeches that are appropriate to a character in a particular situation).

The dynamics of the colonial-imperial situation are also evident in other writings. The scribe (or group of scribes) known as "Enoch," responsible for the Book of Watchers, 1 Enoch 1–36 (12:3–4), occupies a liminal social position. "Enoch" has been educated in certain knowledge and literary genres, yet is at odds with other scribal groups because of a concern with those "from below" who experience the burden of the Ptolemaic system of expropriations of peasant production that the work criticizes. More specifically, Wes Howard-Brook sees Enoch's attack directed toward the socioeconomic exploitation of the poor by Judaea's priestly and scribal elites who collaborated with foreign empires.[26]

The opening of 1 Enoch begins with a revelation of God, the divine warrior, coming to judge the earth, preserving the righteous and destroying the watchers and the wicked (1 En 1–5). Chapters 6–16 define the wicked by quoting from Gen 6:1–4, whereby the "sons of God/heaven" (the fallen watchers) married earthly women and produced giant children (1 En 7:2). These children exercise oppressive and destructive power on the earth, exploitatively consuming resources, spreading war, and causing bloodshed and violence. They "consumed the produce of all people until the people detested feeding them" (1 En 7:3). Their leader Azazel teaches people to make weapons for war, to use cosmetics, and to employ spells and astrology as sources of knowledge (1 En 8:1–4). Adultery, corrupt conduct, bloodshed, and oppression result (1 En 8:2; 9:1, 6, 9). People cry out to God in terms that mimic but also exceed the language used for kings with authority over all (i.e., the language is similar but not quite the same): "Lord of the potentates . . . Lord of Lords . . . God of gods . . . King of kings" (1 En 9:4). The appeals are based on a construction of God as one who imitates but outpowers the rulers.

Yet evil continues on the earth through the "evil spirits" that come from the bodies of the Watchers' slain children, the giants (15:9–11; 16:1). The rest of 1 Enoch 1–36 focuses on the postmortem judgment and abode of the condemned and the righteous.

Various commentators have interpreted these scenarios of the exploitative use of resources and warfare as reflections of and explanations for the political and economic oppression and violence experienced under Hellenistic imperial rule. George Nickelsburg suggests these scenarios correspond to the wars and violence among the successors of Alexander (the *Diadochi*).[27] Richard Horsley does not see any reason to confine the referents to this period.[28] He argues that Jews experienced societal and economic oppression throughout the third-century struggles between the Ptolemies and Seleucids. Enoch presents their rule as being in the control of evil forces/spirits opposed to God's order.

This styling of Hellenistic empires in terms of controlling evil forces counters another native narrative, that of the Deuteronomists who saw in foreign domination divine punishment for the people's sins. Colonizing pressures create fractures among colonized peoples and result in conflict and/or horizontal violence. While Deuteronomists saw divine judgment being worked out in historical events (see 3 Maccabees; also see the book of Tobit, discussed later in the chapter), Enoch's approach is to claim, on the basis of revelatory heavenly tours, the delay of judgment to the period after death. The calamitous events of the present did not constitute judgment on the people either as a whole or as individuals. Rather divine judgment was imagined as a postmortem event directed especially against the wicked and powerful, whether Gentile imperialists or Jewish elites, who caused oppressive damage on earth. Division and contest exist among Judaean provincials as they negotiate imperial rule.

A further version of colonizer-colonized dynamics pre-175 BCE appears in the work of Ben Sira, an upper-level sage/scribe loyal to the Oniad high priest Simon II and temple-centered societal power.[29] Both Ben Sira and Enoch search for "wisdom" or the divine will but in different places. Ben Sira reflects on Torah and creation; Enoch employs revelatory experience along with reflection on Genesis 1–11. While both engage their societal contexts, Ben Sira is more supportive of the status quo than the critical Enoch whose scenes of judgment, fantasies of revenge, and assertions of God's greater sovereignty express considerable native dis-ease with Hellenistic rulers. Their different approaches and evaluations of the imperial status quo reflect the fractures Fanon highlights as common among native populations when imperial power is exerted.

Ben Sira inscribes a hierarchical societal structure in which a small group of powerful and wealthy male rulers and priests preside over Judaean society (Sir 8:1–2). Ben Sira identifies the powerful "famous men" (rulers, counselors, the wealthy)—culminating with the Oniad chief priest Simon who "fortified the temple"—as those who shape this society (44–50). Leo Perdue posits that Ben Sira educated scribal leaders for roles in government, temples, and private houses in the Seleucid colony.[30] Ben Sira recognizes that artisans (e.g., smiths, potters), traders (Sir 37:11), slaves (33:25–33), and especially agricultural workers provide material necessities to sustain this temple-centered structure through hard work and land-derived rents/tributes/tithes and offerings (7:29–31; 35:6–12). In this male-dominated structure, women must submit to male authority with domesticated activities (25–26).

Scribes like Ben Sira serve this hierarchical, priest-ruled temple-state as intellectual retainers. They have the leisure to provide, with appropriate deference to the ruling priestly aristocracy (Sir 4:7; 13:9–10), divinely sanctioned intellectual, cultural, and legal support for priestly rulers to maintain the privileged hierarchical status quo (38:24–39:11). Foundational for the teaching of the Torah-learned scribe (38:34–39:11) is "the fear of the Lord" (10:19–24). Ben Sira's teaching sustains rather than transforms the status quo. He is silent on both structural change and the socioeconomic expropriations effected by the Seleucid empire on peasant farmers.

Yet it would be misleading to construct Ben Sira monolithically as a submissive yet accommodating provincial. One would expect in a colonized context much more complexity including ambivalence and hybridity. Ben Sira brings together Hellenistic culture (Greek language and philosophy)[31] and loyalties to Jewish traditions (Torah, Sir 10:19; 19:20; 24:23; Israel, 17:17) to form an identity of a third "face" that is neither wholly Jewish nor Hellenistic.

Ambivalence also marks Ben Sira's construction of kingly power.[32] He recognizes that kings can rule for good or bad and that an undisciplined or unrestrained king can ruin his people (10:3). Yet God places kings in office, since earthly government is subject to God, who raises up right leaders (Sir 10:3–4), overthrows others, enthrones the lowly, and lays waste to the lands of nations (10:14–16). "Sovereignty passes from nation to nation on account of injustice and insolence and wealth" (10:8). God is the ideal and supreme king, "the Lord" (Sir 1:8), "the king of all" (50:15), the king of kings (51:12 Heb), and, especially, Israel's rightful king (17:17). Ben Sira prays for God to act for Israel against foreign nations to "destroy the adversary and wipe out the enemy" (36:3, 9), to "crush the heads of hostile rulers" (36:12), and to act so that "all who are on earth will know that you are the Lord" (36:22). He locates kings, then, whether Ptolemaic or Seleucid, between power and powerlessness, supreme agency and dependence on and submission to (unrecognized) divine control. Taken together, does Ben Sira offer commonplaces or acerbic commentary on Ptolemaic oppression and support for Seleucid rule? Does he employ ambivalence whereby commonplaces disguise critique?

Ben Sira certainly displays ambivalence toward peasant farmers and other manual workers. From his elevated location, he is aware of the vulnerability of "the poor . . . needy . . . hungry . . . the desperate . . . a supplicant in distress . . . the oppressed . . . orphans" (Sir 4:1–10). He recognizes that, while peasant farmers and manual workers are variously exploited and ignored, and obligated to supply offerings to the temple, they need alms to survive (3:30–4:10; 7:32). He also recognizes a societal hostility between the rich and the poor ("what peace between the rich and the poor?" 13:18) in which the poor are exploited as "feeding grounds for the rich" and are "an abomination to the rich" (13:19–20). The rich are socially prominent while the poor are ignored (13:23), and the poor are vulnerable to the oppressive, powerful elements who withhold their living and wages (34:25–27). Accordingly, he appeals to "the commandment" to attend to the poor (29:9) and asserts that the Lord does not ignore the poor, the wronged, the orphaned, or the widowed (35:15–19). Nor is he reluctant to condemn members of the wealthy and powerful class who oppress, even "murder," the poor by depriving them of resources (34:21–27) or those "unrighteous" elements who corrupt justice (35:14–26). Through such denunciations, Ben Sira occupies the ambivalent space of both sanctioning and attacking those on whom he as a scribe depends.

The scribal author of Ecclesiates or Qohelet, an enigmatic work most scholars place in the late Ptolemaic/third-century era,[33] offers satiric critique of Ptolemaic-era elites, "Hellenistic kings," and retainers including "lower-ranking representatives of political and economic power in Jerusalem and Judaea."[34] This critique exposes even as it reinscribes their practices of domination and excessive wealth.[35] A key rhetorical strategy concerns the construction of Qohelet as King Solomon (Ecc 1:1, 12) who, in Thomas Krüger's terms, is "caricatured" and presented as a "parody" of such figures with wealth, wisdom, status, and power.[36] The rhetoric that constructs a presentation of King Solomon is ambivalent in both boasting of and critiquing accomplishments of power. King Qohelet drinks too much (contrary to Prov 31:4) even as he styles such a project as guided by wisdom (Ecc 2:3). He parades his wealth, power, and status in claiming great works of building—houses and parks—but the rhetorical repetition of "myself" as the object of his efforts of building houses, planting vineyards, establishing gardens and parks, making pools, and acquiring silver, gold and treasures betrays his self-interest and lack of concern for his subjects (2:4–8). More self-deception is evident in the repeated pronoun "I" for the verbs of construction when "everybody knows" that the king's slaves do such work, not the king himself (Ecc 2:7). And the boast that all of this has brought no pleasure seems ironic since elite rulers do not forgo such a lifestyle that is not accessible to nonelites.

But it is the writing's focus on King Qohelet's knowledge that is dominant. As much as military-political-economic domination is evoked, the rhetoric emphasizes and undermines an epistemological assertion of power by means of claims to superior wisdom and knowledge. As Sandoval emphasizes, Qohelet-Solomon boasts of acquiring "great wisdom surpassing all who were over Jerusalem before me" (Ecc 1:16), yet the rhetoric undermines the boast since there was only one person previously "over Jerusalem," his father David. He asserts his superiority over other native perspectives such as the Deuteronomists and other royal and apocalyptic scribes. He admits to seeking to know the work of God but concludes that it cannot be known: "No one can find out what is happening under the sun . . . they cannot find it out" (8:16–17). He seems to polemicize against the claims of the Deuteronomists and/or of received wisdom concerning act and consequence that righteous living results in long life (7:15–17). He seems to reject apocalyptic claims like those of 1 Enoch 1-36 for the authoritative nature of revelations through dreams and visions ("with many dreams come vanities," 5:3, 7). He also seems to reject claims like Enoch's of postmortem judgment ("all turn to dust again . . . who knows whether the human spirit goes upward?" (3:19–21, but also see 12:14). Further, he seems to resist the claim that Ben Sira makes that imperial power and hierarchical society are divinely authorized. For Qohelet, the work of God cannot be known by observing societal order (11:5). He advocates a pragmatic and compliant negotiation of imperializing power. Qohelet recognizes the value of responsible rulers (10:16–17). With their great power such rulers should be obeyed, not because they manifest the divine will but because their power is unchecked and they can punish the disobedient ("Whoever obeys a command will meet no harm," 8:2–5; "Do not curse the king . . . for a bird may carry your voice," 10:20). To submit is a self-protective survival strategy, not one based on enjoying the benefits of good rule. Such horizontal fractures among the colonized reflect, according to Fanon, the impact of vertical imperial power. They also reflect the ambivalent location of the scribal author who benefits from the enforcement of and submission to the political and cultural structures he criticizes.

Qohelet is presented as one with great wealth and slaves (2:4–11) along with leisure to reflect on and write about his society as he experiences it. He is, it seems, without programs or strategies, or even desire, for societal change. He matter-of-factly or cynically recognizes that authoritarian rule damages some people. Those who exercise authority do so "to the other's hurt" (8:9) but he has no interest in assisting the vulnerable poor who are most impacted by imperial extractions. Secure in his own privilege and indifference, he admits to knowing that wickedness exists (2:16) and that oppression brings much pain (4:1), but he does not urge resistance or the transformation of elite ways. In fact he accepts that oppression is inevitable, counseling that one should not be amazed at "the oppression of the poor and the violation of justice" (5:4). Reflecting his privileged location, he can declare that wealth and power cannot match the value of his wisdom (9:11–18). His credo of enjoying food, drink, and work reflects his elite perspective of enjoyment of his privileged status quo, while its lack of viability for most of the population betrays its uselessness. Nonelites cannot presume to enjoy food and drink on a regular basis with their production drained by taxes and tithes. His exhortation to enjoy toil is likewise something that oppressed peasant farmers and laborers would find challenging in the struggle for daily survival (5:18; 9:7).

The book of Tobit, perhaps dating from 250–175 BCE,[37] utilizes a fictional setting in Assyrian exile to engage the question of being faithful to Jewish identity in the midst of foreign power. While the text may have a diaspora provenance, the presence of five copies at Qumran suggests it was accessible to those under Hellenistic power in Judaea/Israel.[38] The text introduces Tobit as an orphan, who is meticulous in paying threefold tithes from his agricultural production to the Jerusalem temple and priests as well as to orphans, widows, and others in need (1:6–8). Tobit is not a priest or ruler; the description of his tithes and almsgiving suggests some wealth from land (1:20) and trade (1:14) until it is confiscated by the exiling Assyrian king (1:20) and he becomes poor (4:21). The exile is, in Deuteronomistic perspective, punishment for sin (3:3b–4; 13:5). It comprises "plunder... death... reproach" (3:4). King Sennacherib violently attacks and kills many Israelites (1:18). Tobit flees for his life, though divine mercy protects and restores him to favor under Esarhaddon (1:19–22; 13:1–17; 14:4–7). Also active in exile are evil spirits like Asmodeus (recall 1 Enoch 1–36), which destroy households, such as the killing of seven of Sarah's husbands (3:7–9).

In exile, Tobit occupies an ambivalent location. Without talk of revolt or refusal, he serves the Assyrian rulers Shalmaneser, Sennacherib, and Esarhaddon. Simultaneously he observes markers of Jewish identity: food purity (Tob 1:10–11), charity in giving food and clothing to the needy (1:17a; 2:2; 4:16), burying the dead (1:17b; 2:3–4), observing festivals (2:1), and praying (3:1). He exhorts almsgiving (4:7–11; 12:8–9) and marriage, not with a foreigner but within one's kinship group (4:12–13). Such actions are not only acts of piety and identity; they are also survival strategies for people under foreign power with limited resources and options. Such acts express practical care, enhance dignity, and maintain communal boundaries.

Tobit's attention to burying the "many Israelites" that King Sennacherib put to death is interpreted by Sennacherib as an act of resistance or defiance (1:18–20). The king searches for Tobit to put him to death, and he confiscates his property. Tobit escapes to survive until Sennacherib's murder (1:21). Does God protect Tobit and thereby sanction his acts of burial? No reason for Sennacherib's actions is given. Perhaps the king resents Tobit's removal of the visual witness to his intimidating, ruthless, and obedience-inducing power.

The writing closes with a further survival strategy comprising mimicry and reversal. Tobit's final prayer is Deuteronomic in acknowledging divine punishment for sin as well as envisioning an act of powerful divine mercy that will regather the exiled and scattered people (13:5) and restore and rebuild Jerusalem (13:9–10) as a theocratic imperial city that dominates the nations. Jerusalem, the "bright light," shines "to all the ends of the earth" and draws "many nations" from all places and generations to Jerusalem with gifts/tributes to worship not idols but God (13:11). Reinforcing this prayerful subversive vision of eternally dominant Jerusalem, Tobit curses those who attack Jerusalem and blesses those who submit to its people and God (13:12–17). Jerusalem's supremacy reflects the supremacy of Israel's God. The prayer constructs God as dominant over all space and time: God's kingdom lasts forever (13:1, 17). He is God forever (13:4), "King of the ages" (13:6, 10), "King of heaven" (13:7, 11), "Lord of the ages" (13:13), and "Lord, the great King" (13:15). This God-King outpowers earthly (Assyrian, Hellenistic) kings in asserting worldwide, imperial domination. The prayer from a subjugated provincial mimics and reinscribes the imperial paradigm, yearning for supreme domination and universal submission while not tolerating different practices and allegiances.

As do Tobit and 3 Maccabees, other writings locate Jews in the midst of assertive Gentile power that threatens Jewish existence and endangers observance of crucial identity markers. These writings often construct Gentiles in part as vicious villains with exiling, imperializing, and even genocidal power.[39] And they offer assurance of powerful divine favor for Jewish faithfulness. So the apocryphal letter of Jeremiah, addressed to Jewish exiles in Babylon, warns against idolatry replacing trust in Israel's God (6:6). Also in exile, Daniel and his companions display faithfulness to food purity, refuse to worship the golden statue or pray to the king, and experience divine protection (Dan 1–6). When divine deliverance from the Assyrian/Babylonian threat is not forthcoming after prayer and fasting, the righteous, brave, and cunning Judith, faithful in all ways including food purity (10:5; 12:19), executes her violent plan to decapitate the Assyrian general Holofernes and deliver the people. In Greek Esther, faithful Mordecai and Esther use their wits and divine intervention to save the people from Haman's destructive plan.[40] While these texts illustrate Collins's claim that cultic practices marked the limits for Hellenization, much more can be said about these texts' negotiations of imperial power, including ambivalent interactions, hybridity, and mimicry in which Israel's God displays destructive and imperializing actions that violently outpower Gentile rulers.

Second-Century Crisis

The first half of the second century BCE is a further context where one can perceive numerous dynamics of colonial-colonized interactions. In 198 BCE, the Seleucid ruler Antiochus III gained control of southern Syria and Judaea after defeating Ptolemaic forces in the Fifth Syrian war (202–199 BCE). Immediately evident are Jewish fractures and factions. A pro-Seleucid faction led by the high priest Onias II, whom Josephus reports had previously refused to pay tribute to the Ptolemies (*Ant* 12.156–159), perhaps welcomed Seleucid power, while others did not. Hybridity marks the interactions of occupier and occupied. Antiochus guarantees Jewish "ancestral laws" and reduces taxes and tributes from Jerusalem though not from surrounding towns (Josephus, *Ant* 12.138–146). Antiochus's *permitting* of Jewish observance asserts imperial domination in replacing the authorization of Jewish observance by long-established native traditions and authoritative texts with the colonizer's permission. The superior and permissive sanction of the imperializer's decree renders local autonomy an illusion. Native traditions intersect with dominant imperial assertions to create a third space of hybridity.[41]

Imperial exploitation of native peoples follows. Josephus notes that Jews underwent "great hardships through the devastation of their land" to support Antiochus's war efforts (Josephus, *Ant* 12.129). The generalized comment masks the taking of crops and animals, hunger, poor nutrition and disease, trade disruption, destruction of property, personal and economic hardship, personal indignities, and divisions among Jews, especially households of poor peasant farmers. Provisioning Antiochus's army included 150 elephants that ate 330–550 pounds of vegetation per elephant per day, an enormous drain on the production of peasant farmers (Josephus, *Ant.* 12.133, 138).[42] The years between circa 200 BCE and circa 170 were not, at least for nonelites, serene and marked by "cordial collaboration" as has been claimed.[43]

Dynastic succession continues the imperializer's power. In 175 BCE, Antiochus IV Epiphanes became king.[44] The subsequent events marked a hostile period of interaction between Judaea/Israel and Seleucid rule. The primary, though disparate, sources are 1 and 2 Maccabees; the focus here is less on the impossible task of trying to reconstruct events and more on the negotiations evident in the texts' narration of the unfolding colonizer-colonized situations. The following discussion prioritizes 2 Maccabees.

- The narrative of 2 Maccabees 4–10 begins not with Antiochus's aggression but with agonistic interactions and fractures among Jerusalem's elite men. The chief priest Onias had repulsed attempts by Heliodorus, an agent of Seleucus IV (d. 175 BCE), and Simon, captain of the temple, to rob the temple's treasury (3:4–8). Thwarted, Simon stirs up opposition to Onias with false accusations. Onias appeals to King Seleucus but the king dies (2 Macc 4:7). Onias's brother Jason takes advantage of the situation to gain the priesthood, promising Antiochus increased and substantial tributes, along with actively promoting "the Greek way of life" in Jerusalem that neglected the divine laws and temple service (2 Macc 4:8–22; cf 1 Macc 1:11–15). Three years later, Menelaus, Simon's brother, displaces Jason by outbidding him for the high priesthood, orders Onias's murder, deputizes Lysimachus who steals from the temple and causes strife and bloodshed in the city, and successfully repulses a counterattack from Jason (4:23–5:10). Agonistic behaviors mean leading provincial men compete for the colonizer Antiochus's favor to occupy Jerusalem's most dominant position. They mimic Antiochus's quest for the dominating power that constitutes masculinity. Evident in these conflicts are numerous dynamics that characterize the multivalent and complex interactions of colonizer and colonized.

- One element concerns the ambivalence and reciprocity of Seleucid negotiation of local Judaean customs and religious practices. On one hand Seleucid tolerance *permits* Jerusalem temple observances; on the other, they interfere with and benefit from replacing traditional sanctions for the chief priesthood by selling it and supporting Jason's faction in promoting "the Greek way of life." The dynamic is not simply a matter of "power over" but rather comprises reciprocity and ambivalence. The colonizer depends on the colonized for economic resources and for controllable, Greek-promoting local leaders, even as it uses these means to exert its own power.
- Jerusalem's chief priests occupy an ambivalent location. As leaders of the Jerusalem temple, they represent native traditions and practices, yet they are deeply indebted to and dependent on Seleucid patronage and benefaction. Some prioritize Jewish practices, others prioritize "the ways of Greek" (Jason is permitted to found a gymnasium). 1 Maccabees condemns their neglecting local practices and preferring Hellenistic traditions by labeling them "renegades" who have "abandoned the holy covenant" (1:11, 15).
- The competition among Jerusalem's male elites expresses their desire for Seleucid favor and power, their mimicry of Seleucid dominating power, and their hybridity as they advocate Greek ways even as they represent traditional Jewish practices. For some (Jason), they mimic what they admire. For others, the violence manifests the ambivalence Fanon observes in the natives' lust for the very power and domination they reject in the colonizer. In Bhabha's terms, some mimic what they detest.
- The conflict and violence among the various elite Jerusalem males and their supporters attest to the fractures and horizontal violence that mark colonized situations where ruling power is asserted. Since direct opposition to ruling power is not possible, colonized groups divert their anger, humiliation, quest for dignity, and thwarted ambition in attacks on other colonized figures and groups while they struggle for power and for the colonizer's favor or defeat. For example, Mattathias kills the Jewish man who seeks to sacrifice at Modein (1 Macc 2:23–24); and Judas, his brothers, and his supporters "gladly fought for Israel" against Antiochus's demands (1 Macc 3:1–2). On the other hand, Simon and Onias (2 Macc 4:1–6) and Simon and Menelaus (2 Macc 4:23–29) resort to violence in their struggle for kingly favor.

- Impacted by the violence, but given minimal attention in the narrative, are the urban crowds of nonelites who are caught up in and exploited and damaged by the struggles and, at times, allied with various figures (2 Macc 5:6, 12–14, 22, 24, 26).

With Jason's attack on the city and fight with Menelaus, Antiochus IV, it seems, constructs the conflict as revolt. He attacks Jerusalem, slaughters "eighty thousand," enslaves many, enters the temple, removes vessels and money, orders a second attack, abolishes law observance (including circumcision and Sabbath observance), rededicates the temple to Olympian Zeus, and requires Jews to participate in Greek customs under penalty of death (2 Macc 5:11–6:26).

What motivated Antiochus's unprecedented attack, contrary to polytheistic tolerance, has provoked numerous explanations. First Maccabees blames his arrogant character as a "sinful root" (1 Macc 1:10, 24). Tacitus (*Hist* 5:8; compare 1 Macc 1:41–50) presents him as a cultural evangelist seeking to "abolish Jewish superstition and to introduce Greek civilization." His devotion to Olympian Zeus is well attested (2 Macc 6:2) but it is not a missionary zeal.[45] Perhaps he acts pragmatically to secure local loyalties and gratitude against the threat of Jason by protecting and maintaining his own economically and politically beneficial alliance with the Menelaus-led Jerusalem faction in promoting their agenda of "the Greek way of life" (2 Macc 4:10). Perhaps he knew that religious disputes (having twice sold the chief priesthood) were destabilizing and that he needed to crush a problematic religion.[46] Perhaps, informed by the ideology of subjugating Hellenistic kingship,[47] he chose to construct the agonistic struggle in Jerusalem as a revolt, which created an opportunity to disorder the status quo by reconquering the people and land and employing "state terror" to massacre, abduct, plunder, shame, parade, ban, and recreate Jerusalem with a dependent and different cultural identity.[48]

Just as native Jerusalem elites have much to gain and lose in agonistic struggles, so too does Antiochus. From selling the priesthood and receiving tribute (2 Macc 4:8–10, 24), he has economic interests to protect and native loyalties and gratitude to secure. Menelaus's refusal to pay the tribute (4:27) and the horizontal violence in Jerusalem provide Antiochus with an opportunity to employ state-terror to reconquer Judaea and recreate Judaean cultural and religious identity (6:1–11). Antiochus employs various strategies of humiliating subjugation: fierce violence, deception (5:25–26), and forced native participation in rituals and parades in honor of Dionysus (6:7–11). James Scott attests to the elite's self-dramatizing and self-hypnotizing use of parades to display the permanence of their rule, stiffen their own spine, and intimidate subjugated natives.[49] Banning Sabbath gatherings removed an opportunity to develop alternative narratives or hidden transcripts that could encourage native boldness.

Both 1 and 2 Maccabees attest to diverse Jewish negotiations of Antiochus's violent assertion of power. Some Judaeans cooperated (1 Macc 1:11–15; 2 Macc 4:10), some refused compliance (2 Macc 6:9–11; 1 Macc 1:62–64), some fled (2 Macc 5:27; 6:11; 1 Macc 2:29–38), some died in ethnic cleansing (2 Macc 5:12–15; 1 Macc 1:62–64) as martyrs (2 Macc 6:18–7:42) or in the violent revolt led by Mattathias and Judas Maccabeus (2 Macc 8–9;

1 Macc 2–4). The violent native opposition mimics Antiochus' violent imperialism in reasserting and reestablishing native dignity, practices, world view, and domination.

First Maccabees also interprets these events with a metanarrative that draws on sacred native traditions as an alternative to that of the Seleucids. While narrating diverse negotiations, it identifies divine involvement on behalf of God's people against the Gentiles to frame a good/evil binary. Against the arrogant "sinful root" Antiochus (1 Macc 1:10, 24), it constructs God as raising up the Hasmonean house as faithful chosen agents whose military actions deliver Judaea/Israel and earn its loyalty.[50] It introduces the priestly Mattathias as a defender of Jerusalem's honor and purity and as having a zeal for the covenant (1 Macc 2). The latter characteristic evokes the zealous Phinehas from Israel's sacred past to sanction military action against the profaning Gentiles (Num 25:6–15; also see 1 Macc 2:51–60). Mattathias gathers supporters faithful to Torah even to death, observing practices of Sabbath observance, circumcision, temple festivals, and food purity. Military action expresses faithfulness to the law and covenant (2:27, 41–50). After Mattathias' death, his son Judas Maccabeus leads the fight and defeats Antiochus, cleanses and rededicates the temple to the worship of God, and reestablishes law observance (1 Macc 3–4). Ambivalence marks the defense of the law, since it requires contravening the Sabbath with fighting to ensure its observance (1 Macc 2:39–41). The resort to violence to secure freedom mimics the colonizer's use of imperializing violence.

Second Maccabees also draws on sacred traditions, including the native Deuteronomist metanarrative that God protects the people and Jerusalem temple in circumstances of faithfulness (2 Macc 3:22–28; 4:2) but allows conquest by Gentiles, not as an abandonment of the people but as a temporary punishment for unfaithfulness (4:16–17; 5:17–20; 6:12–17). The account urges covenant loyalty to God and secures the divine blessing for the nation's security and well-being. This loyalty includes faithful temple service and observing identity markers such as food purity (2 Macc 6:1–19; 7:1–2), Sabbath observance (6:11; 8:26–27), circumcision (6:10), and charity for widows and orphans (8:28). Moreover, the narrative constructs the expectation that obedience extends even to death. The scribe Eleazar refuses submission to Antiochus' decree and is killed (6:18–31) as are the seven brothers (7:1–42). Their martyrdom signals a turning point—a display of covenant faithfulness that seems to absorb divine wrath and provoke God to turn to mercy (7:33–38; 8:5) which results in blessing Judas Maccabeus's military efforts (8–10). The narrative emphasizes that the victory comes not by trusting warfare but by divine intervention (8:18; also 2:21; 8:23; 10:29–30, 38). Further, the brothers announce their confidence that death does not limit God's faithfulness. God will vindicate their faithfulness postmortem by restoring their tortured bodies and reuniting them with each other and their mother as part of the gathering of all Israel (7:9, 14, 23, 27–29). Their resurrection is social, somatic, political, national, and defiant of imperial power in exposing its limits—except when wielded by the more powerful God.

Given that 1 and 2 Maccabees construct colonial imperial dynamics along these particular lines, Daniel 7 takes another approach. Anathea Portier-Young rejects claims that apocalyptic texts are apolitical, arguing that they offer resistant counterdiscourses of divine sovereignty and Jewish allegiance in resisting Antiochus's strategies of terror, conquest, and recreation.[51] The book of Daniel, emerging in 167–164 BCE from and for a circle of wise scribes to teach others (Dan 11:32–35; 12:3, 10), presents the example of Daniel and his companions to exhort nonviolent waiting for God to accomplish a future defeat of Antiochus rather than military action.

- It employs native languages (Hebrew, Aramaic), not Greek, to decolonize native minds, move the audience from collaboration and submission to rejection of Seleucid rule, and to defy Antiochus' decrees.
- It exhorts communal prayer, fasting, and penitence (Dan 9) to express the people's commitments, history, and future, which reflects the Deuteronomic theological narrative of punishment for sin through imperial powers and forgiveness in God's mercy (9:9).
- Its stories of faithfulness against coercive royal power strengthen the native spine to resist even unto death. Daniel and his companions maintain a distinctive Jewish identity in a threatening context. They observe food purity (Dan 1), maintain monotheism by refusing to bow down to the golden image (Dan 3), and refuse to pray to the king (Dan 6). They bravely defy Antiochus and experience divine favor.
- It envisions, in God's timing and ways, God establishing victorious sovereignty and justice over Antiochus.
- It reinterprets Israel's scripture to counter Antiochus's attempts to destroy them. Daniel reinterprets Jeremiah's prophecy of seventy years (Jer 25:11–12; 29:10; Dan 9:20–27), a historical review that provides assurance of God's control of history in which God destroys the new cultic time that Antiochus's edict imposed. The review contextualizes Antiochus's actions, negates his power, creates a counterdiscourse marked by the imminent establishment of God's sovereignty (Dan 7), and sustains active, nonviolent resistance.
- Scott identifies such a "work of negation" as a hidden transcript emerging from locations unauthorized by, yet protected from, the gaze of the powerful where leaders of subordinated groups facilitate the expression of "stifled anger" and the indignities experienced under domination in alternative discourses.[52]

Portier-Young's insightful discussion highlights Daniel's multivalent resistance to Antiochus's program. Yet her analysis overlooks several important dynamics of Daniel's complex negotiation of Seleucid imperial power. For example, Daniel occupies a hybrid location in Babylonian exile, a third space of being accommodated in serving King Nebuchadnezzar while also embracing Jewish identity markers. Nor is the book's metanarrative monolithic in only opposing Antiochus. Evident also is mimicry of the king's imperializing work and imposition of practices. Rooted in native traditions that assert divine sovereignty, the book mimics Antiochus in making total demands (similar but not quite the same). The vision of the assertion of God's victorious and coercive empire over all creation through the designated Son of Man in Dan 7 mimics Antiochus's powerful empire. Yet it out-empires Antiochus in asserting the greater dominance of

God's cosmically and temporally all-encompassing empire and sovereignty that, like Antiochus's empire, leaves no room for dissenters. This Daniel 7 vision—a fantasy of the world turned upside-down–reverses the status quo and fantasizes the different domination of God's victory over the oppressor, even as it assists compliance in the meantime through venting frustration and articulating indignities under domination.[53] The book's scribal teachings are as much about controlling people's minds and bodies, loyalties, and practices as Antiochus's intolerant edicts. The law-sanctioned practices that Daniel advocates shape a communal identity and solidarity that allow for no exceptions—just like Antiochus's program.

This discussion of the conflicts of the 160s BCE under Antiochus IV Epiphanes, while selective and brief, has highlighted some of the diverse dynamics of power and strategies of negotiation—ambivalences, instabilities, mimicries, hybridities, reciprocities, and fractures—employed by colonizer and colonized. Assertions of resistance are simultaneously assertions of counterpower and counternarratives that mimic and reinscribe imperializing strategies.

Independence and Imperial Imitation

The Hasmoneans take advantage of the defeat of Antiochus, the reversal of his edict, the temple's rededication in 164 BCE (1 Macc 4; 2 Macc 10), and inner-Seleucid rivalries to the throne to establish Judaea/Israel's independence. First Maccabees sanctions the Hasmonean line as God's agents of freedom (1 Macc 3:6). They mimic the imperial ways that they had previously resisted, in which they had marinated for centuries, and from which they had learned much. Judas, for example, pursues dominating military action against Idumea, Galilee, and Transjordan to gain territory and secure independence against further Seleucid imperialism. Others led by the high priest Alcimus were willing to support Seleucid rule along with a guarantee to observe native religious practices. There was continuing ambivalence in negotiating Seleucid power and fractures among Jerusalemites, spanning military violence, independence, and dependence.

There was also an emphasis on mimicry. They turn to the past to reinscribe native Judahite priestly and royal dynasties and thereby simultaneously ro imitate the practice of family dynastic succession practiced by the Hellenistic kings. Leadership passes through three of Mattathias' five sons (1 Macc 3–15). With Judas's death (161–143 BCE), his brother Jonathan leads the struggle for independence and territory. His successor, his brother Simon, successfully secures freedom from Seleucid tribute, tax, and military presence (1 Macc 13:41). He "expelled the Gentiles" (14:36) and continued territorial expansion and active "Judaization" in domination over people and land (1 Macc 14:33–34).[54] His further benefactions include protecting the temple and law (14:29–42) and bringing honor to the Jewish people (14:29). Rule became hereditary among Simon's offspring, beginning with his son John Hyrcanus I (chap. 16).

Subsequently Aristobulus I (104–103 BCE) recovers another native institution and simultaneously mimics another Hellenistic practice in declaring himself king, the first Jewish king since 587 BCE (Josephus, *Ant* 13.301). His successor Alexander Jannaeus (103–76 BCE) continues the claim to both kingship and the priesthood and the practice of expanding domination over territory and people. Fractures and infighting, however, bring the assertion of independence to an end. When Aristobulus II comes to power in 67 BCE, his elder brother Hyrcanus II resists him. Both appeal to the Roman Pompey Magnus for the patronage and favor of another imperial power. In the midst of the violence, Pompey installs Hyrcanus as chief priest, executes Aristobulus, and establishes Roman hegemony. That act, declares Josephus, ends "our freedom" (*Ant* 14.74–76; see also *JW* 2.356–57).

NOTES

1. For the contested role of nomenclature for geographical space in colonizer-colonized interactions, see W. Carter, "Judea/Israel under the Greek Empires," in L. Perdue and W. Carter, *Israel and Empire: A Postcolonial History of Israel and Early Judaism* (London: Bloomsbury, 2015), 134–135.
2. S. Cohen, *From the Maccabees to the Mishnah* (Philadelphia: Westminster Press, 1987), 27–59, esp. 36–37.
3. On Alexander's metanarrative/s, see F. W. Walbank, "Monarchy and Monarchic Ideas." in *The Cambridge Ancient History*, 2nd ed., vol. 7, pt. 1, *The Hellenistic World*, edited by F. W. Walbank et al. (Cambridge: Cambridge University Press, 1984), 62–100; M. M. Austin, "Hellenistic Kings, War, and the Economy," *Classical Quarterly* 36 (1986): 450–466; on Alexander's lack of direct contact with Judaea/Israel, see Carter, "Judea/Israel under the Greek Empires," 135–147. For a legend concerning Alexander's submission to Judaea/Israel's God, Josephus, *Ant* 11.304–345.
4. V. Tchherikover, "Jewish Apologetic Literature Reconsidered," *Eos* 48 (1956): 169–193.
5. E. Gruen, "Jewish Perspectives on Greek Culture and Ethnicity," in *Hellenism in the Land of Israel*, edited by J. J. Collins and G. Sterling (Notre Dame: University of Notre Dame Press, 2001), 62–93, esp. 82.
6. J. M. G. Barclay, "Using and Refusing: Jewish Identity Strategies under the Hegemony of Hellenism," in *Ethos und Identität. Einheit und Vielfalt des Judentums in hellenistisch-römischer Zeit*, edited by M. Konradt and U. Steinert (Paderborn: Schöningh, 2002), 13–25.
7. J. J. Collins, *Jewish Cult and Hellenistic Culture: Essays on the Jewish Encounter with Hellenism and Roman Rule* (Leiden: Brill, 2005), 1–43, esp. 15–16.
8. Collins, *Jewish Cult*, 43.
9. S. Cohen, *The Beginnings of Jewishness: Boundaries, Varieties, Uncertainties* (Berkeley: University of California Press, 1999), 69–139.
10. Following Carter, "Judea/Israel Under the Greek Empires," 134–135.
11. See F. W. Walbank, "Sources for the Period," in *The Cambridge Ancient History*, 2nd ed., vol. 7, pt. 1, *The Hellenistic World*, edited by F. W. Walbank, A. E. Astin, M. W. Frederiksen, and R. M. Ogilvie (Cambridge: Cambridge University Press, 1984), 1–22, esp. 1–2; Lester Grabbe, *A History of the Jews and Judaism in the Second Temple Period*, vol. 2, *The Coming of the Greeks: The Early Hellenistic Period (335–175 BCE)* (London: T&T Clark, 2008),

23-24. Andrea M. Berlin, "Between Large Forces: Palestine in the Hellenistic Period," *Biblical Archaeologist* 60 (1997): 2–51.
12. Gayatri Spivak, "Can the Subaltern Speak?" in G. Spivak, *A Critique of Postcolonial Reason: Toward a History of the Vanishing Present* (Cambridge: Harvard University Press, 1999), 266–311.
13. Roger Bagnall, "Decolonizing Ptolemaic Egypt," in *Hellenistic Constructs: Essays in Culture, History, and Historiography*, edited by Paul Cartledge, Peter Guernsey, and Erich Gruen (Berkeley: University of California Press, 1997), 225–241.
14. Fernando Segovia, "Mapping the Postcolonial Optic in Biblical Criticism: Meaning and Scope," in *Postcolonial Biblical Criticism: Interdisciplinary Intersections*, edited by Stephen Moore and Fernando Segovia (London: T&T Clark, 2005), 23–78.
15. Homi Bhabha, *The Location of Culture* (New York: Routledge, 1994), 85ff, 102ff.
16. Frantz Fanon, *The Wretched of the Earth* (1963; reprint, New York: Grove Press, 2004), 16.
17. Bhabha, *Location of Culture*, 90–92.
18. Bhabha, *Location of Culture*, 86.
19. Bhabha, *Location of Culture*, 1–5, 37; on the redefinition of Judaea as "competing versions of tradition negotiated with competing imperial powers," see Mark Kurtz, "The Social Construction of Judea in the Greek Period," *Society of Biblical Literature Seminar Papers* 38 (1999): 54–76.
20. Josephus attests to increasing fractures in Judaea/Israel during the 66–70 war as imperial pressure intensifies (e.g., *JW* 4.377–397; 503–544:84; 5.1–38; Eleazar, John, Simon). Warren Carter argues for the phenomenon in relation to Matthew's Gospel; see "Matthew: Empire, Synagogues, and Horizontal Violence," in *Mark and Matthew I*, edited by Eve-Marie Becker and Anders Runesson, WUNT 271 (Tübingen: Mohr Siebeck, 2011), 285–308, esp. 303–308. For recent European empires, see David Abernethy, *The Dynamics of Global Dominance: European Overseas Empires, 1415–1980* (New Haven: Yale University Press, 2000), 147–161. Abernethy notes horizontal violence between Hindus and Muslims in India and between competing groups in Kenya and Malaya under British imperialism, in Vietnam under French control, and among groups in the former Belgium Congo. For black-on-black violence in South Africa in the 1980s–1990s struggle with apartheid and white power, see Brandon Hamber, "Who Pays for Peace? Implications of the Negotiated Settlement in a Post-Apartheid Settlement in a Post-Apartheid South Africa," in *Ethnopolitical Warfare: Causes, Consequences, and Possible Solutions*, edited by Daniel Chirot and Martin Seligman (Washington, DC: American Psychological Association, 2001), 235–258, esp. 238–241.
21. Fanon, *Wretched of the Earth*, 15–16.
22. R. Horsley, *Scribes, Visionaries, and the Politics of Second Temple Judea* (Louisville: Westminster John Knox, 2007), 34–45; Carter, "Judea/Israel under the Greek Empires," 147–172.
23. Grabbe, *History of the Jews*, 278–287.
24. J. Scott, *Domination and the Arts of Resistance: Hidden Transcripts* (New Haven: Yale University Press, 1990).
25. For discussion, David deSilva, *Introducing the Apocrypha* (Grand Rapids, MI: Baker Academic, 2002), 306–310, 313–315; L. Grabbe, *Judaism from Cyrus to Hadrian*, vol. 1, *The Persian and Greek Periods* (Minneapolis: Fortress, 1992), 177–178; P. Alexander and L. Alexander, "The Image of the Oriental Monarch in the Third Book of Maccabees," in

Jewish Perspectives on Hellenistic Rulers, edited by T. Rajak et al. (Berkeley: University of California Press, 2007), 92–109.
26. W. Howard-Brooks, *Come Out My People: God's Call Out of Empire in the Bible and Beyond* (Maryknoll, NY: Orbis, 2010), 301–302.
27. G. W. Nickelsburg, *1 Enoch 1: A Commentary on the Book of 1 Enoch Chapters 1–36, 81–108*, Hermeneia (Minneapolis: Fortress, 2001) 63, 169–170.
28. Horsley, *Scribes, Visionaries*, 161.
29. deSilva, *Introducing the Apocrypha*, 153–197; Horsley, *Scribes, Visionaries*, 53–149.
30. L. Perdue, *The Sword and the Stylus: An Introduction to Wisdom in the Age of Empires* (Grand Rapids, MI: Eerdmans, 2008), 272–282.
31. Perdue, *Sword and Stylus*, 257–258, for the influence of Greek vocabulary and philosophical themes.
32. For some different emphases, see B. Wright, "Ben Sira on Kings and Kingship," in *Jewish Perspectives on Hellenistic Rulers*, edited by T. Rajak et al. (Berkeley: University of California Press, 2007), 76–91.
33. Perdue, *Sword and Stylus*, 198–255, esp. 219–220; for the second century BCE based on influence from Ben Sira, see C. Whitley, *Koheleth: His Language and Thought* (Berlin and New York: de Gruyter, 1979).
34. Thomas Krüger, *Qoheleth: A Commentary*, Hermeneia (Minneapolis: Fortress, 2004), 62, 66.
35. This discussion follows, with some omissions due to space, an emphasis on epistemological domination; see Timothy Sandoval, "Reconfiguring Solomon in the Royal Fiction of Ecclesiastes," in *On Prophets, Warriors, and Kings: Former Prophets through the Eyes of Their Interpreters*, edited by George Brooke and Ariel Feldman, BZAW 470 (Berlin: de Gruyter, 2016), 3.
36. Krüger, *Qoheleth*, 66.
37. deSilva, *Introducing the Apocrypha*, 63–84, esp. 68–69.
38. deSilva, *Introducing the Apocrypha*, 68.
39. Gruen, "Jewish Perspectives," 62–71.
40. Meredith Stone, *Empire and Gender in LXX Esther* (Atlanta: SBL Press, 2018).
41. J. Ma, "Seleukids and Speech-Acts: Performative Utterances, Legitimacy, and Negotiation in the World of the Maccabees," *Scripta Classica Israelica* 19 (2000): 71–112, esp. 87–89.
42. A. Portier-Young, *Apocalypse against Empire: Theologies of Resistance in Early Judaism* (Grand Rapids: Eerdmans, 2011), 65–66.
43. E. Gruen, "Hellenism and Persecution: Antiochus IV and the Jews," in *Hellenistic History and Culture*, edited by P. Green (Berkeley: University of California Press, 1993), 238–264, esp. 240.
44. Carter, "Judea/Israel under the Greek Empires," 184–215.
45. O. Mørkholm, *Antiochus IV of Syria* (Copenhagen: Gyldendal, 1966), 131–133.
46. J. Goldstein, *1 Maccabees*, AB (Garden City: Doubleday, 1976), 104–160.
47. Walbank, "Monarchy."
48. Portier-Young, *Apocalypse against Empire*, 136–216.
49. Scott, *Domination*, 58–69.
50. deSilva, *Introducing the Apocrypha*, 257.
51. Portier-Young, *Apocalypse against Empire*, 217–218.
52. Scott, *Domination*, 108–135.

53. Scott, *Domination*, 166–172. Portier-Young (*Apocalypse against Empire*, 280–381) discusses two other apocalyptic works: *The Apocalypse of Weeks* (1 Enoch 93:1–10; 91:11–17) and *The Book of Dreams* (1 Enoch 83–90). Space precludes discussion here.
54. Berlin, "Between Large Forces," 28–29.

Bibliography

Alexander, Philip, and Loveday Alexander. "The Image of the Oriental Monarch in the Third Book of Maccabees." In *Jewish Perspectives on Hellenistic Rulers*, edited by Tessa Rajak, Sarah Pearce, James Aitken, and Jennifer Dines, 92–109. Berkeley: University of California Press, 2007.

Austin, M. M. "Hellenistic Kings, War, and the Economy." *Classical Quarterly* 36 (1986): 450–466.

Bagnall, Roger. "Decolonizing Ptolemaic Egypt." In *Hellenistic Constructs: Essays in Culture, History, and Historiography*, edited by Paul Cartledge, Peter Guernsey, and Erich Gruen, 225–241. Berkeley: University of California Press, 1997.

Barclay, John M. G. *Jews in the Mediterranean Diaspora from Alexander to Trajan (323 BCE—117 CE)*. Edinburgh: T&T Clark, 1996.

Barclay, John M. G. "Using and Refusing: Jewish Identity Strategies under the Hegemony of Hellenism." In *Ethos und Identität. Einheit und Vielfalt des Judentums in hellenistisch-römischer Zeit*, edited by Matthias Konradt und Ulrike Steinert, 13–25. Paderborn: Schöningh, 2002.

Berlin, Andrea M. "Between Large Forces: Palestine in the Hellenistic Period." *Biblical Archaeologist* 60 (1997): 2–51.

Bhabha, Homi. *The Location of Culture*. New York: Routledge, 1994.

Carter, Warren. "Judea/Israel under the Greek Empires." In L. Perdue and W. Carter, *Israel and Empire: A Postcolonial History of Israel and Early Judaism*, 129–215. London: Bloomsbury, 2015.

Cohen, Shaye. *From the Maccabees to the Mishnah*. Philadelphia: Westminster Press, 1987.

Collins, John J. *Jewish Cult and Hellenistic Culture: Essays on the Jewish Encounter with Hellenism and Roman Rule*. Leiden: Brill, 2005.

deSilva, David. *Introducing the Apocrypha*. Grand Rapids, MI: Baker Academic, 2002.

Fanon, Frantz. *The Wretched of the Earth*. 1963; reprint, New York: Grove Press, 2004.

Feldman, Louis H., and Meyer Reinhold. *Jewish Life and Thought among Greeks and Romans*. Minneapolis: Fortress, 1996.

Grabbe, Lester. *Judaism from Cyrus to Hadrian*. Vol. 1, *The Persian and Greek Periods*. Minneapolis: Fortress, 1992.

Grabbe, Lester. *A History of the Jews and Judaism in the Second Temple Period*. Vol. 2, *The Coming of the Greeks: The Early Hellenistic Period (335–175 BCE)*. London: T&T Clark, 2008.

Gruen, Erich S. "Hellenism and Persecution: Antiochus IV and the Jews." In *Hellenistic History and Culture*, edited by Peter Green, 238–264. Berkeley: University of California Press, 1993.

Gruen, Erich S. "Jewish Perspectives on Greek Culture and Ethnicity." In *Hellenism in the Land of Israel*, edited by J. J. Collins and G. Sterling, 62–93. Notre Dame: University of Notre Dame Press, 2001.

Gruen, Erich S. *Diaspora: Jews amidst Greeks and Romans*. Cambridge, MA: Harvard University Press, 2002.

Gruen, Erich S. *The Construct of Identity in Hellenistic Judaism: Essays on Early Jewish Literature and History*. Berlin: de Gruyter, 2016.

Hengel, Martin. *Judaism and Hellenism*. Philadelphia: Fortress, 1974.

Horsley, Richard. *Scribes, Visionaries, and the Politics of Second Temple Judea*. Louisville: Westminster John Knox, 2007.

Howard-Brooks, Wes. *Come Out My People: God's Call Out of Empire in the Bible and Beyond*. Maryknoll, NY: Orbis, 2010.

Ma, J. "Seleukids and Speech-Acts: Performative Utterances, Legitimacy, and Negotiation in the World of the Maccabees." *Scripta Classica Israelica* 19 (2000): 71–112.

Nickelsburg, George W. *Jewish Literature between the Bible and the Mishnah*. Philadelphia: Fortress, 1981.

Nickelsburg, George W. *1 Enoch 1: A Commentary on the Book of 1 Enoch Chapters 1–36, 81–108*. Hermeneia. Minneapolis: Fortress, 2001.

Perdue, Leo. *The Sword and the Stylus: An Introduction to Wisdom in the Age of Empires*. Grand Rapids: Eerdmans, 2008.

Portier-Young, Anathea. *Apocalypse against Empire: Theologies of Resistance in Early Judaism*. Grand Rapids, MI: Eerdmans, 2011.

Scott, James. *Domination and the Arts of Resistance. Hidden Transcripts*. New Haven: Yale University Press, 1990.

Segovia, Fernando. "Mapping the Postcolonial Optic in Biblical Criticism: Meaning and Scope." In *Postcolonial Biblical Criticism: Interdisciplinary Intersections*, edited by Stephen Moore and Fernando Segovia, 23–78. London: T&T Clark, 2005.

Spivak, Gayatri. "Can the Subaltern Speak?" In G. Spivak, *A Critique of Postcolonial Reason: Toward a History of the Vanishing Present*, 266–311. Cambridge, MA: Harvard University Press, 1999.

Stone, Meredith. *Empire and Gender in LXX Esther*. Atlanta: SBL Press, 2018.

Stone, Michael. Ed. *Jewish Writings of the Second Temple Period: Apocrypha, Pseudepigrapha, Qumran Sectarian Writings, Philo, Josephus*. Philadelphia: Fortress, 1984.

Tchherikover, Victor. "Jewish Apologetic Literature Reconsidered." *Eos* 48 (1956): 169–193.

Walbank, Frank William. "Monarchy and Monarchic Ideas." In *The Cambridge Ancient History*. 2nd ed. Vol. 7, pt. 1, *The Hellenistic World*, edited by Frank William Walbank, A. E. Astin, M. W. Frederiksen, and R. M. Ogilvie, 62–100. Cambridge: Cambridge University Press, 1984.

Walbank, Frank William. "Sources for the Period." In *The Cambridge Ancient History*. 2nd ed. Vol. 7, pt. 1, *The Hellenistic World*, edited by Frank William Walbank, A. E. Astin, M. W. Frederiksen, and R. M. Ogilvie, 1–22. Cambridge: Cambridge University Press, 1984.

CHAPTER 6

THE ROMAN EMPIRE IN THE SYNOPTIC GOSPELS

JUDITH A. DIEHL

INTRODUCTION

You know that those who are regarded as rulers of the Gentiles lord it over them, and their high officials exercise authority over them. Not so with you. Instead, whoever wants to become great among you must be your servant, and whoever wants to be first must be slave of all. For even the Son of Man did not come to be served, but to serve, and to give his life as a ransom for many.

Words of Jesus (Mark 10:42–45)

AT the center of postcolonial studies is a deliberation on the reaction to and a departure from colonialism, similar to the idea that postmodernism is a reaction to modernism. Generally, postcolonialism presents an ideology or a worldview that is a response to the colonial systems of government, and the social norms of a culture, as well as the notions that undergird those systems. Social-scientific methodologies of biblical interpretation (such as liberation theologies) have been very helpful in making it possible for readers to become aware of the oppression and subjugation of people by domineering regimes or empires. A postcolonial methodology offers at least a "double focus" for studies of the New Testament (NT) Gospels. The first focus is on the past, where the discussion seeks to understand the Roman imperial circumstances that surrounded the Gospels' origins. The second focus involves the present: often modern biblical studies view these Gospels *only* as "religious" texts and therefore fail to fully comprehend them as "anti-imperial literature."[1] Hence, conflating the imperialism in the first century with colonialism in later centuries can determine how the literature of the NT Gospels takes shape within the colonization of Roman imperial culture, not unlike the colonization of people in more recent years. Scholars have noted that, "The economic and cultural effects of Roman imperialism on subjugated peoples are frequently well described by current theories of colonialism, neocolonialism, and postcoloniality."[2]

Moreover, insights into distinctive literary features of the ancient texts lead readers to a fuller understanding of the NT. Stories of Jesus must be understood within the historical and cultural context of Roman imperial ideology. These insights are not in opposition to those who regard the Gospels as written in a Jewish setting, for it is not easy to deny or overlook the Jewish heritage, tone, and ethos that are clearly apparent in the NT Gospels. In terms of literary features, the language and perspectives of the NT authors can be understood as a way to communicate within, and in spite of, the persistent Roman control in their culture, along with a desire to exhort their readers.

The fact that the Christian church grew and spread rapidly in this imperial setting is, indeed, remarkable. Despite the worship of another "god," the early church thrived in a political culture and climate that centered on Roman imperial ideology. Furthermore, if the NT does support any kind of anti-imperial message, it is of great significance for the Christian church of today. This not only affects interpretation of the text but also how the text is applied to current, contemporary social situations. Thus, the main purpose of this discussion is to gain a fuller understanding of the biblical texts, perhaps seeing them in a new light, and to allow a greater understanding of past empires to direct an understanding of vastly different cultures today and in the future.

In their understated manner, the writers of the NT employed what may be considered "anti-imperialism" or "anti-imperial" rhetoric. Because of their immediate social, religious, and political situations, the NT authors had no choice but to engage in a politically charged environment that required them to be guarded about their communications to early Christian communities. Of course, direct language and bold accusations that were opposed to the government or anti-emperor would have been very dangerous and could have led to charges of sedition and even death. Throughout the NT, modern readers can catch a glimpse of a variety of interactions between the first Christians and the ruling powers of Rome. However, this rhetoric has a complicated status among many colonized and postcolonial people in the world today. On the one hand, the Bible has been used by the colonizers to legitimize their authority and control over those people that were colonized. On the other hand, colonized societies have used the Scriptures to better understand their subjugated position, to anticipate their liberation, to bolster their hopes, and to legitimize their resistance to patterns of domination. Thus, there is an interpretive conundrum in discussion of the postcolonial dimension to the NT Gospels.[3]

Historical and Cultural Background of the Roman Empire

While the center of the entire known universe in the first century CE was the city of Rome, the numerous "fringe" provinces, geographically removed from Italy, felt the presence of Rome every day. After Caesar Augustus and during the first century CE, across the vast empire, Rome made her presence known through military soldiers, statues, temples, coinage, forced taxation, and labor conditions.

The regions of Judea and Galilee were smaller provinces in the massive Roman Empire, but they still felt the pressure of her power and authority. At that time, Jesus was a Jew, and he lived and ministered in the ancient land of the Jews. It is true that scholars have noted the Jewish tone of many of Jesus' sayings, Jesus' response to the Jewish Law, and the Jewish ethos of the entire NT. It is important to note that the clashes between Jesus and "the Jews" were primarily with the Jewish leadership—those leaders who had more wealth, power, and position than the common rabble. Thus, by weaving together history, cultures, and social awareness with distinct literary elements, certain biblical passages illustrate the tapestry of life in the Roman Empire for early Christian believers in conjunction with the words and teachings of Jesus.

The Concept of Empire

Questions concerning relationships among the Roman Empire, Jesus, and the first-century CE budding Christian faith should be answered within the context of "empire" in the ancient Near East. It was assumed that a particular nation established itself (usually by force) as the powerful leader at the expense of surrounding, weaker nations. To expand a nation's territory, basically accomplished by the suppression of other lands and peoples, was a sign of superiority and greatness, not only for the controlling nation but also for their national god(s). The overthrow of the conquered people included economic dependence, military force, tributes, taxation, forced labor, and even slavery. Written and oral propaganda was used to encourage the people to accept their fate and their position, thus bringing them into conformity with the conquering empire. This was done by Alexander the Great as he expanded the Greek (Hellenistic) empire years before the Roman conquests.

The concept of empire, therefore, can be considered in two different ways: as history and as theory.[4] After the European colonialism of the nineteenth and twentieth centuries, the term "empire" became associated with human oppression, cultural domination, and the political sovereignty of one nation over another nation. In the twentieth century, a shift in scholarship began to take place. Strictly historical interpretations of the biblical literature were eclipsed by theoretical models. The postmodern concept of empire, then, is associated with concepts of human suppression and resistance to subjugating power; further, the strength of marginalized people enables them to lift themselves out of oppression and into a position of value, merit, and worth. "Empire" thus becomes a pejorative term, and as a result approaches to biblical literature move away from neutral, dispassionate history to disturbing, poignant theoretical studies.

Social Setting

Both history and the writings of the NT reveal a sizable gap between the wealthy, elite class of people and the general population (the nonelites) within the Empire. On the one hand, the most elite and highest-ranking class was the imperial entourage: the emperor himself, his extended family, and all his "satellite" noblemen around him, most of whom were active and retired military officers and/or strategists. Then, each province around the Empire had its own governors and proconsuls who maintained order in the region, squelched uprisings, supported the Empire, and reported to Rome. A small, elite group consisting of about 2 to 3 percent of the population held the most power and wealth, enjoying status and a high quality of life. Power, position, and land were hereditary in the Empire, and these assets were highly protected. The vast Empire was controlled by "coercion," which was, primarily, the Roman army—a firmly established, maintained, and expanded Roman authority throughout the Empire. The elite aristocracy dominated the lower classes of people in all aspects of society: political authority, land ownership, trade and labor agreements, slavery, taxation and tributes, the judicial system, city management, and imperial propaganda (what might now be called "the media").[5]

The fringe areas of the Empire, such as Judea and Galilee, were primarily rural, agrarian areas, producing food and goods for the aristocracy, who consumed the largest portion of the supplies. The nonelites in these areas had very little voice in terms of their quality of life. The power held by Roman authority and associated Jewish elites was implemented politically, economically, socially, militarily, and religiously. Thus it was an act of rebellion to refuse to pay the appropriate taxes to the Roman government, to the Temple in Jerusalem (that is, the priesthood), and to various elite landowners or officials.[6]

Throughout the Empire, society and human relationships existed in an "honor/shame" atmosphere. Public recognition and accomplishments of individuals were of ultimate value and significance. Proper social behavior was expected within the hierarchy; appropriate reciprocation and patronage was the common expectation. Thus, inequality across all levels of society was the rule.[7] Moreover, this attitude was complemented by a view of the aristocratic elites as "benefactors." Necessarily, a person of lower status gave homage to an elite benefactor and expressed loyalty for gracious gifts from the same. Ultimately, the emperor was the highest benefactor to the entire race. The stage was set, then, for a utopian society—an extraordinary, peaceful "kingdom" of divinely chosen, generous, gracious, and caring leadership.

Imperial Cult

The first important aspect of the Roman imperial system was the imperial cult. Basically, the imperial cult was the acknowledgment of the gods' blessings on the emperor and the Empire. Historical accounts demonstrate the deification of the reigning human emperor and the veneration of him and his family. That is, historical writings indicate that in two specific cases by the second century, the powerful Senate voted to consider the Roman emperor (Caesar) to be divine: Caesar Augustus (31 BCE–14 CE) and Claudius (41–54 CE). Even though there were only two *officially* deified emperors in the first century, successive emperors relished this position and their subjects held them in the highest esteem, worshipping them as gods. The emperor Trajan, for example, took it upon himself to confer divinity on his deceased adopted father, the emperor Nerva (98 CE).[8] Worship took place at impressive temples, among statues, incense, and sacrifices. Sacrifices were an expression of loyalty and submission to the emperor by his devoted subjects. The emperor cult, then, was a part of and an addition to the worship of whatever local gods and goddesses were also venerated. With respect to their expressed acts of worship, local elites vied for the most impressive commemorations, and faithful cities competed for the most lavish celebrations.

It is true that, outside of Rome, and especially in the eastern part of the Empire, the worship of the sitting emperor was not a requirement; but many local feasts, festivals, and celebrations honoring the emperor were socially obligatory for everyone. Wealthy men and women of status served as temple priests and personnel. Thus, the worship of the emperor was a symbol of their position, prestige, and power and of their loyalty to the established authority in Rome. Proper worship was related to one's privileged birth and social standing. Those people who could afford it participated in an outward display of public devotion to the emperor and to local gods and goddesses. It was very odd, then, that the Jews and Christians in the Empire worshipped an "unseen" God. They were considered "atheists" and were the object of special scrutiny and suspicion. Within this culture, no wonder they would question how the Christians could worship a peasant Jew who was crucified as a treasonous criminal by the Roman authorities.[9]

The Roman emperor was the leader of military power, financial matters, diplomatic functions, and governmental administration. In his role as leader, he was considered the "Father of the Fatherland" (*Pater Patriae*) and was worshipped as such. This was a competing ideology with the Jewish and Christian belief that their God was the "Father" of his people (see Isaiah 63:16). As the sovereign head of the Empire, the emperor was honored and revered as the strong leader of a male-dominated, male-centered, orderly society.[10] Moreover, the sitting emperor had to demonstrate that he was, indeed, the recipient of divine favors from the gods. This was evident from his military victories as well as displays of amazing signs and wonders. To his loyal subjects, then, the emperor appeared to be a powerful, caring protector and a gracious patron of all the people. The reigning emperor was hailed as a "savior" and "benefactor." The miracles of Jesus, then, were understood in his culture as evidence of his "kingship," and many people (including the threatened leaders) misinterpreted his miracles, his kingdom parables, and his "salvation."

Nevertheless, the ordinary people living in Rome in the 60s CE were suffering from hardships including poor economic conditions and political unrest. There were military defeats resulting in a disgruntled army. Power achieved in the Julio-Claudian dynasty of emperors disintegrated, and the Flavian dynasty took over. There were four emperors in one year, 68–69 CE, causing great unrest and a lack of confidence across the Empire. Emperor Galba was murdered and Otho was forced to commit suicide. The familiar saying is true in this situation: absolute power corrupts absolutely.

Adoption

A second feature of the imperial system in Rome was the unusual acceptance of royal adoption. Julius Caesar died in 44 BCE without an heir, but Augustus (born Gaius Octavius) was adopted as the emperor's son and was made his legal heir. It has been said that Caesar Augustus was the first and most excellent emperor; under his guidance, the Empire reached a "Golden Age."[11] So, the precedent was set, and other key adoptions followed in the line of emperors. The emperor Nero (54–68 CE) was adopted by the emperor Claudius as his son. He was adopted over the emperor's own birth-son, Britannicus, who was rejected as the legal heir to the throne. Of course, this caused apprehension and jealousies on the political scene.[12] Under Nero's leadership, Rome took a turn for the worse. In 64 CE, the Great Fire broke out in Rome. Historians relayed that supposedly Nero set the fire himself and then blamed the city's small Christian community for the carnage. Legend has it that, as a result, Nero had some Christians burned alive and enjoyed the spectacle of seeing them in the flames.[13]

Following Nero, the emperor Galba (68–69 CE) decided to adopt a son in order to assure the continuation of his dynasty. While Galba was not highly successful as a leader, he set another precedent by selecting a man from outside his own family to be his heir. That is, the throne was given on the basis of merit, not on the basis of bloodline.[14] Again, the emperor Nerva (96–98 CE) rejected members of his own family and adopted a man outside of his family to be his successor. Trajan was chosen as the best man for the job, taking office after Nerva in 98 CE. Following Trajan, the next four rulers of the Roman Empire, covering about eighty years, were appointed peacefully to their positions in place of inherited rights.[15] Therefore, if we combine the two imperial concepts of deification and adoption, it naturally leads to the idea that the human emperor was considered the "son of god," by birth or by human selection, and he was revered as such.

Roman Officials

One example of how the NT writers engaged with imperial power and authority is in the portrayal of Roman officials. Both Caesar Augustus and the local client-king Herod the Great were rulers over the region of Palestine at the birth of Jesus (Matt 2:1, 3, 7; Lk 2:1–2). Herod was appointed by the Roman Senate as "king of the Jews" in 40 BCE. Known for his lavish lifestyle, Herod taxed the people of Palestine heavily, and he built massive buildings, temples, and whole cities in honor of Caesar Augustus. Thus, in the Palestine region, the people were paying three levels of financial maintenance: a tribute to the Roman emperor, taxes to Herod to support his administration, and tithes and offerings to the Jerusalem Temple and the high priesthood.[16] A negative view of Herod has been widely accepted in scholarship; he was "ruthless, cruel, one of the most wicked of men, ignorant and insensitive." There may be some scholarly evidence that Herod was not such a monster, but regardless of his expertise and administrative abilities, "King Herod" is portrayed in the NT Gospels as a malevolent person (see Matt 2:3–6, 16–18).[17]

Another key Roman official seen in the Gospels is Pontius Pilate, who was the Roman governor in Jerusalem at the time of Jesus' death. As the prefect of Judea, he was assigned and controlled by the Roman Senate. In both Mark's and Matthew's accounts of Jesus' trials and crucifixion one may see the decisive conflict between Jesus and the ruling authorities. All four Gospels affirm that Jesus was hailed as a king at the time of his triumphal entry into Jerusalem, which occurred before his trial and execution (Mk 11:9–10; Matt 21:5, 9; Lk 19:38; Jn 1:49; 12:13). Yet, the record of Jesus' trial with Pilate (Mk 15:1–15; Matt 27:1–2, 11–26; Lk 23:1–7) is an illustration of the ruling Jewish elites and the powerful Roman governor, Pilate, condemning the poor, powerless, lowly, uneducated, simple Jesus. Some rulers sincerely believed that Jesus was a threat to Rome's authority (Matt 27:11). But, in fact, Jesus was actually a threat to their power, position, wealth, and status. Pilate's role in the Gospels reveals the "self-serving nature of Roman 'justice' that hides behind claims of enacting the public wishes, when it in fact accomplishes its own goals."[18]

Christian Persecution

NT Wright contends that the worst oppression and persecution of Christians does not appear to be full-blown in the Roman Empire until the second century CE, which is after the composition of the NT Gospels and letters. However, while there was no widespread, systematic persecution of Christians, one sees the foundations of second-century attitudes beginning in the first century. The Christians were considered a "subversive sect" related to but not actually members of the Jews.[19] Furthermore, the Christians were considered "cannibals" because of their "corporate ritual meals" where they celebrated the body and blood of Jesus in an "unacceptable" social manner. The persecution of Christians by the emperor Nero was "totally irrational" and was not a widespread, "sustained attack" in the middle of the first century. However, it illustrated that the Roman authorities in power thought very little of the Christians.[20] By about 155–156 CE, when Bishop Polycarp was martyred in Asia Minor, trials and executions of Christians were not uncommon in the Empire. Ultimately, it was the supremacy of Christ over all state and religious deities in the Empire that set up Jesus Christ as a rival monarch, a king, in direct conflict with the dictatorship of the emperor. Christians would not swear to the emperor's "genius" or "lordship" and give devotion to the human rulers; their bold allegiance to Christ set them apart from those who worshipped the pagan gods. A growing number of Christian house-churches met in secret; their gatherings were considered suspicious and viewed as political societies beyond the control of the authorities.[21]

Subversive, Ambiguous Language

Subversion may be defined as "radical interpretation or the undermining of commonly understood images, words, concepts or narratives."[22] Thus, it is the subversion of existing Roman culture that is the key to understanding how the NT Gospel writers "negotiated" the Roman world. Subversive rhetoric may have been started by Jesus himself as he spoke in the Palestinian world and ministered to subjugated people. For example, Jesus' words to the Roman authorities at his trial and before his crucifixion were subversive and ambiguous (Mt 27:11–14; Mk 15:2–5; Lk 23:2–4). The Gospel writers did not fall into "syncretism," but they did reinterpret Greco-Roman philosophies and Jewish imagery into a uniquely Christian rhetoric. The stories and teachings of Jesus circulated among the believers orally and then in writings that were subversive, allowing the narrative to spread throughout the Empire without putting the authors or the readers into dangerous political positions.

Moreover, two very distinguishable aspects of postcolonial literature, that of ambiguity and mimicry, are seen in various passages in the Synoptic Gospels, which contain perplexing ambiguities that raise tensions between clashing cultures. The writers of these Gospels had one foot in the world of Jesus (or the "kingdom of God") and one foot in the imperial world of Rome. To maneuver in both worlds, the writers used ambiguity, intentionally creating a word or phrase signifying two or more ideas or attitudes at the same time. The writers walked a tightrope of domination and subjugation, benefits and injustice, exploitations and cooperation. Familiar, common words and objects were used in new ways and were given double-meanings (such as Jesus' parables). Second, the writers knew that in the world of imperial domination, "envy and mimicry" live in "permanent tension" for those people who were living in a conquered culture. People living with this tension actually seek to have that which is hated and despised (or envied), just like their oppressors, such as material wealth, food, land, and houses. Further, they hoped to duplicate (mimic) for themselves the very things that repressed them, such as power and position in the society.[23]

Hidden Transcripts

In fact, the Gospels may be considered countercultural "hidden transcripts" that challenge public records of the official, elitist power. The Gospels were not intended for public readings on every street corner but rather were developed as specific communications written for and by communities of people who were Jesus-followers in a culture that countered his teachings. The Gospels presented a "hidden message" of the kingdom of God that condemned human domination over subordinated people. Through his words and actions (healings, feedings, and exorcisms), Jesus brought redemption and reparation to an injured, bleeding society. The Gospels offered alternative ways of being a Jesus-follower while still living in the Empire. They provided ways of understanding the society, "*rejecting options of total escape from or total compromise with* Rome's empire."[24] Finally, Jesus' teachings anticipated the ultimate, divine justice of God over all of humanity, which was an encouragement to his followers.[25]

Another example in the Gospels that positions the life and teachings of Jesus above the eminence of human authorities is in references to his "kingdom" and "kingship." Jesus is recognized as "king" in the Gospels by both his followers and his enemies. Evans suggests that in acting in his kingly role, Jesus is therefore established as a rival to Caesar.[26] Repeatedly, Jesus attempted to describe to his followers his kingdom (with his Father God) and how it arrives ("The kingdom of God is like"). God's ultimate power and complete sovereignty provided the basis of Jesus' earthly concerns and his converse message. Yet, it took his followers a long time to fully realize that Jesus was not talking about an earthly kingdom. His kingdom, his discourses, and his actions were not intended to be political threats to the reigning Caesar, despite Roman fears. Jesus was not an earthly, political, revolutionary figure in the manner some thought him to be. What he said and did on earth was a demonstration of his own divinity as *the true Son of God at birth* (even so, at conception, Lk 1:28–33). He conducted his life and his message with boldness, but not with violence, as he confronted both Jewish and Roman authorities. He condemned the corrupt, inept, and abusive leadership as he spoke in (sometimes) cryptic metaphors and parables in order to defy his opponents and to confront evil.

Gospels of Mark and Matthew

Warren Carter contends that the Gospels of Mark and of Matthew are both "works of imperial negotiation." That is, Roman imperialism is evident in the foreground of the writing, not just in the background. These narratives tell the story of Jesus, who was crucified by the Roman authorities because he challenged their power and ideology. The fact that he was raised from the dead revealed the inadequacies of human authority and demonstrated the power of God. These two Gospels navigate the Roman power structure with a "self-protective yet contestive" approach. They offer an "alternative yet imitative (in part)" way of life to the original readers. Mark and Matthew both offer a completely different "social experience" to those readers who were Jesus-followers, primarily by living a life as part of a new, young, and blossoming community that came to be known as "the church."[27] Apart from any earthly kingdom, this new community of believers was a microcosm of the present and future "kingdom of God," promised by Jesus to his followers.

Gospel of Mark

The Gospel of Mark has been generally accepted as the first of the Synoptic Gospels to be written; it has also been suggested that this account was written in Rome during a time of struggle and uncertainty in that city. It was perhaps during this time of unrest that a Jew living in Rome composed a historical account of Jesus.

Tat-siong Benny Liew contends that Mark's Gospel should not be read in a "monolithic way" (i.e., through a white, middle-class, American lens), but he "understands its cultural power to rest precisely on its ability to speak in multiple voices." In general, literary texts "do more than simply reflect history and culture; they also create them."[28] Mark addresses the conflicts surrounding God's "near and coming" kingdom and of leadership and authority in their corrupt culture (both Jewish and Roman). For example, Mark composed a "double parallel" that illustrates Jesus' clash with those in authority. His first trial is before the Jewish authorities, where Jesus is condemned by false witnesses (14:53–65). His second trial is before Pilate, the Roman governor, where the very same agenda is followed (15:1–20). In these parallel trials, Jesus refuses to answer questions about his "kingship," and he is severely mocked and ridiculed. This "double trial" sequence in Mark illustrates that both the Jewish and the Roman leadership were not only corrupt but worked in collaboration with each other.[29] Ironically, Jewish leaders did not believe Jesus was the "Son of God" (15:61), and the Roman leaders were afraid that he was (15:31–32).

Divine Sonship

Michael Peppard analyzes the "metaphor of divine father-son relations" in the Gospel of Mark. This is a key metaphor in the NT Gospels, mimicking a reflection of the "Roman socio-political environment."[30] Caesar Augustus set the precedent of the emperor's role as the *paterfamilias* of a very large family. The *genius Augusti*, the guardian spirit of the imperial *gens*, was considered the "father of the whole human race" (about fifty million people). The residents responded with devoted loyalty to their "father." With great irony, Augustus was actually unable to raise a "natural, begotten son to inherit his power."[31] Thus, when a Christian believer left behind the Roman ideology and accepted a new "Father" (God) and Son (Jesus), he or she was a member of a new family, with new social relations and material blessings. Mark implies that the benefits of this new family are not only "eternal life" in the future but, indeed, rewards in this life as well (10:1–31).[32]

Furthermore, in Mark we see a literary "bookend" that speaks to Jesus' divine sonship. The first expression takes place at Jesus' baptism when God declares that "You are my Son" (1:11). The final, public declaration concerning the sonship of Jesus was recognized by a Roman centurion at the foot of the cross (15:39), which is, perhaps, the best example of "colonial mimicry." Jesus was the "counter-emperor" and the rightful heir to God's "kingdom," who rose to power in a society that "mimicked the imperial power."[33]

Spiritual Battles and Postcolonial Interpretation

In Mark, during his ministry Jesus confronted and exorcised "unclean spirits," which can be interpreted as symbolic of the "Roman colonizers" who were guilty of "convulsing the people of Palestine" (1:21–28; 3:20–30; 5:1–20).[34] In fact, the name given to the demonic spirit in 5:9 is "Legion," a direct reference to the Roman military unit of 6,000 men. The subtle questions are posed by Mark: Who is the ultimate authority in this society? Who is *really* in control? Furthermore, Stephen Moore suggests that, in Mark,

> Rome is merely an instrument of God, his scourge, which he employs to punish the indigenous Judean elites. The ultimate authority would remain remote, unseen and "above the battle" (i.e., the European empires of indirect rule in colonial Africa). Finally, the ultimate authority finds it necessary temporarily to relinquish its god-like remoteness in order to intervene decisively and irresistibly in the corrupt affairs of its creatures, in an attempt to contain the chaos that is own administrative policies created.[35]

The Gospel of Matthew

This Gospel is often considered to be the most Jewish of the NT Gospels. At the time of Jesus' birth, there were a great many "messianic" expectations. The people of Israel expected that eventually God would intervene in the world and reinstate the independent Jewish nation. It was their hope that God (again) would step in and release his people from their position of bondage. With the Romans in control, the future of the Jewish nation was grim. The NT Gospels told of the coming of the promised Messiah, Jesus, who would save his people; however, he was not the political and military savior they were expecting. Matthew quickly modifies the Jewish expectations by redefining them. While it appeared that the Messiah Jesus failed in his mission to avert the tyranny of the Romans (he is crucified), in truth, he was the leader of a new and different kind of "empire."

In spite of its "Jewishness," Matthew's Gospel "offers various strategies for negotiating the elite-dominated, socio-political Roman imperial order."[36] The most likely place of the origin of this Gospel is the area of Antioch in Syria. Taxation, order, and supervision were implemented by the Syrian governor who resided in the capital of Antioch.[37] In contrast, Matthew wrote to encourage his readers, who were a part of God's "empire" (or, typically, the "kingdom of heaven"), while still living under the Roman system. Indeed, while the Christian community to whom Matthew wrote was in conflict with the Roman imperial world, they were also at odds with the Orthodox Jews who rejected Jesus as the promised Messiah. It was necessary, then, for the author and readers to "negotiate" life within the Empire including "accommodation, submission, mimicry," to remain "active but self-protective," with "non-violent resistance, and faithful and hopeful living."[38]

Specifically, Matthew's plot, Christology, eschatology, and ecclesiology all demonstrate interactions that defy the Roman imperial ideology.[39] The plot, of course, is the story of a rebellious Jew who is crucified by the Romans because he was perceived to be a challenge to their established power. In terms of Christology, Matthew insists that Jesus is an agent of God, born of God in the proper lineage (1:16, 17, 20–23) and resurrected by

God (28:7). In fact, the Jewish authorities had to make up a false report about the resurrection events and the incompetency of the Roman guard at the empty tomb (28:4, 11–15). The resurrection of the true King Jesus overpowered and diminished the power of Rome. Matthew's eschatology is the revelation of Jesus' authority "over all the world" (24:14). His ultimate, divine rule and power will be clearly evident at the "end of the age" (24:3, 30–31). Until then, in the present world, Jesus warned his followers about deception, famines, earthquakes and wickedness. They would be hated, persecuted, and put to death ("because of me") (24:4–13; 21–25). Yet, Jesus promised that those who "stand firm" would receive his redemption and salvation. The faithful followers formed a countercultural community under the sovereign rule/reign of God with Jesus (ecclesiology; see 16:16–19; see 18:17). The word "church" is unique to Matthew's Gospel, and in their culture, it implied an assembly of free, voting citizens in a city. Yet, the authorities were suspicious of such gatherings, assuming the members were political schemers. The church stood against Rome, just as much as it did against the false teachings of the Jewish leadership (16:1, 11–12).

The Roman Caesar is particularly mentioned in a highly debated passage, Matthew 22:15–22. The Jewish Pharisees were not in favor of the Roman control of Palestine, and they hated the Herodians, who were wealthy Jews in collaboration with the Roman rulers, the Herods (client-kings). However, the Pharisees went out of their way to enlist the help of the Herodians to trap Jesus in his words. They began with flattery (22:16) and pretended to value Jesus' opinion. If he answered their question about Caesar's taxes in a negative manner, they could report him to the Roman authorities as a traitor. If he answered in a positive manner, the Pharisees could accuse him of being disloyal to his nation of Israel. Knowing their hypocrisy, Jesus asked for a Roman coin. The "denarius" was a common coin, with the imprint of Emperor Tiberius on one side and a Latin inscription on the other side: "Tiberius Caesar Augustus, son of the divine Augustus." Thus, the coin was issued by and belonged to Caesar, and it was to be given back to him in the form of taxation. On the one hand, Jesus makes a clear distinction between the benevolence of God (what is given freely) and the demands of Caesar; and, in doing so, he argues against the false claims in the inscription itself. On the other hand, Jesus' instructions to his hearers to obey the authorities by giving to Caesar what he was due reinforced the idea that Jesus and his followers were not radical revolutionaries attempting to overthrow the imperial government.[40]

While Warren Carter has written extensively on the Gospel of Matthew and the Roman Empire, other writers addressing this topic include H. Bhabha, P. Garnsey and R. Saller, K. C. Hanson and D. E. Oakman, E. Said, and J. Scott.

The Gospel of Luke

The Gospel of Luke is "notably preoccupied with power, pulsing with the energy of charged exchanges between centre and periphery—rich and poor, urban and rural,

Jew and Gentile, Rome and those subjugated under imperial rule." This Gospel and its companion, the Book of Acts, have been interpreted "both as radically subversive and as skillfully accommodationalist in relation to the forces of imperialism and colonialism."[41] In agreement, even more than in Matthew and Mark, Luke is concerned with placing Jesus and his followers squarely within the context of Roman/Jewish political relations. The literary genre of the Gospel of Luke is unique in biblical literature. Luke has been considered the NT "historian," so scholars have labeled his work "historiographic prose."[42] Luke records and interprets real people and real events. He provides his readers with details and reports that do not appear in the other two Synoptic Gospels.

In Luke, the approach of the Roman authorities (who used the domination model) is compared to the social interactions of Jesus (who pictured the humility-service model). Certainly Jesus' emphasis on humility and service was countercultural in the Empire, particularly with those of higher rank and status, both Jewish and Roman. He rebukes discussions about human greatness and position, and he taught the importance of concern for the poor, the disabled, and the infirm. In contrast to accepted Roman norms and values, Jesus affirms those who were classified as "outcasts," such as the Samaritans, women, sinners, and those in poor health (mental and physical).[43] Jesus' humility-service model can be seen clearly in many of his parabolic teachings included in Luke's Gospel. For example, Luke situates three parables in a row that demonstrate Jesus' countercultural teachings (14:7–24). The summation of these parables is in 14:11: "For everyone who exalts himself will be humbled, and he who humbles himself will be exalted."

Birth Story and Crucifixion

Luke is the only evangelist to place the birth of Jesus in a specific time and place (1:5, 2:1–7). "Herod the Great" was a Roman client-king, serving in the area of Palestine, who answered to the Roman Senate. Luke sets the time and the tone of his Gospel by referring to "Caesar Augustus" (2:1), who reigned from 31 BC to 14 AD. This not only limits the approximate date of Jesus' birth, it also sets the stage for the cultural conditions at the time of his birth. The "census" was taken "of the entire Roman world" (2:1) and was employed by the Roman government to compel men into military service and for taxation purposes. The Jews living in Judea and Galilee were exempt from mandatory service in the Roman army, but they were not exempt from paying taxes to Rome.

In direct contrast to the Roman emperors, Luke records the remarkable birth of the one he considered to be *Savior* and *Lord*, born of *God*, and whose reign will bring to people *good news* and *peace*. Luke uses precisely the same titles given to Caesar Augustus for Jesus (2:11, 30–32; cf. Matt 1–2).[44] Matthew, however, places more emphasis on Jesus as the lawful "king" at his birth. Luke includes the song of Mary, the "humble servant" and the mother of Jesus (1:46–55). Matthew emphasized the foreign "kings" (magi) worshipping the baby Jesus, while Luke featured the lowly "shepherds" who were the first to hear of Jesus' birth (2:8–9). Luke establishes Jesus' public ministry within the historic reign of the emperor Tiberius and the governor Pontius Pilate (3:1–2). Other Roman client-kings and local Jewish elites are specifically mentioned by name to create a time frame and authenticity: "Quirinius, the governor of Syria," Herod Antipas, Herod Philip, Lysanias, Annas, and Caiaphas. Luke entwines the lives of these Roman rulers with the lives and ministries of John the Baptist and Jesus. Thus, we see a struggle for power between the dominating forces of Rome and the interceding forces of God. The lives of John the Baptist and Jesus were effectively scrutinized (and ultimately ended) by this triad of Roman rulers: Pilate, the Jewish leaders, and Herod.[45]

In fact, Yamazaki-Ransom states that the birth, life, and crucifixion of Jesus in the Gospel of Luke take place within the cosmic conflict between God and Satan. The latter has dominion over human political institutions, including the government of Rome. Like the other Synoptics, the Jewish leadership was trapped in the same patterns as their Roman tyrants, with their own systems of subjugation and control. Luke tactfully records how the Jewish leaders accommodated the Roman rule for their own wealth and status. Jesus is not unaware of the tyranny of the Roman authorities, but he was also thoroughly dismayed at the manipulation of the Jewish leaders in Jerusalem for their own purposes (19:45–46; 20:9–18).

Luke alone includes the role of the Roman governor Herod Antipas in the interrogation of Jesus before his crucifixion, which may have been initiated by the Jews' question, "Are you the Son of God?" (22:70, which, again, is the same epithet attributed to Caesar). Both Herod and Pilate are strong opponents of God, even though they are completely unaware that they are instruments of God, used to carry out the crucifixion of Jesus. Although he found Jesus innocent of the Jews' charges, Pilate finally takes action against Jesus because his own pride forced him to be more concerned about maintaining order in the city, and his own reputation with Rome, than true justice for Jesus (23:20–25; compare to Mk 15:5; Mt 27:14).[46]

Benevolence

Luke's Jesus acknowledges the controlling tradition of the elite "benefactor," a title and an honor that was highly valued by the Roman rulers. Only Luke uses the title "Benefactor" in 22:25 (see also Mk 10:42 and Matt 20:25). The familiar title used by Jesus is used ironically because, more often than not, people in high positions thought very little about their subjects and more about themselves. So, Jesus said that the "kings of the Gentiles" (the Romans) who were considered "benefactors" actually "lord it over them and exercise authority over them" (22:25). No doubt they considered themselves "the greatest" because of their false benevolence (22:24–26). The point Jesus is making with his disciples is, "For who is greater, the one who is at the table [like Caesar], or the one who serves? But, I am among you as one who serves" (Luke 22:27). Luke seems to show a greater distinction between the challenging message of Jesus and the key political and social leaders of his day.[47]

Political and Economic Factors

Luke's subtle subversions are not only directed at political domination; they also necessarily point out economic injustice as well (although the two are related).[48] The harsh Roman taxation system placed demands on the Palestinian province beyond ration and reason. Luke addresses the social and economic imbalance more than the other Synoptic Gospels. Luke has a version of the "Caesar/coin" story in Matthew 22:15-22. Then, Luke revisits the coin incident in 23:1, when the frustrated Jewish leaders create a bold lie before the Roman governor. They accused Jesus of "subverting the nation" because he "opposes payment of taxes to Caesar and claims to be Christ, the king" (Luke 23:1-2); these are two false accusations in one breath. Jesus never openly called himself "the Christ," perhaps to avoid the misconception that he was an earthly threat to Caesar. By returning the coin to the government, Jesus was making a "covert yet thoroughgoing denunciation of the imposed Roman monetary economy on which imperial exploitation is based."[49]

Luke devised his own list of Beatitudes that are similar to the list found in Matthew's Gospel. Luke, however, intentionally used this list to make subversive comments about the "social injustice of poverty." That is, Luke's Jesus blesses the "poor," blesses the "hungry," and, in contrast, curses the "rich" (Luke 6:20-21, 24-25). His words were a brief view of his "kingdom of God" while addressing the physical needs of his people. In Matthew, however, the message is "spiritualized"; we see the "poor *in spirit*" and those who are "hungering *for righteousness*" (Matt 5:3, 6, emphasis added). Furthermore, Luke is the only Gospel writer to choose to include stories such as the "parable of the rich fool," who is not "rich toward God" (12:15-21), and the tale of Zacchaeus, the wealthy tax-collector who is confronted by Jesus concerning his material riches (Luke 19:1-10). In fact, 19:10 is a key verse in Luke's Gospel because Jesus gives himself the title of "Son of Man" to distinguish himself from the Roman emperors. This title is a fulfillment of the prophesies of Daniel 7:13-14, and this verse also relates Jesus' true intended purpose: "to seek and to save what was lost."[50]

Typically, Luke's Gospel has been interpreted with an historical approach, which is not incorrect. Yet, Burrus contends that a postcolonial (or an "anti-imperialist") approach to Luke allows modern readers to see Luke's stories of Jesus, with all their ambiguities and ambivalences, negotiations and true identities, in a setting of "colonial resistance."[51]

EMPIRE STUDIES

Postcolonialism is a relatively new approach to biblical interpretation. There are numerous related approaches employed by scholars in an attempt to understand the NT as a body of ancient writings and make it relevant in the world today. These include empire studies, liberation theology, and contextual hermeneutics. The latter two approaches can certainly overlap with empire studies and postcolonialism. The hermeneutical categories, therefore, are not rigid by any means. To these categories may be added literary approaches such as critical rhetorical-critical analysis and apocalyptic literary analysis. Thus, it is crucial that scholarship continues to engage with the NT historically, ideologically, and literarily so that scholars can continue to seek to better understand past cultures and empires and apply what they learn to the present culture and hopefully create a better future for humanity.[52]

From a postcolonial point of view, scholars contend that:

> One of the lessons of history is that empires rarely disappear completely. They rise and fall but often resurface in different forms. The current military interventions and territorial occupations in the name of democracy, humanitarianism and liberation are signs of a new form of imperialism. As long as there are empires, dominations, tyrannies and exploitations—either rising or resurfacing—postcolonial criticism will continue to have its vigilant role to play.[53]

This is seen in the post–World War II demise of European empires, which led to criticisms of newer "Western imperialism" (i.e., Britain and America) and to a new image of a Jesus who identified more with marginalized people and resistance movements. Twentieth-century scholarship opened the door to seeing Jesus as "radically different from the dominant one that had been presented over a thousand years."[54] Thoughtful scholarship has presented a variety of opinions about "empire" and anti-imperial rhetoric in the biblical literature—from blatant accommodation and adaptation by biblical authors to "covert, subversive statements to undermine claims of Roman hegemony."[55]

Still, from another point of view, the basic postmodern and postcolonial theories were born out of a noble desire to hear (and liberate) the voices of the disenfranchised, the oppressed and the constructed "other." However, the drawback of some theories is that the intention of the biblical author becomes, at best, a secondary concern, or at worst, an irrelevant (or unknowable) matter.[56]

The difference between empire criticism and postcolonial criticism, then, is intention. In other words, in the NT writings, the *primary* intentions of the authors were not to lead a rebellion against the political situation in the Roman Empire through their writings. One does not see the topics of domination and imperial subjugation over and above any other intentions of the biblical authors. In contrast to the "empire of Caesar," the revelations of the "empire of God" through the words and events of Jesus demonstrate the distinctive features of his message to humanity. The key question is: What is the *purpose* of the Gospel writings? Was the purpose of Jesus' gospel message to resist Rome? Or does the presentation of Jesus' Gospel as an alternate "empire" intentionally promote opposition to Rome and to its authority?

The main trajectory of the NT Gospels is that Jesus taught and displayed a new thing, a new community, and a new way of living that was counter to the existing culture. In fact, Jesus gives two strong commands: love God (as opposed to loving personal power and material possessions) and love one another. He challenged his followers to obey this "double command" to love in spite of opposition, ethical choices, or political motives.[57] This was in contrast not only to the Roman authorities but also to the Jewish leadership (Jesus' own people). The Gospel message Jesus delivered is intended to improve and save lives; it was his intention to elevate humanity toward what God intended. Jesus' silence at his own trials before his execution reveals his true motives were not to overthrow the government. Furthermore, in a military-oriented society, Jesus did not act with violence but with healing and peace. He never raised a sword, physically or metaphorically (Matt 26:52).

Andy Crouch outlines three features that are true about human empires. First, we will always have empires. That is, there will always be human civilizations with a political and economic order and with laws and structures of ideology, philosophies, and theology. Second, empires always come to an end. Human empires rise and fall. Two human drives affect people—expansion throughout the world and reconciliation with one another. This is true of the empire of Rome and the empire of God. Yet, empires are "precarious"; a tension exists because rulers advertise peace and prosperity but rarely deliver on what they promise. While the NT writers seemed to understand the tenuous nature of empires, they reacted to this fact with ambivalence. Granted, empires can be instruments of God's work on earth (we see this in the Old Testament), or they can be impediments of God's rule and reign. Third, not all empires are alike:

> Empires can set themselves up as idols, as the supremely powerful institution. But every idol is the simultaneously exalted and degraded form of a good, created thing. Evil has no resources of its own but must colonize the good. Empires differ in the extent to which they partake in the idolatry of Empire. Consequently, the question is not whether empires will endure (they will not), but what kind of empires we will have [in the future]. Will they succumb to the idolatry of power and lust for domination that comes when human beings explicitly cast off their accountability to the Creator God?[58]

Thus, with all due respect to eminent scholars, the present discussion argues that, in the future, a more accurate approach to NT analysis may be focused on empire studies instead of postcolonialism. The NT should be analyzed in terms of the acute distinctions between two empires, that of Rome and that of God. Certainly missing this sharp contrast, may result in missing the aims and significance of biblical literature. There is no question about whether anti-imperial rhetoric is found in the NT—it most clearly is. But one may question if it is the dominant and controlling idea as some say that it is. The main point of the NT Gospels is to advance a new, *eternal* empire that is far better than any empire created by humans. Jesus did not battle the old system as much as he created a new one that is superior to imperialism in every way: economically, culturally, religiously, socially, and politically. Jesus' "kingdom" was not simply a condemnation of the Roman Empire; it was a criticism of *any* empire (then and now) that seeks to rule its people by tyranny, domination, oppression, and military force.

The only perfectly just and peaceful empire is the divine kingdom promised by God. God's promises for his complete (yet future) reign and rule on the earth raises the dignity of all humans to a level that no human dictator can ever achieve. The continuing study of human empires should help show what is flawed in their power and politics and how people may avoid repeating those mistakes as they try to live together on this planet. In the end, *only* God's kingdom will exist without failings but with the complete peace and justice human beings crave.

Notes

1. Warren Carter, "Matthew and Empire," in *Empire in the New Testament*, edited by Stanley E. Porter and Cynthia Long Westfall (Eugene, OR: Wipf and Stock, 2011), 90–119, 101.
2. Virginia Burrus, "The Gospel of Luke and the Acts of the Apostles," in *A Postcolonial Commentary on the New Testament Writings*, 133–155, edited by F. F. Segovia and R. S. Sugirtharajah (New York: T & T Clark, 2009), 133. See R. S. Sugirtharajah, *Postcolonial Criticism and Biblical Interpretation* (Oxford: Oxford University Press, 2002), 24–28.
3. Philip Esler, "Rome in Apocalyptic and Rabbinic Literature," in *The Gospel of Matthew in Its Roman Imperial Context*, edited by John Riches and David Sim (New York: T&T Clark International, 2005), 10.
4. Michael Smith, "The Empire Theory and the Empires of History – A Review Essay," *Christian Scholar's Review*, 39.3 (2010): 305–322.
5. Warren Carter, *The Roman Empire and the New Testament: An Essential Guide* (Nashville, TN: Abingdon Press, 2006), 3–14. See also Christopher Bryan, *Render to Caesar: Jesus, the Early Church, and the Roman Superpower* (Oxford: Oxford University Press, 2005).
6. Warren Carter, "Matthew and Empire," in *Empire in the New Testament*, 90–119, edited by Stanley E. Porter and Cynthia Long Westfall (Eugene, OR: Wipf and Stock, 2011), 94–95.
7. L. L. Welborn, "Inequity in Roman Corinth," in *The First Urban Churches: Roman Corinth*, 47–84, edited by L. L. Welborn and James R. Harrison (Atlanta: SBL, 2016).
8. "Caligula famously said, 'Let there be one Lord, one king' (Suetonius, *Gauls Caligula* 22), after which he demanded to be treated as a god and began appearing in public dressed as various deities. He once ordered a statue of himself erected in the Jerusalem Temple (Philo, *On the Embassy to Gaius* 30.203)." David Nystrom, "We Have No King but Caesar," in *Jesus Is Lord, Caesar Is Not*, 23–37, edited by Scot McKnight and Joseph B. Modica (Downers Grove: IVP Academic, 2013), 36.
9. Judith A. Diehl, "Anti-Imperial Rhetoric in the New Testament," in *Jesus Is Lord, Caesar Is Not*, 38–81, edited by Scot McKnight and Joseph B. Modica (Downers Grove: IVP Academic, 2013), 44–45.
10. Warren Carter, *The Roman Empire and the New Testament: An Essential Guide* (Nashville, TN: Abingdon Press, 2006), 4.
11. Michael Grant, *The Roman Emperors: A Biographical Guide to the Rulers of Imperial Rome, 31 B.C. to A.D. 476.* (New York: Barnes & Noble Books, 1997), 9–16.
12. Grant, *The Roman Emperors*, 34–35.
13. Grant, *The Roman Emperors*, 34–39.
14. Grant, *The Roman Emperors*, 43–45.
15. Grant, *The Roman Emperors*, 70–71.

16. Richard A. Horsley, *Hearing the Whole Story: the Politics of Plot in Mark's Gospel* (Louisville, KY: Westminster John Knox, 2001), 36.
17. Bryon McCane, "Simply Irresistible: Augustus, Herod and Empire," *Journal of Biblical Literature* 127, no. 4 (2008): 725.
18. Warren Carter, "The Gospel of Matthew," in *A Postcolonial Commentary on the New Testament Writings*, 69–104, edited by F. F. Segovia and R. S. Sugirtharajah (New York: T & T Clark, 2009), 93.
19. N. T. Wright, *The New Testament and the People of God*, vol. 1 (London: SPCK, 1992), 346–347.
20. Wright, *The New Testament and the People of God*, 350–353.
21. Wright, *The New Testament and the People of God*, 350.
22. Brian Godawa, *Word Pictures: Knowing God through Story and Imagination*. (Downers Grove: InterVarsity Press, 2009), 115.
23. Carter, "The Gospel of Matthew," 100.
24. Carter, "The Gospel of Matthew," 12–13, his emphasis.
25. Carter, "The Gospel of Matthew," 99.
26. Craig Evans, "King Jesus and His Ambassadors: Empire and Luke-Acts," in *Empire in the New Testament*, 120–139, edited by Stanley E. Porter and Cynthia Long Westfall (Eugene, OR: Wipf and Stock, 2011), 121–122.
27. Carter, "The Gospel of Matthew," 90.
28. Tat-siong Benny Liew, "The Gospel of Mark," in *A Postcolonial Commentary on the New Testament Writings*, 105–132, edited by F. F. Segovia and R. S. Sugirtharajah (New York: T & T Clark, 2009), 105.
29. Liew, "The Gospel of Mark," 109. See also, C. Clifton Black, *Mark: Images of an Apostolic Interpreter*. (Minneapolis: Fortress Press, 2001), 225–236.
30. Michael Peppard, *The Son of God in the Roman World: Divine Sonship in Its Social and Political Context* (New York: Oxford University Press, 2011), 3.
31. Peppard, *The Son of God in the Roman World*, 66–67.
32. Peppard, *The Son of God in the Roman World*, 126–129.
33. Peppard, *The Son of God in the Roman World*, 130–131.
34. Peppard, *The Son of God in the Roman World*, 130.
35. Stephen D. Moore, *Empire and Apocalypse: Postcolonialism and the New Testament* (Sheffield: Sheffield Phoenix Press, 2006), 35. See also Brian Incigneri, *The Gospel to the Romans: The Setting and Rhetoric of Mark's Gospel* (Leiden: Brill, 2003).
36. Carter, "The Gospel of Matthew," 116.
37. Carter, "The Gospel of Matthew," 69, 75.
38. Carter, "The Gospel of Matthew," 116–117.
39. Carter, "The Gospel of Matthew," 7.
40. Gordon L. Heath, "The Church Fathers and the Roman Empire," in *Empire in the New Testament*, 259–279, edited by Stanley E. Porter and Cynthia Long Westfall (Eugene, OR: Wipf and Stock, 2011), 276.
41. Virginia Burrus, "The Gospel of Luke and the Acts of the Apostles," in *A Postcolonial Commentary on the New Testament Writings*, 133–155, edited by F. F. Segovia and R. S. Sugirtharajah (New York: T & T Clark, 2009), 133.
42. Burrus, "The Gospel of Luke and the Acts of the Apostles," 134.
43. Richard J. Cassidy, *Christians and Roman Rule in the New Testament: New Perspectives* (New York: Crossroads Publishing, 2001), 22.

44. Burrus, "The Gospel of Luke and the Acts of the Apostles," 133.
45. Kazuhiko Yamazaki-Ransom, *The Roman Empire in Luke's Narrative* (New York: T & T International, 2010), 107.
46. Yamazaki-Ransom, *The Roman Empire in Luke's Narrative*, 109–114.
47. Stanley E. Porter and Cynthia Long Westfall, "Introduction: Empire, the New Testament, and Beyond," in *Empire in the New Testament*, 1–16, edited by Stanley E. Porter and Cynthia Long Westfall (Eugene, OR: Wipf and Stock, 2011), 8.
48. Burrus, "The Gospel of Luke and the Acts of the Apostles," 140.
49. Burrus, "The Gospel of Luke and the Acts of the Apostles," 141.
50. Burrus, "The Gospel of Luke and the Acts of the Apostles," 141.
51. Burrus, "The Gospel of Luke and the Acts of the Apostles," 153.
52. Diehl, "Anti-Imperial Rhetoric in the New Testament," 67–74. See also Judith A. Diehl, "Anti-Imperial Rhetoric in the New Testament," *Currents in Biblical Research* 10, no. 1 (2011): 9–52.
53. R. S. Sugirtharajah, "Postcolonial and Biblical Interpretation: The Next Phase," in *A Postcolonial Commentary on the New Testament Writings*, 455–466, edited by F. F. Segovia and R. S. Sugirtharajah (New York: T & T Clark, 2009), 455.
54. Heath, "The Church Fathers and the Roman Empire," 260–261.
55. Heath, "The Church Fathers and the Roman Empire," 262.
56. Heath, "The Church Fathers and the Roman Empire," 276. See also F. F. Segovia, "Introduction: Configurations, Approaches, Findings, Stances," in *A Postcolonial Commentary on the New Testament Writings*, 1–68, edited by F. F. Segovia and R. S. Sugirtharajah (New York: T & T Clark, 2009).
57. Seyoon Kim, *Christ and Caesar: The Gospel and the Roman Empire in the Writings of Paul and Luke* (Grand Rapids: Eerdmans, 2008), 203.
58. Andy Crouch, "Forward," in *Jesus Is Lord, Caesar Is Not*, 7–14, edited by Scot McKnight and Joseph B. Modica (Downers Grove: IVP Academic, 2013), 8–12.

Bibliography

Black, C. Clifton. *Mark: Images of an Apostolic Interpreter*. Minneapolis: Fortress Press, 2001

Bryan, Christopher. *Render to Caesar: Jesus, the Early Church, and the Roman Superpower*. Oxford: Oxford University Press, 2005.

Burrus, Virginia. "The Gospel of Luke and the Acts of the Apostles." In *A Postcolonial Commentary on the New Testament Writings*, edited by F. F. Segovia and R. S. Sugirtharajah, 133–155. New York: T & T Clark, 2009.

Carter, Warren. *The Roman Empire and the New Testament: An Essential Guide*. Nashville, TN: Abingdon Press, 2006.

Carter, Warren. "The Gospel of Matthew." In *A Postcolonial Commentary on the New Testament Writings*, edited by F. F. Segovia and R. S. Sugirtharajah, 69–104. New York: T & T Clark, 2009.

Carter, Warren. "Matthew and Empire." In *Empire in the New Testament*, edited by Stanley E. Porter and Cynthia Long Westfall, 90–119. Eugene, OR: Wipf and Stock, 2011.

Cassidy, Richard J. *Christians and Roman Rule in the New Testament: New Perspectives*. New York: Crossroads Publishing, 2001.

Crouch, Andy. "Forward." In *Jesus Is Lord, Caesar Is Not*, 7–14, edited by Scot McKnight and Joseph B. Modica. Downers Grove: IVP Academic, 2013.

Diehl, Judith A. "Anti-Imperial Rhetoric in the New Testament." *Currents in Biblical Research* 10, no. 1 (2011): 9–52.

Diehl, Judith A. "Anti-Imperial Rhetoric in the New Testament." In *Jesus Is Lord, Caesar Is Not*, edited by Scot McKnight and Joseph B. Modica, 38–81. Downers Grove: IVP Academic, 2013.

Esler, Philip. "Rome in Apocalyptic and Rabbinic Literature," In *The Gospel of Matthew in Its Roman Imperial Context*, edited by John Riches and David Sim, New York: T&T Clark International, 2005.

Evans, Craig A. "King Jesus and His Ambassadors: Empire and Luke-Acts." In *Empire in the New Testament*, edited by Stanley E. Porter and Cynthia Long Westfall, 120–139. Eugene, OR: Wipf and Stock, 2011.

Godawa, Brian. *Word Pictures: Knowing God through Story and Imagination*. Downers Grove: InterVarsity Press, 2009.

Grant, Michael. *The Roman Emperors: A Biographical Guide to the Rulers of Imperial Rome, 31 BC to AD 476*. New York: Barnes & Noble Books, 1997.

Heath, Gordon L. "The Church Fathers and the Roman Empire." In *Empire in the New Testament*, edited by Stanley E. Porter and Cynthia Long Westfall, 259–279. Eugene, OR: Wipf and Stock, 2011.

Horsley, Richard A. *Hearing the Whole Story: The Politics of Plot in Mark's Gospel*. Louisville, KY: Westminster John Knox, 2001.

Incigneri, Brian. *The Gospel to the Romans: The Setting and Rhetoric of Mark's Gospel*, Leiden: Brill, 2003.

Kim, Seyoon. *Christ and Caesar: The Gospel and the Roman Empire in the Writings of Paul and Luke*, Grand Rapids: Eerdmans, 2008.

Liew, Tat-siong Benny. "The Gospel of Mark." In *A Postcolonial Commentary on the New Testament Writings*, edited by F. F. Segovia and R. S. Sugirtharajah, 105–132. New York: T & T Clark, 2009.

McCane, Byron. "Simply Irresistible: Augustus, Herod and Empire." *Journal of Biblical Literature* 127, no. 4 (2008): 725–735.

Moore, Stephen D. *Empire and Apocalypse; Postcolonialism and the New Testament*. Sheffield: Sheffield Phoenix Press, 2006.

Nystrom, David. "We Have No King but Caesar." In *Jesus Is Lord, Caesar Is Not*, edited by Scot McKnight and Joseph B. Modica, 23–37. Downers Grove: IVP Academic, 2013.

Peppard, Michael. *The Son of God in the Roman World: Divine Sonship in Its Social and Political Context*. New York: Oxford University Press, 2011.

Porter, Stanley E., and Cynthia Long Westfall. "Introduction: Empire, the New Testament, and Beyond." In *Empire in the New Testament*, edited by Stanley E. Porter and Cynthia Long Westfall, 1–16. Eugene, OR: Wipf and Stock, 2011.

Segovia, Fernando F. "Introduction: Configurations, Approaches, Findings, Stances." In *A Postcolonial Commentary on the New Testament Writings*, edited by F. F. Segovia and R. S. Sugirtharajah, 1–68. New York: T & T Clark, 2009.

Smith, Michael G. "The Empire Theory and the Empires of History—A Review Essay." *Christian Scholar's Review* 39, no. 3 (2010): 305–322.

Sugirtharajah, R. S. *Postcolonial Criticism and Biblical Interpretation*. Oxford: Oxford University Press, 2002.

Sugirtharajah, R. S. "Postcolonial and Biblical Interpretation: The Next Phase." In *A Postcolonial Commentary on the New Testament Writings*, edited by F. F. Segovia and R. S. Sugirtharajah, 455–466. New York: T & T Clark, 2009.

Welborn, L. L. "Inequity in Roman Corinth." In *The First Urban Churches: Roman Corinth*, edited by L. L. Welborn and James R. Harrison, 47–84. Atlanta: SBL, 2016.

Wright, N. T. *The New Testament and the People of God*. Vol. 1. London: SPCK, 1992.

Yamazaki-Ransom, Kazuhiko. *The Roman Empire in Luke's Narrative*. New York: T & T International, 2010.

CHAPTER 7

JOHN'S WRITINGS AND EMPIRE

Views of Empire Studies and Postcolonial Criticism

JIN YOUNG CHOI

INTRODUCTION

THE purpose of this essay is to provide an overview and assessment of scholarship on John's writings and empire and point toward future directions of empire studies and postcolonial criticism in Johannine studies.[1] The topic of Johannine literature and empire can be discussed in terms of Roman imperial presence *in* the Gospel, the Roman Empire as the socio-political context of the texts, and imperialism-colonialism involved in the production of the Gospel, scholarly construction of or engagement with empire in interpretation, and so forth. I distinguish two disparate but overlapping approaches to the topic: empire studies and postcolonial criticism.

Johannine scholarship has followed the discipline's dominant approach to early Christianity in terms of religion, especially in relation to Judaism, but since the 1980s Johannine scholarship has engaged the Roman Empire in John's writing. Some historical critical scholars explore the Roman Empire as a backdrop of Johannine literature, while limiting their analyses to the text, the author, and authorial intention. Whereas these empire scholars focus on objective historical descriptions, critics who employ literary studies and social studies are more interested in the narrative world of the Gospel, which does not necessarily refer to the historical realities of first-century life. They assume that when John showed characters, people living in the shadow of the empire would have understood John's messages.[2] Both groups of scholars are interested in John's theological understanding of Jesus' superiority over the Roman emperor. Such christological interpretations understand John's Gospel as a counter-narrative that resists Roman imperial rule and ideology.

Ideological criticism and cultural studies, which comprise a variety of approaches to biblical interpretation such as liberation hermeneutics and feminist, minority, and queer criticism, developed in the 1980s through 1990s. In the second half of the 1990s, postcolonial criticism also emerged, focusing on unequal relationships of power in geopolitical terrains.[3] The objects of postcolonial criticism are not only the worlds of the author and the text but also the location and ideological assumptions of the interpreter. Although both imperial-critical studies and postcolonial criticism locate John's writings in the Roman imperial context and involve historical research regarding imperial realities, their perspectives on the text, approaches, and foci are different. I begin with empire studies on Johannine literature.

THE EMPIRE STUDIES ON JOHN AND THE EMPIRE

Despite the predominant view of the Gospel of John primarily as a spiritual or theological book produced in the course of the Johannine community's expulsion from the synagogue, some scholars maintain that the Gospel reflects historical realities in which the community responded to Rome's presence. Other empire studies mainly show how John employs counter-imperial rhetoric or develops high christology to resist the empire or disrupt accommodationist interactions with imperial power.

Foregrounding the Political in John's Writings

The Gospel of John has predominantly been viewed as the most spiritual of the canonical Gospels for two reasons. First, John's Gospel lacks the Synoptic accounts suggesting Roman presence such as: John the Baptist's warning to tax-collectors and the Roman soldiers (Luke 3:12–14), Herod's execution of John (Mark 6:16–29), Jesus' proclamation of the kingdom of God (Mark 1:15), his teaching about imperial and temple taxes (Matt 17:24–27; Mark 12:13–17), his critique of kings of the Gentiles (Luke 22:25), the Sanhedrin's accusation against Jesus as a self-claimed king (Luke 23:2), and so on.[4] Second, what seems distinct in John's Gospel is its spiritualizing tendency toward Jesus' teaching and actions. Jesus rarely speaks about the kingdom of God, and then only as a spiritualized or otherworldly realm when mentioned (John 3:3, 5, 12). Jesus' statement, "my kingdom is not from this world" is often cited to argue that John is apolitical (18:36). Accordingly, John's writings have been interpreted around their theological meanings without considering their wider social contexts. When the historical context is in view, investigations are limited to comparing expressions and ideas in John's writings with religious and philosophical thoughts found in the Greco-Roman or Jewish cultures, such as Gnosticism and Qumran.

Another dominant type of interpretation of John's Gospel is based on a synagogue-exclusion theory.[5] J. Louis Martyn's proposal of the "two-level drama" laid the foundation of the theory by presenting the life of Jesus as intertwined with the Johannine community's exclusion from Jewish local synagogues in the late first century. Since then, Johannine studies has reconstructed the historical context of the community based on the *aposynagōgos* passages (9:22; 12:42; 16:2).[6] Raymond Brown's reconstruction of the community includes the presence of crypto-Christians who were afraid to publicly announce their faith due to the fear of expulsion.[7] Here the fear is of the Jews, not the Romans (7:13; 12:42; 19:38; 20:19). While this expulsion hypothesis can explain John's harsh polemic toward the "Jews" in its social context, interpreting the Gospel as the "the product of an intra-Jewish debate" does not account for John's explicit descriptions of the Roman presence in the Gospel.[8]

Others acknowledge that John is political but attribute this to an apologetic purpose. They contend that John's intention is to demonstrate that "neither Jesus nor the church is a political threat to the Empire."[9] For example, Pilate affirms Jesus' innocence because he does not claim political kingship (18:38; 19:4). Stephen D. Moore, however, argues that by interpreting Jesus' royal claim as "politically unthreatening," scholars promote the depoliticizing of Jesus' kingship.[10] Luise Shottroff also critiques the strong western tradition of interpreting John's Gospel as "the text of an apolitical conventicle and/or an otherworldly Christianity" and alternatively interprets the Gospel "within the Jewish tradition of martyrdom as the way to a political liberation of the people."[11] Only recently have scholars directly raised the question of whether John's Gospel is apolitical. For instance, in responding to an adverse political reality, John's ethics are described as "implicit but real."[12]

Responding to Roman Imperial Realities

One of the earliest attempts to reconstruct the realities of life in the Roman Empire as the background of John's writings is found in Richard J. Cassidy's work. He argues that John's claim of Jesus' sovereignty counters that of the Roman emperors as presented in imperial propaganda.[13] Jesus does not negate his kingship but rather asserts that it is antithetical to Roman kingship built on violence. Jesus' repudiation of Pilate's power to release and crucify him not only appears to directly challenge Roman power but also reflects persecution of Christians (19:10–11) as attested to by correspondence between Pliny the Younger, the governor of Pontus-Bithynia, and the Emperor Trajan around 112 C.E. (Pliny, *Epistles* 10:96–97). In this persecutory context, John portrays Jesus as truly accomplishing the saving of the world and by doing so encouraging his audience to disavow other saviors in the imperial cult. Jesus is a model for those Christians who were indicted before Roman governors.[14]

Yet Warren Carter argues that Rome did not wield power against Christians in the late first century and thus persecution was not at the center of the dynamics that "the Gospel's complex interaction with the empire" created.[15] When the final production of

John's Gospel is associated with Ephesus—the capital of the Roman province of Asia, Roman presence in its social, economic, and military forms is not just a historical backdrop. Rather, all human interactions were conditioned by domination and subordination, and such imperial power appeared to reject God's purposes and agents.[16] John responds to and negotiate such ubiquitous imperial power through resistant or subversive rhetoric even when the Gospel does not specifically address the Roman Empire.

Counter-imperial Rhetoric in Johannine Literature

John adopts and redefines the terminology and language used for the first-century Roman emperors, like "Son of God," to claim that such a title belongs to Jesus (1:34, 49; 3:16–18; 5:25; 10:36; 11:4, 27; 19:7; 20:31). In the Gospel's emphasis on the Father-Son relationship, the Father God is distinguished from Rome's *pater patriae* and his Son Jesus is not sent as a military delegate. The abundant life promised in John is in stark contrast with Rome's prosperity that serves only a handful of the imperial-colonial elite.[17] Along with the "Savior of the world" title, which was used to refer to the Roman emperors in the first century, Jesus is called "Lord" by his disciples and Mary and Martha, as well as by the narrator (4:42; 6:23, 68; 9:38; chaps. 11–14).[18]

Kenneth L. Waters contends that such counter-imperial rhetoric is presented not only in the Gospel of John but also in the Johannine Epistles, by comparing Johannine language and themes to Greco-Roman sources, especially philosophical thoughts and behaviors that shaped Roman imperial politics.[19] Assuming that the Johannine Epistles were written during the reign of Emperor Domitian, Waters contends that the "Savior of the world" title directly counters the claim that the emperor and the imperial dynasty are divinely ordained (1 John 4:14; cf. 2:2).[20] Similarly, Lance B. Richey argues that John sees a fundamental opposition between the Johannine Christians and their Roman persecutors and challenges the imperial ideology by posing a choice between God and Caesar.[21]

In contrast, others argue that John's rhetoric is implicit in that it does not publicly challenge the imperial narrative. Carter maintains that since the Gospel of John contests imperial power by means of narrative, the Gospel is a "text of imperial negotiation" that functions as a "hidden transcript"—a little tradition that contests the imperial great tradition.[22] Taking a critical stance toward Jewish communities in provincial Ephesus that have accommodated to societal participation in the empire, John attempts to separate the followers of Jesus from the synagogue. John's "rhetoric of distance" disrupts the dominant accommodationist interactions, as well as the empire, and urges Jesus-believers to a "distinctive way of life as an antisociety or alternative community."[23] John opts an "alienation of consciousness" or a "revolution of consciousness," as demonstrated in the Samaritans' turning from idolatrous worshipping the world orders to the true God.[24] John not only subverts imperial ideology but also opposes both the zealots' violent resistance and other believers' allegiance to the oppressive orders of the world.

Christology as a Response to the Empire

Tom Thatcher also utilizes the concept of "hidden transcript," which is incorporated in John's christology as a covert form of resistance to domination, and dubs its content "countermemory."[25] John's christology is necessarily "negative" because Christ is best represented by who he is *not* or what he is *greater than*. John's Christ is superior to Caesar and his agents, enabling him to slay the three headed dog of Rome: (1) the Jewish authorities "as auxiliaries of the emperor"; (2) Pilate "*both* as a violent agent of imperial power *and* as a pawn in Christ's plan"; and (3) the cross as "a definitive Christological statement" that reverses Rome's power over the bodies of subject people.[26]

Both Carter and Thatcher explicate the way John illustrates the presence of Rome in the Gospel as either "implicit" or "negative," highlighting John's resistance to the Roman Empire through christological claims. John's eschatology, without an apocalyptic scenario, is a by-product or subtheme of the christology in that Rome has already been conquered and judged in the ministry of Jesus and the faith of his disciples.[27] Waters also draws a similar conclusion regarding the Johannine Epistles, which "proclaim a more complete and correct cosmology, a greater Savior and soteriology, a better pedagogy, a truer doctrine, a sounder *koinonia,* and a more nurturing *paterfamilias* . . . ."[28] Regarding the claim of Christ's superiority, a few of empire studies point out that the rhetoric of resistance not only uses Rome's language and logic subversively but also "ironically mimic[s] the system they resist."[29]

Feminist scholars examine John's presentation of Jesus in light of the Roman Empire's gender ideology. Colleen M. Conway argues that John conforms to the hegemonic masculinity of the empire in which manliness is the ability to control passions as shown in portrayals of the emperor as the ideal man.[30] Additionally, John's "high" christology depicts Jesus as possessing superior masculinity based on his relationship with the Father-God. Others argue that while the glorification via crucifixion follows the rhetoric of glory in the construction of Roman masculinity, Jesus' penetrated body also displays his femininity and by doing so, John's rhetoric subverts the normative masculinity of the empire.[31]

"The Jews" and the Empire

While subverting the ideology of the empire through its christological claims, John imitates the imperial logic in treatment of the Other, particularly the "Jews." While there are neutral descriptions of the Jews in the Gospel, its overall characterization of the Jews is negative and even hostile. One way of explaining John's antagonistic depiction of the Jews in the Roman imperial context is that the Johannine community's expulsion from the synagogues made the believers vulnerable. Since they were no longer Jews, they would be pressed to participate in the imperial cult.[32]

However, it has been also argued that Jesus-believers are still a part of the Jewish community in Ephesus, and the "Jews" are viewed as the privileged elite in the synagogue who conform to the ways of the empire. Thatcher is straightforward in arguing that the Jewish authorities function as a "puppet aristocracy that serves as an interface between the procurator and the masses and thereby attempts to maintain the imperial status quo."[33] In general, empire studies claim that the Gospel's negative portrayal of the "Jews" results from either an intra-Jewish polemic or presents a critical view of the Jewish authorities as localized, not as the entire Jewish people.

Yet Adele Reinhartz contends that John's Gospel obscures the distinction between the authorities and the *ioudaioi*.[34] Additionally, the attempt to justify John's hostile comments about the "Jews" as a response to the trauma of expulsion may secure the Gospel from the charge of anti-Judaism, but it fails to see how such inimical representations are deep-seated in the Gospel's narrative, rhetoric, and symbol system. Rather, John's negative portrayals of the Jews has the rhetorical purpose of persuading the audience, who has deserted the synagogue, not to return to Judaism but to strengthen belief in Jesus as the Messiah. Regardless, she asserts that the text has functioned to foster anti-Judaism in the history of interpretation through its "replacement theology."[35]

John's harsh rhetoric against the "Jews" can be understood in light of postcolonial theory since colonized subjects often denounce one another under the oppression of colonizing powers. The Jews were not the oppressors of the hypothetical historical community, but the acrimonious discord between Jesus and the Jews arose inevitably in the midst of the Roman presence.[36] John's inscription of "horizontal violence and verbal polemic against other Jewish figures and groups" discloses the colonial dynamic deriving from the "vertical pressure of Roman power" in a colonial context after 70 C.E.[37]

Violent Rome

A majority of empire studies of John's Gospel focus on the Passion Narrative because of the evident presence of Rome in Jesus' arrest, trial, and execution while Jewish leadership's role is subsidiary. For example, unlike the descriptions in the Synoptic Gospels, the *speira*—a cohort of Roman troops, commonly consisting of six hundred soldiers, under the authority of a tribune occupies the garden in which Jesus is arrested (18:3, 12). Although Pilate is viewed as a weak character who shows sympathy toward the convict and appears to acquit Jesus, the prefect perfectly embodies Rome.[38]

Pilate manifests Rome's violence. First of all, Pilate's reference to Jesus as "King of the Jews" does not display his noncommittal position regarding the charge (18:33, 37, 39), but rather is a deliberate action to "to ridicule their national hopes by means of Jesus."[39] Then, Jesus' claim in 18:36 by no means implies the negation of the political nature of his kingdom but denotes that, unlike the Roman Empire, his kingship is not based upon violence. Moreover, unlike the Gospels of Mark and Matthew where Jesus is lashed by Pilate after his sentencing, in John Pilate, "as chief inquisitor and head torturer," takes Jesus and scourges (*emastigosen*) him in the trial (19:1).[40] John depicts Pilate as having the authority to crucify Jesus (19:10).

Jennifer A. Glancy specifically discusses the inextricable relationship between empire and torture since the latter is indispensable in maintaining Roman imperial order by controlling subjected bodies. Similarly, crucifixion is an instrument of torture that extracts truth from flesh, but the truth manifest in Jesus' flesh resists the empire of torture.[41] In empire-critical interpretations, the violent death of Jesus reverses the normal logic of Roman crucifixion that rehearses "the physical conquest and psychological denigration of subject peoples" by demonstrating that Jesus is in control, not the imperial power.[42] In this way, one empire is subverted by another.[43]

Reactions and Critiques

Empire studies examine the Roman presence in the Gospel of John or the historical reality in which the Johannine community responded either directly or indirectly to the empire. These studies display the diverse ways that John negotiates imperial power. Some scholars contend that while conscious of the Roman Empire, John attempts to show that Christians are not politically threatening. Others argue that John employs counter-imperial rhetoric to resist the empire or disrupt accommodationist interactions with imperial power. Asserting Christ's sovereignty over Caesar is a discursive way of contesting Rome. A few empire critical studies are akin to postcolonial criticism in that they invalidate simple binaries of domination and subjugation. Instead, they argue that John critiques accommodation to the empire, while simultaneously mimicking the imperial rhetoric—a response of the colonized.[44]

Still, a majority of traditional scholarship ignores, or remains suspicious of, empire-critical studies of Johannine literature. Empire scholarship's argument about John's contact with the Roman world requires "hermeneutical and exegetical caution" lest the Roman backdrop as an "ancillary" component be confused with the story itself.[45] Ironically, their disinterested or apolitical readings of John's Gospel, which emphasize Jewish contexts and themes, often lead them to conclude, "Jesus has come to transcend Jewish expectations."[46] As Carter argues, the dominant readings that highlight John's Jewish relations and spiritual aspects not only make the Roman Empire invisible in the text, but also disguise such readers' political nature and agenda.[47] Besides Christian superiority or supersessionism, western traditional scholarship's failure to situate the readers in their present imperial-colonial contexts hinders the recognition of the Roman presence and the colonized in the Gospel of John.[48]

However, empire studies are also susceptible to similar criticism. R. S. Sugirtharajah critiques empire studies, which employ exclusively philological and comparative historical approaches, concealing the role of the United States in imperial expansion as well as the ideological stance of the interpreter.[49] Empire studies often attempt to rescue "the text from its tainted colonial uses" in a confessional manner.[50] By claiming John's writings chiefly as a resistant discourse, they not only overlook the role of the text in legitimizing oppression and violence but also obscure their complicity in discursive levels of imperial-colonial formations.[51] Postcolonial criticism takes different steps forward from such empire studies in terms of the text, interpretation, and the interpreter.

Postcolonial Criticism of John and the Empire

While empire studies limit their focus to John's authorial intention or rhetoric to resist Roman imperial power through the claim of Christ's superiority, postcolonial criticism not only examines John's writings as liberating, colonial, or imperializing texts but also engages with imperial-colonial formations in the interpreter's geopolitical contexts. Employing multiple reading strategies with the postcolonial optic at heart, postcolonial critics construct their own readings that deal with John's constructions of subjectivity, the other, and the space in which colonial contacts take place and boundaries are crossed.

The Postcolonial Optic in Reading John's Gospel

The increase in the number and production of postcolonial critics from both the non-western world and racial/ethnic minorities in the West has been pronounced over the past quarter century and has influenced the discipline, discourse, and methodology of biblical studies. Particularly, women scholars from the so-called Two-Thirds world have played a leading role in postcolonial criticism of Johannine literature, as notably in Musa W. Dube's extensive work.[52] Fernando F. Segovia formulates a model of postcolonial studies with the concept of "postcolonial optic," which involves a critical analysis of the text and its world, interpretation, and the interpreter all at once. The postcolonial optic is a field of vision that emerges in the wake of imperialism and colonialism and requires consciousness of the continuing power of empire.[53]

First, postcolonial criticism approaches the Gospel of John as a cultural text beyond primarily religious concerns. In the social matrix of the imperial world, John envisions a reality-wide clash of empires involving two spatial realms—an "other-world" as the realm of spirit versus a "this-world" as the realm of flesh. Complex power relations are manifest not only in the coexistence and engagement of these two worlds, but also in the creation of a "colony" of the other-world in this-world.[54] In doing so, John's Gospel appears to both resist imperial oppression and imperialize foreign geographical spaces and inhabitants.[55] With an ambivalent stance toward empire, John exhibits a "highly unstable anti-imperial colonial imperialism."[56] Engaging local and cosmic powers, John negotiates empire on a global and cosmic scale. This geopolitical dimension is critical not only at the level of text or textual production, but also at the level of criticism or textual reception.[57]

Second, postcolonial criticism highlights that all interpretations produce their own Gospels as cultural products.[58] As Dube argues, "imperialisms of different times, forms, and strategies have affected and continue to affect this world on a global scale."[59] Thus, it is imperative to investigate complexities in the colonial exchange in both ancient and present geopolitical worlds. In addition to Johannine scholarship's involvement in various geopolitical matrices, how imperial-colonial frameworks operate in academic reception and production of the Gospel is one of the tasks postcolonial criticism undertakes.[60]

Finally, the flesh-and-blood reader behind interpretation is at the core of postcolonial criticism. Textual reception or criticism cannot be discussed apart from the reader's vision of the self, community, and world in a concrete geopolitical context. Segovia calls the rise of critical awareness regarding the problematic of colonization "conscientization" and reads the Gospel of John as a postcolonial text that scrutinizes the geopolitical relationship of power within imperial-colonial formations across history and culture.[61]

Although postcolonial critics define John's writings in different ways, what is common in their interpretations is that the text emerges as a site of struggle for power. Moreover, the readers engage in their own geographical struggles for liberating power through interpretation. Attending to these convoluted dimensions of the text, interpretation, and reader, the following review of recent Johannine studies employing postcolonial criticism focuses on how each interpretation constructs the Gospel text with a postcolonial optic, engaging geographical spaces or geopolitics.

Productive Potential of Subjectivity in the "Death Zone"

Tat-siong Benny Liew views death as the predominant theme of John's Gospel from its very beginning (1:29, 36). He engages the domain of the "death zone" in which Rome's colonized subjects live a "bare life" conditioned by Rome's sovereign right to kill its subjects (cf. 18:31–32; 19:10). Liew's postcolonial optic emerges out of a concern for the vulnerable other, "particularly the displaced or colonized, both past and present."[62] The Jews under Roman colonization were especially vulnerable, as they experienced war with the Romans in 66–72 and 132–135 C.E., as well as the social death of their separation from the synagogue. The Roman ideology of death, however, was activated not only through military threats but also through the ritualized public forms of death, as in Jesus' death on the cross. The flesh of Jesus, straddling between this and other worlds, represents the bare life of subjected people—the "death-bound subject" (cf. 1:14).[63]

However, Liew's reading of death has productive potential. Given the reality of killing or being killed and unable to actually kill the colonizer, one instead opts to kill oneself or another colonized person. Hence, John's Jesus, a colonized Jew living in the shadow of death, deliberately exercises his agency and will to die, rather than simply remaining a victim of violence. Jesus' death is conceived not only as the consequence of an intra-Jewish power struggle but within the framework of Roman colonialism. For Liew, John's colonial stance is not heightened in the negative depiction of some Jews, but in the emphasis on the vertical relationship between the Father and the Son, which reinscribes imperial sovereignty. In this regard, the Gospel is "an ideological product *and* production that comes out of, as well as seeks to act upon, the ideological structure of its time."[64]

Potential of the Contact Zone and Displacement

The entire volume, *John and Postcolonialism*, edited by Musa W. Dube and Jeffrey L. Staley, engages both the geographical spaces created by the text and the spaces of the interpreters, in which power relations operate in imperial-colonial frameworks.[65] The contributors explore how John constructs "space" by depicting Jesus and other characters as traveling or crossing boundaries. Additionally, such movements engender contested relationships between colonizers and the colonized so that the notion of power emerges in readings.

Based on her borderland experience as a bicultural Mexican-American living in the diaspora, Leticia Guardiola-Sáenz engages the particular space of contact zone—the border in her reading of John 7:53–8:11.[66] While the "Accused," commonly called "the woman caught in adultery," is a border crosser because she does not live within the boundaries enforced by the patriarchal system, Jesus also crosses the religious border as a law breaker. His silent and spoken discourses (8:6–7) mark a hybrid moment that invites the audience, particularly the Pharisees as the border patrol, to re-define their own borders. This story reflects the Johannine community's identity as a border people living on the fringes of their religious community. On the other hand, the leaders who expelled the believers from the sacred space of the synagogue are ironically transformed into the ones expelled from the sacred space Jesus created. Guardiola-Sáenz' reading strategy for survival highlights the liberating power of hybridity, as well as the potential of the contact zone, by illustrating the woman as a free border-crosser in search of better ways of life.

Jeffrey L. Staley's personal history and sense of displacement within the United States impacts his reading of the politics of place in the Johannine text and in scholarship. He engages two Johannine studies that address the politics of place: Gary M. Burge's interpretation of John 15 and Tod Swanson's essay, "To Prepare a Place."[67] While Burge's positive presentation of John's christology that displaces the significance of place has colonial connotations, Swanson argues that John's description of a nonterritorial place for unity functions to delegitimize all other religions based in places. Whereas these two studies address colonialist and hegemonic agendas in an affirmative or negative way, Staley alternatively proposes a resistant reading that views John's postcolonial geography not necessarily as imperialistic but as a witness to the liberation by displacing all without privileging any place.

Constructing Identity, Community, and Nation

Other essays in *John and Postcolonialism* take ambivalent viewpoint of John's Gospel. Reinhartz' geographical location is modern Canada, which is colonizing in relation to marginalized groups such as First Nations, as well as colonized in relation to the United States as a powerful center.[68] This ambiguous positionality leads her to consider Johannine Christianity as the margin, as opposed to the center, of Rome. John's Gospel simultaneously accepts and resists Roman hegemony but because of the power differential between the center and the margin, direct forms of resistance to colonization is impossible. Instead, using colonizing language—both spatial and temporal, Johannine christology places the community at the center through the discourses of the Father and Son relationship and Jesus as the only path to salvation for all humankind, while marginalizing other groups such as the Jews and the Samaritans. In short, the Gospel of John as a text of the colonized can function as a colonizing text, making a claim of absolutism, universalism, and exclusivism.

Liew's essay in the same volume examines the "symbolic" construction of the Johannine community, alongside the construction of US national communities.[69] He argues that John's purpose is building a community that demands consent and confession with a rhetoric of unity and love, over against descent and dissent.[70] Additionally, John promotes the ideology of ascent as represented in Jesus' crucifixion as an up-lifting event. This upward mobility is applied to eternal life for the ever-growing community. Yet this community construction is also ambiguous, as John holds to the ideas of kinship and descent by his depiction of Jesus as a child of God who births a community and of divine rebirth that is not by human will. Moreover, as in other groups, fissures are found in the consensus camp of Jesus (e.g., Judas' betrayal). Similarly, while the US national identity is said to be constructed based on consent and unity, not based on its European roots, its cultural rhetoric of consent and mobility is betrayed when this "immigrant nation" has discriminated through slavery, segregation, and exclusion against non-white people based on their descent. Asian Americans are both included and excluded by white America through the "model minority" myth that appears to affirm upward mobility but actually presents the nation's construction of Asian Americans as an "obscure other." Thus, Liew's stance toward "ambiguous admittance" in the building of the community in both John and in the United States remains itself ambiguous.

In contrast to ambivalent views of the nation taken by Reinhartz and Liew, Zipporah G. Glass' precarious status as an Afro-Deutsch by birth and as an African American by adoption leads her to provide a pointed critique of the vision of identity and community in John 15:1–8.[71] When the modern nation-state pursues homogenization through citizenship and assimilation, a postcolonial intervention is needed through strategies of heterogeneity from the periphery. The Johannine community not only functions as a shifting boundary that divides the frontiers of the Roman Empire, but also emerges as a new center in the frontier by assimilating all diverse groups through expounding an imaginative political vision. In such a vision, John constructs the political body using the metaphor of the vine, which is sustained by binaries such as true/false, inclusion/exclusion, and the universal/particular.

Resisting Cultural Imperialism and Christianity of Missionaries

Whereas Reinhartz, Liew, and Glass focus on John's construction of the community and nation, two other studies in *John and Postcolonialism* are concerned with religious others in interpreting John's Gospel. Francisco Lozada, Jr. critiques the cultural imperialism represented by Johannine scholarship, taking the example of E. W. Huffard's essay "Mission and the Servants of God" (1989) as a colonialist reading based on a theological model of servanthood in John 5.[72] The rhetorical device *anagnorisis* ("recognition") demands true knowledge of Jesus both in the text and for the present reader, which legitimizes the hierarchical relation of superiority and inferiority. In this scheme, Christianity is placed at the top, while denigrating people of different faiths, particularly Muslims, as immoral. Lozada provides an ethical critique of cultural imperialism practiced by means of the biblical text in colonial missionary endeavors and attempts an alternative reading of John 5 that "contributes toward restructuring the world free of colonialism."[73]

Mary Huie-Jolly reads the debate between Jesus and the "Jews" in John 5 in the context of colonization of in New Zealand.[74] The Johannine sonship christology, accompanied by Jesus' identification with God, is akin to the universalizing claims of superiority and dominance by later colonialist Christianity. Upon the loss of their land in the late nineteenth and early twentieth centuries, some of the Maori identified themselves as "Jews"; that is, the enemy of Christians to distinguish themselves from the Christianity of the missionaries and over against the absolute claim to the divine sonship.

Both Lozada and Huie-Jolly interpret the Gospel, particularly John 5, as a colonial text, but they do not specifically examine the Roman Empire. Instead, they deal with the topic of Christian mission and colonialism but in different contexts: cultural imperialism that reinscribes the superiority of Christianity over other religions; and Christianity as the religion of European missionaries which came with colonial domination, respectively. Both Lozada and certain Maori resist the Gospel of John and its universalistic christological claim through their alternative interpretations.

Possibility of Religious Contact

While postcolonial critics, as well as empire scholarship, rarely discuss the Johannine Epistles, Sugirtharajah examines colonial features of the letters' discourse and rhetoric, such as their exclusive truth claim, no tolerance of dissent, and branding opposing views as the sons of Satan or "antichrist" (1 John 2:18, 22; 4:3; 2 John 7).[75] The Epistles also employ hermeneutical strategies that insist on the authenticity of the message of an imperial Christ, as well as the authority of the author. The ethical dualism or binary distinction in Johannine Epistles establishes the hierarchical order through the concept of the father-child relationship, which precipitates silencing the other and controlling the community (1 John 2:7–11; 2:28–3:10; 4:1–6).

Sugirtharajah critiques colonial tendencies of western comparative approaches to Johannine literature, which refer to Jewish and Hellenistic traditions while judging other cultures. Built on the possibility of Buddhist influences in the Johannine Epistles, he instead employs a contrapuntal reading that prioritizes "orally transmitted knowledge" and "conceptual similarities," as well as textual juxtapositions.[76] Theological ideas such as a divine indwelling are found in Mahayana Buddhism, which is believed to have influenced Gnosticism in the Mediterranean world as well as the Johannine worldview (1 John 3:14; 4:4, 15–16). Moreover, the Johannine restricted notion of "love one another" can be complemented by the Buddhist concept of *maitri*, loving kindness extended to those who are not normally liked. Sugirtharajah argues that the Johannine exclusive claim of truth can be genuinely affirmed when the same truth is found in other religions' teachings.

Ambivalence is a postcolonial trait of the Epistles, involving both imperial intentions and a praxis-driven Johannine prescription (2 John 4–6; 3 John 4). While the concealed presence of Buddhist concepts disrupts the imperial-colonial framework, especially alleged purity of Christian tradition and sacred texts, the Epistles' emphasis on ethical engagement or religious activism resonates with postcolonialism's aspiration for praxis (1 John 2:29).

Potential for the Constantinian Religions

Moore argues that John's Gospel denounces Rome as violent, but it depicts the tyrannical empire as the "agent" of divine punishment, rather than the "object" of punishment. Judean leadership is not anxious about God's intervention but about Rome's military intercession, which might be caused by the crowd's enthusiastic response to Jesus' signs (John 11:47–52; 12:12–13). It is Caesar who replaces God in playing the divine role of apocalyptic intervention (19:15). While Jesus is illustrated as the one who dies for the nation and Jewish diaspora (11:51–52), this substitutionary death or atonement is to appease Caesar, only through which God can be appeased.[77]

Johannine Christianity's perception of Rome as God's empire unconsciously displays the colonial desire for the subversion of one empire by another empire—an alternative program of colonization—that is, the "annexation of the world." If Rome acts in place of the world as the object of God's excessive love (3:16), the empire is not rejected but is instead ambitiously taken over by Christianity without the use of armed force. No demise of Caesar's reign in the text signifies Rome's continuation and incorporation into Christianity in the future: "Rome will eventually become Christianity and Christianity will eventually become Rome."[78] Moore's reading of this unconscious dynamic stretches his postcolonial optic from John's perception of the Roman Empire into a future formation of empire, that is, Constantinian Christianity.

In the same vein, John's Jesus betokens later Christianity's supersessionism in replacing the Jerusalem Temple with his body (cf. 2:19). While "Jesus' incessant march up and down the Holy Land in the Fourth Gospel is, in effect, a reconquest of the Holy Land," Moore views the Jewish authorities not as associated with empire, but as "the displaced Jews ... [who] continue to wander the earth homeless."[79] Thatcher disagrees with Moore's arguments not only on John's characterization of the Jewish leadership as victimized by the Roman authorities, but also that John's lack of divine vengeance against Rome opens up the potential for Constantinian Christianity. For Thatcher, John does not need such an apocalyptic eschatology because Rome has already been defeated by Christ.[80] Obviously, this concern with John's "intention" in Thatcher's work is distant from Moore's interest in the meaning potential or the effective history of the Gospel. Yet if John's identification of Rome as the manifestation of God's empire prepared for later Constantinian Christianity, what Moore does not see is not only that Jesus was a colonized Jew, but also that the Holy Land Jesus subdues would also function as a symbol of empire through both Constantinian Judaism[81] and Christian Zionism in future political landscapes.

Feminist Intervention into Nationalism and Imperialism-Colonialism

Feminist interpretations in empire studies that discuss John's presentation of Jesus' gender in light of Rome's construction of hegemonic masculinity arise in the modern US context of muscular Christianity. While their gender analysis is limited to Greco-Roman culture and rhetorical tradition, postcolonial feminist criticism intersects gender construction and national- and geopolitics. Employing a postcolonial feminist and intertextual approach, Jean K. Kim reads the Gospel of John as a patriarchal nationalist discourse that silences women while promoting Jesus as a national hero.[82] Whereas Guardiola-Sáenz' "hybridity" contains a liberating potential of border and border people in reading John 7:53–8:11, Kim reads the same text focusing on the woman's body as a site of hybridity which enables a female reader to claim her own subjectivity.[83] In both Roman military and contemporary US military contexts, native women's bodies in contact with foreign men become the site of cultural corruption, as is presumed to be the case with the woman in John's text. While resisting Roman imperial power by way of nationalism, John's Gospel is a postcolonial text guilty of marginalizing the hybrid woman as immoral. Kim proposes a resistant and ethical reading that removes the story from elite cultural production both in the text and in interpretation and restores the subjectivity of voiceless women through historical contextualization and social memory in ongoing postcolonial and decolonial contexts.

Similarly, Dube's postcolonial feminist interpretation of John emphasizes the geographical expansion of empire, which is often accompanied by using not only native women as the first agents of contact, but also the female gender as representing the colonized to "serve the agendas of constructing hierarchical geographical spaces, races, and cultures."[84]

Imperializing and Decolonial Reading

Dube's postcolonial analysis of John's Gospel arises from the colonial process of the West which takes control of far-off lands in the Two-Thirds World. While imperial expansion is facilitated by the authorization of travel, imperial traveling agents use cultural texts such as the Bible not only to subjugate geographical spaces but also to colonize the minds of native inhabitants. When a foreign power violates the other's territorial and cultural boundaries, the colonized adopts the imperial ideology of expansion, while struggling for their own liberation.[85]

For Dube, John 4 is an imperializing text. Local conflicts between national Jewish groups or within the Johannine community itself demonstrates both the impact of colonialism and the response of the colonized. After losing power in the national competition with the Pharisees (4:9, 20–23), Jesus is manifested as an authoritative traveler superseding other local and historical figure, and then declared as the "Savior of the world" (vv. 38, 42). If the "world" implies foreign geographical spaces across which Jesus and his disciples can traverse, the title "Savior" signifies an imperial ideology of his mission as a saving action for the subjugated. On the other hand, the Samaritans are described as the ripe fields ready to be harvested. As Jesus' encounter with the Samaritan woman exhibits the ideology of hierarchy in racial, gender, and geographical terms, John's alternative vision requires a "rhetoric of concealment" that obscures its own imperialist agendas as victims of imperial expansion.[86]

Dube's postcolonial reading moves from an imperializing to a decolonizing reading. By "decolonizing," she means "the conscious adoption of strategies for resisting imperial domination, as well as the search for alternative ways of liberating interdependence between nations, races, genders, economies, and cultures."[87] As a decolonizing strategy, Dube writes a new narrative of the Samaritan woman using decolonizing texts from Botswana and apartheid South Africa, like *The Victims*, as well as women's interpretations of scripture in African Independent Churches.[88] The rewriting of the story exposes domination and decolonizes hierarchical gender, race and geography while asserting the Two-Thirds World women's dignity and rights to independence and equality.

Assessment of Postcolonial Criticism

Despite the diversity of topics such as constructions of self or subjectivity, community, the other, nation, and empire, one can observe that most postcolonial interpretations emerge from considering the geopolitical relations of domination and subordination. While these studies presuppose the historical construction of the Johannine community as the colonized, they also focus on the colonial or imperializing rhetoric in the text to describe the Father-Son relationship or universal sonship christology. Such rhetoric creates the hierarchical order and marginalization of others, especially through the travel or mission of Jesus and his followers across territorial boundaries. In sum, those studies understand Johannine literature as a cultural product and production, while constructing John's writings as a liberating, colonial, colonizing, or imperializing text. Unlike empire scholarship, however, postcolonial studies rarely engage the material matrix of the text or the material realities of the empire.[89]

As John's writings are shaped by and shape imperial-colonial realities, postcolonial critics engage relations of power at work therein and also in their own geographical spaces, underscoring various contact zones, borders, and boundaries. Ideas developed in postcolonial theory such as traveling, mimicry, hybridity, and ambivalence are employed in constructing those spaces, though most of the studies do not rely overly on postcolonial theory or theorization but instead are concerned with various imperial-colonial formations in current national and international contexts. From the position of the marginalized, their reading strategies vary from resistant, to ambivalent, and on to decolonial. Each reading employs a postcolonial optic with political and ethical ramifications rather than a single interpretive method, but some authors intentionally adopt oppositional reading strategies such as contrapuntal and decolonial to resist the colonial discourse of dominant scholarship.

Future Directions of Empire Studies and Postcolonialism in Johannine Studies

Based on the preceding overview of empire studies and postcolonial criticism in Johannine studies, I envision the following advancements in terms of approaches and topics. First, most empire studies and postcolonial criticism highlight Johannine literature's rhetoric as cultural product, rather than delving into the material conditions under imperial domination. This is partly because John's writings, full of religious or symbolic language, do not directly refer to historical realities. Especially, empire studies use comparative approaches between John's writings and Greco-Roman or Jewish backgrounds. The historical-comparative mode of research limits its source to elite literature, great tradition, and established religious institutions, instead of considering ordinary people's socio-economic conditions, their agency in the social systems, or their religious practices.

Although John's text does not literally reflect historical realities, one can envision a scenario of the social reality of Johannine Christianity in the empire, just as Carter situates the Johannine community in Ephesus as an important imperial center. Sugirtharajah's postulation of Johannine Christianity, which had contact with Buddhism in an eastern Mediterranean region, is another example. Still, beyond exploring Johannine Christians' life situations in conceptual or discursive terms, insights from people's history studies, materialist criticism, or postcolonial archeology would facilitate understanding the material matrix of the text and its cultural production, as well as the socio-economic conditions of Johannine Christianity and its surroundings.

Second, while empire studies' view of John's Gospel as a resistant discourse can reinscribe Christian superiority, postcolonial criticism addresses John's ambiguous stance toward the Roman Empire, at once complicit in imperial-colonial formations and resistant to its specific manifestations. While such an ambivalent position is supported by postcolonial theory, postcolonial studies of Johannine literature will move beyond "the binary mode of production—colonial literary productions supplying the raw material and the West providing the vocabulary and criteria in the form of a neat theory" to bring inspiration from the present struggles of people, as well as the postcolonial literature that emerged from or influenced anti-colonial struggles in the global South.[90]

If postcolonialism has been "accused of its failure as a history" because of its totalizing tendency obscuring the multiplicity of colonial histories, "vernacular hermeneutics" can be a way of resisting such universalizing discourse both in the text and in western Johannine scholarship by using indigenous resources or addresses local conditions of oppression.[91] For instance, reading John's Gospel (2:1–11; 3:5; 4:7–15; 5:1–9; 9:1–14), Jayachitra Lalitha engages the issue of water in the context of postcolonial India in which economic neocolonialism has commodified water so that the poor are deprived of the basic right of free access to water.[92] In this way, she disrupts the interpretation that entirely spiritualizes the water texts in John, instead reading for indigenous people's power struggle to access to wholeness of life.

Last, intersectional analyses of imperial-postcolonial formations in Johannine literature will bring fruitful outcomes to both empire studies and postcolonial criticism. I would like to suggest particular areas that intersects with empire-critical and postcolonial studies, such as feminist, race/ethnicity, disability, and queer studies. As Dube's postcolonial feminist work shows, an exploration of the category of gender/sexuality in John's writings can be extended to complex relations between genders and among empire, nation, and the colonized across history and culture.[93]

While feminist criticism of imperial-colonial frameworks has made significant contributions to Johannine scholarship and beyond, postcolonial criticism in Johannine studies has not seriously engaged race/ethnicity studies despite the Gospel's predominant and distinctive use of racial identities or ethnic markers such as the "Greeks," "Samaritans," and "Galileans," as well as the "Jews." Johannine Christianity's relationship with Judaism is discussed only in terms of religion. Two recent publications employ a "ethnocritical" method and an "*ethnos*-conscious approach," respectively, to interpret race/ethnicity in John's Gospel.[94] While they are conscious of racialization in the US context, they, similar to feminist studies engaging imperial construction of gender, focus on Greco-Roman antiquity in which race was constructed and John's Gospel adopted racializing rhetoric. As a part of Liew's work discusses the colonized "Jews" in the context of Asian Americans' racialization, postcolonial criticism can provide significant insights into topics related to race/ethnicity and empire in John's writings in the intersectional manner.

Imperialism-colonialism exploits strategies of "sexual and racial coding of colonized bodies" as well as the "metaphorical use of sexual and gender tropes in the discourse of nation."[95] With this respect, queer postcolonial analysis is an interesting new area of research not only because John's writings exhibit a strong dualistic understanding of the world that creates the division between the self and the other but also because postcolonialism's preoccupation with binary oppositions leads to the predictable solution of ambivalence or hybridity at best. More than discussing the illustration of the "beloved disciple" leaning on Jesus' bosom (13:23), queer criticism can deal with issues such as how the Roman Empire or John's text regulates gender performance based on the heteronormative ruling of empire.

Though Carter's study on disabled bodies in John 5 does not employ a queer analysis, it has relevant implications because normalcy, health, and civilization mark empire, while the subjugated signify deviance, disability, and deficiency. Carter, as usual, highlights disabled bodies in John's Gospel as sites of the negotiation and contest of imperial power (ex. Jesus' healings as repairing imperial damage), but in this essay he uses postcolonial literature such as the works of Frantz Fanon and Salmon Rushdie to explicate how disabled and diseased human bodies embody the destructive and destructing imperial (dis)order in psychosomatic ways.[96] Being conscious of the risk of reinforcing stereotypes about disabilities through constructions and metaphorization, Carter also pursues the literal "somatic disabling that occurs in collisions between colonizers and colonized through violence, disease, and nutritional limitations."[97]

Disabled bodies in the colonial framework are disposable bodies, which necessarily entail the exercise of sovereignty and thus, violence. As empire-critical and postcolonial interpreters have discussed the violence of the text based on John's claims of Christ's sovereignty, as well as Rome's violence, considering violence, war, and terror seems to be an area demanding of critical analysis.[98] The US military invasion of foreign territories and resultant armed resistance to empire require postcolonial intervention when reading John's writings in the current neocolonial and postcolonial contexts.

I read John's claim of sovereignty, as well as the ascent-descent language, in terms of supremacy as my own life journey has been affected by legacies of Japanese colonialism and the Korean War, ongoing neo-colonial relations between Korea and the United States, and the transnationalism that emerges living as a diaspora in a metropolitan imperial center. For example, John 11 depicts an event between his coming-down and rising-up—one of the most crucial "signs" in his ministry: the raising up of Lazarus. Jesus' intense affective responses are not just because of people's unbelief but are related to the colonial reality in which his work of "raising up" lives would bring about Rome's destructive retaliation (11:50). Critiquing the Christian supremacist ideology embedded in dominant theological and spiritual interpretation of "raising-up" or "lifting-up," I read Jesus' "r[a]ising-up" movement to overcome power of death, which is symbolized by imperial military, the stones threatening or blocking people's lives (11:8, 38–39), and a death cloth attached to skin (cf. 20:5–7). Thus, reading can be an affective intervention into various forms of supremacy including military supremacy and white supremacy. As long as colonial expansionist attempts persist in economic, cultural, and religious domains, postcolonialism has a critical role to play.[99] As Jesus was deeply disturbed by the signs and powers of Death and cried out, "Unbind him, and let him go" (11:44), a postcolonial reading of John observes where unbounded bodies and movements continue to recede—and to rise.

NOTES

1. By "John's writings" and "Johannine literature," which I use interchangeably, I mean the Fourth Gospel and the Johannine Epistles. John as the final author of the Fourth Gospel is also used to refer to the Gospel. Since there are few studies dealing with the Johannine Epistles and empire, this essay primarily focuses on the Gospel of John.
2. Tom Thatcher, *Greater than Caesar: Christology and Empire in the Fourth Gospel* (Minneapolis, MN: Fortress Press, 2008), xiii.
3. Fernando F. Segovia, "The Counterempire of God: Postcolonialism and John," *Princeton Seminary Bulletin* 27, no. 2 (2006): 82–99.
4. Tom Thatcher, "'I Have Conquered the World': The Death of Jesus and the End of Empire in the Gospel of John," in *Empire in the New Testament*, ed. Stanley E. Porter and Cynthia Long Westfall (Eugene, OR: Pickwick, 2011), 141.
5. Warren Carter, *John and Empire: Initial Explorations* (New York: T&T Clark, 2008), 3.
6. J. Louis Martyn, *History and Theology in the Fourth Gospel*, 2nd ed. (Nashville: Abingdon, 1979).
7. Raymond Brown, *Community of the Beloved Disciple: The Life, Love, and Hates of an Individual Church in New Testament Times* (New York: Paulist Press, 1979).
8. It is striking to see that even when an interpretation deals with the apocalyptic in John's Gospel it barely engages the Roman imperial context. Catrin H. Williams and Christopher Rowland, eds. *John's Gospel and Intimations of Apocalyptic* (New York: T&T Clark, 2013).
9. C. H. Dodd, *Historical Tradition in the Fourth Gospel* (Cambridge: Cambridge University Press, 1963), 113–115. See David Rensberger, "The Politics of John: The Trial of Jesus in the Fourth Gospel," *Journal of Biblical Literature* 103, no. 3 (1984): 396–397.
10. Stephen D. Moore, *Empire and Apocalypse: Postcolonialism and the New Testament* (Sheffield: Sheffield Phoenix, 2006), 50–51.
11. Luise Shottroff, "Important Aspects of the Gospel for the Future," in *What Is John: Readers and Readings of the Fourth Gospel*, ed. Fernando F. Segovia (Atlanta: Scholars Press, 1996), 208.
12. Harold Attridge, Warren Carter, and Jan Van Der Watt, "Quaestiones Disputatae: Are John's Ethics Apolitical?" *New Testament Studies* 62 (2016): 484–497.
13. Richard J. Cassidy, *John's Gospel in New Perspective: Christology and the Realities of Roman Power* (Maryknoll, NY: Orbis, 1992).
14. Richard J. Cassidy, *Christians and Roman Rule in the New Testament: New Perspectives* (New York: Crossroad, 2001), 37–50.
15. In addition to persecution under the Emperor Trajan (98–117 C.E.), Carter mentions two other prevalent schemes of persecution: (1) persecution after the loss of the protection of so-called Jewish *religio licita* status when Christians were separated from the synagogue; and (2) persecution by the Emperor Domitian (81–96 C.E.). Carter, *John and Empire*, 69–72. Other scholars also argue that dominant scenarios of persecution under the reigns of Emperors Nero, Domitian, and Trajan are not historically convincing because of the lack

of external evidence of "official persecution of Christians *as Christians*." Greg Carey, "Early Christianity and the Roman Empire," in *The State of New Testament Studies: A Survey of Recent Research*, ed. Scot McKnight and Nijay K. Gupta (Grand Rapids, MI: Bakers Academics, 2019), 22.

16. Carter, *John and Empire*, 488–493.
17. Attridge, Carter, and Watt, "Quaestiones disputatae," 486.
18. Cassidy, *Christians and Roman Rule*, 43–46; Craig R. Koester, "'The Savior of the World' (John 4:42)," *Journal of Biblical Literature* 109, no. 4 (1990): 665–680.
19. Kenneth L. Waters, "Empire and the Johannine Epistles," *Review & Expositor* 114, no. 4 (2017): 542–557.
20. Waters examines ten preeminent themes in the Johannine Epistles, including the *logos* which has "superior authority to guide the lives of the hearers" as opposed to the ideas found in writings of Seneca the Younger, Philo, and Cicero. He extensively refers to philosophical and religious thoughts such as Stoicism, proto-Gnosticism, and Docetism which are inseparable from Roman ideology, as well as political thinkers and documents. Waters, "Empire and the Johannine Epistles," 544.
21. Lance Byron Richey, *Roman Imperial Ideology and the Gospel of John* (Washington, DC: Catholic Biblical Association of America, 2007).
22. Empire-critical scholars often use James C. Scott's concept of "hidden transcripts" to describe the concealed or disguised forms of resistance or "nonviolent acts of protest" of early Christians. This hidden script "affirms the peasant's dignity as one who refuses to be completely subjected. It attests a much larger web of protest against and dissents from the elite's societal order and version of reality." Warren Carter, *Matthew and Roman Empire: Initial Explorations* (Harrisburg, PA: Trinity Press International, 2001), 12.
23. Carter, *John and Empire*, 20, 82.
24. Koester, "Savior of the World," 680; Rensberger, "Politics of John," 411.
25. See chapter 3 of Thatcher, *Greater than Caesar*.
26. Thatcher, *Greater than Caesar*, 17.
27. Jan Van Der Watt contends that the political agenda of John is for the Johannine believers to negotiate actively the incarnation of God's superior and victorious eschatological kingdom in the world in opposition to the other political powers. Attridge, Carter, and Watt, "Quaestiones Disputatae," 493–497.
28. Waters, "Empire and the Johannine Epistles," 557.
29. Attridge, Carter, and Watt, "Quaestiones Disputatae," 488. Wright argues that irony presented in Gospel's arrest, trial, and crucifixion scenes not only critiques elements of imperial power and authority but also mimics Roman imperial ideologies by asserting Jesus' kingship, power, and worldwide empire. Arthur Wright, Jr., *The Governor and the King: Irony, Hidden Transcripts, and Negotiating Empire in the Fourth Gospel* (Eugene, OR: Pickwick Publications, 2019).
30. Colleen M. Conway, *Behold the Man: Jesus and Greco-Roman Masculinity* (New York: Oxford University Press, 2008), 143–158.
31. Jason Ripley, "'Behold the Man'? Subverting Imperial Masculinity in the Gospel of John," *Journal of the Bible and Its Reception* 2, no. 2 (2015): 219–239; Alicia D. Myers, "Gender, Rhetoric and Recognition: Characterizing Jesus and (Re)defining Masculinity in the Gospel of John," *Journal for the Study of the New Testament* 38, no. 2 (2015): 191–218.
32. Richey, *Roman Imperial Ideology*, 52–57.
33. Thatcher, *Greater than Caesar*, 52.

34. Adele Reinhartz, "The Jews of the Fourth Gospel," in *The Oxford Handbook of Johannine Studies*, ed. Judith M. Lieu and Martinus C. de Boer (Oxford: Oxford University Press, 2018), 128.
35. Reinhartz, "Jews of the Fourth Gospel," 131.
36. Colleen M. Conway, "There and Back Again: Johannine History on the Other Side of Literary Criticism," in *Anatomies of Narrative Criticism: The Past, Present, and Futures of the Fourth Gospel as Literature*, ed. Tom Thatcher and Stephen D. Moore (Atlanta: Society of Biblical Literature, 2008), 89.
37. Attridge, Carter, and Watt, "Quaestiones Disputatae," 490.
38. Rensberger, "Politics of John," 401, 406; Moore, *Empire and Apocalypse*, 53, 58.
39. Rensberger, "Politics of John," 402.
40. The NRSV's translation is ambiguous: "Pilate took Jesus and had him flogged." Raymond Brown's chiastic structure comprising seven episodes of the Roman trial narrative (18:28–19:8) supports Moore's argument on Pilate as "the direct agent of the scourging." In the middle of the structure (19:1–3), imperial Rome manifests as the "inquisitor-turning-to torturer" in the person of Pontius Pilate. Moore, *Empire and Apocalypse*, 56–59.
41. Jennifer A. Glancy, "Torture: Flesh, Truth, and the Fourth Gospel," *Biblical Interpretation* 13, no. 2 (2005): 107–136.
42. Thatcher, "I Have Conquered the World," 150–151; Glancy, "Torture," 128.
43. Moore, *Empire and Apocalypse*, 69.
44. Carter attempts to utilize postcolonial studies, particularly the concept of contrapuntal as a reading strategy, in his interpretation, but he does not fully apply such contrapuntal reading to the entire work. *John and Empire*, 77–81.
45. Skinner critiques representative empire studies because their interpretations are "interested" (Carter), "reductionist" (Thatcher), or "balanced" (Richey; because of his inclusion of the Jewish elements). Christopher W. Skinner, "John's Gospel and the Roman Imperial Context," in *Jesus Is Lord, Caesar Is Not: Evaluating Empire in New Testament Studies*, ed. Scot McKnight, Joseph B. Modica, and Andy Crouch (Downers Grove, IL: IVP Academic, 2013), 116–129. A similar criticism is given by Moloney: "But I am not convinced that this world [Roman Empire] has generated the driving hermeneutical principles that produced the final form of the Fourth Gospel." Francis J. Moloney, "Recent Johannine Studies: Part Two: Monographs," *Expository Times* 123, no. 9 (2012): 417–428.
46. Skinner, "John's Gospel," 128; Francis J. Moloney, "God, Eschatology, and 'This World': Ethics in the Gospel of John," in *Johannine Ethics: The Moral World of the Gospel and Epistles of John*, ed. Christopher W. Skinner and Sherri Brown (Minneapolis, MN: Fortress Press, 2017), 207.
47. Carter, *John and Empire*, 3.
48. I am struck by Skinner's paralleling "the specter of Roman Empire cast[ing] its shadow over daily life in first-century Palestine in a way that cannot and should not be ignored" with "the threat of future terrorism and the memory of 9/11 together [that] lie under the surface of everyday life in the United States." Skinner, "John's Gospel," 117.
49. R. S. Sugirtharajah, "Postcolonial Biblical Criticism," in *Voices from the Margin: Interpreting the Bible in the Third World*, 25th anniversary ed., ed. R. S. Sugirtharajah (Maryknoll, NY: Obis Books, 2016), 133–135. Also, see Stephen D. Moore, "Paul After Empire," in *The Colonized Apostle: Paul and Postcolonial Studies*, ed. Christopher D. Stanley (Minneapolis, MN: Fortress Press, 2011), 9–23.

50. Thatcher states, "As a fact of history, there can little doubt that the Gospel of John has been read in support of imperial politics—Roman, European, and more recently, American. Yet I do not believe that John intended to leave the light on for such readings ... and for purposes of the present study I want to focus on John's intentions and his historical context. I confess that this desire reflects my own interests and social location ... [as] an agent of a contemporary faith community." Thatcher, *Greater than Caesar*, 15.

51. A few empire-critical scholars present self-reflective positions in interpreting John and empire in the context of the US empire. For example, the motivation of Glancy's reading of torture in John's Gospel derives from "the horror of a U.S. policy of distilling truth from foreign bodies." Glancy, "Torture," 136. Carey states, "We biblical scholars, who frequently cloak our passions in the language of academic objectivity, often reveal our commitments in assessing how early Christians negotiated their relationship to Rome. Those who are critical of American military, cultural, and economic adventurism ... rely on Scripture as an essential resource for articulating our critiques." Carey, "Early Christianity," 10.

52. Segovia, "Counterempire of God," 82–83. See Musa W. Dube's earliest publications, "Reading for Decolonization (John 4:1–42)," *Semeia* 75 (1996): 37–59; "Savior of the World but Not of This World: A Post-Colonial Reading of Spatial Construction in John," in *The Postcolonial Bible*, ed. R. S. Sugirtharajah (Sheffield: Sheffield Academic Press, 1998), 118–135.

53. Fernando F. Segovia, "Biblical Criticism and Postcolonial Studies: Toward a Postcolonial Optic," in *Postcolonial Bible*, ed. Sugirtharajah, 51.

54. Segovia, "The Gospel of John," in *A Postcolonial Commentary on the New Testament Writings*, ed. Fernando F. Segovia and R. S. Sugirtharajah (New York: T&T Clark, 2007), 156–193.

55. Dube, "Reading for Decolonization," 41.

56. Segovia, "Gospel of John," 192.

57. Fernando F. Segovia, "Johannine Studies and the Geopolitical: Reflections upon Absence and Irruption," in *What We Have Heard from the Beginning: The Past, Present, and Future of Johannine Studies*, ed. Tom Thatcher (Waco, TX: Baylor University Press, 2007), 282–286.

58. Colleen M. Conway, "The Production of the Johannine Community: A New Historicist Perspective," *Journal of Biblical Literature* 121, no. 3 (2002): 479–495. Employing new historicism and cultural materialism, Conway discusses productions of the Gospel by readings that participate in constructing reality for particular groups.

59. Dube, "Reading for Decolonization," 40.

60. Segovia, "Johannine Studies," 284.

61. Segovia, "Gospel of John," 158.

62. Tat-siong Benny Liew, "The Word of Bare Life: Workings of Death and Dream in the Fourth Gospel," in *Anatomies of Narrative Criticism*, ed. Thatcher and Moore, 168–169.

63. Liew, "Word of Bare Life," 175, 182.

64. Liew, "Word of Bare Life," 176. Italics original.

65. Musa W. Dube and Jeffrey L. Staley, ed., *John and Postcolonialism: Travel, Space and Power* (New York: Sheffield Academic Press, 2002). Segovia provides a comprehensive and critical review of the volume in "Johannine Studies." For a postcolonial geographical reading of Jesus' death occasioned by his production of space—a third space that subverts Roman imperial power and empowers the marginalized, see Peter C. Ajer, *The Death of Jesus and Politics of Place in the Gospel of John* (Eugene, OR: Pickwick, 2016).

66. Leticia A. Guardiola-Sáenz, "Border-crossing and its Redemptive Power in John 7:53–8:11: A Cultural Reading of Jesus and the *Accused*," in *John and Postcolonialism*, ed. Dube and Staley, 129–152.
67. Jeffrey L. Staley, "'Dis Place, Man': A Postcolonial Critique of the Vine (the Mountain and the Temple) in the Gospel of John," in *John and Postcolonialism*, ed. Dube and Staley, 32–50. Tod D. Swanson's "To Prepare a Place: Johannine Christianity and the Collapse of Ethnic Territory" is also included as the first chapter in the volume (11–31). Gary M. Burge, "Territorial Religion, Johannine Christology, and the Vine of John 15," in *Jesus of Nazareth, Lord and Christ: Essays on the Historical Jesus and New Testament Christology*, ed. Joel B. Green and Max Turner (Grand Rapids, MN: Eerdmans, 1994), 384–396.
68. Adelle Reinhartz, "The Colonizer as Colonized: Intertextual Dialogue Between John's Gospel and Canadian Identity," in *John and Postcolonialism*, ed. Dube and Staley, 170–192.
69. Tat-siong Benny Liew, "Ambiguous Admittance: Consent and Descent in John's Community of 'Upward' Mobility," in *John and Postcolonialism*, ed. Dube and Staley, 193–224. Reading the Farewell Discourse in her social location of postcolonial Singapore, Tan similarly argues that the Johannine community is an ideological construct, but she highlights that the fluid characterization of the community between the center and margins is a strategy for resistance to imperial-colonial domination. Yak-hwee Tan, *Re-presenting the Johannine Community: A Postcolonial Perspective* (New York: Peter Lang, 2008).
70. John's Christ-centered community is built upon confession and consent by conscious choice, instead of heredity or ancestry (ex. 2:4; 7:1–5; 9:18–23; 19:26; 20:17–18). In other words, the old paradigm of biological descent is replaced with the new paradigm of spiritual consent in the community construction. Liew, "Ambiguous Admittance," 204.
71. Zipporah G. Glass, "Building toward 'Nation-ness' in the Vine: A Postcolonial Critique of John 15:1–8," in *John and Postcolonialism*, ed. Dube and Staley, 153–169.
72. Francisco Lozada, Jr., "Contesting an Interpretation of John 5: Moving Beyond Colonial Evangelism," in *John and Postcolonialism*, ed. Dube and Staley, 76–93. Also, see Francisco Lozada, Jr., *A Literary Reading of John 5: Text as Construction* (New York: Peter Lang, 2000).
73. Lozada, "Contesting an Interpretation of John 5," 78.
74. Mary Huie-Jolly, "Maori 'Jews' and a Resistant Reading of John 5:10–47," in *John and Postcolonialism*, ed. Dube and Staley, 94–110.
75. Sugirtharajah assumes that the Epistles were possibly written by the same person, probably John the elder known as "the beloved disciple" for the community from a city in Asia Minor. R. S. Sugirtharajah, "The First, Second, and Third Letters of John," in *Postcolonial Commentary*, ed. Segovia and Sugirtharajah, 413–415.
76. Sugirtharajah, "First, Second, and Third Letters of John," 418.
77. Moore, *Empire and Apocalypse*, 63–68.
78. Moore, *Empire and Apocalypse*, 73–74.
79. Moore, *Empire and Apocalypse*, 70.
80. Thatcher, *Greater than Caesar*, 15.
81. Jewish liberation theologian, Marc H. Ellis, uses the term Constantinian Judaism to refer to mainstream Jewish life that "has evolved into a new form of Judaism, one that seeks and maintains empire," drawing a close comparison between such Constantinian Judaism and the Constantinian Christianity first promulgated in the fourth century. He asserts, "to dwell in the Holocaust without recognizing the recent history of the Jewish people in Israel and Palestine is to romanticize Jewish suffering as if Jews were only and everywhere

victims." Marc H. Ellis, *Toward a Jewish Theology of Liberation: The Challenge of the 21st Century*, 3rd ed. (Waco, TX: Baylor University Press, 2004), 206, 211.

82. Jean K. Kim, *Woman and Nation: An Intercontextual Reading of the Gospel of John from a Postcolonial Feminist Perspective* (Boston; Leiden: Brill, 2004). Also, see her essay, "A Korean Feminist Reading of John 4:1–42," *Semeia* 78 (1997): 109–119.

83. Jean K. Kim, "Adultery or Hybridity? Reading John 7:53–8:11 from a Postcolonial Context," in *John and Postcolonialism*, ed. Dube and Staley, 111–128.

84. An earlier version of Dube's "Reading for Decolonization (John 4:1–42)" in *John and Postcolonialism* (51–75) appears in *Semeia* 74 (1996), which I cite from now on.

85. Dube, "Savior of the World," 130; "Reading for Decolonization," 51.

86. Dube, "Reading for Decolonization," 47–50.

87. Dube, "Reading for Decolonization," 38.

88. Mositi Torontle, *The Victims* (Gaborone: Botsalo, 1993). For the use of a similar strategy, see Tat-siong Benny Liew, "Margins and (Cutting-) Edges: On the (IL)Legitimacy and Intersections of Race, Ethnicity, and (Post)Colonialism," in *Postcolonial Biblical Criticism: Interdisciplinary Intersections*, ed. Stephen D. Moore and Fernando F. Segovia (New York: T&T Clark International, 2007), 149. Liew engages Korean American author, Theresa Hak Kyung Cha, who interweaves the story of the Samaritan woman with the stories of the female Kore, the nation Korea, in her *Dictee* (Berkeley: University of California Press, 2001). Liew reads her text as multiracial/ethnic and postcolonial text in which Cha attempts at "scriptural in(ter)ventions." Cha's biblical in(ter)ventions become explicit when she inscribes her own words that are made flesh with multiple beginnings and words, instead of the Word made flesh in the beginning (John 1:1, 14).

89. Segovia, "Johannine Studies," 288.

90. Sugirtharajah, "Postcolonial Biblical Criticism," 141–142.

91. Sara Ahmed, *Strange Encounters: Embodied Others in Post-Coloniality* (London: Routledge, 2013), 10. R. S. Sugirtharajah, *Vernacular Hermeneutics* (Sheffield: Sheffield Academic Press, 1999), 11–12.

92. Jayachitra Lalitha, "A Postcolonial Exploration of Water in the Fourth Gospel," *Bangalore Theological Forum* 37, no. 2 (2005): 114–129.

93. Especially, the Johannine Epistles have not been approached in such an intersectional way, even though the Father-Son language in the Gospel is reinscribed in the relationship between the "Elder" and "little children."

94. Rodolfo Galvan Estrada III, *A Pneumatology of Race in the Gospel of John: An Ethnocritical Study* (Eugene, OR: Wipf and Stock Publisher, 2019); Andrew Benko, *Race in John's Gospel: Toward an Ethnos-Conscious Approach* (Minneapolis, MN: Fortress Academic, 2019).

95. Steed Vernyl Davidson, "Writing/Reading the Bible in Postcolonial Perspective," *Brill Research Perspectives in Biblical Interpretation* 2, no. 3 (2017): 72.

96. Warren Carter, "'The Blind, Lame, and Paralyzed' (John 5:3): John's Gospel, Disability Studies, and Postcolonial Perspectives," in *Disability Studies and Biblical Literature*, ed. Candida R. Moss and Jeremy Schipper (New York: Palgrave Macmillan, 2011), 134. Frantz Fanon, *The Wretched of the Earth*, trans. Constance Farrington (New York: Grove, 1968); Salman Rushdie, *Midnight's Children* (New York: Penguin Books, 1991).

97. Carter, "Blind, Lame, and Paralyzed," 146.

98. Davidson, "Writing/Reading the Bible," 75–79. For example, the concept of bare life in the death zone under Rome's sovereignty in Liew's interpretation can be viewed in light of

necropolitics. Mbembe states, "To exercise sovereignty is to exercise control over mortality and to define life as the deployment of manifestations of power." Achille Mbembe, "Necropolitics," *Public Culture* 15, no. 1 (2003): 12.

99. Sugirtharajah, "Postcolonial Biblical Criticism," 142.

Bibliography

Ahmed, Sara. *Strange Encounters: Embodied Others in Post-Coloniality*. London: Routledge, 2013.

Ajer, Peter C. *The Death of Jesus and Politics of Place in the Gospel of John*. Eugene, OR: Pickwick, 2016.

Attridge, Harold, Warren Carter, and Jan Van Der Watt. "Quaestiones Disputatae: Are John's Ethics Apolitical?" *New Testament Studies* 62 (2016): 484–497.

Benko, Andrew. *Race in John's Gospel: Toward an Ethnos-Conscious Approach*. Minneapolis, MN: Fortress Academic, 2019.

Brown, Raymond. *Community of the Beloved Disciple: The Life, Love, and Hates of an Individual Church in New Testament Times*. New York: Paulist Press, 1979.

Burge, Gary M. "Territorial Religion, Johannine Christology, and the Vine of John 15." In *Jesus of Nazareth, Lord and Christ: Essays on the Historical Jesus and New Testament Christology*, edited by Joel B. Green and Max Turner, 384–396. Grand Rapids, MN: Eerdmans, 1994.

Carey, Greg. "Early Christianity and the Roman Empire." In *The State of New Testament Studies: A Survey of Recent Research*, edited by Scot McKnight and Nijay K. Gupta, 9–34. Grand Rapids, MI: Bakers Academics, 2019.

Carter, Warren. *Matthew and Roman Empire: Initial Explorations*. Harrisburg, PA: Trinity Press International, 2001.

Carter, Warren. *John and Empire: Initial Explorations*. New York: T&T Clark, 2008.

Carter, Warren. "'The Blind, Lame, and Paralyzed' (John 5:3): John's Gospel, Disability Studies, and Postcolonial Perspectives." In *Disability Studies and Biblical Literature*, edited by Candida. R. Moss and Jeremy Schipper, 129–150. New York: Palgrave Macmillan, 2011.

Cassidy, Richard J. *John's Gospel in New Perspective: Christology and the Realities of Roman Power*. Maryknoll, NY: Orbis, 1992.

Cassidy, Richard J. *Christians and Roman Rule in the New Testament: New Perspectives*. New York: Crossroad, 2001.

Cha, Theresa Hak Kyung. *Dictee*. Berkeley: University of California Press, 2001.

Conway, Colleen M. *Behold the Man: Jesus and Greco-Roman Masculinity*. New York: Oxford University Press, 2008.

Conway, Colleen M. "There and Back Again: Johannine History on the Other Side of Literary Criticism." In *Anatomies of Narrative Criticism: The Past, Present, and Futures of the Fourth Gospel as Literature*, edited by Tom Thatcher and Stephen D. Moore, 77–91. Atlanta: Society of Biblical Literature, 2008.

Conway, Colleen M. "The Production of the Johannine Community: A New Historicist Perspective." *Journal of Biblical Literature* 121, no. 3 (2002): 479–495.

Davidson, Steed Vernyl. "Writing/Reading the Bible in Postcolonial Perspective." *Brill Research Perspectives in Biblical Interpretation* 2, no. 3 (2017): 1–99.

Diehl, Judy. "Anti-Imperial Rhetoric in the New Testament." *Currents in Biblical Research* 10, no. 1 (2011): 9–52.

Dodd, C. H. *Historical Tradition in the Fourth Gospel*. Cambridge: Cambridge University Press, 1963.

Dube, Musa W. "Reading for Decolonization (John 4:1–42)." *Semeia* 75 (1996): 37–59.

Dube, Musa W. "Savior of the World but Not of This World: A Post-Colonial Reading of Spatial Construction in John." In *The Postcolonial Bible*, ed. R. S. Sugirtharajah, 118–135. Sheffield: Sheffield Academic Press, 1998.

Dube, Musa W., and Jeffrey L. Staley, eds. *John and Postcolonialism: Travel, Space and Power*. New York: Sheffield Academic Press, 2002.

Ellis, Marc H. *Toward a Jewish Theology of Liberation: The Challenge of the 21st Century*, 3rd ed. Waco, TX: Baylor University Press, 2004.

Estrada III, Rodolfo Galvan. *A Pneumatology of Race in the Gospel of John: An Ethnocritical Study*. Eugene, OR: Wipf and Stock Publisher, 2019.

Fanon, Frantz. *The Wretched of the Earth*, translated by Constance Farrington. New York: Grove, 1968.

Glancy, Jennifer A. "Torture: Flesh, Truth, and the Fourth Gospel." *Biblical Interpretation* 13, no. 2 (2005): 107–136.

Glass, Zipporah G. "Building toward 'Nation-ness' in the Vine: A Postcolonial Critique of John 15:1–8." In *John and Postcolonialism: Travel, Space and Power*, edited by Musa W. Dube and Jeffrey L. Staley, 153–169. New York: Sheffield Academic Press, 2002.

Guardiola-Sáenz, Leticia A. "Border-crossing and Its Redemptive Power in John 7:53–8:11: A Cultural Reading of Jesus and the *Accused*." In *John and Postcolonialism: Travel, Space and Power*, edited by Musa W. Dube and Jeffrey L. Staley, 129–152. New York: Sheffield Academic Press, 2002.

Huie-Jolly, Mary. "Maori 'Jews' and a Resistant Reading of John 5:10–47." In *John and Postcolonialism: Travel, Space and Power*, edited by Musa W. Dube and Jeffrey L. Staley, 94–110. New York: Sheffield Academic Press, 2002.

Kim, Jean K. "A Korean Feminist Reading of John 4:1–42." *Semeia* 78 (1997): 109–119.

Kim, Jean K. *Woman and Nation: An Intercontextual Reading of the Gospel of John from a Postcolonial Feminist Perspective*. Boston; Leiden: Brill, 2004.

Kim, Jean K. "Adultery or Hybridity? Reading John 7:53–8:11 from a Postcolonial Context." In *John and Postcolonialism: Travel, Space and Power*, edited by Musa W. Dube and Jeffrey L. Staley, 111–128. New York: Sheffield Academic Press, 2002.

Koester, Craig R. "'The Savior of the World' (John 4:42)." *Journal of Biblical Literature* 109, no. 4 (1990): 665–680.

Lalitha, Jayachitra. "A Postcolonial Exploration of Water in the Fourth Gospel." *Bangalore Theological Forum* 37, no. 2 (2005): 114–129.

Liew, Tat-siong Benny. "Ambiguous Admittance: Consent and Descent in John's Community of 'Upward' Mobility." In *John and Postcolonialism: Travel, Space and Power*, edited by Musa W. Dube and Jeffrey L. Staley, 193–224. New York: Sheffield Academic Press, 2002.

Liew, Tat-siong Benny. "Margins and (Cutting-) Edges: On the (IL)Legitimacy and Intersections of Race, Ethnicity, and (Post)Colonialism." In *Postcolonial Biblical Criticism: Interdisciplinary Intersections*, edited by Stephen D. Moore and Fernando F. Segovia, 114–165. New York: T&T Clark International, 2007.

Liew, Tat-siong Benny. "The Word of Bare Life: Workings of Death and Dream in the Fourth Gospel." In *Anatomies of Narrative Criticism: The Past, Present, and Futures of the Fourth Gospel as Literature*, edited by Tom Thatcher and Stephen D. Moore, 167–194. Atlanta: Society of Biblical Literature, 2008.

Lozada, Jr., Francisco. *A Literary Reading of John 5: Text as Construction*. New York: Peter Lang, 2000.

Lozada, Jr., Francisco. "Contesting an Interpretation of John 5: Moving Beyond Colonial Evangelism." In *John and Postcolonialism: Travel, Space and Power*, edited by Musa W. Dube and Jeffrey L. Staley, 76–93. New York: Sheffield Academic Press, 2002.

Martyn, J. Louis. *History and Theology in the Fourth Gospel*, 2nd ed. Nashville: Abingdon, 1979.

Mbembe, Achille. "Necropolitics." *Public Culture* 15, no. 1 (2003): 11–40.

Moloney, Francis J. "Recent Johannine Studies: Part Two: Monographs." *Expository Times* 123, no. 9 (2012): 417–428.

Moloney, Francis J. "God, Eschatology, and 'This World': Ethics in the Gospel of John." In *Johannine Ethics: The Moral World of the Gospel and Epistles of John*, edited by Christopher W. Skinner and Sherri Brown, 197–218. Minneapolis, MN: Fortress Press, 2017.

Moore, Stephen D. *Empire and Apocalypse: Postcolonialism and the New Testament*. Sheffield: Sheffield Phoenix, 2006.

Moore, Stephen D. "Paul After Empire." In *The Colonized Apostle: Paul and Postcolonial Studies*, edited by Christopher D. Stanley, 9–23. Minneapolis, MN: Fortress Press, 2011.

Myers, Alicia D. "Gender, Rhetoric and Recognition: Characterizing Jesus and (Re)defining Masculinity in the Gospel of John." *Journal for the Study of the New Testament* 38, no. 2 (2015): 191–218.

Reinhartz, Adele. "The Colonizer as Colonized: Intertextual Dialogue Between John's Gospel and Canadian Identity." In *John and Postcolonialism: Travel, Space and Power*, edited by Musa W. Dube and Jeffrey L. Staley, 170–192. New York: Sheffield Academic Press, 2002.

Reinhartz, Adele. "The Jews of the Fourth Gospel." In *The Oxford Handbook of Johannine Studies*, edited by Judith M. Lieu and Martinus C. de Boer, 121–137. Oxford: Oxford University Press, 2018.

Rensberger, David. "The Politics of John: The Trial of Jesus in the Fourth Gospel." *Journal of Biblical Literature* 103, no. 3 (1984): 395–411.

Richey, Lance Byron. *Roman Imperial Ideology and the Gospel of John*. Washington, DC: Catholic Biblical Association of America, 2007.

Ripley, Jason. "'Behold the Man'? Subverting Imperial Masculinity in the Gospel of John." *Journal of the Bible and Its Reception* 2, no. 2 (2015): 219–239.

Rushdie, Salman. *Midnight's Children*. New York: Penguin Books, 1991.

Segovia, Fernando F. "Biblical Criticism and Postcolonial Studies: Toward a Postcolonial Optic." In *The Postcolonial Bible*, edited by R. S. Sugirtharajah, 49–65. Sheffield: Sheffield Academic Press, 1998.

Segovia, Fernando F. "The Counterempire of God: Postcolonialism and John." *Princeton Seminary Bulletin* 27, no. 2 (2006): 82–99.

Segovia, Fernando F. "Johannine Studies and the Geopolitical: Reflections upon Absence and Irruption." In *What We Have Heard from the Beginning: The Past, Present, and Future of Johannine Studies*, edited by Tom Thatcher, 281–306. Waco, TX: Baylor University Press, 2007.

Segovia, Fernando F. "The Gospel of John." In *A Postcolonial Commentary on the New Testament Writings*, edited by Fernando F. Segovia and R. S. Sugirtharajah, 156–193. New York: T&T Clark, 2007.

Shottroff, Luise. "Important Aspects of the Gospel for the Future." In *What Is John: Readers and Readings of the Fourth Gospel*, edited by Fernando F. Segovia, 205–210. Atlanta: Scholars Press, 1996.

Skinner, Christopher W. "John's Gospel and the Roman Imperial Context." In *Jesus Is Lord, Caesar Is Not: Evaluating Empire in New Testament Studies*, edited by Scot McKnight, Joseph B. Modica, and Andy Crouch, 116–129. Downers Grove, IL: IVP Academic, 2013.

Staley, Jeffrey L. "'Dis Place, Man': A Postcolonial Critique of the Vine (the Mountain and the Temple) in the Gospel of John." In *John and Postcolonialism: Travel, Space and Power*, edited by Musa W. Dube and Jeffrey L. Staley, 32–50. New York: Sheffield Academic Press, 2002.

Sugirtharajah, R. S. "A Postcolonial Exploration of Collusion and Construction in Biblical Interpretation." In *The Postcolonial Bible*, edited by R. S. Sugirtharajah, 91–116. Sheffield: Sheffield Academic Press, 1998.

Sugirtharajah, R. S. *Vernacular Hermeneutics*. Sheffield: Sheffield Academic Press, 1999.

Sugirtharajah, R. S. "The First, Second, and Third Letters of John." In *A Postcolonial Commentary on the New Testament Writings*, edited by Fernando F. Segovia and R. S. Sugirtharajah, 413–423. New York: T&T Clark, 2007.

Sugirtharajah, R. S. "Postcolonial Biblical Criticism." In *Voices from the Margin: Interpreting the Bible in the Third World*, 25th anniversary edition, edited by R. S. Sugirtharajah, 129–142. Maryknoll, NY: Orbis Books, 2016.

Swanson, Tod D. "To Prepare a Place: Johannine Christianity and the Collapse of Ethnic Territory." In *John and Postcolonialism: Travel, Space and Power*, edited by Musa W. Dube and Jeffrey L. Staley, 11–31. New York: Sheffield Academic Press, 2002.

Tan, Yak-hwee. *Re-presenting the Johannine Community: A Postcolonial Perspective*. New York: Peter Lang, 2008.

Thatcher, Tom. *Greater than Caesar: Christology and Empire in the Fourth Gospel*. Minneapolis, MN: Fortress Press, 2008.

Thatcher, Tom. "'I Have Conquered the World': The Death of Jesus and the End of Empire in the Gospel of John." In *Empire in the New Testament*, edited by Stanley E. Porter and Cynthia Long Westfall, 140–163. Eugene, OR: Pickwick, 2011.

Torontle, Mositi. *The Victims*. Gaborone: Botsalo, 1993.

Waters, Kenneth L. "Empire and the Johannine Epistles." *Review & Expositor* 114, no. 4 (2017): 542–557.

Williams, Catrin H., and Christopher Rowland, eds. *John's Gospel and Intimations of Apocalyptic*. New York: T&T Clark, 2013.

Wright, Jr., Arthur. *The Governor and the King: Irony, Hidden Transcripts, and Negotiating Empire in the Fourth Gospel*. Eugene, OR: Pickwick Publications, 2019.

CHAPTER 8

THE ROMAN EMPIRE IN PAUL'S LETTERS

TAT-SIONG BENNY LIEW

Paul's letters have been read and studied for a long, long time. Within the canon known as the New Testament, the author of 2 Peter already wrote in the early second century that "there are some things... difficult to understand" in what "our beloved brother Paul wrote" (2 Peter 3:15–16). There is a dominant narrative that academic interpretations of Paul's letters have moved from a Lutheran frame that sees Paul as all about individual guilt and forgiveness (hence the emphasis on "justification by faith") to the "new perspective" that views Paul as engaging with his fellow Jews on the place of Gentiles within the salvation plan of the God of Israel, and finally to a broader understanding that considers Paul and his writings in the political context of the Roman Empire (e.g., Matlock 1998; Punt 2015: 4–6). While this narrative is problematic in its erasure or dismissal of feminist readings of Paul (e.g., Wire 1990; Kittredge 1998), to name just one example, it does point to the fact that Paul's letters read very differently when readers, becoming increasingly aware that religion or theology is inseparable from politics, consider the Roman Empire part of the equation in their approach to Paul.

Before proceeding any further, I must mention two caveats. First, since this chapter is part of a handbook on postcolonial biblical criticism, I must clarify that talking about "the Roman Empire in Paul's Letters" is not the same as talking about postcolonial readings of Paul's letters. My topic does not require me to make a distinction between postcolonial readings and empire critical readings. While the latter is often faulted not only for being ignorant or dismissive of postcolonial theory and criticism but also for engaging in apologetics for presenting biblical writers as completely and purely anti-imperial (e.g., Moore 2000; Harker 2018), its focus on Roman imperial politics can be conducive to further discussion, which I shall explore in this chapter.[1] At the same time, I will not address some postcolonial readings of Paul that aim to challenge certain Western assumptions, ideologies, or hegemonies that do not directly involve the Roman Empire. For instance, K. K. Yeo's work, although included in Anna Runesson's book on "postcolonialism and New Testament studies" (Runesson 2011: subtitle; cf. pp. 168–186), will not fit with my topic because it provides an interpretation of Paul's rhetoric in 1 Corinthians 8 to challenge missionaries' condemnation of Chinese ancestor worship without any mention of the Roman Empire (Yeo 1994). As the title of this chapter indicates, discussion herein refers more narrowly to how the reality, dynamics, and ideology of the Roman Empire function within Paul's letters.

Second, I will take the minimalist approach and limit myself to what most, if not all, scholars consider to be the seven authentic letters written by Paul: namely, Romans, 1 and 2 Corinthians, Galatians, Philippians, 1 Thessalonians, and Philemon. I will also take these letters in their current form, putting aside scholarly arguments of whether some of these letters are composites of different letters that Paul wrote or whether there are later interpolations within Paul's letters.[2] Instead of talking about the Roman Empire in each of these letters one by one, I will use a thematic approach and use different letters by Paul to illustrate each theme.

The Haunting (Omni) Presence of the Roman Empire

Paul's reality as a colonized Jew and an imperial subject of Rome means that the Roman Empire was very much present in his multi-layered world (Wallace and Williams 1998), especially given his frequent travels—likely on Roman roads—to spread the gospel of Jesus Christ to Gentiles of the Roman Empire. Paul's first-century world was basically "determined by the seemingly omnipresent and omnipotent Roman Empire" (Punt 2015: 135). Through monuments, temples, statues, and inscriptions, the Romans "defined, distributed, and ultimately decorated the landscape of their *imperium*" (Ando 2000: 411); through art and architecture, "power was written into the physical fabric of provincial towns" (Revell 2009: 107). In addition, the Romans organized games, parades, and festivals to display their dominion and issued coins with an emperor's image to remind everyone daily of their rule (Lopez 2008: 26–28; Maier 2013: 2–7, 16–31).

The place of the Roman Empire in Paul's letters becomes even more considerable when one realizes that many of the locations in which Paul founded Christ-following communities or assemblies had a long colonial engagement with and under the Roman Empire, including Corinth, Galatia, Philippi, and Thessalonica (e.g., Nasrallah 2014: 428–431; Harker 2018: 31–34, 49–52, 199–203)—not to mention that one of his letters was written to the belly of the beast: Rome. Simply put, Paul's letters were all written and received within the Roman imperial world, so we shall look at how this world is mentioned, referenced, or mirrored in Paul's writings.

Admittedly, Paul rarely makes any direct remarks on the Roman Empire, although he does write a letter to the Christ-following assembly in Rome and, in his letter to the assembly in Philippi, mentions "the emperor's household" (Phil. 4:22) and Rome's "imperial guard" (Phil. 1:13). Even if Paul does not mention the Roman Empire directly, he does refer to "rulers" (Rom. 8:37–39; 13:3–4), "rulers of this age" (1 Cor. 2:6–8), and "authorities" (Rom. 13:1–2, 6–7; Gal. 1:1). Given the Roman colonization of Jews during

Paul's time and Rome's ubiquitous use of imagery and rhetoric within its Empire to reinforce its rule,[3] many scholars have also noticed that many of the terms Paul uses in reference to his gospel about Jesus Christ are exactly the Greek equivalents of those that the Roman Empire employs to talk about itself and to boast of its achievements; these overlaps may suggest, therefore, Paul's presentation or positioning of his gospel as a competing and counter version of Rome's imperial message (e.g., Horsley 1994: 1157; N. Elliott 2008: 14; Wright 2005: 70–71). After all, the term "gospel" or "good news" (e.g., Rom. 1:1, 3, 9, 15–16; 1 Cor. 1:17; 2 Cor. 4:4; Gal. 1:6–9, 11; Phil. 1:5, 7, 12; 1 Thess. 2:2, 4, 8–9; Phlm. 13) was often used by the Romans to announce or celebrate the "peace" (e.g., Rom. 14:17, 19; 1 Cor. 14:33; 2 Cor. 13:11; Gal. 1:3; Phil. 4:7, 9; 1 Thess. 5:23; Phlm. 3), "justice" (e.g., Rom. 3:5, 21–22, 25; 1 Cor. 1:30; 2 Cor. 9:9–10; Gal. 5:5; Phil. 3:6, 9), and hence "salvation" or "security" (e.g., Rom. 1:16; 2 Cor. 1:6; Phil. 1:28; 1 Thess. 5:8–9) that they as "saviors" (Phil. 3:20) had brought to the world. Similarly, Roman emperors often reserved for themselves the title of "lord" (e.g., Rom. 4:8, 24; 1 Cor. 1:2–3, 7–10, 31; 2 Cor. 3:16–18; Gal. 6:14, 18; Phil. 4:2–5, 10, 23; 1 Thess. 3:8, 11–13; Phlm. 3, 5, 16, 20, 25) to whom their subjects owed "faith" or "fidelity" (e.g., Rom. 1:5, 8, 12, 16–17; 1 Cor. 15:14, 17; 2 Cor. 1:24; Gal. 2:16, 20; Phil. 3:9; 1 Thess. 3:2, 5–7, 10; Phlm. 5–6) and "service" (e.g., Rom. 15:16, 27; 1 Cor. 9:13; 2 Cor. 8:23). Augustine was even known as *divi filius* or the "divine son" of Julius Caesar (Rom. 1:4; 2 Cor. 1:19; Gal. 2:20), and Rome's imperial cult of emperor worship was widespread (Hardin 2008; cf. Price 1984; Kahl 2010: 129–167). Paul's word for his "assemblies" (which is often translated as "churches") is also the same term that refers to *political* assembly in which citizens gathered to deliberate on and debate about all kinds of matters—so not merely "religious" ones—that concerned them.[4]

Regardless of Paul's intentions, recipients of his letters might well read his words along this anti-imperial line, given the "empire-saturated context" (Punt 2015: 140) in which they found themselves. In addition to mere terminological parallel or protest, however, the actual contents of and discussions in Paul's letters also show the importance of the Roman Empire in his corpus—although not necessarily or solely in ways that are anti-Rome.[5] For example, given what we know about Rome's imperial cult and view of its rulers as "divine sons," Paul's affirmation that there is only one God and one Lord among many "so-called gods in heaven and on earth" (1 Cor. 8:5–6) clearly comes across as carrying a resonance, and perhaps even a pointed critique, of the Roman Empire (Heilig 2015: 100, 144).

CRITIQUING THE ROMAN EMPIRE

Given the difficulties and frustrations he had with the Corinthians, Paul tried in 2 Corinthians to explain his decision not to visit them. Somewhat suddenly, Paul shifts to a metaphor and writes:

> But thanks be to God, who in Christ always leads us [as captives][6] in triumphal procession, and through us spreads in every place the fragrance that comes from

knowing him. For we are the aroma of Christ to God among those who are being saved and among those who are perishing; to the one a fragrance from death to death, to the other a fragrance from life to life. (2 Cor. 2:14–16)

Paul is describing here a scene that would be familiar to many within the Roman Empire of the first century: namely, a Roman triumph, which was a public parade to celebrate an important military victory and extravagant propaganda to reinforce Roman supremacy—with divine authorization!—by showcasing the spoils of war, including the captives from the defeated nation (cf. Beard 2009).[7] There was Claudius's triumph in 44 CE, but perhaps the most famous and most relevant of these Roman triumphs was the one held by Vespasian and his son Titus, who, after defeating Judea, pulled out all the stops in 71 CE to display the riches he gained from ransacking the Jerusalem temple. There are, of course, two surprises about the triumph being described by Paul in 2 Corinthians. First, the triumph belongs to Christ, the divine son of Israel's God, and not to a Roman emperor—not even Augustus, another "divine son" who "solidified the idea of the [Roman] emperor as the eternal triumphator" (Aus 2005: 8) by restricting and reserving the pageantry to the emperor. Second, Paul presents himself as part of Christ's triumph but as a humiliated captive and not as a celebrating member of the procession. While this might have been Paul's rhetorical move to satirize or appropriate the Corinthians' ridicule of him (cf. 2 Cor. 10:1–10) and/or a convenient way for Paul to shift the responsibility from himself to Christ for missing his promised visit to Corinth because of a change in travel plans (cf. 2 Cor. 1:15–2:13), it actually summarizes a couple of significant pictures of the Roman Empire in Paul's letters.

Paul's Afflictions as Results of Roman Oppression

In addition to talking about himself as a captive in Christ's triumph in connection with his humiliating reception by the Corinthians, Paul gives an expansive account in the same letter of his sufferings on account of the gospel (2 Cor. 11:23–27; cf. Glancy 2010: 24–47). Paul boasts that he has gone through all kinds of near-death dangers; besides risks and problems that inevitably come with travel, Paul says he has experienced "more imprisonments . . . countless floggings," as well as threats from both Jews and Gentiles (cf. 2 Cor. 6:4–10). Although Paul had good reasons for wanting to emphasize his sacrifices to his skeptical recipients in Corinth (cf. 1 Cor. 4:9–13), the Corinthian correspondence is not the only place Paul would speak of these experiences. In his letter to the Romans, he talks about "persecution . . . peril . . . sword," then he quotes Hebrew scriptures with words that are even more descriptive: "we are being killed all day long; we are accounted as sheep to be slaughtered" (Rom. 8:35–36). If there was any confusion as to what this killing "sword" refers to, Paul makes clear that the "sword" is the weapon of the governing power, which Paul also implies is a potential "terror" (Rom. 13:1–4). Although we cannot assume a literal reading of Paul's dramatic and gladiatorial descriptions of his fighting "with wild animals at Ephesus" (1 Cor. 15:32), his repeated use of the word *thlipsis*—variously translated as "affliction" (2 Cor. 1:4, 8; 4:17; 6:4; 7:4; 8:2), "persecution" (1 Thess.

1:6; 3:3, 7), "anguish" (Rom. 2:9), "suffering" (Rom. 5:3; 12:12; Phil. 1:17), "hardship" (Rom. 8:35), or "distress" (1 Cor. 7:28; 2 Cor. 2:4; Phil. 4:14)—paints a picture of someone who is in conflict not only with ordinary people who resist his person and his message but also with imperial officials of Rome, especially when coupled with his numerous personal references to being arrested and imprisoned (Rom. 16:7; 2 Cor. 6:5; 11:23; Phil. 1:7, 13–14, 17; Phlm. 1, 9–10, 13, 23; cf. Cassidy 2001). Moreover, Paul was not shy about comparing his encounters with affliction and danger with those suffered by Jesus Christ, including specifically Jesus's death (2 Cor. 4:7–12; Gal. 6:17). Because Paul refused to let anyone forget that Jesus died from the Roman sentence of crucifixion (Rom. 6:6; 1 Cor. 1:17–18, 23; 2:2, 8; 2 Cor. 13:4; Gal. 5:11; 6:12, 14; Phil. 2:8; 3:18), he may well have linked his own affliction and imprisonment—and perhaps his physical "weakness" (2 Cor. 10:10; 12:10; Gal. 4:13)—with the death-dealing power of imperial Rome. His statement about his own experience of having been "exhibited . . . as though sentenced to death" and "hav[ing] become a spectacle to the world, to angels and mortals" (1 Cor. 4:9) also brings to mind the Roman sentence of crucifixion, which, like lynching of black bodies in the United States, was meant to be "a public spectacle" (Cone 2011: 1; cf. Cook 2012).

Talking about death, Paul expressed in a couple of letters his preference to die (2 Cor. 1:8–9; 5:6–10; Phil. 1:19–26). This rhetoric about contemplating self-killing or suicide (Droge 1988; Croy 2003) was a "cultural cache . . . among first-century upper-class Romans" (Marquis 2013: 50). More significantly for the purposes of this chapter, such rhetoric was often employed when Roman elites had fallen out of favor with the emperor. Finding themselves in trouble with the authorities; they turned to the rhetoric of suicide not only to demonstrate their true freedom and character, but also to avoid the shame and punishments that came with imperial disapproval. This became such a frequent occurrence that Roman jurists discussed whether suicide before trial should be considered a tacit admission of guilt. Arthur Darby Nock refers to a "Stoic cult of suicide," because this "cultural cache" was said to have originated in Cato the Younger's decision to take his own life as a way to refuse Julius Caesar's rule (Nock 1933: 197; Marquis 2013: 61–62, 65). The rhetoric of contemplating suicide, whether carried out or not, thus often functioned in the Roman Empire during Paul's time as a way to assert personal agency in defiance of the emperor's power (Marquis 2013: 65–66). In other words, when Paul talks in his letters about his afflictions and hardships as difficult realities that led him to contemplate or wish for death, both the cause (afflictions and hardships) and the effect (contemplation of suicide) may have been connected with the Roman Empire: while the former was partly the result of Roman oppression, the latter was potentially a refusal of Roman power.

Paul's Apocalyptic Emphasis as Judgment against the Romans

While Paul presents the Philippians as the reason for his decision to stay alive (Phil. 1.21–26) despite his personal preference to die, he gives a different reason for making the same decision in 2 Corinthians: namely, his trust in the final inescapable judgment of God to prove his cause (2 Cor. 1:12–14).

Emphasizing Paul's apocalyptic thinking in his letters (e.g., 1 Cor. 7:29; 15:51–57; 1 Thess. 4:13–18) has not only a long history in the study of his writings (Beker 1982; Matlock 1996), but has also experienced a revival in the 21st century (e.g., Campbell 2009; Blackwell, Goodrich, and Maston 2016; Wasserman 2018; Gaventa 2019). There is also an increasing awareness of the connection between apocalyptic thinking and colonial politics and imperial situations in general (e.g., Liew 1999: 55–63) and of that connection within Paul's letters in particular (e.g., Horsley 1997a: 140–146). When Paul talks about "rulers of this age, who are doomed to perish" and links these "rulers" with the crucifixion of Jesus Christ (1 Cor. 2:6–8), he is clearly referring to the Romans. When he refers in those same verses to a mysterious wisdom of God that God has "decreed before the ages for our glory," Paul is following the scripts of previous Jewish apocalyptic writers—such as Daniel—to declare that God will judge and destroy oppressive foreign empires. In typical Jewish apocalyptic fashion, in other words, Paul is affirming not only God's eventual vindication of and exclusive sovereignty over Israel but also God's control of world history. For Paul, the imperial power of Rome is real but it is only temporary. Even when he is advising the assembly in the belly of the beast to (try to) "live peaceably with all" and to "subject to the governing authorities" (Rom. 12:18; 13:1), he makes a point to bring up God's "wrath," "vengeance," and "judgment" (Rom. 12:19; 13:2). What is different between Paul and his predecessors in Jewish apocalypticism is, of course, Paul's lifting up of Jesus Christ's death and resurrection as *the* key turning points of history. In 1 Cor. 15:20–28, where Paul repeats his point about the inevitable destruction of "every ruler and every authority and power" (1 Cor. 15:24), the passage also highlights not only the resurrection of Jesus Christ from the dead but also this resurrection as "first fruits" (1 Cor. 15:20). While Jesus Christ's own resurrection after his crucifixion demonstrates the impotence and impermanence of Roman power, this resurrection as "first fruits" promises a final and complete apocalyptic victory that will come in the future (1 Cor. 15:23). According to Paul, the Lord's Supper is a proclamation of "Christ death until he comes" (1 Cor. 11:26); it serves as a "dangerous memory" (Morrill 2000), a political reminder that, as we have discussed earlier about Paul's reference to the triumph of Jesus Christ (2 Cor. 2:14–16), Roman power will one day be bowing before and taken over by Jesus Christ (cf. Phil. 2:9–11).

In fact, the Greek term for the (second) coming of Jesus Christ, *parousia* (1 Cor. 15:23; 1 Thess. 2:19; 3:13; 4:15; 5:23), carries political connotations because it is generally used for the visit of a high official, including the advent of an emperor.[8] In 1 Thessalonians, where this term appears most among Paul's letters, Paul addresses whatever hostility or difficulty his recipients have experienced from their "compatriots" by (1) mentioning the death of Jesus Christ, and (2) promising "God's wrath" that will come upon these oppressive compatriots (1 Thess. 2:13–16)—supposedly at the glorious return of the resurrected Jesus Christ (1 Thess. 5:1–11).

Paul's Assemblies as Alternative Communities

As Paul assures the assembly in 1 Corinthians (e.g., 1 Cor. 17:29; 15:20–28) of Christ's apocalyptic victory (which includes the destruction of the Roman Empire), he also advises the assembly not to use the court system of the "unrighteous," because as holy followers of Jesus Christ who will one day judge not only "the world" but also angels, Christ-followers in Corinth are more qualified to judge and settle any grievance or disputes internally among themselves (1 Cor. 6:1–6).

The advice to separate themselves as Christ-followers from the official legal system is one of the reasons that many scholars have long suggested that Paul's assemblies or churches were meant to be alternative communities—alternative in the sense that they should not follow the prevailing ethos and values of the Roman Empire (e.g., Horsley 1997b).[9] What has been said about Rome's "international relations" is also applicable to social relations within the Empire: it was all about "a competition for status" (Mattern 1999: xii; cf. Garnsey and Saller 2015: 209–278). Romans at the time of Paul were most preoccupied with their positions in the Empire's sociopolitical hierarchies. Whether heard by the assemblies that Paul gathered in the name of Jesus Christ or intended by Paul himself, the words in Gal. 3:28 about demolishing the hierarchies based on ethnicity, status, and sex and gender are astounding, especially in light of the rigid hierarchies of the Romans. There were clearly elites at the top, such as the senators, the equestrians, and the decurions; followed by the slaves (who were often captives from war and hence people of another ethnicity) and women towards the bottom of the pyramid.

These hierarchical social relations were being paraded in Roman society all the time through clothes people wore. Senators and their sons were known by their togas with broad purple stripes, for example, while equestrians were identified by their togas with narrow purple stripes. Moreover, in public functions such as banquets, specific seating arrangements displayed and reinforced "proper" social order. One may wonder what Paul meant in this context when he said that those who follow Jesus Christ are all "clothed with Christ" through baptism (Gal. 3:27), especially since this reference was immediately followed by the social leveler we know as Gal. 3:28. Paul's insistence on reordering how the Corinthians consumed the Lord's Supper to avoid division (1 Cor. 11:17–18) was a clear departure from the Roman practice of always prioritizing the elites in public settings, whether these gatherings involved a meal or not. Paul particularly emphasized the need for them to not only remember the meaning of the meal (1 Cor. 11:26) but also start the meal together rather than give priority to those who arrived early or were economically better off (1 Cor. 11:19–22, 33–34).

The thought that Paul wanted those within his assemblies to relate in ways that were different from or contrary to typical Roman practices can further be seen in two letters in which he addresses conflicts or disagreements among his recipients. Whether the issue was marriage (1 Corinthians 7), eating idol-meat (1 Corinthians 8 and 10), the Lord's Supper (1 Corinthians 11:17–34), or spiritual gifts (1 Corinthians 12 and 14),

Paul asked those with greater privilege, power, or freedom (whether in terms of understanding, knowledge, or means) to make accommodations for those with less (Martin 1995: 117–135, 141). As Paul wrote, "[M]embers of the body that seem to be weaker are indispensable" (1 Cor. 12:22), and "God has so arranged the body, giving the greater honor to the inferior member" (1 Cor. 12:24). This same approach is found in Paul's letter to the Romans; whatever the issue might have been in Romans 14 between "the weak" and "the strong," Paul asked those he called "the strong" to "bear with the failings of the weak and not to please [them]selves" (Rom. 15:1). If "Power and Privilege was the way of Rome" (McKnight 2019: 12), then Paul's advice and hope for his assemblies ran contrary to the imperial ethos of the Empire. Rather than modeling his assemblies after Rome's dominating power and masculinist aggression (e.g., Richlin 1992; Lopez 2008: 1–4, 19–22, 29–51), Paul looked to the example of Jesus Christ (1 Cor. 11:1; Rom. 15:3). Perhaps Paul's most detailed explanation of this example by Jesus Christ is in the self-emptying hymn or theme that Paul shared with the Philippians (Phil. 2:1–8)—or what is, in Paul's words, "foolishness to Gentiles" (1 Cor. 1:23). It is worth noting that Paul also talks about "citizenship" in this same letter for the Philippians (Phi. 3:20). However, the citizenship for members of Paul's assemblies was not Roman citizenship that could provide certain legal protections in this fleeting world (cf. 1 Thess. 5:3); their citizenship belonged to a different realm altogether that came with assurance of a final victory and complete transformation (Phil. 3:21). Hence they were also supposed to march by a different drumbeat. As Paul put it in his letter to the assembly in Rome, "Do not be conformed to this world" (Rom. 12:2). To the Corinthians, he used again the death and resurrection of Jesus Christ as an example: as Christ-followers, they were now dead to the world; having become "a new creation," they needed to live for Christ and no longer see people and things from "a human point of view" (2 Cor. 4:16–5:17).

In terms of Roman patriarchy or gender hierarchy, there are *some* indications in Paul's letters that he might have held some different views as well. First of all, Paul at times used female metaphors to talk about himself, such as a woman giving birth (Gal. 4:19; cf. Rom. 8:22), a mother with milk for infants (1 Cor. 3:1–2), or a nurse caring for her children (1 Thess. 2:7; cf. Gaventa 2007; Lopez 2008: 141–146).[10] Paul's recommendation of Phoebe—whom he identified as "a deacon" in the assembly at Cenchreae—to the assembly in Rome and acknowledgment of her as his benefactor (Rom. 16:1–2) are also encouraging, especially if this letter's overall emphasis on not being judgmental (e.g., Rom. 12:3–8) but being welcoming (e.g., Rom. 14:1, 3; 15:7; 16:1–2) was for the purpose of recommending Phoebe and if Phoebe was the trusted courier of his letter to Rome (McKnight 2019: 3–5). The same can be said of Paul's decision to greet many women in the assembly at Rome—including Prisca, Mary, Junia, Tryphaena and Tryhosa, Persis, Rufus's mother, the sisters in Asyncritus's household, Julia, and Nereus's sister—thus signifying Paul's recognition of and respect for their importance and leadership roles among "the saints" there (Rom. 16:3–15).

By embodying an ethos and a set of values different from those of the Roman Empire (including, when necessary, setting themselves apart from the dominant social structures), members of Paul's assemblies, according to Paul's apocalyptic understanding, would also experience a different fortune at the *parousia* of Jesus Christ (Phil. 3:17–21; 1 Thess. 5:1–11). Before the apocalyptic advent of the new age, Paul wanted his assemblies to live in ways that overturned the existing social norms of imperial Rome.

Paul's Collection as a Different Economy and More

The Roman Empire was also characterized by economic exploitation (Garnsey and Saller 2015: 214–216), in keeping with the hierarchical nature of the Empire in general, which was a "system of inequality" (Garnsey and Saller 2015: 231). Part of this exploitative practice included taxation (Goodman 1997: 82–83, 98–101, 113, 142–147, 270–271; N. Elliott 2008: 91–100). In fact, the burden of taxation had led to tax revolts during the time of Claudius and Nero that both emperors had to resort to military might to suppress. As a result, some scholars have argued that Paul's advice to "subject [oneself] to the governing authorities" (Rom. 13:1) was a situational survival strategy, given his mention of the need to pay tax in the immediate literary context of that advice (Rom. 13:6–7; cf. N. Elliott 2008: 152–156; McKnight 2019: 25–26, 46, 58).

Based on the letters we have from Paul, questions of money seem to be following him and besetting his ministry. Traveling teachers or preachers in Paul's time were always under suspicion that they were charlatans talking a good game for material gains (cf. Panayotakis, Schmeling, and Paschalis [eds.] 2015). As his problems with the Corinthian assemblies show, Paul becomes suspect to his recipients (2 Cor. 7:2–3; 8:20–21; 12:17–18) partly because he claims not to ask for financial support (1 Corinthians 9), but asks for money at the same time (1 Cor. 16:3–4).[11] Paul's collection for the Jerusalem assembly seems to occupy a very special place in Paul's understanding of his own work and mission. After all, he specifies that he was asked in his first meeting with the leaders in Jerusalem to "remember the poor" (Gal. 2:10).[12] He also mentions this collection in other letters; namely, 2 Cor. 8:1–9:15 and Rom. 15:25–31, where Paul also expresses an awareness that his trip with the collection to Jerusalem may well spell danger for himself.[13] Paul also refers to "the poor among the saints in Jerusalem" (Rom. 15:26), which may indicate the exploitative nature of Roman economy. How may we read and understand this collection?

New Testament scholars have long suggested that most people in the first-century Mediterranean depended on a patronage system to make life livable for them, given the highly hierarchical society of imperial Rome (J. Elliott 1987; Malina 1988; Chow 1992). While the exchange within a patronage system was reciprocal, the status and power differential between the parties involved as patron and client was asymmetrical, with material resources being given by the patron and services (including public praise of the patron's generosity) by the client. If one looks at the communal nature of Paul's collection, the modest economic status of those within Paul's assemblies (cf. 1 Cor. 16:2; 2 Cor. 8:2, 12) and the promise of multidirectional economic distribution based on need and fairness (so the benefactors at one point in time can become the beneficiaries at another; cf. 2 Cor. 8:13–15), Paul's collection seems to be about redistributing resources among the poor. Hence it was fundamentally different from Roman patronage's reliance on one wealthy individual or family who acted always as the benefactor to cover over the patrons' systematic exploitation of their clients (Friesen 2010: 49–51; cf. McKnight 2019: 38). There are two more reasons to see Paul's collection as different from Rome's patronage system (Wan 2000: 212–215). The fact that the givers were not only communal but also multiple—for example, as Paul emphasizes, from both Macedonia and Corinth (2 Cor. 8:1–4; 9:2–4)— helped break down or decentralize the almost absolute power of a sole giver or benefactor. Moreover, Paul emphasized that whatever resources they had to contribute to the collection, the resources were from God and given to the assembly members by God (2 Cor. 9:8–15). In other words, his assemblies were the conduits rather than the origins of the financial contribution.

More than embodying a different economic system, Paul's collection may have been crucial for Paul because it had to do with ethnic relations in the context of the Roman Empire. At least until the reversal in the fortunes of the Jerusalem and the Gentile assemblies, Paul's collection also served his mission to incorporate Gentiles into the orbit of his Jewish God of the East by making Jerusalem, Paul's "ancestral home" (Charles 2014: 35), the center rather than imperial Rome. There are two additional considerations that would suggest that this collection was even more anti-Rome (Wan 2000: 200–207). First, the collection seems similar to the controversial temple tax that all male Jews above 20 years of age, including proselytes and God-fearers, must pay even if they were in the diaspora. It was "controversial" because the Roman authorities thought this tax drained resources from other provinces to Jerusalem. Second, in light of what we have also discussed about Paul's apocalyptic emphasis, a collection coming from Paul's Gentile assemblies to Jerusalem echoes the eschatological vision in Hebrew scriptures that all the wealth of the nations will one day move into Jerusalem (e.g., Isa. 60:4–7; Micah 4:1–2).[14]

MIRRORING THE ROMAN EMPIRE

Although Paul's collection for the Jerusalem assembly may be interpreted as a subversive act against the Roman Empire, given its apocalyptical allusion and contrast with Rome's patronage system, its similarity to the Jewish temple tax does raise the question of whether we should understand the collection as a taxation system that shared similarities with Rome's tax collection. After all, Paul does seem to have talked out of both sides of his mouth. On the one hand, he said that the contribution is voluntary (2 Cor. 8:10–12; 9:5, 7; Rom. 15:26); on the other hand, he told his assemblies that they "owe" the Jerusalem assembly this collection (Rom. 15:27; cf. Wan 2000: 200, 207–208). The Roman Empire played an ambiguous role within Paul's letters: it was both the target of Paul's critique and as the model of Paul's imitation or mimicry.

Paul's Rhetoric as Similarly Competitive and Hierarchical

We have seen how Paul, in writing to the Corinthians about their collection, brings up the Macedonians' contribution to the project (2 Cor. 8:1–4; 9:2–4). While this may indicate a positive difference between Paul's collection and Roman patronage because it features multiple communal providers of material resources, the mention of the Macedonians is also meant "to goad the Corinthians" (Wan 2000: 194) into doing their part for the collection. We see a similar sentiments and dynamics in not only Paul's praise of the Philippians at the expense of other assemblies (Phil. 4:15–16) but also Paul's explanation in Romans 9–11 about the relationship between Gentiles and Jews in God's plan. For Paul, competition, tension, and jealousy between Jews and Gentiles all worked as an engine that would help engineer and drive God's final goal of saving "all Israel" (Rom. 11:11–27).[15] Paul's portrayal in his letter to the assembly in Rome of Gentiles as morally degenerate and lacking self-mastery (in his diatribe against the Gentiles in Romans 1 and his *prosōpopoiia* or speech-in-character in Romans 6–7) was "a fundamental feature of Jewish self-definition in antiquity" (Stowers 1994: 276; cf. pp. 273–276). Unlike Israelites, who had ancestry, law, and worship, Gentiles only had idols and passions they could not control. Paul's later depiction of Gentiles as "slaves" who became adopted children and heirs (Rom. 8:14–17) was, of course, fitting for his rhetorical purpose, particularly in the context of the ancient household, as it communicated a rather extreme and unlikely change in status (Johnson Hodge 2007: 69); however, calling Gentiles "slaves" might also have been a reference to the Jewish assumption that Gentiles were enslaved to their own idols and passions. With rhetorical sophistry, Paul's logics and logistics of adoption both breached and buttressed the distance between Gentiles and the Jewish people and the Jewish Christ/God: Gentile adoptees who follow Christ are not like Gentiles who don't. His othering of the Gentiles means that he also assumed a particular racial/ethnic hierarchy even, or especially, as he argued for their connection to the same God of Israel: Jews were chosen before and ranked above the Gentiles (Rom. 1:16). As Paul's agricultural metaphor of grafting (Rom. 11: 17–18) shows, the Gentiles "are actually parasitic on [the tree's] richness" (Esler 2003: 124). For Gentiles, therefore, "being 'in Christ' is not ethnically neutral; rather, it falls under the umbrella of Jewishness" (Johnson Hodge 2007: 149), as evidenced by Paul's constant and consistent references to Hebrew scriptures (e.g., Rom. 4:3; 9:17; 10:11; 11:2; cf. Punt 2015: 107–134). Another clear indication of Paul's racial/ethnic ranking is his description in Romans 7 of the Gentile who tries but fails to live by the Jewish law. Here, Paul was using a popular rhetoric within Gentile (Greek) moral tradition but turning it against the Gentiles (Stowers 1994: 148, 271–282). Paul wrote, "We ourselves are Jews by birth and not Gentile sinners" (Gal. 2:15); his very mission to the Gentiles was based on a hierarchical view that sees Gentiles as inferior (e.g., 1 Thess. 4:3–5).

That does not mean, however, that assemblies that Paul established in his mission to the Gentiles were incapable of contending with Paul. Paul's letter suggests that he may have been facing not only competition from outsiders but also resistance from the

Corinthians. Before using the label "false apostles" (2 Cor. 11:13) and "super-apostles" (2 Cor. 11:5; 12:11) to call those whose arrival in Corinth follows his own, Paul wrote,

> We, however, will not boast beyond limits, but will keep within the field that God has assigned to us, to reach out even as far as you. For we were not overstepping our limits when we reached you; we were the first to come all the way to you with the good news of Christ. We do not boast beyond limits, that is, in the labors of others; but our hope is that, as your faith increases, our sphere of action among you may be greatly enlarged, so that we may proclaim the good news in lands beyond you, without boasting of work already done in someone else's sphere of action. (2 Cor. 10:13–16)

This message comes across very differently from the one in 1 Cor. 1:10–17 and 3:1–15, in which Paul addresses divisions among the Corinthians rather than divisions between him and the Corinthians. Granted that we do not know much about either the so-called false apostle that Paul mentioned in 2 Corinthians or Apollos in 1 Corinthians, Paul did seem nevertheless to be willing in his earlier letter to the Corinthians to let God judge the work of a worker, even if someone "builds on the foundation with . . . wood, hay, straw" and not with "gold, silver, precious stones" (1 Cor. 3:12). Paul seemed to get competitive when his standing among the Corinthians begin to look a little shaky (2 Cor. 1:15–23; 7:2–3; 10:1–18; 12:17–18). To show his superiority over these other "apostles," Paul boasted about his ancestral pedigree as a Jew and his personal qualifications as a Christ-following minister, with the latter including not only death-defying sacrifices but also a supernatural journey into heaven and its mysteries (2 Cor. 11:16–12:4). Besides this rather lengthy praise of himself to earn bragging rights, Paul's biting and fighting words against other teachers or leaders can also be found in Gal. 2:11–14 (charging Peter and Barnabas of "hypocrisy") and in Phil. 1:15–17; 3:2 (attacking other preachers of the gospel as "selfish," "dogs," and "evil doers").

Paul's competition with these other teachers or leaders had everything to do with Paul's concern over his own standing within an assembly, as was the case with the Galatians, the Corinthians, and the Philippians.[16] In fact, although Paul may have come across as gentle and humble—or even "weak" (e.g., 2 Cor. 12:10; 13:9)—at times, he assumed more generally a position over his assemblies comparable to that of the *paterfamilias* in a Roman family. Exercising his paternal authority like a *paterfamilias*, Paul did not hesitate to call his recipients "children" (1 Cor. 14:20; 2 Cor. 6:13) or "infants" (1 Cor. 3:1; 14:20); nor was he shy about calling them *his* "children" (1 Cor. 4:14; 2 Cor. 12:14; Gal. 4:19; 1 Thess. 2:7, 11) and calling himself their "father" (1 Cor. 4:15). The Roman Emperor was known, of course, for casting himself as "a sort of *paterfamilias* with very wide discretionary powers" (Lacey 1986: 125). Paul's patriarchal ways are indisputable if one takes into consideration his advice for women in Corinth that they, as women and wives, should be silent in the assembly (1 Cor. 14:33–36) because, despite some expressions of hesitation, he thought that females were created for males and that husbands should be the masters of their wives (1 Cor. 11:2–16).[17] Given the economic concerns that were embedded in Roman ideas of childhood and family, including the expectation that children would provide material support in the future for their parents (Frilingos 2000: 93, 96–97), one may also interpret Paul's "appeal" to his assemblies to support him personally (Phil. 4:15–19) and his collection for Jerusalem (1 Cor. 16:3–4; 2 Cor. 8:1–9:15; Rom. 15:25–31) as part of his benevolent paternalism. Having said that, his emphasis on giving as "voluntary" (2 Cor. 9:5) and on "sharing" financial resources (*metadidōmi* and *didōmi* in Rom. 12:8, 13) functioned to alleviate rather than abolish structural socioeconomic inequity (Oakes 2012: 85).

Paul's letter to Philemon, albeit short, is telling because it involved a conversation—or competition, if you will—between Paul and a *paterfamilias* of a house assembly (Phlm. 1). Paul's admission that he was sending Onesimus back to Philemon because his desire to keep Onesimus needed Philemon's "consent" (Phlm. 12–15) shows clearly that Philemon is the "father" of the family to which Onesimus belongs, whether one interprets Onesimus as Philemon's slave or Philemon's brother.[18] At the same time, by not only claiming Onesimus as his "child" and himself Onesimus's "father" (Phlm. 10) but also presenting Onesimus as Philemon's "beloved brother . . . both in the flesh and in the Lord" (Phlm. 16), Paul was in effect declaring himself Philemon's "father" and the *paterfamilias* of Philemon's house assembly—despite Paul's reference to Philemon also as his "brother" and "partner" (Phlm. 7, 17, 20). Through a rhetorical sleight of hand, "Paul stands at the pinnacle of this domestic triangle, and Philemon and Onesimus are the two points that connect its base" (Frilingos 2000: 103).[19]

In like manner, while Paul seemed to recognize the status—or hierarchy—of "the acknowledged leaders" (Gal. 2:2, 6) or "acknowledged pillars" (Gal. 2:9) he met with in Jerusalem, he added that these so-called leaders mean and contributed nothing to him (Gal. 2:6), because he received his gospel through divine revelation and not from a human source (Gal. 1:11–12, 15–17). He even implied slyly that even his participation in the meeting in Jerusalem was his response to a revelation (Gal. 2:2), so no one should think that he was doing it in response to a summon from any human leaders. If Paul's competitive and hierarchical rhetoric mirrored the Roman drive for status, it may have much to do with Paul's understanding of himself as God's special ambassador.

Paul's Role as God's Primary Ambassador-Slave

If, as it is often assumed, Onesimus was the courier of Paul's letter about him to Philemon, it should be noted that Paul also presented himself as a courier of a letter that recommended Paul himself. In 2 Cor. 3:1–3, Paul claimed to his Corinthian assembly that a recommendation letter "of Christ" was delivered by him and on his behalf. The difference between the NRSV's translation of the passive Greek verb *diakonētheisa* in 2 Cor. 3:3 as "prepared" and a more literal and accurate translation as "delivered" is significant because of what letter couriers did in Paul's time. As is well known, letter couriers in the first-century Mediterranean were often tasked with much more than physically delivering mails to recipients (Klauck 2006: 60–64; McKnight 2019: 5). Couriers often served to explain or elaborate on the meaning of what was written because they basically became a stand-in for the letter writer. Put in this context, by claiming to be the courier of a letter written by Christ to recommend him, Paul was basically asserting his authority as a spokesperson for Christ himself (Marquis 2013: 91–111).

Another image that Paul used to describe his role or relation vis-à-vis Jesus Christ is that of a slave (Rom. 1:1; Gal. 1:10; cf. Gal. 6:17). While the word "slave" may communicate to us today a lowly servile figure, its meaning was more complex and nuanced in Paul's time (Martin 1990: 1–49). Slaves in Paul's time, if they were valued by their masters, could work their way up to become managerial slaves who exercised control over money and properties on behalf of their masters. That was why some people who found themselves in desperate situations during that time were known to have sold themselves into slavery because, at least theoretically, slavery could be an avenue for upward mobility, especially if their master happened to be one of immense wealth, influence, and power. This is not to deny necessarily that slavery in Paul's time was an oppressive institution, but only to stress again the importance of keeping an eye on Paul's first-century imperial context when we read his letters. As "surrogate bodies" (Glancy 2002: 15–16), first-century slaves within the Roman Empire could suffer great physical abuse and harm, but they could also experience positive gains under the right circumstances and with the right master. Of course, the final determining factor on a managerial slave's status was the status of the master. Given Paul's proclamation of Jesus Christ as "son of God" (Rom. 1:4; 2 Cor. 1:19; Gal. 2:20) with "equality with God" (Phil. 2:6), his self-identification as a "slave of Christ" certainly comes across more like a powerful title for an authoritative steward. At the same time, since Paul's own status as a "slave" was dependent on that of his master, we must admit that, despite what has been said about Paul's collection, Paul's letters and rhetoric hardly show a complete rejection of Rome's patronage system. There is no question that Paul's use of slavery as a metaphor for his role in Christ "functioned within the dynamics of Greco-Roman patronage" (Martin 1990: 26).

Yet another telling image Paul used for his role in the gospel of Jesus Christ is "ambassador" (2 Cor. 5:20; cf. Phlm. 9).[20] Although this reference (most likely?) appears only once in Paul's letters, it is a reference loaded with meaning within the context of first-century imperial Rome. Ambassadors during that time were responsible for spreading the news of imperial benevolence and for galvanizing support for the Empire. This they would do by traveling so they could bring "Rome to the provinces and the provinces to Rome" (Marquis 2013: 128). One can readily see the appropriateness of applying this term to Paul, the "apostle to the Gentiles" who traveled around to spread and win followers for the good news of Jesus Christ. In addition, for the purpose of exhibiting the magnanimity of the Empire, ambassadors might at times refuse funding support by a city (Marquis 2013: 129). It is not a coincidence, therefore, that Paul referred to himself and his co-workers as "ambassadors" in his correspondence with the Corinthians (2 Cor. 5:20), given his decision to refuse financial support from them (1 Corinthians 9; 2 Cor. 11:7; 12:11–18; cf. 1 Thess. 2:9).

This idea of Paul as an ambassador for Christ can also be seen in how Paul talked about his mission. We recall that Paul, by his own account, operated under what appeared to be a principle of "first-arrival monopoly" in 2 Corinthians 10; this principle explains perhaps why Paul often recalled his initial visits to his assemblies (e.g., 1 Cor. 2:1–5; Gal. 1:6–9; Phil. 1:3–5; 1 Thess. 2:1–16). Furthermore, this principle is telling because Paul wrote, "We, however, will not boast beyond limits; but will keep within the field that God has assigned to us, to reach out even as far as you" (2 Cor. 10:13). For Paul, then, areas for his mission and his establishment of assemblies were all allotted by God, much like ambassadors in the Roman Empire would go where they were told to go as imperial representatives (cf. Gal. 2:7–9). At the same time, Paul himself would dispatch his co-workers as his own representatives, ambassadors, or "children" to various assemblies to do his bidding (e.g., 1 Cor. 4:17; 16:3–4; 2 Cor. 8:16–18, 22; Phil. 2:19–30; Phlm. 10, 12). The people at local assemblies who received personal greetings from Paul at the end of his letter (e.g., Rom. 16:3–15) might have also functioned as regional power brokers under and on behalf of Paul, just as various local agents were coopted and used by Rome to exercise its rule (Goodman 1997: 100–112; Garnsey and Saller 2015: 3–109; cf. Miles 1990).

Whether Paul presented himself in his letters as a courier, a slave, or an ambassador, he was always presenting himself as a special messenger or "apostle" (Rom. 1:1; 11:13; 1 Cor. 1:1; 9:1–2; 2 Cor. 1:1; Gal. 1:1) sent by Jesus Christ. He was willing and able to not only stand in for his "Lord" as a model for others to imitate (1 Cor. 4:16; 11:1; Gal. 4:12; 1 Thess. 1:6; cf. Castelli 1991) but also speak more authoritatively than angels and any other humans on matters related to the gospel (Gal. 1:8–9); in fact, he even felt free to speak on issues about which his "Lord" did not speak (1 Cor. 7:8–16).

As a result, while he mentioned the principle of following God's allotment of territorial limits in his letter to the Christ-following assembly in Rome (Rom. 15:20–21)—which he did not found—and felt the need to explain or make excuses for his intrusion into the Roman assembly by describing his correspondence with the Roman assembly as something he was doing "boldly" (Rom. 15:15), he showed that he did not necessarily live by his own articulated principle. His letter to the Roman assembly was simply paving the way for his personal visit to Rome (Rom. 15:22–31). Having said that, in the rest of his letter to the Romans Paul held on to another principle of priority that benefited him personally: namely, the subordination or indebtedness of Gentiles to Jews. Not only did he declare this principle rather early in his letter (the gospel is "the power of God for salvation to everyone who has faith, to the Jew first and also to the Greek"; Rom. 1:16), but he also repeated it towards the end when he presented the collection as something the Gentile assemblies "owe" to the Jews (Rom. 15:26–27; cf. Rom. 3:1–2; 9:4–5). Reading Rom. 15:22–29 (especially Rom. 15:24) between the lines, one may well wonder if Paul was not telling the members of the Roman assembly that they were indebted to provide for him and his trip to Spain after he arrived in Rome (cf. 1 Cor. 16:5–9; Phil. 4:15–19).

A shared feature in Paul's self-identification as Jesus Christ's courier, slave, or ambassador, in the context of and in accordance with Roman imperial practices, was Paul's effectual identity as Christ's proxy. That is not to say that there might not be differences between Paul's role and prevalent understandings of these roles in the Roman Empire. For instance, in contrast to Roman ambassadors who generally received requests for peace from places they visited, Paul as a traveling ambassador offered "reconciliation" as initiated by the Christ who sent him (2 Cor. 5:19; cf. Marquis 2013: 129). Whatever differences might have existed between his role and that of Roman ambassadors and between him and recipients of his letter, they did not change Paul's certainty that he was an authoritative representative of Jesus Christ. That is why Paul could suggest that persons who rejected his teachings were in fact rejecting the God who sent Jesus Christ (1 Cor. 14:37–38; 1 Thess. 2:13; 4:1–8). Through his devoted service to Jesus Christ and God, Paul was able to simultaneously achieve status and power for himself.[21]

Paul's God as Another Imperial Ruler

According to Paul's apocalyptic vision, those who reject God—that is, again, those who reject him Paul—will face God's "wrath" (e.g., 1 Thess. 1:9–10; 2:14–16; 5:8–10) and "destruction" (e.g., Phil. 1:27–30; 3:17–21; 1 Thess. 5:1–3). If Paul's God was going to be as dominant and as violent in destroying the Roman Empire and subjecting all competing enemies and kingdoms in the future as was the Roman Empire itself (1 Cor. 15:24–25; Phil. 3:17–21), then this God was in the meantime also as ambitious because, according to Paul, his God-given mission was "to bring about the obedience of faith among *all the Gentiles*" (Rom. 1:5, emphasis added; cf. Rom. 16:25–27). Paul's breadth of territory "from Jerusalem and as far around as Illyricum" (Rom. 15:19), his plan to go to both Rome and Spain (Rom. 15:22–29), and his articulated principle of "not [going] where Christ has already been named" (Rom. 15:20) showed the geographical reach and the ambitious program of this mission to build an "expanding Israel" (McKnight 2019: 98; cf. Marchal 2008: 45–48).[22] Paul might not have appreciated "the rulers of this age" (1 Cor. 2:6, 8) who imprisoned him (Phil. 1:7, 13–14, 17; cf. Phlm. 1, 9–10, 13, 23), but in his role as ambassador, he was in a sense following Rome's colonial style and establishing colonies in different places to help expand the dominion for and of his God, who as "Father" was to sit with "the Lord Jesus Christ" (e.g., Rom. 1:7; 1 Cor. 1:3; 2 Cor. 1:2–3; Gal. 1:3; Phil. 1:2; 1 Thess. 1:1; Phlm. 3) as the new rulers over these assemblies.

Like the masculinist and militaristic Empire of Rome, Paul also used a number of military terms in his letters (Smith 2007: 306, 316; Punt 2016), such as *strateuō* or "to serve as a soldier" (1 Cor. 9:7; 2 Cor. 10:3); *antistrateuomai* or "at war with" (Rom. 7:23); *sustratiōtēs* or "fellow soldier" (Phil. 2:25; Phlm. 2); *stēkō* or "stand firm" (1 Cor. 16:13; Phil. 1:27; 4:1; 1 Thess. 3:8); *hopla* or "weapons" (Rom. 6:13; 13:12; 2 Cor. 6:7; cf. 1 Thess. 5:8). This tendency is arguably most notable in 2 Cor. 10:3–6, where his talk of "waging war" is followed by a rapid succession of references to "weapons," "destroy[ing] strongholds . . . and every proud obstacle," "tak[ing] every thought captive to obey Christ," (2 Cor. 10:5), and "being ready to punish [or avenge] every disobedience." Add to these, Paul's clarification that his weapons "have divine power" (2 Cor. 10:4) and his reference to God parading in a Roman triumph (2 Cor. 2:14) would cause one to conclude that Paul's God is a warrior who is no less formidable than the Roman Emperor. This God and Jesus Christ, Paul says, will empower their followers to become "more than conquerors" (Rom. 8:37).

Conclusion

Given the infusion of the Roman Empire into the visual and material culture of first-century Mediterranean in general and the colonial histories of the cities where Paul founded his Christ-following assemblies in particular, it makes good sense to consider the pervasiveness of the Roman Empire in Paul's letters. However, just as the Roman Empire represents a complex world involving a vast geographical territory and a dense network of economic and sociopolitical manipulations and negotiations, its (direct and indirect) representations in Paul's letters are also intricate and cannot be reduced to simple and one-sided statements such as "Paul's letters endorse the Roman Empire" or "Paul, as a colonized Jew, wrote to defy the Roman Empire." After all, we know that while the books of the Bible were mainly written by Jews living under various colonial situations, these same books have been used by readers for colonial projects. Even if Paul were intentionally referring to the Roman Empire or redeploying Roman rhetoric for his own "religious" or even anti-imperial ends, his words might come across to his readers in different ways. Attempts to pin Paul down regarding his reference to or view of the Roman Empire are unrealistic and reductionistic, because they fail to take into account the complexity of the Roman Empire, of Paul as a person, of language, and of interpretation.

Based on Paul's letters, Paul seems to serve a God who is both a rival and a mirror of the Roman Emperor, and Paul's service to God both causes Paul great problems with the Empire and gives Paul wonderful opportunities to build up his own imperialistic network and authority. Although this chapter, as I stated at the very beginning, is not a postcolonial reading of Paul's letters, nonetheless the postcolonial concepts of ambivalence, mimicry, and hybridity—to the extent that they point to sociopolitical crossings that are entangled and fraught with conflicts, contradictions, and unresolved tensions (cf. Ashcroft, Griffiths, and Tiffin 1998: 10–11, 96–99, 114–116)—are all helpful to our readings and reflections of Paul's letters. What I hope this chapter has shown is that the Roman Empire is both the context and the content of Paul's letters. That is to say, just as Paul's letters appeared in the Roman Empire, the Roman Empire also, as the title of the essay indicates, appears in Paul's letters by affecting Paul's thoughts and words. Even when Paul was not speaking about the Empire or mentioning it by name, the Roman Empire remains always present in his accent.

Notes

1. That is not to say that the definition and parameters of postcolonial biblical criticism is not contested. Richard A. Horsley, who is identified by both Moore and Harker as a scholar of empire-critical readings because of his affirmative readings of Paul as an anti-imperialist, writes, "[T]he most significant way in which a postcolonial reading of Paul disrupts a standard essentialist, individualist, and depoliticized Augustinian-Lutheran

Paul, consists in the rediscovery of the anti-imperial stance and program evident in his letters" (Horsley 1998: 167–168). Furthermore, the particular piece of writing in which Horsley makes this declaration is collected in an anthology entitled *The Postcolonial Bible* (Sugirtharajah [ed.] 1998).
2. Arguments for why certain letters are not deemed to be authentically by Paul and why certain of Paul's authentic letters are viewed as composites (such as 2 Corinthians and Philippians) are readily available in many introductory texts. One passage that has long been suspected as a late interpolation by some scholars is 1 Cor. 14:34–35; for a discussion of this and other possible interpolations in 1 Corinthians, see Murphy-O'Connor 1986.
3. For a discussion of Rome's brutal colonial policies, see Goodman 1997: 85–86; N. Elliott 2008: 27–36; and Liew 2016: 136–141. For a discussion of Rome's use of visual and material culture, see Lopez 2008: 26–28; Kahl 2010: 27–127; and Maier 2013: 2–7, 16–31.
4. As early as the early 20th century, Adolf Deissmann already referred to these terms that appear in the New Testament and talked about "a polemical parallelism between the cult of the emperor and the cult of Christ" (Deissmann 1927: 349; cf. pp. 350–365).
5. Depending mainly on parallel terms as a kind of "hidden echoes" to reveal Paul's anti-Rome stance has been criticized as methodologically "thin" and problematic. For a critique that is more dismissive of Paul's concern with the Roman Empire, see Barclay 2011; for a critique that is more sympathetic with reading Paul as anti-Rome, see Heilig 2015.
6. According to Scott J. Hafemann, the use of *thriambeuō* with a direct object is more or less a technical way to communicate leading captives in a Roman triumph to the punishment of death; see Hafemann 1986: 39. Timothy Luckritz Marquis explains further that Paul's reference to himself as a captive in Christ's triumph is part of his rhetorical strategy to not only explain changes in his travel plans that caused him not to visit Corinth as he had promised (i.e., he is being led by Christ so his travels are basically out of his control) but also turn criticism of his "weakness" into an argument for his sincerity, loyalty, and authority (i.e., his God is a victorious king so acceptance or rejection of Paul carries life-and-death implications). See Marquis 2013: 70–86.
7. The "fragrance" refers to the incense often used in the procession of a triumph; see Marquis 2013: 75.
8. The other term that Paul also uses to talk about the return of Jesus Christ, *apantēsis* (1 Thess. 4:17), similarly comes from political discourse of the Greco-Roman world. It refers to a city's ritual welcome in response to the visit of a high official (Koester 1997: 158–160).
9. The same reason or dynamics may be at work in Paul's advice to the Thessalonians to "lead a quiet life," "mind your own business," and "not be dependent on anybody" (1 Thess. 4:11–12). If so, then Paul thinks that the alternative ethos and value demonstrated by his assemblies can "win respect from outsiders" (1 Thess. 4:12).
10. Given how the Romans feminized nations they conquered, Davina C. Lopez proceeds to argue that Paul's identification with a woman giving birth expresses in effect his solidarity with the nations of vanquished people within the Roman Empire. See Lopez 2008.
11. Despite what Paul says in 1 Corinthians 9, he acknowledges receiving financial help from the Philippians in Phil. 3:15–20.
12. There have been some scholarly discussions about the socio-economic makeup of Paul's assemblies; see, for example, Meggit 1998; and Friesen 2004.
13. Other passages—such as 2 Cor. 1:15–16; 12:17–18—have been read as alluding to the collection as well, even if the collection is not explicitly mentioned; see Wan 2000: 194. Wan

further suggests, on the basis of Rom. 15:22–31, that Paul sees the collection "as a point of departure, literally and figuratively, for his future endeavors"—that is, his mission to Spain (Wan 2000: 194–195).

14. Wan is careful to argue that the collection should not be read as Paul's ethno- or cultural chauvinism. He does so by contrasting Paul's collection with exclusionary attempts by some first-century Jews to refuse Gentile gifts or sacrifices for the temple, and by attending to Paul's emphasis on equity between Jews and his Gentile assemblies in Paul's discussion of the collection (cf. 2 Cor. 8:13–14). See Wan 2000: 202–203, 210–212.
15. Given what Paul has said regarding how God uses the jealous competition between Gentiles and Jews to save both peoples, it is ironic that Paul ends his letter to the Romans persuading his Gentile readers not to look down on or be in competition with others but be accepting of others, including those of a different race/ethnicity (Romans 12–15). Scot McKnight also wonders if Paul's collection for Jerusalem from assemblies in Gentile territories is not related to what Paul calls "the full number of the Gentiles" or "the fullness of the Gentiles" (Rom. 11:25) and hence functioning to "provoke nonbelieving Jews in Jerusalem to jealousy and to embrace the Messiah" (McKnight 2019: 82).
16. Paul's problems with the Galatians over circumcision and with the Corinthians over his credibility (because of his changing travel plans and the question of money) are clear from his letters; less so is his problems with the Philippians. According to Cynthia Briggs Kittredge, Paul's imprisonment (Phil. 1:7, 13) might have caused the assembly in Philippi to turn to Euodia and Syntyche as their new leaders, and these women were leading the assembly in ways that Paul did not approve (Phil. 4:2); as a result, Paul wrote to the Philippians to send Timothy and Epaphroditus to replace the women as leaders of the assembly (Phil. 2:19–30). See Kittredge 1998.
17. Some scholars argue that both of these passages in 1 Corinthians are later interpolations, and so they were not penned by Paul. See again Murphy-O'Connor 1986.
18. Most scholars have of course assumed Onesimus to be Philemon's slave because of Phlm. 16. For a recent work that uses Phlm. 16 to read Onesimus as Philemon's brother, see Callahan 1997.
19. Paul's superiority to Philemon is also subtly suggested by (1) Philemon's inability to make Onesimus "useful" as Paul does (Phlm. 11); (2) Philemon's "duty" to follow Paul's "command" (Phlm. 8); (3) Philemon's obligation to provide "service" to Paul during Paul's imprisonment (Phlm. 13); and (4) Philemon's indebtedness to Paul (Phlm. 19).
20. There has been considerable discussion about whether the Greek word in Phlm. 9 should be *presbytēs* ("old man") or *presbeutēs* ("an ambassador"). Allen Callahan contends that while manuscript traditions favor *presbytēs*, "Paul's rhetorical tone is precisely that of an ambassador" (Callahan 1997: 31); this is one of the reasons that Callahan titles his book on Philemon *Embassy of Onesimus* (Callahan 1997: title).
21. This has caused many feminist scholars to call for the need to "decenter Paul"; see especially Schüssler Fiorenza 1999: 31–55, 105–194. See also Marchal (ed.) 2015 for an attempt to do so with the assembly at Philippi; and Nasrallah 2019 with Paul's various assemblies through archaeology.
22. McKnight himself does not address the irony of this expression, because his argument about Romans focuses on an alternative understanding of peace being provided by Paul against *Pax Romana*. See McKnight 2019.

References

Ando, Clifford. *Imperial Ideology and Provincial Loyalty in the Roman Empire.* Berkeley: University of California Press, 2000.

Ashcroft, Bill, Gareth Griffiths, and Helen Tiffin. *Post-colonial Studies: The Key Concepts.* New York: Routledge, 1998.

Aus, Roger David. *Imagery of Triumph and Rebellion in 2 Corinthians 2:14–17 and Elsewhere in the Epistles: An Example of the Combination of Greco-Roman and Judaic Traditions in the Apostle Paul.* Lanham: University Press of America, 2005.

Barclay, John M. G. "Why the Roman Empire Was Insignificant to Paul." In *Pauline Churches and Diaspora Jews,* edited by John M. G. Barclay, 363–387. Tübingen: Mohr Siebeck, 2011.

Beard, Mary. *Roman Triumph.* Cambridge: Harvard University Press, 2009.

Beker, J. Christiaan. *Paul's Apocalyptic Gospel: The Coming Triumph of God* Minneapolis: Augsburg Fortress, 1982.

Blackwell, Ben C., John K. Goodrich, and Jason Maston, Eds. *Paul and the Apocalyptic Imagination.* Minneapolis: Fortress, 2016.

Callahan, Allen Dwight, *Embassy of Onesimus: The Letter of Paul to Philemon.* Harrisburg, PA: Trinity International, 1997.

Campbell, Douglas A. *The Deliverance of God: An Apocalyptic Rereading of Justification in Paul.* Grand Rapids: Wm. B. Eerdmans, 2009.

Cassidy, Richard. *Paul in Chains: Roman Imprisonment and the Letters of Paul.* New York: Crossroad, 2001.

Castelli, Elizabeth A. *Imitating Paul: A Discourse of Power.* Louisville: Westminster John Knox, 1991.

Charles, Ronald. *Paul and the Politics of Diaspora.* Minneapolis: Fortress, 2014.

Chow, John K. *Patronage and Power: A Study of Social Networks in Corinth* (Sheffield: Sheffield Academic, 1992.

Cone, James H. *The Cross and the Lynching Tree.* Maryknoll: Orbis, 1992.

Cone, James H. *The Cross and the Lynching Tree.* Maryknoll: Orbis, 2011.

Cook, John Granger. "Crucifixion as Spectacle in Roman Campania." *Novum Testamentum* 54 (2012): 68–100.

Croy, N. Clayton. "'To Die Is Gain' (Philippians 1:19–26): Does Paul Contemplate Suicide?" *Journal of Biblical Literature* 122 (2003): 517–531.

Deissmann, Adolf. *Light from the Ancient East: The New Testament Illustrated by Recently Discovered Texts of the Graeco-Roman World.* New York: Harper & Brothers, 1927.

Droge, Arthur J. "*Mori Lucrum*: Paul and Ancient Theories of Suicide." *Novum Testamentum* 30 (1988): 262–286.

Elliott, John H. "Patronage and Clientism in Early Christian Society: A Short Reading Guide." *Forum* 3 (1987): 39–48.

Elliott, Neil. *The Arrogance of Nations: Reading Romans in the Shadow of Empire.* Minneapolis: Fortress, 2008.

Esler, Philip F. "Ancient Oleiculture and Ethnic Differentiation: The Meaning of the Olive-Tree Image in Romans 1." *Journal for the Study of the New Testament* 26, no.1 (2003) : 103–124.

Friesen, Steven J. "Poverty in Pauline Studies: Beyond the So-Called New Consensus." *Journal for the Study of the New Testament* 26 (2004): 323–361.

Friesen, Steven J. "Paul and Economics: The Jerusalem Collection as an Alternative to Patronage." In *Paul Unbound: Other Perspectives on the Apostle*, edited by Mark D. Given, 27–54., Peabody: Hendrickson, 2010.

Frilingos, Chris. "'For My Child, Onesimus': Paul and Domestic Power in Philemon." *Journal of Biblical Literature* 119 (2000): 91–104.

Garnsey, Peter and Richard Saller. 2015. *The Roman Society: Economy, Society and Culture* (Berkeley: University of California Press, 2nd edn).

Garnsey, Peter and Richard Saller. *The Roman Society: Economy, Society and Culture*, 2nd ed. Berkeley: University of California Press, 2019.

Gaventa, Beverly Roberts. *Our Mother Saint Paul*. Louisville: Westminster John Knox, 2007.

Gaventa, Beverly Roberts. *Apocalyptic Paul: Cosmos and Anthropos in Romans 5–8*. Waco: Baylor University Press, 2019.

Glancy, Jennifer. *Slavery in Early Christianity*. New York: Oxford University Press, 2002.

Glancy, Jennifer. *Corporal Knowledge: Early Christian Bodies*. New York: Oxford University Press, 2010.

Goodman, Martin. *The Roman World: 44 BC–AD 180*. New York: Routledge, 1997.

Hafemann, Scott J. *Suffering and the Spirit: An Exegetical Study of 2 Cor 2:14–3:3 within the Context of the Corinthian Correspondence*, Tübingen: Mohr Siebeck, 1986.

Hardin, Justin K. *Galatians and the Imperial Cult: A Critical Analysis of the First-Century Social Context of Paul's Letter*. Tübingen: Mohr Siebeck, 2008.

Harker, Christina. *The Colonizers' Idols: Paul, Galatia, and Empire in New Testament Studies*. Tübingen: Mohr Siebeck, 2018.

Heilig, Christoph. *Hidden Criticism? The Methodology and Plausibility of the Search for a Counter-Imperial Subtest in Paul*. Tübingen: Mohr Siebeck, 2015.

Horsley, Richard A. "Innovation in Search of Reorientation: New Testament Studies Rediscovering Its Subject Matter." *Journal of the American Academy of Religion* 62 (1994): 1127–1166.

Horsley, Richard A. "Paul's Counter-Imperial Gospel: Introduction." In *Paul and Empire: Religion and Power in Roman Imperial Society*, edited by Richard A. Horsley, 140–147. Harrisburg, PA: Trinity International, 1997a.

Horsley, Richard A. "1 Corinthians: A Case Study of Paul's Assembly as an Alternative Society." In *Paul and Empire: Religion and Power in Roman Imperial Society*, edited by Richard A. Horsley, 242–252. Harrisburg, PA: Trinity International, 1997b.

Horsley, Richard A. "Submerged Biblical Histories and Imperial Biblical Studies." In *The Postcolonial Bible*, edited by R. S. Sugirtharajah, 152–173. Sheffield, UK: Sheffield Academic, 1998.

Horsley, Richard A., ed. *Paul and Empire: Religion and Power in Roman Imperial Society*. Harrisburg, PA: Trinity International, 1997.

Horsley, Richard A., ed. *Paul and Politics: Eklessia, Israel, Imperium, Interpretation: Essays in Honor of Krister Stendahl*. Harrisburg, PA: Trinity International, 2000.

Johnson Hodge, Caroline. *If Sons, Then Heirs: A Study of Kinship and Ethnicity in the Letters of Paul*. New York: Oxford University Press, 2007.

Kahl, Brigitte. *Galatians Re-Imagined: Reading with the Eyes of the Vanquished*. Minneapolis: Fortress, 2007.

Kahl, Brigitte. *Galatians Re-Imagined: Reading with the Eyes of the Vanquished*. Minneapolis: Fortress, 2010.

Kittredge, Cynthia B. *Community and Authority: The Rhetoric of Obedience in the Pauline Tradition*. Harrisburg, PA: Trinity International, 1998.

Klauck, Hans-Josef. *Ancient Letters and the New Testament: A Guide to Context and Exegesis*, translated by Daniel P. Bailey. Waco, TX: Baylor University Press, 2006.

Koester, Helmut. "Imperial Ideology and Paul's Eschatology in 1 Thessalonians." In *Paul and Empire: Religion and Power in Roman Imperial Society*, edited by Richard A. Horsley, 158–166. Harrisburg, PA: Trinity International, 1997.

Lacey, W. K. "*Patria Potestas*." In *The Family in Ancient Rome: New Perspectives*, edited by Beryl Rawson, 121–144. London: Croom Helm, 1986.

Liew, Tat-siong Benny. *Politics of Parousia: Reading Mark Inter(con)textually*. Leiden: Brill, 1999.

Liew, Tat-siong Benny. "The Gospel of Bare Life: Reading Death, Dream, and Desire through John's Jesus." In *Psychoanalytic Mediations between Marxist and Postcolonial Readings of the Bible*, edited by Tat-siong Benny Liew and Erin Runions, 129–170, Atlanta: SBL Press, 2016.

Lopez, Davina C. *The Apostle to the Conquered: Reimagining Paul's Mission*. Minneapolis: Fortress, 2008.

Maier, Harry O. *Picturing Paul in Empire: Imperial Image, Text and Persuasion in Colossians, Ephesians and the Pastoral Epistles*. New York: T&T Clark, 2013.

Malina, Bruce J. "Patron and Client: The Analogy behind Synoptic Theology." *Forum* 4 (1988): 1–32.

Marchal, Joseph A. *The Politics of Heaven: Women, Gender, and Empire in the Study of Paul*. Minneapolis: Fortress, 2008.

Marchal, Joseph A., ed. *The People beside Paul: The Philippian Assembly and History from Below*. Atlanta: SBL Press, 2015.

Martin, Dale B. *Slavery as Salvation: The Metaphor of Slavery in Pauline Christianity*. New Haven: Yale University Press, 1990.

Martin, Dale B. *The Corinthian Body*. New Haven: Yale University Press, 1995.

Marquis, Timothy Luckritz. *Transient Apostle: Paul, Travel, and the Rhetoric of Empire*. New Haven: Yale University Press, 2013.

Matlock, Barry. *Unveiling the Apocalyptic Paul: Paul's Interpreters and the Rhetoric of Criticism*. Sheffield: Sheffield Academic, 1996.

Matlock, Barry. "Almost Cultural Studies? Reflections on the 'New Perspective' on Paul." In *Biblical Studies/Cultural Studies: The Third Sheffield Colloquium*, edited by Cheryl Exum and Stephen D. Moore, 433–459. Sheffield: Sheffield Academic, 1998.

Mattern, Susan P. *Rome and the Enemy: Imperial Strategy in the Principate* Berkeley: University of California Press, 1999.

McKnight, Scot. *Reading Romans Backwards: A Gospel of Peace in the Midst of Empire*. Waco: Baylor University Press, 2019.

Meggit, Justin J. *Paul, Poverty and Survival*. New York: T&T Clark, 1998.

Miles, Gary B. 1990. "Roman and Modern Imperialism: A Reassessment." *Comparative Studies in Society and History* 32.4: 629–659.

Moore, Stephen D. "Postcolonialism." In *A Handbook for Postmodern Biblical Interpretation*, edited by A. K. M. Adam, 182–188. St. Louis: Chalice, 2000.

Morrill, Bruce T. *Anamnesis as Dangerous Memory: Political and Liturgical Theology in Dialogue*. Collegeville: Liturgical, 2000.

Murphy-O'Connor, Jerome. "Interpolations in 1 Corinthians." *Catholic Biblical Quarterly* 48 (1986): 81–94.

Nasrallah, Laura Salah. "1 Corinthians." In *The New Testament: Fortress Commentary on the Bible*, edited by Margaret Aymer, Cynthia Briggs Kittredge, and David A. Sánchez, 427–471. Minneapolis: Fortress, 2014.

Nasrallah, Laura Salah. *Archaeology and the Letters of Paul*. New York: Oxford University Press, 2019.

Nock, Arthur Darby. *Conversion: The Old and the New in Religion from Alexander the Great to Augustine of Hippo*. New York: Oxford University Press, 1933.

Oakes, Peter S. "Economic Approaches: Scarce Resources and Interpretive Opportunities." In *Studying Paul's Letters: Contemporary Perspectives and Methods*, edited by Joseph A. Marchal, 75–91. Minneapolis: Fortress, 2012.

Panayotakis, Stelios, Gareth Schmeling, and Michael Paschalis, eds. *Holy Men and Charlatans in Ancient Novel*. Eelde: Barkhuis, 2015.

Price, Simon R. F. *Rituals and Power: The Roman Imperial Cult in Asia Minor*. New York: Cambridge University Press, 1984.

Punt, Jeremy. *Postcolonial Biblical Interpretation: Reframing Paul*. Leiden: Brill, 2015.

Punt, Jeremy. "Paul, Military Image and Social Disadvantage," *Acta Theologica* 23 (2016): 201–224.

Revell, Louise. *Roman Imperialism and Local Identities*. New York: Cambridge University Press, 2009.

Richlin, Amy. *The Garden of Priapus: Sexuality and Aggression in Roman Humor*, revised ed. New York: Oxford University Press, 1992.

Runesson, Anna. *Exegesis in the Making: Postcolonialism and New Testament Studies*. Leiden: Brill, 2011.

Schüssler Fiorenza, Elisabeth. *Rhetoric and Ethics: The Politics of Biblical Studies'* Minneapolis: Fortress, 1999.

Smith, Abraham. "The First and Second Letters to the Thessalonians." In *A Postcolonial Commentary on the New Testament Writings*, edited by Fernando F. Segovia and R. S. Sugirtharajah, 294–322. New York: T & T Clark, 2007.

Stowers, Stanley K. *A Rereading of Romans: Justice, Jews, and Gentiles*. New Haven: Yale University Press, 1994.

Sugirtharajah, R. S., ed. *The Postcolonial Bible*. Sheffield, UK: Sheffield Academic, 1994.

Wallace, Richard, and Wynne Williams. *The Three Worlds of Paul of Tarsus*. New York: Routledge, 1998.

Wan, Sze-kar. "Collection for the Saints as Anticolonial Act: Implications of Paul's Ethnic Reconstruction." In *Paul and Politics: Eklessia, Israel, Imperium, Interpretation: Essays in Honor of Krister Stendahl*, edited by Richard A. Horsley, 191–215. Harrisburg, PA: Trinity International, 2000.

Wasserman, Emma. *Apocalypse as Holy War: Divine Politics and Polemics in the Letters of Paul*. New Haven: Yale University Press, 2018.

Wire, Antoinette Clark. *The Corinthian Women Prophets: A Reconstruction through Paul's Rhetoric*. Minneapolis: Fortress, 1990.

Wright, N. T. *Paul: In Fresh Perspective*. London: SPCK, 2005.

Yeo, Khiok-Khng. "The Rhetorical Hermeneutic of 1 Corinthians 8 and Chinese Ancestor Worship." *Biblical Interpretation* 2 (1994): 294–311.

CHAPTER 9

THE ROMAN EMPIRE IN THE BOOK OF REVELATION

JACQUELINE M. HIDALGO

INTRODUCTION

FILLED with so many hard-to-interpret visions that it is often just called "Revelations" in popular discourse, the Book of Revelation (singular), also known as the Apocalypse of John (or "the Apocalypse"), has both mystified and intrigued generations. One of the most controversial books of the Christian Testament, the Book of Revelation is so full of verbal and visual evocations of Roman imperial practices, motifs, and myths that one could write an entire book just listing and tracing these parallels.[1] Yet, as a product of a minoritized community, the Apocalypse also depends completely on earlier Jewish texts and traditions, including texts that did not make it into the Jewish canon. How does understanding the Roman Empire help us understand the Book of Revelation, its history, and its circulation? How do we make sense of this text's hybridity?

This brief essay surveys key trends in the study of the Roman Empire in Revelation from the last thirty years of biblical scholarship, particularly those strands of biblical scholarship shaped by postcolonial literary critical approaches and questions. On the one hand, this essay summarizes scholarship that describes much of the fantastic imagery in the Book of Revelation as playing with and responding to Roman imperial histories, rituals, propaganda, and images. On the other hand, this essay also charts contemporary scholarly debates over the *meaning* of Rome in Revelation. I break down the patterns of interpretation that scholars pursue, showing how scholars turn to the Roman Empire as a way to decode Revelation's imagery but also wrestle with Rome and Revelation in order to grapple with their own views on empire (ancient and modern), resistance, and the ethics of interpretation.

Because it is outside this essay's purview to survey reception history, I take for granted the import of the world of interpreters, a world that comes after five hundred years of Western European and Euro-diasporic U.S. imperialism around the world. I do not think there is a simple correlation between the presence of the Roman Empire in the Book of Revelation and the spread of modern European and Euro-descended empires throughout the world.[2] Nor do I think there is a direct trajectory from Roman imperial motifs in the Apocalypse to modern European/Euro-diasporic imperial uses of the Book of Revelation, though others have made compelling cases for the import of Revelation to modern imperialism.[3]

As an additional caveat to this essay, I wish to note that our questions about empire and biblical texts have changed as more descendants of the Global South studied and wrote about the Book of Revelation in academic settings, especially in the postcolonial era of the second half of the twentieth century. At the same time many postcolonial biblical critics do not hail from the Global South. Regardless, scholarly experiences with imperial metropolises as well as within settler colonial nations have drawn attention to the reception history of the Book of Revelation as a text that justified imperialism and settler colonialism in modernity but also served as a resource for colonized populations as they imagined and struggled for a world otherwise. As a daughter of Latin America (born in Costa Rica), I grew up in and work in the United States. Thus my own experiences with the persistent presence of multiple imperial histories in the Western hemisphere—and their subversion—have always shaped the questions I ask. I hope that readers of this essay similarly reflect on how their contexts factor into how they read Rome, Revelation, or other texts.

REVELATIONS OF EMPIRE: THE ROMAN EMPIRE AS A CONTEXT FOR THE APOCALYPSE

At the start of the twenty-first century, Harry O. Maier described the Apocalypse "as a revelation of empire and one's place within it."[4] Scholars in the last few decades have particularly focused on how empire in general and the Roman Empire in particular appear in the Apocalypse. Since empire is so pervasive and multivalent, it would be difficult to trace all the different ways that Rome appears in Revelation. We also must remember that empire is and was a multisensory experience. Sight, sound, food, money, trade, sanctity, divinity, and other facets of Roman culture are all themes in Revelation's narrative, message, and performance. The earliest audiences of Revelation mostly *heard* and *saw* the text performed out loud, likely as a form of liturgical and potentially ecstatic worship. Hearing the Apocalypse was thus also a multisensory experience that could affect a sense of divine communion while enabling marginalized participants to feel themselves to be central figures in a great mythscape.[5] Even as we privately read for the Roman Empire in Revelation, we need to remember that written discourse would not have been the first or most important encounter the earliest auditors had with this text.

Although we cannot know the actual author of this text, we can follow the claimed author, John, as a "rhetorical device."[6] When I refer to Revelation's "author" in this essay, I am referencing the implied author-as-character rather than any real historical figure. In Revelation 1:9, the author names himself as John, "your brother and partner in the oppression, the kingdom, and the endurance in Jesus." We know that the character narrating Revelation is identified with a community following Jesus—a community of shared oppression but also a community that endures. Furthermore, John was "on the island called Patmos on account of the word of God and the testimony of Jesus." John may be residing in some form of exile, though it is hardly clear whether it is a self-chosen exile, some form of political punishment, or merely a form of self-description.[7] Nevertheless, the rhetorical author has positioned himself in some sort of adverse relationship to Rome.

Although we tend to treat the Apocalypse as a "Christian" text, cognizant of the absence of the word "Christian" anywhere in the Book of Revelation, we should understand the Apocalypse to be an ancient Jewish text.[8] Jewish experiences with diaspora and Roman Empire thus provide significant context to Revelation. There have been scholarly debates over whether to date Revelation anywhere from the 60s to the 90s (or even a little later); most place the text during the reign of Roman emperor Domitian (81–96 CE).[9] In the late 60s CE Judea revolted against Roman imperial power, and Rome responded forcefully, massacring many, deporting others, and destroying the Second Temple in Jerusalem in 70 CE.[10] Regardless of the text's exact date, the text frames itself within a Jewish community that remains antagonistic to Roman domination even if it is also produced in and through the cultural life of Roman Asia.

Revelation's epistolary framing as a letter "to the seven assemblies that are in Asia" (Rev 1:4) relies on political terrain. The word regularly translated as "churches" (ἐκκλησία) in political contexts referred to the assemblies of citizens of a particular city-state. The seven cities addressed—Ephesus, Smyrna, Pergamum, Thyatira, Sardis, Philadelphia, and Laodicea (Rev 1:11)—were cities that played important roles in the Roman governance of Asia for more than two centuries. These opening letters also mimic the form of imperial edicts.[11] By framing the Apocalypse with a focus on these seven cities, the rhetorical author is addressing a rhetorical audience composed of colonized territories known for the successful spread of Roman religion, economy, and ideology. The presence of Roman imperialism as an important backdrop to the text stretches from the geographical imagination of the author in exile, to the cities of address in the opening letters, and on into the closing blessings and curses on readers who keep this text and readers who alter it (Rev 22:18–19).[12]

Nested within Revelation's epistolary structure is a recounting of a heavenly vision filled with multivalent symbolism, motifs of divine leadership, and regular intervals of sung praise, which further underscore the Apocalypse's history of liturgical performance. Although Revelation is an incredibly complex, metaphorically rich, and visually and sonically evocative text, when it comes to Rome in Revelation, one way to interpret the Apocalypse is through Gayatri Chakravorty Spivak's notion of catachresis, where the colonized "strategically" use imperial myths so as to turn those myths against the oppressors.[13] Where Rome claims eternal power over the earth, particularly through the authorization of Jupiter and the gods, Revelation describes Rome as a minion of Satan that blasphemes against the real ruler of all creation, God, while persecuting those witnesses who remain faithful to God's sovereignty. Rome and its practices appear as a target of blatant critique in several key passages and characters, and it is notable that these passages often also rhetorically evoke gender (stereotyped representations of femininity or masculinity) and/or sex. These passages include criticisms against local churches in the opening letters (and especially against John's antagonists such as the Nicolaitans, Jezebel, Balaam, and the synagogue of Satan), the throne room (Rev 4–5), the woman in heaven (Rev 12), the Beasts of land and sea (Rev 13), the 144,000 virgins (Rev 14), the woman Babylon (Rev 17–19), and the new Jerusalem (Rev 21–22).

For instance, the most obvious allusion to Rome appears in the woman Babylon (Rev 17–18). She is "clothed in purple and scarlet" (Rev 17:4) and pretty decisively describes the city of Rome: the woman Babylon sits on seven hills (Rev 17:9), a common descriptor of Rome, and is "the great city that rules over the kings of the earth" (Rev 17:18). Though she has promised "to never see mourning" (18:7), an allusion to Rome's promise of eternal peace, she will fall. Instead of Rome's claims to offer peace, security, salvation, and global power, God is the ultimate source of "salvation and glory and power" (19:1). Although the name Babylon may seem like a coded message, given that the author of this text could not have named Rome directly, a first-century diasporic Jewish audience would have clearly heard "Babylon" and known that Babylon meant Rome, since Babylon stands for another imperial "enemy" that had destroyed the First Jerusalem Temple in 587/586 BCE.[14]

The Roman Imperial Cult as Apocalyptic Decoder Ring

One of the most straightforward ways that scholars approach Rome's appearance in Revelation is to turn to Rome as the "decoder ring" that clarifies some of Revelation's most mystifying images, especially its images that have appeared in popular appropriations of Revelation. For example, given popular fascination with "the number of the beast," scholars regularly decode 666 (Rev 13:18) through gematria, or traditional Hebrew play with letters and numbers, and they argue that this number is actually a coded way to name the Roman emperor Nero.[15] Yet, scholars are not just interested in decoding these specific popular images; they see Rome, especially Roman ideology, as a key to the entire mythscape of the text.

Rome portrayed itself as a world ruler and a bringer of order, a Pax Romana that was heavenly, earthly, and universal.[16] Such claims are not only political or ideological but also religious. Scholars have often suggested that Jewish diasporic communities may have seen Rome's self-rhetoric as blasphemous. The imperial cult in particular has served as a focus for decoding Revelation in part because these imperial devotions tie together religion, politics, and economics so well.[17] Religious devotions to the emperors also incorporated reiterations of mythic ideologies that justified Roman domination.

Economic relationships as well as political positions could be allocated to faithful participants in imperial cult devotions, and coins carried religious inscriptions and images.[18]

Through a system of binaries that ultimately divide followers of God and of Satan—bear in mind there is no anti-Christ mentioned in Revelation—John inscribes an ideological conflict between the followers of the Lamb and the imperial temple cult.[19] Here Revelation's rhetorical geography is again relevant. The cities named as Revelation's audience were cities that participated in the imperial cult. The first imperial cult temple in Asia was built in Pergamum in 29 BCE. Smyrna's dates to 45 CE, Philadelphia to 55 CE, Sardis to 56 CE, and Laodicea to 87 CE. If we date Revelation to the 90s, it may respond to the recent buildup of the imperial cult in the region; for instance, Ephesus dedicated the Temple of the Sebastoi around 89/90 CE.[20]

One concrete example of using the imperial cult to decode Revelation would be decrypting the beasts in Revelation 13. The beast from the sea appears to have political, military, and economic power. Followers of the Lamb are distinguished specifically by their refusal to worship the beast from the sea (Rev 14:9–11; 20:4).[21] Rome dominated its Asian province by sea; the Roman governor would have arrived by sea.[22] The beast from the land also has power but specifically works to deceive people into worshipping the first beast, and it does so through theatrical practices that may be related to the imperial cult: "it performs great signs, namely making fire from heaven come down to earth" (Rev 13:13). Because such dramatic plays with fire could be associated with imperial cult ritual, the beast from the land probably describes the priesthood of the imperial cult.[23]

The ways the imperial cult pervaded daily economic life have particularly interested those scholars who use the imperial cult to decode Revelation. For instance, David E. Aune points to the place of the goddess Roma on an Asian coin from 71 CE, which shows the goddess Roma sitting on seven hills with the river Tiber, and he connects this to representations of the woman Babylon found in Revelation 17:1 and 17:9.[24] The beast from the land also works to ensure that only those bearing the beast's "mark" can buy or sell (Rev 13:16–17), which could refer to carrying Roman coins that are stamped with these "religious" symbols.

Because actual Roman settlers were a minority of the local populace, Rome relied on colonies of occupation where local elites cooperated in many facets of colonial governance.[25] Local elites derived both economic gains and political capital—for themselves or their descendants—from their staged performances of acquiescence.[26] Steven J. Friesen argues that the imperial cult figured importantly in daily life in critical ways, such as "worship, processions, festivals, delegations, sports, governance, inscriptions and coinage," and that we must assume people widely celebrated and participated in imperial cult practices in Asia Minor.[27] Local elites would participate in rituals such as animal sacrifice (and its ultimate consumption) as well as devotional oaths conveying loyalty to the emperor and empire. Cities themselves would compete for the title of *neokoros*, a form of official recognition as an imperial cultic center, as a means of competing for power and prestige. According to Jean-Pierre Ruiz, we should understand Asia Minor's imperial cult practices as a means of "sorting out their colonial entanglements."[28]

Participants derived economic benefits from the imperial cult. Thus a lack of participation would have increased economic hardship, and John's calls for endurance may refer to enduring those economic hardships rather than any formal "persecution."[29] For instance, John criticizes people in his own communities who "eat food sacrificed to idols" (Rev 2:14; 2:17; 2:20). Perhaps community members ate food sacrificed to idols as part of their participation in trade guilds or civic honors to the Roman emperors.[30] Eating idol food also drew community members into an economic and political tangle with Rome.

Sex, Gender, and Imperial Visuality

Because we have access to archaeological remains, while in similar ways we cannot access other facets of ancient Roman imperial life (and also because visual rhetoric was so important to Rome), scholars particularly look at how Revelation's visually evocative language conjures comparison to Roman images. Long before there was an imperial cult, there were temples throughout Asia Minor dedicated to the divine personification of Rome—the goddess Roma. The first temple to Rome antedates the Roman province of Asia since it was built in Smyrna in 195 BCE.[31] Temples to Roma were one way that peoples could understand, relate to, and negotiate a dominating power, and thus the temples could be places specifically for worshipping strength, which is what the word "Rome" meant in Greek.[32] Visually speaking, Revelation's Babylon can be understood as a caricature of the goddess Roma, whose representation was based on Athena and the Amazons, and she generally wore "military dress."[33]

Imperial cult temples themselves visually represented the power and legitimacy of Roman rule in a way that nonparticipating passersby would have observed.[34] For temples within the imperial cult that honored Augustus in particular, he had commanded that temples to him or his adoptive father must also include devotion to the goddess Roma, so her image was also prominent in imperial cult temples.[35] However, after Augustus's death, this decree began to fade from memory, and it was common to find other divinities or a "local patron deity" as an accompaniment in imperial cult temple dedications.[36] As archaeologist Benjamin B. Rubin argues, the deities invoked in the imperial cult temples' visual repertoire further underscored a Roman cosmovision where Jupiter was the highest god, the emperor was an intermediary who manifested divine will on earth, and the emperor ruled over the spirit of the local people.[37] Perhaps John responds to temple representations of this cosmovision in Revelation 2:13, where the "throne of Satan" may refer to the altar of Zeus amid the imperial cult in Pergamum.[38]

Gender, family, and sexual metaphors were all important to Roman rhetoric and visual propaganda. The social construction of gender—as distinct from biological sex—was a way of thinking about and representing power in the Roman world (and in our present one) even if such representations did not always break in ways that are either biological or neatly binaristic.

Scholars tend to examine "active" and "passive" as the categories that are generally gendered "masculine" and "feminine," but, as Bernadette J. Brooten explains, Romans "described passive men as effeminate and active women as masculine."[39] However, at the most basic level, masculinity was defined as penetrating others and not being penetrated, or being active and not passive. Again, this gendering did not always simply rely on the ways we define men and women. Rome used "women," such as the Vestal Virgins, in order to represent its impenetrability and "inviolability."[40] Nevertheless, being the ones who penetrated but were not themselves penetrated served as a potent gender and sexual metaphor for Roman virility and power.

These metaphors were often presented visually. The Sebasteion, a first-century imperial temple complex in Aphrodisias, provides insight into how Romans visualized gender and power. In one relief that scholars often discuss, the emperor Claudius towers over a bare-breasted feminine figure, Britannia, representing Britain, whose body lays beneath Claudius. As Davina C. López has argued, such a portrayal was part of Roman imperial propaganda where a representation of "sexual humiliation and violence" underscores that Britain is vulnerable and conquered while emperor Claudius, and thus Rome, penetrates while remaining "impenetrable."[41] Gender representations and sexual violence functioned as both literal and metaphorical forms of conquest and colonization.[42]

Given the prominence of Roman visual representations of gender and sexual domination, the depictions of Jezebel and Babylon on the one hand, and the virginal 144,000 and bridal new Jerusalem on the other, can also be understood within the logics of gender and sexuality as representations of power. Revelation's gender and sex acts do not necessarily refer to literal women and/or sexual practices; rather, sexual practices such as seduction (Jezebel), prostitution (Babylon), abstinence (the 144,000), or preparation for marriage can be understood as serving rhetorical purposes. For example, the 144,000 "virgins" (Rev 14:4) may represent strength through a form of masculinity, as they are impenetrable, but their abstinence may also signal a refusal of Roman masculinity because they abstain from penetrating "women."[43]

The Ethics of Reading the Roman Empire in Revelation

For many biblical scholars, reading Revelation is not simply a matter of using Roman imperial contexts in order to "decode" hidden meanings. As the example of the 144,000 shows, scholars also seek to understand John's perspective on empire. As a consequence, scholars ask about how Revelation, early Christian communities, and more modern readers understand and relate to empire, both ancient and modern, as well as specific (e.g., the Babylonian Empire, the Roman Empire, the British Empire, the United States) and general ideologies. As Luis Menéndez-Antuña has argued, interpreters thus pose questions of ethics.[44] Partially because most scholars are deeply concerned about the ethics of our own responses to empire, we ask: What is the ethical relationship to empire that John posits? What are the ethics of reading Revelation in the midst of contemporary empires?

Because Rome appears as both a target of criticism but also a source of influential rhetoric and imagery, most (but not all) contemporary scholars approach Revelation as a response to Rome born out of hybrid traditions, even if the character of the author seems unconscious of his hybridity. Hybridity, as a "Third Space" for the making and unmaking of cultures, is the not necessarily resistant byproduct of negotiations between colonizing and colonized cultures. Although too often understood, or even celebrated, as the effects of cultural mixture, Homi K. Bhabha defines hybridity around an ambivalent core; in fact hybridity is "the effect of an ambivalence produced within the rules of recognition of dominant discourse as they articulate the signs of cultural difference."[45] Although John's binaristic rhetoric seems to desire a community of Jewish Jesus followers purified of Rome, for Bhabha, any claims of "essentialist" cultural purity (on the part of colonizer or colonized) are impossible.[46]

Ultimately I would argue that, especially for those of us residing in imperial metropolises, in ethical terms we have to read Revelation amid a self-reflective ambivalence: Revelation's resistance to empire relies on violent imagery of upheaval and domination. In the remainder of this essay, I trace three main strains in interpreting Revelation's ethics among postcolonial critics: (1) examining Revelation's literary and performance strategies of resistance; (2) underscoring the extent to which the Book of Revelation mimics and thereby also encodes and idealizes Roman imperialism and practices of hierarchal domination; and (3) turning to the Book of Revelation as a locus for thinking about our own practices of interpretation. These three main approaches are not mutually exclusive, though some scholars tend to emphasize one approach more than another.

Revelations against Empire: The Subversion of Roman Myths and Practices

To some extent, I have already framed Revelation as a countermythology that specifically criticizes community participation in Roman religion, politics, and economy. Through an interlocking set of binaries, Revelation demands community members adhere to the practices of God and avoid the practices of Satan, generally aligned with the Roman Empire. In underscoring Revelation as a critique of Rome, scholars often portray John and the earliest receiving communities as minoritized Roman subjects negotiating their own hybridity amid territorial and cultural colonization.

That does not mean Revelation responds to immediate violence in Asia Minor. A Roman state-sanctioned "persecution" does not account for the social situation in which this text was written and initially circulated. The Apocalypse is more likely a Jewish diasporic response to the first Jewish Roman War (66–73 CE), a response crafted either during or in the decades after the war. Thusly, we can approach John as practicing his own "diasporic hermeneutics." For R. S. Sugirtharajah, diasporic hermeneutics tries "to address the state of 'homelessness' ... to find a home for those people who have been made homeless."[47] As I argue elsewhere, if we see this text as a Jewish diasporic response to the Roman destruction of the Temple, we might see how the Apocalypse crafts an imaginative, diasporically mobile temple accessed during the ritualized performance of this text.[48] In this regard, the Apocalypse may function as a diasporic "homing device," a way of creating a mobile home through text and ritual performance. If participants felt unhomed by empire, the work of making home together is itself an act of resistance to empire.

The very language of Revelation, a sort of Aramaized Greek, may be a sign of this kind of diasporic resistance. Revelation's hybrid language in which eastern Mediterranean Jews may have been conversant can be analogized to the ways that Latina/o/xs in the United States often speak a hybrid mixture of Spanish and English. Allen Dwight Callahan describes John's contorted Greek as a reflection of the "subaltern" situation wherein a minoritized author is forced "to appropriate [mainstream discourse's] articulations simply to be understood." John then intentionally broke the rules of Greek grammar "as an exercise of his own discursive power."[49]

As a way of making home, Revelation also draws on earlier Jewish texts. The Apocalypse of John plays with language, tropes, and structures found in earlier Jewish resistance literature, such as Jewish "apocalyptic" texts, Qumran literature, and Hebrew biblical prophetic texts. These earlier Jewish apocalyptic texts have been characterized as "resistance literature" that critically challenged Hellenistic political domination and cultural hegemony.[50] According to Brian K. Blount, John's use of earlier Jewish texts can be compared with "sampling" wherein a "rap artist recalls the past in a way that encourages resistance to the present. In doing so, however, rap is not originating something new but building upon a musical legacy."[51] As a practice of musical memory, the performance of apocalyptic sampling of Jewish traditions serves as a resistant way of making diasporic home by recalling past, successful struggles for survival.

Yet, it is not only that Revelation turns to Jewish traditions to make home and remember a history of resistance. Blount sees Revelation as a call to an active form of nonviolent resistance because of Revelation's call to testimony and bearing witness to God while calling out the evil practices of the Roman Empire.[52] In bearing witness to empire, Revelation underscores the violence of Roman domination found in its economics, its politics, its culture, and its epistemology. For example, Dagoberto Ramírez Fernández examines Revelation 17–18 as an indictment of the dehumanizing practices of Roman economics.[53] Likewise, Clarice J. Martin examines the list of imperial merchandise (18:11–13) and its conclusion with "slaves and human lives."[54] By reversing Ezekiel's list of cargo (27:12–25), John demonstrates that Rome valued slaves and human beings less than precious stones, livestock, or cinnamon.[55] Yet John's list underscores the inherent human value of slaves because it pairs the word "slaves" with the term for "human souls" or "human lives." In this way, John refuses the Aristotelian description of slaves as "defectively souled." Moreover, the communities of God, including angels, elevated through their connection to God, are regularly identified through inflections of the noun δοῦλος, which we should translate as "slave."[56]

This sense that Revelation works through strategic reversals, valuing precisely those practices and people devalued by Rome, has also shaped how scholars understand Revelation's rhetoric. A focus on rhetoric that attacks Roman values has also been a way that scholars have sought to make sense of John's use of misogynistic metaphors, such as Babylon as a "whore." Elisabeth Schüssler Fiorenza is perhaps one of the earliest and most prominent scholars to adapt this strategy, arguing that we cannot take Babylon as a literal woman but as a figural representation. With Babylon, John uses the gendered logic of the time to criticize Rome; fundamentally, though, Babylon represents the home of demons while the new Jerusalem represents the city of God.[57] Barbara Rossing follows this argument even further by examining an ancient Roman, Hellenistic, and Jewish rhetorical device, "the choice between two cities," with each city figured as a woman—a bad woman and a good woman. Revelation 17–22 manifests this sort of choice between two cities. The new Jerusalem, adorned like a bride (Rev 21:2), contrasts symbolically with Babylon, the ravaged and destroyed enslaved prostitute, drawing Revelation's historical audiences into an imaginative reversal of their contemporary historical situation.[58]

Looking at this rhetorical reversal has allowed scholars to see Babylon as a dystopian imagination that stridently depicts the evils of empire, while the new Jerusalem is the utopian counterimagination that eliminates imperial domination. Where Babylon trades in human lives, the new Jerusalem ends the exploitative Roman economy.[59] The troubling image that "the sea was no more" in Revelation 21:1 may emphasize the end of Rome's "shipping economy."[60] The new Jerusalem parodies Greco-Roman ideals of wealth when it descends shining, covered in stones, and with streets of gold.[61] These precious jewels and metals now serve the public good rather than private luxury, even as they make the new Jerusalem appear wealthy.[62]

The reversals found in the binary of Babylon/new Jerusalem may also encode critiques of Roman political practices. The sea is the space that divides Revelation's earliest communities from its Judean homeland; eliminating the sea eliminates the space that separates the diaspora from home. Instead of diaspora, now there is one central city, where all nations can enter and bring their "glory" (Rev 21:24). Where Roman citizenship made all peoples into one people, the new Jerusalem's peoples (λαοί) remain plural (Rev 21:3).[63] Babylon's destruction and the final rule of the new Jerusalem refutes Rome's claims to eternal domination. John interrupts the temporal narrative Rome provided, where Rome was, in a sense, "the end of history."[64]

In constructing a utopian vision beyond the present oppressive histories that Rome relies upon, then, John does not rely only on rhetoric to reject Roman economic and political practices. He also draws auditors into the language of myth and, through catachresis, John directly subverts Roman myths and epistemological practices.[65] For example, David A. Sánchez argues that the Apocalypse appropriates the dominant myths of Rome and turns them to the advantage of Revelation's audience. James C. Scott has described how dominated peoples speak in "hidden transcripts"—transcripts that must provide lip-service to dominant rhetoric even as they work to subvert the myths dominant powers tell about themselves.[66] Because of the power dynamics of empire, the writers and readers of Revelation must necessarily speak through coded language, and they must know Rome's myths well even as they work to undermine those myths. Revelation takes up the myths that justify Roman domination, and flips those myths on their head by promising Rome's destruction and the elevation of those who suffer under Roman imperial rule.

Sánchez carefully examines Revelation 12 as a central passage that takes over the Roman imperial myth of Apollo-Leto-Python, which served a significant role in Roman imperial propaganda under Augustus and Nero.[67] This story in which a chaos monster threatens a divine mother and her child was quite familiar in the ancient world. Rome understood itself to be heir to Apollo, the child who defeats chaos represented as the serpent; Rome was the divine bringer of order. However, in Revelation 12:3, the Roman Empire is now symbolically identified with the dragon, the chaos monster. The message of Revelation 12 becomes that the Satanic empire of chaos has already been defeated in heaven and its earthly agent, Rome, will also lose. The myths that once justified Roman imperial divinity and eternal authority are transformed so that now they describe the eternal sovereign power of God's alter-empire and the Lamb/Christ.[68] Rome is a slave of Satan that will be crushed by God, the true bringer of order.

The Mimic Monster: Revelation's Encoding of Empire as Ideal

That the Apocalypse presents an alter-empire rather than an anti-empire brings forth several questions about the logics of hybridity. Has John's mimicry and mockery of Roman forms led the Apocalypse simply to dethrone Rome while adapting the ideology of the Roman Empire? Are not binaristic hierarchies and drives for purity actually imperial ideologies?

Perhaps one of the best-known proponents of this view is feminist critic Tina Pippin. She ultimately argues that women can find no liberation in Revelation because, even if John rejects the literal Roman Empire, John offers no resistance to Roman ideologies of hierarchical oppression. In fact, he mimics the patriarchal norms of his time and denigrates women in his attack on Rome. For Pippin, the metaphoric women of Revelation are all patriarchal stereotypes: the rival prophet dubbed "Jezebel" (Rev 3), the Woman Clothed with the Sun (Rev 12), the woman Babylon (Rev 17–19), and the bride as new Jerusalem (Rev 20–21). Women briefly appear in 14:4, but only so the text can exhort the faithful to avoid women's bodies as they might defile themselves in relationship to them.[69] Rossing's rhetorical choice between two cities can also be understood as a patriarchal form of dividing up and nurturing conflict between women. For Pippin the representation of Babylon symbolizes a masculinist desire for women's destruction. Babylon/Rome is figured as a woman abused, ravaged, and destroyed by men, and her being a critique of Rome offers us no liberation. The positive representations of mother and bride do not help us much either.[70]

In this reading of Revelation, John simply desires and mimics the structures of Roman power—structures that are represented through hierarchal gender domination. For instance, the *Ara Pacis Augustae* (Altar of Augustan Peace) frieze, commissioned in 13 BCE to honor the emperor Augustus, portrayed Augustus as father of a Roman Empire whose "subjects" were all "children."[71] Similar representations could be found on temples in Asia Minor. These familial representations reinforced domestic hierarchies and the hierarchies of the state. As divinely sanctioned fathers, Romans positioned themselves along a trajectory familiar to contemporary colonized subjects. Rome presented its citizens as the bearers of true humanity and the bringers of real civilization to those they ruled; moreover, such civilization was nurtured in others because Rome served as the father figure of the lands they ruled, where these lands became women, children, and enslaved household members.[72] Even the seemingly positive feminine figure of the new Jerusalem of Revelation 21–22 encodes a visual mapping of the pater familias structure (22:1–3), with God and the Lamb merely replacing the Augustus Caesar from the *Ara Pacis*.

The only woman referenced in the text who may be based on a historical woman is the rival prophet, dubbed Jezebel and thus reduced to a negative stereotype from Jewish tradition. A study of interpretive debates around Jezebel helps us to understand the limits of any simple valorization of Revelation as a text of resistance. In the letter to Thyatira (Rev 2:18–29), Jesus (as relayed by John) praises the assembly, including their "endurance" (2:19), but then he quickly criticizes them: "you allow the woman Jezebel, who calls herself a prophet, to teach and seduce my slaves to act the harlot and to eat food offered to idols" (2:20). Jezebel seductively leads people to πορνεύω, "to act the harlot," which references the sexual metaphor of infidelity to God but also connects to the woman Babylon (Rev 17–18), a πόρνη ("harlot" or "whore").

When scholars read Revelation with an emphasis on resistance, they see a call for endurance. Attention to food in this letter reminds the Thyatirans to continue enduring. John's critique of eating idol food could be understood as both a literal and metaphorical demand to reject Rome. For example, Roberto Mata examines Revelation's use of Exodus in its discourses around food. Whereas Rome offers food that has been sacrificed to idols, those who conquer and endure an "eschatological migration" toward the new Jerusalem will be rewarded with hidden *manna* (2:17).[73] Because eating is and represents consumption, to eat food sacrificed to idols is to consume the products of imperial domination and to participate both physically and metaphorically in the worship of Rome's demonic powers. Since a meal or a eucharistic celebration may also have been part of a liturgical encounter with Revelation, textual attention to food seems all the more potent. Alluding to Exodus calls upon the memory of earlier Jewish resistance and survival, and this letter calls for resistance through the sustaining of Jewish traditions among community members who have come together for a shared meal.

For interpreters who focus on the resistant edge of Revelation, John plays with a long tradition of both Jewish prophetic and Roman rhetorical uses of gender and sexuality to signal allegiance and betrayal. In English, the term "faithful" can signify belief, but the word may also describe sexual fidelity. The utopian new Jerusalem as a bride points to the potential of a loving "marriage" between God and the faithfully enduring followers of Jesus. Revelation draws on other Jewish prophetic literature here; for instance, Second Isaiah (Isaiah 54, for instance) depicts Israel as a communal wife to a loving God.[74] In Revelation, metaphors of "fornication" generally describe and denounce participation in practices of Roman culture and domination that the author opposes. Practices such as eating idol food put people into a seemingly unfaithful allegiance with Rome: to side with Rome is to be "in bed" with the enemy. Thus John worries that Jezebel will seduce followers to be promiscuous, to collude with Rome, and to be unfaithful to God.

However, this metaphoric representation plays right into Roman norms of gender, sexuality, and power. Unfaithful women and enslaved household members undermine God's masculinity because they demonstrate a lack of divine control. Adulterous Jezebel (Rev 2:22) may be punished through rape ("I throw her onto a bed") and the murder of "her children" (2:23), which recollects some of the friezes representing Roman domination, such as Claudius's domination of Britannia at the Sebasteion in Aphrodisias. Moreover, living women today can still recognize and fear the terms of this violence. The portrayals of Jezebel and Babylon/Rome replicate the threat of gendered, colonizing sexual violence and perpetuate representations of sex work as shameful. Thus the contemporary sex workers, with whom Avaren Ipsen reads Revelation, see themselves as the denigrated and threatened antagonists in John's imaginary.[75]

Moreover, in totally refusing any accommodation to Rome, might this form of resistance rely on the logics of empire? Does it partially rely on concerns with purity mobilized in a dominant culture? Stephen D. Moore characterizes Jezebel, Balaam, and the Nicolaitans with their accommodating practices as representing "the threat of the hybrid" in Revelation's universe, and in this regard John's binaristic structure replicates Roman concerns with purity.[76]

By fearing hybridity and threatening his own community members with alter-imperial violence, John seems to fall into a trap outlined by Paulo Freire in *Pedagogy of the Oppressed* (1968). Colonized ambivalence can instigate "a type of horizontal violence, striking out at their own comrades for the pettiest of reasons....Because the oppressor exists within their oppressed comrades, when they attack those comrades they are indirectly attacking the oppressor as well."[77] Moreover, according to Freire, when an oppressed population has regularly been denigrated, humiliated, and dehumanized by a dominating population, their depressed self-esteem and sense of alienation may also lend itself to a desire to imitate the dominant group, to simply reverse the roles of colonizer and colonized, of dominator and dominated, of oppressor and oppressed.[78]

Perhaps John pursues a resistance that only imitates Roman domination. Lynne St. Clair Darden elucidates how the throne scene (Rev 4–5) imitates representations and performances of Roman imperial governance and devotion.[79] Thus an imperial ideology still holds sway. John's throne of God resembles Rome's throne and, according to Moore, its ideology: "incomparable glory and authority, overwhelming power and punitive wrath."[80] Additionally, God, the Lamb, and their agents practice the activities of empire: war, territorial expansion, and the elimination of those who do not succumb to their dominating power. Followers of Jesus remain enslaved subjects of a dominating "Lord." Moore further examines the raging hypermasculinity attributed to the alter-imperial figures of the one seated on the throne and the Lamb, and he points out the ways that divine hypermasculinity imitates Roman discourses as well. Moore's work often demonstrates the extent to which, "in contrast to the scenario adduced by Bhabha in which systemic mimicry of the agents and institutions of imperialism perpetually threatens to teeter over into parody or mockery, Revelation presents us with a reverse scenario in which parody or mockery of the imperial order constantly threatens to keel over into mimicry, imitation, and replication."[81]

Ambiveilence and the Reader of Revelation's Rome

That Revelation's mimicry may merely replicate Roman imperialism seems to make sense of its history as a Christian imperial text par excellence from Constantine to George W. Bush. Ultimately, Darden depicts Revelation as a warning to colonized populations: "It is imperative for a marginalized community to be aware of the possibility of reinscribing the oppressive elements of their own contemporary society. This reinscription, I argue, is inevitable if marginalized members of the community are unconscious of their ambivalent identity construction."[82] In lifting up the fundamental ambivalence of John as a colonized subject, Darden does not really focus on John's ethics. More importantly, she asks, how does *our* ambivalence interact with John's? Can a self-critical awareness of ambivalence keep us from simply replicating empires when we critique them?

This question of how to read for and understand our own ambivalence haunts postcolonial interpretations of Revelation, especially interpretations of the figure Babylon. Probably because so many scholars write from within imperial metropolises, Babylon serves as a potent locus for identification and disidentification. On the one hand, Babylon, as discussed above, is clearly a parody of Rome. And yet, she is ultimately mauled by her consorts. Merchants will weep for the end of their trade (18:11), and she will be stripped, burnt, and dismembered. The angel promises her destruction will be violent (18:21). This parody represents the desire for the fall of the empire, a discourse on the religious, economic, political, and militaristic violence by which Rome has governed. Where Rome claimed to be an imperial pater familias, a paragon of masculine self-control who promised eternal rule, instead Babylon/Rome is a promiscuous, easily destroyed, and abandoned woman. Since Babylon/Rome has promised peace through violence, so too will she reap violence in her destruction. God will judge Babylon/Rome and "avenge on her the blood of [God's] slaves" (19:2).[83] And yet, many contemporary readers cannot help but wonder about the ambivalent desire for empire that seems to appear in this depiction of a desirable, enslaved prostitute.

One way to think about this ambivalent desire is to examine the call to "look" that pervades the Book of Revelation. For Christopher A. Frilingos, the scene of Babylon's destruction recalls the effects of Roman spectacle. Throughout the Empire, from the Coliseum in Rome to local theaters in Asia Minor, a variety of beasts and humans, often engaged in violent struggles, were put on display as a way of demonstrating Rome's expansive dominion and its capacity for domination.[84] One could demonstrate an aptitude for self-mastery in viewing these spectacles precisely by controlling oneself as a viewer, and yet one was always being viewed by others.[85] The strong, like the Lamb, can watch with self-mastery; they are not "amazed" (14:9–10).[86] Those who "conquer," especially who demonstrate such self-mastery will enter the "new Jerusalem."[87] Yet, John is "amazed" (17:6), and the angel chastises him for it (17:7) and uses John's amazement to explain to the audience who Babylon really is and what will happen to her. In this way, John may recognize his own ambivalence—the colonized subject's desire for the colonizer even as he also desires Rome's destruction.

Yet, it is not only within the textual spectacle that we struggle with an ambivalence of desire that breaks down a simple binary of colonizer/colonized. Partially it comes about through our own process of identification and disidentification. For example, Lynn R. Huber recognizes in Babylon another queer woman whose sexual practices as a "whore" break with heteronormativity.[88] On account of this queering of norms, Babylon also shares in the threat of death that has been leveled against so many flesh-and-blood LGBTQ readers in our contemporary world.[89] Huber identifies with Babylon the Whore and fears a shared fate of violence. Yet she also disidentifies with her. Huber recognizes in Babylon an indictment of empire and the ways that minoritized subjects can also be assimilated into and made complicit with empire's violence.[90] For Huber, then, gazing at Babylon as Whore becomes an opportunity for critical self-reflection. We should wonder about how we have become complicit in empire but also how, in reading Revelation, we risk rejecting empire in ways that simply replicate it.[91]

Encountering our own ambivalence in reading Babylon should press us to reconsider the very act of reading itself. Challenging prior interpretations, Stephen D. Moore and Jennifer Glancy have argued that we must see Babylon complexly precisely because she is labeled a "brothel slave" (πόρνη) rather than a wealthier and more autonomous "courtesan" (ἑταίρα).[92] Thus, she may appear in the clothing of wealth and power, but she is also an enslaved woman, a victim of and participant in empire.[93] In reading Babylon as an imperially dressed but enslaved prostitute, Shanell T. Smith recognizes herself, a woman who descends from enslaved Africans but also, on account of her socioeconomic positioning and citizenship within the United States, benefits from U.S. empire. Smith's encounter with Babylon is an opportunity to rip the veil on her own existence and to see her own dual nature. Smith reads Revelation in order to think about the practice of interpretation itself; she offers a critical reading practice that she terms "ambi*veil*ence."[94] She bridges Bhabha's notion of ambivalence with W. E. B. DuBois's conception of the "veil."[95] Ambiveilent readings see the doubleness of Revelation, its antagonism to Rome, its desire for Rome, and its rootedness in the experience of a colonized and minoritized community that longs for and participates in Roman Empire. Yet ambiveilence also pushes us to read ourselves, similarly struggling with our own layers of double consciousness because of our place within the structures of empire.

Not unlike Smith, Erin Runions's encounter with Babylon presses her to offer up an alternative interpretive approach that refuses simple binaries. In looking at Revelation in historical context, Runions argues that colonized subjects desire Babylon, despise her, and despise their "own stereotyped gendering through her."[96] The conflict of despising/desiring Babylon does not stop in the ancient world, though. Runions examines histories of popular and political uses of Babylon as trope. In studying diverse histories of interpretation and their ambivalent desire for and destruction of Babylon, she proposes a "queerly sublime ethics of reading" that holds onto a fundamental "opacity" and "indeterminability" of meaning in biblical texts. Confronting ambiveilence not only in Revelation but also in the history of interpretation requires that contemporary readers embrace ambivalence and dwell with the ambiguities and tensions of the text, what we know about the ancient world, and what we know about reception history. Rather than pass ethical judgment on Revelation as text, it is our own ethics as readers that must be scrutinized. We must seek unfixed and never finalized meaning even as we live with textual opacity, the indeterminability of meaning, and our own indeterminability.

The Futures of Empire in the Study of Revelation

I would prefer that future biblical interpreters employ a queerly sublime ethics of reading grounded in ambiveilence. Future scholarship need not further decode the Roman Empire in Revelation, though that is certainly one task that biblical scholars will continue to pursue. Yet such decoding often relies too much on a myth of stable meaning. But how can meanings be stable when readers change? As imperialism looks different in this century, different themes of empire must command our focus. For example, especially as we confront global environmental crises, scholarship could shift from an attention to questions of identity and instead examine how imperial environmental practices have appeared and shaped Revelation, its writing and circulation, and its reception histories.[97] However, we must learn to ask these new questions through examining the interplay of diverse meanings.

Previous scholarship has often focused on a binary of resistance versus mimicry in assessing Revelation's relationship to empire. Yet, the text cannot do anything on its own. Revelation's readers have made it a myth of resistance or a tale of minoritized victory easily translatable to the hands of later generations of colonizers. Another future for the study of empire in Revelation will take for granted the fraught hybridity of the text, and then start with the ambivalence of the reader and of Revelation's reading history. Resisting Revelation's seeming call for closure, "readers become as important as texts."[98] Readers learn to speak in their own tongues but also remain open to reading and perceiving those tongues critically, in part through "critical dialogue among the many tongues."[99] The demands of our present moment, where we witness the rise of far-right nationalist parties and governments who wish to quell the world's diversity, should press us further to read with and across difference, embracing plurivocal interpretations and critically examining, together, the plural revelations that the Book of Revelation has inspired.

One other future might take the Apocalypse as a conversation partner for decolonial thought. Its multivalent and horrifying imagery may press us to explode our earlier categories and particularly to think beyond imperialism's structuring vocabulary of binaries. In using Revelation as a conversation point in thinking beyond binaries, we could study "apocalypso" rather than the Apocalypse. Afro–Puerto Rican decolonial critic Yomaira C. Figueroa describes "apocalypso," a mash-up of "apocalypse" and "calypso," as a confrontation of the realities of coloniality that explodes the categories we have inherited.[100] It particularly explodes any simple binaries of Self and Other, because apocalypso is what happens when "the Other appears to be the One."[101] Apocalypso, as a refusal of modern imperial binaries, relies on Latin American and Latina/o/x reflections on modern coloniality and decolonial thought.[102]

Recognizing the coloniality of knowledge, we may use the Book of Revelation as a jumping-off point for thinking through the histories of spectacular and spectacularly violent epistemologies that rely on hierarchal binaries to assert value while encompassing extractive relationships between dominating persons and those lands, peoples, and texts who are dominated. Ethicist Melissa Pagán has described a *"hermeneutics of el grito,"* a listening to the screams (*gritos*) of present and past "struggles against colonial power."[103] A hermeneutics of *el grito* "challenges us to listen and recognize how our current categories inhibit rather than facilitate liberative possibilities."[104] We can read Revelation, and its history of interpretation, in order to reflect on how the epistemological binaries of coloniality structure violent and extractive relationships, including the relationships we biblical scholars have taken with our texts, which we often treat as "resources." How, for instance, have our uses of Revelation, whether to justify imperialism or as a resource for our resistance, actually relied on extractive logics?

Starting from a hermeneutics of *el grito*, we do not need to judge Revelation as an ally or an enemy in the struggle for a better world. Instead we need to attend to ourselves and read Revelation as an opportunity to reflect further on how empire has shaped us and our very definitions of the human, how we have responded to empire, and how we might yet respond to empire in ways for which there is no prior script. We may direct our questions at the histories and practices of "meaning seeking" in relationship to Revelation without thinking Revelation anticipates our current situation or prescribes a usable model for navigating empire.[105] Revelation, and the place of Rome within it, becomes but one conversation partner with which to rethink and transform the categories and cosmologies we have inherited after millennia of plurivocal revelations.

Notes

1. Stephen D. Moore, "The Revelation to John," *A Postcolonial Commentary on the New Testament Writings*, ed. R. S. Sugirtharajah and Fernando F. Segovia, The Bible & Postcolonialism (London and New York: T&T Clark/Continuum, 2009 [2007]), 436–454; 443. Scholars have long commented on the appearance of Roman rhetoric and imagery in Revelation. For instance, Adolf Deissmann outlined parallels between devotions to Caesar and to Christ. Adolf Deissmann, *Licht vom Osten: Das Neue Testament und die neuentdeckten Texte der hellenistisch-römischen Welt*, 4th ed. (Tübingen: Mohr Siebeck, 1923), 290.

2. On the problematic uses of simple correlation as a hermeneutical strategy that too often flattens the diversity of both ancient and contemporary contexts, see Jean-Pierre Ruiz, *Reading from the Edges: The Bible and People on the Move* (Maryknoll, NY: Orbis, 2011), 17.
3. For example, much work examines the Spanish, the Book of Revelation, and the conquest of the New World. I discuss some of the ways Revelation served as a touchstone for Spanish and U.S. imperialism in *Revelation in Aztlán: Scriptures, Utopias, and the Chicano Movement* (New York: Palgrave Macmillan, 2016), 7, 105–112, 175–176, 261–271. Also see, for instance, Jean-Pierre Ruiz's essays on Guadalupe and on Christopher Columbus; Ruiz, *Reading*, 123–135; and Ruiz, "The Bible and U.S. Hispanic American Theological Discourse: Lessons from a Non-Innocent History," in *From the Heart of Our People: Latino/a Explorations in Catholic Systematic Theology*, ed. Orlando O. Espín and Miguel H. Díaz (Maryknoll, NY: Orbis, 1999), 100–120. See also David A. Sánchez, *From Patmos to the Barrio: Subverting Imperial Myths* (Minneapolis: Fortress Press, 2008), 47–82; and Alain Milhou, "*Mundus novus et renovatio mundi*: Messianic and Utopian Currents in the Indies of Castile," trans. Nadia Benabid, in *Utopia: The Search for the Ideal Society*, ed. Roland Schaer, Gregory Claeys, and Lyman Tower Sargent (New York: New York Public Library/Oxford University Press, 2000), 140–151. The Getty Museum in Los Angeles also produced an intriguing exploration of the ways the Spanish mapped their ideas of the Roman Empire onto the Aztecs. John M. D. Pohl and Claire L. Lyons, *The Aztec Pantheon and the Art of Empire* (Los Angeles, CA: Getty Publications, 2010).
4. Harry O. Maier, *Apocalypse Recalled: The Book of Revelation after Christendom* (Minneapolis: Fortress Press, 2002), 37–38.
5. José Adriano Filho, "The Apocalypse of John as an Account of a Visionary Experience: Notes on the Book's Structure," *Journal for the Study of the New Testament* 25, no. 2 (2002): 213.
6. Several scholars have argued that Revelation might contain different books composed in different eras, so we cannot think about a simple, singular author. For Greg Carey, it is more useful to think of the author as a rhetorical device, that is, as a character in the larger narrative we encounter, rather than applying a reference to any particular human author. Greg Carey, *Elusive Apocalypse: Reading Authority in the Revelation to John* (Macon, GA: Mercer University Press, 1999), 7.
7. For the idea that John chose this exile, see Leonard L. Thompson, *The Book of Revelation: Apocalypse and Empire* (New York: Oxford University Press, 1990), 173. Although no one knows of Patmos as some sort of "penal colony," if John was a formal "exile" that would also suggest a higher social status since exile could be "permitted those of higher status who had been condemned to death, but they were usually subsequently deprived of both citizenship and property." See David E. Aune, *Revelation 1–5*, Word Biblical Commentary, 52 (Nashville, TN: Thomas Nelson Publishers, 1997), 79. David A. Sánchez identifies the rhetorical author as an exile, *relegatio in insulam*, a specific kind of banishment for those who have somehow "threatened public interest and security." See Sánchez, *From Patmos to the Barrio*, 37–38.
8. The term "Christian" only seems to emerge after the Book of Revelation. See arguments in John W. Marshall, *Parables of War: Reading John's Jewish Apocalypse* (Waterloo, Canada: Wilfrid Laurier University Press, 2001). There are also significant debates about using the modern term "Jewish" in discussing the ancient world, but I follow the arguments of Adele Reinhartz in using the term because of the impact of the Christian bible on modern Jewish lives. See Adele Reinhartz, "The Vanishing Jews of Antiquity," *Marginalia—the Los Angeles Review of Books (2014)*. Accessible at https://marginalia.lareviewofbooks.org/vanishing-jews-antiquity-adele-reinhartz/.

9. For a thorough examination of the different possibilities for dating the Apocalypse, see Steven J. Friesen, *Imperial Cults and the Apocalypse of John: Reading Revelation in the Ruins* (New York: Oxford University Press, 2006), 136–151.
10. Rome is not the only empire that appears in Revelation or to which it responds. Lynne St. Clair Darden examined the lingering cultural impact of Achaemenid Persian imperialism, which had dominated ancient Anatolia in certain eras; moreover, the Parthian empire remained proximate. Both empires held sway in Greek and Roman imaginations at large and impacted Rome's Asian province in particular. This legacy of empire must also be added onto the memories of Babylonian, neo-Assyrian, and Hellenistic empires contained within Jewish diasporic traditions. Lynne St. Clair Darden, *Scripturalizing Revelation: An African American Postcolonial Reading of Empire* (Atlanta, GA: Society of Biblical Literature, 2015), 112–113, 116, 132.
11. David E. Aune, "The Form and Function of the Proclamation to the Seven Churches (Revelation 2–3)," *New Testament Studies* 36 (1990): 199–204.
12. Although Robert Royalty has convincingly demonstrated that Revelation 22:18–19 connects to Deuteronomy 4:2 and 29:19–30:8, W. C. Smith also observed how this part of Revelation parallels the Bisitun inscription of Emperor Darius. Smith suggests that this Persian imperial format of blessing those who preserve words and cursing those who destroy them was widely imitated by many Greek and Roman inscriptions. Robert M. Royalty Jr., "Don't Touch *This* Book! Revelation 22:18–19 and the Rhetoric of Reading (in) the Apocalypse of John," *Biblical Interpretation* 12 (2004): 291. W. C. Smith, *What Is Scripture? A Comparative Approach* (Minneapolis: Fortress Press, 1993), 63, 277n73. Benjamin Rubin's work likewise demonstrates the longstanding impact of Darius's Bisitun monument on representations of kingship in Anatolia, especially through his examination of the Sebasteion at Aphrodisias. See Benjamin B. Rubin, "(Re)presenting Empire: The Roman Imperial Cult in Asia Minor, 31 BC–AD 68," (PhD diss., Classical Art and Archaeology, University of Michigan, 2008), 72–116.
13. Gayatri Chakravorty Spivak, "Poststructuralism, Marginality, Postcoloniality and Value," in *Literary Theory Today*, ed. Peter Collier and Helga Geyer-Ryan (London: Polity Press, 1990), 228.
14. An identification of Babylon with Rome might antedate the Temple's destruction and reach back to 66 or 67 when the Romans began their siege of Jerusalem. See George H. van Kooten, "The Year of the Four Emperors and the Revelation of John: The 'Pro-Neronian' Emperors Otho and Vitellius, and the Images and Colossus of Nero in Rome," *Journal for the Study of the New Testament* 30 (2007): 220.
15. This point has been debated among many scholars, but for a simple summation, see Elaine Pagels, *Revelations: Visions, Prophecy, and Politics in the Book of Revelation* (New York: Penguin, 2012), 32–33.
16. Darden, *Scripturalizing Revelation*, 128.
17. Although there are good reasons to problematize the term "cult" here, that argument is outside the purview of this essay, and so I follow the most common scholarly terminology. The "imperial cult" does not refer to any single or standardized system or practice. See James Rives, *Religion in the Roman Empire* (Malden, MA: Blackwell, 2007), 148–156.
18. The struggle over the definition of/boundary between "religion" and "politics" also shaped classical scholarship on ancient Roman imperialism. For instance, see Michael Naylor's discussion of debates over the "religious" and "political" dimensions of imperial

cults for much of the twentieth century; Michael Naylor, "The Roman Imperial Cult and Revelation," *Currents in Biblical Research* 8, no. 2 (2010): 209.

19. David A. deSilva, "The Revelation to John: A Case Study in Apocalyptic Propaganda and the Maintenance of Sectarian Identity," *Sociological Analysis* 53 (1991): 375–395. Also see Friesen, *Imperial*, 133–217.
20. Jean-Pierre Ruiz, "Taking a Stand on the Seashore: A Postcolonial Exploration of Revelation 13," *Reading the Book of Revelation: A Resource for Students*, ed. David L. Barr (Atlanta, GA: Society of Biblical Literature, 2003), 126.
21. Steven J. Scherrer, "Signs and Wonders in the Imperial Cult: A New Look at a Roman Religious Institution in the Light of Rev 13:13–15," *Journal of Biblical Literature* 103, no. 4 (1984): 1984.
22. Ruiz, "Seashore," 131.
23. Naylor, "Roman Imperial Cult," 217.
24. David E. Aune, *Revelation 17–22*, Word Biblical Commentary, 52C (Nashville, TN: Thomas Nelson Publishers, 1998), 919–928.
25. Moore, "Revelation," 438. As Moore argues, that is another reason that a simple correlation with the Americas, a hemisphere broadly composed of settler colonial nations, would be impossible.
26. Wes Howard-Brook and Anthony Gwyther, *Unveiling Empire: Reading Revelation Then and Now* (Maryknoll, NY: Orbis, 1999), 116.
27. As Friesen argues, "in critiquing imperial worship . . . [John] spoke as a minority in his society, and perhaps even as a minority in the churches." Steven J. Friesen, "The Cult of the Roman Emperors in Ephesos: Temple Wardens, City Titles, and the Interpretation of the Revelation of John," in *Ephesos Metropolis of Asia: An Interdisciplinary Approach to Its Archaeology, Religion, and Culture*, ed. Helmut Koester (Valley Forge, PA: Trinity Press International, 1995), 250.
28. Ruiz, "Seashore," 130–131.
29. J. Nelson Kraybill, *Imperial Cult and Commerce in John's Apocalypse* (Sheffield, UK: Sheffield Academic Press, 1996), passim, for this argument.
30. Kraybill, *Imperial Cult*, 140.
31. Stephen D. Moore, *Untold Tales from the Book of Revelation: Sex and Gender, Empire and Ecology* (Atlanta, GA: Society of Biblical Literature, 2014), 129.
32. Moore, *Untold Tales*, 130.
33. Moore, *Untold Tales*, 131.
34. Local elites adapted Roman imperial ideology through local visual repertoires, creating a hybrid visuality that drew not only on Roman representation but also on more local histories of representation. Steven J. Friesen, *Twice Neokoros: Ephesus, Asia, and the Cult of the Flavian Imperial Family* (Leiden: Brill, 1993), 75.
35. See Dio Cassius, 51.20.6–9.
36. Rubin, "(Re)presenting Empire," 63.
37. Rubin, "(Re)presenting Empire," 70.
38. Naylor, "Roman Imperial Cult," 216.
39. Bernadette J. Brooten, *Love between Women: Early Christian Responses to Female Homoeroticism* (Chicago: University of Chicago Press, 1996), 116. This simple binary of active/passive can break down and fail to capture some of the complex arrays of gender and sexuality in Rome. For a critique sensitive to the limits of the active/passive binary in early Christian discourse, see Maia Kotrosits, "Penetration and Its Discontents: Greco-Roman

Sexuality, the *Acts of Paul and Thecla*, and Theorizing Eros without the Wound," *Journal of the History of Sexuality* 27, no. 3 (2018): 343–366.

40. Lynn R. Huber, *Thinking and Seeing with Women in Revelation* (New York: Bloomsbury, 2013), 47.
41. Davina C. López, *Apostle to the Conquered: Reimagining Paul's Mission* (Minneapolis: Fortress Press, 2008), 44.
42. This point may present a connection between ancient Roman imperialism and modern U.S. settler colonialism. Andrea Smith, "Not an Indian Tradition: The Sexual Colonization of Native Peoples," *Hypatia* 18, no. 2 (Spring 2003): 70; also A. Smith, "Queer Theory and Native Studies," 61.
43. Lynn R. Huber, "Sexually Explicit? Re-reading Revelation's 144,00 Virgins as a Response to Roman Discourses," *Journal of Men, Masculinities and Spirituality* 2, no. 1 (January 2008): 3–28; available online www.jmmsweb.org.
44. Luis Menéndez-Antuña, *Thinking Sex with the Great Whore: Deviant Sexualities and Empire in the Book of Revelation* (New York: Routledge, 2018), chap. 1, Kindle.
45. Homi K. Bhabha, *The Location of Culture* (New York: Routledge, 1994), 110.
46. Bhabha, *The Location of Culture*, 58.
47. R. S. Sugirtharajah, *Postcolonial Criticism and Biblical Interpretation* (New York: Oxford University Press, 2002), 191.
48. For my arguments about how Revelation itself can function as a temple, particularly through its representation of the new Jerusalem, see Jacqueline M. Hidalgo, *Revelation in Aztlán: Scriptures, Utopias, and the Chicano Movement* (New York: Palgrave Macmillan, 2016), 85–95.
49. Allen Dwight Callahan, "The Language of Apocalypse," *Harvard Theological Review* 88, no. 4 (1995): 464.
50. See discussions in Richard A. Horsley, *Revolt of the Scribes: Resistance and Apocalyptic Origins* (Minneapolis: Fortress Press, 2010); and Anathea E. Portier-Young, *Apocalypse against Empire: Theologies of Resistance in Early Judaism* (Grand Rapids, MI: William B. Eerdmans, 2011).
51. Brian K. Blount, *Can I Get a Witness? Reading Revelation through African American Culture* (Louisville, KY: Westminster John Knox Press, 2005), 109.
52. See Blount, *Can I Get a Witness?*, passim, but one example is on p. 38.
53. Dagoberto Ramírez Fernández, "The Judgment of God on the Multinationals: Revelation 18," *Subversive Scriptures: Revolutionary Readings of the Christian Bible in Latin America*, ed. Leif E. Vaage (Valley Forge, PA: Trinity Press International, 1997), 97.
54. Clarice J. Martin, "Polishing the Unclouded Mirror: A Womanist Reading of Revelation 18:13," in *From Every People and Nation: The Book of Revelation in Intercultural Perspective*, ed. David Rhoads (Minneapolis: Fortress Press, 2005), 82–109.
55. Martin, "Polishing the Unclouded Mirror," 99.
56. The term δοῦλος appears in 1:1 as a categorization for John and the intended audience of this revelation. More work on the ambivalent use of metaphorical enslavement in Revelation is currently underway. See Marvin Suber Williams, "Early Christian Formation as a Paradigm of Liberation: Studying the Role of Δοῦλος in Revelation 21.1–22.5," in *Text and Community: Essays in Memory of Bruce M. Metzger*, ed. J. Harold Ellens, vol. 1 (Sheffield, UK: Sheffield Phoenix Press, 2007), 282.
57. Elisabeth Schüssler Fiorenza, *The Book of Revelation: Justice and Judgment*, 2nd ed. (Minneapolis: Fortress Press, 1998), 26.

58. Klaus Wengst, "Babylon the Great and the New Jerusalem: The Visionary View of Political Reality in the Revelation of John," in *Politics and Theopolitics in the Bible and Postbiblical Literature*, ed. Yair Hoffman, Benjamin Uffenheimer, and Henning Graf Reventlow (Sheffield, UK: Sheffield Academic Press, 1994), 197.
59. Pablo Richard, *Apocalypse: A People's Commentary on the Book of Revelation*, trans. Phillip Berryman (Maryknoll, NY: Orbis, 1998), 166.
60. Barbara R. Rossing, *The Choice between Two Cities: Whore, Bride, and Empire in the Apocalypse* (Harrisburg, PA: Trinity Press International, 1999), 146.
61. Maier, *Apocalypse Recalled*, 194–197.
62. Eric J. Gilchrest, *Revelation 21–22 in Light of Jewish and Greco-Roman Utopianism* (Leiden: Brill, 2013), 223.
63. Wengst, "Babylon the Great and the New Jerusalem," 199.
64. My allusion to Francis Fukuyama's *The End of History* (the 1989 essay and the 1992 book) is intended. See my discussion of Revelation's temporality, Hidalgo, *Revelation in Aztlán*, 90–95.
65. In the interest of space, this essay focuses on David A. Sánchez's discussion of mythic subversion, but I also outline other forms of Roman knowledge, specifically the use of spectacle, seeing, and text in Hidalgo, *Revelation in Aztlán*, 102–104.
66. James C. Scott, *Domination and the Arts of Resistance: Hidden Transcripts* (New Haven: Yale University Press, 1990).
67. Sánchez, *From Patmos to the Barrio*, 9–10.
68. Margaret Aymer describes Revelation's perspective as "alter-imperial, rather than anti-imperial, for all the rhetorics of empire pertain." Margaret P. Aymer, "Empire, Alter-Empire, and the Twenty-First Century," *Union Seminary Quarterly Review* 59, nos. 3–4 (2005): 145.
69. Tina Pippin, *Death and Desire: The Rhetoric of Gender in the Apocalypse of John* (Louisville, KY: Westminster John Knox Press, 1992), 70.
70. Tina Pippin, *Apocalyptic Bodies: The Biblical End of the World in Text and Image* (New York: Routledge, 1999), 123.
71. Christopher A. Frilingos, *Spectacles of Empire: Monsters, Martyrs, and the Book of Revelation* (Philadelphia: University of Pennsylvania Press, 2004), 21.
72. Rubin, "(Re)presenting Empire," 18. As an example of this discourse, Rubin reads Pliny the Elder (21–79 CE) in his *Natural History*, where one particularly sees the representation of Rome as parent to other nations.
73. Roberto Mata, "Border Crossing into the Promised Land: The Eschatological Migration of God's People in Revelation 2:1–3:22," in *Latinxs, the Bible, and Migration*, ed. Efraín Agosto and Jacqueline M. Hidalgo (New York: Palgrave Macmillan, 2018), 180–181.
74. Rossing, *The Choice Between Two Cities*, 137.
75. Avaren Ipsen, *Sex Working and the Bible* (Oakville, CT: Equinox, 2009).
76. Moore, "Revelation," 449.
77. Paulo Freire, *Pedagogy of the Oppressed*, trans. Myra Bergman Ramos (New York: Continuum, 1990 [1970/1968]), 48.
78. Freire, *Pedagogy of the Oppressed*, 49.
79. Darden, *Scripturalizing Revelation*, 135–156.
80. Moore, "Revelation," 451.
81. Moore, "Revelation," 446.
82. Darden, *Scripturalizing Revelation*, 157.

83. For discussion of the potential power of cathartic reversal, see Adela Yarbro Collins, *Crisis and Catharsis: The Power of the Apocalypse* (Philadelphia: Westminster Press, 1984).
84. Frilingos, *Spectacles of Empire*, 30.
85. Frilingos, *Spectacles of Empire*, 36–37.
86. Frilingos, *Spectacles of Empire*, 81.
87. Gilchrest outlines this promise in the opening letters: "For example, the 'conquerors' from Ephesus are given access to the tree of life and the paradise of God (2:7); Smyrna's conquerors are not hurt by the second death (2:11); Sardis receives white robes and a place in the book of life (3:5); Philadelphians have a place in the new Jerusalem (3:12); and the Laodiceans get the chance to sit on the throne of Jesus, perhaps that throne that sits in the middle of the city in Rev 22:3 (3:21)." See Gilchrest, *Revelation 21–22*, 222.
88. Lynn R. Huber, "Gazing at the Whore: Reading Revelation Queerly," in *Bible Trouble: Queer Reading at the Boundaries of Biblical Scholarship*, ed. Teresa J. Hornsby and Ken Stone (Atlanta, GA: Society of Biblical Literature, 2011), 307, 309.
89. Huber, "Gazing," 314.
90. Huber, "Gazing," 314–316.
91. Huber, "Gazing," 317.
92. Jennifer A. Glancy and Stephen D. Moore, "How Typical a Roman Prostitute Is Revelation's 'Great Whore'?" *Journal of Biblical Literature* 130 (2011): 551–552, 557.
93. Although she does not focus on the word πόρνη, Jean K. Kim had earlier identified Babylon's potentially ambiguous representation as both colonizer and colonized. Jean K. Kim, "'Uncovering Her Wickedness': An Inter(Con)Textual Reading of Revelation 17 from a Postcolonial Feminist Perspective," *Journal for the Study of the New Testament* 73 (1999): 61–81.
94. Shanell T. Smith, *The Woman Babylon and the Marks of Empire: Reading Revelation with a Postcolonial Womanist Hermeneutics of Ambiveilence* (Minneapolis: Fortress Press, 2014), 67–69; 131–133.
95. S. T. Smith, *The Woman Babylon*, 3, 56–67, 70. Work on colonial ambivalence tends to draw upon Bhabha's essay "Of Mimicry and Man: The Ambivalence of Colonial Discourse," 85–92. Also see W. E. B. Du Bois, *The Souls of Black Folk* (Rockville, MD: Arc Manor, 2008), 12.
96. Erin Runions, *The Babylon Complex: Theopolitical Fantasies of War, Sex, and Sovereignty* (New York: Fordham University Press, 2014), 240.
97. Barbara Rossing's work has turned in this direction. A recent example of this work can be found in Micah D. Kiel, *Apocalyptic Ecology: The Book of Revelation, the Earth, and the Future* (Collegeville, MN: Liturgical Press, 2017).
98. Fernando F. Segovia, "'And They Began to Speak in Other Tongues': Competing Modes of Discourse in Contemporary Biblical Criticism," in *Reading from This Place*, vol. 1, *Social Location and Biblical Interpretation in the United States*, ed. Fernando F. Segovia and Mary Ann Tolbert (Minneapolis: Fortress Press, 1995), 32.
99. Segovia, "Other Tongues," 31.
100. Yomaira C. Figueroa-Vásquez, *Decolonizing Diasporas: Radical Mappings of Afro-Atlantic Literature* (Evanston, IL: Northwestern University Press, 2020), 159–160.
101. Figueroa draws on pale, Afro-Jamaican writer Michelle Cliff's term "apocalypso," which she uses to name the way that she explodes binaries of black and white racial division. Michelle Cliff, "In My Heart, a Darkness," in *If I Could Write This in Fire* (Minneapolis: University of Minnesota Press, 2008), 87.

102. Many works, such as those of Aníbal Quijano or Walter Mignolo would be important to examine in future scholarship on Revelation. But perhaps the most important for thinking through the problems of how coloniality has structured the way we think would be the works of Nelson Maldonado-Torres and María Lugones.
103. Melissa Pagán, "Puerto Rico Forum Reflection #3: Cultivating a Hermeneutics of 'El Grito' in the Eye of the Storm," *Perspectivas* 15 (2018): 72; http://perspectivasonline.com/downloads/cultivating-a-hermeneutics-of-el-grito-in-the-eye-of-the-storm/.
104. Pagán, "Hermeneutics of 'El Grito,'" 72.
105. Vincent L. Wimbush, "Introduction: TEXTureS, Gestures, Power: Orientation to Radical Excavation," in *Theorizing Scriptures: New Critical Orientations to a Cultural Phenomenon*, ed. Vincent L. Wimbush (New Brunswick, NJ: Rutgers University Press, 2008), 4–5.

Bibliography

Agosto, Efraín, and Jacqueline M. Hidalgo. Eds. *Latinxs, the Bible, and Migration*. New York: Palgrave Macmillan, 2018.

Aune, David E. *Revelation*. Word Biblical Commentary. Vol. 52. Nashville, TN: Thomas Nelson Publishers, 1997–1998.

Aymer, Margaret P. "Empire, Alter-Empire, and the Twenty-First Century." *Union Seminary Quarterly Review* 59, nos. 3–4 (2005): 140–146.

Barr, David L. Ed. *Reading the Book of Revelation: A Resource for Students*. Atlanta, GA: Society of Biblical Literature, 2003.

Blount, Brian K. *Can I Get a Witness? Reading Revelation through African American Culture*. Louisville: Westminster John Knox Press, 2005.

Carey, Greg. *Elusive Apocalypse: Reading Authority in the Revelation to John*. Macon, GA: Mercer University Press, 1999.

Darden, Lynne St. Clair. *Scripturalizing Revelation: An African American Postcolonial Reading of Empire*. Atlanta, GA: Society of Biblical Literature, 2015.

Figueroa, Yomaira C. "Reparation as Transformation: Radical Literary (Re)imaginings of Futurities through Decolonial Love." *Decolonization: Indigeneity, Education & Society* 4, no. 1 (2015): 41–58. https://jps.library.utoronto.ca/index.php/des/article/view/22151.

Figueroa-Vásquez, Yomaira C. *Decolonizing Diasporas: Radical Mappings of Afro-Atlantic Literature*. Evanston, IL: Northwestern University Press, 2020.

Frilingos, Christopher A. *Spectacles of Empire: Monsters, Martyrs, and the Book of Revelation*. Philadelphia: University of Pennsylvania Press, 2004.

Gilchrest, Eric J. *Revelation 21–22 in Light of Jewish and Greco-Roman Utopianism*. Leiden: Brill, 2013.

Glancy, Jennifer A., and Stephen D. Moore. "How Typical a Roman Prostitute Is Revelation's 'Great Whore'?" *Journal of Biblical Literature* 130 (2011): 551–569.

Hidalgo, Jacqueline M. *Revelation in Aztlán: Scriptures, Utopias, and the Chicano Movement*. New York: Palgrave Macmillan, 2016.

Hornsby, Teresa J., and Ken Stone. Eds. *Bible Trouble: Queer Reading at the Boundaries of Biblical Scholarship* Atlanta, GA: Society of Biblical Literature, 2011.

Horsley, Richard A. *Revolt of the Scribes: Resistance and Apocalyptic Origins*. Minneapolis: Fortress Press, 2010.

Howard-Brook, Wes, and Anthony Gwyther. *Unveiling Empire: Reading Revelation Then and Now*. Maryknoll, NY: Orbis Books, 1999.

Huber, Lynn R. *Thinking and Seeing with Women in Revelation*. New York: Bloomsbury, 2013.

Ipsen, Avaren. *Sex Working and the Bible*. Oakville, CT: Equinox, 2009.

Kiel, Micah D. *Apocalyptic Ecology: The Book of Revelation, the Earth, and the Future*. Collegeville, MN: Liturgical Press, 2017.

Kim, Jean K. "'Uncovering Her Wickedness': An Inter(Con)Textual Reading of Revelation 17 from a Postcolonial Feminist Perspective." *Journal for the Study of the New Testament* 73 (1999): 61–81.

Kotrosits, Maia. "Penetration and Its Discontents: Greco-Roman Sexuality, the *Acts of Paul and Thecla*, and Theorizing Eros without the Wound." *Journal of the History of Sexuality* 27, no. 3 (2018): 343–366.

López, Davina C. *Apostle to the Conquered: Reimagining Paul's Mission*. Minneapolis: Fortress Press, 2008.

Maier, Harry O. *Apocalypse Recalled: The Book of Revelation after Christendom*. Minneapolis: Fortress Press, 2002.

Marshall, John W. *Parables of War: Reading John's Jewish Apocalypse*. Waterloo, Canada: Wilfrid Laurier University Press, 2001.

Menéndez-Antuña, Luis. *Thinking Sex with the Great Whore: Deviant Sexualities and Empire in the Book of Revelation*. New York: Routledge, 2018.

Moore, Stephen D. *Untold Tales from the Book of Revelation: Sex and Gender, Empire and Ecology*. Atlanta, GA: Society of Biblical Literature, 2014.

Pagán, Melissa. "Puerto Rico Forum Reflection #3: Cultivating a Hermeneutics of 'El Grito' in the Eye of the Storm." *Perspectivas* 15 (2018): 68–73.

Pagels, Elaine. *Revelations: Visions, Prophecy, and Politics in the Book of Revelation*. New York: Penguin, 2012.

Pippin, Tina. *Death and Desire: The Rhetoric of Gender in the Apocalypse of John*. Louisville: Westminster/John Knox Press, 1992.

Pippin, Tina. *Apocalyptic Bodies: The Biblical End of the World in Text and Image*. New York: Routledge, 1999.

Portier-Young, Anathea E. *Apocalypse against Empire: Theologies of Resistance in Early Judaism* Grand Rapids, MI: William B. Eerdmans, 2011.

Reinhartz, Adele. "The Vanishing Jews of Antiquity," *Marginalia—the Los Angeles Review of Books*. 2014. Accessible at https://marginalia.lareviewofbooks.org/ vanishing-jews-antiquity-adele-reinhartz/.

Rhoads, David. Ed. *From Every People and Nation: The Book of Revelation in Intercultural Perspective*. Minneapolis: Fortress Press, 2005.

Richard, Pablo. *Apocalypse: A People's Commentary on the Book of Revelation*. Translated by Phillip Berryman. Maryknoll, NY: Orbis Books, 1998.

Rives, James. *Religion in the Roman Empire*. Malden, MA: Blackwell, 2007.

Rossing, Barbara R. *The Choice between Two Cities: Whore, Bride, and Empire in the Apocalypse*. Harrisburg, PA: Trinity Press International, 1999.

Ruiz, Jean-Pierre. *Reading from the Edges: The Bible and People on the Move*. Maryknoll, NY: Orbis Books, 2011.

Runions, Erin. *The Babylon Complex: Theopolitical Fantasies of War, Sex, and Sovereignty*. New York: Fordham University Press, 2014.

Sánchez, David A. *From Patmos to the Barrio: Subverting Imperial Myths*. Minneapolis: Fortress Press, 2008.

Schüssler Fiorenza, Elisabeth. *The Book of Revelation: Justice and Judgment*. 2nd ed. Minneapolis: Fortress Press, 1998.

Segovia, Fernando F., and Mary Ann Tolbert. Eds. *Reading from This Place*. Vol. 1, *Social Location and Biblical Interpretation in the United States*. Minneapolis: Fortress Press, 1995.

Sugirtharajah, R. S., and Fernando F. Segovia. Eds. *A Postcolonial Commentary on the New Testament Writings*. London: T&T Clark/Continuum, 2009 (2007).

Thompson, Leonard L. *The Book of Revelation: Apocalypse and Empire*. New York: Oxford University Press, 1990.

Wimbush, Vincent L. Ed. *Theorizing Scriptures: New Critical Orientations to a Cultural Phenomenon*. New Brunswick, NJ: Rutgers University Press, 2008.

Yarbro Collins, Adela. *Crisis and Catharsis: The Power of the Apocalypse*. Philadelphia: Westminster Press, 1984.

CHAPTER 10

THE APOCRYPHAL ACTS OF THOMAS AND EMPIRE

CLARA A. B. JOSEPH

Introduction

The Christian Apocrypha reflect the complexities of the cultures and societies of the time and the pervasiveness of Empire in the early Christian period. Scholars observe that not just the content of the Apocrypha but also its relegation to the category of the apocryphal—the genre of doubtful authenticity—indicate the persistence of empire even as the empire changed titles—from the "Roman Empire" to the "Christian Empire." While covering the aforementioned discussions, this essay extends the argument to note that modern-day scholarship on the Apocrypha, specifically the Acts of Thomas is often overdetermined by imperial discourse. I focus on the Acts of Thomas also because it is the only Apocryphal manuscript within the genre of the Apocryphal Acts that is available in full and has a living community of Christians claiming apostolic heritage through Saint Thomas. I contend that scholarship on the Apocryphal Acts of Thomas is often Eurocentric because it overlooks the anti-imperial discourse that formulates both heresy and fiction. Overall, the essay proposes that empire studies can benefit from a review of Apocryphal literature and its historical and social exchanges.

The discussion signifies a relationship between genre and society. To an extent, the genres of the Apocrypha and their historical hiddenness account for how Christians and the academy have responded to this literature. The Apocrypha revealed itself in various forms, as gospels, acts, epistles, and apocalypses—the very genres that defined the New Testament canon, which, nevertheless, alludes to the tug of war between the Apocryphal and the canonical and their survival as discrete entities. Similarly, and as the etymology makes clear, the Apocrypha have been a category of the secret (i.e., that which is hidden). The secret words that Thomas perceives and reports in the Gospel of Thomas are one instance of this hiddenness. Accusations of Gnosticism that have been the predicament of several Apocrypha—including the Acts of Thomas, which shows the influence of the Gospel of Thomas—point to another aspect of this hiddenness. Both in their existence as forms of literature and as the theologically unknown the Apocrypha are, thus, a threat to the powers that be. Therefore, a reading of the Apocrypha prompts discussions on the empire and scrutiny of its discourse.

The methodology involves reading primary and secondary sources to unravel ideologies of the empire and thus falls under what has come to be known as postcolonial reading, although the essay will not engage with canonical postcolonial scholars per se. In this, I follow the footsteps of R. S. Sugirtharajah, who introduces the method in *The Bible and Empire: Postcolonial Explorations* as follows: "Postcolonialism is used here as an interventionist instrument which refuses to take the dominant reading as an uncomplicated representation of the past and introduces an alternative reading. Postcolonialism allows silenced and often marginalized people to find their own voices when they are at logger heads with the dominant readings."[1] The essay takes Sugirtharajah's method of reading to early Christian texts and to contemporary scholarship on those texts and contexts. The essay will first consider some of the prominent ways in which the empire is known to have interfaced with the genre of the Christian Apocrypha. The relegation of the genre to the heretical is the subject of the next section. Here, with the focus turning to the Acts of Thomas, I deliberate the heretical, however, as instances of resistance to the empire. Section three examines scholarship on the Acts of Thomas and its relationship to the Thomas Christians, a community that continues to have some significant connections with the tradition of that text. The purpose of this section is to show how imperial discourse continues into the post-colonial period in the scholarship. It is, indeed, a matter of some curiosity that the category of the Christian Apocrypha uncovers a sustained engagement with dominant powers down the ages.

Empire, Apocrypha, and the Politics of Genre

Studies on the early Christian period and texts tend to focus on the Roman Empire often to the exclusion of Eastern empires that historically maintained ongoing interactions of trade, treaties, and war. It is a problem in discussions of the Acts of Thomas, with its setting in India, and references both in the Apocryphal text and in other historical documents to the Apostle Thomas having visited either Parthia or India. According to Leonardo Gregoratti, the "Parthian monarchy had no strong centralized power, nor a strong imperial apparatus. It had no official orthodox religion and lacked a rooted and extensive presence on the territory. Nevertheless, in the middle of the first century BC Parthian rule stretched from the Euphrates to northwest India, including Mesopotamia, Iran and all the territories lying between the Persian Gulf and the Indian Ocean to the south and the Caspian Sea and the Caucasus to the north."[2] Gregoratti suggests the pervasiveness of the Parthian Empire on account of its geographical and cultural reach.

This section considers some of the historical and discursive instances and implications for the center-margin struggle, as it manifests in recent scholarship on the Apocrypha, to indicate a problem with scholarship that is West-oriented.

On Privileging the Roman Empire

For Helen C. Rhee, Apocryphal sources, such as the Apocryphal Acts and Martyr's Acts, deserve to be studied as more than "purely literary" works for they are as historical as the Apologies (the other genre that she studies) in determining Christian identities and ideals in the crucial early Christian period, namely the second and third centuries.[3] Rhee goes on to discuss the five oldest and major Acts: Acts of John, Acts of Paul, Acts of Peter, Acts of Andrew, and Acts of Thomas. A key area of determination of the Apocrypha (the Acts and the Martyr's Acts) involved the conflict between Christianity and the Empire,[4] where the empire—for Rhee—is always the Roman Empire.[5] According to such scholarship, the genre of the Apocrypha turns out to be a classic instance of resistance to the empire, but it positions this empire as solely Roman. Rhee, for instance, elides the location and cultural geography of the Acts of Thomas in its essential relationship to the Parthian and Sasanian empires. Early on in the book, she acknowledges the Eastern origin of the Acts of Thomas and the Acts of Andrew.[6] In a footnote, she refers to Jan Bremmer's theory that only the Acts of Thomas lies outside Western Asia Minor. However, as far as Rhee is concerned, the impact of the Apocryphal acts was on the Mediterranean region, the "Greco-Roman" world.[7] By focusing mainly on the Roman Empire, Rhee inadvertently obstructs what she sets out to do—study how the Apocryphal sources functioned "historically" in shaping realities. Briefly, her work does not recognize historical identities and ideals in Eastern Christianity and, thus, in the East.

Not only is it that Rhee's is no exception, but the imperialist trajectory of this kind of research becomes only more evident when the Roman Empire is privileged in the study of early Christianity. Scholarship on early Christianity, including the period following the third century, privileges the Roman Empire to bring about the conclusion—"Christians could speak of themselves as Romans."[8] Here, Jeremy M. Schott proposes a postcolonial analysis of late antiquity in his study on the dynamics of Christianity and empire and its "material consequences of domination."[9] The direction is already clear: the movement from Pax Romana to Pax Britannica (and to Pax Americana, for Ian Morris)[10] is such that the empires would be labeled "Christian." The thesis of Schott's book is that "the discourse of Christian imperialism was effective precisely because it developed out of, rather than erased, earlier imperial discourses."[11] Where many scholars are apt to trace the genealogy of religion to European colonialism, then, for Schott, that genealogy in fact goes further back to a Christian Roman imperialism: "If, as a number of contemporary scholars have noted, the category 'religion' emerges largely as a product (and instrument) of the subjugation of native cultures by (Christian) European imperialism, then exploring the interrelationship between Christian apologetic discourse and Roman imperialism suggests that we might locate the seeds of this process in the early fourth century as 'religion' was emerging as both the primary marker of ethnic and cultural identity and the central basis for (Christian) Roman imperial power."[12] In such studies of early Christianity, the Roman Empire—whether termed "Western Empire," "Eastern Empire," or "Roman Empire"—is for all practical purposes comprehended as at once Wstern and European and, consequently, Christianity itself remains at bottom Western, as the term signifies in its modern-day widespread use.

A Problem in the Study of the Apocrypha

The Acts of Thomas illustrates why such privileging of the Roman Empire is a problem. In the second edition of his study of the Acts of Thomas, the eminent New Testament and Apocrypha scholar, A. F. J. Klijn, continues to rely on the Syriac edition of William Wright's *Apocryphal Acts of the Apostles*, published in 1871. Klijn justifies his choice by noting that scholars, in general, concur that the Acts of Thomas was written in Syriac. At times, where additions occur, Klijn refers to Greek versions where the instance points to a prior tradition in the textual history. For, according to him, "the Acts were written in a bilingual environment in which both the Syriac and Greek versions originated simultaneously."[13] This note on a bilingual environment is also a caution against assuming that a monolithic "empire" overruled a highly heterogeneous ground reality.

The heterogeneity concerned the tug of war that involved more than the Roman Empire, historically—the Seleucid, Parthian, Kushan, and Sasanian empires, where the various empires often functioned in palimpsest even long after the official end of a period. Of these, the Parthian Empire is of particular significance for the Acts of Thomas. In this regard, Eivind Heldaas Seland writes, "Although the Acts [Acts of Thomas] themselves must be considered legendary, Gondophares[14] is numismatically attested to have ruled an Indo-Parthian kingdom in the Indus Valley ca.20–45 ce. The geographical and chronological context of the narrative is not implausible, and there are strong Indian traditions tracing the origins of Christianity on the subcontinent to the first century, traditions that may have resurfaced in the Acts of Thomas."[15] I will discuss the Indian traditions later, but here my purpose in citing Seland is to point to the importance of studying the Parthian Empire and to recognize that binaries of Rome versus its other (Parthia) are, simply put, ahistorical.[16]

Furthermore, an understanding of the Acts of Thomas requires a study of both the Syriac and Greek translations (regardless of the controversy on which came first), for often what is missing in one can be found or clarified in the other. Thus the initial reference to the merchant, who eventually hires Thomas as the carpenter to build the palace of King Gudnaphar (Syriac) or Gundaphares/Gondaphoros (Greek), is to his arrival from "(illegible)[sic]" and "from the south country" (both in Syriac) and "from India" (in the Greek text).[17] Through a careful reading of these various texts and, likely, an earlier reference to the merchant as an "Indian," Klijn concludes by conflating: "We suppose that the original Syriac text read 'from the south country, from India.'"[18] Similarly, a remarkable scene—of Thomas baptizing the king and his brother, Gad, appears with noticeable variation in the different translations.[19] The Greek translation names the king as Gondaphoros and details at length the ceremony of anointing,[20] which was part of the baptism (according to the Greek version); in the Syriac translation, the anointing precedes baptism.[21] This kind of intertextuality is a metaphor for the world outside the previously mentioned Eurocentric binary of Rome and its other.

The Role of Genre

The Apocrypha function to expose the Empire even as the genre, defined noncanonical and (hence) marginalized, bears the intertextuality and heterogeneity. In his review of Hans-Josef Klauck's *The Apocryphal Acts of the Apostles: An Introduction*, Michael J. Kruger observes that scholars are "fascinated with alternate versions of the history of Early Christianity."[22] In this context, he points especially to the Nag Hammadi discoveries of Apocryphal Gospels. The Apocryphal Acts, he complains, are "largely overlooked,"[23] but he states that Klauck's book fills that gap. Klauck's book, initially published in German and then, three years later, in an English translation, covers The Acts of John, The Acts of Paul, The Acts of Peter, The Acts of Andrew, The Acts of Thomas, The Acts of Peter and the Twelve Apostles, The Pseudo-Clementines, and, in a single chapter, the lesser-known sources such as The Acts of Philip, The Acts of Matthew, The Acts of Matthias, and others. The translation points to a readership out there. Charles Cosgrove writes about the original readers, "In the case of the readership of Acts of Thomas, we must contemplate members of Thomasine Christian communities who are well-versed in Thomasine beliefs and practices, as well as readers who have not been initiated into the Thomasine way. Bremmer contemplates the following possible audiences for the apocryphal acts: the author's own 'immediate circle,' the author's church, and a (somewhat) wider audience through publication of the book."[24] The demand, for Klauck's book, denotes a readership that entertains the noncanonical genre, which can be interpreted to some extent as the continued competition of the genres as a symptom of the center-margin struggle.

However, one of the captivating aspects of the Apocrypha, as presented by Klauck, is its proximity to the ancient Greek novel: "the Hellenistic love novel" (Klauck cites Plumacher here),[25] for instance. He also quotes Bremmer: "In fact, the intertextuality of the AAA[p] with the novel cannot be doubted, if we look at the cumulation of similar motifs, as collected by [Rosa] Soder: shipwreck, brigands, sale into slavery, putting girls in brothels, unruly crowds, travel around the empire, thinking of suicide, sending messages, corrupting a servant, trials, locking up in tombs, endless journeys and loving couples (Platonic or not)."[26] Soder culls her list, however, not to establish the link between the Greek novel and the Apocryphal Acts. She rather concludes that witnesses of old folk tales of the adventures, wonders, and love affairs of great men are likely the source of and influence on the Acts, a point Bremmer dismisses.[27] Klauck himself, on the other hand, points to other influences on the genre of the Acts—"the traditions about Jesus in the gospels . . . Luke's Acts of the Apostles . . . other community traditions."[28]

Interestingly, none of the mentioned sources cogitates the influence of Parthian literature and literary traditions on the Apocrypha. In her book *Parthian Writing and Literature*, Mary Boyce refers to "women's minstrelsy," "singing girls," and the "lyre" as motifs in the literature of the Sasanian period.[29] She also discusses at length the oral tradition that would have contributed to the rich poetry and music of Parthia. Yet, apart from Boyce's early edition, *The Manichean Hymn-Cycle in Parthian*, and a few others,[30] it is difficult to come by scholarly discussions on Parthian literary traditions in the Acts of Thomas. This too is a symptom of the center-margin struggle.

Additionally, it is an aspect of what Vijay K. Bhatia terms "the politics of genre." According to him, the limits that are part of any genre, the advanced awareness of those limits (even limitations) that empowers specific "discourse communities," and their exploitation by scholars toward set goals constitute the politics of genre.[31] It denotes legitimacy in attempts "to maintain solidarity within a disciplinary community" and (Bhatia does not say "illegitimacy in") strategies in keeping "outsiders at a respectable distance."[32]

The legendary format of the Apocrypha with its talking animals and its themes that privilege the enlightened have historically formed a closed readership. The genre and its style also have, as this essay aims to demonstrate, shaped in turn the Empire, including a community of scholars that deploys the politics of genre. In short, if genre has a politics, even more so the genre that is in the margins.

A crucial aspect of the politics of genre is the noncanonicity of the Apocrypha, which is based on charges of heresy and the heretical. For Paul Foster, however, the "[n]oncanonical gospels are . . . a powerful witness to the diversity of early Christianity itself."[33] Taken thus, the heretical becomes a problem of the binary where the "gnostic," for instance, falls under the realm not of Rome but its other. A focus on the identities and ideals in the East becomes the need of the day. It, therefore, becomes imperative to privilege the intertextual and the other traditions instead strategically.

Heresy as Resistance to the Empire

Gnosticism, Encratism, and Manichaeanism are only some of the heretical categories liberally applied to Apocryphal sources. According to Thomas Aquinas, heresy is "a species of infidelity in men who, having professed the faith of Christ, corrupt its dogmas."[34] This definition, applied retroactively, together with the Greek etymology of "heresy" that implies choosing, points to the illicitness of choosing that the Apocryphal community might engage in. Viewed thus, charges of heresy are intensely political on the side of the accuser as well as the accused. Both truth and its representation cannot be interpreted except within the dynamics of the Empire. In what follows, I reconsider some of the charges, specifically of Encratism and magic, against the Acts of Thomas in the context of empire studies and suggest its significance for heresiology.

Encratism and Empire

In "Canonical and Apocryphal 'Acts of the Apostles,'" Francois Bovon explains that all Apocryphal acts are not encratic and that representations of restraint in sex are not encratic in themselves.[35] Nevertheless, he identifies Encratism in the Acts of Thomas.[36] He remarks, "Careful readers see strong divergences in christology (docetism can be present in certain passages of the *Acts of John*, incarnation underlined in the *Acts of Philip*) or in the realm of asceticism (marriage can be banned all together in the *Acts of Thomas* in favor of encratism and purity; marriage can be accepted if combined with strict morality in other apocryphal Acts)."[37] Whereas being continent in itself is not heretical, the denial of marriage is. Klijn, on the other hand, does not interpret the Acts of Thomas in this manner: "We can not [sic] say that they are rejecting marriage, although it should not be consummated, which is supposed to be a 'deed of shame.'"[38] Yves Tissot similarly concludes that it would be Encratism only when "sexual continence is not proposed 'in order to be closer to God' . . . but imposed on every baptized person as a requirement of the faith."[39] In making this point, Tissot rejects those who label Apocryphal works as encratic. Specifically, he raises objections to opposing conclusions in Geboren Takashi Onuki as well as to Georges Blond's labeling of the Acts of Thomas as a "vehemently Encratite work."[40] My paraphrase of the plot in the Acts of Thomas, next, however, points to another dimension of the so-called Encratism or continence—the empire.

Renouncing sex, as well as meat and wine, are indeed telltale signs of Encratism. The Acts of Thomas presents almost all of these situations and, thus, is vulnerable to ruthless categorizing. The apostle Thomas's first encounter after boarding ship is with a situation of marriage and sex. According to the Acts of Thomas, the setting is the port city of Sandaruk (Syriac) or Andrapolis (Greek). Scholars differ in locating the city in Syria[41] or Andhra in India[42] but agree that the region was under Parthian rule. In this city, Habban, King Gondophares' agent who purchased Thomas from Jesus for twenty pieces of silver, and Thomas are invited to the wedding feast of the local king's daughter. After the feast, in the course of which Thomas performs a miracle or two, the king further invites him to the palace in the following manner: "[C]ome with me and pray for my daughter, because she is my only one, and today I am giving her away in marriage."[43] Thomas is reluctant as he has not yet received a sign from the Lord; but, "the king carried him off by force to the bridal chamber."[44] Once in the presence of the young couple, Thomas prays, invoking the Lord who is "the discloser of hidden secrets, and the revealer of mysterious sayings" and concludes with an innocent benediction: "I ask of you on behalf of these young people, that whatever you know to be beneficial for them, you will do for them."[45] He lays his hand upon them, and says to them: "Our Lord be with you," and he leaves them. However, the consequence of that prayer is that Jesus, whose look-alike Thomas ("the twin") is, himself appears to the hapless couple and counsels them against "filthy intercourse" so that they can become "pure temples."[46] The young couple follows the instructions to the letter, and Thomas is left to the mercies of an enraged king. Similar situations, involving royals and nobles, recur once Thomas arrives at his destination in India. Klijn concludes that Thomas was executed for imposing sexual abstinence on married couples.[47] Thus Encratism or heresy would have to be understood in the context of the empire.

Heresy and the Family

The preceding discussion of the plot proposes that Thomas's/Jesus' reformations strike at the very foundation of the worldly empire, that is, the family. Whereas royalty and nobility actively seek to raise families with several children, Jesus and Thomas (in other scenes) equally dissuade the creation of children. Sexual union is "filthy" because it leads to procreation, which triggers a series of immoralities, and as Jesus tells the newlyweds, "if you have children, for their sakes you will become oppressors and robbers and smiters of orphans and wringers of widows, and you will be grievously tortured for their injuries."[48] It appears Jesus has deliberately laid out the series of crimes repeated by the Empire—oppression, robbery, and injustice—which come with a terrible consequence. The juxtaposition of the worldly and heavenly kingdoms ("the true wedding feast") cannot get sharper. The heavenly kingdom aims to subdue the worldly kingdom by invading the bridal chamber, and the Empire reacts: Thomas is imprisoned. Later on, having arrived at his destination in India, Thomas's influence on the women of the palace, which results in these women abstaining from sex with their husbands, culminates in the execution of Thomas. About two millennia later, another "great soul" reformed his own life and that of numerous others, including newly married couples,[49] by simultaneously advocating sexual abstinence and an equally sacrificial stance against the British Empire. Were Mahatma Gandhi a Christian, the British could have added against him the charge of Encratism on top of sedition. In other words, the later charge of Encratism by scholars of the Acts of Thomas would be misleading to the extent that the crime of Thomas is not against religion but the Empire.

Heresiology and Empire

Another reason for suspecting Encratism in the Acts of Thomas has been the manner in which the Eucharist is celebrated. Even this may have to be reconsidered within empire politics. Klijn notices a trend in the Syriac to avoid associating not only the Eucharist but also any allusions to wine elsewhere. He draws attention to the phrase in the Acts of Thomas—"drunk of the life" in Syriac instead of "drunk of the wine" in Greek—to note that "it agrees with a tendency to avoid using wine at the Eucharist."[50] A cup of water, rather than wine, is used in the ceremony. For Susan E. Myers, "the avoidance of wine for the Eucharist is probably in keeping with the encratite tendencies of the document."[51] As much as Encratism is imaginable, the geopolitical situation would also have encouraged Christians of the East who were fighting a not-yet-converted Roman

Empire by renouncing, even denouncing, an essential item of trade—wine. Again, the utter poverty that the marginalized community experienced, whether voluntarily or not, would also have compelled the use of an inexpensive and available drink—water. The Thomas of the Acts, who moved his abode from a region of the Roman Empire to that of Parthia, would be responding to these political, economic, and ethical situations whether he was defining or only observing the Eucharistic ritual. Interestingly enough, during the period of Portuguese colonization, the then bishop of the Thomas Christians was forced to replace the dry grapes (raisins) and water mix of the Eucharistic ritual of the Thomas Christians with imported Portuguese wine.[52] According to the document known as "The Narratives of Joseph the Indian" (1501), the raisins came from China.[53] Portuguese items competed with products of East Asia and the Levant, and this competition manifested itself also in the liturgy. Both in the study of the early Christian period and the period of the Reformation and the Counter-Reformation, empire studies has the potential to force a rethinking of heresiology.

Magic or Resistance

Allegations of plain magic in the Acts of Thomas too can be revisited in the context of the politics of the Empire. In "'Magic or Miracle'? Some Second Century Instances," Harold Remus observes, "Christians who ate the flesh of a crucified man and employed the cross in various ways might well be suspected of magic. Some Christians for their part stressed the potency of the cross, the Eucharistic bread, and other ritual elements in a way that pagans might consider magical."[54] In the Acts of Thomas, the king's wife, Tertia, repeats to Thomas the happenings of that day to which Jesus, whom she mistakes for Thomas, was a witness: "King Mazdai sent and had me Tertia brought to him and he said to me: 'That conjuror has not yet got power over you, because I have heard that he bewitches with oil and water and bread and wine and he has not yet bewitched you. ... For I know that as long as he has not given to you water and oil and bread and wine he has not yet got full power over you."[55] Thus, King Mazdai interprets the elements of the sacraments as magic. Remus proceeds to discuss specific "magical" scenes in the Acts of Thomas. A scene that he does not refer to but that is equally magical is of the queen and a noble's wife and maid exiting a sealed prison to congregate with Thomas, who has similarly left his prison, and then returning unnoticed to their respective cells. Those in charge of Thomas's prison complain to the king: "Our lord the king either let this sorcerer go or imprison him in another place for we are unable to guard him because twice your good fortune has guarded the prisoners otherwise they would all have escaped for we shut the doors and we find them open."[56] The prison guards can only conclude that the king's magic (good fortune) withstood Thomas's. However, when the king has Thomas stripped and brought to him wearing a girdle to cover his loins, his response to the king's question, whether he is a slave or a freeman, is: "I am a slave but you have no power whatever over me."[57] Bremmer wonders if the Roman Empire's sanctions on magic have resulted in increased literary representations of magic, as in some of the Apocrypha. He cites the Acts of Peter and the Acts of Andrew in this regard.[58] By presenting Christians who defy the prison system by leaving and then returning autonomously, the Acts of Thomas stages not just magic but also an instance of nonviolent resistance to the Empire.

In concluding this section, I shall quote William Young, who presents before us an intricate and complicated network of power that accompanied accusations of heresy: "Roman Emperors like Constantine the Great, Constantius and Theodosius had laid down what the Church was to believe, and declared heretical or schismatic worship to be illegal. Later the Roman Catholic Church was to try 'heretics' and hand them over to the 'secular arm' for punishment, while in the Byzantine Empire Justinian was to order the Governors of his Eparchies, under threat of the death penalty for disobedience, to see to it that metropolitans and bishops carried out their duties to the letter."[59] In his dissertation, Young is discussing the happenings of the fifth century. Young's research focused on the Roman Empire, both the Western and the Eastern. Nonetheless, his analysis is a useful clue to the extent to which empires, in general, would have influenced heresiology in the preceding (and following) centuries, including the verdict of the third-century church historian and polemicist, Eusebius of Caesarea, that the Acts of Thomas is heretical. Schott observes that apologetics became a discourse that continued, rather unchanged (Augustine adopting Eusebius, for instance), and, furthermore, "Early Christian apologetics—as an historical-ethnographic discourse— also proved useful well beyond late antiquity."[60] Schott, in particular, means how European colonialism deployed the earlier apologetic discourse. The preceding discussions advise that charges of "heresy" in the Acts of Thomas, and likely other Apocrypha, should not be taken at face value but ought to be reread and amended to "imperial discourse."

THE ACTS OF THOMAS AND THE THOMAS CHRISTIANS OF INDIA

The heretical as well as the fictional status of the Acts of Thomas defined how scholars interpreted what Mundadan refers to as its "historical nucleus."[61] But how scholars interpreted this signifies the West's ideological position with regard to the other. The ground reality of the historical core is the living tradition of the Thomas Christians, a community that claims apostolic heritage through the Apostle Thomas, who lived in the first century. Today, the size of this community is "about nine million."[62] Some scholars have considered the Acts of Thomas as the urtext of this community. Andrade, for example, claims that Thomas Christians themselves look to this text for proof of the antiquity of their church.[63] In what follows, I examine the scholarship of George Huxley, Lourens P. Van den Bosch, Andrade, Mathias Mundadan, Xavier Koodapuzha, and

George Nedungatt, who present cases for and against the presence of Christianity in antiquity in India and its relationship to the Acts of Thomas. Their scholarship is recent and relevant in covering related issues of historiography and literary and cultural critique. One of the critical questions posed by these scholars concerns the historical relationship between the Acts of Thomas and India and reflects the cartographic and ideological aspirations of the West.

Thomas to India

The Acts of Thomas makes clear right from the start that the mission of Thomas is to no other place but India. Thus, the initial scene, involving Jesus and Thomas, centers on the division of the countries of the world among the apostles and the allotment of India to Thomas:

> And when all the Apostles had been for a time in Jerusalem,— Simon Cephas and Andrew, and Jacob (James) and John, and Philip and Bartholomew, and Thomas and Matthew the publican, and Jacob the son of Alphaeus, and Simon the Kananite, and Judas the son of Jacob (James),—they divided the countries among them, in order that each one of them might preach in the region which fell to him and in the place to which his Lord sent him. And India fell by lot and division to Judas Thomas the Apostle. And he was not willing to go, saying: "I have not strength enough for this, because I am weak. And I am a Hebrew: how can I teach the Indians?" And whilst Judas was reasoning thus, our Lord appeared to him in a vision of the night, and said to him: "Fear not, Thomas, because my grace is with you." But he would not be persuaded at all, saying: "Whithersoever you will, our Lord, send me; only to India I will not go."[64]

The preceding narrative is a somewhat doleful version of the Great Commission of the canonical gospel, Matt 28:16–20: "And Jesus came and said to them, 'All authority in heaven and on earth has been given to me. Go therefore and make disciples of all nations, baptizing them in the name of the Father and of the Son and of the Holy Spirit, and teaching them to obey everything that I have commanded you. And remember, I am with you always, to the end of the age'" (NRSV). Whereas the canonical version might—at least in the popular imagination—suggest a heroic enactment of the commission from start to finish, the Acts of Thomas presents to us an apostle who is fearful and hesitant at the prospect of not necessarily the commission but the specific locale given to him—India. According to the Apocryphal Acts of Philip (as per information Philip receives from John in Parthia), Thomas was indeed sent to India. In the Acts of Thomas, Jesus makes a special appearance to Thomas to reassure him in his unique impasse, but to no avail. The stubbornness and ultimate bathos of Thomas's reply makes one suspect that Thomas knew precisely where he was being sent—to which India he was headed.

Which India?

"Which India?" is a motif in colonial and post-colonial scholarship that denotes either the uncertainty or denial of the geographical destination as or including the region of present-day India. The motif appears rather consistently in Western scholarship and necessitates scrutiny on account of its relevance for the study of the Acts of Thomas and its relationship to the Thomas Christians. As such, "which India?" is a problem for the history of geography and, equally, for empire studies. In his essay, "Geography in the *Acts of Thomas*," Huxley proposes to demonstrate how the geography narrated in the Acts of Thomas assists an understanding of the composition and adaptation of that text. However, the essay provides little clarity on this goal; instead, it focuses on what Huxley proposes not to do, "the question of the historicity of St Thomas's missionary journeys."[65] A key concern of this question is whether the India referenced in the Acts of Thomas was indeed India. To scholars who interpret the "town of Sandaruk,"[66] where Habban and Thomas disembark for the first time during their journey, as "Andhra" (the region of the present-day state in India by that name), Huxley replies simply that that association "must also be questioned."[67] He continues, challenging the links that some scholars have made to the possibility that the place name might refer to North-West India, "Nor are we required to connect SNDRWK [Sandaruk] with Sindh."[68] As to the mention of the Parthian king, Gondophares, Huxley remarks that the alignment of the period of Gondophares' rule and Thomas's alleged visit demonstrates "not that Thomas went to India in the second quarter of the first century A.D., but that the author of the Acts knew the date of Gondophernes."[69] Here, Huxley is referring to the numismatic evidence and the evidence provided in the Takht-i-Bahi inscription about Gondophares, which brought scholars to an agreement that the kingdom of Parthia extended into India around the first century CE.[70] He concludes that the fictional location is in southern Arabia.[71] However, a literary problem—with or without a "historical nucleus"—remains: Why did the author of the Acts of Thomas send Thomas to, of all places, India?[72]

Tradition First or Book First

Like Huxley, Van den Bosch also presumes that the Thomas Christian tradition of India has been derived from the Apocryphal Acts of Thomas.[73] According to him, the Thomas Christian tradition is untenable in this case because the Acts of Thomas "relate the journey of the apostle Thomas and his missionary activities in India in a 'romantic' way ... [and is] the result of a rich imagination of the author."[74] Thus, not just its pseudepigraphical status but also the literary nature of the Acts of Thomas automatically determines and proves the spuriousness of the Thomas Christian tradition. Ironically, he acknowledges that another Apocryphal source, The Passion of Bartholomew, "a highly legendry [sic] text," presents the evangelization of India by Bartholomew and yet "we do not hear about the existence of Christian communities in India that appealed to

Bartholomew as their founder."[75] Van den Bosch does not explain why, in his theory, the Acts of Thomas created a Thomas tradition and yet the Passion of Bartholomew failed to create a parallel Bartholomew tradition in India. According to the Thomas Christian Church historian, Xavier Koodapuzha, the Thomas Christian tradition is not derived from the Acts of Thomas. Rather, this tradition was prevalent in India well before the Acts of Thomas was compiled.[76] Nevertheless, unlike Huxley, Van den Bosch believes that Christianity entered North-West India in antiquity and that the foreign names in the Acts of Thomas "may at best refer to the northwestern part of India with its Greek, Parthian and Persian influences."[77] In the conclusion of his essay, he casually wonders about "the deeper motives of the Portuguese" and proposes that the tradition associated with the tomb of Thomas at Mylapore, in South-East India, was a Portuguese political invention built strategically onto the equally fictitious beginnings of the Thomas Christian tradition in the Acts of Thomas.[78] Van den Bosch ignores the evidence that an oft-cited source of his, A. Mathias Mundadan's *History of Christianity in India*, provides establishing the reputation of the tomb of Thomas in India prior to 1517, the year that Diego Femandes (Fernandes), "the first Portuguese informant," wrote to his king about the tomb in Mylapore.[79] Mundadan, for instance, points to related evidence in the edited collection of Georg Schurhammer, specifically the "Three Letters of Mar Jacob" (the letters were written in 1504), which indicate that the East Syrian prelate of the Thomas Christians was aware of the tradition of the tomb of Thomas in Mylapore at the turn of the fifteenth century, before the time of Van den Bosch's "informant." Mundadan also refers to the document known as the "Narrative of Joseph the Indian," containing the information that the Thomas Christian priest, Joseph, provided as he traveled in the ship with Pedro Alvares Cabral in 1501.[80] Thus, whereas Van den Bosch at times relents in saying that there were Christian communities in India in the first and second centuries,[81] he cannot consider the plausibility of Thomas having traveled to present-day India. For him, the "fact" of Thomas evangelizing Parthia was mixed with the "fiction" of Thomas evangelizing India; the author of the Acts of Thomas, accordingly, only connoted that "with his missions to India the apostle Thomas had preached his gospel unto the ends of the earth."[82] A little later, Van den Bosch interprets Thomas's reluctance to go to India as meaning he "did not like to travel to remote countries."[83] However, to make this statement, he has to evade Thomas's words, "Whithersoever you will, our Lord, send me."[84] In the introduction to his translation of the Acts of Thomas, Klijn approves of Van den Bosch's study as "well balanced."[85] Yet, India within such critique is not a country but a synecdoche.

The Thomas Christian Strikes Back

In his monograph, *Quest for the Historical Thomas Apostle of India: A Re-reading of the Evidence*, Nedungatt painstakingly responds to several Western authors who summarily dismiss the probability of the Apostle Thomas having visited India. In a footnote, Nedungatt, for instance, takes objection to Van den Bosch's study as follows:

"His 'reconstruction of Christianity in India'[86] is guided by historicism, contains convenient theories of 'interpolation'[87] and ignores the Indian tradition while speaking of 'the ancient imagination of Thomas's visit to India.'"[88] To explain Nedungatt's assessment, the charge of historicism signifies in particular the insistence on contemporary documents—that is, the pedantic position that since there are no documents available from the Apostle Thomas's own time and situation, and because the Acts of Thomas is dated to the third century, it can be concluded that there is no proof of Thomas ever having traveled to India. Van den Bosch dismisses a ninth-century allusion to the "House of Thomas" (Bethuma or Batuma) in an Islamic source on India as likely an interpolation. The House of Thomas, according to this source, "can be reached in 10 days from Quilon."[89] (Mundadan, otherwise, is a source that Van den Bosch uses amply.) Moreover, Van den Bosch does not take into account the Indian tradition. His insistence on documentary corroboration can be safely interpreted as his reluctance to admit of any oral and performance sources, a crucial mistake in historical methodology.[90] Again, responding to a scholar of the British colonial period in India, Nedungatt writes:

> A British writer [James Hough], who was chaplain to the British East India Company at Madras, asserted in his *History of Christianity in India* the "improbability of any Apostles having preached in India." His reasoning was as follows. ["]Considering the tedious mode of communication with that country, and the ancients' limited knowledge of its inhabitants until towards the close of the first century, it is not probable that any of the Apostles of our Lord embarked on such a voyage.["] With this assertion the writer showed not only his own very "limited knowledge" of ancient India but betrayed a naive colonial myopia and prejudice such as had not afflicted the ancients.[91]

Thus, Nedungatt challenges both the theoretical methodology and the discourse in scholarship, such as of Van den Bosch and Hough, which he concludes is ultimately imperial.

To the question as to which India was the mission of the Apostle Thomas, Nedungatt categorically concludes that it is indeed the region of present-day India. For this, he does not rely on the Acts of Thomas, which he, like the authors mentioned previously, dismisses as unhistorical. Instead, he cites Herodotus and Xenophon, among others, for their knowledge of both "Kush [Ethiopia] and Hindu [India]" (whereas later writers, and with persistence in the colonial and post-colonial periods, confused the two).[92] He recalls the writings of the Church Fathers, including Origen, who would not have seen the Acts of Thomas and yet refers to Thomas being assigned Parthia. Nedungatt also draws his conclusions from what he calls a "multifocus Indian tradition" consisting of Taxila (Sirkap, Pakistan)[93]—"the capital of the Parthian kingdom of Gundaphar called India by the author of the *ATh*";[94] Udayapur (central India), where an eleventh-century inscription alludes to there having been a church; Mylapore (in Tamil Nadu) that claims the tomb of the Apostle Thomas; and Malabar (Kerala) with the community of Thomas Christians and their living tradition spanning two millennia.[95] Nedungatt's research points to the palimpsest of empires—Parthia to post-colonial India—and unmasks the persistent colonial discourse that pervades present-day scholarship on India and its Christians.

In conclusion, the modern-day scholarship that veers toward seeing Christianity as centered in Rome and the Roman Empire as "really" Western also tends to ignore the role of Parthia and other empires in determining the literature, culture, and history of the Apocrypha. To the extent that it allows for a consideration of the East, the scholarship focuses on the western regions of that region in the East, specifically the Levant. As a result, a text such as the Acts of Thomas and a living community linked to that tradition are often subjected to misreading that is also (racially?) biased. A critical analysis of the noncanonical status of the text and its genre points to a political battleground that perhaps is more intense precisely on account of the marginality of the genre in question. Such marginality has both caused and resulted in charges of heresy. A close reading of the Apocryphal text confirms many oddities in dogma and doings; yet, when approached critically within empire studies, the same text connotes anti-imperial discourse. What is more, such a discourse has historically challenged not only the early Christian period but also the colonial and later periods. Ultimately, an important implication of such readings is that heresiology would have to be reconsidered within the framework of empire studies. Furthermore, the Acts of Thomas asks why the text's central location is India. The heretical and fictional characteristics of the Acts of Thomas have shaped how most Western scholars have assessed the history and tradition of the Thomas Christians. Their assessments take on a Eurocentric direction and have duly been countered by Indian church historians. Future research would benefit from a detailed study of the exchanges between the various empires and its consequences for the text in question; the narrative or counternarrative offered by the women characters; the relevance of the conversion narrative in world and India politics today; and enlightenment, Gibbonian, or postcolonial views of Christian triumphalism rising from the text. This essay, through a rereading of the Acts of Thomas, however, has pointed to the persistence of imperial discourse on the one hand and the equally dogged resistance to it beginning with the saint, if not Jesus, himself.

Notes

1. R. S. Sugirtharajah, *The Bible and Empire: Postcolonial Explorations* (Cambridge: Cambridge University Press, 2005), 3.
2. Leonardo Gregoratti, "Sinews of the Other Empire: The Parthian Great Kin's Rule over Vassal Kingdoms," in Hakon Fiane Teigen and Eivind Heldaas Seland, 95–104. *Sinews of Empire: Networks in the Roman Near East and Beyond* (Philadelphia: Oxbow Books, 2017), 103.
3. Helen Rhee, *Early Christian Literature Christ and Culture in the Second and Third Centuries* (London: Routledge, 2005), 2.
4. Rhee, *Early Christian Literature*, 187.
5. Rhee, *Early Christian Literature*, 7.

6. Rhee, *Early Christian Literature*, 3.
7. Rhee, *Early Christian Literature*, 124.
8. Jeremy M. Schott, *Christianity, Empire, and the Making of Religion in Late Antiquity* (Philadelphia: University of Pennsylvania Press, 2008), 1.
9. Schott, *Christianity*, 10.
10. Ian Morris, *War! What Is It Good For? Conflict and the Progress of Civilization from Primates to Robots* (New York: Farrar, Straus & Giroux, 2014).
11. Schott, *Christianity*, 10.
12. Schott, *Christianity*, 14.
13. A. F. J. Klijn, *The Acts of Thomas: Introduction, Text, and Commentary* (Leiden; Boston: Brill, 2003), 3.
14. "Gondophares" is rendered as "Gundaphoros" in Klijn, *Acts of Thomas*, 75.
15. Eivind Heldaas Seland, "Trade and Christianity in the Indian Ocean during Late Antiquity," *Journal of Late Antiquity* 5, no. 1 (2012): 79.
16. Grant Parker, "India, Egypt and Parthia in Augustan Verse: The Post-orientalist Turn," *Dictynna: Revue de Poetique latine* 8 (2011): 5.
17. Klijn, *Acts of Thomas*, 21.
18. Klijn, *Acts of Thomas*, 20.
19. Klijn, *Acts of Thomas*, 75.
20. Klijn, *Acts of Thomas*, 75–76.
21. Klijn, *Acts of Thomas*, 78.
22. Michael J. Kruger, "Review: The Apocryphal Acts of the Apostles: An Introduction by Hans-Josef Klauck," *Journal of the Evangelical Theological Society* 52, no. 2 (2009): 395.
23. Kruger, "Review," 395.
24. Charles H. Cosgrove, "Singing Thomas: Anatomy of a Sympotic Scene in Acts of Thomas," *Vigilaw Christianae: A Review of Early Christian Life and Language* 69, no. 3 (2015): 257.
25. Hans-Josef Klauck, *The Apocryphal Acts of the Apostles: An Introduction* (Waco, TX: Baylor University Press, 2008), 13.
26. Jan N. Bremmer, "The Five Major Apocryphal Acts: Authors, Place, Time and Readership," in *The Apocryphal Acts of Thomas*, 164, quoted in Hans-Josef Klauck, *The Apocryphal Acts of the Apostles: An Introduction* (Waco, TX: Baylor University Press, 2008), 13.
27. Jan N. Bremmer, "Five Major Apocryphal Acts," 164.
28. Klauck, *Apocryphal Acts of the Apostles*, 14.
29. Mary Boyce, *The Manichean Hymn-Cycle in Parthian* (London: Oxford University Press, 1954), 1158.
30. For instance, Kathleen E. McVey examines the "Hymn of the Bride" in the Acts of Thomas as a madrasa that Thomas chants but also feels compelled to allude to Ephrem's reference to the madrasa of Mani and, thus, its heretical strain (194). Kathleen E. McVey, "Were the Earliest Madrase Songs or Recitations?" in *After Bardaisan: Studies on Continuity and Change in Syriac Christianity in Honour of Professor Han J. W. Drijvers* (Leuven: Peeters Publishers, 1999), 185–200. Also see: Yiphtah Zur, "Parallels between Acts of Thomas 6–7 and 4Q184," *Revue De Qumran* 16, no. 1 (1993): 103–107; Charles H. Cosgrove, "Singing Thomas: Anatomy of a Sympotic Scene in Acts of Thomas," *Vigilae Christianae: A Review of Early Christian Life and Language* 69, no. 3 (2015): 256–275
31. Vijay K. Bhatia, "The Power and Politics of Genre," *World Englishes* 16, no. 3 (1997): 359–371.
32. Bhatia, "Power and Politics of Genre," 367.

33. Paul Foster, *The Apocryphal Gospels: A Very Short Introduction* (Oxford; New York: Oxford University Press, 2009), 110.
34. Thomas Aquinas, *Summa* II.II:11:1.
35. Francois Bovon, "Canonical and Apocryphal 'Acts of the Apostles,'" *Journal of Early Christian Studies* 11, no. 2 (2003): 181.
36. Bovon, "Canonical and Apocryphal 'Acts of the Apostles,'" 193.
37. Bovon, "Canonical and Apocryphal 'Acts of the Apostles,'" 192–193.
38. Klijn, *Acts of Thomas*, 10.
39. Yves Tissot, *The Oxford Handbook of Early Christian Apocrypha*, ed. Andrew Gregory (Oxford: Oxford University Press, 2015), 408.
40. George Blond, quoted in Yves Tissot, *The Oxford Handbook of Early Christian Apocrypha* (Oxford: Oxford University Press, 2015), 410.
41. George Huxley, "Geography in the Acts of Thomas," *Greek, Roman, and Byzantine Studies* 24 (1983): 71–80.
42. Klijn, *Acts of Thomas*, 24; George Nedungatt, *Quest for theHistorical Thomas Apostle of India: A Re-reading of the Evidence* (Bangalore: Theological Publications in India, 2008), 248–249.
43. Klijn, *Acts of Thomas*, 41–42.
44. Klijn, *Acts of Thomas*, 42.
45. Klijn, *Acts of Thomas*, 43.
46. Klijn, *Acts of Thomas*, 52.
47. Klijn, *The Acts of Thomas*, 10.
48. Klijn, *Acts of Thomas*, 53.
49. Jawaharlal Nehru's sister, Vijaya Lakshmi Pandit, testifies that she and her husband, Ranjit Sitaram Pandit, as newlyweds, were advised by Gandhi to forgo sex. In this matter, they disobeyed. Vijaya Lakshmi Pandit, *The Scope of Happiness: A Personal Memoir* (London: Weidenfeld and Nicolson, 1979), 73–74.
50. Klijn, *Acts of Thomas*, 38.
51. Susan E. Myers, *Spirit Epicleses in the Acts of Thomas* (Tubingen: Mohr Siebeck, 2010), 2.
52. Pius Malekandathil, *Jornada of Dom Alexis de Menezes: A Portuguese Account of the Sixteenth Century Malabar* (Delhi: LRC Publications, 2003), 33; Scaria Zacharia, *The Acts and Decrees of the Synod of Diamper 1599* (Edamattam: Indian Insitute of Christian Studies, 1994), 139–140.
53. William Brooks Greenlee, "The Account of Priest Joseph," in *The Voyages of Pedro Alvaes Cabral to Brazil and India* (Nendeln/Liechtenstein: Kraus Reprinted Limited, 1967), 104.
54. Harold Remus, "'Magic or Miracle'? Some Second Century Instances," *The Second Century: A Journal of Early Christian Studies* 2, no. 3 (1982): 140.
55. Klijn, *Acts of Thomas*, 236.
56. Klijn, *Acts of Thomas*, 246.
57. Klijn, *Acts of Thomas*, 246.
58. Jan N. Bremmer and Jan R. Veenstra, *The Metamorphosis of Magic from Late Antiquity to Early Modern Period* (Leuven-Paris: Peeters, 2002), 52.
59. William Young, *Patriarch, Shah and Caliph: A Study of the Relationships of the Church of the East with the Sassanid Empire and the Early Caliphates up to 820 A.D. with Special Reference to Available Translated Syriac Sources, with Handbook of Source-Materials for Students of Church History up to 650 A.D.* (Doctoral diss., University of Glasgow, 1972), 68.

60. Jeremy M. Schott, *Christianity, Empire, and the Making of religion in Late Antiquity* (Philadelphia: University of Pennsylvania Press, 2008), 171.
61. Mathias A. Mundadan, *History of Christianity in India: From the Beginning ip to the Middle of the Sixteenth Century (up to 1542)*, Vol. 1 (Bangalore: Church History Association of India, 2001), 23; Xavier Koodapuzha, *Bharathasabhacharithram*, 2nd enlarged ed. (Kottayam and Murinjapuzha, Kerala: Oriental Institute of Religious Studies, India and Mar Thoma Sleeha Dayara Publications, 2018), 181–184; James F. McGrath, "History and Fiction in the Acts of Thomas: The State of the Question," *Journal for the Study of the Pseudepigrapha* (2008): 310.
62. Errol D'Lima SJ, *A Concise Encyclopaedia of Christianity in India* (Pune: Jnana-Deepa Vidyapeeth, 2014), 700.
63. J. Nathanael Andrade, *The Journey of Christianity to India in Late Antiquity: Networks and the Movement of Culture* (Cambridge: Cambridge University Press, 2018), 2.
64. Klijn, *Acts of Thomas*, 17.
65. Huxley, "Geography," 80.
66. Klijn, *Acts of Thomas*, 23.
67. Huxley, "Geography," 73.
68. Huxley, "Geography," 73.
69. Huxley, "Geography," 75.
70. Koodapuzha, *Bharathasabhacharithram*, 180–181.
71. Huxley, "Geography," 80.
72. Andrade (see 54–60, but esp. 55) claims that Parthian regions (surprisingly) desired not the apostle but his disciple, Addai, and that therefore Thomas was "sent" to India. This does not satisfactorily answer the "why India?" question. On the other hand, Andrade's definition of Manichaeanism—as "an eclectic and cosmopolitan religion that interwove Christian, Zoroastrian, Jain, and Buddhist religious strands"—that many scholars, including Andrade, consider as having influenced the Acts of Thomas, provides an answer to the "which India?" question. Ironically, this would be another instance wherein the marginal genre of the apocrypha functions as a counternarrative to Eurocentric scholarship. See Nathanael J. Andrade, *The Journey of Christianity to India in Late Antiquity: Networks and the Movement of Culture* (Cambridge: Cambridge University Press, 2018), x. See also Andrade, *The Journey of Christianity to India in Late Antiquity*, 54–60.
73. Lourens Van den Bosch, "India and the Apostolate of St. Thomas," in *The Apocryphal Acts of Thomas*, ed. Jan N. Bremmer (Leuven: Uitgeverij Peeters, 2001), 126; Andrade, *Journey of Christianity*, 2–4 and 221–222.
74. Bosch, "India," 126; also see Andrade, *Journey of Christianity*, 16.
75. Bosch, "India," 142.
76. Koodapuzha, *Bharathasabhacharithram*, 184.
77. Bosch, "India," 135.
78. Bosch, "India," 148.
79. Bosch, "India," 147.
80. Mundadan, *History of Christianity in India*, 403–405.
81. Bosch, "India," 141.
82. Bosch, "India," 137.
83. Bosch, "India," 138.
84. Klijn, *Acts of Thomas*, 17.
85. Klijn, *Acts of Thomas*, viii.
86. Bosch, "India," 143–148.

87. Bosch, "India," 148.
88. Bosch, "India," 125, 148; Nedungatt, *Quest*, 96.
89. Mundadan, *History of Christianity in India*, 56.
90. Jan Vansina, *Oral Tradition: A Study in Historical Methodology* (New York: Routledge, 2017).
91. Nedungatt, *Quest*, 80.
92. Nedungatt, *Quest*, 67.
93. Nedungatt, *Quest*, 405.
94. Nedungatt, *Quest*, 405.
95. Nedungatt, *Quest*, 406.

Bibliography

Andrade, J. Nathanael. *The Journey of Christianity to India in Late Antiquity: Networks and the Movement of Culture*. Cambridge: Cambridge University Press, 2018.

Aquinas, Thomas. *Summa Theologica* II.II:11:1., trans. Fathers of the English Dominican Province. Allen, TX: Christian Classics, [1911] 1981.

Bhatia, Vijay K. "The Power and Politics of Genre." *World Englishes* 16, no. 3 (1997): 359–371.

Bovon, Francois. "Canonical and Apocryphal 'Acts of the Apostles.'" *Journal of Early Christian Studies* 11, no. 2 (2003): 165–194.

Boyce, Mary. *The Manichean Hymn-Cycle in Parthian*. London: Oxford University Press, 1954.

Bremmer, Jan N. *The Apocryphal Acts of Thomas*. Edited by Jan N. Bremmer. Leuven: Uitgeverij Peeters, 2001.

Bremmer, Jan N. "The Five Major Apocryphal Acts: Authors, Place, Time and Readership." In *The Apocryphal Acts of Thomas*. Edited by Jan N. Bremmer, 149–170. Leuven: Uitgeverij Peeters, 2001.

Bremmer, Jan N., and Jan R. Veenstra. *The Metamorphosis of Magic from Late Antiquity to the Early Modern Period*. Leuven-Paris: Peeters, 2002.

Cosgrove, Charles H. "Singing Thomas: Anatomy of a Sympotic Scene in Acts of Thomas." *Vigiliae Christianae: A Review of Early Christian Life and Language* 69, no. 3 (2015): 256–275.

D'Lima, Errol, SJ. *A Concise Encyclopaedia of Christianity in India*. Edited by Jnana-Deepa Vidyapeeth. Pune: Jnana-Deepa Vidyapeeth Pontifical Institute of Philosophy and Religion and St. Pauls, Mumbai, 2014.

Foster, Paul. *The Apocryphal Gospels: A Very Short Introduction*. Oxford; New York: Oxford University Press, 2009.

Greenlee, William Brooks. "The Account of Priest Joseph." In *The Voyages of Pedro Alvares Cabral to Brazil and India*. C. 1505. Translated by William Brooks Greenlee, 95–113. Nendeln/Liechtenstein: Kraus Reprint Limited, 1967.

Gregoratti, Leonardo. "Sinews of the Other Empire: The Parthian Great King's Rule over Vassal Kingdoms." In *Sinews of Empire: Networks in the Roman Near East and Beyond*. Edited by Hakon Fiane Teigen and Eivind Heldaas Seland, 102–111. Pennsylvania: Oxbow Books, 2017.

Huxley, George. "Geography in the Acts of Thomas." *Greek, Roman, and Byzantine Studies* 24 (1983): 71–80.

Klauck, Hans-Josef. *The Apocryphal Acts of the Apostles: An Introduction*. Translated by Brian McNeil. Waco, TX: Baylor University Press, 2008.

Klijn, A. F. J. [Albertus Frederik Johannes.] *The Acts of Thomas: Introduction, Text, and Commentary*. Leiden; Boston: Brill, 2003.

Koodapuzha, Xavier. *Bharathasabhacharithram*. 2nd enlarged ed. Kottayam and Murinjapuzha, Kerala: Oriental Institute of Religious Studies, 2018.

Kruger, Michael J. "Review: *The Apocryphal Acts of the Apostles: An Introduction* by Hans-Josef Klauck." *Journal of the Evangelical Theological Society* 52, no. 2 (2009): 395–396.

Malekandathil, Pius. Ed. *Jornada of Dom Alexis de Menezes: A Portuguese Account of the Sixteenth Century Malabar*. Delhi: LRC Publications, 2003.

McGrath, James F. "History and Fiction in the Acts of Thomas: The State of the Question." *Journal for the Study of the Pseudepigrapha* 17, no. 4 (2008): 297–311.

McVey, Kathleen E. "Were the Earliest Madrase Songs or Recitations?" In *After Bardaisan: Studies on Continuity and Change in Syriac Christianity in Honour of Professor Han J. W. Drijvers*. Edited by G. J. Reinink and A. C. Klugkist, 185–200. Leuven: Peeters Publishers, 1999.

Morris, Ian. *War! What Is It Good For? Conflict and the Progress of Civilization from Primates to Robots*. New York: Farrar, Straus & Giroux, 2014.

Mundadan, Mathias A. *History of Christianity in India: From the Beginning up to the Middle of the Sixteenth Century (up to 1542)*. Vol. 1. Bangalore: Church History Association of India, 2001.

Myers, Susan E. *Spirit Epicleses in the Acts of Thomas*. Tubingen: Mohr Siebeck, 2010.

Nedungatt, George. *Quest for the Historical Thomas Apostle of India: A Re-reading of the Evidence*. Bangalore: Theological Publications in India, 2008.

Pandit, Vijaya Lakshmi. *The Scope of Happiness: A Personal Memoir*. London: Weidenfeld and Nicolson, 1979.

Parker, Grant. "India, Egypt and Parthia in Augustan Verse: The Post-Orientalist Turn." *Dictynna: Revue de Poetique latine* 8 (2011): 1–16.

Remus, Harold. "'Magic or Miracle'? Some Second Century Instances." *The Second Century: A Journal of Early Christian Studies* 2, no. 3 (1982): 127–156.

Rhee, Helen. *Early Christian Literature: Christ and Culture in the Second and Third Centuries*. London: Routledge, 2005.

Schott, Jeremy M. *Christianity, Empire, and the Making of Religion in Late Antiquity*. Philadelphia: University of Pennsylvania Press, 2008.

Seland, Eivind Heldaas. "Trade and Christianity in the Indian Ocean during Late Antiquity." *Journal of Late Antiquity* 5, no. 1 (2012): 72–86.

Sugirtharajah, R. S. *The Bible and Empire: Postcolonial Explorations*. Cambridge: Cambridge University Press, 2005.

Tissot, Yves. *The Oxford Handbook of Early Christian Apocrypha*. Edited by Andrew Gregory, Tobias Nicklas, Christopher M. Tuckett, and Joseph Verheyden, 407–423. Oxford: Oxford University Press, 2015.

Van den Bosch, Lourens. "India and the Apostolate of St. Thomas." In *The Apocryphal Acts of Thomas*. Edited by Jan N. Bremmer, 125–148. Leuven: Uitgeverij Peeters, 2001.

Vansina, Jan. *Oral Tradition: A Study in Historical Methodology*. New York: Routledge, 2017.

Young, William. "Patriarch, Shah and Caliph: A Study of the Relationships of the Church of the East with the Sassanid Empire and the Early Caliphates up to 820 A.D. with Special Reference to Available Translated Syriac Sources, with Handbook of Source-Materials for Students of Church History up to 650 A.D." Doctoral diss., University of Glasgow, 1972.

Zacharia, Scaria. *The Acts and Decrees of the Synod of Diamper 1599*. Edamattam: Indian Institute of Christian Studies, 1994.

Zur, Yiphtah. "Parallels between Acts of Thomas 6–7 and 4Q184." *Revue De Qumran* 16, no. 1 (1993): 103–107.

PART II

MODERN EUROPEAN AND ASIAN EMPIRES

CHAPTER 11

SCRIPTURAL BATTLEFIELDS

The Old Testament, Legal Culture, and the Polemics of the Spanish New World Empire, 1492–1821

JORGE CAÑIZARES-ESGUERRA AND
ADRIAN MASTERS

ABRAHAM and Joshua conquered America. When Martín Fernández Enciso left for Darién in 1514 in the company of military commander Pedrarias Dávila, this veteran of Caribbean colonization had almost a decade of conquest experience under his belt. This time, however, Enciso's search for the South Sea was constrained by new royal orders regulating invasions. Beginning in 1514, the conquistadors had to read a document to indigenous communities before an assault: the infamous *requerimiento*. A committee of expert jurists and theologians, who had assembled in Burgos and Valladolid to evaluate the legality of wars of captivity and enslavement, introduced this rule.[1] They formulated a document that all conquistadors had to communicate to Indians. The *requerimiento* explained that the Pope had universal spiritual sovereignty over their souls; that the Church had transferred such authority to the monarch; and that if they rejected conversion they would suffer death, captivity, and slavery. Those who willingly accepted the monarch, however, would become vassals.

Enciso thought these new procedures absurd, viewing them as burdensome regulations formulated by ivory tower theologians who were detached from the realities of war. However, the *requerimiento* had not been proposed by these aloof ministers but by Dominican friars in Hispaniola. The friars' campaign in favor of the Indians had begun with a sermon by Friar Antonio de Montesinos, who threatened the settlers with excommunication for their sins against Indians during Advent masses in December 1511.[2]

The Dominicans triggered a debate in the highest echelons of imperial governance, which centered around the Old Testament. Up until the juntas of Burgos and Valladolid, there was absolute consensus over the Pope's right to transfer spiritual sovereignty to the Catholic monarchs and the right of Spaniards to enslave idolaters. In his later writing opposing the *requerimiento*, Enciso forcefully summarized the Old Testament foundations of both rights. In the same way that God had "promised" Abraham the land of Israel to grow his lineage, the Pope had conceded the New World to the kings. And in the same way that Joshua took the Israelites into the Promised Land by warring against and enslaving Canaanites, Spanish conquistadors had the authority to raid and enslave indigenous communities.

The jurists who wrote the new laws of Burgos and the *requerimiento* did not challenge these two principles. Indeed, the magistrate Juan López de Palacios Rubios proffered the *requerimiento* as an Old Testament solution to the problem.[3] Passages of Deuteronomy demanded Joshua and the Israelites read the Canaanites a text before their onslaught, sparing these idolatrous enemies from slavery and extermination if they surrendered peacefully (D 20, 10–14).

The cases of Enciso and López de Palacios reveal the importance of the Pentateuch in the twin pillars of conquest and colonization. Luther's Reformation, however, forced Spain to abandon the doctrine of transfer of spiritual sovereignties to temporal authorities along with the idea that idolatry was sufficient to justify the loss of life and liberty, for these principles could now be easily turned against the church and Catholic monarchs. By the 1530s, the Neo-Scholastic School of Salamanca led by Francisco de Vitoria abolished the idea that the Pope could transfer dominium of polities at will. The Reformation also emphasized the difference between Christ's Gospel of Grace and the belligerent moral code of the God of the Pentateuch.

Yet Spaniards did not abandon their faith in the Old Testament as the foundation of colonization in the famous debate of Valladolid of 1540. Juan Ginés de Sepúlveda, for example, sought to prove that the new loving gospel of Christ also authorized violence against reluctant idolaters, for both the new law of Christ and the old laws of Moses were based on Natural Law. According to Natural Law, slavery was the rightful punishment for Indian idolatry, cannibalism, sodomy, and bestiality. Although Sepúlveda had no use for the papal transfer of sovereignty in the New World, he believed that the Old Testament subordinated Charles V to the Pope's authority. If Abraham and Saul had bowed to the supreme spiritual authority of Melchizedek and Samuel respectively, so too should the Holy Roman Emperor follow the will of the Pope in the New World.

The famed Dominican friar and advocate of Indian protection, Bartolomé de las Casas, responded to Ginés de Sepúlveda with a scriptural counterargument. The story of God's promise to Abraham and Joshua's violence against the reluctant Canaanites applied solely to the Israelites, because they had no land of their own. Clearly, this was not the case with the Iberians, who already had a homeland. Moreover, Las Casas drew a clear distinction between Christ's new law of love and Moses' old law of captivity and violence. The Act of the Apostles demonstrated how to draw peoples to the Gospel voluntarily through preaching. The Apostles won over the Romans' faith through persuasion, not violence. Yet Las Casas did not abandon the Israelite analogy entirely; in fact, he reversed it. The Dominican found the natives to be far more pious than the Romans, and therefore closer to the Israelites in God's favor. Las Casas's sophisticated interpretation of the Old Testament shows that this book's role in Spanish imperial expansion would by no means be straightforward.

The Old Testament and the New World

The Old Testament informed innumerable aspects of Spanish imperialism—encompassing its institutions, conquest, enslavement, reform, and rebellion. In this essay, we will focus only on select aspects of the Empire's relationship to the Old Testament, especially the cornerstones of imperial administration legislation (*gobierno*), privileges and status (*gracia*), and litigious justice (*justicia*). The Spanish Empire was a petitioning state that allowed vast amounts of political debate within select bureaucratic channels, meaning that citizens mobilized arguments drawn from the Old Testament (among other sources) to prompt new laws and policies. While engaging with this hierarchical but vibrant petition-and-response system, imperial subjects found in the Old Testament both affirmation and precedent. For many, in fact, the very bureaucratic institutions upon which the global Spanish monarchy relied originated in biblical models of justice and governance. Just as important, these petitioners and officials, always enveloped in epistolary disputes over policies and privileges, continuously drew on the Old Testament for prefigurations, tropes, images of just society, and cautionary tales of moral and civilizational collapse.

This essay explores how Spanish officials and vassals understood debates over justice, new institutions, new legislation, and the status of the New World itself through the lens of the Old Testament. We show that Moses, the kings of the House of David, and other Israelite leaders provided models for some of the most important institutions of the Spanish monarchy, like the Royal Council, the Council of the Indies, the Escorial, and the Inquisition. The legitimacy of the conquest itself, as well the specific legal practices of conquistadors such as the infamous *requerimiento* declaration, frequently hinged upon Scripture. During and beyond the conquest, those asserting the legitimacy of Spanish imperialism, just slavery, taxation, and forced Indian tribute could find in the Jewish Bible numerous prophecies and authorizations. Arguments that the New World had been an Old Testament colony of the House of David legitimated miners' exploitation of its resources. Crown authorities used the Book to stress Indians' duty to render tribute and of all subjects' responsibility to pay taxes. Women's subordinate status due to Eve's original sin all but cemented Scripture's power to conserve the Indies' subordination to Spanish patriarchy.

Scripture was not merely a tool of a statist, imperialist patriarchy, however. Critics often fired back against these readings, employing counterarguments from the same text. They argued for the absurdity of the permanent social inferiority of the Indian, noted the excellence of women by pointing to the matriarchs of Israel, and even imaged Hebraic utopias with robust republican elections and no private property. The New World could be a Paradise, a realm of riches central to global history like the biblical Ophir, and its pre-conquest Indian leaders could parallel the greatest ancient Israelites. Even the Marian apparitions of the New World, especially that of the famed Virgin of Guadalupe, had been prefigured in the Old Testament. For every passage alleging the inferiority of the Indies and its people, there was another proclaiming their excellence and equality with Europe. Little wonder, then, that when violence erupted in the early 1800s throughout the New World, with many subjects renouncing the Crown in the name of new republics, both sides claimed to have the correct interpretation of Scripture. The Book was not merely a legitimating agent of the birth of the Spanish Empire in the New World and a force for reform—it was also an intellectual vehicle of its demise.

The Inquisition

Without the Old Testament, early modern Iberian culture and New World history are both unintelligible. The central role of this text remains nevertheless historiographically invisible, largely due to the narrative of an Iberian Inquisition committed to eradicating Judaism from the polity. Yet it is relatively easy to demonstrate that even the Spanish Inquisition was born in the late fifteenth century out of the efforts of the descendants of Jews who converted to Christianity (the conversos) to demonstrate that faithful, noble former Jews were better Christians than Iberian descendants of Roman pagans and Goths.

For this first generation of conversos, the solution to Nicodemism was to harshly punish conversos engaging in deception. Foremost first-generation conversos, including Grand Inquisitor Tomás de Torquemada, found in the Old Testament typological prefigurations of the Inquisition. The very first Inquisitor was God himself, who held the original auto de fe in Paradise against Adam and Eve. The Jewish Bible itself justified the Inquisition.

Others were of a similar mind. For instance, in the 1598 book *De origine et progressv officii sanctae inqvisitionis*, Inquisitor Luis de Páramo interpreted God's punishment of Adam as the first Inquisition. In his view, Adam and Eve's sins, and God's guilty verdict in the world's First Age, had ensured that all of humanity already inherited its mark of shame, a metaphysical *sanbenito* (penitential garment).[4] For Páramo, there was no mistaking the similarities between the Inquisitors and God's trial of Adam; he explicitly noted, "*Sancti Officii Inquisitores modum procedendi à Deo mutuantur & eundem observant* (Inquisitors observe and follow the same procedures of God)."[5]

The Inquisition was therefore legitimated by the Old Testament. Yet, somewhat paradoxically to readers today, one of the Mosaic inquisitors' tasks was the prosecution of those non-Catholics who rejected Jesus and continued to live in the "law of Moses."[6] The institution was even hostile toward the dissemination of vulgate and heterodox translations of the Book.[7] In 1558, for example, the Crown decreed the death penalty for printing any works that had not been approved by its ministers and censors, including vulgate Bibles.[8] Since at least the 1580s, royal decrees prohibited subjects from possessing rabbinical or Islamic commentaries on Scripture.[9]

In Spain, the Inquisition guarded these intellectuals' glosses in their libraries under lock and key. They were reserved for the eyes of scholars only—though scholars and universities complained that this practice thwarted theological inquiry.[10] Still, throughout the viceregal New World, the Inquisition discovered a number of cases in which humble and ordinary subjects sold and bought copies of Bibles and commentaries.[11] This was a war pitting an Old Testament institution against the readers of the very same book—a very tangible New World struggle over the metaphysical powers of an ancient "Jewish" text.

Yet the Hebrew Bible was disseminated all over the land. The very anthropomorphic Catholic images of the Divine that appeared painted on the walls of thousands of chapels and churches were very often organized around Old Testament tropes, stories, and typologies. Mary, mother of Christ, became both Tabernacle and Ark, a veritable physical container of the living Torah that was the new Law, Christ. Stories of Samson and Joseph illuminated many churches, as their struggles prefigured those of Christ. Images of Israelite heroines like Judith and Yael, who slaughtered Assyrian and Canaanite generals, stood in temples as anticipations of the Virgin Mary and as models for nuns as the vanguard of God. Sacristies of Catholic basilicas had paintings of Melchizedek offering blessings, bread, and wine to Abraham, and getting the right to the tithe in return (Gen 14:17–44 and Heb 7), which served as Old Testament prefigurations of the appropriate relationship between secular and religious authorities. The same sacristies also featured images of the angel that gave bread and water to a fleeing Elijah (1 Kings 19:4–8), the Paschal Supper (Exod 12–13; Lev 23:15–14), or the Israelites gathering manna in the desert (a prefiguration of the Eucharist), among countless other examples.[12]

Indeed, many of these images were painted by Europeans, but other murals featuring the figures of Scripture were also painted by Indians.[13] The Inquisition might have prohibited the use of written reproductions of the Bible, but it did so while promoting the promiscuous use of Old Testament imagery in plays, sermons, and walls. Scriptural tropes and biblically inspired thinking thus were part of everyday life well beyond the lettered fortresses of inquisitors and theologians.

INSTITUTIONS

These two debates—about the Indians in the early 1500s and the legitimacy of the Inquisition—were merely subsets of the rich, overlapping world of the Old Testament and Crown justice. Indeed, in the 1500s the monarchy envisioned its mission to spread justice and Christianity as deeply tied to Scripture. By the 1520s and 1530s, royal and local officials, hoping to ensure law and order, oversaw complex paper-based institutions, answering vassals' *gobierno*, *gracia*, and *justicia* petitions in enormous numbers. Kings and subjects were profoundly concerned with sculpting the growing Empire according to the examples of antiquity, finding within them lessons to guide their institutions and policies through difficult times.

Throughout Iberia's Christian history, the Israelites always loomed large in thinkers' and legislators' minds, for they simultaneously provided models of governance worth emulating. Many argued they also had a direct historical link to the Spanish Crown. Since antiquity, pagan, Jewish, and Christian thinkers had traced the twin institutions of writing and lawgiving to the Hebrew people. According to many early Christian and scholastic authorities, the world's ancient and unbroken genealogy of writing, counseling, and lawgiving reached back to Moses.[14] They often cited Exodus 18, in which the priest Jethro petitioned his son-in-law Moses to not be "consumed by foolish labor," for he had noticed the prophet-leader was weary from judging the people of Israel "from morning till night." Moses was to henceforth "provide from the whole people tribunes, rulers of hundreds, rulers of fifties and rulers of tens, to judge the people," delegating his authority to his council ministers and to local judiciaries throughout the land.

The Exodus 18 story of Moses' development of the world's first council was very influential in Spanish government by the late Middle Ages. In 1385, King John I of Castile signed the kingdom's *Ordenanzas*, which pointed to this passage as theologians had done before.[15] It noted that Jethro had petitioned Moses, advising him that the leader's dedication to resolving the people's "affairs or litigations or quarrels" (*negoçios o pleitos o querellas*) was "consuming" his health—just as it was wearing down John I. Moses was to appoint to this council the wisest of the Israelites:

> [C]ertain powerful men and without avarice, to listen to and dispatch all the lawsuits (*demandas*) and quarrels (*querellas*) and petitions (*petiçiones*) of the people, and if any grave thing should arise among them which they could not resolve, that they send a report to him [Moses], and that he dispatch it; and in so doing they would obey the commandments of God . . . and the said Moses, having heard this counsel, was much pleased and put this later into effect, for which the people of Israel was well ruled in its time.[16]

This was not the only Old Testament episode to provide inspiration for European governance. True, Moses had received the divine gift of writing from God, had been the first in world history to judge his people, and created the first council to ensure justice. However, Mosaic governance had not yet reached its apogee. Centuries later, by divine grace, the House of David took the integrity and justice of the Hebrews to new heights. David, a soldier of lowly station, had risen through his heroics to become king of Israel. He soon promised God a temple from which his dynasty would rule. His son, Solomon, who would for centuries be the embodiment of the wise ruler, completed this Temple of Jerusalem.

Admiration for these Hebrew leaders had widespread European roots, appearing in mirrors of princes for Charlemagne as early as the 830s CE among the Germanic kings.[17]

Unsurprisingly, then, Castilian kings turned frequently to the House of David when devising their iconography. Sancho IV, Enrique II, Juan I, and Enrique IV often used Solomonic imagery—a king upon a throne with lions—as the Old Testament repeatedly described him.[18]

If the medieval Castilians establishing a system of councils deliberately looked to Moses and the House of David as paragons of just rule, the Habsburgs went one step further. They claimed jurisdiction over David's line itself, and over the Temple of Jerusalem, through a complex dynastic inheritance.[19] When the Habsburgs finalized their incorporation of the Crowns of Castile and Aragon in the 1510s, Charles V also inherited the Aragonese claim to Jerusalem. Despite the frequent modern refrain that the Holy Roman Empire was not holy, Roman, or an empire, its dynastic claims to Jerusalem and the House of David made this Roman dynasty holy indeed.[20]

Charles V's understanding of his own duties as legislator and giver of justice was to be intimately tied to the Old Testament. He would surely have heard stories of the Hebrew kings as a young prince, especially from his tutor Erasmus.[21] During the Austrian's earliest tours of Europe, subjects often gifted him with the parables of David and Solomon.[22] After Charles's 1530 anointment as Holy Roman Emperor, he would have worn the Imperial Crown of the Holy Roman Empire, the *Reichskrone*, fashioned in 960 for Otto I. It contained images of Kings David and Solomon, as well as the lesser-known but virtuous King Hezekiah and the Prophet Isaiah, as well as numerous Old Testament admonishments for kings to follow the just deeds of the kings of Israel.[23]

The Royal Palace and the Monastery of the Escorial

Charles had always embraced and entertained Solomonism to a certain extent. His courtiers also lavished him with comparisons to Greco-Roman mythological figures, Roman and other ancient emperors, and Christ.[24] By contrast, it was his more contemplative son Philip who most often appeared as a wise new Solomon, and it was he who both tacitly approved of and directly sponsored Solomonism.[25] As King Philip II, he would express this emulation of Hebrew justice in the arts and architecture.

By the 1540s Philip took up a strong interest in restoring Spain's crumbling royal palaces, despite his father's insistence that "kings do not need to have residences."[26] He would soon select a permanent home base for this growing empire—Madrid.[27] There, his palace walls were decorated with scenes of the Old Testament by Spain's and Europe's leading masters, featuring themes as diverse as Adam and Eve, Noah's Ark, the travails of Moses, Abraham, Jacob, and Job, the rape of Susanna by the Elders, the regicide of the woman Judith slaying Holofernes, the blinding of Samson, and, of course, the deeds of David and Solomon.[28] Hebrew ancients were quite literally looking over the shoulders of kings, secretaries, and ministers as they ruled.

Thirty-five miles to the northwest of Madrid, Philip would also build a second, private base of operations—the Monastery of San Lorenzo, located in the village of El Escorial. This would become Philip's enormous palace, begun in 1562 and finalized in 1584.[29] His architects sought to frame the Escorial as a hybrid of classical and Hebrew architecture and ideology and a demonstration of the wisdom he inherited from this ancient dynasty.[30]

The Escorial, argued the Jeronomite José de Sigüenza (1544–1606) in 1600, was the architectural fulfillment of several biblical prefigurations. Like Noah's Ark, it saved "countless souls fleeing from the deluge of the world." Like Moses' Tabernacle, "it kept the ark in which God himself dwelled, protecting and disseminating His laws." And like the Temple of Solomon, it specialized "day and night in the praising of the Lord, the continuous performance of sacrifices, the burning of incense, the keeping of perpetual fire and fresh bread in front of the divine presence, and the preservation of the ashes and bones of those who sacrificed for Christ."[31]

The façade of the Escorial's basilica had statues by Juan Bautista Monegro (1545–1621), featuring those kings of Judah who, in ascending order of piety, either destroyed pagan temples or built the Temple of Jerusalem: Jehoshaphat and the repentant Manasseh (outer flanks), Hezekiah and Josiah (outer middle), and David and Solomon (center). All were prefigurations of the Habsburgs' Counter-Reformation zeal and of the piety and wisdom of Charles V and Philip II in particular.[32]

Finally, in the courtyard of the Escorial stood a fountain and four "rivers" in the middle, each flanked by Monegro's statues of Matthew, Mark, Luke, and John, a scene prefiguring both Paradise and the expansion of the Catholic monarchy into Asia, Africa, Europe, and the "new America."[33] In the Tower of the Prior, a ceiling featured a fresco by Francisco de Urbino depicting the Judgment of Solomon.[34] Philip would also sponsor the Jesuit books of mathematician-architect Juan Bautista Villalpando and biblical expert Jerónimo del Prado, who would by 1605 publish their *In Ezechielem Explanationes et Apparatus Urbis, ac Templu Hierosolymitani* (Explanations of the Book of Ezekiel, and the Urban Layout and Temple of Jerusalem).[35]

For early modern Christians, the personal wisdom of the Hebrew patriarchs was not enough to provide justice to the Israelite multitudes. These ancient kings also needed writing, scribes, and palace courts. The massive bureaucracies of the Escorial and the Madrid Royal Palace were thus completely compatible with the Old Testament councils. Juan de Sevilla Pineda's 1609 *De Rebus Salomonis Regis* (On the Matters of King Solomon) would provide a sweeping overview of the Spanish Crown as the House of David. Sevilla viewed David and Solomon as the emblematic just kings (*reges iustitiae*), citing Wisdom 8–14 and Proverbs 8–14.[36] They especially meted out fair court cases and distributed grace and mercy among the people, as in Proverbs 20–28.[37]

Sevilla went to great pains to establish parallels between these Hebrew kings' chancelleries and contemporary—and especially Spanish—institutional practices. He conjectured that the Temple of Solomon was divided exactly as the Royal Palace of Madrid: "[Q]uod apud nos in eadem regali domo vulgatissimum est nominare; *El quarto del Rey, el quarto de la reyna, y el patio de los consejos*" (italics his) (Which is the same as we call in the royal household very popularly: The chamber of the King, the chamber of the Queen, and the Courtyard of the Councils).[38] King Solomon had a council of ministers, as 1 Chronicles 26 established.[39] Sevilla pointed to Moses' introduction of divine writing to the world by way of Saint Augustine's *City of God*, arguing that David and Solomon had a "flourishing" scribal staff.[40] The Temple thronged with bureaucrat-officials, including council ministers, translators, and scribes—"*los secretarios de la cifra*" (italics his) (The secretaries of the cypher).[41] These officials oversaw a towering, incorruptible repository of holy works and other papers—an archive that helped the kings maintain "legis incorrupta intelligentia" (uncorrupted knowledge of the law).[42] The wise kings of the House of David thus meted out perfect justice and grace thanks to their mighty bureaucracy, which operated from the ideal palace, the Temple of Jerusalem. Spain had resurrected the ideal government of the Hebrew people and created a Temple from which the new Chosen Ones were to rule the world.

The Growth of the Mosaic Council System

If Sevilla drew rather far-fetched parallels between an early modern Spanish bureaucracy and the ancient Hebrew Temple of Jerusalem, he also was making a profound observation about Old World governance, in which Mosaic writing was at the heart of virtually all systems of law and justice. During Columbus's time, administrative paperwork was surging.[43] The Catholic kings created new and more specialized councils to respond to this flood of petitions: the Councils of Brotherhoods (1476–1498), Inquisition (1488), Aragon (1494), Military Orders (1495), House of Trade (1503), and Crusade (1509). The young Charles V approved Spaniards' requests for the creation of the Council of the Indies, previously a subcommittee of the Royal Council.[44] The Council of the Indies formally began operations in 1524.[45]

This Council understood its own day-to-day functions through a paperwork trinity. *Justicia* court cases resolved conflicts between two or more parties but did not produce legislation. The *gobierno* channel generated imperial policies and almost always began at the behest of petitioners. Vassals could also seek privileges by submitting requests via the *gracia* channel. As the Empire expanded its local institutions, the High Courts came to oversee *justicia*, and the viceroys, presidents, and governors oversaw *gobierno* and *gracia*.

Officials did not base all or even most of their *gobierno*, *gracia*, and *justicia* decision-making on the Old Testament. In theory ministers could draw from any sources at their disposal. However, the documentary record suggests that in practice these officials had time constraints that limited the number of references they could turn to, and that they preferred the Crown's own legal documents—royal decrees and compilations. Nonetheless, some Council ministers had theological training and knowledge that they may have employed in their everyday reasoning. Minister Gregorio López's 1555 published commentaries on the medieval lawbook of the *Siete Partidas* demonstrates his profound knowledge of this religious text and his vision of Castilian law as a reflection of Israelite government.[46] Moreover, an anonymous document produced within the Council early in its existence, probably the 1520s, suggested that ministers should know the "Testaments Old and New" and carry with them breviaries for quick reference.[47] The Inquisitor-cum-Council of the Indies president Juan de Ovando, who reformed New World governance between 1571 and his 1575 death, also owned a Bible and numerous glosses in his personal library.[48]

Many ministers were doubtless following these guidelines throughout the Council's history, without necessarily applying Scripture's contents rigorously to their policies and adjudications.

PROPHECY AND COLONIZATION

The Old Testament did not remain in the theological ivory tower. Indeed, it was central to Christians' appraisals of the New World from the beginning. Scriptural prophecy was among the foremost lenses that Iberians used to comprehend what they beheld. Friars came to the New World armed with this medieval science; they used prefigurations in the Old Testament to find the basis of a history of conquest. Europe's first full practitioner of this science of wildly creative and meticulous Pentecostal prophecy was Joachim of Fiore, a twelfth-century Calabrian abbot. Joachim thought that the Old Testament included seven periods that prefigured those of the history of Christianity, with parallel heroes, wars, tragedies, and rewards. Joachim added complexity to his model by reading history as an unfolding of the "laws" of the Trinity: Father (Mosaic Law), Son (Christ's new law), and Spirt (of millenarian Pentecostal liberation from all temporal and spiritual hierarchies, including popes).

Thus, when the Portuguese and Spanish monarchies began exporting the Gospel to Africa, India, and the New World, dozens of Joachimite writers turned to the Old Testament for insight and prophetic prefiguration. These included the Dominican Giles of Viterbo, Amadeus of Portugal, and the Cardinal Bernardino López de Carvajal. These three inaugurated a vast imperial archive of writings on Old Testament prophecy on the Catholic Church's global expansion. They provided ideological ammunition for Iberian monarchies seeking to justify expansion in the late 1400s and early 1500s, and in the process they transformed the Papacy, the curia, and even Vatican architecture.[49]

Mexico and Peru witnessed dozens of these mendicants' prophetic debates around interpretations of textual fragments of the Old Testament. Take, for example, the case of the Dominican Domingo de Betanzos, who began his career as a radical critic of Spanish colonization in Hispaniola, alongside Bartolomé de las Casas. As Betanzos experienced the demographic collapse of the indigenous populations of the Caribbean and later those of Mexico, he turned to Deuteronomy (4, 28, 32) and Isaiah (20, 28, 28, 32) as well as Jeremiah, Hezekiah, and Micah for explanation.

Old Testament prophets, Betanzos argued, had long prefigured the death and destruction of the natives as the fate awaiting the lost Ten Tribes of Israel for their devolution into idolatry. The natives were the long-lost Israelites, Betanzos concluded, and should consequently be treated as such. He went to Rome as a *procurador* (legal representative) of the Dominicans to lobby on behalf of Spanish tribute-masters and slavers of Indians.

In Rome, however, Betanzos met the coordinated efforts of Franciscans like Jacobo de Testera and the Dominican Bernardino de Minaya. These pro-Indian agents successfully lobbied the Pope to pass the 1537 bull *Sublimus Deus* and silence Betanzos. *Sublimus* explicitly denounced Betanzos as Satan's paralegal agent and unequivocally sided with the abolitionist pro-Indian party in the Indies.[50]

There were dozens of authors who dug into Old Testament passages of Isaiah, Daniel, Amos, Obadiah, Ezekiel, Jeremiah, and many others for prefigurative traces of Iberian conquest and expansion.[51] For every zealot Joachimite Dominican prophesizing doom and negativity, however, there were dozens of wildly optimistic Joachimite Franciscans and Jesuits foretelling breathtaking continental millenarian triumphs.[52] Old Testament prophecy could have justified violence and destruction in Iberian imperial expansion and in the conquest of idolaters, but the documentary record suggests that policymakers did not eagerly embrace these prophetic arguments. As the case of the Dominican Betanzos and the Franciscan lobby in 1530s Rome suggests, these arguments formed a central part of the theological and paralegal backdrop of the imperial enterprise and served as a cornerstone of the debate on the legal status of the Indian.

Genealogical connections that readers traced from the Old Testament to the present shared with prophecy the power to shape subjects' understandings of group status and other legal issues. Iberian society viewed genealogy as a crucial element of self-identity and status. Saint Isidore of Seville had stated in the seventh century that many during his time linked Iberia to Tubal. In this interpretation of Genesis 10, Noah's son Japheth inherited Europe, and Japheth's fifth son Tubal engendered the Celtiberians in Spain.[53] Three centuries later another Iberian chronicler, ʿArīb ibn Saʿīd al-Kātib al-Qurṭubī, suggested Spain had been founded by Tufayl Ibn Yafit ibn Nuh, that is, Tubal, son of Japheth, son of Noah.[54] Jiménez de Rada's circa 1243 *Opera* and King Alfonso X's thirteenth-century *Estoria de España* both asserted that Noah's son Japheth inherited Europe, and that Japheth's fifth son Noah engendered the first men to arrive in Spain, the Celtiberians.[55]

The Tubal connection often had political implications. By the 1400s this narrative began to play a political role, with Castile employing it to argue for its eminence and antiquity in Europe.[56] In the late 1400s and 1500s, as Castile and Aragón's joint might was transforming European politics, Tubal allowed Spain a deeper and more dignified origin than the barbarian Goths who had nearly destroyed Roman civilization.[57] Indeed, the Dominican Annio da Viterbo argued in his 1498 *Commentaria* that he had proven that the Spanish monarchy descended directly from Tubal and had even been visited by Noah in person, making its lineage the greatest pedigree in Europe.[58]

Tubal's genealogy gave Spain an important paralegal privilege in Europe. He also gave Spain certain characteristics and honors. In 1541, Florián de Ocampo expounded on the significance of Tubal in his *Crónica de España*, making this ancient figure not only the founder of Iberia in 2163 BCE but also the first master of science, astrology, geometry, music, agriculture, laws, and moral philosophy.[59] Noah's grandson, not the Romans, had ensured that "our Spaniards were among the first men to know the sciences and music, and of the first to have knowledge of good living."[60]

This construction of Iberians as descendants of Japheth's son had two facets—one establishing their European pedigree, and the other cementing their inheritance of dominion over the world and its other peoples. For just as there were blessed lineages like that of Japheth and the House of David, there were cursed ones as well. According to European Christian tradition based on Genesis 10, Noah's sons inherited different traits and also had legitimate claims to specific world regions. Japheth dominated Europe, Shem dominated Asia, and Ham was to receive Africa. Many argued that Ham was the accursed son, punished by God for a sinful but mysterious encounter with his drunken father (Gen 9:20–27).

This theory was ubiquitous in theologians' justifications of the enslavement of sub-Saharan Africans and non-Christians more generally, until the Council of the Indies prohibited most enslavement of Indians in various decrees throughout the 1500s. Nonetheless, others like Juan Suárez de Peralta, in his 1589 *Treatise on the Discovery of the Indies*, suggested the Indians were likely descended from the accursed Cham (whom he called Chanaan), who "engendered the idolatrous descendants of Canaan."[61] A similar genealogical argument from the Book of Exodus would have it that the strong but unintelligent Issachar and his descendants were doomed to hard slave labor.[62]

Even when Spaniards were not making direct genealogical arguments about the status of non-European peoples, they could arrange their pre-Hispanic histories according to the Old Testament narrative structure. In 1590 the Jesuit José de Acosta popularized the notion that the Mexica were Satan's elected. He argued that the resemblances of the southbound migration of the Mexica from Azatlán to central Mexico eerily mirrored that of the Israelites from Egypt to Canaan. Like the Israelites, the Mexicans carried a Tabernacle and Ark of their deity, Huitzilopochtli.[63] Dominicans like Gregorio García further fleshed out this narrative: Satan, mimicking how God had fed the Israelites in the wilderness, caused bread to rain from the sky and water to gush from rocks, sustaining the Mexica during their own exodus.[64] The Mexica also had their own versions of Moses and Aaron in their leaders. By the early seventeenth century, Jesuits, Dominicans, and Franciscans saw the Mexica as the satanic mirror image of that of the Israelites. Along with an Exodus, Canaanite oppression, and an age of monarchies and prophets for Mexico, they interpreted the fall of Tenochtitlan as the equivalent to the fall of Jerusalem.[65]

Exactly how the many indigenous peoples of the New World responded to these scriptural reconstructions of the New World past is not clear. However, in the 1554 *Title of Totonicapán*, a Mayan K'iche community genealogically connected subgroups of the Nima K'iche', Tamub', and Ilokab' to the Israelites, Canaanites, and Hebrews. They concluded, "We are the grandchildren and sons of Israelites and holy Moses... Babylon has been... [the] root of our grandfathers' and fathers' lineage."[66] Here, an Israelite genealogy served not to argue for some blessed or accursed lineage but to establish the legitimacy of K'iche' locals' historical claims to the region.

THE NEW WORLD AS AN OLD TESTAMENT LANDSCAPE

Not only the Indians but the very geography of the New World itself divulged parallels to the Old Testament. This engendered rich scriptural debates about the legitimacy of empire. Columbus had sought Paradise itself there. He also noted that Solomon had built his Temple of Jerusalem using the faraway mines of Ophir and Tarshish (see, e.g., 2 Chron 9:21 and 1 Kings 22:48). Peru's enormous silver deposits only reinforced the common belief that Solomon's colonies were at hand. One French scholar, Guillaume Postel, had already suggested in 1561 that Peru was Ophir. The renowned Spanish author Benito Arias Montano identified Peru with both Ophir and the mysterious Old Testament land of Parva'im, also one of Solomon's mines, and the Indians as lost Israelites.[67]

The image of a wise Israelite king conquering lands overseas to build his palace in Jerusalem was a parallel many could not help but make. The House of David's mines were back in its Habsburg descendants' possession after being lost for millennia. But this was no mere return—it was the beginning of an even brighter era. Lawyer and scholar Doctor Francisco de Monzón would write sometime before his 1571 death about the remarkable efficiency and splendor of Solomon's court, and how it thronged with innumerable foreigners—including the awestruck Queen of Sheba. This Temple was possible because of the king's overseas dominions—but now, Monzón noted, King Philip would soon overshadow the Hebrew ruler, for he would shortly be the master of "parts of Africa, and the Indies... which are not less than what King Solomon had."[68]

One of the most adamant advocates of this theory was Licenciado Fernando de Montesinos (whose last name means "Mount Sinai"). He had arrived in Peru in 1628 with the entourage of the newly appointed Viceroy Count of Chinchón, a grandee determined to reform the monarchy along the lines first suggested by the Count-Duke of Olivares, the so-called *valido* (prime minister) of King Philip IV.[69] Montesinos argued in his circa 1644 *Ophir de España* that, just as Ophir had once provided the raw materials for the Temple of Jerusalem for Solomon, these mines had now reappeared 2,542 years later in Peru to help Spain consolidate global dominion.[70] A number of Old Testament figures, including David himself, had also prophesized this revelation.[71] This left no doubt about Spain's "mysterious rights of possession" over the New World.[72] It also made Peru central to world history. Montesinos seamlessly connected the entirety of the history of ancient Israel and the Old Testament to that of the new Israel that was the Spanish Monarchy via the history of Peru.

The Old Testament at the Heart of the Polemic of the New World

With so many conquerors using the Old Testament to justify the conquest, it is little wonder the Crown's ministers often weighed scriptural arguments in its special committees or juntas. As one theologian in the 1530s wrote these officials, the Old Testament itself called rulers to consult theologians. He cited Deuteronomy 17, which stated that "thou shalt come unto the priests the Levites, and unto the judge that shall be in those days, and enquire."[73]

Among the most important of these committees were the 1510s juntas, in which the Royal Council debated the legality of Spanish behaviors in the Caribbean. In 1512, Dominican Friar Montesinos voiced many Dominicans' disgust with the system of Indian enslavement that was depopulating the islands and mainland of the Indies. Friars and settlers sent petitions and procurators back to the court to promote their reforms. Dominicans won the ear of the Crown, bringing about reforms in the Royal Council's Juntas of 1512 and 1513. These birthed, as we have seen, the Deuteronomical *requerimiento*.[74]

Not all readings of Deuteronomy legitimated conquest in these juntas. As abuses against Indians once again became an issue of concern for the Crown in the late 1530s, Francisco de Vitoria rejected the doctrine that sinners could not have political dominion (whose adherents, he said, cited Kings 1:15–16). He noted that King David himself was a sinner but did not lose sovereignty.[75] Indians, he concluded, had legitimate claims to sovereignty over the New World.[76] Even the Habsburgs' claims to universal monarchy were invalid, he argued, citing a number of passages in Genesis in which God approved of the existence of multiple leaders and nations regardless of their creed.[77]

By the 1540s and 1550s, however, the Council of the Indies began to lean less often on theologians to make major decisions regarding New World policy. The Old Testament, the New Testament, Aristotle, Saint Thomas, and the other scholastic sources had reached their limits in the Council's decision-making process; ministers' accumulated experience and their subtler divide-and-conquer strategy rose to the fore.[78] Ministers themselves began to articulate a preference for experience over theology, especially after their righteous but politically disastrous 1542 New Laws engendered major conquistador revolts in Peru.[79]

In the Council's efforts to weaken the Peruvian warlords' power, the Old Testament may have also played a continuing role in legitimizing the expansion of Crown authority. An extensive juridical scrapbook produced by one of its officials, probably their royal attorney or *fiscal*, featured heavy annotations to biblical and juridical sources. This book likely served to help the *fiscales* and their assistants take subjects to court in *justicia* cases.[80] The Council seems to have used this scripturally informed dossier to strip power from the very men who used the Old Testament to claim it in the New World.

The Council also invoked the Old Testament to legitimate its policies under extraordinary circumstances. The important *fiscal* Antonio de León Pinelo, for example, did so in his 1630 *Confirmaciones reales de encomiendas* (Royal Confirmations of *Encomiendas*), a work discussing royal grants of Indian tribute (*encomiendas*). Its frontispiece featured images of Peru and New Spain accompanied by Old Testament passages. Citing Genesis 49:15, the attorney linked Peruvian Indians to Issachar, the perpetual "servant unto tribute."[81] He linked the Mexica to a similar passage from Deuteronomy 20, in which a defeated people render tribute to the Israelites for eternity.[82] The eminent jurist and Council minister Juan de Solórzano y Pereira also wrote in his 1647 *Política Indiana* that both Indians and Afro-descendants had inherited the curse of Noah's second son Ham, whose misdeeds damned his lineage to eternal servitude.[83]

Petitioners and the Old Testament

Vassals often employed the Jewish Bible when they sent the Council their *gobierno* and *gracia* petitions. In efforts to create new imperial *gobierno* policymaking, they often employed creative rhetorical allusions to Scripture. Some flattered the kings and Council ministers with favorable references to the patriarchs of Israel. Friar Pedro Suárez de Escobar likened his letter to the monarch to 1 Kings 17, in which the Prophet Elijah pleaded that God bring a sick child back to health.[84] High Judge Diego de Soto, writing from New Granada in 1587, justified the king's role as supreme justice and defender of the realm by invoking Isaiah 32:1, "Behold, a king shall reign in righteousness, and princes shall rule in judgment."

Others warned the king not to ignore the example of the Hebrew kings and prophets, lest the kingdom fall into injustice. A Spanish bishop named Garay warned King Philip II not to seek riches but "the glory of eternal justice," quoting King Solomon in Ecclesiastes 5:10, "He that loveth silver shall not be satisfied with silver, nor he that loveth abundance with increase: this is also vanity."[85] One Miguel de Villanueva wrote from Bolivia with a parable from 2 Kings 5 in which the poor prophet Elisha approached the king of Syria and offered to cure one of his generals of leprosy. The king was so angered at this impudent offer that he tore at his own clothes. Yet when Elisha convinced the afflicted general to wash in the River Jordan, the leprosy miraculously faded away. Humbled and ashamed, the king conceded that he had wrongly ignored the poor prophet's advice. Villanueva concluded, "if the words of council are good, they must be heeded without regarding who offers them."[86] The famed friar Gerónimo de Mendieta wrote from Mexico in 1587 that King Solomon described monarchs' hearts as sitting in the palm of the Lord, inclining them to heed, love, and improve their imperfect vassals.[87]

Others still used references to Old Testament justice to bolster their own authority as prophets and undermine their rival petitioners' claims. Friar Melchor de San José's undated petition offered the Council a biblical passage to drive his reforms home and denigrate his enemies simultaneously. He cited Isaiah 29:13, in which the Lord declares that "forasmuch as this people draw near me with their mouth, and with their lips do honour me, but have removed their heart far from me."[88] He also recalled the Prophet's cry in Isaiah 6:5, "Woe is me! For I am undone; because I am a man of unclean lips, and I dwell in the midst of a people of unclean lips."[89] Petitioners also often cast themselves as Israelites under the yoke of the Pharaoh, awaiting the justice of the king to deliver them from their burdens, often in the context of denouncing local authorities' abuses.[90]

The *Arbitrios* and Paralegal Commentaries

As the Council became increasingly crowded with petitions, a new genre of extended and elaborate suggestions for government reform (*arbitrios*) arose in the late 1500s and early 1600s. These were part-petitions, part-treatises that aimed both to interest the public and to sway imperial policy. Some sought to legitimate the conquest. Soldier Bernardo de Vargas Machuca's 1603 *Defense of the Western Conquests* would bluntly claim that "the inhabitants of the Promised Land were destroyed for idolatries as well as for human sacrifice, as the Holy Scriptures say in Deuteronomy, chapters 9, 12, and 20, and Leviticus, 18 and 20."[91] He also cited Psalm 138:4, "All the kings of the earth shall praise thee" to disprove Las Casas's claim that non-Christians had sovereignty.[92]

Other *arbitrios* were reform-minded. By the 1600s, after all, the Empire was facing major challenges to its economic and military integrity. The social models of Scripture once again loomed large in reform projects, with powerful administrators and ecclesiastics in the Indies envisioning this ancient social order as the key to imperial reorganization. Sucre-born Gaspar de Escalona Agüero's influential 1647 book on taxation, *Gazophilatium Regium Peruvicum* (Treasury of the Peruvian Realm) (1647), for instance, did so repeatedly when tackling the issue of officials' behavior. Its frontispiece referred to the ever-present idea that Peru was King Solomon's mines of Ophir, rendered the viceroyalty's treasury the Tabernacle of Moses, and suggested the figure of the royal official as another Job forced to resist temptation.[93]

In 1640, the powerful bishop-grandee Juan de Palafox y Mendoza arrived in Mexico in 1640 as Bishop of Puebla and inspector (*visitador*), charged with overseeing both departing and newly elected viceroys.[94] Rodríguez de León became Palafox's most trusted theological adviser, and he would correct and expand the bishop's treatise on political philosophy, the 1642 *Historia Real Sagrada: Luz de principes y Subditos* (Sacred Royal History: Light of princes and subjects). This was an extended commentary and mirror of princes drawing from the Old Testament books of Genesis, Exodus, Kings, and Chronicles. Palafox considered Rodríguez de León to be a sage given the latter's formidable command of Old Testament Scripture. Palafox's and Rodríguez's commentary on Israelite leaders and monarchies was a treatise on imperial reform and served as a manual to help the Crown reclaim its fading power in the wake of the revolts of Portugal, Cataluña, and Naples.[95]

The Old Testament often provided a model for commentators to hold Spaniards accountable for their misdeeds and even to critique the core tenets of the New World economy. As the mining industry became increasingly prominent, some turned the narrative of God-ordained Solomonic mining on its head. The Peru-born Augustinian friar Augustín de Calancha did so as he recounted the Chunbibilcan Indian Gualca's discovery of the mines of Potosí—the silver-rich mountain that would become "the admiration of the world, which enrichens all."[96] Calancha tied the institution of mining itself back to Tubalcain, the sixth descendant of Cain, calling him the first miner, idolater, and warmonger.[97] After all, the three practices were connected—man's new ability to claim mastery over metals engendered weapon-making and the creation of statues of false gods. Tubalcain's evil innovations were everywhere on display at Potosí, for this was "the town in the world where there are ... the headquarters of the wars and struggles ... where against the Indians we see the cruelties of the greedy."[98] Gualca's discovery had inadvertently heralded in a new era of idolatry—an idolatry of mineral wealth that was Spanish by way of Tubalcain.

For Calancha and many others, the question of whether Spaniards had the authority to enslave Indians also related to the latter's possible descent from a disgraced Old Testament lineage. However, he took the opposite route: one could, using historical and ethnographic information, *disprove* Indians' cursed descents just as easily as others could prove them. He pointed to the widespread theory among chroniclers of Peru that its Indians descended from Ham.[99] However, he noted, these authors had not read the Old Testament well, for three of Ham's sons were not eternal slaves; only the Canaanites were to be, and these were only to be slaves of select Israelites.[100]

Could Spaniards enslave at all? Calancha winkingly noted that those who would yoke the Indians would have to "negotiate" their pure Christian lineages. By claiming the Old Testament as authority to enslave, they had not only made the Indians Canaanites but made themselves Jews.[101] He also angrily rejected the arguments that the Indians were descendants of Issachar—for was there not a class of Issachars in every society?[102] This reasoning shows that, for many intellectuals, Old Testament lineages were important, perhaps not for the day-to-day adjudication and legislation of the Empire but for the paralegal contexts of polemics about imperial reform.

Scripture as a Font of Radicalism?

In rare cases, utopian visions critical of earthly society and of Spanish policies could also look to Scripture for a radical new vision of the future. In the anonymous text *Sinapia* (possibly late 1600s–1700s), the author imagined a world with both Far Eastern and New World characteristics in which all subjects lived without private property in perfect harmony. In this faraway land of Sinapia, whose name mirrored *Hispania*, the church resembled less the Roman model of the present than the biblical priesthood of Israel. Children were to learn the proverbs of Solomon from a young age, and all would attend a temple adorned with the "stories and saints of the Old Testament" that were painted outside and inside the central church. Priests would wear the Old Testament breastplates, and they would adhere to Scripture by growing long hair and beards and by shunning mixed clothes.[103] Though *Sinapia*'s vision maintained slaveholding and strict gender hierarchies, its call for a strong electoral democracy and shared property shows that the Old Testament could also provide a model for bold new visions of society.

Thinkers at the time also debated the status of women, in part through the prism of the Old Testament. Just as the curse of Ham and Isaachar "the strong ass" seemed to condemn whole peoples into slavery, so too were women cursed by Eve's original sin of eating from the Tree of Knowledge. But not all scholars accepted this as a straightforward confirmation of women's exile from greatness. For instance, in 1627 Martín Carrillo's *History or Elegy of Women* discussed fifty-four important female protagonists in the Old Testament.[104] He reversed the predominant script by arguing that "there is no industry, genius, ability, nor art, that a women cannot reach and know, in matters of good, as well as in evil."[105] He argued that though Eve had sinned, she was also a prefiguration of the immaculate Virgin Mary as God's chosen vessel.[106] He also defended, albeit in nonegalitarian tones, women's participation in politics. When recounting the case of how the prophetess Huldah discovered the Law Books of Moses in the Temple of Jerusalem in 2 Kings and 2 Chronicles, Carrillo produced the following stanza:

> That for the prudence of the Council
> It is good that the King listen even to women,
> For she [Huldah], showed with her sacrosanct wisdom,
> (Which she used to teach the Lettered to read)
> That sometimes women are manly indeed.[107]

Doña María de Guevara, a rare female *arbitrista*, also cited the Old Testament to justify women's participation in imperial governance in her 1664 *Disenchantments at the Court and Valorous Women*. She did so in even more pointed terms than Carrillo, citing (among others) the intelligent rule of Queen Michal during a time of crisis to prove that "a government of women is at times better than that of many men."[108] Many passages of the Old Testament could thus be invoked against its own genealogical determinism.

These visions met one of their highest expressions in the writings of the famed Mexican nun Sor Juana Inés de la Cruz. In 1691, Sor Juana penned her *Answer to Sister Filotea de la Cruz* in which she supported the Mexican theologian Juan Díaz de Arce's argument that women were the most able to interpret the deep, prophetic meanings of the Bible. Sor Juana was encouraged by "Deborah, issuing laws, military as well as political, and governing the people among whom there were so many learned men" as well as "the exceedingly knowledgeable Queen of Sheba, so learned she dares to test the wisdom of the wisest of all wise men."[109]

Indeed, the Old Testament had been a gateway to Sor Juana's own breadth of learning. To achieve her understanding of theology, she observed, "it seemed to me necessary to ascend by the ladder of the humane arts and sciences"—without music, how could one understand David's songs?[110] Without arithmetic, how could she understand the reckoning of the days in Daniel, or the Ark of the Covenant and Jerusalem without geometry and architecture?

The Old Testament could also allow New World patriots to critique imperial institutions and propose a more meritocratic treatment of Creoles and Indians. By the 1600s, Indies subjects developed more elaborate visions of the Old Testament past, often arguing that the Council should honor America's inhabitants more than it had done in the previous century. The Mexican jurist and theologian Juan Zapata y Sandoval's 1609 *Disquisition on Distributive Justice* not only made this argument but also showed the power of the Old Testament to produce sophisticated readings of imperial justice and its apparent paradoxes. Zapata's treatise heavily employed the Old Testament to explain the apparent inconsistencies of the Spanish legal system's mix of norms and norm-circumventing privileges. He noted that, on the one hand, laws existed to be universally binding—this was the field of *justicia legal*, which consisted of rules that all in the community must obey. There was also *justicia comutativa*, in which individuals mutually pacted with one another as equals. Then there was the justice of the whole to its parts, *justicia distributiva*, or what the Council variously called *gracia* and *méritos*—that is, the world of merit and privilege.

Zapata was particularly concerned with this last type of justice's relation to the whole. He argued that too often, both the petitioner and the judge assigned little importance to the circumstance of the case and focused rather on the individual who sought the privilege—a flaw he referred to as *ascepción*. God did indeed sometimes appear to consider the individual rather than the circumstance—as in the case of the bereaved Job before God in Job:42, and the Prophet Isaiah before King David in 2 Kings 19.[111] In reality, Zapata argued, these cases were not proof of God's bias toward individuals but expressions of a functional system of *justicia distributiva* in which the extraordinary actions of otherwise ordinary vassals earned them privileged status and resources within society.[112] God had been clear: in Leviticus 19 He instructed Moses to treat all equally without exception. This sophisticated treatise thus used the Old Testament (and other sources) to reconcile the Empire's legal system. Sandoval even took the argument one step further, implying that if *acepción* were to fall and *justicia distributiva* were to take its rightful place, all those born in the New World—perhaps even Indians—should be eligible for the priesthood and other honors.[113]

Indigenous writers sometimes followed a similar line of argument. The Quechua chronicler Guamán Poma de Ayala, writing in 1616, cited the passage Psalm 74:4, "I bear the pillars," confirming the legitimacy not of Spanish but of Indian rule over Peru.[114] In 1748, the part-Indian, part-Spanish Friar Calixto de San José submitted a somewhat similar polemic to King Ferdinand VI, the *Exclamation of the American Indians*. The friar deliberately styled the treatise off of the laments of the Prophet Jeremiah (Jeremiah 5).[115] He called for a sweeping overhaul of imperial Indian policies, calling for their equal treatment. Just as the Old Testament could allow friars to argue that Indians were eternal servants, others could use the text to structure opposite arguments—equality or special preference for New World inhabitants in general, or Indians in particular.

One paralegal strategy that patriots pursued was the use of the Old Testament to vindicate the New World's pre-Hispanic past. Authors could cast Indian rulers, not Spanish ones, as Old Testament kings to drive this point home. In the late 1600s, the famed Mexican patriot Carlos Sigüenza y Góngora drew new, numerous parallels between Moses and the Mexica rulers, calling attention to their virtues and edifying examples.[116]

In order for the New World to become the Old World's equal, however, it would need to redeem more than just Indian kings. The Americas would need to become a cradle of Christianity that could rival Europe and the Middle East. The royal privileges of a town, city, province, or even an entire realm depended not only on its heroes' deeds but also on the saints and virgins who proved its place in the hierarchy of spiritual favor. Here is where the hermeneutical tradition of locating prefigurations in the Old Testament became important to New World patriots. Canonization of New World saints was a legal process which also drew from the Old Testament. In *Breve teatro de las acciones más notables del bienaventurado Toribio, arzobispo de Lima* (Rome, 1683), friar Francisco Antonio de Montalvo drew constant parallels between Moses and Saint Toribio de Mogrovejo (1538–1606), Archbishop of Lima. Montalvo commissioned the images to promote the canonization dossier of Mogrovejo after his beatification in 1679. The Vatican canonized Mogrovejo in 1726. The Archbishop's miracles were distinctly Biblical. Like Moses, Mogrovejo survives a river crossing on his way to Peru, parts the waters of a river during a pastoral visitation to the Indians of Peru, draws water from a rock to allow Indians to battle a drought, and delivers the new covenant in the Sinai that Peru to ensure the conversion of Indians to Christianity (Figure 11.1). The images in the *Breve teatro* typify viceregal hagiographies that presented New World saints as Old Testament heroes.

Hagiographical constructions of male and female sainthood and prayer were permeated by Biblical references. In fact, saints were often manifestations of Old Testament heroes and vice versa. This was because any exceptional individuals could be simultaneously manifestations of the Israelite Law of Moses and the Christian Law of Grace. We find these references in numerous texts, especially in hagiographies and little-explored *novena* prints (Figure 11.2).[117] These show that the Granada-born Saint John of God (1495–1550) could appear as a fulfillment of Abraham of the Law of Moses (Figure 11.2a). In a 1674 hagiography, the Peruvian Mercedarian Pedro Urraca was a Job of the Age of Grace (Figure 11.2c). Christians thus became Hebrew exemplars. But Israelites could also become Christian saints, A 1774 *novena* published in Cartagena de Indias presents the Old Testament Prophet Elijah as a saint (Figure 11.2b) and Saint Moses appears in Francisco de Holanda's *De Aetatibues mundi imagines* (ca. 1545) (Figure 11.2d).[118] Ideas not only of canonization but sainthood itself were profoundly influenced by Scripture.

FIGURE 11.1: Saint Toribio Mogrovejo recapitulates life and miracles of Moses. Francisco Antonio de Montalvo *Breve teatro de las acciones más notables del bienaventurado Toribio, arzobispo de Lima* (Rome, 1683). Public Domain.

For patriots seeking to ennoble the New World with Scripture, the theological discipline of Mariology would become a critical asset. In the Catholic tradition, the cult of Mary elevated her status through prefigurative readings, linking her especially to the Israelite cults of heroines such as Judith, Esther, Deborah, Sarah, Jael, and Rebecca. The

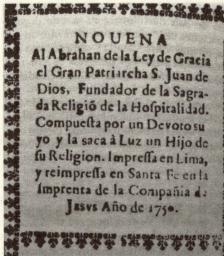
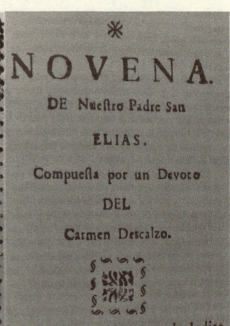

FIGURE 11.2: Old Testament heroes as Catholic Saints and Catholic Saints as Old Testament Heroes. (a) *Novena al Abrahan de la Ley de Gracia al Gran Patriarcha San Juan de Dios* (Lima: Imprenta Compañía de Jesús, 1750). (b) A *Novena de nuestro padre San Elias, compuesto por un devoto del Carmen Descalzo* (Cartagena de Indias: Imprenta de Antonio Espinoza de los Monteros, 1774). (c) Fray Felipe Colombo, *El Job De La Ley De Gracia, Retratado en la Admirable Vida Del Siervo De Dios Venerable Padre Fray Pedro Urraca* (Madrid: Imprenta Real, 1674). (d) Francisco de Holanda. *De Aetatibues Mundi imagines* (ca. 1545), 35v. Biblioteca Nacional de Madrid. MS DIB.1426. Public Domain.

Spanish were more invested in the Marian tradition than others in the wider Catholic Mediterranean.[119] In the New World, patriotic contemporaries rarely failed to note the typological connections of these apparitions to the Old Testament. Marian apparitions proved the Indies' virtue and clarified their place in the arc of human history.

For instance, in Miguel Sánchez's 1648 *Imagen de la Virgen María de Dios de Guadalupe*, the famous apparition of the Virgin of Guadalupe on the Mexican hill of Tepeyac paralleled and fulfilled God's delivery of the Ten Commandments to Moses on Mount Sinai—only this time, the leader of the Israelites was the Indian Juan Diego.[120] Indeed, first in the 1680s and especially in the 1740s and 1750s, as this Virgin was in the process of becoming the patroness of Mexico, her devotees acclaimed her special authority over the world and the people of Mexico, citing Psalm 147:20, "He hath not dealt so with any nation: and as for his judgments, they have not known them."[121] This religious fervor had elevated Mexico in a very real way within Catholicism's social and legal economy of grace, a status shown in the Pope's official 1754 confirmation of her status as the patroness of the viceroyalty.[122]

The Scriptural Battlefield

By the late 1700s, then, the Old Testament was a sword that cut both ways. It not only justified the inferiority of the New World, its Indians, and its women but also ennobled the New World's people and landscapes. This came to a head in the era of imperial troubles of the late 1700s. In the early 1800s Wars of Independence, the Old Testament once again came to play a part in the paralegal legitimation of both sides' causes, meeting quite literally on the battlefield.

In New Spain in 1810, as rebel priest Miguel Hidalgo y Costilla laid siege to Mexico City under the banner of the Virgin of Guadalupe, the royalist defenders turned to the Virgin of los Remedios. Hidalgo had superior armaments but disastrously decided not to attack, dooming his efforts. In a cathedral sermon commemorating this providential outcome the following year, the orator Juan Bautista Díaz Calvillo sought to provide an explanation. He made use of a series of events narrated by the Book of Judges. It told of the wicked king of Israel, Abimelech, who ignored the words of the prophet Jotham and, during an ill-advised attack, met his doom when a woman in a tower crushed his skull with a rock. Hidalgo was Abimelech, and the woman who annihilated him at the last minute was the Virgin of los Remedios.[123]

The Virgin was not only a loving and self-sacrificing mother but also, above all, a warrior-woman. She had her prefiguration in the Old Testament in the actions of Judith, who lopped off the head of Holofernes the Assyrian general (Judith 10), and by Jael, who smote the Caananite general Sisera with a nail (Judges 4). She was also the fulfillment of Old Testament enemies of heresy. In a 1791 allegorical painting by Andrés López in the Basilica of the Virgin of Guadalupe, Our Lady of Mount Carmel is the royalists' weapon against the French Revolution. Upon her lap is the Ark of the Alliance that holds the written Law of Moses, which in reality is an anticipation of the Body of Christ. The Ark prefigures the womb of Mary. Here, the Virgin appears constantly as a recipient or vessel, as she does frequently in Mariological analyses. She is, for example, the throne upon which Christ sits, which is at the same time none other than the podium of King Solomon, with six stairs flanked by pairs of statues of lions (1 Kings 10:18–20). In López's painting, Mary-as-warrior, defender of the royalist cause, was also prefigured by Elijah, the prophet and slayer of heretics.[124]

For the royalists, Bolívar and other liberals often appeared as biblical false idols. In the Peruvian lowland tropics of Maynas, Bishop Franciscan Hipólito Sánchez Rangel de Fayas y Quiroz encountered resisting Indians, whom he likened to Israel's enemies the Canaanites, Jebusites, Amorites, and Philistines of Gaza, Ashdod, Ashkelon, Gath, and Ekron.[125] But his Old Testament rivals would soon shapeshift into liberals.

Republican forces laid siege to the region in 1819–1821, led by Commander General Pedro Pascacio Noriega. Sánchez found himself ousted as Absalom had been by King David in 2 Samuel 15. Noriega met the same fate as Absalom, executed on May 10, 1821, while the bishop was in Brazil.

The Old Testament also permitted Sánchez to present himself before King Ferdinand VII as Nehemiah, the prophet who during his exile convinced the king of Babylon to permit him to return to Israel and rebuild the walls of Jerusalem, which were falling apart (2 Esdras 1.11). From exile, Sánchez denounced Bolívar, San Martín, and their commanders as false prophets, the equivalent of priest-killer Queen Jezebel. Sánchez called on King Ferdinand VII to take up the mantle of the warrior Elijah who slayed the enemies of God: "Yes, Spaniards, and our beloved countrymen, the King of Spain the Catholic and our Monarch Lord don Fernando VII, this is the Elijah placed by God before us . . . to defend his Church and the integrity of his monarchy, beheading all who oppose its execution of its duty."[126]

Republicans also offered their contrasting Old Testament responses. For every biblical example amenable to the Spanish monarchy there was another of republican character. A month before Díaz Calvillo pronounced his sermon in 1810, Juan Germán Roscio wrote to the residents of Nirgua, commanding them to join the Junta of Caracas to convert Venezuela into a republic like that in Judges. The letter of Roscio to Nirgua is a little-studied document. It reveals the fundamentally religious nature of the republican project that our historiographies have not known how to recognize, in part because they have understood Roscio and his allies, Francisco Miranda and Bolívar, as Enlightenment liberals.[127] His letter urged the people of Nirgua to rid themselves of kings, for this was the true message of the Bible. It was a tall order—the town's largely Afro-indigenous population had found the Crown to be a faithful protector of their interests against Spanish encroachment.[128]

Roscio thought that the institution of the monarchy had been one of the most severe forms God used to punish sin. Since creation, God excoriated men time and time again, from the expulsion from Paradise to the Flood and Babel's confusion of tongues. But of all these punishments, the worst was the introduction of kings to the peoples.

In his interpretation of the Bible, Roscio found that for most of history humanity lived without kings. God had created Man in His image and with free will, which made it impossible that men would be disposed to abandon their right to choose, protest, and elect. Why, then, had monarchies become the world's most prevalent institution? For Roscio the answer had to be found in the sin of idolatry, which permitted certain humans to convince others that they were deities that had the right to command obedience. Most people turned to kings just as they did to idolatry. However, God's Chosen Ones did not: Roscio deemed God's election of Abraham and his progeny to constitute history's first republican resistance against the plague of monarchies. For over eight hundred years the Israelites rejected kings and were ruled by judges. They remained free and republican until the era of Samuel, the priest-prophet, when, in opposition to the wishes of God, they picked Saul as their first monarch.

Roscio interpreted the circumstances surrounding the coronation of Saul as king, from the first book of Samuel, as a dramatic twist in the history of Israel. Yet for Roscio the republican spirit of Israel was not altogether lost. When Roboam, as a good son of Samuel, decided to demand more tribute, ten of the twelve tribes rebelled and created a new political community under Jeroboam, "the Patriot."

It should surprise no one, therefore, that in the mouths of innumerable holy orators the rebellion against the Spanish monarch was one led by Jeroboam, the patriot, Simón Bolívar. The Liberator also became the Israelite hero Simon Maccabeus.[129] For example, the magister-deacon Mariano Talavera of the cathedral of Bogotá delivered 1824 and 1825 sermons organizing the life and actions of Bolívar around those of Simon Maccabeus and of specific passages: 1 Maccabeus 15:33–34 and 1 Maccabeus 13:6–9. Maccabeus was the quintessential Jewish revolutionary, and the royalists were the wicked Seleucids, the oppressors of the Israelites.

Conclusions

New World vassals and royal officials' interpretations of the Old Testament are as diverse as the Spanish Empire itself. Institutions like the Council system, the Inquisition, and the monarchy itself invited countless parallels to ancient Hebrew justice. The Empire's understanding of its legal geography followed suit, with the Solomonic Royal Palace and Escorial viewed as parallel to Paradise and King Solomon's mines of Ophir. The Book shaped debates about the nature of the New World past; the legitimacy of the conquest; and questions of mining, taxation, and other major issues. The Council's ministers, familiar with theological reasoning, nonetheless invited petitions and summoned Juntas where Indians, friars, conquistadors, and intellectuals cited this work's passages to underscore their reasoning. In the world of *gracia*, conquerors and pessimists could depict the New World and its peoples as the antithesis of Israel and the Israelites, while activists, patriots, and women flipped the script with aplomb. And as republicans defeated royalists in the nineteenth century, these divergent readings of the Book had their day on the battlefield itself.

This article has not covered all or most of the relationship between Spanish imperial law, legal culture, and the Old Testament. There are surely many other institutions and crises that vassals and officials envisioned through this lens. For example, we have not touched upon the role and transformations of Scholastic thought, a major force in Spanish imperial law, which often provided vassals and royal officials with other sophisticated commentaries on Scripture's relationship with the New World. We have only fleetingly touched upon how proto-ethnographic writings used the Old Testament to understand and evaluate Indians and have only briefly considered the Indian response. Moreover, the question of Jewish, New Christian, Muslim, and Morisco visions of the Old Testament remain ripe subjects for exploration. Lastly, the question of whether Spanish theologians and others commented at length upon the Americas' Afro-descendants, variously free and enslaved, remains a rich field for scholars to investigate.

What should be clear from these pages, nonetheless, is that the historiography has underestimated the Old Testament's versatility as a master text of Iberian and New World legal culture. An empire's institutions, politics, juridical culture, polemics, literature, architecture, and iconographies remain ripe for reevaluation. If scholars continue to ignore this rich and complex master text, the history of the Empire will remain not only incomplete, but incomprehensible.

Notes

1. For the committee (Junta) texts, see Archive of the Indies (henceforth AGI), Indiferente General 419, 83r and Justicia 299, 603r–621v. For transcriptions and studies, see Rafael Altamira "El texto de las Leyes de Burgos de 1512," *Revista de Historia de América* 4, (1938): 6–79. Antonio Moro Orejón has found in the Archivo de Simancas (henceforth AGS) printed editions of the ordenanzas of 1512 and of the modifications (*moderaciones*) of 1513; see "Ordenanzas reales sobre los Indios, (Las Leyes de 1512–1513)," trascripción, estudios y notas de Antonio Moro Orejón, *Anuario de Estudios Americanos* 13 (1956): 317–371.
2. The best study of the trans-Atlantic debates that the Dominican sermon triggered until 1523 are the two volumes by Manuel Giménez Fernández, *Bartolomé de la Casas: Delegado de Cisneros para la reformación de las Indias (1516–1517)* (Sevilla: CSIC 1953); and *Bartolomé de la Casas: Capellán de SM Carlos I poblador de Cumaná (1517–1523)* (Sevilla: CSIC, 1960).
3. Juan López de Palacios Rubios, *Libellus de insulis oceanis*, Biblioteca Nacional de Madrid (henceforth BNM) Mss. 17641, 1-89v. It has been translated and edited as *De las islas del mar océano = Libellus de insulis oceanis*: Introducción, texto crítico y traducción de Paulino Castañeda Delgado, José Carlos Martín de la Hoz, y Eduardo Fernández (Pamplona: EUNSA, 2013). Other jurists in the Junta also wrote treatises on slavery and just war drawing from Scripture. See Matías de Paz," Libellus circa dominium regum Hispaniae super indos [1512]/*Acerca del dominio sobre los indios*, Bilingual edition, with introduction and critical translation by Paulino Castañeda, José Carlos Martín de la Hoz, y Eduardo Fernández (Salamanca: Editorial San Esteban, 2018).

4. Luis de Páramo, *De origine et progressv officii sanctae inqvisitionis* (Madrid: Typographía Regia, 1598), 27–30. On Páramo, see Kimberly Lynn, *Between Court and Confessional. The Politics of Spanish Inquisitors* (Cambridge: Cambridge University Press, 2013), 140-190.
5. Ibid., 30 (*Inquisitors imitate and follow the same procedures of God*). Other segments of the Old Testament drove Páramo's point home, including Psalm 14:1–5, in which God surveys all from the Heavens and puts the unbelievers who say "there is no God" into "great fear, for God is the generation of the righteous." Páramo also cited Psalm 35, which included a prayer that "the angel of the Lord chase" the wicked for their sins.
6. Henry Kamen, *The Spanish Inquisition: A Historical Revision* (New Haven: Yale University Press, 1998 [1997]), 286.
7. José Luis González Novalín, *El inquisidor general Fernando de Valdés (1483–1568): su vida y su obra* (Oviedo: Universidad de Oviedo, 2008), 259–268.
8. Ibid., 268–269.
9. Elvira Pérez Ferreiro, *Glosas rabínicas y sagrada escritura* (Salamanca: Editorial San Esteban, 2004), 38–39.
10. Luis de Páramo, *De origine et progressv officii sanctae inqvisitionis* (Madrid: Typographía Regia, 1598), 27–30.
11. Stuart Schwartz, *All Can be Saved* (New Haven: Yale University Press, 2008), 145–149.
12. José de Sigüenza, *La fundación del Monasterio del Escorial* [1600–1605] (Madrid: n.p., 1963), 343–344. The use of at least three of the images at the Escorial (the gathering of the manna, Jews and the Paschal Lamb, and Melchizedek and Abraham) as a prefiguration of the Eucharist was a well-established medieval tradition. For example, see them clustered in Albert C. Labriola and John W. Smeltz, eds., *The Mirror of Salvation [Speculum Humanae Salvationis]: An Edition of British Library Blockbook G. 11784*, (Cambridge: Clarke, 2002), 48–49. See also Kelly Donahue-Wallace, *Art and Architecture of Viceregal Latin America* (Albuquerque: University of New Mexico Press, 2008), 1521–1821, 28, 43, 87, 186.
13. Samuel Y. Edgerton, *Theaters of Conversion: Religious Architecture and Indian Artisans in Colonial Mexico* (Albuquerque: University of New Mexico Press, 2001), 141, 156, 223, 233, 243.
14. Ben Zion Wacholder, *Eupolemus: A Study of Judaeo-Greek Literature* (Cincinnati: Hebrew Union College, 1974), 56–68, 72–74, quote on 78, 84–91. In Augustine, *The City of God, Books XVII–XXII (The Fathers of the Church)*, trans. Gerald G. Walsh S. J., and Daniel J. Honan (Washington, DC: Catholic University of America Press, 2008 [1954]), Book 18, chap. 39.
15. Salustiano De Dios, "Ordenanzas del Consejo Real de Castilla (1385–1490)," *Historia. Instituciones. Documentos* 7 (1980): 269–320, 271–272.
16. Dios, "Ordenanzas," 272: "establesçiese çiertos ommes poderosos sabios e syn codiçá, los quales oyesen e librasen todas las demandas e querellas e petiçiones del pueblo, e que sy alguna grave cosa oviese en que ellos non pudiesen poner cobro, que fiziesen rrelaçion dello ael, e quela librase el; e que asy faziendo, que cunpliria los mandamientos de Dios. . . . E el dicho Moysen oydo este consejo, plogole mucho del e pusolo luego por obra, por lo qual el pueblo de Ysrrael ffue bien regido en su tienpo."
17. Hannelor Zug Tucci, "Le incoronazioni imperiali nel medioevo," in *Per me reges regnant: La regalità sacra nell'Europa medieval*, ed. Franco Cardini and Maria Saltarelli, 119–136 (Siena: Il Cerchio, 2002), here 105, and 128. Some Christian scholars would argue that these ancient patriarchs were not merely worthy of admiration, but bestowed divine authority upon their descendants. The papacy claimed indirect institutional descent from

Moses and the House of David, not through its dynast Jesus of Nazareth but through His Apostle Saint Peter. Others cherished what they believed to be their relics, like the Eastern Romans, who held that crusaders had brought Solomon's throne and the staff of Moses intact to Constantinople. See Antonio Carile, "La sacralità ritual dei ΒΑΣΙΛΕΙΣ bizantini," in *Per me reges regnant: La regalità sacra nell'Europa medieval*, ed. Franco Cardini and Maria Saltarelli, 53–96 (Siena: Il Cerchio, 2002), here 62, and 83.

18. Victor Mínguez, "El rey de España se sienta en el trono de Salomón. Parentescos simbólicos entre la Casa de David y la Casa de Austrias," in Víctor Mínguez, ed., *Visiones de la monarquía hispánica*, 19–55 (Castellón: Universitat Jaume I, 2007), here 25. Solomon appears in his adjudication between two women claiming maternity over a child (1 Kings 3:16–28) in a 1391 book ostensibly by King Sancho himself in *Castigos y documentos del rey don Sancho*; see BNM, Mss. 3995, 13r. In the 1475 *Doctrinal de príncipes*, courtier and intellectual Diego de Valera would point to the Old Testament and Alfonso X's *Siete partidas* to recommend that kings seek the "Solomonic" advice of ministers; see BNM, Mss. 2953, 10r.

19. They did so through the Duke of Lorraine's long-gone Latin Kingdom of Jerusalem, whose titles passed to the Kingdom of the Two Sicilies and ultimately to the Holy Roman Empire; see Mínguez, "El rey de España," 19.

20. Mínguez, "El rey de España," 2–24.

21. Desiderius Erasmus, *Collected Works of Erasmus*, vol. 66, ed. John W. O'Malley (Toronto: University of Toronto Press, 1988), i.e., 196.

22. Jaime Lara, "Feathered Psalms: Old World Forms in a New World Garb," in *Psalms in Community: Jewish and Christian Textual, Liturgical, and Artistic Traditions*, Harold W. Attridge and Margot Elsbeth Fassler, 293–312 (Leiden and Boston: Brill, 2004), 299–302.

23. Hubert Herkommer, "Typus Christi—Typus Regis. David als politische Legitimationsfigur," in *König David—biblische Schlüsselfigur und europäische Leitgestalt*, ed. Walter Dietrich and Hubert Herkommer, 383–436 (Stuttgart: W. Kohlhammer Verlag, 2003), here 404. The Crown also featured the passage from Proverbs 8:15: "By me kings reign, and princes decree justice." These point to Proverbs 8:14, "Counsel is mine, and sound wisdom: I am understanding; I have strength," as well as Proverbs 8:16, "By me princes rule, and nobles, even all the judges of the earth." Solomon himself holds a banner reading, "*Timete domunum et recede a malo*"—from Psalm 3:7, "Be not wise in thine own eyes: fear the Lord, and depart from evil."

24. Fernando Checa Cremades, *Carlos V y la imágen del héroe en el Renacimiento* (Madrid: Tauris, 1987).

25. Mínguez, "El rey de España," 26.

26. William S. Maltby, *The Reign of Charles V* (New York: Palgrave, 2002), 65.

27. Henry Kamen, *Philip of Spain* (New Haven: Yale University Press, 1998), 178–180.

28. Gloria Martínez Leiva and Ángel Rodríguez Rebollo, *El Inventario del Alcázar de Madrid de 1666: Felipe IV y su colección artística* (Madrid: Museo del Prado, 2015), 245–624.

29. Geoffrey Parker, *Imprudent King: A New Life of Philip II* (New Haven: Yale University Press, 2014), 100–105.

30. Mínguez, "El rey de España," 29.

31. José de Sigüenza, *La fundación del Monasterio del Escorial* [1600–1605] (Madrid: n.p., 1963), 6. The literature on the Escorial is vast. Pioneering in calling attention to the role of the Temple of Solomon as the organizing metaphor of the Escorial (albeit with too much emphasis on Neo-Platonism and Rosicrucian symbolisms) is René Taylor, *Arquitectura y magia: Consideraciones sobre la idea de El Escorial* (Madrid: Siruela, 1992). For a more

balanced approach that does not overlook the importance of the Temple of Solomon as a prefiguration of the Escorial, see Cornelia von der Osten Sacken, *El Escorial como estudio iconológico* (Madrid: Xarait, 1984). Most studies, however, have not paid sufficient attention to how the typologies of Noah's Ark and Moses's Tabernacle influenced the design and function of the building.

32. Sigüenza, *Fundación*, 213–216. On the image of King Solomon and other biblical heroes, such as Gideon, as prefigurations of the emperors of the Holy Roman Empire from Charlemagne to Philip II, see Marie Tanner, *The Last Descendant of Aeneas: The Hapsburgs and the Mythic Image of the Emperor* (New Haven: Yale University Press, 1993). On the statues see also Manuel Rincón Álvarez, *Claves para comprender el Monasterio de San Lorenzo de el Escorial* (Salamanca: Ediciones Universidad de Salamanca, 2007), 124.
33. Sigüenza, *Fundación*, 247.
34. Rincón Álvarez, *Claves*, 124.
35. Ibid., 177.
36. Johannes de Sevilla Pineda, *Ad suos in Salomonem commentarios Salomon praevius i.e.: de Rebus Salomonis Praevius, id est, de Rebus Salomonis Regis Libri Octo* (Lugduni: Apuv Horatium Cardon, 1609), 255.
37. Sevilla Pineda, *De Rebus Salomonis*, 286.
38. Ibid., 363.
39. Ibid., 346.
40. Ibid., 389.
41. Ibid., 392.
42. Ibid., 392.
43. Pedro Luis Lorenzo Cadarso, *El documento real en la época de los Austrias (1516–1700)* Cáceres: Universidad de Extremadura, 2002, 36.
44. AGS, Patronato leg. 70, doc. 9, 51r-v.
45. Ernesto Schäfer, *El Consejo Real y Supremo de las Indias: Su historia, organización y labor aministrativa hasta la terminación de la Casa de Austria*, vol 1 (Madrid: Marcial Pons Historia, 2003).
46. Gregorio López, *Las siete partidas del sabio rey Don Alonso el Nono, nuevamente glosadas* (Salamanca: Andrea de Portonaris, 1555).
47. BNM, Mss. 904, "Papeles references al gobierno de España," 263v.
48. Instituto Valencia don Juan, Colección Altamira, Envío 54, Caja 71, N.385, 342r.
49. The literature on Joachim of Fiore and Joachimite prophecy is immense. We have relied specially on the writings of Marjorie Reeves, *The Influence of Prophecy in the Later Middle Ages: A Study in Joachimism* (Oxford: Oxford University Press, 1969); and *Joachim of Fiore and the Prophetic Future* (London: Harper & Row, 1977). See also Marjorie Reeves, ed., *Prophetic Rome in the High Renaissance: Essays* (Oxford: Oxford University Press, 1999). On Viterbo and the Portuguese expansion, see John O'Malley, "Fulfillment of the Christian Golden Age under Pope Julius II: Text of a Discourse of Giles of Viterbo, 1507," *Tradition* 25 (1969): 265–338. On Amadeus of Portugal, see José Adriano de Carvalho, "Achegas ao Estudo da Influência da *Arbor Vitae Crucifixae* e da *Apocalypsis Nova* no século XVI em Portugal," *Via spiritus* 1 (1994): 55–109. On Spain, Rome, and Bernardino de Carvajal, see Nelson Minnich,"The Role of Prophecy in the Enigmatic Luis López de Carvajal," in *Prophetic Rome in the High Renaissance: Essays*, ed. Marjorie Reeves, 111-120 (Oxford: Oxford University Press, 1999).

50. Carlos Sempat Assadourian, "Hacia la 'Sublimis Deus:' las discordias entre los dominicos indianos y el enfrentamiento del franciscano padre Testera con el padre Betanzos," in *Historia Mexicana* 47(3) (1998): 465–536.
51. See, for example, Rui Grillo Capelo, *Profetismo e esoterismo: A Arte do prognóstico en Portugal (séculos xvii–xviii)* (Coimbra: Minerva, 1994); José van den Basselaar, *António Vieria: Profecia e polemica* (Rio de Janeiro: EDUERJ, 2002); Plinio Freire Gomez, *Un herege vai ai paraíso. Cosmologia de un excolono condenado pela Inquisição (1680–1744)* (Sao Paulo: Companhia das Letras, 1997); Adriana Romeiro, *Un visionário na corte de Dom João* (Belo Horizonte: UFMG, 2001); Ronald Cueto, *Quimeras y sueños. Los profetas y la Monarquía Católica de Felipe IV* (Valladolid: Universidad de Valladolid, 1994); Richard Kagan, *Lucrecia's Dreams Politics and Prophecy in Sixteenth-Century Spain* (Berkeley: University of California Press, 1990); Eulàlia Duran and Joan Requesens, eds., *Profecia i poder al Renaixement Texts profètics catalans favorables a Ferran el Catòlic* (Valencia: Elisei Climent Editor, 1997).
52. John Leddy Phelan, *The Millennial Kingdom of the Franciscans in the New World* (Berkeley: University of California Press, 1979); and Marjorie Reeves, "Joachim di Fiore and the Society of Jesuits," in *Joachim di Fiore in Christian Thought*, ed. Delno West, vol. 2 (New York: Burt Franklin, 1975), 209–227.
53. Mateo Bellester Rodríguez, "La estirpe de Tubal: Relato bíblico e identidad nacional en España," *Historia y Política* 29 (January–June 2013): 219–246, here 223–224.
54. Ibid., 224 and Jon Juaristi, *El reino del ocaso: España como sueño ancestral*. Madrid: Espasa Calpe, 2004, 81.
55. For Jiménez de Rada's *Opera*, also known as the *Historia de rebus Hispaniae*, see BNM, VITR/4/3, 7v and for Alfonso's *Estoria* see BNM, Mss. 5795, 2r.
56. Rodríguez, "La estirpe de Tubal," 226.
57. Ibid., 227.
58. Ibid., 227; and Richard L. Kagan, "Clio and the Crown," in *Spain, Europe and the Atlantic: Essays in Honour of John H. Elliott*, ed. Richard L. Kagan and Geoffrey Parker, 73–100 (Cambridge: Cambridge University Press, 2002 [1995]), here 77.
59. Florián de Ocampo, *Las quatro partes enteras dela Cronica de España* (Zamora: Augustín de Paz y Juan Picardo, 1541), vii verso and xxi verso.
60. Ibid., xxii recto.
61. Juan Suárez de Peralta, *Tratado del descubrimiento de las Yndias y su conquista*, 1589 BNM, Mss. 20143, 25r–26r.
62. For example, Franciscan friar Pedro Simón suggested that the Indians resembled Issachar due to their tendency to shoulder great burdens in his *Noticias historiales de las conquistas de Tierra firme* (Cuenca: Casa de Domingo de la Yglesia, 1626), 40. Solórzano, Calancha, and others would reject the Issachar theory; see Lee Eldridge Huddleston, *Origins of the American Indians: European Concepts, 1492–1729* (Austin: University of Texas Press, 1967).
63. José de Acosta, *Historia natural y moral de las Indias*, Book 7 (Madrid: Juan Berrillo, 1608), 459–460.
64. Gregorio García, *Origen de los indios de el Nuevo Mundo, e Indias Occidentales* (Valencia: Pedro Patricio May, 1607), Book 3, Ch. 3, sec. 3, f.234.
65. For a more detailed account of this mendicant biblical narrative of Mexica satanic election, see Jorge Cañizares-Esguerra, "The Structure of a Shared Demonological Discourse," in *Puritan Conquistadors: Iberianizing the Atlantic, 1550–1700*, 83–119 (Stanford: Stanford University Press, 2006).

66. Garry Sparks, ed. and trans., with Frauke Sachse and Sergio Romero, *The Americas' First Theologies: Early Sources of Post-Contact Indigenous Religion* (Oxford: Oxford University Press, 2017), 235–236.
67. James Romm, "Biblical History and the Americas: The Legend of Solomon's Ophir, 1492–1591," in *The Jews and the Expansion of Europe to the West, 1450–1800*, ed. Bernardini Paolo and Fiering Norman, 27–46 (New York: Berghahn Books, 2001), 34–40.
68. BNM, Mss. 8547, cxlv.
69. To reconstruct Montesinos's career, we have relied on "Servicios del Licenciado Don Fernando de Montesinos, Presbítero, 1644," in *Papeles varios*, Biblioteca de la Universidad de Sevilla, A 332/124, documento 41, ff. 472–500. For Olivares, see John H. Elliott, *The Count-Duke of Olivares: The Statesman in an Age of Decline* (New Haven: Yale University Press, 1989).
70. Fernando de Montesinos, *Ophir de España. Memorias historiales y políticas del Pirv*, Manuscript in the Biblioteca de la Universidad de Sevilla, A 332/124, documento 41, 1r.
71. Ibid., 144r–183v.
72. Ibid., 1r.
73. Francisco de Vitoria, *Relecciones sobre los indios y el derecho de guerra*, Tercera edición (Madrid: Colección Austral 1975 [1946]), 35 and 38.
74. See n, 1.
75. De Vitoria, *Relecciones sobre los indios y el derecho de guerra*, 42.
76. Ibid., 52.
77. Ibid., 57–58.
78. This is not to say that theological Juntas disappeared entirely. For instance, we find the Council once again consulted about certain papal bulls for raising funds around 1564; see AGI, Patronato 170, R.49. Moreover, Vitoria would employ theological arguments in yet another Junta on the *encomienda*, the 1554 Junta of London; see Bibliothèque nationale de France, Espagnol 325, 347r–348v.
79. For the revolts see James Lockhart, *Spanish Peru, 1532–1560: A Social History* (Madison: University of Wisconsin Press, 1994), 5. For ministers' comments see LOC, Kraus Collection, 1542, Digital ID mespk k13800, LOC, Hans P. Kraus Collection, Digital ID mespk k13200.
80. AGI, Indiferente, 532, L.1
81. Jorge Cañizares-Esguerra, "Typology in the Atlantic World: Early Modern Readings of Colonization," in, *Soundings in Atlantic History: Latent Structures and Intellectual Currents, 1500–1830* (Cambridge: Harvard University Press, 2009), 248.
82. Ibid.
83. Juan de Solórzano y Pereira, *Política Indiana* (Madrid: Diego Díaz de la Carrera, 1647), Book 1, Chap. V, 22
84. AGI, Patronato, 171, N.2, R.1, "El espiritu consolador," undated.
85. AGI, Patronato 171, N.2, R.6.
86. AGI, Lima 270, "Algunas vezes he considerado," April 15, 1564.
87. AGI, Mexico 107, "La experiencia cierta," October 15, 1584.
88. King James Bible.
89. AGI, Mexico 282, "Postquam," undated, 694r-v.
90. AGI, Mexico 105, "Por la divina ordenacion," November 20 1581, Bachiller Luis González.
91. Bernardo de Vargas Machuca, *Defending the Conquest: Bernardo de Vargas Machuca's Defense and Discourse of the Western Conquests*, ed. Kris Lane, trans. Timothy F. Johnson (University Park: Pennsylvania State University, 2010), 42.

92. Ibid., 43.
93. Jorge Cañizares-Esguerra, "Typology in the Atlantic World: Early Modern Readings of Colonization," in Bernard Bailyn and Patricia L. Denault, eds, *Soundings in Atlantic History: Latent Structures and Intellectual Currents, 1500–1830*. Cambridge: Harvard University Press, 2009.
94. On Palafox's projects of strengthening the Empire by granting fueros and establishing a Creole kingdom in New Spain, see Cayetana Álvarez de Toledo, *Politics and Reform in Spain and Viceregal Mexico: The Life and Thought of Juan de Palafox, 1600–1659* (Oxford and New York: Oxford University Press, 2004).
95. Álvarez de Toledo offers a very partial interpretation of the Historia, shorn of all theological and typological dimension.
96. Antonio de la Calancha, *Coronica Moralizada del Orden de San Avgvstin en el Perv*, Primer Tomo (Barcelona: Pedro Lacavalleria, 1639), 745.
97. Ibid., 364 and 745–746.
98. Ibid., 746.
99. Ibid., 36.
100. Ibid., 37.
101. Ibid.
102. Ibid., 40.
103. Anonymous, *Descripción de la Sinapia, península en la tierra austral*, ed. Miguel Avilés Fernández (Madrid: Brizzolis, 2011), 76.
104. Rosilie Hernández, "The Politics of Exemplarity: Biblical Women and the Education of the Spanish Lady in Martín Carrillo, Sebastián de Herrera Barnuevo, and María de Guevara," in *Women's Literacy in Early Modern Spain and the New World*, ed. Anne J. Cruz and Rosilie Hernández, 225–242 (Farnham: Ashgate, 2011), here 225.
105. Martin Carrillo, *Historia o Elogios de las Mugeres insignes de que trata la Sagrada Escritura* (Huesca: Pedro Blusón, 1627), 6v.
106. Ibid., 2v–3r.
107. Ibid., 226v.
108. María de Guevara, *Warnings to the Kings and Advice on Restoring Spain: A Bilingual Edition*, ed. and trans. Nieves Romero-Díaz (Chicago: University of Chicago Press, 2007), 71.
109. Sor Juana Inés de la Cruz, *The Answer/La Respuesta*, exp. ed., ed. and trans. Electa Arenal and Amanda Powell (New York: Feminist Press, 2009), 109.
110. Ibid., 53.
111. Juan Zapata y Sandoval, *Disceptación sobre justicia distributiva y sobre la acepción de personas a ella opuesta*, primera parte, ed. Arturo Ramírez Trejo and Paula López Cruz (Mexico: UNAM, 1994), 43.
112. Ibid., 49–50.
113. Juan Zapata y Sandoval, *Disceptación sobre justicia distributiva y sobre la acepción de personas a ella opuesta*, segunda parte, ed. Arturo Ramírez Trejo and Paula López Cruz (Mexico: UNAM, 1994), ci.
114. Jorge Cañizares-Esguerra, "Typology in the Atlantic World: Early Modern Readings of Colonization," in Bernard Bailyn and Patricia L. Denault, eds *Soundings in Atlantic History: Latent Structures and Intellectual Currents, 1500–1830* (Cambridge, MA: Harvard University Press, 2009), 259.

115. In Martin Lienhard, *Testimonios, cartas y manifiestos indígenas: desde la conquista hasta comienzos del siglo XX* (Caracas: Biblioteca Ayacucho, 1992), 242–254, here 242.
116. Jorge Cañizares-Esguerra, "Typology in the Atlantic World: Early Modern Readings of Colonization," in Bernard Bailyn and Patricia L. Denault, eds *Soundings in Atlantic History: Latent Structures and Intellectual Currents, 1500–1830* (Cambridge, MA: Harvard University Press, 2009), 262–263.
117. Anonymous, *Nouena al Abrahan de la Ley de Gracia* (Santa Fé: Compañía de Jesus, 1750). Anonymous, *Novena de nuestro padre San Elías* (Cartagena de Indias: Antonio Espinosa de los Monteros, 1774). Felipe Colombo, *El Iob de la ley de gracia* (Madrid: Imprenta Real, 1674), and Biblioteca Nacional de España. MS DIB.1426.
118. Biblioteca Nacional de España. MS DIB.1426.
119. See, for example, *Regla de N[uestro] P[adre] S[an] Agustín, águila de los doctores, luz de la iglesia. Manual y espejo espiritual de sus hijas, por la línea recta de nuestro gran Padre Santo Domingo, y herederas lejíitimas del espíritu de ambos santísimos patriarcas, místicos Abraham y Jacob; Job y Moyses; Rechab y Jonadab* (Granada: Imprenta Real, 1677); and Martin Carrillo, *Elogios de mugeres insignes del viejo testamento* (Huesca: Pedro Blusón, 1627). Although the topic is not explicitly broached, Erin Kathleen Rowe's *Saint and Nation: Santiago, Teresa of Avila, and Plural Identities in Early Modern Spain* (University Park: Pennsylvania University Press, 2011) demonstrates the importance that the Crown, city council, and cathedral chapters assigned to female saints like Saint Theresa as Jewish warriors, plausible co-patrons of Spain, along with St James, the Moor slayer.
120. Jorge Cañizares-Esguerra, "Typology in the Atlantic World: Early Modern Readings of Colonization," in Bernard Bailyn, Patricia L. Denault, eds *Soundings in Atlantic History: Latent Structures and Intellectual Currents, 1500–1830*, (Cambridge, MA: Harvard University Press, 2009), 255.
121. Timothy Matovina, *Theologies of Guadalupe: From the Era of Conquest to Pope Francis* (Oxford: Oxford University Press, 2018), 109; and Jorge Cañizares-Esguerra, "Typology in the Atlantic World: Early Modern Readings of Colonization," in Bernard Bailyn, Patricia L. Denault, eds *Soundings in Atlantic History: Latent Structures and Intellectual Currents, 1500–1830*, (Cambridge, MA: Harvard University Press, 2009), 256.
122. Timothy Matovina, *Theologies of Guadalupe: From the Era of Conquest to Pope Francis* (Oxford: Oxford University Press, 2018), 112, 204.
123. Juan Bautista Díaz Calvillo, *Sermón que en el aniversario solemne de gracias a María Santísima de los Remedios, celebrado en esta santa iglesia catedral el día 30 de octubre de 1811 por la victoria del Monte de las Cruces* (México: Imprenta de Arizpe, 1811).
124. Jaime Cuadriello, "Estudio preliminar," in Fray Francisco de Jesús María/Andrés López, *Cuaderno en que se explica la Novísima y Singularísima Imagen de la Virgen Santísima del Carmen, 1794 (edición facsimilar)*, con estudio preliminar de Jaime Cuadriello (Morelia: Museo de la Basílica de Guadalupe y Honorable Ayuntamiento de Morelia, 2009), 30.
125. Hipólito Sánchez Rangel de Fayas y Quiros, *Pastoral religioso-política-geográfica* (Lugo: Imprenta de Pujol, 1827), 6.
126. Ibid., 48.
127. See, for example, the important study on Miranda as an Enlightened, liberal cosmopolitan, straddling both Atlantic worlds: Karen Racine, *Francisco de Miranda: A Transatlantic Life in the Age of Revolution* (Wilmington: Scholarly Resources, 2003).

128. Irma Medina Mendoza, "El cabildo de Pardos en Nirgua: Siglos XVII y XVIII," *Anuario de Estudios Bolivarianos* 4 (1995): 95–120. Regarding popular support for the royalist cause in nearby areas, see Marcela Echeverri, "Popular Royalists, Empire, and Politics in Southwestern New Granada, 1809–1819," *Hispanic American Historical Review* 91 (2011): 237–269.

129. See, for example, Mariano Talavera, magister-deacon (*canónigo magistral*) of the cathedral of Bogotá, who in his December 25, 1824 and June 25, 1825 sermons, the latter responding to the victory at Ayacucho, organizes the life and actions of Bolívar around that of Simon Maccabeus and of specific passages: 1 Maccabeus 15: 33–34 and 1 Maccabeus 13: 6–9. Talavera, *Oración que en la festividad decretada por el Congreso de Colombia por los triunfos que en el Perú pronuncio el 24 de Junio de este año* (Bogotá: Imprenta de Espinosa, 1825); and *Oración que en las fiestas nacionales pronunció en la Iglesia Metropolitana de Bogotá el 25 de diciembre de 1824* (Bogotá: Imprenta de la República por Nicomedes Lora, 1825).

Bibliography

Bellester Rodríguez, Mateo. "La estirpe de Tubal: Relato bíblico e identidad nacional en España." *Historia y Política* 29 (January–June 2013): 219–246.

Cañizares-Esguerra, Jorge. "Typology in the Atlantic World: Early Modern Readings of Colonization." In Bernard Bailyn, Patricia L. Denault, eds *Soundings in Atlantic History: Latent Structures and Intellectual Currents, 1500–1830.* 237–264. Cambridge, MA: Harvard University Press, 2009.

Caudriello, Jaime. "Estudio preliminar." In *Cuaderno en que se explica la Novísima y Singularísima Imagen de la Virgen Santísima del Carmen, 1794*, ed. Fray Francisco de Jesús María/Andrés López *(edición facsimilar)* (Morelia: Museo de la Basílica de Guadalupe y Honorable Ayuntamiento de Morelia, 2009).

Domínguez-Matito, Franciso and Juan Antonio Berbel, eds. *La Biblia en teatro español.* Vigo: Editorial Academia del Hispanismo, 2012.

Hernández, Rosilie. "The Politics of Exemplarity: Biblical Women and the Education of the Spanish Lady in Martín Carrillo, Sebastián de Herrera Barnuevo, and María de Guevara." In *Women's Literacy in Early Modern Spain and the New World*, edited by Anne J. Cruz and Rosilie Hernández, 225–242. Farnham: Ashgate, 2011.

Jon Juaristi, *El reino del ocaso: España como sueño ancestral.* Madrid: Espasa Calpe, 2004.

Kagan, Richard L. "Clio and the Crown." In *Spain, Europe and the Atlantic: Essays in Honour of John H. Elliott.* edited by Richard L. Kagan and Geoffrey Parker, 73–100. Cambridge: Cambridge University Press, 2002 [1995].

Lara, Jaime. "Feathered Psalms: Old World Forms in a New World Garb." In *Psalms in Community: Jewish and Christian Textual, Liturgical, and Artistic Traditions*, ed. Harold W. Attridge and Margot Elsbeth Fassler, 293–312. Leiden and Boston: Brill, 2004.

Leddy Phelan, John. *The Millennial Kingdom of the Franciscans in the New World.* Berkeley: University of California Press, 1979.

Machuca, Bernardo de Vargas. *Defending the Conquest: Bernardo de Vargas Machuca's Defense and Discourse of the Western Conquests.* Edited by Kris Lane. Translated by Timothy F. Johnson. University Park: Pennsylvania State University, 2010.

Matovina, Timothy. *Theologies of Guadalupe: From the Era of Conquest to Pope Francis.* Oxford: Oxford University Press, 2018.
Navarro-Durán, Rosa, ed. *El Siglo de Oro.* Volume 2 of *La Biblia en la literatura española,* Gregorio del Olmo Lete, general editor. Madrid: Editorial Trotta, 2008.
O'Reilly, Terence. *The Bible in the Literary Imagination of the Spanish Golden Age. Images and Texts from Columbus to Velázquez.* Philadelphia: Saint Joseph's University Press, 2010.
Rincón Álvarez, Manuel. *Claves para comprender el Monasterio de San Lorenzo de el Escorial.* Salamanca: Ediciones Universidad de Salamanca, 2007.
Romm, James. "Biblical History and the Americas: The Legend of Solomon's Ophir, 1492–1591." In *The Jews and the Expansion of Europe to the West, 1450–1800,* edited by Bernardini Paolo and Fiering Norman, 27–46. New York: Berghahn Books, 2001.
Sparks, Garry. Ed. and trans., with Frauke Sachse and Sergio Romero. *The Americas' First Theologies: Early Sources of Post-Contact Indigenous Religion.* Oxford: Oxford University Press, 2017.
Tanner, Marie. *The Last Descendant of Aeneas: The Hapsburgs and the Mythic Image of the Emperor.* New Haven: Yale University Press, 1993.

CHAPTER 12

THE BIBLE AND THE DUTCH EMPIRE

JANNEKE STEGEMAN

The Bible and the Dutch Empire

In the Dutch Republic, religious, national and legal identity developed in interaction. The revolt of the Eighty Years war (or Dutch Revolt, 1568–1648) was a catalyst for the development a Dutch empire. The Reformation stimulated the struggle for independence, and helped shape Dutch national identity:[1] in 1618 Reformed theologians from all over Europe met in Dordt to resolve a theological conflict.[2] At the Synod, Reformed Christianity became the Dutch state religion and slavery and colonialism were debated from a theological point of view.

Religion and empire were the constitutive forces of nation building, economic expansion, and identity formation in the early modern era in Europe in general.[3] In the Dutch context, the Eighty Years' War for Dutch independence began with an uprising against the Spanish ruler that was led by the prince of Orange. Prince William succeeded in uniting the seven Dutch provinces in support for the uprising.[4] The war was fought out on sea and on land, including in and around Spanish colonial possessions. Ships containing enslaved people were captured, as well as Spanish and Portuguese[5] colonial possessions. The Dutch declared their independence over their Catholic Spanish rulers in 1581 and formed the Dutch Republic. In 1583, the Reformed religion was proclaimed as the only permitted religion.[6] The Republic soon became a colonial power and the Dutch began to participate in the trade in enslaved people and in setting up plantations. The period between 1590–1670 became known as the "Golden Age," the height of the Dutch Empire.

Early modern Europe's worldview was based on Scripture. Early Protestant exegesis moved away from symbolic and allegoric readings to more literal interpretations. The Hebrew Bible in particular "provided a vivid template for the explorations and conquests of the great European Age of Discovery."[7] The biblical narratives offered both spiritual guidance and "geoeschatology,"[8] as colonial projects led to questions of orientation in time and space. The way the Bible was read and understood transformed too: colonial encounters challenged the existing Bible-based world view. Scriptural authority was questioned also as a result of upcoming biblical philology in the second half of the seventeenth century.[9] Colonial nations had to redefine their own place in an "expanding" world and adapt their worldview to accommodate newly "discovered" peoples and continents. Western Christian worldviews, hermeneutical and dogmatic concepts, practices and self-understanding were transformed through the colonial experience. Concepts and practices were also redefined by their appropriation by the subjects of Dutch colonial rule and through translation of the Bible into non-European languages.[10]

Scripture was foundational for the Dutch Empire's cultural archive specifically. The Republic as a Calvinist nation positioned itself within the biblical narrative and colonial experiences too were understood within this framework. For instance, the Dutch colony of New Netherland was described as a land of milk and honey, using a biblical metaphor for the Promised Land.[11] Dutch national identity developed in interaction with unfolding Dutch colonialism, even if Holland and Zeeland were the two provinces the most involved in maritime and colonial activity. Strategies to exploit, control and categorize the colonized produced racialized identities that also shaped Dutch self-understanding.

A paradox has often been pointed out: the Dutch prided themselves in their hard-fought freedom, their tolerance and the "Dutch Republic's avowed commitment to the principle of liberty."[12] Slavery was forbidden on Dutch soil.[13] Nevertheless, the Dutch dominated, enslaved and violated hundreds of thousands of people in colonial contexts.[14] The propaganda of the revolt vilified Catholic Spaniards as evil, lazy and addicted to luxury, forcing enslaved people to do their work, while by contrast Calvinist were depicted as sober, hardworking and modest. The Dutch contested Catholic colonial claims and expressed doubts about colonial practices of war and enslavement, or even strongly denounced these, again pressed by their anti-Spain ideology. William of Orange for instance wrote that the Spaniards committed "horrible excesses" against the "Indians"[15] and regarded enslavement as "papist."[16] Shareholders of the VOC worried it was morally wrong for Christians to wage war.[17] However, initial abstention from slave trade (of the WIC) changed when the WIC controlled parts of Brazil and labor became a bottleneck.[18] Ideology changed: theologians and philosophers increasingly began to defend colonialism and slavery.

The Dutch Empire: West India Company and East India Company

The Dutch Empire encompassed continents and centuries. It was an active power in the Atlantic and Indian Ocean for most of the seventeenth and eighteenth centuries.

The Dutch controlled the South East Asian slave trade for the main part of these two centuries and often controlled Atlantic slave trade. Dutch colonial enterprises West of the Cape were in the hands of the West India Company (*West Indische Compagnie*, WIC),[19] while the East India Company (Vereenigde Oostindische Compagnie, VOC) controlled colonies, trading posts and settlements on Mauritius, present-day Indonesia, on the Indian subcontinent and several other places in Southeast Asia. Also, it controlled the Dutch Cape Colony in present-day South Africa.[20] WIC and VOC were multinational corporations while also functioning as the international arm of the Dutch Republic: the cooperations possessed quasi-governmental powers.

In 1594, a Dutch fleet succeeded in breaking the Portuguese monopoly on spice trade in the East Indies by bringing back a small cargo of pepper from Bantam.[21] This is considered as the (violent) beginning of Dutch colonization in the East. In 1602, various competing East India companies were brought together in the Dutch East India Company.[22] It was the VOC's aim to expand its control and establish a monopoly through pressure, conquest and diplomacy. It fought natives and also other European empires in order to achieve this. Territorial expansion was rarely the intention. Batavia became the Dutch economic and administrative center in the region, acting as a sovereign of a vast number of (semi-) client states. The VOC used indigenous structures of governance and made alliances with local rulers.

In the Atlantic world, the Dutch was the first Protestant nation to develop an empire. Initially, the goal of the WIC was to inflict damage on the colonial resources of the Iberian enemy.[23] The Dutch attempted to break the Spanish and Portuguese monopoly on sugar. In 1613, the Dutch settled on the coast between the Orinoco and the Amazon. The Dutch West Indies Company was established in 1621, right after the end of the Twelve Years' Truce with Spain. During its first 30 years, WIC waged war against its Catholic enemy which resulted in territorial expansion. Trading posts were set up and the first Dutch plantation was established in the Americas in 1628. The WIC carried out triangular slave trade: carrying slaves, cash crops, and manufactured goods between West Africa, Caribbean, Surinam and American colonies, and the European colonial powers.[24] In 1674 the Company was dissolved, as it could not pay its debts. The New West India Company was established in 1675 in order to continue colonial endeavors and slave trade.

Existing Research

Scholarship on Dutch colonialism is in a defining stage of its development. Older generations of Dutch academics often studied Dutch colonialism from what was considered a neutral perspective, but reflected the generally positive and proud attitude of Dutch society towards the Dutch empire and the "Golden age."[25] In addition, while the Atlantic slave trade has at least been researched rather intensely, Indian Ocean slavery has been under researched and portrayed as "relatively 'benign' compared to its Atlantic plantation counterpart."[26]

Protestant and Catholic mission and colonial churches have been studied rather thoroughly, although mostly by scholars in theology and religious studies and not from a postcolonial perspective. Such works often do not escape what Porter calls a "tendency to hagiography or institutional piety."[27] In research on the Dutch empire, only recently scholars are beginning to study mission in the Dutch empire from a postcolonial/decolonial perspective.[28] Internationally, a postcolonial perspective is often more developed. Protestant mission is studied from a postcolonial perspective by for instance Kidd, Porter, Stanley and Gerbner. Stanley (1990) and Porter (2014) addressed Protestant mission within British imperialism.[29] Stanley criticized dismissive attitudes towards mission, as if Bible and imperialism always went hand in hand and addresses the ambiguities of mission. Missionaries are not just "faceless imperialist agent[s]" but actively influenced colonial policies as well as Christian practices and ideas. Missionaries sometimes attempted to "convert" colonialism,[30] while national and religious identities were transformed through colonial experiences. Porter investigated the interplay of mission and empire in their mutual dependencies. Colonized people transformed Christian practices and ideas and created their own Christianities. Porter criticized historians of imperial Britain for not taking religion into account. Kidd demonstrated how colonial appropriation of the Bible racialized the texts, uncovering the colonial encounters and anxieties that led to these reinterpretations.[31] Gerbner in her important book on Christian slavery compared Protestant practices of conversion in Atlantic colonialism, including Dutch colonialism, also indicating how the Dutch empire is connected to other Protestant Empires.[32]

Since the last decade, a more critical postcolonial perspective is surfacing in more mainstream Dutch scholarship.[33] In these approaches, the entanglement of churches and missionaries with the colonial state is studied, although a secular perspective is often still dominant.[34] The so-called "secular-religious divide" tends to obscure interactions of Dutch Calvinist churches and missionaries with the state and colonial rule. Theological thinking was crucial in the development of colonial hierarchies, racialization and "race" though. The connection between religion and race requires more attention in the Dutch context, as well as the intersections of class, race, religion and gender.

Lastly, overemphasis of the colonial paradigm silences indigenous agents and ignores how they "translated" the gospel.[35] Also in the case of the Dutch empire, resistance of the enslaved and indigenous and their reception of the Bible and of Christianity is hardly documented and researched. Colonized and enslaved people who embraced Christianity appropriated and transformed Christian worldviews and practices and forced colonial powers to reconsider the relationship between religion, freedom and slavery. Sometimes Bible and Christianity stimulated resistance and rebellion, for instance among the converted Africans who fought for their manumission, as described above. For some enslaved people, Christianity was a means to gain at least some agency.[36] Here I focus on the colonizers' use of the Bible, specifically, Dutch Reformed colonial use of the Bible.

Dutch Early Empire and Its Ideology

The Dutch did not create a legally and ideologically consistent system of colonialism and slavery.[37] In different Dutch colonies, different systems or customs developed, changing over time. The Dutch largely took over colonial territories that were in Catholic Iberian control, adapting aspects of the existing imperial systems and slave trade. Also, the majority of those enslaved by the WIC were acculturated in a Catholic Portuguese context.[38] Other aspects of the Dutch approach were unique for a Protestant nation, such as initial eagerness of the Dutch Reformed Church to evangelize and baptize among the enslaved.[39] A physical and psychological distance separated the Dutch from the overseas reality of slavery. In spite of colonialism, the Netherlands remained almost entirely white until the twentieth century. It was less acute to come to terms with colonialism in the metropolis.[40]

Initially, the States-General encouraged the VOC to trade with the East Indies in order to challenge to monopoly and power of its oppressor. Slave trade took place incidentally when ships of the enemy were captured. In 1596, a boat with 130 enslaved Africans probably captured from a Portuguese ship arrived in the port of Middelburg. The plan was probably to sell the enslaved on the local market, but protests from Middelburg's citizens prevented this.[41] In 1603, the East India Company captured a Portuguese ship in the Strait of Malacca thus challenging the Portuguese monopoly. A Dutch Admiralty Court condemned this. The East India Company asked the Dutch lawyer Hugo Grotius (1583–1645), one of Europe's prominent intellectuals, to legitimize the act. A modified version of Grotius's response was published in 1609 as Mare Liberum. This work dealt with the Republic's relationship to the Spanish monarchy and its right to commercial activities in South East Asia. Grotius argued that as the ship was captured in a "just war" the spills taken were legitimate. The Republic however was not at war with African people. Grotius had to defend that this battle indeed was a war, and, again, also that this war between two Christian nations was just.[42] Grotius's solution was that the many "just wars" within Africa legitimized enslavement.

Following natural law tradition, Grotius condoned the institution of slavery "within natural limits," such as humane treatment, moderate punishment, and the provision of proper nourishment and other necessities of life.[43] It was better to enslave "prisoners of war" than to kill them, he argued. International law justified enslavement, especially of "barbarians and savages."[44] Slavery was not for everyone though; it was understood as not part of the natural order, but a consequence of original sin.[45] In the late medieval time enslavement of Christians was a taboo—a perspective Grotius holds on to. Grotius's political theory is based on a hierarchical social system. Although indigenous peoples were in theory free and sui juris (legally competent), in practice they could easily loose this freedom.[46]

In spite of their initial hesitation, both in East and West Dutch colonial powers soon became convinced enslavement was necessary to make colonies profitable.

In Asia, already in 1615 authorities argued that enslaved people were indispensable to the Company for the construction of fortifications and other activities involving heavy physical labor under tropical conditions.[47] Indian Ocean slavery was multi-ethnic in character.[48] Enslavement and slave trade found wide acceptance among self-righteous religious, military, and civil officials of the Dutch East India Company. Private and Company slaves served as general laborers and were used in a wide variety of occupations in the Dutch settlements across the Indian Ocean Basin. The trade in enslaved people in South East Asia too was urban-cantered: enslaved people worked mainly in households. In the Cape Colony, Jan van Riebeeck decided in 1658 on the basis of his knowledge of the company's experiences in Batavia and Ceylon that the introduction of enslaved people would be the most efficient answer to the colony's labor needs. Here, most of the enslaved worked in agricultural production.

In Dutch Brazil, labor was a bottleneck, also because the Dutch did not enslave indigenous people.[49] The first decision of the directors of the WIC to ship enslaved people from the African coast to Dutch Brazil was taken in 1635.[50] In 1637 Elmina, the most important Portuguese slave port on the African coast, was captured.[51] Brazil became the center of Dutch slave operations in the Americas and the colony became a model for how to deal with enslaved people.[52]

Theologians Debating Slavery

Most theologians remained silent on the issues of slavery and colonialism. Initially, a number of Dutch theologians criticized or even outright rejected slavery. Others contributed to the theological defense of enslavement and colonialism that became part of the ideology of the Dutch empire. They relied on the Bible, and also on classical and legal sources such as Grotius.[53] They sometimes wrote on the instigation of WIC and VOC as for the companies too theological legitimization mattered.

The European theologians meeting at Dordt in 1618 also debated current issues, including mission and slave trade. Some delegates spoke out against slavery. Hommius, one of the contra-Remonstrants, argued that slavery was a form of theft to be punished by the government: God had ordained that "whoever steals a man, whether he sells him or is found in possession of him, shall be put to death." Hommius based this on Exodus 21:16.[54] He specified that the term theft of humans included the abduction of free people and sale of slaves, "thus depriving them of their most precious possession, which is freedom." Nevertheless, Hommius held the common opinion of his day that slave trade was allowed under certain circumstances.[55] Under the right conditions, enslavement was a life-saving act of Christian compassion. Hommius thus already allowed space for the later "solution" of Christian slavery that is discussed next.

Probably informed by Hommius's views, the classes of Walcheren and Amsterdam, the Reformed classes most involved in Dutch colonialism, wrote to the WIC in response to its request for advice in 1628 that it was not a Christian practice to have "lyffeygene."[56] Slavery, they argued, was "unedifying and not permitted among the Christians in the Indies." The classes did wonder if international law allowed for exceptions, for instance in the case of prisoners of war. The church council of Batavia led by Justus Heurnius who served as a minister in the East Indies responded. It stated that "as it seems natural for our nation to aspire to golden freedom," Asians have a different nature: because of their "servile character," freedom and self-government would be worse for them than slavery.[57] In addition, the enslaved were thought to convert to Islam if they were emancipated.

Around 1640 slavery and slave trade had become an established practice in the Dutch empire. The majority of theologians accepted slavery, although most remained silent on issues of colonialism and slavery. A factor may have been that because of the "physical and psychological separation," there was hardly any need to come to terms with colonial slavery for the majority of Dutch people.[58] In a sense, the discussion on slavery remained a theoretical discussion. Nevertheless, a number of theologians continued to debate enslavement and slave trade in the course of the seventeenth and eighteenth centuries, some mainly more orthodox voices continued to criticize (the excesses of) enslavement.

Foundational for Dutch Protestant ideology of slavery became the work *The Spiritual Rudder of the Merchant Ship*[59] written by Udemans. He expressed his views on the Eighty Year's War, colonialism, colonial war and slavery on the request of VOC and WIC. The ultimate goal of any trade from him was the expansion of the Kingdom of God. In the eyes of Udemans, it was not by coincidence that Dutch colonial expansion and the Reformation coincided: the time had come to preach the gospel in the entire world.[60]

Udemans based his ideas on the Bible, on Grotius and on theologians like Augustine. The concept of just war was important in his thinking on colonialism: peaceful strategies to end conflict had to be explored first, Udemans wrote, as is for instance commanded in Deuteronomy 20.[61] The war had to be initiated by the government, as the government received the sword from God (Romans 13: 1–4). The concept of just war also creates opportunity for enslavement: "heathens and Turks" can be enslaved, "if captured in a just war."[62]

However, Udemans seems to wrestle with slavery, "it is somewhat allowed and somewhat not."[63] One reason seems to be that the Bible is not clear on the issue: some texts seem to accept (certain forms of) slavery, others do not. As man is created in the image of God, both spiritual and physical slavery are not natural in the eyes on Udemans.[64] All who are born Christian, are born free, Udemans asserted. Although "our saviour Jesus Christ only freed us from spiritual slavery," and spiritual freedom is of higher value than physical slaver,[65] for Christians physical freedom is a great treasure. In freedom one can "better serve God."[66] Christians could therefore not be enslaved or sold. This freedom ("like our free Dutchmen") was out of grace, since all people deserve enslavement as a consequence of sin (John 8: 34, Romans 6: 16, and 2 Peter 2:19).

Enslaved people have to be treated in a Christian manner, which first of all means that their souls have to be taken care of. The enslaved cannot be "brought into a more miserable state, either physically or spiritually, than they were in before: because that is in conflict with love and justice"—Udemans based this on the Golden Rule in Matthew 7:12. "Loyal slaves, especially those who become pious Christians" have to be emancipated after a certain time, "so that they will not become discouraged."[67]

Udemans mentioned the curses that befell Ham and his son Canaan, as well as the Gibeonites whom Joshua curses when they had betrayed the Israelites. "Indians, Egyptians, Moors etc." come from "the lineage of Ham, like the Jews are from the lineage of Shem, and we are from the lineage of Japheth."[68] Udemans also remarked that "the son shall not suffer for the iniquity of the father" (Ezekiel 18:20), suggesting that enslavement is not simply the inherited curse of the descendants of Ham. God sometimes allowed slavery to humiliate and teach "his own people and his dearest children," like God did with Joseph and "the children of Israel in Egypt":[69] for Udemans, slavery is not the fate of a certain group of people. He does not categorize "Indians" and "Moors" as essentially different from European Christians. As far as they are different, it is because they are heathens, and therefore "estranged from the citizenship of Israel, the testaments of promises and without hope."[70] Udemans reminds his readers that "we were heathens" too.[71] In Udemans's reading, the Bible does not prove Christian and/or Dutch superiority. Rather, the "heathen" represents what "people are by nature without the knowledge of Christ." Udemans stressed that all humanity was created out of one man (Acts 17: 26).[72]

Most theologians who criticize the cruelties of enslavement allow for an idealized form of slavery, as we see below in the discussions at Dordt and in the work of Grotius and Udemans. A radical Reformed Biblicist attitude sometimes functioned as an antidote against this Reformed concept of slavery as a Christian task under utopian circumstances though. We see this in a heated controversy that took place a few decades after Dordt between followers of Voetius (Voetians; such as Hondius, De Raad, and Smytegelt) and Cocceius (Cocceians) about freedom of the will.[73, 74] The orthodox Voetians rejected the "theft of humans." They based this on their understanding of biblical texts like Exodus 20:15 ("thou shalt not steal") and Exodus 21: 16 and emphasized the natural equality of humans. Cocceius interpreted the Exodus text differently based on the Mishna: he argued it only applied to kidnapping among the Israelites.[75]

Jacobus Hondius and Georgius de Raad, both followers of Voetius and ministers in the second half of the seventeenth century in cities important for slave trade both underlined that enslaved people are created after God's image too. Hondius included slavery in his list of sins of his age.[76] De Raad discussed whether it is allowed to sell an enslaved to a catholic, an important question at the time. [77] His answer was negative: the Pope is the Antichrist. Risking people's souls by bringing them closer to Catholicism, is a grave sin. De Raad also considered enslavement—provided that the enslaved were captured in a "just war" and are to receive Christian education—a good thing, as it presents the "heathen" with a chance to convert to the true Reformed religion. De Raad, however, doubted whether the merchants give "highest consideration" to the soul, as they should. [78] He seems to suggest such "beneficial" enslavement is impossible in practice.[79]

Smytegelt, an orthodox Reformed minister who preached in Middelburg (1665–1739), criticized slavery in a sermon on the eighth commandment "thou shalt not steal": "Isn't that sad: the Christians made a business out of that. O! May those people, who are transported and often killed, once speak; wouldn't they say like Joseph did once; 'I was thievishly stolen from my land.'" Smytegelt, too, based his rejection of slavery on Exodus 21: 16: "*die eenen mensche steelt, zeid God, zal zeekerlyk gedood worden.*"[80] Like Udemans and in good Reformed fashion, Smytegelt underlined the sorry and sinful state of all humankind: "'man is a miserable subject [. . .] not only those who live far away in Indie, the barbarians, we should [also] think about ourselves."[81]

An example of a non-Voetian theologian criticizing slave trade is minister Johannes de Mey, who witnessed slave trade on St. Eustatius and in the East. Like De Raad, he counters arguments of slave traders who claim it is better to sell a heathen enslaved person to a "Papists," so that they would at least gain some knowledge of Christianity. De Mey too stressed that "all humans share the same nature."[82]

Both proponents and opponents of slavery and colonialism based their views on the Bible. Exodus 20 and 21, for instance, are used by both. It is not a coincidence that orthodox Calvinists more often criticized or rejected slavery and slave trade. Their orthodox focus on the sinful state of humankind prevented these theologians from idealizing European Christians and elevating them above "heathens." In addition, as we will see below, biblical authority was at stake.

Three concepts based on scriptural argumentation that we already encountered in the work of Udemans need to be discussed: Calvinist Dutch exceptionalism or election (that implies replacement and racialization of the Jews); the idea that a specific sin brought the curse or punishment of slavery upon certain groups of people; and lastly the concept of Christian freedom and what it entailed. Being Dutch and being Christian were both strongly associated with freedom. Yet the church had to express what this implied in a colonial context. In the work of Udemans we already see how this could lead to tensions: Christians ought to be physically free, and enslaved people ought to be taught the gospel. I discuss these concepts next, beginning with how baptism functioned to create Protestant exceptionalism.

Baptism and Other Colonial Dilemmas

Baptism was a central concern in the discussions about slavery and colonialism. In the Catholic colonial world, in theory, every enslaved person had to be baptized first. Baptism superficially included the enslaved into the Christian community.[83] Those who were baptized, however, rarely received education about Christianity.[84] While Catholicism aimed for (superficial) inclusion through baptism in colonial contexts, Protestants made baptism exclusive.[85] In the Reformed colonial world, baptism had always provided "a structure for creating difference and partitioning the Christian from the infidel." It now functioned to construct that partition in different ways. Reformed baptism was a religious signifier that also provided a legal identity: baptism into the Reformed church had important civic consequences, such as the right to marry and inheritance rights.[86] As a result, baptism and civic rights were associated. It finally resulted in a theology of race in which "Christian and infidel identity were engendered less by sacraments than by genealogy and biological kinship." Conversion never became entirely impossible, but it was increasingly seen as an anomaly. The first step, however, was the development of Protestant supremacy that constricted the Dutch Reformed Christian community.[87] The synod of Dordt and its conversations on baptism were crucial in this development.

Initially, access to Protestantism was not policed strictly in Dutch colonial contexts. When the Dutch arrived in colonial spaces, they often found existing communities that included segregated enslaved and free black and brown Catholic Christians[88] or brought in enslaved people who had been baptized catholic. Initially, the Dutch attempted to convert them.[89] The expectation was that Christianity could be a "useful tool to foster slave loyalty."[90] But soon conversions and baptisms in colonial contexts led to dilemmas. Such dilemmas occupied all colonial Reformed churches, not only the Dutch, during the seventeenth and eighteenth centuries.[91]

At Dordt, the doctrine of election was connected to the necessity of mission, as the Canons of Dordt expressed a deep concern for salvation. It was debated whether or not Dutch Christian slave owners were responsible to evangelize their enslaved, and whether they could remain enslaved once converted and baptized. The direct occasion for this conversation at Dordt was a letter Rev. A. J. Hulsebos, minister at Jakarta, wrote in 1609 to the Amsterdam Classis, asking what was to be done with "household slaves" within Christian households, since in East Asia as well as in New Amsterdam and in other Dutch colonies local and enslaved people had been introduced to Catholicism under a century of catholic colonialism. Added was the question whether children, born of heathen parents who had become members of Christian households, ought to be baptized when the householder promised to bring the child up in the Christian faith.[92]

The Dordt delegates did not achieve full consensus on the issue, but the eighteen discrete opinions from church delegations were preserved in the document *De Ethnicorum Pueris Baptizandis*. Although these did not become part of the Canons of Dordt, they proved vitally important in the development of colonial policies. The biblical narrative in which Abraham is commanded to circumcise all males in his household, including those bought with money (Gen. 17:11–13), was understood as the central precedent: baptism was understood as the equivalent of circumcision.[93] Therefore, all children in a Reformed household, including the enslaved, had to be given access to baptism.[94] Baptism, which was "a clerical imperative for the Catholic church," became a "household imperative" at Dordt.[95] The synod agreed that baptism could not be forced onto children; children could only be baptized after proper catechetical instruction and confession of faith, and once baptized, they should be set free from slavery.[96] However, delegates from North Holland, South Holland, and Helvetia wanted to limit baptism to "ethnic"[97] children in the age of discretion, since "they were not born within the Covenant." For them, education had to precede baptism, so that "Christian genealogy became a requisite for infant baptism."[98] "Ethnics" were not regarded as infidels like Jews and Muslims, towards whom Europeans were hostile as they allegedly knew Christ but rejected him, but as adherents of primal religions.[99]

De Ethnicorum instigated further debates. According to the Genevan delegate Giovanni Deodatus, an enslaved person who was baptized "should enjoy equal right of liberty with all other Christians" and could not "be sold to another," because of the danger of apostasy. Unclear was whether Deodatus meant "another heathen" or "another person."[100] This question became a crucial issue: if he meant 'person,' the enslaved would no longer be transferable property and therefore no longer a slave in the sense of Roman law.[101] Apart from the lack of clarity, Dordt did associate Reformed baptism of an enslaved person with limitations on selling. This resulted in increasing opposition to conversion among planters.[102]

In the eyes of protestant Dutch slaveholders, the status of being enslaved and that of being Christian became less and less compatible. Colonial Protestants increasingly claimed Christianity for themselves, creating an exclusive ideal of religion based on ethnicity: Protestant identity was fundamental to their status as masters. The material interests of every slave-owner were central and the debate over Reformed baptism lost its theological context.[103] Baptism became a "primary symbol for civic incorporation or exclusion for slaves and people not of Christian descent."[104]

It is not always clear what the influence of *De Ethnicorum* on colonial practices was or when the Dordt deliberations reached the colonies. The first known reference to Dordt at the Cape is in 1664 when the council of Batavia and the governor-general mention Dordt and the "example of the Patriarch Abraham" in reference to "many disputes" about whether the children of unbelieving parents should be admitted to baptism.[105] The lack of clarity of *De Ethnicorum* led to a variety of interpretations and practices. In the Cape colony, WIC administrators baptized and sometimes educated the enslaved, following instructions from Batavia. Private slave owners, however, judged it safer to prevent their enslaved from being baptized so that they would remain marketable. This resulted in empty benches "reserved for slaves in the Groote Kerk in Cape Town" by the end of the eighteenth century.[106] Periodic reminders from Batavia and after 1731 from the Republic to baptize slaves were ignored.[107]

In New Netherland the WIC wanted to develop a settler colony. It therefore expanded its territory on Manhattan in the 1620s. Because of insufficient numbers of Dutch and other European immigrants, the WIC acquired enslaved laborers.[108] The enslaved, some of whom had been baptized Catholic, were often allowed to marry and have their children baptized in the Dutch Reformed Church. In the 1640s, eleven enslaved persons petitioned against the WIC for manumission on the basis of their baptism. The result in this case, and in several others, was a half-freedom, meaning that the enslaved were emancipated but their freedom was not hereditary, and their provisional freedom ended as soon as the WIC needed them.[109] Some slaves of individual owners were able to emancipate themselves. In the 1660s the situation had changed. Reverend Selyns,[110] the first minister of the Dutch Reformed Church in New Amsterdam, rejected demands from the Classis of Amsterdam to catechize the enslaved, because "blacks wanted nothing else than to deliver their children from bodily slavery, without striving for piety and Christian virtues."[111]

In Dutch Brazil (1630–1654) slavery was already an important element of society when it was captured by the Dutch. The initial goal of the Reformed Church was to usurp Catholicism and convert people of European descent as well as indigenous populations. Making the Americas truly Christian was initially seen as a divinely ordained task of Dutch Calvinists.[112] The classis of Recife expected their ministers not only to work among the Dutch, but also to evangelize among indigenous Americans, black people, and Portuguese.[113] In practice, this ideal was never realized, partially because of a shortage of ministers and the disinterest among the European population, but also because of changing attitudes toward the conversion and baptism of enslaved people. When the English conquered Dutch Brazil in 1654, the Dutch Reformed Church had to reconsider its destiny, and it lost its all-embracing spirit and became more strict.[114] By then, Reformed ministers had virtually ceased baptizing black people in Dutch Brazil.[115]

As church authorities increasingly began to doubt the practice of baptism of enslaved people, baptism became an exclusive sacrament. Some criticized this. Johannes van der Kemp, who went to the Cape colony as a missionary in 1797, wrote that the "pernicious laws of baptism" were at the root of the colony's problems. "There is an ardent desire among them to know the word of God, . . . but customs and rules of this country do not allow them to be baptized."[116] In 1770 the council of Batavia prohibited the transfer of the converted enslaved, and a British governor wrote that this "completely stopped the progress of the Christian religion" among the enslaved.[117] In the early nineteenth century, the missionary Joseph Kam had different reasons to oppose baptismal exclusivism in the Dutch Indies. He strategically baptized large numbers of children on the Moluccan island of Luang in order to stop the spread of Islam.[118] In 1733, the first law regulating manumission was issued in Surinam. Manumission now had to be previously approved by the Court. The enslaved had to be educated and brought up in the Christian religion.[119] In Suriname, the few black children who were baptized received the sacrament separately from white children. Baptized blacks, who were mostly emancipated enslaved or of mixed descent, had to sit in the back rows.[120]

By policing the access to baptism, colonial Reformed Christianity became an exclusive religion. Being Christian gave access to rights and privileges, and access to Christianity was gained through baptism. In the eyes of the Dutch, being Christian implied having access to the privileges of being European. Gerbner coined the term 'Protestant Supremacy,' as the predecessor of White Supremacy, to indicate the exclusive nature of Protestantism based on ethnicity.[121]

Some of black people—either enslaved with higher and more intimate positions or free—still received access to Christianity, thus implicitly undermining Protestant supremacy.[122] This necessitated a more elaborate theological justification and rationalization of enslavement that allowed for the enslaved to become Christian, but without that being a ground for emancipation. Slavery was increasingly defined in racial rather than in religious terms. The concept that emerged by the end of the seventeenth century in order to differentiate between European and colonized Christians and to rationalize the physical freedom of the former, was that of whiteness. 'White' was not a new category, it replaced and grew out of 'Christian' as an "indicator of freedom and mastery."[123]

Although white supremacy replaced Protestant supremacy, Protestantism continued to be conceptualized as an exclusive institution that was accessible for 'cultured people' only. [124] Cultural literacy and competence were other factors in play for determining racial membership.[125] People were categorized on the basis of their closeness to and remoteness from a normative European Christian identity. Race cannot be understood in separation from religion, class, education and geographic origin. Being Christian remained one of the factors determining one's place in society; other factors were class, race, and gender.[126]

In the WIC colonies where the European colonial population was stronger and the sex ratios more balanced, a more rigid line was drawn between black and white. In Asia, only higher-ranking VOC employees were permitted to bring their wives with them. Men in lower positions often married women of Portuguese-Asian descent or lived with concubines—such marriages and relations were at best tolerated but were nevertheless very common. A class-based society emerged, in which racial-ethnic boundaries were porous. Many intermediate categories existed between being enslaved and being free.[127]

The constructions of Protestant and white supremacy can be better understood against the background of biblical appropriation, specifically the narrative of Canaan's curse and Dutch Reformed identification with Israel.

THE DUTCH ISRAELITES

Dutch Protestants identified as the new Israel, or 'Neerlants Israel' (Israel of the Netherlands).[128] The identification with Israel was not exclusively Dutch, but was a shared characteristic of ethnic and national identities being shaped in Europe.[129] Supersessionist historiography was particularly strong among Protestants.[130] Protestants identified as 'the spiritual Israel' that was thought to supersede 'Israel in the flesh,' Judaism. This "spiritual Israel" became part of emerging national identities. The narrative not only of Dutch Calvinists, but also of the Dutch Republic as a whole was one of a miraculous victory of a Protestant, superior, chosen people over a mighty empire.[131] The Calvinist notion of election enforced this identification.[132] Connected to this was a 'siege mentality' that was carried into colonial contexts: the Dutch saw themselves as isolated and alone, heroically struggling against enemies overwhelming in numbers and power.[133]

The Reformed Church was described as "adopted as God's special people, like Israel at Sinai";[134] William of Orange was a new Moses; Spain the new Egypt.[135] Not only theologians made such comparisons: they became part of a political theology used by artist, professors, and regents alike. In 1580 Marnix van St. Aldegonde, a Calvinist

Humanist and secretary to William of Orange, published a translation of the Psalms that opens with a dedicatory poem to the states of Holland and Zeeland, in which he compared Dutch suffering under Spanish rule with that of the Israelites under Egypt and Babylon.[136] The later identification of the Dutch with Israel (Neerlants Israel) usually referred to the Dutch Reformed Church, but sometimes it included the Republic. The reference is mostly found in the works of orthodox ministers but is also used by their adversaries.

This supersessionist appropriation of biblical texts served as a model for colonial Christianity. Colonial racialization built on existing notions of Semitic otherness that placed Semites outside of Christian Europe. Europeans centered themselves as the chosen and the norm, a position from which they could categorize others, according to transcendental and comparable categories, to which eventually the concept of race became central.[137]

Calvinist interpretations of Scripture did not only claim the notion of chosen people. Geographical locations such as Zion and the (promised) land too were appropriated and decontextualized, detaching biblical texts from their particular geographies.[138] Colonial spaces were appropriated as part of Neerlants Israel, while local Dutch churches were named, for instance, het Dordtse Zion (Zion of Dordt)[139] and 'het Utrechtse Zion (Zion of Utrecht). A colonial example is a text above the door of the Reformed church of Elmina that reads:

> Zion is des Heeren ruste/ Dit is Syn woonplaetse in eeuwigheyt.
> (Zion is the resting place of the Lord/ This is his dwelling for ever)

It is taken from Psalm 132: 13–14, which reads:

> For the Lord hath chosen Zion; he hath desired it for his habitation.
> This is my rest for ever: here will I dwell[140]

In the Psalm, Zion is presented as a resting place chosen by God. The quote above the door in Elmina relocates Zion. In the adapted quote God does not choose a habitation, but the Dutch declare Elmina as a new dwelling for God. In this supersessionist framework the spatial context of the Psalm is lost, while Elmina is incorporated into the Dutch empire. In Dutch colonial hermeneutics, scripture becomes a device of claiming the colonial spaces.

Canaan's Curse

Colonial "discoveries" of new continents and civilizations challenged the "intellectual and theological coherence of Christianity and the credibility of the Bible."[141] Why was America not mentioned in the Bible? How was it peopled? Theological conceptualization on the basis of Genesis 9:20–27 played a crucial role in answering these questions. It became one of the most important narratives to explain that slavery was not part of the natural order but was of God's making. Initially, colonial 'others' were linked to either Shem or Ham of Japheth, like Udemans did. He contrasted the religious attitudes of the descendants of Noah's sons, but stressed that the son shall not suffer the iniquities of his father. Picardt began to distinguish between the descendants of Noah's sons on the basis of "physical" characteristics: he thought Europeans to be "more richly blessed in soul and body."[142] Ham and his descendants were now associated with black skin and seen as fundamentally different. After Ham's misconduct, enslavement became the natural state of "Canaanites, Philistines, Arabians, Egyptians [. . .] and all Moors of Africa. As they are incapable to live in freedom and govern themselves, enslavement and harsh treatment is beneficial to them," wrote Picardt.[143] He identified Europeans, "except for the Jews," as "Japheten," the offspring of the biblical Japheth.[144] Europe is "Japheths patrimonie en erfdeel" (Japheth's patrimony and share), gifted with the Christian faith and the knowledge of the only true God, as is visible in Europe's *"heylsame en well-gefondeerde wettten,"* in its many learned men, its artists, its pure spirit, its many heroes and its dominance over other parts of the world.[145] "In summa," writes Picardt, Europe is a queen over Africa, Asia and America."[146] Blackness came to be associated with degeneration and barbarity, whiteness with civilization and, of course, Christianity. In this line of thinking the Bible becomes the book of white European Christian superiority.

The Biblical narrative prescribed the unity of humans as descendants of Adam and Eve. As the concept of race developed, "races" were increasingly understood as fundamentally different to the point of challenging the biblical notion of monogenesis. As we saw, Voetius and like-minded more strict theologians underlined that all people are of the same nature. The suggestion of polygenesis of for instance the French theologian La Peyrère was met with severe criticism.[147] Voetius instigated censure against La Peyrère's book.[148] The works of La Peyrère instigated discussions among wider audiences and were a factor in the emergence of radical biblical criticism in the Republic.[149]

Christian Slavery: The Position of Missionaries

It was the conviction of the Reformed Church and Dutch nation that it was their God-given task to spread the gospel. Already in 1611, the *Sovrat ACB* was published in Malay to provide a basic understanding of Reformed Christianity for the indigenous in the East Indies.[150] Heurnius urged the VOC to promote Reformed Protestantism by building schools and supporting the translation of the Bible.[151] However, mission was mostly limited to the inhabitants of the Moluccas who had been influenced by Catholicism. The VOC also encouraged conversion in places where Dutch rule was shaky, hoping Christianity would stimulate docile attitudes. Mission among the Muslim population was avoided. The VOC and WIC, too, professed their task was to protect and spread the Reformed doctrine. In practice, however, the orthodox Calvinists were hardly active in mission. Since according to Dordt, the householder was primarily responsible for baptism, the role of clergy and missionaries became less important. The Dutch did not undertake mission in any serious and systematic manner until the nineteenth century. Important contributions to mission came from Herrnhutter and Catholic and missionaries, as in the eighteenth century they were admitted to the Dutch colonies.

While most theologians were removed from the realities of colonialism and enslavement, missionaries had a special position in the debates on slavery and conversion. They contributed to the reconciliation of Protestantism and its notions of civility and freedom with enslavement.[152] The competing interest of church, planters, VOC, and WIC were bridged by missionaries. Slaveholders were often outright hostile toward missionaries. In response, missionaries created the concept of Christian slavery: it was possible to be enslaved and Christian at the same time.

Colonial power was both weary about the emancipatory effects of conversion and hopeful about its potential to make the colonized easier to control. Missionaries emphasized the benefits of conversion: enslaved Christians would be more productive and docile.[153] They used "Christian humanitarian" arguments also found in the work of Udemans, for instance. Dutch company officials were eager to cast themselves as saviors, portraying the enslavement of Asians in Batavia and Ceylon as a "work of compassion."[154] This view became dominant in the eighteenth and nineteenth century as Dutch colonialism became increasingly paternalistic.

Of importance in the debate on the compatibility of Christianity and slavery was the voice of Jacobus Eliza Capitein, minister of Elmina from 1742–1747. Capitein, who was kidnapped as a child, was given as a present to Van Goch a WIC merchant living at Elmina around 1725. When he was around eleven, the family returned to The Hague in 1728. Jacobus was treated as a protégé and given support to study theology when he expressed a desire to return to Africa as a missionary. The classis Amsterdam then gave him permission to return to Elmina to serve the Dutch Reformed Church of Elmina, a position paid by the WIC. He became the first minister at Elmina with the explicit responsibility not only to take care of the religious well-being of the Dutch Reformed community, but also to convert Africans. Although Capitein's position is not unique—it is in harmony with many of his contemporaries and with Herrnhutter views—he gained fame in the Republic as a defender of Christian slavery of African descent. He was seen as the living proof of missionary success and its legitimacy.

Capitein published two works in which he discussed slavery: "De Vocatione Ethnicorum" (1742) and "Political-Theological Dissertation on Slavery, as Being Not in Conflict with Christian Freedom" (1742). Capitein counters those saying that Christians ought to free enslaved when they convert: there is nothing in the gospel that suggests slavery in itself is wrong, he argues, how could we otherwise understand the slave-master language used by Paul? Manumission was an option but not a Christian plight: Christian freedom is inner freedom, not physical.

In the eighteenth century, Herrnhutter mission reached the Dutch colonial world.[155] In 1735 Herrnhutters came to Surinam, in 1769 they received permission to baptize enslaved people.[156] For the white Reformed elite it was more acceptable that a society separate from their Reformed Church undertook mission: they did not want to go to church with enslaved black people.[157] It was hoped for that Herrnhutter mission would silence voices criticizing enslavement, although plantation owners still feared for rebellion. Although Herrnhutters opposed slavery in Surinam on moral grounds, based on Paul's command in Romans 13 to submit to authorities they did not consider slavery as illegitimate and taught the enslaved to resign to their fate.[158] The Herrnhutter mission society in Zeist stressed that the enslaved in Surinam had to be taught about Christianity from an early age, given their "stupidity."[159]

Criticism on Christian slavery was voiced for instance by Marten Douwe Teenstra who worked for the colonial government in Surinam. For Teenstra, Christianity and slavery were not compatible: the enslaved had to be emancipated and then Christianized. He criticized the hypocrisy of Catholic and Moravian missionaries in Curacao and Suriname for trading and holding enslaved people and for teaching the enslaved submission.[160]

CIVILIZATION AND DECOLONIZATION

In the (ongoing) process of Dutch decolonization, external forces played an important role. Within the Netherlands a fundamental revision of Dutch self-understanding or interpretation of key texts rarely took place. The role of Scripture did change. The Bible no longer functioned as a blueprint for understanding the world, but rather as an ethical guideline that provided practical advice on mission as well. In the end of eighteenth century individuals often from smaller Protestant denominations such as Remonstrants and Dutch Mennonites dominated the still very limited protest that again did not have much effect.[161] In 1797 the Mennonite minister Willem de Vos published a work against slavery. In the preface the publisher, the Mennonite minister Jan van Geuns, remarked that Noah did not curse Canaan and his descendants. Noah only predicted the fates of three different tribes.[162] Theologically, Van Geuns was far removed from orthodox Reformed arguments against slavery. His focus was on the "doctrine of Jesus" and its "pure and extensive love for humanity," not discriminating in "class, wealth, nation, religion, etc."[163]

Around 1840, the Protestant movement of the Reveil, a Calvinist response to the Enlightenment, arose. Most Reveil theologians did not reject slavery categorically, as the Bible seemed ambivalent about it. Isaac da Costa even described abolitionism as one of the dangers of his time. Some Reveil representatives like Groen van Prinsterer campaigned against enslavement because it resulted in such cruelty that it could not be tolerated. Mission to free people would be more effective, while Christian workers were expected to be more productive, he argued.

In this period, even defenders of slavery realized that in the end abolition could not be stopped. They focused on underlining perceived risks of abolition.[164] In the debates on abolition of slavery and later on decolonization, the Dutch identified as an enlightened and ethical Christian people. Dutch attitudes remained paternalistic and racist, and profit remained a powerful driving force. The call "come over and help us," taken from Acts 16:9, where a Macedonian man begs Paul for help, expressed Dutch self-understanding: the Dutch were, of course, Paul. The Macedonians were their colonial subjects, helpless, poor, lost, uneducated, and unsaved. Their needs are understood as spiritual in nature, to be met by Christianity and civilization.[165] A minority raised a more prophetic voice that, again, was not very influential. An example was the Reformed theologian and missionary Verkuyl.[166] Verkuyl referred to prophetic literature: prophets like Amos and Jeremiah would not have condoned the imbalances in Indonesia, or have praised the Dutch, saying "that we are the best colonial power in the world" but rather have "uttered their prophetic indignation."[167] Quoting the Bible seems (also) a rhetorical device here, in a genre in which scriptural argumentation is expected. The style of arguing is markedly different from the days of Udemans. Udemans wove a thread of Bible quotes through his arguments, while Verkuyl constructed a political argument, rarely referring to the Bible.

It is quite typical that in the Dutch context protests against slavery remained limited in scale, while for instance in the United Kingdom a large organized movement protested enslavement. The debates were dominated by paternalistic feelings of superiority and pragmatic arguments and external pressure rather than fundamental rejection were decisive in ending enslavement and the breakdown of colonialism.

When in 1814 the Netherlands signed an international agreement to end the slave trade, the practice was already in decline. The trade declined significantly in the end of the eighteenth century as a result of recession and war with Great Britain.[168] In 1791, the WIC was dissolved. Colonial endeavors and possessions came under state control and were framed in the patronizing terms of a paternal relationship. Slavery itself was abolished only in 1860 in Dutch colonies in the East and in the West in 1863 under English pressure. Abolishment was pushed not only by international pressure, but also by the notion that slavery was inefficient. Ending it might stimulate colonial agriculture and trade, it was thought.[169] After the abolition, the enslaved were forced to continue their plantation work on a contract basis and were released only in 1873. To replace them, the Dutch introduced the system of Asian indentured labor, recruiting people from then British India and Netherlands East Indies. In 1975 Surinam gained its independence. Asian indentured labor stopped in 1917.

In the end of the eighteenth and beginning of the nineteenth century, the Dutch Indies changed drastically. The colonies became isolated because of political turmoil in the Republic. After the demise of the VOC 1800, the areas that belonged to the VOC become the possession of the Dutch state. In 1816, the state colonized the Dutch Indies. In this so-called "ethical" phase[170] convictions of the responsibilities of the state and ideas on Christian superiority were interwoven. The Dutch Indies officially became a colony. In the eyes of the Dutch, their task was to civilize the "uncivilized" through Christianization and transfer of Western culture.[171]

Churches played a role of importance in the debate on decolonization. After the Second World War, the Dutch Reformed Church reflected on how to be present in society. A report of the Dutch Reformed church spoke of the calling of the church to remind the government of God's laws.[172] Although the Dutch Reformed Church claimed it supported Indonesian independence, the Synod sided with the policy of the Dutch state. The missionary responsibilities of both church and state were used as arguments against decolonization. Indonesia declared its independence in 1945. The Dutch very violently attempted to restore their control. Indonesian independence was accepted only in 1949 under international pressure.[173] The Dutch government, however, refused to hand over West New Guinea to the Indonesian regime. The issue was framed in developmental language and support for Papuan self-determination.[174] In fact, the Dutch government was afraid to lose its colonial prestige and hoped to transform West New Guinea into a prosperous settler colony. Most Dutch missionaries were not happy with this, but few protested.

With respect to Surinam, too, Dutch attitudes were racially prejudiced and paternalistic: the Dutch colonizer was morally obliged to guarantee public order and stability.[175] Only the hard hand of Europeans could bring civilization and prosperity to the colony. Finally, in 1954 when the Charter for the Kingdom of the Netherlands was signed, the Netherlands, Surinam and the Netherlands Antilles became equal partners, at least on paper. In 1975, Surinam left the Kingdom of the Netherlands and became an independent state. One of the motivations of the Dutch was that they had begun fearing the consequences of continued colonial commitment.[176]

Toni Morrison wrote in *Beloved*: "Slavery broke the world in half, it broke it in every way. It broke Europe. It made them into something else, it made them slave masters, it made them crazy. You can't do that for hundreds of years and it not take a toll. They had to dehumanize, not just the slaved but themselves. They have had to reconstruct everything in order to make that system appear true." This complicated system in which religious, legal, ethnic, and racist notions are intertwined continues to influence Dutch realities, often in hidden ways. In spite of legal equality, in contemporary debates on integration and citizenship, the positions of Dutch citizens with colonial roots continue to be challenged. Racial, linguistic, religious, and historical notions are part of how Dutch citizenship is conceptualized.[177] "Genuine" Dutchness remains to be associated with Christianity and whiteness. Now that finally these discussions on Dutch colonial heritage and its continuing influence are gaining momentum, it is important to also include Bible and Christianity in the analyses. In order to deconstruct how notions rooted in the history of Dutch Christian identity continue to play a role in Dutch society today, it is necessary to pay attention to the role of the Bible.

Notes

1. William T. Cavanaugh, *The Myth of Religious Violence*, Oxford: Oxford University Press 2009.
2. The Synod of Dordt was held in 1618 and 1619 on the authority of the States-General of the Dutch Republic to resolve a conflict on the doctrine predestination that had arisen at Leiden's theological faculty in 1602. A second goal was to enforce the unity of the United Provinces in a crucial stage of the Eighty Years' War (1568–1648). The synod strongly influenced not only Dutch Reformed theology and religious life, but also contributed to Dutch cultural identity and its colonial ideology.
3. Linda Gregerson and Susan Juster, eds., *Empires of God: Religious Encounters in the Modern Atlantic* (Philadelphia: University of Pennsylvania Press, 2019), 4.
4. When in 1584 William was assassinated, power passed to Grand Pensionary Johan van Oldenbarnevelt and Prince Maurice, who took over military command. The seven northern provinces separated from the southern provinces that continued under Habsburg Spain until 1714.
5. Between 1580 and 1640 the Spanish and Portuguese dynasties were united.
6. Even though Calvinists were never a majority, they did dominate government and trade, given that such positions were reserved for those of the upper-middle class professing orthodox Calvinism.
7. Gregerson and Juster, *Empires of God*, 1.
8. Delno West coined the term 'geoeschatology'; see Carol Delaney, "Columbus Ultimate Goal: Jerusalem," *Comparative Studies in Society and History* 48, no. 2 (2006): 280.
9. For instance, critical editions of the Greek New Testament showed the instability of the text. As biblical studies were increasingly published in the vernacular, this sometimes led to public conflicts ('presses were running hot') for instance on the character of the Sabbath, the antiquity of the world and the origin of nations that eventually all had to do with the authority of Scripture. Dirk van Miert, *The Emancipation of Biblical Philology in the Dutch Republic, 1590–1670* (Oxford: Oxford University Press 2018), xvii, 220, 229.
10. Katharine Gerbner, "Theorizing Conversion: Christianity, Colonization, and Consciousness in the Early Modern Atlantic World," *History Compass* 13, no. 3 (2015): 143.
11. Jaap Jacobs, *New Netherland: A Dutch Colony in Seventeenth-Century America* (Leiden: Brill, 2005), 7.
12. Thelma Wills Foote, *Black and White Manhattan: The History of Racial Formation in Colonial New York City* (Oxford: Oxford University Press, 2004), 48.
13. Katherine Gerbner, *Christian Slavery: Conversion and Race in the Protestant Atlantic World* (Philadelphia: University of Pennsylvania Press, 2018), 22.
14. Rik van Welie, "Slave Trading and Slavery in the Dutch Colonial Empire: A Global Comparison," *NWIG, New West Indian Guide*, 82, no. 1/2 (2008): 49.
15. David Brion Davis, and Steven Mintz, eds., *The Boisterous Sea of Liberty: A Documentary History of America from Discovery through the Civil War* (Oxford: Oxford University Press, 1998), 39.
16. William of Orange wrote in his "Apologie" (1580) that the Spaniards killed 20 million Indians, as part of the propaganda of the revolt. This was initially used as an argument against slave trade. William declared that Spain "committed such horrible excesses that all the barbarities, cruelties and tyrannies ever perpetrated before are only games in comparison to what happened to the poor Indians." David, and Mintz, eds., *Boisterous Sea*, 39.

17. G. Edmond, "The Freedom of Histories: Reassessessing Grotius on the Sea," *Law Text Culture*, 2 (1995): 194–196.
18. Robin Blackburn, *The Making of New World Slavery: From the Baroque to the Modern, 1492–1800* (London: Verso, 1998), 193.
19. The WIC controlled settlements and trading posts on the coast of West Africa and West Central Africa, in North America, in the Caribbean and in South America.
20. Only in Java, Moluccas, Ceylon, Formosa the VOC became a territorial power. The VOC was also the only company in the world to trade with Japan after 1640.
21. After the Spanish and Portuguese closed their ports to Dutch ships in 1585 because of the Eighty Years War, the Dutch were depended on contraband colonial good, such as spices.
22. The VOC was given the right to build fortresses and wage defensive war by the States General. Subscriptions came from all over the Netherlands, and sometimes also from abroad.
23. Jacobs, *New Netherland*, 2.
24. The Dutch part in the Atlantic slave trade is estimated at 5-7 percent, or some 550,000-600,000 Africans.
25. Van Welie, "Slave Trading," 48. Van Welie points out that the VOC especially is admiringly remembered, while negative aspects of colonialism are mainly connected to WIC. He notes that "the historiography of Indian Ocean World slavery in general is still in an embryonic phase" (p. 50). Baay, too, points out that slavery in the East is often considered less relevant, or as "a fairly 'innocent' form of slavery"; (Reggie Baay, *Daar Werd wat Gruwelijks Verricht* (Amsterdam 2015) 13.
26. M. P. M. Vink, "'The World's Oldest Trade': Dutch Slavery and Slave Trade in the Indian Ocean in the Seventeenth Century," *Journal of World History*, 14, no. 2 (2003): 132, 134.
27. Andrew Porter, *Religion versus Empire?: British Protestant Missionaries and Overseas Expansion, 1700–1914* (Manchester: Manchester University Press 2014), 5.
28. See for instance the research of Iris Busschers on mission, religion, and empire.
29. Porter, *Religion versus Empire?*; Brian Stanley, *The Bible and the Flag: Protestant Missions and British Imperialism in the Nineteenth and Twentieth Centuries* (Trowbridge: Apollos, 1990).
30. Dana L. Robert, ed., *Converting Colonialism: Vision and Realities in Mission History*, 1706–1914 (Grand Rapids: Willem B. Eerdmans Publishing Company, 2008), 3.
31. Colin Kidd, *The Forging of Races: Race and Scripture in the Protestant Atlantic World, 1600–2000* (Cambridge: Cambridge University Press, 2006).
32. Gerbner, *Christian Slavery*.
33. Gloria Wekker, Philomena Essed, and Kwame Nimako are examples of (black) Dutch researchers who since have long voiced a critical postcolonial perspective but were largely ignored by mainstream academia. Numerous activists and/or researchers (sometimes outside of academia) also contributed to the process of dismantling a more Eurocentric colonial perspective on the history of the Dutch empire. Examples are Patricia D. Gomes and Jeffrey Pondaag.
34. Historians of Empire, not only in the Dutch context, were mostly interested in political, economic, and constitutional aspects. Porter, *Religion versus Empire?*
35. Sanneh in Robert, ed., Converting Colonialism, 4.
36. For instance, Sensbach describes the life and work of Rebecca Protten (1718–1780), a black free woman born on the island of St. Thomas whose mission it was to spread the gospel. John F. Sensbach, *Rebecca's Revival: Creating Black Christianity in the Atlantic World*

(Cambridge: Harvard University Press, 2005). Dutch and Danish planters responded with aggression to Rebecca's evangelization efforts, even though Rebecca and her husband, as Moravians, did not oppose slavery. They were persecuted and imprisoned. Rebecca's efforts led to a vibrant community of black Protestants on St Thomas.

37. Alan Watson, *Slave Law in the Americas* (Athens, US: University of Georgia Press, 1989), 39.
38. Jeroen Dewulf, "Emulating a Portuguese Model, the Slave Policy of the West India Company and the Dutch Reformed Church in Brazil (1630–1654) and New Netherland (1614–1664) in Comparative Perspective," *Journal of Early American History* 4 (2014): 9.
39. Jacobs, *New Netherland*, 314–317.
40. Van Welie, "Slave Trading," 50.
41. Van Welie, "Slave Trading," 49.
42. Knud Haakonssen, "Introduction," *The Free See, Natural Law and Enlightenment Classics*. Knud Haakonssen, ed. (Indianapolis 2004), xiii. Whether a war is just could be derived from two natural laws according to Grotius: that of self-defence and that of self-preservation.
43. Marcus P. M. Vink, "'A Work of Compassion?' Dutch Slavery and the Slave Trade in the Indian Ocean in the Seventeenth Century," The History Cooperative, accessed September 20, 2019, https://www.historycooperative.org/proceedings/seascapes/vink.html.
44. Gerbner, *Christian Slavery*, 22.
45. Europeans did not find it morally acceptable to enslave fellow Europeans. In the Americas under Spanish rule, indigenous people were deemed unsuitable for enslavement. According to Columbus the natives could be 'converted to our Holy Faith by love [better than] by force. Enslaved Africans were brought over instead. The Dutch too were hesitant to enslave indigenous peoples in the Americas: they were deemed fragile children who had to be protected against Spanish tyranny (Angelie Sens, *Mensaap, Heiden, Slaaf* (The Hague: SDU, 2001), 103, 104). Sometimes, native Americans were regarded as a lost tribe of Israel.
46. Elizabeth A. Sutton, *Capitalism and Cartography in the Dutch Golden Age* (Chicago: University of Chicago Press, 2015), 95, 96.
47. 'We cannot extract the necessary labor from our nation in these districts […]. I have already experienced, that one slave produces more work than two or more of our nation. If only I could get slaves, I would know how to employ them well in our service' (Vink, "A Work of Compassion?").
48. Enslaved Africans were brought in, and also Asians from different regions were enslaved, Van Welie, "Slave Trading," 68, 69. In spite of ethnic stereotyping (African enslaved were for instance considered best for hard work, Balinese for domestic work and as potential partners or concubines), the identity of the enslaved was never 'encapsulated in one clear racial qualification' (69). Van Welie points out that the documentation of Asian slave trade is incomplete and anecdotal (67).
49. Blackburn, *New World Slavery*, 195.
50. Van Welie, "Slave Trading," 58.
51. The Dutch operated from some 10 fortresses along the Gold Coast (now Ghana), from which slaves were shipped across the Atlantic.
52. Dewulf, "Emulating a Portuguese Model," 8. When Brazil was returned to Portugal in 1654, Curacao became the central depot of enslaved people of the WIC.
53. Vink, "A Work of Compassion?"; See also Van Ittersum, "The Long Goodbye: Hugo Grotius' Justification of Dutch Expansion Overseas, 1615–1645, *History of European Ideas* 36, 4 (2010): 386–411.

54. Hommius increased the number of biblical references forbidding the theft of humans. He added Deuteronomy 24:7 that forbids Israelites to enslave each other, and 1 Timothy 1:10 in which slave traders are mentioned as an example of sinners.
55. Vink, "'A Work of Compassion?"
56. G. J. Schutte, *Het Calvinistsch Nederland, Mythe en Werkelijkheid* (Hilversum: Verloren, 2000), 34.
57. Heurnius, in *De Legatione Evangelica (1618)*, cited in Vink, "A Work of Compassion?"
58. Van Welie, "Slave Trading," 50.
59. Godefridus Udemans, *'t Geestelyck Roer van 't Coopmans Schip*, Dordrecht: Françoys Boels, 1655.
60. Udemans, *'t Geestelyck Roer van 't Coopmans Schip*.
61. Udemans, *'t Geestelyck Roer van 't Coopmans Schip*, folia 550b.
62. Udemans, *'t Geestelyck Roer van 't Coopmans Schip*, folia 316b.
63. Udemans, *'t Geestelyck Roer van 't Coopmans Schip*, folia 316b.
64. Udemans, *'t Geestelyck Roer van 't Coopmans Schip*, folia 314a, b.
65. The conviction that Christian freedom is spiritual freedom in the first place is already found in the work of Calvin: one cannot appeal to Christian liberty for political revolution. Henk van den Belt, "Spiritual and Bodily Freedom," *Journal of Reformed Theology*, 9, no. 2 (2015): 151.
66. Udemans, *'t Geestelyck Roer*, folia 316a.
67. Udemans, *'t Geestelyck Roer*, 318a.
68. Udemans, *'t Geestelyck Roer*, folia 104a.
69. Udemans, *'t Geestelyck Roer*, folia 315a, b. Udemans added that this proves that in John 8:33 the Jews "lie impudently" by saying they have never been slaves: "the Old Testament proves that their forefathers were slaves many times."
70. Udemans, *'t Geestelyck Roer*, folia 102a.
71. Udemans refers to Efese 2: 12 ("remember that you were at that time separated from Christ, alienated from the commonwealth of Israel and strangers to the covenants of promise, having no hope and without God in the world").
72. Udemans, *'t Geestelyck Roer*, folia 115b.
73. Voetians wanted a larger role for church and religion in politics, while Cocceians were more accepting of the subordination of the church in the Dutch Republic and its colonies. It was also a debate on hermeneutics: Cocceians advocated a philological explanation of the Bible, while they regarded Voetian hermeneutics as based on systematic theology.
74. This was the heated controversy between orthodox and moderate Calvinists a few decades after Dordt centered on freedom. The orthodox group, so-called Voetians, wanted a larger role for religion in politics, whereas the opposing group of Cocceians was more accepting of the subordination of the church in the Dutch Republic and the overseas world. It was also a debate on hermeneutics.
75. The Misnna reads: 'whoever kills an Israelite, transgresses the negative precept: thou shalt not steal' (Laws on Theft 9:1). Cocceius's use of Mishna is indicative of the popularity of rabbinic sources in the Renaissance: Christian Hebraists like Cocceius attempted to understand Christian faith through the eyes of Jews. Yehonathan Elazar-DeMota, "Slavery Debates in the Seventeenth-Century Dutch Republic: Misinterpretations of the Torah?" Asser Institute, accessed January 8, 2020, https:www.asser.nl/global-city/news-and-events/slavery-debates-in-the-seventeenth-century-dutch-republic-misinterpretations-of-the-torah.

76. Jacobus Hondius, *Swart Register van duysent Sonden* (Amsterdam: Gerardus Borstius, 1679), 363–364.
77. Georgius de Raad, *Bedenckingen over den Guineeschen Slaef-Handel der Gereformeerde met de Papisten* (Vlissingen: Abraham van Laren, 1665), 157, 158.
78. de Raad, *Bedenckingen over den Guineeschen Slaef-Handel*, 126.
79. de Raad, *Bedenckingen over den Guineeschen Slaef-Handel*, 161, 168. ("It is impossible to do mercy through evil. Aren't we all Christians?")
80. Bernardus Smytegelt, *Des Christens Eenige Troost in Leven en Sterven* (The Hague: Ottho en Pieter van Tol, 1747), 636.
81. Smytegelt, *Des Christens Eenige Troost*, 17.
82. Johannes de Mey, *Alle de Neder-Duitsche Wercken* (Middelburg: Johannis Meertens, 1681), 305.
83. In the pre-colonial age, baptism through conversion was used to define and police the borders of Christian identity. For instance, converted Jews (conversos) and Muslims (moriscos) became Christians by force, but never became full members of Catholic Iberian society.
84. Robert C. H. Shell, "Religion, Civic Status and Slavery from Dordt to the Trek," *Kronos* 19 (1992): 28.
85. Gerbner, *Christian Slavery*, 26–28. Exclusion of black Africans from Protestantism was implicit. Concepts of power, race, and paternalism have deep roots in European history, but small-scale narratives still need to be written (151).
86. Shell, "Religion, Civic Status, and Slavery," 29.
87. Gerbner, *Christian Slavery*, 25–27.
88. Gerbner, *Christian Slavery*, 3.
89. Gerbner, *Christian Slavery*, 25. There were no plantages yet. The enslaved belonged to the WIC and were exploited to build the colony. They were allowed to own property and to marry, they could earn wages and sometimes claimed property rights.
90. Dewulf, "Emulating a Portuguese Model," 20.
91. Shell, "Religion, Civic Status, and Slavery," 30. In this period the religious and legal identity of the Netherlands took shape, Shell notes, as this synod defining the Dutch Reformed Church coincided with the dilemmas of colonialism and the struggle against catholic Iberian hegemony.
92. The scholars were asked to hurry up, since the VOC's outward-bound fleets were ready to sail and awaiting the answer. Shell, "Religion, Civic Status, and Slavery," 30–33.
93. Dewulf, "Emulating a Portuguese Model," 22.
94. The responsibility of Reformed clergy only extended to their own households. They had no evangelical duties. The clergy had the right to refuse baptism. The large majority of enslaved people in Dutch Brazil had already been baptized into Catholicism (Dewulf, "Emulating a Portuguese Model," 24).
95. Shell, "Religion, Civic Status, and Slavery, 31.
96. Gideon van der Watt, "Voetius," *In die Skriflig/In Luce Verbi* 53, no. 3 (2019): 3, https://doi.org/10.4102/ids.v53i3.2449
97. As Daniels points out, the term 'ethnic' (ethnicorum in Latin) was used in this period in contrast to Christianity as a true religion, referring to religions beyond Christianity, Judaism and Islam. David D. Daniels, "The Global South: The Synod of Dordt on Baptizing 'Ethnics,'" in *The Protestant Reformation and World Christianity: Global Perspectives*, ed. Dale T. Irvin (Grand Rapids: Willem B. Eerdmans Publishing Company, 2017), 99.

98. Daniels, "The Global South, 105.
99. Daniels, "The Global South, 98.
100. These rights are not specified, but probably included the rights to testify in court, enter into Christian matrimony, inherit, and have burial in a Christian graveyard. Shell, "Religion, Civic Status, and Slavery," 31, 32.
101. Shell, "Religion, Civic Status, and Slavery," 32.
102. Shell, "Religion, Civic Status, and Slavery," 33.
103. Gerbner, *Christian Slavery*, 29.
104. Shell, "Religion, Civic Status, and Slavery," 33.
105. Shell, "Religion, Civic Status, and Slavery, 39.
106. Shell, "Religion, Civic Status, and Slavery, 45. When sometimes private slave owners did allow baptism, the purpose was often to legitimize and enable the freedom of their offspring (38).
107. Shell, "Religion, Civic Status, and Slavery, 43.
108. Enslaved Africans came from captured ships or from other Dutch colonies in the West Indies. In 1652 the import of enslaved directly from Africa was allowed by the directors of the company. Company slaves were initially not sold to private owners. After the loss of Brazil to Portugal, Curacao became the company's entrepot of enslaved people.
109. Foote, *Black and White*, 39.
110. Sometimes spelled as 'Selijns,' 'Selwyns,' or 'Selwyn.'
111. Ira Berlin, "From Creole to African: Atlantic Creoles and the Origins of African-American Society in Mainland North America," in The Slavery Reader, Volume 1, ed. Gad J. Heumen and James Walvin (London: Routledge, 2003), 438.
112. Voetius is regarded as the first Protestant to develop a comprehensive theology of mission. Gideon van der Watt, "Voetius," *In die Skriflig—In Luce Verbi* 53(3): 2019. https://doi.org/10.4102/ids.v53i3.2449.
113. Dewulf, Emulating a Portuguese Model," 20.
114. Dewulf, "Emulating a Portuguese Model," 18–20.
115. Graham Russell Hodges, Slavery and Freedom in the Rural North: African Americans in Monmouth Country, 1665–1865 (Lanham: Rowman & Littlefield Publishers, 1997), 26.
116. Shell, "Religion, Civic Status, and Slavery," 49. Also, Le Boucq wrote that baptism was scandalously misused at the Cape: "ministers do not determine whether the fathers or mothers are Christian . . . simply baptize as the pope does . . . the third misuse is that baptized salves and their baptized children . . . are often sold and used in slavery which is against Christian liberty" (Shell, "Religion, Civic Status, and Slavery," 42).
117. Shell, "Religion, Civic Status, and Slavery," 50.
118. Sens, *Mensaap, Heiden*, 87. The stipulation that a baptized slave could not be sold also stimulated the spread of Islam in the Cape colony, as slave owners prevented Christian education. Conversion to Islam would distance them from emancipation (Shell, "Religion, Civic Status, and Slavery," 56).
119. Rosemary Brana-Shute, "The Manumission of Slaves in Suriname, 1760–1828," (PhD diss., University of Florida, 1985), 108.
120. Joop Vernooij, "Mapping Religious Surinam," *Exchange* 31, no. 3 (2002): 231.
121. Gerbner, *Christian Slavery*, 2.
122. Gerbner, *Christian Slavery*, 76, 80. For instance, children conceived by masters with enslaved women. Also, the most trusted enslaved were sometimes "privileged" with access to baptism. In rare cases, favored enslaved were manumitted.

123. Gerbner, *Christian Slavery*, 12.
124. Gerbner, *Christian Slavery*, 48.
125. Race, blackness, and whiteness were slippery and flexible concepts. Stoler points out that the porousness we assign to the contemporary concept of race may be fluidity fundamental to the concept itself and not a hallmark of our postmodern moment. (Ann Laura Stoler, *Carnal Knowledge and Imperial Power: Race and the Intimate in Colonial Rule* (Berkeley: University of California Press, 2010).
126. Stoler considers racism "an inherent product of the colonial encounter," but the character and intensity of racism varies widely among different times and locales. Stoler, *Carnal Knowledge and Imperial Power*.
127. Van Welie, "Slave Trading," 88.
128. Some historians do not share the view that Dutch Calvinists considered themselves as the inhabitants of a new Israel. See G. Groenhuis, "Calvinism and National Consciousness: The Dutch Republic as the New Israel," in *Britain and the Netherlands, Papers Delivered to the Seventh Anglo-Dutch Historical Conference*, Church and State Since the Reformation (Volume 7), ed. A. C. Duke and C. A. Tamse (The Hague: Springer, 1982).
129. See for instance Robert Smith, *More Desired than Our Owne Salvation, the Roots of Christian Zionism* (Oxford: Oxford University Press, 2013).
130. While medieval theologians tried to embrace many interpretations of biblical texts, theologians of the Reformation emphasized the literal, grammatical, and historical interpretation of texts. History became a lens for interpreting scripture. The Iberian empire understood itself as the new chosen people, elected to execute a Divine plan in which Jews played a crucial role. Columbus's ideal was to re-conquer Jerusalem and convert all peoples to the Christian faith—Jews did still play a figurant role in Christian eschatology. Many of his contemporaries embraced the same apocalyptic scenario (Delaney, "Columbus," 287).
131. Dunkelgrün points out that the Dutch Israel uniquely unifies the Dutch beyond Calvinist circles only. Theodor Dunkelgrün, "'Neerlands Israel': Political Theology, Christian Hebraism, Biblical Antiquarianism, and Historical Myth," *Myth in History, History in Myth*, ed. Laura Cruz and Willem Frijhoff (Leiden: Brill, 2009), 208.
132. See G. Groenhuis, *De Predikanten. De Sociale Positie van de Gereformeerde Predikanten in de Republiek der Verenigde Nederlanden voor ± 1700* (Groningen: Wolters-Noordhoff, 1977), 85.
133. Markus P. M. Vink, *Encounters on the Opposite Coast, The Dutch East India Company and the Nayaka State of Madurai in the Seventeenth Century European Expansion and Indigenous Response* (Leiden: Brill, 2016), 117.
134. C. Huisman, *Neerlands Israël, Het Natiebesef der Traditioneel-Gereformeerden in de Achttiende Eeuw* (Middelburg: Stichting de Gihonbron, 2006), 52.
135. See, for instance, a poem by the orthodox Calvinist Revius that celebrates the 1609 truce, Dunkelgrün, "Neerlands Israel," 202.
136. Dunkelgrün, "Neerlands Israel," 219. Marnix's mastery of Hebrew is indicative of the central position of the Hebrew Bible in Dutch Protestant national consciousness.
137. Geraldine Heng points out that for a long time, the Middle Ages were left out of the history of the concept of race, thus resulting in a focus on race as it was understood in the nineteenth century. However, race-making and racialization began with the racialization of Muslims and Jews. Geraldine Heng, *The Invention of Race in the European Middle Ages* (Cambridge: Cambridge University Press, 2018). See also Dennis Austin Britton,

Becoming Christian: Race, Reformation, and Early Modern English Romance (New York: Fordham University Press, 2014). Britton points at race as a category of identity in early modern Protestant understandings of salvation.
138. Westerduin uses the term 'supersessionist geographies' to refer to the process in which Christian identity became a transcendental category, disconnected from place. Matthea Westerduin, *Displacement and Loss in the Muslim Question. Re-membering the Making of Race, Religion, and Whiteness in Europe and Its Colonies* (PhD diss., VU University Amsterdam, forthcoming).
139. It is interesting that on a medal given by the States General to all participants of the Synod of Dordt, Dordt is identified as another Zion. Dunkelgrün, "Neerlands Israel," 213.
140. Translation: New King James Version.
141. Kidd, *The Forging of Races*, 12.
142. Johan Picardt, *Korte Beschrijving van Eenige Vergetene en Verborgene Antiquiteiten*, 1660, reprint (Leiden: Sidestone Press), 7.
143. Picardt, *Korte Beschrijving van Eenige Vergetene*, p. 9.
144. Picardt, *Korte Beschrijving van Eenige Vergetene*, p. 7.
145. Picardt, *Korte Beschrijving van Eenige Vergetene*, p. 8.
146. Picardt explained explains that the 'Japheten' were planted in the tents of the descendants of Shem, who were driven out after "crucifying their own Messias," thus fulfilling Genesis 9: 27. Picardt warned that dark clouds hung above Christianity and that God would punish them as he punished the Jews. Cham and his progeny were destined to be servants and slaves, Shem and his progeny would be cast away from the God's sanctuary, Japheth's children would not only be miraculously multiplied above the others and be blessed in many other respects, but they would also finally be gathered in the church and the community of God. European supremacy was proven in the "lamentable histories of black people and Jews," Picardt argued.
147. Isaac La Peyrère, *Praeadamitae* (Amsterdam: Lodewijk Elzevier and Daniel Elzevier, 1655). La Peyrère divided human history into four phases. The pre-Adamite phase was followed by three phases of sacred history.
148. La Peyrère challenged the authority of scripture also by claiming the Pentateuch could never have been written by Moses. To strict Protestants like Voetius, the Bible was the transcendent Word of God and (had to be) entirely unproblematic.
149. Erik Jorink, "'Horrible and Blasphemous.' Isaac de la Peyrère and the Emergence of Radical Biblical Criticism in the Dutch Republic," in *Nature and Scripture in the Abrahamic Religions: Up to 1700*, ed. Jitse M. van der Meer and Scott Mandelbrote (Leiden: Brill, 2008) 445, 446. Vossius, Descartes, and Spinoza were central figures in this process, in which the Republic played an important role. The humanist turn *ad fontes* enhanced the status of the Bible. Only in the nineteenth century the Bible lost its status as viable academic source. (Kidd, *The Forging of Races*, 56).
150. Yudha Thianto, *The Way to Heaven: Catechisms and Sermons in the Establishment of the Dutch Reformed Church in the Est Indies* (Eugene: Wipf & Stock, 2014), 13. The book included the Malay translation of the Ten Commandments, the Lord's Prayer, the Apostle's' Creed, and several standard prayers.
151. Donald F. Lach, and Edwin J. Van Kley, eds., *A Century of Advance*, Book One: Trade, Missions, Literature, Asia in the Making of Europe, Vol. 3 (Chicago: University of Chicago Press, 1993), 275.
152. Gerbner, *Christian Slavery*, 3.

153. "Conversion:" is a term to be "used with caution," as it suggests converts "abandoned one belief system for another." It also fixes our attention on missionary intentions rather than on the agency of Native Americans, Africans, and Asians choosing Christianity. Gerbner, *Christian Slavery*, 6–12, 7.
154. Vink, "A Work of Compassion?" Such ideas were also found in the Statutes of Batavia and in slave ordinances.
155. The Reformed Church considered Herrnhutters apostates and a threat to the true church and blocked their missionary attempts, for instance, in Ceylon and South Africa. Others defended them because of their impeccable and exemplary behavior. The Paramaribo mission encountered resistance from clergy and colonial officials too.
156. Sens, *Mensaap, Heiden*, 91. Only in 1786 were priests allowed in Surinam, and in 1817 a Catholic mission arrived in Surinam. On Curacao, Catholicism was regarded as Christianity for the enslaved: Catholicism was considered simpler and therefore more suitable for black people. In Surinam, the Catholic community grew mainly among Europeans, as missionaries were not allowed on plantations.
157. Susan Legêne, *De bagage van Blomhoff en Van Breugel, Japan, Java, Tripoli en Suriname in de Negentiende-Eeuwse Nederlandse Cultuur van het I mperialisme* (Amsterdam: Koninklijk Instituut voor de Tropen, 1998), 155.
158. Legêne, *De bagage*, 156. Paragraph 61 in the Herrnhutter mission instruction quotes Romans 13: 1–2. The verses apply to the missionaries who have to be obedient to the authorities, as well as to the enslaved taught by them.
159. "Berigten uit de Heidenwereld," Zendeling-Genootschap Zeist, 2 (1851), 2.
160. Marten Douwes Teenstra, *De Negerslaven in de Kolonie Suriname en De Uitbreiding van het Christendom onder de Heidensche Bevolking* (Dordrecht: H. Lagerweij, 1842), cited in Armando Lampe, *Mission or Submission? Moravian and Catholic Missionaries in the Dutch Caribbean During the 19th Century* (Göttingen: Vandenhoek & Ruprecht, 2001), 23.
161. Patricia D. Gomes, *Over 'Natuurgenoten' en 'Onwillige Honden': Beeldvorming als Instrument Voor Uitbuiting en Onderdrukking in Suriname 1842–1862* (Amsterdam: Uitgeverij Maklu, 2003), 60.
162. Legêne, *De Bagage*, 126, 127. Jan van Geuns, Preface to Philalethes Eleutherus [pseudonym of Willem de Vos], *Over den Slaaven-stand* (Amsterdam: Jan Van Geuns, 1797), xxvii.
163. Jan van Geuns, *Philalethes Eleutherus* 1797, VII. De Vos and Van Geuns pled to add an article against slavery in the first constitution of the Batatian Republic—in 1795, the Batavian Revolution ended the Republic of the Seven United Provinces. The 1798 constitution turned the United Provinces into a centralized nation-state. After 1806, the Netherlands became a Kingdom, although between 1810 and 1813 it was a French province. In 1816 the House of Orange was reinstalled.
164. Legêne, *De Bagage*, 120.
165. See for instance I. H. Enklaar, *Kom Over en Help Ons!* (The Hague: Boekencentrum, 1981), 5.
166. In the early twentieth century, groups that had separated from the Dutch Reformed church merged into the Reformed Churches in the Netherlands.
167. Johannes Verkuyl, *De Achtergrond van het Indonesisch Vraagstuk* (Den Haag: D. A. Daamen, 1946), 24.
168. Johannes Postma, *The Dutch in the Atlantic Slave Trade, 1600–1815* (Cambridge: Cambridge University Press, 2009), 284.

169. Sens, *Mensaap, Heiden*, 117-119.
170. In 1901, the Dutch queen Wilhelmina said in her annual speech from the throne that the Netherlands have a *zedelijke roeping* (a moral calling) toward the people in colonies. Other terms used were *eereschuld* (honorary debt) and *zedelijke verplichting* (moral plight).
171. The *cultuurstelsel*, a system of forced cultivation of cash crops, was implemented, primarily on Java. It was framed as beneficial to local farmers, but in practice it meant more oppression and exploitation. Some of the income the Dutch derived from the Indies was now used to 'elevate' the colonial subjects. An unintended consequence was that the educational program that was part of the plan stimulated Indonesian nationalism. The *cultuurstelsel* in the Dutch Indies was ended in 1870.
172. Hans van de Wal, *Een aanvechtbare en onzekere situatie. De Nederlandse Hervormde Kerk en Nieuw-Guinea 1949-1962* (Hilversum: Verloren, 2006), 52.
173. Today, the Dutch state still does not recognize 1945 as the year of Indonesia's independence.
174. Vincent Kuitenbrouwer, "Beyond the 'Trauma of Decolonisation': Dutch Cultural Diplomacy during the West New Guinea Question (1950-1962)," *The Journal of Imperial and Commonwealth History*, 44, no. 2 (2016): 322. Supposed "racial differences" between Papuans and Indonesians were used by the Dutch to enforce their claim.
175. Rosemarijn Hoefte, "The Last Convulsions of Colonialism: The Suriname Experiment in the 1930s," (Inaugural Lecture, University of Amsterdam, March 16, 2018, accessed February 14, 2019), 7, 8. [https://www.kitlv.nl/online-inaugural-lecture-oratie-rosemarijn-hoefte/]
176. Bob Moore, "Decolonization by Default: Suriname and the Dutch Retreat from Empire," *Journal of Imperial and Commonwealth History* 28, no. 3 (2000): 228.
177. See Willem Schinkel, "De Virtualisering van Burgerschap en de Paternalistische Staat," *Sociologie* 5, no. 1 (2009), and Charlotte Laarman, Oude Onbekenden: het Politieke en Publieke Debat over Postkoloniale Migranten, 1945-2005, Ph.D. Diss. Leiden University 2013, [http://hdl.handle.net/1887/21049]

Bibliography

Amponsah, David Kofi. "Christian Slavery, Colonialism, and Violence: The Life and Writings of an African Ex-Slave, 1717-1747." *Journal of Africana Religions* 1, no. 4 (2013): 431-457.

van den Belt, Henk. "Spiritual and Bodily Freedom." *Journal of Reformed Theology* 9, no. 2 (2015): 148-165.

Berlin, Ira. "From Creole to African: Atlantic Creoles and the Origins of African-American Society in Mainland North America." In *The Slavery Reader*, edited by Gad J. Heumen and James Walvin, 122-154. London: Routledge, 2003.

Blackburn, Robin. *The Making of New World Slavery: From the Baroque to the Modern, 1492-1800*. London: Verso, 1998.

Bijl, Paul. "Colonial Memory and forgetting in the Netherlands and Indonesia." *Journal of Genocide Research* 14, no. 3-4 (2012): 441-461.

Bloembergen, Marijke, and Remco Raben, "Wegen Naar het Nieuwe Indië 1890-1950." In *Het Koloniale Beschavingsoffensief: Wegen naar Het Nieuwe Indië 1890-1950*, edited by Marijke Bloembergen, and Remco Raben, 7-24. Leiden: KITLV Press, 2009.

Bosma, Ulbe, and Remco Raben, *Being Dutch in the Indies: A History of Creolisation and Empire, 1500–1920*. Athens, 2008.

Boxer, Charles Ralph. *The Dutch in Brazil, 1624–1654*, Oxford, 1973.

Brana-Shute, Rosemary. "The Manumission of Slaves in Suriname, 1760–1828." PhD diss., University of Florida, 1985. https://ufdc.ufl.edu/AA00047769/00001.

Britton, Dennis Austin. *Becoming Christian: Race, Reformation, and Early Modern English Romance*. New York: Fordham University Press, 2014.

Cavanaugh, William T. *The Myth of Religious Violence*. Oxford: Oxford University Press, 2009.

Daniels, David D. "The Global South: The Synod of Dordt on Baptizing 'Ethnics.'" In *The Protestant Reformation and World Christianity: Global Perspectives*, edited by Dale T. Irvin, 96–119. Grand Rapids: Willem B. Eerdmans Publishing Company, 2017.

Davis, David Brion, and Steven Mintz, eds. *The Boisterous Sea of Liberty: A Documentary History of America from Discovery through the Civil War*. New York; Oxford University Press, 1998.

Delaney, Carol. "Columbus Ultimate Goal: Jerusalem." In *Comparative Studies in Society and History*, 48, no. 2 (2006): 260–292.

Dewulf, Jeroen. "Emulating a Portuguese Model, the Slave Policy of the West India Company and the Dutch Reformed Church in Brazil (1630–1654) and New Netherland (1614–1664) in Comparative Perspective." *Journal of Early American History* 4 (2014): 3–36.

Draper, Andrew T. *A Theology of Race and Place: Liberation and Reconciliation in the Works of Jennings and Carter*. Eugene: Pickwick Publications, 2016.

Dubois, Laurent, and John D. Garrigus. *Slave Revolution in the Carribean, 1789–1804: A Brief History with Documents*. Bedfort: Palgrave Macmillian, 2006.

Dunkelgrün, Theodor. "'Neerlands Israel': Political Theology, Christian Hebraism, Biblical Antiquarianism and Historical Myth." In *Myth in History, History in Myth*, edited by Laura Cruz and Willem Frijhoff, 201–236. Leiden: Brill, 2009.

Edmond, G. "The Freedom of Histories: Reassessing Grotius on the Sea." In *Law Text Culture* 2 (1995): 179–217.

Elazar-DeMota, Yehonathan. "Slavery Debates in the Seventeenth-Century Dutch Republic: Misinterpretations of the Torah?" Asser Institute, accessed January 8, 2020, https://www.asser.nl/global-city/news-and-events/slavery-debates-in-the-seventeenth-century-dutch-republic-misinterpretations-of-the-torah/.

Enklaar, I. H. *Kom over en Help Ons!* The Hague: Boekencentrum, 1981.

Foote, Thelma Wills. *Black and White Manhattan: The History of Racial Formation in Colonial New York City*. Oxford: Oxford University Press, 2004.

Gerbner, Katherine. "Theorizing Conversion: Christianity, Colonization, and Consciousness in the Early Modern Atlantic World." *History Compass* 13, no. 3 (2015): 134–147.

Gerbner, Katherine. *Christian Slavery: Conversion and Race in the Protestant Atlantic World*. Philadelphia: University of Pennsylvania Press, 2018.

van Geuns, Jan. Preface to Philalethes Eleutherus [pseudonym of Willem de Vos], *Over den Slaaven-Stand*. Amsterdam: Jan van Geuns, 1797.

Gomes, Patricia D. *Over 'Natuurgenoten' en 'Onwillig Honden': Beeldvorming als Instrument voor Uitbuiting en Onderdrukking in Suriname 1842–1862*. Amsterdam: Uitgeverij Maklu, 2003.

Gouda, Frances. *Dutch Culture Overseas: Colonial Practice in the Netherlans Indies 1900–1942*, Jakarta, 2008.

Gregerson, Lydia, and Susan Juster, eds. *Empires of God: Religious Encounters in the Modern Atlantic*. Philadelphia: University of Pennsylvania Press, 2019.

Groenhuis, G. *De Predikanten. De Sociale Positie van de Gereformeerde Predikanten in de Republiek der Verenigde Nederlanden voor ± 1700*. Groningen: Wolters-Noordhoff, 1977.

Groenhuis, G. "Calvinism and National Consciousness: The Dutch Republic as the New Israel." In *Britain and the Netherlands, Papers Delivered to the Seventh Anglo-Dutch Historical Conference*, Church and State Since the Reformation (Volume 7), edited by A. C. Duke, and C. A. Tamse, 118–133. The Hague: Springer, 1982.

Haakonssen, Knud, ed. *The Free See, Natural Law and Enlightenment Classics*. Indianapolis, 2004.

Haefeli, Evan. *New Netherland and the Dutch Origins of American Religious Liberty*, Philadelphia, 2012.

Heng, Geraldine. *The Invention of Race in the European Middle Ages*. Cambridge: Cambridge University Press, 2018.

Hodges, Graham Russell. *Slavery and Freedom in the Rural North: African Americans in Monmouth Country, New Jersey, 1665–1865*. Lanham: Rowman & Littlefield Publishers, 1997.

Hoefte, Rosemarijn. "The Last Convulsions of Colonialism: The Suriname Experiment in the 1930s." Inaugural Lecture, University of Amsterdam, March 16, 2018. KITLV/Royal Netherlands Institute of Southeast Asian and Caribbean Studies, accessed February 14, 2019, https://www.kitlv.nl/online-inaugural-lecture-oratie-rosemarijn-hoefte/.

Hondius, Jacobus. *Swart Register Van Duysent Sonden*. Amsterdam: Gerardus Borstius, 1679.

Huisman, G. *Neerlands Israël: Het Natiebesef der Traditioneel-Gereformeerden in de Achttiende Eeuw*. Middelburg: Stichting de Gihonbron, 2006.

Israel, Jonathan Irvine. "The Intellectual Debate about Toleration in the Dutch Republic." *The Emergence of Tolerance in the Dutch Republic*, edited by Christiane Berkvens-Stevelinck, Jonathan Irvine Israel, and G.H.M. Posthumus Meyjes: Leiden: Brill, 1997.

Israel, Jonathan Irvine, and Stuart B. Schwartz. *The Expansion of Tolerance: Religion in Dutch Brazil (1624–1654)*. Amsterdam, 2007.

van Ittersum, Martine Julia. "The Long Goodbye: Hugo Grotius' Justification of Dutch Expansion Overseas, 1615–1645." *History of European Ideas* 36, 4 (2010): 386–411.

Jacobs, Jaap. *New Netherland: A Dutch Colony in Seventeenth-Century America*. Leiden: Brill, 2005.

Jongeneel, Jan A.B. *Nederlandse Zendingsgeschiedenis, Ontmoeting van Protestantse Christenen met Andere Godsdiensten en Geloven (1601–1917)*. Boekencentrum, 2015.

Joosse, Leendert Jan. *Geloof in de Nieuwe Wereld: Ontmoetingen met Afrikanen en Indianen (1600–1700)*, Kampen, 2008.

Jorink, Eric. "'Horrible and Blasphemous.' Isaac de la Peyrère and the Emergence of Radical Biblical Criticism in the Dutch Republic." In *Nature and Scripture in the Abrahamic Religions: Up to 1700*, edited by Jitse M. van der Meer and Scott Mandelbrote, 429–450. Leiden: Brill, 2008.

Kidd, Colin. *The Forging of Races: Race and Scripture in the Protestant Atlantic World, 1600–2000*. Cambridge: Cambridge University Press, 2006.

Kuitenbrouwer, Vincent. "Beyond the 'Trauma of Decolonisation': Dutch Cultural Diplomacy during the West New Guinea Question (1950–62)." *Journal of Imperial and Commonwealth History*, 44, no. 2 (2016): 306–327.

Charlotte Laarman, Oude Onbekenden: Het Politieke en Publieke Debat over Postkoloniale Migranten, 1945–2005, Ph.D. Diss. Leiden University, 2013 [http://hdl.handle.net/1887/21049].

Lach, Donald F., and Edwin J. Van Kley, eds. *A Century of Advance*, Book One: Trade, Missions, Literature, Asia in the Making of Europe Vol. 3. Chicago: the University of Chicago Press, 1993.

Lampe, Armando. *Mission or Submission? Moravian and Catholic Missionaries in the Dutch Caribbean During the 19th Century*. Göttingen: Vandenhoek & Ruprecht, 2001.

Legêne, Susan. *De bagage van Blomhoff en Van Breugel, Japan, Java, Tripoli en Suriname in de Negentiende-Eeuwse Nederlandse Cultuur van het Imperialisme*. Amsterdam: Koninklijk Instituut voor de Tropen, 1998.

Meijer, Hans. "'Het Uitverkoren Land.' De Lotgevallen van de Indo-Europese Kolonisten op Nieuw-Guinea 1949–1962." *Tijdschrift voor Geschiedenis* 112 (1999): 353–384.

De Mey, Johannes. *Alle de Neder-Duitsche Wercken*. Middelburg: Johannis Meertens, 1681.

Meyer, Eric Daryl. "The Ineradicable Supersessionism of the Christian Imagination," see https://itself.blog/2015/02/08/the-ineradicable-supersessionism-of-the-christian-imagination.

van Miert, Dirk. *The Emancipation of Biblical Philology in the Dutch Republic, 1590–1670*. Oxford: Oxford University Press, 2018.

Moore, Bob. "Decolonization by Default: Suriname and the Dutch Retreat from Empire." *Journal of Imperial and Commonwealth History* 28, no. 3 (2000): 228–250.

la Peyrère, Isaac. *Praeadamitae*. Amsterdam: Lodewijk Elzevier and Daniel Elzevier, 1655.

Picardt, Johan. *Korte Beschrijving van Eenige Vergetene en Verborgene Antiquiteiten*. 1660. Reprint, Leiden: Sidestone Press, 2008.

Porter, Andrew. *Religion versus Empire? British Protestant Missionaries and Overseas Expansion, 1700–1914*, Manchester: Manchester University Press, 2014.

Postma, Johannes. *The Dutch in the Atlantic Slave Trade, 1600–1815*, Cambridge: Cambridge University Press, 2009.

Protschky, Susie. "Race, Class and Gender: Debates over the Character of Social Hierarchies in the Netherlands Indies, circa 1600–1942," in *Bijdragen tot de Land-, Taal en Volkenkunde* 167, no. 4 (2011): 543–556.

de Raad, Georgius. *Bedenckingen over den Guineeschen slaef-handel der Gereformeerde met de Papisten*. Vlissingen: Abraham van Laren, 1665.

Raben, Remco. "A New Dutch Imperial History? Perambulations in a Prospective Field." *Bijdragen en Mededelingen Betreffende de Geschiedenis der Nederlanden* 128, no. 1 (2013): 5–30. https://doi.org/10.18352/bmgn-lchr.8353.

Robert, Dana L., ed. *Converting Colonialism: Visions and Realities in Mission History, 1706–1914*. Grand Rapids: Willem B. Eerdmans Publishing Company, 2008.

Schinkel, Willem. "De Virtualisering van Burgerschap en de Paternalistische Staat." *Sociologie* 5, no. 1 (2009): 48–68.

Schutte, G. J. *Het Calvinistisch Nederland, Mythe en Werkelijkheid*. Hilversum: Verloren, 2000.

Schwartz, Stuart B., ed. *Early Brazil, a Documentary Collection to 1700*. Cambridge: Cambridge University Press, 2009.

Sens, Angelie. *Mensaap, Heiden, Slaaf: Nederlandse Visies op de Wereld Rond 1800*. The Hague: SDU, 2001.

Sensbach, John F. *Rebecca's Revival: Creating Black Christianity in the Atlantic World*. Cambridge: Harvard University Press, 2005.

Shell, Robert C. H. "Religion, Civic Status and Slavery from Dordt to the Trek." *Kronos* 19 (1992): 28–64.

Slabodsky, Santiago. *Decolonial Judaism: Triumphal Failures of Barbaric Thinking*. Springer, 2014.

Smith, Robert. *More Desired than Our Owne Salvation: The Roots of Christian Zionism*. Oxford: Oxford University Press, 2013.

Smytegelt, Bernardus. *Des Christens Eenige Troost in Leven en Sterven*. The Hague: Ottho en Pieter van Thol, 1747.

Stanley, Brian. *The Bible and the Flag: Protestant Missions and British Imperialism in the Nineteenth and Twentieth Centuries*. Trowbridge: Apollos, 1990.

Stoler, Ann Laura. *Carnal Knowledge and Imperial Power: Race and the Intimate in Colonial Rule*. Berkeley: University of California Press, 2010.

Sutton, Elizabeth A. *Capitalism and Cartography in the Dutch Golden Age*. Chicago: University of Chicago Press, 2015.

Thianto, Yudha. *The Way to Heaven: Catechisms and Sermons in the Estabishment of the Dutch Reformed Church in the Est Indies*. Eugene: Wipf & Stock, 2014.

Udemans, Godefridus. *'t Geestelyck Roer van 't Coopmans Schip*. Dordrecht: Françoys Boels, 1665.

Verkuyl, Johannes. *De Achtergrond van het Indonesisch Vraagstuk*. Den Haag: D. A. Daamen, 1946.

Vernooij, Joop. "Mapping Religious Surinam." *Exchange*, 31, no. 3 (2002): 230–238.

Vink, Markus P. M. "'The World's Oldest Trade': Dutch Slavery and Slave Trade in the Indian Ocean in the Seventeenth Century." *Journal of World History*, 14, no. 2 (2003): 131–177.

Vink, Markus P. M. *Encounters on the Opposite Coast: The Dutch East India Company and the Nayaka State of Madurai in the Seventeenth Century*. Leiden: Brill, 2016.

Vink, Markus P. M. "'A Work of Compassion?' Dutch Slavery and Slave Trade in the Indian Ocean in the Seventeenth Century." The History Cooperative, accessed September 20, 2019. https://www.historycooperative.org/proceedings/seascapes/vink.html.

Vossius, Isaac. *Dissertatio de vera aetate mundi*, 1659.

van de Wal, Hans. *Een aanvechtbare en onzekere situatie. De Nederlandse Hervormde Kerk en Nieuw-Guinea 1949-1962*. Hilversum: Verloren, 2006.

Watson, Alan. *Slave Law in the Americas*. Athens, GA: University of Georgia Press, 1989.

van der Watt, Gideon. "Voetius." *In die Skriflig/ In Luce Verbi* 53, no. 3 (2019), https://doi.org/10.4102/ids.v53i3.2449.

van Welie, Rik. "Slave Trading and Slavery in the Dutch Empire." *New West Indian Guide* 81, no. 1-2 (2008): 47–96.

Westerduin, Matthea. "Displacement and Loss in the Muslim Question. Re-membering the Making of Race, Religion, and Whiteness in Europe and Its Colonies." PhD diss., VU University Amsterdam, forthcoming.

CHAPTER 13

THE BIBLE AND THE BRITISH EMPIRE

RALPH BROADBENT

Talking about Scholarship

EVERY academic discipline has a backstory—a myth, a legend, an ideology—that informs its self-understanding. In the case of biblical studies, part of this backstory is the myth of rigorous scientific neutrality. But as various schools of biblical interpretation in recent years have shown (for example, feminist scholarship, liberation hermeneutics, and indeed postcolonial hermeneutics), neither the biblical text itself nor biblical scholarship are entirely innocent. Both are problematic. Similar discussions have gone on with regard to the history of empire and imperialism. Historians have debated whether empire was generally a good thing, and if so for whom. Who has supported empire and who has called it into question? Is history a neutral discipline? Is it sometimes rewritten as propaganda?

It will be necessary to touch on all these questions to understand some aspects of the role of the Bible and biblical scholarship in relation to the British Empire. While unpicking some of these things, an important point must be made. Imperial attitudes cannot be properly understood without some reference to the English class system. In the Victorian era, at the top of the pyramid was the monarchy, then the aristocracy, then various levels of what we would now call the middle classes. After this would come the poor, divided hierarchically into the "deserving" and "undeserving" poor. Finally, at the bottom, would come the colonized, the natives, the orientals, etc. Women tended to fit into this scheme below their husbands or fathers. In the use of the Bible and its interpretation, this hierarchy is always there, either implicitly or explicitly.

THE BRITISH EMPIRE

The idea of the British Empire is deeply embedded in British cultural life, in virtually every field from literature to politics. Twenty-first-century politicians still fantasize about Britain "punching above its weight" on the world stage and its "special relationship" with the United States. Service to the nation is recognized by the award of various medals—the Order of the British Empire, Member of the British Empire, and, at the bottom of the pile, the British Empire Medal.[1] The latter had fallen into disuse in the early 1990s, but was revived in 2011 by the then prime minister, David Cameron, despite the empire having long vanished in the real world.

The British Empire in its Victorian and early twentieth-century form was very real. It was an empire on which it was said that "the sun never set." Such was its magnitude that it is impossible to give a "one size fits all" description. It has also varied through the centuries. From our perspective, however, it is instructive to look at how historians have interpreted it retrospectively.[2] At the risk of some simplification, there are three main positions. Position one is that the empire was, on the whole, a good thing that brought many benefits to the various colonized countries. Position two is not dissimilar, but acknowledges that there were various serious problems with imperial colonization for the colonized. Rather less common is position three, which holds that empire was a bad thing.

A leading modern exponent of "the empire as a good thing" is the conservative historian Niall Ferguson. In his book *Empire*, Ferguson sets out some of the typical arguments used in favor of empire. First, economic, claiming "there is good evidence that the imposition of British-style institutions has tended to enhance a country's economic prospects, particularly in settings where indigenous cultures were relatively weak," and that "the notion that British imperialism tended to impoverish colonized countries seems inherently problematic."[3] This claim is not uncontested. The British historian Linda Colley notes that the "immediate impact of British imperial free-trading was often the collapse of local indigenous industries which were in no position to compete, and a consequent destruction of livelihoods and communities."[4] Second, Ferguson claims, "we should not underestimate the benefits conferred by British law and administration." And, with a swipe at the French, British "common-law countries have the strongest, and French-civil-law countries the weakest, legal protections of investors."[5] Third, "British governance was remarkably cheap and efficient," and its "sins were generally sins of omission, not commission."[6] Ferguson concludes that "the British Empire proved ... that empire is a form of international government that can work—and not just for the ruling power. It sought to globalize not just an economic but a legal and ultimately a political system too."[7] Looking around the world, one might be tempted to wonder how accurate that conclusion might be.

As might be expected, other historians are more nuanced. Ashley Jackson wryly notes that "a history involving violence, dispossession, and even atrocity cannot be abridged in the rush to start telling the 'good news' story about railways and the global economy."[8] Jackson draws attention to the fact that the "story of Britain's rise as a global power became a standard part of school history texts and national self-image."[9] Through these texts and elsewhere, the great imperial empire builders were "lionized" and passed on to the next generation. In 1908, J. W. Willis, Education Chairman of Worcester County Council, wrote that the curriculum should "bring before the children the lives and work of English people who serve God in Church and State, to show that they did this by courage, endurance, and self-sacrifice, that as a result the British Empire was founded and extended and that it behoved every child to emulate them."[10] The story of empire was portrayed as a British story, the "subject peoples were largely passive." Jackson points out that the highly influential British historian Hugh Trevor-Roper (1914–2003), sometime Regius Professor of Modern History at the University of Oxford and later Master of Peterhouse, Cambridge, claimed that "Africa had no history prior to the arrival of Europeans; it was nothing more, he wrote, than the 'unedifying gyrations of barbarous tribes in picturesque but irrelevant corners of the globe.'"[11]

As noted above, empire still permeates British folk memory. Any British person of a certain age will remember reading at school the stories of British imperial heroes. General James Wolfe from the 1700s who died heroically, fighting the French on the battlefield of Quebec in Canada. From India, in the same period, Clive of India who opened up the East for the East India Company. And, from the late Victorian period, General Gordon of Khartoum, famously portrayed by Charlton Heston in the 1960s film epic. Adroitly glossed over was the rapacious treatment of India by Clive and his trial by the British Parliament. Likewise, Gordon's slaughter of the natives was glossed over and he was portrayed as a saint and a Christian martyr. One woman did make it into the lists of British heroes. Florence Nightingale, famously known as the Lady with the Lamp, nursed the wounded during the Crimean War, a war famous for another act of imperial manliness, the Charge of the Light Brigade, again, immortalized in celluloid.[12]

Now, it might be thought that these memories of and ways of thinking about empire might be gradually fading into the sunset. But the myths persist. Two twenty-first-century British prime ministers, and Labour ones, have picked up these imperial themes. Gordon Brown, then Chancellor of the Exchequer, said on a visit to Africa in 2005 that "[the] days of Britain having to apologise for its colonial history are over. . . . We should talk, and rightly so, about British values that are enduring, because they stand for some of the greatest ideas in history: tolerance, liberty, civic duty, that grew in Britain and influenced the rest of the world." Tony Blair, speaking a few years earlier in 1999, claimed that if "we can establish and spread the values of liberty, the rule of law, human rights and an open society then that is in our national interests too. The spread of our values makes us safer."[13] More recently, Brexit, Britain's departure from the European Union, has brought imperial themes to the fore. It has been widely noted that Brexit "is fuelled by fantasies of 'Empire 2.0,' a reconstructed global mercantilist trading empire in which the old white colonies will be reconnected to the mother country."[14]

A Trip to Oxford

Anyone taking a trip to Oxford recently would find a new attraction: a guided tour of the city's imperial history, devised by two enterprising history doctoral students.[15] One of the stops on this walking tour is Oriel College, which found itself the center of unwelcome publicity in 2015–2016. The college has a statue and a plaque dedicated to Cecil Rhodes, who (in)famously founded the British colony of Rhodesia (now Zimbabwe and Zambia). Rhodes became hugely wealthy through his business interests, particularly diamond mining, and this wealth continues to support Rhodes scholarships to the University of Oxford. He was a thorough-going imperialist who believed in the superiority of the white, and particularly the British, race. Following protests at the University of Cape Town, which led to the removal of a statue of Rhodes, the protest spread to Oxford, where some students very vocally demanded that his statue and plaque be likewise removed. They claimed that the values that Rhodes represented were incompatible with the values of a modern university, and that the university history curriculum should be suitably modernized, to "decolonise the space, curriculum and institutional memory" and expunge the memory of a man who they claim was a "racist and murderous colonialist."[16] There was predictable outrage from right-wing British newspapers such as the *Daily Mail* and the *Daily Telegraph*. Academics also joined the fray. Mary Beard, the famous classical scholar, weighed in. She had sympathy with the need to consider the university curriculum. However, she was unable to support the removal of the statue, as that would be to rewrite history. Much better, she claims, "to look history in the eye and reflect on our awkward relationship to it." She goes on to say that "the battle isn't won by taking the statue away and pretending those people didn't exist. It's won by empowering those students to look up at Rhodes and friends with a cheery and self confident sense of *unbatterability—much* as I find myself looking up at the statues of all those hundreds of men in history who would vehemently have objected to women having the vote, let alone the kind of job I have."[17]

Also entering into the fray was Nigel Biggar, Regius Professor of Moral and Pastoral Theology at Oxford. Writing in *The Times* newspaper, Biggar claimed that Rhodes was not "your stereotypical racist." In fact, he "was not a racist. He was an imperialist, but only because he believed in the modernity and progress that the British empire of his time represented." In fact, Biggar claims, "whether in terms of science or technology or communications or commerce or liberal political institutions and mores, late 19th century Britain was light years ahead of any indigenous African society."[18] Biggar was to return to his theme a couple of years later, this time referencing an online article by Bruce Gilley, "The Case for Colonialism."[19] Gilley argues that decolonized countries have often descended into chaos. In arguments reflecting Niall Ferguson, he contends that things were often better for countries during colonial times. He goes further and suggests that failing ex-colonies would do well to replicate "the colonial governance of their pasts," that those which cannot manage this should invite Western powers to "recolonise some areas," and that in certain circumstances it might be possible to "build new Western colonies from scratch." Gilley concludes with a cri de coeur, that a "hundred years of disaster is enough. It is time to make the case for colonialism again."[20] This is, so to speak, music to Biggar's ears. He waxes lyrical about political order and state institutions. At the very least, we should "moderate our post-imperial guilt." So, "[p]ride at the Royal Navy's century-long suppression of the Atlantic slave trade, for example, will not be entirely obscured by shame at the slaughter of innocents at Amritsar in 1919. And while we might well be moved to think with care about how to intervene abroad successfully, we won't simply abandon the world to its own devices."[21]

On the subject of guilt and pride, Biggar need not have worried. In a YouGov poll, 59 percent thought that the British Empire was something of which to be more proud than ashamed, and 34 percent said they would like it if Britain had an empire today.[22] Nor did Rhodes fall at Oriel. Whatever the arguments, money talked. It was reported that Oriel lost one donation of half a million pounds, and one other donation of three quarters of a million and a legacy of £100 million were in question.[23]

What should have been of more concern to Biggar was that his interventions drew attention to the Oxford-based research project he had initiated called "Ethics and Empire." This five-year research project's main objective was to develop "a nuanced and historically intelligent Christian ethic of empire." It was endowed by an American foundation, the McDonald Agape Foundation, whose rubric is "Encouraging distinguished scholars for Christ." The project came under heavy criticism from a whole range of academic sources. A large group of Biggar's Oxford colleagues published a withering open letter ("Ethics and empire: an open letter from Oxford scholars") criticizing the whole project for its naivety and poor historical scholarship.[24] The letter argues that Biggar's project "asks the wrong questions, using the wrong terms, and for the wrong purposes." It concludes that we "have never believed it is sufficient to dismiss imperialism as simply 'wicked.' Nor do we believe it can or should be rehabilitated because some of it was 'good.'" The outcome of this and other criticism was that Biggar felt obliged to hold his academic seminars in secret.[25] *The Times* continued to support him, publishing a rather tendentiously titled article "Censorship on campus 'is Stalinist,'" written by its arts correspondent.[26] Biggar did appear in public, however, and continued to press his case. At the Cheltenham Literary Festival, in 2018, he claimed that the empire "wasn't only about racial contempt; it was also about inter-racial admiration, affection and love."[27]

Other commentators are more critical of empire. Richard Gott draws attention to the violence within the empire and native opposition to it. His conclusion is blunt: the "rulers of the empire may one day be perceived to rank with the dictators of the 20th century as the authors of crimes against humanity."[28] William Dalrymple mentions approvingly a book by Shashi Tharoor, *Inglorious Empire* (2017), which, while making some mistakes on Indian economic matters, still makes "compelling the argument that the whole enterprise of the Raj was a vast British-run exercise in loot and plunder that reduced a previously great and wealthy nation to beggary and despair." Dalrymple goes on to note that "this debate has now bounced back to the ivory towers of our universities, where passions are running high over the legacy of Cecil Rhodes and over often uncritical teaching of British imperialism."[29]

However, many historical figures were well aware of imperial shortcomings. Bishop Reginald Heber (1783–1826), who was bishop of Calcutta, reported that "the peasantry in the Company's provinces are, on the whole, worse off, poorer and more dispirited than the subjects of the native princes." It was, in modern terms, an "extractive colony."[30] Slightly later in the nineteenth century, in 1876, the Marquis of Salisbury passed comment on the British proposal to establish an Indian peerage similar to that of Britain. He noted: "Whether the Indian aristocracy themselves are very powerful may be doubted ... but ... their goodwill and co-operation, if we can obtain it, will at all events serve to hide to the eyes of our own people & perhaps of the growing literary class in India *the nakedness of the sword upon which we rely*."[31] David Reynolds draws attention to Winston Churchill, famously a great supporter of empire, who wrote a memorandum in 1914. In it, Churchill said: "We are not a young people with *an innocent record and* a scanty inheritance. We have got all we wanted in territory and our claim to be left in the unmolested enjoyment of vast and splendid possessions, *mainly acquired by violence, largely maintained by force*, often seems less reasonable to others than to us." Reynolds notes that when it came to quoting this memorandum in his war memoirs, Churchill omitted the italicized phrases, "a sign, presumably, of his awareness that they did not accord with what the British like to present as their principled love of peace."[32]

It was not only politicians and academics who disputed the prevailing imperial ideology. Writers also contested it. Joseph Conrad's *The Heart of Darkness*, E. M. Forster's *A Passage to India*, George Orwell's *Burmese Days*, and many others called empire into question. Such writings and statements by politicians help lay to rest an often quoted position—that it is anachronistic to judge the empire and imperialism by today's standards. There is no particular need to use today's standards, as the past gives enough voices to critique empire with (past) contemporary standards.[33] As Gopal points out: "Dissenters from the imperial status quo may not have carried the day, but they were no lone wolves either."[34]

POSTCOLONIALISM

It will not have escaped notice that in all the discussion about empire so far, "native" voices, the voices of the colonized, have been largely absent. This is where postcolonial criticism makes its appearance. It makes space for their voices. As a discipline it is not unproblematic. It "covers such a wide ground, and is so incoherent internally, that even those who endow it with the status of theory fail to explain what such a theory might look like."[35] Nonetheless, it provides an important tool to interrogate both empire, the Bible, and biblical studies. This part of the chapter will set out some of its main themes.[36]

Probably the most famous writer in the field of postcolonialism is Edward Said. In his book *Orientalism*, he claimed that Western ideas about the Orient were often false and did not match reality. This was achieved in three ways. Anyone who writes or researches about the Orient, academic anthropologists, historians, philologists, (and, we might add, biblical scholars), "is an Orientalist, and what he or she does is Orientalism." Secondly, "Orientalism is a style of thought based on an ontological and epistemological distinction made between 'the Orient' and (most of the time) 'the Occident.'" In other words, the West and the East and their respective peoples are essentially different. Finally, Orientalism is a way of dealing with the Orient "by making statements about it, authorizing views of it, describing it, by teaching it, settling it, ruling over it: in short, Orientalism as a Western style for dominating, restructuring, and having authority over the Orient."[37] This domination was achieved through the study of ancient (oriental) manuscripts and texts, which were seen as defining the essence of the Orient. "Proper knowledge of the Orient proceeded from a thorough study of the classical texts, and only after that to an application of those texts to the modern Orient."[38] The classical texts are read with the assumption that oriental people are "irrational, depraved (fallen), childlike, 'different'; thus the European is rational, virtuous, mature, 'normal.'"[39] The Orient itself is described in terms of sensuality, despotism, aberrant mentality, and backwardness.[40] The outcome of all this is the imperial imperative: the East must be ruled for its own sake as well as for the prestige of Europe.[41]

Of course, there had been others well before Said who had begun to unpack the imperial project from the viewpoint of the colonized. Frantz Fanon, a psychiatrist from the French colony of Martinique, began to unpack the psychological devastation wreaked upon the colonized.[42] It is, however, Fanon's older compatriot Aimé Césaire who can give an insight into what was being written in this era. Césaire went to France for his higher education. On his return to Martinique, he started work on a long poem, "Return to My Native Land," published in the late 1930s.[43] It pulled no punches. He described colonial poverty: "[T]he hungry West Indies, pitted with smallpox, dynamited with alcohol, stranded in the mud of the bay."[44] Also, the brutality of the colonizer, "[t]he famine-man, the insult-man, the torture-man [who] can at any moment seize, beat up or kill—yes, really kill—without having to account to anybody, without having to excuse oneself to anyone."[45] And in all this inflicted brutality, the colonized man or woman blames himself or herself rather than the colonizer. It is the fault of the colonized and punishment is necessary. "I know my crimes; there is nothing to be said in my defence. Dances. Idols. Backsliding. Me too. I have assassinated God with my laziness with my words with my gestures with my obscene songs ... the flogged Negro who says: 'Pardon, my master' and the twenty-nine blows of the legal whip and the cell four feet high and the spiked iron collar."[46]

In a later work, *Discourse on Colonialism*, Césaire worked on these themes in more detail. He saw Christianity as the basic driving force behind colonialism. The chief culprit was "Christian pedantry, which laid down the dishonest equations *Christianity = civilization, paganism = savagery*, from which there could not but ensue abominable colonialist and racist consequences, whose victims were to be the Indians, the yellow peoples, and the Negroes."[47] These consequences involve "force, brutality, cruelty, sadism, conflict, and, in a parody of education, the hasty manufacture of a few thousand subordinate functionaries, 'boys,' artisans, office clerks, and interpreters necessary for the smooth operation of business."[48] Césaire says much more on colonialism, but a final point is worth noting—the effect of colonialism on the colonizer. It "works to *decivilize* the colonizer, to *brutalize* him in the true sense of the word, to degrade him, to awaken him to buried instincts, to covetousness, violence, race hatred, and moral relativism ... a poison has been instilled into the veins of Europe and, slowly but surely, the continent proceeds toward *savagery*."[49] He compares colonialism to Nazism. Europe tolerated this when it was applied to non-Europeans and only objected when Nazism/colonialism was applied at home.[50] His book was published at precisely the same time as the British authorities were torturing (including castration and burning alive), killing, and using concentration camps in Kenya during the Mau Mau uprising.[51] With all this in mind, we will turn now to the Bible. The material is vast, so in order to give a taste of things, we will look at three brief snapshots of interpretation, the early Victorian era, the late Victorian era, and, lastly, aspects of the twentieth century.

THE BIBLE IN THE EARLY VICTORIAN ERA

In the early part of the nineteenth century, the study of the Bible was not the separate academic discipline into which it has subsequently evolved. It is also important to note that scholarship in the period was heavily class-biased. The ruling classes had been unnerved by events such as the French Revolution, and also by the rising middle classes at home who were demanding a political voice. Leading churchmen were part of the ruling-class fight-back.

One such was John Bird Sumner (1780–1862), who was educated at Eton and King's College, Cambridge. In due course he became archbishop of Canterbury. He was influenced by Thomas Malthus's (in)famous "Essay on Population." This was brutally simple. There is only so much food in a country. The poor are given to overbreeding. When this happens, starvation is the inevitable result until the food supply and population are once more in equilibrium. In 1816, Sumner published his *The Records of Creation*.[52] Making use of Genesis, and linking to the ideas of Malthus, Sumner argued that the natural rules that govern nature must also apply to the human population.[53] With a nod to the French Revolution, Sumner asked, rhetorically, if equality within society might be a good thing. His answer was that wherever "equality is found to exist ... mankind are in the lowest and most savage state."[54] This poverty is due to the absence of monarchy and social superiors—"to the absence of this palace and these superiors, he owes the misery of his hut of reeds, and the insufficiency of his scanty clothing."[55] Colonization brings the benefits of monarchy and social superiors to foreign lands, which speeds up the natural progress of primitive nations and civilization.[56] Furthermore, colonization provides space for the emigration of the surplus poor if they cannot be persuaded to restrain their natural desire to multiply.[57] If equality were introduced in England, there would be no incentive for anyone to "preserve all the roads, the mines, the canals," and the country would degenerate to the condition of the native races and become fixed in a "stationary barbarism."[58] The English would become like "the native Indians of North and South America," whose "highest enjoyment is indolence," or like the "savages of the Caribee islands, who barter their hammock in the morning for some trifling satisfaction."[59]

Sumner was not alone in using the Bible to support the monarchy, class, and empire. His contemporary, Richard Whately (1787–1863), was to become, following undergraduate life and a fellowship at Oriel College, Oxford, archbishop of Dublin. He was every bit as severe as his Canterbury colleague. For the starving poor, Whately believed that food should only be given to them as a reward for "*extraordinary* sobriety, industry, and general good-conduct."[60] He believed that any woman requiring Poor Law relief "should have her hair cut off; it may seem trifling, but . . . [a] good head of hair will fetch from 5s. to 10s., which would perhaps be a fortnight's maintenance."[61] Even at the height of the potato famine, he was against poor relief.[62] He viewed Ireland in imperial terms. In 1837, he wrote to Bishop Stanley of Norwich that "if the Sovereign can be brought to visit Ireland—not once for all, like George IV, but as a resident for at least a month or two every year or two—Ireland may become a really valuable portion of the British Empire, instead of a sort of morbid excrescence."[63]

Whately helped set this imperial incorporation via education. He was head of the commission, appointed in 1831, to administer a new system of united, national education within Ireland. This included, at school-level, a course in "Scripture Extracts" and some "Introductory Lessons on Christian Evidences," based on Paley. He made Irish children sing "The Stately Homes of England" and his goal was to make every pupil "a happy English child." At a more advanced educational level, he specifically excluded from the curriculum Irish literature and history, regarding Plato, Aristotle, Bacon, Shakespeare, Jane Austen, and Paley as universal writers.[64] This educational policy was used throughout the empire.[65]

The Bible in the Later Victorian Era

Although critical biblical scholarship as we might recognize it today had been bubbling away in the background, it became an almost unstoppable force from about the 1860s, though many tried to roll things back. Figures such as Herbert Marsh, Connop Thirlwall, Henry Milman, Thomas Arnold, John Colenso, and Arthur Stanley were all influenced by the Enlightenment and German scholarship. This exploded into the mainstream with the publication of *Essays and Reviews* in 1860. A central figure was Benjamin Jowett (1817–1893). He went to Balliol College, Oxford, as an undergraduate and stayed there for the rest of his life, eventually becoming Master. In his contribution, Jowett pointed out (among many other things), that his object was "to read Scripture like any other book."[66] He also pointed out that the study of "the language of the New Testament has suffered . . . by following too much in the track of classical scholarship," and that "the discussions respecting the chronology of St. Paul's life and his second imprisonment . . . or in another department, respecting the Greek article, have gone far beyond the line of utility."[67] Observations that might well be applied to some areas of contemporary scholarship.

However "advanced" his views on the Bible appear, Jowett was very traditional when it came to matters such as the role of women and the place of the working classes. Ideally, women should remain at home for their education, with "home life and education going on together, each influencing the other." If women insisted on being educated away from home, then he wanted "the Ladies' Colleges [in Oxford] to be distinguished as places of society and good manners."[68] On the subject of the biblical injunctions to sell all, Jowett wrote that to "take them literally would be injurious to ourselves and to society." The classes should be properly separated. "It will not do to make a great supper, and mingle at the same board the two ends of society, as modern phraseology calls them, fetching in 'the poor, the maimed, the lame, the blind,' to fill the vacant places of noble guests. That would be eccentric in modern times, and even hurtful."[69]

Jowett was also heavily involved in the preparation of candidates for the Indian Civil Service. Unsurprisingly, the exams the candidates had to pass gave Greek and Latin twice as many marks as modern and oriental languages.[70] Laying the foundation stone for the "Indian Institute" at Oxford University, Jowett remarked that the study of Sanskrit, Arabic, and Persian "can hardly be made the basis of education in the same way as the classics, nor can they enter into our religious life as the Hebrew Scriptures do."[71] Three of Jowett's pupils held the Viceroyalty of India in succession.[72] And in a letter to Florence Nightingale, he wrote: "I should like to govern the world through my pupils."[73]

Jowett realized that the Bible was a book of the East, as it "speaks the language and has the feeling of Eastern lands."[74] Despite having produced the Bible, oriental nations have "literal and servile habits of mind," they "have no history of their own," and they should not be allowed to have the "Book of Scripture . . . but the truth of the Book, the mind of Christ and His Apostles."[75] So, the Bible was produced in the Orient by Orientals. Yet these unchanging Orientals have somehow changed and lost the ability to interpret their own book. So the West must interpret it for them and should give them, not the Bible itself, but some sort of simplified moral code.

No snapshot of this late Victorian era would be complete without some mention of the famous Cambridge trio of Joseph Barber Lightfoot (1828–1889), Brooke Foss Westcott (1825–1901), and Fenton John Anthony Hort (1828–1892). Their scholarship, involving a very cautious use of German critical scholarship, set the pattern of British scholarship, which arguably still dominates today.[76] The first of the three, Lightfoot, studied at Trinity College, Cambridge, became in due course Hulsean Professor, and was finally bishop of Durham. He was chaplain to Queen Victoria and Prince Albert, and had a close relationship with the future Edward VII, whom he had tutored at Trinity.[77] This closeness to royalty was reflected in a sermon he preached in 1887, the year of Queen Victoria's golden jubilee, based on Isaiah 11:12, titled "An Ensign for the Nations." He believed that "the one prominent idea which impressed all thoughtful minds was the imperial destiny of England—her world-wide interests and responsibilities." England possesses a "spirit of adventure" and has "exceptional fecundity." The empire was not to be neglected, because to do so would have "an almost immediate effect on commerce and manufacture, and so on the material prosperity of the country." Likewise, there is a special place for the Anglican Church. There is a "unique destiny which in God's providence seems to be reserved for the Anglican community in shaping the future of Christendom."[78]

Lightfoot's attitude to women was not dissimilar to Jowett's position. Women could receive some education, and he was supportive of founding a women's college in Hitchen, but when there was an attempt to have it incorporated into the university, he withdrew his support.[79] This withdrawal reflected Lightfoot's general attitude to women.[80] However, he regarded this (Christian) treatment of women as very advanced. Only "when we turn to the harem and the zenana do we learn to estimate what the Gospel has achieved, and still has to achieve, in the emancipation of woman, and her lawful place in the social order."[81] Something similar is reflected in Lightfoot's view of slavery. Discussing slavery in his commentary on Philemon, he claims that for Christians to attack slavery "would tear society into shreds" and lead to "a servile war." However, Christianity had dealt it a fatal blow by having both slave and master kneeling "at the same holy table." This abolition had taken quite a few centuries, but Lightfoot believed that the "abolition of slavery throughout the British Empire at enormous material sacrifice [was] one of the greatest moral conquests which England has ever achieved." He likewise approved the abolition of serfdom under the Russian tsar, Alexander II, as well as the "emancipation of the negro in the vast republic of the New World."[82]

Westcott, perhaps most famously known for his work on the Revised Version of the Bible, seen as a replacement for the King James Bible, was equally enamored by empire and all it involved.[83] He was firmly of the view that women should be educated separately from men and that the "family is the woman's realm."[84] His commentary on Ephesians, published posthumously, noted that the "Church offers to Christ the devotion of subjection, as the wife to the husband."[85] It was the role of men to take the lead in other matters. Once men, educated in the universities, had understood the Christian faith, "then will England be prepared to fulfil her mission for which . . . the world is now waiting. Then will she be able to interpret and harmonize the East and West in virtue of her history, of her character, of her spirit."[86] God, according to Westcott, had "fitted us as a people and as a church to be the missionaries of the world."[87] Westcott's own family fulfilled this missionary call. Six of his seven sons were ordained, four of whom went to India, where two became bishops. The authoritarian family also had imperial implications. In the past, a "constitution and laws reared on a lofty estimate of the Family gave Rome the sovereignty of the world."[88] The church "embodies the Imperial idea, and hallows it."[89] This missionary work is literally the "white man's burden."[90] A successful outcome would be "the victorious universality of our own faith," with India being "organised in distinct nations under our paramount power," and providing the "victory over Asia."[91]

Should there be any financial burden from running the empire, this would not be a problem, as the "Colonies and India alike spontaneously placed their resources at the disposal of the Mother Country, and at once the Empire was revealed."[92] While the colonized were able to be spontaneously generous, they nonetheless needed to be disciplined and kept under authority, as they were "[c]hildren and childly races."[93] Like Corinth at the time of St. Paul, Calcutta, Benares, Cawnpore, Delhi, and Lahore were "beset by idolatry and unbelief and corruption."[94] Part of the problem was "the sterile theism of Islam and the shadowy vagueness of Hindu philosophy," and the fact that Indians had no "historic sense."[95] If the East was childlike, corrupt, and idolatrous, England was different. She was "the mother and the mistress of the nations."[96]

There is much more in Westcott's writings. He was a fervent supporter of the Boer War. The Boers were to surrender or war would follow and it would be a just war. "The duty of fulfilling a trust is not a matter for arbitration, and if need be, [war] must be preferred to the maintenance of peace."[97] He regarded American Independence as a mistake. "The old argument that the Colonies will fall from the parent stem like fruit when they are ripe is no longer current. We have learnt that the separation of the United States is a warning and not a precedent."[98] On the home front, his views on poverty reflected his earlier episcopal colleagues—in 1895 he delivered an address on "The Deserving Unemployed and how to help them." He speculated that the materially rich were often as badly off as the poor, since they lacked spiritual resources. In reply to this, *The Spectator* was moved to discourse on "the rich poor" and "the busy unemployed."[99]

Hort, unsurprisingly, took a very similar view to the other members of the trio. He thought that the idea of universal suffrage and votes for women "plainly set aside the idea of the family."[100] Also, if there is universal suffrage, then monarchs will only have their authority granted "by the free-will of their subjects."[101] This undoes the divine right of monarchy and, in turn, implies that the headship of husband over wife is likewise a voluntary arrangement rather than something built into creation by God. With a clear echo of rendering to Caesar, Hort notes that "[s]ubmission to *de facto* rule is a duty."[102] In a sermon on Ephesians 5:22–24, Hort approvingly mentions that St. Paul "believed it to be part of God's unchanged and unchangeable order that in some ways the husband should be over the wife, and have a right to her obedience."[103]

Hort was not only concerned with the "home front." He saw the power of a united USA as a threat to Europe, "a standing menace to the whole civilization of Europe," and hoped that the American Civil War would pull the Union apart.[104] The continuation of slavery in the American South would be an acceptable price to pay for the destruction of the Union. He wrote, "I care more for England and for Europe than for America, how much more than for all the niggers in the world!"[105] Hort claimed to hate slavery, but this was "much more for its influence on the whites than on the niggers themselves. The refusal of education to them is abominable; how far they are capable of being ennobled by it is not so clear. As yet *everywhere* (not in slavery only) they have surely shown themselves only as an immeasurably inferior race, just human and no more, their religion frothy and sensuous, their highest virtues those of a good Newfoundland dog."[106] Hort used the bestiary elsewhere, describing one of his cats "as a domestic nigger, fat, greedy, and stupid."[107] He referred, approvingly, to an article on the West Indies which claimed that "the W. Indies are going to rack and ruin, for laborers won't work; niggers like pumpkin and idleness; niggers never did any good yet, have no enterprise, no nothing. Man's highest business is work; if niggers won't work, they must be made to work."[108]

Hort was an enthusiastic supporter of the Cambridge Mission to Delhi, active in the recruitment of missionaries for India, and, after his death, some of his books were sent to the Cambridge Mission.[109]

The Bible in the Twentieth Century

The earlier years of the twentieth century can be seen as a time of transition. Scholarship continued to slowly evolve under the influence of German scholarship. Figures such as Arthur Headlam (1862–1947), joint author of the ICC commentary on Romans and eventually bishop of Gloucester, represent the transition from the Victorian era to more modern times. His 1923 work, *The Life and Teaching of Jesus the Christ*, was dedicated "to the memory of the men of the British Empire who in the Great War laid down their lives for that Holy Land where Jesus lived and taught and died."[110] As late as the beginning of the Second World War, reflecting that England was ill-prepared, he noted that a "wave of sentimentalism, of pacifism, and love of economy had made us forget our duty as guardians of a great empire and the inheritors of the command of the sea."[111] But figures such as Headlam became rare for various reasons—the decline of the Anglican Church, as well as the expansion of university education, leading to some broadening of the class origins of those who became biblical scholars. But a brief look at the biographical details of many twentieth-century scholars shows that many of them were educated in the classics, often at public schools, in the same way as their predecessors, before moving into the field of biblical scholarship. We also lose the insights given by the voluminous correspondence and books of sermons that previous generations produced. Indeed, biblical scholarship was often detached from religious faith and became professionalized. So we have to try to unpick from commentaries, etc., if the hierarchical ideology of the Victorian era—monarchy, aristocracy, the lower classes, the poor, women, and the imperial other—continues in more recent scholarship. Four areas suggest this might be the case.

Firstly, there is the role of hierarchy and the state, in particular the "render-to Caesar" and Romans 13 mosaic of texts. The Torch commentary on St. Mark claimed that "there was much to be said for the Roman government; to its subject peoples it brought, on the whole, peace and even-handed justice."[112] Vincent Taylor, predictably, wrote that "the acceptance and use of Caesar's coinage implicitly acknowledge his authority and therefore the obligation to pay taxes."[113] Numerous other commentaries take a similar line. This type of interpretation is not limited to the First World. The TEF study guides designed for a Third World audience efficiently export this exegesis: "*The taxes we pay are not a gift to the state, but a debt we pay back:* ... We receive the benefits of a government, e.g., roads, law-courts, etc. Christians admit this and pay for them by taxes: in fact a man becomes a more loyal citizen than he was before when he becomes a Christian."[114] Commentaries on Romans 13:1–7 (with support from 1Tim 2:1–2, Titus 3:1, and 1 Pet 2:13–17) show, almost universally, similar hierarchical points of view. A handful of writers waver a little when considering the passages in the light of resistance to the Nazi regime, but even they see this as very much the exception to the rule.[115]

It takes a colonial voice to puncture this mainstream British position. The Indian Jesuit Samuel Rayan describes this render-to-Caesar exegesis as one whose "entire atmosphere, horizon and perspective throughout are those of the dominant classes and in keeping with the age of imperialism and colonial aggression." He makes the important point that "[t]he use of Caesar's coin argues no recognition of Caesar's claims. Those who have lived under colonial domination know that they have no choice in such vital economic matters.... That Caesar was God's delegated authority, that he had rights, that his prescriptions were lawful are all ideologically conditioned positions."[116]

Secondly, there are the views on wealth and poverty. In earlier periods, the division of wealth was seen as God-given. This essentially continues as before, as any browse through any number of commentaries will show. For example, the story of the rich young ruler in the Gospels draws such comments as "experience has taught us that giving money or food or clothing to the poor often does more harm than good," and in fact, "the rich man is to be pitied" and "rich men may have to keep their riches and bear the burden of using them wisely for the kingdom of God."[117] Moving to the Pastoral Epistles, similar positions are taken by commentators. From an Indian context, we read that wealth "is a very heavy responsibility. Sharing it is not as simple as it sounds, for the one who does so is apt to become an easy prey to all sorts of deceivers and ne'er-do-wells."[118] In Britain, the ICC commentary on the Pastoral Epistles feels obliged to argue: "It has to be remembered that, on the whole, simply redistributing the existing wealth will not make for a vast change in the lives of the poor; the solution generally lies in increased productivity and ensuring that the poor get their fair share of the proceeds."[119] No evidence is given for this claim.

Thirdly, there is the place of women. In mainstream scholarship, not much has changed since Victorian times. The subordinationist, "separate-spheres" ideology is very clear and runs on through the century, despite votes for women, women's roles in industry in the Second World War, the women's movement, and the advent of feminist scholarship. At the start of the century (on 1 Cor 11:3ff), Robinson and Plummer tell us that "it is by the original ordinance of God that the husband has control of the wife."[120] In the second half of the century, Margaret Thrall regards the same passage as "a very trivial matter," and feels no need to argue with it.[121] C. K. Barrett believes that a woman who wears her hair long "is fulfilling her role in creation."[122] In 2000, Thiselton was arguing that gender distinction was from God and not a human construction, and that this "still speaks today when many ascribe gender distinctions largely ... to social construction."[123] Caird tells us of the "natural structure of the family," and that in "the home there must, to be sure, be one head of the household, whose authority is accepted by the rest."[124] Muddiman does not deal with this matter at all. His bibliography has no mention of feminist biblical scholarship.[125] The nineteenth century has extended its grip into the twenty-first.

Fourthly, there is Orientalism. It is true to say that Orientalism becomes less obvious during the twentieth century. There are still plenty of scattered references to oriental customs, but commentators do not usually draw direct inferences concerning the inferiority of Eastern customs or those who keep them. But there are glimpses of the "other" being written out of history. In 1 Corinthians 13:3, does Paul hand his body over so that he "may boast," or should it read, with the textual variant, "to be burned"? The textual choice is important, because the variant would probably be a reference to an Indian who burned himself to death in Athens a few years before Paul was in the city. Likewise, the story of the Ethiopian eunuch (Acts 8:26–40). As Clarice Martin has pointed out, despite "prodigious classical evidence" showing that "Ethiopian" is virtually synonymous with "negro," this fact escapes comment.[126] Given the love of all things classical of most NT scholars, one might have expected this to receive a mention. It does not. C. K. Barrett, writing five years after Martin, has a long section with numerous classical quotations, but has no mention of race.[127] Perhaps "the other" is to be written out of the NT.

Some Conclusions

It seems clear that the Bible, in British scholarship, has been used to support the building and maintenance of the British Empire. It has done this by supporting an interlocking system of ideology from monarchy, via aristocracy, to the oriental other. In part, this was driven by self-interest. The earlier scholars were, either by birth or education, part of the ruling class, and their exegesis was far from disinterested. Later interpretations of the Bible, in the main, followed the same pattern. Now, it might be objected that we cannot judge yesterday by the standards of today. This is nonsense. Alternative views were available. For earlier scholars, Thomas Paine presented a different perspective on wealth and its redistribution to the poor. Malthus was chosen instead. Mary Wollstonecraft presented an alternative view of the place and role of women. Subjection and headship were chosen instead. John William Colenso, sometime bishop of Natal in the Victorian period, had a high view of the African people among whom he worked. His fellow scholars portrayed subjects of empire as either savages or children. And if we come to more modern scholarship, despite the efforts of Latin American liberation theologians on behalf of the poor, feminist theologians on behalf of women, and postcolonial biblical scholars on the subject of empire and Orientalism, the framework remains largely intact and alternative perspectives are ignored. This is despite each of these areas now having produced a considerable body of scholarship.[128]

The picture sketched out in this chapter is, of course, just that—a sketch. There is considerably more work to be done, particularly on imperial expansion before, say, the time of the French Revolution. What role did the Bible play in the conquest of North America? What role did it play in the slave trade? There are many other gaps to be researched in this area of Bible and empire. Perhaps Oxford could host a research institute named "The Bible and the British Empire" based on postcolonial principles, though it is doubtful if it would attract the necessary funding from wealthy sources.

And this raises a final conundrum—the position of the Bible in twenty-first-century Britain. Firstly, it has become increasingly irrelevant as Christianity has weakened, both numerically and as part of the social fabric. Secondly, while liberation, feminist, and postcolonial approaches have sought to see behind the prevailing ideologies of biblical interpretation, their goal has been to rescue the biblical text and make it usable for a modern readership. Subaltern voices have also made themselves heard. But what if the Bible cannot be repositioned? What if the text itself is actually inherently hierarchical in various ways? Perhaps as the British Empire has come to an end, so too has the Bible, in some ways, run its course, an imperial text in a post-imperial age. Only time will tell.

Notes

1. There are others as well.
2. For a brief but comprehensive overview, see Ashley Jackson, *The British Empire: A Very Short Introduction* (Oxford: Oxford University Press, 2013).
3. Niall Ferguson, *Empire: How Britain Made the Modern World* (London: Penguin, 2003), 368–69.
4. Quoted in Jackson, *The British Empire*, 127.
5. Ferguson, *Empire*, 369.
6. Ferguson, *Empire*, 370.
7. Ferguson, *Empire*, 371.
8. Jackson, *The British Empire*, 118. The building of railways in some colonies is often seen as one of the huge benefits of empire. The irony of this claim for imperial improvement is often missed.
9. Jackson, *The British Empire*, 102.
10. Jackson, *The British Empire*, 103. It is perhaps no coincidence that the city of Worcester possesses a large and very visible public memorial, on the grounds of its cathedral, to the fallen of the Boer War in South Africa, which had concluded only a few years previously. As is well known, the British made extensive use of concentration camps during this war.
11. Jackson, *The British Empire*, 104.
12. Interestingly, Nightingale was very interested in theological matters, being unimpressed by eternal damnation and open to non-Christian faiths.
13. Quoted in Priyamvada Gopal, *Insurgent Empire: Anticolonial Resistance and British Dissent* (London and New York: Verso, 2019), 447.
14. Fintan O'Toole, *Heroic Failure: Brexit and the Politics of Pain* (London: Head of Zeus, 2019), 3.
15. Patrick Kidd, "Meander through Oxford's Dark Past is More Than a Woke Walk," *The Times*, January 25, 2020.
16. Amelia Jenne, "Mary Beard Says Drive to Remove Cecil Rhodes Statue from Oxford University Is a 'Dangerous Attempt to Erase the Past,'" *The Independent*, December 22, 2015.
17. Mary Beard, "Cecil Rhodes and Oriel College, Oxford," *Times Literary Supplement*, December 20, 2015.
18. Nigel Biggar, "Message to Students: Rhodes Was No Racist," *The Times*, December 22, 2015.
19. Bruce Gilley, "The Case for Colonialism," *Third World Quarterly* (Online, September 8, 2017), 1–17.

20. Gilley, "The Case for Colonialism," 11.
21. Nigel Biggar, "Don't Feel Guilty about Our Colonial History." *The Times*, November 30, 2017.
22. Amia Srinivasan, "Under Rhodes," *London Review of Books*, March 31, 2016.
23. Srinivasan, "Under Rhodes."
24. Copies, from multiple sources, are readily available on the Internet.
25. Sumantra Maitra, "'If I Want to Hold Seminars on the Topic of Empire, I Will Do So Privately': An Interview with Nigel Biggar." *Quillette*, June 7, 2018.
26. David Sanderson, "Censorship on Campus 'Is Stalinist,'" *The Times*, October 8, 2018.
27. Fuller remarks can be found in "Censorship and the Complexities of Empire" in the News section of the McDonald Centre website, at https://www.mcdonaldcentre.org.uk/news/censorship-and-complexities-empire.
28. Richard Gott, "Let's End the Myths of Britain's Imperial Past," *The Guardian*, October 19, 2011.
29. William Dalrymple, "*The British in India* by David Gilmour Review—Three Centuries of Ambition and Experience," *The Guardian*, September 27, 2018.
30. Ferdinand Mount, "Umbrageousness," *London Review of Books* 39, no. 17 (2017): 3–8.
31. Quoted in Paul Smith, "Refuge of the Aristocracy," *London Review of Books* 23, no. 12 (2001). Italics added.
32. David Reynolds, *Island Stories: Britain and Its History in the Age of Brexit* (London: William Collins, 2019), 74.
33. In an essay written in 1929, "How a Nation Is Exploited: The British Empire in Burma," Orwell wrote: "the British are stealing from Burma in two ways: In the first place, they pillage her natural resources; secondly, they grant themselves the exclusive right to sell her the manufactured products she now needs." Peter Davison, ed., *Orwell and Politics* (London: Penguin, 2001), 7. This is the same technique was used to extract raw cotton from India to Britain and then send back manufactured goods for profit.
34. Gopal, *Insurgent Empire*, 455.
35. Arif Dirlik, "Response to the Responses: Thoughts on the Postcolonial," *Interventions* 1, no. 2 (1999), 286.
36. It will, for obvious reasons, be highly selective and compressed.
37. Edward W. Said, *Orientalism: Western Conceptions of the Orient, with a New Afterword* (London: Penguin, 1995), 2–3.
38. Said, *Orientalism*, 79.
39. Said, *Orientalism*, 40.
40. Said, *Orientalism*, 205.
41. Said, *Orientalism*, 30.
42. See especially Frantz Fanon, *Peau Noire, Masques Blancs* (Paris: Éditions du Seuil, 1952); and *Les Damnés De La Terre* (Paris: F. Maspero, 1961).
43. Aimé Césaire, *Return to My Native Land* (Paris: Présence Africaine, 1968).
44. Césaire, *Return to My Native Land*, 11.
45. Césaire, *Return to My Native Land*, 37.
46. Césaire, *Return to My Native Land*, 59, 115.
47. Aimé Césaire, *Discourse on Colonialism* (New York: Monthly Review Press, 1972), 11.
48. Césaire, *Discourse on Colonialism*, 21.
49. Césaire, *Discourse on Colonialism*, 13. Italics original.
50. Césaire, *Discourse on Colonialism*, 14.

51. See, for example, Caroline Elkins, *Imperial Reckoning: The Untold Story of Britain's Gulag in Kenya* (London: Pimlico, 2005). The colonial attorney general in Kenya saw that what was happening resembled Nazi Germany, but agreed to draw up legislation that allowed beatings, as long as they were kept secret. He wrote in a memo, "If we are to sin, we must sin quietly." Also, see Ian Cobain and Jessica Hatcher, "Kenyan Mau Mau Victims in Talks with UK Government over Legal Settlement," *The Guardian*, May 5, 2013.
52. John Bird Sumner, *A Treatise on the Records of the Creation and on the Moral Attributes of the Creator; With Particular Reference to the Jewish History, and to the Consistency of the Principle of Population With the Wisdom and Goodness of the Deity* (London: J. Hatchard and Son, 1816).
53. Sumner, *The Records of Creation*, 172–177.
54. Sumner, *The Records of Creation*, 187.
55. Sumner, *The Records of Creation*, 193.
56. Sumner, *The Records of Creation*, 266–267.
57. Sumner, *The Records of Creation*, 237.
58. Sumner, *The Records of Creation*, 211–212.
59. Sumner, *The Records of Creation*, 188–190.
60. E. Jane Whately, *Life and Correspondence of Richard Whately, D.D., Late Archbishop of Dublin, in Two Volumes* (London: Longmans, Green, 1866), I:77. Italics original.
61. Whately, *Life and Correspondence of Richard Whately*, I:163.
62. Whately, *Life and Correspondence of Richard Whately*, II:115.
63. Whately, *Life and Correspondence of Richard Whately*, I:378.
64. Norman Vance, "Improving Ireland: Richard Whately, Theology, and Political Economy," in *Economy, Polity, and Society: British Intellectual History, 1750–1950*, ed. Stefan Collini, Richard Whatmore, and B. W. Young (Cambridge: Cambridge University Press, 2000), 193.
65. Macaulay's famous "Minute on Indian Education" of 1835 stated that "a single shelf of a good European library was worth the whole native literature of India and Arabia." C. L. R. James (1901–1989), born in Trinidad, who was to become an important anticolonial figure, described himself as being a "British intellectual long before I was ten, already an alien in my own environment among my own people, even my own family." His secondary education reinforced this. "I studied Latin with Virgil, Caesar and Horace, and wrote Latin verses. I studied Greek with Euripides and Thucydides. I did elementary and applied mathematics, French and French literature, English and English literature, English history, ancient and modern European history... it was a very good school, though it would have been more suitable to Portsmouth than to Port of Spain." See *Beyond a Boundary* (London: Serpent's Tail, 1994), 18, 28.
66. Benjamin Jowett, "On the Interpretation of Scripture," in *Essays and Reviews: The 1860 Text and Its Reading*, ed. Victor Shea and William Whitla (Charlottesville: University Press of Virginia, 2000), 482.
67. Jowett, "On the Interpretation of Scripture," 512, 513.
68. Evelyn Abbott and Lewis Campbell, *The Life and Letters of Benjamin Jowett, M.A. Master of Balliol College, Oxford with Portraits and Other Illustrations in Two Volumes* (London: John Murray, 1897), II:158, 316.
69. Jowett, "On the Interpretation of Scripture," 495.
70. See Peter Hinchliff, *Benjamin Jowett and the Christian Religion* (Oxford: Clarendon Press, 1987).
71. Abbott and Campbell, *The Life and Letters of Benjamin Jowett*, II:227.

72. Richard Symonds, *Oxford and Empire: The Last Lost Cause?* (London: Macmillan, 1986), 27.
73. Symonds, *Oxford and Empire*, 24.
74. Jowett, "On the Interpretation of Scripture," 498.
75. Jowett, "On the Interpretation of Scripture," 532–533.
76. So, C. K. Barrett wrote on Lightfoot's *Galatians*, "Lightfoot is not out of date, and it is difficult to see that he ever will be." On Westcott's *Hebrews*, "This is a great book." Charles Kingsley Barrett, "New Testament Commentaries III: Epistles and Revelation," *Expository Times* 65, no. 6 (1954), 178, 179.
77. Bruce N. Kaye, "Lightfoot and Baur on Early Christianity," *Novum Testamentum* 26, no. 3 (1984), 198.
78. Joseph Barber Lightfoot, *Sermons Preached on Special Occasions* (London: Macmillan, 1891).
79. Geoffrey R. Treloar, *Lightfoot the Historian: The Nature and Role of History in the Life and Thought of J. B. Lightfoot (1828–1889) as Churchman and Scholar* (Tübingen: Mohr Siebeck, 1998), 184.
80. The nature of Lightfoot's commentaries, with their emphasis on grammar and ancient literary allusions, means that there is often little direct comment on women. Perhaps he could assume that the passages concerning women were readily understandable and would ensure their continuing subordination. See, for example, Lightfoot's exegesis of Colossians 3:18, "Wives obey your husbands." *Saint Paul's Epistles to the Colossians and to Philemon* (London: Macmillan, 1875).
81. Joseph Barber Lightfoot, *Sermons by the Late Right Rev. J. B. Lightfoot. D.D., D.C.L., Lord Bishop of Durham* (London: Swan Sonnenschein, 1892), 119.
82. Lightfoot, *Saint Paul's Epistles to the Colossians and to Philemon*, 320–327.
83. The RV was criticized for having "converted every Englishman's copy of the New Testament into a partial and one-sided Introduction to the Critical Difficulties of the Greek text." And, it was claimed, "Our Authorized Version is the one religious link which at present binds together ninety millions of English-speaking men scattered over the earth's surface. Is it reasonable that so precious a bond should be endangered, for the sake of . . . getting rid of a few archaisms?" "New Testament Revision: Westcott and Hort's Textual Theory," *Quarterly Review* 153, no. 306 (1882), 311; "New Testament Revision: The New English Version," *Quarterly Review* 153, no. 305 (1882), 1.
84. Brooke Foss Westcott, *The Incarnation and the Common Life* (London: Macmillan, 1893), 163.
85. Brooke Foss Westcott, *Saint Paul's Epistle to the Ephesians: The Greek Text with Notes and Addenda* (London: Macmillan, 1906), 84.
86. Brooke Foss Westcott, *On Some Points in the Religious Office of the Universities* (London: Macmillan, 1873), 75.
87. Westcott, *On Some Points in the Religious Office*, 88.
88. Brooke Foss Westcott, *Social Aspects of Christianity* (London: Macmillan, 1887), 22.
89. Brooke Foss Westcott, *Lessons from Work* (London: Macmillan, 1901), 381.
90. Westcott, *Lessons from Work*, 376.
91. Arthur Westcott, *Life and Letters of Brooke Foss Westcott: In Two Volumes* (London: Macmillan, 1903), II:291; Westcott, *Lessons from Work*, 380.
92. Westcott, *Lessons from Work*, 374.
93. Westcott, *Lessons from Work*, 37.

94. Westcott, *Lessons from Work*, 205.
95. Brooke Foss Westcott, *Christian Aspects of Life* (London: Macmillan, 1897), 166, 170.
96. Westcott, *Christian Aspects of Life*, 144.
97. Westcott, *Life and Letters of Brooke Foss Westcott*, II:287.
98. Westcott, *Lessons from Work*, 374.
99. Westcott, *Life and Letters of Brooke Foss Westcott*, II:193–194.
100. Arthur Fenton Hort, *Life and Letters of Fenton John Anthony Hort* (London: Macmillan, 1896), I:134.
101. Hort, *Life and Letters of Hort*, I:137.
102. Hort, *Life and Letters of Hort*, I:144–145.
103. Fenton John Anthony Hort, *Village Sermons in Outline* (London: Macmillan, 1898), 126–127.
104. Hort, *Life and Letters of Hort*, I:459.
105. Hort, *Life and Letters of Hort*, I:459.
106. Hort, *Life and Letters of Hort*, I:458.
107. Hort, *Life and Letters of Hort*, I:388.
108. Hort, *Life and Letters of Hort*, I:128.
109. Hort, *Life and Letters of Hort*, II: 223, 321, 458.
110. Arthur Cayley Headlam, *The Life and Teaching of Jesus the Christ* (London: John Murray, 1923).
111. Ronald Jasper, *Arthur Cayley Headlam: The Life and Letters of a Bishop* (London: Faith Press, 1960), 317.
112. Archibald Macbride Hunter, *The Gospel according to Saint Matthew* (London: SCM Press, 1949), 116.
113. Vincent Taylor, *The Gospel according to St. Mark* (London: Macmillan, 1952), 480.
114. John Hargreaves, *A Guide to St Mark's Gospel* (London: SPCK, 1969), 199. Italics original.
115. C. E. B. Cranfield, *The Service of God* (London: Epworth Press, 1965), 55–62; John A. Ziesler, *Paul's Letter to the Romans* (London: SCM Press, 1989), 308.
116. Samuel Rayan, "Caesar versus God," in *Jesus Today*, ed. Stephen Kappen (Madras: AICUF, 1985), 91–93.
117. Alfred Plummer, *An Exegetical Commentary on the Gospel according to S. Matthew* (London: Elliot Stock, 1909), 268; and similarly, Sherman Elbridge Johnson, *A Commentary on the Gospel according to St. Mark* (London: A & C Black, 1960), 175; C. E. B. Cranfield, *The Gospel according to Saint Mark* (Cambridge: Cambridge University Press, 1963), 331; Charles Francis Digby Moule, *The Gospel according to Mark* (Cambridge: Cambridge University Press, 1965), 80.
118. Maxwell R. Robinson, *A Commentary on the Pastoral Epistles* (Madras: Christian Literature Society, 1962), 69.
119. I. Howard Marshall, *A Critical and Exegetical Commentary on the Pastoral Epistles* (Edinburgh: T & T Clark, 1999), 670.
120. Archibald Robertson and Alfred Plummer, *A Critical and Exegetical Commentary on the First Epistle of St Paul to the Corinthians* (Edinburgh: T & T Clark, 1911), 231.
121. Margaret E. Thrall, *The First and Second Letters of Paul to the Corinthians* (Cambridge: Cambridge University Press, 1965), 78.
122. Charles Kingsley Barrett, *A Commentary on the First Epistle to the Corinthians* (London: A & C Black, 1968), 257. Perhaps we should be grateful that it is no longer suggested that women sell their hair—see above on Whately.

123. Anthony C. Thiselton, *The First Epistle to the Corinthians: A Commentary on the Greek Text* (Grand Rapids, MI: Eerdmans, 2000), 846.
124. George Bradford Caird, *Paul's Letters From Prison (Ephesians, Philippians, Colossians, Philemon) in the Revised Standard Version* (Oxford: Oxford University Press, 1976), 87.
125. John B. Muddiman, *A Commentary on the Epistle to the Hebrews* (London and New York: Continuum, 2001).
126. Clarice J. Martin, "A Chamberlain's Journey and the Challenge of Interpretation for Liberation," *Semeia* 47 (1989), 110–111.
127. Charles Kingsley Barrett, *A Critical and Exegetical Commentary on the Acts of the Apostles in Two Volumes* (Edinburgh: T & T Clark, 1994), 420–436.
128. On this last area, see, for instance, Fernando F. Segovia and R. S. Sugirtharajah, *A Postcolonial Commentary on the New Testament Writings* (London and New York: T & T Clark, 2007); R. S. Sugirtharajah, ed., *Still at the Margins: Biblical Scholarship Fifteen Years after "Voices from the Margin"* (London and New York: T & T Clark, 2008).

Bibliography

Abbott, Evelyn, and Lewis Campbell. *The Life and Letters of Benjamin Jowett, M.A. Master of Balliol College, Oxford with Portraits and Other Illustrations in Two Volumes.* London: John Murray, 1897.
Barrett, Charles Kingsley. "New Testament Commentaries III: Epistles and Revelation." *Expository Times* 65, no. 6 (1954): 177–180.
Barrett, Charles Kingsley. *A Commentary on the First Epistle to the Corinthians.* London: A & C Black, 1968.
Barrett, Charles Kingsley. *A Critical and Exegetical Commentary on the Acts of the Apostles in Two Volumes.* Edinburgh: T & T Clark, 1994.
Beard, Mary. "Cecil Rhodes and Oriel College, Oxford." *Times Literary Supplement*, December 20, 2015.
Biggar, Nigel. "Message to Students: Rhodes Was No Racist." *The Times*, December 22, 2015.
Biggar, Nigel. "Don't Feel Guilty about Our Colonial History." *The Times*, November 30, 2017.
Caird, George Bradford. *Paul's Letters from Prison (Ephesians, Philippians, Colossians, Philemon) in the Revised Standard Version.* Oxford: Oxford University Press, 1976.
Césaire, Aimé. *Return to My Native Land.* Paris: Présence Africaine, 1968.
Césaire, Aimé. *Discourse on Colonialism.* New York: Monthly Review Press, 1972.
Cobain, Ian, and Jessica Hatcher. "Kenyan Mau Mau Victims in Talks with UK Government over Legal Settlement." *The Guardian*, May 5, 2013.
Cranfield, C. E. B. *The Gospel according to Saint Mark.* Cambridge: Cambridge University Press, 1963.
Cranfield, C. E. B. *The Service of God.* London: Epworth Press, 1965.
Dalrymple, William. "*The British in India* by David Gilmour Review—Three Centuries of Ambition and Experience." *The Guardian*, September 27, 2018.
Davison, Peter, ed. *Orwell and Politics* London: Penguin, 2001.
Dirlik, Arif. "Response to the Responses: Thoughts on the Postcolonial." *Interventions* 1, no. 2 (1999): 286–290.
Elkins, Caroline. *Imperial Reckoning: the Untold Story of Britain's Gulag in Kenya.* London: Pimlico, 2005.

Fanon, Frantz. *Peau Noire, Masques Blancs*. Paris: Éditions du Seuil, 1952.
Fanon, Frantz. *Les Damnés de la Terre*. Paris: F. Maspero, 1961.
Ferguson, Niall. *Empire: How Britain Made the Modern World*. London: Penguin, 2003.
Gilley, Bruce. "The Case for Colonialism." *Third World Quarterly* (Online, September 8, 2017): 1–17.
Gopal, Priyamvada. *Insurgent Empire: Anticolonial Resistance and British Dissent*. London and New York: Verso, 2019.
Gott, Richard. "Let's End the Myths of Britain's Imperial Past." *The Guardian*, October 19, 2011.
Hargreaves, John. *A Guide to St Mark's Gospel*. London: SPCK, 1969.
Headlam, Arthur Cayley. *The Life and Teaching of Jesus the Christ*. London: John Murray, 1923.
Hinchliff, Peter. *Benjamin Jowett and the Christian Religion*. Oxford: Clarendon Press, 1987.
Hort, Arthur Fenton. *Life and Letters of Fenton John Anthony Hort*. London: Macmillan, 1896.
Hort, Fenton John Anthony. *Village Sermons in Outline*. London: Macmillan, 1898.
Hunter, Archibald Macbride. *The Gospel according to Saint Matthew*. London: SCM Press, 1949.
Jackson, Ashley. *The British Empire: A Very Short Introduction*. Oxford: Oxford University Press, 2013.
James, Cyril Lionel Robert. *Beyond a Boundary*. London: Serpent's Tail, 1994.
Jasper, Ronald. *Arthur Cayley Headlam: The Life and Letters of a Bishop*. London: Faith Press, 1960.
Jenne, Amelia. "Mary Beard Says Drive to Remove Cecil Rhodes Statue from Oxford University Is a 'Dangerous Attempt to Erase the Past.'" *The Independent*, December 22, 2015.
Johnson, Sherman Elbridge. *A Commentary on the Gospel according to St. Mark*. London: A & C Black, 1960.
Jowett, Benjamin. "On the Interpretation of Scripture." In *Essays and Reviews: The 1860 Text and Its Reading*, edited by Victor Shea and William Whitla, 477–536. Charlottesville: University Press of Virginia, 2000.
Kaye, Bruce N. "Lightfoot and Baur on Early Christianity." *Novum Testamentum* 26, no. 3 (1984): 193–224.
Kidd, Patrick. "Meander through Oxford's Dark Past is More Than a Woke Walk." *The Times*, January 25, 2020.
Lightfoot, Joseph Barber. *Saint Paul's Epistles to the Colossians and to Philemon*. London: Macmillan, 1875.
Lightfoot, Joseph Barber. *Sermons Preached on Special Occasions*. London: Macmillan, 1891.
Lightfoot, Joseph Barber. *Sermons by the Late Right Rev. J. B. Lightfoot. D.D., D.C.L., Lord Bishop of Durham*. London: Swan Sonnenschein, 1892.
Maitra, Sumantra. "'If I Want to Hold Seminars on the Topic of Empire, I Will Do So Privately': An Interview with Nigel Biggar." *Quillette*, June 7, 2018.
Marshall, I. Howard. *A Critical and Exegetical Commentary on the Pastoral Epistles*. Edinburgh: T & T Clark, 1999.
Martin, Clarice J. "A Chamberlain's Journey and the Challenge of Interpretation for Liberation." *Semeia* 47 (1989): 105–135.
Moule, Charles Francis Digby. *The Gospel according to Mark*. Cambridge: Cambridge University Press, 1965.
Mount, Ferdinand. "Umbrageousness." *London Review of Books* 39, no. 17 (2017): 3–8.
Muddiman, John B. *A Commentary on the Epistle to the Hebrews*. London and New York: Continuum, 2001.

"New Testament Revision: The New English Version." *Quarterly Review* 153, no. 305 (1882): 1–63.

"New Testament Revision: Westcott and Hort's Textual Theory." *Quarterly Review* 153, no. 306 (1882): 309–377.

O'Toole, Fintan. *Heroic Failure: Brexit and the Politics of Pain*. London: Head of Zeus, 2019.

Plummer, Alfred. *An Exegetical Commentary on the Gospel according to S. Matthew*. London: Elliot Stock, 1909.

Rayan, Samuel. "Caesar versus God." In *Jesus Today*, edited by Stephen Kappen, 88–97. Madras: AICUF, 1985.

Reynolds, David. *Island Stories: Britain and Its History in the Age of Brexit*. London: William Collins, 2019.

Robertson, Archibald, and Alfred Plummer. *A Critical and Exegetical Commentary on the First Epistle of St Paul to the Corinthians*. Edinburgh: T & T Clark, 1911.

Robinson, Maxwell R. *A Commentary on the Pastoral Epistles*. Madras: Christian Literature Society, 1962.

Said, Edward W. *Orientalism: Western Conceptions of the Orient, with a New Afterword*. London: Penguin, 1995.

Sanderson, David. "Censorship on Campus 'Is Stalinist.'" *The Times*, October 8, 2018.

Segovia, Fernando F., and R. S. Sugirtharajah. *A Postcolonial Commentary on the New Testament Writings*. London and New York: T & T Clark, 2007.

Smith, Paul. "Refuge of the Aristocracy." *London Review of Books* 23, no. 12 (June 21, 2001).

Srinivasan, Amia. "Under Rhodes." *London Review of Books* 38, no. 7 (March 31, 2016).

Sugirtharajah, R. S., ed. *Still at the Margins: Biblical Scholarship Fifteen Years after "Voices from the Margin."* London and New York: T & T Clark, 2008.

Sumner, John Bird. *A Treatise on the Records of the Creation and on the Moral Attributes of the Creator; With Particular Reference to the Jewish History, and to the Consistency of the Principle of Population with the Wisdom and Goodness of the Deity*. London: J. Hatchard and Son, 1816.

Symonds, Richard. *Oxford and Empire: The Last Lost Cause?* London: Macmillan, 1986.

Taylor, Vincent. *The Gospel according to St. Mark*. London: Macmillan, 1952.

Thiselton, Anthony C. *The First Epistle to the Corinthians: A Commentary on the Greek Text*. Grand Rapids, MI: Eerdmans, 2000.

Thrall, Margaret E. *The First and Second Letters of Paul to the Corinthians*. Cambridge: Cambridge University Press, 1965.

Treloar, Geoffrey R. *Lightfoot the Historian: The Nature and Role of History in the Life and Thought of J. B. Lightfoot (1828–1889) as Churchman and Scholar*. Tübingen: Mohr Siebeck, 1998.

Vance, Norman. "Improving Ireland: Richard Whately, Theology, and Political Economy," In *Economy, Polity, and Society: British Intellectual History, 1750–1950*, edited by Stefan Collini, Richard Whatmore, and B. W. Young, 181–202. Cambridge: Cambridge University Press, 2000.

Westcott, Arthur. *Life and Letters of Brooke Foss Westcott: In Two Volumes*. London: Macmillan, 1903.

Westcott, Brooke Foss. *On Some Points in the Religious Office of the Universities*. London: Macmillan, 1873.

Westcott, Brooke Foss. *Social Aspects of Christianity*. London: Macmillan, 1887.

Westcott, Brooke Foss. *The Incarnation and the Common Life*. London: Macmillan, 1893.

Westcott, Brooke Foss. *Christian Aspects of Life*. London: Macmillan, 1897.
Westcott, Brooke Foss. *Lessons from Work*. London: Macmillan, 1901.
Westcott, Brooke Foss. *Saint Paul's Epistle to the Ephesians: The Greek Text with Notes and Addenda*. London: Macmillan, 1906.
Whately, E. Jane. *Life and Correspondence of Richard Whately, D.D., Late Archbishop of Dublin, in Two Volumes*. London: Longmans, Green, 1866.
Ziesler, John A. *Paul's Letter to the Romans*. London: SCM Press, 1989.

CHAPTER 14

WHITE WOMAN'S BURDEN AND THE BIBLE DURING THE BRITISH OCCUPATION OF SINGAPORE

CHIN MING STEPHEN LIM

> You must not say to Him "what doest Thou?" He is your *absolute* Sovereign. All you possess is at His will. And you must obey Him; if He say "Go," you must go; "Come" you must come; "Do this," you must do it. Your will must be His. *You are His servant—His willing Bondsman.*
>
> The Christian in Singapore: A Religious Magazine

INTRODUCTION

THIS essay is an attempt to "muddl[e] along at the margins" by exploring the use of the Bible in one periphery of the British Empire of the nineteenth century: Singapore as part of the region of Southeast Asia.[1] In particular, the discussion focuses on the intersection of two margins: (1) the geopolitical aspect, as Singapore was considered peripheral to missionary interests in the East Asian region;[2] and (2) gender as seen in the work of woman missionaries and their protégés.[3] This is in order to assess the extent to which the "reader rebelled, the past was liberated and the text was made problematic" in the hands of those seen as operating in the margins of the British Empire.[4]

Among the key functions that women performed in the mission field during the nineteenth century, education of local women and children arguably had the greatest impact on the societies of the colonized.[5] One of the major centers of education in Southeast

Asia was Singapore, especially during the period when missions in China had yet to take off. In the interest of space, this essay surveys the work of women missionaries, especially Sophia Cooke at the Chinese Girls' School in Singapore, which was touted as the "best piece of Episcopalian mission work in Malaya."[6] In the imagination of white missionaries, this school was the model of British benevolence in the region and supplied a broadly inclusive, progressive curriculum to women of all ages.[7] Singapore is also an interesting site of study because women missionaries were not only engaged in the restricted domain of education but also participated in general education. Among these efforts in the public sphere was the Ladies Bible and Tract Society, which published a quarterly periodical titled *The Christian in Singapore: A Religious Magazine*. The periodical had explicit intentions to educate the Christian masses. The key line of inquiry in this essay is to see how far what Antoinette Burton outlines as the "white woman's burden" manifested itself in the Singaporean context through use of the Bible. Therefore, this essay begins with a discussion of how the work of white women is entangled with interests of the Empire before analyzing the periodical *The Christian in Singapore* and a regional publication, *India's Women and China's Daughters*. This is followed by a closer look at education and women in periodicals published by the Church Missionary Society (henceforth, CMS), particularly as an aspect of the biography of Sophia Cooke, a prominent missionary in Singapore.

CHURCH AND EMPIRE: WHITE WOMEN MANUFACTURING DOCILE SUBJECTS

According to Antoinette Burton, liberal bourgeois feminism of nineteenth-century Britain was a major impetus for women's involvement in civilizing missions, what Burton calls the "White Woman's Burden." In her assessment, the movement has more in common with the imperial ethos of the Empire than what one would expect.[8] First, even though women were regarded as the weaker sex within Victorian sexual ideology, they were often thought of as having moral superiority, given their roles in bringing up children. This perception was successfully utilized by Victorian feminists to establish their place in social concerns outside the home. Second, feminists were able to rebut the accusation that the feminist movement destabilized families (and by implication the Anglo-Saxon race as a whole) by redirecting their energies from their domestic space to the wider political arena. In response, British feminists argued that, on the contrary, they were the "mothers of the race" and "enthusiastically claimed racial responsibility as part of their strategy to legitimize themselves as responsible and important imperial citizens."[9] Such a claim was often made on the basis of not only racial but also religious and cultural grounds. Finally, the Empire at large provided a raison d'être for the women's movement in Britain of the nineteenth century. When it came to civilizing the Empire, most feminist reformers saw themselves as the most ideal candidates or, in Burton's words, "the guarantor of social progress, the agent of civilization."[10]

Howard Le Couteur also identifies education and countering indigenous religious beliefs and practices in the colonies as key approaches in the colonial expansion of Empire.[11] Furthermore, in exchange for continued support and funding by the Empire, the Anglican Church became a chief organ to cultivate loyalty among the colonies through religious education, especially in church-affiliated schools. Le Couteur writes that these schools would "inculcat[e] values such as deference, civil obedience, respect for authority, and attachment to the Crown and Church," which ultimately served to establish "a well-regulated, civilized colonial society."[12] In so doing, we find that the women under the broader umbrella of the church were important facilitators in building what Hilary Carey has called "transnational spiritual networks that aimed to transcend the cultural constraints and legal proscriptions of the past."[13]

In addition, Catherine Hall points out that the pressure to produce colonial subjects through education was brought about by several factors: the slow outmoding of the slave trade in both the United Kingdom and the emerging United States of America; increasing numbers of people within British colonies who were not slaves; and critique from prominent economists like Adam Smith.[14] As she highlights, education as governance was not unique to the British Empire but had been preferred by many empires to violent force in producing subservient, obedient subjects in a process that often entailed erasure of their previous indigenous identities. What is of importance to this essay is how Hall demonstrates a clear movement from "an evangelical and conservative vision of Empire" to "a reforming liberal and secular one."[15] This secularizing movement coincided with the woman's movement in Britain that allowed women to come out as single missionaries, traversing the globe and being part of God's work beyond the confines of Britain.[16]

So, it is in light of the entanglements of the white woman's burden with Empire that the next section explores an important periodical by the Ladies Tract and Bible Society in Singapore.

The Christian in Singapore

As far as I am able to find, there are two surviving copies of *The Christian in Singapore: A Religious Magazine*, which are the first and second issues. This publication was put together by the Ladies Bible and Tract Society founded by Sophia Cooke and a few other (presumably white) women for the general education of audiences who could read English. This included both British white Christians who had migrated to Singapore and the local converts who had an English education.[17] In addition to what seem like opinion essays, there were also portions that explicitly aimed to educate—be it in terms of the history of missions, updates of missionary efforts, hymns presumably for general use, or explaining and translating different parts of Scripture. It also appeared that the intention was for the publication to be circulated around the Straits Settlements and possibly parts of China like Hong Kong, as there were sections devoted to the history of missions such as in Malacca or scattered references to these areas.[18] This could be especially so since, in the imagination of the British Empire, Singapore as a Chinese majority state was often conflated with Hong Kong, Macau, and China (and arguably the other Straits Settlements of Penang and Malacca were seen in similar ways).

The inaugural issue of *The Christian in Singapore* was published in April 1861. While it was produced under the auspices of the Ladies Bible and Tract Society, it is hard to tell who the authors really were as they were not named on most article contributions. It would be presumed for the purposes of this essay that these articles were at the very least endorsed and approved by white women missionaries in Singapore,[19] and therefore they represented fairly their views, ideas, and attitudes toward the local population that was the ostensible target audience of these publications.

Singapore as Another America?

In establishing the purpose of this periodical, the editors (presumably from the Ladies Bible and Tract Society) unequivocally wrote in the introduction that this publication served as "edification" to the readers to remember their status as God's "bondsman."[20] Being God's "servant," as it were, applied not only to the setting of a religious community but also in "your business, in society, in family circle."[21] Since the readers were nothing but "weak and ignorant child[ren]" who could "never do enough for such a Master," they must "gladly open [their] ear to instruction" and be obedient to His will. It seemed this would include devotion to the missionary cause and the propagation of its message in Singapore.[22] Therefore the so-called edification within the periodical was really a form of a check on their loyalty to the cause of the church. It is important to note that the authors made an attempt to differentiate the Christian *in* Singapore from the Christian *of* Singapore where the former were Christians "of European extraction" and the latter the inhabitants. The purpose of presumably British Christians was to be "spiritual father[s]" to the inhabitants who had converted to Christianity. Admission into the ranks of "Christians in Singapore" could be extended to locals if they had been believers for more than thirty years.[23] It would seem here that women missionaries were asserting a form of authority over not only other white women but also white men, even though the slippage into patriarchal language was clear here. Nonetheless, a spiritual hierarchy was put in place where whiteness doubtlessly occupied the upper rungs.

The opening article of this publication, titled "The Source of Power," was written in light of South Carolina and other states seceding from the American Union.[24] The authors wanted to take the opportunity to highlight a key fallacy of Republican institutions regarding their belief in democracy so as to point out that the true source of (political) power was God. Still, the editors were careful to lay out the ambivalence about the periodical's role in politics. It made clear that it did not wish to take part in "local questions with which the daily and weekly press are concerned."[25] That being said, it recognized that, since "God is the God of nations," it cannot completely overlook such matters, but rather saw its role *primarily* in bringing the Bible to shed light on these issues.[26]

The article begins with the assertion of God as "the King of all the Earth," and therefore a schema of government that worked toward any form of independence where subjects could choose their rulers was anathema to this grand scheme. The readers were then reminded that such forms of governance owed their success to "advance[s] in civilization" and "train[ing] by Religion to a willing respect for law and order."[27] In fact, the most ideal form of government this article supported was a theocracy. Such an idea was based on a reading of the nation of Israel as one that forsook its God in favor of a human king. The Israelites preferred a human king to the Mosaic Law, which formed the basis of their nation-state that demonstrated their loss of "the fear of God."[28] As a result, anarchy and chaos ensued as "each man would do 'what was right in his own eyes' (Judges 21.25)."[29] Ultimately the eventual concession God made for Israel was contingent on this form of government "recogniz[ing] that *God is the only source of power*."[30]

It would not be too far a stretch to assume that the authors had in mind Britain as the "truly pious and God fearing nation."[31] This could be illustrated in the 1860s by Thomas Jones Barker's famous painting *The Secret of England's Success*, where, as Rasiah Sugirtharajah describes, the Bible was portrayed as "England's greatest cultural product ... [that] will be distributed throughout the world as an icon containing civilizing properties."[32] In this instance, it seemed that the law of the Empire was analogous to the "Mosaic Law" of which religion played a vital role in upholding. If that were true, then the opening article of a magazine instructing Christians in the local populace was meant to set the tone for the British Empire, serving as a sharp reminder that creating another "Republic" in Singapore would be tantamount to disobeying God Almighty himself who had set up the rulers of this great Christian nation. The basic legitimation for such a claim was found in the very pages of the Bible itself in the experience of the "Republic" of Israel that abandoned its "theocracy." Such a warning was not only to local elites but also to British settlers who might have entertained similar thoughts like those who migrated to the Americas.

Yet at the same time, there seems to be an ambivalence that attends this writing. In negotiating the secularizing turn of British society mentioned earlier, there was an insistence on acknowledging that the "sovereigns of modern states," who could also include those of the British Empire, lived on "God's providence" for the ultimate pleasure of God himself. They too were bound by "loyalty and willing obedience" if they expected "Divine favor" over them and their nation-states. They are expected to uphold "Law or Order" as constituted by "God's ordinance" rather than the works of man.[33]

That being said, rebellion was discouraged in every way:

> [I]n the event of bad government, it is not the right of the people to be impatient, or to take the matter into their own hands; but to humble themselves under their trial as affliction sent from above; because good government is God's blessing, and bad government is His chastening for national sin.[34]

Here, the authors were possibly alluding to Romans 13 and 1 Peter 2 even though no explicit biblical reference was made. The Bible, however, was quoted to conclude the call of the Christian in the midst of such chaos—that is, to practice more personal piety such as faithfully attending church and spreading the gospel. Citing Hosea 8:4 and Ezekiel 21:26–27, the article ended with a resounding claim that God alone had the power to "overturn, overturn, overturn" the current rulers and would give the right to rule to Him when "He comes whose right it is."[35]

As Carl Trocki points out, Stamford Raffles, who established Singapore as a free port, was a key catalyst in putting the city at the center of the opium trade in the East and Southeast Asian regions.[36] In fact, he goes so far as to demonstrate that opium was the major item of trade in Singapore in the nineteenth century and that it connected the economies of the British and the Chinese.[37] The complexities of these economic relationships should not detain us. Of relevance to this essay, opium abuse was a major problem among the Chinese population. This was even acknowledged in the missionary archives. For instance, Reverend W. C. Burns wrote in 1861 that the problem of opium was so bad that "the race of Chinese in Singapore would, in two or three generations become extinct."[38] Therefore it would be surprising that these white women were unaware of this, especially since those like Sophia Cooke would come into intimate contact with the local Chinese population. It is of course difficult to speculate, but there is at least one indication of the reason why. In a possibly rare moment of critical reflexivity, Miss Hessie Newcombe, who was a missionary to China, conceded the complicity of Christians with the opium trade. After being confronted about the "poison [of opium] . . . from England," she wrote, "I did not dare to tell her the whole truth, that our Christian Government obtained a portion of its revenue from its sale."[39] Notwithstanding the preceding discussion, modern readers ought to be curious that, rather than dealing with the issue of opium abuse their Empire brought to the shores of East Asia, including Singapore, the article seemed to be more concerned with the potential ills of a country that became independent of the Empire so far away.

On a related note, Anne Foster points out that opium generated a significant proportion of the revenue needed for running different colonial empires in the Southeast Asian region where Singapore was likely most dependent.[40] In terms of the British Empire's trade interests in Singapore, opium was most certainly one of the main attractions.[41] Yet in dealing with wealth, the periodical was overtly more concerned with how money was spent rather than where it came from. For instance, the difficult passage in Luke 16:9, where Jesus tells of a parable exhorting his hearers to "make to yourselves friends of the mammon of unrighteousness," was paraphrased as "[b]ut do ye use even the things of the world not in the service of the world, but as *subsidiary* to your *faithful use* of the true riches."[42] As a result, the entire parable was interpreted precisely as saying that, because one cannot have two Masters, "Mammon must be used for the purposes of God."[43] This was reinforced by contributions to the section in the periodical called "The Gleaner,"[44] which reduced the idea of serving "one Master" as a matter of "conscience," "break[ing] the chains of self" and "sav[ing] the soul."[45] Of course, such spiritualizing away the problems of wealth by avoiding the question of where it came from, and obsessing over how it was used, should not be surprising given that to read and speak English was a sure sign of white class privilege and those who had the good fortune to share in it. Yet in the backdrop of Empire and opium, such interpretations of Scripture with the veneer of authority went a long way to entrench systemic ignorance regarding problems of British occupation.

Overall, the expected result of such discursive use of the Bible by this periodical was to inculcate docility and submission in the subjects through deferring all political power and, by implication, agency to God himself. The obsession of the Christian in Singapore has to be located elsewhere in questions of assurance of salvation, personal sin,[46] reliability of the Scriptures,[47] and servility to the God of the Bible. It is hard to miss the subtle irony of the Marxist axiom of religion as the opiate of the masses in a city ravaged by opium itself.

If we are to understand *The Christian in Singapore* more generously, the Ladies Tract and Bible Society was an intermediary communicating the desires of presumably white men in power within the metropoles of Britain to subjects of the colony. A more cynical take would be that they were, as Barbara Ramusack writes, maternal imperialists— claiming what would be essentially patriarchal authority to discipline subjects, including white male settlers, into upholding their responsibilities to the Empire in the peripheral colonies.[48] In other words, they were leveraging their moral superiority to discipline the masses into submission to God and his ordained Empire. Perhaps surprisingly, given the rising role of white women in Britain during the course of the nineteenth century, is that the dimension of gender was largely missing in these opening issues.

WOMEN'S MISSIONS AND EDUCATION

This section takes a closer look at the work of white woman missionaries in the schools they had set up. In the East and Southeast Asian contexts, Valerie Griffiths traces the inception of woman's education to Robert Morrison's return to Britain in 1824.[49] Influenced by growing concern within Britain for equal education for both boys and girls, he sought support for the commissioning of single women to go out to East and Southeast Asia to educate girls. He even took it upon himself to teach a few women the Chinese language at his home in Hackney. Among his students was Maria Tarn Dyer, who went on to found the Chinese Girls' School in Singapore in 1842. One of the most notable headmistresses, Sophia Cooke, took over in 1854 and ran the school for the next forty-two years. Under her charge, the school grew exponentially.[50] Ryan Dunch sums up the functions of women's education in the East Asian region, which would include Chinese-majority settlements in Southeast Asia like Singapore, as "the need for converts to read the Bible, the need to procure educated wives for church workers, and the aspirations of converts for their daughters."[51]

Furthermore, setting up schools in the Southeast Asian region was a pragmatic move because, at this time, China was closed to all missionaries. In the years to come, as Griffiths traces, the Chinese Girls' School in Singapore would become an important source of sending women into China as Biblewomen.[52] In the highly gendered societies of East Asia, these Biblewomen could serve their husbands and bring up their children. In addition, the exigencies of ministry to non-Christian women in societies that adhere to strict gender segregration facilitated the move of these women out of their homes and into rural villages to perform the roles that men would have.[53]

In the interest of space, the next section explores the story of one such prominent Biblewoman within the CMS Periodicals—Chitnio, who trained under Sophia Cooke in Singapore. This discussion will also be supplemented with stories from E. A. Walker's biography, *Sophia Cooke; or Forty-Two Years' Work in Singapore*, and reports in the regional periodical *India's Women and China's Daughters*.

CHITNIO: MODEL BIBLEWOMAN

One name that stands out in the writings of both white men and white women during this period is Chitnio, or Mrs. Ling. So celebrated was she as the model Biblewoman that an extended write-up was devoted to her in the regional periodical *India's Women and China's Daughters*.[54] Why it is particularly pertinent in this essay is the seemingly extraordinary effort on the part of the periodicals to mention her time of training under Sophia Cooke at the Chinese Girls' School. Through the eyes of the British Empire, Chitnio arguably represented one of the Western church's greatest achievements in civilizing the native.[55]

As mentioned earlier, Chitnio was trained at the Chinese Girls' School in Singapore under the headship of Sophia Cooke. Like many Biblewomen, she was eventually matched up with a clergyman in Foochow who was a catechist with CMS.[56] Unfortunately her husband died two years after the marriage when he was arrested and tortured to death by the Chinese government.[57] According to early-twentieth-century records, Chitnio had risen to a position as prominent matron of a training school for Biblewomen in Foochow while it was still under the headship of white women.[58] What follows is an analysis of an account by Chitnio, which was supposedly published "with very slight revision."[59]

From Darkness to Light

Chitnio's autobiographical account was prefaced by a conflict between the "the great Empire of China" and the "Church of Christ in China."[60] Where the future of the former was "subject of speculation," the latter was not "a matter . . . of speculation" but "of reasonable certainty."[61] Therefore in the eyes of the colonialists, a battle was being waged within this seemingly insignificant account of a Chinese woman abandoning her Chinese roots to become a Christian. Chitnio's account echoed this when she alluded to

1 Peter 2:9 in her conclusion that "God has called me out of darkness into His marvellous light."[62] This is supplemented by another allusion to Colossians 1:13 where she thanked God who "hath delivered me from the power of darkness, and hath translated me into the kingdom of His dear Son."[63]

In Chitnio's autobiographical accounts, her previous world was constantly shrouded in darkness. Her family were "all heathen" (she herself readily accepted this label), deep in the "worshipping [of] the idols" and "very, very ignorant."[64] Not only were they trapped in the darkness but also they did not allow anyone to leave it. Her father opposed her going to the Chinese Girls' School to the point that she could only go literally over his dead body: "As long as I live I will not let you go. If I die, I should not see you; then you may do what you like."[65] Writing in a style reminiscent of a kind of apathy one might encounter in Old Testament accounts of death during war, Chitnio quite blandly stated, "[a] few weeks after that he died, knowing nothing of the doctrine of Christ."[66] Her elder brother also opposed her going but was eventually persuaded to bring her there. Miss J. Bushel summarized the mounting hostility from Chitnio's family as moving from "entreaties" to "wrath" where they threatened to cut her material inheritance, which seemed to suggest how the Chinese were money-minded. In order to reflect a kind of childlike faith that obedient natives were presumed to have, Bushel showed how easily Chitnio abandoned her previous beliefs when her teacher simply led her to see that only God could create her hand so "beautifully" and "wonderfully."[67] The opposition of her family was also mentioned by Chitnio. One could say that she went further, dramatizing her family's attempt to frighten her with claims that only the "heathens" would concoct, such as saying that "when a Christian died his eyes were pulled out, and his feet and hands cut off."[68]

Such dark tropes of the Chinese world found similar expressions in other parts of the archives. First, Chinese families were touted to be poor places for the nurturing of young girls, and they were depicted as being excessively disciplined with the use of the "rod"[69] and running the risk of abandonment should they fall too ill. When it came to marriage, Chinese girls were "often sold by their heartless parents to Malay sailors for a mere trifle," which then meant that one "happy result of Singapore under British rule" was that they could seek refuge in the schools that they had set up for them.[70] Given the prevalence of opium abuse in Singapore, it is curious that it was never numbered among the "sins" of the Chinese in these accounts about and by Chinese women.

Second, as the account of Chitnio seemed to imply, the Chinese world was full of idols and superstitions. With regard to this issue, there was a greater prevalence of the use of the Bible, which in this case was mainly Psalms 115, especially verses 4 to 7. The students, mostly girls, were challenged to test the veracity of the verses that claimed idols were substantially nothing. There were different attempts to test whether the idols were real, such as poking them with a fork[71] or smashing them to see if there were any true consequences.[72]

Therefore, the Bible served to frame the world into binary, irreconcilable opposites of light and darkness. The world of darkness was explicit with its false idols and wanton cultural practices. These vilifications then often implicitly suggested the world of light represented by the British Empire and its subjects as the ideal opposite. In this synthesis, the Bible gave Biblewomen such as Chitnio the hermeneutical resources needed to depict their Chineseness as a set of dangerous superstitions and, as seen in the next section, the tools to debunk it.

Bible as Source of Empowerment

Seemingly unfazed by the deaths of two close relatives within less than six months, Chitnio's struggle centered on becoming a devout Christian. It is here that her account was lit up with references from the Bible such as "the light of Jesus Christ shone into [Chitnio's] heart."[73] The Lord's Prayer and the Ten Commandments were mobilized as counterdiscourses to the pagan superstitions of her community. When her family begged her not to get baptized, she prayed (presumably with the aid of the Lord's Prayer) that she would be "faithful, and not deny Christ."[74]

Furthermore, the Bible became an important place of refuge as Chitnio weathered her departure from the "darkness" of the Chinese world. Citing from Jeremiah 31:3, she gained assurance that God loved her with "an everlasting love." In response, she evoked Psalms 101:1 to "[b]less the Lord . . . [and] His Holy Name" in hope that in "suffer[ing] with Him, [she] shall also reign with Him (2 Timothy 2:12)."[75] Therefore, she used these symbolic footholds to scale the walls that her family and traditions had erected around her so as to escape her captivity to the "darkness."

Another instance of using the Bible as a means to endure such struggles was Anleang, a woman who told missionaries that, despite strong opposition in her family, she felt assured by the word of God that her salvation was "bought, not 'with corruptible things, as silver and gold, but with the precious blood of Christ,'" presumably alluding to 1 Peter 1:18–20.[76] Therefore, the Bible gave many of these girls the will to persevere through these trials so as to become "Chinese Fellow Soldier[s] of Jesus Christ."[77]

Colonial Mimicry or Imitation?

What is perhaps salient in Chitnio's correspondence and writings is a possibly high level of what Homi Bhabha calls "mimicry."[78] To him, in order to better satisfy his proposal of colonial mimicry, there has to be also "the desire for a reformed, recognizable Other, as *a subject of a difference that is almost the same, but not quite.*"[79] One finds similar teachings about idols using Psalms 115 and the Ten Commandments by British women themselves.[80] Yet there are also slippages in the accounts of her work, such as the time Chitnio was defending her husband's death. She pointed out that many saw them as working for the English when in actuality they perceived themselves as working for God.[81]

That being said, it would seem such a view hardly permeated Chitnio's uses of the Bible as illustrated earlier. This might be attributed to the nature of the material consulted since much of it was found within the established archives of British institutions.

Therefore, one has to remain highly skeptical of how much it represents the subaltern during the British occupation.[82] Another possible reason is that she cites from the Bible, which she might have perceived as the white man's (and white woman's) text—a tradition to which she could not imagine herself as an heir but rather as an adoptee, where the feeling of being an outsider continued to linger and haunt her writings. Given the fragmentary nature of the evidence, it would be hard to arrive at a definitive conclusion.

Some Conclusions

This short essay explores the different tropes that influenced biblical interpretation among white women and the Biblewomen they trained in the British colony of Singapore in relation to Empire. First, the Bible was constantly called upon to frame the world into biblical-sounding tropes of light and darkness in accounts of both white women and their disciples. Second, the Bible was used to understand Chinese religions as idolatrous and patently false. In contrast, the Bible offered refuge, as it "calls our feeble women from the very depths of idolatry and misery, enables them to live such lovely lives, and to die such fearless and blessed deaths!"[83] In other words, it claimed to help them weather their exodus out of their Egypt called "the Chinese world." The end result of these maneuvers produced the third function of the Bible, which was to facilitate submission to the Empire lest the colonies fall into the times of Judges where everyone did "what was right in his own eyes." In addition to being a warning against judgment, the Bible also exhorted subjects to "sit like Mary at the feet of Jesus and obey his will in all things" rather than remaining "in the midst of [their] rebellion and stout-heartedness."[84]

Thus we find the Bible embroiled in efforts of white women to produce docile subjects among young Chinese women. The liberation of white women to form missionary societies in the colonies, such as the Ladies Bible and Tract Society that enjoyed relative autonomy in running women's education, does not necessarily translate into similar liberation of the colonized Other. Rather this emancipation subtly fulfills what Madhavi Kale describes very aptly as "the missionaries' role in the consolidation of imperial modernity [and] the production of modern, colonial governmentality," or what has been discussed earlier as the white woman's burden through maternal imperialism.[85]

Despite these efforts, the use of the Bible was usually marginal at best. It was often referred to vaguely and sometimes interchangeably with the word "Gospel." There were very few references to specific verses or even particular stories and teachings in the Bible. Very often, the Bible had to be emptied of its contents in order to allow for greater mobility in the discourse of missionaries in the service of church expansion and empire building. In doing so, the power of the Bible could be used with relatively greater ease to *sacralize* the damaging essentialist ideas of the Chinese as being steeped in idolatry and holding on to archaic ways of living, especially with respect to religious views like the afterlife. Different adherents engaged in various rhetorics of representation, in which the Chinese were likened to the ancient Near Eastern peoples of old who hang on to false gods—to which white women held out the Bible as the bastion of universal, moral truth. The end-result of such discursive claims on Scripture would ultimately serve to cement these tropes about the Chinese frozen in darkness and white women as their saviors.

Finally, the benefits of women's education that missionaries like Sophia Cooke brought cannot be denied. It most certainly gave many women an opportunity to learn that they would not otherwise have easily accessed. In all likelihood, these white women perceived themselves, very much like Chitnio, to be doing "God's work" rather than the Empire's work. Perhaps a more generous way of looking at this is that, while being sandwiched between positive associations with whiteness and Empire and negative connections to gender constructions, these white women, through their use of the Bible, reproduced the very subordination they claimed to be fighting against. A more cynical take would be that the peripheries provided opportunities for white women to exercise power and control over the colonized in Singapore and, by implication, the East Asian context. Having once entered the fold of the church, the colonized, especially women and children, would become ripe for the Empire to reap for their loyalty and devotion. How the Empire capitalized on the work of white women is a subject for future study, but at the very least one could see the great potential for that to happen.

In 2019, Singapore committed the entire year to commemorate 200 years since the arrival of the British in 1819, making it one of the few countries in the world that gives such importance to its colonial past. While relatively muted, the legacies of Sophia Cooke and other white women are still remembered and celebrated.[86] In light of this, the essay presents myself as a Singaporean reader, as it were of another time who resists in hope to liberate in some small measure the past by problematizing the use of the Bible in the hands of white women and their disciples.

Notes

I would like to thank Hong Kong Baptist University Library's Special Collections and Archives for allowing me access to the Church Missionary Society Periodicals.

1. The opening epigraph is from "To the Reader," *The Christian in Singapore: A Religious Magazine* 1, no. 1 (1861): 3, emphasis theirs. Rasiah S. Sugirtharjah, "Muddling along the Margins," in *Still at the Margins: Biblical Scholarship Fifteen Years after the Voices from the Margin*, ed. Rasiah S. Sugirtharajah (London: T&T Clark, 2008), 8–22.
2. Robbie Goh, *Christianity in Southeast Asia* (Singapore: Institute of Southeast Asian Studies, 2005), 35–37.
3. Wai-Ching Angela Wong and Patricia P. K. Chiu, "Introduction," in *Christian Women in Chinese Society: The Anglican Story*, ed. Wai-Ching Angela Wong and Patricia P. K. Chiu (Hong Kong: Hong Kong University Press, 2018), 2–3.
4. Sugirtharajah, "Muddling along the Margins," 13.
5. Patricia Grimshaw and Peter Sherlock, "Women and Cultural Exchange," in *Missions and Empire*, ed. Norman Etherington (Oxford; New York: Oxford University Press, 2005), 173–193 (180).

6. "Notices of Books: Sunny Singapore," *The Church Missionary Review* 58 (1907): 499. See also "Editorial Notes," *India's Women and China's Daughters* (1900): 26–27; http://eresources.nlb.gov.sg/infopedia/articles/SIP_2014-12-16_105929.html (last accessed January 29, 2023).
7. "The Chinese Girls' School, Singapore—An Interesting Extract," *India's Women and China's Daughters* 56, no. 589 (1936): 35.
8. Antoinette Burton, "The White Woman's Burden: British Feminists and the 'Indian Woman,' 1865–1915," in *Western Women and Imperialism: Complicity and Resistance*, ed. Nupur Chaudhuri and Margaret Strobel (Bloomington: Indiana University Press, 1992), 137–157.
9. Ibid., 138.
10. Ibid., 139.
11. Howard Le Couteur, "Anglican High Churchmen and the Expansion of Empire," *Journal of Religious History* 32, no. 2 (2008): 194.
12. Ibid., 202.
13. Hilary M. Carey, *God's Empire: Religion and Colonialism in the British World, C. 1801–1908* (Cambridge; New York: Cambridge University Press, 2011), 4.
14. Catherine Hall, "Making Colonial Subjects: Education in the Age of Empire," *History of Education* 37, no. 6 (2008): 774.
15. Ibid., 784, 787.
16. Wong and Chiu, "Introduction," 5.
17. Bobby E. K. Sng, *In His Good Time: The Story of the Church in Singapore 1819–1992*, 2nd ed. (Singapore: Graduate Christian Fellowship, 1993), 71.
18. "Malacca," *The Christian in Singapore* 1, no. 1 (1861): 28–35.
19. There are signs that contributions could be from both men and women. For instance in one article, the author makes special reference to "our lady readers" while remarking "we men" within the same paragraph. It is hard to tell if "men" is used generically as humankind or in the gendered sense of the word. "Natura—Nature, Prophetic of Her Restitution," *The Christian in Singapore* 1, no. 1 (1861): 14.
20. "To the Reader," 3.
21. Ibid., 3.
22. Ibid., 4.
23. Ibid., 5.
24. "The Source of Power," *The Christian in Singapore* 1, no. 1 (1861): 7–10.
25. "To the Reader," 6.
26. Ibid., 6.
27. "The Source of Power," 7.
28. Ibid., 8.
29. Ibid.
30. Ibid., 9, emphasis theirs.
31. Ibid., 8.
32. Rasiah S. Sugirtarajah, *The Postcolonial Bible* (Sheffield: Sheffield Academic, 1998), 14–15.
33. "The Source of Power," 9.
34. Ibid., 10.
35. Ibid.
36. Carl A. Trocki, *Opium and Empire: Chinese Society in Colonial Singapore, 1800–1910* (Ithaca; London: Cornell University Press, 1990), 1.
37. Ibid., 2–6.

38. "The Present State: The Opium Trade with China," *Scottish Review* (1860): 12.
39. Hessie Newcombe, "Foo-Chow—Much Land to be Possessed," *India's Women and China's Daughters* 10, no. 59 (1890): 274.
40. Anne L. Foster, "Opium, The United States and the Civilizing Mission in Southeast Asia," *Social History of Alcohol and Drugs* 24, no. 1 (2010): 8–9. See also Trocki, *Opium and Empire*, 70–78.
41. Trocki, *Opium and Empire*, 50–57.
42. "The Annotator," *The Christian in Singapore* 1, no. 1 (1861): 37–38, emphasis mine.
43. Ibid., 38.
44. The section featured contributions from "several kind friends" of the Ladies Bible and Tract Society. This particular issue focused on reflections of people's private experiences, including some who presumably had passed away. *The Christian in Singapore* 1, no. 1 (1861): 41.
45. "No Man Can Serve Two Masters," *The Christian in Singapore* 1, no. 1 (1861): 41.
46. See for instance, "On the Eternity of Punishment," *The Christian in Singapore* 1, no. 2 (1861): 72–80, which deals with the question of God's benevolence and his punishment of sin.
47. See for instance, "Bible History of Creation," *The Christian in Singapore* 1, no. 2 (1861): 63–71, which looks at why the creation account need not satisfy the rules of physical science to be true.
48. Barbara Ramusack, "Cultural Missionaries, Maternal Imperialists and Feminist Allies: British Women Activists in India, 1865–1945," in *Western Women and Imperialism: Complicity and Resistance*, ed. Nupur Chaudhuri and Margaret Strobel (Bloomington: Indiana University Press, 1992), 119–136.
49. Valerie Griffith, "Biblewomen from London to China: The Transnational Appropriation of a Female Mission Idea," *Women's History Review* 17, no. 4 (2008): 521–541.
50. Ibid., 523, 525. See also Sng, *In His Good Time*, 65–69.
51. Ryan Dunch, "'Mothers to Our Country': Conversion, Education, and Ideology among Chinese Protestant Women, 1870–1930," in *Pioneer Chinese Christian Women: Gender, Christianity, and Social Mobility*, ed. Jessie Gregory Lutz (Bethlehem: Lehigh University Press, 2010), 336–337. See also Wong and Chiu, "Introduction," 5–6.
52. Griffith, "Biblewomen from London to China," 525–526.
53. Dunch, "'Mothers to Our Country,'" 336.
54. "Chitnio's Story," *India's Women and China's Daughters* 7, no. 69 (1892): 99–102.
55. Her training in the school in Singapore remains an almost undetachable label in many correspondences, one that she could not shake off even after her death. See for instance, "China," *India's Women and China's Daughters* 17, no. 138 (1897): 274. Her other association was to her husband who was often celebrated as a martyr in the records. See for instance, "Our Anniversary: Our Afternoon Meeting," *India's Women and China's Daughters* Supplement (1897): 10.
56. Emilie Stevens, "The Olives, Foochow," *India's Women and China's Daughters* 17, no. 138 (1897): 274–276.
57. "Chitnio's Story," 99.
58. Emilie Stevens, "News from Foochow," *India's Women and China's Daughters* September (1902): 211.
59. "Chitnio's Story," 99.
60. Ibid.
61. Ibid.

62. Ibid., 102.
63. Ibid.
64. Ibid., 100.
65. Ibid.
66. Ibid.
67. J. Bushel, "Chitnio," *The Church Missionary Quarterly Token*, no. 210 (1908): 7.
68. "Chitnio's Story," 100.
69. E. A. Walker, *Sophia Cooke; or Forty Two Years' Work in Singapore* (London: Elliot Stock, 1899), 15.
70. Ibid., 36
71. Ibid., 14–15.
72. Ibid., 22.
73. "Chitnio's Story," 100.
74. Ibid., 101.
75. Ibid., 102.
76. Walker, *Sophia Cooke*, 16.
77. "Chitnio's Story," 102.
78. Homi Bhabha, "Of Mimicry and Man: The Ambivalence of Colonial Discourse," in *Tensions of Empire: Colonial Cultures in a Bourgeois World*, ed. Frederick Cooper and Ann Laura Stoler (Berkeley: University of California Press, 1997), 152–160.
79. Ibid., 153, emphasis his.
80. See for instance, Miss Collisson, "Miss Collisson's Report," *India's Women and China's Daughters* 2, no. 8 (1889): 84.
81. "Lin Sieng-Sing's Trials at Kiong-Ning Fu: Communicated by His Wife Chitnio," *The Church Missionary Gleaner* 5, no. 50 (1878): 20. Another instance that also betrayed her own ambivalence toward the British would be when she had to educate them on Chinese etiquette such as what to do in a Chinese home. See F. I. Codrington and A. M. Robinson, "Birds on the Wing: Chapter 4—50 Years Ago!" *Church of England Zenana Missionary Society: Homes of the East* 31, no. 132 (1934): 40–41.
82. See Ryan Dunch, "'Mothers to Our Country,'" 326–329. Here he discusses the difficulties in navigating primary sources largely written by men and focused on the work and achievements of men to find the voice of subaltern women.
83. Walker, *Sophia Cooke*, 48.
84. Ibid., 27.
85. Madhavi Kale, "Subject to Question: Empire and Catherine Hall's Civilizing Subjects," *Small Axe* 7, no. 2 (2003): 134.
86. See for instance, https://www.bible.org.sg/women-advancing-gods-word/ (last accessed January 29, 2023).

Bibliography

Bhabha, Homi. "Of Mimicry and Man: The Ambivalence of Colonial Discourse." In *Tensions of Empire: Colonial Cultures in a Bourgeois World*, edited by Frederick Cooper and Ann Laura Stoler. Berkeley: University of California Press, 1997, 152–160.

"Bible History of Creation." *The Christian in Singapore* 1, no. 2 (1861): 63–71.

Burton, Antoinette. "The White Woman's Burden: British Feminists and the 'Indian Woman,' 1865–1915." In *Western Women and Imperialism: Complicity and Resistance*, edited by Nupur Chaudhuri and Margaret Strobel. Bloomington: Indiana University Press, 1992, 137–157.

Bushel, J. "Chitnio." *The Church Missionary Quarterly Token*, no. 210 (1908): 7–8.

Carey, Hilary M. *God's Empire: Religion and Colonialism in the British World, c. 1801–1908.* Cambridge; New York: Cambridge University Press, 2011.

"China." *India's Women and China's Daughters* 17, no. 138 (1897): 274.

"The Chinese Girls' School, Singapore—An Interesting Extract." *India's Women and China's Daughters* 56, no. 589 (1936): 35.

"Chitnio's Story." *India's Women and China's Daughters* 7, no. 69 (1892): 99–102.

Codrington, F. I., and A. M. Robinson. "Birds on the Wing: Chapter 4—50 Years Ago!" *Church of England Zenana Missionary Society: Homes of the East* 31, no. 132 (1934): 37–42.

Dunch, Ryan. "'Mothers to Our Country': Conversion, Education, and Ideology among Chinese Protestant Women, 1870–1930." In *Pioneer Chinese Christian Women: Gender, Christianity, and Social Mobility*, edited by Jessie Gregory Lutz. Bethlehem: Lehigh University Press, 2010, 324–350.

"Editorial Notes." *India's Women and China's Daughters* February (1900): 25–27.

Foster, Anne L. "Opium, the United States and the Civilizing Mission in Southeast Asia." *Social History of Alcohol and Drugs* 24, no. 1 (2010): 6–19

Goh, Robbie. *Christianity in Southeast Asia*. Singapore: Institute of Southeast Asian Studies, 2005.

Griffith, Valerie. "Biblewomen from London to China: The Transnational Appropriation of a Female Mission Idea." *Women's History Review* 17, no. 4 (2008): 521–541.

Grimshaw, Patricia, and Peter Sherlock. "Women and Cultural Exchange." In *Missions and Empire*, edited by Norman Etherington. Oxford; New York: Oxford University Press, 2005, 173–193.

Hall, Catherine. "Making Colonial Subjects: Education in the Age of Empire." *History of Education* 37, no. 6 (2008): 773–787.

Kale, Madhavi. "Subject to Question: Empire and Catherine Hall's Civilizing Subjects." *Small Axe* 7, no. 2 (2003): 127–136.

Le Couteur, Howard. "Anglican High Churchmen and the Expansion of Empire." *Journal of Religious History* 32, no. 2 (2008): 193–215.

"Lin Sieng-Sing's Trials at Kiong-Ning Fu: Communicated by His Wife Chitnio." *The Church Missionary Gleaner* 5, no. 50 (1878): 20.

Miss Collisson, "Miss Collisson's Report." *India's Women and China's Daughters* 2, no. 8 (1882): 83–88.

"Malacca." *The Christian in Singapore* 1, no. 1 (1861): 28–35.

"Natura—Nature, Prophetic of Her Restitution." *The Christian in Singapore* 1, no. 1 (1861): 14.

Newcombe, Hessie. "Foo-Chow—Much Land to be Possessed." *India's Women and China's Daughters* 10, no. 59 (1890): 273–274.

"No Man Can Serve Two Masters." *The Christian in Singapore* 1, no. 1 (1861): 41.

"Notices of Books: Sunny Singapore." *The Church Missionary Review* 58 (1907): 499.

"On the Eternity of Punishment." *The Christian in Singapore* 1, no. 2 (1861): 72–80.

"Our Anniversary: Our Afternoon Meeting." *India's Women and China's Daughters* Supplement (1897): 2–13.

"The Annotator." *The Christian in Singapore* 1, no. 1 (1861): 36–40.

"The Present State: The Opium Trade with China." Extracted from *Scottish Review* January (1860): 3–16.

"The Source of Power." *The Christian in Singapore* 1, no. 1 (1861): 7–10.

"To the Reader." *The Christian in Singapore* 1, no. 1 (1861): 3–6.

Ramusack, Barbara. "Cultural Missionaries, Maternal Imperialists and Feminist Allies: British Women Activists in India, 1865–1945." In *Western Women and Imperialism: Complicity and Resistance*, edited by Nupur Chaudhuri and Margaret Strobel. Bloomington: Indiana University Press, 1992, 119–136.

Sng, Bobby E. K. *In His Good Time: The Story of the Church in Singapore 1819–1992*. 2nd ed. Singapore: Graduate Christian Fellowship, 1993.

Stevens, Emilie. "The Olives, Foochow." *India's Women and China's Daughters* 17, no. 138 (1897): 274–276.

Stevens, Emilie. "News from Foochow." *India's Women and China's Daughters* September (1902): 211.

Sugirtharajah, Rasiah S. *The Postcolonial Bible*. Sheffield: Sheffield Academic, 1998.

Sugirtharajah, Rasiah S. "Muddling along the Margins." In *Still at the Margins: Biblical Scholarship Fifteen Years after the Voices from the Margin*. edited by Rasiah S. Sugirtharajah. London: T&T Clark, 2008, 8–22.

Trocki, Carl A. *Opium and Empire: Chinese Society in Colonial Singapore, 1800–1910*. Ithaca; London: Cornell University Press, 1990.

Walker, E. A. *Sophia Cooke; or Forty Two Years' Work in Singapore*. London: Elliot Stock, 1899.

Wong, Wai-Ching Angela, and Patricia P. K. Chiu. "Introduction." In *Christian Women in Chinese Society: The Anglican Story*, edited by Wai-Ching Angela Wong and Patricia P. K. Chiu. Hong Kong: Hong Kong University Press, 2018, 1–16.

CHAPTER 15

THE BIBLE IN THE GERMAN EMPIRE

JOERG RIEGER

German Imperialism

GERMAN imperialism is a surprisingly complex topic, still underexplored, as research in German history has focused more on German fascism, National Socialism, World War II, and the Holocaust. Despite Germany's reputation as a substantial influence in the world and one of the centers of what is now often called Eurocentrism, its history as an actual colonial power lasted only thirty years from 1884 to 1914 (ending at the beginning of World War I). By the time of the Versailles Treaty in 1919, Germany had lost all of its colonies.[1] Further complexity is added by the fact that Germany became a nation-state only in 1871—the so-called *deutsche Reich* (German Empire).

Mindful of this complexity, the following chapter attempts to provide historical background as well as a variety of glimpses into the context in which the Bible was used in Germany in the nineteenth century, which leads up to the short duration of Germany's colonial powers. If imperialism is defined as central control of governments over colonies, and colonialism is defined as activities in the colonies that are not under the direct control of government,[2] then we need to bring both perspectives together when dealing with the German Empire. The words of Bradley Naranch set the stage for our inquiry: "When it comes to colonialism, there are no marginal players and no protected places entirely free of its impact."[3]

Furthermore, we also agree with Geoff Ely: "While not formally *about* colonialism, certain works become extremely suggestive once viewed in that light."[4] In order to get as much of a grasp on the Bible in the German Empire as possible, we will deal with different writings, not only academic exegesis but also sermons, devotionals, and other theological reflections that deal with core themes of the Bible. In so doing, the discussion will be limited to Protestant authors, who, in the German context, reflect the German spirit more straightforwardly than Roman Catholic authors who are shaped by theological perspectives that emerge from a broader international context linked to Rome.

When examining the German Empire, it is crucial to keep in mind the various shapes of empire. Empire is most visible in its harder forms. Conquest, slavery, military aggression, genocide, and even economic exploitation are, for the most part, openly visible. Yet empire also exists in softer forms that are often not considered in imperial terms: exploration, education, and development. The churches' missionary efforts have been linked to both harder and softer forms of empire, although German missionary efforts were usually of the softer kind and were often tied to charitable and developmental efforts, especially before 1884 and after the genocide of the Herero in 1904.

Cultural and Historical Perspectives

Recent historical studies have once again emphasized the complexity of dealing with the German Empire and colonialism. In conversation with Edward Said's ground-breaking book *Orientalism*, which investigates developments in Britain and England but does not address Germany, Suzanne Marchand has produced a monumental study of German orientalism in which she presents many different and often contradictory developments, from academics in love with their subject matter who resisted efforts to instrumentalize their knowledge to other academics, missionaries, and public officials who pursued more practical interests and those simply not interested in colonial relations.[5] Marchand and other scholars thus challenge discourses on Orientalism that are focused too narrowly and that overlook the complexity of what is going on. This group of scholars insists that talking about German imperialism or colonialism is, in general, not helpful because the phenomena that are supposedly described by these terms are too disparate.

Despite this complexity, however, other investigations of the broader historical and cultural situation have identified common tendencies and themes. Even though Germany did not have colonies as such from the seventeenth century until the second half of the nineteenth century, widespread colonial fantasies point to a colonial spirit that pervades the age. Susanne Zantop refers to this "latent colonialism." It is found not so much in statements of intent as much as in "an unspecific drive for colonial possession" subconsciously embedded in ideas of romantic relationships between colonizer and colonized (some of them sexual as well).[6] These stories became embedded in Germany's collective imagination, creating some cultural cohesion, and they could be activated in different ways at different times. Here lies the origin of modern notions of race and gender as hierarchical, biological, intellectual, and moral markers, defining the dominance of white German males both abroad and at home.[7] We might add that these developments are bound to include class differentials as well, which requires further study.

Zantop disputes Said's notion that the initial lack of colonies made German colonialist discourse more abstract and less influential, arguing that the opposite is the case. The absence of colonial subjects precludes challenges, and the lack of colonial possessions produces a sense of entitlement of such future possessions, allowing German thinkers to assume a moral high ground.[8] In the German situation, imaginary colonialism preceded actual imperialism and combined with a dream of nationhood that preceded actual nationhood. The magnitude of these colonial fantasies' eventual power is exemplified by business interests picking them up in order to market products like coffee, cigars, clothing, and mouthwash, some of which had nothing to do with colonial products. These marketing campaigns thematized the tensions between savagery and civilization as well as escapism and adventure.[9]

Colonial fantasies were further promoted by exploration and discovery abroad, which became topics of popular literature—even a theologian like Friedrich Schleiermacher was moved to contribute a four-volume history on the settlement of New Holland in Australia. While missionaries were often not taken seriously for various reasons, missionary activities increased in the nineteenth century and were linked with budding colonial activities. The so-called *Missionsfeste* put on by the churches drew crowds that were interested in learning what was happening in faraway exotic places.[10] Even those who did not officially participate in colonial enterprises or colonial discourses were operating within these force fields, and an awareness of this context helps throw light on how they deal with the texts of the Bible and how their theologies shape up.

As time went by, the colonial idea was also promoted by growing numbers of German emigrants to North and South America—as many as five million, due to population growth and failed revolutions—along with missionaries and merchants who established outposts for their businesses, much like tobacco merchant Adolf Lüderitz in the early 1880s in Southwest Africa.[11]

In 1884, Germany officially entered into the colonial race. Reasons included becoming a unified nation in 1871 under the hegemony of Prussia and industrial expansion, which began in the middle of the nineteenth century. While Chancellor Otto von Bismarck was originally reluctant, believing colonies to be expensive luxuries, popular interest in the expansion of national prestige added to the push for colonies.[12] Some structures were already in place that would support the acquisition of colonies. When in 1884 Southwest Africa was declared a German protectorate, German missionaries were already present, welcoming the move and assuming the role as mediator with the people.[13] Further complexifying this history are currents that sought to integrate Africans into the colonial structures as a "plantation proletariat," which included a sense that Africans were "capable of becoming reasonable facsimiles of Europeans."[14] In this way, the structures of colonialism and capitalism went hand in hand, developing a colonialism that was not genocidal but deeply racist.

COLONIAL AND IMPERIAL IDENTITIES

While the Bible in the German Empire was certainly linked to the complexities of German imperialism and colonialism, starting with colonial fantasies and including both harder and softer forms of expansion, it must also be understood as the heart of culture and the emerging German nation. While colonialism and imperialism are matters of relationship with others—particularly with those outside of one's own location (nation, economy, culture, religion)—those relationships are always linked to relationships within one's own location. This will be demonstrated by engaging a variety of influential takes on biblical themes and the Bible during this time, including those whose thinking was influenced by colonial fantasies like Schleiermacher, those involved in missionary enterprises like Buss, those involved in what has become known as social Christianity like Naumann, and academics who did not voice explicit colonial interests like Wellhausen. The dynamics of colonialism and empire are not merely additional or exceptional matters; they are tied to basic matters of identity and suffuse all aspects of life, including what is considered public and private.

We need to keep in mind, however, that while colonial policy is based on "an image of the native's essential distance from, or proximity to, the culture of the colonizer," there was never a unified style of German colonialism and imperialism. Natives could be conceived on a spectrum ranging between absolute difference, similarity, and even identity. Colonialism and imperialism ranged from assimilation to genocide to more egalitarian partnerships and everything in between.[15]

Colonial Fantasies: The Beginnings of Liberal Theology

For most of the nineteenth century, when neighboring European countries built colonial empires, German-speaking regions harbored what historians have called "colonial fantasies." During the late eighteenth and early nineteenth centuries, such colonial fantasies took shape, for instance, in a flood of popular travel writings and reports, some of them written by authors who never traveled abroad, others by Germans explorers like Alexander von Humboldt. In part these fantasies were based on interest in what was happening elsewhere, in a sense that Germans, if given the chance at colonization, would bring education and civilization to the world rather than conquest and violence (like the Spaniards of previous centuries) or commerce and trade (like contemporary British colonialism). And Germans sincerely believed that they would not be as cold-hearted as the Dutch.[16]

Emerging colonial fantasies, just like the budding German identity, came mostly from members of the educated middle class, the so-called *Bildungsbürgertum*. This class was in control of the press and was able to shape the tastes of the reading public through the national literature. Because colonialism found expression in fantasies rather than the messiness of reality, Germans felt they were in a position to critique other colonial enterprises and imagined themselves as superior.[17] As educated Germans expanded their horizons, visions of others, especially in the Orient, and recovering the classics went hand in hand.[18]

Unfortunately, little investigative research has been done on the fact that modern German theology's beginning coincided with these early colonial phantasies. Friedrich Schleiermacher (1768–1834), often considered the father of liberal theology, was so intrigued by colonial developments that he authored a four-volume opus on the settlement of New Holland in Australia. Like many of the travel writers of his day, Schleiermacher relied on reports of travelers rather than firsthand experience. Unfortunately, much of this work has been lost, but the remaining fragments grant us some insight into how Germany's theological, colonial fantasy shaped up.[19]

Colonialism and imperialism are not immediately obvious in Schleiermacher's work. His theology, as well as his readings of the Bible, is characterized by a benevolent spirit that acknowledges the divine in others who are culturally and religiously different. God-consciousness is not limited to Christians or Germans, and Schleiermacher references Romans 1:21ff and Acts 17:27–30 to make his case. The latter text, which references Paul's speech in Athens and the passage that "in [God] we live and move and have our being," will be referenced by many other interpreters of the Bible during colonial times, as we shall see.[20]

A fundamental characteristic of Schleiermacher's interpretation of the work of Christ is his rejection of coercion. Christ does not operate with force and violence, unlike certain colonizers and missionaries. Rather, Christ is at work through "attraction" and "pervasive influence." Schleiermacher describes Christ's work as "impulses [that] flow to us from Him," which operate to pull us into "His sphere of living influence" through "attractive power." Biblical confirmation of this argument includes "all those passages in Scripture which speak of Christ being and living in us, including Gal. 2:20; Rom.8:10, John 17:23, 2. Cor 13:6."[21] Schleiermacher thus provides an alternative to the colonial and imperial positions that identify Christ's power with the top-down coercion of crude military and political power. Yet are colonial relationships really overcome here?

In his *Christian Faith*, Schleiermacher draws on the example of teacher and student when he talks about the "attractive power" of those "to whose educative intellectual influence we gladly submit ourselves," an influence that is not only "person-forming" but also "world-forming."[22] Yet this attractive power assumes a hierarchy that can perhaps be most clearly seen in his taxonomy of religion. While Schleiermacher acknowledges other religions outside of Christianity, he also insists on a classification that allows for "different states of development,"[23] with European Protestantism at the highest level. Elsewhere, he talks about a "most manifold gradation of life, from the lowest and most imperfect forms up to the highest and most perfect." This gradation, he argues, is willed and put in place by God, "the divine good-pleasure," which is to be received in "quiet acceptance." Both human nature and the "sphere of spiritual life" are permeated by this gradation.[24] This same logic applies to the colonial enterprises of the British in Australia that Schleiermacher describes in the remaining fragments of his lost four-volume work.[25] Christ's attractive power works because of his superiority and a differential of power. One might wonder which differentials are greater—the ones between Christ and the European Christians or the ones between European Christians and Native Australians.

The colonial spirit of biblical and theological interpretation frequently shows in the discussion of miracles. The Old Testament prophets, Schleiermacher explains, needed to perform miracles as "special proof of their authority," not least because their speech challenged society and the status quo.[26] The situation of contemporary Christians is different from both the Old Testament and the times of Jesus, Schleiermacher argues. Our advantage over the contemporaries of Christ is that we can see beyond individual miracles to the "general spiritual miracle, which begins with the person of the Redeemer and is completed with the completion of His Kingdom."[27] Christ transcends both the Jewish limitations and the limitations of the present and is, thus, both the "climax" and the "end of miracle."[28] Schleiermacher's conclusion regarding miracles firmly reinforces the framework of the colonial fantasy: "Even if it cannot be strictly proved that the Church's power of working miracles has died out . . . yet in general it is undeniable that, in view of the great advantage in power and civilization which the Christian peoples possess over the non-Christian . . . the preachers of to-day do not need such signs."[29] Miracles are unnecessary because of the "power and civilization" of the Christian nations when compared to non-Christians. In other words, Christianity itself is the divine miracle, and its colonial history is proof. Even the Jewish-Christian relationship testifies to this. While Christ is the climax and end of teaching, prophecy, and miracle, Prussian Christianity is closest to Christ; it is closer than the Jewish religion and certainly closer than the rest of world.[30]

Schleiermacher's thoughts on mission further reflect a colonial fantasy, noting that "it is an essential of our faith that every nation will sooner or later become Christian."[31] God does indeed care about all of humanity, not only about Prussian Christians, but "God regards all men only in Christ."[32] Still, Christian mission must proceed by attraction and not coercion. Schleiermacher argues that missionary coercion is the main reason, despite centuries of exchange between Christians and non-Christians, that no desire (*Neigung*) for Christianity has developed. Without the use of force, Schleiermacher maintains, the "benign tribes" would have become Christians by now, and this is "a disgrace for the Christian peoples."[33] Patterned after Christ's power, which works through attraction rather than sheer force, Schleiermacher identifies a Christian desire to act and a desire to receive by those who do not yet know Christ.[34] "An institution, like in the [Roman] Catholic Church, which is called 'Mission,'" is unnecessary because Christianity spreads quite naturally through colonial expansion and other connections based on "worldly interest." Christian missionary activities are required only to the degree that colonialism is unable to contribute to the spread of Christianity. In general, Christian missions should be related to points where the civilizing mission is already at work.[35]

Christ's divinity guarantees the "essential equality" of all members of the church, since what matters is the relation of individual Christians to him who is absolutely superior.[36] Even non-Christians are included in this vision since the difference is only temporal: some already have the Holy Spirit, others not yet.[37] Schleiermacher's pedagogy is linked to this insight and shows emancipatory traits that might help push against colonialism to some degree. While the ethical action of children is supposed to be that of obedience, Schleiermacher rejects punishment and reward as educational tools because they fail to acknowledge the stronger power of Christ's Spirit, referencing Colossians 3:21 and

Ephesians 6:4.[38] This can be considered a progressive move even today and runs counter to colonizing efforts. Others in Schleiermacher's day who promoted colonial models of education, like Joachim Heinrich Campe in his 1779 German version of *Robinson Crusoe*, merely promote "paternal kindness" and provide a "model for domesticating little 'savages' in Germany." The inevitable result of Campe's approach is the annihilation of Native Culture.[39] Since the "special mission of Germans to educate" is one of the pillars of German colonialism in the nineteenth century, Schleiermacher's insights might be somewhat of a counterweight.[40]

Nevertheless, the basic theme that runs like a common thread through this discourse is that the lower is attracted by the higher—a principle that Schleiermacher would have considered to be a force for good in the world but that turns out to be the basis for the colonization of others in all its various forms. Despite considerable differences, this theme remains present through almost all the other discourses of the nineteenth century. And, beyond the purview of this chapter, one might wonder how this theme continued through the German fascism of the Nazi era and into the present, legitimizing various neocolonialisms.

BETWEEN COLONIAL FANTASIES AND EMPIRE: MISSION

It is striking that those born into the colonial fantasies of the nineteenth century often perpetuated these sentiments without much firsthand experience. Many, Schleiermacher included, never traveled abroad. This is even true for those who spent their careers exploring other religions. Friedrich Max Müller (1823–1900), for instance, the German-born father of Indian studies and comparative religion who worked in England for most of his life, immersed himself in Sanskrit and Indian religions without ever traveling to India. At the same time, as Kwok Pui Lan and Laura Donaldson have pointed out, "Müller believed he could understand and represent the Indian past better than the Indians. The Indians could not be trusted to represent themselves; they had to be represented."[41] Many other scholars of religion, including interpreters of the Bible located at the universities, likewise never left Europe. Surprisingly, neither did some of the most prominent directors of mission and advocates of colonialism, such as Friedrich Fabri, the director of the Rhenish Mission.

Before Germany officially acquired its own colonies in 1884, it was German missionaries (and some businesspeople) who maintained the connections to faraway places. Most of this work was done through independent missionary societies, which sent missionaries into various parts of the world long before the official churches did. The declared goal was to convert people to faith in Christ rather than to plant subsidies of churches. Because the standards of these missionary efforts were developed through biblical interpretation, Bible societies and mission societies were inextricably linked.[42]

The missionary spirit that gained ground in Germany in the nineteenth century was linked to a religious awakening that split the German population. While liberal ideas and the values of the Enlightenment were perpetuated by the intellectuals and the bourgeoisie, others, including the nobility, the petite bourgeoisie, and peasants, were moved by the awakening.[43] This split mission, according to David Bosch, became "the hobby of rather simple and unsophisticated people on the margins of the established church." For this reason, Bosch concludes, "the entire period of German Protestant missions until shortly before the 1880s may, with reference to the issues of 'mission and colonialism,' be called a period of innocence."[44] This is, of course, no excuse for German colonialism, but it reminds us of the complexity of the situation and that resistance to dominant interests was also an option. It is no accident that these circles, while contributing to colonial developments, also tended to push back against developments of Culture Protestantism at home and the union of religion and nation.[45]

Since missionaries were not intellectuals or members of the bourgeoisie, they were often belittled and not taken seriously back home. According to Gustav Warneck (1834–1919), the father of German missiology, the book of Acts (Acts 4:13, 17:18) resonates with this experience in that the apostles were treated in the same way. In the nineteenth century, missionaries were mostly volunteers and therefore could not expect material gain or financial security. They, for the most part, did not hold clergy status in their sending churches,[46] and by the middle of the nineteenth century up to two-thirds of missionaries were women, which only furthered the lowly status of missionaries.[47] At the same time, these missionaries made substantial contributions to German colonial and imperial developments, increasing the knowledge about other peoples, places, and languages. Their firsthand study of ethnology, linguistics, history of religions, and geography would become useful for academic work back home–and later to colonial enterprises.[48] Already in the 1870s, the Bible had been translated into 180 languages, and missionaries were at the forefront of that work.[49]

Even though these missionaries rarely gained wealth or power from their work, they created stability for German business interests abroad. Warneck proudly states that the "army of missionaries" functions as a protective force (*Schutzmacht*) in foreign countries, which is more effective in securing world trade than gunboats. Merchant boats can land peacefully whereever the missionaries have done their work, and, Warneck adds, all of this service is done for free.[50] Despite these contributions to colonial power, it was only after the colonial system was established in 1884 that Germans would find overseas service to be stepping stones for careers.[51]

Still, the numbers of German missionaries were lower than those of other countries since Germany did not have colonies until 1884, and German missionaries often worked for foreign missionary agencies. The missionary activity of Germans was, on the whole, substantially less developed than missionary activity in the English-speaking world.[52] At the end of the nineteenth century, 1,060 missionaries were British, 502 German, 460 North American, and 110 stemmed from all other European countries combined.[53]

The earliest German missions go back to 1706 in Tranquebar, India, with Bartholomäus Ziegenbalg (1682–1719) and Heinrich Plütschau, both of whom were students of the Pietist

August Hermann Francke. These missionaries sought to be respectful of Indian culture and studied local languages, culture, and religions. The new church in India, they felt, should be an Indian church.[54] In India, Ziegenbalg produced the first Tamil dictionary and translated the Bible and some of Luther's writings into Tamil. Yet his study of Hindu practices was seen as "too objective," failing to impress his ecclesial supporters as well as Franke, who refused to publish them.[55]

Biblical texts like Acts 4:12, which states, "There is salvation in no one else, for there is no other name under heaven given among mortals by which we must be saved," were important in subsequent missionary efforts. This text serves as the foundation of the father of missiology Gustav Warneck's 1876 reflections on mission.[56] Liberal Protestantism, he argues, has given up on mission because it is not worth bothering to carry a gospel across the oceans that has eradicated the validity of this passage and thus the exclusivity of Christianity.[57] Still, Warneck's approach to mission is pragmatic. Comparing mission in apostolic and modern times, Warneck finds the basis of modern mission to be communication and exchange with smaller and larger European settlements and colonial enterprises all over the world. This is the work of God, he claimed, and the result was that mission acquired "power and expanse" greater than any other period in history.[58]

Using military language, Warneck talks about the armies (of missionaries) moving further and further into enemy territories, some of which were dangerous due to the climate and crudeness (*Rohheit*) of its population.[59] In addition, Warneck notes the differences of cultures and the hard work required to learn languages and customs, and he respects efforts to "acclimate intellectually," which he argues may excuse some of the mistakes that have been made by missionaries. Despite the lower status of missionaries at home, missionaries "dominate" on the basis of their superior education even among the "cultured peoples." This cultural superiority is said to spread "true culture," but it has its limits in that it makes the missionaries appear foreign to the natives and makes them dependent.[60] Damage is done by those Europeans who neglect to embody this culture, perpetuating the various slave and opium trades.[61] In general, evangelization and civilization go hand in hand,[62] and the lower seems to be attracted by the higher.

Miracles become part of the conversation once again, and Warneck provides a long list of biblical passages that reference them. Yet while mission in the early days was supported by miracles, they are no longer available to the missionaries of today, and even modern medicine is not impressive enough to count as a miracle. Warneck notes, tongue-in-cheek, that we should be glad that contemporaries believe in spite of miracles, since those are questioned by modern minds.[63] Nevertheless, even though the missionary work began small, Warneck highlights its rapid growth and projects even faster growth for the future.[64]

Concluding his reflections on mission, Warneck picks up the famous passage from 1 Corinthians 1:26–27: "Consider your own call, brothers and sisters: not many of you were wise by human standards, not many were powerful, not many were of noble birth. But God chose what is foolish in the world to shame the wise; God chose what is weak in the world to shame the strong." The experience of the early church seems to match the experience of contemporary missionaries and their converts, who are usually poor rather than wealthy.[65] This means, according to Warneck, that God works from the bottom up, as power is being made perfect in weakness (allusion to 2 Cor 12:9, without reference). Warneck observed that in India the missionaries are most successful among the untouchables and in the minority communities, and the same is true in China.[66]

Here is an example of a colonial interpretation of the Bible that potentially pushes against the values of colonialism, but the concern of Warneck's interpretation is not solidarity with the foolish and the weak but raising them up. Noting that many of the new Christians are lower than the early Christians, the missionary effort has to do with raising them up to higher stages—presumably those of the missionaries and eventually those who sent them.[67]

Immediately before Germany became a colonial empire in 1884, the Swiss pastor Ernst Buss (1843–1928), president of the General Evangelical Protestant Mission Association (*Allgemeiner Evangelisch-protestantischer Missionsverein*), developed an understanding of mission as linking civilization and Christianization. Drawing on Troeltsch's idea of an open-minded Protestantism,[68] Buss argues that Jesus' call to mission and Paul's embodiment of that call must be pursued differently in different cultural situations.

Following the model of Paul in front of the Areopagus in Athens and the example of later apologists, the guiding texts are Acts 17:22f and 27–29.[69] Mission has to start with what both sides share in common. For the cultured nations (*Culturvölker*),[70] Christianity would grow out of a dialogue as something that is not foreign or imported, corresponding with the respective national characters and perhaps taking forms that are "totally foreign" (*völlig fremd*).[71] Buss's missionary organization was founded on those ideas and was particularly active in China.[72] In other cases where nations have little or no culture,[73] civilization has to go ahead of Christianization. In these situations, he argues that it may be necessary to send farmers and artisans before sending missionaries.

Mark 1:15—"The time is fulfilled, and the kingdom of God has come near"—is the biblical basis of Buss's approach to missions. He understands this passage to mean that Jesus proclaims the religion of the fulfillment of time and projects "dominion over all of humanity." Christian dominion must be understood in contrast with the domination of the Roman Empire, yet not in terms of quality but quantity. Buss notes that the dominion proclaimed by Jesus will be greater in terms of "expanse, power, and duration" than anything the world has ever seen.[74] What is true for Christianity and the Roman Empire is also true for Christianity and other religions: their accomplishments and their truths are gathered up and absorbed in Christianity, which satisfies all religious needs and is therefore the "absolute religion."[75] This means, according to Buss, that Christianity's universal character has to be realized in history and must expand geographically so that Christianity will become the general religion of the world.[76] Any obligation for Christians to engage in missionary activity is based on this insight.

According to Acts 19:21, Paul sets the stage for Christian mission, as his goal is to go to Rome in order to tie into the elements of truth at work there (according to Acts 17:22–23, the altar of the unknown God).[77] Like Paul, Christianity needs to go to the capitals of the world. Once those are won over for Christianity, everything else will follow. This is why for Buss, India, China, and India are the central places for mission.[78] It is not hard to see how German colonialism and even imperialism are building here, because while Buss's argument displays an awareness of the value of other cultures, he draws a clear distinction in the value of what he would consider higher and lower cultures. In the end, however, no culture can reach Christianity.

Friedrich Fabri (1824–1891), director of the Rhenish Mission Society since 1857 and father of the German colonial movement, caused a stir with his 1879 piece on whether Germany needed colonies. Fabri was ahead of the curve—even the German chancellor Bismarck still opposed colonial engagement of Germany.

The biblical foundation of Fabri's approach is developed in an earlier text of 1861 and based on various biblical passages: "The human spirit is the lamp of the Lord, searching every innermost part" (Prov 20:27); Jesus' insistence, in the Sermon on the Mount, that light can be found in every human being (Matt 6:23); and John's claim that the light shines in darkness for every human being (John 1:5).[79] Fabri's position is grounded in an optimistic understanding of humanity possessing what he calls a "*sensus communis*," a drive of all that is natural toward God and a general feeling of equity, law, and truth.[80] This *sensus communis* is present in all of humanity, even though to varying degrees and levels; Fabri even grants it to Native Americans.[81] It matters, though, that his examples are taken from the patriarchal family and the factory: the power and authority of the patriarch and the factory owner influence everything, so that the order of the house and of the factory is vital and effective. The same is true for all ethical and natural areas of life.[82] Jesus communicated with people by drawing on this *sensus communis*, and only in a few cases did he have to confront people who shut him out, like the Pharisees. Fabri is not worried that too many people would do that. However, entrance into the kingdom of God demands that the general feeling of truth is combined with going through the narrow gate and a new birth, and so Christians have an edge.[83]

It is this edge that appears to be the foundation of his 1879 piece demanding German colonies. Colonies are within reach and necessary, Fabri notes, due to Germany's economic position after becoming a nation in 1871, a crisis in tariff and trade policy, and a growing naval fleet.[84] German emigrants led the way, but they were always forced to adapt to English language and habits, losing their language, nationality, and culture. Germany, he therefore claims, has much catching up to do in relation to the other colonial powers. Initially, the mother country would have to support colonial efforts, but it would eventually gain from them.[85] Colonization will take care of the problems of unemployment and problems like social-democratic materialism that misled people into thinking that they could be happy. He argues that Germany needs to embrace cultural mission, which is made possible by the fact that it is no longer merely an intellectual and literary force. It has become a political force as well. Cultural tasks (ethical, moral, and economic) go hand in hand with political colonialization.[86] Thus it is necessary to "learn from the colonial skill of our Anglo-Saxon cousins" and to engage in "peaceful competition."[87] It is stunning to see the fierce colonial thrust built on a theological optimism about human nature that takes an early start with Schleiermacher (although Fabri does not reference him in his reflections on the *sensus communis*).

Fortunately, the Rhenish Mission refused to accommodate to the budding colonial empire completely. In 1884, Fabri was forced to resign as director because his colonial-imperial fervor went too far.[88] In 1904, after the Herero Rebellion in the German colony of Southwest Africa (Namibia) and General Lothar von Trotta's "extermination order," which cost the lives of 80 percent of Herero,[89] the Rhenish Mission took the sides of the Africans, pointing out the injustice of colonial exploitation and the business practices that defrauded Africans. The colonizers accused the missionaries of colluding with Africans. However, despite the disagreements, the legitimacy of colonialism itself went unquestioned.[90]

German theologian Dieter Schellong summarizes the emerging colonial spirit and subsequent practice: "Since the Enlightenment, 'good' means to know that is 'good' for *others*, and to impose it on them."[91] What changed as the nineteenth century went on were the forms of imposition, and softer forms of colonialism tended to become harder ones. This included increasing racism. According to Bosch, it was only after 1884 that German missionaries operated with a more sustained consciousness of the superiority of the white race and of Germany in particular.[92] In fact, "racialized thinking forged in the colonies simultaneously subsisted on social experience back in the metropolis."[93] Some of this racism materialized in anti-Semitism.

Empire Proper: Academic Developments and Mainline Protestantism

In the latter half of the nineteenth century, a line emerged between the "useful orientalism" of missionaries and diplomats and the less engaged oriental interests of the academics, who considered the knowledge of the former as superficial at best. More practically interested institutes at German universities were founded for the production of knowledge that would support colonial enterprises, like studying languages and colonial realities, but these institutions were considered inferior by the academic elites and were relegated to tracks separate from traditional academic disciplines. Other efforts to start institutions of higher learning related to colonialism were only moderately successful and could not be maintained in the long term.[94] For what it is worth, class differentials played a role once again, as those who held university positions came mostly from the bourgeois middle classes (often from liberal Protestant or Jewish circles); socialists and left liberals were generally excluded.[95] In contrast, many German colonial officials—looked down upon by the academics—had advanced university degrees but little inherited cultural and economic capital, and they used their colonial positions to move up in the world.[96]

In the nineteenth century, the academic enterprise—*Wissenschaft* and *Bildung*—was more narrowly defined. Marchand talks about "post-romantic narrowing and professionalizing tactics,"[97] which resulted in theology giving way to philology. These developments were matched by a sense that most Germans did not seem to be "suited to be missionaries or colonizers," as a contemporary observed in 1819, even though their deep knowledge of world-historical, philological, and philosophical insights was often unmatched by scholars elsewhere. Readings of the Bible informed by "Higher Criticism" took off in the early 1800s and led to a synergy between liberal Protestantism and orientalism.[98] In biblical studies, the methods of the history of religions school broadened the perspectives further as the century went on. Modernizing ways of reading the Bible informed by this synergy brought religion and culture together in what has become known as "Culture Protestantism," a phenomenon that still needs to be studied in its relation to colonial realities.

Still, at the time Germany acquired colonies in 1884, many academics were slow to embrace the new imperial realities. Academic exegesis of the time still displayed a rather narrow focus on typical questions of the Enlightenment, and, except for a push against everything considered as Judaism, there seems to have been little explicit engagement with topics related to colonization or empire. Orientalist scholarship, in which some of the biblical scholarship participated, while not in the forefront of German colonization, was useful in the implementation of "indirect" colonialism that proceeded via studying languages, local customs, and cultures. The currency of these methods rose after initial, hard approaches to colonialism had failed, including the genocidal massacres by German troops in the African colonies in 1904–1905.[99] In other words, biblical scholars' approaches to Judaism and the Orient more generally became useful in the colonial enterprise.

Julius Wellhausen (1844–1918) was among those moving from theology to *Wissenschaft*, dedicating himself more to what he considered realism and history than to romantic idealism and the embrace of orientalist interests. Like the previous generation of scholars, such as Heinrich Ewald, he believed that early Israelite religion was pristine and powerful, that German Protestant Christianity was its heir, and that its monotheism laid the foundation for contemporary monotheism.[100] The early Israelites, for Wellhausen, embodied liberal values such as individual liberty, freedom of conscience, and political autonomy—values that he also found in Arab history. In 1882 he shifted from a position as senior professor of Old Testament in Greifswald to junior professor in the philosophical faculty of the University of Halle. He then moved to the Marburg and Göttingen universities, where he became a professor of oriental languages in 1892, concentrating on the study of Arabic and the history of Islam.[101] In Göttingen he moved on to the study of the New Testament in 1902.

Wellhausen's commentaries on the gospels indicate how the Bible was read in the academy at the height of the German Empire proper. These readings hardly provide a sense that Wellhausen supported Bismarck's imperial realpolitik, and the search for a colonial spirit is frustrated at first sight. Only a few blatant statements stand out that might betray Wellhausen's attitudes toward colonialism. Perhaps the strangest one is a comment on Matthew 25, where—out of the blue and without any context—he notes that in Palestine the sheep are mostly white and the goats are black.[102] While there is indeed a breed of Syrian goats that are black, one wonders about the deeper levels of meaning in this comment at a time when racism had become a key part of German colonial discourse. Little asides also express his sense of the differential between higher and lower cultures. For instance, he notes that "orientals have no trouble finding a seat" (in response to a reference in Mark 3:34 about people sitting around Jesus),[103] insinuating that these so-called orientals do not mind sitting on the floor.

Wellhausen argues that Jesus' question in Mark 8:27, "Who do people say that I am?" was based on the assumption of a "sharp contrast" between the Jewish and the Christian Messiah. The old Jewish idea of the Messiah stood in stark contrast to a suffering and crucified Messiah. Christ was crucified for trying to liberate people from priestly hierarchies and the rule of the law rather than his resistance against the Romans.[104] In addition, the Christian message picks up a path that late Judaism prepared: life after death, a stronger focus on the individual, and a focus on another world.[105] Following Jesus is a "quiet way of life" (*stiller Wandel*) that does not challenge any dominant status quo.[106] Still, Jesus is more defined by what is non-Jewish and human in general than by what is Jewish.[107] In the relation of Judaism and Christianity, a colonial sense of superiority is affirmed and deepened.

Colonial attitudes also appear in the interpretation of miracles. Commenting on Mark 1:21–28, where Jesus heals a man with an unclean spirit, Wellhausen affirms that Jesus was a healer and notes his giftedness. Demon possession is part of Jesus' healings, but it is a lower-class phenomenon, typical for New Testament literature produced by less noble writers and therefore less prominent in the Hebrew Bible, according to Wellhausen.[108] In his interpretation of Mark 2:21–22, Wellhausen claims that the old cloak and the old wineskin cannot be anything but forms of Judaism (*die Form des Judentums*).[109] Despite its lowly beginnings in the New Testament, Christianity—presumably coming into its own in its modern German Protestant forms—is on its way up in the world and is destined to replace older religious traditions. The dynamic of Christianity is its move from the lower to the higher: Jesus' healing of the Gerasene Demoniac is characterized as a "farce" (*Schwank*) because it dwells on the loss of 2,000 unclean animals and the cheating of demons, who lost their dwelling place as soon as they entered the pigs. Wellhausen wonders how such an odd story could have become attached to Jesus.[110]

On the whole, Wellhausen assumes a scale of religion. Starting from the assumption that monotheism is the highest form of religion, Christianity is seen as the highest form because it improves on other monotheisms like Judaism. A case in point is Jesus' improvement of the Ten Commandments in Mark 10:19.[111] The ongoing challenge of these colonial interpretations, all the way back to Schleiermacher, is finding a way to appreciate other religions while maintaining the superiority of Christianity.

The history of religions school (*religionsgeschichtliche Schule*), the next generation of scholars after Wellhausen, broadened the purview of biblical studies by engaging religions of the ancient world, including the popular backgrounds of religion and archaeology. A new, inclusive spirit emerged that also reshaped the study of the Bible. Orientalist interests in the academy broadly conceived also increased interest in the historical and cultural contexts of the Hebrew Bible, taking hold in New Testament studies slightly later in the work of scholars like Wilhelm Bousset and Wilhelm Heitmüller.[112]

Wilhelm Bousset (1865–1920) abandons narrow and unhistorical methods and interprets Jesus instead on the backdrop of the intellectual and emotional world (*Gedanken- und Stimmungs-Welt*) of late Judaism (*Spätjudentum*). His work is founded on a broad picture of late Judaism that consists of two epochs before and after the Syrian persecution and the Maccabean uprising. The ideology of late Judaism is characterized by an eschatological bent and a national-political character of its piety.[113]

While the notion of God in Israel keeps expanding in late Judaism, adding images of omnipotence and rulership of the world, Bousset argues that it does not have the "inner vitality" (*innere Lebenskraft*) to give concrete shape to such an idea, and so the image of God moves away from the world and from engagement with it. Although there was still some inspiration in the first epoch of Judaism, late Judaism had no "lasting vitality" (*dauernde Lebenskraft*) and degenerated into legalism.[114] The core of late Judaism was a strict distinction between present and future, with the present being evil and the future located in another world. There is no bridge between this world and the other, and no human activity can bring in the future.[115] This tendency to emphasize the transcendent and the supernatural led to "Pharisaism,"[116] where piety became an external matter that lacks a living piety (*lebendige Frömmigkeit*) which penetrates life.[117] Bousset's general assessment that later Hellenistic Judaism was degenerate but that early Judaism possessed spirit and faith parallels that of Wellhausen and reflects part of the colonial spirit of the time.[118]

In Jesus something new emerges, a forceful piety (*kräftige Frömmigkeit*) able to survive the destruction of Jerusalem, which has to be understood in direct contrast to Judaism. A new foundation was necessary.[119] Key to the proclamation and life of Jesus is the faith in God as father. Even though early Israel may have had a sense of this as well, Jesus is the one who embodies this faith. This faith does not carry nationalist and political traits and deletes everything that is nature-identified, earthly, and passionate (*alles naturhafte irdische leidenschaftliche*).[120] Judaism serves as a foil for Bousset's ideas about Jesus. While in old Israel God was a powerful and passionate hero, in Jesus God is a constant goodness, a justice that cannot be swayed, a holiness that is not full of wrath or hate but insists on a clear either-or.[121] The world is not a place devoid of God; it reflects God—there is no "sick longing for the other world." God gives rain to good and bad and clothes the lilies in the field.[122]

Becoming like children (Mark 10:15) means absolute and immediate dedication to God and light-filled happiness and freshness, which was not experienced even by the greatest of the old covenant.[123] In contrast, the otherworldliness of late Judaism gave up on the world and is full of hate against the status quo—especially the rich, the powerful, and the kings. This contrast between Jesus and Judaism informs Bousset's reading of the Bible. Passages that do not fit this model are rejected. Luke 6:24, Jesus' proclamation of woe to the rich, was interpreted as a distortion of Jesus' message. Instead of hatred against the rich, Bousset claims, Jesus is full of compassion.[124] Even without explicitly supporting colonialism, this message becomes good news to the colonizers. Likewise, Bousset's argument that Jesus' message is universal supports the dominant status quo: even the Hebrew prophets, whom Bousset appreciates and who might offer some counterpoints to the dominant status quo, are seen as too narrowly tied to the horizon of the people.[125] Supersessionism in relation to the Jewish religion implies supersessionism in relation to all religions—the break with the particularism of the faith of Israel can be translated into the break with the particularism of all other faiths.

Matt 6:33—"strive first for the kingdom of God and his righteousness"—defines the main concern of Jesus, starting with the encounter with God and the beginning of the kingdom of God. Bousset points to echoes of this throughout the Gospels, including Matthew 12:28, Luke 17:20f, Matthew 11:11, Matthew 21, 31, and Mark 10:15.[126] Rather than miracles, the center is Jesus' new hope for justice.[127] Left open, however, is the question of what justice means. Is it the justice of the status quo and its legal system or something else? Despite modernity's hope in human development, Bousset rejects the idea of an increasing perfection of the world, assuming instead that (German) humanity has reached a certain height in its development.[128]

In the end, Bousset normalized Jesus in terms of the status quo of his time, according to the precepts of Culture Protestantism, whose colonial underpinnings are becoming increasingly clear. This goes hand in hand with more explicit efforts to normalize other religions like Islam in the German academy for the purposes of colonizing Africa. This move rests on the assumption that there is a dynamic hierarchy of religions whereby the lower assimilates to the higher.[129]

The work of Wilhelm Heitmüller (1869–1926) displays similar tendencies. His interpretation of the Johannine tradition of the Samaritan woman at the well (John 4:4–26) also betrays signs of this dynamic hierarchy of religions, expressed in terms of Christian (and male) superiority. While readers have a sense of the higher meaning of Jesus' words, he claimed, "it can obviously not be expected of the Samaritan women that she grasps this higher meaning."[130] And although salvation comes through the Jews (Heitmüller emphasizes that Jesus refers to "the Jews," perhaps implying that Jesus disassociates himself from Jewish traditions), the true worship of God is not accomplished by the Jews either. Heitmüller argued that the worship of God has to be purely inner, spiritual, and therefore universal. In conclusion, the woman cannot fathom such great prophetic announcements—"they transcend her understanding."[131] In Heitmüller's interpretation, the woman is not an individual but a representative of the Samaritan people,[132] who, it seems, are just as underdeveloped.

In this approach, Christianity becomes "the purely spiritual religion of humanity, liberated from all national and local barriers."[133] Once again, universality is that which transcends those who adhere to simpler religions, whether the Samaritans in the past or the Jews throughout history. It is not hard to imagine what Heitmüller would have to say about other religions of the present and how this supports the colonial spirit of the time. Interpreting Jesus' claim to be the way, the truth, and the life (John 14:6), Heitmüller proclaims that Christianity is the "absolute religion," without need for further explanation.[134] In this context, his emphasis on the progressive nature of the Gospel of John in the context of early Christianity supported the colonial-imperial system, even if he was not fully aware of it. The Johannine emphasis on eternal life beginning here and now, and that life after death is only a continuation of this life, is crucial. But it all depends on how this life shapes up—is it the Prussian-Germanic way of life or something else? The colonial implications of Heitmüller's concern for an inner grasp of God, God's being, and community with God—parallel to Bousset's interpretation—depend entirely on what his God looks like.[135] Claiming universality will not do the trick, as empty universals are quickly taken over by the dominant forces.

Interpretations of the Bible that provide alternatives to academic orthodoxy in the era of the German Empire proper were provided by two very different theologians who are often identified with the concerns of social Christianity, Friedrich Naumann (1860–1919) and Christoph Friedrich Blumhardt, to whom we will return below. Naumann's social Christianity promoted respect for the struggling working class, yet his social liberalism proved more attractive to the educated strata of society than to the masses of working people.[136] Bousset was among those who supported Naumann, which led to Bousset being rejected for an academic post in Berlin. Even the fairly moderate liberalism of Naumann (despite sometimes being classified as a "left liberal") was obviously considered too radical by the liberal academic status quo.[137]

Naumann's published devotionals, written from 1895 to 1902, provide another glimpse into biblical interpretation at the height of German colonial imperialism. In a reflection on Matthew 25:45 at the turn of the twentieth century, Naumann deplores that the nineteenth century lacked creativity in matters of faith and love and that Christian doctrine was easy rather than challenging—thus pushing against the Culture Protestantism of his age.[138] In another comment on this passage, Naumann makes it clear that the divine final judgment is not based on knowledge but on what people (not only Christians) did in support of the least of these.[139] However, care for the less fortunate can be expressed as attraction of the lower to the higher, in sync with all the other nineteenth-century interpretations we have discussed so far. Naumann interprets Christ's claim to be the way (John 14:6) in terms of a law of spiritual attraction to Jesus. This is how the lowly are raised up, he concluded, exemplified by Jesus' disciples who were lifted to such heights that today it takes large universities to study the spirits of Peter and John.[140] Still, Naumann retains an edge as he challenges the wealthy who put their own pecuniary success above the common good, and he reinforces Jesus' warning that it is impossible to serve God and Mammon (Matt 6:24).[141] Referencing Matthew 23:14, he advised people of faith to fight cruel economic laws that favor wealthy investors over poor widows, claiming that faith and business cannot be separated.[142]

The colonial spirit of Naumann is most clear in his political advice. When commenting on Luke 20:25—"give to the emperor the things that are the emperor's and to God the things that are God's"—he affirms that, for Germans, paying taxes to the emperor would be easier than it was for Jesus' contemporaries because Germans belong to the same nation as the emperor, because they speak the same language, and because the emperor is a Protestant. It never even occurs to him that Jesus might have challenged the emperor. The emperor simply needs to be reminded that no one is without error and to serve God in a spirit of love of neighbor and faithfulness (*Nächstenliebe und Treue*).[143] Commenting on war (based on Mark 9:23, "all things can be done for the one who believes"), Naumann affirms that it is the "natural order of God" to fight for one's existence. In war, both sides may pray to God with integrity, thus being obedient to God's order while avoiding unnecessary cruelty and despair.[144] In the war against China, Naumann allowed that the Gods of the Chinese are the same as the Christian God—the Germans simply need to remain steadfast in their prayers and duties.[145] In the war against France, Naumann once again affirms that the Germans and the French pray to the same God, yet that God will abandon any nation that does not have the energy of life, creativity (*Lebenskraft, Schaffenskraft*), or love for family or the poor. The same principle applies to trade wars.[146] Here, a universal vision of God upholds the colonial-imperial system as well as budding capitalist relations, as the winners are seen as blessed by God. When advising a soldier (drawing on Rom 14:8), Naumann issued the call to "Go with God," affirming that God is everywhere there is a sacrifice for a great cause, like the cause of Germany.[147]

The colonial spirit also shines through in Naumann's interpretation of Jesus' great commission in Mark 16:15, wherein he observes that faith cannot be a private matter. It is all or nothing for Naumann, as a religion needs to be either the truth for all or die. As a result, he challenges his readers to "Make your truth to be universal truth."[148] This truth is not necessarily a German one, however, as Naumann resists a national savior who has black hair but blue eyes and a German heart. In order to know Jesus, we must learn what little we can know about the "oriental Jesus" and the confessions of the past, he argues, and even if those confessions are foreign for Germans our own confession is shaped in relation to them.[149]

Appreciation for mission was growing in Germany at the turn of the century. Two decades after Warneck's concern that mission was not respected, Naumann reports that mission was drawing great interest from the public. Mission, under the conditions of active colonialism and imperialism, is praised for making up for the bad influences of Europe where it brought alcoholism and immorality. Naumann acknowledges a two-way street, as conversions abroad can spark conversions back home and revitalize the faith of Germans. The only remaining challenge, according to Naumann, is to make mission mainstream to such a degree that the two-thirds of humanity not yet Christian would join Christianity as well.[150]

Christoph Friedrich Blumhardt (1842–1919), finally, presents a perspective that differs from most of the others in the nineteenth century. Also concerned with the growing social problems of his time, Blumhardt is more open than Naumann to the agency of those on the receiving end, both at home and abroad. His advice to his son-in-law Richard Wilhelm en route to China was not to convert people but to show empathy and minister to their needs. This was his approach to working people at home as well.[151]

Reflecting on Revelation 21:5, "Behold, I make all things new," Blumhardt insinuates that his contemporaries lacked faith that this could happen. Instead, they "call everything God."[152] In sync with Culture Protestantism and the colonial predilections of most of the other interpreters of the Bible of his age, Blumhardt's charge that the role of Christians is "to be fighters and to bring the world under God's feet"[153] may sound like yet another colonial-imperial claim but, depending on what is understood as "the world," it can also be anticolonial and anti-imperial. When Christ claims to be the light of the world (John 8:12), he poses a challenge not only to personal or religious affairs ("don't draw me into all your petty affairs") but to the world as a whole.[154] The problem with dominant Christianity is that it does not challenge the world of the status quo any more, and Blumhardt identified a conflict whenever the kingdom of God is proclaimed as dynamic and living[155] (reflections on John 7:44–53 where the chief priests and the Pharisees seek to arrest Jesus). Yet God does not overpower the world like a colonial-imperial force. Commenting on Matthew 16:13–19, where Jesus promises the keys of the kingdom to Peter, Blumhardt emphasizes that Jesus will not build the kingdom of God without human engagement.[156]

Blumhardt's Jesus takes sides, but he does so differently than the colonial Jesus who takes the sides of absolute and colonial Christianity: "Jesus intervenes on the level of those who are ignored by the history of the nations and of society. These miserable people who have never come to the light are the very ones whose side Jesus takes." This is not an easy task, and "any other, who has not come from God, cannot take up the cause of this class of people to this very day." People who care about education, philosophy, and science do not care, Blumhardt notes, because it is the educated who have created the gap between the educated and uneducated, rich and poor, high and low.[157] Blumhardt has a sense that colonialism is not just a matter of politics and economics—it suffuses everything. Picking up Matthew 25, "I was poor, I was hungry, I was imprisoned, and you came to me, to the poor Savior," Blumhardt argues that we can only follow Jesus if we accept him in the company of the poor. It is from there "that the power comes which will overthrow the world."[158] While many are afraid of the collapse of the world of the well-intentioned elites, good kings, ministers, prelates, and popes, Blumhardt confesses that he is looking forward to it.[159] Here, an anticolonial and anti-imperial spirit, rather unusual for its time, shines through.

A bigger and more sustained critique of colonialism and imperialism emerges from this: "We are incapable of building up a civilization without killing people" because "everything we do is done at the cost of others."[160] Blumhardt's motto, therefore, is "keep to the lowly"; "only out of the large, uneducated masses can true help for the world come."[161] Putting a final nail in the coffin of even the most benevolent colonialism, Blumhardt argues that the agency for transformation does not come from the elites but from the masses; the problem is that the church has abandoned them.[162]

Conclusions

Marchand agrees with Said that European orientalism was supported by imperial ventures but, discussing German orientalism, she questions whether orientalism is always about European culture "setting itself off against the Orient," and she doubts that imperial experience shaped everything. She furthermore argues that that knowledge of the other "can also lead to appreciation, dialogue, self-critique, perspectival reorientation, and personal and cultural enrichment."[163] Our survey of German ways of reading the Bible in the nineteenth century, in part, affirms these claims. Schleiermacher's efforts to appreciate other religions, missionary efforts to engage other cultures, and the history-of-religions school's efforts to broaden the horizon of biblical interpretation by incorporating insights from other religions all exemplify the benefits of a certain openness to the other. Nevertheless, in each of these examples we have also observed that the self is defined in relation to the other and that imperial sensitivities go deep, sometimes in more positive ways (when comparing advanced cultures) and sometimes in more negative ways (when putting down late Judaism or primitive cultures).

What matters most in this development is the location of power. While true colonial and imperial power accrues to Germans only in the short period from 1884 to 1914, the semiotic and cultural power of deep-seated colonial fantasies and missionary enterprises, and even the occasional German-led explorations and business ventures, should not be underestimated. One can, of course, distinguish between different forms of power—violent and peaceful ones, political and cultural ones, economic and religious ones, more supportive and less supportive ones—but as long as tropes of higher and lower, more developed and less developed, universal and parochial are at work, the spirit of colonialism and imperialism poses problems.

Even the discourse of love, usually seen as a positive one and cherished in eighteenth-century colonial discourse, can be fraught with problems in colonial-imperial situations: love can establish natural boundaries, improve the races that need improving, and even legitimize the colonial enterprise. One of the prominent colonial fantasies of love was the educational and patriarchal relation between father and child, and this relation seems to have been a model of German colonial fantasies.[164] The notion of love as such therefore does not overcome the colonial system.

What about alternatives? There is resistance within the colonial situation itself, often emerging from places where it is least expected. Missionaries, who were at the forefront of colonial dynamics, often became part of this resistance in small ways. Nevertheless, even the liberals among the bourgeoisie were generally pro-colonial, and only more progressive spirits such as social democrats and others on the left were anticolonial.[165] This throws some light on the disappointing role of the academics whose interpretations of the Bible, for the most part, were developed as if colonialism did not exist. It also throws some light on why people like Blumhardt were different—he was tied to his relation to working people and social democracy (when he was elected to the Württemberg legislature he was asked to resign as a pastor).

Still, even some Germans who went abroad developed more critical perspectives on colonialism and imperialism, as the example of physician Erwin Bälz shows. As German culture considers others with contempt, he notes, a German who goes abroad and finds that he has been misinformed turns to the other extreme. Unfortunately, Bälz concludes, "one who, having gone abroad, remains a good German and wants to enlighten his fellow-countrymen is not understood at home and is despitefully used."[166]

Why have so few German scholars dealt with this complex history of German colonialism and imperialism? While we are experiencing a renaissance of historical studies of this period, biblical scholars still have to catch up. The notion of "a general amnesia about colonialism"[167] remains a problem for Germany. Recall that Germany lost its colonies not due to resistance from the colonies but as a result of World War I, when the other colonial powers took over the former German colonies. As a result, Germans never had to deal firsthand with anticolonial and anti-imperial resistance, and so colonialism and decolonization appeared to be the problems of others. German colonial fantasies even survived World War II and the Holocaust, as Germans after 1945 identified colonialism and imperialism with fascism and National Socialism that they had defeated successfully. Much work remains to be done.

Notes

1. German colonies included German East Africa, Togoland, German Southwest Africa, Cameroon, German New Guinea, Samoa, Chinese Kiaochow, and some small islands. These colonies were occupied by other European colonial forces soon after the beginning of World War I. Charles Lansing, "German Colonial Empire," *Europe since 1914: Encyclopedia of the Age of War and Reconstruction*, ed. John Merriman and Jay Winter (Detroit: Charles Scribner's Sons, 2006), 1209; 1208–1210.
2. Robert J. C. Young, *Postcolonialism: An Historical Introduction* (Oxford: Blackwell, 2001), 16–17.
3. Bradley Naranch, "German Colonialism Made Simple," in *German Colonialism in a Global Age*, ed. Bradley Naranch and Geoff Ely (Durham: Duke University Press, 2014), 9; 1–18.
4. Geoff Ely, "Empire by Land or Sea? Germany's Imperial Imaginary, 1849–1945," in: *German Colonialism in a Global Age*, ed. Bradley Naranch and Geoff Ely (Durham: Duke University Press, 2014), 22; 19–45.
5. Suzanne L. Marchand, *German Orientalism in the Age of Empire: Religion, Race, and Scholarship* (Cambridge: Cambridge University Press, 2009).
6. Susanne Zantop, *Colonial Fantasies: Conquest, Family, and Nation in Precolonial Germany, 1770–1870* (Durham: Duke University Press, 1997), 2–3; Zantop claims that these fantasies provide acces to the "political unconscious" of a nation; ibid., 4.
7. Ibid., 5.
8. Ibid., 7–8.
9. Janne Lathi, "German Colonialism and the Age of Global Empire," *Journal of Colonialism and Colonial History* 17, no. 1 (Spring 2016): n.p.
10. See Friedrich Naumann, *Gotteshilfe: Gesamtausgabe der Andachten aus den Jahren 1895-1919 sachlich geordnet*, 6th ed. (Göttingen: Vandenhoeck und Ruprecht, 1926), 556.
11. Sara Friedrichsmeyer, Sara Lennox, and Susanne Zantop, "Introduction," in: *The Imperialist Imagination: German Colonialism and Its Legacy*, ed. Sara Friedrichsmeyer, Sara Lennox, and Susanne Zantop (Ann Arbor: University of Michigan Press, 1998), 9; 1–29.
12. Stephen Neill, *Colonialism and Christian Missions* (New York: McGraw-Hill, 1966), 386, 389.
13. Neill, *Colonialism and Christian Missions*, 391–392.
14. George Ndege, "Africa: German Colonies," in *Encyclopedia of Race and Racism*, vol. 1, 2nd ed., ed. Patrick L. Mason (Detroit: Macmillan Reference, 2013), 45; 43–47.
15. George Steinmetz, "'The Devil's Handwriting': Precolonial Discourse, Ethnographic Acuity, and Cross-Identification in German Colonialism," *Comparative Studies in Society and History* 45, no. 1 (January 2003): 46–47; 41–95. In Samoa and Southwest Africa,

for instance, the difference between the natives and colonizers was emphasized, even though natives were seen as "noble savages." Chinese Quingado, by contrast, was framed as a culture in decline, beginning with active efforts of separation but shifting to a later sense that Chinese and German civilizations could be considered as equal. Ibid., 48–50. Acknowledgment of difference in a place like Samoa could mean that Samoans were encouraged to continue practicing their culture. Ibid., 56–66.

16. Johann Gottfried Herder, reference in Joerg Rieger, *Christ and Empire: From Paul to Postcolonial Times* (Minneapolis: Fortress Press, 2007), 224.
17. Friedrichsmeyer, Lennox, and Zantop, "Introduction," 19–20.
18. Marchand, *German Orientalism*, 54–55.
19. See Rieger, *Christ and Empire*, chap. 5.
20. Friedrich Schleiermacher, *The Christian Faith*, ed. H. R. Mackintosh and J. S. Stewart (Edinburgh: T.&T. Clark, 1986), 34. Other texts include Rom 1:18ff; ibid., 55. The Bible is at times referenced to make his case, even though not always with specific references. See, for instance, ibid., 24: "An uninterrupted sequence of religious emotions can be required of us, as indeed Scripture actually requires it."
21. Schleiermacher, *The Christian Faith*, 425, 426, 427.
22. Ibid., 427.
23. Ibid., 31. He explicitly rejects the view that "Christian religion (piety) should adopt towards at least most other forms of piety the attitude of the true towards the false."
24. Schleiermacher, *The Christian Faith*, 556–557.
25. The focus of Schleiermacher's study is on New South Wales on the east coast of Australia, originally called New Holland (*Neuholland*) in honor of the Dutch ships that discovered the coast of Australia in the seventeenth century. Schleiermacher worked on this project, which was under contract but never published, between 1799 and 1802. It has been characterized as a major project among his literary endeavors of that time. Günter Meckenstock in his introduction calls it *gewichtig* (substantial); Friedrich Daniel Ernst Schleiermacher, *Schriften aus der Berliner Zeit 1800–1802*, ed. Günter Meckenstock, Kritische Gesamtausgabe, and Hans-Joachim Birkner et al., Abt. 1, vol. 3 (Berlin: Walter de Gruyter, 1988), lxxxv; vii–cxxvi. Schleiermacher's descriptions of the original inhabitants of Australia are even more telling than his description of the land and help us dig deeper into the underlying colonial mentality. The Aboriginals, he judges, are arrested at the "lowest rung of pleasure and action," and therefore they would not pose any threats or prevent the colonizers from owning the treasures of the land. Ibid., 278.
26. Schleiermacher, *The Christian Faith*, 441.
27. Ibid., 449.
28. Ibid.
29. Ibid., 450.
30. The Jewish other presents a highly developed yet somewhat lower position than the Christian, a judgment that can also be found in Schleiermacher's typology of religion. In the final account, the Jewish other is different, and this difference is where the problem lies; consequently, "whatever is most definitely Jewish" in the Old Testament has "least value"; Schleiermacher, *The Christian Faith*, 62.
31. Ibid., 558–559.
32. Ibid., 560; 527. Schleiermacher argues that "only that part of the world which is united to the Christian Church is for us the place of attained perfection, or of the good, and– relatively to quiescent self-consciousness—the place of blessedness."

33. Friedrich Schleiermacher, *Die Christliche Sitte nach den Grundsätzen der evangelischen Kirche im Zusammenhang dargestellt* (Waltrop: Spenner, 1999), 288–290.
34. Schleiermacher, *Christliche Sitte*, 370–371. The Christians experience a *"religiöse Lust"* (religious desire) and the non-Christians desire to receive *"den wahren Gegenstand ihres Verlangens."*
35. Ibid., 381, 382.
36. Ibid., 518. This is another example where the Protestant and Roman Catholic churches differ, as the latter does not assume this basic equality. Ibid., 519.
37. Ibid., 514.
38. Ibid., 234–236.
39. Zantop, *Colonial Fantasies*, 14, 105, 114–115. Nevertheless, there are also parallels between the approaches. The "perfectibility of *all* humans" is a core belief of both Campe and Schleiermacher.
40. Neither world trade nor sea power are the primary goal of Germany, but rather their aim is "the cultivation of natural peoples and natural territories"; Zantop, ibid., 199, quoting Heinrich Hübbe-Schleiden.
41. Laura E. Donaldson and Kwok Pui-lan, "Introduction," in *Postcolonialism, Feminism, and Religious Discourse*, ed. Laura E. Donaldson and Kwok Pui-lan (New York: Routledge, 2002), 19; 1–38.
42. Hans-Werner Gensichen, *Die Missionsgeschichte der neueren Zeit* (Göttingen: Vandenhoeck und Ruprecht, 1961), 31–36.
43. Kurt Dietrich Schmidt, *Grundriß der Kirchengeschichte*, eigth edition (Göttingen: Vandenhoeck und Ruprecht, 1984), 470–471.
44. David J. Bosch, *Transforming Mission: Paradigm Shifts in Theology of Mission* (Maryknoll: Orbis Books, 1991), 308.
45. Schmidt, *Grundriß der Kirchengeschichte*, 505–506.
46. Gustav Warneck, *Die apostolische und die moderne Mission: Eine apologetische Parallele* (Gütersloh: Bertelsmann, 1876), 22–23.
47. Gensichen, *Die Missionsgeschichte der neueren Zeit*, 42.
48. Warneck, *Die apostolische und die moderne Mission*, 31.
49. Ibid., 18.
50. Warneck, *Die apostolische und die moderne Mission*, 46.
51. See, for instance, the career of Wilhelm Solf, governor of Samoa and later secretary of the German Colonial Office, who supported "scientific colonialism" without war and exploitation—and who challenged the kaiser and the finance industry for the last dozen years before World War I. Marchand, *German Orientalism*, 346–347.
52. Gensichen, *Die Missionsgeschichte der neueren Zeit*, 40.
53. Warneck, *Die apostolische und die moderne Mission*, 22.
54. Gensichen, *Die Missionsgeschichte der neueren Zeit*, 17.
55. Marchand, *German Orientalism*, 8.
56. Gustav Warneck, *Die apostolische und die moderne Mission: Eine apologetische Parallele* (Gütersloh: C. Bertelsmann, 1876), 3.
57. Warneck, *Die apostolische und die moderne Mission*, 4n1.
58. ibid., 12–13.
59. Ibid., 16.
60. Ibid., 18–19.
61. Ibid., 21n1.

62. Ibid., 45.
63. Ibid., 24–25.
64. Ibid., 66.
65. Ibid., 80.
66. Ibid., 83.
67. Ibid., 88–92.
68. Gensichen, *Die Missionsgeschichte der neueren Zeit*, 44.
69. Ernst Buss, *Die Mission einst und jetzt* (Frankfurt am Main: Diesterweg, 1883), 55.
70. *Culturvölker*, Buss, *Die Mission einst und jetzt*, 54.
71. Buss, *Die Mission einst und jetzt*, 58.
72. Gensichen, *Die Missionsgeschichte der neueren Zeit*, 44.
73. Buss, *Die Mission einst und jetzt*, 52.
74. Ibid., 1.
75. Ibid., 1–2.
76. Ibid., 2
77. Ibid., 6.
78. Ibid., 51,
79. Friedrich Fabri, *Der sensus communis, das Organ der Offenbarung Gottes in allen Menschen: Eine biblisch-psychologische Betrachtung zur Beleuchtung der Stellung des Christen zur Welt* (Barmen: W. Langewiesche, 1861), 10. Fabri references texts from the Bible without providing chapter and verse without reference to the books but not chapter and verse.
80. Fabri, *Der sensus communis*, 7.
81. Ibid., 11, 35, 53.
82. Ibid., 16–17.
83. Ibid., 42, 44. While Fabri supports mission, he is suspicious of indiscriminate awakenings such as in the United States, where rapid growth of Christianity seems superficial and of short duration. Friedrich Fabri, *Die neuesten Erweckungen in Amerika, Irland und anderen Ländern* (Barmen: W. Langewiesche, 1860), 20. He is especially concerned about emotional reactions such as people being "stricken down" (a phrase he quotes in English; ibid., 24). The problem, he argues, is that such awakenings are not real and lack fundamental conversions; ibid., 30.
84. Friedrich Fabri, *Does Germany Need Colonies?* Original German text and English translation reprinted in Friedrich Fabri, *Bedarf Deutschland der Colonien?/Does Germany Need Colonies? Eine politische-ökonomische Betrachtung von Friedrich Fabri*, ed., trans., and intro. E. C. M. Breuning and M. Chamberlain, *Studies in German Thought and History*, no. 2. (Lewiston: Edwin Mellen Press, 1998), 46–59, 78–79, 82–85, 148–153, 178–181. The following page numbers are from an abbreviated edition in *German History in Documents and Images*, 1, available online: http://germanhistorydocs.ghi-dc.org/sub_document.cfm?document_id=1867.
85. Ibid., 4–5.
86. Ibid., 6–7.
87. Ibid., 8.
88. Bosch, *Transforming Mission*, 309.
89. Michelle R. Moyd, "German Empire," in *Encyclopedia of African Colonial Conflicts*, ed. Timothy J. Stapleton, vol. 1 (Santa Barbara: ABC-CLIO, 2017), 312; 309–312.
90. Bosch, *Transforming Mission*, 311–312.

91. Reference in ibid., 313.
92. Bosch, *Transforming Mission*, 310.
93. Ely, "Empire by Land or Sea?" 33.
94. Marchand, *German Orientalism*, xxxiii, 337, 353–354.
95. Ibid., 343.
96. Steinmetz, "'The Devil's Handwriting,'" 52–53. In the colonies, Wilhelm Solf as governor of Samoa exemplifies what colonialism could do for educated Westerners: his appreciation of and support for Samoan culture helped him accrue cultural capital as an enlightened official in the eyes of fellow Germans and to exercise control over Samoans, most of whom were supportive of him. Ibid., 55–66.
97. Marchand, *German Orientalism*, 58.
98. Ibid., 76, 78.
99. See also Ibid., 334–335 and 346.
100. Ibid., 180–181.
101. Ibid., 184–185. See the references in ibid., 183.
102. Julius Wellhausen, *Evangelienkommentare: Das Evangelium Matthaei*, reprint of 2nd ed., 1914 (Berlin: Walter de Gruyter, 1987), 127–128.
103. Julius Wellhausen, *Evangelienkommentare: Das Evangelium Marci*, reprint of 2nd ed., 1909 (Berlin: Walter de Gruyter, 1987), 15.
104. Julius Wellhausen, *Einleitung in die drei ersten Evangelien*, reprint of 2nd ed., 1911 (Berlin: Walter de Gruyter, 1987), 80–83.
105. Wellhausen, *Evangelienkommentare: Einleitung*, 90–91.
106. Ibid., 104.
107. "Man darf das Nichtjüdische in ihm, das Menschliche, für charakteristischer halten, als das Jüdische," in ibid., 103.
108. Wellhausen, *Evangelienkommentare: Das Evangelium Marci*, 11
109. Ibid., 19.
110. Ibid., 39.
111. Ibid., 97.
112. Another interest in ancient sources emerged via the appreciation for the universal spirit of the ancient Greeks, represented by scholars like Albrecht Ritschl and Adolf von Harnack, whose work will not be discussed further here.
113. Wilhelm Bousset, *Jesu Predigt in ihrem Gegensatz zum Judentum: Ein religionsgeschichtlicher Vergleich* (Göttingen: Vandenhoeck und Ruprecht, 1892), 10, 11.
114. Bousset, *Jesu Predigt*, 13–14, 15, 18–19.
115. God can no longer be found in the world. Ibid., 22, 23.
116. Ibid., 27, 29. According to Bousset, there are no exceptions, Judaism is Pharisaism and Pharisaism is Judaism; ibid., 32.
117. This would have required a moral power and a creative spirit that late Judaism lacked. Ibid., 35–36, 38.
118. "Das Evangelium entwickelt verborgene Triebe des alten Testamentes aber es protestiert gegen die herrschende Richtung des Judentums," in ibid., 130.
119. Ibid., 39, 41. The agreement with Wellhausen is noted explicitly.
120. Ibid., 41–42.
121. The contrast is the abstract transcendence of ancient Judaism. Ibid., 42–43.
122. Ibid., 44. The allusion is to Matt 6:28, even though the passage is note referenced.
123. Ibid., 45.

124. Ibid., 46–47; 47n2.
125. Ibid., 50, 85.
126. Ibid., 89–96.
127. Ibid., 99.
128. Ibid., 103, 103n2.
129. Europeanized Islam would be useful for the conversion of Africans as it was in closer proximity to them, according to Carl Becker. See Marchand, *German Orientalism*, 361–367.
130. Wilhelm Heitmüller, "Johannes-Evangelium," in *Die Schriften des Neuen Testaments neu übersetzt und für die Gegenwart erklärt*, ed. Otto Baumgarten et al., vol. 4 (Göttingen: Vandehoeck und Ruprecht, 1918), 76.
131. Ibid., 77–78.
132. Ibid., 81.
133. Ibid., 80.
134. Ibid., 149.
135. Ibid., 83.
136. Schmidt, *Grundriß der Kirchengeschichte*, 502–503.
137. Marchand, *German Orientalism*, 289.
138. Friedrich Naumann, *Gotteshilfe: Gesamtausgabe der Andachten aus den Jahren 1895–192 sachlich geordnet*, 6th ed. (Göttingen: Vandenhoeck und Ruprecht, 1926), 47.
139. Ibid., 468.
140. Ibid., 252.
141. Ibid., 471.
142. Ibid., 472–473.
143. Ibid., 518. The German term *Treue* references a political relation of swearing allegiance.
144. Ibid., 523.
145. Ibid., 526.
146. Ibid., 527.
147. Ibid., 524.
148. Ibid., 534.
149. Ibid., 537.
150. Ibid., 556–557.
151. Reference in Marchand, *German Orientalism*, 464–467.
152. *Christoph Blumhardt and His Message*, ed. R. Lejeune (Woodcrest: The Plough Publishing House, 1963), 113.
153. Ibid., 103.
154. Ibid., 136.
155. Ibid., 146.
156. Ibid., 161.
157. Ibid., 189.
158. Ibid., 190.
159. Ibid., 191.
160. Ibid., 191.
161. Ibid., 194, 195.
162. Ibid., 195.
163. Marchand, *German Orientalism*, xxv.
164. Zantop, *Colonial Fantasies*, 100–101.

165. Lathi, "German Colonialism and the Age of Global Empire," n.p.
166. Quoted in Marchand, *German Orientalism*, 386.
167. Friedrichsmeyer, Lennox, and Zantop, "Introduction," 24–25.

FURTHER READING

Bosch, David J. *Transforming Mission: Paradigm Shifts in Theology of Mission*. Maryknoll: Orbis Books, 1991.

Friedrichsmeyer, Sara, Sara Lennox, and Susanne Zantop. Eds. *The Imperialist Imagination: German Colonialism and Its Legacy*. Ann Arbor: University of Michigan Press, 1998.

Gensichen, Hans-Werner. *Die Missionsgeschichte der neueren Zeit*. Göttingen: Vandenhoeck und Ruprecht, 1961.

Marchand, Suzanne L. *German Orientalism in the Age of Empire: Religion, Race, and Scholarship*. Cambridge: Cambridge University Press, 2009.

Naranch, Bradley, and Geoff Ely. *German Colonialism in a Global Age*. Durham: Duke University Press, 2014.

Rieger, Joerg. *Christ and Empire: From Paul to Postcolonial Times*. Minneapolis: Fortress Press, 2007.

Young, Robert J. C. *Postcolonialism: An Historical Introduction*. Oxford: Blackwell, 2001.

Zantop, Susanne. *Colonial Fantasies: Conquest, Family, and Nation in Precolonial Germany, 1770–1870*. Durham: Duke University Press, 1997.

CHAPTER 16

THE BIBLE AND AMERICAN EMPIRE

JUDITH H. NEWMAN

FROM political stump speech to inaugural address, American presidents have often evoked the Puritan leader John Winthrop's famous vision of a shining "city on a hill," a phrase drawn from Jesus's Sermon on the Mount. Presidents as diverse as Bill Clinton, Ronald Reagan, and Barack Obama have deployed that phrase to evoke the exceptional character of the United States as a model for other nations with its unique destiny in history. Many Americans continue to idealize the country as a chosen nation, a beacon of freedom to the world, a Republic born of a rebellion that stands against oppressive regimes abroad.

The sustaining public myth of the United States does not admit of being an empire. The imperial character of the United States in its colonization of the continent and its expanded domination around the globe has already been discussed extensively. The burden of this chapter is to emphasize that the empire's defining character in regard to both Native Americans and African Americans was shaped by biblical discourse, especially in the nineteenth century. In the unfolding of that century, Anglo-American citizens of the new country gained control of a vast expanse of western lands and exploited African Americans for labor in the south.

In order to offer a contrapuntal reading in the spirit of Edward Said, one that offers an alternative perspective to a triumphalist or self-congratulatory nationalism, I focus instead on the disempowered within the larger political and economic system.[1] My account is partial and incomplete, but it is written in keeping with the perspective of R. S. Sugirtharajah, "not with the intention of idealizing and glorifying them [Indigenous or "othered" people] but to make it clear that the narrative is complicated and disputed."[2] In effect, it is to reread history by humanizing those who have been considered less than fully human and to reincorporate cultural knowledge and perspectives that have either been ignored or denigrated in systemic ways.[3]

Scripturalizing Foundations: The Puritan Land Claims in the New Israel

A well-known painting by George Henry Boughton, famous for his renderings of Puritans, depicts a group walking in the snow on their way to church (Figure 16.1). Each Pilgrim is armed with either a rifle or a Bible. Dating to 1867, the image hearkens back to the colonial period but at the same time reflects the contemporary reality of post-Civil War America. The men with guns are alert to dangers in the wilds of the woods, be they beasts or Indian "savages." The amount of personal property depicted is anachronistic. In the seventeenth century each person would not own their own Bible, but in the colonial period and early America, the Bible was the most authoritative, available, and familiar book.[4] If a Christian household possessed any book at all, it would have been a Bible, and by the nineteenth century the King James Bible would have been a family mainstay.[5] Boughton's painting also anticipates the America of the twenty-first century in which gun-ownership is at an all-time high and bibles retain their iconic power in public spaces, whether in swearing-in ceremonies or more ominous situations. The image is echoed in the menacing actions of an American president who was always ready to stage a photo op, Donald Trump, as he used gun-toting troops to clear Lafayette Square in order to hold up a Bible in front of a church to appeal to his evangelical supporters.[6]

In today's more secular and religiously diverse country awash with all kinds of print, most Americans are less familiar with the Bible than they were in Boughton's day. In

FIGURE 16.1. *Pilgrims Going to Church*, by George Henry Boughton, 1867.
Available from New York Historical Society (https://www.nyhistory.org/exhibit/pilgrims-going-church-0) and Wikimedia Commons (https://commons.wikimedia.org/w/index.php?curid=308136).

early America, biblical concepts and language circulated through sermons and various forms of print and oral media, but also through other means of communication and signification. It permeated all cultural arenas, providing insights and frameworks for law, politics, civil government, and other areas of life.[7] A high degree of biblical literacy was true not only of elite "founding fathers" of the United States but also of the population more generally, such regional elites as ministers and state-level politicians.[8] In the earliest days of European settlement, Puritans claimed their identity as a newly liberated Israel, an elect, covenant people guided by divine providence and delivered into a Promised Land. By the mid-nineteenth century, the white Anglo-Protestant majority would come to understand this history as a "manifest destiny," a purposeful and divinely ordained spread of a righteous nation.[9]

At the same time, Boughton's retrojection of a pure Pilgrim past masked the reality of contemporary conflict among settlers, pioneers, ranchers, and Native American groups in the West, not to mention the divisive issues of slavery and Catholic immigration roiling the South and East.[10] This Christian ethos was frequently enmeshed with an ideology of white ethnic supremacy on the part of the new citizen-settlers all the while championing religious freedom and tolerance as civic virtues. As Tisa Wenger has observed, in the late eighteenth and nineteenth century a cultural perspective born of liberal universalism viewed the rational, civilized white male subject as superior to racialized or gendered "others" who were irrational, primitive, child-like. In her words, "These liberal thinkers defended empire as justifiable, even laudable and benevolent, because it provided a way to bring the values and virtues of freedom and civilization to the racialized subjects of colonial rule."[11] Settler colonialism can be understood as one mode of imperialism in which the means of expansion were made through claiming and settling land, displacement of Indigenous peoples, and extraction of resources.

Mapping Western Lands: Lewis, Clark, Sacagewa, and Native Knowledge

The science of cartography was another European import used by the United States for imperial ends. In 1803, Thomas Jefferson paid $15 million to France for the Louisiana Purchase, a huge expanse of land west of the Mississippi River that doubled the then size of the country. Jefferson realized that for maximum use to the new nation, the newly purchased region required exploration and mapping. This was in keeping with the spirit of scientific inquiry so characteristic of the "Age of Reason." As John Rennie Short has observed: The land required survey in all the subtle meanings of that term, including knowing, surveillance and control."[12] Jefferson promptly commissioned Meriwether Lewis and William A. Clark as a "Corps of Discovery" to launch an expedition with two aims related to capitalist ventures. One was to find a water route from the Missouri River to the Pacific in order to enable a trade passage. The second was to explore the land to see what valuable goods might be found, whether new discoveries of minerals, animals, or plants.

The expedition of Lewis and Clark has been extensively chronicled. Less often considered is the role of Native American knowledge of the land in making the journey and its mapping possible. "Colonial map-making was not a one-way process," observes Pamela Klassen, " . . . but a hybrid process combining Indigenous territorial knowledge with the techniques and motives of colonial surveyors."[13] The Corps comprised fifty men, including one named York who was enslaved by Clark, and a Lemhi Shoshone woman, Sacagewa, married to a Quebecois trapper Toussaint Charbonneau. Sacagewa, who bore her first child on the journey at age seventeen, represents not only a tale of strength and endurance, but also intercultural dexterity. Sacagewa's involvement was a crucial part of the expedition in the complex cultural encounters with native tribes. She served as translator to the over seventy native tribes they encountered, and she had knowledge of the land in an existential way that differed from the explorers. Canadian novelist Thomas King captures essential distinctions:

> Land has always been a defining element of Aboriginal culture. Land contains the languages, the stories, and the histories of a people. It provides water, air, shelter, and food. Land participates in the ceremonies and the songs. And land is home. Not in an abstract way . . . For non-Natives, land is primarily a commodity, something that has value for what you can take from it or what you can get from it.[14]

King's point about the land's participation in ritual life underscores the embedded relationship between native tribes and the land on which they live and the skies they look to for signs. Mountains and streams can have agency, not unlike in biblical literature, in which mountains burst into song and trees clap their hands (Isa 55:12); the sun and moon stand still (Joshua 10:12); and stars are exhorted to praise their creator (Psa 148:3). Mapping practices of the Native Americans reflect the intimate connection with the land, and not just any land, but the particular places they inhabit.[15]

At least thirty Native American maps appear in the archives of Lewis and Clark, and information gathering from natives is recorded throughout their official journal.[16] The common thread in these indigenous maps is that they reflect deep knowledge and experience of the land. Moreover, they were not based on the experience of one individual but on accumulated and shared knowledge among tribal members, who knew the currents in the streams and rivers, who had studied the habits of the moose they wanted to hunt, and visited the place where the most abundant stands of wild rice could be found, not to mention the most expedient route from the hunting spot or trading post to home.[17] As a result of their traditional oral cultures and the concentration of knowledge in tribal elders or other individuals, Native American "maps" were more often verbal, gestural, or performative, rather than graphic representations on durable media.

This intimacy with the earth and natural agency is reflected as well in native place names. In Louise Erdrich's novel, *The Last Report on the Miracles at Little No Horse*, the Anishinaabe storyteller Nanapush contrasts the naming practices of white settlers, who name places after men, for military leaders or entrepreneurs, and the Ojibwe who name places for what grows there or what is found. Native naming, and native mapping, require indigenous local knowledge of the land and their engagement and history with it.[18] Native cartography can also have a cosmological significance. This arises from a sense of sacred geography, and it might be manifest by positing a sacred center, an "*axis mundi*" to use Mircea Eliade's term.[19] Such a center might be the *Nanih Waiya* "mother mound" of the Choctaw of Mississippi, or it might be the sacred post in the sweat lodge of the Yurok people of northern California they thought to be the world's first redwood tree, or it might be another spot.[20] Cosmogonic maps allow a community to find orientation in history and in values, past, present, and future by providing meaning and direction in life.

By contrast, European maps provide a bird's eye view of territory by surveying, quantifying, demarcating, and charting according to longitude and latitude in order to gain perspective on a commodified land. Matthew Edney characterizes such modern settler mapping practices as "imperial mapping," which "manifest a dramatic irony in which imperial actors map a territory not for the benefit of the territory's inhabitants—who do not participate within and who largely remain ignorant of the discourse—but for a knowing, empowered, imperial audience."[21] Mapping states, territories, townships, in short, indicating borders and boundaries on a flat surface in this manner alongside topographical features, served as a means of asserting political and economic power. The Lewis and Clark exploration resulted in the well-known "Track Map" (Figure 16.2) that, while not yet defining fixed boundaries, would serve as an imperial map. Although it contains Indian tribal names, it is a map of erasure of native presence with no trade routes, sacred places, or settlements included. Here indeed was a visual assertion of

FIGURE 16.2. A map of Lewis and Clark's track, across the western portion of North America from the Mississippi to the Pacific Ocean: By order of the executive of the United States in 1804, 5 & 6.

Courtesy of Library of Congress, Geography and Map Division, Louisiana: European Explorations and the Louisiana Purchase.

"*terra nullius*" that lay at the heart of the "doctrine of discovery," a land emptied of the long history of native habitation.[22]

After the return of the Corps of Discovery, William Clark served as brigadier general for the militia in Louisiana territory and eventually as Superintendent of Indian Affairs from 1822 to 1838. Although sympathetic to the Indians and their cultures, he also held the prevailing assimilationist view. As Superintendent, he would enact policies that forced the depopulation of Native Americans from their ancestral lands, especially President Andrew Jackson's "Indian Removal Act" of 1830. During Clark's tenure, the Cherokee, Chickasaw, Choctaw, Delaware, Kickapoo, Miami, Osage, Ottowa, Potowatomi, Quapaw, Seneca, Shawnee, and Wynadot were all forcibly removed.[23] The federal move to push Natives from the tribal lands was not met without stiff resistance, especially from those who identified themselves with the "Friends of the Indian" movement, composed especially of Protestant clergy and advocates. One of the prominent Indian rights groups was the American Board of Commissioners for Foreign Missions (ABCFM). Jeremy Evarts, a leader of the ABCFM and a staunch opponent of Jackson's plans for Indian removal, drew from the Bible to express his disdain, likening the actions to King Ahab and Queen Jezebel's theft of Naboth's vineyard.[24]

In spite of the opposition of the ABCFM and other parties, Jackson and his party were unmoved. The discovery of gold in Georgia and the booming cotton trade throughout the southeast meant that white settlers wanted to claim the land for themselves. Congress appropriated $500,000 for the relocation of Cherokees. The forced march of some 16,000 Cherokees to a newly created "Indian Territory" beyond the Mississippi was called by the Cherokees *nunna daul isunyi*, "the trail where we cried." Indian Territory was steadily diminished and eventually whittled down to an area in present-day eastern Oklahoma. The setting of boundaries and settling of territories in the nineteenth century also included the vast expanse of territory to the south and west of "Indian Territory."[25] Into the region stretching from Texas to the Pacific Ocean would enter a new religious movement rooted in biblical revelation and born in the United States.

A Blueprint for the New Zion: The Utopian Geography of the Latter-Day Saints

In its missionary zeal for global reach, its entrepreneurial spirit, and its commitment to commerce and productivity, the Church of Jesus Christ of Latter-Day Saints (LDS) is quintessentially American. Arising in the midst of the Second Great Awakening, the Mormons provided a new rationale for claiming territory in a new Israel. If, as in the famous observation by Sacvan Bercovitch, the Puritans "discovered America in the Bible," the LDS upped the ante by "discovering" their own scriptures as well.[26] The self-proclaimed prophet Joseph Smith launched his movement with the publication of the Book of Mormon in upstate New York in 1830, the same year the Indian Removal Act was signed into law. An American scripture for a uniquely American religion, the Book of Mormon was itself scripturalized. The book lodged its own authority not only in claims to new prophecy but in the use of the language and style of the Authorized Version, peppered with "thees" and "thous" and liberally salted with "And when it came to passes." If the new religion was similar in certain respects to that of the Puritans in its strong identification with ancient Israel, its distinctive beliefs and practices would result in persecution, if not their own "trail of tears."

The Mormons provided both a new beginning and a new ending for American history. The Book of Mormon includes an account of the tribal ancestor Lehi whose sons were the righteous Nephi and the duplicitous Laman. Mormons held that the native peoples were "Lamanites," none other than descendants of the ten lost tribes of ancient Israel exiled at the time of the Assyrian conquest in the eighth century BCE.[27] The end time would include the conversion of the Lamanites and the full restoration of the church. Mormons were not alone in identifying the Native Americans as the ten lost tribes, but this was a new twist.[28] In the initial years up through their time in Nauvoo, Illinois, they anticipated a return of Christ to America, where according to doctrine he had once made a post-resurrection experience. There was thus no need to dispossess the Native Americans who would be redeemed along with the LDS.[29]

The Mormon blueprint for their new Zion was infused by utopian fervor yet at the same time was utilitarian and informed by contemporary urban planning. In the words of John Reps, a historian of city planning: "the Church of Jesus Christ of Latter-Day Saints—or the Mormons, as they were soon called—became the most successful city builder [sic] of all the religious and utopian societies."[30] The biblical vision for this new urban model was laid out in the Mormon *Doctrine and Covenants*: "And it shall be called the New Jerusalem, a land of peace, a city of refuge, a place of safety for the Saints of the Most High God. And the glory of the Lord shall be there, and the terror of the Lord shall be there, insomuch that the wicked will not come unto it, and it shall be called Zion."[31] In 1833, Joseph Smith sent his community a letter with exact plans for the "Plat of the City of Zion": "When this square is thus laid off and supplied, lay off another in the same way, and so fill up the world in these last days; and let every man live in this city for this is the City of Zion."[32] The square plan (Figure 16.3) was drawn from a scaled-down version of the heavenly city of Revelation but also inspired by the plans for cities of the Levites mentioned in Numbers 35, Leviticus 25, as well as the Ezekiel's vision of the restoration of the Israelite tribes to the land in Ezekiel 47–48.[33]

Ezekiel's perspective focuses on the cultic center of priestly power in the Temple of Jerusalem. This Zion theology envisions Jerusalem as the *axis mundi*, the center not only of the land of Israel, but of the world. The new Jerusalem, a vision taken up again in the book of Revelation, will be a symmetrically shaped community.

The city plan combined the utopian ideals of the Puritan settlers with their concern for cultivating and improving the land according to the mandate of Genesis 1:27 with the practicality for which the settler Mormons would be known.[34] The houses were to

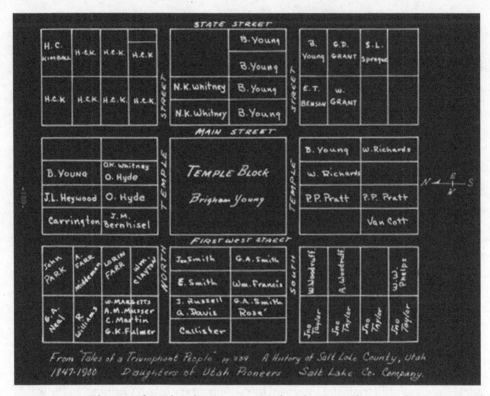

FIGURE 16.3. Blueprint for Salt Lake City. *From Tales of a Triumphant People: A History of Salt Like County, Utah, 1847–1900.* Salt Lake City: Daughters of Utah Pioneers and Salt Lake Co. Company, 339.

be planned in a grid with each house to be placed twenty feet back from the street to allow for cultivation of gardens in the front. Streets were to be 132 feet wide, allowing for a team of oxen to turn around. Agrarian areas would belt the town. In one sense, this city planning followed the American adaptation of the grid pattern laid down in New York City in 1811 and in Washington, D.C. (Figure 16.4). The grid with its numbered or lettered streets enabled quick navigation of the city. Whereas the grid plan on the island of Manhattan was made for purely pragmatic reasons, Pierre L'Enfant's plan for the nation's capital aimed at something more monumental, placing the Capitol building, the American temple of democracy, as its orientational center. Both city plans, however, were secular, except to the degree that the United States and its government can be understood to have a civil religion. Salt Lake City, by contrast, was and remains unapologetically theocentric, with the Temple topped by Joseph Smith's revealing angel Moroni as the central point of navigation. This City of Zion was envisioned as a new Jerusalem, from whence the Mormons would go out to proselytize the world two-by-two on their missions, but also as a place of the ultimate ingathering. Rather than an eschatological vision of the Jewish Passover with its hope for a diasporic return in the "next

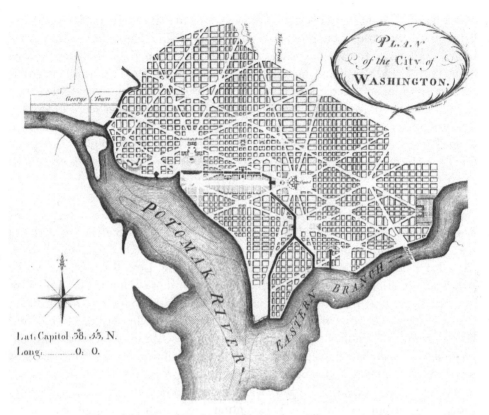

FIGURE 16.4. "Plan of the City of Washington," by Andrew Ellicott, revised from Pierre (Peter) Charles L'Enfant. Thackara & Vallance: Philadelphia, 1792.

Available from Library of Congress.

year in Jerusalem," however, those summoned for the ultimate return to Salt Lake City would be the new converts to the LDS Church, joining the "new Israel" in the restored homeland.[35]

The LDS were not the only ones holding utopian views or the understanding that the Indians were the ten lost tribes of Israel. Jewish American Mordecai Manuel Noah also sought to bolster the identification. As a major Tammany Hall figure, newspaper publisher, and one-time ambassador to Tunis, in 1820 he sought to establish a Hebrew city of refuge named Ararat on the 17,381-acre Grand Island on the Niagara River close to Buffalo, New York.[36] Although he planned his colonization idea for several years, the attempt was short-lived because the persecuted European and Palestinian Jews he wished to migrate never materialized. But where Noah failed, the Mormon initiative proved enduring.

The Mormons did not originally fix the place of the ideal settlement but awaited further prophecies from their leaders. They first settled in Kirtland, Ohio, then in far west Missouri, and from there, Nauvoo, Illinois where the city planning was begun, complete with a Temple.[37] When controversies in Nauvoo resulted in the murder of Joseph Smith, Brigham Young arose as the prophet-leader of the religion. He undertook a massive project of resettling the Mormons from Illinois to Utah. More than any other religious group in America, Mormons sought literally to chart and implant their millennial and utopian vision of an ordered scriptural society directly on the land they settled. This was reflected not only in their City of Zion plan, but on the broader scope of western territory. The original proposal submitted to Utah did not lack for ambition. Brigham Young had in mind a Mormon empire if also religiously democratic, a pilgrimage place for all the Mormons and their converts. The original "State of Deseret" envisioned most of what is now Nevada, Utah, Arizona, and parts of five other states, including southern California all the way to the Pacific in order to gain access to a seaport.

Mizpah, Jericho, Bethel, Hebron, Zion, Jordan, Gilead—these and many other biblical toponyms appear not once but many times on the map of America, but Utah has the highest percentage of biblical place names in the United States. To count places in Utah that include biblical allusions, like Temple Mountain, Three Patriarchs, or Noah's Ark, would multiply the number. Like the colonial Puritans of New England, many of the names were drawn from the Bible but Mormons settling in their new Zion added their own toponyms drawn from the Book of Mormon: Lehi, Nephi, Moroni, and Kolob Valley.[38] Mormons have long understood themselves as a righteous remnant, providentially mandated. Ensign Peak, north of the Capitol building in Salt Lake City, was named by Brigham Young because he said it was a proper place "to raise an ensign to the nations" (Isa 5:26, 11:10, 12 KJV) signaling an end to their Exile with a return to Zion.[39] The missionary zeal of the LDS continues with their program of sending out pairs of disciples throughout the world to make new converts for the church's empire of souls. In the center, however, stands the City of Zion, as the LDS await the climactic Second Coming.

While Mormons held religious views of sacred space and social organization that distinguished them from other Christians, in other respects they were very much a part of white culture in respect to tolerance of slavery. Three black enslaved people, Green Flake, Hark Lay, and Oscar Crosby, arrived with the original Mormon colonizers in 1847.[40] Because Native Americans were understood to be Lamanites, the lost tribes of Israel and thus Mormon kin, Indian slavery was forbidden by the LDS Church. On the other hand, African American slavery was condoned. An interview recorded between abolitionist Horace Greeley and Brigham Young includes the following exchange:

H.G.: What is the position of your church with respect to slavery?
B.Y.: We consider it of divine institution, and not to be abolished until the curse pronounced upon Ham shall have been removed from his descendants.[41]

As we shall see, the Mormon acceptance of the "curse of Ham" found in Genesis 9 as a rationale for the perpetual subordination of African Americans was very much in accord with the southern Zeitgeist.

Talking Back to the Talking Book: From the Myth of Ham to New Exodus

Beginning in the late eighteenth and into the nineteenth century, the publication of slave narratives popularized the trope of the "Talking Book," in which a formerly enslaved author describes their first encounter while still illiterate with someone reading a book, imagining that the book itself could speak.[42] On one hand, the book represented the power of the Bible as a potent book. On the other, the trope reinforced the status of the now literate evangelical author. The Great Awakening and the revival movements of the late eighteenth and early nineteenth century spawned not only the visionary Mormon movement, but galvanized Baptists, Methodists, and Presbyterians to evangelical action not only in New England and the "Burned-over District" of western New York, on fire with spiritual fervor, but also in the south among the enslaved. Indeed, Black Baptist preachers began to pastor their own people beginning already in the late eighteenth century. As Albert Raboteau observes about the liberating potential of their scriptural interpretation: "They were able to interpret the stories, symbols, and events of the Bible to fit the day-to-day lives of those held in bondage. And whites—try as they might—could not control this interpretation or determine its 'accuracy.' "[43] While not all the enslaved may have been able to read the "Talking Book," they recognized the power and moral authority it held over their masters in the broader Protestant culture of the South. They learned its characters, stories, and lessons and engaged them.

If the Mormons headed west for their Promised Land in settling Utah Territory, enslaved African Americans looked to the North Star for theirs. For the many who adopted Christianity, the power of the Exodus story and Israel's long trek through the wilderness toward Canaan held deep meaning.[44] Their main concern was not settling land, however, but the liberation of their long-suffering souls and exploited bodies from the Peculiar Institution of slavery as it took shape in the expanding empire. Slave labor was used in domestic settings, as well as specialized trades like blacksmithing or shoemaking, and in agriculture to harvest rice, tobacco, and indigo, but the major labor demand came from the booming production and export of cotton that drove the engine and global financial reach of the American empire. The brutality of American capitalism thus begins with the plantation in service to the growth of the industrial revolution in Great Britain and elsewhere (Figure 16.5).[45]

Enslaved people were exploited for not only for their labor but for the commodification of their bodies which were treated as human capital to be traded, trafficked, and mortgaged. Thomas Jefferson, for example, mortgaged one hundred-fifty of his enslaved workers to build his plantation Monticello, and his practice was typical. While Jefferson admitted to the evils of slavery, other southern planters found legitimation for their views of African Americans as cursed in the Bible even as ever-increasing numbers of their enslaved workers became "Bible-believing" Christians themselves. The Bible assumes the existence of slavery, and pro-slavery Christians often cited Eph 6:5–9, Gal

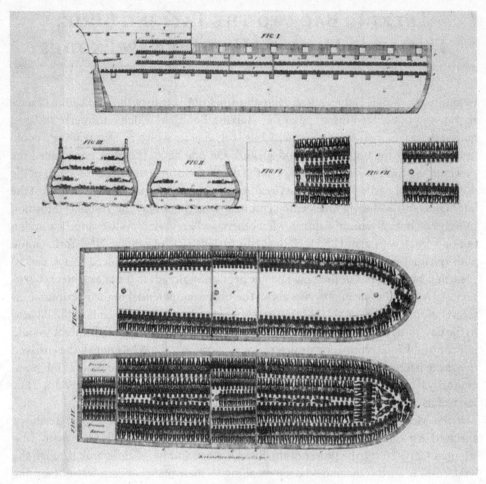

FIGURE 16.5. A Trans-Atlantic ship with four slave decks for transporting human beings like cargo. By Printer: Boek- en steendrukkerij v. C.A. Spin, Amsterdam.

Available from Peace Palace Library, The Hague.

3:28, or Col 3: 22–4:1 in support of their views; however, the racialized view of slavery in America as part of divinely ordered nature was related primarily to one story from Genesis. Opponents were forced to contest dominant interpretations about racial origins rooted in the story of Noah's cursing of his grandson Ham.[46]

COUNTERING THE CURSE OF HAM

For all Protestants in early America, the Bible was held to be an accurate account of the origins of the world and its peoples. Before the discoveries of the *Enuma Elish* and the *Gilgamesh Epic* could provide rival accounts of universal origins, the first chapters of Genesis were understood as the one true story of God's plan for the world. Noah, who together with his three sons, Ham, Shem, and Japheth survived the flood, were thus the ancestors of all humanity. Whether pro-slavery or abolitionist, enslaved or free, Christians accepted the idea that Ham was the ancestor of the "Negro race."[47]

The story in Genesis 9 in which Noah curses Ham's son Canaan after Ham sees Noah's nakedness was interpreted differently, however, by pro-slavery proponents and abolitionists. White enslavers argued for slavery as part of a "natural" set of hierarchies in which females were subordinate to males, and blacks to whites, thus elevating the white male slaveholder as the highest in the status hierarchy.[48] English planters in particular were resistant to letting their enslaved population receive instruction in Christianity. In the words of Albert Raboteau: "It seemed that the Christian commission to preach the gospel to all nations ran directly counter to the economic interest of the Christian slave owner."[49]

African Americans, on the other hand, who accepted this biblical claim of racial origins, argued that the three great ancient civilizations produced by Ham's descendants in Ethiopia, Babylonia, and Egypt, proved the brilliance of their dark-sinned ancestors. They used this to bolster their case against the white supremacist view that blacks were inherently inferior. A number of influential African American biblical scholars offered nuanced interpretations of the Genesis account that countered racist perspectives, including the idea that the *divine blessing* over Noah and his three sons, Shem, Ham, and Japheth was much stronger and enduring than Noah's curse. Noah's human curse of Canaan, pronounced while he was inebriated, was in effect a false prophecy, according to the Rev. George Washington Williams.[50]

Another alternative and ingenious interpretation of the Bible was offered by William J. Anderson. Rather than look for the origins of the so-called black race, he examined the scriptures for the origins of the white race and found it in the story of Naaman's healing by Elisha in 2 Kings 5.[51] In that story, the Syrian captain Naaman seeks out Elisha to heal him and Elisha promptly does so. Rather than accept payment, he sends Naaman away. Elisha's servant Gehazi thereby tried secretly to wrest payment from Naaman and is cursed by Elisha with the same "disease" as Naaman, with Gehazi becoming "white as snow." A more common reading of 2 Kings 5 by contemporary expositors indicted Gehazi for his greed. Anderson's interpretation implicitly highlighted the selective and inconsistent reading by many in antebellum America who narrowly sought the origins of "blackness" in the Bible while ignoring other relevant texts. Yet as Emerson Powery points out, "Had Anderson's reading of 2 Kings 5 prevailed, the understanding of 'whiteness' as a curse on Gehazi and his "seed forever," brought about because of greed, might have served as a potent condemnation of a system that dehumanized darker peoples for the financial benefit of lighter peoples and perhaps even fostered conversation about such economic exploitation."[52]

African Americans found means to combat white supremacy aside from the Bible. The outlawing of slavery in England in 1807 and the American prohibition of the importation of slaves in the same year led to perverse results. Social reformer and abolitionist Frederick Douglass recognized that the idea of a "pure African" simply did not make sense in the context of the Peculiar Institution in which slave-holding men frequently raped enslaved women in order to produce more "commodities" for their enrichment. Writing in the context of his time, he points out another debased fact of plantation life: "If the lineal descendants of Ham are only to be enslaved, according to the scriptures, slavery in this country will soon become an unscriptural institution; for thousands are ushered into the world annually, who—like myself—owe their existence to white fathers."[53] In the words of Douglass, "this arrangement admits of the greatest license to brutal slaveholders, and their profligate sons, brothers, relations and friends, and gives to the pleasure of sin, the additional attraction of profit."[54]

The renowned author Harriet Jacobs, herself of mixed race, chronicled her life and experience of enslavement. She made a similar point: "They seem to satisfy their consciences with the doctrine that God created the Africans to be slaves. What a libel upon the heavenly Father, who made of one blood all nations of men!' And then who *are* Africans? Who can measure the amount of Anglo-Saxon blood coursing in the veins of American slaves?"[55] Like other abolitionists, Jacobs refers to a verse from Paul's address in Athens on the Areopagus (Acts 17:27) to argue for the basic commonality of all humans. Like Douglass she also points to the malignant pervasiveness of sexual abuse by so many enslavers.

Aside from responding to the commonly used interpretation of the curse of Ham, many African American interpreters of scripture felt free to challenge traditional and prevalent interpretations. Abolitionist Sojourner Truth often drew from the Bible in her speeches such as her famous address, "Ain't I a Woman" at the 1851 Women's Rights Convention in Akron, Ohio. With acerbic wit she offered counter readings to prevailing interpretations, including that concerning "original sin" in this defiant response: "If Eve's sin so upset the world, she herself should have the chance to set it right again."[56] Her independent feminist spirit shined through as well with her observation that Jesus arrived in the world by the power of God and a woman without benefit of a man.[57] Sojourner Truth's ironic "sass" shares the same spirit as a twentieth-century African American James Baldwin, who sought to call his country to account for their racial sins.

THE CODED LANGUAGE OF THE SPIRITUALS

The title of James Baldwin's jeremiad *The Fire Next Time* anticipates its final words: "If we do not now dare everything, the fulfillment of that prophecy, recreated from the Bible in song by a slave, is upon us: *God gave Noah the rainbow sign, No more water, the fire next time!*"[58] Drawing on a well-known spiritual, his book issues a prophetic and apocalyptic warning to white America of the cost of continuing to ignore deep injustices of racial inequity embedded in society. Published on the hundredth anniversary of the Emancipation Proclamation and at the height of the civil rights movement, he wrote in the form of a letter to his nephew but by extension to all black boys and beyond to all

Americans, to warn them about the dangerous legacy of racism rooted in its original sin of slavery.

Baldwin, the eloquent former preacher, draws from the well of his own experience about the strictures of living in a dominant, oppressive culture that neither sees nor hears the marginalized. Freed from "the man" in the company of other African Americans, he can be liberated: "This is the freedom that one hears in some gospel songs, for example, and in jazz. In all jazz, and especially in the blues, there is something tart and ironic, authoritative and double-edged."[59] That same freedom and character is found in the Negro spirituals, which is a freedom that exposits and expounds on scripture in a sinuous and often double-edged way. The spiritual Baldwin cites is at once a reference to the eternal covenant God makes with Noah in Genesis 9 after the punishment of all humanity for their wickedness through flood, and the fiery punishment of the damned from the Christian Bible's culmination in Revelation 20. The second level of meaning inheres in Baldwin's own critique of the American empire, implicitly compared with the divine punishment of the Babylonian/Roman empire in John's prophetic Apocalypse.

If William Anderson sought to undermine the prevalent "curse of Ham" and its toxic effects through close exegesis and prose, a very different hermeneutical engagement with scripture is found in the poetic form and soaring imagination of Negro spirituals.[60] One of the earliest reflections on the cultural significance of these compositions was offered by W.E.B. Dubois. He referred to them as the "Sorrow Songs" that "tell in word and music of trouble and exile, of strike and hiding, they grope toward some unseen power and sign for rest in the End."[61] The tragic ongoing reality of broken-up families, of young children wrenched from the arms of their mothers to be sold on the auction block to the highest bidder, of a husband sold "down river" never to see his wife again, led to such desolate words as these: "Sometimes I feel like a motherless chile, I'm a long ways from home." The sorrow expresses a solitude and sadness born of endemic family dislocation. On the level of engagement with scripture, it is clear the degree to which the characters, events, and narratives of the Bible became fully present, interwoven into the current lives of the enslaved. Jacob, Sarah, Joshua, Daniel, all came alive to be engaged in song. DuBois characterized their transformation of scripture: "Especially is this true of Bible phrases. 'Weep, O captive daughter of Zion,' is quaintly turned into 'Zion, weep-a-low,' and the wheels of Ezekiel are turned every way in the mystic dreaming of the slave, till he says: 'There's a little wheel a-turnin' in-a-my heart.' "[62]

Spirituals represent a hybrid cultural phenomenon, borrowing from traditional African tunes and songs. One feature of this borrowing was the coded meaning so many of them contained. The lyrics could hold more than one level of meaning. "Much of the verbal art of West Africans and many of the folk tales of their American descendants were characterized by indirect, veiled social comment and criticism, a technique appropriately described as 'hitting a straight lick with a crooked stick,' " writes Raboteau.[63] Baldwin's use of the spiritual in his book reflects such an encrypted meaning. For those in the ante-bellum south, the coded meeting was linked with an abiding hope for escape from slavery whether in this life or the next. This hope was most often then linked to an identification with the ancient Israelites. Frederick Douglass recalls this trickster double-meaning of the spirituals from his own experience of enslavement before his escape in Baltimore:

> At certain moments, we had an extraordinary spiritedness, we sang hymns, we shouted for joy, on a tone that was almost as triumphant as if it were already secure in a land of freedom. An attentive observer would have been able to see in the repetition of 'O Canaan, sweet Canaan, I'm goin' to the land of Canaan' something more than the hope to reach heaven. In it we expressed our hope to reach the North and the North was our Canaan.[64]

The code was not difficult to parse for those "in the know." The longed-for destination was the Promised Land, Canaan, or Heaven. Pharoah would be the system of slavery and white supremacy, and the South would be the Egypt from whence to escape. The Jordan River would represent the mighty Ohio River, which allowed safe passage. Neither the creation of these lyrics nor the coded language required literacy, just an active imagination. The escape to freedom, for those enslaved souls who dared to escape on the Underground Railroad, however, required great audacity. Even more daring and risk was required of the "conductors" who accompanied those who had escaped on their journey following the North Star.

Most famous of the conductors is Harriet Tubman whose favorite spiritual was said to be "Go down Moses."[65]

> When Israel was in Egypt's land
> Let my people go
> Oppressed so hard they could not stand
> Let my people go
>
> Go down, Moses
> Way down in Egypt's land
> Tell old Pharaoh
> Let my people go

She never learned to read or write, but she was learned in moral courage, fearlessly making numerous trips to the eastern shore of Maryland where she had first been enslaved. Like Moses, Tubman had no rival. But unlike Moses, she kept returning to that "Egypt" in order to lead more groups to their freedom up north in Canaan, to Canada. She packed her own pistol and fiercely warned her "passengers" when they got cold feet and thought about returning to life in slavery: "a live runaway could do great harm by going back, but that a dead one could tell no secrets."[66]

Other spirituals might weave together characters and stories from the Old and New Testaments to create a kind of timeless fusion:

> Oh, Mary, don't you weep, don't you mourn
> Pharoah's army got drownded

> Oh, Mary, don't you weep
> One of these mornings, it won't be long
> You're gonna call my name but I'll be gone...

This famous spiritual contains allusions to the lament of Mary over Jesus's death and to the crossing of the Red Sea. Built into the song is a typology that relates the first liberation through Exodus with the death of Jesus as a new liberation. Both will result in the drowning of the enemy, the forces of chaos and oppression, whether Pharoah or the satan of sin. Yet the song also hints in coded terms at the departure of the one who is going to escape for freedom soon. In an inventive spin and double-edged indirection, the songs thus give voice to lament in the present but express an assured hope for a better future.

A second borrowing from the African ancestors relates to their performance. The liberating role of spirituals for the enslaved cannot be understood simply from the words and notes on a page.[67] These songs need to be understood as performed. There was of course first the imaginative creation of the lyrics, but there was also spontaneity, variety, and interchange with the community in their enactment. In the antebellum period when they were first being composed and performed, the songs were shouted, danced in the ring shout, with singing accompanied by jubilant motion, clapping of hands, tapping of feet. A leader would call out a verse or a spiritual, and the others would sing a response shuffle-dance, in rhythmic motion, always counter-clockwise.[68] The songs and dance were a communal performance.[69] Although slaves might be allowed to attend white services in which they sat segregated by themselves, secret prayer meetings offered another means of spiritual and physical release. In this shadow religion that occurred in the cloak of darkness, in woods or swamps, thickets or caves, the enslaved might "steal away to Jesus" to a sacred place where they could "escape" spiritually and "escape" by anticipating their future freedom from slavery. "Steal away home. I ain't got long to stay here" thus might represent all at once that home in the sky with Jesus, a future divine reckoning in which all the righteous will be summoned home, or that future home of freedom in the great North away from the shackles of slavery. "The famous 'Steal Away,' with its apocalyptic scenes, is a kind of exaltation of flight."[70] Secret meetings might equally lead to other means of political resistance to that brutal system. Clandestine gatherings might be a time to learn to read or to plan an escape or a rebellion against the oppressive forces of the Egyptian empire.

Conclusion

Like the ideal City of Zion in Mormon history, John Winthrop's "city on a hill" was mobile, but the city continues to exist as a metonymy, the idea of America itself in the imaginations of Americans. The "city on a hill" represents a beacon to others, but its rhetorical use carries the risk of overweening national exceptionalism. The Founding

Fathers did not choose Winthrop's Boston as the nation's capital but considered Philadelphia and New York in the Empire State before settling on Washington, D.C.

At Washington's heart and abutting the Capitol building is the National Mall edged by the museums of its Smithsonian Institution, a central site of American cultural memory. The Air and Space Museum is the most popular, with its commemoration of America's ventures to explore and conquer space. But the two most recent additions signal a degree of reckoning with a different history of conquest, the tragedies of dispossession and enslavement alongside a history of violence and cultural decimation. The National Museum of the American Indian is housed in a curvilinear limestone building meant to evoke the long-term forces of nature on rock formations. The architecture and its landscaping are a continuing reminder of the intimate native relationship to the land. The style of the Museum of African American History and Culture fuses aspects of classical architecture with strong African influences. A visit there begins in the basement, like a slave ship's hold, with the story of the Middle Passage, and moves ever upward to arrive finally at the rich cultural contributions of African Americans.

Another new addition to the neighborhood is the Museum of the Bible, built with a $400 million sponsorship by a conservative evangelical billionaire. Its location away and apart from the Mall reflects how the relationship of the Bible and American empire has changed in the twenty-first century.[71] The renovated 1922 brick building is most distinctive for its aspiration to be at the political center with a top floor clearstory that overlooks the Capitol building.[72] The permanent exhibit tells "the" history of the Bible but does not consider the complex and contested history of its interpretations. It is a narrative nostalgic for a time when the King James Bible alone reigned supreme, a story of prosaic simplicity rather than poetic complication, a story unconcerned with the imperial domination that we have considered here. One of the ironies of American history is that its dreams and ideals are so often thwarted by its actions, especially as the nation has grown ever more powerful. "Imperialism is a perennial problem of human existence," writes Reinhold Niebuhr, "for powerful nations and individuals inevitably tend to use the weak as instruments of their purposes."[73]

The steps of the Capitol building by the National Mall are the site of presidential inaugurations. An iconic use of the Bible accompanies the swearing in by the Chief Justice of the United States, but as we have seen, the power of that book lies not in its iconic status, but in its interpretative use that can deal in both death and life. In keeping with the hope for change that is brought about with each inauguration, National Youth Poet Laureate Amanda Gorman, a descendant of slaves, offered these verses in 2021, which serve as a suitable coda to this chapter:

> Scripture tells us to envision
> that everyone shall sit under their own vine and fig tree
> and no one shall make them afraid.
> If we're to live up to our own time,
> then victory won't lie in the blade.
> But in all the bridges we've made,

> that is the promise to glade,
> the hill we climb.
> If only we dare.
> It's because being American is more than a pride we inherit,
> it's the past we step into
> and how we repair it.[74]

Notes

1. On contrapuntal reading, see Edward W. Said, *Culture and Imperialism* (New York: Vintage, 1994), especially the second chapter, which draws attention to the unsavory imperial exploitation that makes the life of the main characters in Jane Austen's *Mansfield Park* possible. R. S. Sugirtharajah provides a lucid introduction to developments in postcolonialism as it has developed and been adopted in biblical studies with a helpful caution against excessive theorizing, *Exploring Postcolonial Biblical Criticism: History, Method, Practice* (Oxford: Wiley-Blackwell, 2011), 7–30 Thanks are due to Marc Brettler, Gabriel Holt, Sebastian Holt, Néstor Medina, Jorunn Økland, and Jeremy Schipper for their comments and suggestions that helped to improve this chapter.
2. Sugirtharajah, *Exploring Postcolonial Biblical Criticism*, 26.
3. There is much more work that could be done on the role of scriptural interpretation connected to the extension of American Christian nationalism in the present, such as Christian Zionists, whose uncritical "support" of Israel is intertwined with both messianic/millennial expectations and American politics.
4. The status that has been well documented by scholars. See for example, James P. Byrd, *Sacred Scripture, Sacred War: The Bible and the American Revolution* (Oxford, UK: Oxford University Press, 2013); Eran Shalev, *American Zion: The Old Testament as a Political Text from the Revolution to the Civil War* (New Haven, CT: Yale University Press, 2013); Mark A. Noll, *In the Beginning Was the Word: The Bible in American Public Life, 1492–1783* (Oxford, UK: Oxford University Press, 2015).
5. Harry S. Stout makes the argument that the Puritans' shift from reliance on the Geneva Bible of 1560 to the Authorized Version of 1611 bespoke the increased influence of the movement fixed on establishing a this-worldly social order rooted in scriptural blueprints, "Word and Order in Colonial New England," *The Bible in America: Essays in Cultural History* (New York: Basic Books, 2017). The Douay-Rheims Bible translation made in support of the Counter-reformation and published in an American edition in 1790 did not have the same cachet; Seth Perry, *Bible Culture and Authority in the Early United States* (Princeton, NJ: Princeton University Press, 2018), 11–12.
6. It is ironic that the bible was an NRSV translation, an ecumenical venture considered suspect by many of those same evangelicals. The event occurred on June 1, 2020, at a tense time in American history. It was in the midst of the global COVID pandemic after weeks of civil disruption following the death of George Floyd, an unarmed black man, at the hands of the police in Minneapolis and the emergence of the Black Lives Matter movement. In reactions provoked by Trump's actions, Mariann Budde, the Episcopal bishop with oversight of St. John's Lafayette Square, denounced him publicly, and Washington, D.C. mayor Muriel Bowser renamed two adjacent blocks of 16th Street, N.W., "Black Lives Matter Plaza."

7. Like scholarship on American empire, the bibliography on the role of religion and the use of the Bible in American history is extensive, some of which is contained in Mark A. Noll, *In the Beginning Was the Word: The Bible in American Public Life, 1492–1783* (Oxford, UK: Oxford University Press, 2015). On the broader range of communication and "scripturalizing" and "socio-cultural signifying practices" by which the Bible has and continues to influence American culture, see Vincent L. Wimbush, "Introduction: Textures, Gestures, Power: Orientation to Radical Excavation," in *Theorizing Scriptures: New Critical Orientations to a Cultural Phenomenon*, ed. Vincent L. Wimbush (New Brunswick, NJ: Rutgers University Press, 2008), 1–20.
8. David L. Driesbach, *Reading the Bible with the Founding Fathers* (New York: Oxford University Press, 2016).
9. On the concept of manifest destiny, see the classic collection of Conrad Cherry, ed., *God's New Israel: Religious Interpretations of American Destiny* (Revised and updated edition; Chapel Hill: University of North Carolina Press, 1998).
10. David Morgan "The Image of the Protestant Bible in America," in *The Bible in the Public Square: Its Enduring Influence in American Life*, ed. Mark A. Chancey, Carol Meyers, and Eric M. Meyers (Atlanta, GA: SBL Press, 2016).
11. Tisa Wenger, *Religious Freedom: The Contested History of an American Ideal* (Chapel Hill, NC: University of North Carolina Press, 2017), 10. The evangelical movements accelerating from the Second Great Awakening qualifies this for the second half of the 19th century, and its influential role on free black churches will be considered further.
12. Short, John Rennie. *Cartographic Encounters: Indigenous Peoples and the Exploration of the New World* (London, UK: Reaktion Books, 2009), 59.
13. Pamela E. Klassen, *The Story of Radio Mind: A Missionary's Journey on Indigenous Land* (Chicago, IL: University of Chicago Press, 2018), 91.
14. Thomas King is of Cherokee and Greek ancestry and thus, bi-cultural himself, understands its nuances, *The Inconvenient Indian: A Curious Account of Native People in North America* (Anchor Canada, 2013), 218.
15. This is not to suggest that Native Americans did not also have a long-term ecological impact on their environments. On the legacy of indigenous use on diversity in forest garden eco-systems, see C. Armstrong, J. Miller, A. C. McAlvay, P. M. Ritchie, and D. Lepofsky, "Historical Indigenous Land-Use Explains Plant Functional Trait Diversity," *Ecology and Society* 26, no. 2 (2021): 6. https://doi.org/10.5751/ES-12322-260206 Many thanks to Gabriel and Sebastian Holt for drawing this research to my attention.
16. Short, *Cartographic Encounters*, 60–61.
17. Malcom G. Lewis, "Maps, Mapmaking, and Map Use by Native North Americans," *The History of Cartography. Volume 2, Book 3: Cartography in the Traditional African, American, Arctic, Australian, and Pacific Societies*, ed. David Woodward and G. Malcolm Lewis (Chicago: University of Chicago Press, 1998), 51–182, at 99. Cf. also Malcolm G. Lewis, "Recent and Current Encounters," in *Cartographic Encounters: Perspectives on Native American Map-making and Map Use*, ed. G. Malcolm Lewis (Chicago: University of Chicago Press, 1998), 71–110.
18. This reference to Erdrich's book is found in Kelli Lyon Johnson, "Writing Deeper Maps: Mapmaking, Local Indigenous Knowledges, and Literary Nationalism in Native Women's Writing," *Studies in American Indian Literatures* (Winter 2007): 103–120, at 103.
19. Eliade's concept has been reconsidered by Jonathan Z. Smith, "The Wobbling Pivot," *Map Is Not Territory* (Chicago, IL: University of Chicago Press, 1978). Smith's binary between

"locative" and "diasporic" categories can be challenged, however, because it does not recognize the "locative" itself can be "diasporic" in the case of American imagination in which the "imperial center" of Zion is mobile, as has been the case with Mormons and their temple or Native Americans whose migrations have occasioned a reconfiguration of center. Cf. also Yi-Fu Tuan, *Man and Nature*, Resources Paper no. 10 (Washington, D.C.: Commission on College Geography, 1971).

20. Peter Nabokov, "Orientations from Their Side: Dimensions of Native American Cartographic Discourse," in *Cartographic Encounters: Perspectives on Native American Mapmaking and Map Use*, ed. G. Malcolm Lewis (Chicago: University of Chicago Press, 1998), 241–269, at 249–250.
21. Matthew W. Edney, "The Irony of Imperial Mapping," *The Imperial Map: Cartography and the Mastery of Empire* (Chicago: University of Chicago Press, 2009), 11–45, at 40.
22. For a brief account of this issue particularly as it relates to biblical interpretation, see Judith H. Newman, "Tracing the Use of the Bible in Colonial Land Claims in North America," *The Bible in Political Debate: What Does It Really Say?* ed. Rodney Werline and Frances Flannery (T&T Clark, 2016), 127–140. A statement made by the Assembly of First Nations in Canada that maps a process for dismantling the Doctrine of Discovery can be found online at https://www.afn.ca/wp-content/uploads/2018/02/18-01-22-Dismantling-the-Doctrine-of-Discovery-EN.pdf
23. Short, *Cartographic Encounters*, 65.
24. Jennifer Graber, *The Gods of Indian Country: Religion and the Struggle for the American West* (New York: Oxford University Press, 2018), 31.
25. Indigenous peoples of North America have also worked to "reclaim" land through such remapping projects as https://native-land.ca/ which includes information about territories, languages, and treaties.
26. Sacvan Bercovitch, "The Biblical Basis of the American Myth" in *The Bible and American Arts and Letters*, ed. Giles Gunn (Philadelphia: Fortress; Chico, CA: Scholars, 1983), 221–32, at 23.
27. The Mormons were by no means the first to identify Indigenous peoples with the ten lost tribes of Israel in the "New World." One of the earliest accounts is found in a book by an Amsterdam rabbi, Menasseh ben Israel, *The Hope of Israel* published in 1650 that circulated in Europe. Menasseh incorporates an earlier work by Antonio de Montezinos, a Marrano Sephardic Jew, that described his travels in South America and his encounter with Indians he identified as descendants of the ten lost tribes. For modern edition of the 1652 English translation by Moses Wall, see *The Hope of Israel*, ed. Henry Méchoulan, and Gérard Nahon (New York: Littman Library for Oxford University Press, 1987). Many thanks to my colleague Néstor Medina for drawing my attention to this work.
28. For other details, see Eran Shalev, *American Zion*, 136–138.
29. Matthew Dougherty, *Lost Tribes Found: Israelite Indians and Religious Nationalism in Early America* (Norman, OK: University of Oklahoma Press, 2021).
30. John W. Reps, *The Making of Urban America: A History of City Planning in the United States*, Rev. ed. (Princeton, NJ: Princeton University Press, 1992), 466. Smith's map and letter are also available online: https://www.josephsmithpapers.org/paper-summary/plat-of-the-city-of-zion-circa-early-june-25-june-1833/1
31. Dougherty, *Lost Tribes*.
32. Reps, *The Making of Urban America*, 468.
33. Reps, *The Making of Urban America*, 472.

34. For the distinctively English interpretation of Gen 1:27 to cultivate the land by fencing it, see Patricia Seed, *Ceremonies of Possession in Europe's Conquest of the New World 1492–1640* (New York: Cambridge University Press, 1995), 35, or my discussion of this in relation to the Puritans in "Tracing the Use of the Bible in Colonial Land Claims in North America."
35. Richard Francaviglia, *The Mapmakers of New Zion: A Cartographic History of Mormonism* (Salt Lake City, UT: University of Utah Press, 2015), 31.
36. Eran Shalev provides an account of Mordecai Noah in *American Zion: The Old Testament as a Political Text from the Revolution to the Civil War* (New Haven, CT: Yale University Press, 2013), 76–82, 139–144.
37. The town's name Nauvoo is an anglicized version of the Hebrew for "beautiful" taken from Isaiah 52:7a: "How beautiful upon the mountain are the feet of the messenger who proclaims peace."
38. John Leighly, "Biblical Place-Names in the United States" *Names: A Journal of Onomastics* 27, no. 1 (1979): 46–59 at 58.
39. The LDS Church's financial management division is likewise called "Ensign Peak Advisors." As of 2019, they had amassed some $100 billion of their members contributions. In addition, Church real estate alone is worth billions of dollars.
40. James B. Christensen, "Negro Slavery in the Utah Territory," *The Phylon Quarterly* 18, no. 3 (1957): 298–305, at 298. Cf. also Newell G. Bringhurst, "The Mormons and Slavery: A Closer Look" *Pacific Historical Review* 50, no. 3 (1981): 329–338.
41. Christensen, "Negro Slavery in the Utah Territory," 300. The Utah Territory Slave Code passed in 1852 forbid any sexual intercourse between slaveowners and their black slaves and provided eighteen months of schooling for them. https://www.blackpast.org/african-american-history/primary-documents-african-american-history/utah-slave-code-1852/
42. The "double-voicing" this narrative trope represents, as both the voice of the former self and the now literate self speaking to European culture, was first propounded by Henry Louis Gates. The first use of such a trope is found in the narrative of James Albert Ukawsaw Gronniosaw, but the most well-known slave narrative may be that of Olaudah Equiano whose astute work in giving voice to his "slave self" Gates characterizes: "Under the guise of representation of his naïve self, he is naming or reading Western culture closely, underlining relationships between subjects and objects that are implicit in commodity cultures." *The Signifying Monkey: A Theory of Afro-American Literary Criticism* (New York: Oxford University Press, 1988), 156. Equiano had a major impact on the British law abolishing the slave trade; see Vincent Carretta, *Equiano the African: Biography of a Self-Made Man* (Athens, GA: University of Georgia Press, 2005). Many thanks to Jorunn Øklund for first drawing my attention to Equiano.
43. Albert Raboteau, *Slave Religion: The "Invisible Institution" in the Antebellum South* (New York: Oxford University Press, 1978), 6.
44. For consideration of the socio-political dimensions of African American use of the Exodus from the ante-bellum period through the Obama presidency, see Herbert Robinson Marbury, *Pillars of Cloud and Fire: The Politics of Exodus in African American Biblical Interpretation*. Religion and Social Transformation, 8 (New York: NYU Press, 2015).
45. Matthew Desmond, "American Capitalism Is Brutal. You Can Trace that to the Plantation." *The New York Times Magazine* August 14, 2019. Desmond's article was part of *The New York Times Magazine*'s 1619 Project, which sought to assess the impact of slavery on the 400th anniversary of the first enslaved Africans to North America to the British colony of Virginia.

46. Another view about racial origins was connected with the "mark" that God gave Cain after killing Abel. See David M. Goldenberg, *Black and Slave: The Origins and History of the Curse of Ham. Studies of the Bible and Its Reception*. (Berlin: Walter de Gruyter, 2017). Cf. as well the more recent discussion of Nyasha Junior, "The Mark of Cain and White Violence," *JBL* 139, no. 4 (2020): 661–673.
47. Sylvester A. Johnson, *The Myth of Ham in Nineteenth-Century American Christianity* (New York: Palgrave Macmillan, 2004). Not all white Americans saw the dark skin of Ham as a curse, however. Virginia physician John Mitchell viewed the darker pigmentation of African skin as a development for a hot climate; Colin Kidd, *The Forging of Races: Race and Scripture in the Protestant Atlantic World, 1600-2000* (New York: Cambridge University Press, 2006), 76.
48. Stephen R. Haynes, *Noah's Curse: The Biblical Justification of American Slavery* (New York: Oxford University Press, 2002), 87–101. There was also an anti-miscegenation argument rooted in a convoluted interpretation around the very minor figure of Naamah mentioned in Gen. 4: 20–22, who some understood to be married to Ham and bear the mark of Cain (as blackness). Jeremy Schipper offers a fascinating treatment of this in "Religion, Race, and the Wife of Ham," *Journal of Religion* 100, no. 3 (2020): 386–401.
49. Raboteau, *Slave Religion*, 99.
50. For a careful consideration of the exegetical arguments of Williams, James W.C. Pennington, Alexander Crummell, and Benjamin Tucker Tanner, see Jeremy Schipper, "The Blessing of Ham: Genesis 9:1 in Early African American Biblical Scholarship," *Biblical Interpretation* 28, no.5 (2021): 1–16.
51. For an extended and more nuanced treatment, see Powery, "The Origins of Whiteness and the Black (Biblical) Imagination," and cf. *The Genesis of Liberation: Biblical Interpretation in the Antebellum Narratives of the Enslaved* (Louisville, KY: Westminster John Knox, 2016).
52. Powery, "The Origins of Whiteness," 87.
53. David W. Blight, *Frederick Douglass: Prophet of Freedom* (New York: Simon & Schuster, 2018), 46.
54. Blight, *Frederick Douglass*, 16, quoting Douglass in *My Bondage and My Freedom* (1855; repr., New Haven, CT: Yale University Press, 2014), 47.
55. Harriet Jacobs, *Incidents in the Life of a Slave Girl* (Boston, 1861), 69.
56. Claudia Setzer, "The Bible and the Legacy of First Wave Feminism," in *The Bible in American Life*, ed. Philip Goff, Arthur E. Farnsley II, and Peter J. Thuesen (New York: Oxford University Press, 2017), 183–191, at 186.
57. Sojourner Truth is now seen as a social critic attentive to "intersectional" identity issues of race, class, gender, ability, and old-age, *avant la lettre*. See for example, Corinne T. Field, "Old-Age Justice and Black Feminist History: Sojourner Truth's and Harriet Tubman's Intersectional Legacies," *Radical History Review* 137, no.1 (2021): 37–51.
58. James Baldwin, *The Fire Next Time* (New York: Vintage Books/Random House, 1993; orig. pub. New York: Dial Press, 1963), 106.
59. Baldwin, *The Fire Next Time*, 41–42.
60. The first known collection of spirituals was gathered during the Reconstruction era by three northern abolitionists, William Francis Allen, Charles Wave, and Lucy Garrison, eds. *Slave Songs of the United States* (New York: Allen Simpson, 1867). For an overview of African American music, see Hansonia L. Caldwell, *African American Music: A Chronology: 1619–1995* (Los Angeles, CA: Ikoro Communications, 1995).
61. W. E. B. DuBois, "Of the Sorrow Songs" the final chapter of *The Souls of Black Folk: Essays and Sketches* (orig. pub., Chicago, IL: A.C. McClurg and Co, 1903).

62. W. E. B. DuBois, "Of the Sorrow Songs," the closing chapter of *The Souls of Black Folk* https://www.gutenberg.org/files/408/408-h/408-h.htm#chap14.
63. Raboteau, *Slave Religion*, 249–250.
64. Frederick Douglass, *The Life and Times of Frederick Douglass* (1892; reprint, New York: Collier, 1962), 159.
65. Caldwell, *African American Music*, 45.
66. William Still. *The Underground Rail Road. A Record.* (Philadelphia, PA: Porter & Coates, 1872), 297.
67. Raboteau, *Slave Religion*, 246.
68. The Gullah-Geechee, an isolated group living on the coastal lowlands and Sea Islands of South Carolina and Georgia, descended from West African transplants to South Carolina, preserved the ring shout longer than other groups. Traditional performers such as the McIntosh County Shouters from Georgia still preserve the performance: https://www.youtube.com/watch?v=uxPU5517u8c&ab_channel=LibraryofCongress
69. Albert Raboteau, *Slave Religion*, 244–245.
70. Bruno Chenu, *The Trouble I've Seen: The Bible Book of Negro Spirituals* Translated by Eugene V. LaPlante (Valley Forge, PA: Judson Press, 2003), 119.
71. The empire has morphed to include global spheres of dominion through financial, military, and technological means. This globalized military and financial empire includes territories acquired that are not part of the "logo map" of the United States. Daniel Immerwahr uses the term "pointillist empire" to describe the territorial sphere of domination that was carefully constructed to include territories that are not governed by the US Constitution and where quasi-legal ventures are carried out, including the detentions at Guantanamo Bay in Cuba. The territories include Guam, Puerto Rico, the Philippines, American Samoa, the Northern Marianna Islands; Daniel Immerwahr, *How to Hide an Empire: A History of the Greater United States* (New York: Farrar, Straus, and Giroux, 2019).
72. In a further irony, the museum's architects, SmithGroupJJR pointedly describe their aims in terms that challenge the fundamentalist views of its founder: "The building avoids the easy, literal symbolism that is often associated with biblical representation, in favor of rich but subtle allusions. The result is a work of architecture that is simultaneously timeless and of-the-moment, both universal and place-specific. And it reflects a concerted effort to allow for, and even encourage, a multiplicity of views, interpretations, and experiences." https://www.architectmagazine.com/project-gallery/museum-of-the-bible_o
73. Reinhold Niebuhr. *The Irony of American History* (New York: Charles Scribner's Sons, 1952), 113.
74. This is an excerpt of her much longer poem "The Hill We Climb" recited at the inauguration of president Joseph Biden. The allusion to Micah 4:4 in this excerpt of her poem also reflects cultural scripturalization. The verse was a favorite of George Washington that he used frequently in his correspondence and speeches. More recently the address was recycled in "One Last Time," the final song of Lin-Manuel Miranda's hit musical "Hamilton" that premiered in 2015. The song with its allusion was later remixed as "One Last Time (44 Remix)" with former President Barack Obama reciting Washington's words. On Washington's use of Micah 4:4, see Daniel L. Dreisbach, "The 'Vine and Fig Tree' in George Washington's Letters: Reflections on a Biblical Motif in the Literature of the American Founding Era," *Anglican and Episcopal History* 76, no. 3 (September 2007): 299–326.

Bibliography

Adelman, Jeremy, and Stephen Aron. "From Borderlands to Bordered Land: Empires, Nation States, and the People in between in American History." *The American Historical Review* 104, no. 3 (1999): 814–841.

Allen, James. *Without Sanctuary: Lynching Photography in America*. Santa Fe, NM: Twin Palms, 2000.

Allen, William Francis, Charles Wave, and Lucy Garrison, eds. *Slave Songs of the United States*. New York: A. Simpson & Co., 1867.

Anderson, Benedict. *Imagined Communities: Reflections on the Origins and Spread of Nationalism*. Rev. ed. London: Verso, 2006.

Armstrong, C., J. Miller, A. C. McAlvay, P. M. Ritchie, and D. Lepofsky. "Historical Indigenous Land-Use Explains Plant Functional Trait Diversity." *Ecology and Society* 26, no. 2 (2021): 6. https://doi.org/10.5751/ES-12322-260206

Baldwin, James. *The Fire Next Time*. New York: Vintage Books/Random House, 1993. First published New York: Dial Press, 1963.

Banner, Stuart. *How the Indians Lost their Land: Law and Power on the Frontier*. Cambridge, MA: Harvard University Press, 2007.

Baptist, Edward E. *The Half Has Never Been Told: Slavery and the Making of American Capitalism*. New York: Basic Books, 2014.

Ben Israel, Menasseh. *The Hope of Israel*, edited by Henry Méchoulan and Gérard Nahon. New York: Littman Library for Oxford University Press, 1987.

Berkovitch, Sacvan. "The Biblical Basis of the American Myth," in *The Bible and American Arts and Letters*, edited by Giles Gunn, 221–232. Philadelphia: Fortress; Chico, CA: Scholars, 1983.

Boelhower, William. *Through a Glass Darkly: Ethnic Semiosis in American Literature*. New York: Oxford, 1987.

Blight, David W., ed. *Passages to Freedom* Washington, D.C.: Smithsonian Books, 2004.

Blight, David W. *Frederick Douglass: Prophet of Freedom*. New York: Simon & Schuster, 2018.

Blount, Brian K., ed. *True to Our Native Land: An African American New Testament Commentary*. Minneapolis, MN: Fortress, 2007.

Bradford, Sarah H. *Harriet Tubman: The Moses of Her People*. (Originally published as *Scenes in the Life of Harriet Tubman*. Auburn, NY: W. J. Moses Printer, 1869).

Bringhurst, Newell G. "The Mormons and Slavery: A Closer Look" *Pacific Historical Review* 50.3 (1981): 329–338

Brooks, David. "Obama, Gospel and Verse." *New York Times* April 27, 2007.

Brown, Kelly Douglas. *Stand Your Ground* (p. 170). Maryknoll, NY: Orbis. Kindle Edition, 2015.

Byrd, James P. *Sacred Scripture, Sacred War: The Bible and the American Revolution*. Oxford, UK: Oxford University Press, 2013.

Byron, Gay L., and Vanessa Lovelace, eds. *Womanist Interpretations of the Bible: Expanding the Discourse* Semeia 85. Atlanta, GA: SBL Press, 2016.

Caldwell, Hansonia L. *African American Music: A Chronology: 1619–1995*. Los Angeles, CA: Ikoro Communications, 1995.

Callahan, Allen Dwight, *The Talking Book: African Americans and the Bible*. New Haven, CT: Yale University Press, 2006.

Carretta, Vincent. *Equiano the African: Biography of a Self-Made Man*. Athens, GA: University of Georgia Press, 2005.

Case, David S., and David A. Voluck. *Alaska Natives and American Laws*. 2nd ed. Fairbanks, AK: University of Alaska Press, 2002.

Chancey, Mark A., Carol Meyers, and Eric M. Meyers, eds. *The Bible in the Public Square: Its Enduring Influence in American Life*. Atlanta, GA: SBL Press, 2016.

Christensen, James B. "Negro Slavery in the Utah Territory." *The Phylon Quarterly* 18, no. 3 (1957): 298–305.

Curtis, Adrian, Herbert G. May. *Oxford Bible Atlas*. 4th ed. New York: Oxford University Press, 2007.

De Certeau, Michael. *The Practice of Everyday Life*. Translated by Steven Rendall. Berkeley: University of California Press, 1984.

Desmond, Matthew. "American Capitalism Is Brutal. You Can Trace that to the Plantation." *New York Times Magazine*. August 14, 2019.

Dougherty, Matthew W. *Lost Tribes Found: Israelite Indians and Religious Nationalism in Early America*. Norman, OK: University of Oklahoma Press, 2021.

Douglas, Kelly Brown, *Stand Your Ground: Black Bodies* (p. 170). Maryknoll, NY: Orbis. Kindle Edition, 2015.

Dozeman, Thomas B. "Biblical Geography and Critical Spatial Studies," in *Constructions of Space I: Theory, Geography, and Narrative*, edited by Jon L. Berquist and Claudia V. Camp, 87–108. New York: T&T Clark, 2007.

Dreisbach, Daniel L. "The 'Vine and Fig Tree' in George Washington's Letters: Reflections on a Biblical Motif in the Literature of the American Founding Era." *Anglican and Episcopal History* 76, no. 3 (September 2007): 299–326.

Driesbach, David L. *Reading the Bible with the Founding Fathers*. New York: Oxford University Press, 2016.

Edney, Matthew H. "The Irony of Imperial Mapping," in *The Imperial Map: Cartography and the Mastery of Empire*, edited by James R. Akerman, 11–45. Chicago: University of Chicago Press, 2009.

Edney, Matthew H. "Map History: Discourse and Process" in *The Routledge Handbook of Mapping and Cartography*, edited by Alexander J. Kent and Peter Vujokovic, 68–79. New York: Routledge, 2018.

von Ehrenkrook, Jason. "The Inaugural Bible: Presidential Rhetoric and the Politics of Scripture." *The Journal of the Bible and Its Reception* 7, no. 2 (2020): 205–240.

Fea, John. *Believe Me: The Evangelical Road to Donald Trump*. Grand Rapids, MI: Eerdmans, 2018.

Felder, Cain Hope, ed. *Stony the Road We Trod: African American Biblical Interpretation*. Philadelphia: Fortress Press, 1991.

Field, Corinne T. "Old-Age Justice and Black Feminist History: Sojourner Truth's and Harriet Tubman's Intersectional Legacies." *Radical History Review* 137, no. 1 (2021): 37–51.

Foner, Eric. *Gateway to Freedom: The Hidden History of the Underground Railroad*. New York: W.W. Norton, 2015.

Francaviglia, Richard. *The Mapmakers of New Zion: A Cartographic History of Mormonism*. Salt Lake City, UT: University of Utah Press, 2015.

Frankel, David. *The Land of Canaan and the Destiny of Israel: Theologies of Territory in the Hebrew Bible*. Siphrut 4. Winona Lake, IN: Eisenbrauns, 2011.

Franks, Mary Ann. *The Cult of the Constitution: Our Deadly Devotion to Guns and Free Speech*. Palo Alto, CA: Stanford University Press, 2019.

Frymer, Paul. *Building an American Empire: The Era of Territorial and Political Expansion*. Princeton, NJ: Princeton University Press, 2017.

Gates, Jr., Henry Louis. *The Signifying Monkey: A Theory of Afro-American Literary Criticism.* New York: Oxford University Press, 1988.

Gates, Jr., Henry Louis. *Stony the Road: Reconstruction, White Supremacy, and the Rise of Jim Crow.* Penguin, 2019.

Go, Julian. *Patterns of Empire: The British and American Empires, 1688 to Present.* New York: Cambridge University Press, 2011.

Goff, Philip, Arthur E. Farnsley II, and Peter J. Thuesen, eds. *The Bible in American Life.* New York: Oxford University Press, 2017.

Goldenberg, David M. *The Curse of Ham: Race and Slavery in Early Judaism, Christianity, and Islam.* Princeton: Princeton University Press, 2003.

Goldenberg, David M. *Black and Slave: The Origins and History of the Curse of Ham. Studies of the Bible and Its Reception.* Berlin: Walter de Gruyter, 2017.

Graber, Jennifer. *The Gods of Indian Country: Religion and the Struggle for the American West.* New York: Oxford University Press, 2018.

Gray, Christina, and Daniel Rück. "Reclaiming Indigenous Place Names." Yellowhead Institute Policy Brief 40. October 7, 2019. www.yellowheadinstitute.org

Gutjahr, Paul, ed. *Oxford Handbook of the Bible in America.* New York: Oxford University Press, 2017.

Hanson, Paul D. *A Political History of the Bible in America.* Louisville, KY: Westminster John Knox, 2015.

Harriss, M. Cooper. "On the Eirobiblical: Critical Mimesis and Ironic Resistance, in *The Confessions of Nat Turner.*" *Biblical Interpretation* 21, no. 4–5 (2013): 469–93.

Harley, J. B. "New England Cartography and the Native Americans," in *American Beginnings: Exploration, Culture, and Cartography in the Land of Norumbega*, edited by Emerson W. Baker, Edwin A. Churchill, Richard S. D'Abate, Kristine L. Jones, Victor Konrad, and Harald E. L. Prins, 287–313. Lincoln, NE: University of Nebraska Press, 1994.

Hietala, Thomas, *Manifest Design: American Exceptionalism and Empire.* Rev. ed. Ithaca, NY: Cornell University Press, 2003.

Immerwahr, Daniel. *How to Hide an Empire: A History of the Greater United States.* New York: Farrar, Straus, and Giroux, 2019.

Johnson, Kelli Lyon. "Writing Deeper Maps: Mapmaking, Local Indigenous Knowledges, and Literary Nationalism in Native Women's Writing." *Studies in American Indian Literatures* 19, no. 4 (2007): 103–120.

Johnson, Sylvester A. *The Myth of Ham in Nineteenth-Century American Christianity: Race, Heathens, and the People of God.* Palgrave Macmillan, 2004.

Johnson, Sylvester A. *African American Religions, 1500–2000: Colonialism, Democracy, and Freedom.* New York: Cambridge University Press, 2015.

Kidd, Colin. *The Forging of Races: Race and Scripture in the Protestant Atlantic World, 1600–2000.* New York: Cambridge University Press, 2006.

Klassen, Pamela E. *The Story of Radio Mind: A Missionary's Journey on Indigenous Land.* Chicago, IL: University of Chicago Press, 2018.

Krieger, Alex. *City on a Hill: Urban Idealism in America from the Puritans to the Present.* Cambridge, MA: Harvard University Press, 2019.

Langston, Scott M. "Joshua and the Israelite Conquest in American History," in *On Prophets, Warriors, and Kings: Former Prophets through the Eyes of Their Interpreters*, edited by George J. Brooke and Ariel Feldman, 229–263. BZAW 470. Berlin: Walter de Gruyter, 2016.

Leca, Radu. "Cartography and the 'Age of Discovery,'" in *The Routledge Handbook of Mapping and Cartography*, edited by Alexander J. Kent and Peter Vujokovic, 134–144. New York: Routledge, 2018.

Leighly, John. "Biblical Place-Names in the United States." *Names: A Journal of Onomastics* 27, no. 1 (1979): 46–59.

Lewis, G. Malcolm. "Maps, Mapmaking, and Map Use by Native North Americans." *The History of Cartography*. Volume 2, Book 3: *Cartography in the Traditional African, American, Arctic, Australian, and Pacific Societies*, edited by David Woodward and G. Malcolm Lewis, 51–182. Chicago: University of Chicago Press, 1998.

Lewis, G. Malcolm, "Recent and Current Encounters," in *Cartographic Encounters: Perspectives on Native American Map-making and Map Use*, edited by G. Malcolm Lewis. Chicago: University of Chicago Press, 1998.

Liew, Tat-siong Benny. "Postcolonial Approaches," *The Oxford Encyclopedia of the Bible and Gender Studies*. Julia O'Brien, ed. New York: Oxford University Press, 2009.

Lipka, Michael. "Half of Americans Say Bible Should Influence U.S. Laws, Including 28% Who Favor It Over the Will of the People." Pew Fact Tank: News in the Numbers, July 25, 2020 https://www.pewresearch.org/fact-tank/2020/04/13/half-of-americans-say-bible-should-influence-u-s-laws-including-28-who-favor-it-over-the-will-of-the-people/.

Lupu, Ira, and Robert W. Tuttle. *Secular Government, Religious People*. Grand Rapids, MI: Eerdmans, 2014.

Maps of tribal territories: https://native-land.ca/ Government of Canada: https://www.aadnc-aandc.gc.ca/eng/1290453474688/1290453673970; https://www.tribalnationsmaps.com/

Marbury, Herbert Robinson. *Pillars of Cloud and Fire: The Politics of Exodus in African American Biblical Interpretation*. Religion and Social Transformation 8. New York: NYU Press, 2015.

Martin, Bonnie, and James F. Brooks, eds. *Linking the Histories of Slavery: North America and Its Borderlands*. Santa Fe, NM: School for Advanced Research Press, 2015.

Martin, Bonnie. "Slavery's Invisible Engine: Mortgaging Human Property," *Journal of Southern History* 76, no. 4 (2010): 817–866.

Meadows, William C. "Black Goose's Map of the Kiowa-Comanche-Apache Reservation in Oklahoma Territory" *Great Plains Quarterly* 71 (2006): 265–282.

Medina, Néstor. *Christianity, Empire, and the Spirit (Re)Configuring Faith and the Cultural*. Leiden: Brill, 2018.

https://native-land.ca/ founded by Victor Temprano

Nabokov, Peter. "Orientations from Their Side: Dimensions of Native American Cartographic Discourse." *Cartographic Encounters: Perspectives on Native American Map-making and Map Use*, edited by G. Malcolm Lewis, 241–269. Chicago: University of Chicago Press, 1998.

Nabokov, Peter. *A Forest of Time: American Indian Ways of History*. New York: Cambridge University Press, 2002.

Newman, Judith H. "Tracing the Use of the Bible in Colonial Land Claims in North America," in *The Bible in Political Debate: What Does It Really Say?*, edited by Rodney Werline and Frances Flannery, 127–140. T&T Clark, 2016.

Niebuhr, Reinhold. *The Irony of American History*. New York: Charles Scribner's Sons, 1952.

Noll, Mark A. "Reflections on the Bible and American Political Life," in *Faithful Narratives: Historians, Religion, and the Challenge of Objectivity*, edited by Andrea Sterk and Nina Caputo, 214–230. Ithaca, NY: Cornell University Press, 2014.

Noll, Mark A. *In the Beginning Was the Word: The Bible in American Public Life, 1492–1783.* Oxford, UK: Oxford University Press, 2015.

Painter, Nell Irvin. "Millenarian Aspects of the Exodus to Kansas of 1879." *Journal of Social History* 9 (1976): 331–338.

Painter, Nell Irvin. *Exodusters: Black Migration to Kansas after Reconstruction.* New York: Alfred A. Knopf, 1977.

Perry, Seth. *Bible Culture and Authority in the Early United States* (Princeton, NJ: Princeton University Press, 2018).

Piketty, Thomas. *Capital and Ideology.* Trans. Arthur Goldhammer (Cambridge, MA: Belknap Harvard University Press, 2020).

Powery, Emerson B. and Rodney S. Sadler Jr., eds. *The Genesis of Liberation: Biblical Interpretation in the Antebellum Narratives of the Enslaved* (Louisville, KY: Westminster John Knox, 2016).

Preston, Douglas. *Talking to the Ground: One Family's Journey on Horseback across the Sacred Land of the Navajo* (New York: Simon & Schuster, 1995).

Raboteau, Albert J. *Slave Religion: The "Invisible Institution" in the Antebellum South* (New York: Oxford University Press, 1978).

Raboteau, Albert. "African Americans, Exodus, and the American Israel," in *African American Christianity: Essays in History*, Paul E. Johnson, ed. (Berkeley: California, 1994), 1–17.

Reagan, Ronald, "Election Eve Address: 'A Vision for America,'" November 1980. Retrieved from: https://www.presidency.ucsb.edu/documents/election-eve-address-vision-for-america

Reps, John W. *The Making of Urban America: A History of City Planning in the United States.* Rev. ed. Princeton, NJ: Princeton University Press, 1992.

Rifkin, Mark. *Manifesting America: The Imperial Construction of U.S. National Space.* New York: Oxford University Press, 2009.

Said, Edward W. *Orientalism.* New York: Pantheon, 1978.

Said, Edward W. *Culture and Imperialism.* New York: Vintage, 1994.

Schipper, Jeremy. "Religion, Race, and the Wife of Ham." *Journal of Religion* 100, no. 3 (2020): 386–401.

Schipper, Jeremy. "The Blessing of Ham: Genesis 9:1 in Early African American Biblical Scholarship." *Biblical Interpretation* 28, no. 5 (2021): 1–16.

Seed, Patricia. *Ceremonies of Possession in Europe's Conquest of the New World, 1492–1640.* New York: Cambridge University Press, 1995.

Seed, Patricia. *American Pentimento: The Invention of Indians and the Pursuit of Riches.* Minneapolis, MN: University of Minnesota Press, 2001.

Sellers, Charles L. "Early Mormon Community Planning." *Journal of the American Institute of Planners* 28 (1962): 24–30.

Shalev, Eran. *American Zion: The Old Testament as a Political Text from the Revolution to the Civil War.* New Haven, CT: Yale University Press, 2013.

Short, John Rennie. *Cartographic Encounters: Indigenous Peoples and the Exploration of the New World.* London, UK: Reaktion Books, 2009.

Stout, Harry S. *American Aristocrats: A Family, a Fortune, and the Making of American Capitalism.* New York: Basic Books, 2017.

Still, William. *The Underground Rail Road: A Record.* Philadelphia, PA: Porter & Coates, 1872.

Sugirtharajah, R. S. *The Bible and Empire: Postcolonial Explorations.* New York: Cambridge University Press, 2005.

Sugirtharajah, R. S. *Exploring Postcolonial Biblical Criticism: History, Method, Practice*. Oxford: Wiley-Blackwell, 2011.

Warrior, Robert. "A Native American Perspective: Canaanites, Cowboys, and Indians," in *Voices from the Margin: Interpreting the Bible in the Third World*, edited by R. S. Sugirtharajah. New York/London: Orbis/SPCK, 1995.

Wenger, Tisa. *Religious Freedom: The Contested History of a Religious Ideal*. Chapel Hill, NC: University of North Carolina Press, 2017.

Wilkerson, Isabel. *Caste: The Origins of Our Discontents*. New York: Random House, 2020.

Wimbush, Vincent. *Theorizing Scriptures: New Critical Orientations to a Cultural Phenomenon*. New Brunswick, NJ: Rutgers University Press, 2008.

Wimbush, Vincent L., ed., with the assistance of Lalruatkima and Melissa Renee Reid. *Misreading America: Scriptures and Difference*. New York: Oxford University Press, 2013.

Woodward, David. "Cartography and the Renaissance: Continuity and Change." *The History of Cartography*. Vol. 3, edited by J. B. Harley and David Woodward, 3–24. Chicago: University of Chicago Press, 1987.

CHAPTER 17

THE COLONIZING OTHER

The Japanese Challenge for Postcolonial Biblical Criticism

EMILY ANDERSON

THE case of Japan, which expanded into a colonial empire beginning in 1895, immediately presents a categorical challenge to scholars of modern empire and religion.[1] While Japan is a non-Western country, it resisted the efforts of Western imperial powers to impose overt control over it and eventually became a colonial empire in its own right. Nonetheless, as a nonwhite nation, Japan failed to attain the respect and inclusion it sought from other imperial powers. Until recently, the Japanese empire has been viewed as a failed empire whose inadequacies were largely due to a lack of understanding of the systems and institutions it vainly attempted to imitate.[2] Among Japan's failures, according to this line of reasoning, the greatest is the Japanese government's reliance on religious devotion to an emperor to ensure the absolute loyalty of its subjects. Although State Shinto ideology was seen as a nonreligious form of civic ritual, it nonetheless operated like a religion, making the Japanese empire decidedly unmodern. This characterization of the Japanese empire has not only consigned it to a perpetual "exception" category in discussions of imperialism and empires. But it has also obscured the diversity and complexity of the religious landscape of the time and relegates all other religious beliefs, customs, and practices to a secondary and limited role.

Applying a postcolonial critique to the Japanese context breaks with multiple assumptions about the relationship between the West and "the rest." First, Japan is both and neither. While not a Western, white empire, Japan nonetheless behaved like one, colonizing multiple places and imposing its rule on others. At the same time, it remained anxious about its relatively unequal status vis-à-vis the West. Japan championed its supposed supremacy but also claimed to celebrate a Pan-Asianism that would oppose Western domination.[3] This ambiguity also shaped how Christianity was received, interpreted, and treated. Unlike other empires, in the case of Japan,

Christianity was considered a foreign religion. Japanese converts often faced derision, and their loyalty to the state and emperor was considered suspect. Briefly, Christianity was associated with a West that needed to be emulated; but this period was short-lived as Japanese society generally shifted toward embracing a putative notion of Japanese tradition and rejecting a wholesale adoption of the West. Furthermore, Japan's Christians were often at the forefront of challenging the boundaries of the limits of religious freedom allowed by the state, as well as the boundaries of what constituted the behavior and beliefs of a loyal subject of the emperor.

A Brief Overview of Christianity in Japan

The fraught history of Christianity in Japan highlights the tension at the heart of Japan's place in world history. Japan first encountered Christianity in the form of Roman Catholicism amid a period of internecine war and turmoil during the sixteenth century. As a series of powerful generals attempted to gain ultimate supremacy over competing domains, European explorers and missionaries—mainly Portuguese—began appearing on Japan's shores. While the leaders of this period demonstrated considerable interest in both the guns and the teachings of what they called the "barbarians from the south," they also viewed the activities of the missionaries and the growing number of converts with suspicion. Their distrust was not simply a matter of disliking the foreign or unfamiliar; it was in fact grounded in a shrewd recognition that religions that demanded unconditional belief or that amassed considerable resources possessed the power to compete with them for temporal authority. The first of these military leaders, Oda Nobunaga, destroyed the temple complex of Tendai Buddhism in the hills neighboring the imperial capital of Kyoto, and he also decimated the Ikko sect of True Pure Land Buddhism because of the devotion of its adherents. The second military leader, Toyotomi Hideyoshi, who had initially welcomed the European missionaries, turned on them, initiating the first execution of missionaries and Japanese converts and issuing the first set of decrees targeting Christians. Tokugawa Ieyasu, the last of the military leaders whose victory over competing domanial armies in 1600 ushered in a new era and the unification of the domains in a loose confederation, issued the final decrees that outlawed the practice of Christianity and expelled missionaries from Japan.[4]

Under Ieyasu and his descendants, the Tokugawa family maintained tenuous control over a realm of domains. To fend off the ascendancy of competing domains that might unseat them from power, the ruling family instituted a number of key policies. Relevant to this discussion is their continued absolute opposition to Christianity. The rulers were not concerned with the particulars of Christian belief so much as they were with the consequences of religious devotion: Christian converts, they feared, might not only assert themselves as a competing regime but also allow in European powers who would subjugate Japan to foreign control. Japanese converts were subjected to persecution and execution, and the regime required all households to register with a Buddhist temple to demonstrate their disavowal of Christianity.[5]

Japan's second encounter with Christianity, this time dominated by American Protestants, also coincided with a period of domestic turmoil and uncertainty. After two centuries of peaceful rule, the Tokugawa family's hold on its authority had begun to weaken by the early nineteenth century. At the same time, increased Western imperial attention to the region jeopardized Japan's longstanding policy of limiting contact with the outside world. Maintaining political control through limiting outside influences was no longer tenable, and in 1854, Japan was forced into its first unequal treaty through the gunboat diplomacy of the United States. By the 1860s, treaty ports were established along Japan's coast. American merchants were joined by the French, the British, the Dutch, and Russians, whose countries secured their own unequal treaties. Conversion to Christianity was still punishable by death for Japanese, but the unequal treaties guaranteed the foreigners in treaty ports the right to practice their religion. Japan became accessible to the outside just as foreign missions became a central concern of religious Christians in the West. Not easily dissuaded, missionaries found ways to enter Japan. The Japanese government was eager to gain access to Western education and medicine and so it welcomed teachers and doctors. The earliest missionaries arrived with these practical skills and used their schools and practices as useful sites of contact with what they hoped would be converts to Christianity.[6]

Soon after missionaries began to arrive in Japan, long-simmering domestic tensions finally erupted. Several domains joined forces to overthrow the Tokugawa government and finally declared victory in 1868. They claimed to restore rightful rule to the emperor, but actually the new regime was established by an oligarchy composed of leaders of the victorious domains, their sympathizers, and some members of the previous regime. From the outset, the newly constituted government was concerned with both securing Japanese independence from Western influence and achieving greater centralization and influence over the populace in order to create a strong, unified, and modern nation that would be acknowledged as an equal by the West.

The orchestrators of the modern Japanese governing structure recognized that religion presented a significant challenge to their authority and could limit how much loyalty they could demand of Japanese subjects. As Trent Maxey effectively demonstrates, the short-lived Great Promulgation Campaign, a state-led effort to "evangelize" a newly constructed set of religious doctrines asserting the divinity of the emperor and the duty of each imperial subject to "believe" in the emperor, was abandoned when the new leaders of modern Japan realized that this created the problem that some might choose to believe something else. Loyalty to the state—the purpose, after all, of demanding belief in the emperor—needed to be segregated from the uncertainties of individual belief. This also led these leaders to engage in a study of how the Western powers addressed the problem of religious belief, which led to the eventual inclusion of a conditional guarantee of religious freedom in the 1889 Constitution.[7] Their awareness also highlights another significant point: the emergence of the veneer of secularism among Western powers, or at least the promise of religious toleration, even while certain religious traditions continued to be dominant during this period. Thus, when Japan adopted a constitution (presented to the public as a gift of the emperor) that promised a limited freedom of religious practice, there was little difference, in reality, from how the Western powers dealt with religious diversity. In other words, religion, broadly construed, caused considerable consternation for modern empires.[8] In the case of Japan, however, Christianity presented a particularly unique and interesting case.

Made aware that continuing to prohibit Christian conversion would prolong its unequal status with the West, the government rescinded the Christian prohibition in 1873. The missionaries, aware that their popularity depended on the perception that they represented the West, attempted to impart to their charges a distinctly conventional Christian interpretation of the world. This effort failed with the arrival of Western educators opposed to Christian beliefs, especially scientists and other scholars who accepted Darwinism, while the missionaries did not. Nonetheless, many of the missionaries in Japan tried to present a notion of uniform Christian beliefs and biblical exegesis.[9] In turn, the version of theology and doctrine they presented was itself a critique of the rising influence of ideas, such as German higher criticism that challenged their more orthodox beliefs.

In the case of Japan, denominational divisions were often the result of geography. The missionaries who first arrived in Japan very quickly chose different geographical regions in which to focus their work to avoid unnecessary competition. As a result, the Presbyterian and Reformed missionaries focused on the Tokyo and Yokohama areas, the Congregationalists (ABCFM) focused on the Osaka-Kyoto-Kobe area to the West, and the Methodists also settled in Tokyo. There were missionaries representing other denominations, including even Unitarians, but these three were the most prominent. This was partly because they founded schools in each of these areas through which they were able to establish contact with Japanese. Furthermore, their students primarily came from the samurai class, young men (and, very occasionally, some remarkably brave young women) who sought to elevate their access to the ranks of power in the new government through gaining knowledge of the English language and a Western education. These divisions, of course, were fluid, but the most influential ministers and theologians of each group first encountered Christianity in some form through these Western schools. Converts who maintained their connection to Christianity tended to retain their original affiliations with a few exceptions, the most significant being the embrace of higher criticism by some of the Congregationalists in defiance of American missionaries' caution against this stance. The development marked an important moment of Japanese independence from missionary influence.[10]

The particular way by which the first generation of Japanese Christians were introduced to Christianity and to the significance of things like denominational authority, the authority of scripture, and orthodoxy shaped the ways they expressed themselves as they matured. While Reformed and Methodist leaders followed those traditions, the Congregationalists reflected their decentralized nature, with leaders advocating everything from orthodox theology to liberal theology influenced by German higher criticism. Further, theological disagreements were shaped by two general forces: disagreements among Japanese converts and disagreements between Japanese converts and the missionaries who influenced them.

Within this context, Japan's Christians developed their beliefs and practices, uneasy with their relationship with Western missionaries and self-conscious about their differences with other Japanese, even while envisioning a critical role for themselves in transforming Japan. This complexity informed their approach to reading and interpreting scripture, their choice of passages they chose to relate to and identify with, and how they used different texts to exhort, admonish, and condemn. Biblical exegesis became an important site through which Japan's Christians demonstrated their independence from Western missionaries, asserted and refined their own beliefs, and expounded their visions for the nation and empire.

Any discussion of how Japanese Christians understood, interpreted, and employed the Bible in modern Japan must take into account this fundamental tension. As both a colonizing and non-Western nation whose subjects experienced white racism, Japanese Christians attempted to find justification for expansion and liberation from subjugation not only from the same source but also from a source of dissent against an increasingly oppressive regime. Ultimately, however, as militarism came to subsume the nation under its totalizing control, dissent was silenced (at least publicly), and Christian interpretations of belief stepped in line with the increasing extremism of the state. After the Japanese empire suffered nearly cataclysmic defeat and was stripped of its colonial territories, Japan's Christians struggled with the role they had played in defending and legitimizing a regime that was oppressive at home and that engaged in a destructive war abroad. The United Church of Christ in Japan—the denomination to which most Japanese Protestant churches now belong—issued a statement of confession in 1966. While the statement was controversial to some, it nonetheless reflected the regret many Japanese Christians felt. The sense that their Christian predecessors had failed to behave according to their beliefs has also shaped the way Japanese scholars evaluate the work of the earlier generation. Many layers of colonial and imperial relationships inform and influence how the Bible was interpreted and how these interpretations were subsequently evaluated.[11]

Applying a Postcolonial Biblical Perspective

The unique position of Japan as both a colonizing nation and a nonwhite nation subjected to unequal treaties, discriminatory laws, and racist rhetoric offers the opportunity for new avenues of postcolonial biblical criticism.[12] Furthermore, the Japanese empire's colonies were for the most part countries and territories closest to it, populated by people that shared important and longstanding cultural similarities and connections, which adds a level of complexity to the common assumption that perceived difference, as well as race and ethnicity, are obvious sources of contention and inequality. Of course, Japanese asserted their relative superiority to the people they colonized; at the same time, they deployed a logic of sameness—or the possibility of eventual absolute assimilation—in rationalizing the legitimacy of its expansion.[13] In other words, the case of Japan does not diminish the importance of perceived racial or ethnic difference as a driving force behind imperialism. What it does do is offer a case for the extent to which difference can be more insidious and the promise of eventual acceptance even more elusive. In multiple ways, Japan confounds attempts to subject it to the type of postcolonial critique usually used to examine Western empires, just as it cannot simply be restored or reclaimed the way a colonized country or territory might be.

In the sense that postcolonial criticism also seeks to counter Eurocentric history, however, Japan offers a unique opportunity to more deeply examine the contours of imperialism and its effects. These factors include the inadvertent complicity of different actors who are seduced by colonialism and the limitations of certain ideals to provide redemption, restoration, and emancipation from the constricting effects of capitalism, power, and violence. The Japanese empire confounds the claim that, as one scholar puts it, the political stance of postcolonialism is "about the impact created by Western colonization on individuals, communities, and cultures."[14] Japan complicates the binarization that is often at the center of imperial relationships. Even with the rise of subaltern studies and the recognition that there is more at work than colonizer/colonized or complicity/resistance, a binary logic often defines how we approach the history of modern imperialism. In other words, for Japanese to refuse Western influence or assert a type of Japanese Christianity independent of Western missionaries cannot be simply taken as an act of defying imperial authority. It could just as easily be an act of defending Japanese imperialism. Japanese could claim that they have been on the receiving end of Western colonization—and, indeed, this argument is raised whenever Japan's neighbors decry its colonial past and violence, even while Japan itself colonized a substantial part of Asia by the 1930s.[15] It would be easy to dismiss Japan's expansionist and aggressive actions as simply efforts to find acceptance by an indifferent and racist West. But this type of reductive argument does not account for the capacity people have for violence and assertions of unequal power, just as it does not allow for people in the same population to arrive at very different conclusions about how to respond to claims of power and superiority. The differences that Japan represents also allow for the inclusion of greater diversity in how we as scholars consider the interactions and relationships between colonized and colonizer, the interactions between dominant and minority religions, and the ways that power and influence rarely are absolute but rely on constellations of existing, complicated, and unequal relationships and networks.

This chapter examines the ways Japanese Christians, specifically those who consciously grappled with Japan's contradictory place in the imperial landscape, approached scripture or biblical imagery to validate and promote their positions. Not all Christians were principally concerned with the wider context of empire. But for those who were, the fate of the empire seemed inextricably linked with the fate of Christianity within it. While their non-Christian contemporaries—and indeed many who have come after them—dismissed these Christians as an ineffectual and marginalized minority, they claimed for themselves a central place in a historic and global Christian drama. Far from viewing their battles and controversies as the insignificant struggles of a few at the edge of the Christian map, they argued that Japanese Christianity was the culmination of centuries of Christian attempts at reform and redemption. But whether they insisted Japan would be the fulcrum of God's kingdom on earth, or that through becoming a small country Japan would emulate a perfect Christian community, these ministers and public intellectuals superimposed Christian debates onto their visions for the Japanese empire.

Existing Scholarship

There is substantially more Japanese-language than English-language scholarship on all aspects of Japanese Christianity, and particularly with regards to biblical exegesis, hermeneutics, and theology. However, many of the scholars who specialize in these areas assess their historical subjects according to two broadly defined sets of ideals: adherence to an idealized notion of Christian living or an idealized idea of opposition to imperialism. This is largely due to a general sense of responsibility on the part of scholars to indict pre–World War II Christians who succumbed to the allure of imperialism and failed to oppose the government's increasingly restrictive, oppressive, and often violent policies.[16]

Given the state of the field, and the overwhelming amount of scholarship in Japanese, I will offer a few comments here, even though I will reserve most of this overview for English-language scholarship. The question of how leading Christian figures addressed imperialism, broadly defined, is a dominant concern for Japanese scholars who must take into account the Japanese military and colonial aggression that started in the 1930s. Many scholars who work on Christianity are concerned with exposing past sins of pre–World War II leaders—who failed to sufficiently oppose the government—or attempt to elevate the reputations of those who have otherwise been considered passive or actively supportive of imperialism or colonialism.[17] The problem with this approach is that it is overdetermined by the extremes of Japanese militarism that are often anachronistically applied to earlier periods when the eventual conclusion of Japan's trajectory in the early twentieth century was not set or certain.

Scant attention has been paid outside of the mission world to Japanese theology. Even the little that exists in English is limited in scope and shaped by an overarching concern with the degree to which the theologies examined conform to a normative or proper set of beliefs and doctrines. Existing English-language scholarship tends to fall into two broad camps, both of which reflect limiting sets of concerns: missiological studies that introduce the reader to the state of the field in Japan and are therefore skewed by a certain view of what Christianity *ought* to be;[18] and social-historical studies that evaluate the social contributions and significance of Christianity without much consideration for the ideas and beliefs that drove adherents. The bulk of research was published in the 1960s and 1970s, and until recently little attention was paid to Christianity in Japan by scholars of history or religious studies.[19]

For example, in *A History of Japanese Theology*, edited by Yasuo Furuya, the chapter by Dohi Akio on the first generation of Japanese converts (itself an English adaptation of a chapter in the scholar's seminal history of Japanese Protestantism) limits its scope to four figures, each of whom is quite unusual or iconoclastic, while also influential: Ebina Danjō and Kozaki Hiromichi of the Kumiai Kyōkai, or Congregational Church; Uemura Masahisa of the Nihon Kirisuto Kyōkai, associated with the Reformed and Presbyterian churches; and Uchimura Kanzō, who founded the Mukyōkai, or nonchurch movement.[20] In what is probably the only single-author monograph on Japanese theology, *Protestant Theologies in Modern Japan*, also published in the 1960s, C. H. Germany evaluates the quality of the theologies he examines according to their adherence to conventional Protestant doctrines. For example, he criticizes Ebina Danjō for his concern for society—influenced by the German theologian Friedrich Schleiermacher—over individual salvation.[21] This scholar's preoccupation with how a particular figure's beliefs conform to a predetermined set of normative standards limits this work's contributions.

Within this rather thin body of existing scholarship, certain general observations can still be made. First, English-language scholarship tends to focus on the relationship between Western missionaries and Japanese converts; it frames the place of Christianity in Japan as an issue of Westernization or the inherent challenge (even impossibility) of a non-Western culture absorbing a Western religion and belief system. What is important, and relevant, in this body of work is what it reveals about the initial biblical education given to Japanese converts. But by focusing on the relationship between missionaries and converts, this scholarship reinforces the notion that Japanese converted to Christianity out of a desire to become more Western, and that the West must remain the primary frame of reference for the non-West regardless of experience or context.

One figure who frequently emerges as a proponent of a uniquely Japanese form of Christianity that embraced intense biblical study as the central practice is Uchimura Kanzō, and his iconoclastic Mukyōkai (nonchurch movement). The son of a samurai in the small domain of Takasaki in the northern Kanto Plains, Uchimura encountered Christianity while he was a student at the Sapporo Agricultural College on the northern island of Hokkaido. He wrote later that he felt pressured to declare his faith in Christianity prematurely at the school but later underwent what might be called a genuine conversion experience. Perhaps most importantly, or most relevant to this discussion, he became one of the most visible faces of Japanese Christianity to English-speaking audiences during his lifetime. Taking advantage of his education not only in Sapporo but also at Amherst where he later studied, Uchimura wrote in English to assert that in Japan, a different kind of Christianity superior to Western Christianity could be established, fulfilling the reformation that did not quite take place under the leadership of Luther. He advocated an alternative to denominational allegiance that involved small-scale meetings of like-minded people who studied scripture together. These Mukyōkai meetings, filled primarily by highly educated men, were cerebral affairs. He also published a journal called *Seisho no kenkyū* (The Study of the Bible) through which he and other followers of Mukyōkai published their ideas about the Bible and theology.

Uchimura's reputation has also been shaped by a number of notorious incidents in which he was involved that have been interpreted as proof of his resolute stance against the rise of the oppressive and repressive government that eventually led Japan into cataclysmic war. The first, known as the *fukei jiken*, or lèse majesté incident, cemented his public reputation. In 1891, when the Imperial Rescript on Education, a brief document detailing the government's expectations for how education would transform imperial subjects into loyal subjects of the emperor, was unveiled at schools across the country, Uchimura, then a teacher at the prestigious First Higher School in Tokyo, failed to fully bow at the ceremony. He later explained that his hesitation stemmed from a sense of uncertainty rather than resolute refusal to perform an act of worship of the emperor at the ceremony. Those around him, and public pundits, jumped on his behavior as evidence that Christians were incapable of being trustworthy subjects.[22] Forced to resign from his position, Uchimura eventually made his way to the *Yorozu chōhō*, the most popular daily newspaper, where he worked alongside some of Japan's best-known early socialists. As tensions between Japan and Russia began to build as each vied for greater influence over Korea, Uchimura and his socialist colleagues resigned their positions in protest over the newspaper's prowar stance. This cemented his reputation, as one scholar phrases it, as "a powerful critic famous for his newspaper editorials and their opposition to government authoritarianism."[23]

Uchimura's idiosyncrasies, and his reluctance to support Japan's increasing expansion and military interventions, have made him a popular subject of study. Further, his establishment of an explicitly nonecclesiastical form of Christian fellowship and his insistence that he embraced the core of Christianity while rejecting Western interpretations of it, have made him attractive to those who seek to identify a uniquely Japanese form of Christianity that sought to reconcile seemingly incompatible cultural norms and beliefs successfully. This position is succinctly captured in the statement most often associated with him, that is, his professed love for "two J's": Jesus and Japan.[24]

The fascination with Uchimura, and the handful of other figures like him who gained international reputations through unconventional ministries and positions, has predominated in the limited scholarship on Japanese Christianity in both English and Japanese. In fact, Uchimura's self-assigned role as the Japanese interlocutor to Western Christianity, and his promotion of a uniquely Japanese Christianity, have also elevated his reputation in Japan. (When I was conducting my dissertation research in Kyoto, Japan, in 2007, I attended several Fulbright receptions that were also attended by Japanese alumni of the Fulbright program. Without fail, when I explained that I was studying Japanese Christianity and imperialism, they asked me if I was aware of Uchimura and mentioned that I should focus on him).

While at first glance Uchimura's career might appear to represent the type of reaction to Western influence that resonates with postcolonial biblical critiques, it also serves to reinforce assumptions rooted in an imperial logic. First, while Uchimura is known for his refusal to work with foreign missionaries and rarely interacted with them, his well-known assertion belies a preoccupation with cultivating a foreign audience. The alliterative impact of "the two J's," after all, can only work in English; in Japanese, "Jesus" is *Iesu* and "Japan" is *Nihon*.[25] While Uchimura has been called courageous, even heroic, by some scholars for his stance during the *fukei jiken* and his opposition to the Russo-Japanese War, in fact it is probably more accurate to call him apolitical.[26]

The problem with Uchimura is that he fulfills the expectations of those who assume there would be, and perhaps should be, a Japanese Christianity that is drastically different from the conventional, chauvinistic form. But Uchimura's supposed antiwar stance makes his chauvinism a kind of anti-West position instead of a form of imperialistic arrogance directed toward the rest of Asia. Far from taking a strong stance against the government's increasingly aggressive stance toward its neighbors, however, Uchimura withdrew from public life. A young man sought Uchimura's support when he planned to refuse his conscription orders, but Uchimura instead discouraged him, urging him that Christians had a duty to obey earthly authorities. Following the death of a daughter, he fixated on the Second Coming as the solution to world peace, embracing premillennial dispensationalism. While he was critical of Japanese Christians who advocated establishing a mission in Korea after it had been made a Japanese colony, this seemed more associated with his expectation of divine retribution than concern for Japan's rising imperialism.[27]

While Uchimura is credited with taking a firm stance against Japanese imperialism, in fact, much of his work fails to acknowledge the imperial context that shaped the Japan he declared to love so much. His confident assertion as a unique spokesperson for a Japanese Christianity with no need for foreign interference has made him popular with Japanese- and English-language scholars alike, but their expectation of assertions of Japanese chauvinism lead them to grant Uchimura greater credit than the evidence warrants.

THE BIBLE FOR THE JAPANESE EMPIRE

This is not to say that Japanese Christians of the first half of the twentieth century failed to directly address the imperial context of their world or that they did not grapple with how their place as Christians in the Japanese empire imposed challenges on their beliefs and practices. Most Japanese Protestant leaders were more conventional than someone like Uchimura and were ministers of churches or authors associated with mainstream denominations. Among these Christians, divergent opinions about how the Bible should be interpreted served as a point of contention between Japanese Christians and

Western missionaries and reflected the power struggle at the heart of Japan's ambivalent position as both colonizer and colonized.

Not every Christian minister, educator, or public intellectual actively grappled with Japan's rise as an empire and the role of Christians within it. But for those who did, and particularly for those who viewed this rise as God-ordained, scripture and doctrine became a way to distance themselves from the missionaries who initially influenced them, even as they sought justification for Japan's actions in the region and the world in the same sources.

As can be seen from the name assigned to the incident in which Uchimura failed to bow appropriately in front of the imperial portrait, his act is often treated as *the* Christian act challenging the state's insistence that imperial subjects demonstrate their loyalty through a nonreligious act of worship of the emperor. In fact, there were numerous reports across the country accusing Christians of demonstrating a lack of respect for emperor and country that prompted a frenetic exchange of editorials and articles in both the most read and lesser known publications across the country debating whether or not Christians could be good imperial subjects. Accusations were lobbed at Christians from Buddhist priests eager to reestablish their supremacy as Japan's moral and religious leaders as well as from intellectuals educated in Europe and influenced by philosophers skeptical or contemptuous of Christian influence and beliefs. In other words, for some of their accusers—including the most prominent, Inoue Tetsujirō, who was chair of the philosophy department of Tokyo Imperial University—what made Uchimura and the other Christians' refusal to swear their absolute allegiance to the emperor on religious grounds was the arcane nature of religious belief itself. This was not a rejection of Christianity because it was Western and foreign, but rather a rejection of religion as outdated and no longer appropriate for an emerging modern nation and empire.[28]

Japan's in-between status meant that early in its renewed contact with the West, it reached out to the West for knowledge and influence. But this was only temporary, and soon Japan began to assert its independence from the West and claimed parity, even superiority, with it. Regardless of religious affiliation, most well-educated Japanese in the Meiji period had a familiarity with the Bible and with basic Christian doctrine. As they also discovered other types of Western thought—especially that opposed to religion or literal interpretations of scripture—these intellectuals accused Christians of being backward and unsophisticated. Thus, how Christians interpreted scripture was not simply a matter of being right about doctrine, but it was also about demonstrating to non-Christian intellectuals that Japanese Christians, unlike the American missionaries, were intellectually sophisticated and rational.

For example, one such intellectual, Katō Hiroyuki, former president of Tokyo Imperial University, went so far as to publish a full volume devoted to debunking Christianity as nothing more than superstitious belief in myth and spirits. Watase Tsuneyoshi, a disciple of Ebina Danjō and a figure rising in prominence in the the Kirisuto Kyōkai, responded with his own book. Significantly, the terms of Watase's rebuttal focused on correcting what he claimed was Katō's mistaken perception of

Christianity. Far from the arcane and superstitious hindrance to modernity Kato made it out to be, according to Watase, "the new Christianity... was informed by the latest scholarship in comparative religion and guided by a more enlightened theology based on biblical criticism or new scholarship of the Bible."[29] For at least some of Japan's Christians, demonstrating their acceptability as sophisticated and critical consumers of modern thought—as opposed to recipients of the orthodox theology espoused by American missionaries—was a crucial way of demonstrating their legitimacy in a nation aspiring to attain parity with the West.[30]

JAPANESE COLONIAL CHRISTIANITY

As Japanese Christians debated and grappled with their place in Japan and in Christendom, a few in particular championed a vision for Christians as the moral leaders of the Japanese empire. They pointed to both scriptural references and biblical imagery as precedents for their unique position in world history. The most prominent of these was a controversial Congregational minister, Ebina Danjō. As a youth, he had first been exposed to Christianity at the Kumamoto School for Western Learning in the southern island of Kyushu, where the head teacher, the American Civil War veteran Captain L. L. Janes, patterned his strict instruction after his alma mater, West Point. Unlike the missionaries who were concerned with imparting denominational doctrine as the only interpretation of Christianity, Janes encouraged his students to be curious, to embrace science, and to think independently. When he began leading Bible studies outside of class time, a group of boys converted. Ebina was among these. He quickly emerged as a leader among this group—called the Kumamoto Band—and developed a reputation for liberal, even heretical ideas and a dynamic presence.[31]

Disagreements over interpretations of scripture and doctrine occurred among Christians themselves, the most significant and notorious being the debate between Ebina and Uemura Masahisa of the Nihon Kirisuto Kyōkai, which was affiliated with the Presbyterian and Reformed churches. Prompted by disagreements over who would be allowed to join an ecumenical evangelistic group, this theology debate centered on whether or not God had become man—in other words, whether or not to affirm the Nicean Creed. While not specifically a matter of biblical interpretation, the substance of this debate imperiled one of the central tenets of Protestant Christianity. Ebina criticized Uemura's adherence to this belief as outdated and dependent on irrational beliefs that were no longer relevant.[32] He dismissed trinitarianism as irrational and contradictory, calling it a form of "tri-theism" instead. He later went so far as to claim that trinitarianism had served a useful function historically for the early church, as a way of reconciling the monotheism of Judaism with the need to accommodate both God the father and Jesus.[33] In a newly modern nation and a time of progress, however, such ideas were no longer needed or even appropriate.[34]

While on the surface this debate appeared to be a contest over two giants of Japanese Protestantism vying for the upper hand, for Ebina, it was also a show of independence from the theology espoused by the American Board of Commissioners of Foreign Missions, the missionaries with which his Kumiai Kyōkai was most associated. By asserting that some of the most central doctrines of conventional Protestantism, like trinitarianism, were a result of historical contingencies, not a reflection of absolute truth, he claimed for himself—and for Japanese Christians more generally—the prerogative to evaluate Western Christian teaching on its own terms. Furthermore, he suggested that strict adherence to such doctrine was outdated, implying that his controversial positions were in fact the result of a modern and more civilized outlook. Ebina further reinforced these points in his sermons at his church, which was located only meters away from Tokyo Imperial University, where he lauded German theologians such as Friedrich Schleiermacher, Gotthold Lessing, and Albrecht Ritschl as guides for a "scientific" understanding of the Bible for a new era.[35] His regular references to these German theologians also signaled to missionaries that his rejection of missionary influence was thus not simply a disavowal of the West but was instead an expression of his right to rely on those ideas he found most convincing.

Ebina's assertion of independence had broader implications, for he also envisioned a unique role for Japanese Christians in the empire. Far from rejecting imperialism or withdrawing from public life, Ebina proposed that through integrating themselves into the mechanism of imperial expansion, Japanese Christians would accomplish what Western Christians had failed to: establishing God's kingdom on earth. He began by advocating for missions, but he ultimately envisioned a grand role for Japan in the history of Christendom. He argued that missionaries, especially the American ones with whom he had the most contact, imparted a Christianity that was no longer relevant.[36] Unlike the West, which had attempted but ultimately failed to establish God's kingdom on earth, Ebina proclaimed that God had called Japan's Christians to transform the Japanese empire and through it to create God's kingdom on earth. At the basis of this idea was a parting of ways with the missionaries and an assertiveness on the part of Japanese Christians that they had the prerogative to interpret scripture and develop doctrine on their own.[37]

Once Japan had successfully colonized Korea in 1910, Ebina began promoting the importance of Japanese Christian evangelism to Koreans in earnest. His efforts were evidence of the maturation of Japanese Christianity and also served as an important first practical step in Christianizing the empire itself. In 1910, as the Japanese government forced the Korean government to sign a treaty formalizing annexation, Ebina gave a sermon at his church in Tokyo on the significance of overseas missions. For this, he used as his primary Bible quotation a passage in the gospel of Luke that describes Jesus's first interaction with Simon Peter, John, and James as they return from a futile night of fishing on the Sea of Galilee. He explained to his congregation that this passage was a metaphor for the importance of going abroad; "He explained that the Sea of Galilee represented the world, the shores Judea, and Peter's reluctance to return to sea his aversion to evangelizing to Gentiles due to his patriotic (ethno)nationalism. As told by Luke,

Peter's boat becomes so full of fish that he has to call for help; in Ebina's telling, the boat that comes to his aid represents Paul, who was better equipped than Peter to evangelize to Gentiles."[38] This sermon, delivered just as Japan was finalizing its colonization of Korea, attempted to provide biblical justification to a new phase for Japan's Protestants: overseas missionary work.

What made Japanese Christians better able to impart to Koreans a kind of civilizing influence was precisely the in-between status of Japan. While not a Western nation, it had already undergone "civilizing" through Western influence, but as a fellow Asian country with a shared heritage, its subjects were better positioned to sympathize and communicate with Koreans. Japanese Christians were even more suited for this intermediary and influential role, and through successfully achieving the cooperation and friendship of Korean Christians, they would together begin the even more important work of transforming the Japanese empire into a Christian one.

In 1911, the Kumiai church founded its mission in Korea with Watase Tsuneyoshi as the director. It was financially supported by a substantial annual allocation from the colonial government as well as donations from some of Japan's most prominent business conglomerates. Watase relied on biblical imagery and references to interpret his experiences there and to narrate them to supporters at home. On Watase's first trip into the Korean countryside—guided by Korean Christians who had sought affiliation with the mission—he conflated the landscape he witnessed with the New Testament. Noting that women carrying large jars on their heads made him think of Judea, he remarked that he felt as though he had been taken back to Palestine in the time of Christ.[39] He also associated what he described as the rustic charm of the countryside to Palestine, implying that rural Korea was temporally separate from Japan. As he visited small Korean congregations, he even claimed that he could understand how Jesus must have felt preaching to the people.[40]

Watase's frequent reliance on biblical imagery to establish a temporal and cultural distance between himself and the Koreans with whom he had contact is an impulse easily recognizable as typical of Western missionaries. Not only did he animate his patronizing attitude toward Korean colonial subjects this way, but he also reconciled the violence of colonial rule with Christian belief by asserting that Japan would elevate the place of Koreans—and especially Korean Christians—through civilizing them. This would not only rescue Koreans from their benighted state—a frequent claim of Japanese to justify colonizing Korea—but, once united, Japanese and Korean Christians would transform the rest of Asia, possibly even the world. The Christianization of the colonial slogan of *naisen ittai*, or Japanese-Korean unification, promised to fulfill colonial goals and Christian ones at the same time. Or at least that is what Watase promised when he first arrived in Korea, and what he continued to assert he was accomplishing to his supporters back in the colonial metropole.

Watase's vision of a peaceful synthesis of Japanese and Korean Christians joined in unified promotion of the Japanese empire was disrupted by the reality of subaltern anger through the March First Movement, a series of protests that spread across the Korean peninsula in 1919. Enduring nearly a decade of oppressive rule by the Japanese colonial government, Koreans expressed their desire for independence; the colonial government suppressed it through violence. Watase and the Kumiai Kyōkai had promised the authorities that they would secure the cooperation of Korean Christians, a group considered to be mostly responsible for anti-Japanese sentiment. With the outbreak of this peninsula-wide rejection of Japanese rule, the colonial authorities concluded that Watase's promises were nothing but a naïve pipe dream. They withdrew their financial support, forcing Watase and most of the other Japanese missionaries to return to Japan. Some missionaries were sent instead to areas in China under Japanese influence. But this Kumiai attempt to align its ministries to the empire's activities ended in failure.

THE BIBLE AND A VOICE IN THE WILDERNESS

Of course, Christians were not united in promoting the expansion of the Japanese empire. There were some who concluded that opposing restrictive policies at home and violent expansion abroad was the logical conclusion of applying biblical teaching to their lives and ministries. A fellow Kumiai minister, Kashiwagi Gien, is an excellent example of the use of the Bible as a tool of dissent. Kashiwagi, like Watase, had once been a disciple of Ebina. In fact, he became the minister of the church in the town of Annaka where Ebina had cut his teeth as an evangelist while he was still a student. Unlike Watase and Ebina, however, Kashiwagi found in the Bible evidence that Japan should aspire to be a small country, concerned with the needs of the least, instead of a colonial empire continuing expansion in the name of progress and civilization.

Kashiwagi was the minister of a modest congregation. But through a monthly regional newsletter that Kashiwagi published he became a dissenting voice, within both his denomination and society in general. He established his stance as an independent voice early in his career, insisting on his right to practice his religion without state interference and denouncing Japan's entry into war with Russia in 1904. In addition to this antiwar stance, he also publicly aligned himself with the nascent socialist movement, encouraging readers of his newsletter to subscribe to *Heimin shinbun*, the first socialist weekly newspaper that was also the leading voice against the war until it was dismantled by the government in 1905. Kashiwagi also put his weight behind criticizing Watase's work in Korea, and he questioned Watase's motives for establishing the mission. After all, Kashiwagi argued, Korea was already home to numerous missionaries and converts. If conversion was indeed the goal, as Watase claimed, expending precious Japanese resources that might be better invested at home made no sense. He accused Watase of supporting imperial expansion instead. Kashiwagi argued that imperial expansion violated God's law.[41]

Whereas Ebina and Watase embraced the idea of a powerful and modern Japan transformed through imperial expansion and the other results of modernization and civilization, Kashiwagi denounced imperialism as one branch of the grasping reach of capitalism. While others insisted Japan required a strong military in order to attain parity with Western powers, Kashiwagi argued that wars were waged and militaries raised to support the never-ending greed of capitalists, not for national security. He denounced capitalism as an evil that disposed of people with ease and promoted inequalities and the impoverishment of too many.

Kashiwagi's efforts to come to terms with the suffering of the poor and what he believed to be God's benevolence can be observed in two editorials on the parable of the rich man and Lazarus, published nine years apart. In 1910, Kashiwagi offered the parable as scriptural encouragement to the poor to consider their present toil as a precursor to eternal rewards. While expressing sympathy with the poor, he offered nothing besides a call to patient suffering. However, in 1919, when he revisited this parable, he excoriated the wealthy for twisting their purpose and pursuing their own comfort and pleasure instead of promoting the good of all.[42]

The time span between Kashiwagi's first and second approaches to the rich man and Lazarus coincided with the beginning of Japanese rule in Korea and the outbreak of the March First Movement. Never convinced that the Korea Mission was anything besides a way to curry favor with the government and tainted through its acceptance of substantial financial support from the colonial authorities, Kashiwagi was outraged to hear that Watase and his subordinates sided with the colonial authorities as Japanese engaged in violent suppression of Korean protesters. His denunciation of the colonial mission and of capitalism—as represented by the rich man in the parable—were inextricably linked. Capitalism required the expansive reach of imperialism, and imperialism was fueled with the investments gained through capitalism. This was the lesson he drew from the fate of the rich man in Luke.[43]

Conclusion

Japan may appear to be an enigma in modern history: it was one of the few nations to resist Western domination, then emerged as an empire in its own right while retaining a reputation as somehow completely other to the West. The continued preoccupation with the West as the frame of reference for engaging in postcolonial critiques, especially of Christianity and interpretations of the Bible, fail to account for the exception that Japan represents. On one hand, Japan was influenced by the hegemony of the West in the ways it established its new modern government and social structures and the means by which it attempted to achieve parity with the West. But to assign to Japan a position of perpetual disadvantage to the West elides Japan's engagement with imperialism as well as the ways that Japan's Christians grappled with synthesizing their belief in an ostensibly foreign religion and their position as imperial subjects in an emerging empire in the early twentieth century.

This chapter has only touched on a few examples of Japanese Christians who confound some of the more conventional approaches, even of postcolonial biblical criticism, to restore or resuscitate the vibrancy of non-Western Christian positions, interpretations, and aspirations. Examinations of figures like Ebina, Watase, and Kashiwagi are only the beginning of reconsidering the complexity of the intersection of Japanese imperialism with Christianity. This case offers possibilities to more fully explore the effects of imperial ideology and actions, the complicity of Christian belief and missions, and the emancipatory potential of dissent and liberation rooted in the gospel.

Notes

1. While Taiwan, acquired as part of the war indemnity China owed Japan following the conclusion of the First Sino-Japanese War, is generally considered Japan's first colony, it would perhaps be more accurate to say that Japan had already colonized two territories, Okinawa and Hokkaido, by this time. Although incorporated into Japan proper as prefectures, both were only loosely associated with Japan before the establishment of the modern government in 1868. Okinawa, then the Kingdom of the Ryukyus, paid tribute both to Qing China and the Japanese domain of Satsuma. While there was a Japanese outpost, Matsumae, on the northern island of Hokkaido, until the modern period it was not considered part of Japan proper and was instead treated as a "barbarian frontier."
2. For example, in the introduction to the first volume to take up Japanese imperialism in a substantive way, Mark Peattie evaluates Japan's colonial policies against that of Western empires, and he concludes that its colonial ambitions had failed in part because of an inadequate understanding of how to rationally govern other populations and properly civilize them. Mark Peattie, "Introduction," in *The Japanese Colonial Empire, 1895–1945*, edited by Ramon H. Myers and Mark R. Peattie, 3–52 (Princeton: Princeton University Press, 1985).
3. One excellent examination of Pan-Asianism is Cemil Aydin, *The Politics of Anti-Westernism in Asia: Visions of World Order in Pan-Islamic and Pan-Asian Thought* (New York: Columbia University Press, 2007).
4. On this period of Roman Catholicism in Japan as well as the persecution of Japanese Catholics that followed, see, e.g., George Elison, *Deus Destroyed: The Image of Christianity in Early Modern Japan* (Cambridge, MA: Harvard East Asian Monographs, 1988); and Neil Fujita, *Japanese Encounter with Christianity: The Catholic Mission in Pre-Modern Japan* (Paulist Press, 1991).
5. This is obviously a simplified summary of the factors at work in the ways the Tokugawa government outlawed and maintained opposition to Christianity in the early modern period. On the Buddhist temple registration system, see Nam-lin Hur, *Death and Social Order in Tokugawa Japan: Buddhism, Christianity, and the Danka System* (Cambridge, MA: Harvard University Asia Center, 2007). One key aspect I am excluding is the relationship between the regulation of neo-Confucian orthodoxy and the continuous publication of tracts and chapbooks ridiculing Christianity. For an excellent discussion of this aspect, as well as how this context shaped anti-Christian opinion in the modern period, see Kiri Paramore, *Ideology and Christianity in Japan* (London and New York: Routledge, 2009).
6. For a succinct summary of the early years of missionary work in this period, see, e.g., for example Richard H. Drummond, *A History of Christianity in Japan* (Grand Rapids, MI: Eerdmans, 1971), 145–162.

7. Trent Maxey, *The "Greatest Problem": Religion and State Formation in Meiji Japan* (Cambridge, MA: Harvard University Asia Center, 2014).
8. For an excellent discussion of this issue, see Gauri Viswanathan, *Outside the Fold: Conversion, Modernity, and Belief* (Princeton: Princeton University Press, 1998), esp. 3–43.
9. See, e.g., Helen Ballhatchet, "The Religion of the West versus the Science of the West: The Evolution Controversy in Late Nineteenth Century Japan," in *Japan and Christianity: Impacts and Responses*, edited by John Breen and Mark Williams, 107–121 (New York: St. Martin's Press, 1996).
10. For a brief summary of this, see Dohi Akio, "The First Generation," in *A History of Japanese Theology*, edited by Yasuo Furuya, 19–22 (Grand Rapids, MI: Eerdmans, 1997).
11. See, e.g., Emily Anderson, *Christianity and Imperialism in Modern Japan: Empire for God* (London: Bloomsbury, 2014), 242–243.
12. I am basing my understanding of postcolonial biblical criticism on those points introduced and discussed in works such as Fernando F. Segovia and Stephen D. Moore, *Postcolonial Biblical Criticism: Interdisciplinary Intersections* (London: T&T Clark International, 2005); and R. S. Sugirtharajah, *Exploring Postcolonial Biblical Criticism: History, Method, Practice* (Chichester, UK: Wiley-Blackwell, 2012).
13. On the logic of sameness at the root of Japanese imperialism, see the following studies: Oguma Eiji, trans. David Askew, *A Geneology of "Japanese" Self-Images* (Melbourne: Trans Pacific Press, 2002); Todd A. Henry, *Assimilating Seoul: Japanese Rule and the Politics of the Public Sphere in Colonial Korea, 1910–1945* (Berkeley and Los Angeles: University of California Press, 2014); Mark Caprio, *Japanese Assimilation Policies in Colonial Korea, 1910–1945* (Seattle: University of Washington Press, 2009).
14. R. S. Sugirtharajah, *Exploring Postcolonial Biblical Criticism* (Wiley-Blackwell, 2012), 13.
15. On what might be termed a type of historical amnesia about Japan's imperial aggression, see, e.g., Yoshikuni Igarashi, *Bodies of Memory: Narratives of War in Postwar Japanese Culture, 1945–1970* (Princeton: Princeton University Press, 2000).
16. This sensibility has affected everything from which figures are overwhelmingly studied by scholars, to the tone of scholarship, to the selection of themes. For instance, Ebina Danjō, who was the senior pastor of the influential Hongō Church in Tokyo and later served as president of Dōshisha University, has not been made the subject of a collection of major works, which is very common for well-known public figures in Japan. Many of his contemporaries are represented by complete or partial collections of works, like Uemura Masahisa, and even Ibuka Kajinosuke, who is not as prominent or influential.
17. For example, in an article on the Reformed Church leader Uemura Masahisa, the author argues that while he did not explicitly oppose Japan's engagement in war, he nonetheless did, but without offering substantial evidence to support this conclusion. See Yoshinare Akiko, "Uemura Masahisa no Nichi-Ro sensōron: kasenron ni okeru bunmei, sensō, kirisutokyō," *Jinbun kagaku kenkyu kiyō* 48 (December 2015): 139–165.
18. For a recent example of this type of work, see Scott W. Sunquist, *Explorations in Asian Christianity: History, Theology, Mission* (Downers Grove, IL: IVP Academic, 2017).
19. Some of the key monographs on Japanese Christianity from this period are Ernest Best, *Christian Faith and Cultural Crisis: The Japanese Case* (Leiden: E. J. Brill, 1966); Irwin Scheiner, *Christian Converts and Social Protest in Meiji Japan* (Berkeley and Los Angeles: University of California Press, 1970); Drummond, *A History of Christianity in Japan*; George Bikle, *The New Jerusalem: Aspects of Utopianism in the Thought of Kagawa Toyohiko*

(Tuscon, AZ: University of Arizona Press, 1976); and Carlo Caldarola, *Christianity: The Japanese Way* (Leiden: E. J. Brill, 1979).

20. Akio Dohi, "The First Generation: Christian Leaders in the First Period," in *A History of Japanese Theology*, edited by Yasuo Furuya, 11–42 (Grand Rapids, MI: William B. Eerdmans, 1997). The Japanese original is "Meiji-ki no shingaku shisō," in *Ebina Danjo, Nihon purotesutanto kirisutokyōshi*, 170–194 (N.p.: Shinkyō shuppansha, 2004 [fifth printing]).
21. C. H. Germany, *Protestant Theologies in Modern Japan: A History of Dominant Theological Currents from 1920–1960* (Tokyo: IISR Press, 1965), 19–29.
22. On the greater significance of the Imperial Rescript on Education for Christians, see Anderson, *Christianity and Imperialism in Modern Japan*, esp. 27–50.
23. John F. Howes, *Japan's Modern Prophet: Uchimura Kanzō, 1861–1930* (Vancouver: UBC Press, 2005), 75.
24. Uchimura Kanzō, "Two J's," *Japan Christian Intelligencer* 1, no. 7 (September 9, 1926): n.p., quoted in Hiroshi Miura, *The Life and Thought of Kanzo Uchimura, 1861–1930* (Grand Rapids, MI: Eerdmans, 1996), 52.
25. I want to thank the scholar Ōta Yūzō, the author of *Uchimura Kanzō to sono jidai*, for pointing this out during a Q&A session at a conference on Christianity and Japan at University of British Columbia in 2005.
26. See, e.g., Howes, *Japan's Modern Prophet*, 1.
27. See, e.g., Yakushige Yoshihiro, "Uchimura Kanzō no sairin undō ni okeru shionizumuron to shokuminchi shugi," *Ningen Kankyōgaku* 21 (2012): 195, 198, 201.
28. For a complete discussion of the larger debate, see Anderson, *Christianity and Imperialism in Modern Japan*, esp. 27–50.
29. Anderson, *Christianity and Imperialism in Modern Japan*, 56.
30. For a full overview of the debate between Katō and Christians, see Anderson, *Christianity and Imperialism in Modern Japan*, 50–60.
31. For a detailed account of Janes and the Kumamoto School for Western Learning, see Fred Notehelfer, *American Samurai: Captain L. L. Janes and Japan* (Princeton: Princeton University Press, 1985).
32. Emily Anderson, "Christianity in the Japanese Empire: Nationalism, Conscience, and Faith in Meiji and Taisho Japan" (PhD diss., UCLA, 2010), 109.
33. Anderson, "Christianity in the Japanese Empire," 112–113.
34. Anderson, "Christianity in the Japanese Empire," 114.
35. Anderson, *Christianity and Imperialism in Modern Japan*, 69.
36. Emily Anderson, "Developing an Imperial Theology: Transforming 'Others' into 'Brothers in Christ' for a Multiethnic Empire," in *Belief and Practice in Imperial Japan and Colonial Korea*, edited by Emily Anderson (Singapore: Palgrave, 2017), 125.
37. Anderson, "Developing an Imperial Theology," 128.
38. Anderson, "Developing an Imperial Theology," 120.
39. Anderson, *Christianity and Imperialism in Modern Japan*, 134–135.
40. On the Korea Mission, see Anderson, *Christianity and Imperialism in Modern Japan*, 123–158.
41. On Kashiwagi's criticism of Watase and the Korea Mission, see Anderson, *Christianity and Imperialism in Modern Japan*, 146–149.
42. Anderson, "Christianity in the Japanese Empire," 393–394.
43. Anderson, "Christianity in the Japanese Empire," 390–394.

Bibliography

Akiko, Yoshinare. "Uemura Masahisa no Nichi-Ro sensōron: kasenron ni okeru bunmei, sensō, kirisutokyō." *Jinbun kagaku kenkyu kiyō* 48 (December 2015): 139–165.

Akio, Dohi. "The First Generation." In *A History of Japanese Theology*, edited by Yasuo Furuya, 19–22. Grand Rapids, MI: Eerdmans, 1997.

Anderson, Emily. "Christianity in the Japanese Empire: Nationalism, Conscience, and Faith in Meiji and Taisho Japan." PhD diss., UCLA, 2010, 390–394

Anderson, Emily. *Christianity and Imperialism in Modern Japan*. New York: Bloomsbury, 2014.

Aydin, Cemil. *The Politics of Anti-Westernism in Asia: Visions of World Order in Pan-Islamic and Pan-Asian Thought*. New York: Columbia University Press, 2007.

Ballhatchet, Helen. "The Religion of the West versus the Science of the West: The Evolution Controversy in Late Nineteenth Century Japan." In *Japan and Christianity: Impacts and Responses*, edited by John Breen and Mark Williams, 107–121. New York: St. Martin's Press, 1996.

Best, Ernest. *Christian Faith and Cultural Crisis: The Japanese Case*. Leiden: E. J. Brill, 1966.

Caprio, Mark. *Japanese Assimilation Policies in Colonial Korea, 1910–1945*. Seattle: University of Washington Press, 2009.

Carlo Caldarola, *Christianity: The Japanese Way* Leiden: E. J. Brill, 1979.

Dohi, Akio. "The First Generation: Christian Leaders in the First Period." In *A History of Japanese Theology*, edited by Yasuo Furuya, 11–42. Grand Rapids, MI: Eerdmans, 1997. The Japanese original is "Meiji-ki no shingaku shisō," in *Ebina Danjo, Nihon purotesutanto kirisutokyōshi*, 170–194. 5th printing. N.p.: Shinkyō shuppansha, 2004.

Drummond, Richard H. *A History of Christianity in Japan*. Grand Rapids, MI: Eerdmans, 1971, 145–162.

Elison, George. *Deus Destroyed: The Image of Christianity in Early Modern Japan*. Cambridge, MA: Harvard East Asian Monographs, 1988. Fujita, Neil. *Japan's Encounter with Christianity: The Catholic Mission in Pre-Modern Japan*. New York: Paulist Press, 1991.

George Bikle, *The New Jerusalem: Aspects of Utopianism in the Thought of Kagawa Toyohiko*. Tuscon, AZ: University of Arizona Press, 1976.

Germanyt, C. H. *Protestant Theologies in Modern Japan: A History of Dominant Theological Currents from 1920–1960*. Tokyo: IISR Press, 1965, 19–29.

Henry, Todd A. *Assimilating Seoul: Japanese Rule and the Politics of the Public Sphere in Colonial Korea, 1910–1945*. Berkeley and Los Angeles: University of California Press, 2014.

Howes, John F. *Japan's Modern Prophet: Uchimura Kanzō, 1861–1930*. Vancouver: UBC Press, 2005, 75.

Igarashi, Yoshikuni. *Bodies of Memory: Narratives of War in Postwar Japanese Culture, 1945–1970*. Princeton: Princeton University Press, 2000.

Hur, Nam-lin. *Death and Social Order in Tokugawa Japan: Buddhism, Christianity, and the Danka System*. Cambridge, MA: Harvard University Asia Center, 2007.

Kanzō, Uchimura, "Two J's." *Japan Christian Intelligencer* 1, no. 7 (September 9, 1926): n.p., quoted in Hiroshi Miura, *The Life and Thought of Kanzo Uchimura, 1861–1930*. Grand Rapids, MI: Eerdmans, 1996, 52.

Maxey, Trent. *The "Greatest Problem": Religion and State Formation in Meiji Japan*. Cambridge, MA: Harvard University Asia Center, 2014.

Notehelfer, Fred. *American Samurai: Captain L. L. Janes and Japan*. Princeton: Princeton University Press, 1985.

Oguma, Eiji. Trans. David Askew. *A Geneology of "Japanese" Self-Images*. Melbourne: Trans Pacific Press, 2002.

Paramore, Kiri. *Ideology and Christianity in Japan*. London and New York: Routledge, 2009.

Peattie, Mark. "Introduction." In *The Japanese Colonial Empire, 1895–1945*, edited by Ramon H. Myers and Mark R. Peattie, 3–52. Princeton: Princeton University Press, 1985.

Scheiner, Irwin. *Christian Converts and Social Protest in Meiji Japan*. Berkeley and Los Angeles: University of California Press, 1970.

Segovia, Fernando F., and Stephen D. Moore. *Postcolonial Biblical Criticism: Interdisciplinary Intersections*. London: T&T Clark International, 2005).

Sugirtharajah, R. S. *Exploring Postcolonial Biblical Criticism: History, Method, Practice*. Chichester, UK: Wiley-Blackwell, 2012.

Sugirtharajah, R. S. *Exploring Postcolonial Biblical Criticism*. Chichester, UK: Wiley-Blackwell, 2012, 13.

Sunquist, Scott W. *Explorations in Asian Christianity: History, Theology, Mission*. Downers Grove, IL: IVP Academic, 2017.

Viswanathan, Gauri. *Outside the Fold: Conversion, Modernity, and Belief*. Princeton: Princeton University Press, 1998.

Yoshihiro, Yakushige. "Uchimura Kanzō no sairin undō ni okeru shionizumuron to shokuminchi shugi." *Ningen Kankyōgaku* 21 (2012): 195, 198, 201.

CHAPTER 18

THE BIBLE IN THE KOREAN RESISTANCE AGAINST THE JAPANESE EMPIRE (1910–1945)

JINA KANG

ANY discussion of the relationship between Christianity (or, more specifically, Protestantism) and Korean nationalism during the decades of the Japanese occupation (1910–1945) must be a multicentered one. Nationalist movements during this tumultuous period took on various forms (e.g., cultural nationalism,[1] economic nationalism,[2] and gendered forms of nationalism[3]). However, the unifying goal of these nationalist movements during the decades of Japanese occupation was to restore the political sovereignty of Korea against foreign occupation. Timothy S. Lee summarizes the overarching aims of various forms of Korean nationalist movements during this period as "Korea for, by, and of Koreans."[4] As such, Christianity was but one stimulus to the movement, just as other factors (e.g., Buddhism, Chŏndogyo,[5] socialism, and Western democracy) had utility to the conceptualization of Korean nationalism and what a renewed Korean state should look like. As much as there was not a singular form of "Korean nationalism," there was not a singular way in which Christianity influenced nationalist discourses during this period. In fact, when Christianity intersected with nationalism, it contributed to complex conceptualizations of Korean identity, assessments of Korea's place in geopolitics, and engagement with the Japanese Empire. This study focuses on how the Christian Bible was interpreted to build momentum for nationalist movements for Korean sovereignty.

THE EMERGENCE OF CHRISTIANITY IN THE KOREAN PENINSULA: A BRIEF HISTORY

In 1905, the Japan-Korea Treaty officially declared Korea a protectorate of Japan. This was followed by a formal annexation in 1910, which established Japanese colonial control over the Korean Peninsula under the Government-General of Korea. Considered within a context of the tense geopolitical struggle for power and power balance in the region, Japan's successive victories in the Sino-Japanese War (1894–1895) and Russo-Japanese War (1904–1905) all but secured Japanese dominance in the region. This dominance was further secured through agreements with the Western powers, including the United States and England, such as the Taft-Katsura Agreement (1905) (with the United States) and the renewed Anglo-Japanese Alliance (1902, 1905) (with England). These agreements assured the Western powers' recognition of Japanese claims to the Korean Peninsula. The geopolitical interest in the Korean Peninsula was significant for the island nation as it would serve as a strategic staging ground, both militarily and economically, for securing Japanese expansion in the region. The formal abdication of the Korean emperor in August 1910 brought an end to the half-century of *Chŏsun* rule in the Korean Peninsula. These conditions catalyzed the March First Movement (*samil undong*) in 1919, which set off months of nationalist demonstrations across the peninsula and mobilized nationalist movements to restore Korean sovereignty.

While nationalist discourse was heightened by resistance movements against Japanese occupying forces, there were already developing nationalist movements under the ruling Yi Dynasty. Nationalist movements began to emerge in reaction to growing socioeconomic inequities of a stratified caste system[6] as well as the negligence of the ruling classes who were paralyzed by competing factions. This is particularly seen in the *Tonghak* ("eastern learning") rebellion of 1894–1895,[7] which mobilized a populace who were too often victimized by a widespread system of abuse that was attributable to pandering by the ruling factions to outside agents (i.e., Japan and Russia) at the expense of the large peasant population.[8] While this popular nationalist movement failed to bring about the intended reforms or resistance to eventual foreign occupation, these early movements began to reawaken a Korean nationalist consciousness. They also introduced some important figures who would play key roles in the March First Movement, which catalyzed nationalist movements for Korean sovereignty during the decades of Japanese occupation. These prominent individuals included those who would lead independence movements in the diaspora, such as Sŏ Chae-p'il (who would later attain U.S. citizenship and take the anglicized name Philip Jaisohn), Yi Sŭng-man, and An Ch'ang-ho.

Within this context of growing or heightened nationalist discourses and movements, Christianity (and, more specifically, Protestantism) emerged on the peninsula and became an efficacious tool for the movement. In some regard, the earlier *Tonghak* rebellion indicated the presence of Christianity as it was motivated by a syncretic consolidation of traditional religious systems (e.g., Confucianism, Buddhism, and shamanism) with Catholicism, which was known as *Sŏhak* ("western learning") at the time. Prior to annexation, the ruling Yi Dynasty had a long-established resistance to opening Korea to the outside world (hence, the moniker "Hermit Kingdom"), with the exception of vassal relations with China. When Catholicism first made landfall in Korea, it was not via Western missionaries but through Korean emissaries who returned with Christian writings when they came into contact with Jesuit missionaries in China. These writings of *Sŏhak* first caught the interest of Korean scholars. Eventually, Christian teachings of equality before God as "children of God" appealed to the larger populace, who were unduly marginalized in a stratified socioeconomic system. One of the unique aspects of the history of Christianity in Korea is that the spread of the religion was neither initiated nor led by Western missionaries; instead, its rise is largely credited to local converts and self-evangelization. This will be a crucial factor in the impact and role of Christianity in the nationalist struggle for independence in later decades. Christianity was neither overtly seen as a foreign import (or imposition) nor associated with the colonizing powers.[9] In other words, the process reveals the early development of a Korean-led and Korean form of Christianity. Therefore, it was seen as a propitious tool for shaping the Korean national consciousness at a time when the failures of the domestic systems of rule as well as foreign occupying forces had thrown the nation into tumult.

By the time the first Catholic missionaries made landfall in the Hermit Kingdom in the late eighteenth century, they encountered periodic persecution by *Chŏsun* rulers for perceived foreign subversion of traditional practices (such as the important Confucian rite of ancestral memorial, called *chesa*, which many Christian converts refused to perform as a form of idolatry) and, by extension, subversion of the authority of the ruling classes.[10] James Huntley Grayson observes that the early periods of persecution and execution of converts as well as foreign missionaries led to the emergence of a "Catholic ghetto mentality," which focused on institutional growth and limited engagement with "social outreach and little awareness of the historical events taking place around them."[11] By the time of formal Japanese occupation in 1910, the Catholic Church in Korea had largely removed itself from Korean social (and political) affairs. Thus, Catholic influence on the nationalist discourse and resistance movements against Japanese occupation was limited if not avoided. Grayson further notes that the hesitation of the Catholic Church to give any public impression of support to politically motivated movements against the Japanese Empire was influenced by a concordat signed between the Vatican and the Japanese imperial government in 1936. The concordat safely secured a Catholic presence in Japan in exchange for the Church's recognition of *Shinto* rites as expressly not idolatrous.[12] Therefore, any perception of Catholic defiance or subversion of the Japanese authorities could potentially disrupt the overall missionary endeavors of the Catholic Church in the region. While Catholicism has a longer history than its Protestant counterpart in Korea, its influence in the region during the Japanese occupation was visibly limited but certainly cannot be overlooked. Even during the years of state-led persecutions (e.g., Sinyu persecutions in 1801, Ŭrhae persecutions in 1815, Chŏnhae persecutions in 1827, Kihae persecutions in 1839, and the years of the Great Persecution in 1866–1871), the Korean Catholic Church saw a steady growth of converts, primarily led by efforts of local converts to fill in the gaps left by removal of foreign missionaries.[13] Protestantism, on the other hand, escaped a history of conflicts in the peninsula and the traumatic impact of historical persecution and went on to play an observable role in nationalist movements during the decades of Japanese occupation.[14]

By the time Protestant missionaries entered the peninsula in the mid-1880s, they built on the self-evangelizing efforts of local converts, which culminated in Protestant missionaries of various denominations adapting what became known as the Nevius Method. The Nevius Method shifted responsibility and self-determinative potential toward local converts to support (including financially) the church and to self-evangelize.[15] In this regard, Protestantism was not seen as a foreign imposition but was established in a Korean form. Protestantism had also by accident entered Korea at an auspicious time to be seen as a modernizing force, especially in opposition to the apparent failures of the domestic system of rule. Yi Kwang-su, who emerged as one of the leaders of the nationalist movement, notes in July 1917:

> Toward the end of the Korean [Chŏsun] regime, politics was not the only corrupt element. Commerce, the economy and education were faltering. As the political administration deteriorated, social morality was also becoming corrupt. Extravagance, selfishness, dishonesty and jealousy swept through Korea like the wind.... In other words, within the Korean lifestyle, there were no ideals, morality or standards.... To the chaotic and evil society, Christianity brought a high ideal of life and the dignity of virtue. Intemperance and immorality were forbidden. Dishonesty was denounced. Human traffic was discouraged. To worship God, to seek after his righteousness, to teach new ways of living a pure, ideal life, all this has been the gift of Christianity. It is Christianity that has enabled nearly three hundred thousand souls to enjoy religious consolations and to strive after a morally pure life.[16]

Internal and international affairs played key roles in creating the "right" environment for Protestantism to stake out an important role in nationalist movements against Japanese occupation. As the above quote indicates, the decline in the effectiveness, if not legitimacy, of the Yi Dynasty and the ruling classes set the stage for a renewed desire for a better social imagination in Korea.[17] Neither marred by associations with the failing Yi Dynasty nor the foreign occupying Japanese colonial government, Protestantism lent itself to providing a new language to imagine what a "better Korea" or "new Korea" should look like. As Philip Jaisohn, president of the First Korean Congress, remarked when the Congress gathered diasporic nationalist leaders in response to the March First Movement: "This is not old Korea; this is new Korea."[18] As Korean Christianity began to take shape in Korea, Christianity lent the emerging nationalist movements a way to re-imagine a "new Korea."

Presbyterian and Methodist denominations had a particularly visible impact on the landscape of Korean Christianity by establishing social services such as hospitals, private schools, and universities. In the intervening years of Japanese occupation, these locales became important meeting places for resistance movements despite the objections of Western missionaries. In fact, when Japan formally annexed Korea, Western missionaries accepted (if not welcomed) the change in expectation that the Japanese imperial government would be friendly to their missionary agenda. In a letter written by Arthur Brown, the board secretary of the Presbyterian mission in Korea, he remarks:

> What is the attitude of the missionaries toward the Japanese?... loyal recognition, is I believe, the sound position. It is in accord with the example of Christ, who loyally submitted himself and advised His apostles to submit themselves to a far

worse government than the Japanese and it is in line with the teaching of Paul in Romans xiii.[19]

Compliance with occupying forces was advised as not only prudent but also following the example of Jesus Christ (Matt 22:15–22) as well as the teachings of Paul the Apostle in Romans 13.[20] While theological motivations influenced Western missionaries' stance regarding foreign occupiers in Korea, they were also motivated by expectations that the Japanese presence would bring about technological, medical (hygienic), and infrastructural developments to the benefit of Korea.[21] All in all, Western missionaries and their respective denominations expected to encounter a friendly state in the Japanese Empire—perhaps a far better state than the one encountered by Jesus in the Roman Empire. Such expectations gradually declined in the intervening years of Japanese occupation, which brought about various policies that restricted missionary endeavors of education and social services in Korea.[22] For example, an ordinance issued in 1915 prohibited the use of the Bible in school curricula, including schools founded by missionaries, as well as banning teaching in the Korean language. The intent of such ordinances was to suppress a perceived Christian impetus for developing nationalist/anti-Japanese sentiments among Koreans. Later, missionaries who reported on the violent response of the Japanese police and military to the March First Movement would identify these restrictions amid the many grievances for which they sought reprieve.[23] However, there is no doubt that missionaries as Western agents were afforded a cautious response from Japanese officials who wanted to avoid conflict with their representative Western nations in the international arena.[24] One may surmise an underlying mutual cautiousness for the sake of avoiding undue conflict between competing imperial powers. Eventually, the Western missionary posture of "loyal recognition" became problematic following the March First Movement. The undeniably violent response of Japanese officials to what started as a peaceful protest compelled cautious moral objections from Western missionaries.[25]

As Japanese dominance in the region culminated in a formal annexation, diasporic Koreans in the United States, China (Shanghai), and Japan[26] began to independently organize. As World War I began in 1914, Korean nationalist leaders exiled abroad began to calculate opportunities to reclaim Korean sovereignty. President Woodrow Wilson's Fourteen Points provided such an opportunity. The Fourteen Points, outlining a principle of national self-determination, provided the impulse for international (in particular, American) support for reclaiming Korean sovereignty. The Korean National Association, first established by Korean immigrants in Hawai'i, met in San Francisco and unsuccessfully attempted to send Yi Sŭng-man and Chŏng Han-gyŏng (Henry Chung) as delegates to the Paris Peace Conference in 1919. The U.S. State Department had rejected the men's requests for passports because Korea was an annexed state of Japan. Therefore, the State Department redirected the petitioners to request passports through Japanese authorities. However, Korean nationalist leaders in China (Shanghai) were able to successfully organize to send Kim Kyu-sik to Paris to represent the case for Korean independence among the gathered nations. Distant both geographically and politically from the reach of the Japanese imperial state, diasporic Koreans found themselves in unique positions of subverting imperial censors, surveillance, and even arrest.[27]

Meanwhile, on the Korean Peninsula, nationalist movements for Korea's independence were forming but a unified effort had yet to be seen. However, on January 22, 1919, the last surviving monarch of the Yi Dynasty suddenly died. As rumors began to circulate speculating on nefarious Japanese involvement in the monarch's untimely death, funeral arrangements for the late monarch were scheduled for March 3, 1919. The funeral provided the opportunity and cover for covert preparations for a public declaration of independence. Organizers strategized that Japanese police would be expecting masses to congregate in Seoul for the official funeral ceremony and, thereby, would be less suspicious of the movements of the Korean populace. Religious leaders of Christian denominations, Buddhists, and *Chŏndogyo* sects were key to the organizing efforts. On the afternoon of March 1, 1919, masses gathered at Pagoda Park in Seoul surprising not only Japanese forces but also Western missionaries who were deliberately kept in the dark. It is not difficult to surmise the calculus of the organizers; they likely expected the Western missionaries' stance of "loyal recognition" to discourage such demonstrations as resistance to "governing authorities" (Rom 13:1, NRSV). As demonstrators gathered, a copy of the Declaration of Independence was dispatched to the Japanese governor-general and read aloud at Pagoda Square, which was followed by resounding cries of the crowd: "*Daehandonglip manse!*" ("Long live an independent Korea!"). The expressed intent of the demonstration was nonviolent, and the Declaration itself asserted in moderate terms the claim for Korean sovereignty.[28] The Declaration was not expressly a Christian document, but the perception of Christian influence in the movement was not overlooked by Japanese authorities as fifteen of the thirty-three signatories were Christian.[29] A commission of the Federal Council of the Churches of Christ in America, who composed a report in the months following the March First Movement, assessed: "No more remarkable 'revolution' has taken place in recent history than that which occurred in Korea beginning March 1, 1919. The plan was to secure independence by moral force, without resorting to violence."[30]

However, the response from Japanese police was one that "bordered on hysteria."[31] The Japanese did not expect such a mass gathering let alone that the Korean populace would be capable of such organization. It seems the Japanese officials were blinded by an imperial paradigm of the superiority of the colonizers over the delinquency of the colonized. The violent response of Japanese police and military, intending to quickly suppress the movement with deadly force,[32] only fanned the flames. Japanese records indicate that in the ensuing months disturbances were reported across the counties in Korea and scores were killed, tortured, and arrested.[33] Japanese authorities suspected Christian influence in the demonstrations. Even prior to the March First Movement, Government-General officials had demonstrated wariness regarding possible Christian-led, if not Christian-motivated, attempts to subvert the colonizers. The growing number of converts and a wave of revival campaigns for a "million souls for Christ" in 1909 only exacerbated Japanese nervousness. In 1912, 124 people were arrested, of whom 98 were Christian, based on the unsubstantiated suspicion of organizing a plot to assassinate the Governor-General Terauchi Masatake, and these events culminated in what became known as the Conspiracy Trial of 1912. While the vast majority of the accused were eventually acquitted through a series of trials, "there is little historical question that those prosecuting the Conspiracy Case concocted evidence and that Japanese government officials were unable to prove any conspiracy on the part of Christians in Korea."[34] Japanese intent to (violently) suppress the momentum of Christian influence on nationalist movements only further solidified Christian resolve to resist Japanese occupation of Korea and, ironically, also legitimized Christianity as a tool for nationalist movements.[35]

The March First Movement also prompted a reconstitution of the Japanese Empire in its relationship with Japanese Christians in Korea. Emily Anderson's seminal study examines the role of the Japanese missionary endeavor in Korea. The Government-General supported (including financially) the Korean Mission of the *Kumiai Kyōkai* to provide "religious coercion"[36] to compel Korean Christians to be compliant and loyal subjects of the Japanese Empire. Therefore, the mission of the *Kumiai Kyōkai* was to convert Koreans to a Japanese form of Christianity that expressly tied the notion of being a true Christian to being a loyal subject integrated into the Japanese Empire. Anderson refers to the observation of Watase Tsuneyoshi, director of the *Kumiai Kyōkai* Korea Mission, during the mission's first annual conference that was attended by Korean converts and Japanese Christians:

> I heard the sound of people thanking God for the labor of brothers and sisters in the *naichi* [Japan], as well as those fervently asking God for the unity of Koreans and Japanese (*naisen ittai*), and there was an exchange of sympathy that transcended ethnic and racial lines; it was a truly joyous meeting.[37]

While the *Kumiai Kyōkai* had limited impact on Korean Christianity, the presence of a Japanese Christian mission supported by the Government-General expressly highlights the intersections between empire and religion. While the Government-General vehemently (and violently) opposed Korean Christianity and suppressed its influence on Korean nationalist movements, imperial strategies for dominance and control over the colony included converting Korean Christians to a distinct form of Japanese Christianity in hopes of creating compliant subjects of the Empire. Religion, therefore, was not only a tool for the colonized but also used in the service of the imperial agenda. By 1932, the policy of the Government-General required all school personnel, including faculty and students, to observe state-sponsored ceremonies at *Shinto* shrines. For many Korean Christians, this ceremony was perceived as a form of idolatry that further highlighted the incompatibility between an authentic Korean Christian faith and compliance with occupying forces.[38] It seems the Government-General's initial attempts to utilize Japanese Christianity introduced an idiosyncratic tool to assuage (or coerce) Korean Christians into compliance by forging compatibility between their faith and the Empire. Not unlike the colonial rhetoric of justifying occupation with the promise of advances in technology, economy, infrastructure, and overall modernization for Korea, the Japanese form of Christianity was harnessed as a tool for securing the expansionist agenda of the Japanese Empire. However, the March First Movement proved the ineffectiveness, if not the failures, of the *Kumiai Kyōkai* mission as many Korean Christians took to the streets in protest against Japanese occupation. In response, the Government-General seized financial support of the mission, which quietly dissipated the mission in the peninsula.

The history of Protestantism (Christianity) in Korea from the end of the *Chŏsun* state to the rise of the Japanese Empire shows the complex and multicentered intersections between Christianity and the nationalist movements of this time period. In the following section, this study will now turn its attention to how interpretations of the Christian Bible affected Korean nationalism.

Korean Nationalism and the Bible

While the March First Movement was unsuccessful in negotiating the restoration of the sovereignty of Korea, it was nonetheless an important stimulus that aroused a renewed sense of Korean consciousness and motivation for the growing independence movements. An increased sense of nationalism is dangerous for any imperial enterprise because it poses a powerful counter-rhetoric to the notion of a unified empire of compliant subjects. In response to the growing nationalist movements, Government-General officials enacted various strategies to suppress nationalist sentiments (including censorship, educational policies, and economic controls) and to coerce the Korean populace to submissively integrate into the Empire. Within such a framework, the intersectionality between citizenship and theology yielded a dynamic conceptualization of Korean nationalism. The Bible became an influential and compelling tool for that purpose.

Christian nationalists saw a natural compatibility in their Christian and Korean identities. The Christian notion of equality of all people as children of God provided a language to counter the inequities of and abuses within a stratified caste system. After the formal loss of sovereignty, the idea of being "children of God" was seamlessly merged with Korean nationalist sentiments. In a sermon titled "Cultivation of the Second-Generation Korean (*jeikukminŭi yangsŏng*)," Yi Man-jip, a pastor and nationalist leader in Daegu, drew inspiration from Ephesians 6:4 to highlight the importance of raising the next generation of Koreans as Christians.

> What do we mean by body and spirit (*yŏngyuk*)? It does not mean other than that God is in us and that God is our father. It teaches us that we are God's children.... In the same way, the second-generation Korean should be educated within Christ's church. When we see the growth of 500,000, 1,000,000 people who have been nurtured within Christ's church and within families of Christ's disciples, there is no doubt that we have entered an age in which we have mastered our Korean consciousness (*chosŏnui chŏngshinkye*).[39]

At a time when all the vestiges of legitimate political claims to a national identity were disrupted by empire, Christian nationalist leaders reoriented the Korean consciousness (*chosŏnui chŏngshinkye*) or Korean identity around the familial language of Christianity. If God is father, then Christ's followers are God's children, securing their sense of self—both body and spirit—in this renewed identity as Korean Christians. In this way, Christianity provided a new language to redefine a transformed sense of being Korean. As such, Timothy S. Lee highlights the political opportunities that afforded Protestantism's successful integration with the Korean nationalist movements:

> That there was a political dimension to the success of Protestantism in Korea is not difficult to surmise. For if we take Hintze's observation as an interpretive warrant—that an ideal succeeds in history only in so far as it becomes associated with the real interests of the people to whom it is exposed—it must also be granted that an ideal-driven religion like Protestantism could have succeeded in Korea only because it somehow became associated with the real interests of the Koreans.[40]

The loss of national sovereignty could be mitigated with an identity secured in God who is "in us." Imperial policies and rhetoric to suppress Korean identity into compliant Japanese subjects could be covertly resisted with faithful devotion to raising the next generation as children of God.

An Ch'ang-ho was a Christian nationalist leader who was instrumental in the formation of the Provisional Government in Shanghai.[41] While he mostly worked in the diaspora, he returned to Korea and later died in 1938 after suffering prison torture. In a message simply titled, "Love," An Ch'ang-ho reflects on the meaning of John 1:3 as a way of inspiring the youth involved in the nationalist movement in Korea.[42]

> How can our spirit be in God and God's spirit in us? Just as the sunlight can only enter if there is a hole, there is no one who has seen God, but when we love one another God is in us. So, a person with godly love is a godly person. Jesus taught of love for three years. While he was on earth, he experienced hunger, cold, and did not have a place to lay his head. Then, he demonstrated true love by shedding his blood on the cross. . . . Now, those who diligently labor for independence are indeed truly godly. At a time when life and death is uncertain, those who sacrifice resources (money) and life are indeed true godly believers.[43]

Not unlike Yi Man-jip's sermon on Ephesians 4:6, An Ch'ang-ho also finds solace in an identity secured in God dwelling "in us." He refers to Jesus' life of suffering and rejection that culminated in his death on the cross. He connects the suffering of Christ to the suffering of those involved in the independence movement. Monetary sacrifice and even the sacrifice of life not only connects the faithful with Jesus but also places the independence movement within a redemptive Christological framework. The convergence of Jesus' ministry with the struggle for independence established a theological legitimacy to the movement and assured that suffering (even death) was not without purpose. The struggle for independence was not just a matter of patriotism alone but a means of demonstrating genuine devotion and love of God. Participation—in fact, suffering and sacrificing—in the nationalist cause was seen as a marker of genuine Christian faith and Christian identity as one in whom God dwells.

For nationalist leaders like Yi Man-jip and An Ch'ang-ho, the picture of a suffering Christ provided purpose, legitimacy, and impetus for the independence movement. Just as Christ suffered, the faithful disciples of Christ were suffering for the independence of Korea. However, the suffering Christ model also proved that the world was a place of suffering and that there was futility in resisting such reality. In a sermon on the Lukan account of Jesus' crucifixion (Luke 23:39–43), Kil Sŏn-ju points to the confession of one of two criminals executed alongside Jesus: "Jesus, remember me when you come into your kingdom" (verse 42).

> Believing in eternal life and awaiting Jesus' second coming, he [the criminal] demonstrated an utmost faith. Although it is easy to despair and be disheartened that life is usually filled with suffering and sin, he rather hoped in the future even while suffering. He awaited eternal life even while facing imminent death. He confessed his past sins because he believed and hoped that only if he could receive Jesus' forgiveness that he would become a citizen of heaven.[44]

Kil Sŏn-ju was an early leader of the March First Movement, was one of the signatories of the Declaration of Independence, and was imprisoned for three years for his role in the movement. He became an ardent preacher of an apocalyptic message until his death in 1935. His son and biographer, Kil Chin-gyŏng, recalls that his father found solace in the Bible and, in particular, the Apocalypse of John during his time of imprisonment.[45] Kil saw neither an immediate redemptive purpose nor an imminent end in the suffering of the criminal in the Lukan account. Rather, the criminal proved his faith by hoping for a paradisiacal world to come. The March First Movement had sparked months of protests, arrests, and losses across the peninsula; however, the movement ultimately failed to usher in independence. Such a reality proved the futility of resisting or even awaiting an imminent end to suffering (i.e., Japanese oppressive policies). Therefore, in light of such realities, Kil seems to have "turned his gaze away from the Korean nation to the Kingdom of God."[46] Kil's apocalyptic message offered solace not in assigning purpose to the suffering and death of protesters; rather, Kil reconceptualized his hope in the eventual in-breaking of the Kingdom of God.[47] He reimagined and reoriented the Korean Christian identity as citizenship in the Kingdom of God to come.

In the apocalyptic message of Kil, the Kingdom of God was an anticipated oasis that would eventually bring an end to the suffering endemic to this world. However, the language of the Kingdom of God also united theology with the political aims for a sovereign Korean state for others in the nationalist movement. The news of the March First Movement prompted diasporic Korean nationalists to mobilize to consolidate their efforts with those on the peninsula. One such key movement in the diaspora was actualized in the meeting of the First Korean Congress, which gathered in Philadelphia on April 14–16, 1919. One resolution drafted and adapted by the Congress was called "An Appeal to America":

> We appeal to you for support and sympathy because we know you love justice; you also fought for liberty and democracy; you stand for Christianity and humanity. Our cause is a just one before the laws of God and man. Our aim is freedom from militaristic autocracy; our object is democracy for Asia; our hope is universal Christianity. Therefore we feel that our appeal merits your consideration.[48]

The goal of the resolution was multifaceted. One of the expressed intentions of the Congress was to spread the news of the plight of the Korean people. In addition, the resolution appeals to the history of America's own fight for "liberty and democracy" to make the case that support for Korean independence was support for democracy. Democracy, according to this resolution, stood in diametric opposition to militaristic autocracy. The not-so-veiled logic is that America must naturally—"before the laws of God and man"—stand on the side of Korean independence since, to do otherwise, is to stand for what is arguably un-American. The resolution negotiates a convergence of Christianity and democracy, which established for the delegates a common cause and shared identity between American Christians and Korean Christians. As seen in the sermons of Christian nationalist leaders such as Yi Man-sik, An Ch'ang-ho, and Kil Sŏn-ju, Christianity and a Christian identity offered a language and a means to negotiate a renewed Korean identity at a time when national sovereignty had been lost. In addition, the reference to the "Kingdom of God" connected Korean Christians with potential allies in the Western world to compel sympathy and support for Korean sovereignty.

While the resolution did not make explicit mention of the "Kingdom of God," it does refer to a "universal Christianity." It suggests that establishing a sovereign, democratic state in Korea will support the missionary endeavor to spread or "universalize" Christianity. On the second day of the Congress, a resolution titled "To the Thinking People of Japan" was drafted and adapted. The resolution asked the Japanese people to correct the wrongs of Japanese hostility and forcible annexation of Korea.[49] In discussing the resolution, Philip Jaisohn, president of the Congress, overtly refers to this missionizing potential of the Korean nationalist movement:

> If you send this message to the people of Japan it will be laughed at by a large majority of the Japanese. They will scorn and scoff at you. All right. When Christ preached the Gospel at different places they scoffed at Him. Just the same, that didn't stop Him from preaching. You have two great missions to perform and you are adapted for it. You are just the people. The first mission is to Christianize the Orient, and the second is to democratize the Orient. With the first, let us begin with our worst enemy, Japan.[50]

Jaisohn, too, refers to a picture of a suffering Christ. Again, the rejection of Christ was likened to the efforts of the nationalist movement. For Christian nationalist leaders, the matter of reestablishing Korean sovereignty was a microcosm of a greater vision for ushering in the Kingdom of God on earth. The twofold task to "Christianize" and "democratize" suggests not only an appeal for political support from Western nations but also an evangelistic goal of expanding the Kingdom of God. Establishing Korean sovereignty was a matter of theological and geopolitical significance.

On the side of the nationalist movement, the Kingdom of God established a pivotal point for a renewed sense of Korean identity, shared interests with potential allies in the global arena, and expansion of the Kingdom. However, such aims were also tools for the Empire. Japanese imperial policies were intended to suppress any distinct Korean nationalist sentiments in order to create a unified Empire. For some time, the Government-General supported Japanese Christian (*Kumiai Kyōkai*) missionary endeavors to spread a Japanese form of Christianity that preached the compatibility of compliance to the Japanese Empire as a way of Christian devotion. In the aftermath of the March First Movement, the perspective of a Japanese Christian in Korea was published in the *Missionary Review of the World*:

> Chosenese [a Japanese reference to Koreans] are human beings. They have their national pride, their love of native land. Japanese have no monopoly over patriotism. With our shameless swagger and brandishing of "Japanism" how can we quiet their opposition? If we do not get rid of this spirit and take our stand upon conduct growing out of the love which "loves the neighbor as oneself" I do not think we can long hold our position as lord of the East.[51]

The perspective of the writer is neither to criticize patriotism for one's native land (including Korea) nor to negate Japanese imperial domination over their regional neighbors ("lord of the East"). The former is a natural human inclination. Therefore, his intention was not to criticize or even be surprised by the Korean response to Japanese occupation. For the writer, the failure of the Japanese Empire was a failure of loving one's neighbors. The moral failures against the Korean people not only betrayed the imperial agenda of inspiring compliant subjects but also failed to demonstrate Christian love for neighbors. Therefore, the writer concludes, "*By all means Japan must be born again.* Therefore, there is today no enterprise which compares in urgency with the work of evangelization."[52] If part of the "mission" of Korean nationalists was to expand the Kingdom of God, this message could also be harnessed in service of the expansionist agenda of the Japanese Empire.[53]

In this way, it may be seen that the Bible was not only a tool for the Korean nationalist movements but also a tool for Empire. Ultimately, the dispersion of the *Kumiai Kyōkai* in Korea suggests that the rhetoric was ineffective in persuading Koreans and imperial officials alike. Nonetheless, the potential utility of the Bible for those standing on either side of empire suggests the complexity of hermeneutics when nationalism comes into contact with empire. As the Bible became an increasingly pervasive literary presence in Korea, it also caught the attention of a Marxist literary critic and nationalist writer, Kim Namchŏn, who did not consider himself to be Christian.

In an essay titled "The Judas within and Literature," Kim finds inspiration in the disciple who betrayed Jesus:

> These are desperate times, and writers have been brought to the realization that they cannot do anything at all without first resolving the problem of the self. This may be the reason why the attempt to expose the Judas within and to grapple uncompromisingly with it as the first step in the process of creative practice becomes the moral [obligation] of the modern writer. The writer must insist on the path of self-perusal, self-negation, and self-criticism, struggling with the Judas within to the very end until a conclusion is reached, right or wrong. This is also the reason why literary self-accusation by writers of a petit-bourgeois background represents one of the directions the literature of accusation (*kobal munhak*) must adopt.[54]

Kim, interested in the Bible from a literary point of view, takes particular note of the lack of details regarding Judas' state of mind at Jesus' last supper with his disciples when the master makes a direct accusation of Judas' intent to betray him (John 13:21–30) and at the moments leading to Judas' suicide (Matt 27:3–5). Kim remarks: "To me, this death is no less valuable than the holy acts of the other disciples."[55] Kim found, in the figure of Judas, a welcome model of self-introspection fit for the times. Even under brutal suppression and censorship, Kim saw the possibility for literature as a way for political action to prevent complacency and inadvertent compliance under the oppressive policies of the Japanese Empire. The Bible provided literary opportunity for exposing the national subconscious while subverting the Empire. If outward and public expressions of nationalism would be met with suppression by way of censorship and persecution, Kim offers a literary critique of the Bible that compels continued self-introspection and internal reflection on the Korean nationalist consciousness—thereby keeping the nationalist sentiment alive. In Kim's literary critique, we see a unique intersection between the Bible (Christianity) and Korean nationalism. Rather than the Bible simply serving as a source of inspiration for Korean nationalist movements, it was the reawakened sense of Korean nationalism that inspired a unique Korean hermeneutic to critical interpretation of the Bible.

Conclusion

The Bible, whether in the hands of Korean Christian nationalists, Japanese Christians, or Marxist activists, yields utility. The Kingdom of God is a powerful tool for a people who find themselves suddenly stateless. Their sense of belonging and citizenship is redefined within the universal domain of the Kingdom of God. Such rhetoric has the potential to catalyze momentum for a struggle for independence as well as to stimulate hope for a future paradise. Simultaneously, the political motivations of appealing to the Kingdom of God for the sake of establishing important allies is not any less theologically motivated. Furthermore, the intersectionality between a sovereign, democratic Korea and the Kingdom of God was calculated by nationalist leaders as a means of evangelization in the region. However, this same rhetoric was adaptable to the expansionist agenda of the Japanese Empire. If Kim Namchŏn's essay offers a model, the Bible was a way of reflecting on and engaging with a hostile world. In the Korean nationalist struggle for independence, the Bible was an inspiration not only for the March First Movement but also for the nationalist struggle, becoming a hermeneutical lens to reflect on and engage with empire.

Notes

1. Michael Robison, "Ideological Schism in the Korean Nationalist Movement, 1920–1930: Cultural Nationalism and the Radical Critique," *Journal of Korean Studies* 4 (1982–1983): 241–268; Michael Edson Robinson, *Cultural Nationalism in Colonial Korea, 1920–1925* (Seattle and London: University of Washington Press, 1988); Jacqueline Pak, "The An Ch'angho Controversy: Gradualist-Pacifism, Cultural Nationalism, or Revolutionary-Democracy," *International Journal of Korean Studies* 6 (2002): 109–135; Jun-Hyeok Kwak, "Domination through Subordination: Yi Kwangsu's Collaboration in Colonial Korea," *Korea Observer* 39 (2008): 427–452.
2. K. M. Wells, "The Rationale of Korean Economic Nationalism under Japanese Colonial Rule, 1922–1932: The Case of Cho Man-sik's Products Promotion Society," *Modern Asian Studies* 19 (1985): 823–859; Albert L. Park, "A Vision of Modernity: The Gospel of Wealth and Protestantism in Early Modern Korea (1885–1919)," in *Korean Christianity in Korea-U.S. and Korea-Canada Relations*, ed. Sung Deuk Oak (Los Angeles: UCLA Center for Korean Studies, 2009), 5–22.
3. The role of women in the independence movement and the impact of the independence movement on feminist consciousness have been addressed in growing bodies of works. See "Address by Nodie Dora Kim at the First Korean Congress," in minutes of *The First Korean Congress Held in The Little Theatre 17th and Delancey Streets April 14, 15, 16* (Philadelphia: n.p., 1919), 17–18; Yung-hee Kim, "Under the Mandate of Nationalism: Development of Feminist Enterprises in Modern Korea, 1860–1910," *Journal of Women's History* 7 (1995): 120–136; Elain H. Kim and Chungmoo Choi, eds., *Dangerous Women: Gender and Korean Nationalism* (New York: Routledge, 1998); Mi-Soon Im, "Gender Empowerment and Korean Nationalism: A Case Study of the Influence of Single Female Missionaries of the Methodist Episcopal Church, South, during the Japanese Occupation, 1897–1920," in *Korean Christianity in Korea-U.S. and Korea-Canada Relations*, ed. Sung Deuk Oak (Los Angeles: UCLA Center for Korean Studies, 2009), 24–44; Donald N. Clark, "Mothers, Daughters, Biblewomen, and Sisters: An Account of 'Women's Work' in the Korea Mission Field," in *Christianity in Korea*, ed. Robert E. Buswell Jr. and Timothy S. Lee (Honolulu: University of Hawai'i Press, 2006), 167–192; Hyaeweol Choi, *New Women in Colonial Korea: A Sourcebook* (New York: Routledge, 2012); Jooyeon Rhee, "'No Country for the New Woman': Rethinking Gender and Cultural Nationalism in Colonial Korea through Kim Myŏngsun," *Acta Koreana* 17 (2014): 399–427.
4. See note 7 in Timothy S. Lee, "A Political Factor in the Rise of Protestantism in Korea: Protestantism and the March First Movement," *Church History* 69 (2000): 119.
5. *Chŏndogyo* is a syncretic form of Korean traditional religion with Catholicism that has its roots in the *Tonghak* movement of 1894–1895 (see also n. 8) and is closely associated with its founder, Ch'oe Che'u. See Grayson, *Korea—A Religious History*, 198–202; Cho Kyu-t'ae, *Chŏndogyo ui minjok undong yon'gu* (Seoul: Sŏnin, 2006).

6. See Carter J. Eckert et al., *Korea Old and New: A History* (Seoul: Ilchokak Publishers for the Korea Institute, Harvard University, 1990), 107-154.
7. See Chong-Sik Lee, *The Politics of Korean Nationalism* (Berkeley and Los Angeles: University of California Press, 1963), 19-33; Michael F. Robinson and Michael E. Robinson, "Nationalism and the Korean Tradition, 1896-1920: Iconoclasm, Reform, and National Identity," *Korean Studies* 10 (1986): 35-53; Eckert et al., *Korea Old and New*, 214-230; Andrew Schmid, *Korea between Empires, 1895-1919* (New York: Colombia University Press, 2002), 23-54.
8. The four-point manifesto of a leader in the *Tonghak* movement, Chŏng Pong-jun, summarizes the twofold goals of domestic reform and resistance against foreign forces: (1) Do not kill the [innocent] people; do not destroy [the people's] properties; (2) Fulfill the duties of loyalty [to the sovereign] and filial piety [to parents]; sustain the nation and provide for the people; (3) Drive out and eliminate the Japanese barbarians and thereby restore the Way of the [Confucian] Sages; and (4) Storm into the capital in force and thoroughly cleanse [the government of] the powerful families—so as to strengthen [Confucian] moral relationships, to rectify names and roles, and to realize the teachings of the Sages. Translated in Eckert et. al., *Korea Old and New*, 218.
9. While Japan was not a "Christian" empire, this did not preclude imperial strategies that utilized Christianity as a tool for empire-building. Japanese Christians of the *Kumiai Kyōkai* denomination were supported by the Government-General in Korea to provide a religious impulse for "converting" Korean Christians to becoming loyal subjects of the Japanese Empire. See Emily Anderson, *Christianity and Imperialism in Modern Japan: Empire for God*, SOAS Studies in Modern and Contemporary Japan (London and New York: Bloomsbury Academic, 2014), 1-62; Andre Schmid, "Colonialism and the 'Korea Problem' in the Historiography of Modern Japan: A Review Article," *Journal of Asian Studies* 59 (2000): 951-976.
10. Wi Jo Kang attributes the eventual breakdown of the *Chŏsun* isolationist policy in part to the persistence of Catholic missionaries to gain access to the "Hermit Kingdom." See Wi Jo Kang, *Christ and Caesar in Modern Korea: A History of Christianity and Politics*, SUNY Series in Korean Studies (Albany: State University of New York Press, 1997), 1-8.
11. James Huntley Grayson, "A Quarter-Millennium of Christianity in Korea," in *Christianity in Korea*, ed. Robert E. Buswell Jr. and Timothy S. Lee (Honolulu: University of Hawai'i Press, 2006), 11-12. See also Chai-Shin Yu, *The Founding of Catholic Tradition in Korea* (Fremont, CA: Asian Humanities Press, 2004); Charlotte Horlyck and Michael J. Pettid, *Death, Mourning, and the Afterlife in Korea: Ancient to Contemporary Times* (Honolulu: University of Hawai'i Press, 2014), 213-235.
12. James Huntley Grayson, *Korea—A Religious History*, rev. ed. (London: Routledge Curzon, 2002), 172-173.
13. Grayson, "A Quarter-Millennium of Christianity in Korea," 12; Sebastian C. H. Kim and Kirsteen Kim, *A History of Korean Christianity* (Cambridge: Cambridge University Press, 2015), 60-62; Don Baker, *Catholics and Anti-Catholicism in Chosŏn Korea* (Honolulu: University of Hawai'i Press, 2017).
14. Historiographies of the emergence of Protestantism and Protestant missionaries in Korea often include the story of Dr. Horace N. Allen. Allen arrived in Korea in 1884 as one of the first Protestant (Presbyterian) missionaries to establish residency in Korea. An attempted coup to force out the powerful Min family (backed by the queen) ended in the nephew of the queen, Min Yong-ik, being gravely injured. Despite the efforts of court doctors, the

queen's nephew remained in grave condition. Allen, however, was able to nurse him to recovery. This afforded Allen a place in the Korean court as well as gaining permission to open a hospital in Korea. Allen's favor with the Yi court opened the door for the arrival of other Protestant missionaries including Horace G. Underwood (Presbyterian) and Henry Appenzeller (Methodist) who would become pioneers of Western Protestant missionary endeavors in Korea.

15. The Nevius Method was developed by Dr. John L. Nevius who was part of the Northern Presbyterian Mission in China. This method was later adapted by other denominations, including the Methodist mission in Korea. John L. Nevius, *Methods for Mission Work* (New York: Foreign Mission Library, 1895). See also Charles Allen Clark, *The Nevius Plan for Mission Work in Korea* (Seoul: Christian Literature Society, 1937).
16. Yi Kwang-su, "Yesugyo ui Choson e chun Unhye," *Chungch'un* 9 (July 1917): 18. Translated by Tun Chi'i-ho in Park, "A Vision of Modernity," 7–8.
17. Lee, "Political Factor in the Rise of Protestantism in Korea," 123–138.
18. *First Korean Congress*, 31.
19. Letter from Arthur J. Brown to Masanao Hanihara, dated February 16, 1912, in the Presbyterian Library, New York.
20. "Let every person be subject to the governing authorities; for there is no authority except from God, and those authorities that exist have been instituted by God. Therefore whoever resists authority resists what God has appointed, and those who resist will incur judgment" (Romans 13:1–2, NRSV).
21. Albert L. Park argues that, while Japan did bring these developmental efforts to Korea, they were introduced in pursuit of Japanese imperial goals and certainly did not prioritize benefit to the local economy or people. In fact, Park argues that Japanese economic policies stood to take advantage of the resources in Korea for the primary benefit of the Japanese economy (rice production). In addition, Park observes that such developments in infrastructure and technologies in support of agricultural production were already developing in Korea before annexation. See Park, "Vision of Modernity," 5–22.
22. See Wi Jo Kang, "Church and State Relations in the Japanese Colonial Period," in *Christianity in Korea*, ed. Robert E. Buswell Jr. and Timothy S. Lee, 97–115 (Honolulu: University of Hawai'i Press, 2006).
23. See the letter sent by the Federal Council of Western missionaries in Korea to Saitō Makoto, who was appointed as governor-general following the nationalist uprising in Korea, in Federal Council of the Churches of Christ in America, *The Korean Situation: Authentic Accounts of Recent Events by Eye Witnesses* (New York: The Commission, 1919–1920), 9–12.
24. An example of such cautiousness is seen during the early years of Japanese occupation when there was an effective press blackout through strict suppression of publication. Most Korean publishers of newspapers were shut down in the first years after formal annexation with the exception of *Taehan Maeil Shinbo* (*Korea Daily News*), which included as one of its founders Ernest T. Bethell, a British citizen. *Taehan Maeil Shinbo* was allowed to continue publication under scrutiny of the imperial government until the death of Bethell. See Eckert et al., *Korea Old and New*, 246–247.
25. The *Korean Situation* includes statistical data on affected Christian villages and churches as well as the number of Korean Presbyterians who were arrested, beaten, or killed during the demonstrations (see *Korean Situation*, 4–5). Along with these statistics, there is an overriding tenor of cautiousness to condemn the violence without outright condemnation of

the Japanese Empire. In fact, after these statistics, the report follows with the assessment: "We have rejoiced in the many improvements brought about in Korea since that country came under the authority of the Japanese Government. We do not wish to condone any mistakes the Korean people may have made nor do we disregard the inherent difficulty always attached to such an administrative task as that in hand in Korea." *Korean Situation*, 6.

26. There was an influx of exchange students to Japan seeking educational opportunities, especially under restrictive and discriminatory educational policies in Korea. The compulsion to head to Japan for study was multifaceted and included proximity as well as restrictive opportunities to travel elsewhere under the colonial government. See Dongyoun Hwang, *Anarchism in Korea: Independence, Transnationalism, and the Question of National Development, 1919–1984* (Albany: State University of New York Press, 2016).

27. Anderson refers to a group of Korean political exiles in Shanghai who were able to seek asylum at the French Concession and thus avoided arrest. See Anderson, *Christianity and Imperialism in Modern Japan*, 162–168. See also Erik Esselstrom, *Crossing Empire's Edge: Foreign Ministry Police and Japanese Expansionism in Northeast Asia*, The World of East Asia (Honolulu: University of Hawai'i Press, 2009).

28. Part of the Declaration reads: "Independence for Korea today shall not only enable Koreans to lead a normal, prosperous life, as is their due; it will also guide Japan to leave its evil path and perform its great task of supporting the cause of the East, liberating China from a gnawing uneasiness and fear and helping the cause of world peace and happiness for mankind, which depends greatly on peace in the East. How can this be considered a trivial issue of mere sentiment?" See Yŏngho Ch'oe, Peter H. Lee, and William Theodore de Bary, eds., *Sources of Korean Tradition*, vol. 2 (New York: Columbia University Press, 2000), 338.

29. Among the religious ranks of the organizers of the March First Movement included those of a syncretic domestic religion called *Cheondogyo* as well as Buddhists.

30. *Korean Situation*, 3. See also n. 28.

31. Eckert et al., *Korea Old and New*, 279.

32. *Korean Situation* reports: "Though fired upon by the police, sabred, bayonetted, arrested, beaten, tortured, and punished by court judgments, the persistence of the movement has been phenomenal, and the slight amount of retaliation by the Koreans has been amazing." *Korean Situation*, 3.

33. Japanese records indicate upward of 1,000,000 participants in the ensuing demonstrations following March 1, 1919. See tables on the distribution of arrests across provinces, religious affiliation, education level, age, occupation in Lee, *Politics of Korean Nationalism*, 115–118.

34. Kang, "Church and State Relations in the Japanese Colonial Period," 100.

35. In his dissertation, Matsutani contends that the Protestant churches led by Western missionaries maintained an incompatible relationship with Korean Christian nationalists, which often compelled departure or resulted in dismissal from the church. See Motokazu Matsutani, "Church over Nation: Christian Missionaries and Korean Christians in Colonial Korea" (PhD diss., Harvard University, 2012).

36. Anderson, *Christianity and Imperialism in Modern Japan*, 158.

37. Translated in Anderson, *Christianity and Imperialism in Modern Japan*, 143.

38. Sung-gun Kim, "The Shinto Shrine Issue in Korean Christianity under Japanese Colonialism," *Journal of Church and State* 39 (1997): 503–521.

39. Kyŏng-ho Chŏng, "Kyohoewa sahoewa minjokŭl sŏmkin taeku kyŏngpukŭi kŏin Yi Man-jip moksa" in *YMCA inmul k'onsŏt'ŭ: Y-wa sahoerŭl ilkun salamdŭl* (Seoul: Han'guk Kidokkyo Yŏksa Yŏn'guso, 2014), 69.

40. Lee, "A Political Factor in the Rise of Protestantism in Korea," 118.
41. Hyung-chan Kim, *Tosan Ahn Ch'ang-ho: A Profile of a Prophetic Patriot* (Los Angeles: Academia Koreana, Keimyung-Baylo University, 1996); Jacqueline Pak, "Cradle of the Covenant," in *Christianity in Korea*, ed. Robert E. Buswell Jr. and Timothy S. Lee, 116–148. (Honolulu: University of Hawai'i Press, 2006).
42. "All things came into being through him, and without him not only things came into being" (John 1:3, NRSV).
43. An Ch'ang-ho, *Na ŭi sarang hanŭn chŏlmŭnidŭl ege* (Seoul: Chisŏng Munhwasa, 1987), 46–47.
44. Kil Sŏn-ju (comp. Han'guk Kodŭng Sinhak Yŏn'guwŏn), *Kil Sŏn-ju: Han'guk Kidokkyo chidoja kangdan* sŏlgyo (Seoul: Hongsŏngsa, 2008), 32.
45. His firstborn son died in the spring of 1918 and he received news of the arrest (and subsequent torture) of his second son while he was under arrest. Kil Chin-gyŏng, *Kil Sŏn-ju: puhŭng ŭi saebyŏk ŭl yŏlta* (Seoul: Turanno Sŏwŏn, 2007), 191–213.
46. Chong Bum Kim, "Preaching the Apocalypse in Colonial Korea: The Protestant Millennialism of Kil Sŏn-ju," in *Christianity in Korea*, ed. Robert E. Buswell Jr. and Timothy S. Lee, 152 (Honolulu: University of Hawai'i Press, 2006).
47. For discussion on Kil's delineation of a three-tier apocalyptic world after the last judgment of a heavenly paradise, earthly paradise, and hell, see Kim, "Preaching the Apocalypse in Colonial Korea," 154–157; Hŏ ho-ik, *Kil Sŏn-ju Moksa ŭi mokhoe wa sinhak sasang* (Seoul: Taehan Kidokkyo Sŏhoe, 2009), 341–351.
48. *First Korean Congress*, 29–30.
49. "First you must right the wrong you have done to Korea. Give her absolute freedom, keep your hands from the politics of the peninsula. You will find that Korea will develop into a peaceful, democratic and industrial nation, which will be absolutely neutral in her foreign policies, will be a buffer between your country, China and Russia. The interest of your country requires a friendly buffer state in this region instead of a territory inhabited by sullen, resentful people in whose hearts hatred for you and your government will always exist as long as you try to govern them by force, cruelty and injustice." *First Korean Congress*, 46.
50. *First Korean Congress*, 49.
51. Takashi Suzuki, "The Emergency in Chosen," *Missionary Review of the World* 42 (1919): 661.
52. Suzuki, "Emergency in Chosen," 663. Emphasis in original.
53. The compatibility between Christianity and the Empire was a debated issue amongst Japanese Christians. See discussion in Anderson, *Christianity and Imperialism in Modern Japan*, 5–25, 123–158.
54. Translated in Youngju Rhu, "Kim Namchŏn," in *Imperatives of Culture: Selected Essays on Korean History, Literature, and Society from the Japanese Colonial Era*, ed. Christopher P. Hanscom, Walter K. Lew, and Youngju Ryu, 191 (Honolulu: University Hawai'i Press, 2013).
55. Rhu, "Kim Namchŏn," 189.

Bibliography

An, Ch'ang-ho. *Na ŭi sarang hanŭn chŏlmŭnidŭl ege*. Seoul: Chisŏng Munhwasa, 1987.
Anderson, Emily. *Christianity and Imperialism in Modern Japan: Empire for God*. SOAS Studies in Modern and Contemporary Japan. London and New York: Bloomsbury Academic, 2014.
Baker, Don. *Catholics and Anti-Catholicism in Chosŏn Korea*. Honolulu: University of Hawai'i Press, 2017.

Buswell, Robert E., Jr., and Timothy S. Lee. Eds. *Christianity in Korea*. Honolulu: University of Hawai'i Press, 2006.

Cho, Kyu-t'ae. *Chŏndogyo ŭi minjok undong yŏn'gu*. Seoul: Sŏnin, 2006.

Ch'oe, Yŏngho, Peter H. Lee, and William Theodore de Bary. Eds. *Sources of Korean Tradition*. Vol. 2. New York: Columbia University Press, 2000.

Choi, Hyaeweol. *New Women in Colonial Korea: A Sourcebook*. New York: Routledge, 2012.

Clark, Charles Allen. *The Nevius Plan for Mission Work in Korea*. Seoul: Christian Literature Society, 1937.

Eckert, Carter J., et al. *Korea Old and New: A History*. Seoul: Ilchokak Publishers for the Korea Institute, Harvard University, 1990.

Esselstrom, Erik. *Crossing Empire's Edge: Foreign Ministry Police and Japanese Expansionism in Northeast Asia*. The World of East Asia. Honolulu: University of Hawai'i Press, 2009.

Federal Council of the Churches of Christ in America. *The Korean Situation: Authentic Accounts of Recent Events by Eye Witnesses*. New York: The Commission, 1919–1920.

Grayson, James Hutley. *Korea—A Religious History*. Rev. ed. London: Routledge Curzon, 2002.

Hanscom, Christopher P., Walter K. Lew, and Youngju Ryu. Eds. *Imperatives of Culture: Selected Essays on Korean History, Literature, and Society from the Japanese Colonial Era*. Honolulu: University Hawai'i Press, 2013.

Hŏ, Ho-ik. *Kil Sŏn-ju Moksa ŭi mokhoe wa sinhak sasang*. Seoul: Taehan Kidokkyo Sŏhoe, 2009.

Horlyck, Charlotte, and Michael J. Pettid. *Death, Mourning, and the Afterlife in Korea: Ancient to Contemporary Times*. Honolulu: University of Hawai'i Press, 2014.

Hwang, Dongyoun. *Anarchism in Korea: Independence, Transnationalism, and the Question of National Development, 1919–1984*. Albany: State University of New York Press, 2016.

Kang, Wi Jo. *Christ and Caesar in Modern Korea: A History of Christianity and Politics*. SUNY Series in Korean Studies. Albany: State University of New York Press, 1997.

Kil, Chin-gyŏng. *Kil Sŏn-ju: puhŭng ŭi saebyŏk ŭl yŏlta*. Seoul: Turanno Sŏwŏn, 2007.

Kil, Sŏn-ju. Comp. Han'guk Kodŭng Sinhak Yŏn'guwŏn. *Kil Sŏn-ju: Han'guk Kidokkyo chidoja kangdan sŏlgyo*. Seoul: Hongsŏngsa, 2008.

Kim, Elain H., and Chungmoo Choi. Eds. *Dangerous Women: Gender and Korean Nationalism*. New York: Routledge, 1998.

Kim, Hyung-chan. *Tosan Ahn Ch'ang-ho: A Profile of a Prophetic Patriot*. Los Angeles: Academia Koreana, Keimyung-Baylo University, 1996.

Kim, Sebastian C. H., and Kirsteen Kim. *A History of Korean Christianity*. Cambridge: Cambridge University Press, 2015.

Kim, Sung-gun. "The Shinto Shrine Issue in Korean Christianity under Japanese Colonialism." *Journal of Church and State* 39 (1997): 503–521.

Kim, Yung-hee. "Under the Mandate of Nationalism: Development of Feminist Enterprises in Modern Korea, 1860–1910." *Journal of Women's History* 7 (1995): 120–136.

Korean Congress. *The First Korean Congress Held in the Little Theatre 17th and Delancey Streets April 14, 15, 16*. Philadelphia: n.p., 1919.

Kwak, Jun-Hyeok. "Domination through Subordination: Yi Kwangsu's Collaboration in Colonial Korea." *Korea Observer* 39 (2008): 427–452.

Lee, Chong-Sik. *The Politics of Korean Nationalism*. Berkeley and Los Angeles: University of California Press, 1963.

Lee, Timothy S. "A Political Factor in the Rise of Protestantism in Korea: Protestantism and the 1919 March First Movement." *Church History* 69 (2000): 116–142.

Matsutani, Motokazu. "Church over Nation: Christian Missionaries and Korean Christians in Colonial Korea." PhD diss., Harvard University, 2012.

Nevius, John L. *Methods for Mission Work*. New York: Foreign Mission Library, 1895.

Oak, Sung Deuk. Ed. *Korean Christianity in Korea-U.S. and Korea-Canada Relations*. Los Angeles: UCLA Center for Korean Studies, 2009.

Pak, Jacqueline. "The An Ch'angho Controversy: Gradualism-Pacifism, Cultural Nationalism, or Revolutionary-Democracy." *International Journal of Korean Studies* 6 (2002): 109–135.

Rhee, Jooyeon. "'No Country for the New Woman': Rethinking Gender and Cultural Nationalism in Colonial Korea through Kim Myŏngsun." *Acta Koreana* 17 (2014): 399–427.

Robison, Michael. "Ideological Schism in the Korean Nationalist Movement, 1920–1930: Cultural Nationalism and the Radical Critique." *Journal of Korean Studies* 4 (1982–1983): 241–268.

Robinson, Michael Edison. *Cultural Nationalism in Colonial Korea, 1920–1925*. Seattle and London: University of Washington Press, 1988.

Robinson, Michael F., and Michael E. Robinson. "Nationalism and the Korean Tradition, 1896–1920: Iconoclasm, Reform, and National Identity." *Korean Studies* 10 (1986): 35–53.

Schmid, Andrew. "Colonialism and the 'Korea Problem' in the Historiography of Modern Japan: A Review Article." *Journal of Asian Studies* 59 (2000): 951–976.

Schmid, Andrew. *Korea Between Empires, 1895–1919*. New York: Columbia University Press, 2002.

Suzuki, Takashi. "The Emergency in Chosen." *Missionary Review of the World* 42 (1919): 661–663.

Wells, K. M. "The Rationale of Korean Economic Nationalism under Japanese Colonial Rule, 1922–1932: The Case of Cho Man-sik's Products Promotion Society." *Modern Asian Studies* 19 (1985): 823–859.

Yu, Chai-Shin. *The Founding of Catholic Tradition in Korea*. Fremont: Asian Humanities Press, 2004.

Yun, Kyŏng-no. *YMCA inmul k'onsŏt'ŭ: Y-wa sahoerŭl ilkun salamdŭl*. Seoul: Han'guk Kidokkyo Yŏksa Yŏn'guso, 2014.

PART III
EMPIRES AND TRANSLATIONS

CHAPTER 19

COMPETING NARRATIVES ON BIBLE TRANSLATION IN INDIA

Missionary Linguistics, Postcolonial Criticism, and Translation Studies

HEPHZIBAH ISRAEL

INTRODUCTION

Despite its long history of dissemination through translation, Bible translation has not typically been considered a form of biblical criticism in India or elsewhere. The act of translation, however, is primarily an act of interpretation. The kind of close textual analysis that is traditionally assigned to biblical hermeneutics applies in equal degree to the process of Bible translation. Yet, translation as an interpretative act that offers only *one* out of a range of potential "meanings" or interpretations is mostly viewed in narrow terms of linguistic choice rather than as a significant hermeneutical strategy that has considerable and wide-ranging ideological implications. The primary scholarly focus on the selection of terminology in Bible translation disempowers translation's potential in consolidating or challenging dominant ideological structures. All translation projects, including that of Bible translation, participate in a network of interpretative choice and effect, which when examined carefully indicate the work of translation as a key interpretative framework much as biblical criticism. This chapter focuses on Bible translation in India and how this history, as far as it is possible to reconstruct it, may be seen to intersect with colonial and postcolonial interests. It is important to state this at the outset because this history in relation to Indian-language Bibles has so far been commissioned by the Bible Society[1] or written from the perspective of mission studies, which has by and large ignored developments in translation studies or postcolonial studies. This chapter therefore engages with Bible translation from these alternative critical perspectives apart from evaluating a few key approaches in current studies of Bible translation.

But before engaging with some of the critical themes and issues that emerge from the history of Bible translation in Indian languages, it would be valuable to examine how translation and postcolonial studies intersect, and more specifically, to ask what a distinctly postcolonial translation studies perspective brings to this handbook's focus on postcolonial biblical criticism. It is apposite at this point to clarify that the use of the category "postcolonial" in this chapter refers to the entire period from the first occasion of cultural contact with European traders and colonizers until after the political independence of India from the British. This both avoids reference to political independence as a sharp and artificial break from a colonial past, dividing preindependent from postindependent history, while also acknowledging that resistance to colonialism was part of the fabric of colonial experience right from the start and not just a movement that gained momentum in the lead-up to the Indian nationalist struggle for independence.

Postcolonial Translation Studies and the Study of Religion

Translation studies has a relatively short history as an academic discipline (from the early 1970s) and coincides more or less with the emergence in the 1970s of a critical intervention from literary scholars that eventually came to be known as Postcolonial Studies. The 1990s saw a few key studies that drew attention to the converging scholarly concerns of translation and postcolonial studies.[2] These scholarly engagements, focusing mainly on literary translation, highlighted that, far from being a neutral act of transfer across languages, translation is a political act with both immediate and long-term repercussions. They remind us that while translation served imperial interests in colonizing more effectively, it was equally available as a tool of resistance to challenge colonial rule and lead to various forms of decolonization. One important concern that these scholars share, and pertinent to the focus of this chapter, is that of the unequal relations of power such that the supposed hierarchy between an "original" and its "translation" in Western intellectual history has been compared to the hierarchy assumed between the superior colonizing "West" and the lesser colonized "non-West": the colony was imagined for all intents and purposes as an inferior copy much as a translation is taken to be. A second point that these scholars make is with regards to the hierarchy of languages and the effects this has on translation projects and their reception among audiences. The direction of translation, whether from a perceived "higher" language to a "less developed" one, or the other way round, directly impacts the translation choices adopted, which then inevitably influence the way the translation is received or experienced in a colonial context. Often, underlying Eurocentric assumptions or purposes have been shown to be at work through translation, subtly promoting the viewpoint of one culture as superior to others. The decision to translate or to leave words or parts of the text untranslated were strategic choices to promote one point of view over others. The choice of translation strategies and decisions are thus considered either to have perpetrated "violence" of one kind or another (ethnic, cultural, religious) on the colonized or used to challenge colonial authority, providing a powerful impetus to challenge colonial rule and assist in various forms of "decolonization."

The majority of postcolonial translation scholarship has however not engaged fully with religion or religious identities, texts, or practices within colonial contexts. The aspect of religion *in translation* has more recently been attracting attention from scholars in other disciplines, such as religious studies, anthropology of religion, and translation studies. These scholars are particularly interested in the role of translation in the construction *of* religion as a category in colonial encounters, in the production of knowledge *about* religions within the colonial context, and the effects of these *on* religious identities. There is, for instance, a growing body of work focusing on Jesuit translations in East Asia, South Asia, and South America and the effects of their linguistic conversion on the languages and communities of the peoples encountered. One of the earliest was Vicente Rafael's study of Jesuit translation projects in Tagalog societies during the sixteenth century in the Philippines.[3] Rafael argued that translation was a conceptual tool in the hands of the Spanish Jesuits with which they did not just "convey" the Christian message to the Tagalog but sought to mold their self-conceptualization as *Catholic* Tagalogs. By not translating key terms into Tagalog, the Jesuits attempted to control the meaning and use of Catholic terminology but by the same token opened these up to some radical appropriations by the Tagalogs. The outstanding study by linguistic anthropologist William Hanks on Jesuit translation among the Maya of Yucatán in Mesoamerica argues that although this has been presented as a peaceful conquest, the forms of linguistic translation that were undertaken "were actually forms of *reducción* in the strong sense of systematically re-forming their object."[4] Hanks states that translation served, for all intents and purposes, as a process of *reducción*, convincing and putting to better order three key aspects of Mayan life: a reordering of their towns, their conduct, and their language. In Hanks's view, translation was the framework within which the social, religious, and political institutions of the Maya were reordered to agree with Spanish and Catholic systems of organizing civil society:

> [T]he tie to language runs deeper still, since the indigenous languages were the objects, and not only the instruments, of *reducción*. The missionaries sought to *reducir* the Indian languages, including Yucatec Maya, by describing them in terms of rules and patterns. The result of this kind of *reducción* is a grammar, or a set of rules that specify the structure and regularity of the language. In the overall project, town layout, regional governance, civility of conduct, grammar, and proper speech are of a single cloth.[5]

Jesuit translations served to reform and reorder Yucatec Maya from a language referring to "false words of idolatry and superstition" into "build[ing] cathedrals of meaning around their triune god."[6] In a similar study of Jesuit translations in India, Zupanov's examination of Jesuits in South India points to their use of translation as a mode by which Christian concepts could be presented in "pagan" languages such as Tamil in a transparent and simplistic manner to control language for Jesuit purposes.[7] Zupanov argues that, for instance, Henriquez's sixteenth-century *Arte Malabar* was

> a Christian missionary grammar since the choice of its interior linguistic apparatus is geared to keeping the conversion machine going. It comes as no surprise then that the verb employed to demonstrate the conjugation paradigm ... in Tamil was vicuvadi, to believe. On more than thirty sheets, this verb spreads faith in all its forms—participles, verbal nouns, imperatives, conditionals, and so on. Sentence examples in Tamil and Portuguese translation cover almost all that can be said and done with the word *to believe* in two languages and often in two scripts.[8]

Studying a range of sixteenth- and seventeenth-century interlinear translations of key Catholic texts—the catechism, creed, prayers, and missionary grammars—Zupanov contends that translation in practice proved a disorderly instrument that altered both Tamil and Portuguese. In a further study of what Xavier and Zupanov term "Catholic Orientalism," they point to the collusion between Portuguese colonial and missionary interests: "The process of 'grammaticalization' of Indian languages—on the basis of Portuguese and Latin grammatical rules—which inaugurated translation of Christian doctrine and extraction of useful information was far from an innocent intervention."[9] But, they argue, these "translation instruments" of imperial agents worked both ways, on the one hand allowing the ordering, classification, and objectification of Indian languages to facilitate Portuguese imperial interests but also offering Indians ways to redefine and express new idioms and metaphors.

Apart from scholarship on Jesuit translation projects, other scholars have examined the role of sacred text translation in the trajectories of other religious traditions active in India. These include studies of translations undertaken by both European and Indian translators and the effects these have had on religious scriptures, communities, and identities. Mandair points to a philosophy of "generalized translation" that emerged as a key conceptual matrix in the colonial encounter between South Asia and the West.[10] Critically engaging with postcolonial theory and political theology, Mandair demonstrates how this philosophy of translation constructed a specific formulation of Sikh tradition and identity in colonial South Asia that continues to have repercussions for the religious identity of the Sikh community in South Asia and in the diaspora. Herling's study of Herder and Friedrich Schlegel's translations of the Bhagavadgita into Latin points to translation strategies that presented it as a classical text that offered a powerful Romantic synthesis between continental philosophy and Indian religion and culture.[11] In his view, by refraining from nonphilological commentary, Schlegel in his full Latin translation of 1823

> resists the temptation to impose some cultural or philosophical agenda on his rendering. This move reveals that a new interpretive structure is at work in the examination of Indian sources: that of philological science. The hermeneutical issues, the interpretive questions that prompted response and further inquiry within this

discursive community, were concentrated within the language itself; they resided within the translator's choices, and these become the more technical sites of inquiry that anchored the practice of interpretation in the era of Indology.[12]

Herling makes an important observation about the ideological function of philology here, a point to which I will return to in the context of scholarly discussions of Bible translation later in this chapter. Although these were translations in the opposite direction, from Indian to European cultural contexts, Herling's study of German Indological engagements and translations complements the numerous other translation projects undertaken by the English, French, and Portuguese in India, which related to several other religions observed in the subcontinent. Numark, for instance, argues that Scottish missionary translations of Hindu, Zoroastrian, Jain, and Buddhist sacred texts and inscriptions led to an increasingly comparative approach to the study of religions in India, among which Christianity by then featured prominently.[13]

Why offer this whistle-stop tour of colonial translations of a range of sacred texts[14] in a chapter on Bible translation and postcolonial criticism? First, while postcolonial criticism may not have sufficiently engaged with religion, its critical interventions offer valuable lines of inquiry with which to approach translations of sacred texts in colonial contexts as part of a larger history of postcolonial translation and transmission. Second, posing questions drawn from the different strands of postcolonial criticism, including postcolonial translation, opens up the study of the Bible in India to its translation history as embedded within a wider cultural context of translation, where translation decisions taken to present the Bible in Indian languages were directly influenced by nonbiblical translation activities that were taking place simultaneously in other religious and cultural contexts. This therefore allows us to see the Bible's material and cultural presence as a sacred text in interaction with many other sacred and nonsacred texts in the subcontinent and in the context of the number of different ways communities have interacted with it. Such studies of the translated Bible as imbricated in wider social, political, and cultural contexts have rarely been undertaken; instead, Bible translation in South Asia, historic or current, is mostly examined as distinct from all other literary writing and translation activity that is carried on in parallel. In the following section, I briefly discuss three strands of scholarly debates where such a wider focus can be seen to offer valuable interventions in the current scholarly approaches to the study of Bible translation in India.

Three Approaches to the Study of Bible Translation and Three Areas of Intervention

There is a longstanding difference in critical perspective on the study of Bible translation between the philological approach, mainly exemplified in the work of scholarship that has more recently come to be known as "missionary linguistics," and the more discursive, postcolonial approaches, among which also fall scholars who more recently self-identify with an alternative approach they term "colonial linguistics." The main scholarly aims of missionary linguistics is to retrieve and recuperate the extensive labor of missionaries in writing, translating, and preparing grammars and dictionaries by comparing Latin and one of the European vernaculars such as Spanish, English, German, or French with a non-European language. They acknowledge imperial ideology and colonialism but treat these as a composite and somewhat neutral backdrop against which missionary translations and linguistic activities take place. This means that they do not engage critically with the extent to which missionary linguist-translators may have been influenced by the historical and political contexts within which they were working. As Stolz and Warnke point out, "ML [Missionary Linguistics] is largely a 'monodisciplinary' project which aims at determining the impact the linguistic work of missionaries has had on the development of linguistics in general."[15] By continuing in the vein of missionary scholars, that is, by only digging deep into languages to compare linguistic structures, grammars and vocabulary at the expense of wider political contexts that shape language use as well as its study, scholars of missionary linguistics can be said to perpetuate a critical perspective that constructs linguistic histories without reference to issues of power, whether material, economic, or ideological. By not acknowledging that the logic of colonialism ideologically informed linguistic treatment and by isolating linguistic work from wider cultural networks, scholars of missionary linguistics ignore the relations of power that affect how languages mutate in relation to each other and how such an academic study of languages can effectively maintain imbalances in power long after political control by European empires have ceased. One of the effects of the current limited focus of missionary linguistics is that it constructs the European missionary linguist, with the Bible in one hand and the Latin grammar in the other, as the sole "expert" who brings order and organization to the disorderly, unsystematic, and intuitive "users" of non-European languages.

Further, scholars of missionary linguistics study linguistic activity in erstwhile colonies as if missionaries were the sole scholars studying languages systematically. But a careful consideration of the social history of linguistic work reveals the situation to be otherwise: first, there were many other European scholars and linguists besides missionaries—colonial administrators, civil servants, sailors, merchants, and travelers—although the latter may have dominated language study in specific periods; and second, Europeans almost never worked on their own but always in conjunction with local scholars. Many, such as James[16] or Jeyaraj,[17] discussing missionary study of Tamil and Bible translation, show little interest in perspectives from local non-Christian scholars or users of the translated Bibles, both Christian and non-Christian. If local language scholars are mentioned at all, it is usually in passing and without equal consideration of their works or critical perspectives *along with* that of missionary scholars.

This unidirectional focus is challenged by scholars of colonial linguistics, who call for a bidirectional study of languages to take into account that missionary linguistics was heavily influenced by a range of colonial discourses that were operating within the same space and time. Colonial linguistics "counts among its tasks (ideally) the entire range of phenomenon which interconnect language and colonialism, most of which are irrelevant for the goals of ML. Colonialism in CL [colonial linguistics] therefore is no background phenomenon for an interest in languages but a precondition for linguistic constellations, from language contact through to language politics and finally language analysis and documentation."[18] Colonial linguists are interested, for instance, in the phenomenon that Latin invariably served as the main reference point against which all non-European languages were compared, resulting in the presentation of a "lack" in the latter in terms of vocabulary, grammar, or orthography. They point out that this perceived lack was then used to confirm the assumed inferiority of the language community. By the same token, a further challenge is posed to missionary linguistics if nonlinguistic factors influencing languages and the social uses of languages are taken into account. Just as languages never develop in isolation, the systematic study of languages is never undertaken without reference to the social and ideological imperatives that shape language use. Some recent scholars such as Muru do suggest that it would be valuable for future studies to consider the perspectives of Tamil language users and what they thought of missionary linguistic activities but she does not herself undertake this in her article.[19]

A second difference in critical perspective centers on whether or not Bible translation projects are viewed as implicated in colonial history and as influenced by imperial trading interests and colonial conquest. There are three main scholars who have argued against viewing Bible translation as linked to colonial contexts: Brian Stanley (1990) in the *Bible and the Flag*, Lamin Sanneh ([1989] 2009) in *Translating the Message*, and William Smalley (1991) in *Translation as Mission*. The three scholars focus on Protestant Bible translation projects undertaken by missionaries in Africa and Asia. Stanley critiques the argument that British missionaries were agents of European colonialism and argues instead that rather than commercial gain, it was the Christian revivals of eighteenth- and nineteenth-century Britain that fueled British missionary interest in Asia. While the focus of his book is not Bible translation alone, this argument reinforces the scholarly treatment of Bible translation as distinct from colonial interests and discourses. Smalley argues that Bible translations undertaken by missionaries put "local languages and the relevant parts of local culture ... on a par with the missionary language and culture,"[20] which presumes that all non-European languages were inferior to European languages and needed to be "made" equal through Bible translation. Such an interpretation is problematic from a postcolonial perspective. Lamin Sanneh, theologian and World Christianity scholar with a special interest in West African Christianity, has dominated the debate on African Christianity, Bible translation, and colonialism.[21] Although he too offers a positive account of Bible translation as one that renewed indigenous African languages and cultures, his arguments contest the standpoint of Stanley and Smalley in important ways. On the one hand, the position he sets out in his introduction is not that different: "Persisting through all this material is the idea that specific Christian translation projects have helped to create an overarching series of cultural experiences, with hitherto obscure and marginal cultural systems being drawn into the general stream of universal history."[22] Sanneh's reading of the history of biblical translations and the interactions of Christian cultures outside the Western world is one where non-Christian religious cultures enter into a Christian "stream of universal history" without coercion, conflict, or resistance. Although this may seem like wishful thinking on his part, Sanneh is also strongly critical of those European missionaries with short-sighted and paternalistic attitudes, who were often undone in his view by their own inability to set aside cultural superiority. He argues that the power and cultural chauvinism of missionaries and of Western Christianity were dismantled by Christianity's inherent "force of translatability," which challenged the missionary enterprise:

> Translation creates a pluralistic environment of incredible variety and possibility, and invests culture with an ethical and qualitative power. That power may be defined as the capacity to participate in intercultural and interpersonal exchange, as the recognition that whatever and however we are doing now, we can do differently and, under certain circumstances, we must do differently in order to live ethically as neighbours.... Christianity promotes two sorts of universal appeal in its mission: the universal truth of one God is represented by the ethics of commitment to local specificity.[23]

Sanneh is convinced that the "vernacular translation" of the missionaries "overshadowed colonial assumption and presumptions" and "outdistanced and outlasted the forces of ephemeral colonial rule."[24] Sanneh's theological interpretation of the politics of Bible translation as an intrinsically egalitarian process has been welcomed by many Christian theologians for reorienting critical attention on the peoples and languages of Christianity in the Global South. However, his wholehearted celebration of translation in the "African vernaculars" is also based on an acceptance of the claim (unethical, some might say) that these cultures and languages were inherently inferior in the first place, needing "religious renewal and indigenous revitalisation."[25] By arguing that the "vernacular Bible was the divine imprimatur on otherwise inferior cultures,"[26] Sanneh offers a theological solution to redress the perceived inequality and inferiority of African languages, apparently stimulated and renewed by the superior power of Christianity: "There is radical pluralism associated with vernacular translation wherein all languages and cultures are in principle equal in expressing the word of God."[27] However, Sanneh does not at any point challenge the cultural representation of African languages as inferior in the first place. Despite his strong reservations, Sanneh draws a picture of (missionary) translators undone by (Bible) translation while all the time preserving the message of God intact because his *Christian* ethics dictate that biblical meaning is transferred faithfully and independently of colonial inequalities. He also relies uncritically on definitions of translation he inherits from Western philosophical traditions and biblical translation that emphasize equivalence and faithfulness in translation,[28] a notion that is not central to conceptions of translation in other parts of the world. Thus, his celebratory view of Bible translation's rejuvenating effects in Christianity's history in the Global South remains fragmented by contradictions.

It is left to other African theologians to offer a more challenging view to Sanneh's. Kwame Bediako, a Ghanian theologian, taking his cue from Sanneh, argues for the increasing need for a "mother-tongue theology" to ensure translation is not based on simple "word equivalents" as opposed to "theology" shaped by "Western Christian history and experience" that rejects Ghanian idioms and images as inappropriate.[29] Kinyua argues that "Bible translation in colonial Africa, though in most cases defended as a neutral, legitimate, and benevolent act of redemption, disguises the colonial power situation."[30] He examines the extent to which Bible translation, leading to the standardization of languages such as Gĩkũyũ, "was a hegemonic process that facilitated the domestication as well as homogenization of the idiom through the predetermined process of cooption and expansion of the linguistic tools. Since the Africans were not consulted or involved in the decision-making process it was also an obvious act of imposition."[31] Bringing to attention the work of parallel African translators, whose work was not accepted by the Bible Society, he also argues that "translation was not immune to the ambivalence and contradictions of the discourse of colonialism. Like any other colonial discourse, Bible translation betrays instability. By choosing to translate the Bible into the vernacular languages, the colonial church flung wide open the interrogatory interstices where biblical texts, hermeneutics, doctrines, culture, and power could be negotiated, contested, and hybridized."[32] For Kinyua, like Rafael, the instability of languages and their resistance to translation's reordering of semantics meant that the African Christian could be read as an active translator rather than a passive recipient (perhaps even, victim) of translation, leading to translation becoming "a performative act of decolonization."[33] Similarly, writing largely on the Asian context, theologian R. S. Sugirtharajah has consistently offered postcolonial critiques of missionary handling of the Bible in colonial encounters.[34] He has revitalized theological debates by recovering marginalized narratives of biblical interpretation and alternative theological forays by Indians and by analyzing them from postcolonial perspectives. Although he does not discuss biblical translation, his argument regarding biblical criticism can as easily be applied to Bible translation.

The third critical difference pertains particularly to the scholarship on Bible translation in India. For too long the study of Bible translation and biblical criticism in India has been conducted as an isolated, self-contained, and self-defensive object of study. Either the translation history of the Bible in individual languages has been studied independently or, if any comparative study is undertaken, it is with reference to Bible translation in "neighboring" Indian languages or English translations. In the case of discussions of Christian terminology, and there are plentiful examples of this, most studies focus on whether a particular term was accepted or rejected on the grounds of being a perceived "Hindu" soteriological term. This usually plays out as a rather limited "inculturation" or "interfaith dialogue" argument that I will elaborate on further in the next section. Little effort is made to locate the history of Bible translation in India as part of a larger history of textual transmission and translation involving numerous other sacred texts and literary traditions. As some of the scholarship cited in this chapter shows, translations of other sacred and nonsacred texts directly or indirectly impacted Bible translation throughout the postcolonial period, from the earliest contact to the postindependent present. Moreover, any serious study of Bible translation should also situate it within the long history of sacred text translation[35] traditions of South Asia that predated European contact. Not taking into account these two intersecting vectors circumscribes the critical lenses with which one views the specifics of Bible translation, resulting in a partial engagement with translation history in India. Moreover, there is no effort to engage with translation studies as a discipline that directly relates to this field of inquiry despite historic connections between translation studies and Bible translation.[36] The consequence of such a blinkered approach is that the scholarship on Bible translation in India remains detached from other literary and cultural studies, apparently representing the "minority" scholarly interests of a "minority" religious community. While there are a few exceptions to this, and I will elaborate on these further in the following section, much of the treatment of Bible translation, whether by Anglo-American historians of mission or by Indian theologians, tends to incorporate its history within conventional Christian apologetics, which limits the potential of this field of study.

THE STUDY OF BIBLE TRANSLATION IN INDIA

Much of the scholarly study of Bible translation, limited as it is, focuses mainly on the nineteenth century with disproportionate attention paid to the Serampore Baptist missionaries in Bengal and later the British and Foreign Bible Society (hereafter BFBS) that followed soon after. This, accompanied by the assumption that the Baptists' printing press at Serampore inaugurated the birth of print technology in India, has helped to convey the mistaken notion that the history of the Bible and Bible translation in India only started in nineteenth-century Bengal. Neither are factually correct. The Bible is believed to have existed in the Syriac in the western state of Kerala in South India since the second century CE with at least one extant version that dates between the ninth and twelfth centuries CE.[37] The earliest known translation of the Bible in India was undertaken at Agra in the Mughal courts at the invitation of the emperor Akbar (r. 1556–1605), who ordered a Persian version to be prepared to satisfy his interest in Christianity. The Jesuit, Jerome Xavier, and Akbar's courtier Abd al-Sattar together prepared a translation under the title *Mirat al-Quds* or the "Mirror of Holiness," which combined events from the four New Testament Gospels with a biography of Jesus' life. Presented first to Akbar in 1602 as a "Life of Christ" and later to his son Jehangir (r. 1605–1627), this was a collaborative Persian translation arrived at from a combination of "source texts"—the Latin Vulgate, Greek, Syriac, and Arabic translations—that were available to them in India at the time. Whatever its limitations,[38] the existence of this Jesuit version demonstrates that this early version of the Bible extant in India was supported by royal invitation and patronage and available to an elite audience at least two hundred years before the Baptists started operating the printing press at Serampore. It is also important at this point to take into account that the New Testament was only one among a range of sacred texts translated into Persian in the imperial translation bureaus of Akbar and Jehangir. Besides the New Testament, the *Ramayana* and the *Mahabharata*, for instance, were also translated into Persian under Mughal patronage. Whatever proselytizing intentions the Jesuit Xavier may have had, the Mughal interest in supporting the translation of sacred texts, including the New Testament, indicates, as Alam and Subrahmanyam[39] and Truschke[40] argue, not just a desire to synthesize the best from all religions into the "universal" religion *din-i-ilahi* (as is represented in popular historiography) but also to participate in imperial image-making where the Moghuls wished to project themselves as sophisticated and well-versed in a range of philosophical and religious disputations.

Jesuit translations of parts of the Bible in Goa on the western coast and in Tamilnadu on the eastern coast through the sixteenth and seventeenth centuries have been well documented.[41] There is evidence that the Catholic translation of the catechism *Doctrina Christam* in Tamil was first printed in Quilon in South India in 1578. A few Dutch translation efforts in Sri Lanka of sections of the Bible (mainly Phillipus Baldeus's Gospel of St Matthew, which he was unable to print) preceded the first complete translation of the New Testament in Tamil published in 1714–1715 in Tranquebar, located a few miles south of Madras. This was undertaken by the German Pietist Bartholomeus Ziegenbalg under the patronage of the Danish king, with a printing press shipped by the Society for the Propagation of Christian Knowledge and Tamil fonts produced in Halle. This major translation in Tamil print and subsequent translation history undertaken by German Lutheran missionaries, along with their rivalry with the Jesuits working in neighboring areas,[42] has been well documented by Tamil theologians and scholars of Tamil translation and print history.[43] These translation efforts thrived a good hundred years before the arrival of print in Bengal with the Baptists (1793) and later the British and Foreign Bible Society (in 1811). However, as I have argued previously,[44] once they entered the scene, the nature and degree of Bible translation in India changed from small translation teams working on individual language pairs. Instead, the Baptist mission and the BFBS undertook several Indian-language translations in swift succession and very quickly established an intricate network among translators, printers, colporteurs, and readers. They worked to standardize Protestant terminology and publish "standard" translations in each of the languages. This is not to say that the two societies worked in conjunction with each other. They battled over the translation of key terms, and chief among them was the appropriate term for "baptism" across the languages.[45] Much of these lexical disputes and discussions dominate nineteenth-century archival documents—reports, minutes of translation committee meetings, prefaces to dictionaries, and "scriptural lexicons"[46]—and appear to be repetitive, transferring to the colonial stage the theological and hermeneutical arguments that dogged British Christianity throughout the eighteenth and nineteenth centuries.

Current examination of Bible translation in India continues this focus on detailed discussions of individual terms and of the merits of one equivalent over others, not dissimilar to the scholarship on missionary linguistics delineated in the preceding section. Such a focus, however, has limited potential. From a translation studies perspective, it is pertinent to emphasize that the focus on the translation of individual lexical items can only offer a partial and limited picture of the complex social and cultural interaction that translation involves. This is in fact merely the first stage in the building blocks of translation research since it is recognized in the discipline that pointing to the different nuances in meaning across different languages or pointing to the "lack" of equivalents does not take a scholarly argument very far. This scholarship is almost solely interested in proving that some terms successfully "inculturate" Christianity, usually understood as bringing it closer to a high, philosophical register of Hinduism, while others do not achieve this "interfaith dialogue." Take for instance, Bror Tilliander's study,[47] along with Kulendran[48] and Packiamuthu[49] writing in Tamil; these offer classic examples of this genre in relation to the Tamil Bible, focusing mainly on which terms brought the Christian message closer to Hindu concepts and usage without "diluting" the Christian message. Similarly, Ulla Sandgren[50] offers a short study of selected passages of the New Testament in seven Tamil translations. Sandgren follows in the tradition of Tiliander in comparing terms and passages from the Tamil Bible but there is much less effort than Tiliander at offering an analysis of how the terms work in each translation context. Sandgren's textual and linguistic comparisons, as of the others, are useful perhaps to the translator but the lack of a contextualized analysis limits its value. Brekke[51] on the Bengali Bible and the conflict over the choice to represent "baptism," and Peter Dass's[52] more recent consideration of Protestant translations of the Bible in Hindi where he discusses the merits of representing the incarnation of Christ as *avatar* over *dehadharan*, operate along a similar vein, although Dass does point to the blurring of distinctions between the two religions in the use of some terms. However, such a focus on differences in specific terminology across languages at the expense of other considerations limits the scholar to a display of philological and grammatical flair in specific languages rather than the politics of asymmetrical power between languages. It is the political implications of lexical choice, what meanings are marginalized, and a consideration of who has the power to make such lexical choices for whom and how this plays out in the ideological battleground over the correct interpretation of scripture that by far constitute the more valuable focus in translation research. For instance, standardization of terminology, not just within each language but across all Indian languages, was seen as key to establishing the Bible as "scripture" in nineteenth-century BFBS discourse. But to achieve this, all languages had to be remolded with reference to Sanskrit and Protestant requirements, in order to arrive as one standard Protestant vocabulary even when some languages, such as Tamil, had a separate lineage from the Sanskrit.[53]

If the "inculturation" model must be used, it would be worthwhile to engage more critically with what definitions of "culture" scholars are working with. By far, there is a tendency among scholars of biblical terminology and translation to focus on individual Sanskrit terms as the etymological foundations of a single extensive bank of sacred terminology underlying modern Indian languages available to modern-day translators. This is possible because they take their cue from the nineteenth-century missionary and orientalist distinction between the perceived "high," philosophical, and more acceptable form of Hinduism (as religion) from the "low," ritualistic Hinduism observed in practice.[54] The repeated focus on Sanskrit, as a language of both classical and sacred provenance, served and continues to service the argument of conceptual commensurability between European Christianity and Indian Hinduism. As a result, terminology in each of the modern Indian languages that could trace roots back to a Sanskrit term is usually preferred over lower registers of the languages. Such an emphasis therefore obviates the study of other languages, including demotic or subaltern registers of languages used for sacred purposes for centuries within Hinduism, let alone in the context of Bible translation for Christian communities. This further succeeds in reifying the assumption of a homogenous "high-caste" Hinduism and a monolithic postulation of Indian culture with which Christianity must primarily engage with, which also functions to marginalize sections of Indian society that were historically denied the right to participate in Sanskritic high culture even before they converted to Christianity. It also effectively marginalizes language communities, such as those of North-East India that do not trace their lineage to Sanskrit, from mainstream scholarly examinations of Bible translation in India. The philological focus on individual lexical items examined through the lens of missionary linguistics continues to facilitate textual study at the expense of situating the text at the intersections of race, class, and gender politics.

By way of contrast, a more valuable form of "inculturation" (again if one must needs use this term) is where Bible translation, past and present, is situated squarely within the politics of class and caste difference—within the pulls of regional nationalisms in postindependent India or the challenge posed by feminist scholars critically engaging with the deployment of religions as social forms of control. There are currently just a handful of scholars who have attempted to offer such analyses of the role of Bible translation in the political lives of language communities. Longkumer's[55] recent study of Christianity's persistence as a form of political articulation in contemporary Nagaland includes a section on Bible translation and print, as a legacy from the American Baptists that has had long-reaching effects. In his analysis, the decision of the Baptists to represent the numerous Naga languages in the Roman script functioned to unify the different tribes that previously had no standardized lingua franca. The romanization of Naga languages had three important ideological effects according to Longkumer: first, the decision to simplify and contain linguistic diversity led to a greater spread of literacy, centralized education in English, and upward social mobility among the Naga; second, that it resulted in Bible translation and text production in the Naga languages; and third, it led to greater intertribal solidarity amongst the different Naga groups. Drawing on Anderson's (1983) thesis of "imagined communities," Longkumer argues that it was not monolingualism but the use of a single script in print, first introduced through Bible translation, that enabled the Nagas to imagine themselves as a unified "Naga nation" and as different from other social and linguistic groupings in India. While Longkumer warns that it would be erroneous to privilege print over orality and performance, especially in the Naga context, he argues that Bible translation and its print played an important role through "the adoption of the Roman script, and not [a] dependence on a unitary vernacular. The script unified the linguistic landscape in terms of its mutual and strategic practicalities, but it did not obliterate local vernaculars in the case of the polyglot Nagas."[56] Barkataki-Ruscheweyh too analyzes the politics of Bible language choice and translation among the Tangsa groups in North-East India, arguing that the fracturing of the Tangsa communities was the result not of theological disagreements but the role played by "differences over the choice of (Tangsa) language for translation of the Bible... that caused these splits."[57] Unlike the Naga situation, the Tangsa versions of the Bible had neither a common language nor a common script, which could be used to read the Bible across the language family and that led to disputes between the different groups. There is potential for Bible translation scholarship in other Indian languages to be examined in like manner with reference to language, print and book history at the regional and national levels, and how these aspects intersected with religious, social, caste, and political identities; however, there have been few such studies.

Therefore, rather than once again summarize the available literature focusing on terminological choice in the history of the Bible in Indian-language translations, I propose, in the spirit of this chapter's objective to challenge and advance mainstream scholarship on Bible translation, to present translations of parts of the Bible that for long have been marginalized, both in the historical narratives constructed by the BFBS and the more recent academic studies of the translated Bible. In the following section I recuperate verse translations of the Bible that have been paid little attention in the history of the Bible in Indian languages and comment on reasons for their marginalization. By recovering such translations from obscurity, I construct an alternative politics of biblical poetics and theology in India.

Verse Translations of the Bible

Of what significance is the choice of genre in the history of the Bible in Indian-language translations and in its function as a sacred text? The conceptual difference between prose and verse translation is an important one to keep in mind since texts considered "scriptural" by one faith community when translated without sufficient consideration of the cultural significance of textual genres may not even be recognized as "scripture" by receiving audiences. The predominant scholarly interest in the "meanings" that lexical items carry with them precludes critical consideration of the importance of literary genre in the shaping of biblical scripture and the politics of translation choice implied. Prose translations of the Bible in Indian languages have always been recognized as the "authorized" and official translations of the Bible and have consistently been treated as "sacred texts" in Christian ritual life. In contrast, verse translations have been appreciated more for their aesthetical appeal as *literary* texts, and while they did not serve a sacred function, these translations have instead been called upon to represent the successful "inculturation" of Christianity in India. It is these verse translations that are inevitably and conveniently exhibited in any discussions of "interfaith dialogue" or "Christian syncretism." Authored almost exclusively by Indian Christians and non-Christians (there are just a couple of European Jesuits who also chose verse genres), verse translations have been dismissed as charming poetry at best and as bordering on heretical similarities with "misleading" sacred poetry of other religious groups at worst. Prose translations however are simply *the Bible* in an Indian language and are meant to function primarily as sacred scripture.

I first highlighted the significance of examining verse or poetic versions of the Bible as "translations" when I discussed Tamil verse translations in *Religious Transactions in Colonial South India*.[58] I argued that, despite repeated and widespread observation that the verse was assigned the highest sacred and literary status in most Indian languages and that the "Indian mind" was persuaded best by sacred texts in verse, Protestant missionaries and the BFBS approved only prose translations for publication. In the British Protestant missionary imagination, prose was the form of rational, sacred truth and clearly to be separated from verse, seen as the domain of rival Hindu and Catholic poets. Spats between Catholic and Protestant missionaries over verse translations, as I have discussed there,[59] reveal an important difference in translation strategy. Examining a nineteenth-century controversy over the Jesuit Constantin Beschi's *Tempavani*, a Tamil epic (composed 1726–29?), narrating portions of the Old and New Testament in the literary style of the Tamil classic *Kamparamayana*, my contention was that Christian verse translations of the Bible were suppressed precisely because Protestant detractors recognized the aesthetic power of sacred verse and its cultural significance in the religious lives of Indian communities. In poetry's place, Protestant interlocutors wished to instate prose as the discursive form best able to convey Christian truth. Yelle's argument that the Protestant "disenchantment" of Sanskrit in colonial India was a continuation of Reformation's movement toward literalism is equally applicable to the context of Bible translation: because it meant "both a valorization of the semantic content of language and a devaluation of its poetic and magical functions, which contributed to the rise of polemics against both ritual and mythological language."[60] Verse genres were associated strongly with the aesthetic/emotive, magical/mythological, and erotic, three features that Protestant translators were determined to keep out of the Bible.

This bias in favor of prose, strong in the nineteenth century, has survived in current scholarly examinations of the Bible in Indian languages. There are but a handful of scholars (including myself) who have commented on the significance of verse translations. Among these, those working on early Jesuit materials have been most interested in verse translations. For instance, Županov writing on Tamil Jesuit and Malayalam works comments that "Jesuit versified translations, communicating Christian message while at the same time referring back to local literary traditions, were the most successful. Some poems such as Tempavani and Johann Ernst Hanxleden's *Puthen pana* (New Hymn in Malayalam), retelling the life of Christ in twelve cantos are still recited on the radio and read in Christian families. Others are invisibly incorporated into folk literature such as the popular stories of guru Paramarta."[61] Annie George[62] has more recently worked on the Marathi verse translation *Kristapuranam* by the English Jesuit, Thomas Stephens. Composed in the sixteenth and seventeenth centuries, Beschi's Tamil *Tempavani* and Stephens's Marathi *Kristapuranam* were serious efforts to engage with the sacred idioms, metaphors, and genres of religious poetry they encountered in the South Asian literary and religious landscapes. Neither Jesuit poet displays a similar attention to the transfer of meaning across lexical units as Protestant translators do, harnessing instead the sacred potential of verse traditions for Christian purpose, which led to reinterpretations of both biblical and Hindu narratives.

However, with the onset of Protestant translation projects from the early eighteenth century, there was deliberate eschewal of verse in missionary translations. But conversely, or perhaps *because* of this suppression of poetry in standard published versions of the Bible, the mantle of poetry was picked up, by and large, by Indian converts to Christianity. From the second half of the nineteenth century and well into the twentieth, there were several Protestant poets who translated parts of the Bible into verse. I have compiled a list of titles across different languages to show that there are a good number of these verse translations that can be culled from catalogues of Christian literature.[63] I have not included here the vast body of Christian hymns and poetical literature but only those that purport to offer a specific book of the Bible in verse translation:

Bengali

- *Srigurucharitamrita. Luke in Verse.* 1916. Calcutta: Bible Translation Society (Auxiliary of the Baptist Missionary Society).
- *Guru Māhātyma.* 1919. *Matthew in Verse.* Calcutta: Bible Translation Society (Auxiliary of the Baptist Missionary Society).
- *Gurucharit. Mark in Verse.* 1920. Calcutta: Bible Translation Society (Auxiliary of the Baptist Missionary Society).

Oriya

- Gaṅgādhara Ratha. 1912. *The Precious Story of Jesus: A Poetical Rendering of the Gospel of John.* Cuttack: Bible Translation Society.
- Mukanda Das, 1883. *Verse Translations of the Four Gospels, the Psalms, and Proverbs.*

Malayalam

- K. V. Simon. 1931. *Veda Viharam.* Translations of the book of Genesis.

Marathi

- Thomas Stevens. *Kristapuranam.* First printed in 1616.

Sanskrit

- William Mill. [Book 1. 1831.] 1842. *Śrī Khṛshṭasaṃgītā.* English introduction to the Christa-Sangítá or the Sacred History of Our Lord Jesus Christ in Sanscrit verse, etc.
- P. C. Devassia. 1977. *Kristubhagavatam: A Mahakavya in Sanskrit based on the life of Jesus Christ.* Trivandrum.

Tamil

- Constantin Beschi. *Tembavani* (composed 1726–29).
- E. Evarts Kanakasabai, 1866. *Tiruvakkupuranam: A Poetical Version in Tamil of the Holy Scriptures.* Ed. Rev. C Macarthur. Jaffna, The Editor, 1866.

- Cāminātappiḷḷai, C., and Irāmacāmi Nāyuṭu. 1908. *Mattēyu cuvicēṭ veṇpā*. Kāñcīpuram. Madras: Christian Literature Society.
- K. K. Estasan Joseph. 1922. *Yopu-Carittiram* [The Story of the Patriarch Job in Tamil Lyrics]. Cunoor. [pp. 11] 14170.aaa.30
- M. Peter of Rayapet, Madras. 1915. *Suvisesha sallapa-kadal sindu* [A Metrical Version of the Gospel Story]. Ed. C. S. Iniya-nathar. Madras: n.p.
- Narasimullu Kavirayar. 1849. *Poetical Version of the Book of Genesis*. Madras: n.p.
- V. J. Cinnatambi Piḷḷai. 1914. *Tiruvākkuppurāṇam*. [*Tiruvakkupuranam: A Metrical Version of the Book of Ruth*. With preface by Pillai. Maturai.

Telugu

- Bhujanga Rao. 1913–1920. *New Testament*.
- Tatavarthi Narayaṇaswamy. 1914. *Dēvatanayaśatakamu*. The Gospel of St. John in Telugu verse. Nellore: n.p.
- Yēsudāsan Siṅgu. 1926. *Yobu Caritramy: Harikatha Rupamu*. Candragiri: n.p.

This list is by no means complete and needs attention from scholars working with other Indian languages. However, these titles are included here merely to indicate the number of such translation projects that were undertaken to translate prose into poetry within the same language, which suggests the perceived significance of this task among Indian writers and translators. Why were so many writers translating the Bible or parts of it into verse? And why are these not catalogued under "Bible translation" in print?[64]

I deliberately employ the category of translation to draw attention to the texts and to emphasize that these "metrical" or "poetical" versions were as much a form of translation as established prose translations of the Bible. In some cases, such as *Tempavani* and *Kristapuranam*, there is considerable poetic license exercised in terms of selection of narratives incorporated and the specific saints focused on. But in other instances, such as Kanagasabai's *Tiruvakkupuranam*, the poet takes care to indicate correspondence between chapter and verse of the Tamil prose Bible in his translation. In my opinion, his careful attempt to follow the structure of the prose source text was a means to indicate that, although he was translating into verse, Kanagasabai wanted his verse translation to be taken as seriously as any prose translation of the Bible in Tamil. Each poet-translator used traditional and complex verse genres (such as the Tamil veṇpa) and narrative structures (such as the purana) from existing religious literatures in India to translate the Bible. It is important to attend to what the poets are signaling to their contemporaries and not dismiss them as mere amateur attempts to express the Christian message or theology through literary tropes. By continuing to ignore such translation attempts or not recognize them as "Bible translation," the current scholarship on biblical criticism and missionary history is marginalizing a whole body of translations that were undertaken to signal different types of cultural allegiances to the Protestant prose project. Although many poetic translations have been incorporated by the Christian communities into church worship and music, however controversial at some points,[65] by not offering them official status as "translations" of the Bible, they remain secondary to prose translations, which are often criticized for stiff, unnatural, and ungrammatical use of Indian languages.

Conclusion

There is currently little research on the rich history of Bible translation in the many languages of India and how it intersects with wider literary and religious histories. What does exist is atomized and circumscribed within each language, lacking a more comparative perspective. Although this may pose some difficulties, since most scholars may have limited access to more than two languages, collaborative research projects can overcome the challenge of comparative research across a range of languages. Collaborative work may also make it possible to include experts in the literary cultures of each language, so that it is possible to study how the Bible in Indian-language translation intersects with other sacred texts, literary translations, and religious landscapes. This has potential not only to exploit postcolonial criticism but also to contribute further to postcolonial translation studies by drawing attention to the significance of attending to the cultural histories of sacred texts as they traveled across languages.

It must be acknowledged in conclusion that the effects of the power imbalances generated by colonialism and empire on Bible translation is only one area that needs further examination. There are several other power imbalances at play in contemporary India that continue to intersect and impact on Bible translation as interpretation that urgently need scholarly attention. For instance, while Dalit theologians have engaged constructively with liberation theology to challenge continuing caste hierarchies within the Christian community, they have not yet turned critical attention to Bible translation as an important aspect of biblical criticism. This is despite the engagement of key Dalit theologians in the *process* of Bible translation. For instance, James Massey (1943–2015), one of the few Dalit theologians who also translated the Bible on his own (he spent approximately ten years between 1970 and 1980 in translating the Bible into Punjabi), does not comment on whether and to what extent Dalit liberation theology impacted his translation strategy in an article he wrote on the Punjabi Bible and his translation.[66] Similarly, there are hardly any Indian feminist studies of Bible translation or studies of translations undertaken by women. A significant example here is Ramabai's translation of the New Testament into Marathi, published in 1912, which has not been studied either by feminist scholars examining Ramabai's life and ouvre or by feminist theologians studying Christianity in India.

Whether engaging with postcolonial criticism or not, it is important that scholars examining Bible translation in India recognize that translation is a process of intervention—of contrived commensurability that suits specific purposes at specific historical junctures. Taking full cognizance of this invites scholars to engage critically with political contexts, such as postcolonial encounters, rather than to ignore or vilify the study of Bible translation from postcolonial perspectives as dangerous to or undermining

Christianity in India.[67] Ultimately, looking beyond missionary linguistics and philology to the politics of translation opens up new ways of engaging with the Bible in postcolonial contexts, especially of how it *becomes* "sacred" in and through translation.

NOTES

1. I use this as a generic category to refer both to the BFBS that was a key player in Bible translation from the early nineteenth century to Indian Independence and the Bible Society of India after 1947. For a critique of the BFBS's historiography, see Sue Zemca, "The Holy Book of Empire: Translations of the British and Foreign Bible Society," 1991; and Israel, *Religious Translations in Colonial South India*, chap. 1.
2. Tejaswani Niranjana, *Siting Translation: History, Post-structuralism, and the Colonial Context*, 1992; Douglas Robinson *Translation and Empire: Postcolonial Theories Explained*, 1997; Bassnett and Trivedi, *Post-colonial Translation: Theory and Practice*, 1999; Maria Tymoczko, *Translation in a Postcolonial Context: Early Irish Literature in English Translation*, 1999; Tarek Shamma, *Translation and the Manipulation of Difference: Arabic Literature in Nineteenth-century England*, 2009.
3. See Vicente L. Rafael, *Contracting Colonialism: Translation and Christian Conversion in Tagalog Society under Early Spanish Rule* [1988] 1993.
4. See William F. Hanks, *Converting Words: Maya in the Age of the Cross*, 2010.
5. Hanks, *Converting Words*, 2010, 4.
6. Hanks, *Converting Words*, 2010, 3.
7. Ines G. Županov, *Missionary Tropics: The Catholic Frontier in India, 16th-17th Centuries*, 2005.
8. Županov, *Missionary Tropics*, 2005, 251
9. Ângela Barreto Xavier, and Ines G. Županov, *Catholic Orientalism: Portuguese Empire, Indian Knowledge (16th-18th Centuries)*, 2015, 204.
10. Arvind-Pal S. Mandair, *Religion and the Specter of the West: Sikhism, India, Postcoloniality, and the Politics of Translation*, 2009.
11. Bradley L. Herling, *The German Gita: Hermeneutics and Discipline in the German Reception of Indian Thought 1778–1831*, 2009; "Either a Hermeneutical Consciousness or a Critical Consciousness: Renegotiating Theories of the Germany-India Encounter," *The Comparatist* 34 (2010): 63–79.
12. Herling, "Either a Hermeneutical Consciousness or a Critical Consciousness," 2010, 70.
13. Mitch Numark, "Translating Dharma: Scottish Missionary-Orientalists and the Politics of Religious Understanding in Nineteenth-Century Bombay," *Journal of Asian Studies* 70 (2011): 471–500.
14. The category "sacred text" is defined here as any text perceived as sacred or used for any purpose considered sacred by a faith community. This includes both the written and oral text, as well as sacred texts as objects of veneration and so "handled" in special or ritualized ways.
15. Thomas Stolz and Ingo H. Warnke, "From Missionary Linguistics to Colonial Linguistics," in Klaus Zimmermann and Birte Kellermeier-Rehbein ed. *Colonialism and Missionary Linguistics*, 2015, 12.
16. Gregory James, "The Terminology of Declension in Early Missionary Grammars of Tamil," in Otto Zwartjes, Gregory James, and Emilio Ridruejo ed. *Missionary Linguistics III*, 2007, 167–190.

17. Daniel Jeyaraj, "Embodying Memories: Early Bible Translations in Tranquebar and Serampore," *International Bulletin of Mission Research* 40, no. 1 (2016): 42–59.
18. Stolz and Wanke, "From Missionary Linguistics to Colonial Linguistics," 2015, 13.
19. Cristina Muru, "Shaping minds and Cultures: The Impact of Missionary Translations in Southern India," in Otto Zwartjes, Klaus Zimmermann, and Martina Schrader-Kniffki ed. *Missionary Linguistics V*, 2014, 203–230.
20. William Smalley, *Translation as Mission: Bible Translation in the Modern Missionary Movement*, 1991, 244.
21. Lamin Sanneh, *Translating the Message: The Missionary Impact on Culture*, [1989]2009.
22. Sanneh 2009, 3.
23. Sanneh 2009, 242.
24. Sanneh 2009, 163.
25. Sanneh 2009, 219.
26. Sanneh 2009, 193.
27. Sanneh 2009, 251.
28. Maria Tymoczko, "Western Metaphorical Discourses Implicit in Translation Studies," in *Thinking Through Translation with Metaphors*, edited by James St. Andre, Manchester: St. Jerome Publishing, 2010, pp. 109-143.
29. Kwame Bediako, Bediako, "The Doctrine of Christ and the Significance of Vernacular Terminology," 1998, 110.
30. Johnson Kiriaku Kinyua, "A Postcolonial Analysis of Bible Translation and its Effectiveness in Shaping and Enhancing the Discourse of Colonialism and the Discourse of Resistance: The Gĩkũyũ New Testament—A Case Study," 2013, 58–59.
31. Kinyua, 2013, 84.
32. Kinyua, 2013, 65.
33. Kinyua, 2013, 84–85.
34. R. S. Sugirtharajah, *The Bible and Empire: Postcolonial Explorations*, 2005.
35. Sacred text translation refers to the translation and/or verbal interpreting of any text considered sacred, through any medium or mode of communication.
36. For instance, most Translation Studies scholars take into account statements on translation by key Bible translators such as fourth-century CE Jerome, who translated the Latin Vulgate and Eugene Nida (1914–2011), who contributed considerably to the development of the study of translation in the twentieth century.
37. Claudius Buchanan is reported to have presented to Cambridge University Library in the nineteenth century this manuscript of the Bible in Syriac, which has come to be known as the "Buchanan Bible."
38. See R. S. Sugirtharajah, *Jesus in Asia*, 2018 for an extended discussion.
39. Muzaffar Alam and Sanjay Subhrahmanyam, "Frank Disputations: Catholics and Muslims in the Court of Jahangir (1608–11)," *Indian Economic and Social History Review* 46, no. 4 (2009): 457–511.
40. Audrey Truschke, *Culture of Encounters: Sanskrit at the Mughal Court*, 2016.
41. Županov, *Missionary Tropics*, 2005; Xavier and Županov, *Catholic Orientalism*, 2015.
42. The most recent study of the rivalry between the two is presented in the coauthored article by Will Sweetman and Ines Zupanov, "Rival Mission, Rival Science? Jesuits and Pietists in Seventeenth- and Eighteenth-Century South India," *Comparative Studies in Society and History* 61, no. 3 (July 2019): 624-653.

43. See Stuart Blackburn, *Print, Folklore and Nationalism in Colonial South India*. Delhi: Permanent Black, 2003; Vēṅkaṭācalapati, Ā. Irā. *The Province of the Book: Scholars, Scribes, and Scribblers in Colonial Tamilnadu*. Ranikhet: Permanent Black, 2012.
44. Israel 2011
45. See Torkel Brekke, "Mission Impossible? Baptism and the Politics of Bible Translation in the Early Protestant Mission in Bengal," *History of Religions* 45, no. 3 (2006): 213–233 (for Bengali); Israel 2011 (for Tamil).
46. William Hodge Mill, *Proposed Version of Theological Terms with a View to Uniformity in Translations of the Holy Scriptures etc. into the Various Languages of India* (Calcutta: Bishop's College Press, 1828); John Murdoch, *Renderings of Important Scriptural Terms in the Principal Languages of India* (Madras: Christian Vernacular Education Society, 1867).
47. Bror Tilliander, *Christian and Hindu Terminology: A Study in Their Mutual Relations with Special Reference to the Tamil Area*, 1974.
48. Sabapathy Kulendran, *Kiristava Tamil Vētākamattin Varalāru* [A History of the Tamil Bible], 1967.
49. Sarojini Packiamuthu, *Viviliyamum Tamilum* [Bible and Tamil], 2000.
50. Ulla Sandgren, *The Tamil New Testament and Bartholomaüs Ziegenbalg*, 1991.
51. Brekke, "Mission Impossible?," 2006.
52. Rakesh Peter Dass, "Translating with Care: An Essay on Hindi Protestant Christian Writings," *International Journal of Hindu Studies* 21, no. 1 (2017): 83–98.
53. Hephzibah Israel, "Translating the Bible in Nineteenth-Century India: Protestant Missionary Translation and the Standard Tamil Version." *Translating Others*. Ed. Theo Hermans. Vol. 2. 2006, 441–459.
54. Geoffrey A. Oddie, *Imagined Hinduism: British Protestant Missionary Constructions of Hinduism, 1793–1900*, 2006.
55. Arkotong Longkumer, "Along Kingdom's Highway: The Proliferation of Christianity, Education, and Print amongst the Nagas in Northeast India," *Contemporary South Asia* 27, no. 2 (2019): 160–178.
56. Longkumer, "Along Kingdom's Highway," 2019, 173.
57. Meenaxi Barkataki-Ruscheweyh, "Fractured Christianity amongst the Tangsa in Northeast India—Bible Language Politics and the Charm of Ecstatic Experiences," *South Asia: Journal of South Asian Studies* 41 (1) (2018): 213.
58. Israel 2011.
59. See Israel, *Religious Transactions in Colonial India*, chap. 4.
60. Robert A. Yelle, *The Language of Disenchantment: Protestant Literalism and Colonial Discourse in British India*, 2012, 26.
61. Xavier and Županov, *Catholic Orientalism*, 2015, 230–231.
62. Annie Rachel George and Arnapurna Rath, "'Must among Perfumes:' Creative Christianity in Thomas Stephens's *Kristapurana*," *Church History and Religious Culture* Vol. 96, Issue 3 (2016): 304-324 ; "Translation, Transformation and Genre in the *Kristapurana*," *Asia Pacific Translation and Intercultural Studies* Vol. 3 (Issue 3) (2016): 280–293.
63. I have used only English and Tamil-language catalogues to compile this list. I believe a search through each of the language catalogues would yield more such verse translations, but this is something I am unable to do without access to the different languages.
64. See discussion on Tamil verse translations of the Bible in Israel 2011, Chapter 4.

65. H. Israel, "Authority, Patronage and Customary Practices: Protestant Devotion and the Development of the Tamil Hymn in Colonial South India," in Chad Bauman, Richard Fox Young ed. *Constructing Indian Christianities: Culture, Conversion and Caste*, 2014.
66. James Massey, "Presbyterian Missionaries and the Development of Punjabi Language and Literature, 1834–1984," *Journal of Presbyterian History (1962–1985)* 62, no. 3, Fall 1984: 258–261.
67. Richard Fox Young, "Was the Sanskrit Bible the 'English Bible-in-Disguise'?: Postcolonialism meets Philology in William Carey's *Dharmapustaka* (1808)," *International Journal of Asian Christianity* 1 (2018): 177–197.

References

Alam, Muzaffar, and Sanjay Subhrahmanyam. "Frank Disputations: Catholics and Muslims in the Court of Jahangir (1608–11)." *Indian Economic and Social History Review* 46, no. 4 (2009): 457–511.

Anderson, Benedict. *Imagined Communities : Reflections on the Origin and Spread of Nationalism*. London: Verso, 1983.

Barkataki-Ruscheweyh, Meenaxi. "Fractured Christianity amongst the Tangsa in Northeast India—Bible Language Politics and the Charm of Ecstatic Experiences." *South Asia: Journal of South Asian Studies* 41, no. 1 (2018): 212–226.

Bassnett, Susan, and Harish Trivedi. *Post-colonial Translation: Theory and Practice*. London: Routledge, 1999.

Bediako, Kwame. "The Doctrine of Christ and the Significance of Vernacular Terminology." *International Bulletin of Missionary Research* (1998): 110–111.

Blackburn, Stuart. *Print, Folklore and Nationalism in Colonial South India*. Delhi: Permanent Black, 2003.

Brekke, Torkel. "Mission Impossible? Baptism and the Politics of Bible Translation in the Early Protestant Mission in Bengal." *History of Religions* 45, no. 3 (2006): 213–233.

Dass, Rakesh Peter. "Translating with Care: An Essay on Hindi Protestant Christian Writings." *International Journal of Hindu Studies* 21, no. 1 (2017): 83–98.

Dhavamony, Mariasusai. "The Lord's Prayer in the Sanskrit Bible." *Gregorianum* 68, nos. 3/4: 639–670.

George, Annie Rachel, and Arnapurna Rath. "'Must among Perfumes': Creative Christianity in Thomas Stephens's *Kristapurana*." *Church History and Religious Culture* 96 (2016): 304–324.

George, Annie Rachel. "Translation, Transformation and Genre in the *Kristapurana*." *Asia Pacific Translation and Intercultural Studies*.

Hanks, William F. *Converting Words: Maya in the Age of the Cross*. Berkeley; London: University of California Press, 2010.

Herling, Bradley L. *The German Gita: Hermeneutics and Discipline in the German Reception of Indian Thought 1778–1831*. New York; London: Routledge, 2009.

Herling, Bradley L. "Either a Hermeneutical Consciousness or a Critical Consciousness": Renegotiating Theories of the Germany-India Encounter." *The Comparatist* 34 (2010): 63–79.

Israel, Hephzibah. "Translating the Bible in Nineteenth-Century India: Protestant Missionary Translation and the Standard Tamil Version." In *Translating Others*, edited by Theo Hermans, 441–459. Vol. 2. Manchester: St. Jerome: 2006.

Israel, Hephzibah. *Religious Transactions in Colonial South India: Language, Translation and the Making of Protestant Identity.* Palgrave Studies in Cultural and Intellectual History. Basingstoke; New York: Palgrave Macmillan, 2011.

Israel, Hephzibah. "Authority, Patronage and Customary Practices: Protestant Devotion and the Development of the Tamil Hymn in Colonial South India." In *Constructing Indian Christianities: Culture, Conversion and Caste*, edited by Chad Bauman and Richard Fox Young, 86–109. New Delhi; London: Routledge, 2014.

James, Gregory. "The Terminology of Declension in Early Missionary Grammars of Tamil." In *Missionary Linguistics III*, edited by Otto Zwartjes, Gregory James, and Emilio Ridruejo, 167–190. Amsterdam; Philadelphia: John Benjamins, 2007.

Jeyaraj, Daniel. "Embodying Memories: Early Bible Translations in Tranquebar and Serampore." *International Bulletin of Mission Research* 40, no. 1 (2016): 42–59.

Kinyua, Johnson Kiriaku. "A Postcolonial Analysis of Bible Translation and Its Effectiveness in Shaping and Enhancing the Discourse of Colonialism and the Discourse of Resistance: The Gĩkũyũ New Testament—A Case Study." In *Black Theology* 11, no. 1 (2013): 58–95.

Kulendran, Sabapathy. *Kiristava Tamiḻ Vētākamattin Varalāṟu* [A History of the Tamil Bible]. Bangalore: Bible Society of India, 1967.

Longkumer, Arkotong. "'Along Kingdom's Highway': The Proliferation of Christianity, Education, and Print amongst the Nagas in Northeast India." *Contemporary South Asia* 27, no. 2: (2019): 160–178.

Mandair, Arvind-Pal S. *Religion and the Specter of the West: Sikhism, India, Postcoloniality, and the Politics of Translation.* New York: Columbia University Press, 2009.

Massey, James. "Presbyterian Missionaries and the Development of Punjabi Language and Literature, 1834–1984." *Journal of Presbyterian History (1962–1985)* 62, no. 3 (1984): 258–261.

Muru, Cristina. "Shaping Minds and Cultures: The Impact of Missionary Translations in Southern India." In *Missionary Linguistics V*, edited by Otto Zwartjes, Klaus Zimmermann, and Martina Schrader-Kniffki, 203–230. Amsterdam; Philadelphia: John Benjamins, 2014.

Niranjana, Tejaswini. *Siting Translation: History, Post-Structuralism, and the Colonial Context.* Berkeley; Oxford: University of California Press, 1992.

Numark, Mitch. "Translating Dharma: Scottish Missionary-Orientalists and the Politics of Religious Understanding in Nineteenth-Century Bombay." *Journal of Asian Studies* 70, no. 2 (2011): 471–500.

Oddie, Geoffrey A. *Imagined Hinduism: British Protestant Missionary Constructions of Hinduism, 1793–1900.* New Delhi; Thousand Oaks, CA: Sage Publications, 2006.

Packiamuthu, Sarojini. *Viviliyamum Tamilum* [Bible and Tamil]. Cittamparam: Meyappan Tamilayvah Veliyittu, 2000.

Rafael, Vicente L. *Contracting Colonialism: Translation and Christian Conversion in Tagalog Society under Early Spanish Rule.* 1st paperback ed. Durham: Duke University Press, [1988] 1993.

Richard, H. L. "Some Observations on William Carey's Bible Translations." *International Bulletin of Mission Research* 42, no. 3 (2018): 241–250.

Robinson, Douglas. *Translation and Empire: Postcolonial Theories Explained.* Manchester: St. Jerome Publishing, 1997.

Sandgren, Ulla. *The Tamil New Testament and Bartholomäus Ziegenbalg: A Short Study of Some Tamil Translations of the New Testament.* Missions no. 1. Uppsala: Swedish Institute of Missionary Research, 1991.

Sanneh, Lamin. *Translating the Message: The Missionary Impact on Culture*. 2nd ed. Maryknoll, NY: Orbis Books, [1989]2009.

Shamma, Tarek. *Translation and the Manipulation of Difference: Arabic Literature in Nineteenth-Century England*. Manchester: St. Jerome, 2009.

Smalley, William. *Translation as Mission: Bible Translation in the Modern Missionary Movement*. Macon, GA: Mercer University Press, 1991.

Stanley, B. *The Bible and the Flag: Protestant Missions and British Imperialism in the Nineteenth and Twentieth Centuries*. Apollos, 1990.

Stolz, Thomas, and Ingo H. Warnke. "From Missionary Linguistics to Colonial Linguistics." In *Colonialism and Missionary Linguistics*, edited by Klaus Zimmermann and Birte Kellermeier-Rehbein, 3–25. Berlin; Munster: De Gruyter, 2015.

Sugirtharajah, R. S. *The Bible and Empire: Postcolonial Explorations*. Cambridge: Cambridge University Press, 2005.

Sugirtharajah, R. S. *Jesus in Asia*. Cambridge: Harvard University Press, 2018.

Tilliander, Bror. *Christian and Hindu Terminology: A Study in Their Mutual Relations with Special Reference to the Tamil Area*. Almqvist & Wiksell, 1974.

Truschke, Audrey. *Culture of Encounters: Sanskrit at the Mughal Court*. New York: Columbia University Press, 2016.

Tymoczko, Maria. *Translation in a Postcolonial Context: Early Irish Literature in English Translation*. Manchester: St. Jerome, 1999.

Vēṅkaṭācalapati, Ā. Irā. *The Province of the Book: Scholars, Scribes, and Scribblers in Colonial Tamilnadu*. Ranikhet: Permanent Black, 2012

Xavier, Ângela Barreto, and Ines G. Županov. *Catholic Orientalism: Portuguese Empire, Indian Knowledge (16th–18th Centuries)*. 1st ed. New Delhi: Oxford University Press, 2015.

Yelle, Robert A. *The Language of Disenchantment: Protestant Literalism and Colonial Discourse in British India*. Oxford: Oxford University Press, 2012.

Young, Richard Fox. "Was the Sanskrit Bible the 'English Bible-in-Disguise'?: Postcolonialism Meets Philology in William Carey's *Dharmapustaka* (1808)." *International Journal of Asian Christianity* 1 (2018): 177–197.

Zemca, Sue. "The Holy Book of Empire: Translations of the British and Foreign Bible Society." In *Macropolitics of Nineteenth Century Literature: Nationalism, Exoticism, Imperialism*, edited by Jonathan Arac and Harriet Ritvo. Philadelphia: University of Pennsylvania Press, 1991.

Županov, Ines G. *Missionary Tropics: The Catholic Frontier in India, 16th–17th Centuries*. Ann Arbor: University of Michigan Press, 2005.

CHAPTER 20

BIBLE TRANSLATION IN THE COLONIAL PROJECT IN AFRICA AND ITS IMPACT ON AFRICAN LANGUAGES AND CULTURES

DORA R. MBUWAYESANGO

THE Bible entered Africa initially as a translated oral message. Later it appeared as a written, translated text, which was carried by European missionaries during the modern colonial period. Bible translation study is characterized by two broad aims—inculturation/contextualization and decolonization. While inculturation glorifies the seeming translatability of biblical or Christian concepts and messages into the African worldview, decolonization critiques the colonial ideology and agenda that was and continues to be inherent in Bible translation in Africa. For the purpose of inculturation, Bible translation garners favorable evaluation and its impact is seen as having a positive impact on African languages and cultures as a preservation and revitalization tool.[1] In the decolonization approach, however, Bible translation is problematized through postcolonial analysis as a powerful imperial tool of European colonization and subjugation of African peoples that distorted African languages for the purpose of obliterating African cultures and religions.

Consequently, postcolonial analysis of Bible translation in Africa shatters the image of the Christian mission as a peaceful civilizing force. In this view, Bible translation is a part of the violent imperial dispossession and colonization of African peoples. Through postcolonial analysis from different but related angles, Bible translation is critiqued on the colonial ideology that informed its process and content. The inseparable link between language and culture is laid bare in the process of colonial Bible translation that continues to this day. Through translation, the religious and cultural colonization of the people is carried out through the colonization of African languages.

The role of Bible translation in Africa is investigated through postcolonial analysis that places translation in its colonial context. This analysis, rooted in the problematization of Bible translation, is still in its infancy in the development of African biblical scholarship.[2] It seeks to investigate how the colonial context and agenda influenced the translation of the Bible into African indigenous languages and the impact of translated Bibles on African cultures and religions. Thus far, at least three areas of focus highlight the role of Bible translation in the colonial project in Africa: (1) negative distortions of religio-cultural meanings, (2) adoption of the indigenous names of gods, and (3) rejection of culturally charged words. Each of these areas are analyzed in ways that reveal the colonial biases of the missionary translators and the negative impact on African cultures then and now. After a brief overview of Bible translation in Africa, this essay highlights significant aspects within the three areas of impact of Bible translation.

A Brief General Overview of Bible Translation in Africa

Bible translation into indigenous languages began during the European colonization of Africa, which was part of the scramble for Africa in the nineteenth century and continues to this day. The translation of the Bible happened during two phases in the colonial history of Africa. In the first phase, the precolonial, missionaries were part of the harbingers of colonialism in the company of traders and explorers who began at the African coast and made their way into the hinterland of Africa. This phase was marked by the activities of legendary missionary-explorer figures such as David Livingstone, John Mackenzie, and John Campbell in Southern Africa.[3] In this phase, Bible translation was informal and oral in form and entailed the interaction of the missionaries, who did not know the indigenous languages, and indigenous interpreters, whose command of the European languages was very minimal, if not totally absent.

The challenges inherent in these early translation endeavors of the Bible and its message are illustrated in Moffat's assessment of it:

> The interpreter, who cannot himself read, and who understands very partially what he is translating, if he is not a very humble one, will, as I have heard, introduce a cartwheel, or an ox-tail into some passage of simple sublimity of Holy Writ, just because some word in the sentence had a similar sound. Thus the passage, "The salvation of the soul is a great and important subject;" The salvation of the soul is a very great sack, must sound strange indeed.[4]

Moffat also clearly articulated the distrust of indigenous translators/interpreters that missionaries harbored as he stated,

> I have been very much troubled in my mind on hearing the most erroneous renderings having been given to what I have said. Since acquiring the language, I

have had opportunities of discovering this with my own ears, by hearing sentences translated which at one moment were calculated to excite no more than a smile, while others would produce intense agony of mind from their bordering on blasphemy, and which the interpreter gave as the word of God.[5]

Before the establishment of colonial rule, missionaries were thus informally engaged in Bible translation as they attempted to proselytize to the African peoples. In many cases, it was through these attempts at conveying the Christian message to the Africans, especially to the African royalty, that missionaries gained African trust, which was utilized by colonial agents in the dispossession of Africans from their land. For example, Reverend Helm of the Christian Missionary Society (CMS) misled Lobengula, the Ndebele king, into signing a document that gave away all the Ndebele land to the British South Africa (BSA) Company led by Cecil John Rhodes.[6] It is quite evident that Charles Daniel Helm took advantage of the trust and friendship cultivated through his proselytizing attempts in Ndebeleland. Similarly, Antonio Barroso persuaded Dom Pedro V, king of Congo, to sign a note in 1884 that was actually an oath of loyalty and submission to the king of Portugal, presented as a letter of gratitude for a gold-decked chair.[7]

The second phase of Bible translation, the formal written form, commenced aggressively once the Europeans had succeeded in the military conquests of the Africans that led to their displacement from their lands. Colonial authorities granted lands to the missionaries among the Africans where the missionaries set up their mission stations. Bible translation played a significant role in the consolidation of colonial rule. It can be argued that it facilitated the Africans' acceptance of colonial control and governance. The missionaries valued the security provided by the colonial governments and were very much willing agents in that regard. The missionaries may have not set out to consolidate colonial governments as their focus was on saving the souls of Africans, but that was the ultimate result of the translation of the Bible into African languages. The missionaries realized that for the biblical message to take root and make a lasting impact on the African peoples, the Bible had to be presented in written form in African indigenous languages.

As African languages were mostly oral, the first step toward the translation of the Bible was to establish a writing system for the languages. Consequently, the missionaries commenced to reduce African languages into written form by developing orthographies and dictionaries. It was missionaries who had sole autonomy to determine the written form according to African sounds. This autonomy, however, met robust contestation in some parts of Africa as demonstrated by the response of the Batswana to the first Setswana Bible.[8] A written translated Bible meant that Africans had to be equipped with the necessary skills to read it. Literacy became one of the primary goals for the missionaries; however, it proved difficult or nearly impossible to introduce literacy to African adults, so the missionaries focused on the education of African children. The establishment of mission schools to impart the gospel message to African children led to the establishment of an African elite class who were more prone to break away from African ways of thinking in favor of Western ways. Awolalu suggests that the educated African converts, who were mostly teachers and pastors, were encouraged to flout authority by breaking taboos.⁹ The translated Bible became the textbook for education in the mission schools. African active resistance to colonial rule was suppressed as missionary education promoted Western supremacy and the missionary-educated elite became the intermediaries of colonial governments.

The assessment of the role of Bible translation in the missionary projects and its impact on African languages and cultures varies depending on the discipline. In the missiology discipline, the impact of Bible translation is evaluated positively as a tool that made the Bible accessible to Africans and resulted in the positive transformation of indigenous cultures (Lamin Sanneh, John Mbiti, Kwame Bediako).[10] Some distinction between Christianity and colonialism is made as emphasis is placed on the Africanization of Christianity. Translation is seen as a catalyst in the transfer of control of the Bible and its message from Western to African control, which resulted in the establishment and growth of Christianity in Africa. For example, Sanneh considers the rise of African Independent churches as strong evidence for the positive role of Bible translation in making Christianity an African religion.[11] Literacy, which is a direct outgrowth of Bible translation, is given much credit for the rise of political anticolonial consciousness since many of the recognized anticolonization leaders were educated at mission schools.

Yet, others see the Western Christian mission as different sides of the imperial/colonial coin who were working together collaboratively with political colonizers in the project of turning Africans into strangers in their own land. While political colonizers ultimately resorted to military force to subdue the Africans and dispossess them of lands, the Bible was the weapon for the missionaries. In this regard, the missionaries are seen as agents of colonialism who used Bible translation to achieve the colonial agenda, while those who do not see missionaries as agents of colonialism saw them as the preservers of African languages and cultures through Bible translation.

Adoption of Indigenous Divine Names

The problematization of Bible translation is a recent development in African scholarship. The issue of biblical translation has often surfaced as the issue of translatability of biblical or Christian concepts in the area of missiology. One issue is whether or not African cultures or religions are compatible with Christianity. Another is the translatability of biblical concepts into African culture. Although there are scholars who question the compatibility of some aspects of biblical and African concepts, scholars who use the comparative approach seek to establish points of agreement between the Bible and African religions and cultures. In the inculturation agenda, the issues of translation of the biblical text is tangential because the focus is mostly on cultural elements. Although most of the concepts discussed have implications for Bible translation, the inculturation does not cross over to the quest for proper indigenous terms in the biblical text. In this regard, the African religions and cultures are regarded as inferior and needing to measure up to the Bible's supremacy. As it is articulated by Justin Ukpong, "Inculturation hermeneutics sees the bible as a document of faith and therefore demands entry into and sharing the faith of the biblical community expressed in the text."[12] Various cultural and religious concepts are lifted up for comparison. For example, Temba Mafico argues for the compatibility of the concept of the God of the Fathers in the Hebrew Bible and African Ancestors; Gomang Seratwa Ntloedibe compares the liberative role of the biblical Jesus and the Ngaka—an indigenous healer—in African religion.[13] This comparative approach seeks to establish continuity of concepts and practices between biblical and African cultures. For example, John Mbiti sees African indigenous religions as the forerunner to biblical religion. Thus, precolonial religions of Africa were to be replaced by the full revelation of the gospel situated in the Bible.

One of the most significant concepts with some direct connection to Bible translation is the concept of the Supreme Being in the context of inculturation, especially with regards to the adoption of indigenous names for the biblical deity. Although the pioneer missionaries did not initially see the compatibility of the indigenous gods to the biblical god, they eventually concluded that it was prudent to accept them for the sake of gaining African conversion. The idea that African concepts of the deity is incompatible with the biblical god continues to this day among some Eurocentric translators on the African continent, as demonstrated by Hermanson's statement:

> It would seem that the cultural baggage attached to traditional names for God in other languages does not necessarily degrade the God of the Bible. Rather the revelation in the Bible of the true nature of God can transform the words so that the original connotation becomes completely obliterated in a new knowledge of and personal with the one true living God.[14]

Some missionaries even claimed that it was necessary to first purge the bad connotations inherent in these indigenous names for God. African scholars like John Mbiti argued very strongly for the compatibility of African indigenous gods. In fact, he saw them as one and the same deity as he states:

> I have no doubt whatsoever that God the Father of our Lord Jesus Christ is the same God who for thousands of years has been known and worshipped in various ways within the religious life of African peoples. He is known by various names, and there are innumerable attributes about him which are largely identical or close to biblical attributes about God.[15]

Although he seemed to acknowledge later that there were some profound theological issues with translating indigenous divine names into the Bible, he still insisted that equation was automatic:

> Even when translators make use of the existing word for God in African (and other) languages, profound theological issues remain. What does it mean when translations employ ancient (traditional) names by which people have named, acknowledged, and worshipped God in their own languages? Would that be talking of the same God,

as named both in these languages and in the Bible? In the minds and life-practice of the Akamba and other African peoples, the answer is unequivocally YES. The very translation of the word God into an indigenous language automatically merges the two worlds as they name the same God, in both the Biblical and African worlds (languages).[16]

Scriptural translation is also credited with the preservation of the indigenous divine names and the religious social worlds that undergirded them. This opinion is asserted strongly by Sanneh as he contrasts the impact of Christianity and Islam: "For example, Hausa or Fulani Muslims have, to all intents and purposes, allowed Allah to displace the gods of pre-Islamic times."[17] Hence there is much effort to demonstrate that the indigenous concepts about the Supreme Being are similar to those reflected in the Bible, fueled by the desire to endorse or advocate for the equation of the indigenous gods to the biblical god. Others in the inculturation/contextualization approach, however, argue that the adoption of indigenous names for deities results in their transformation and the implication is that their biblical location somehow makes them better. For example, J. O. Kombo states:

> The Christianized *Modimo* for the Sotho-Tswana is no longer "enabler" or "midwife" in the story of creation. The name *Modimo* for God, that is baptized in the Biblical and Christian theological content and meaning will be known in the Son and be worshipped in the Spirit.[18]

Similarly, Bosch, speaking of the Zulu deity Nkulunkulu, asserts that the name and "robe" of Nkulunkulu are to remain but the "content" of Nkulunkulu is to become different from the indigenous meaning. For him, "the traditional gods must give themselves up. The old God has to die, in order to rise again to a new life."[19] The goal of inculturation is thus to replace the African concepts of God, considered inferior, with biblical ones, considered civilized and advanced.

The politics of Bible translation into African languages is also analyzed in ways that problematize the adoption of the names of indigenous deities for the biblical deity. The missionaries were unwilling to give any value to the African religious epistemology. In almost every case in Africa, the missionaries went through a process that began with a rejection of the equation of the biblical and African dieities.[20] But as history shows, the missionaries eventually came to the decision that, for their mission to have any success, they had to accept the names but not African conceptions of the deities. Thus, contrary to the positive view that the adoption of the African names in Bible translation has contributed to their preservation, the adoption was to separate African peoples from their God in a way that renders African religious epistemology worthless. Thus postcolonial analysis exposes this adoption of African deities as a colonizing strategy.

In the context of the Shona peoples of Zimbabwe and the Batswana people of Botswana, I and Gomang Seratwa Ntloedibe-Kuswani argue that, rather than preserving the African dieties, the God of the Bible replaced the Mwari of the Shona and Modimo of the Batswana in the Shona and Setwana Bibles respectively[21]. In fact and in effect, this adoption was a religious colonization of the Shona people. As I assert:

> The missionary translation of the Bible was aimed at replacing the Shona Mwari with the biblical God in everything else but the name.... The adoption of the Shona name Mwari for the biblical God was in reality the religious usrurpation of the Shona. The missionaries took the Shona captive by colonizing the Shona Supreme Being.[22]

And according to Aloo Osotsi Mojola and Ntloedibe-Kuswani, this adoption of African divine names was practically a hijacking of African cultures.[23] Mojola states, "[T]he local gods, religious terminology, and categories are usually hijacked and christianised, or infused with new biblical meaning."[24] So the act of translation divorces the African gods from their indigenous and traditional contexts. This adoption of the African gods into the Bible devalues African ways of knowing and relating to their gods. As demonstrated by the case of Mwari, "for the Shona to relate to their god, they had to abandon their Shona identity and become Western. Their religious traditions suddenly were deemed incompatible with *Mwari*."[25]

But more significantly, the adoption of the African gods in Bible translation resulted in the anthropomorphizing and patriarchalizing of the African gods.[26] Using the depiction of the biblical god in Genesis 1:26–27, I illustrate how Mwari, who had no gender or form, is given human form and gender. And Ntloedibe-Kuswani demonstrates the same with Modimo's adoption into the Setswana Bible, tracing the translation of the divine in both the Hebrew Bible and the New Testament.[27] She points out how the Batswana avoided any references that would equate Modimo with human form or experience but preferred to use a neuter system or use.[28] This Batswana belief and practice is jeopardized when Modimo's genderlessness is completely erased on becoming the biblical God who only is known through the Bible. According to Ntloedibe-Kuswani, this adoption of Modimo in Bible translation results in the "colonization and gendering of Modimo, the hijacking of Setswana traditions."[29] This hijacking of African traditions means they are no longer serving African interests but colonial interests.

The patriarchalizing of the African gods in the indigenous Bibles has resulted in devastating consequences for African women in all spheres of life. Many of the biblical concepts about women's status in family and society introduced a higher degree of marginalization and oppression of women while simultenously emboldening African patrirachy. Women were marginalized in the political, religious, economic, and social spheres. The translation of the Bible into African languages also introduced a more narrow and oppressive view of gender and sexuality that has led to a dangerous intolerance of diversity that was not part of African thought and practice. As Ifi Amadiume demonstrates in the context of the Igbo people of Nigeria, the binary view of gender did not exist in Africa prior to the colonial imposition of sexual difference as constructed in Western culture.[30] She aptly demonstrates this common phenomenon in Africa through the practices of "*nhanye*—officialy placing a daughter in the position of son, that is, making her a male" and of "*igba ohu*—woman-to-woman marriage."[31] In that regard, for example, the translation of Genesis 1:26–27 into African indigenous languages not only introduced a Western gender ideology alien to African practice and thought but also imposed Western gender norms onto African cultures with the power of the Bible.

One of the positive results of Bible translation highlighted in the missiology discipline is the standardization of African dialects where a language was characterized by existing in a variety of dialects. Standardization is viewed as a positive development that promoted a sense of "nationalism" thought to be previously lacking in Africa. Thus, Sanneh endorses this view by quoting Keatley:

> The missionaries followed up by adopting the language of Manganja, Chi-Nyanja, and employed it as the lingua franca of the country. By this action the missionaries were "creating a sense of Nyasa nationalism . . . the missionaries gave the Nyasas a heritage of national unity and of deep regard for learning that was to serve them in the political battles of the 1950s and 1960s."[32]

This positive view of the standardization of African languages falls into the realm of viewing Africans as primitive and uncivilized and needing the intervention of Western civilization. But even more significantly, such ideas are based on the erroneous view that different dialects in African languages was a sign of divisiveness, which ignores how much was lost through the standardization of African languages. This move by missionaries is even more sinister considering that they took upon themselves the role of teaching Africans their own language. The damage done to African languages and cultures becomes evident in the postcolonial examination of Bible translation discussed in the following section.

Negative Distortions of Religio-Cultural Meanings

Hidden within African vernacular Bibles are violent attacks against African cultures and religions. While reading the book of Matthew with a group of Batswana women, Musa W. Dube discovered that Wooley's revised earliest Setswana Bible (the women's preferred version) translated "*Badimo*" as "demons" whom Jesus cast out. As Dube explains:

> The word *Badimo* literally means the "High Ones" or "Ancestors" in Setswana cultures. *Badimo* are sacred personalities who are mediators between God and the living in Setswana cultures. They consist of the dead members of the society and the very old members of the family who are attributed with divine status and sacred role.[33]

Consequently, she expresses the personal impact of such a discovery of the demonization of ancestors or ancestral spirits as follows:

> The reading experience was chilling to say the least. My reading moment was a violent experience which accelerated my heartbeat. The text exploded, shattering the very centre of my cultural world view. It invited me to see myself and my society as people who had believed and depended on the demons and devils before the coming of Christianity.[34]

Dube points out that *Badimo* is not the logical rendering of the Greek word as found in the book of Matthew; rather it was a deliberate distortion, "a structural device of alienating natives from their cultures."[35] The guarantee of the effectiveness of this agenda was not just the translated Bible, but the rendering of this demonization was moved into the arena of everyday language in dictionaries. This rendering of the *Badimo* as demons was put in the Brown Dictionary compiled after the Wooley Bible, which continued to be in use until 1993. Not only where the Setswana readers of the Bible subjected to this negative depiction of their beliefs, but its sphere of influence and impact was broadened with its inclusion in the dictionaries. These dictionaries were part of the resources used to teach English to the Setswana as part of the education system. The creation of these dictionaries that defined indigenous words and concepts in ways influenced by the use of the Bible as an evangelizing tool was the standard in sub-Saharan Africa. Hence, indigenous languages did not have meaning aside from the Christian context and ideology.

Following Dube's example, Lovemore Togarasei investigates politics involved in the translation process in Shona colonial Bible translation, focusing on the translation of "banquetings" (1 Peter 4:3) into the oldest Shona Bible, the *Union Shona Bible*, which dates to 1949/1950.[36] In this earliest complete translation of the Bible into Shona, the word was rendered *mabira*, a central ritual for communicating with ancestors on issues affecting both family and community. This distorted translation is contrasted to the 2005 *Testamente Itsva MuChishona Chanhasi* (The Testament in Today's Shona), which features an accurate rendering of "banqueting" into *kuraradza*, "excessive drinking." Thus, this new translation removes the term "banqueting" from the realm of ancestral veneration that had been imposed on it. In the earlier Shona Bible, *mabira* was demonized and turned into a vice that African Christians were to avoid. Togarasei discusses the politics involved in the translation process in colonial Shona Bible translation. In his analysis, the term "politics" refers "to strategies used by Bible translators to influence the meaning of texts to the recipients of the translated texts."[37] In addition, Togarasei asserts that the attack on the *mabira* resulted in the division of the Shona people and links that to the conquest of the Shona by the missionaries:

> Translating banqueting into *mabira* has succeeded not only in demonizing the Shona culture and religion but also in dividing Shona families.... With its demonisation, the extended family has been broken up and in some cases rivalries created. Christians who no longer want to take part in *mabira* are often accused of witchcraft

by their traditional relatives. Since they do not participate in the honour of the departed, family misfortunes are attributed to them. Divided, the Shona have therefore been conquered by the missionary translation of banquentings into *mabira*.[38]

Like Dube, Togarasei does not see any other objective for the negative reduction of significant Shona religious ceremony to "drinking" or "drinking partying" as nothing less than an effort to alienate the Shona from their culture. The strong message through the translation was that time for *mabira* (Shona religious observance) was to cease because that practice was put in the same realm as worshipping idols in the Christian context. Thus the missionaries did not respect the Shona culture and religion, and their energy was not on preservation but total obliteration.

J. Kabamba Kiboko analyzes 1 Samuel 28 and problematizes its translation history in English and Kisanga as to "unmask and challenge translations that undermine the value of divinatory practices in the text." According to her, "the vocabulary of divination in this passage and beyond has been mistranslated in authorized English translations" from the King James Version to the Revised Standard Version to the New Revised Standard Version. She argues that these mistranslations were influenced by the negative extrabiblical views of magic in the Christian European culture. Gender is also judged to have played a big role in the representation of the woman in the passage as a witch.[39] She engages in a creative, interpretive act of translation in which she offers a translation of the passage in English, French, and Kisanga. The Kisanga translation is "both faithful to the original text, more fitting for the African pro-divinatory Christian context, and more appropriate to an inculturated African Christian hermeneutics, theology, and praxis."[40] Thus like Dube, Kiboko seeks to decolonize and depatriarchalize the translation of terms and concepts that are weapons against African cultures.

REJECTION OF SIGNIFICANT CULTURALLY CHARGED TERMS

Bible translation was not only limited to the adoption of African deities while demonizing important aspects of African religions and cultures but also included the rejection of terms and concepts that were judged to have negative impacts on the Bible message. Lovemore Togarasei examines the reasons for transliteration of the term "prophet" as *muprofita* in the earliest Shona Bible.[41] This practice of transliterating English words in Bible translation in Africa was commonplace. For example, the term "prophet" was transliterated in Ndebele, Setswana, Zulu, and Chewa to name just a few. Togarasei examines the significance of the prophet as a key figure in divine manifestation and argues that theological and ideological implications for transliterating to *muporofita*. He explores "the Hebrew world of the term prophet, reflect[s] on the Shona world of the term *svikiro* and then conclude[s] that *svikiro* was supposed to be used to translate the word prophet into Shona."[42] Thus, the choice to transliterate was based on the missionaries' overwhelming agenda to annihilate African religion and cultures. Togarasei undescores the fact that this choice to transliterate was not an innocent gesture, and he concludes, "they decided to use the name Mwari for [the biblical] God, while *svikiro* was clearly the best translation for *prophet*. The missionaries' decision not to use this term can therefore only be explained in terms of their negative attitude towards the traditional religion."[43] I would conlude even further that both adoption of Mwari and rejection of *svikiro* functioned to rob the Shona of their culture. While *svikiro* was removed from meaningful circulation, Mwari was translated into a non-Shona meaning.

While Togarasei discusses the colonization of African cultures and religions through the practice of transliteration in Southern and Central Africa, Mojola discusses how missionary translators addressed the issue of unacceptable terms in the case of the Swahili Bible in East Africa.[44] He demonstrates that the missionary translators opted to use Arabic words and Islamic religious concepts rather than the suitable Swahili terms of Bantu origin. Mojola asserts:

> For example, words for priest, prophet, spirit, holy, sacrifice, altar, offering, life, blood, impure, sin, cleanse, condemn, believe, faith, hope, human being, good news, book, psalm, glory, blessed, earth, and numerous others, in these translations are all derived from Arabic. Even in cases where a particular term was not in use in Swahili Islamic discourse, these translators invented one derived from Arabic.[45]

In addition, when Bantu terms with religious senses were retained in the translations, they were given Islamic meanings. All these translation choices were colonial strategies that were designed to undermine African religions and cultures through language. As in the case of transliteration in Southern Africa, the privileging of Arabic and Islamic terms removed those terms from the Swahili-Bantu world.

Conclusion

The impacts of Bible translation on African cultures and languages have so far been evaluated through three main translation practices of the missionaries, namely, the adoption of indigenous names for deities, negative distortions of religio-cultural terms, and rejection of significantly cultural terms. The adoption of indigenous deity names was a colonizing strategy that devalued African ways of knowing and relating to their gods. In addition, this practice negatively impacted African women by introducing biblical concepts that have resulted in a higher degree of political, religious, economic, and social marginalization and oppression of women. The negative distortions of religio-cultural terms changed the meanings of these terms in ways that made them weapons against African religious and cultural practices as in the case of *Badimo* in Setswana and *mabira* in Shona. Finally, the rejection of significant culturally charged terms introduced foreign terms while making extinct important African terms. Bible translation was also characterized by standardization, which negatively impacted African languages with many different dialects.

The exposition and documentation of the colonizing and patriarchalizing of Bible translation in Africa is a very new development in the study of the impact of the Bible on African cultures and languages. In fact, until very recently African biblical scholars have not critically examined the African translated Bibles for their content and studied how they relate to the original languages of Hebrew, Aramaic, and Greek. All three areas highlighted in this essay regarding the politics of Bible translation in African need critical analysis. African biblical scholars need to exegete indigenous Bibles for indigenous readers so as to contribute to how the Bible is read and applied in African contexts. The marketing of the Bible to peoples who had their own religions and cultures, started by colonial missionaries during the scramble for Africa, continues today. The translation of the Bible is still being utilized as a weapon against indigenous cultures and religions.

Notes

1. For example, Lamin Sanneh, *Translating the Message: The Missionary Impact on Culture* (Maryknoll: Orbis, 1989; reprint ed., 2004); John Mbiti, *Bible and Theology in African Christianity* (Nairobi: Oxford Press, 1986);
2. Musa W. Dube's 1999 publication, "Consuming a Cultural Bomb: Translating '*Badimo*' into 'Demons' in the Setswana Bible," marks the beginning of postcolonial investigation of Bible translation by African biblical scholars.
3. See J. H. Worcester Jr., *David Livingstone: First to Cross with the Gospel* (Chicago: Moody, 1990); Anthony Dachs, *Papers of John Mackenzie* (Johannesburg: Witwatersrand University Press, 1975); John Campbell, *Travels in South Africa: Undertaken at the Request of the Missionary Society* (London: Black, Parry & Co., 1815; reprint ed., Cape Town: Struik, 1974); Elizabeth Isichei, *A History of Christianity in Africa: From Antiquity to the Present* (Grand Rapids: W. B. Eerdmans, 1995).
4. Robert Moffat, *Missionary Labours and Scenes in Southern Africa* (London: John Snow, Paternoster-Row, 1842), 294.
5. Ibid.
6. Robert Rotberg, *The Founder: Cecil Rhodes and the Pursuit of Power* (New York/Oxford: Oxford University Press, 1988), 262–264; Scott T. Noth, "Assessing the Matabele Wars: An Exercise in Understanding the Perspective of 'the Other,' " *Historia* 4 (1995): 54–65.
7. Miguel Bandeira Jeronimo, "The 'Congo Question': Ecclesiastical and Political Rivalries and the Internationalization of African Affairs," in *Colonialism and Imperialism: Between Ideologies and Practices*, ed. Diogo Ramada Curto and Alexis Rappas (Fiesole, Italy: European University Institute, 2006) 20–22; http://cadmus.eui.eu/bitstream/handle/1814/4159/HIST_2006_01.pdf.
8. Musa W. Dube, "The Bible in the Bush: The First 'Literate' Batswana Readers," *Translation* 2 (2013): 79–103; and in *Postcoloniality, Translation, and the Bible in Africa*, ed. Musa W. Dube and R. S. Wafula, 159–175 (Eugene, OR: Pickwick, 2017).

9. J. O. Awolalu, "The Encounter between African Traditional Religion and Other Religions in Nigeria," in *African Traditional Religions in Contemporary Society*, ed. J. K. Olupona, 111–118 (Minnesota: Paragon House, 1991); Also see B. Datta, *Education and Society: A Sociology of African Education* (London: Macmillan, 1984); A. Moumouni, *Education in Africa* (London: Andre Deutsch, 1992).
10. Sanneh, *Translating the Message*; John Mbiti, *The Bible and Theology in African Christianity* (Nairobi: Oxford University Press, 1986); Kwame Bediako, *Jesus and the Gospel in Africa: History and Experience* (Maryknoll: Orbis Books, 2004); Paul J. Gifford, *Christianity in Africa: The Renewal of Non-Western Religion* (Maryknoll: Orbis Books, 1996).
11. Sanneh, *Translating the Message*, 168–169.
12. Justin Ukpong, "Rereading the Bible with African Eyes: Inculturation and Hermeneutics," *Journal of Theology for Southern Africa* 91 (1995): 10
13. For example, Temba Mafico, "The Biblical God of the Fathers and African Ancestors," in *The Bible in Africa: Transactions, Trajectories and Trends*, ed. Gerald O. West and Musa W. Dube, 481–489 (Boston/Leiben: 2001); "Ngaka and Jesus as Liberators: A Comparative Reading," in *The Bible in Africa: Transactions, Trajectories and Trends*, ed. Gerald O. West and Musa W. Dube, 498–510 (Boston/Leiben: 2001).
14. Eric Hermanson, "Missionary Translations of the Bible in Zulu" in *Bible, Translation and African Languages*, ed. Gosnell L. O. R. Yorke and Peter Renju, 41–58 (Nairobi: Acton, 2004), 55.
15. John Mbiti, "On the Article of John W. Kinney: A Comment," *Occasional Bulletin of Missionary Research* 3(2) (1979): 68.
16. John Mbiti, "Challenges of Language, Culture, and Interpretation in Translating the Greek New Testament," *Swedish Missiological Themes* 97(2) (2009): 151.
17. Sanneh, *Translating the Message*, 181.
18. J. O. Kombo, "The Doctrine of God in African Christian Thought: An Assessment of African Inculturation Theology from a Trinitarian Perspective," DTh. Dissertation, University of Stellenbosch, 2000, 219.
19. Discussed and quoted in Tiina Ahonen, *Transformation through Compassionate Mission: David Bosch's Theology of Contextualization* (Helnsiki: Luther-Agricola Society, 2003), 193–200.
20. For examples of discussion of the early missionary rejection of African deity names see Dora R. Mbuwayesango, "How Local Divine Powers Were Suppressed: The Case of Mwari of the Shona," in *Other Ways of Reading: African Women and the Bible*, ed. Musa W. Dube, 63–77 (Atlanta: Society of Biblical Literature, 2001); Eric Hermason, "Missionary Translations of the Bible in Zulu," in *Bible, Translation and African Languages*, ed. Gosnell L. O. R. Yorke and Peter Renju, 41–58 (Nairobi: Acton, 2004).
21. Mbuwayesango, "How Local Divine Powers Were Suppressed": Gomang Seratwa Ntloedibe-Kuswani, "Translating the Divine: The Case of Modimo in the Setswana Bible," in *Other Ways of Reading: African Women and the Bible*, ed. Musa W. Dube, 78–97 (Atlanta: Society of Biblical Literature, 2001).
22. Mbuwayesango, "How Local Divine Powers Were Suppressed," 119.
23. Aloo Osotsi Mojola, "Bible Translation," in *Dictionary of Third World Theologies*, ed. Virginia Fabella and R. S. Sugirtharajah, 30–31 (Maryknoll: Orbis, 2000); Ntloedibe-Kuswani, "Translating the Divine," 99.
24. Mojola, "Bible Translation," 31.

25. Mbuwayesango, "How Local Divine Powers Were Suppressed," 125.
26. Ibid., 69, 121; Ntloedibe-Kuswani, "Translating the Divine," 84–86.
27. Ibid., 88–91.
28. Ibid., 82–85.
29. Ibid., 88.
30. Ifi Amadiume, *Male Daughters and Female Husbands: Gender and Sex in an African Society* (London: Zed Books, 2015).
31. Ibid., 218–219.
32. Sanneh, *Translating the Message*, 113.
33. Musa W. Dube, "Consuming A Colonial Cultural Bomb: Translating '*Badimo*' into 'Demons' in Setswana Bible," *Journal for the Study of the New Testament* 73 (1999): 40.
34. Ibid.
35. Musa W. Dube, "Consuming A Colonial Cultural Bomb: Translating '*Badimo*' into 'Demons,'" in *Postcoloniality, Translation, and the Bible in Africa*, ed. Musa W. Dube and R. S. Wafula (Eugene, OR: Pickwick, 2017), 10.
36. Lovemore Togarasei, "The Shona Bible and the Politics of Translation," in *Postcolonial Perspectives in African Biblical Interpretation*, ed. Musa W. Dube, Andrew M. Mbuvi, and Dora R. Mbuwayesango, 185–198 (Atlanta: Society of Biblical Literature, 2012).
37. Ibid., 191.
38. Ibid., 195.
39. J. Kabamba Kiboko, *Divining the Woman of Endor: African Culture, Postcolonial Hermeneutics, and the Politics of Biblical Translation* (London, UK: T & T Clark, 2017), 13–14.
40. Ibid., 21.
41. Lovemore Togarasei, "The Prophet and the Divine Manifestations: On the Translation of the Word 'Prophet' in the Shona Union Bible," *Old Testament Essays* 30(2) (2017): 821–834.
42. Ibid., 824.
43. Ibid., 834.
44. Aloo Osotsi, Mojola, "Postcolonial Translation Theory and the Swahili Bible," in *Bible, Translation and African Languages*, ed. Gosnell L. O. R. Yorke and Peter Renju, 77–104 (Nairobi: Acton, 2004); and Dube and Wafula, *Postcoloniality, Translation, and the Bible in Africa*, 26–56.
45. Mojola, "Postcolonial Translation Theory," 43.

Selected Bibliograpy

Amadiume, Ifi. *Male Daughters and Female Husbands: Gender and Sex in an African Society*. London: Zed Books, 2015.

Dube, Musa W. "Consuming a Cultural Bomb: Translating 'Badimo' into 'Demons' in the Setswana Bible." *Journal for the Study of the New Testament* 21(73) (1999): 33–59.

Dube, Musa W. "Consuming A Colonial Cultural Bomb: Translating 'Badimo' into 'Demons' in the Setswana Bible." In *Postcoloniality, Translation, and the Bible in Africa*, edited by Musa W. Dube and R. S. Wafula. Eugene, OR: Pickwick, 2017.

Dube, Musa W. "The Bible in the Bush: The First 'Literate' Batswana Bible Readers." In *Postcoloniality, Translation, and the Bible in Africa*, edited by Musa W. Dube and R. S. Wafula. Eugene, OR: Pickwick, 2017.

Hermason, Eric. "Missionary Translations of the Bible in Zulu." In *Bible, Translation and African Languages*, edited by Gosnell L. O. R. Yorke and Peter Renju, 41–58. Nairobi: Acton, 2004.

Isichei, Elizabeth. *A History of Christianity in Africa: From Antiquity to the Present*. Grand Rapids: W. B. Eerdmans, 1995.

Jeronimo, Miguel Bandeira. *The "Congo Question": Ecclesiastical and Political Rivalries and the Internationalization of African Affairs*. In *Colonialism and Imperialism: Between Ideologies and Practices*, edited by Diogo Ramada Curto and Alexis Rappas, 20–22. European University Institute, 2006. http://cadmus.eui.eu/bitstream/handle/1814/4159/HIST_2006_01.pdf. Accessed February 28, 2019.

Kiboko, J. Kabamba. *Divining the Woman of Endor: African Culture, Postcolonial Hermeneutics, and the Politics of Biblical Translation*. London, UK: T & T Clark, 2017.

Mbuwayesango, Dora R. "How Local Divine Powers Were Suppressed: The Case of Mwari of the Shona." In *Postcoloniality, Translation, and the Bible in Africa*, edited by Musa W. Dube and R. S. Wafula, 115–128. Eugene, OR: Pickwick, 2017.

Mojola, Aloo Osotsi. "Postcolonial Translation Theory and the Swahili Bible in East Africa." In *Postcoloniality, Translation, and the Bible in Africa*, edited by Musa W. Dube and R. S. Wafula, 26–56. Eugene, OR: Pickwick, 2017.

Mojola, Aloo Ostotsi. "Translation Theory and the Swahili Bible." In *Bible Translation and African Languages*, edited by Gosnell L. O. R. Yorke and Peter M. Renju, 77–104. Nairobi: Acton, 2004.

Noth, Scott T. "Assessing the Matabele Wars: An Exercise in Understanding the Perspective of 'the Other.'" *Historia* 4 (1995): 54–65.

Ntloedibe-Kuswani, Gomang Seratwa. "Translating the Divine: The Case of Modimo in the Setswana Bible." In *Postcoloniality, Translation, and the Bible in Africa*, edited by Musa W. Dube and R. S. Wafula, 97–114. Eugene, OR: Pickwick, 2017.

Rotberg, Robert. *The Founder: Cecil Rhodes and the Pursuit of Power*. New York/Oxford: Oxford University Press, 1988, 262–264.

Togarasei, Lovemore. "The Shona Bible and the Politics of Bible Translation." In *Postcolonial Perspective in African Biblical Interpretation*, edited by Musa W. Dube, Andrew M. Mbuvi, and Dora R. Mbuwayesango. Atlanta: Society of Biblical Literature, 2012.

Togarasei, Lovemore. "The Prophet and Divine Manifestations: On the Translation of the Word 'Prophet' in the Shona Union Bible." *Old Testament Essays* 30(3) (2017): 821–834.

Ukpong, Justin. "Rereading the Bible with African Eyes: Inculturation and Hermeneutics." *Journal of Theology For Southern Africa* 91 (1995): 3–14.

CHAPTER 21

CROSS-TEXTUAL INTERPRETATION AS POSTCOLONIAL STRATEGY IN BIBLE TRANSLATION IN ASIA

ARCHIE C. C. LEE

Introduction

CHRISTIANITY is essentially "a religion of translation" as most of its followers have mainly read the Bible in translation in various native languages.[1] The Hebrew Old Testament and the Greek New Testament, though easily accessible, are not readily understood by ordinary readers who rely on translations to read the Word of God. To assist in understanding the phenomenon of Bible translation, a key observation was made at the Bicentenary of the British Foreign Bible Society by Rowan Williams, Archbishop of Canterbury, who said that "Christians have been convinced that every language can become the bearer of scriptural revelation" and that Bible translation "represents an enormous act of faith."[2] This "act of faith" is contingent on a couple of significant factors at work in the production of any attempt to translate the Bible into the vernacular.

The first consideration is the tension between a declared quest for fidelity to the text and the difficulties encountered in the ambiguities of the original text when interpretative options are open, not to mention the number of manuscripts with unresolved variants or numerous fragments available to the translator for consultation. Furthermore, the doctrinal disposition or theological assertion held by translators will sometimes overrule the intended fidelity to the text. Most translation projects of the Bible will at the very outset proclaim the purposes of translation in following the text closely. Fidelity to religious texts is assumed by readers who expect credibility in the translated version.[3]

A second factor that affects Bible translation involves contextual and ideological issues of translation with regard to the initiator, the patron, and/or the translator of a particular translation project. There is increasing attention paid to the religio-cultural perspective and the sociopolitical setting of the translators. This is especially obvious when missionaries are involved in translating the Bible into the language of the colonized in the mission field. Missionaries are inevitably part and parcel of the empire-building project, not to mention the fact that they may, consciously or unconsciously, be agents of the colonizing enterprise. It is the assumption of Bible translators that they could reproduce the Bible from its original text into the target language for local people with the declared mission of communicating the Gospel in its pure form to gentiles. Though the endeavor may be respectful and admirable, the impossibility of exact reproduction without deconstructing and reconstructing processes has not always come into the purview of the missionary translators, who would not admit that their social worldviews, their political positions, and their attitudes toward religious traditions of the colonized had been shaped by their doctrinal confessions and imperialist colonial backgrounds. These factors have had an impact on the resultant translation work.

This chapter will focus on these two factors involving Bible translation from the perspective of ideological criticism offered by postcolonial studies, engaging the Bible and its translation as sites of contestation and negotiation. For a more focused study, the chapter will concentrate on the translation of the Bible in East Asia in general and in China in particular and highlight two aspects of translation: (1) how the Biblical God is to be named; and (2) how God's opponents are understood in a Chinese context. From a postcolonial perspective, the issues of naming God and demonizing other people's cultures as opposing God are sites that would reveal the translator's imperialistic and colonial mindset. The most salutatory legitimization for colonization, as seen by Vicente Rafael, lies in its claim to convert and save lost souls and barbaric heathens through a noble, ethical imperative to "Christianize them so that light is shed on their miserable state of total darkness."[4] In this perspective, translation that works hand in hand with conversion represents "the triumph of universal civilization over the particularizing destructiveness of barbarism in whatever religious, political or cultural guise it takes."[5] What is proposed at the end of this chapter is a cross-textual approach to Bible translation that will affirm the hybridized identity of the colonized and provide a creative site for negotiation between Asian texts and biblical texts in the process of translation.

Scriptural Imperialism in the Empire's Civilizing Mission

Despite its complicated process, Bible translation by missionaries as seen from a postcolonial critical perspective is mostly "a one-way flow from a superior race to an inferior one" and usually aims "at the moral and intellectual improvement of the natives."[6]

Though the contribution of native assistants (sometimes referred to by the missionaries as "teachers") cannot be overlooked as they have contributed to the editing and polishing of initial drafts of the missionaries' translations,[7] their significant role is often forgotten and their identities are not duly recognized. Many of these assistants' names are not fully recorded and some have remained nameless in the historical records. The Bible is mainly taken by the missionary enterprise as playing an indispensable role in their mission to civilize the heathens. The colonized are often perceived as the Other, not only as uncivilized and barbaric but also as ignorant and inherently idolatrous. The texts of the colonized are seen as distorted and even demonic, constituting a threat to the advanced and progressive religion of Christianity. What underlies this conception and imagery is the evolutionary idea of history and the notion of difference between the colonizer and the colonized.

The dominant image at work is of the Tower of Babel (Gen 11), which to the missionaries represents sin and punishment. The rebellious people at Babel received tragic results through the proliferation of languages and their dispersion over the earth. It is not surprising that such an interpretation has been employed and manipulated to caricature the foreignness of strange languages that are not fully controllable by the Western Christian world. Some of these Protestant missionaries during the colonial era in China adopted an orientalist interpretation of the Babel story to demonize strange religious practices and difficult native languages. They superimposed this negative view onto the Chinese culture, which, according to the civilized West, is merely an embodiment of abomination and idolatry. In missionary writings and reports, the colonial discourses exhibited a construct of otherness in terms of differences and impurity. An orientalist view of the East in binary terms of "us and them" is upheld to differentiate the two worlds.[8] It is typical for missionary literature to describe China as a land of idols populated by uncivilized and backward people—the opposite of the Christian West. The cultural and religious "Other" represents great transgression and utter corruption, which is fatally in need of Christian conversion and salvation. There are examples of Western missionaries' perceptions of China as a homogeneous entity, consisting of only sinful and rebellious people, as condemned in the story of the Tower of Babel (Gen 11). Two well-known missionaries—Andrew Patton Happer (1818–1894), the founder of Canton Christian College in 1886 and a missionary educator to Guangzhou, and Thomas Booth McClatchie (1814–1885), the founder of the Church Missionary Society in China—both adopted the powerful colonial image and imperial reading of the narrative of the Tower of Babel to highlight the irreconcilable cultural and linguistic differences between the Christian West and the pagan East.[9]

William Remfry Hunts from the United Christian Missionary Society (a missionary to Jiangsu, China in 1900–1932) had a special interest in the class of literati who could benefit from reading the Bible. When a few of these literati began to read the colonial book, Hunts expressed delight and reported that it was "encouraging to know that the sacred page is filtering through the empire, securing attention and arousing inquiry in the minds of the already awakened Chinese."[10] At the end of his report he went further and said: "It is also encouraging to know that these millions of people, devoted to the learning and aided by the wonderful means of communication in unity of language, even though bewildered by the confused mythic meanings of Buddhistic, Confucianistic, and Taoistic imaginations, are more ready than ever to search our 'classics' if haply they might find the truth."[11]

Though he had appreciation for the Chinese literary heritage, Hunt was convinced of the superiority of Christianity and its Bible over all other religions and scriptures in Asia. A sort of religious imperialism accompanied by his faith in the universality of the text of the Bible informed his experience and expectation that "in all other non-Christian lands" that "the best religion will come to the front" and Christianity as a universal religion "has supplied a universal book."[12] The divine word in the book, he said, will promise a bright morning to "the shadow of the Asian night" and, in respect to China, "guarantee[s] animation to, and accelerate[s] the regeneration of, one of the greatest nations of antiquity."[13]

One of the great outgrowths from the missionary endeavor in the translation of the Bible is the creation of a writing system for people who formerly communicated only orally without any form of written language. Missionaries became inventors of local languages for some small ethnic groups in the southwestern part of China and the hill countries of Thailand, Burma, and northeast India. They helped to produce dictionaries and grammar books that initially were used for their own learning process of the language. Faced with the burden of overcoming difficulties of a native language, which is often taken as the "terrible obstacle to missionary enterprise,"[14] missionaries engaged with the challenge of having to master the native language of the colonized and imperialized. In turn, missionaries helped to promote the partial eradication of illiteracy, especially in raising the status of women via increased opportunities for education through women's schools and colleges. Women's colleges and universities in Korea, Japan, China, and other Asian countries strongly bear witness to this aspect of the emancipation of women. For indigenous people otherwise deprived of the privilege to read and write, the Bible was the first book they read because it was printed in their vernaculars.

In order to overcome the difficulties of native language missionaries who manipulated the "clumsy" and "complicated" written form, as proposed by C. E. Trevelyan for Indian languages, the introduction of the Romanization system served two purposes: making the vernaculars accessible to foreign missions; and introducing the English language.[15] The colonial project of standardizing and unifying the local languages and dialects is seen as "the pathway to progress and civilization."[16] For the native vernaculars "to become the instruments for the word of God, they had first to be reconstructed and codified" and the grammatical features resituated "within the grid of Latin grammatical terms."[17] Such a colonial project contributed to communication between communities formerly separated and isolated due to the language barrier and led subsequently to the unification of a people or a nation in certain communities. The colonized seemed better off in terms of economic gains, social development, and class mobility, albeit at the expense of losing their language's diversity and cultural richness.

The noble missionary course of providing the Bible in native languages was often counteracted with the inadequacy of vernacular languages to convey the truth of the Christian message. Missionaries sometimes refused to render key Christian conceptions into the vernacular or insisted that some thoughts were untranslatable with no local equivalent. The rendering of the biblical God into native languages is a good case in point as a few of the missionaries were afraid of having "the possibility of confusing and corrupting 'God' with pagan associations."[18] For example, the omission of certain terms for Christian ideas of sin and salvation led to the perception that some local cultures of the third world were uncivilized and had to be "Christianized."[19] In addition, a translator's incapability to find a counterpart for a biblical concept was often taken as a deficiency of the language "to convey the inner, vital truth of the Word" in addition to "the difficulties in native modes of thought, the peculiar moral ideas of duty to Heaven and man, and the rigid, primary meaning of Chinese characters, which too often resist adaptation to Scriptural uses."[20]

Besides the problem of adopting local religious terminology, there was also the issue of whether to translate literally or to supply a meaning as understood and interpreted by the translator. J. C. Hepburn in his lecture to the General Conference of the Missionaries of Japan at Osaka on April 16–21, 1883, stated that "ambiguous phrases should be rendered ambiguously."[21] He was in favor of the literal approach of the Bridgman-Culbertson translation as against the Delegates Version. A strong supporter of Hepburn, Hugh Waddell expressed his opinion thus: "We must translate literally. When the text is ambiguous, the translation should be ambiguous also. The translator has no right to give the sense according to his own interpretation or idea."[22] It is, however, not always easy to practice the claim of adhering faithfully to the original text in its literal sense. Textual authority is sometimes undermined by the diehard doctrinal proclamation of *Sola Scriptura*. Calvin Mateer, missionary to Shandong, China and chairman of the Committee on the Translation of CUV (1919) has advocated for a Chinese Bible "just as it is written" without "any doctoring at the hands of translators."[23]

The colonial preoccupation with mechanical literal accuracy or rigid theological claims in the translation of the Bible is "a way of assuming control" and a means to insulate the Bible from any religious and philosophical influences that are regarded as contaminating or dangerously pagan. This negative attitude toward the target language and local culture have been seen as turning the Bible into a closed book, which does not enlighten the rich Asian world of religion and philosophy, nor does it open any space for contribution of the nonbiblical world to engender meaning in the Bible. Colonial translation of the Bible ignores the validity of local religions and their scriptures since the primacy of Christianity must be upheld even at the expense of purging the native culture of its religious content and uprooting its very existence. This effort to advocate one's identity through prejudicial attitudes toward other peoples is what John Hull termed as "religionism."[24]

In such a perspective, adopting any Confucian, Daoist, and Buddhist terminology in rendering concepts of the Bible into Chinese would raise criticism.[25] The fear of overstepping the line between what is proper inculturation, appropriate accommodation, and acceptable contextualization and what constitutes undesirable distortion of the gospel message is not easy to define.[26] An anonymous author (signed "K"), writing on the revision of the Bible in China, maintains the superiority of the Bible by his unwillingness to make "the ignorance of Confucianism the gauge by which to determine" the validity of Biblical notions.[27]

Despite the missionary conception of language hierarchy and the difference in approach to translating, the very fact that local vernaculars are adopted as media for translating the Bible is a way of "canonizing" and "elevating" the vernaculars.[28] A process of negotiation that involves the Bible and the entire spectrum of Asian cultural-religious reality should be taking place in the translation of the Bible in Asia. The following discussion examines the issue of naming God and the rendering of the biblical "sea monster[s]" in China to assess some of the questions in how missionary translators have approached Chinese culture and religion in the colonial context.

Naming God and the Superiority of the Empire

The issue of naming God in Asia is a major problem in what has been mentioned as the "one-way flow" in Bible translation and the otherness of the uncivilized Other. When it comes to the discussion of the paramount issue of translation of the Bible in Asia, the problem of how the Christian God is to be rendered in the native language can never be overstated. How can the biblical God, *Elohim*, and YHWH be named without undermining the authority, power, and supremacy of the monotheistic deity who is the creator of heaven and earth? This so-called term question has surfaced in almost all translation projects in Asia and has aroused debates and discussions from the outset of translation.[29] The basic question boils down to whether the translation will use names of the local Supreme Being or native terms for the deities. After all, this very basic issue is not merely a technical one of finding an appropriate "term" for God. It hinges on the significant presupposition of the whole missionary movement of spreading the Gospel and the foundation of the colonial project of trade and military expansion in the name of civilizing lost souls. Many missionaries objected to the adoption of native terms as that would give an impression that the native people had the notion of the one true God in their cultural makeup.[30] The reality is that every culture and its language have terminology for a supreme deity, but the polytheistic context of a hierarchical pantheon is unacceptable to Christianity in encountering Asian culture and religion. The understanding of non-Christian culture as being derogatory and demonic will almost determine the outcome of the search for an appropriate term in naming God. Behind the claim of there being no current or ancient term in the target language that can be used to name the Christian God is an absolute imperial claim of superiority for both the divine and the human missionary agent. Missionaries with such a mind advocate the creation of a new term or adoption of a generic name for the category of the divine. Sometimes qualifying the generic terminology by adding the word "true" is the usual practice in East Asia.

Lillias H. Underwood, the wife of H. G. Underwood, the first missionary to Korea, stated the following position on naming God in East Asia:

> Throughout China, Japan and Korea it has been a vexed question among missionaries what word they should teach the native Christians to use for our word for "God." The people of all those countries have some name for their chief deity from the ancient classics or in the religious traditions that are passed down to them from history. But many missionaries hold that the use of this word is likely to lead to error, since the people have been accustomed not only to worship that particular god, but at the same time many other gods. The use of the name of any one of their gods implies the possibility of other deities, but a generic term may be so used as to exclude all others.[31]

The concern expressed in this statement exhibits the basic position among missionaries to not only exclude all other deities but also categorically reject all Asian religions and cultures. The first missionary Bible translators were open to quite a few divine names, but usually by the second or third generations these names would have been eliminated. In the first period of Korean missionary history, "as many as eight words were used for 'God': *Hananim, Hananim, Haneunim, Tyunju, Sin* ('God' or 'Spirit'), *Sangdje, Sangdje-nim*, or *Chansin* ('Real God' or 'Real Spirit')."[32]

Doing away with all existent terms in the native language for naming the biblical God will leave the translator with only one option: using the collective term for Elohim and a transliteration for YHWH (based on the pronunciation in the Hebrew Bible as "Jehovah"). For the goal of winning Asian people to the Christian faith and converting them from the "perverted" religions, "no other God" has been at the core of the missionary attitude toward other religions. In the history of Chinese Bible translation, "*Shangdi*" ("the Lord on High"), the name adopted in the Chinese classics and used by Chinese religious traditions, has been argued by some European and British missionaries as the proper name for the Hebrew term for Elohim. Strong opposition, however, was launched from a group of missionaries, mostly from America, under the leadership of the Episcopal Bishop Boone who was in favor of the generic term "*Shen*" (meaning "divine," "spirit," and "a deity" or "deities") for God. This resulted in a long debate in China in the 1860s.[33] Even up till today the two versions (called "*Shangdi* version" and "*Shen* version") of the Chinese Bible are still in print. In close examination, there is the problem of some passages where a name of God is expected. *Elohim* as God's name in Psalm 109 is a case in point when it is written that "YHWH is Elohim." The Chinese option for "YHWH is *Shangdi*" and "YHWH is *Shen*" communicate different meanings. The former conveys a meaning that YHWH is *Shangdi* in the Chinese context while the latter asserts that YHWH is divine.

From a postcolonial stance, there should be a variety of ways to name the divine as the biblical traditions have preserved different names for God, especially in the Old Testament (e.g., *El, Elohim, Eloah*; see Gen 33:20; 46:3; Dan 2:47). For Chinese Christians, "by and large, the status quo" of usage of different names for God (*Shangdi* and *Shen* in the Protestant tradition, *Tianzu* in the Catholic tradition, and *Shangzhu* for ecumenical services) is mostly acceptable.[34] The Old Testament was translated into Mandarin by Joseph Schereschewsky and published by the American Bible Society in 1875 and the British and Foreign Bible Society in 1878; the 1866 version of the New Testament was jointly translated by Schereschewsky and John S. Burden, Joseph Edkins, Henry Blodget, and William A. P. Martin.[35] These translations use the Catholic term "*Tianzhu*" for the Greek "*Theos*," a divergence from the well-established rendering of "*Shen*" initiated by Bishop William Boone, Schereschewsky's predecessor.

The use of multiple names for God in Chinese Christian communities, even across denominational boundaries, represents a postcolonial subversion of the imposition of only one name for God in Asia. The presence of Asian religions embedded in Asian culture presents a great challenge to the claim of the Gospel for an exclusive monopoly on human spirituality and truth proclamation. The reality of multiple religious belongings and the plurality of religious classics in Asia would give an impetus to Asian Christians to seek ways to go even beyond the statement of Sundar Singh (1889—1929), who acknowledges the role of Hinduism in "digging channels" and the fulfillment of Christianity in Christ as being "the water to flow through these channels."[36] There are missionaries who are open to crossing the boundary and incorporating local religious tradition into Bible translation. Adoniram Judson (1788–1850), an American Baptist missionary, holds a negative view of Buddhism, yet adopts its religious terms for his translation of the Bible into Burmese.[37] This is an important step forward.

THE DRAGON AND THE DEMONIZING OF THE OTHER

In the history of translation of the Bible in China, there is great dissonance among Chinese Christians on the subject of the "dragon" that appears in the King James Version (KJV) and the Chinese Bible. The tension is between the common Chinese celebratory perspective of the *long* as representing the source of blessings and the demonic notion of a biblical dragon, translated into *long* as God's enemy, in the Old Testament and as Satan in the New Testament. In all Chinese-English and English-Chinese dictionaries, the Chinese character for *long* (龙) is rendered in English as "dragon." The misconception of Chinese auspicious image of *long* as demonic is rooted in translation of the mythic Satanic creature called "dragon" in the Greek language of the Book of Revelation (12–13, 16, 20). Chinese Christianity has preserved the alliance of the two original terms into one.[38]

Long, the dragon, is popularly imagined as an auspicious and beneficent animal. It is usually taken as both real in natural existence and as a marvelous creature with immense size, gigantic might, and supernatural powers over the fate of people in all aspects of life. Therefore, the *long* is duly held in reverence and even worshipped as the Lord of Rain as it rides on the cloud in the sky. All over China, temples are built in dedication to the dragon deity depicted as *Long Wang* (the Dragon King) who is often implored in times of drought. *Long* fares prominently in China at all levels in art, literature, architecture, and, not least, political realms as an imperial symbol. The great ancestor of the Chinese, the Yellow Emperor, is said to be taken to heaven upon the back of a huge dragon after reigning for 110 years.[39] According to Newton Hayes, the *long* of the Chinese differs from the generally accepted Western idea of "the dragon" in three striking particulars: appearance, disposition, and the regard in which it is held.[40]

However, the *long*, being identified as the dragon, is presented by missionaries to the Chinese as demonic, a cruel monster, the personification of all that is evil, and the enemy of God. This notion of the dragon may have helped the Jesuits to convince the Chinese of their ability as exorcists.[41] Protestant missionaries have also capitalized on the negative image of the dragon and asserted the image as, in the words of Hampden Du Bose, "an emblem of China and its state church."[42] Du Bose mocked China as "the land of demons"[43] and sarcastically constructed the Chinese rejoicing cry to Mara, the Lord of Hades, as "Hosanna to the son of darkness; Hosanna in the lowest!"[44] In the conclusion he also remarked on the situation of the Chinese from the Christian point of view: "As we witness the downward progress of their systems from the school to the temple, from philosophy to demonolatry, and from asceticism to devil-worship, we instinctively cry, 'The night is far spent!' [T]he night of superstition and idolatry, and call to the heralds on Zion's towers, 'Watchman, what of the night?' The watchman saith. 'The morning cometh! The Sun of Righteousness arises.'"[45]

Seeing the procession of the dragon in Macau, G. Tradescant Lay, a British naturalist, accused the Chinese of being faithful to "the abominable worship of Satan"[46] O. G. Hertzog, another Protestant missionary to China, while confessing that he was impressed by the vastness of the land of China and the density of its population, perceived the great problem of China as being "bound by the chain of superstition and idolatry."[47] His negative comment described China as a land of the dragon under the control of Satan and the Old Serpent to be eventually destroyed by Christ according to the Book of Revelation. He caricatured China as an ancient state with not only deep-seated political and religious prejudices but also the following problem:

> Its symbol is the dragon, and over its portal is written, "None may enter here." But this is but a challenge to the herald of the Cross. Has not God said that He would lay hold on the dragon, that old serpent, the devil, and Satan, and bind him a thousand year, and that the seed of the woman should bruise the serpent's head.[48]

Through Christianizing China, Hertzog believed that the whole of Asia would be "dominated by the Cross, and not by the Crescent or by the Dragon."[49] To assert the new identity of newly converted Chinese Christians, missionaries and preachers in China propagated the distinctive mark of separation between the idolatrous Chinese public and the redeemed souls of the church. This has intensified the foreignness and the claimed superiority of Christianity, underlined the conflict between new converts and Chinese society in general, and increased an unsettling perception of "the saved" and "the condemned" in local communities. The dissonance would never be resolved without delinking the two concepts by adopting two different terms.

The theme of a demonic dragon/*long* was taken up by the leaders of the Taiping Heavenly Kingdom, which conquered from the southern part of China to central China up to the Yangtze River, with Nanjing as the Heavenly Capital, in 1853–1864.⁵⁰ The legacy of both images—an imperial image of the dragon, representing the power of the Taiping emperor, and the Protestant missionary caricature of Chinese culture as embodying the red dragon—exists side by side in the Taiping Kingdom, and the negative view has been further developed by native Christians up to very recent times.⁵¹

The Chinese Bible has been influenced by the Empire's Bible, the authoritative English translation of the KJV, which has been around since 1611 and has shaped many of the missionaries' translations in terms of the reading of the Bible and the literary style adopted for translation. Robert Morrison was the first missionary to China and the first in China⁵² to render the whole Bible into Chinese (published in 1823) with the assistance of William Milne, the second missionary to China. They adopted the Chinese character *long* for all the twenty-eight occurrences of the Greek "dragon" in the New Testament. In the Old Testament, Morrison only followed five of the six occurrences of "dragon" (in the singular) in the KJV, both for the singular (וְתַנִּ֖ית) and plural (תַנִּ֖ה; לוֹדָגֹ ם) terms, into *long*. He renders the term for "dragon" in Isa 27:1 as "sea monster" (海之妖兽).⁵³ Going through the various Chinese translations from 1823 to 1919, the dragon disappears, except in the New Testament where the Greek word for "dragon" is used. Though in the Old Testament the term "dragon" has mostly disappeared in recent translations, the notion of the dragon as Satan and God's enemy has been fixated in the mind of many Chinese Christians. In fact, the evil perceptions of the sea monster/creature in the Hebrew Bible is far from being monolithic. There are passages on sea creatures as not being entirely God's opponents to be confined and finally conquered but as part of God's creation (Gen 1:21) and as being playful, tamed, and naturalized (Ps 104:26). But the dimensions of the monstrous and the horrific as divine opponents in the structuring of other people's religion by the missionaries and in the constructing of self-identity by the native Christians are so powerful that the issue is still real in contemporary China, and the conflict is internal and deep-rooted. The "Red Dragon" as used in the Book of Revelation has also been applied to Communist rule in the late 1940s and early 1950s. The Communist rule is thus caricatured as the "Red Dragon over China"⁵⁴ and Hong Kong is said to return to the dragon in 1997.⁵⁵ The missionary translation of the Bible by demonizing the Other as God's enemy may be better understood with the observation of Timothy K. Beal that, by demonizing monsters as God's opponents, "we keep God on our side."⁵⁶

Cross-Textual Translation and the Reclamation of Asian Culture

In colonial times, the printing technology that makes the Bible available in printed form in local languages has contributed to the "development of self-awareness through literacy" in the post-Reformation European context.[57] It has also been noted by the historian Adrian Hastings that Bible translation has become the source of modern nationhood and the development of cultural identities.[58] This is particularly true in some remote parts of Asia, where Bible translation has become an instrument of modernizing societies in purging inhumane practices and customs.

Retrospectively, one may accuse some of the missionaries of being both advocates of imperialism and destroyers of indigenous cultures.[59] Andrew Porter is of the opinion that missionaries may not advocate empire, "but were often associated with institutions and beliefs identified by the local peoples with imperialism."[60] One ambiguous case concerns the role of mission schools established by missionary boards, which have contributed to the spread of literacy and knowledge and have successfully achieved liberating impacts and a widening of horizons for locals to contest both traditional values and colonial assumptions.[61] There is no doubt that missionaries have created writing systems for Asian-minority communities, introduced literacy to remote and isolated peoples, and promoted emancipation of women in Asian societies. But in derogative attitudes toward other people's religion in the translation and interpretation of the Bible, there is a serious severing from local textual-cultural configurations that undermines the process of Bible reading. Translation of the Bible into the vernacular can be a way to reduce the image of the Bible as a "foreign book" of invaders, colonizers, and imperialists, but most of the native people persist in holding general hostility and negative attitudes toward the Bible. The enterprise of translation has promoted the Bible as a colonial book, but its status as a sacred book has been much denied in China.

Viewed from a postcolonial perspective, it must be recognized that there is a great variety of missionaries, and the generalization of all of them being "imperial and colonizing agents" may not reflect the true picture. The language ability and knowledge of the native culture may have shaped missionaries' attitudes, affected their experiences, and determined their mission strategies.[62] Many must struggle to adopt the right approach in encountering "other people's culture," which is basically foreign and at times alienating. This has cast a long shadow onto their comprehension of what "accommodation" really means existentially even if they are convinced of it being the most appropriate way.

The liberalization of Christianity in China during the first few decades of the 1900s has great cultural and theological impacts on the conception of the Christian mission and its stance on non-Christian religions. Instead of the unreserved enthusiasm for conversion of heathens in darkness in the previous century, there is "a rethinking of mission," which is also the title of an influential book that incorporates the report of the Layman's Foreign Mission Inquiry.[63] The document advocates recognition in the Western world of light and insights in the so-called pagan religions in the East and presents a great challenge in departing from the former assertion of finality of the Christian faith. There are missionaries who have been "converted" from fundamentalist hostile attitudes toward pagan religion to being more liberal in their outlook of appreciation of the value of religions of the Other. Many have called for Christian cooperation with non-Christian religions instead of the traditional missionary position of fierce competition and aggressive replacement.[64] More liberal missionaries have realized the importance of decentering the West, the need to eliminate any form of hegemony, and the imperative to engage in dialogue with other peoples' texts and faith traditions.[65] This should also include resolving the tension between the Biblical language and that of the vernaculars in the translation process.

Kosuke Koyama, a prominent Japanese theologian, has tried to reconceive this issue in his discussion on the work of Bible translation as having the experience of hierophany. Coming to the truth involves "the manifestation of the sacred" in both the states of revelation (discontinuity) and enlightenment (continuity).[66] Though he sees that the two sets of language in the Bible and in Asia are different in nature, they have equal status in expressing the truth. "In Asia, Bible translation," according to Koyama, "is mostly the activity to adopt the language of enlightenment to render the language of revelation."[67] From a postcolonial critical point of view in affirming the hybridity of Asian Christian identity, the Asian textual tradition should play a further role in the production of a Bible translation with cross-textual practices that affirm Asian religiosity and social reality.[68] It is proposed that the approach of cross-reading of the Asian text (Text A) and the Biblical text (Text B) would open a new site for creative and enriching negotiation in Bible translation in Asia.

A conceptual notion and an operational practice comprise the process of cross-textual translation: namely "contextual notion" and "contesting practice," respectively. Cross-textual translation involves a complicated process of due recognition of the plurality of text in context. The textual plurality in Asia has presented a great challenge to translators. Asia should not be seen only as a missionary field of evangelistic work in biblical interpretation and translation. There are multiple texts of scriptural status that have nurtured the peoples of Asia for centuries and are still profoundly influential at present, shaping the thinking and lifestyles of Asians. Assuming there is a "pure," linguistically defined Asian language to be adopted as an instrument cannot reflect the cultural context of Asia and its religion. This is not to say that traditional Bible translators did not understand the impact of Asian languages on Bible translation. On the contrary, they have known of it all too well, setting up preventive measures to avoid "contaminating" the Bible, and intending to achieve the "one-way flow" of translation discussed previously. In the perspective of cross-textual translation, due attention should be paid to the interactive process of the biblical text with Asian texts to the extent that the latter may have played a contributing role rather than merely functioning as a communicative tool. In this sense, cross-textual translation helps to bring out previously unrecognized levels of meaning embedded in the biblical text.

Translation is, therefore, truly an interpretation involving a conglomeration of the source text and many other texts in the target language. The "con" in the word "con/text" may have four major meanings.[69] First, it conveys the idea of "being with/coming together" as expressed in the prefix "con-" ("concord"). Second, it indicates an "argument against" as in "pro and con." Third, it includes the meaning of researching and studying intensively; and lastly, it implies the effort to direct and take action to steer as in the case of conning a ship. Critical research on the literature and history of the Bible has also revealed the complicated processes of the formation of the biblical text in responding to the context of ancient West Asia, which was full of "texts." The Bible is consequential to the "contesting process" in terms of "receiving," "rejecting," "reversing," and "reformulating" (the 4Rs) of different texts that have been recovered from ancient libraries in archaeological excavations. Cross-textual translation in Asia should involve this contesting practice in dealing with the Bible and Asian texts. In this way, translation is a "con/textual" exercise of conning both the embedded texts in the Bible and the texts of the target language.

In cross-textual translation in Asia, translators should come to terms with the plurality of the names of God(s) in both the biblical tradition and in Asian culture and its religions. Furthermore, translators must come to terms with the importance of religious images in Asian religion, lest they fall into a destruction of Asian religious tradition as experienced in disastrous iconoclastic movements; the Taiping Heavenly Kingdom is one of the sad cases.[70]

There is a need to revisit the aniconic tradition (Exod 20:4) of making no images or representation for YHWH in contrast to idol worship and the meaning of idolatry. Bible translators, especially those of the Old Testament, are invited to rethink the issue of the monotheistic formulation, which in fact takes stages and successive contexts to accomplish, while passages that do not express the monotheistic notion are not to be subjected to the Judeo-Christian doctrinal imposition. Cross-textual translation will make a distinction with precise nuances of polytheism, henotheism, and monotheism. Passages that are not straightly monotheistic (Exod 20:3), as has been pointed out by scholars, will have to be reconsidered and the different contexts of the faith of Israel within the world of ancient West Asia (Mesopotamia and Canaan) and Egypt should be respected.

Cross-textual interpretation has revealed a conception of the divine-human continuum in both Asian religions and the biblical world. This should have implications for the translation of the Hebrew Bible text of human beings being created a little lower than "Elohim" (God or Gods). It should be so rendered. The apparent theological assertion of the absolute supremacy of God over a presumed abject and insignificant humanity, as shown in the rendering Elohim into "angels" by the ancient translations (Greek, Syriac, Latin, etc.), should not dictate the translation.

When Asian mythology is brought in to the cross-textual reading of Genesis 1, a new perspective presents itself in the understanding and translation of the first two verses. Similar to the ancient West Asian creation myths, the ancient East Asian myths usually begin with a pre-creation situation of chaos or conflicts. Order is then introduced or restored in creation. More and more scholars have arrived at this reading of Genesis 1 as expressed in NRSV: "In the beginning when God created the heavens and the earth, the earth was a formless void and darkness covered the face of the deep, while a wind from God swept over the face of the waters."[71] This is contrary to the King James Version (KJV) and Revised Standard Version (RSV), which assert the theological position of *creation ex nihilo*. Asian mythology also affirms similar ideas of chaos, void, darkness, and the deep as being the pre-creation state to be overcome by the creator. The NRSV has added a note to "while a wind from God," which reads: "Or while the spirit of God or while a mighty wind." Besides the word "Elohim," the Hebrew word רוח is open to at least three different translations: "wind," "spirit," and "breath." Cross-textual translation of the word in Genesis 1:2 into Chinese adopts the Daoist perception of the primordial *qi* (气), which sustains the whole universe, the myriad things and living creatures, including animals and human beings from the beginning, as an appropriate option. *Qi* conveys the meaning of the passage better than the conventional renderings of *ling* (灵) and *Shen* (神) by the Protestants and the Catholics respectively. The two different words mean "spirit" and again they are associated with the doctrine of the Holy Spirit in the Trinity in the two traditions of Chinese Protestantism and Catholicism, which the Hebrew Bible does not presuppose.

In conclusion, the cross-textual approach to Bible translation as proposed here is an appropriate means to affirm the hybridized identity of the colonized by providing a creative site for negotiation between the Asian text and the biblical text. It allows Asians to reclaim their religious-cultural texts in the reading, interpretative, and translation process. It also challenges the word of Bishop Rowan Williams of Canterbury, cited at the beginning of the chapter, that "every language can become the bearer of scriptural revelation." On the one hand, Asian languages have been the bearer of revelation in the Bible, but on the other, the culture embodied in Asian languages will contribute to the revelatory truth by going beyond the role of the bearer. Asia will and has been enriched through understanding of the Bible. Cross-textual translation responds to the earnest call of George Soares-Prabhu, an Indian biblical scholar, to engage Bible translation with the Indian religiosity of "the ashramites" and the conscientizing work of "the liberationists."[72] It is this spirit of openness to Asian texts and the practice of negotiation that constitutes a meaningful postcolonial strategy in Bible translation in Asia.

Notes

1. Carlos F. Cardoza-Orlandi and Justo L. Gonzalez, *To All Nations from All Nations: A History of the Christian Missionary Movement* (Nashville: Abingdon Press, 2013), 20.
2. Rowan Williams, "Forward," in *Sowing the Word: The Cultural Impact of British and Foreign Bible Society, 1804–2004*, edited by Stephen Batalden, Kathleen Cann, and John Dean (Sheffield: Sheffield Phoenix Press, 2004), x.
3. The research of this paper is supported by the National Social Science Fund of China on "The Hebrew Literary Classics in the Cultural Context of Ancient Mediterranean" (Project No. 15ZDB088).
4. Vicente L. Rafael, "Betraying Empire: Translation and Ideology of Conquest," *Translation Studies* 8, no. 1 (2015): 82–93, 88.
5. Rafael, "Betraying Empire," 83. Nietzsche has already alluded to how the Roman Empire's practice of translation of ancient Greek texts is to be understood as conquest actualizing in violation. He is quoted by Rafael (on the same page) as saying: "Indeed translation was a form of conquest. Not only did one omit what was historical, one also added allusions to the present and above all, struck out the name of the poet and replaced it with one's own—not with any sense of theft, but with the very best confidence of *imperium Romanum*."
6. The term "scriptural imperialism" is used by R. S. Sugirtharajah, *The Bible and the Third World: Precolonial, Colonial and Postcolonial Encounters*, (Cambridge: Cambridge

University Press, 2001), 45, 52, 60. The quote is from R. S. Sugirtharajah, *Asian Biblical Hermeneutics and Postcolonialism* (Sheffield: Sheffield Academic Press, 1999), 87.

7. For the Meiji Translation in Japan, see Doron B. Cohen, *Japanese Translations of the Hebrew Bible: History, Inventory and Analysis*, (Leiden and Boston: Brill, 2013), 154.
8. Edward Said, *Orientalism* (New York: Vintage Books), 1978, 299, 335. See a recent critique of binarism from the perspective of Asian theology: Simon Shui-Man Kwan, *Postcolonial Resistance and Asian Theology* (London and New York: Routledge, 2014), 12–13, 28–30, 54–59.
9. These two missionaries applied the Tower of Babel to the Chinese people, who were said to be punished more severely for having a very difficult language; see A. P. Happer, "A Visit to Peking," *Chinese Recorder* 10 (1879): 23–47; and Thomas McClatchie, "Paganism, v," *Chinese Recorder* 8 (1877): 56. Details of their views are discussed in Archie C. C. Lee, "Engaging the Context of the Tower of Babel and Listening to the Voices in the Text," in *Wrestling with God in Context: Revisiting the Theology and Social Vision of Shoki Coe*, edited by M.P. Joseph, Po Ho Huang and Victor Hsu *of Shoki Coe* (Fortress Press, forthcoming).
10. Rev. W. Remfry Hunt, "Bible Societies and Colportage," *Chinese Recorder and Missionary Journal* 31, (July 1, 1900) 341n.p.
11. Hunt, "Bible Societies and Colportage," 343.
12. Hunt, "Bible Societies and Colportage," 343.
13. Hunt, "Bible Societies and Colportage," 344.
14. Quoted by R. S. Sugirtharajah, *Postcolonial Criticism and Biblical Interpretation* (Oxford: Oxford University Press, 2002, 158).
15. Sugirthurajah, *Postcolonial Criticism*, 159.
16. Sugirtharajah, *Postcolonial Criticism*, 158.
17. Rafael, "Betraying Empire," 88.
18. Rafael, "Betraying Empire," 88.
19. Surgirtharajah, *Postcolonial Criticism*, 58–59.
20. CCB, "Notices of Recent Publications: Aids to the Understanding of the Bible in the Chinese Written Language," *Chinese Recorder and Missionary Journal*, March 1, 1883, 152.
21. Quoted by Cohen, *Japanese Translations of the Hebrew Bible*, 404.
22. Cohen, *Japanese Translations of the Hebrew Bible*, 405.
23. Calvin W. Mateer, "Lessons Learned in Translating the Bible into Mandarin," *Chinese Recorder* 39, November 1908, 608.
24. John Hull, "The Transmission of Religious Prejudice," *British Journal of Education* 14, no. 2 (1992): 69–72. Referred to by Sugirtharajah, *Asian Biblical Hermeneutics and Postcolonialism*, 93.
25. Examples are cited by Sugirtharajah regarding the translation of Christian ideas in the so-called Nestorian Monument unearthed in 1623 in Xian, West China. See Sugirtharajah, *Postcolonial Criticism*, 22–30. The stone is said to have been erected in 781 CE revealing the story of the arrival of the Syrian priest named Alopen (Aluoben) in China during the time of Tang Taizong in 635. The traditional reference to him and his church as being "Nestorian" may not be appropriate in view of the history of Syrian Christianity and its self-designation.
26. Sugirtharajah, *The Bible and the Third World*, 28.
27. Anonymous, "Bible Revision," *The Chinese Recorder and Missionary Journal* 22, November 1891, 501.
28. Rafael, "Betraying Empire," 91.

29. Archie C. C. Lee, "Naming God in Asia: Cross-Textual Reading in Multi-Cultural Context," *Quest: An Interdisciplinary Journal for Asian Christian Scholars* 3, no. 1 (2004): 21–42.
30. Archie C. C. Lee, "The Politico-Cultural Dynamics of Rendering the Biblical God in Asia," *Humanities: Christianity and Culture* 37 (March 2006): 75–89; and Archie C. C. Lee, "The Names of God and Bible Translation: Engaging the Chinese Term Question in the Context of Scriptural Interpretation," *Journal of Theologies and Cultures in Asia* 5 (2006): 1–17.
31. Quoted by Sung-Wook Hong, *Naming God in Korea: The Case of Protestant Christianity* (Oxford: Regnum Books International, 2008), 96. Hong discusses the topic of God in Korean Bibles, 95–104, and on God in the 1960s, 105–126.
32. Hong, *Naming God in Korea*, 101.
33. See the contribution of Chinese Christians to the discussion in *The Globe Magazine*, collected in *Discourses on Naming God: Debate on the Chinese Name of the Christian God in The Globe Magazine in Late Qing Dynasty* (《聖號論衡: 晚清〈萬國公報〉基督教"聖號論爭"文獻滙編》), edited by Archie C. C. Lee (Shanghai: Guji Publication, 2008).
34. Paul L. King reveals a survey of 161 native speakers of Chinese in New York City and reported in "Chinese Names for God," *The Bible Translator* 29, no. 3 (1978): 338. The phrase adopted by King for the Chinese response to the current usage is "vindicated."
35. See Irene Eber, *The Jewish Bishop and the Chinese Bible: S.I.J. Schereschewsky (1831–1906)* (Leiden, Boston, and Koln: Brill, 1999), 115–116; Irene Eber, *Bible in Modern China: The Literary and Intellectual Impact*, edited by Irene Eber, Sze-kar Wan, and Knut Walf (New York: Routledge, 1999), 151. See also Irene Eber, "Translating the Ancestors: S. I. J. Schereschewsky's 1875 Chinese Version of Genesis," *Bulletin of the School of Oriental and African Studies* 56, no. 2 (1993): 219–233.
36. Quoted by Kosuke Koyama, "The Role of Translation in Developing Indigenous Theologies—An Asian View," in *Bible Translation and the Spread of the Church, The Last 200 Years*, edited by Philip C. Stine (Leiden: E. J. Brill, 1990), 102.
37. David Thang Moe, "Adoniram Judson: A Dialectical Missionary Who Brought the Gospel (Not God) and Gave the Bible to the Burmese," *Missiology: An International Review* 45, no. 3 (2017): 265–282.
38. Examples of the impact on ordinary Chinese Christians are cited by Yang Donglong, "The Issue of Contextualization of 'Dragon' and Bible Translation," *Nanjing Theological Review* (2001/2002): 44–46.
39. L. Newton Hayes, *The Chinese Dragon* (Shanghai: Commercial Press, 1923), 11. Hayes studied the Chinese dragon in over half of the provinces in China for fourteen years before composing the book.
40. Hayes, *The Chinese Dragon*, 40–41.
41. Emily Dunn, "The Big Red Dragon and Indigenization of Christianity in China," *East Asian History* 36 (December 2008); 75.
42. Hampden C. Du Bose, *Dragon, Image and Demon: The Three Religions of China, Confucianism, Buddhism and Taoism, Giving an Account of the Mythology, Idolatry and Demonolatry* (London: S. W. Partridge, 1886), 8.
43. Du Bose, *Dragon, Image and Demon*, 457.
44. Du Bose, *Dragon, Image and Demon*, 461.
45. Du Bose, *Dragon, Image and Demon*, 462.
46. G. Tradescant Lay, *The Chinese as They Are: Their Moral, Social, and Literary Character* (London: William Ball, Paternoster Row, 1841).

47. O. G. Hertzog, "Some Opportunities and Possibilities in China," *The Chinese Recorder* 43, 1912, 33–40, 33.
48. Hertzog, "Some Opportunities and Possibilities in China," 34.
49. Hertzog, "Some Opportunities and Possibilities in China," 35.
50. Archie C. C. Lee, "The Bible in China: Religion of God's Chinese Son," *Princeton Seminary Bulletin* 29 (2008): 21–38.
51. Emily Dunn, "The Red Dragon and Indigenization of Christianity in China," *East Asian History* 36 (2008): 73–85.
52. Joshua Marshman in collaboration with Joannes Lassar, an Armenian Christian from Macau published the first full Chinese translation of the Bible in Serampore College, India in 1822. See Zhao Xiaoyang, "An Examination of the Relationship among the Marshman, Morrison, and Basset Versions of the Bible," *Chinese Studies in History*, 46 (2012), 6–34. For a detailed study of the history of the Chinese Bible, see Jost Oliver Zetzsche, *Bible in China: The History of the Union Version or The Culmination of Protestant Missionary Bible Translation in China* (Nettetal: Monumenta Serica, 1999)
53. Joshua Marshman also renders five of the six appearances of "dragon" in the KJV as "long." He translates the "dragon" of KJV in Jeremiah 51:34 into "big serpent" (大蛇).
54. Harold H. Martinson, *Red Dragon over China* (Minneapolis: Augsburg Publishing House, 1956). This is a collection of terrifying stories told by Chinese refugees and foreigners who escaped from China.
55. Betty Ann Maheu, "Hong Kong Returns to the Dragon," *Tripod* 113 (1999): 44–50.
56. Timothy K. Beal, *Religion and Its Monsters* (New York and London: Routledge, 2002), 6. He advocates the importance of knowing something of a religion by studying its monsters and learning of monsters by going to the religious background of monsters; see the Introduction and structure of his book, 4.
57. Dana L. Robert, *Christian Mission: How Christianity Became a World Religion* (Oxford: Wiley-Blackwell, 2009), 35. Robert cites a reference on this idea by Carter Lindberg, *The European Reformations* (Oxford: Blackwell, 1996), 39.
58. Adrian Hastings, *The Construction of Nationhood: Ethnicity, Religion and Nationalism* (Cambridge: Cambridge University Press, 1997), 12.
59. Quoted by Andrew Porter from an Oxford University sermon delivered by Krishnan Srinivasan ("Mission and Message," The Ramsden Sermon 17 November 2002) in *Religion Versus Empire? British Protestant Missionaries and Overseas Expansion, 1700–1914* (Manchester and New York: Manchester University Press, 2014), 316.
60. Porter, "Mission and Message," 316.
61. Porter, "Mission and Message," 318.
62. See the discussion of the difficulties faced by missionaries in China in Lin Mei Mei, "Samuel I. J. Schereschewsky and the Appropriation of Mission Strategies of the Protestant Episcopal China Mission: The Encounter and Dialogue between American Protestantism and Chinese Culture in the 19th Century," *Donghua Journal of Humanities* 4 (2002): 31–80.
63. This is the title of an influential book in recognizing insights in the so-called pagan religions: William Ernest Hocking, *Re-thinking Mission: A Layman's Inquiry after One Hundred Years* (New York and London: Harper & Brothers, 1932).
64. Lian Xi, *The Conversion of the Missionaries: Liberalism in American Protestant Missions in China, 1907–1932* (University Park: Pennsylvania State University Press, 1997).

65. See the analysis of the new approach on "The Crack within a missionary discourse" in Kwan, *Postcolonial Resistance and Asian Theology*, 76–82.
66. Koyama, "The Role of Translation in Developing Indigenous Theologies," 95.
67. Koyama, "The Role of Translation in Developing Indigenous Theologies," 96.
68. Archie C. C. Lee, "Scriptural Translations and Cross-textual Hermeneutics," *Oxford Handbook of Christianity in Asia*, edited Felix Wilfred (Oxford: Oxford University Press, 2014), 121–133.
69. There are other meanings of the word "con," which are not applicable to the present discussion, such as "cheating someone with a trick," a member of the conservative party in Britain, or an abbreviation for a "convict."
70. Archie C. C. Lee, "Reading Iconoclastic Stipulations in Number 33:50–56 from the Pluralistic Religious Context of China," *Leviticus and Numbers: Text @ Context*, edited by Athalya Brenner and Archie Lee (Minneapolis: Fortress Press, 2013), 213–226.
71. NRSV adds a note: "Or when God began to create or In the beginning God created."
72. George Soares-Prabhu, "Towards an Indian Interpretation of the Bible," in *Biblical Themes for a Contextual Theology Today*, edited by Isaac Pudinjarekuttu (Pune: Jnana-Deepa Vidyapeeth Theology Series 1999), 218.

Bibliography

Anonymous. "Bible Revision." *The Chinese Recorder and Missionary Journal* 22, (November 1891): 499–508.
Beal, Timothy K. *Religion and Its Monsters*. New York and London: Routledge, 2002.
Cardoza-Orlandi, Carlos F. and Justo L. Gonzalez, *To All Nations from All Nations: A History of the Christian Missionary Movement*. Nashville: Abingdon Press, 2013.
CCB. "Notices of Recent Publications: Aids to the Understanding of the Bible in the Chinese Written Language." *The Chinese Recorder and Missionary Journal*, (March 1, 1883): 152–162.
Cohen, Doron B. *Japanese Translations of the Hebrew Bible: History, Inventory and Analysis*. Leiden and Boston: Brill, 2013.
Du Bose, Hampden C. *Dragon, Image and Demon: The Three Religions of China, Confucianism, Buddhism and Taoism, Giving an Account of the Mythology, Idolatry and Demonolatry*. London: S. W. Partridge, 1886.
Dunn, Emily. "The Big Red Dragon and Indigenization of Christianity in China." *East Asian History* 36 (December 2008); 73–85.
Eber, Irene. "Translating the Ancestors: S. I. J. Schereschewsky's 1875 Chinese Version of Genesis." *Bulletin of the School of Oriental and African Studies* 56, no. 2 (1993): 219–233.
Eber, Irene. *The Jewish Bishop and the Chinese Bible: S.I.J. Schereschewsky (1831–1906)*. Leiden, Boston, and Koln: Brill, 1999.
Eber, Irene. *Bible in Modern China: The Literary and Intellectual Impact*, edited by Irene Eber, Sze-kar Wan, and Knut Walf. New York: Routledge, 1999.
Happer, A. P. "A Visit to Peking." *The Chinese Recorder and Missionary Journal* 10 (1879): 23–47.
Hastings, Adrian. *The Construction of Nationhood: Ethnicity, Religion and Nationalism*. Cambridge: Cambridge University Press, 1997.
Hayes, L. Newton. *The Chinese Dragon*. Shanghai: Commercial Press, 1923.
Hertzog, O. G. "Some Opportunities and Possibilities in China." *The Chinese Recorder and Missionary Journal* 43, (1912): 33–40.

Hocking, William Ernest. *Re-thinking Mission: A Layman's Inquiry after One Hundred Years*. New York and London: Harper & Brothers, 1932.

Hong, Sung-Wook. *Naming God in Korea: The Case of Protestant Christianity*. Oxford: Regnum Books International, 2008.

Hull, John. "The Transmission of Religious Prejudice." *British Journal of Education* 14, no. 2 (1992): 69–72.

Hunt, Rev. W. Remfry. "Bible Societies and Colportage." *The Chinese Recorder and Missionary Journal* 31, (July, 1900): 340–344.

King, Paul L. "Chinese Names for God." *The Bible Translator* 29, no. 3 (1978): 338.

Kwan, Simon Shui-Man. *Postcolonial Resistance and Asian Theology*. London and New York: Routledge, 2014.

Koyama, Kosuke. "The Role of Translation in Developing Indigenous Theologies—An Asian View." In *Bible Translation and the Spread of the Church, The Last 200 Years*, edited by Philip C. Stine. Leiden: E. J. Brill, 1990.

Lay, G. Tradescant. *The Chinese as They Are: Their Moral, Social, and Literary Character*. London: William Ball, Paternoster Row, 1841.

Lee, Archie C. C. "Naming God in Asia: Cross-Textual Reading in Multi-Cultural Context." *Quest: An Interdisciplinary Journal for Asian Christian Scholars* 3, no. 1 (2004): 21–42.

Lee, Archie C. C. "The Politico-Cultural Dynamics of Rendering the Biblical God in Asia." *Humanities: Christianity and Culture* 37 (March 2006): 75–89.

Lee, Archie C. C. "The Names of God and Bible Translation: Engaging the Chinese Term Question in the Context of Scriptural Interpretation." *Journal of Theologies and Cultures in Asia* 5 (2006): 1–17.

Lee, Archie C. C. *Discourses on Naming God: Debate on the Chinese Name of the Christian God in The Globe Magazine in Late Qing Dynasty* (《聖號論衡: 晚清〈萬國公報〉基督教 "聖號論争" 文獻滙編》). Shanghai: Guji Publication, 2008.

Lee, Archie C. C. "The Bible in China: Religion of God's Chinese Son." *Princeton Seminary Bulletin* 29 (2008): 21–38.

Lee, Archie C. C. "Reading Iconoclastic Stipulations in Number 33:50–56 from the Pluralistic Religious Context of China." In *Leviticus and Numbers: Text @ Context*, edited by Athalya Brenner and Archie Lee, 213–226. Minneapolis: Fortress Press, 2013.

Lee, Archie C. C. "Scriptural Translations and Cross-textual Hermeneutics." In *Oxford Handbook of Christianity in Asia*, edited Felix Wilfred, 121–133. Oxford: Oxford University Press, 2014.

Lee, Archie C. C. "Engaging the Context of the Tower of Babel and Listening to the Voices in the Text." In *Wrestling with God in Context: Revisiting the Theology and Social Vision of Shoki Coe*, edited by M. P. Joseph, Po Ho Huang and Victor Hsu. Fortress Press, forthcoming.

Lin Mei Mei. "Samuel I. J. Schereschewsky and the Appropriation of Mission Strategies of the Protestant Episcopal China Mission: The Encounter and Dialogue between American Protestantism and Chinese Culture in the 19th Century." *Donghua Journal of Humanities* 4 (2002): 31–80.

Lian Xi. *The Conversion of the Missionaries: Liberalism in American Protestant Missions in China, 1907–1932*. University Park: Pennsylvania State University Press, 1997.

Maheu, Betty Ann. "Hong Kong Returns to the Dragon." *Tripod* 113 (1999): 44–50.

Martinson, Harold H. *Red Dragon over China*. Minneapolis: Augsburg Publishing House, 1956.

McClatchie, Thomas. "Paganism, v." *The Chinese Recorder and Missionary Journal* 8, (January 1877): 54–65.

Mateer, Calvin W. "Lessons Learned in Translating the Bible into Mandarin." *The Chinese Recorder and Missionary Journal* 39, (November 1908): 603–609.

Moe, David Thang. "Adoniram Judson: A Dialectical Missionary Who Brought the Gospel (Not God) and Gave the Bible to the Burmese." *Missiology: An International Review* 45, no. 3 (2017): 265–282.

Porter, Andrew. *Religion Versus Empire? British Protestant Missionaries and Overseas Expansion, 1700–1914.* Manchester and New York: Manchester University Press, 2014.

Rafael, Vicente L. "Betraying Empire: Translation and Ideology of Conquest." *Translation Studies* 8, no. 1 (2015): 82–93.

Robert, Dana L. *Christian Mission: How Christianity Became a World Religion.* Oxford: Wiley-Blackwell, 2009.

Said, Edward. *Orientalism.* New York: Vintage Books, 1978.

Soares-Prabhu, George. "Towards an Indian Interpretation of the Bible." In *Biblical Themes for a Contextual Theology Today*, edited by Isaac Pudinjarekuttu, 207–222. Pune: Jnana-Deepa Vidyapeeth Theology Series, 1999.

Sugirtharajah, R. S. *Asian Biblical Hermeneutics and Postcolonialism.* Sheffield: Sheffield Academic Press, 1999.

Sugirtharajah, R. S. *The Bible and the Third World: Precolonial, Colonial and Postcolonial Encounters.* Cambridge: Cambridge University Press, 2001.

Sugirthurajah, R. S. *Postcolonial Criticism and Biblical Interpretation.* Oxford: Oxford University Press, 2002.

Williams, Rowan. "Forward." In *Sowing the Word: The Cultural Impact of British and Foreign Bible Society, 1804–2004*, edited by Stephen Batalden, Kathleen Cann, and John Dean, x–xii. Sheffield: Sheffield Phoenix Press, 2004.

Yang Donglong. "The Issue of Contextualization of 'Dragon' and Bible Translation." *Nanjing Theological Review* (2001/2002): 44–46.

Zetzsche, Jost Oliver. *Bible in China: The History of the Union Version or the Culmination of Protestant Missionary Bible Translation in China.* Nettetal: Monumenta Serica, 1999.

Zhao Xiaoyang. "An Examination of the Relationship among the Marshman, Morrison, and Basset Versions of the Bible." *Chinese Studies in History*, 46 (2012): 6–34.

PART IV
POSTCOLONIAL SOCIAL AND ETHICAL CONCERNS

PART IV

CHAPTER 22

POSTCOLONIAL BIBLICAL CRITICISM AND QUEER STUDIES

JEREMY PUNT

INTRODUCTION

Recognizing the intercadence between postcolonial and queer studies is often easier than fully explaining the reasons for associating the two fields of study or comprehensively describing the nature, scope, and elements constituting the connections. Part of the challenge in describing the possible connections is the recurrent contentiousness in describing either of the two. The strongest links between postcolonial and queer theory (but not necessarily the simplest to explain) are related to their particular focus on dissent and their take on power. Postcolonial and queer approaches trace those social configurations of power that have led and continue to lead to the establishment of people as subjugated Others (Spivak) and their perpetual, continuing marginalization. Concerned with the well-being of Others, both approaches invoke theoretical frameworks for understanding but also for circumventing and working toward eradicating networks of power that (continue to) subjugate marginalized people. With regard to sex and gender, queer theory destabilizes the self-evidence of power and marginality, center and periphery, and related notions that are central to postcolonial theory.[1] Both postcolonial studies and queer work constitute a move away from identity to subjectivity that implies detachment from biological, national, cultural, or other essentialisms. This move marks a critical theoretical departure from previous definitions of identity and refocuses attention on "the complex, intersecting ways in which people are embedded within multiple, conflicted discourses, practices, and institutions" (Oleksy 2009: 1). The nonessentialist, intersectional move avoids the extremes of bland detachment or partisan activism. In the case of biblical studies, postcolonial and queer theorists engage the different ways in which Othering takes place in and around biblical texts, in the reception history of the Bible, and in the scholarly guild. They stay alert to prevailing hermeneutics but are also intent on exploring alternative, and to some extent restorative, hermeneutics and textual readings.

This contribution explores a number of links, relations, and intersections between postcolonial and queer criticisms, trying to understand wherein such links may be situated and also how queer theory, or better, theories function with regard to postcolonial biblical criticism. Some of the alignments are evident, such as postcolonial and queer theories' seeming shared predilection for technical theoretical apparatuses at the surface level, their social constructionist angles, and the identification of the discursive nature of power relations. Other aspects are less self-evident, such as the interconnections brought about by queer theory's sociopolitical implications and how queerness impacts on and plays out in sociopolitical terms. Such interconnections may be related to postcolonial theory's (at times reluctant) inclusion of sex and gender and its attention to how unequal power relations both inform and are impacted by sex and gender. In the end, both postcolonial and queer work seem to be driven by common concerns, such as power, identity, difference, mimicry, agency, and the quest for a new world order.[2] This contribution aims to explore the postcolonial queer relationship with such questions in mind. The discussion starts with a brief account of the two approaches.

Lay of the Land: Accounting for Two Approaches

Postcolonial and queer criticism, as well as its biblical studies variants, are notoriously difficult to describe. Queer biblical criticism typically serves as an "umbrella term" for a variety of critical approaches, which includes wide-ranging perspectives such as gay, lesbian, bisexual, intersexed, and transgendered experiences, and also "a theoretical sensibility that pivots on transgression or permanent rebellion" (Seidman 1996: 11).[3] While Foucault was in the past often posited as the primary originator of queer theory, a growing sentiment relates queer beginnings rather to sociopolitical forces that resisted its emergence. Various dissenting groups and voices, as well as conflictual and confrontational aspects, contributed in different ways to the rise of this field of knowledge.[4] Queer approaches combine elements from gender studies and are characterized by their questioning and destabilizing of sexual identities and countering cultural prejudice against sexual minorities (Donovan 2001: 266 n72). Queer theories denounce sexuality as a universal and eternal drive but affirm it as an important social construct.[5] Queer theorists in particular challenge the conventional framework for human sexuality that produces heterosexuality and homosexuality, as binaries, and considers religious ideas as the cultural means of production for that system[6] (Schneider 2000a: 3; 2000b: 208). Queer biblical criticism engages the interpretation of the biblical material on corporeality and the body, on sex and sexuality, and on gender and gender performativity. It focuses on meaning generated through the queering of texts, often alert to their historical contexts but without allowing the latter to regulate or establish some sort of Archimedean point. Queer biblical criticism is all about investigating the ways in which sex and gender function within and are (taken to be) constitutive of power grids in biblical texts and associated sociohistorical settings.

Postcolonial biblical criticism has been around slightly longer and is in a similar way a collective term, in the sense of a broader approach, rather than encapsulating a proliferation of discrete, self-contained hermeneutical or exegetical methods. Although descriptions differ, as essays in this volume will illustrate, it is often taken to refer to a variety of different methodologies, characterized by their overt political nature and ideological agenda, whose textual politics ultimately concerns both a hermeneutic of suspicion and a hermeneutic of retrieval or restoration.[7] While little agreement may exist on terminology, certain broader patterns that have evolved within postcolonial biblical criticism can be identified. Postcolonial work interacts with colonial history and its aftermath(s), which concerns histories of both repression and of repudiation, but it also deals with exposé, with restoration, and with transformation. Not only lamenting the past, postcolonial work allows for other voices from the texts but also from other, marginalized contexts, ancient and more recent, to surface. Postcolonial theorists, such as Said with orientalism, Bhabha with hybridity and mimicry, and Spivak with othering, have contributed to a vocabulary for describing encounters with empire and colonialization, alert to the prevailing ambivalence of such encounters.[8] While postcolonial approaches admit various perspectives in method and of orientation, scope, and level, an overly generous use of postcolonial notions runs the risk of deflating its specific value for biblical studies. In fact, postcolonial work would exclude some traditional scholarly methods because of their hegemonic positions and imperialist stances. Like queer biblical criticism, postcolonial biblical criticism is about a different focus and purpose, rather than a different hermeneutical method per se, and it reserves special attention for ideology criticism and a hermeneutics of suspicion (Punt 2015: 74–76).

Just over a decade ago, the alignment between approaches such as queer theory and postcolonial theory on theoretical grounds as much as for their sociopolitical thrust was acknowledged: "theory-savvy critical movements that all, to a greater or lesser degree, bring critical sensibilities forged in the crucible of an often generic poststructuralism to bear upon assorted 'material' domains" (Moore 2005: 82). However, such acknowledgment has not meant that queer has been associated self-evidently or consistently with postcolonial work, which explains, respectively, the absence of the one in recent commentaries dedicated to the other. While the editors make it clear in their preface to *The Queer Bible Commentary* (Guest, Goss, West, and Bohache 2006: xiii) that contributions to this volume are informed also by postcolonial studies, the volume offers no sustained discussion of possible areas of contact. So too, in *A Postcolonial Commentary of the New Testament Writings* (Segovia and Sugirtharajah 2007), robust discussions of queer are lacking, and the few instances where queer is used seem to suggest that the intersections between postcolonial and queer studies are not deemed crucial for postcolonial work.

Intersections between postcolonial and queer approaches reach beyond their theoretical acumen and dissenting stance. The political nature of queer theory is most evident perhaps in its critique of heteronormativity, the mainstay of modern society and contemporary culture (Moore 1998: 259). Increasingly, race- and class-consciousness are palpable in queer theory,[9] and the depth of significance and the inseparability of race, class, ethnicity, and gender in queer theorizing gives queer theory its cutting edge (Schneider 2000b: 211; see Spurlin 2001: 185). So too, the criticism that postcolonial studies have by and large ignored how heterosexism and homophobia in many ways contributed to the shaping of the world of hegemonic power (Spurlin 2001: 185) suggests some latent if still neglected connections between postcolonial and queer work. Queer and postcolonial biblical criticisms, then, are neither versions of each other nor singular, exegetical models of some sort, but rather broader hermeneutical frameworks that provide heuristic epistemologies for interpreting biblical texts.[10]

Primary Encounters: Significant Primary Research Foci

Postcolonial and queer encounter each other in biblical criticism in a number of significant areas. Queer theories' skepticism about gender or sexual identity relies on the notion not only that the prevalent alignment of sex and gender is artificial but also that regulatory regimes use such sex- and gender-informed identity categories, whether as repressive structures or as reclaimed positions to resist those very repressive structures.[11] Postcolonial queer biblical criticism concerns itself with sex and gender discourses generated and maintained through biblical interpretation, associated considerations of hegemony and power, and related ongoing ideological impact—indicated here in terms of six important areas.

Sexualized Social Hierarchy

Queer studies and postcolonial work feed into each other already in plotting the sexualized social hierarchies of biblical times, trying to understand the intricate relationship between sex and power in ancient communities. A queer or queerying reading of Paul's letter to the Romans, and Rom 1:26–27 in particular, teases out the difference in perceiving sex and gender in the first century and today (Moore 1998: 250–274; 2001: 133–172).[12] A study of contemporary first-century authors shows an understanding of homoeroticism that differs radically from modern perceptions, not the least because ancient sexuality was not separated by a homosexual-heterosexual dividing line but adhered to boundaries informed by social status and determined by activity and passivity. Freeborn males ruled the roost and asserted their masculinity through (sexual) activity, by penetration, in contrast to being soft and being penetrated, which was a role reserved for those lower down on the social ladder, regardless of their sex, including women, slaves, effeminate males, eunuchs, "barbarians," and "captives."[13] "The reduction of sexual relations to the act of penetration enables sex to become a simple yet effective instrument for expressing hierarchical relations" (Moore 1998: 271). Gender and social status in the first-century Greek and Roman world were interlinked, rendering "class-infused views of masculinity" (Moore 1998: 266–267; Vorster 2000: 103–124), and relegated femininity and women along with other nondominant groups as subsidiaries to free men. Modern binaries fail to address this situation, which already suggests the need for and potential value of the queerying of sex, gender, and sexuality.

Apart from modern binaries being inadequate markers for ancient gender and sex, in the first century CE single people were sexual minorities. Notwithstanding sociocultural as well as legal pressure, especially since Augustus's attempts to regulate marriage and childbirth in 17/18 BCE, and the marginalization that accompanied singleness, indications are that most biblical authors nevertheless were single (Hanks 2000: 148–149; 177, 182ff). While Jesus' marital status is never in focus in the New Testament, Paul made his preference for singleness and celibacy abundantly explicit (1 Cor 7:6–8, 26, 37–38). Paul's option for celibacy disenables a simplistic ascription to him of either a strict gender differentiation based on sex and gender or an absolute, heterosexist position regarding procreative sex. It further bears reminding that the Pauline and other references to biblical texts were of course, amid all the accompanying variety and subtle differences, ensconced in the androcentric, patriarchal, and heteronormative sociocultural societies of the ancient Mediterranean. Operating at a metaphorical level, living in and through textual embodiments, these arrangements of and for sex and gender are replete with social embodiment, indicative of the societal, physiological, and other material and concrete manifestations of human living in biblical times.

Bodies and Empire: The Political Nature of Sex and Gender

A primary concern of postcolonial biblical criticism is the significance of empires for (if not always explicitly in) the biblical documents. It investigates the presence and impact of Assyrian, Egyptian, Persian, Greek, and Roman empires on the social, cultural, and political framework in which biblical documents came into being. While earlier work probes empire as part of the broader sociohistorical setting of the Bible, postcolonial criticism looks at empire from a different perspective, which is informed by postcolonial theory and its apparatus. It considers the depiction of empire, its role in the lives of people, and the ways in which they are portrayed in biblical texts (Sugirtharajah 2012: 46–51). The relationship between politics and sex is confirmed by the countless gendered body metaphors that informed imperial and colonial enterprises, often using sexual imagery of conquering, penetration, and ravishing to express its hegemonic gain or hold over the colonized worlds.

The preponderance of the Bible's body-metaphors, and to some extent kinship-metaphors, suggests postcolonial and queer theories as viable options for the analysis of biblical texts. Furthermore, the corporeality of human existence constitutes an obvious but primary link between sex, gender, and politics. It is in and through bodies as sexual and gendered entities, within communities and societal systems at large, that the biblical texts are constituted and, today, read and interpreted.[14] Although often presented as oppositional spheres of public versus private, politics and sex nevertheless stand in close proximity to each other at the geopolitical level, where land and body are reciprocally inscribed by the colonizers. "Sexual desire mobilises people's concept of citizenship and of justice. In political discourse, sex counts and in political theology, it is an essential resource" (Althaus-Reid 2000: 139).

In the extension of its focus on corporeality are issues caused by the movement of people, such as diaspora, migrancy, multiculturalism, hybridity, and nationhood, brought about by colonialism and postcolonialism (Sugirtharajah 2012: 50–51). It is the gendered and sexual nature of the movement of people-issues that queer studies wants to focus on, not only how their embodied, gendered, and sexualized makeup gives rise to people on the move but also how the sex and gender configurations determine and affect—and queer—such movement of people. In the biblical context, the Rahab and Ruth narratives of the Hebrew Bible render a masculinized woman sex-worker and an Israelite woman using sexual wiles to achieve her goals (see, e.g., Runions 2011: 45–74; Darden 2012: 63–71). So too in the New Testament (NT), movement of people is central, exemplified by the restless Jesus of the Gospel generally traveling with his band of brothers, the disciples. On the one hand, the patriarchal society of the time certainly legitimated public male-male congregation, with male friendship a particularly highly rated virtue in the Greek and Roman society. On the other hand, such relationships necessarily stood within the tensions of male honor, prescribed gender status and roles, and so forth, rendering homoeroticism ambivalent at the best of times. And so in the NT also, the male bias in public association, even when overlaid by aspirations to honor, aided the thrust of people movement.

Both postcolonial and queer theories emphasize the corporal and therefore the political but they venture beyond conventional, naturalized binaries and, adopting an ideological critical posture, investigate the sources, nature, and scope of power and its exercise.[15] Both theoretical approaches work toward the demystification of material bodies encapsulated in conventional, normal, or traditional; both are intensely interested also in understanding how concepts and categories claiming universality were formed or constructed, the nature of their interdependency and often reciprocal convergence, and in whose interest and for whose benefit they were constructed. Queer theory works to move away from and to desist from either homogenizing same-sex love in a white, Western, capitalist, and male gay model, and from its inverse, of orientalizing that is exoticising and othering, reducing otherness to undifferentiated blandness (see Punt 2008: 2).

Challenging Heteronormativity

The despotic of the conventional sex and gender regime resonates with the dictatorial imperialisms and colonialisms identified in postcolonial work. Queer theories' challenge to the imperializing nature of heteronormativity is a political act. Queer theories gather under their wings many critical positions regarding sex and gender, and at times also radical dispositions, all of which are directed against "*normative* consolidations of sex, gender and sexuality—and that, consequently, is critical of all those versions of identity, community, and politics that are believed to evolve 'naturally' from such consolidations" (Jagose 1996: 99). The connections between queer and postcolonial theories are probably most explicit in the engagement of queer theories with the totalitarian and universally acclaimed regime of heteronormativity. So too, the inherent ambivalence of ascribed transgressivity is reclaimed as both right and challenge and informs both postcolonial and queer biblical interpretation: "it is in this non-denial, yet challenge that discourses of dissent are produced" (Vorster 2012: 605)—of which both queer and postcolonial discourses are good examples.

More than a descriptive category, heterosexuality is a social and political organizing principle, imbued with a politics of knowledge and difference (Seidman 1996: 9), fraught with the danger of becoming totalitarian heteronormativity. While heteronormativity relies upon established and fixed sex and gender patterns, queer theories do not simply tolerate ambivalence but anticipate and actively celebrate sex and gender differences. Queer biblical criticism shows that gender patterns in the Bible at times become obscure and challenge heteronormative positions. Gender is queered in the reference to Epimenides, who was a gay shaman from Crete (sixth century BCE) and who is quoted twice, favorably, in the NT (Ac 17:28; Ti 1:12–13).[16] The inclusiveness toward eunuchs in the Bible is particularly remarkable: the prohibition on admitting eunuchs into the people of God (Deut 23:1) is superseded in Is 56:31–35. And in the NT, Jesus spoke favorably of eunuchs (Mt 19:12), and Philip as an early leader of the church brought a eunuch into the Jesus follower community through baptism (Ac 8:26–80; Mollenkott 2003: 192–193). The binary of masculinity and femininity is a social construction, serving political hegemonic purposes rather than reflecting the inevitable nature of men or women as supposedly buttressed by a divinely ordained Bible. In contrast to dominant readings that attribute binaries such as strong–weak, intelligent–stupid, or outgoing–domestic to men and women respectively, Genesis portrays Jacob's gender performance as unbefitting for an ancient Israelite man. Jacob associates primarily with his mother and lives in her domestic space. However, when Israel is named, it is not for Esau as the manly type but for Jacob who is at home in the kitchen (Stone 2016: 4). In all its disruptiveness and transgressiveness, queer theories produce difference through questioning the conventional and anticipating alternatives.

The Queer God's Impact on Social Arrangements

The biblical image of the divine is not as masculine and patriarchal as suggested by its normalized version. Already in the Hebrew Bible, and in the Genesis accounts specifically, God is described in terms of an all-inclusive gender (Gen 1:26; 5:1-2). Given the importance of sex and gender for sociocultural worldviews, the use of sex and gender constructions to justify conventions, and how communities and societies organized themselves, the dual-gendered depiction of God was bound to contribute to destabilizing, countercultural notions and to challenge prevailing male-female gender constructions.[17] The earliest Jewish commentaries on Genesis referred to Adam, created in the likeness of God, as at first being created as a bisexual and thus was a hermaphrodite. However, the biblical notion of a sexless God did not win out against Christian theology's later development of a male God, who soon became established as the traditional God-image (e.g., Loughlin 2005: 9-27; Stone 2005: 23-45).[18]

As has become clear already, tracing the relationship between sex, gender, and power requires attention for intersectionality. In biblical times, the household or family functioned as the foundational unit of the state,[19] and it was supported by household codes that served as a model for the political order.[20] Human nature was thought of as a hierarchically ordered unity, served by the male and female distinction that provided the framework for procreation but that, through marriage and "family" (in the sense of household), also provided continuity and stability in the social order.[21] Social arrangements depend on sex and gender categories and their naturalization, crucial aspects of which are heteronormativity and ascribing different roles to women and men. However, queer critics point out that, in the Hebrew Bible, the male patriarchs perceive themselves collectively with the people of ancient Israel as the consort of God. Sex and gender are already implicit in social arrangements, but when human orderings are endorsed in the name of the divine, the political roles of sex and gender become even more pronounced. The patriarchs of Israel are wife to God as husband, as described also by the prophets Hosea, Jeremiah, and Ezekiel (Loughlin 2005: 23). Later in the prophetic material, detailed graphics describe how the relationship between God and Israel is sexually consummated (Ezek 16:4-9). "God washes away the blood of Israel's 'deflowering'; and male circumcision becomes the mark, in her flesh, of God's possession" (Loughlin 2005: 24). The consequence of inscribing God sexually meant that God was portrayed in a way that queered the men of Israel and left them with a choice between having become like women or like men sleeping with men as with women (Lev 18:20).[22] But this all-male affair leaves women peculiarly not only outside these relationships but even outside full humanity. Cut off from the divine by not sharing a similar connection with the divine, women are by and large excluded from social power.[23]

The normalized convention of household codes in Colossians 3:18-25 and Ephesians 5:22-6:9, and similar instructions in the Pastoral Epistles and 1 Peter 2:18-3:7, reflect a prevalent slaveholder morality.[24] The gospels, though, suggest that Jesus anticipated the dissolving of family bonds (Mt 10:35-36; Lk 12:53), taking his cue from Micah 7:6. In the implied disruption of the household for the sake of the gospel,[25] Jesus re-envisioned the composition and function of the household, its social place, and its social roles.[26] Jesus referred to his followers in household terms—as brother, sister, and mother—but not as father or wife and thus without notions of authority, procreation, or patriarchy. In this way the household is queered in the kingdom, and so too is Jesus queered.[27] Amid sociopolitical developments such as Herod Antipas' attempt to establish a new Greek- and Roman-style economy, which favored cities and the elite,[28] Jesus was portrayed as breaking through established social boundaries, offering an alternative social environment for the household. In the ancient context, where households were an elemental version of the larger community and the building blocks of the empire, any challenge to households was political and potentially anti-empire.

Queer(ed) Believers: Upsetting Social Values

Not only did a queer God impact on and disrupt conventional social arrangements, so too did queer(ed) believers upset reigning social values, politically inscribed in public structures and systems. The NT authors used a wide variety of sex and gender images to describe the Jesus followers, as well as their relationships to God and Jesus and among themselves. Many of these images conjured up queer notions, challenged reigning sociopolitical norms, and needed to be hidden from sight amid imperial or colonial conquests. Such conquests not only relied upon unambiguous, clear gender and sex values for their own ideological claims, but they claimed to further such values as part of their missio-political quest. However, such clear-cut notions are not representative of much of the NT, when the sex and gender of early followers of Jesus are queered by men's portrayals as the metaphorical brides of Christ (Eph 5:29–32) or by women believers included among Jesus' brothers (Rom 8:28–29) in the early Jesus communities. "If only at a symbolic level, all Christian [sic] men are queer" (Loughlin 2005: 24), and such queerness also applies to women as a matter of fact. The call upon the whole (female) church "to grow in every way into him who is head" (Eph 4:15) also suggests that gender is not conceptualized as a simple binary.[29] So too in the NT, cross-dressing metaphors are used in positive contexts (Col 3:9–10; Rom 13:14). Abraham's fatherhood is defined through motherhood in Gal 4:21–5:1 (see also Kahl 2000: 45), and transgendering is taken up without blinking so that Paul becomes a mother giving birth (Gal 4:19),[30] and male–female polarities are listed as a dichotomy that should ideally be overcome (Gal 3:28).[31] Particularly with such a self-presentation in Galatians within a context where the supramasculine sign of circumcision was the discourse marker and symbol par excellence, which further included "his shamefully 'unmanly' boasting of weakness as something to be imitated (4:12–15), his rejection of male honor and image games (5:26; 6:12), his nasty remark concerning castration, [and] his model of a 'household of faith' without patriarchal authority (6:10)," makes Paul appear positively queer (see Kahl 2000: 49). Queer and postcolonial biblical criticisms pursue such contrapuntal readings, not only challenging gender and sex norms as anything but stable but also decentering them in their sociopolitical positioning of hegemonic cultural and political practices.

At other times, Pauline queerness is on the back-foot as, for example, in his affirmation of first-century conventions when he correlated people's sexual relations to their relations with God. In Romans, Paul's depiction of homoeroticism as the result of the failure to acknowledge God fits in well with the Greek and Roman world's hypernormativity in a phallofixated system: "a sex-gender system in which every sexual act *must* involve a masculine and a feminine partner—to the extent that when an anatomically female partner is lacking, an anatomically male partner must be conscripted to play the woman" (Moore 2001: 170). Gender hierarchy is maintained by and through sex, confirming the superiority of man and inferiority of woman, to the extent that same-sex encounters become expressions of misogyny. Since Paul's theology, writ small, was not only inflected but partly produced by the prevailing sex and gender notions, reversals of the latter would have serious implications for his theological convictions. Together with postcolonial biblical criticism, at such times queer biblical criticism has to acknowledge the compromised nature of the biblical texts and how they are implicated in hegemonic practices of the past and the present. Moreover, the transmission of the Bible in a colonial context had to strive to avoid the conveyance of any such socially disturbing notions, which was one of the important factors impacting on Bible translations for the "new world."

Betrayful Translations

Access to the Bible and its translatability are two sides of the same coin and characterize the Christian scriptures (e.g., Sanneh 1989; Schaaf 1994). But biblical access and translatability are ambivalently situated with regard to interpretive hegemonies, at times serving a hegemony while at others working against it.[32] Access to the Bible has brought about the decentering of interpretation, so that queering is no longer found among trained interpreters only. Attentive readers in various contexts find significant instances of queering sex and gender in the biblical texts. However, queer texts have all but disappeared in modern Bibles through either careless or ideological translations. In both instances, translations impose modern figurations on ancient, biblical bodies to make them present in new but unbiblical and irresponsible—at least as far as the original texts are concerned—personages.[33] In this regard, queer and postcolonial criticism, for cultural as much as for theological reasons, show upon shortcomings in Bible translations of past and present while acknowledging translations' often constructive role in rejuvenating indigenous languages (e.g., Schaaf 1994; cf Dube 2001). Queer studies, like postcolonial work, seeks to reverse the cultural impact of biblical translation as much as interpretation of blurred local cultures' egalitarian values (Sugirtharajah 2012: 46–51). In one of the lesbigay six-shooter or clobber texts, Rom 1:26–27, Paul's emphasis on *nature* (natural) is far removed from the scientific-biological model of the twenty-first century. In ancient literature, φύσις or φυσικός was generally used to mean either "constitution" or, in medical-technical and vulgar language, referred to the genitals. "Natural *relations*" is not a proper translation of τὴν φυσικὲν χρῆσιν, which means "natural *use/act*," that is, an act that is in accordance with the social hierarchy of society, the conventional way of acting.[34] Paul's use of "unnatural" with reference to *action* is borne out by his reference to desire and shows a typical first-century concern for the "natural use" of sex to contain passions (Martin 1995: 341–342). Using words such as "homosexuality" or "unnatural relations" in Bible translations of Romans 1 does it an injustice, enslaving it to a modern and heteronormative worldview,[35] and thus it misleads Bible readers.

Such translations are particularly harmful in colonized settings. Same-sex relationships in precolonial Africa tolerated many different approaches to sexual behavior. In precolonial society, sex and gender did not necessarily coincide, as Ifi Amadiume reminded us, and gender roles were neither rigidly masculinized nor feminized.[36] Same-sex relations that existed without infringing upon social norms changed with the onset of colonization (see also Punt 2014), where the political nature of sex and gender became even more pronounced. Translation comprises more than moving notions between different languages; it also reveals how such notions are conceptualized. Translated Bibles play a particularly important role in conveying (new) understandings of the text, for example, by not obscuring the remarkable queerness of Jesus Christ with its claims to be an imprint of God (Phil 2:6; Heb 1:3) and, according to the gospel narrative, an offspring of a virgin (Lk 1:26–35).[37] Jesus' parthenogenetic birth suggests him having two X-chromosomes, although the first-century audiences understood it differently given the dominance of an androcentric physiology (e.g., Laqueur 1990; Mollenkott 2003: 192). The focus on Jesus' virgin birth holds interesting if unintended possibilities for understanding the significance of his gender today.[38] Does the ascription of masculinity to Jesus require some form of sex reversal in the male phenotype, or should Jesus Christ be understood as not in the first instance a male but rather an intersexual savior? When the act of (re)translating concerns a far-reaching reformatting of the text for a new context and not mere dependence upon the past (Sugirtharajah 1998: 97), the postcolonial-queer intersection insists on looking beyond the conventional and the established—of which some contributions and directions can be considered now.

Queer(y)ing Contributions and Directions

In this chapter's brief assessment of queer studies' relation to postcolonial biblical criticism, two important if rather subtle aspects emerge, defining the nature of the task at hand rather than constituting its contents. One, connections between politics writ large and various other aspects of human life, and sex and gender in particular, require more attention to the intersectionality of the work done in these (and other) areas in various historical and contextual dimensions. Two, queer studies' growing importance relates to the capability of such work in opening up understanding through destabilizing sex and gender and revealing these aspects as being ostensibly both stable and the building blocks of human lives and, in particular, of society.[39] In both instances, namely the sex, gender, and politics intersectionality as well as the socially constitutive aspects of sex and gender, these considerations apply to ancient as well as modern contexts albeit that they are sociopolitically inscribed differently across time-lines. These two general but vital aspects frame four more specific areas where queer studies provide interesting perspectives in conjunction with postcolonial biblical criticism.

First, queer studies, like postcolonial work, has vested interests in *claiming and reclaiming identity*, not in the sense or for the purpose of identity politics but rather as retrievals of a sort. Postcolonial and queer biblical critics' resistance against identity politics have led to accusations of intellectual insularity and social irrelevance (Punt 2015: 84–86). However, in reclaiming queer from its past derogatory use, queer theory extends beyond similar restorations such as "gay," which recover erotic interests, because queer criticism reclaims a broader spectrum of marginalized interests.[40] This understanding of queer not only shows it as a positive and affirmative designation but also reveals its critical and political dimension. Not to decry the legitimacy or need of lesbigay movements' focus on identity politics for their political interventionist strategies, the queer response to identity categories is more mediated. Queer work assists in showing the provisional and contingent nature of such categories and their growing political curtailment in a postmodern world; however, queer increasingly serves self-identification and political organization purposes (Brown 2001: 371).

Postcolonial biblical criticism is invested in retrieval hermeneutics, often described through three tasks: retrieving those deliberately marginalized and silenced figures or incidents and restoring them to dignity; exploring and retelling the stories of those who, often imaginatively, resisted hegemony; and recovering the skeptical reactions of the co-opted yet ambivalent agents of colonization (Sugirtharajah 2012: 46–51). Queer theories similarly do not chase after some perceived original, authentic (if divergent) sex and gender. Retrieval hermeneutics is, however, also not excluded in queer studies, especially as far as precolonial sex and gender patterns and identities are concerned. Here too intersectional approaches, with economics and politics playing roles in sociocultural values regarding the "originals" but also in their manufacturing and reformatting by the colonists, as well as interdisciplinary work, are considered vital for queer work.[41] Although to some extent already implicit in the previous areas, postcolonial and queer criticisms show what can be called a militant sensitivity to historic silences and crude universalisms.

Second, *issues of power and their intersectionality* largely continue to determine the focus and programs of postcolonial and queer approaches. In as much as postcolonial biblical criticism explores how biblical interpreters (re)present empire, whether under the past influence of empire and colonization or the continuing hegemonic patterns such as neocolonialism (Sugirtharajah 2012: 46–51), queer biblical scholars consider the powerful impact of historical and enduring sex and gender patterns on biblical interpretation. Eschewing the ever popular but banal battle-of-the-sexes notion, very real and ongoing contestations characterize gender performativity and constructions of sex. The nature of power becomes clearer especially when its interworkings with the construction of meaning is considered: "a deepened understanding of the discursive structures and representational systems that determine the production of sexual meanings, and that micromanage individual perceptions, in ways which serve to maintain and reproduce the underpinnings of heterosexist privilege" (Halperin 1995: 32).

Postcolonial and queer rub shoulders even stronger in their at times all too comfortable link with globalization, often the neocolonization of our time, but also that which blurs borders and renders nation-states irrelevant.[42] On the other hand, nation-states that are affirmed in postcolonial studies amid the dangers of global and globalizaing (read, Western) homogenizing and universalizing often find it difficult to deal with what is perceived as sexual dissidence. In short, queer and postcolonial theories at times do not reckon strongly enough with empire's "inclusionary mechanism," with its centripetal pull, so that their theorists "who advocate a politics of difference, fluidity, and hybridity in order to challenge the binaries and essentialism of modern sovereignty have been outflanked by the strategies of power" (Hardt and Negri in Hawley 2001: 9).[43] The danger is that Othering increases beyond politics, sex, or gender to include Othering due to class or other social formations as well as intersectional Othering. The entanglement of gender with socioeconomic processes has received more attention than the intersection between sex and economics, apart from issues such as transactional sex. However, as in a recent collection of essays on queering the economy, scholars increasingly investigate economic processes by pointing to perspectives based on, and connections between, desire and justice. The volatile, interrelated combination of colonial legacies, exploitative relations, and hierarchical arrangements based on sex and gender are impacted by a complex mixture of forces and relations of power, domination, and violence, which sees economy as a vital component in the vigorous interaction between subjectivity, signification, and governance (Dhawan et al. 2015).

Third, integral to postcolonial and queer work is a strong element of *denaturalization*. "The theory of performativity largely underwrites the 'queer' project. Like it, 'queer' opts for denaturalization as its primary strategy" (Brown 2001: 373). What Morgensen argues for in anthropological work, applied more broadly as well, is that queer both uncovers and disrupts colonial conditions of epistemology and methodology. "Just as queer accounts must analyze the violences of colonial modernity, thinking with qualities evoked by this term disturbs the colonial structuration of knowledge and invites unanticipated thought" (Morgensen 2016: 607). By denaturalization, queer's applicability reaches beyond sex and gender, at least beyond sex and gender in isolation, to also include the investigation of other identity negotiation discourses such as race, ethnicity, and postcolonial nationality, whether they establish or rupture identity processes. "By problematizing normative consolidations of sex, gender, and sexuality, 'queer' is most productive in its critique and disruption of all those versions of identity, community, and politics that are popularly believed to evolve 'naturally' from such consolidations, and, for these reasons, it has been, and is, indispensable for the present and future of postcolonial studies" (Brown 2001: 374).

However, neither queer sexualities nor denaturalization tend to sit equally well in the postcolonial context or among all postcolonial agents. In 1995, the then president of Zimbabwe, Robert Mugabe, banned the Gays and Lesbians of Zimbabwe (GALZ) organization from participating in the Zimbabwe International Book Fair; he referred to them as "worse than dogs or pigs" and not entitled to basic human rights because of their ""unnatural perversion" (Human Rights Watch)." It also bears reminding that African writers and leaders like Jomo Kenyatta, Julius Nyerere, and Frantz Fanon on the one hand discredited so many of the racist ideas promoted by colonialism and apartheid, but on the other hand they were complicit in propagating the entangling myth of a "heterosexual Africa" (Epprecht 2008).[44]

Four, for both postcolonial and queer biblical criticisms, *the Bible and associated Christian religions are part of the problem*, at least at times. In the relationship of politics and sex, and the resultant hegemonies created, liminality is the order of the day, as well as in communities of faith laying claim to the Bible. On the one hand, people continuously find themselves falling between the sexual and political cracks. Liminality, marginalization, and exclusion are regulated according to sexuality with systems of power prescribing and constructing sexuality, and thus rewarding, punishing, encouraging, or suppressing certain practices and identities (Rubin 1993: 34). On the other hand, the liminality of gender constructions at the same time challenges and deconstructs the simplistic binaries of heteronormativity (see Dayal 2001: 309). In the interrelated crisis pertaining to the pillaged land and violated body in the colonizing enterprise, the third, connecting element was religion and, in particular, the Christian religion.[45] Although not their enemy, the handling of the Bible poses challenges to those affected by colonialism and imperialism and their effects, also and especially where the hegemony is sexually and gender-imposed.

FUTURE QUEER EXPECTATIONS

By way of conclusion, it may be worthwhile—if precarious—to point toward a few areas that may receive further attention in queer biblical studies in future. Neither postcolonial nor queer biblical criticism aspires to being locked into a singular mode or definition or incorporating diversity to the point of elusiveness.[46] However, not only is the theoretical basis of postcolonial queer work plural, so too are its possible future directions, which could include the following concerns. A *first* important future challenge for queer theories, especially in conjunction with postcolonial work, is to deal with a range of *tensions*. How does one effectively deploy queer approaches in texts from contexts where sex was regulated but often also conceived through social power and cultural convention and where, so to speak, sex was powered rather than gendered? Can one indeed use queer discernment separately from postcolonial insights? And these questions do not simply relate to the past, since while sex and power intersections are differently constituted in the present, they are by no means absent. Queer theory's critique of heteronormativity as the central pillar of modern, contemporary culture makes the political evident (Moore 1998: 259), but "queer" is all too often still seen as an epithet only (or even more) appropriate to white and the middle class. In addition, queer theory sits with the dilemma that as soon as "queer," which refers to what lies outside the norm, is defined it becomes domesticated, "rendering queer no longer outside of anything, and so no longer queer—in theory at least" (Schneider 2000b: 206). In this way "queer" stands to lose its claim to the outsider position in the heteronormative society and its power arrangements in particular.

Queer biblical criticism, especially in its intersections with postcolonial work, in the second place, poses questions for the understanding of *categories of bodily identity*. The postcolonial-queer reframing and recoding of these categories impacts on the study of religion and gender (Schippert 2011: 84). Identity politics is best replaced by invoking the notion of subjectivities, which on the one hand is unencumbered by the normative constraints of traditional and humanistic thought but on the other hand retains a focus on the gendered social locations of biblical interpretation. Making room for subjectivities in biblical interpretation allows also for what others would call their body politics.[47] The move away from identity to subjectivity implies detachment from biological, national, cultural, or other essentialisms, which marks "a critical theoretical departure from previous definitions of identity" and refocuses attention on "the complex, intersecting ways in which people are embedded within multiple, conflicted discourses, practices, and institutions" (Oleksy 2009: 1).[48] More often than not, however, contemporary societies' discursive practices of Othering renders a contested body in the form of the body of a gendered, sexual, religious, or ethnic other, engraved with related dichotomies such as West–East, male–female, religious–secular, straight–gay, and their power relations. "The deconstruction of the normative regulation and representation of the body should therefore not be investigated along the lines of the public-private divide, but in a manner that questions this divide" (Van den Berg, Van den Bogert, Korte 2017: 181). People's creative and nonconforming bodily practices challenge the disciplining through both institutionalized religion and secularism with their ideologies and politics of gender, sexuality, and ethnicity.

In a related way, a third dimension of future postcolonial queer biblical criticism is to expand *beyond* engaging predominantly with *societal structures* such as marriage, including notions of childbearing and the lives of children.[49] The ostensibly positive roles ascribed to children in the NT, notwithstanding a setting where children's sex and gender were considered fluid at best, raise interesting considerations but also many questions. Does the kingdom that belongs to children and those like children align with the notion of no sex in heaven? (Stuart 1997: 185–204). What more does Jesus' overturning of familial structures in society (Mk 12: 18–27) signal, beyond critiquing social systems of exclusion and privatized love and suggesting the radical equality of the reign of God? How can postcolonial critique of pervasive hegemonic structures and queer criticism of ownership-based monogamy contribute toward inclusive friendship, with faithfulness defined in the well-being, empowerment, and fulfillment of all?

Four, the continued implication of *knowledge systems and their use in the identification and exercise of powers*, whether through indirect and restrained inferiorization or by direct and blatant claims upon power, continues unabated amid a global thrust toward a spectrum of political goals including political correctness.[50] Nancy Fraser's warning of two decades ago seems to have gone unheeded—to not separate injustices of distribution and injustices of recognition, and to not derogate either of the two: "the point is to conceptualize two equally primary, serious, and real kinds of harm that any morally defensible social order must eradicate" (Fraser 1997: 280). Both, and jointly, postcolonial and queer interpreters resist the reduction of political power to material or class distinctions, and gender or sexuality to cultural or representation distinctions, but in the process they raise important questions for existing critical theories and methodologies in biblical studies.

Finally, some of the most difficult aspects to address in postcolonial and queer work are not only the ambivalence of social life but also the extent to which *all people*, oppressors and subjugated, perpetrators and victims alike, *participate in social life* and are unable to distance themselves from the polluting effects of power. "Colonialism infiltrates the ways in which both colonizer and colonized express themselves and corrupts even the process of forming a strategy for resistance" (Hiddleston 2009: 65, referring to Ashis Nandy's work). The push and pull of empire, whether that of imperialist sex and gender regimes or the political use of sex and gender, strain onto the foreground amid defiant deference, collusion, and contestation and recall Gramsci's definition of hegemony as domination by consent. While "gender and power are not easily mapped out in religion and culture as they are lived" (Roden 2009: 8), postcolonial queer biblical criticism's bias in the end is situated in its interest in both the embedded and conventional but also in the more elusive constructions of sex and gender, particularly where they are used either for sustaining and legitimizing the powerful or in the interest of scripting and controlling liminality, marginalization, and exclusion.

Notes

1. As argued elsewhere, and without detracting from the importance of social relations or gender performativity—in fact, emphasizing both of the former—the relationship between place and gender must be acknowledged more overtly and beyond naturalized clichés like "a woman's place is in the kitchen" or "this is a man's world." Gender is about more than social relations and involves also spatial dimensions (Punt 2011: 322).
2. In an earlier study (Punt 2008: 24.1–24.16), the focus was on theoretical points of connection between postcolonial and queer theoretical approaches in biblical studies. Without losing the theoretical altogether, the emphasis here shifts to the interwoven nature and operational alignments of such approaches in encountering biblical texts.
3. Scholars use queer theory with a broad spectrum of meanings and across a wide range, which is understandable "because the status of sexual identity itself is part of the question, the scope of queer studies is necessarily diffuse" (Schneider 2000b: 209). For the same reason, some scholars prefer to use the plural, queer *theories* (Hall 2003). Teresa de

Lauretis, a feminist film scholar, coined the term "queer theory" in the nineties to get beyond simplistic binaries and static, isolated categories and to challenge their ideological confines; "queer," in the words of De Lauretis (1991: iv), "marks a certain critical distance" from the terms "gay" and "lesbian."
4. The important association with Michel Foucault and his *History of Sexuality*'s emphasis on the social and historical contingency of sexuality to theorizing queer, with the origins of wider queer theory notwithstanding, see Garton (2004: 22–24) and Vorster (2012: 604) for arguments in favor of a broader context for the germination of queer theory; cf Schneider (2000a: 3).
5. Sexuality and erotic desire in particular only exist within and not above or beyond history, and therefore they are always to be interpreted within history (Stuart 1997: 3; see also Seidman 1996: 8–9).
6. "The central tenet of queer theory is a resistance to the normativity that demands the binary opposition, hetero/homo" (Hawley 2001: 3).
7. "It must be stressed that it [postcolonialism] is not a homogenous project, but a hermeneutical salmagundi, consisting of extremely varied methods, materials, historical entanglements, geographical locations, political affiliations, cultural identities, and economic predicaments" (Sugirtharajah 1998: 15).
8. Earlier, important publications, which also brought these and a range of other helpful terms and expressions to the scholarly discussion, include Bhabha (1994); Said (1994), Spivak (1995).
9. Even if "queer" may all too often still be regarded as an epithet appropriate to whites and the middle class, a sentiment intersecting with the notion that people from other groups exuding a queer identity are suffering from "white disease" (Kumashiro 2000: 146). For a queer of color critique's focus on the intersections of race, political economy, gender, and sexuality, see, e.g., Ferguson (2018).
10. A decade and a half ago, Schneider (2000b: 211) was not altogether convinced that queer theory should aspire toward disciplinary status: "It is still new enough, and contested enough on every level, that beyond Foucauldian critiques of naturalized sexuality queer theory has not, and perhaps should not yet, resolve into a 'discipline' with an absolute priority of theoretical considerations."
11. Butler warns against the "prospect of identity becoming an instrument of the power one opposes" (Butler 1990: xxviii; also Milani 2014: 261).
12. Queerying refers to investigations that, given the social construction of sex and gender, trace the theoretical and political interests of such constructions and their involvement in social dynamics and power.
13. Others object to this description; e.g., "I must applaud recent studies that have shown unequal-status and active/passive aspects to be a culturally sustained component of an ancient world portrait of homosexuality. But interjecting equal-status or covenant into the equation fails to side-step the problem. The deepest issue for the biblical authors was the breaking of sexual boundaries between male and female." However, Webb's statement betrays his bias through his imposition of context-foreign material onto the biblical authors' frame of reference, claiming it as their theological position in abstraction while in effect discounting their own sociocultural context and the extent to which their context predisposed their theological understanding of human sexuality (Webb 2001: e.g., 251).
14. Over the centuries and to this day, many communities the world over confirm with Loughlin (2005: 10) that "the Bible writes our flesh, its meanings and possibilities."

15. "In the quest for the obliteration of binarisms (such as the bipolar gender system), such openness to multiplicity and challenge to any gay unitary identity may position queer theorists surprisingly near non-Western postcolonial theorists" (Hawley 2001: 14).
16. Clement of Alexandria ascribed the references, which is different from the original in not being in poetic meter or even the expected dialect, to Epimenides (poet from Crete, ca. 600 BCE); however, as the plural (ποιητῶν, poets) in Ac 17:28 suggests, other Stoics may also have been referenced, e.g., Aratus's *Phaenomena* 5; or even Cleanthes' *Hymn to Zeus*.
17. See also Sheffield (2008: 233–258), who reinterprets the Chalcedonian formulation of the relationship of Jesus and God as an Augustinian reading of Gen 1–3, posing instead a multigendered and multisexed Jesus at the center.
18. Others argue that in Gen 1 and 2 the emphasis is on a "no-body" God. They connect it to monotheistic isolation and the absence of a physical body, and similarly raise questions as to whether God should be conceived of in terms of sexuality or sex (e.g., Eilberg-Schwartz 1997: 34–55). Ancient rabbis understood Gen 1:27–28 to refer to Adam being created intersexed, not just male or female but both. This is the image of God in which humankind was created, and God divided Adam into male and female only at a later stage (Gross 2000: 13).
19. "The empire itself was envisioned as a great household, and the emperor therefore the 'father of the fatherland,' the benefactor or patron of all" (Hollingshead 1998: 109). In the Ptolemaic state, Egypt was the king's estate (οἶκος), with corresponding household terms used for officials (financial manager, διοικητής; submanager, ὑποδιοικητής; steward of an individual district, οἰκονόμος) (White 1999: 173–176).
20. Greek rulers and later Roman emperors used father identity, incorporating priestly responsibilities into fatherly duties on behalf of the imperial household. It was not long before the Roman emperor's public image was seen to be constituted by the threefold authority of political leader, priestly lord, and beneficial head of a communal family (White 1999: 173–206).
21. Musonius Rufus XIV claimed: "Thus whoever destroys human marriage destroys the home, the city, and the whole human race."
22. See Hornsby (2005: 157): "Paul's imaging of God as masculine not only creates gendered ambiguity, particularly for men . . . but engenders the concept of 'sinner' as already more feminine."
23. In the words of Loughlin (2005: 13): "But biology is cultural, and our ideas of sex are gendered, and God's gender affects his sex, and this becomes all too evident when divinity is used to underwrite certain human orderings, and most notably those that exclude women from certain kinds of power . . . we discover that women are not fully human because not really divine—in the way that men are. We discover that gender neutrality is a ruse of male partiality."
24. These codes did not acknowledge the moral agency of women, slaves, or children but, to the contrary, promoted moral dependency rather than moral maturity.
25. As mitigation and in a reconciliatory gesture, Luke wrote the mother of Jesus into the infancy narrative in a prophetic role, and he suggested continuation of family ties by putting Jesus' mother as present at the Pentecost and portraying James, brother of Jesus, as a leader in the Jerusalem community (see Osiek 2005: 218).
26. Traditional interpretations often failed to appreciate the countercultural, radical implications of Jesus' appeal on young men, barren women, and little children to join and thereby redefine the kingdom of heaven contrary to societal conventions. The transformed

household, with its transgression of roles and order, is encapsulated in Jesus' saying about himself and his male followers who became "eunuchs for the sake of the kingdom of heaven" (Mt 19:12), since the eunuch figure infracted masculine identity (Moxnes 2003: 72–90).

27. A queer Jesus protested fixed categories and affirmed the historical and social construction of all categories of identity: "Jesus was an ascetic who transgressed the boundaries of what it meant to be male in first-century Palestine. Moreover, he introduced that transgression as characteristic of the kingdom" (Moxnes 2003: 105).

28. Moxnes (2003: 151) challenges Horsley's notion that Jesus wanted to revitalize village life according to traditional values, and he contends that Jesus also broke with local authority and customs, as reflected in his disputes in the villages that often broached issues about identity. Since Jesus also came into conflict with the elite, his role was ambiguous (Moxnes 2003: 154).

29. In medieval times, female mysticism was a consequence of women's exclusion brought on by increased clericalism, which again was the result of increased ecclesial activity through the sacraments, relics, and other ways to deal with the body and suspicions against it. Female mysticism fed off deeply embodied, erotically charged encounters between women and Christ. Medieval women "subverted the patriarchal association of fleshiness with femaleness by obtaining bodily knowledge of Christ in their own flesh" (Isherwood and Stuart 1998: 69).

30. Maybe even more interesting is that Paul's self-claimed transgendered status hardly evoked comments from biblical scholars, except for, e.g., Gaventa (1990: 189–210), but her focus was more on the maternal metaphor and its significance than on the transgression of gender lines; but see Martyn (1997: 424–431); Osiek (1992: 333–337). See also Stewart (2017: 305–308) on the queer and transgender intersection in the Hebrew Bible.

31. Arguing strongly for the eradication of hierarchies and accompanying marginalization as Paul's position in Galatians (esp. 3:28)—following Martyn's position on the στοιχεῖα τοῦ κόσμου as "universal polarities that the Greeks and others thought to be the basis of the cosmos, structuring reality in binary oppositional pairs"—Kahl's claim that Paul did not "proclaim the erasure of sexual (or any other difference, but the end of the social hierarchies and exclusions (re)produced by it" (Kahl 2000: 44), may be too ideologically loaded in defense of the apostle.

32. As Sugirtharajah (1998: 97) explains: "Translation in a postcolonial context is not merely seeking dynamic equivalence or aiming for linguistic exactness, but desires to rewrite and retranslate the texts, as well as the concepts, against the grain. Rewriting and retranslating are not a simple dependence upon the past, but a radical remolding of the text to meet new situations and demands."

33. "Thus homosexuals appear in the Bible, but only in modern, twentieth-century Bibles, as when the New English Bible finds 'homosexual perversion' in Corinth, or the New Revised Standard Version discovers 'sodomites' in the same place (1 Cor. 6.9)" (Loughlin 2005: 12).

34. Paul's argument is not about the wrong object choice but the problem of uncontrolled desire. Interestingly, in other instances where Paul used an appeal to φύσις (nature) in his argument (e.g., 1 Cor 11:13–15, regarding hairstyles; Rom 11:17–24 (esp. 24), on the unnaturalness of the inclusion of Gentiles among believers), biblical interpreters generally agree on its contextually determined nature and relevance.

35. Various terms for illicit sexual activity, expressed in different ways in the NT, and including various technical terms such as μοιχεία (adultery), ἀσέλγεια (sexual immorality,

2 Cor 2:21; Gal 5:19; Rom 13:13), or, in particular, πορνεία (sexual immorality), do not appear in Rom 1. However, Paul did use the word ἀκαθαρσία (Rom 1:24) to describe his belief that God delivered those who refused to acknowledge him into "uncleanness" or "impurity." The Pauline word for "impurity" appears in settings of sexual immorality (e.g., 1 Th 4:7; 2 Cor 12:21; Gal 5:19; Rom 1:24; 6:19; and cf. Eph 4:19; 5:3; Col 3:5). Elsewhere in the NT, ἀκαθαρσία appears only in Mt 23:27. But "impurity" is used as part of the broader argument of Rom 1:18–32, which describes the results of and not the reason for of idolatry (Punt 2008).

36. In Nigerian Igbo society, women could become "female husbands" if they accumulated the same amount of status and wealth as a male and fulfilled the gender norms associated with being male. While such same-sex relationships resembled the male and female gender norms of heterosexual relationships, they did not amount to a new social identity or meaning (Amadiume 1987).

37. In the context of the Roman Empire, divine fatherhood was intended to sanction political authority rather than simply express genealogical relation; however, emperors' appeals to childhood derived from the gods provided fertile ground for framing Jesus' origins, which queer theory can exploit further.

38. Extrapolating the notion of a dual-genderedness is important, given also the importance of invoking parthenogenetic birth for many other important figures of the first century.

39. "Mary with her crying infant is a perfect figure for queer theology. She is a virgin who yet gives birth; a mother for whom there is no father other than the one she comes to see in her son. And her son, when grown into the Christ of faith and heart, in turn gives birth to her, to the *ecclesia* he feeds with his blood as once he was fed with her milk. And then this son takes her—his mother and child—as his bride and queen, so that we can hardly say who comes from whom, who lives in whom, or how we have come to find our own bodies remade in Christ's: fed with his flesh which is also Mary's" (Loughlin 2007: 32).

40. However, ironically, "]t finds itself curiously central to culture at large, disavowed but necessary for a heterosexual normalcy that defines itself in terms of what it rejects" (Loughlin 2007: 8).

41. It is as much a misunderstanding to see such retrieval work as affirmation of the very elements that constitute the object of postcolonial and queer critique, namely the involvement, or even complicity, of the biblical texts and their use in imperialist-colonialist and sexist-homophobic endeavors.

42. "The nation-state is a machine that produces Others, creates racial difference, and raises boundaries that delimit and support the modern subject of sovereignty" (Hardt and Negri in Hawley 2001: 9). According to Appadurai, "the modern nation-state . . . grows less out of natural facts—such as language, blood, soil and race—and more out of a quintessential cultural product, a product of collective imagination" (in Hawley 2001: 10).

43. The resultant commercialization, proliferation of target markets, and the spreading of corporate capital have led to the so-called Americanization of lesbigay lifestyles by co-opting lesbigay consumers and thus fixing their lifestyles and the liberatory potential of postcolonial discourse, which is limited to the wealthy, elite population (Hawley 2001: 10).

44. Their heteronormativity probably had its roots in struggles to reestablish a sense of African masculinity that was largely discredited through slavery and colonialist practices and in the disavowal of all colonialist-associated, demeaning practices. Then also, the successful anticolonial political struggles prepared the way for struggles for the emancipation of women as well as LGBTQIA rights.

45. Reverting to central theological complexes does not resolve the difficulties of plotting sex and gender: "Neither the Law of the Father nor the Christian articulation of the conquest by the Son (on behalf of the Father) gives a final word to understanding the place of gender in either Judaism or Christianity. Just as gender cannot be easily scripted with respect to power in either Judaism or Christianity, neither can those religious discourses or identities be plotted simplistically with respect to one another on a continuum of power" (Roden 2009: 8).
46. "Like any other theoretical framework developed in 'post-' or 'late' conditions (i.e., poststructuralism, postmodernism, late modernity, etc.), queer theory is not a consistent, coherent, and all-encompassing conceptual apparatus. In short, there is no such thing as a queer theory in the singular. Rather, queer theory consists of many, very different, slippery, and at times apparently incoherent approaches" (Milani 2014: 261).
47. For Mignolo (2007: 449–514), "the body-politics of knowledge includes the re-inscription per Fanon for example, of the history inscribed in the black body in a cosmology dominated by the white body beneath the theo- and ego-politics of knowledge."
48. In this regard Povinelli's (e.g., 2011) work, which among others differentiates between corporeality and carnality, engages the materiality of late-liberal forms of power and corporeality in postessentialist thought. She moves beyond the critique of metaphysics of substance, no longer striving to find and describe substances in their prediscursive authenticity but rather trying to understand how and for what and whose purposes such substances are produced.
49. For the construction of "biblical family values" and dangers associated with it, see, e.g., Punt (2010: 152–175).
50. Sugirtharajah (2012: 46–51) has indicated also postcolonialism's scrutiny of the public nature of biblical studies through its professionalized and specialised guilds and bodies as one of its major concerns. Such scrutiny includes attention to the nature and composition of these organizations, the overt and other interests they serve, the religious ideology they reflect, the critical theories and reading practices they encourage, and the extent to which alternative and minority hermeneutics are encouraged in mainstream work.

Bibliography

Althaus-Reid, M. 2000. *Indecent Theology: Theological Perversions in Sex, Gender and Politics*. London and New York: Routledge.

Amadiume, I. 1987. *Male Daughters, Female Husbands: Gender and Sex in an African Society*. London: Zed.

Bhabha, H. K. 1994. *The Location of Culture*. London and New York: Routledge.

Brown, J. N. 2001. "Queer." In *Encyclopedia of Postcolonial Studies*, edited by J. C. Hawley, 370–374. Westport, CT: Greenwood.

Butler, Judith. 1990. *Gender Trouble: Feminism and the Subversion of Identity*. 2nd ed. Thinking Gender. Vol. 2. New York: Routledge.

Darden, L. 2012. "Hanging out with Rahab: An Examination of Musa Dube's Hermeneutical Approach with a Postcolonial Touch." In *Postcolonial Perspectives in African Biblical Interpretations*, edited by M. W. Dube, A. M. Mbuvi, and D. Mbuwayesango, 63–71. Global Perspectives on Biblical Scholarship. Vol. 13. Atlanta: Society of Biblical Literature.

Dayal, S. 2001. "By Way of an Afterword." In *Postcolonial, Queer: Theoretical Intersections*, edited by J. C. Hawley, 205–325. SUNY Series: Explorations in Postcolonial Studies. Albany: State University of New York Press.

De Lauretis, T. 1991. "Queer Theory: Lesbian and Gay Sexualities: An Introduction." *differences: A Journal of Feminist Cultural Studies* 3(2): i–xviii.

Dhawan, N., A. Engel, C. F. E. Holzhey, and V. Woltersdorff. Eds. 2015. *Global Justice and Desire: Queering Economy*. Social Justice Series. London and New York: Routledge.

Donovan, J. 2001. *Feminist Theory: The Intellectual Traditions*. 3rd ed. New York and London: Continuum.

Dube, M. W. 2001. "'What I Have Written, I Have Written' (John 19:22)?" In *Interpreting the New Testament in Africa*, edited by M. N. Getui, T. S. Maluleke, and J. S. Ukpong, 145–163. Nairobi: Acton.

Eilberg-Schwartz, H. 1997. "The Problem of the Body for the People of the Book." In *Reading Bibles, Writing Bodies: Identity and the Book*, edited by T. K. Beal and D. M. Gunn, 34–55. Biblical Limits. London and New York: Routledge.

Epprecht, M. 2008. *Heterosexual Africa? The History of an Idea from the Age of Exploration to the Age of AIDS*. New African Histories Series. Athens: Ohio University Press.

Ferguson, R. A. 2018. "Queer of Color Critique." *Oxford Research Encyclopedia of Literature*. http://literature.oxfordre.com/view/10.1093/acrefore/9780190201098.001.0001/acrefore-9780190201098-e-33 (accessed August 29, 2018).

Fraser, N. 1997. "Heterosexism, Misrecognition, and Capitalism: A Response to Judith Butler." *Social Text* 52/53, 15(3 and 4): 279–289.

Garton, S. 2004. *Histories of Sexuality. From Antiquity to Sexual Revolution*. Critical Histories of Subjectivity and Culture. London: Equinox.

Gaventa, B. R. 1990. The Maternity of Paul: An Exegetical Study of Galatians 4:19. In *The Conversation Continues: Studies in John & Paul. In Honor of J Louis Martyn*, eds. R. T. Fortna and B. R. Gaventa, 189–201. Nashville: Abingdon Press.

Gross, S. 2000. Male *and* Female God Created Them. *Challenge* 59: 12–13.

Guest, D. R. E. Goss, M. West, and T. Bohache. Eds. 2006. *The Queer Bible Commentary*. London: SCM.

Hall, D. E. 2003. "Queer Theories." In Transitions, edited by J. Wolfreys. Basingstoke, UK, and New York: Palgrave Macmillan.

Halperin, D. M. 1995. Saint Foucault: Towards a Gay Hagiography. New York: Oxford.

Hanks, T. 2000. The Subversive Gospel. A New Testament Commentary of Liberation, trans. J. P. Doner. Cleveland: Pilgrim Press.

Hawley, J. C. 2001. "Introduction." In *Postcolonial, Queer: Theoretical Intersections*, edited by J. C. Hawley, 1–18. SUNY Series: Explorations in Postcolonial Studies. Albany: State University of New York Press.

Hiddleston, J. 2009. *Understanding Postcolonialism*. Understanding Movements in Modern Thought. Stocksfield: Acumen.

Hollingshead, J. R. 1998. *The Household of Caesar and the Body of Christ: A Political Interpretation of the Letters from Paul*. Lanham, MD: University Press of America.

Hornsby, T. J. 2005. The Gendered Sinner in Romans 1–7. In *Gender, Tradition and Romans. Shared Ground, Uncertain Borders*, eds. C. Grenholm and D. Patte, 143–166. Romans through history and cultures Series. New York & London: T&T Clark.

Isherwood, L. and E. Stuart. 1998. *Introducing Body Theology*. Introductions in Feminist Theology. Cleveland: Pilgrim.

Jagose, A. 1996. *Queer Theory: An Introduction*. New York: New York University Press.
Kahl, B. 2000. "No Longer Male: Masculinity's Struggles behind Galatians 3.28?" *Journal for the Study of the New Testament* 79: 37–49.
Kumashiro, K. 2000. Review of *Queer Theory in Education*, by William F Pinar (ed). In *Journal of homosexuality* 39(1): 144–152.
Laqueur, T. 1990. *Making Sex. Body and Gender from the Greeks to Freud*. Cambridge & London: Harvard University Press.
Loughlin, G. 2005. "Biblical Bodies." *Theology & Sexuality* 12(1): 9–27.
Loughlin, G. 2007. "Introduction: The End of Sex." In *Queer Theology: Rethinking the Western Body*, edited by G. Loughlin, 1–34. Malden MA, Oxford, Carlton: Blackwell.
Martin, D. B. 1995. "Heterosexism and the Interpretation of Romans 1:18–32." *Biblical Interpretation* 3(3): 332–355.
Martyn, J. L. 1997. *Galatians*. Anchor Bible. New York: Doubleday.
Mignolo, W. D. 2007. "Delinking: The Rhetoric of Modernity, the Logic of Coloniality and the Grammar of De-Coloniality." *Cultural Studies* 21(2): 449–514.
Milani, T. M. 2014. "Queering Masculinities." In *The Handbook of Language, Gender, and Sexuality*, edited by S. Ehrlich, M. Meyerhoff, and J. Holmes, 260–278. Blackwell Handbooks in Linguistics. Chichester: Wiley-Blackwell.
Mollenkott, V. R. 2003. "Crossing Gender Borders: Towards a New Paradigm." In *Body and Soul: Rethinking Sexuality as Justice-Love*, edited by M. M. Ellison and S. Thorson-Smith, 1–22. Cleveland: Pilgrim.
Moore, S. D. 1998. "Que(e)rying Paul: Preliminary Questions." In *Auguries: The Jubilee Volume of the Sheffield Department of Biblical Studies*, edited by D. J. A. Clines and S. D. Moore, 250–274. JSOTSS 269. Sheffield: Sheffield Academic Press.
Moore, S. D. 2001. *God's Beauty Parlor: And Other Queer Spaces in and Around the Bible*. Contraventions: Jews and Other Differences. Stanford: Stanford University Press.
Moore, S. D. 2005. "Questions of Biblical Ambivalence and Authority under a Tree outside Delhi; Or, the Postcolonial and the Postmodern." In *Postcolonial Biblical Criticism: Interdisciplinary Intersections*, edited by S. D. Moore and F. F. Segovia, 79–96. The Bible and Postcolonialism. London: T & T Clark International.
Morgensen, S. L. 2016. "Encountering Indeterminacy: Colonial Contexts and Queer Imagining." *Cultural Anthropology* 31(4): 607–616.
Moxnes, H. 2003. *Putting Jesus in His Place: A Radical Vision of Household and Kingdom*. Louisville: Westminster John Knox.
Oleksy, E. H,. Ed. 2009. *Intimate Citizenships: Gender, Sexualities, Politics*. New York and London: Routledge.
Osiek, C. 1992. Galatians. In *The Women's Bible Commentary*, eds. CA Newsom and SH Ringe, 333–337. Louisville: Westminster/John Knox.
Osiek, C. 2005. "Family Matters." In *Christian Origins*, edited by R. A. Horsley, 201–220. A People's History of Christianity. Vol. 1. Minneapolis: Fortress.
Povinelli, E. 2011. *Economies of Abandonment: Social Belonging and Endurance in Late Liberalism*. Durham and London: Duke University Press.
Punt, J. 2008. "Intersections in Queer Theory and Postcolonial Theory, and Hermeneutical Spin-Offs." *The Bible and Critical Theory* 4(2): 24.1–24.16.
Punt, J. 2010. "'All in the Family?' The Social Location of New Testament Households and Christian Claims on 'Traditional Family Values.'" *Acta Patristica et Byzantica* 21(2): 152–175.

Punt, J. 2011. "Queer Theory, Postcolonial Theory, and Biblical Interpretation: A Preliminary Exploration of Some Intersections." In *Bible Trouble: Queer Reading at the Boundaries of Biblical Scholarship*, edited by T. J. Hornsby and K. Stone, 321–341. Semeia Studies. Vol 67. Atlanta: SBL.

Punt, J. 2014. "Countering Bible-based, Culturally-Ensconced Homophobia: Un-African Meets Unambiguous!" *Journal of Theology in Southern Africa* 149: 5–24.

Punt, J. 2015. *Postcolonial Biblical Interpretation: Reframing Paul*. STAR. Vol. 20. Leiden: Brill.

Roden, F. S. 2009. "Introduction: Jewish/Christian/Queer: Crossroads and Identities." In *Jewish/Christian/Queer: Crossroads and Identities*, edited by F. S. Roden, 1–18. Queer Interventions. Farnham: Ashgate.

Rubin, G. S. 1993. "Thinking Sex: Notes for a Radical Theory of the Politics of Sexuality." In *The Lesbian and Gay Studies Reader*, edited by H. Abelove, M. A. Barale, and D. M. Halperin, 3–44. New York and London: Routledge.

Runions, E. 2011. "From Disgust to Humor: Rahab's Queer Effect." In *Bible Trouble: Queer Reading at the Boundaries of Biblical Scholarship*, edited by T. J. Hornsby and K. Stone, 45–74. Semeia Studies. Vol. 67. Atlanta: SBL.

Said, E. 1994. *Orientalism*. 2nd ed. New York: Vintage.

Sanneh, L 1989. *Translating the Message: The Missionary Impact on Culture*. American Society of Missiology Series, 13. Maryknoll, NY: Orbis.

Schaaf, Y. 1994. *On Their Way Rejoicing: The History and the Role of the Bible in Africa*. Trans. P. Ellingworth. African Challenge Series. Carlisle: Paternoster.

Schippert, C. 2011. "Implications of Queer Theory for the Study of Religion and Gender: Entering the Third Decade." *Religion & Gender* 1(1): 66–84.

Schneider, L. C. 2000a. "Homosexuality, Queer Theory, and Christian Theology." *Religious Studies Review* 26(1): 3–12.

Schneider, L. C. 2000b. "Queer Theory." In *Handbook of Postmodern Biblical Interpretation*, edited by A. K. M. Adam, 206–212. St. Louis: Chalice.

Segovia, F. F., and R. S. Sugirtharajah. Eds. 2007. *A Postcolonial Commentary on the New Testament Writings*. The Bible and Postcolonialism. New York: T & T Clark.

Seidman, S. 1996. "Introduction." In *Queer Theory/Sociology*, edited by S. Seidman, 1–29. Twentieth-Century Social Theory. Oxford: Blackwell.

Sheffield, T. 2008. "Performing Jesus: A Queer Counternarrative of Embodied Transgression." *Theology and Sexuality* 14(2): 233–258

Spivak, G. C. 1995. "Can the Subaltern Speak?" In *The Post-Colonial Studies Reader*, edited by B. Ashcroft, G. Griffiths, and H. Tiffin, 24–28. London ad New York: Routledge.

Spurlin, W. J. 2001. "Broadening Postcolonial Studies/Decolonizing Queer Studies." In *Postcolonial, Queer: Theoretical Intersections*, edited by J. C. Hawley, 185–205. SUNY Series: Explorations in Postcolonial Studies. Albany: State University of New York Press.

Stuart, E. 1997. "Sex in Heaven: The Queering of Theological Discourse on Sexuality." In *Sex These Days: Essays on Theology, Sexuality and Society*, edited by J. Davies and G. Loughlin, 185–204. Studies in Theology and Sexuality. Sheffield: Sheffield Academic Press.

Stewart, David T. 2017. "LGBT/Queer Hermeneutics and the Hebrew Bible." *Currents in Biblical Research* 15(3): 289–314.

Stone, K. 2005. *Practicing Safer Texts: Food, Sex and Bible in Queer Perspective*. Queering Theology Series. London and New York: T & T Clark International.

Stone, K. 2016. "Queer Criticism and Queer Theory." In *Oxford Encyclopedia of Biblical Interpretation*. Oxford Biblical Studies Online, http://www.oxfordreference.com/abstr

act/10.1093/acref:obso/9780199832262.001.0001/acref-9780199832262-e-78?rskey=nmN Qi4&result=78.

Sugirtharajah, R. S. 1998. *Asian Biblical Hermeneutics and Postcolonialism: Contesting the Interpretations*. The Bible and Liberation series. Maryknoll, NY: Orbis.

Sugirtharajah, R. S. 2012. *Exploring Postcolonial Biblical Criticism: History, Method, Practice*. Chichester: Wiley-Blackwell.

Van den Berg, M., K. Van den Bogert, and A. Korte. 2017. "Editorial: Religion, Gender, and Body Politics." *Religion & Gender* 7(2): 18–183.

Vorster, J. N. 2000. (E)mpersonating the bodies of Early Christianity. *Neotestamentica* 34(1): 103–124.

Vorster, J. N. 2012. "The Queering of Biblical Discourse." *Scriptura* 111(3): 602–620.

Webb, W. J. 2001. Slaves, Women & Homosexuals. Exploring the Hermeneutics of Cultural Analysis. Downers Grove: IVP.

White, J. L. 1999. *The Apostle of God: Paul and the Promise of Abraham*. Peabody: Hendrickson.

CHAPTER 23

RACE, SCRIPTURES, AND THE POSTCOLONIAL WORLD

VINCENT L. WIMBUSH

General Framework and Problematics

For at least sixty years, scholars of the Bible have claimed to be situated in and influenced by the assumptions and politics of the postcolonial world.[1] Although these scholars have been of different ethnic backgrounds, genders, and nationalities and have been differently oriented in terms of academic training and intellectual orientation, "race" has been at times broached by them—even if warily, haltingly, inconsistently, and timidly—as an important, complex issue or problem to be addressed. Reflecting a kind of anxiety of engagement, the situation as described is part of the deep but mostly unacknowledged challenges of the local and national societies in which these scholars have worked. But it is also striking evidence of a longstanding, deeply rooted, and larger set of fears, assumptions, collusions, orientations, and politics that have organized and haunted (if not paralyzed) the entire Western world, including its discourses associated with academic fields and disciplines and, among such, not least the academic field of biblical studies. Complicating and at times conflicting tendencies at the nexus of antiquarianist/textual/philological and religious/theological interests and practices, and the politics of social quiescence, obfuscations, and ambivalences, have taken their toll on the academic identity and larger world political impact, cache, relevance, and social-cultural power of biblical studies, now rather widely situated in various domains, contexts, and institutions throughout the world colonized by the West.

The toll comes from the now widely recognized muted or stuttering voice of biblical studies, which it shares with most other academic fields, even as it faces some special or even unique challenges. To what and for whom—in whose real and sustained interest—has the field of biblical studies historically spoken (long before and far beyond the late nineteenth century as the time of guild-organizational founding in the United States and Europe)? And to what and for whom does it now speak? Does it belong mostly or only to the academy, the church, high culture as the legatee in part of Western classical traditions, or to elite male (Jewish/Protestant/Catholic) clerical arrogations and interests? To what time period is it oriented—our time and its headlines, challenges, and complexities—or to an invented past and its invented issues?

Until well into the twentieth century, into the decades of the late 1960s if not the 1970s, the default character, substantive interests, and agenda of the field (as is evident in the demographics of the largest organization of such scholars, represented by the U.S.-based Society of Biblical Literature) were for the most part arguably identified with predominantly Euro-American attitudes and highly inflected by Protestantism and white male clerical intellectualism. Such an inflected orientation was made dominant and embraced and imitated over many decades, notwithstanding the belated inclusion and participation of Catholic, Jewish, and religiously nonaffiliated and noncommitted persons, along with female and non-European ("Third World") scholars of different orientations and nationalities in much smaller numbers.

As was the case with almost all academic guilds situated in North America and Europe, the 1980s ushered in an encouraging and exciting uptick (in the minds of some) or explosion (according to the nervous and threatened sensibilities of others) of gender and racial-ethnic diversity in membership demographics, including those among the heretofore rarely seen or heard "minoritized" or self-ascribed, impatient "minorities," mostly persons of color. Many in these latter categories began quite intentionally to embrace and associate themselves in their scholarship with some strongly articulated consciousness-raising and political questions and issues and with some programmatic and new political-intellectual filiations and perspectives in their guilds.[2] Various new and explicitly named advocacy committees—such as feminist and nonwhite/communities of color—associated with the American Academy of Religion and the Society of Biblical Literature, beginning in the 1980s, serve as evidence.

But soon thereafter, in the early twenty-first century, a change not so much caused by the period of the Obama presidency in the United States (2009–2017), but reaching a fever pitch and poignantly somewhat overlapping with the era, became apparent in the United States. This was also reverberated throughout the North Atlantic world in the form of backlashes, political obstruction, resistance, and outspokenness among white nativist and conservative groups. There was a longing for a return to the immediate pre-Obama era, certainly, but mostly for a pre–civil rights and pre–women's liberation movement past, with the aim of forcing the slowdown or abandonment of sociopolitical and economic reform along with ongoing diversification in participation throughout all domains of society and culture on the part of various racial, ethnic, and immigrant groups. The result in parts of the United States and in various countries in Europe was heightened, sharper, and more deeply felt divisions and conflicts, accompanied by a deep sense of white fear and anxiety. In addition to the Obama presidency as a trigger for white grievance and irrational shock and threat, in the United States there was fear based on knowledge for some or a hunch for others that "soon" the country would no longer be or look majority-white.

The Western academy and guilds have not been immune to this development. These institutions have in fact been major sites of incitement—in some places even laboratories and think tanks—for the roiling and questioning that defined the conflict and tense situation. In light of changes in demographics and consciousness, schools, colleges, and universities have had to raise questions about what type of education or formation is now needed, what curriculum is best, who should be read and how to read. There were discussions about whether there should be a canon and if so for whom. Who/what should be in the canon? Who are the guardians of the canon? What must the educated person in this changed world be expected to know? Or should all now be expected to know the same things in the same ways? Who should be admitted into the most elite universities, and on what bases or sets of criteria? What about merit? What about centuries of exclusion of some from the academy? Should this history be factored in? How? What about affirmative action? These were among the questions and issues still being raised.

The default position for many institutions and for many academic guilds, including students of religion and theology—most especially those focused on the study of the Bible—involves a rather complicated juggling of commitment, continued stable/conservative big tent growth, and diversification of participation in authorized, guild-credentialed interpretive practice. Such juggling reflects a politically and intellectually timid, muffled, and ill-defined collective guild organizational mindset and agenda evident in terms of decisions made about leadership, budget, programming, and politics; it would seem to add up to (so to say almost literally, if not cheekily) hiding behind "the text." The textualist or text-fetish agenda, sensibilities, and practices demanded by many came to be seen and appealed to over a long, fraught period in Western history as the fulcrum around which stasis in the guild, and through the guild in society at large, is maintained. All important matters and issues are addressed only as they can be argued or claimed to appear in the texts.[3]

There was a critical response to this textualist orientation and all that pertained to and was associated with it. Thus, in the wake of black consciousness movements in the United States and in Africa during the 1960s and 1970s—and in the push for human and civil rights in many places around the world in subsequent decades—there was the development of a heightened awareness of, and fairly serious interest in, the topics of race and racisms. This was the case even in some academic and other professional circles.

The actual direction of social and political pressure and influence, it should be made clear, was generally from the streets to the academy—not the reverse. The pressure and influence led to efforts among some intellectuals and academics in some places to move race/racism beyond the confines and control of institutional, disciplinary, and field guardrails, shadows, and silences and into larger open arenas of cross-field/cross-disciplinary and broader extra-academic cultural crosswinds and exchanges. Yet scholars for the most part seemed to pull up the rear: many slowly followed other sectors, such as sports, entertainment, and the arts in general in joining the resistance. Establishment of many ethnic studies department and programs in the United States and United Kingdom came from persistent protests, not from academic-intellectual conceptualizations, long-term planning, and administrative execution. Even if not everywhere, in every field, or with the same clarity of acknowledgment, interest, and commitment, since the 1970s and 1980s the topic of race and racial inequality has in many places been let out of the academic fields' discursive cage—that is to say, discussion has not been controlled and framed by the usual dynamics and considerations that control fields and their control over canonical texts or problems.[4]

Before declaring anything approaching a change in field orientation or politics in regard to issues raised here, however, a consideration of what persists as default practice and sentiment is in order. In addressing race and racialist discourses as part of modern scholars' interests and agenda, practices in the field of biblical (and related) studies have historically entailed mining among those books assumed to enjoy special canonical status those passages that include admonitions, terms, or narratives of racial/racist terror. Examples include the curse of Ham as the curse of black peoples, most notably, in the Old Testament; but also, of course, the practice of and indifference to slavery in the New Testament. Other texts seem to speak to the yearning for or possibility of social elevation and reform, including a hoped-for racial harmony (e.g., Exodus traditions, Jesus' teachings, and early church communalism).[5]

But in light of what is often assumed or declared to be the postcolonial situation, it is now necessary to question whether this cherry-picking/indexical-philological approach can any longer be intellectually justified or even be deemed broadly (that is, outside guild circles) illuminating or compelling, not to mention politically and psychically freeing. To be sure, the text-topical interest in and uses of certain texts in order to find the issue/phenomenon "x" is traditional. This type of interpretive operation has traditionally been practiced in a number of humanities fields and disciplines and even in popular domains, such as within English, literary criticism, or philology, and in that field of operations that is broadly labeled "biblical exegesis" (with scriptural-textual studies serving as a useful, and in some cases usefully infamous, metonym). Investigative journalism and legal scholarship/jurisprudence, whether originalist or not, are examples of other domains in which the practices are similar. As is the case with any other area of scholarship, this kind of intellectual project is carried out with mixed results cross-corresponding to mixed levels of investment, creativity, and sophistication.

One of the problems with this scriptural operation sketched above is that it has tended not to address—indeed, usually it does not even provide an opportunity to address— some important critical pre- or extratextual issues, namely, the broader issues already operating, influencing, and directing the interpreter before s/he engages texts. Exegesis is an operation done or discourse performed by specialists who, for the most part, sometimes complexly or naively position themselves inside the scriptural circle—religious, ethnic, legal, literary, rhetorical, cultural-political—and who work to guard the circle and make clear to members the meaning of (belonging to) the circle and the psycho-social-cultural and political work it models. This has historically been a clerical-scholastic-apologetic project, although laypersons have arrogated to themselves more opportunities and authority in more recent times. Such authority does not differ from the older regime. Whatever the status within the circle, one may be intentional about working against the grain—that is, against the performance of the exegetical. But the question that ought to be raised is why it is that one who may be oriented toward basic or radical critical questioning would want to (continue to) participate in, model, and perform the exegetical project.

Inspired or provoked to pursue "race" as a fraught topic—or, possibly, stumbling onto it and then being forced to do so—the question for those critics facing the challenges and problems of the twenty-first century concerns the relevance of the work of exegesis as scholarly operation. No matter how well executed according to accepted rules and assumptions of style, approaches, and methods—or how creative, dazzling, or avant-garde the arguments and insights—the issue is the adequacy or relevance of the operation in the interest of getting beyond the ultimate defense of any particular canon or tribe as reading formation. This explains why there is at times chagrin over the fact that in spite of what seems like profound differences in interpretative arguments and conclusions between liberal and conservative exegetes, there are really only minor differences—if any at all—in the protocols of the basic exegetical operations and orientation to or assumptions about the operation itself. Part of the explanation lies in mimetics.[6] Cultural practices represent fealty to and fetish for the text or a certain politics of language on the part of all groups—indeed, on the part of all Western moderns. In terms of modern Western centering politics, all is exegesis, everything runs on the basis of exegesis of canonical texts, and much cultural power lies with the exegete.[7] The persistent bottom line, the basis of reality, and the touchstone of power is the text—always "the text." The one—historically a male—who wields the text controls the textually woven, textually mimetic world.

The implications (for thinking about thinking) and ramifications (for action and politics) of this situation are obviously necessarily significant and beg continued exploration and analysis. Sustained or persistent collective critical exploration and analysis of such—what I would argue is possible in, even if not so far consistently evident of, the postcolonial situation—require in terms of orientation and action the turn away from the exegetical-textualist mode of operation. That is, it is important to go beyond the obsession with *meaning* of the lexical/indexical/content of the text to focus instead on the *textural*/gestural, on the human, on psycho-social relations, on what "work" we make texts do. Focus should be placed on the critical historical (*not* the historical-critical), and with it contemporary/real time social-cultural-political interpretation into the functions, politics, and psycho-socio-cultural logics involved, *not* the structure and contours of an invented text-canonical antiquity.

The work of scripture-making can be summed up with the term *scripturalization*,[8] a shorthand reference to a regime of knowledge/language/discourse/media control and authorization. The personal and social-cultural corporate pieties and acts of violence, the politics, and the social psycho-socio-cultural logics appertaining to scriptures that have come to be associated with the "world religions" and their devotees, and the civilizations with which they are complexly imbricated, are but one example of the phenomenon of scripturalization, located within one (artificially separated) domain of modern life ("religion"). That this phenomenon is arguably metonymic of operations and orientations from other domains of modern life in the Western world explains what is apt and compelling about the capacious and elastic term as a category of modern world critical comparative description and analysis.

Partly in response to social pressures, partly on the basis of the reflexivity provoked by textual content (certain terms, figures, etc.), at times in response to the need to confront its own constructions, race/racism was from the beginning a subject of the modernist standard textual-exegetical operation, evident in all the old fields of academic study.[9] But as part of a somewhat naïve but persistent textualist agenda, absent a critical studies commitment to problematization of categories and operations and self- and cultural-interrogation, the default protocol was and remains this puzzling situation—where the already chosen text appears or is assumed to address "race," the interpreter is assumed to be equipped to address the matter. But this addressing is understood by most academic (and most other) exegetes to be appropriately controlled, limited, and anachronistic—understood to be part of the distant (biblical-mythic or otherwise civilizational-mythic) past and place—over there—not the here of the interpreter and the world of the interpreter's readers. Much that is described as academic biblical scholarship is carried out in this framework. Race/racism is engaged within the bounds of the text. And the general thinking is that the matter that may be found to be in the text is either naively about us or (depending on the issue) not really (directly, at least) about "us." It does not take much training in or general play with psychology to recognize that the forced effort to maintain such control, distance, or intimacy can in times of distress collapse upon itself in all sorts of unexpected ways and then lead to unusual, ill-considered compensatory proposals and agenda. The texts can be made to do the socio-psycho-cultural and political duty required—and this without the consciousness or intervention of the text critics.

The postcolonial era and situation, and the consciousness that may appertain to it, is not a surety of change in this situation, but it appears to be an opportunity to make interrogation of the Bible and its relationship to race/racism more layered and complex. Insofar as it requires going beyond traditional orientations and practices and interrogating the colonial as modernist exegetical discourse to make the whole phenomenon of reading—texts, people, worlds—again strange or unfamiliar, it represents the possibility of heightened or sharper consciousness and deeper insight.[10] How odd is it to make and accept the (usually radical) claims made in relationship to the Bible (and other texts similarly positioned in other religio-cultural circles and worlds)? It is the postcolonial situation—with its shakeup if not breakup and breakdown of systems and regimes—that affords opportunity for the reconsideration of the basic assumptions, categories, and terminology framing and ordering colonialist/modernist (scriptural) discourse and politics. Efforts to clarify what are the complex connections and relationships that obtain among the three fraught categories repeatedly referenced above and serving as the focus of this essay are assumed to facilitate deeper, more layered, and expansive trans-disciplinary critical questioning and analysis—of social formation and social conscientization—far beyond the narrow conceptualization of each term, as though what each represents exists, could ever exist, or has ever existed, in isolation. Critical thinking about the complex connectedness and functions of the categories at issue should provide a strong springboard for a thicker historical-social-cultural analysis. This approach can be argued to be more illuminating and compelling than the typical approach in articles, essays, and books in which the author cherry-picks specific fraught terms from fraught texts in philological (dis)play that nevertheless fails to move discussion beyond the colonial world agenda of cultural-rhetorical-discursive and political stability for the sake of establishing and maintaining dominance and a certain "order of things."

What follows below in this essay is a necessarily limited discussion about the fraught categories the "postcolonial" (world), "the Bible," and "race"—how they are complexly interrelated, how the one sets conditions for the others, and how they invent, define, and delimit one another and thereby shape thinking, discourse, and politics. The foregoing has been an argument that the categories of focus for this essay are not inert or flat backdrops, backgrounds, or contexts against which one then engages texts; they are themselves complex phenomena and dynamic "texts" that have to be excavated. The challenge ahead has to do with how the imbrication of the intertextual dynamics will be perceived. What follows is an attempt in our enormously complex times to demonstrate a defensible way forward that entails exploding rather sinking into traditional notions about the textual. This involves focus on the textural and the politics and social-psychologics that appertain thereto. Put more simply, it entails focus on lives, social relations, and power dynamics.

Scripturalization Up Close

If the prefix "post" in the term "postcolonial" means anything, it must mean (among other things) *not* the end or aftermath of the colonial but the opportunity to reexamine everything wrought by the colonial situation. The "post" in postcolonial thus refers not to something in the past or something left behind. To the contrary, if not ironically, "post" may signal no more than a situation of even more evidence of the colonial such that it forces a break(down)—an explosion, perhaps, or a revolt toward radical reorientation—and the chance to face, name, and challenge the colonial as the establishment or center of power. The same argument may be applied with respect to the terms "postliberal," "postchristian," "postdemocratic," and so on. There have been historical situations aplenty so extreme and so persistent that they have provoked revolt, not least in orientation and consciousness. Such a description is more apt and accurate in regard to the situation that "postcolonial" references than the notion of ending, going beyond, leaving behind, and the like. It will be appropriate to return below to the matter of what the postcolonial world ushers in, but it is even more important first to point to what were the complex relationships and dynamics ushered forth by the colonial world.

The *colonial* in the postcolonial situation perdures—perhaps, in some respects, ever more intensely, if at times and in some contexts also subtly and deeply, such as can be discerned in terms of social-cultural (including academic-intellectual) and political-economic sedimentation. What is basically at issue in the colonial situation is of course the control—of mind and body--of populations. This control is managed through a complex of strategies or tools—military, economic, and so forth. By no means is the least of the strategies socio-cultural-psychological and linguistic-discursive.

The eighteenth-century classic *Robinson Crusoe* is a useful window—albeit on a smaller and simpler scale—onto what obtains in such situations. It is possible—perhaps, remotely possible—for Crusoe to have physically overpowered Crusoe; but what was far more narratologically realistic, effective, and politically compelling was Crusoe's display of cultural imperialism quite evident in his rhetorical/discursive trickery or what I have termed "white men's magic." Of course, the Crusoe story for a number of reasons is not typical—again, the scale of things is relevant—of the actual historical-colonial situation. That is, except for the window it opens onto what is inside and drawn from the colonial master's toolbox, namely, socio-cultural-psychological trickery as language play.

Another fascinating example even more useful to think about the phenomenon and dynamics—the textures and politics of scriptualization—can be found in Chinua Achebe's acclaimed novel *Things Fall Apart* (hereafter *TFA*).[11] What we are provided in this mid-twentieth-century, first-of-its-kind novel, written at the early dawn of African resistance to the colonial and postcolonial awakening, is a more realistic and authentic picture of how a particular form of colonialism worked within a local West African community in the advanced stages of domination. What falls apart—not through gunfire or other forms of physical warfare—are local traditions and through them the local people's capacity to define themselves as a world and face the antagonisms and brutalities of the larger colonial world pressing in on them. What was destroyed was their voice, their language, their ability to speak to and for themselves. Perhaps, it is going too far to interpret the tragic major character Obierika with his suicide as the fate of the entire village of Umuofia (and beyond it the whole of black Africa); but Obierika's dyspeptic reactions, his stuttering and eventual choking and silence in the face of the changes ordered by the white men, say much if not all about what was being described. The colonial situation for the Umuofians meant having their identities and voices taken away. It entailed being "pacified," being written up. Few shots were fired in Umuofia. Yet the writing up of the Umuofians as "primitives" was violent, deadly, and decisive. They were thereby (re)invented.

"Colonial" may reference (different types of) historical regimes held together (over the long term) not so much by brute physical force but as part of a game of illusion and misrecognition played especially with and through language/discourse and with media of all types claimed to be and presented as culturally authoritative. These types of media can be called "scriptures" or more poignantly the "regime of the scriptural."[12]

I call the language regime "scripturalization" as a way of calling attention to the dynamics and real effects of the politics of language in operation. That we have to do with language and the games played with such should not confuse anyone regarding matters of real impact: the language games evident and relevant are actually deadly serious, with impact in all aspects of life. Of course, this argument is not hard to make when the phenomenon of the scriptural is understood here in the most expansive terms possible, that is, in terms of mediatization.[13] Associating the latter with scripturalization makes clear the nature of the extent of the influence and effect at issue here.

The colonial is provocative shorthand for a type of regime of power in history, usually but not strictly associated with (the ushering in of) modernity. There can be easily established a certain connection between the colonial and the need for and uses of scriptures or the scriptural. The latter was needed to help to maintain and manage control over subjects. This was done through particular uses of the scriptural, through a politics of language, a control over discourse/speech, all legitimated media, all communication, thinking itself, and through such, even the bodies of those manipulated and dominated. Such uses doubtless always obtained where there was the technology of writing. But modernity seemed to be different in terms of the larger scale and the wider range of type of politics brought to bear on the situation.

The colonial control of the benighted Others, of course, necessarily, operated within and (for the most part) with the ideological support of the newly separate domain we now call—due to the influence of the European self-ascribed Enlightened Ones—"religion." The latter has never been and could never be outside the politics of control or management of the colonial regime. In fact, a more accurate and compelling critical analysis of "religion" should involve viewing it in terms of "scripturalism," that is, as ideology that turns around fetishization of the written and the establishment of various "reading formations."[14]

The "world religions" have always represented examples of such ideologies and formations. The general consolidation or firm establishment of "world religions" as concepts and social movements in the nineteenth century is tied to the translation of the "sacred books" project led by Sanskrit scholar and comparativist F. Max Müller, which resulted in the collection, translation, publication, and wider dissemination of the texts by which each exemplum and the category as phenomenon is now clearly classified.[15] The publication and dissemination of such texts is just one example of how the colonial empires provide the conditions for the development and growth of scripturalism in terms of the development of world religions as part or reflection of advanced civilization. These religions also seemed to serve as metonyms or certainly powerful examples of scriptural formation and politics, conveniently (mis)recognized and (un)acknowledged according to what proved to be politically practical and useful. Moreover, they also provided a sort of blueprint or guide for social and political formation and control.[16] Obviously, what is now popularly known and referred to as "the Bible" is the central text of the world religions of the Western world. But it must be stressed at this point that there is no text that is independent and free-floating: all texts are products and projections of—and thereby complexly imbedded and imbricated in—different historical-social and material conditions,[17] including the different circles of formations that are represented by empire and (the "scriptural"="world") religions.

Scriptural religion/s may serve several different types of functions in the context of colonial empire, but they must consistently contribute to some degree and in some respects to the stability of the colonial order. This is always understood, even if not honestly acknowledged. Notwithstanding some historical conflicts, the two types of formations are normally less at odds than complementary, relating more like the dynamics obtaining with concentric circles. Even more important, it is evident that the contribution of the smaller circle to the larger lies less in supplying declarative ideological propositions or pronouncements, that is, in terms of message or meaning conveyed (McGann), than in terms of the phenomenal (event) or in terms of dynamics, inflections, practices, performances, and politics. More plainly, this means colonial regimes have vested interests in scriptural religions on account of the social-political stasis and styles and justifications for authority they model and promote. The politics and social practices of scriptural religions have even been imitated by the modern-world colonial regimes. The wide range or swings of scriptural politics—what I call "scripturalectics," the management of all that is or can be subsumed under the scriptural, including knowledge, discourse, and communication—are imitated as a part of colonial control and management. This situation betrays the scriptural as a phenomenon that goes beyond even as it includes religion, ironically, in spite of the modern-era tendency to make religion a separate social-cultural domain. The sacred-secular divide is scrambled and made problematic by the scriptural. Scriptural religions may be thought by some to have been put aside, to have been surpassed, but not so what is most "fundamental"(!) about them—scripturalism and scripturalectics, modernist ideology, and the management of relations.

What needs further consideration is the matter of the basic ongoing work of the scriptural as it is located and made to work within the context of the colonial system. That basic function is classification, ordering, and hierarchialization. The term "classification" can be argued to be a most apt descriptor of the originary impetus for the work of the scriptural, that is, of writing systems. Lévi-Strauss made the point some time ago that the impetus for writing was the inventorying/classifying of possessions—animals, slaves, property, and the like. So from its beginning writing was implicated in power dynamics and structuring enslavement.[18] The drive behind the scriptural is social-psychological, a will to "classify and conquer" (*dividé et impera*, Müller's chilling translation of an ancient phrase that he took as definition of his sacred books project).[19]

Achebe's novel *TFA* can be read as a window onto the dynamics of consciousness and social relations that are being called here "scripturalectics."[20] The last line of his last chapter—"Pacification of the Primitive Tribes"—includes terms that cry out for unpacking or critical analysis of what is at issue with the scriptural in the modern world, specifically in this case, the British colonial project at end of century in the "Lower Niger." These strange and now haunting famous words constitute the title of the book that the British colonial District Commissioner (DC) was contemplating. The title is jarring, freighted, even a bit frightening. It is the book the DC intends to write about the natives in the region being occupied that will be forever transformed by the British. The plan is for the book to include "material" about the ways of the Umuofian natives and to chronicle a particular example—mostly exemplary, of course, even with missteps here and there—of late-nineteenth/early-twentieth-century British colonial sub-Saharan African management styles and policies. The narrator makes the DC indicate what "point" in the book would be "stress[ed]": it would be generally framed as a record of British "pacification," wry British racialized euphemy for manipulation and control of the "primitives."

The term "pacification" barely masks contempt of the British for those dominated by the British. It seems to be used to deflect reality and make it easier for the dominated to accept the dominance and the contempt that attends it. Most likely, the term is used both by dominants within the narrative and by Achebe himself to speak to the psychology of dominance and management of others.

Regarding primitive tribes, the rationalization among those invading and colonizing must be that only those who are backward and without civilization can and should be managed. We know now that the fixed ideology of modern antiblack racism was cultivated in the aftermath of the European slave trade. In the throes of the monstrous trade, notwithstanding all that it had wrought in commercial terms and in the expansion of European capital(ism), it had to be rationalized in the collective mind of the civilization of slavers. Naming, theorizing, and ideologizing the sub-Saharan black Africans, enslaved as children, as retarded and backward peoples requiring European discipline and governance was the way to explain and justify the trade. All those beyond Christianism were deemed savages; among such could be included some European tribes and Muslims and varieties of Asians, with their various religious traditions, some of which were scriptural traditions that might be comparable but ultimately in the most important respects inferior to Christian traditions. Those outside European modernity and enlightenment were deemed "primitives." They were considered to be benighted and cursed because they were without (European-recognized) writing traditions.[21]

Now regarding books, including The (Holy) Book. And writing. And reading. This is what distinguishes the higher from the lower, civilization from existence as primitives. The book is the modern-world technology and medium by which dominance is established and extended, the most powerful and available means by which social-cultural and political-economic transcendence is realized. With the book, after all, the Christian god is approached and engaged as the ubiquitous and the all-powerful. Seen clearly enough by the stranger, the outsider—including the narrator of *TFA*—the book is for the British (and Europeans, more generally) a—*the*(?) —"fetish." Associated with it is power, "magic," to effect all sorts of outcomes, in addition to the "government" of local native peoples.

It is the book (and reading/writing) that is a stand-in for British networks and systems of communication in the most general terms. It is clearly the British scriptures that Achebe made the major site of controversy in *TFA*: missionaries were depicted as being among the front-line soldiers in the Empire's advance in Africa and beyond. Their offensive weapon was the English Bible. It was made to signify the mysterious power of the British. It explained their power to lure locals away from their traditions and accounted for their powers of healing. And it explained their claims to know so many things, to accomplish so many things, including their very presence in Umuofia.

The appearance of white men—mostly the missionaries—is registered most dramatically in terms of the appearance and uses of the Bible. The strange men are heard making outrageous statements and strange claims that not even typical translation challenges and the particular awkwardnesses of the local situation could address or overcome. Umuofians were told about "this new God, the Creator of all the world and all the men and women." They were also told in the key of great certainty and hubris that Umuofians worshipped "false gods, gods of wood and stone."[22] In spite of the disturbing response— "A deep murmur went through the crowd"—the harangues continued. Umuofians were strongly exhorted to "leave your wicked ways and false gods and turn to Him so that you may be saved." That this rhetoric is clearly (British-inflected) biblical in origins and in intonation—reflecting the imperial times—is without question. Questions and counterarguments are not countenanced and do not prevail: "Which god is the god referenced?" "There is only one true God" (*TFA*, 84). A breathtaking claim. But even more breathtaking is the degree to which we among the civilizations of the scriptural religions have come/been made to accept the attitude as natural.

The narrator has little need to name explicitly or have any characters point out the source of authority (or arrogance) in evidence. Biblical references are embedded in the rhetoric of the British missionaries so regularly and naturally to the point of appearing not to be separate from their persons. The Bible is conveyed not only in the colonialists' apodictic statements of religious discourse, including the hymns taught the locals (*TFA*, 85), it was also embedded in other types of discourse. In response to questions raised about any subject or issue—even those far beyond (the Europeanist modern separate realm of) "religion" —answers are provided that are themselves reflective of absolutist biblical rhetorics. After the missionaries—"crazy men" —had spent some time among villagers, saying and doing many things that "puzzled," the narrator summed up the generally held view of them—"that the white man's fetish had unbelievable power" (*TFA*, 86). There should be little doubt that here with the term "fetish" Achebe is signifying on—capping on, reversing—white men's already long history of projecting "Africans" as "primitives" peculiarly prone to fetishizing practices. The object that need not be named here is the white men's book, "the Bible," "the scriptures," "the Word of God." It was generally agreed, even taken for granted among "white men"—certainly, the white men who were the British—that through such an object God spoke and made things happen. Indeed, all books were more or less thought to be significant. Therein lies their "unbelievable power"—insofar as they projected in association with The Book such unprecedented, seemingly ridiculous certainty and confidence: "There is only one true God" (*TFA*, 84); "worship the [one] true God" (*TFA*, 87).

The book that was the Bible was itself part—the most important part, to be sure—of a larger system, what might be thought about in terms of a language system or regime (so scripturalization.) That Achebe thought in terms of structure can be seen at the point when he had his narrator indicate that stories had circulated among villagers that the white man "had not only brought a religion but also a *government*" (*TFA*, 89; emphasis mine). I take this term to capture Achebe's view that the influence of the British in the life of the village of Umuofia was encompassing. "Religion" was not enough to capture the radical changes wrought by the British "presence." The change was already—from the perspective of the narrator—multidimensional, sedimented, and broad-based, felt in every sector of life. "Government"—"white man's government"—aptly described the capture (*TFA*, 89, 99).

The establishment of "white man's government" in Umouofia was accomplished primarily not through warfare, but "quietly," via the more devastatingly powerful psycho-socio-cultural weapon. And the latter was first and most effectively wielded primarily through "religion," the sort that had been made transcendent, that is, transported through the agency of scriptures, namely, *things written*, as political and as social-cultural power—the "only true Word of God." Such power was in evidence in every domain of life in British and European worlds—from ritual ("religion" as separate domain) to commerce to the courts. As such, it was also deeply settled in the individual's and the corporate body's "head." One of the village elders who was also a major character in the novel points to how what we might call socialization and formation were accomplished—and with what consequences:

> Our own brothers who have taken up his religion also say that our customs are bad. How do you think we can fight when our own brothers have turned against us? The white man is very clever. He came *quietly* and *peaceably* with his *religion*. We were amused at his foolishness and allowed him to stay. Now he has won our brothers, and our clan can no longer act like one. He has put a knife on the things that held us together and we have *fallen apart*. (*TFA*, 100)

This assault on the traditional was far-reaching and profound and elicited a note of the ironic. The "falling apart" was in evidence no matter the attitude or discretionary policies of the white men, encountered as missionaries or as commissioners. It happened under the more severe policies of the hard-liner Reverend Mr. Smith. But it also happened with the relatively moderate attitudes and policies of the missionary Mr. Brown. When a local fanatical convert named Enoch "murdered"—unmasked—an elder (*egwugwu*), the decision was made to retaliate by burning down the white men's "shrine." Mr. Smith "stood his ground" against the threat of the eventual burning of the church. And when the *egwugwu* retreated as though satisfied that with the retaliatory burning the assault had been curtailed, the narrator, in concluding his report about this incident, suggested that "for the moment" the clan was "pacified" (*TFA*, 108).

But the term "pacified" is here rather odd. The reader knows that this cannot possibly be the end of the story. It feels rather like the beginning of something shaky, if not horrible, something to make one rather ill at ease. Things were far from being at peace. The clan had not at all been pacified. White men with such power could not possibly be turned around or routed in this way. There was an unquiet about the quiet.

The major heroic and tragic character Okonkwo was determined to take action to change the situation. He met with other elders about the situation. At Okonkwo's compound, "in a flash," he killed a messenger who had been sent by the DC to inform all gathered to cease and desist their rumblings. Confusion ensued. Okonkwo fled. When the dust had settled and the DC had arrived on the scene, Okonkwo's body was found behind his compound "dangling" from a tree (*TFA*, 117).

In response to the request from the wise and sober Obierika for assistance in handling the body, the DC, knowing Okonkwo's death had put an end to the acute tension and conflict, began to make himself a "student" of "primitive customs." This turn of interest on his part, to study the wise and not so wise steps in British colonial rule—through study of the "primitives"—is critical. It provides perspective on how British colonial rule is established and maintained, mostly in connection with writing. Not only is writing the means by which colonial rule communicates with, and takes direction from, the metropole, it is also the means by which "primitives" are "pacified." This latter term is significant: it takes us back to the valences of the term I discussed above; it also recalls earlier use of the term in Achebe's novel. There was fateful, almost haunting irony in the "pacification" that ensued in the wake of the assault on the white men's shrine. Such "peace" was fleeting. But in the wake of Okonkwo's suicide, as all things had clearly already fallen apart for Umuofia, there is another eerie "peace" that is referenced—the type easily assumed on the part of the DC to obtain in and define that particular colonial situation. This is the "peace" that was colonial rule. The pacification in this context has to do with dominating/managing/reorienting the primitives, ensuring that British rule is able to reap as much of the economic and other benefits from its efforts. From the perspective of the narrator, it is a fraught, cynical, and bitter peace. And it is maintained through the violence of forms of communication, even as it is, by the likes of Achebe, honestly, chillingly, and disturbingly described—through (highly conscientized and artful) writing.

How is writing made to do the work of managing the Umuofians (and all others beyond *TFA*—colonized and enslaved Africans)? And what makes it a type of violence? As is indicated in Achebe's story, pacification-as-management is accomplished by naming, defining, overdetermining, flattening, and circumscribing the Umuofians. They are first of all pronounced *"primitives."* And they are *enscripturalized*[23]—made to be what they are on account of being written up, that is, made official and real—in the white men's records in their papers and books. The Umuofians are through British language inscribed and invented as a different people for the sake of British rule. And given the reach and fixity of writing, the inscription and invention would remain, notwithstanding independence.

The phenomenon of what now can only be understood in terms of the ironic and sardonic pacification in relationship to the Umuofians—and beyond, or more generally throughout the colonial regime—works on at least two different planes. First, as we have already seen, there are the ("religious") scriptures, understood in the narrow terms of the object deployed or manipulated by the missionaries. The latter carried and deployed—read from, pointed out, projected, quoted from, paraphrased—the English Bible as scriptures as advancement not only of the strictly religious-evangelical but also, simultaneously and coextensively, the broader socio-cultural-economic-political colonial formation agenda. There was no simple or honest way or reason for Achebe and his contemporary cohorts who shared his sensibilities and political commitments to separate out the different agendas among different social-cultural and political groups and interests that defined and contributed to the big agenda of the colonial project. Thus, "scriptures" in Umuofia and throughout the English world was also shorthand, understood to refer to writing in general, books, other documents/texts/colonial schooling and communication in general. In other more pointed, perhaps disturbing, words, those scriptures represented what the late-eighteenth-century figure Olaudah Equiano called "white men's magic," what Achebe called "pacification," and what in this essay is analyzed as the phenomenon of scripturalization in modern-world history. As such, scriptures not only captured the politics and practices of the colonials but also the terms around which the colonized and enslaved engaged in complex mimetics.[24]

Summary: Reading Scripturalectics (*Not* Scriptures) as Critical Orientation and Agency

The Bible functions most widely and powerfully for all within the Western world, as well as those beyond the West but under its influence, as a discursive police. Insofar as it is a complex of representations and social-cultural-political (reading/interpretive) practices put in place ("donated") by the colonial order of things, engagement of the Bible should be presumed to be in terms of originating politics and psychology in support of the colonial order. It is fundamentally a part of the colonial order, and thus it is one of the means by which such an order was established and was and is maintained.

The colonial donation still determines the Bible—what it is, how it works, and the terms on which it is viewed and engaged. This development has taken place without much of a fight or without sustained and effective resistance because the situation that obtains has hardly been recognized and taken seriously. It is difficult to resist that which is taken to be natural and all too obvious.

A critical approach of the type argued for here suggests a need not for exegesis or deconstruction of the texts or the letters but for defamiliarization—of the *entire phenomenon of the invention and mimetic uses and politics of scriptures (or: critical analyses of the dynamics that are scripturalectics: scripturalizing, scripturalization, scripturalizing)*. We need to be able to get out of and beyond the "box," what Bourdieu calls *doxa*, within which are "texts" the engagement of which represents pursuit of lexical-cultural/theological/religious meanings. The modern-world colonialist structures require obsession over texts or meaning for the sake of control. As our example of scriptures as cultural phenomena and dynamics, the Bible has been historically engaged through mimetic practices inside the box. Stepping outside the box is a matter not so much of the fetishistic pursuit in mimetic practices of the meaning of this or that text—which registers as the familiar cultural practice or operation intended to result in stasis—but the questioning of the *donation* of the text in the first place, that is, what it is, how it has come about, and *its meaning in connection with meaning*, including its politics. Such orientation is easier said/written about than accomplished, to be sure. The occlusion from the naturalization of the textual is akin to a type of sleep, a lack of consciousness, and so it is difficult to scrutinize. There is much at stake in being awake or provoking an awakening. A good beginning in wakefulness should entail giving more attention to the social textures, stories, or sojourns of peoples (the likes of which are Achebe's Umuofians) to discern how they are coping and responding to efforts—persistent efforts—to determine the shape of their formation (as readers, as humans) through control and management of communications, knowledges, and scriptures. Agency and freedom, then, must include a capacity for reading scripturalectics—the dynamics, mimetic practices, politics, forms of violence, forms of resistance, and (social-cultural-political) transcendence that appertain to the imposition of scriptures.

Notes

1. The foremost scholar in this area of inquiry is R. S. Sugirtharajah. For wide perspective one might begin with his edited collection of essays by a wide circle of scholars, *Postcolonial Biblical Reader* (Oxford, UK: Wiley-Blackwell, 2005).
2. See as simply one example from one community—and the earliest of such publications in the United States—*Stony the Road We Trod: African American Biblical Interpretation*, ed. Cain H. Felder (Philadelphia: Fortress Press, 1991). See now also: Francisco Lozada Jr. and Fernando F. Segovia, eds., *Latino/a Biblical Hermeneutics* (Semeia Studies 68; Atlanta: SBL Press, 2014); R. S. Sugirtharajah, *Jesus in Asia* (Cambridge, MA: Harvard University Press, 2018); Benny Tat-siong Liew, *What Is Asian American Biblical Hermeneutics? Reading the New Testament* (Honolulu: University of Hawaii Press, 2007); Michael Joseph Brown, *Blackening of the Bible: Aims of African American Biblical Interpretation* (Harrisburg: Trinity Press International, 2004); and *They Were All in One Place? Toward Minority Biblical Criticism*, ed. Randall C. Bailey, Benny Tat-Siong Liew, and Fernando F. Segovia (Semeia Studies 57; Atlanta: SBL Press, 2009).
3. On this point Michel de Certeau, *Writing of History* (New York: Columbia University Press, 1988), is most provocative as he charts the change in orientation of culture (eighteenth-century French as example) by focusing on the exclusive authority the clerical class arrogated to itself in interpretation of scriptures—both narrowly and broadly understood.
4. Several examples may serve to make this point. No example is more powerful than the work of Martin Bernal and the roilings caused in the classics field by his work *Black Athena: The Afroasiatic Roots of Classical Civilization*, 3 vols. (New Brunswick: Rutgers University Press, 1987, 1991, 2006).
5. For a useful if not totally satisfying single-volume treatment of some of the major issues and problems engaged over a long historical period, see Colin Kidd, *Forging of Races: Race and Scripture in the Protestant Atlantic World, 1600-2000* (Cambridge: Cambridge University Press, 2006). Here one comes to understand the reality of interpretation of the Bible—especially in the Protestant world—becoming the work or play that everyone invested in social criticism engaged.
6. For provocative argument and very useful perspectives on this phenomenon, see Nidesh Lawtoo, *Conrad's Shadow: Catastrophe, Mimesis, Theory* (East Lansing: Michigan State University Press, 2016).

7. Or the one wielding the *skeptron*. See, for insightful analysis, Pierre Bourdieu, *Language and Symbolic Power* (Malden MA: Polity Press, 1991), passim.
8. See Vincent L. Wimbush, *White Men's Magic: Scripturalization as Slavery* (New York: Oxford University Press, 2012), for introduction to and critical discussion of the term and concept.
9. For helpful perspective, see Ivan Hannaford, *Race: The History of an Idea in the West* (Baltimore: Johns Hopkins University Press, 1996); Joel Kovel, *White Racism* (New York: Columbia University Press, 1984); and Nell Irvin Painter, *The History of White People* (New York: W. W. Norton, 2010).
10. Note that in this article the three categories—Bible; race/racism; and postcolonial—have been placed within quotation marks in order to make the point that they all beg or require considerable sustained conceptual unpacking or defamiliarization as part of complex theoretic engagement. With the term "defamiliarization" I mean simply that this article is conceptualized around and driven by the stance that these fraught terms and categories we use are too much taken for granted, rendered too flat and simple, as though we are all in agreement about what the terms refer to and what we are communicating. This can hardly be the case. There is in fact among us far too much conflict and talking past one another for this to be true! We must, therefore, essentially make these categories again (and again?) foreign to our thinking, step back, and take stock of what we assume is at stake and is basic. This (ascetical) gesture—of disciplined and sensitive listening to others, of forbearance and tolerance—is required in order that we might open up and keep open conversation, debate, and courageous thinking about how we are or might be constituted as a world. Reconsideration of the categories above would need to be part of such an interest.
11. The text hereafter quoted from and cited in this essay is *Things Fall Apart: Authoritative Text, Contexts and Criticism*, ed. F. A. Irele (New York: W. W. Norton, 2009) (hereafter *TFA*). For a more elaborate analytical discussion of *TFA*, see my *Scripturalectics: Management of Meaning* (New York: Oxford University Press, 2017).
12. Here I note the influence of M. de Certeau, *Practice of Everyday Life* (Berkeley: University of California Press, 1984) and his *Writing of History*; Pierre Bourdieu, *Outline of a Theory of Practice* (Cambridge: Cambridge University Press, 1977); Yuri Lotman, *Universe of the Mind: A Semiotic Theory of Culture* (Bloomington: Indiana University Press, 2001); Alekse Semenko, *The Texture of Culture: An Introduction to Yuri Lotman's Semiotic Theory* (New York: Palgrave Macmillan, 2012).
13. See Stig Hjarvard, *Mediatization of Culture and Society* (London: Routledge, 2013).
14. For more discussion about "scripturalism," see *Scripturalectics* 74– 75, 153, 155. In re: "reading formations," see Tony Bennett, "Texts, Readers, Reading Formations," *Bulletin of the Midwest Modern Language Association* 16, no. 1 (Spring 1983): 3–17.
15. See *Sacred Books of the East* (multiple volumes). For illuminating background and critical perspective, see Tomoko Matsuzawa, *The Invention of World Religions: Or, How European Universalism Was Preserved in the Language of Pluralism* (Chicago: University of Chicago Press, 2005), chap. 7.
16. See Francois Furstenberg, *In the Name of the Father: Washington's Legacy, Slavery, and the Making of the Nation* (New York: Penguin Books, 2007), for argument about the United States as scriptural formation, both in terms of textual-content and mimetic practices.
17. See Jerome J. McGann, *The Textual Condition* (Princeton: Princeton University Press, 1991), esp. Part One, for important perspectives on how text and textualities work in society and culture.

18. See *Conversations with Claude Lévi-Strauss*, ed. G. Charbonnier, trans. John and Doreen Weightman (London: Jonathan Cape, 1969), esp. chap. 2 ("Primitive Peoples and 'Civilized' Peoples").
19. See n. 15 (in re: Matsuzawa).
20. Elaboration can be found in *Scripturalectics*, passim.
21. See n. 18.
22. See on the phenomenon of certainty, Wendy James, ed., *The Pursuit of Certainty: Religious and Cultural Formations* (London and New York: Routledge, 1995).
23. See in re: related concept of "entextualization," Webb Keane, *Christian Moderns: Freedom and Fetish in the Mission Encounter* (Berkeley: University of California Press, 2007), 14, 171, 261.
24. See fascinating arguments made by Lawtoo, *Conrad's Shadow: Catastrophe, Mimesis*, esp. chap. 5, in re: Achebe's *TFA*.

Bibliography

Bailey, Randall C., Benny Tat-Siong Liew, and Fernando F. Segovia, Eds. *They Were All in One Place? Toward Minority Biblical Criticism*. Semeia Studies 57; Atlanta: SBL Press, 2009.

Bourdieu, Pierre. *Language and Symbolic Power*. Malden, MA: Polity Press, 1991.

Bourdieu, Pierre. *Writing of History: Outline of a Theory of Practice*. Cambridge: Cambridge University Press, 1977.

Brown, Michael Joseph. *Blackening of the Bible: Aims of African American Biblical Interpretation*. Harrisburg: Trinity Press International, 2004.

de Certeau, Michel. *Practice of Everyday Life*. Berkeley: University of California Press, 1984.

de Certeau, Michel. *Writing of History*. New York: Columbia University Press, 1988.

Charbonnier, G., Ed. Trans. John and Doreen Weightman. *Conversations with Claude Lévi-Strauss*. London: Jonathan Cape, 1969.

Felder, Cain H., Ed. *Stony the Road We Trod: African American Biblical Interpretation*. Philadelphia: Fortress Press, 1991.

Hannaford, Ivan. *Race: The History of an Idea in the West*. Baltimore: Johns Hopkins University Press, 1996.

Hjarvard, Stig. *Mediatization of Culture and Society*. London: Routledge, 2013.

James, Wendy, Ed. *The Pursuit of Certainty: Religious and Cultural Formations*. London and New York: Routledge, 1995.

Keane, Webb. *Christian Moderns: Freedom and Fetish in the Mission Encounter*. Berkeley: University of California Press, 2007.

Kidd, Colin. *Forging of Races: Race and Scripture in the Protestant Atlantic World, 1600–2000* Cambridge: Cambridge University Press, 2006.

Kovel, Joel. *White Racism*. New York: Columbia University Press, 1984.

Liew, Benny Tat-siong. *What Is Asian American Biblical Hermeneutics? Reading the New Testament*. Honolulu: University of Hawaii Press, 2007.

Lotman, Yuri. *Universe of the Mind: A Semiotic Theory of Culture*. Bloomington: Indiana University Press, 2001.

Lozada, Francsico, Jr., and Fernando F. Segovia, Eds. *Latino/a Biblical Hermeneutics*. Semeia Studies 68; Atlanta: SBL Press, 2014.

Matsuzawa, Tomoko. *The Invention of World Religions: Or, How European Universalism Was Preserved in the Language of Pluralism*. Chicago: University of Chicago Press, 2005.

McGann, Jerome J. *The Textual Condition*. Princeton: Princeton University Press, 1991.
Painter, Nell Irvin. *The History of White People*. New York: W. W. Norton, 2010.
Sugirtharajah, R. S. *Postcolonial Biblical Reader*. Oxford, UK: Wiley-Blackwell, 2005.
Wimbush, Vincent L. *Scripturalectics: Management of Meaning*. New York: Oxford University Press, 2017.
Wimbush, Vincent L. *White Men's Magic: Scripturalization as Slavery*. New York: Oxford University Press, 2012.

CHAPTER 24

ECOLOGY AND POSTCOLONIAL BIBLICAL CRITICISM

ELLEN F. DAVIS

ECOLOGICAL and postcolonial studies are complementary angles of vision on the Bible. Fundamental to both is the critique of exercises of human power that may have destructive consequences on a massive scale. While postcolonial studies have named the imperialism of nation-states as a persistent social phenomenon, ecological studies have drawn attention to the new and related phenomenon of geophysical imperialism. Humans now operate as a geological force, both intentionally and inadvertently imposing change on a planetary scale. Here I propose to address the concerns of both areas of study by outlining an eco-agrarian approach to ancient Israel's Scriptures, which focuses on the multifaceted interdependency of arable land, animals, and human communities in all their particular places. Such an approach can be both exegetically accurate and theologically rich, because the worldview of many or most biblical writers is agrarian; the Bible itself, and especially the Hebrew Bible, may be the most extensive and nuanced collection of agrarian writings extant from the premodern world.[1] Therefore, in order to comprehend the various understandings of God and humanity represented there, we must reckon with an awareness that is deeply inscribed on page after page of Israel's scriptures: wellbeing —a complex concept evoked by such terms as *shalom*, *tsedaqah* (righteousness), and *yeshu'ah* (salvation)—is a condition of life that can be achieved only by and for the whole indivisible community of humans and non-human creatures, including land, water, and sky. After a long period of cultural amnesia, industrialized Westerners like me must labor to regain that awareness if we humans are to flourish for countless generations into the future.

Eco-agrarian readings of Scripture focus attention on the essential material substrate of human existence, including what we sometimes call our "spiritual life"—a dubious phrase if it is meant to imply a realm of experience distinct from our material existence. A postcolonial perspective augments such readings by highlighting the crucial element of social dynamics, especially how the exercise of oppressive force is a near-constant in human societies and therefore in biblical texts—be it as a sharp and indelible memory, an imminent threat, or a dominant reality. This essay attempts to reread a few familiar texts, with explicit attention to both perspectives in light of significant scholarly works and interpretive conversations that have emerged over the last forty years. My own work as a biblical interpreter has for several decades been informed by the fairly large body of literature produced by neo-agrarian writers, of whom Wendell Berry is the best known. I begin here with a brief example of how my own agrarian reading of a text I thought I knew well has recently been deepened by more attention to the dynamics of force that seem to underlie it.

Saving the Farm

"Humans and animals you *save*, YHWH!" (Ps 36:7 Heb., some translations 36:6), exclaimed by one praying poet, is a remarkably concise expression of the agrarian connection between human and nonhuman creatures. Only here is the common Hebrew verb for acts of divine deliverance (*y-sh-ʿ*) applied to animals along with humans—although some translators mute the parallel with other accounts of YHWH's salvific acts by choosing a different English verb: "preserve" (KJV, NIV) or "rescue" (Alter).[2] The poet's imagination turns to the temple ("your house," 36:9 or 36:8) in Jerusalem, where God provides safe shelter and drink "from the torrent of your *delights*"—*ʿadaneykha*, literally "your Edens." The temple is conceived as the original garden of delight, now replanted in Jerusalem. In the ideology of pilgrimage, it is the one place on Earth where humans, God, and the garden itself may coexist in perfect harmony, if only for a few days each year.

These several observations are the start of an eco-agrarian reading, which is as far as I had previously gone with this psalm. What they fail to take into account is the strong element of fear that frames this Edenic picture on either side. The psalm opens with a detailed picture of the wicked person who

> plots iniquity on his bed,
> sets himself on a course that is no good,
> does not reject evil. (Ps 36:5 or 36:4)

Then, turning to YHWH, the psalmist enters into a different imaginary, in which the core realities are covenant-loyalty and divine faithfulness that reach "to the clouds," "righteousness like mighty mountains," divine justice like "the great Deep" (36:6–7 or 36:5–6). Those bedrock realities anchor the affirmation that follows immediately of the creation-wide scope of God's salvific action, for both humans and animals (*behemah*); likely the psalmist thinks in the first instance of the domestic animals present in every Israelite household.[3] However, the psalmist's household is currently under siege. The final lines of the poem-prayer are a plea that the imagined deliverance be actualized *now*, and that plea seems to be uttered in the face of an attempted land-grab:

> May the foot of pride not overtake me,
> nor the hand of the wicked displace me. (36:12 or 36:11)[4]

In characteristically lapidary language, the psalm echoes the prophet Micah's more detailed denunciation of those who plot evil "on their beds" (Mic 2:1; cf. Ps 36:5)—that is, as a leisure-time activity:

> By the morning light, they execute it—
> for theirs is an almighty hand.
> They covet fields and appropriate them—
> and houses, and take them away.
> They oppress a landowner and his household,
> an individual and his family-land. (Mic 2:1–2)

The eighth-century prophet depicts a scene of domestic colonialization, portraying the legalized crimes of the powerful who can buy court decisions (7:3). Micah anticipates a day when a God of searing "salvation" (7:7) will strip the royal cities, Samaria and Jerusalem, of their fortresses, when their sites will be planted like any farmer's field (1:6, 3:12), and plowshares will be valued over swords (4:3).

Reading Psalm 36 in light of Micah's description of land appropriation, it is clear that that experience, which was all too common for smallhold farmers in Iron Age Israel, grounds (in the strong sense) the psalmist's notion of salvation. Saving humans and animals alike means preserving their shared habitat, namely the family farm. Further, keeping their bodies in place generation after generation means perpetuating a wealth of knowledge about land care that is (in Daniel Stulac's apt phrase) "calibrated to its local context."[5] No place requires such precise knowledge more than the uplands of Canaan, a steep, fragile, and semiarid agricultural zone with wide variations in rainfall and exposure to the sun and winds. This zone can be farmed successfully only by experienced farmers who know the possibilities and limits of each particular piece of land.[6] A vision of salvation that happens on the ground and extends to both humans and animals is congruent with the psalmist's further affirmation of how God's protective presence guarantees the dynamic stability of the created order: "For with you is the fountain of life" (Ps 36:10 or 36:9). "The fountain of life"—that metaphor gives accurate insight into the nature of the order of living beings. Or perhaps it is not a metaphor at all but simply the most straightforward description of creaturely habitat, an ancient farmer-poet's formulation that is echoed in the modern dictum of pioneer ecologist Aldo Leopold: "Land ... is not merely soil; it is *a fountain of energy* flowing through a circuit of soils, plants, and animals."[7] Like Micah and the psalmist, Leopold articulated his own scientific and ethical vision under the shadow of land loss. Watching soil sent "helter-skelter downriver," plant communities exterminated, and animal species extirpated, he called for a land ethic that "changes the role of *Homo sapiens* from conqueror of the land-community to plain member and citizen of it."[8]

The eco-agrarian perspective articulated by Leopold adds an important dimension to the conversation about land that was initiated by African biblical scholars in the first decade of the new millennium.[9] Temba Mafico's essay, "Land Concept and Tenure in Israel and African Tradition," is a profound lament informed by both biblical understandings and recent history in Zimbabwe, which breaks down any simple dichotomizing between the colonial and postindependence eras. Not only was arable land forcibly appropriated during the period of European control, colonialization also worked deep ideological changes within African communities. The traditional understanding of land as the property of an extended family through its generations, which Mafico equates with the biblical concept of *naḥalah*, was assailed and replaced in the minds of many with the notion of land as a salable commodity. Along with that ideological shift came the erosion of social cohesion in a quest for private gain. "Instead of redistributing land, the black aristocratic class who campaigned for independence under the guise of a socialistic society, has grabbed the European farms for themselves. Many black Zimbabweans, as a result, fare as badly, if not worse, in post-independence Zimbabwe as they did in Rhodesia prior to independence."[10]

The complementary insight of eco-agrarianism is that land itself fares badly when deprived of traditional knowledge and inhabitants capable of affection for the land and respect for its long-term health. As Stulac notes, such respect is expressed in the common practice of aboriginal cultures of "adapt[ing] to the character of the places in which they subsist, employing subsistence strategies based on highly specific, locally relevant knowledge rather than on universal principles,"[11] which are developed and applied with the aim of maximizing short-term production and profitability for a few. By contrast, a sustainable economy "must match itself to natural systems" in all their particularity, "or to rephrase the same idea theologically, the human economy must seek analogical compatibility with God's economy."[12] Manna is of course the biblical symbol for a divinely contrived and mandated food economy that is adapted to the particularities of a certain place and aims at sustainable provision for a whole community over time and in adverse circumstances. It is telling that the manna economy is the first institution prescribed for the Israelites after crossing the Re(e)d Sea. The implication would seem to be that living and eating thus is to be freed of "all the sickness that [YHWH] inflicted upon Egypt" (Exod 15:26)—Egypt itself being the foremost biblical symbol of imperial control and ultimately destruction of land, animals, and people.[13]

These voices both biblical and modern, reflecting experience on three continents, attest to how an eco-agrarian focus on the health of land and its inhabitants contrasts with widespread colonialist practices and ideologies. The biblical writers themselves underscore that contrast; while most of them espouse agrarian perspectives, they represent colonialism as a constant threat or vicious reality. Therefore the following features of colonialization should be regularly considered in the interpretation of biblical texts:

1. A fundamental move of colonialization is to force a degree of separation between a people and the land on which their life depends, with the intent of changing a people's sense of history and their identity. The essential action of colonialization is to declare to those who live on the land that *the land is somebody else's business*. Even if they are not removed from ancestral land but rather made to work it for the benefit of colonizers, indigenous peoples are deprived of control with respect to how the land is used and its produce distributed.
2. Colonialization is a political-economic-military move that necessarily has ecological consequences. People who work colonized land are rarely the same people who make major decisions about how to work it, that is, decisions about its use or abuse. Moreover, the factors that most often lead to and follow from colonialization—that is, war and maximally extractive economic practices—are inevitably destructive of both land and human communities over the long term.
3. The experience of subjugation and alienation from control of the land was normative for most residents of Israel and Judah through most of the period in which the biblical texts, both canonical and deutero-canonical, were composed. Domestic colonization by the kings of Israel and Judah likely began in the ninth or early eighth centuries in the forms of land appropriation, commandeering of produce, and military and corvée labor drafts for farmers. The even heavier hand of imperial control was established with the Neo-Assyrian incursions in the last quarter of the eighth century. Control by successive empires continued, with only brief interruptions of home rule, throughout the rest of the biblical period.
4. Most readers, hearers, and scholars of the Bible live in societies in which the effects of colonialization, as a recent or current phenomenon, are strongly felt in both the cultural and the physical environments. Although most European and North American scholars do not generally count themselves (ourselves) among either the colonized or the colonizers, the biblical accounts may well illumine dynamics of land possession and dispossession, use and abuse, in which we participate.

The rest of this essay develops the thesis that, from a perspective widely attested in the Bible, land can never be safely construed as somebody else's business. From the first chapters of Genesis, the land/earth (*erets*) is constantly in view, and the initial view is comprehensive and interactive. Humans and nonhuman creatures together constitute the biotic unity that Leopold called the "land-community" and the psalmist, the "fountain of life." All its members are subject to divine *blessing* (Gen 1:22, 1:28); divine commitment to their flourishing is built into the structure of the world. Moving further into Genesis, Israel's own story begins with the call and blessing of Abraham, who is charged to be a source of blessing to "all the families of the fertile-soil (*adamah*)" (12:3). The formulation of the blessing (uniquely phrased here) is unmistakably agrarian, and its scope is explicitly not limited to Israelite families. In short, both biblically and ecologically speaking, the land—be it family farm, wilderness, Jerusalem and its environs, or what we now call the planet—is everybody's business.

Relearning Bible and Land

As is well known, forty years is the period by which biblical writers characterize the experience of a generation, long enough to witness substantial change in how a whole group of people thinks and acts. It may then be more than coincidence that, approximately forty years ago, an intellectual shift occurred that laid the groundwork for the approach I take here. More accurately, several nearly simultaneous shifts can now be seen as mutually reinforcing. Within the space of about a year, three remarkable books appeared: Walter Brueggemann's *The Land* (1977), Wendell Berry's *The Unsettling of America* (1977), and Edward Said's *Orientalism* (1978). In time, this trio would make it "theoretically" possible, even necessary, to think about Bible, ecology, and colonialist practices together.

In his relatively early work, Brueggemann explicitly sets out to change the categories of biblical theology with his proposition that land is "a central, if not *the central theme* of biblical faith."[14] *The Land* is written as a response not to the ecological crisis but to a modern social crisis that he identifies as "a deep sense of rootlessness."[15] Seeking an alternative to the (then) dominant categories of biblical theology, Brueggemann looks for a new kind of epistemology that does not focus on "transforming discontinuities" whereby God is discerned or revealed, either in an existentialist experience or through the "mighty deeds of God in history."[16] Instead of reading the Bible as narrating a series of events, the historicity of which might be debated among scholars, he shows how a variety of texts, both narrative and poetic, reveal certain cultural dispositions and dynamics operative in the ancient world and in our own. Land as gift, Israel's faithless and abusive practices in the land and exile from it, the possibility of healing and restoration—these are the themes that are central to Israel's account of its own concrete experience.

Berry's *The Unsettling of America* names the ecological crisis as a crisis of American culture and character, manifested in the agricultural "orthodoxy" that became dominant in North America during the second half of the twentieth century: "Get big or get out!"[17] He reviews industrialized economics and practices that are exploitive of farming families and communities, contemptuous of human bodies and their labor, and ultimately destructive of the land itself. If readers happened to engage both Brueggemann's and Berry's books in 1977, might they have noted a convergence in their insights about cultures ancient and modern that are forgetful of the land on which their life depends, along with the people who work the land?[18] Did they note a common recognition that wilderness is indispensable as both religious symbol and cultural model, because it sets a just limit on human use of the world and our presumption to control it?[19] Wilderness for Berry denotes neither wasteland nor (merely) pretty scenery; rather, it points to "natural forces within the climate and within the soil that have never in any meaningful sense been controlled or conquered."[20] Citing *King Lear*, the Book of Job, and Chinese landscape painting, Berry asserts that until modern times "we have focused a great deal of the best of our thought" upon wilderness as a measure of what it is to be truly human, a "tiny member of a world [we] cannot comprehend or master or in any final sense possess." Such a perception of ourselves is a check against either imagining ourselves to be gods or becoming fiends, with a willingness to participate in "the final despair of destructiveness" toward Creation itself.[21] Creation (with a capital "C") is a central point of reference for Berry's critique of American agriculture, because "our culture now simply lacks the means for thinking of it."[22]

In *Unsettling* and elsewhere, Berry's periodic references to biblical texts are generally brief, but his work consistently points to what is implied and at stake in the Bible's countless references, both literal and metaphorical, to soil, water, earth, seed and grain, wine and oil, sheep and goats. Berry and other contemporary agrarians have awakened in me and other biblical scholars a different kind of interest in the history of the biblical period.[23] A new generation of archaeologists, soil scientists, and social scientists focuses attention less on singular persons and events (monarchs and battles) than on the material and economic experience of the vast majority of the population.[24] Almost all Israelites were smallhold farmers, for whom soil and its products, animal and vegetable, were the elements of daily existence. Therefore those were key elements of religious practice—festal celebrations, animal and cereal sacrifices, consumption of animal flesh within prescribed limits (see especially Lev 11), household healing practices,[25] and theological reflection.

Berry is keenly attuned to the reality of a corporation-driven colonial economy in contemporary North America, an economy that "takes everything—the produce of the land, the work of the people, the young people—and gives back as near as possible to nothing."[26] Such observations have guided my own inquiry into the power arrangements of ancient West Asian royals and the surrounding empires. Narrative accounts of Solomon's forced labor practices and massive extractions of agricultural products for his banqueting table; prophetic denunciations of the tiny Israelite elite class from the eighth-century agrarians Amos, Hosea, Micah, and Isaiah; legal prescriptions aimed at limiting the terms of service for debt slaves and countering permanent alienation of family land—these and many other texts point to the relentless pursuit of arable land and its products, as well as of indentured or enslaved Israelite labor, by both Israelite and foreign kings.

Said was born in Jerusalem in 1935, a member of a Palestinian Christian family that was forcibly displaced to Egypt in 1948. He lived the rest of his life in the diaspora, most of it in the Ivy League exile of Princeton, Harvard, and Columbia universities, where he taught English and comparative literature. In *Orientalism*, he explores the cultural and intellectual rationale that undergirded European and later American domination of the Eastern Mediterranean for more than three centuries, namely the perception of "the Orient" or "Middle East" (from what geographic point of reference?) as inherently weak and irrational. He shows how scholarly institutions and intellectual practices serve to stabilize political power configurations by legitimating some forms of knowledge and devaluing others. Orientalism is a failure both ethical and intellectual; it represents the inability to recognize as human the culture, people, and experience of a whole region that was (is?) identified as irreducibly alien.[27] Although Said does not treat biblical texts directly, his work warrants mention here because of its seminal role in the development of postcolonial criticism.[28] By challenging the modes of knowledge fostered by colonial power arrangements, Said encouraged a kind of engagement that is generated largely "at the margins," from outside the academic power centers of the majority world, and includes a variety of nonacademic social and cultural arenas such as the arts, popular culture, and the traditional practices of indigenous communities.

My own work has benefited from the wisdom of rural communities in the Great Lakes region of East Africa, where I have for some years studied biblical texts with colleagues. A few of my study partners are scholars; more are clergy, other ministerial professionals, or lay workers in their communities. Some have years of formal theological education; others have a few weeks of it, or none. Probably all of them were born in farming villages and reared there, if they were not among the millions of children who fled through the bush during the wars that ravaged the countryside and populations of South[ern] Sudan, Rwanda, Burundi, Congo, and the Democratic Republic of Congo, and then spent much of their adolescence in refugee camps. The Bible's agrarian ethos is deeply familiar to them. Nonetheless, the individualized and spiritualized interpretations of Scripture long promoted by missionary teachers and preachers from the West, and later indigenized within African churches, did not equip them to draw connections between the text and the agrarian traditions of their people over centuries, nor to interpret texts out of their extensive knowledge of the physical environment and nonhuman creatures. Yet when they are encouraged to draw such connections, they prove to be perceptive, critical, and self-critical readers, who sometimes negotiate with ease issues that present problems to Westernized readers, including those with postcolonial or ecological sympathies.

For instance, if East African Christians are not scandalized by the divine mandate in the creation story for humans to "exercise skilled mastery among" the nonhuman creatures (Gen 1:26, 1:28), that is because they do not labor under an ideological bias, either positive or negative, engendered by the phenomenon of technological domination of the nonhuman world. That cultural phenomenon has not yet eradicated or completely changed their relationship to the nonhuman world. Yet they often discover that the text gives focus to their own sense of loss and human failure. One group of South Sudanese educators readily inferred from Adam's naming of the animals (Gen 2:19–20) that people are meant to have a genuine relationship with beasts both domestic and wild. They acknowledged that this value was honored more in pre-Christian villages than is currently the case in towns populated by churchgoers—where, for instance, donkeys are often harshly treated. Similarly, they spoke with sensitivity, even personal pain, about the problem of alienation from animals, which Genesis represents as an effect of human disobedience (Gen 3:15, cf. 9:2–3): "How," they asked, "can we live in harmony with snakes and scorpions? What should we do about the Nile leopard?"—beautiful, endangered, yet also threatening to their children and domestic animals. Most participants accepted as a matter of fact that, during the war, live snakes would lie as pillows under the heads of collapsed refugees. "But that would no longer happen," they said, "now they are afraid of us again." One bishop said that whenever there is a rat infestation in the house, the first thing they do is pray that they may recognize and resolve whatever disharmony obtains in their family and community life—and then they stop up the holes!

Because they are steeped in a storytelling culture, Sudanese Christians know that an important story generally has a complex history and multiple layers of meaning. The historical-critical proposal that the first two chapters of Genesis come from different sources, reflecting somewhat different perspectives on the human place in the created order, is unsurprising to a group of readers that includes Nuer and Dinka, Zande and Shilluk, since they are familiar with different yet complementary accounts of creation from their several ancestral traditions. Again, they find in Genesis 1, with its pronounced emphasis on "seed" (vv. 11–12, 29), a value they understand and share. It reminds them painfully of the loss of ancient seed stock when crops and trees were deliberately destroyed in wartime by the scorched-earth policies of both the Government of Sudan and the Sudanese People's Liberation Army. Equally, it evokes in their minds Jesus Christ as the seed of a new humanity, who extends to all peoples the "earthy" blessing conferred upon Abraham (cf. Gal 3:14, 16).

Certainly one of the challenges for biblical scholarship in this generation is to widen the possibilities for cooperative work across continents and between readers who bring to the text experience that is in various ways essential for comprehending its linguistic, literary, and historical character and the values it articulates, as well as the kind of social and material knowledge—the wisdom belonging to an agrarian culture—that underlies most of Israel's Scriptures.

Relationships within the Earth Community

If the core insight of ecological thinking is that humans must learn again how to live as members and citizens of what Leopold calls the land-community, then we are challenged to reimagine our relationships with the other, nonhuman members. We must imagine a style of relationality that differs fundamentally from the crass profiteering from so-called natural resources that has so profoundly damaged the whole order of creatures, including ourselves. The term "ecology," coined by Ernst Haeckel in 1866, refers to "the science of relations between organisms and their environment."[29] Accordingly, the Hebrew Bible is surely one of the richest resources for the ecological imagination and reconceiving our relationships with other living things, because in almost every book the writers give close attention to the actions and specific qualities of nonhuman creatures: the domestic animals with which Israelites lived intimately and also fields and forests, rivers and rainfall, seeds and stars.

In a recent comprehensive study of biblical descriptions of nonanimal subjects, Mari Jørstad demonstrates that all major sections of the Hebrew Bible attest to "conceptualizations of liveliness that fall outside the range of what modernism allows."[30] Mountains and hills burst into jubilation, and trees clap their hands in response to YHWH (Isa 55:12). The land of Israel observes Sabbath rest, as do domestic and wild animals (Lev 19:10; 25:2–7). Jørstad argues that these are not empty metaphors but rather indications of sociality, emotion, and moral responsibility—modes of subjectivity that in the biblical imaginary extend far beyond the human sphere. In sum, "the concept of personhood encompasses humans, but is not limited to us."[31] "A person is someone who relates, and relationships make persons."[32]

Viewing nonhuman members of the Earth community as subjects is the central hermeneutical tenet of *The Earth Bible* series, initiated by Australian scholar Norman Habel at the dawn of the new millennium.[33] There and in subsequent publications he introduced the hermeneutical stance he calls "reading from the perspective of Earth." Inspired by multiple biblical texts and challenging others, *The Earth Bible* articulates basic "ecojustice principles" that identify Earth as "a community of interconnected living things," each with intrinsic worth. Earth (the total ecosystem) has a distinctive perspective and agency; it is "capable of raising its voice in celebration and against injustice" and actively resisting acts of injustice at the human hands.[34] Likewise the authors of the multiauthored volumes eschew the vaunted objective stance of historical criticism and adopt a stance that is avowedly passionate, perspectival, and resistant; "a disinterested approach is of little use in a crisis."[35]

In later studies Habel explicitly articulates "a radical new way of reading" that proceeds from the core suspicion that "most interpreters in the past and probably most biblical writers themselves have written from an anthropocentric perspective."[36] Out of identification and empathy with Earth, Habel draws an ethical distinction between texts he categorizes as either "green" or "grey":

> Green texts are those texts where nature, creation, or the Earth community is affirmed, valued and recognized as having a role and a voice. Grey texts are those texts where nature, creation or the Earth community is devalued, oppressed, deprived of a voice or made subject to various forms of injustice at the hands of humans or God.[37]

Habel reads the first two chapters of the Bible as epitomizing that distinction. He takes Genesis 1:26–28 to be a grey text that mandates humans to dominate Earth; by contrast, the "green" account in Genesis 2:15 intends humans to serve and guard it. Habel challenges those who follow Jesus of Nazareth to declare that "the grey texts of the Old Testament are superseded and are no longer valid as expressions of our faith in Christ."[38]

It is notable that Mark Brett, another Australian scholar who shares with Habel a strong commitment to honor indigenous perspectives and land claims in a postcolonial context, does not categorically reject the mandate to "fill the earth and subdue it" (Gen 1:28), although he acknowledges that through the nineteenth and twentieth centuries that verse was used to undergird the Australian settler movement, which claimed that uncultivated land was effectively uninhabited.[39] Brett argues for reading the two creation stories in counterpoint, not for choosing between them. Viewed in historical and literary context, the notion that humans are created in God's image, as unique arbiters of power, represents "a democratization of human dignity"; in the priestly imaginary of the Persian period, it implies a critique of monarchic or imperial sovereignty as Israel knew it. Further, the first part of the creation account implies not just power but also human responsibility within a web of relations. Brett infers from the summary formula that concludes the seven days—"These are the generations of the heavens and the earth" (2:4)—that "the humans belong to the vast lineage systems of creation, and human wellbeing is inextricably tied to the wellbeing of non-human creatures."[40] Moreover, in the second part of the account, it is implied that in this family, "the land is the parent," the figure of authority![41] The notion of humans "serving" the land (2:15) is a deliberately ironic editorial inversion of the charge to subdue the Earth, which "potentially undermines any inflated version of human supremacy."[42]

Habel's assertion of Earth's subjectivity is the hermeneutical key also to his treatments of the bloodying of the Nile (Exod 7:19–25) and the parting of the Sea (Exod 14–15) in the war between Pharaoh and YHWH, where he "dare[s] to identify with the waters."[43] He treats the Nile as "a living subject in the narrative" and "a massive ecosystem that sustains both humans and nonhumans" along its length.[44] By his reading, the plague account shows "innocent domains of nature" suffering divine assault.[45] "In the Exodus narrative, YHWH's mighty acts of deliverance for Israel are at the same time mighty acts of destruction for nature."[46]

The question that needs to be asked is whether the waterways of Egypt do in fact function as "nature" within the literary context of Exodus. There is no biblical word or concept that corresponds closely to the modern notion of a natural world. The Bible represents a world of creatures, God's "works" (e.g., Ps 145:4, 9, 10, 17), both human and nonhuman. Yet when the prophet Ezekiel speaks of the Nile, he represents it as the creature of Pharaoh—an acute irony and a theological impossibility. Thus Ezekiel mocks the Egyptian ruler's foolish pretense to be creator and owner of the great river on which his power depends:

> Here I am against you, Pharaoh, King of Egypt,
> the great sea-serpent who crouches in the midst of his Nile,
> who said, "My Nile is my own; I am the one who made it for myself."
> || because he said, "The Nile is mine; I am the one who made it"—so, here I am coming at you and your Nile-channels, and I will turn the land of Egypt into waste places.
>
> (Ezek. 29:3, 9–10)

Pharaoh claims the Nile as his creation and habitat; it is the base from which he launches his acts of aggression. Therefore (pace Habel) it cannot be construed as "innocent."

However, within the book of Exodus itself, the identity of the Nile and other waters of Egypt is more ambiguous. In his well-known study of the plagues as "ecological signs of historical disaster," Terence Fretheim observes that the bloody waters "throughout the whole land of Egypt" (Exod 7:19, 21) have "sign value," signaling the disaster (for Egypt) that lies ahead at the Sea.[47] One could add that blood in the water also recalls the beginning of the story, when baby boys born to Hebrew women were thrown into the Nile to die (1:22). Within the context of Exodus, the Nile is first the instrument of death and then the vehicle of Moses' deliverance. Pharaoh's daughter "draws him out" (2:10) from the water, in the same way he will eventually draw Israel out of the Sea.

In both Exodus and Ezekiel, the waters of Egypt are both more and less than natural ecosystems. They are symbols, inherently partial and mutable representations of reality, and as such they point beyond physical entities and historical events. Because their meaning varies according to the social, cultural, and (in this case) literary contexts in which they are embedded, interpreting them involves selecting the *few* aspects that are relevant to any given usage. Reading the Nile of Exodus as an ecosystem involves something analogous to what James Barr has called an "illegitimate totality transfer," importing "the total series of relations" associated with a given word into every instance of its occurrence.[48] Habel treats the "water events" of Exodus as instances of "divine pollution" with disastrous effects; they are "mighty acts of destruction for nature."[49] However, the narrative of the Sea crossing seems explicitly to discourage a naturalistic reading. There is no permanent disruption or damage: "The Sea returned at daybreak to its steady [or primeval] course" (*le'etano*, Exod 14:27; cf. Mic 6:2). Far from being destroyed or polluted, the returning waters perform a crucial function in destroying Pharaoh's army. If readers look to see the Sea as a subject here, then the poetics of the narrative would suggest that the Sea is an active agent of resistance to empire. In what is generally considered to be one of the earliest pieces of Israelite literature, the poet declares to YHWH:

> You stretched out your right hand;
> Earth [*erets*] swallowed them. (15:12)

Jørstad comments: "At the tipping point of the poem, the moment at which Israel transforms from a group escaping Egypt into a community journeying toward their new home, the writer points to the sympathetic involvement of the non-animal world."[50] Rather than YHWH's assault victim (so Habel), Earth is a willing ally. Moreover, its action is theologically consequential; it helps effect a critical change of perception among the Israelites. As they move from one shore to the other through the Sea's protective walls, they experience a healthy refocusing of their fear, a conversion from fearing Pharaoh (Exod 14:10) to fearing YHWH (14:31).

In the context of the Exodus story, the waters are instruments and subjects in a theologically driven narrative; their roles in the story are the key to evaluating what happens to and through them. I have consistently observed that South Sudanese Christians living along the banks of the Nile have no difficulty distinguishing between the river in the story and the river as the natural ecosystem of which they themselves are a part, upon which they depend daily for water, food, and transport. At the same time, one aspect of their experience enables them to appreciate how the Nile of the Exodus story functions to represent pharaonic power; they have themselves seen enemy soldiers pull baby baskets from the heads of mothers, bayonet the infants (and especially the boys), and throw them into the Nile. Tragically, that role for the river remained unchanged from pharaonic times to the twenty-first century.

Elements of a Prophetic Ecology

The eco-agrarian perspective of the Bible is not a universal farmer's perspective (as though there were such a thing). Rather it is a way of viewing land that takes account of the distinctive characteristics of one particular place—its geophysical character, its social history, and the religious understandings that it has generated. Viewed as an ecological niche and agrarian environment, Canaan/Israel/Palestine is a small and fragile place, "a strip of land between two seas": water on one side and the equally trackless desert on the other. Farmers, especially in the hill country, have always contended with the threats of water scarcity, erosion, and short- and long-term desertification. Viewed as a political environment, that land has been from ancient times to the present among the world's most highly contested territories, scarred by repeated ethnic and national conflicts over the limited and precious resource—or gift, as the biblical writers and neo-agrarians such as Berry would call it—of arable land located at the juncture of three continents. Viewed as a religious environment, the territory whose center-point is Jerusalem is designated as "the holy land" at least once within the Bible (Zech 2:16 and Heb 2:12 [some translations]) and often in common parlance. While its extent may be unclear and disputed, that territory is thus marked as a space where God's presence may be experienced as palpable and transformative. These several angles of vision—geophysical, political, and religious—bear on any biblically informed conversation between eco-agrarianism and postcolonialism. The prophetic corpus of the Bible draws on all three to give insight into the complex interaction among humans, God, and that particular land-community. Therefore this essay concludes by highlighting several passages in Former and Latter Prophets that may illumine elements of a prophetic ecology, offering a visionary perspective for dwelling in that land.

It is in the book of Joshua that a location within the land of Canaan is first designated as "holy" (Josh 5:15). Joshua is at Jericho, just prior to the non-battle that will deliver the city into his hands (cf. Josh 6:2), when this unexpected encounter occurs:

> He looked and here—a man standing with a drawn sword in his hand, and Joshua went up to him and said to him, "Are you for us or for our opponents?" But he said, "No, for I am Commander of YHWH's army; I have just arrived...." And the Commander of YHWH's army said to Joshua, "Remove your sandals from your feet, for the place on which you are standing is holy."
>
> (Josh 5:13–15)

In this liminal moment, there is a clear echo of the paradigmatic prophetic encounter between Moses and YHWH at the burning bush (cf. Exod 3:5), which was the first step toward Israel's rescue from bondage in Egypt. Yet now the divine warrior does not even acknowledge the impending conflict between Israel and its so-called opponents, let alone take a side. What is important is that Joshua himself acknowledges the holiness of the land where he has at last set foot. Could it be that one thing that marks this place as holy is the destabilization of any neat opposition between Israelites and Canaanites—that is, destabilization of the idea that God gives the land exclusively to one political or ethnic group? Moreover, Joshua is to stand unshod, with not even a piece of leather between him and the Earth. Perhaps that direct contact (however brief) with the Earth is what moved the ancient rabbis to see Joshua as an Israelite agrarian, the first to concern himself with proper use of the land. It was he who laid down stipulations regarding the pasturing of herds and tending of trees, fields, and water sources on both public and private land, so that human needs might be met while also maintaining habitats for plants, animals, and fish.[51]

A second suggestive passage from Former Prophets is the Song of Deborah (Judg 5), evidently one of the earliest sacred poems or songs preserved by Israel. The poem, like the immediately preceding prose account of the same event (Judg 4) describes two cultures and economies in conflict: the small farmers of the Jezreel Valley going to war against the kings of Canaan (5:19) and their professional army. The soldiers of "Israel" depicted here are not a great national force but rather an ill-equipped "remnant" (5:13), inhabitants of small hamlets (5:7, 11) without shields or spears (5:8).[52] They marched on foot; the wealthiest of them rode on asses (5:10), while Sisera's chariotry and cavalry were equipped out of the royal Canaanite armory and stables. Some of Israel's most powerful tribes must have given up the cause as lost in advance. Reuben and Dan sent no troops, and likewise Gilead/Gad and Asher "sat still" (5:16–17); Judah, Levi, and Simeon go unmentioned. Yet despite that indifferent showing, the Canaanite general Sisera was undone by YHWH's special forces:

> From the skies the stars fought; from their courses they fought with Sisera.
> The torrent swept them away—ancient torrent, torrent Kishon.
>
> (Judg 5:20–21)

The heavy iron chariots, the fighter jets of the ancient world, foundered when the fertile plain flooded into marshland. Here and elsewhere in the Former Prophets, war is the main context in which the subjectivity of the nonhuman world expresses itself in action (cf. Josh 10:12–13; 2 Sam 18:8).[53] As at the Re(e)d Sea and later in the wilderness (see Judg 5:4–5), threatened Israelites were rescued by the nonhuman creatures of YHWH. Thus the pride of the empire was washed away:

> So may all your enemies vanish, YHWH,
> and those who love [you] be like the sun going forth in its power!
>
> (Judg 5:31)

This is the victory cry of the villagers of Israel, the people of the land who in the Late Bronze Age gradually separated from the city-state system of Canaan, which in the thirteenth century was under the control of Egypt's New Kingdom. The new entity Israel emerged by a process of self-differentiation, both religious—"when new gods were chosen" (Judg 5:8)—and socioeconomic. Scores of unwalled farming villages appeared, especially in the hill country—unwalled, because this was marginal agricultural land that the empire did not want. In other words, an ancient version of postcolonialism is part of the biblical DNA.

However, it is not self-evident who in the ancient world, or even now, might identify with "Israel" as it is represented here and who is excluded. As we have seen, the ethos of this poem is not primarily nationalistic; most Israelite tribes played no role. Moreover, those that sat out the battle were the herders (Reuben and Gilead) and seafarers (Asher and Dan)—that is, those who depended heavily on trade with urban populations. The confrontation described is thus less between two clearly distinct political and ethnic groups than it is between two social locations and economies, indeed two ways of living in relation to the land: "Israelite" villagers and seminomads maintaining themselves, their fields and flocks, at subsistence level, versus "Canaanites," powerfully equipped for war and living in Bronze Age luxury.[54] The difference between them is epitomized by the contrasting portraits of women with which the poem concludes. Here is the tent-dweller Yael, striking down the Canaanite general with a peg and a pounder, the tools at hand (Judg 5:24–27), while Sisera's mother looks out the latticed window of a palatial home, anxious at his delayed return. Her "wise" attendants distract her by helping her to imagine the soldiers dividing the spoils of war—including sexual spoils, women captives, "a womb or two for every man" (5:30). If that is how any of those women first came into Sisera's household, they have put the memory behind them in order to inhabit the world of the supposed victors, whose chief representative now lies dead on the floor of Yael's tent.

The location of the battle in Deborah's Song is the rich agricultural district of Jezreel, which became legendary in Israel as a place where farmers strove to defend their smallholdings against incursions from the royal sector. Those who fought against Sisera were the ancestors of Naboth, who faced off against Ahab and Jezebel in the ninth century and were legally murdered as a result (1 Kings 21). A century later the agrarian prophet Hosea would remember "the blood of Jezreel" and hold it against the royal house of Israel, a domestic source of oppression that no longer merits YHWH's compassion (Hos 1:4–6).[55] In the twenty-first century, the Palestinian Christian theologian Mitri Raheb reminds us that the native people of the land represented here and elsewhere are his own ancestors, and that "the entire Bible, both Old and New Testaments, struggles to find a faithful response to various and recurring empires."[56]

Raheb makes an important theological and historical advance in drawing the line of continuity between contemporary Palestinians and the smallholder farmers who were the majority population in the biblical period, for whose cause the Former and Latter Prophets repeatedly advocate. However, the challenge that remains for contemporary Palestinians and Jews is to recognize each other in the land of their common origin and unbreakable attachment and, further, to recognize that an eco-agrarian sensibility, linking the *shalom* of the land with adequate provision for its human inhabitants, is essential for peace.[57] This is of course not a new vision for that land and its inhabitants. The agrarians Isaiah and Micah each preserve the tradition of *torah*, divine instruction, and going forth from Zion. This is a *torah* for recrafting weapons into agricultural instruments and unlearning the skills of war (Isa 2:2–4; Mic 4:1–3), and so it can be no coincidence that both prophets tell of divine instruction yielding reliable food provision for smallholder farmers (Isa 28:24–29; Mic 4:4). Daniel Stulac observes that the vision of the wise farmer in Isaiah 28, which is paradigmatic for the whole book, "is born from and remains responsible to the prophetic community's *local attention to the land*."[58]

Not just the Prophets, but virtually every book of the Hebrew Bible, draws vital connections between human flourishing and attention to the land on which all life depends. The ubiquity of the land is reflective of the geographic and geopolitical realities of the place from which the Bible emanates: a narrow temperate zone strategically located at the juncture of three continents, rich in biodiversity, with marginally adequate supplies of water and fertile soil, capable of yielding agricultural sustenance over the long term to those who tend it wisely. Those advantages, and the sanctity ascribed to that place, have made it contested space, often an occupied land, from ancient times to the present. Perhaps its sanctity is in no small part due to the fact that the possibility of living there in *shalom*, prosperity and peace, can never be taken for granted.

The Bible's preoccupation with matters of land is surely part of the *torah* it offers readers in our own time. People everywhere must learn to draw the essential connections between human flourishing and the particular gifts and limits of the places we inhabit, in a world where the degradation of arable land and the competition for it are more acute than ever. "For us, agriculture is the only alternative to war," said a South Sudanese man with whom I had struck up a casual conversation in a Juba café—echoing Isaiah and Micah, deliberately or not. I had mentioned that I was working with the Episcopal Church of Sudan and South Sudan to integrate community health and community agriculture into the theological education curriculum for clergy and lay leaders at regional colleges. I did not need to explain to him why that was important for the revival and survival of a people who had endured some fifty years of war and a generation of genocide. More than two million lives were lost, along with most of the traditional village-based infrastructure and much local knowledge and practice. Like Amos and Jeremiah, my lunch companion in Juba immediately recognized the connection between responsible religious leadership and the need for responsible agriculture, along with the presence and protection of subsistence-level farming communities as a central part of the restoration of a land torn by war and the depredations of empire (see Amos 9:11–15; Jer 32).[59] Whatever his particular knowledge of the biblical Prophets may have been, he intuited that prophetic *torah*; his deep cultural heritage and direct experience enabled him to comprehend something that a Western biblical scholar such as I will spend the rest of my life laboring to grasp.

Notes

1. See Ellen F. Davis, *Scripture, Culture, and Agriculture: An Agrarian Reading of the Bible* (New York: Cambridge University Press, 2009).
2. Robert Alter, *The Book of Psalms: A Translation with Commentary* (New York: W. W. Norton, 2007), 127.
3. Ellen F. Davis, "Identity and Eating," *Studies in Christian Ethics* 30, no. 1 (2017): 1-12, http://sce.sagepub.com/content/early/2016/10/19/0953946816674145.full.pdf?ijkey=BNLEEl2LfFeicJT&keytype=finite
4. The reference to land loss in Psalm 36 is strongly underscored by the two psalms that frame it on either side, which speak in detail about acts of depredation against the "poor and vulnerable" (35:10), with the expectation that "the humble will inherit land" (37:11)—a more concrete promise than the traditional translation, "the meek shall inherit the earth" (KJV), might seem to suggest.
5. Daniel Stulac identifies the notion of "the creaturely body in place" as lying at the core of an agrarian epistemology; see his sensitive discussion in Daniel J. Stulac, *History and Hope: The Agrarian Wisdom of Isaiah 28-35* (University Park, PA: Eisenbrauns, 2018), 8-21 (for the phrase cited, see 16).
6. James C. Scott carefully develops the contrast between what he calls *mētis*, practical or "situated knowledge" and "imperial knowledge," with its "thin simplifications" and "standardized formulas legible only from the center"; see James C. Scott, *Seeing Like a State: How Certain Schemes to Improve the Human Condition Have Failed* (New Haven: Yale University Press, 1998), 309-341.
7. Aldo Leopold, "The Land Ethic," in *A Sand County Almanac* (New York: Oxford University Press, 1966), 253; italics added.
8. Ibid., 240; italics original.
9. It is notable that "Reading the Bible and Land" is the focus of one of eight sections in the volume *Postcolonial Perspectives in African Biblical Interpretations*, ed. Musa W. Dube, Andrew M. Mbuvi, and Dora R. Mbuwayesango (Atlanta, GA: Society of Biblical Literature, 2012), pp. 221-56. Between 2004 and 2010, the essays were presented as papers in the African Biblical Hermeneutics section of the Society of Biblical Literature.
10. Temba L. J. Mafico, "Land Concept and Tenure in Israel and African Tradition," in *Postcolonial Perspectives in African Biblical Interpretations*, ed. Musa W. Dube, Andrew M. Mbuvi, and Dora R. Mbuwayesango (Atlanta, GA: Society of Biblical Literature, 2012), 243.
11. Stulac, *History and Hope*, 15.
12. Ibid., 15-16.
13. See Ellen F. Davis, "Leaving Egypt Behind, Embracing the Wilderness Economy," in Davis, *Scripture, Culture, and Agriculture: An Agrarian Reading of the Bible* (New York: Cambridge University Press, 2009), 66-79.
14. Walter Brueggemann, *The Land: Place as Gift, Promise, and Challenge in Biblical Faith* (Philadelphia: Fortress Press, 1977), 3; italics original.
15. Ibid., xv.
16. Ibid., 3.
17. The phrase "Get big or get out!" is credited to Earl Butz, U.S. Secretary of Agriculture from 1971 to 1976 (under Richard Nixon and Gerald Ford). See Michael Carlson, "Obituary: Earl Butz," The Guardian, February 7, 2008.

18. Brueggemann cites Wendell Berry and American mismanagement of land in his Preface to the second edition of *The Land* (Minneapolis: Fortress Press, 2002), xxii–xxiii.
19. See Wendell Berry, *The Unsettling of America: Culture and Agriculture* (San Francisco: Sierra Club Books, 1977), 30. See also Brueggemann, *Land*, 28-44.
20. Berry, *Unsettling*, 100.
21. Ibid., 99.
22. Ibid., 22.
23. Theodore Hiebert may have been the first biblical scholar to write from an avowedly agrarian perspective; see his *The Yahwist's Landscape: Nature and Religion in Early Israel* (New York: Oxford University Press, 1996). A seminal early publication by theologians and church leaders was *Theology of the Land*, ed. Leonard J. Weber, Bernard F. Evans, and Gregory D. Cusack (Collegeville, MN: Liturgical Press, 1987); it includes an essay by Brueggemann. For a related kind of inquiry from a biblical exegete, see Nathan MacDonald, *What Did the Ancient Israelites Eat? Diet in Biblical Times* (Grand Rapids, MI: Eerdmans, 2008).
24. See, e.g., Philip J. King and Lawrence E. Stager, *Life in Biblical Israel* (Louisville, KY: Westminster John Knox Press, 2001); Oded Borowski, *Daily Life in Biblical Times* (Atlanta, GA: Society of Biblical Literature, 2003); and *Agriculture in Iron Age Israel* (Winona Lake, IN: Eisenbrauns, 1987); Daniel Hillel, *The Natural History of the Bible: An Environmental Exploration of the Hebrew Scriptures* (New York: Columbia University Press, 2006); Carol L. Meyers, *Rediscovering Eve: Ancient Israelite Women in Context* (New York: Oxford University Press, 2013); and Roland Boer, *The Sacred Economy of Ancient Israel* (Louisville, KY: Westminster John Knox Press, 2015).
25. On the religious dimensions of household practices such as preparing food and treating illness and wounds, see Meyers, *Rediscovering Eve*, 147-170.
26. See Wendell Berry, *The Art of Loading Brush: New Agrarian Writings* (Berkeley, CA: Counterpoint, 2017), 77.
27. See Edward Said, *Orientalism* (New York: Pantheon Books, 1978), 327-328.
28. See, e.g., Leela Gandhi, *Postcolonial Theory: A Critical Introduction* (New York: Columbia University Press, 1998), 64-80 and passim; R. S. Sugirtharajah, *The Bible and the Third World: Precolonial, Colonial, and Postcolonial Encounters* (Cambridge: Cambridge University Press, 2001), 247-248.
29. Cited by Norman Wirzba, *The Paradise of God: Renewing Religion in an Ecological Age* (New York: Oxford University Press, 2003), 100. The connection between ecology and relationality lies at the heart of Terence E. Fretheim's study, *God and World in the Old Testament: A Relational Theology of Creation* (Nashville, TN: Abingdon Press, 2005).
30. See chap. 2 of Mari Jørstad, *The Hebrew Bible and Environmental Ethics: Humans, Non-Humans, and the Living Landscape* (New York: Cambridge University Press, forthcoming 2019).
31. Ibid.
32. Ibid.
33. The first volume in *The Earth Bible* series is *Readings from the Perspective of Earth*, ed. Norman C. Habel (Sheffield, UK: Sheffield Academic Press, 2000). Four other volumes followed in that series (2000-2002); and later, the *Earth Bible Commentary*. The first publication in that series is Norman Habel's *The Birth, the Curse, and the Greening of Earth* (Sheffield, UK: Sheffield Phoenix Press, 2011).
34. Habel, *Readings from the Perspective of Earth*, 24.

35. Ibid., 14.
36. Norman Habel, *An Inconvenient Text: Is a Green Reading of the Bible Possible?* (Adelaide: ATF Press, 2009), xx, 116.
37. Habel, *The Birth, the Curse, and the Greening of Earth*, 3.
38. Habel, *An Inconvenient Text*, 77.
39. Mark G. Brett, *Political Trauma and Healing: Biblical Ethics for a Postcolonial World* (Grand Rapids, MI: Eerdmans, 2016), 50-51.
40. Ibid., 184-185.
41. Mark G. Brett, *Genesis: Procreation and the Politics of Identity* (New York: Routledge, 2000), 31.
42. Ibid., 30. Cf. Brett, *Political Trauma*, 185.
43. Habel, *An Inconvenient Text*, 17. In addition to his short published treatment of the Exodus passages, Habel also treated both the Nile and the Sea in a lengthy unpublished paper, "An Ecological Reading of the Exodus Tradition," presented in the 2007 Ecological Hermeneutics section of the Society of Biblical Literature (San Diego).
44. Habel, *An Inconvenient Text*, 17-18.
45. Ibid., 20.
46. Ibid., 19.
47. Terence E. Fretheim, *God and the World in the Old Testament: A Relational Theology of Creation* (Nashville, TN: Abingdon Press, 2005), 116. See also his commentary, *Exodus, Interpretation: A Bible Commentary for Teaching and Preaching* (Louisville, KY: John Knox Press, 1991), 105-132.
48. James Barr, *The Semantics of Biblical Language* (London: SCM Press, 1983), 218.
49. Habel, *An Inconvenient Text*, 19.
50. Jørstad, *Hebrew Bible and Environmental Ethics*, chap. 3.
51. Babylonian Talmud Bava Kamma 81a-81b and Tosefta Bava Kamma 8:17; see Hayim Nahman Bialik and Yehoshua Hana Ravnitzky, eds., *The Book of Legends: Sefer Ha-Aggadah* (New York: Schocken Books, 1992), 107.
52. Susan Niditch translates *perazon* (Jud 5:7, 11) as "unwalled towns," connecting it with a related form denoting an "open region, hamlet." See Susan Niditch, *Judges*, The Old Testament Library (Louisville, KY: Westminster John Knox Press, 2008), 71-72.
53. See Jørstad, *Hebrew Bible and Environmental Ethics*, chap. 4.
54. See Jo Ann Hackett, "'There Was No King in Israel': The Era of the Judges," in *The Oxford History of the Biblical World*, ed. Michael D. Coogan (New York: Oxford University Press, 1998), 149-150.
55. On the agrarian orientation of the eighth-century prophets Hosea, Amos, Micah, and Isaiah, see Davis, *Scripture, Culture, and Agriculture*, 120-138.
56. Mitri Raheb, *Faith in the Face of Empire: The Bible through Palestinian Eyes* (Maryknoll, NY: Orbis, 2014), 11.
57. Recent studies that argue for critical rereadings of biblical and Jewish traditions about territory in support of peace between Palestinians and Israeli Jews include David Frankel, *The Land of Canaan and the Destiny of Israel: Theologies of Territory in the Hebrew Bible* (Winona Lake, IN: Eisenbrauns, 2011); and Salim J. Munayer and Lisa Loden, eds., *The Land Cries Out: Theology of the Land in the Israeli-Palestinian Context* (Eugene, OR: Cascade, 2012). See also Yossi Klein Halevi, *Letters to My Palestinian Neighbor* (New York: HarperCollins, 2018).
58. Stulac, *History and Hope*, 225; italics original.

59. On Jeremiah 32 and the restoration of land and community, see Ellen F. Davis, *Biblical Prophecy: Perspectives for Christian Theology, Discipleship, and Ministry* (Louisville, KY: Westminster John Knox Press, 2014), 163-166.

Bibliography

Alter, Robert. *The Book of Psalms: A Translation with Commentary*. New York: W. W. Norton, 2007.
Barr, James. *The Semantics of Biblical Language*. London: SCM Press, 1983.
Berry, Wendell. *The Art of Loading Brush: New Agrarian Writings*. Berkeley, CA: Counterpoint, 2017.
Berry, Wendell. *The Unsettling of America: Culture and Agriculture*. San Francisco: Sierra Club Books, 1977.
Bialik, Hayim Nahma, and Yehoshua Hana Ravnitzky, eds. *The Book of Legends: Sefer Ha-Aggadah*. New York: Schocken Books, 1992.
Boer, Roland. *The Sacred Economy of Ancient Israel*. Louisville, KY: Westminster John Knox Press, 2015.
Borowski, Oded. *Agriculture in Iron Age Israel*. Winona Lake, IN: Eisenbrauns, 1987.
Borowski, Oded. *Daily Life in Biblical Times*. Atlanta: Society of Biblical Literature, 2003.
Brett, Mark G. *Genesis: Procreation and the Politics of Identity*. New York: Routledge, 2000.
Brett, Mark G. *Political Trauma and Healing: Biblical Ethics for a Postcolonial World*. Grand Rapids, MI: Eerdmans, 2016.
Brueggemann, Walter. *The Land: Place as Gift, Promise, and Challenge in Biblical Faith*. Philadelphia: Fortress Press, 1977.
Carlson, Michael. "Obituary: Earl Butz." *The Guardian*. February 7, 2008.
Davis, Ellen F. "Identity and Eating." *Studies in Christian Ethics* 30, no.1 (2017): 1-12. http://sce.sagepub.com/content/early/2016/10/19/0953946816674145.full.pdf?ijkey=BNLEEl2LfFeicJT&keytype=finite.
Davis, Ellen F. "Leaving Egypt Behind, Embracing the Wilderness Economy." In *Scripture, Culture, and Agriculture: An Agrarian Reading of the Bible*, 66-79. New York: Cambridge University Press, 2009.
Davis, Ellen F. *Biblical Prophecy: Perspectives for Christian Theology, Discipleship, and Ministry*. Louisville, KY: Westminster John Knox, 2014.
Davis, Ellen F. *Scripture, Culture, and Agriculture: An Agrarian Reading of the Bible*. New York: Cambridge University Press, 2009.
Dube, Musa W., Andrew M. Mbuvi, and Dora R. Mbuwayesango, eds. *Postcolonial Perspectives in African Biblical Interpretations*. Atlanta: Society of Biblical Literature, 2012.
Frankel, David. *The Land of Canaan and the Destiny of Israel: Theologies of Territory in the Hebrew Bible*. Winona Lake, IN: Eisenbrauns, 2011.
Fretheim, Terence E. *Exodus*. Interpretation: A Bible Commentary for Teaching and Preaching. Louisville, KY: John Knox Press, 1991.
Fretheim, Terence E. *God and the World in the Old Testament: A Relational Theology of Creation*. Nashville: Abingdon Press, 2005.
Gandhi, Leela. *Postcolonial Theory: A Critical Introduction*. New York: Columbia University Press, 1998.

Habel, Norman C. "An Ecological Reading of the Exodus Tradition." Paper presented in the Ecological Hermeneutics section of the Society of Biblical Literature, San Diego, 2007.

Habel, Norman C. *An Inconvenient Text: Is a Green Reading of the Bible Possible?* Adelaide: ATF Press, 2009.

Habel, Norman C. *The Birth, the Curse, and the Greening of Earth.* Sheffield: Sheffield Phoenix Press, 2011.

Habel, Norman C., ed. *Readings from the Perspective of Earth.* Sheffield: Sheffield Academic Press, 2000.

Hackett, Jo Ann. "'There Was No King in Israel': The Era of the Judges." In *The Oxford History of the Biblical World*, edited by Michael D. Coogan, 132-64. New York: Oxford University Press, 1998.

Halevi, Yossi Klein. *Letters to My Palestinian Neighbor.* New York: HarperCollins, 2018.

Hiebert, Theodore. *The Yahwist's Landscape: Nature and Religion in Early Israel.* New York: Oxford University Press, 1996.

Hillel, Daniel. *The Natural History of the Bible: An Environmental Exploration of the Hebrew Scriptures.* New York: Columbia University Press, 2006.

Joerstad, Mari. *The Hebrew Bible and Environmental Ethics: Humans, Non-Humans, and the Living Landscape.* New York: Cambridge University Press, Forthcoming.

King, Philip J., and Lawrence E. Stager. *Life in Biblical Israel.* Louisville, KY: Westminster John Knox, 2001.

Leopold, Aldo. "The Land Ethic." In *A Sand County Almanac.* New York: Oxford University Press, 1966.

MacDonald, Nathan. *What Did the Ancient Israelites Eat? Diet in Biblical Times.* Grand Rapids, MI: Eerdmans, 2008.

CHAPTER 25

BIBLE, EMPIRE, LIBERALISM, AND RACIAL CAPITALISM

STEED VERNYL DAVIDSON

BOTH empire and the Bible are shifty concepts. Not only have the experiences of empire varied from one European manifestation to the next but also, over time, empire has adapted to ensure its perpetuation. Given such mutations, postcolonial discussions need to attend to historical effects as well as the continued legacies of empire as reflected in local and global movements across time and space. This attention becomes even more urgent with regard to contemporary realities since empire tends to mask itself. The Bible poses similar conceptual challenges given the tendency to think of it as a near-eternal text with an inert quality. Despite its appearance as static, the movement of the Bible from a disparate set of texts to particular canonized collections exercising normalizing functions over the ordering of life in societies around the world indicates its fluid nature, at least at some points in its history. Arguably, this fluidity continues in its current form. In any event, these two shape-shifting entities have coexisted in a century's long, somewhat codependent relationship where one enhances rather than creates the power of the other.

In this article I work with the presumption that the modern will to empire does not directly arise from the Bible. Rather the Bible accompanies the territorial expansion of modern European states in order to sanctify these actions and to subsequently gain support for them both at home and abroad. Despite several similarities between the discourse of empire present in the Bible and the actual practices of European imperial expansion, the varying degrees of separation between church and state among European nations suggest different motivations for the will to empire. In this regard, Catholic nations such as Spain and Portugal reflect closer allegiance to religious authorities in their practices than Protestant nations such as Britain and France.[1] However, religious inspiration for empire building does not equal strict adherence to biblical texts. Clear use of theological and biblical ideas guide the Spanish in their imperial ventures and these represent some of the more overt uses of biblical material. Among the British, imperial officials were reluctant to be seen as operating by religious values even though the religious beliefs of individuals shaped their public life.[2] The Bible plays, therefore, a different though not diminished role in the construction of the British Empire. I characterize this role as manufacturing consent for empire, though I acknowledge that the Bible functioned in other ways.

Several elements contribute to building modern empires. The intersection of race and capitalism that develops first within Europe, but whose intertwined logic guides the imperial project overseas,[3] offers an interesting site for reading the Bible's supporting role in imperial construction. Race and capitalism draw upon different theological notions needed to define humanity on the one hand and on the other to rationalize the use of labor needed to fuel the engines of empire. Biblical scripts provide ways to articulate these ideas in relation to the indigenous people in the Americas that draw upon older biblical tropes already in use in relation to Jews and Moors.[4] The logics of race as a marker of humanity practiced in Europe also expand to include Africans and Asians as capitalist and territorial advancement occur. Empire as a global system of domination and control over the lands, resources, and bodies of non-Europeans established for the benefit of Europeans draws upon several virtues and ideals. The liberal discourse of the nineteenth century offers one way of ennobling the practice of empire. Here empire is seen as a form of uplift and advancement for people stunted along the path of human progress. As a European discourse, liberalism outlines a single path, a single historical trajectory, and a singular set of ideals of what development and progress look like. Empire with its agents of race and capitalism positions peoples at different points on this path and sets out to manipulate their movement along the path. If liberalism offered a secular theology for empire among Protestant nations (*mission civilisatrice* for the French), the church had its own religious forms of development, such as Christian conversion among the Spanish. Biblical discourses, therefore, easily situate within these two centers to legalize and legitimize imperial practices and to commend the benefits that accrue from empire.

Empire faced opposition from those on its receiving end from the beginning. Over the centuries of modern European empires, imperialized peoples employed different tactics aimed at dismantling empire. These political and discursive forms of native resistances draw upon different local sources as well as those used by Europeans to advance empire. As equally as the fierce inspiration of Voodoo ideologies, liberal discourses of equality empowered Haitian revolutionaries. Yet as the case of Haiti shows, even after the defeat of the French Empire, the concept of empire still remains in effect. What actually constitutes effective resistance or efforts to dismantle empire is a question that swirls around the discussion in this essay. If the deep underpinnings of modern empire are sustained by race and capitalism, to what extent do biblical texts in their forms as European sacred texts effectively challenge and dismantle empire? As a foreign and imposed text, the Bible provides discursive resistance to empire among indigenous peoples beset by the combined projects of imperialism and Christianization. Seemingly the same text, as far as words are concerned, resistant biblical readings developed from a necessary set of deconstructive steps that resituate the Bible. In part, this involved disrupting the Bible as a European product that facilitates white mythologies, one of which Robert Young names as "History."[5]

This essay explores two different poles of the Bible in the midst of empire—the polarities of justification and resistance. The first part of the essay examines how race and capital form strong motivations for empire, which sets the stage for the second section that describes how the Bible provides justification for empire. At the heart of the essay is the notion of the Bible's function as a mechanism for the manufacturing of consent to empire at home and abroad. I examine this in the form of sermons preached in London in 1857 in response to the uprising in India that unsettled the British Empire. In the third section, I look at the decolonization struggle in southern Africa that illustrates the case of a set of important gains that relieve the oppression of empire that led to a retreat rather than a retrenchment of empire. The final section of the essay offers a treatment of Rastafari textual traditions that function as an overt rejection of the Bible as an example of the disruption of the logic of empire.

Race, Capital, and Empire

For the purposes of this essay I treat race and capitalism as somewhat conjoined entities. My claim here is not that they create each other or even have a common temporal origin. Rather, following the lead of several scholars, I offer that race and capitalism become both constitutive and operative logics in the service of what will become empire. Admittedly, locating a single story of origins for the specter of modern imperialism is well nigh impossible. This impossibility does not exclude the examination of the relationship between several of the key loyalties that play out in the construction and maintenance of modern European empires. Empire represents an assemblage of different ideologies and practices marked by force and violence in varying forms. Empire, as Michael Hardt and Antonio Negri read it in its modern incarnation, "is formed not on the basis of force itself but on the basis of the capacity to present force as being in the service of right and peace."[6] The Bible performs an important service as one of the textual apparatuses that builds and holds empire together as a force for good in the world.

The arena of modern European imperial activities takes place largely outside of Europe. That these sites of imperial endeavor coincide with non-European races may seem like pure happenstance. However, considering the incentives of greater territory, exploitation of natural resources, and the potential for vast quantities of unfree labor in these non-European spaces, the locations of imperial construction do not appear that accidental. Economics and secondarily religion served as the drivers of European territorial expansion. In either case race provided part of the logic of these impulses. Cedric Robinson views European capitalist expansion as "racial capitalism . . . [pursuing] essentially racial directions, so too did social ideology."[7] Similarly, Walter Mignolo locates imperial impulses in the sixteenth-century expansions of Spain and Portugal under the guise of the "world universal Church,"[8] which was intent on eradicating difference, particularly religious difference as seen in the struggles against the Moors on the Iberian peninsula. Race, capitalism, and religion are constituent elements assembled in the layers of modern empire.

Both Robinson and Mignolo usefully situate the genesis of modern imperial logics in the sixteenth century rather than the eighteenth century, as is the custom of most postcolonial scholarship.[9] By doing so they avoid focusing attention on historical periods that more visibly characterize the shape of the modern world created by European territorial expansion where some of the crass impulses of race and greed have already become normative and therefore somewhat hidden. Instead, the sixteenth century reveals the way capitalism in its burgeoning phase at that time already took advantage of social relations of inequality within Europe. Robinson, in particular, demonstrates that the social classifications that developed in the sixteenth century also consisted of cultural and ethnic distinctions that overlapped with economic categories made sensible from a capitalist point of view that included proletariats, mercenaries, peasants, and slaves.[10] These categories were not merely socially constructed but sustained to facilitate capitalist gains.

Capitalism as an engine of empire requires access to cheap labor, preferably free labor in the form of slaves. Who should occupy the social role of the slave has been an ongoing debate from the time of Aristotle.[11] However, with the parallel developments of capitalism and race, the ethnic groups determined as inferior provide the answer to the question of the ideal slave. By the sixteenth century both the language and practice of slavery equated the ideal slave with particular ethnic groups. At this time Slavs were equated with bond labor used in large-scale production of sugar.[12] Tartars in Italian cities provide another instance of the racial capitalist logic of enslavement.[13] Ultimately, sub-Saharan Africans fill out the ancient question of the ideal slave due to various forms of anti-black racism.[14] Though David Davis attributes the eventual firm equation of sub-Saharan Africans with slavery as a function of racism, the fact remains that slavery facilitated the capitalist impulses of empire. The logic of darkness as the ideal expression of slavery created not simply a class of permanent slaves but hierarchies of unfree labor that would characterize European empires across four continents.[15]

Capitalism and race together provide a concentrated plank that sustains modern empire. From one perspective, race and capitalism identify the groups of people suited for the exploitative structures of empire. Thomas McCarthy sees the organization of colonial systems as taking place along racial lines.[16] These racial grids premised upon liberal ideas of differential civilizational development in turn form the basis for what Jodi Byrd regards as "discourses of savagery"[17] that would "simultaneously ... other and abject entire peoples so they can be enslaved, excluded, removed, and killed in the name of progress and capitalism."[18] While the animus of pure racism cannot be easily excluded as a motivating factor, the exploitation of cheap labor sits beneath the liberal "conceptions of development, enlightenment, civilization and progress."[19] Additionally, this exploited cheap labor fuels the capitalist enterprise that is at the heart of modern empire in some form. While more light tends to be shed upon the enslavement of Africans as the most grotesque form of exploitation of modern European imperialism, Lowe points out that the near extermination of indigenous people in the Caribbean provided the conditions for the introduction of slave labor from Africa. She also notes that the formal end of slavery in the British Empire accelerated the practice of indigenous labor from Asia (i.e., India and China). Lowe understands these interlocked, though not necessarily causal, histories as creating an intimacy of four continents upon which settler and colonial capitalism is built. The cheap labor that moved the engines of empire "produced the assets for the bourgeois republics of Europe and North America."[20] Race and capitalism as a result are not simply the ingredient spices that flavor local forms of imperialism, they form the pot of modern empire.

Race and capitalism as constitutive elements of empire enact their coercive forces upon human bodies, among other things. Precisely because they are disciplinary regimes, they require more than simply force in their practices and maintenance. They need the consent of actors and those acted upon for their success. While several intersecting imperial discourses may have served this purpose, I am interested here with civilizing discourses and the way they draw upon secular and biblical ideologies for their content. These ideologies subsume the racial logics under idealistic conceptions of human development and therefore find the Bible a suitable site to situate aspects of these discourses. At the same time, the material profits of empire conscript beneficiaries to maintain the system by appealing to benevolent ideals and the language of necessity. On the surface, civilizing discourses do not always draw direct links between race, capitalism, and empire. Therefore, my argument here largely sits upon the use of biblical texts and ideas to offer general support and justification as a perpetuation of the foundational elements of empire. Impact rather than intent is my concern, since discerning intention is both difficult to ascertain and serves as a distraction.

Biblical Justifications of Empire

In setting out the role of the Bible in empire, the relationship between Christianization and imperial expansion also requires examination. The apparent close relationship gives the impression of the two operating as coordinated systems. Whatever the historical relationship may have been during the period of formal colonialism, the continued growth of Christianity beyond the earlier mutations of empire suggests to some scholars that Christianity became disconnected from empire prior to the end of colonialism or may not have been as closely tied as previously suspected.[21] Despite this apparent distance, European missionaries served as bearers of culture and the political project of colonialism. Norman Etherington views "the mission stations as a microcosm or trope of Empire" in the way they functioned as promoters of the "spread of modernization, globalization, and Western cultural hegemony [replicating] . . . political and economic imperialism."[22] Christianization therefore was not separate and immune from the complexities of race and capitalism that fueled imperial expansions and practices. Christian missions, as Comaroff and Comaroff indicate, sat within the cleavages of "colonizing populations; how they were related to distinctions, at home and abroad, of class, gender, and nation; how, over time, they played across the racial line between ruler and ruled."[23]

Both imperial and missionary discourses reflect the common theme of uplift centering on different emphases. For missionaries, the adoption of Christian culture marked developmental progress, and for secular colonialists the adoption of European culture was evidence of civilizational advancement. These ideologies rest upon racial constructs that express the dominance of whiteness as the pinnacle of human civilization to which other races and people should aspire. The liberal discourses of progress that offered support for the necessity of empire, in the attempt to hold together a coherent notion of history, advance the idea of reform "for societies that have been stunted through history."[24] As Uday Singh Mehta puts it, "the empire, one might say, is an engine that tows societies stalled in their past into contemporary time and history."[25] Mehta points to the resemblances between liberalism's progress and the evangelical belief in eschatology that fuels Christian missions. They both share "a deep impulse to reform the world."[26] As a result of these shared values, biblical discourses can do double-duty in supporting Christianization as well as the general political policy of aiding native progress.

The use of biblical material in the sermons of Christian preachers in London in reaction to the Indian rebellion of 1857 provides an instance where the political and religious discourses of uplift occur. The sermons offer insight into the use of biblical material in support of empire. These sermons, which were preached on the day that Queen Victoria proclaimed on September 25, 1857 as "A Day of Humiliation," "a public day of solemn fast, humiliation, and prayer,"[27] draw upon various biblical texts that are pressed into service to decry what is presented as the Indians' rejection of British munificence. The failure of effective evangelism appears as one of the main themes in the sermons. This neglect and failure therefore leads to uprising and not to the restrained civility as envisaged by either imperialism or Christianization.

Texts and citations proclaim an expansive and universal Christian imperium raised for listeners of the sermons on the value of the British presence in India.[28] Canon Dale preaching at St. Paul's Cathedral from Isaiah 26:9 (cited as 26:7) leans into the theme of righteousness as a global reality. Dale adopts a capacious geography of divine action and challenges hearers not to fall prey to the notion that the creator of the earth is limited to particular spaces and particular peoples. Implicitly here Dale rejects a flat theological relativity since he inveighs particularly against theists who require recognition of Indian native religious sensibilities.[29] That Dale lacks any patience to accommodate a non-Christian view of morals and acting in the world is seen in the collection of texts that he brings together to strengthen his claim. He gathers Amos 3:6 to talk of the universality of God. He adds Isaiah 45:7 to point to the timelessness and breadth of God as well as Psalm 105:7 to affirm the universal judgment of God. With this assemblage, Dale presents Christian imperialism as a reality of India.[30]

The civic value of the observance naturally presents the opportunity for preachers to display an overt political theology. This theology offers full support of empire and articulates how imperial goals were consistent with evangelistic goals. Sermons acknowledged the benefits of empire to India. Rev. F. J. Stainforth points to the provision of "education and liberty" to India, a benefaction offered to "an ignorant and slavish race."[31] The views here are consistent with the liberal values that advocated for empire as the means to ensure "the higher accomplishments of civilization."[32] To the extent that preachers critiqued this position, they did so to point out that secular liberalism was an insufficient goal that required a more robust Christian application or what Rev. Stainforth views as "the principles of religion."[33] For Stainforth the events in India resemble the chaos that resulted from the secular liberalism of the French Revolution. At a Town Hall meeting, the Bishop of Durham also noted that "England in all her dealings with her empire in India had not been true to the Christian principles and faith she professed."[34] The bishop expressed regret that a more vigorous, and perhaps narrow, liberal agenda was not followed: "If they had civilized, if they had Christianized . . . they would not have been exposed to those calamities which had befallen them."[35]

The biblical discourse in the sermons amplifies the conceptions of liberal imperialism. Rev. Stainforth in his selected texts of Ezra 8:21–23 notes Ezra's task of handling the transfer of treasures from the King's storehouse along with the establishment of religion in Jerusalem. He explains that this dual task was such an awesome responsibility that Ezra needed to spend time in fasting in order to acquire the necessary divine help for this duty.[36] Empire in the face of the challenges in India needed similar divine input. Rev. R. W. Browne provides his hearers with a sizable list of British accomplishments in India, but his observation that "we have not done a tithe of what we might have done" serves as an indicator that outstanding debt is religious duty.[37] Canon Dale also picks up the theme of British benefaction in India. However, he spends more time on the religious changes that Christians already accomplished in India. For him, prior to the British presence, India resembled the hapless state of Jerusalem in the days of Jeremiah as described in Jeremiah 5:1. The lack of righteousness no longer exists. As a result of these accomplishments the empire must remain, since a premature British withdrawal would imperil the gains already established and leave no trace of the Christian presence.[38] The concern to stay the course in terms of evangelism in India reflects the liberal justification to fulfill "a tutelary duty to assist it, . . . in passing from social childhood to social maturity."[39]

The sermons also express a profound sense that Britain and its Christian citizens were given a divine duty in the form of empire. Preachers spoke affectionately of the imperial relations as a divine bequest. Rev. Browne acknowledges the divine bequest of "that great empire which Almighty God has entrusted to our care during 100 years."[40] Phrases that speak to "the hand of God," not simply as determining the course of events (here the Bishop of Durham and Rev. Browne preaching from Psa. 20:7) but particularly in the divine grant of responsibility to the more enlightened people of Britain, appear in some sermons. Biblical texts perform the task of shaming the nation and hearers in the congregation of the national and personal failure. Dr. Croly preaching from Psalm 79:8–9 adopts the penitent position suitable to the day but delineates the national sin as the abandonment of the sacred tasks of empire. He reminds his hearers: "as possessors of a vast empire we were charged with the just duties of empire."[41] Here these duties of

Christians in the context pertain to civic religion that blends evangelism with cultural assimilation. Rev. Browne seamlessly integrates the "right hand of God" from Psalm 20:7 with several secular functions of empire: "to protect, to civilize, to regenerate, to educate, to raise them to the scale of nations until they are fitted for our institutions."[42]

The sermons provide a thick description of what Byrd calls "Indianness." While Byrd conceptualizes Indianness via US settler imperial logic, her thinking applies equally well to the other India that lent its name to the indigenous people in the western Atlantic. For Byrd, Indianness "moves not through absence but through reiteration, through meme, as theories circulate and fracture, quote and build."[43] The sermons collect evidence of savagery as reliable ethnographic research to build out for hearers and readers what constitutes Indianness. Given that "national imaginaries ... served to united disparate populations around putative commonalities of origin and descent, language and tradition, custom and culture increasingly overlapped with racial imaginaries in the course of the nineteenth century,"[44] the thick descriptions of Indianness function also as affirmations of racist presumptions. On one hand, equating Canaanites with Indianness constructs what Byrd sees as the conflation of "racialization and colonization" that quite often permits the use of violence that leads to populations being "enslaved, excluded, removed, and killed in the name of progress and capitalism."[45] Militaristic images pervade several sermons with their calls for divine vengeance. However, the invocation of biblical narratives of conquest inserts a racialized rhetoric of violence.

At least four of the preachers make reference to the Canaanites in their sermons using it as a nod to racial difference. Rev. M. Gibbs preached at Christ Church, Newgate-Street, calling attention to the failure of the Israelites to follow the virulent instructions to destroy the religious symbols as reported in Judges 2:1–5. At the West London Synagogue for British Jews, Mr. Marks preached from Psalm 3 but appears to focus mostly upon the rebellion of Absalom against his father David in 2 Samuel 15. Outraged by the events as seen in his use of the story of familial betrayal, Mr. Marks calls for the annihilation of the movement: "The abominations of the Sepoys were equaled only by the crimes of the Canaanite, and, like them, they should be exterminated."[46] Rev. R. Bickerdike, preaching at St. Saviour's Southwark, takes a similar path by using the comparative assessment of the fortunes of Japheth and Shem in Genesis 9:27. The text enables him to advance racist ideas as biblically ordered and the use of progress as an arbiter of dominance. In his exposition of the text, the superiority of Japheth over Shem is not simply about sibling rivalry but also racial superiority as evidenced in the Roman triumph over "the land of Canaan and other Asiatic countries" and more recently the "English dwelling in Hindostan."[47]

A vigorous evangelism takes its biblical warrant from Matthew 28:18–20. This so-called Great Commission contains both the sending and travel requirements that place destinations like India in view. The text calls these destinations "nations" (εθνη), a nineteenth-century conception not undifferentiated from race. Yet as McCarthy offers the nineteenth-century European notion of race "comprised a congeries of elements, including not only other 'material' factors such as geographical origin and genealogical descent, but also a shifting array of 'mental' characteristics such as cognitive ability and moral character, as well as a mobile host of cultural and behavioral traits."[48] India, in this case, looms large precisely because of the many ways race is refracted in the church's evangelical mission. Race determines secular and religious missions in their most idealistic goals of progress and conversion. The liberal notions of history, progress, uplift, and civilizational development appear in both discourses. While Christian leaders may have thought of themselves as distant from the world of bringing European culture and political dominance to other nations, Maxwell notes that "despite their increasing democratic sensibilities, missionaries became a pillar of colonial rule."[49] In fact, Comaroff and Comaroff believe that contact with non-Western peoples inevitably resulted in the assertion of an ethnocentric core from which missionaries "honed a sense of themselves as gendered, national citizens, as Godly, right-bearing individuals, and as agents of Western reason."[50] The thrust to develop a nation that knows righteousness, as Canon Dale advocated in his sermon, takes on the apparatus of empire and suborns the aims of empire with biblical language.

Maintaining the Logic of Empire

This section turns to the period of decolonization. I select two southern African personalities involved in the struggle against the remnants of imperialism that stubbornly persists in the twentieth-century form of white minority rule in Zimbabwe and apartheid in South Africa. The political and religious contexts of southern Africa in addition to these personalities make for a compelling example of the central point that I provide in this essay. Here we see how a more progressive biblical discourse that supports a drive for racial and other forms of justice continues earlier versions of the discourse of uplift that argued for the necessity of empire.

The demand for decolonization rests upon justice. The end of colonial rule and the handover of political control to indigenous and local leaders would not only be just but also timely. A cadre of local leaders, educated and trained in imperial political structures, makes the case for local control of their nation. In effect, the requests rest upon the maintenance of the logic of imperial rule and the structures that support that logic—we are capable of running a nation as Europeans have constructed the idea of a nation. Decolonization in many respects challenged imperial power and gained many benefits for racialized groups particularly in the form of legal rights previously denied. Yet at the same time, despite decolonization, "many forms of *de facto* inequality remained in place—deeply entrenched in the beliefs and values, symbols and images, practices and institutions, structures and functions of national and global society."[51] Local leaders inherited the governance of formerly imperialized nations situated within a global community that operated upon the imperialist presumptions of civilizational development, which in the decolonization period also meant economic development. Decolonization did not substantially alter the alignment of global power. In the same vein, the presumptions of racial uplift through evangelization still structured the mission of the church even as deeper and more overt political involvement placed emerging local church leaders in the forefront of the struggle for decolonization and development.

The uneasy relationship between evangelization and imperialism takes on a peculiar form in southern Africa that shapes the way the Bible functions during the decolonization period. Some Christian missionaries perceived themselves as different and separate from the political agendas of imperialists, finding refuge in interpretations of Romans 13:1–7. The separatist views of this text appear in Sugirtharajah's summation that Paul "occasionally . . . censures the evils of the Empire, but offers no political strategy or practical solution for its liquidation."[52] If missionaries cultivated a safe distance from the imperial state that enabled the fiction of their cultural neutrality, burgeoning nationalist movements exposed their complicity with imperial culture but only to the extent that this collusion enabled crass racial injustices.

Romans 13:1–7 served to justify the implicit and explicit expressions of imperial logic grounded in liberal understandings of civilizational development. The empire and in later stages the state exercised the paternalistic role to ensure the progress of those requiring more development and therefore the maintenance of the subtle and not so subtle racial distinctions in society. This biblical text encourages a bifurcation that leaves unfettered control of the political arena to the state along with the silent assent of Christian voices. Yet such silence did not mean absence from social spaces as religious leaders engaged social space in the performance of works aimed at human development, narrowly confined to spaces such as health and education. Consequently, the church practiced a deep involvement in social development, as distinct from political activity, with the thought of building a "kingdom" far superior to what imperialists had envisaged. A generation of southern African Christians comfortable in the public square, using the Bible as a means to inveigh against the racist ideologies of holdover settler imperialism, marked the decolonization period.

Nationalist movements during the period of decolonization drew upon biblical texts, particularly in the articulation of their vision of a more just society. In his Nobel Lecture, the South African nationalist leader Albert Luthuli proclaimed the moment as "Africa's age—the dawn of fulfillment,"[53] then explicitly cited Isaiah 60:1 (KJV) to make the case for an independent Africa to be a stabilizing force in a world marked by disorder. This text not only matches Luthuli's sense of the dawning of a new day and hence the call to "Arise and shine for thy light is come" but also draws upon the liberal and evangelical rhetoric of bringing light to a dark space of earth. In this citation, Luthuli is able to announce that the light of Africa has been lit not because of European intervention but as a result of destiny placed upon Africa. The light that has come represents Africa's moment in the world, as Luthuli points out the damages incurred by imperialism and evangelization: "Though robbed of her lands, her independence and opportunities to become—this, oddly enough, often in the name of civilization and even Christianity."[54] Luthuli, though, does not set aside the liberal claim of the singular history and path of development that puts Europe ahead of everyone else even though he challenges this. His challenge consists of making a case for Africa to be included on that path of civilizational development—not as one to be helped but as a leader. Hence his sense of the destiny for Africa in the form of the light informed by that Isaian vision of the new opportunity: "should she not see her destiny as that of making a distinctive contribution to human progress and human relationships with a peculiar new Africa flavor enriched by the diversity of cultures she enjoys."[55] The themes of progress and development, foundational aspects of modern empire, are in fact reaffirmed but with the assertion of African inclusion into the conception of the singular path of development and progress.

Luthuli further articulates a vision of an Africa free of the clutches of white minority rule that rests upon development in the key areas of economics, education, and social movement. Here he ties freedom to development. In doing so he resorts again to Isaiah to point out the benefits of disarmament for global development. Citing Isaiah 2:4 (cf. Mic. 4:3) he indicates how Africa's penchant for peace can address issues of starvation and illiteracy. In the process, Luthuli indicts European histories of conquest by implicitly contrasting Africa's way of being in the world with an unnamed comparison: "Africa's qualification for this noble task is incontestable, for her own fight has never been and is not now a fight for conquest of land, for accumulation of wealth or domination of peoples, but for the recognition and the preservation of the rights of man and the establishment of a truly free world."[56] Informed by a biblical vision of peace as a pathway to human development, Luthuli carves out a justification for his leadership of a movement of nonviolence as the route to decolonization. While he begins his lecture noting the necessity for peace, his vision for peace rests upon the unmistakable dismantling of the forces of oppression. Here he does not draw upon any explicit biblical reference but instead resorts to liberal principles of equality. His lecture, though, opens with a clear declaration of human dignity as a consequence of divine creation and his own embrace of this precept as a Christian. The striking feature of his declaration lies in his recognition that the biblical narrative of creation requires that he neither accept racism nor remain neutral: "To remain neutral in a situation where the laws of the land virtually criticized God for having created men of color was the sort thing I could not, as a Christian, tolerate."[57] In some regard, Luthuli's lecture functions as an effective valedictory that embraces the major themes of liberalism that structure modern empire.

The conviction that Christianity and the Bible provide the tools and vision for a just society marks several leaders of the African decolonization movement. As the new generation of Christians, in what in essence is a young church,[58] these leaders experience the ambiguities of the benefits from mission churches that provide schools and hospitals to transform their societies but at the same time suffer under the racism engendered by these churches. As Maxwell observes education and healthcare was the ambivalent space where mission churches exercised ministry to local populations under the naïve assumption that they were apolitical and therefore unlike the imperialists. Yet ironically these were the two areas where "mission and colonialism came closest together."[59] However, it is the space from which the biblical rhetoric is used to critique the excesses of empire rather than its foundational structure. The obvious injustice of racial oppression stands in front of the more problematic aspects of the implications of liberalism that enables modern empire.

The Zimbabwean church leader, activist, and for a brief time Prime Minister, Bishop Abel Muzorewa encounters some of the tensions generated by the ambivalent zone of church social involvement and withdrawal in a visit to New York in March 1970. In this ambivalent zone, race alone gets amplified and its links to broader capitalist and imperialist structures remain hidden. During this meeting with young Zimbabweans living and studying in New York Muzorewa receives streams of bitterness regarding the church in Zimbabwe largely centered around the racist practices of mission churches. Muzorewa responds acknowledging the validity of the criticisms but with the observation: " 'But that is only one side of the missionaries' impact on us and our people,' I went on. 'Here we sit condemning the Church, yet without the church schools which each of us have attended we would not be here today.' "[60] Like Luthuli who grew up a beneficiary of the Anglo-American mission activity that Wallace Mills locates as starting in the late 1790s and continuing until the postmillennial fervor, Muzorewa received an orientation to Christianity that saw the need to improve the world through evangelism either in response to or in preparation for God's reign of peace.[61] Here Muzorewa places special emphasis upon the notion of white generosity and misses how these actions stand upon the liberal imperialist logic of backwardness. That the benefits of European education were not widely distributed or that a dysfunctional educational system was the imperial legacy would be critical areas that animated Muzorewa's political activism. This activism stems from an optimistic viewpoint that was dangled before African Christians. The thought of a better Africa came with a disposition toward the Bible as a text that witnesses God's transformation of the world. Admittedly, this vision resembled the ideals of liberal imperialism that advocated for racial equality and justice but within the worldview framed by European Enlightenment principles.

In his reading of the Bible, Muzorewa puts critical distance between the traditional interpretations of Romans 13:1–7 and adopts what he later comes to recognize as Liberation Theology.[62] The intimate identification of the church with the state stemming precisely from the church's work in education, where "ninety percent of African pupils attend 'mission' schools run by the churches, but financed and supervised by the State," meant a future of "vigorous confrontation with the State."[63] As Hazel Ngoshi puts it, "In that vocation he marries the gospel of Christian salvation to nationalist liberation politics."[64] Biblical texts like Luke 4:18–19 and the Exodus narrative, standard fare in Liberation Theology, provide him with a way to spread a message based upon a demand for justice. He reports that his preaching from Luke 4:18–19 reflects his insistence on the need for a "total gospel"[65] and his frustration with the highly spiritualized preaching of the church. In this regard, Muzorewa stresses the importance of embodiment: "God created a man, or a woman, as a total person, having a body, a mind and a spirit; and that our Heavenly Father would save that total person. I believed, and preached, that to love as God loves means to be in total service to the total man. That includes politics."[66] The political edges of his reading of the Bible appears in the parallels he makes between the Israelites in the Exodus narrative and Zimbabweans, offering the observation that "as God led His children out of bondage in Egypt into a promised land, so he will lead his children in Zimbabwe if they are faithful to Him."[67]

While Muzorewa seems comfortable with the vocation of herald for divine justice, the implications of abusing divine and political power appears to trouble him. He quickly explains his added qualification of his reading of the Exodus narrative with the inclusion "if they are faithful to Him." For Muzorewa this condition is necessary in order to guard against the "excesses" that can occur in the "revolutionary struggle." Unwilling to access divine blessing for every aspect of the revolution, lest this justifies further oppression, he positions the church to perform the work of reconciliation on the realization of liberation.[68] Muzorewa's vision rests largely upon the realization of liberal values of justice and equality. He walks in the path of European liberals who embrace the ideals of equality and strongly critique aspects of imperial policy such as the slave trade and slavery.[69] Muzorewa firmly believes that the Bible provides the church with a vision of an inclusive society as seen in texts like John 14:2. Reacting to what he regards as a misinterpretation of the text by the Minister of Justice, Law and Order who was invited to preach at the Salisbury Cathedral, Muzorewa gathers up descriptions of the Minister's defense of apartheid as "'Irresponsible,' 'provocative,' 'shameful,' 'shocking.'"[70] Having been denied by the Dean of Cathedral to preach at the Cathedral some time after the Minister of Justice, he instead preaches before a congregation at St. Peter's in Harare on "Christian Unity," marveling at the presence of white attendees in the congregation. His reading of Jesus' declaration of the multiple mansions in God's house as stated in John 14:2 offers a capacious vision of inclusion that he sees possible in the church that could in turn serve as a model for the nation. This model of the church, conflated into the nation,[71] reflects "human freedom which will allow its members to speak freely irrespective of their colour, sex or age."[72] This transracial vision undergirded by the hard work of reconciliation draws upon the deep wells of liberal optimism that guided Muzorewa's reading of the Bible.

The visions of liberal optimism enabled Christians in southern Africa imbued by a wave of postmillennial missions to engage social issues during the period of decolonization. Mills dates the advent of postmillennialism in South Africa to the rise of British rule.[73] This period also coincides with significant growth in Christianity in South Africa at the beginning of the twentieth century.[74] This numerical growth occurs in large part due to indigenizing processes that involved local people in various places.[75] Even the strong influx of postmillennial teaching took on a decidedly African character that would shape both the church and the political culture of South Africa.[76] In general, this meant a reading of the Bible that harnessed the expectation of a renovated world and the possibilities for the transformation of the oppressed. That history was moving toward this grand moment of liberation can be seen in the application of biblical material to the processes of decolonization. In the southern African context, decolonization meant the dismantling of a social structure that made explicit the racist constructions of liberal imperialism. Contours of oppression could be easily sketched from biblical material and the teleological hope of God's kingdom depicted in the real world conditions of the betterment of black Africans. From this perspective the Bible serves as a useful force to dismantle the injustices of racism that denied the claims of equality and human community in order to advance the development of the society.

Despite the open opposition to empire and the racist expressions of empire, the biblical anti-imperial rhetoric maintained the logic of modern empire in its racist and capitalist configurations. The clear rejection of racial oppression and the embrace of the idea of human equality notwithstanding, the presumption of civilizational progress and the necessity for non-European nations to catch up to the more developed nations still remained in place after decolonization. The biblical telos makes progress an attractive way to read history and economic and social development as realizable forms of justice. The shifts in empire that accompanied decolonization represent the success of nationalist movements to address key areas of concern. Empire however mutated into another form and "did not imply a radical change of socioeconomic structure."[77] The biblical critique of empire supported what Mills and other scholars regard as the three Cs: Christianity, civilization, and commerce. These elements "closely interlinked and reinforced each other" where the message of Christian evangelism ensured conversion to Eurocentric worldviews and culture that paved the way for a civilization that resembles European cultural norms under the guise of development and that in turn stimulates commercial activity.[78]

Rastafari: Rejecting Empire

In this section, I turn to the third case of the use of the Bible in empire. I select Rastafari as one of the more striking examples of anti-imperial biblical discourse. The Rastafari case is not without its difficulties and therefore I am not advocating for it as an ideal. However, the departures from both the orthodoxies of European Christianity and sociality provide it with more room to undermine some of the features of empire, particularly as these are hidden within the discourses of liberalism.

On the surface, Rastafari may not be that different from other millennial-inspired biblical critiques of empire in southern Africa. They both have in common a decidedly antiracist, justice-seeking, liberationist perspective. Rastafari though represents a striking rejection of key elements of modern empire, particularly the liberal underpinnings that bring together race and capitalism. The rejection of the notion of the unitary nature of history that allows for the conception of civilizational progress allows Rastafari to stand outside of the presumptions of empire. The appeal to an alternative history that does not intersect with the singular historical liberal narrative disrupts the claim of civilizational progress and much of the racist discourse that springs from it. This rejection also puts Rastafari in a different relation to the Bible since they do not accept any of the explicit and implicit claims of the Bible. As a religion with a decidedly millennial bent but one that is also world denying, particularly the world as constructed by Europe, Rastafari lacks the type of optimism that leads to social engagement and that can support capitalist activity.

The church, viewed as an agent of empire, along with its sacred text, forms one of the key areas where that Rastafari challenges empire. As a product of the Jamaican urban underclass during the twentieth-century version of the British Empire, nascent Rastafari encounter the Bible in the Protestant King James Version. This tool of English enculturation that exercised a strong formative influence is noted for its unique canonical content. That it differs from the Catholic and Orthodox Bibles immediately sets it apart as suspect because of its reduced canon. Rastafari would reject the King James Bible for the absence of the book of Maccabees, largely standing in as a symbol of European manipulation of the Bible. Max Romeo's "Maccabee Version" captures the belief of the King James Bible as one that "belongs to the white man," but by contrast it is the "Maccabee Version that God gave to black man."[79]

The rejection of the Bible, albeit a particular English Bible, represents Rastafari's abandonment of a critical source that forms European identity and the consequent teleological ideas that feed into liberalism. Rastafari therefore adopts an alternative conception of history and does not attempt to jostle for a place of recognition within the historical schema established by European thinking as most anti-imperial and antiracist struggles have done. The collection of sacred and authoritative texts acknowledged by Rastafari assert a counternarrative that quite often details the strength of African civilization independent of the European presence. In addition to the purported Maccabee Bible—in essence an expanded Christian canon—Rastafari draws upon the *Kebra Nagast*, *The Royal Parchment Scroll of Black Supremacy* (1926?), *The Holy Piby* (1924), and other minor texts and teachings to build out a resistant black space against the Eurocentric imagination. The *Kebra Nagast*, a fourteenth-century text, presents the claim of Ethiopian kings as direct descendants of Solomon. Rastafari amplify what at first is the *Kebra Nagast*'s nationalist posturing into a frontal challenge to 1 Kings 10:1–10 and the notion of the Queen of Sheba's subordination to Solomon. The *Kebra Nagast*'s version of events therefore functions as a replacement text for the biblical account. In essence, this African canonical text highlights an incontrovertible alternative history that would not be subsumed into European history. *The Royal Parchment Scroll*, written by Fitz Balintine Pettersburgh in Jamaica, grounds its thinking in Ethiopianism and anticipates that African descendants in Jamaica will serve as a remnant from which Africa will be resurrected. The essential challenge where Pettersburgh calls for "a new dictionary and a new Bible and new board of education and a new money mint represents what Clinton Hutton views as "a new episteme, pedagogy and ontology in which the apotheosis of self was rooted in the realm of a black Almighty."[80] Also among the texts deemed sacred is *The Holy Piby*, published by Robert Athlyi Rogers from Anguilla, which advances similar Ethiopianist claims with a sharp refusal to be subsumed into a European project: "O people of Ethiopia boast not the progress of the white race, believing that you are part of the project."[81]

Rastafari grew out of movements of Ethiopianism that developed in Africa and reverberated throughout the African diaspora toward the end of the nineteenth century as a product of the interpretation of Psalm 68:31 by several preachers and thinkers of African descent.[82] Read as a prophetic text and a predictor of African greatness, the psalm verse provided an orientation for African revolutionary thought in an age where African enslavement around the world was complemented by an imperial land grab in Africa. Ethiopianism as an interpretation of what was seen as biblical veneration of Ethiopia (read Africa) may have begun as a source of pride, but Kalu suggests that by 1872, Ethiopianism takes the form of resistance and the demand for liberation of enslaved Africans around the world.[83] Marcus Garvey, a pivotal thought leader in the emergence of Rastafari, draws upon several streams of intellectual and religious traditions (for instance, the preaching of George Liele,[84] and Edward Blyden's exploration of Ethiopia and the Bible[85]) to meld an Africa-centered reading of the Bible with contemporary politics that led to the assertion of Selassie as the fulfillment of Psalm 68:31.[86] Leonard Howell's organizational work and public addresses went further than Garvey ventured[87] to advance the idea of the deification of Selassie in Jamaica[88] and to kick-start Rastafari. Rastafari not only challenges the validity of the biblical texts but also offers a completely oppositional theological proposition in the deification of Selassie; as Bob Marley sang, "almighty God is a living man" (and, importantly, he was African). This theological assertion when taken in the context of the British Empire's perception of its transcendence contains several bold elements, chief among them being what Rex Nettleford regards as the "Africanization of consciousness."[89] To build consciousness outside of the epistemologies presented by Europe marked a vital departure from cultural, educational, and religious norms entrenched by European colonization. Ultimately, to embrace an Africanized consciousness as detailed by Rastafari means a departure from the logics of empire. Biblical texts serve as one of the spaces where Rastafari mounts this particular challenge.

Three main texts represent an expanded Rastafari biblical canon. *The Holy Piby*, *The Royal Parchment Scroll*, and *The Promised Key* set the stage for later developments of the interpretive tradition that can offer a preliminary insight into the rage against imperialism and the destabilization of the Bible as a means to undermine empire. Leonard Howell, writing under the pseudonym G. G. Maragh, draws upon the previously published *Holy Piby* and *Royal Parchment Scroll* in *The Promised Key*. He follows the Ethiopia-centered reading of the Bible set forth in the previous documents but outlines a vision of the world as ruled under the auspices of the Ethiopian emperor, Ras Tafari. In doing so, Howell sets aside the claims of British imperial supremacy by transferring biblical texts onto the Ethiopian ruling family. Central to Howell's claims are the theopolitical interpretations of biblical texts that leave no room for abstractions. Howell interprets the Duke of Gloucester's participation in the coronation of Ras Tafari as the capitulation of the British Empire to the rule of Ethiopia. In a deft move that draws together the ceremonies of statecraft and prophetic reading of biblical texts, Howell presents the duke as not only openly doing obeisance to Ras Tafari and pledging his fealty but also showing that these acts represent the fulfillment of Psalm 72:9–11 and Gen. 49:10: "The Duke fell down on bending knees before His Majesty Ras Tafari the King of Kings and Lord of Lords and spoke in a loud voice and said, 'Master, Master, my father has sent me to represent him sir. He is unable to come and he said that he will serve you to the end Master.'"[90] Rather than expressly citing the biblical texts, Howell merely offers them up as references, primarily because he inserts several strong biblical allusions in the surrounding text. Allusions such as "her hands reach unto God" (Psa 68:31) and "king of kings" (Rev 19:16) become standard fare in Rastafari biblical discourse that affirms not only Ethiopia's destiny but also Haile Selassie's divinity.

Despite Howell's substantial use of biblical texts, his theopolitical views draw more upon *The Holy Piby*, which presents itself as an alternative authoritative source to the Bible. Rogers crafts *The Holy Piby* by imitating the genre of sacred writings set out by the King James Bible. Phrases such as "And it came to pass," "Verily I say unto you," "For as much as," and "Woe be unto you" appear frequently in the text. Even the structuring of the work adopts the general plot-line of the Bible that begins with creation, the proclamation of law, a pivotal turn to a human messenger in the form of Marcus Garvey, and considerations of heaven and hell as a sort of telos. Rogers does not so much reread the Bible as rewrite it in order to center Ethiopia and critical African personalities as the basis of an alternative scriptural tradition. The preface of the writing understands the work of the gospel that it announces, spearheaded by "Shepherd Athlyi, apostle Marcus Garvey and colleague," saying that it would "lay the foundation of industry, liberty and justice unto the generations of Ethiopia."[91] Rogers's account of the Creation follows the pattern of six days of creation and the seventh day of rest as in Genesis 1. Rather than providing the sequential details, he hurries through to focus on the creation of humans on the sixth day and harmonizes aspects of Genesis 1:26 with Genesis 2:20–25. Precisely because Rogers understands that the Bible, as a tool of British imperialism, is presented under the assumption of white normativity, he includes a comment on the racial character of the first humans: "And God called the man Adam and the woman Eve. They were of a mixed complexion."[92] The precise identification here remains uncertain since Howell takes a somewhat different view of this text. Howell rejects black descent from Adam and Eve and situates a different line of descent for Africans since "King Alpha and Queen Omega said they are our parents.... He and his wife are not any family at all to Adam and Eve and Abraham, and Isaac and the Anglo Saxon Slave Owners."[93] In any event, both Rogers and Howell as they rewrite these texts establish alternative historical myths to the dominant European ones that they understand serve to diminish African dignity.

The insertion of characters of African descent and the centering of African redemption are notable features of Rogers's reformation of sacred texts. He receives constant revelation and interpretation of divine messages from an angel identified as Douglas. Subsequent to the text, Rogers claimed that Douglas here is Frederick Douglass, who "came to him as an angel and said to him not until black people embraced the divinity of Ethiopia there was any hope of their liberation."[94] Rogers's use of Douglass as a messenger of liberation beatifies him and joins his struggle into a historical fight for African liberation. This invasion into Christianity's settled orthodoxies with such overt blackness shows up the harsh critique that Howell levels against the church that he views as "speaking lies ... and let the people walk in darkness."[95] Douglass as a trusted authoritative source of black wisdom proves suitable and needed in order to redeem the discredited religious forms that these texts use quite freely.

These proto-Rastafari texts comfortably appropriate scriptural practices such as a list of commandments. Rogers enunciates for Ethiopians a twelve-point list of "Holy Commandments,"[96] unlike those in Exodus 20 and Deuteronomy 5. The notable difference lies in the decidedly communal nature of these commandments that are unconcerned about individualistic moralisms. The commandments aim at building particular communal attributes such as industry, thrift, social solidarity, honesty, punctuality, and pride. The twelfth and final commandment demonstrates Rogers's selectivity with the biblical text. Rogers merges the biblical commandment against idolatry and the one enjoining the observance of the Sabbath. Communal appeal of Rogers's commandments contrasts with the biblical commandments that address only propertied males. *The Holy Piby* also contains a prayer that appropriates the language of the Prayer of Jesus in Matthew 6:9–13 and other popular forms. Like the Holy Commandments, this prayer reflects a concern for Ethiopia and is addressed to "O God of Ethiopia." The prayer is titled "The Shepherd's Prayer by Athlyi,"[97] positioning Rogers in the role of Jesus. The prayer's vocabulary draws upon the biblical text, reusing key words and phrases like "lead us," "forgive," "on earth as in Heaven," "deliver us," and "forever and forever. Amen." This prayer adopts some of the same departures from a narrow piety in order to encourage an outward set of actions aimed at strengthening the community. In place of the biblical petition "lead us not into temptation" (KJV), the *Piby* has "lead us, help us to forgive that we may be forgiven." To the extent that the petition touches on personal piety, it quickly moves on to request instruction that grants wisdom that sustains a life of social solidarity: "that the hungry be fed, the naked clothed, the sick nourished, the aged protected and the infants cared for."

These foundational texts set up Rastafari not only as an oppositional force to Christianity and its textual traditions but as a frontal challenge to imperialism. The emergence of Rastafari in the early efforts of decolonization suggests dissatisfaction with the state of nationalist movements that offered continuities of imperialist logic. Rastafari rejects the presuppositions of Christianity even while freely drawing upon its forms. However, this rejection marks a refusal to be co-opted into the liberal logic of history, progress, and development that privilege European culture. The acceptance of Christianity with its European logic, European authoritative texts, and European leadership structure, among other things, Rastafari suggests, means a perpetuation of the power of the religious imagination that sees Africans as a deficit race. The rejection and then recreation of sacred texts that establish a different basis of authority outside of the liberal constructs of history enable Rastafari, as least at the level of rhetoric, to step outside the power of what Bhabha sees as colonial mimicry. Rather than normalizing the forms of imperial power as represented in the state, in the Bible, in the given logic of reality, and so on, Rastafari avoids becoming the "recognizable Other, *as a subject of a difference that is almost the same, but not quite.*"[98] Despite the resemblances in the textual forms, the mere centering of Ethiopia and the evaluation of Africans in these sacred texts render them unrecognizable to the logic upon which empire rests.

Conclusion

The Bible despite its fixed canon becomes malleable in particular contexts to prevailing ideas. Arguably, the constructs of power, particularly the imperial-sized notions of power as depicted in divine power, make the Bible specially suited to the discourses of empire. The Bible in its broad scope facilitates the fiction of the benevolent purposes of power. Rather than trouble or unsettle large concentrations of power, the Bible convinces its readers that power should be facilitated in order to do good in the world. Of course, the fact that the real impetus for doing good can be largely self-serving remains hidden in order to appeal to readers' higher motivations. The liberal discourse that accompanies modern empire intersects with the biblical discourses that shape Christian evangelization. Both see authorization of travel to other parts of the world to improve and uplift people as signal goals. However, both represent unreflected analyses of their purported altruistic virtues.

Empire as a hydra with several heads is a somewhat close description of the manifestations of modern empire. This descriptor points to both the complexity of empire and, as a result of its complexity, its adaptability. Mehta details some of the elements that constitute empire: "multiple purposes of power, commerce, cultural and religious influence, and the imperatives of progress, along with the myriad subsidiary motives of pride, jealousy, compassion, curiosity, adventure, and resistance."[99] Precisely this complexity and fluidity means that addressing one aspect of empire successfully does not result in an end to empire. Decolonization successfully removed the physical presence of empire builders but not until empire had been studied, taught, caught, enculturated, and sanctified by those who sought to get rid of it. The effective challenge to the racist practices of empire resulted in greater participatory democracy in formerly colonized nations. Yet the structures of empire embedded in the global economy that transferred and generated wealth to imperializing nations remained intact.

In the use of the Bible against empire, Rastafari demonstrates a useful model of rejection and refusal. By simply moving outside of the singular history of Enlightenment rationality that feeds liberalism and its consequent racialized hierarchies that suggest the civilizing mission, Rastafari undermines one of the pillars of empire. The daring move to reject Christianity and the presuppositions of European culture by normalizing African values, cultures, and personalities—and in the process promoting the Africanization of consciousness—Rastafari offers a new path of resistance that is not simply about fighting for inclusion in a system constructed to favor Europeans. Their challenge to the racial capitalism of empire appears in their frontal attacks on several institutions of empire—education, religion, politics, and culture. Since the Bible threads its way through these institutions and their logics, the muting of the power of the Bible and replacing it with alternative sacred texts can have a destabilizing effect. Rastafari may not in the end be the imperial antidote, but it does help expose the ways the Bible has accompanied and still stands in support of empire.

Notes

1. Hilary M. Carey, "Introduction: Empires of Religion," in *Empires of Religion*, ed. Hilary M. Carey, Cambridge Imperial and Post-Colonial Studies (Hampshire, UK: Palgrave Macmillan, 2008), pp. 1–21.
2. Carey, "Introduction: Empires of Religion," 1, 5.
3. Uday Singh Mehta, *Liberalism and Empire: A Study in Nineteenth-Century Britisih Liberal Thought* (Chicago: University of Chicago Press, 1999), 81.
4. Walter D. Mignolo, *Local Histories/Global Designs: Coloniality, Subaltern Knowledges, and Border Thinking* (Princeton, NJ: Princeton University Press, 2000), 27.
5. Robert J. C. Young, *White Mythologies: Writing History and the West* 2nd ed. (London: Routledge, 2004), 2.
6. Michael Hardt and Antonio Negri, *Empire* (Cambridge, MA: Harvard University Press, 2000), 15.
7. Cedric J. Robinson, *Black Marxism: The Making of the Black Radical Tradition* (Chapel Hill, NC: University of North Carolina Press, 2000), 2.
8. Mignolo, *Local Histories*, 21.
9. Robinson, *Black Marxism*, 19; Mignolo, *Local Histories*.
10. Robinson, *Black Marxism*, 25.
11. David Brion Davis, *Inhuman Bondage: The Rise and Fall of Slavery in the New World* (Oxford: Oxford University Press, 2006), 33.
12. Davis, *Inhuman Bondage*, 39.
13. R. S. Sugirtharajah, *The Bible and Empire: Postcolonial Explorations* (Cambridge: Cambridge University Press, 2005), 83.
14. Davis, *Inhuman Bondage*, 48–76.
15. Lisa Lowe, *The Intimacies of Four Continents* (Durham, NC: Duke University Press, 2015), 10, 20.
16. Thomas McCarthy, *Race, Empire and the Idea of Human Development* (Cambridge: Cambridge University Press, 2009), 1.
17. Jodi A. Byrd, *The Transit of Empire: Indigenous Critiques of Colonialism* (Minneapolis: University of Minnesota Press, 2011), xxi.
18. Byrd, *Transit of Empire*, xxiii.
19. McCarthy, *Race, Empire*, 166.
20. Lowe, *Intimacies of Four Continents*, 20.
21. David Maxwell, "Decolonization," in *Missions and Empire*, ed. Norman Etherington (Oxford: Oxford University Press, 2005), pp. 285–306.
22. Norman Etherington, "Introduction," in *Missions and Empire*, ed. Norman Etherington (Oxford: Oxford University Press, 2005), pp. 1–18.
23. Jean Comaroff and John L. Comaroff, *Of Revelation and Revolution: Christianity, Colonialism, and Consciousness in South Africa*, vol. 1 (Chicago: University of Chicago Press, 1991), 10.
24. Mehta, *Liberalism and Empire*, 81.
25. Mehta, *Liberalism and Empire*, 82.
26. Mehta, *Liberalism and Empire*, 79.
27. "A Proclamation for a Day of Solemn Fast, Humiliation, and Prayer," *The Times*, September 28, 1857, sec. b, 4.
28. "Proclamation for a Day of Solemn Fast," p. 6, col. d.

29. "Proclamation for a Day of Solemn Fast," p. 6, col. b.
30. "Proclamation for a Day of Solemn Fast," p. 6, col. b.
31. "Proclamation for a Day of Solemn Fast," p. 6, col. d.
32. Mehta, *Liberalism and Empire*, 81.
33. "Proclamation for a Day of Solemn Fast," p. 6, col. d.
34. "The India Relief Fund," *The Times*, October 5, 1857, p. 7, col. c.
35. "India Relief Fund," p. 7, col. c.
36. "Proclamation for a Day of Solemn Fast," p. 6, col. d.
37. "Proclamation for a Day of Solemn Fast," p. 6, col. e.
38. "Proclamation for a Day of Solemn Fast," col. b.
39. McCarthy, *Race, Empire*, 168.
40. "Proclamation for a Day of Solemn Fast," p. 6, col. e.
41. "Proclamation for a Day of Solemn Fast," p. 6, col. e.
42. "Proclamation for a Day of Solemn Fast," p. 6, col. e.
43. Byrd, *Transit of Empire*, xviii.
44. McCarthy, *Race, Empire*, 9.
45. Byrd, *Transit of Empire*, xxiii.
46. "Proclamation for a Day of Solemn Fast," p. 8, col. f.
47. "Proclamation for a Day of Solemn Fast," p. 8, col. b.
48. McCarthy, *Race, Empire*, 6.
49. Maxwell, "Decolonization," 289.
50. Jean Comaroff and John L. Comaroff, *Of Revelation and Revolution: The Dialectics of Modernity on a South African Frontier*, vol. 2 (Chicago: University of Chicago Press, 1991), 6.
51. McCarthy, *Race, Empire*, 30.
52. R. S. Sugirtharajah, *Asian Biblical Hermeneutics and Postcolonialism*, Biblical Seminar (Sheffield: Sheffield Academic Press, 1999), 20.
53. "Excerpts from Nobel Lecture by Luthuli in Oslo," *New York Times*, December 12, 1961, sec. b-g, col. e.
54. "Excerpts from Nobel Lecture by Luthuli in Oslo," p. 12, col. b.
55. "Excerpts from Nobel Lecture by Luthuli in Oslo," p. 12, col. g.
56. "Excerpts from Nobel Lecture by Luthuli in Oslo," p. 12, col. g.
57. "Excerpts from Nobel Lecture by Luthuli in Oslo," p. 12, col. b.
58. David Chidester, Judy Tobler, and Darrel Wratten, *Christianity in South Africa: An Annotated Bibliography* (Westport, CT: Greenwood, 1997), 2.
59. Maxwell, "Decolonization," 289.
60. Bishop Abel Tendekai Muzorewa, *Rise Up and Walk: An Autobiography*, ed. Norman E. Thomas (London: Evans Brothers, 1978), 74.
61. Wallace G. Mills, "Millennial Christianity, British Imperialism, and African Nationalism," in *Christianity in South Africa: A Political, Social and Cultural History*, ed. Richard Elphick and Rodney Davenport (Berkeley: University of California Press, 1997), pp. 327–346.
62. Muzorewa, *Rise Up*, 62.
63. Muzorewa, *Rise Up*, 75.
64. Hazel Tafadzwa Ngoshi, "Portrait of a Political Liberation Theologian: Liberation Theology and the Making of Abel Muzorewa's Autobiographical Subjectivity in Rise Up and Walk," *Imbizo* 5 (2014): 101, 97–113.
65. Muzorewa, *Rise Up*, 55.

66. Muzorewa, *Rise Up*, 56.
67. Muzorewa, *Rise Up*, 185.
68. Muzorewa, *Rise Up*, 185.
69. Mills, "Millennial Christianity," 338.
70. Muzorewa, *Rise Up*, 130.
71. Ngoshi, "Portrait of a Political Liberation Theologian," 108.
72. Muzorewa, *Rise Up*, 70.
73. Mills, "Millennial Christianity," 338.
74. Chidester, Tobler, and Wratten, *Christianity in South Africa*, 2.
75. Peggy Brock, "New Christians as Evangelists," in *Missions and Empire*, ed. Norman Etherington (Oxford: Oxford University Press, 2005), pp. 132–152; Chidester, Tobler, and Wratten, *Christianity in South Africa*.
76. Chidester, Tobler, and Wratten, *Christianity in South Africa*, 12.
77. Ogbu U. Kalu, "Passive Revolution and Its Saboteurs: African Christian Initiative in the Era of Decolonization, 1955–1975," in *Missions, Nationalism, and the End of Empire*, ed. Brian Stanley, Studies in the History of Christian Missions (Grand Rapids, MI: Eerdmans, 2003), pp. 250–277.
78. Mills, "Millennial Christianity," 340.
79. Erna Brodber, "Reggae as Black Space," in *Global Reggae*, ed. Carolyn Cooper (Kingston: Canoe, 2012), pp. 21–36.
80. Clinton A. Hutton, "Leonard Howell Announcing God: Conditions That Gave Birth to Rastafari in Jamaica," in *Leonard Percival Howell and the Genesis of Rastafari*, ed. Clinton A. Hutton et al. (Kingston: University of the West Indies Press, 2015), pp. 9–52.
81. Hutton, "Leonard Howell Announcing God," 21.
82. Barry Chevannes, *Rastafari: Roots and Ideology* (Syracuse, NY: Syracuse University Press, 1994), 232; Ogbu U. Kalu, "Ethiopianism in African Christianity," in *African Christianity: An African Story*, ed. Ogbu U. Kalu (Trenton, NJ: Africa World, 2007), 137, pp. 229–243; Ken Post, "The Bible as Ideology: Ethiopianism in Jamaica, 1930–38," in *African Perspectives: Papers in the History, Politics and Economics of Africa Presented to Thomas Hodgkin*, ed. Christopher Allen and R. W. Johnson (Cambridge: Cambridge University Press, 1970), pp. 185–207.
83. Kalu, "Ethiopianism in African Christianity," 232.
84. Ennis Barrington Edmonds, *Rastafari: From Outcasts to Culture Bearers* (New York: Oxford University Press, 2003), 34.
85. Edward W. Blyden, *Christianity, Islam and the Negro Race* (Edinburgh: Edinburgh University Press, 1967).
86. Noel Leo Erskine, *From Garvey to Marley: Rastafari Theology* (Gainesville: University Press of Florida, 2005), 120.
87. Erskine, *From Garvey to Marley*, 120.
88. Hutton, "Leonard Howell Announcing God," 10.
89. Rex Nettleford, "From the Cross to the Throne," in *Let Us Start with Africa: Foundations of Rastafari Scholarship*, ed. Jahlani A. H. Niaah and Erin Macleod (Kingston: University of the West Indies Press, 2013), 18, pp. 10–21.
90. G. G. Maragh, *The Promised Key* (Hogarth Blake, 2008), 5.
91. Robert Athlyi Rogers, *The Holy Piby* (Hogarth Blake, 2008), 6.
92. Rogers, *Holy Piby*, 8.
93. Maragh, *Promised Key*, 19.

94. Robert A. Hill, "Leonard Howell and Rastafari Origins," in *The Encyclopedia of Caribbean Religions*, ed. Patrick Taylor and Frederick I. Case, vol. 1 (Champaign, IL: University of Illinois Press, 2013), 767.
95. Maragh, *Promised Key*, 7.
96. Rogers, *Holy Piby*, 15–16.
97. Rogers, *Holy Piby*, 17.
98. Bhabha, *Location of Culture*, 122. Emphasis in the original.
99. Mehta, *Liberalism and Empire*, 1.

Selected Bibliography

Blyden, Edward W. *Christianity, Islam, and the Negro Race*. Edinburgh: Edinburgh University Press, 1967.

Byrd, Jodi A. *The Transit of Empire: Indigenous Critiques of Colonialism*. Minneapolis: University of Minnesota Press, 2011.

Carey, Hilary M. "Introduction: Empires of Religion." In *Empires of Religion*, edited by Hilary M. Carey, 1–21. Hampshire, UK: Palgrave Macmillan, 2008.

Chevannes, Barry. *Rastafari: Roots and Ideology*. Syracuse, NY: Syracuse University Press, 1994.

Davis, David Brion. *Inhuman Bondage: The Rise and Fall of Slavery in the New World*. Oxford: Oxford University Press, 2006.

Edmonds, Ennis Barrington. *Rastafari: From Outcasts to Culture Bearers*. New York: Oxford University Press, 2003.

Erskine, Noel Leo. *From Garvey to Marley: Rastafari Theology*. Gainesville: University Press of Florida, 2005.

Hutton, Clinton A. "Leonard Howell Announcing God: Conditions That Gave Birth to Rastafari in Jamaica." In *Leonard Percival Howell and the Genesis of Rastafari*, edited by Clinton A. Hutton, Michael A. Barnett, D. A. Dunkley, and Jahlani A. H. Niaah, 9–15. Kingston: University of the West Indies Press, 2015.

Lowe, Lisa. *The Intimacies of Four Continents*. Durham, NC: Duke University Press, 2015.

Maxwell, David. "Decolonization." In *Missions and Empire*, edited by Norman Etherington, 285–306. Oxford: Oxford University Press, 2005.

McCarthy, Thomas. *Race, Empire and the Idea of Human Development*. Cambridge: Cambridge University Press, 2009.

Mehta, Uday Singh. *Liberalism and Empire: A Study in Nineteenth-Century British Liberal Thought*. Chicago: University of Chicago Press, 1999.

Mignolo, Walter D. *Local Histories/Global Designs: Coloniality, Subaltern Knowledges, and Border Thinking*. Princeton, NJ: Princeton University Press, 2000.

Robinson, Cedric J. *Black Marxism: The Making of the Black Radical Tradition*. Chapel Hill: University of North Carolina Press, 2000.

PART V

POSTCOLONIAL BIBLICAL CRITICISM AND COGNATE DISCIPLINES

CHAPTER 26

POSTCOLONIAL BIBLICAL CRITICISM AND FEMINIST STUDIES

SUSANNE SCHOLZ

THE study of the postcolonial "imagination" has become prevalent outside and inside biblical studies since the late 1980s. As Bible scholar R. S. Sugirtharajah puts it: "At its simplest: it is about the impact created by Western colonization on individuals, communities, and cultures."[1] For sure, postcolonial Bible scholars did not invent this intellectually significant and transformative project. They learned about it from their personal experiences, as many of them originate from, grew up in, or sometimes still live in countries that wrestled off colonial powers, such as Britain and France, since the 1950s. Most importantly, postcolonial biblical scholars have studied the works of postcolonial thinkers, such as Frantz Fanon, Aimé Césaire, Edward Said, Gayatri Spivak, Chandra Talpade Mohanty, and Homi K. Bhabha.[2] All of them were Western-educated but of non-Western heritage or origins. They challenge Western complacency to postcolonial dynamics and advance scholarly scrutiny of the histories, politics, traditions, and ongoing worldwide effects of the colonial era.

In the 1990s, Two-Thirds World Bible scholars connected postcolonial theories with their biblical research. Once they made this connection, they asserted that colonialism sits at the heart of biblical scholarship. After all, modern biblical exegesis developed exactly within the same 500 years in which the West colonized many Two-Thirds World countries. In the 1990s Sugirtharajah became one of the first postcolonial Bible scholars to trace the connections between colonialism and the Bible.[3] Sugirtharajah and other postcolonial critics have analyzed how biblical texts and their interpretations contributed to geopolitical exploitation, expansion, and domination of many Two-Thirds World countries and people.[4] They reject as colonizing any exegetical postures of political neutrality or intellectual objectivity, and they investigate the Bible's contributions to colonial hegemony in past and present society, culture, and religion.

Male thinkers initiated the intellectual discourse on postcolonial analysis, but feminist scholars have also made important contributions to analyzing the link between postcolonialism and gender oppression. Already in 1988, Chandra Talpade Mohanty criticized the Western feminist inclination to universalize the analytic category "woman" as if all women, anywhere and at any time, face the same traditions, structures, and histories of gender oppression.[5] Characteristic for postcolonial theorists, Mohanty rejected a monolithic gender analysis, especially because the Western feminist tendency to generalize the category of "woman" has covered up differences among women in terms of race, class, ethnicity, religion, or national identity. According to Mohanty, the universalizing tendency must be understood as part of the totalizing tendencies characteristic of the colonizing West. Postcolonial feminist theorists like Mohanty criticize this intellectual convention and insist that women face structures of domination differently due to different colonial contexts, histories, and cultures.

Since approximately 2000, postcolonial feminist exegetes have made major contributions to biblical scholarship. Like many postcolonial theorists in general, postcolonial feminist Bible interpreters, too, have experienced colonial oppression in their own lives and societies. Their countries suffered through the political, economic, and social realities of colonialism and postcolonialism, and so they know firsthand that a monolithic analysis based on gender alone is insufficient for understanding histories, cultures, politics, and traditions of past and present geopolitical dynamics. The link with sexism and other forms of discrimination is inherently obvious to them, and so they reject studying the Bible for academic purposes alone. They practice biblical exegesis as a way of fostering political, economic, social, and religious change in women's lives and the lives of those people close to them. After forty years of feminist biblical interpretation, then, the feminist biblical conversation has turned global, foregrounding social responsibility and change.

This essay elaborates on the emergence and development of postcolonial feminist biblical scholarship. The first section outlines major theories in postcolonial feminist biblical scholarship, followed by a second section that organizes the large amount of scholarly literature in postcolonial feminist studies by discussing three areas of concentration. Some postcolonial feminist exegetes focus on a biblical book, others on a biblical chapter, and still others on a biblical theme or character. One example in each area illustrates the combined inquiries into gender and postcolonial hermeneutics as a productive exegetical approach. The third section explores how to move postcolonial feminist scholarship beyond biblical texts to research the biblical interpretation histories. A conclusion summarizes the main findings and offers some ideas for future directions in postcolonial feminist biblical studies.

THREE MAJOR THEORIES IN POSTCOLONIAL FEMINIST EXEGESIS

Several exegetes have articulated their hermeneutical theories about the interpretation of the Bible as a postcolonial feminist text. Among them are Musa W. Dube, Kwok

Pui-lan, and Judith E. McKinlay.[6] One of the earliest and wide-reaching hermeneutical theories comes from the Botswanian Bible exegete, Musa W. Dube.[7] She developed the concept of "Rahab's reading prism" to articulate that the female character of Joshua 2, Rahab, submits to the imperial power of biblical Israel, thus illustrating the complex position of Two-Thirds World women today. To Dube, Rahab is a politically problematic female character with whom postcolonial feminists should not identify. Yet Rahab is significant because her story illustrates the multiple positioning of colonized women. They are like Rahab. She encounters the Israelite spies and negotiates her own and her family's survival with them, even converting to their culture and religion.

Since Rahab's position in the biblical story illustrates the geopolitical complexities of colonized women's struggles for survival, postcolonial feminist readers need to consider various hermeneutical elements from her story. Dube's concept of Rahab's reading prism aims to provide such exegetical guidance. Three features stand out. First, Rahab's reading prism consists of "a postcolonial feminist eye of many angles and of seeing, reading, and hearing literary texts," and it also resists "imperial and patriarchal oppressive structures and ideologies."[8] Second, Rahab's reading prism "enlightens women on how to form political coalitions that do not invite double-colonized women to the table as parroting Rahabs [i.e., women submitting to colonizing forms of oppression]." Third, the prism "demands the radical transgression of boundaries by embracing a multicultural canon, which does not continue to privilege imperializing canons." In other words, Rahab's reading prism is a way of reading biblical texts to "revolutionize the structural oppression" and to "cultivate reading-writings of liberative interdependence, where differences, equality, and justice for various cultures, religions, genders, classes, sexualities, ethnicities, and races can be subject to constant reevaluation and celebration in the interconnectedness of our relationships."

Another element defines Dube's theorizing on postcolonial feminist exegesis that aligns with postcolonial feminist theory in general. She asserts that the feminist postcolonial interpretation of the Bible needs to reject the homogenizing and universalizing use of the category "woman" that ruled supreme in Western feminist biblical studies from the 1970s to the 1990s and is still prevalent among Christian right readers today.[9] Like other postcolonial feminist exegetes, Dube insists that patriarchal oppression takes many different forms, and women of different social locations experience patriarchy differently. Most importantly, women who live under imperial oppression are at least doubly oppressed. Both gender and imperial oppression needs to be considered in any biblical reading because colonization overlaps with patriarchal domination, executed by both colonized native males and the colonizing power. Feminist biblical interpreters have to be aware of the combined effect of gender and empire, creating so-called double colonization.[10] Postcolonial feminist exegetes thus uncover and oppose the many forms of social, political, and economic forms of exploitation. They assume and recognize the multivalent layers of domination. Different women in different lands experience patriarchy differently, and so contextualized analyses are required. Finally, Dube aims for broad and all-inclusive biblical interpretation that is located deliberately within the political, cultural, and religious conditions of an interpreter's time and space. Such exegesis recognizes the multilayered dimensions of human structures of power. It participates in justice-seeking projects of politically and socially progressive movements. Dube's proposal resonates among many postcolonial feminist scholars, and a quote from Malebogo Kgalemang illustrates its general acceptance:

> Postcolonial feminist analysis of the Bible "reads" and "writes" woman at the collusion and intersection of patriarchy, imperialism, neocolonialism, gender, nation, and religion in the Bible. It is rooted in postcolonial feminist theory, in postcolonial biblical interpretation, and in feminist interpretation of the Bible.[11]

Another postcolonial feminist scholar, Kwok Pui-lan, offers important theoretical ideas about the practice of postcolonial feminist exegesis. Born in Hong Kong and teaching Christian systematic theology in the United States, Kwok views postcolonial feminist biblical interpretation as an approach that creates "a space" so that women living in colonized and semicolonized countries, such as China, "can be remembered in order to enliven our historical and moral imagination."[12] She tells the story of an almost illiterate Chinese woman, living at the turn of the twentieth century, who used a hairpin to cut from the Bible the verses of Paul instructing women to be submissive and remain silent in church. Kwok explains that "this story demonstrates how oppressed women have turned the Bible, a product introduced by the colonial officials, missionaries, and educators, into a site of contestation and resistance for their own emancipation."[13]

Kwok explains that postcolonial feminist exegesis has a twofold task. Postcolonial feminist interpreters need to recover the interpretative insights from ordinary women like the Chinese woman in the early 1900s, and they also must "unmask the myriad ways in which biblical scholars, feminists among them, have been complicit with or oblivious to colonialism and neocolonialism."[14] Kwok refers to an Asian American Old Testament exegete, Gale Yee, to emphasize the need for studying gender in the Bible with the sociopolitical categories of race, class, and colonial status. Such an intersectional analysis has much to contribute to biblical exegesis, Kwok explains, as many male postcolonial critics ignore gender in their works on colonialism, postcolonialism, decolonialism, and neocolonialism.[15] After all, so Kwok, androcentric power and ideology have played a major role in colonial processes and biblical exegetes need to account for it, but they often neglect the aspect of gender.

Kwok elaborates on four additional areas of investigation that postcolonial feminist interpreters need to consider in their biblical interpretations. They have to listen to biblical women living in the "contact zone" and develop counternarratives of those women's stories. Kwok explains that contact zones are spaces in which the colonial encounters between people of different geopolitical backgrounds meet. When postcolonial feminist exegetes focus on the encounters of biblical characters in the contact zone, new narratives emerge that "speak of equality and freedom."[16] Yet another area of investigation that postcolonial feminist exegetes ought to explore pertains to the careful analysis of "metropolitan interpretations."[17] Postcolonial feminist exegetes have to investigate if and how biblical interpretations endorse colonizing ideologies, gloss over imperial contexts and assumptions, or contribute to decolonizing texts that favor empire over liberation. Still another area of investigation ensures that the exegetical focus moves from dominant Western patriarchal readings to the roles and contributions of ordinary readers. Postcolonial feminist interpreters need to favor Bible readers with "suppressed knowledges that academic elites often dismiss."[18] Finally, Kwok urges postcolonial feminist exegetes to attend to "the politics and poetics of location."[19] This idea, which is indebted to New Testament scholar Mary Ann Tolbert, recognizes that the social background of interpreters is always complex. Hence the "politics of location" accounts for the mixture of gender, race, sexual orientation, one's national and institutional setting, and economic and educational features. Interpreters need to be clear on how they bring their backgrounds into the interpretive analysis. They also need to consider the theological and ethical impact of their readings, which refers to the poetics of location. These four theoretical convictions determine how Kwok approaches biblical exegesis, and she asks others to take them into account, too. As Kwok states: "We have the challenge to turn the postcolonial 'contact zones' into places of mutual learning, and places for trying out new ideas and strategies for the emancipation of all."[20] A proponent of a dialogically defined postcolonial feminist hermeneutics, Kwok invites exegetes and theologians alike to engage in this kind of biblical interpretation.

A third postcolonial feminist exegete, Judith E. McKinlay, offers ideas about the nature, purpose, and goals of postcolonial feminist biblical hermeneutics. McKinlay acknowledges her own personal involvement in developing a postcolonial feminist biblical hermeneutics. She explains: "I have become very interested in the processes of Othering, so often linked with the imposition and maintenance of opposing orthodoxies. I begin with the I, for my interest is personal."[21] She discloses biographical information about growing up and living in the former British colony, New Zealand: "As a woman, and a feminist, I know a little about Othering from the underside, but, as a white New Zealander (a Pakeha) belonging to the dominant culture in a postcolonial society, I am also aware of its binary opposite."[22] She asserts that personal reflections on a biblical character have political implications. Thus, she is very precise and direct in referring to her personal background:

> Geographically I am a New Zealander, living at the south of the Pacific. But if I expand that to say that I live in Aotearoa New Zealand that already hints at more to be said. For I am a *Pakeha*, non-Maori, living in a country originally settled by Maori, but subsequently entered by Europeans, first arriving in significant numbers in the nineteenth century, as whalers, traders and settlers. On my father's side my roots in this land go back four generations. My ancestors left Scotland under the leadership of a somewhat charismatic religious figure, Norman McLeod, who had had a number of disputes with his church authorities, and had decided to emigrate to Nova Scotia in Canada. There they settled and formed a self-identified Presbyterian community. Then, in the 1850s, a significant number, including McLeod, left Nova Scotia and travelled on again to New Zealand. The family history that has been passed down to my generation begins with the highland clearances and the enforced landlessness of disposed crofters, followed both by the failing herring trade in Scotland and divisive church disputes. Those that set sail again from Nova Scotia arrived in New

Zealand as settlers with the land-buying power of a self-contained Gaelic speaking community, an identity that was carefully maintained for a generation or two and still remembered in Waipu, the original area of settlement, which celebrates this tradition with Highland Games each January. On my mother's side, however, I claim Yorkshire ancestry, my mother having arrived here in the 1920s with her parents, who were looking for better business opportunities. This mix of early and more recent arrivals is a typically New Zealand heritage.[23]

In her view, then, postcolonial feminist readers cannot pretend to read biblical texts and characters from a distant, uninvolved, and objective position. Thus, she "will be reading this text from within the worldview I inhabit" and "this is true of all readers, whether we are conscious of it or not."[24] She ponders how to read the specific narratives about Jezebel in 1 Kings, asking whether she should follow "those later scribes in Judah, Babylon, or even Yehud scratching their heads and planning their countermoves."[25] The story is mainly about Ahab, the king of Israel, and the academic diachronic study deciphers more about him than about Jezebel.[26] Yet McKinlay warns that those scribes can "be turned and twisted around" to serve almost any purpose.[27] She knows that the original writers do not merely transmit a neutrally toned message from the northern kingdom. Instead, they set up the story to fit their ideological interests that were heavily invested in the politics of empire and patriarchy. Since the original writers were not on the side of the queen, postcolonial feminist readers must be wary about the historical meaning of this text. As a feminist exegete coming from the side of the colonizing empire, McKinlay recognizes this fact, and so she takes herself as a reader seriously.[28]

Attention to her stance as a reader means that she is suspicious of historical claims of the biblical writers. She wants to tell the stories about Jezebel on the basis of "creative imagination."[29] Accordingly, she gives voice to the "othered" female character. The attempt to retell the story from Jezebel's perspective demonstrates to McKinlay that the biblical text others the female character almost beyond recognition. We can hardly imagine her beyond the colonizing-androcentric depiction and a "happy ending for such an evil Other" is impossible.[30] McKinlay's "interventionist" approach that tries to reimagine the suppressed and distorted character suggests that the "textualization" of Jezebel eradicates her from the collective memory.[31] Since McKinlay reads the Bible from her postcolonial context of Aotearoa New Zealand, she advises not to get stuck in the biblical text but to connect it with other texts, such as letters and journals from Protestant Evangelical missionaries in New Zealand of the early nineteenth century. McKinlay explains that "my interest here is in how these early missionaries reacted when faced with a different culture, different spirituality, and different cosmology."[32] Did they, too, erase the "other" from memory?

In a second theoretical move, McKinlay expands the canon beyond the Bible by including texts from the history of interpretation. Her goal is to elaborate on the othering processes involved in the elimination of female biblical figures. The result is unsurprising. As the missionaries advanced the othering of female characters, so they sidelined femininity in the indigenous religion and culture of the Maori people.

McKinlay diagnoses that the missionaries colonized intellectually the nonliterate culture. They textualized and marginalized it beyond recognition.[33] In short, McKinlay's theoretical move to integrate accounts from the Christian missionary movement in New Zealand enabled her to correlate the invisibility of female characters, such as Jezebel, with the invisibility of female aspects in the Maori traditions. The hermeneutical clarity gained is profoundly disturbing, and so McKinlay acknowledges: "There is such sadness in looking and reading back through these feminist postcolonial lenses."[34]

The theoretical idea to correlate the Bible with other texts is a core postcolonial procedure. Called a "contrapuntal" reading, it requires bringing one's own postcolonial context into conversation with the biblical text. It teaches to read biblical texts as "warning signs." It indicates that "this issue is not to be left enclosed in the world of biblical academic study, allowing us to close the book, reshelve it, and carry on with our lives unaffected."[35] It also teaches that notions of Otherness and orthodoxies, of right belief, are still "very much alive."[36]

In sum, postcolonial feminist interpreters of the Bible have developed distinct but related theories about the nature, purpose, and goals of postcolonial feminist exegesis. The theories of Dube, Kwok, and McKinlay exemplify the wide array of proposals to guide the practice of postcolonial feminist exegesis. Most postcolonial feminist exegetes, however, prefer to dive into specific biblical texts without much theoretical reflection.

Postcolonial Feminist Exegesis of Biblical Books, Texts, and Themes or Characters

While postcolonial feminist Bible scholars have expanded theoretical notions about the nature, purpose, and goals of biblical exegesis and defined it as an intersectional, nonessentializing, and geopolitically located practice of feminist reading, they have also interpreted countless biblical texts ranging from entire biblical books to specific biblical chapters and themes or characters. In the exegetical process, they have established various strategies of interpretation. Jeremy Punt identifies five approaches that he classifies as standing at (1) the intersection of colonization and gender, (2) colonial domination and subordination invoking divine agency and sanction, (3) women and colonial hybridity, (4) contrapuntal reading strategies, and (5) challenges of textual "property rights."[37] Except perhaps for the last approach, Punt's approaches center on biblical texts, even though they also attempt "to open up religion to other discourses."[38]

Other strategies exist. In my discussion of postcolonial feminist interpretations, I identified three strategies employed by postcolonial feminist interpreters.[39] One strategy correlates the lot of biblical women with the sociopolitical contexts of postcolonial feminist exegetes. They read biblical women as women "like us" and align themselves with the "other" women in the texts. Another strategy favors ordinary Two-Thirds World women who are not usually academically trained but nevertheless read the Bible from their experiences and viewpoints. When postcolonial feminist exegetes rely on this strategy, they assert that ordinary readers have much to contribute to the biblical meaning-making process and that academics better listen to the interpretations of ordinary readers. Yet another strategy locates feminist biblical meaning within (post)colonial histories and interprets biblical women with the respective historical, postcolonial contexts in mind. McKinlay describes this strategy as "spinning hybrid interpretations within (post)colonial theory." It makes visible imperial storytelling in the Bible and in the world, exposing binary, othering, and colonizing notions as part of settler narratives that harm society to this very day.

In light of the large amount of books, essays, and journal articles, three examples shall illustrate the wide range of biblical interpretations that postcolonial feminist exegetes have produced during the past twenty years. Many publications focus on a biblical book,[40] a biblical chapter,[41] or a biblical theme or character.[42] The following discussion presents one example for each category. Joseph A. Marchal's examination of Paul's letter to the Philippians illustrates a postcolonial feminist study of a biblical book. Marcella María Althaus-Reid's interpretation of Joshua 2 exemplifies a postcolonial feminist reading of a biblical chapter. Madipoane Masenya's discussion on levirate marriage in the book of Ruth and among South African Pentecostal single women illustrates a postcolonial feminist interpretation of a biblical theme.

First, Marchal examines Paul's letter to the Philippians on the basis of four metalevel questions, developed by Musa Dube, "to evaluate ancient texts on their literary-rhetorical grounds."[43] The questions are: "1. Does this text have a clear stance against the political imperialism of its time? 2. Does this text encourage travel to distant and inhabited lands and how does it justify itself? 3. How does this text construct difference: Is there dialogue and liberating interdependence, or condemnation of all that is foreign? 4. Does this text employ gender and divine representations to construct relationships of subordination and domination?"[44] Marchal's examination shows that "Paul reinscribes and mimics the imperialism of his time in the letter to the Philippians" by "cod[ing] the community as colonized and feminine, in need of his divinely approved model and authority."[45]

As Marchal scrutinizes the intersection between a particular New Testament book—the Pauline letter to the Philippians—and imperial language and gender, he stresses that the ancient city of Philippi was "an ancient imperial contact zone"[46] and thus an ethnically, religiously, politically, and geographically diverse place. Paul relies on the colonizing strategy of mimicry and his travels within the Roman Empire, and he always writes from a distance to his various audiences, including the Philippian community. Paul repeatedly states that he made "progress" in convincing people of his message of Christ. Accordingly, Marchal finds that Paul's letter to the Philippians is rhetorically very similar to Roman Empire rhetoric. Both assert that "empire is for the good of the subjects, a paternalistic, civilizing force of advancement."[47] The passages in 3:14–17 and 4:8–9 illustrate that both the Pauline message and Paul himself travel from place to place. Moreover, Paul encourages the Philippians to imitate him and to mime his imperial discourse about Christ, just as the empire of their time and place asks them to be loyal subjects, to submit to authority, and to be obedient and compliant to the emperor.

Importantly, so Marchal, Paul constructs difference by "rul[ing] out arguing, questioning, or dialogue between the community and himself."[48] Paul's arguments are "dualistic and violently condemnatory," and his vision is "exclusive, absolutist."[49] In fact, Marchal asserts that the Pauline message is "compatible with the colonizers narrative of 'civilization.'"[50] For instance, Paul advises in Philippians 2:15 that the community be "silent, compliant, obedient subjects in opposition to the base, perverted, and savage surrounding world."[51] Paul even rejects resistance as dangerous and positions himself "as a provincial governor or colonial administrator for the divine imperator."[52] Importantly, Paul's rhetoric always imagines the superiors as male, whether they are Paul, Christ, or God. In short, Marchal's postcolonial feminist analysis of the letter to the Philippians uncovers a colonial, phallogocentric order that is both hierarchical and gendered. This order creates "fear and trembling"[53] in its adherents while Paul receives "an elevated position . . . in this imperial and patriarchal hierarchy."[54] Consequently, Paul's theological rhetoric is deeply complicit with gender-oppressive and empire-friendly concepts.

Still, Marchal comes to a "nuanced answer"[55] when he ponders Dube's question: Does the text take a clear stance against the political imperialism of its time? Yes and no, he concludes. On the one hand, Paul argues in favor of the empire of his time when he condemns enemies and outsiders. Paul relies on a "violently dualistic way,"[56] characteristic of colonizing thinking. On the other hand, even if one were to believe that Paul argued subversively, his writing would allow others to co-opt and assimilate his rhetoric in support of colonizing interests. Marchal quotes Kwok to sum up the postcolonial difficulties with Paul's letter: "Though Kwok might locate this tendency [of imperial co-optation of his letter] to the period of Constantine and Nicaea, her words aptly describe Paul's efforts in Philippians 'to maintain its symbolic unity and to marginalize ambiguous and polarized differences.'"[57] Marchal thus wonders what to do with Pauline studies in light of this particular Pauline letter. He almost seems despairing about the exegetical result when he asks:

> What kinds of approaches do we wish to see in Pauline studies? Which intersections can be found or connections made in feminist interpretation? What coalitions are still possible among those who study feminism, postcolonialism, and Roman imperialism? What kinds of inquiries are still to come?[58]

In sum, Marchal worries about the future of reading Pauline texts with postcolonial feminist concerns in mind. In an earlier study, he suggests that "what biblical interpretation needs is a healthy appreciation of its own conflicted, unstable, and ambivalent processes of identification with and through biblical materials,"[59] with the full recognition that biblical interpretation "cannot be assumed to have a univocally positive function for our futures."[60] We need to recognize that it is difficult to find clear-cut traces of anticolonial resistance in the colonial contact zone that the Pauline letters represent.

Second, Althaus-Reid's interpretation of Joshua 2 relies on the lenses of queer theory to illustrate the postcolonial feminist preference of investigating particular biblical chapters. Discussing the postcolonial and gender-queer significance of Joshua 2,[61] she finds this narrative "one of the most intriguing texts in the Scriptures in terms of sexual epistemologies of confrontation and struggle."[62] As she provocatively puts it, "sexual terrorism and guerrilla struggles reach their peak" in this biblical chapter, which she titles "The Origin of Queer Betrayal."[63] In Althaus-Reid's reading, Rahab emerges as a Canaanite woman, a sexual "other," who lives "a bisexual praxis of thinking and living in the frontier."[64] Althaus-Reid asserts that Rahab moves into the "heterosexual mono-loving mentality of only one nation, one God and one faith,"[65] as Rahab betrays her own people. Said differently, Althaus-Reid observes that Rahab moves from the frontier and the queer "Other" to the center, the place of the insider, the straight and colonial position. Understood within the dynamics of the queering and normalizing poles, Joshua 2 is "a deeply, frontier-like bisexual text" that offers limited possibilities for uncovering "the 'real queer lives' " of Rahab and the Canaanite people.[66] The queer positioning enables Rahab to live out her life in a way that does not require betrayal of herself in order to find acceptance; it is a life outside colonial expectations, structures, and institutions. Yet in the biblical tale Rahab betrays her queerness for colonial acceptance and inclusion, as she manages to survive the conquest of the frontier land. She leaves "the frontier by declaring herself heterosexual," an Israelite and a believer in "the mono-God."[67] Rahab's conversion follows "the love/logic of imperialism," Althaus-Reid explains. Rahab becomes "normalized," abandons her Canaanite life, and submits to "the God of the Market."[68]

Does anything of the "queer" Rahab, the Canaanite, the "Other," or the "wise, sexually and economically independent" woman survive the conversion as told in Joshua 2?[69] Was Rahab perhaps "a willing victim"?[70] Althaus-Reid finds that very little is left of the queer Rahab, and so this postcolonial and gender-queer interpreter imagines catching a glimpse of Rahab in the "transgressive women" and transvestites in Buenos Aires who have "blonde hair done up in a bun, publicly identifying themselves with Eva Perón, in a display of political transgression which was also a transgression of the silencing of the right to difference."[71] In Althaus-Reid's reading, the queer Rahab falls prey to imperial forces that attempt to eliminate her from memory. The textual report ensures that the conversion of the Canaanite, liberated, empowered, and dignified woman signifies the end of her material and spiritual independence. After the conversion, the formerly free woman is burdened with colonizing expectations and restrictions. Showing up in the Matthean genealogy of Jesus (Matt 1:5), she is even characterized as being "saved," but this characterization signifies her queer death. She becomes the Israelite Rahab who leads a colonized, heteronormative, and alienated life. In short, Althaus-Reid's postcolonial and gender-queer reading of Joshua 2 offers a radical critique of conventional Jewish and Christian readings. It turns the textual view of Rahab upside down, inviting readers to not forget Althaus-Reid's postcolonial, gender-queer reading of Joshua 2.

Third, some postcolonial feminist exegetes focus on biblical themes or characters in their work. Masenya develops such a study on levirate marriage in the book of Ruth and correlates it with South African Pentecostal Christian unmarried women. She observes that fundamentalist readings of the book of Ruth perpetuate not only patriarchal but also Western imperialist views about marriage.[72] She argues that these views do not only foster a "Western, individualistic, African-unfriendly outlook" but appeal to "Westernized and individualized African minds" and to "gender-sensitive biblical scholars [who] claim that a Western, individualistic outlook is found to be liberating and affirming toward many a subordinated African woman."[73] Thus, Masenya raises an important question: "What if that which is claimed to be a legitimate, biblical, and liberating reading is not affirming to many a single woman within African Pentecostal churches?"[74]

To answer her question, Masenya rereads the story of Ruth to evaluate if Ruth's levirate marriage with Boaz would be suitable for African women who are unmarried but disallowed from enjoying sex outside of marriage. Masenya wonders whether perhaps this kind of biblical marriage would allow African women, whose indigenous African marriage customs were vilified by colonialism and apartheid, to move beyond the rigid ideas about the heterosexual monogamous marriage as the only legitimate form of marriage for Pentecostal Christians, a view heavily indebted to the former African colonial power. Masenya's postcolonial feminist goal is to affirm single Pentecostal women as sexual beings, and so their dilemma, colloquially characterized as "stuck in the waiting room," is at the forefront of Masenya's discussion. Taking seriously "the context of marriage-obsessed African Pentecostal Christianity,"[75] she reads the biblical text with her characteristic *bosadi* hermeneutic that is grounded in "the unique experiences of an African South African woman, with a commitment to her liberation."[76] Masenya identifies compatible characteristics of levirate marriage, as described in the book of Ruth and as practiced in the African context. For instance, she finds that both the biblical tale and the African context connect marriage to matters of inheritance, "notions of family, communality, *botho/ḥesed*, and the desire for (male) progeny."[77] Masenya thus argues that "the gist of the levirate arrangement as presented in the book of Ruth would make sense within an African (traditional) setting."[78] At the same time she is also careful to emphasize that "a reenvisioned levirate union" requires that "*all the parties* consent to the union."[79]

Yet she also identifies incompatible elements between the biblical and African notions of levirate marriage. African levirate arrangements often resemble polygynous marriages, and Boas does not live in an extended family unlike African men. He is "[a] rich elderly, kind man" who seems to be "a loner, with no extended family, no nuclear family."[80] Most importantly, some of the interviewed Pentecostal women do not resonate with the biblical tale. Only 20 percent of them affirm that a levirate marriage "could serve as a means to address some of the challenges experienced by single women in Pentecostal churches."[81] Masenya recommends that ministers preach and teach about "other possible forms of heterosexual marriage" to accommodate the needs of their women congregants and begin to address contemporary practices of levirate arrangements, polygamy, polygyny, and "sexual starvation."[82] With the help of the biblical levirate theme, then, Masenya encourages her Christian African sisters and brothers to tackle "unconventional form[s] of marriage." She urges them to realize that polygynous or monogamous marriages define a woman's status but "it is the dependence and domination mentalities of the women and men sharing marriage."[83] In her view, the latter are in dire need of transformation.

In sum, postcolonial feminist Bible scholars tackle a wide array of biblical books, chapters, and themes in their exegetical work. A multifaceted and wide-ranging potpourri of biblical interpretations challenge rigid, monolithic, a-contextual, and colonizing biblical meanings that serve past or present empires and gender stereotypes. Exegetical creativity, ethical commitment, and geopolitical perspectives inform the postcolonial feminist work, whether it focuses on a large or a small part of the Bible. However, another crucial aspect of postcolonial feminist exegesis must be considered. It pertains to investigating the complex and varied interpretation histories that have normalized colonizing and gender-discriminatory biblical meanings. Investigations of biblical interpretation histories are important because they assist in nurturing decolonial, gender-egalitarian, and justice-oriented readings of the Bible.

INVESTIGATING THE POSTCOLONIAL-GENDERED INTERPRETATION HISTORIES OF THE BIBLE

Research of biblical literature's interpretation histories in various global places and during various time periods, with a focus on gender in its various manifestations, is strangely absent in postcolonial feminist Bible scholarship. Even postcolonial feminist theologian Kwok Pui-lan, who demands "a radical reappraisal of the biblical heritage" due to the Bible's "prominent position" in the Christian tradition,[84] moves straight into the biblical text when she is looking to find Ruth a "home," not based on "traditional Jewish or Christian interpretations" but in line with "the experiences of those whose lives have been marginalized and oppressed by the Bible."[85] Kwok's interpretation mentions postcolonial feminist and Jewish feminist exegetes, but her goal is to offer a reading that takes account of "its broader cultural and political impact on shaping the values, norms, and actions of society."[86] Her "search for new ways of interpreting the Bible for the contemporary world"[87] remains steadfastly focused on the biblical text, and so the Bible's postcolonial and gendered interpretation histories are not part of the inquiry. Since Kwok works primarily as a Christian systematic theologian, she discusses postcolonial feminist issues in more general ways when she moves beyond specific interpretations of the Bible.[88]

Some postcolonial biblical scholars examine postcolonial interpretation histories, though not from feminist perspectives. It is particularly bourgeoning in the area of African biblical translation studies. For instance, the anthology *Postcoloniality, Translation, and the Bible in Africa*, edited by Musa W. Dube and R. S. Wafula,[89] features some of the biblical interpretation histories to understand the literary and political contexts and power dynamics of various African Bible translations. Translations, such as the Swahili Bible, provide unique hermeneutical insight into the colonial attitudes toward African concepts and languages. It becomes clear that missionary translators tailored their Bible translations according to local African power struggles. Since Western male missionaries and indigenous male translators produced the various translations, the translated Bibles always advanced particular colonial and patriarchal notions. For instance, formerly nongendered concepts about deities were masculinized in the process of translating the Bible into local African languages. In recent years, therefore, African postcolonial biblical scholars have produced enormously important insights into the Bible's African interpretation histories that go far beyond a text-focused hermeneutics. The significance of African biblical translation studies in the understanding of (post)colonial African Christianity, history, and politics is obvious, and so Dube demands correctly that "translation studies should no longer be in the periphery of African and biblical studies as a whole."[90]

The original impetus to investigating the Bible's interpretation histories as part of the postcolonial biblical project goes back to one of the founding fathers of biblical postcolonialism, R. S. Sugirtharajah. In fact, his book entitled *Jesus in Asia* presents the history of Jesus research among Asian theologians and writers, providing Asian interpretation history on this most central Christian figure.[91] The study's premise is that "just as the Bible in Asia is not a stand-alone text but has to be read in conjunction with religious texts of the East, so, too, Jesus has to be understood in relation to the region's spiritual sages."[92] Sugirtharajah has always recognized the significance of the study of biblical interpretation histories. For instance, he warns of the theopolitical dangers of unconsciously perpetuating missionary patterns imposed on biblical texts during the European colonial period, and so he invites "a reorientation in both our missiological assumptions and our exegetical conclusions" when "there are widespread virulent forms of religious fanaticism."[93] Said differently, he invites reading biblical texts within their reading traditions.

In his view, the historical understanding of biblical texts within their colonial interpretation histories precludes proselytizing tendencies and missionary fervor that fundamentalist religious Bible-reading groups adhere to. He finds it important that "[a] postcolonial critic's role is not simply limited to textual dealings or literary concerns."[94] Accordingly, his research has always included the excavation of the Bible's interpretation histories in (post)colonial settings. For instance, his book, titled *Asian Biblical Hermeneutics and Postcolonialism: Contesting the Interpretations*,[95] presents the reading of the Bible as a colonial project that led to contested readings by the colonial subjects in the form of "The Brahmin's Bible" and "The Heathen and his Hermeneutics."[96] He therefore investigates the imperial biblical commentaries written in colonial India to decipher the influence of the commentators' allegiance to the empire. By reading the Bible with Sugirtharajah, we encounter the Bible's interpretation histories as well as the politics, economics, and cultures of those who read biblical texts.[97] Yet his work does not cover research on the gendered interpretation histories of the Bible in Asian lands. Thus, postcolonial feminist Bible exegetes face the huge task to exhume the unknown colonial and postcolonial interpretation histories as they pertain to gender in its intersectional manifestations.

Moving Beyond the Western Colonial Text Fetish: Concluding Remarks

The development of postcolonial feminist studies has invigorated biblical exegetes from around the globe as they produced biblical interpretations sensitive to the intersectionality of colonialism and gender. These scholars have articulated various theories on the nature, purpose, and goals of postcolonial feminist biblical studies. Yet most postcolonial feminist interpreters prefer to focus on biblical texts, which is a typical preference in the field of biblical studies as a whole. Accordingly, whether they develop biblical meanings behind, within, or in front of the text, countless postcolonial feminist readings center on the biblical text. Sometimes they interpret entire biblical books, sometimes they engage particular biblical chapters, and sometimes they highlight particular biblical themes or characters. In contrast, the postcolonial feminist concern for biblical interpretation histories leaves much room for further exploration. Importantly, some postcolonial Bible scholars who do not advance a feminist hermeneutical perspective have begun to explore biblical interpretation histories. Postcolonial feminist exegetes ought to consider researching biblical interpretation histories around the globe with their various hermeneutical convictions in mind. Much work remains to be done in this area.

This final section offers four comments in the spirit of dialogical feminist conversation to highlight important issues for the ongoing development of postcolonial feminist Bible scholarship. First, postcolonial feminist exegesis seems to hold on to rather simplistic notions about the West and the state of postcolonialism today. Sugirtharajah makes an important observation about the lack of recognition that European colonial empires of the nineteenth and twentieth centuries are indeed a fact of the past. He states:

> What we need to be aware of is the change of scenario in the theological firmament. The hegemonic Western theologies which took upon themselves the mantle to speak for all, and invaded our space, have lost their nerve.... We have not only lost an enemy but also have been pushed further to the periphery in the name of postmodern celebration of the local and the different. We need to pay attention to the fact that over the years not only the Master himself has changed, but along with him, his language of discourse, too, has modified. The master discourse no more talks about civilizing mission. The new lexicon is not about rescuing the benighted natives but concerns the universal ethics of human rights.... The failure to note this moral shift may mean ... that we are barking up the wrong tree.... [I]n fact we may be boxing a straw West entirely of our making.[98]

His concern is powerful. Do postcolonial feminist exegetes perhaps bark up the wrong tree and box a "straw West"? Sugirtharajah urges postcolonial Bible scholars to reconsider whether the colonial boundaries are still as clear-cut in the early part of the twenty-first century, when neocolonialism and neoliberalism reign supreme around the globe, as they were in the past. At stake is how today's postcolonial feminist exegetes connect biblical scholarship with contemporary neocolonial and neoliberal realities in which the West is not a separate geopolitical entity from the East and the North is enmeshed with the South, thanks to digital communication tools, means of transportation, and global trade. Do we still explain Mumbai's luxury condos, built on the edge of the sprawling slums, with nineteenth-century colonialism? How do today's global economies reinforce the colonial/colonized binary within the same country and implemented by its own political and economic leaders, sometimes even elected by the people? What do postcolonial feminist Bible scholars say about corrupt constellations in formerly colonized lands? Sugirtharajah's observation that Western power dynamics have shifted reminds biblical exegetes from every land that strawmen discussions have limited value for understanding the world so that people's perceptions can change "to make people see more, feel more and rekindle the fist of resistance."[99]

Second, postcolonial feminist exegetes say little about the illusion of innocence among the descendants of colonial oppression. I am not sure how to interpret this situation, but few of us who write on the destruction and damage of colonizing Bible readings have actually lived under colonial political structures. Many postcolonial feminist readers are the children, children's children, or even children of the children's children of everyday colonial life. Since claims about one's innocence are rarely productive in any conversation or analysis, the reticence to acknowledge one's own benefits from the current sociopolitical and economic status quo is questionable. All exegetes, engaging in postcolonial and feminist readings of the Bible, dream of justice, peace, and the integrity of creation. Moreover, nobody ought to be sitting on a high horse when it comes to the trauma, suffering, and destruction done in the past. We are the inheritors of a difficult, painful, and disturbing past. As a Protestant, post-Holocaust, diasporic German and U.S.-"naturalized" feminist exegete, I am convinced of the truth of this statement. In my view, then, the key question for biblical scholars engaged in the postcolonial feminist hermeneutical enterprise is this: How do we use our privilege as Bible scholars to unmask the neocolonial structures of oppression when it comes to gender in its various manifestations? Also, how can we develop ways of studying the Bible that recognize the ambiguity not only of the biblical text but also of the interpretation histories and our locations in them? One thing is certain. This is not the time for the descendants of the colonial powers to take intellectual or political revenge. It is time to foster cooperation and collaboration against the geopolitical structures of domination so that the poor and oppressed remain on our collective exegetical horizon.

Already in 1998, Sugirtharajah reminds his postcolonial colleagues not to lose focus on what matters most: "Although postcolonialism is an important political and cultural agenda, we have other equally important issues to grapple with, such as poverty, nationalism, communalism, casteism, patriarchy, internal exiles, all of which may or may not be linked to colonialism. In our eagerness to produce a resistance theory, we may ignore the minorities without our societies."[100] My intention is not to present Sugirtharajah's positions as the only or most important guide for postcolonial feminist exegetes. I quote him because of his significant hermeneutical, cultural, and exegetical insights into the various double-binding dynamics involved when postcolonial feminist exegetes read the Bible. After all, the mother of Western Christian feminist theologizing, Mary Daly, exclaimed decades ago that "the obvious corruption and cooptation of women under patriarchy can function to weaken Female-identified Outrage in women who are sincerely struggling to live a metapatriarchal morality."[101] Or as the U.S.-American Christian feminist ethicist Beverly W. Harrison put it: "Human alienation and sin live on so ferociously from one generation to the next because evil, injustice, or wrong and distorted relationships are patterned or institutionalized over time.... When social inequities, structured over time, continue, the result is great disparities of power between persons and groups and the violation of one group over another."[102] The renowned post-Holocaust German sociologist, Christina Thürmer-Rohr, also refers to the co-optation of women when she states:

> Frauen werden nicht nur unterdrückt, missbraucht und in ein schädigendes System verstrickt, sondern steigen auch eigentätig ein, gewinnen Privilegien, ernten fragwürdige Anerkennung und profitieren von ihren Rollen, sofern sie sie erfüllen. Frauen sind nicht nur durch gemeinsame Leiderfahrungen geprägt, sondern auch durch direkte und indirekte Zustimmung zur Höherwertung des Mannes und zur Enlastung gesellschaftlicher Täter. Diese Bereitschaft zur Duldung, Unterstützung oder Nichtzuständigkeit ist der Triumpf, den die Patriarchate feiern können.[103]

My point is that the illusion of innocence is real both for those standing in the colonizing intellectual traditions and for those hailing from colonized lands. There simply is no postcolonial feminist purity, and postcolonial feminist Bible interpreters ought to talk more with each other about this important insight that goes beyond personalized and individualized moments of confession.

Third, biblical studies has been a colonizing enterprise, but research efforts on the emergence of the field as a colonial endeavor are still few and far between. A case in point is historical criticism and its ongoing hegemonic status in biblical studies. Although scholars such as Stephen D. Moore and Yvonne Sherwood explain definitively how the field of biblical studies was invented as part of the modern nation-state and at exactly the moment of colonial European expansion,[104] biblical scholars still use and prefer the very methods and tools invented during this time. The umbrella term for these exegetical methods is historical criticism. Even the systematic theologian, Kwok Pui-lan, observes correctly that "postcolonial criticism does not reject the insights of historical criticism."[105] Doubly curious, then, is why even in most recent publications postcolonial feminist Bible scholars still employ historical criticism despite its apparent connections to colonialism. For instance, Kwok maintains that historical criticism provides "understanding of the 'worldliness' of the text, that is, the material and ideological background from which the text emerged and to which the texts responded."[106] Although she also acknowledges that "postcolonial critics pose new questions about the historical and literary contexts and thereby enlarge the moral imagination of the interpretive process,"[107] she accepts the merits of the intellectual framework ("the quest for origins"), set by the exegetical umbrella procedure called "historical criticism" and established within the Western European colonial intellectual contexts of the modern era. In other words and in my view, the acceptance of historical criticism buys into the colonial and colonizing project of the modern West, even if in a slightly modified fashion, namely by raising "new questions about this historical and literary contexts" with the goal of "enlarging the moral imagination."[108] What is missing, then, are critical postcolonial feminist studies that excavate the historical details about the developments of historical criticism as an intellectually colonial and gender-discriminatory enterprise. Perhaps such research ought to be the task for Western postcolonial feminist scholars living in European lands today.[109]

Fourth, for the past few years Vincent L. Wimbush has brought to our attention the issue of the text fetish. As he explains: "My call (the 'scream') is for a different orientation to interpretation itself, using the engagement of scriptures as a cultural practice and site of struggle to think with."[110] He proposes that during modernity the Bible was revered as fetish, an artifact invested with enormous powers to shape modern ideologies and practices. He thus urges scholars to study "the making and ongoing uses of Scriptures as fetish,"[111] not by producing yet another exegesis of this or that biblical text, but by "theorizing scriptures, signifying [on] scriptures, or critical comparative scriptures."[112] So the question is why postcolonial feminist exegetes are still laboring over individual biblical text after individual biblical text, as if they did not see the forest for the trees. Do they still believe they can explain the neocolonizing structures of domination with one more minutiae exegesis done in the text-fetishized ways invented by the colonial Western fathers? When will it be enough? With Wimbush, then, I urge postcolonial feminist Bible scholars to develop interdisciplinary projects that do not reduce the scholarly task to one more text study, whether it proceeds with an empiricist-antiquarian, a literary, or a cultural hermeneutics, but to join the conversation about "a different orientation to interpretation itself" that is multidisciplinary and investigates "the practices and gestures and ideas and associations and affiliations that have to do with being oriented in the world."[113] In conclusion, postcolonial feminist exegetes continue to be called to make important scholarly contributions in solidarity with the ongoing struggles of bringing justice, peace, and the integrity of creation into the world.

Notes

1. R. S. Sugirtharajah, *Exploring Postcolonial Biblical Criticism: History, Method, Practice* (Malden, MA: Wiley-Blackwell, 2012), 13.
2. See, e.g., Frantz Fanon, *The Wretched of the Earth* (trans. Richard Philcox; New York: Grove Press, 1963, 2004); Aimé Césaire, *Discourse on Colonialism* (trans. Joan Pinkham; New York: Monthly Review Press, 1972, 2000); Edward W. Said, *Orientalism* (New York: Vintage, 1979); Gayatri Spivak, "Can the Subaltern Speak?," in Cary Nelson and Larry Grossberg,

eds., *Marxism and the Interpretation of Culture* (Chicago: University of Illinois Press, 1988), 271–313; Chandra Talpade Mohanty, "Under Western Eyes: Feminist Scholarship and Colonial Discourses," *Feminist Review* 30 (Autumn 1988): 60–88; Homi K. Bhabha, *The Location of Culture* (London: Routledge, 1994).

3. Among his many publications are: R. S. Sugirtharajah, *The Bible and Asia: From the Pre-Christian Era to the Postcolonial Age* (Cambridge, MA: Harvard University Press, 2013); *Postcolonial Criticism and Biblical Interpretation* (Oxford/New York: Oxford University Press, 2002); *The Bible and the Third World: Precolonial, Colonial, and Postcolonial Encounters* (Cambridge/New York: Cambridge University Press, 2001); *Vernacular Hermeneutics* (ed.; Sheffield: Sheffield Academic Press, 1999); *Asian Biblical Hermeneutics and Postcolonialism: Contesting the Interpretations* (Maryknoll, NY: Orbis Books, 1998); *The Postcolonial Bible* (ed.; Sheffield: Sheffield Academic Press, 1998).

4. For other important postcolonial Bible critics, see, e.g., Fernando F. Segovia, *Decolonizing Biblical Studies: A View from the Margins* (Maryknoll, NY: Orbis Books, 2000); Fernando F. Segovia, *Interpreting Beyond Borders* (The Bible and Postcolonialism 3; Sheffield: Sheffield Academic Press, 2000); Stephen D. Moore and Fernando F. Segovia, eds., *Postcolonial Biblical Criticism: Interdisciplinary Intersections* (London: T&T Clark International, 2005).

5. Mohanty, "Under Western Eyes."

6. The following discussion focuses on the proposals of the succinct theories of three prominent feminist exegetes and theologians. Other postcolonial feminist researchers could have been included, such as Laura E. Donaldson, a retired English professor at Cornell University, whose postcolonial feminist work discusses the book of Ruth within her Native American context; see "The Sign of Orpah: Reading Ruth through Native Eyes," in *Ruth and Esther: A Feminist Companion to the Bible (Second Series)*, ed. Athalya Brenner (Sheffield: Sheffield Academic Press, 1999). Another prominent feminist Bible scholar is Elisabeth Schüssler Fiorenza; see, e.g., her book titled *The Power of the Word: Scripture and the Rhetoric of Empire* (Minneapolis: Fortress Press, 2007). For an examination of various postcolonial feminist hermeneutical approaches, see also Susanne Scholz, "Ruth, Jezebel, and Rahab as 'Other' Women: Integrating Postcolonial Perspectives," in *Introducing the Women's Hebrew Bible: Feminism, Gender Justice, and the Study of the Old Testament*, ed. Susanne Scholz (2nd rev. and exp. ed.; London/New York: Bloomsbury T&T Clark, 2017).

7. See especially Musa W. Dube, *Postcolonial Feminist Interpretation of the Bible* (St. Louis, KY: Chalice Press, 2000).

8. Ibid., 123. This and the following quotes are from this page.

9. For an analysis of the latter, see Susanne Scholz, "Essentializing 'Woman': Three Neoliberal Strategies in Christian Right's Interpretations on Women in the Bible," in *Introducing the Women's Hebrew Bible: Feminism, Gender Justice, and the Study of the Old Testament*, ed. Susanne Scholz (2nd rev. and exp. ed.; London/New York: Bloomsbury T&T Clark, 2017), 149–169.

10. Dube, *Postcolonial Feminist Interpretation of the Bible*, 121.

11. Malebogo Kgalemang, "A Postcolonial Feminist Reading of Mark 14–16," in *Postcolonial Perspectives on African Biblical Interpretations*, ed. Musa W. Dube, Andrew M. Mbuvi, and Dora R. Mbuwayesango (Atlanta: SBL, 2012), 442.

12. Kwok Pui-lan, "Making the Connections: Postcolonial Studies and Feminist Biblical Interpretation," in *Postcolonial Imagination and Feminist Theology*, ed. Kwok Pui-lan (Louisville, KY: Westminster John Knox, 2005), 77.

13. Ibid., 77–78.

14. Ibid., 78.
15. For an informative discussion of these terms, see Fernando F. Segovia, *Decolonizing Biblical Studies: A View from the Margins* (Maryknoll, NY: Orbis Books, 2000).
16. Kwok, "Making the Connections," 82.
17. Ibid., 83.
18. Ibid.
19. Ibid., 84.
20. Ibid., 99.
21. Judith E. McKinlay, "Jezebel and the Feminine Divine in Feminist Postcolonial Focus," in *Feminist Frameworks and the Bible: Power, Ambiguity, and Intersectionality*, ed. L. Juliana Claassens and Carolyn J. Sharp (Library of Hebrew Bible/Old Testament Studies 630; London: Bloomsbury T&T Clark, 2017), 59.
22. Ibid., 60.
23. Judith E. McKinlay, "A Matter of Difference," in *Reframing Her: Biblical Women in Postcolonial Focus*, ed. Judith E. McKinlay (Sheffield: Sheffield Phoenix Press, 2004), 16–17.
24. McKinlay, "Jezebel and the Feminine Divine," 60.
25. Ibid., 61.
26. Ibid.
27. Ibid.
28. For an expanded exploration of McKinlay's journey from historical criticism to a postcolonial feminist hermeneutics, see her "First Step: Moving Off with Wisdom," in *Reframing Her: Biblical Women in Postcolonial Focus*, ed. Judith E. McKinlay (Sheffield: Sheffield Phoenix Press, 2004), 1–15.
29. McKinlay, "Jezebel and the Feminine Divine," 64.
30. Ibid., 65.
31. Ibid., 66.
32. Ibid., 67.
33. Ibid, 70.
34. Ibid., 71.
35. Ibid., 72.
36. Ibid.
37. Jeremy Punt, "Dealing with Empire and Negotiating Hegemony: Developments in Postcolonial Feminist Hebrew Bible Criticism," in *Feminist Interpretation of the Hebrew Bible in Retrospect: Volume III: Methods*, ed. Susanne Scholz (Recent Research in Biblical Studies 9; Sheffield: Sheffield Phoenix Press, 2016), 278–303, esp. 283–295.
38. Ibid., 294.
39. Susanne Scholz, "Ruth, Jezebel, and Rahab as 'Other' Women: Integrating Postcolonial Perspectives," in *Introducing the Women's Hebrew Bible: Feminism, Gender Justice, and the Study of the Old Testament*, ed. Susanne Scholz (London: Bloomsbury T&T Clark, 2017), esp. 114–125.
40. For scholarly publications on biblical books, see, e.g., Jin Young Choi, *Postcolonial Discipleship of Embodiment: An Asian and Asian American Feminist Reading of the Gospel of Mark* (New York: Palgrave Macmillan, 2015); Michele A. Connolly, *Disorderly Women and the Order of God: An Australian Feminist Reading of the Gospel of Mark* (London/New York: Bloomsbury T&T Clark, 2018); Jean Kyoung Kim, *Woman and Nation: An Intercontextual Reading of the Gospel of John from a Postcolonial Feminist Perspective* (Boston: Brill Academic Publishers, 2004); Christl M. Maier and Carolyn

Sharp, eds., *Prophecy and Power: Jeremiah in Feminist and Postcolonial Perspective* (The Library of Hebrew Bible/Old Testament Studies 577; London: T&T Clark, 2015); Dora R. Mbuwayesango, "Canaanite Women and Israelite Women in Deuteronomy: The Intersection of Sexism and Imperialism," in *Postcolonial Interventions: Essays in Honor of R. S. Sugirtharajah*, ed. Tat-Siong Benny Liew (Sheffield: Sheffield Phoenix Press, 2009), 45–57; Stephen D. Moore, *Untold Tales from the Book of Revelation: Sex and Gender, Empire and Ecology* (Atlanta: SBL Press, 2014); Itumeleng J. Mosala, "The Implications of the Text of Esther for African Women's Struggle for Liberation in South Africa," in *The Postcolonial Biblical Reader*, ed. R. S. Sugirtharajah (Oxford/Malden, MA/Carlton, Victoria, Australia: Blackwell, 2006), 134–141.

41. For scholarly publications on biblical chapters, see, e.g., Ulrike Auga and Bertram J. Schirr, "Do Not Conform to the Patterns of This World! A Postcolonial Investigation of Performativity, Metamorphoses and Bodily Materiality in Romans 12," *Feminist Theology* 23, no. 1 (September 2014): 37–54; Lynne St. Clair Darden, "A Womanist-Postcolonial Reading of the Samaritan Woman at the Well and Mary Magdalene at the Tomb," in *I Found God in Me: A Womanist Biblical Hermeneutics Reader*, ed. Mitzi J. Smith (Eugene, OR: Cascade Books, 2015), 183–202; Malebogo Kgalemang, "A Postcolonial Feminist Reading of Mark 14–16," in *Postcolonial Perspectives in African Biblical Interpretations*, ed. Musa W. Dube, Andrew M. Mbuvi, Dora R. Mbuwayesango (Atlanta: SBL, 2013), 441–464; Seong Hee Kim, "Our (Neither) Mother and (Nor) Father in Heaven: A Postcolonial Reading of the Lord's Prayer," in *Korean Feminists in Conversation with the Bible, Church and Society*, ed. Kyung Sook Lee and Kyung Mi Park (The Bible in the Modern World 24; Sheffield: Sheffield Phoenix Press, 2011), 66–80; Surekha Nelavala, "God as 'the King' and His Act of Reconciliation: Hope! Despair! A Postcolonial Dalit Feminist Re-interpretation of 'The Vineyard and the Laborers,'" *Currents in Theology and Mission* 43, no. 3 (July 2016): 8–11; Makhosazana Nzimande, "Reconfiguring Jezebel: A Postcolonial *imbokodo* Reading of the Story of Naboth's Vineyard (1 Kings 21:1–16)," in *African and European Readers of the Bible in Dialogue: In Quest of a Shared Meaning*, ed. Hans de Wit and Gerald O. West (Leiden: Boston: Brill, 2008), 223–258; Jeremy Punt, "Power and Liminality, Sex and Gender, and Gal. 3:28: A Postcolonial, Queer Reading of an Influential Text," *Neotestamentica* 44, no. 1 (2010): 140–166; Carolyn J. Sharp, "'Are You for Us, or for Our Adversaries?' A Feminist and Postcolonial Interrogation of Joshua 2–12 for the Contemporary Church," *Interpretation: A Journal of Bible and Theology* 66, no. 2 (2012): 141–152; Jeffrey L. Staley, "Changing Woman: Toward a Postcolonial Postfeminist Interpretation of Acts 16.6–40," in *A Feminist Companion to the Acts of the Apostles*, ed. Amy-Jill Levine and Marianne Blickenstaff (London/New York: T&T Clark, 2004), 177–192; Caroline Vander Stichele and Todd C. Penner, eds., *Her Master's Tools? Feminist and Postcolonial Engagements of Historical-Critical Discourse* (Leiden/Boston: Brill, 2005); Alice Y. Yafeh-Deigh, "The Liberative Power of Silent Agency: A Postcolonial Afro-Feminist-Womanist Reading of Luke 10:38–42," in *Postcolonial Perspectives in African Biblical Interpretations*, ed. Musa W. Dube, Andrew M. Mbuvi, and Dora R. Mbuwayesango (Atlanta: SBL, 2013), 417–440.

42. For examples of scholarly publications on biblical themes and characters, see, e.g., Bradley L. Crowell, "Good Girl, Bad Girl: Foreign Women of the Deuteronomistic History in Postcolonial Perspective," *Biblical Interpretation* 21, no. 3 (2013): 1–18; Steed V. Davidson, "Gazing (at) Native Women: Rahab and Jael in Imperializing and Postcolonial Discourses," in *Postcolonialism and the Hebrew Bible: The Next Step*, ed. Roland Boer (Atlanta: Society of

Biblical Literature, 2013), 69–92; Laura E. Donaldson, "The Sign of Orpah: Reading Ruth Through Native Eyes," in *The Postcolonial Biblical Reader*, ed. R. S. Sugirtharajah (Oxford/Malden, MA: Carlton, Victoria, Australia: Sheffield/Blackwell Sheffield Academic Press, 2006), 159–170; Musa W. Dube, "Rahab Says Hello to Judith: A Decolonizing Feminist Reading," in *The Postcolonial Biblical Reader*, ed. R. S. Sugirtharajah (Oxford/Malden, MA/Carlton, Victoria, Australia/Maryknoll, NY: Blackwell/Orbis Books, 2005), 142–158; Esther Fuchs, "Jephthah's Daugher: A Feminist Postcolonial Approach," in *Feminist Theory and the Bible: Interrogating the Sources*, ed. Esther Fuchs (Lanham, MD: Lexington Books, 2016), 71–94; Wilda C. M. Gafney, "A Prophet-Terrorist(a) and an Imperial Sympathizer: An Empire-Critical, Postcolonial Reading of the Noʻadyah/Nechemyah Conflict," *Black Theology* 9, no. 2 (August 2011): 161–176; Musa W. Dube, "Boundaries and Bridges: Journeys of a Postcolonial Feminist in Biblical Studies," *Journal of the European Society of Women in Theological Research* 22 (2014): 139–156; L. Javachitra, "A Postcolonial Feminist Biblical Interpretation: Mary Magdalene and Canonization." *Bangalore Theological Forum* 38, no. 1 (June 2006): 93–107; Seong Hee Kim, Mark, *Women and Empire: A Korean Postcolonial Perspective* (Sheffield: Sheffield Phoenix Press, 2010); Jayachitra Lalitha, "Postcolonial Feminism, the Bible and the Native Indian Women," in *Evangelical Postcolonial Conversations: Global Awakenings in Theology and Praxis*, ed. Kay H. Smith, Jayachitra Lalitha, and L. Daniel Hawk (Downers Grove, IL: InterVarsity Press, 2014); Shiju Mathew, "Law, Land, and Gender in the Hebrew Bible: A Postcolonial Womanist Reading," *Asia Journal of Theology* 30, no. 2 (October 2016): 177–192; Judith E. McKinlay, *Troubling Women and Land: Reading Biblical Texts in Aotearoa New Zealand* (Sheffield: Sheffield Phoenix Press, 2014); Shanell T. Smith, *The Woman Babylon and the Marks of Empire: Reading Revelation with a Postcolonial Womanist Hermeneutics of Ambivalence* (Minneapolis: Fortress Press, 2014).

43. Joseph A. Marchal, "Imperial Intersections and Initial Inquiries: Toward a Feminist, Postcolonial Analysis of Philippians," *Journal of Feminist Study of Religion* 22, no. 2 (2006): 18. For his extensive discussion on the Pauline letters in general, see Joseph A. Marchal, *The Politics of Heaven: Women, Gender and Empire in the Study of Paul* (Minneapolis: Fortress Press, 2008).
44. Ibid., 18–19.
45. Ibid., 31.
46. Ibid., 32.
47. Ibid., 21.
48. Ibid., 23.
49. Ibid. 24.
50. Ibid.
51. Ibid.
52. Ibid., 25.
53. Ibid., 27.
54. Ibid., 29.
55. Ibid., 30.
56. Ibid.
57. Ibid.
58. Ibid., 32.
59. Marchal, *The Politics of Heaven*, 73.
60. Ibid., 74.

61. For a theoretical discussion on the relationship between queer and postcolonial studies, see, e.g., Jeremy Punt, "Queer Theory, Postcolonial Theory, and Biblical Interpretation: A Preliminary Exploration of Some Intersections," in *Queer Reading at the Boundaries of Biblical Scholarship*, ed. Teresa J. Hornsby and Ken Stone (Atlanta: SBL Press, 2011), 321–339. He explains on p. 329: "The strongest connection between queer and postcolonial theories is, I contend, in their concern about the contemporary politics of identity, regarding the categories and institutions, the knowledge(s) and the power plays by means of which social dynamics and people are structured and regulated."
62. Marcella María Althaus-Reid, "Searching for a Queer Sophia-Wisdom: The Post-Colonial Rahab," in *Patriarchs, Prophets and Other Villains*, ed. Lisa Isherwood (London/Oakville: Equinox, 2007), 132.
63. Ibid., 138.
64. Ibid., 132.
65. Ibid., 134.
66. Ibid.
67. Ibid., 137.
68. Ibid., 140.
69. Ibid., 139.
70. Ibid., 138.
71. Ibid., 139.
72. Madipoane Masenya (ngawan'a Mphahlele), "Stuck between the Waiting Room and the Reconfigured Levirate Entity: Reading Ruth in Marriage-Obsessed African Christian Contexts," in *Feminist Frameworks and the Bible: Power, Ambiguity, and Intersectionality*, ed. L. Juliana Claassens and Carolyn J. Sharp (London: Bloomsbury T&T Clark, 2017), 163–175.
73. Ibid., 164.
74. Ibid.
75. Ibid., 166.
76. Ibid.
77. Ibid., 167.
78. Ibid., 169.
79. Ibid., 171 (emphasis in original).
80. Ibid.
81. Ibid.
82. Ibid.
83. Ibid.
84. Kwok, *Postcolonial Imagination*, 7.
85. Ibid., 121.
86. Ibid., 113.
87. Ibid., 121.
88. See, e.g., Kwok, "The Bible, the Critic, and the Theologian," in *Discovering the Bible in the Non-Biblical World*, ed. Kwok Pui-lan (Maryknoll, NY: Orbis, 1995); "Searching for Wisdom: Sources for Postcolonial Feminist Theology," in *Postcolonial Imagination* ed. Kwok Pui-lan. Kwok also rehearses the interpretation history as it pertains to European and Western historical Jesus research in the nineteenth century, see her "Touching the Taboo: On the Sexuality of Jesus," in *Sexuality and the Sacred: Sources for Theological Reflection*, ed. Marvin Mahan Ellison and Kelly Brown Douglas (2nd ed.; Louisville, KY: Westminster John Knox, 2010), 119–134.

89. Musa W. Dube and R. S. Wafula, eds., *Postcoloniality, Translation, and the Bible in Africa* (Eugene, OR: Wipf and Stock, 2017).
90. Ibid., xxvii. For other recent publications in African biblical translation studies, see, e.g., Johanna Stiebert and Musa W. Dube, eds., *The Bible, Centres and Margins: Dialogues between Postcolonial African and British Biblical Scholars* (London: Bloomsbury T&T Clark, 2018). See also Gerald O. West, *The Stolen Bible: From Tool of Imperialism to African Icon* (Biblical Interpretation Series 144; Leiden/Boston: Brill Academic, 2016).
91. R. S. Sugirtharajah, *Jesus in Asia* (Cambridge, MA: Harvard University Press, 2018).
92. Ibid., 249.
93. See, e.g., R. S. Sugirtharajah, "A Postcolonial Exploration of Collusion and Construction in Biblical Interpretation," in *Postcolonial Reconfigurations: An Alternative Way of Reading the Bible and Doing Theology* (St. Louis, MO: Chalice Press, 2003), 91–116 (esp. 107).
94. Ibid., 113.
95. R. S. Sugirtharajah, *Asian Biblical Hermeneutics and Postcolonialism: Contesting the Interpretations* (Maryknoll, NY: Orbis, 1999).
96. These are two chapter titles in the book.
97. For a scholarly exploration of the colonial connections between European German-speaking Bible scholars and their preference for historical criticism, see Simon Wiesgickl, "Gefangen in uralten Phantasmen: Über das koloniale Erbe der deutschen alttestamentlischen Wissenschaft," in *Postkoloniale Theologien II: Perspektiven aus dem deutschsprachigen Raum*, ed. Andreas Nehring and Simon Wiesgickl (Stuttgart: Kohlhammer, 2018), 171–185; Simon Wiesgickl, *Das Alte Testament als deutsche Kolonie: Die Neuerfindung des Alten Testaments um 1800* (BWANT 214; Stuttgart: Kohlhammer, 2018).
98. Sugirtharajah, *Postcolonial Reconfigurations*, 122–123.
99. Ibid., 125.
100. Sugirtharajah, "A Postcolonial Exploration of Collusion," 112.
101. Mary Daly, "Be-Friending: The Lust to Share Happiness," in *The Mary Daly Reader*, ed. Jennifer Rycenga and Linda Barufaldi (New York: New York University Press, 2017), 297.
102. Beverly Wildung Harrison, *Making the Connections: Essays in Feminist Social Ethics*, ed. Carol S. Robb (Boston: Beacon Press, 1985), 154.
103. Christina Thürmer-Rohr, "Mittäterschaft von Frauen: Die Komplizenschaft mit der Unterdrückung," in *Handbuch Frauen- und Geschlechterforschung: Theorie, Methoden, Empire*, ed. Ruth Becker and Beate Koretndiek (3rd exp. and updated ed.; Geschlecht & Gesellschaft 35; Wiesbaden: VS Verlag für Sozialwissenschaften, 2010), 89. My translation of the quote into English: "Women are not only oppressed, abused, and entangled into a harmful system, but they actively engage with it, earn privileges in it, gain questionable recognition from it, and profit from their roles if they accept them. Thus women do not only share common experiences of pain, but they also directly or indirectly approve of the higher status of men and exonerate (male) perpetrators. This willingness to tolerate, support, und ignore is the triumph celebrated by the patriarchs."
104. *Stephen D. Moore* and Yvonne Sherwood, *The Invention of the Biblical Scholar: A Critical Manifesto* (Minneapolis: Fortress Press, 2011).
105. Kwok, Pui-lan, "Making the Connections," 78.
106. Ibid.
107. Ibid.

108. Ibid. In a different area of scholarly inquiry, Kwok offers some critical assessment of historical criticism; see Kwok Pui-lan, "Touching the Taboo: Sexuality of Jesus," in *Sexuality and the Sacred: Sources for Theological Reflection*, ed. Marvin M. Ellison and Kelly Brown Douglas (2nd ed.; Louisville, KY: Westminster John Knox, 2010), 119–134.
109. For an earnest beginning, see, e.g., Wiesgickl, *Das Alte Testament als deutsche Kolonie* See also Susanne Scholz, "Von der Dekolonisation deutschsprachiger Bibelexegese träumen," in *Von Peripherien und Zentren, Mächten und Gewalten: Jerusalemer Ansätze für eine postkoloniale Theologie*, ed. Ulrich Winkler, Christian Boerger and Joel Klenk (JThF 44. Münster: Aschendorff Verlag, 2021), 93–113.
110. Vincent L. Wimbush, "It's Scripturalization, Colleagues," *Journal of Africana Religions* 3, no. 2 (2015): 194.
111. Vincent L. Wimbush, "Signifying on the Fetish: Mapping a New Critical Orientation," in *The Future of the Biblical Past: Envisioning Biblical Studies on a Global Key*, ed. Roland Boer (Semeia Studies 66; Atlanta: Society of Biblical Literature, 2012), 338.
112. Wimbush, "It's Scripturalization," 194.
113. Ibid., 197.

Bibliography

Anderson, Cheryl B. *Ancient Laws and Contemporary Controversies*. Oxford/New York: Oxford University Press, 2009.

Dube Shomonah, and Musa W., Ed. *Other Ways of Reading: African Women and the Bible*. Atlanta, GA: SBL Press, 2001.

Fuchs, Esther. *Feminist Theory and the Bible: Interrogating the Sources*. Lanham, MD: Lexington Books, 2016.

Hawley, John C., Ed. *Postcolonial, Queer: Theoretical Intersections*. New York: SUNY Press, 2001.

Moore, Stephen D. *The Bible in Theory: Critical and Postcritical Essays*. Atlanta, GA: SBL Press, 2010.

Schroer, Silvia, and Sophia Bietenhardt, Eds. *Feminist Interpretation of the Bible and the Hermeneutics of Liberation*. London/New York: Sheffield Academic Press, 2003.

Schüssler Fiorenza, Elisabeth, Ed. *Feminist Biblical Studies in the Twentieth Century: Scholarship and Movement*. The Bible and Women: An Encyclopedia of Exegesis and Cultural History: The Contemporary Period, vol. 9.1. Atlanta, GA: Society of Biblical Literature, 2014.

Schüssler Fiorenza, Elisabeth. *The Power of the Word: Scripture and the Rhetoric of Empire*. Minneapolis, MN: Fortress, 2007.

Smith, Shanell T. *The Woman Babylon and the Marks of Empire: Reading Revelations with a Postcolonial Womanist Hermeneutics of Ambivalence*. Minneapolis, MN: Fortress, 2014.

Yee, Gale A. *The Hebrew Bible: Feminist and Intersectional Perspectives*. Minneapolis, MN: Fortress Press, 2018.

CHAPTER 27

POSTCOLONIAL LIBERATION

Decolonizing Biblical Studies in the South African Postcolony

GERALD O. WEST

INTRODUCTION

THERE has been some reflection on the intersections between liberation and postcolonial biblical hermeneutics, with R. S. Sugirtharajah even positing a hyphenated term to link the two in a form of hybrid discourse: "liberation-postcolonial."[1] This hybridization is helpful in recognizing sister relationships and a two-way movement of mutual engagement. Significantly, liberation and postcolonial biblical hermaneutics are rather late discourse descriptors within African biblical hermeneutics. The precursor to both, in significant respects, is African inculturation biblical hermeneutics.

In his studies that map African biblical scholarship—and it is important to note here that this "map" is drawn by Africans—Justin Ukpong locates the emergence of the discipline within inculturation through a comparative biblical interpretation in the 1930s.[2] In his confirmation of Ukpong's analysis, Eric Anum makes it clear how inculturation through comparative biblical hermeneutics is postcolonial in its orientation:

> The comparative method arose as a response to a colonial conception of African Traditional Religion and culture on the part of missionaries who believed that African cultures were satanic and pagan and needed to be totally abandoned if Christianity was to thrive in Africa. Thus, what African biblical scholars tried to do was to identify similarities between the biblical world and African religio-cultural practices and to use their scholarly and scientific tools to show the relationship between African Traditional Religion and Christianity.[3]

The emphasis here is not only on resonance but also on political import, as Knut Holter recognizes, arguing that inculturation through comparative biblical hermeneutics "legitimized African religion and culture vis-à-vis the Western tradition through comparative studies."[4] African biblical scholarship was properly postcolonial from its inception.[5]

While the discussion here hesitates to distinguish South African biblical hermeneutics from African biblical hermeneutics more generally, there are significant features of the South African postcolony that require a special type of postcolonial-liberation. Indeed, part of the argument in this essay is that grand narratives of liberation or postcolonialism should be replaced by more careful and specific analyses of particular postcolonies.

A Postcolony of a Special Type

The South African postcolony, among other African postcolonies, is distinctive. The variant form of colonialism is "colonialism of a special type," which includes, according to the South African Communist Party (SACP) in the early 1960s, the following elements: "a relatively extensive European settler occupation of the territory; the survival of indigenous African people and their societies as an oppressed but overwhelming majority; and the decisive factor—the imperialist implantation of a highly developed 'mature' capitalist system into this colonial setting."[6]

This essay argues that the three features identified by the SACP provide a useful set of distinctive features for hyphenating the hybrid term "postcolonial-liberation." First, the European settlers' occupation of the territory offers three related elements: land, race, and the Bible/Christianity. Land has been an enduring site of South African struggle since 1652.[7] From the moment the landing party of the Vereenigde Oostindische Compagnie (VOC) (Dutch East India Company) set foot on the Cape on the morning of April 7, 1652, the land became contested. Indeed, specific instructions had been given to these first settlers that stated, "[as] soon as you, and the people who have landed with you, are in such a state of defence, that you cannot be surprised by any one, you will proceed to select a proper place to be appropriated as Gardens, taking for this purpose all the best and richest ground, where whatever is sown or planted can thrive well, which Gardens (according to circumstances and situation) ought to be fenced round."[8]

Colonial land occupation continued over the centuries. For example, the Natives Land Act, 1913, represented

> not the final act of dispossession but, rather, the formalization of a dual system of property rights whereby the majority black population would be granted limited and conditional access to land, greatly inferior to those of their white counterparts, in urban areas, on white-owned farms and, above all, in the ethnically based "Native

Areas" (later Bantustans) that eventually accounted for [only] 13 per cent of the national territory.[9]

The lack of significant progress in land restitution since South African liberation in 1994 has recently come to a head,[10] with the ruling African National Congress (ANC) supporting a parliamentary motion by the Economic Freedom Fighters (EFF) for land "expropriation without compensation" on May 26, 2016.[11]

Race remains a site of struggle. The settlers in their two most substantial forms, the Dutch and the English, are white. The racial capitalism of the British, refined and legislated as "apartheid" by Afrikaners,[12] has indelibly inscribed South Africa as a racialized reality. And while liberation has brought South Africa significant change at the legal and political levels, and some change at the economic level, race remains a distinctive feature of the contemporary South African postcolony two decades after liberation.[13]

Missionary-driven colonial Christianity is a site of struggle as well, though not overtly distinguished by the SACP, but the conflicts are implicit in the European settler occupation of the southern part of the African continent. The early Dutch settlers, though driven by trade, were being shaped by an emerging Reformed Christian religion in which the Bible occupied a constrained but distinctive presence.[14] When the British colonialists took control of the Cape in 1806 all British possessions fell under the episcopal management of the bishop of London. After 1810 civil and colonial chaplains were appointed and paid by the Colonial Office in London "to minister to the spiritual needs of the British settlers at the Cape."[15] Initially, the Church of England in South Africa was concentrated on the colonial rim of the continent and focused almost entirely on white colonists. But as the demands of empire shifted, so too did the focus of the Anglican church. The British government used the opportunity presented by the depression in Europe and Britain after the Napoleonic Wars to bring British settlers to the Cape in 1820 with the aim "to be settled along the Eastern Frontier, to act as a buffer between the colony and the [indigenous] Xhosas."[16] As these settlers moved into the interior, so too did their Anglican clergymen.

Pursuing a related but quite different path, the Nonconformist British missionaries focused on the emerging chain of mission stations that led into the "interior" of South Africa, bearing a more overt Bible.[17] These missionaries believed that "the simple reading and study of the Bible alone will convert the world" and that the task of the missionary therefore was "to gain for it [the Bible] admission and attention, and then let it speak for itself."[18] But like their Church of England cousins, Nonconformist missionaries were part of the imperial project of taking hold, quite literally, of African territories and resources. Thus these missionaries prepared Africans for their entry into the Christian commonwealth, which included being inducted into God's economic order.[19]

These three elements—land, race, and Bible/Christianity—cohere in a well-known African anecdote: "When the white man came to our country he had the Bible and we had the land. The white man said to us, 'let us pray.' After the prayer, the white man had the land and we had the Bible."[20] The chapter will analyze this African anecdote more fully later in the chapter, but here the discussion continues with an overview of the remaining two distinctive features of the South African postcolony.

"[T]he survival of indigenous African people and their societies as an oppressed but overwhelming majority" (SACP 2012) offers a second distinctive feature, here referred to as the question of indigenous culture. While there has always been an expressed need for the recognition and recovery of indigenous African culture, politics and economics have dominated the South African liberation struggle and thus the postcolony as well. In the South African postcolony there is a "return" to culture,[21] and so to the more familiar territory of "postcolonialism."

Third, foregrounded by the SACP, is "the imperialist implantation of a highly developed 'mature' capitalist system into this colonial setting." (SACP 2012). This third distinctive feature of the South African postcolony is vital, for it intersects with each of the others in critical ways. This essay follows Sampie Terreblanche's characterization of the imperial-colonial economic systems that constitute South Africa—not in a linear manner but across the "entangled time" that is the African postcolony.[22] Terreblanche identifies a number of successive but entangled systemic periods in South African history, beginning with "the mercantilistic and feudal system institutionalised by Dutch colonialism during the second half of the 17th and most of the 18th century (1652–1795),"[23] followed by the system of British colonial and racial capitalism (1795–1890) and a related system of British colonial and mineral capitalism (1890–1948). Exploitative, coercive racist labor patterns were intensified when the Afrikaner-oriented National Party won the general election of 1948. Although the National Party "did not drastically transform the economic system of racial capitalism institutionalised by the English establishment, it used its political and ideological power to institutionalise a new version of it." "Since 1990," continues Terreblanche, "we have experienced a transition from the politico-economic system of white political domination and racial capitalism to a new system of democratic capitalism."[24]

These, then, are the three distinctive features that constitute postcolonial-liberation in the South African postcolony. Drawing on the discourse of the South African postcolony's contemporary time, this chapter will designate the form of postcolonial-liberation constituted by these three distinctive features as "decolonization," replacing the hyphenated hybrid term with a single, unified term.

Decolonization

The recent (2015–2018) #FeesMustFall movement, originating among South African university students, has reclaimed and reinvigorated decolonization, making a threefold demand for free tertiary education, quality tertiary education, and decolonized tertiary education. An eloquent and engaged articulation of this form of decolonization can be found in Leigh-Ann Naidoo's 2016 "Ruth First Lecture: On Revolution and the Rainbow Nation," delivered on August 17, 2016 at the University of the Witwatersrand in Johannesburg, South Africa. The title of her lecture, within the overall rubric of "Violence and Rage," was "Hallucinations."[25] Naidoo reiterated aspects of her argument in a lecture at the author's own university, the University of KwaZulu-Natal, on November 10, 2016 as part of the College of Humanities Transformation and Leadership Lecture Series, while our campuses were in the midst of a mass student mobilisation: "Decolonising the Curriculum by Centering the Black Intellectual."[26]

Naidoo locates her analysis within the postliberation, postapartheid South African postcolony, refusing to heed the constraining voices of "an older generation of anti-apartheid activists." She cautioned the student movement in saying

> "We are not in a time of revolution," as they shake their heads, knowingly. Or they say, with certainty, "you cannot justify such action because we are far from the conditions of revolution," "it's not the time for this or that because we are already in democracy," "we have already achieved liberation." Or perhaps most earnestly, they say "there is no need for revolutionary action because the laws and institutions of post-apartheid are sufficient."[27]

Naidoo insists that "*we are living in different times*. Or at least, our time is disjointed, out of sync, plagued by a generational fault line that scrambles historicity. The spectre of revolution, of radical change, is in young peoples' minds and politics, and it is almost nowhere in the politics of the anti-apartheid generation."[28] "What time *is* it?," she asks, acknowledging, "Yet to tell the time is a complex matter in this society. We are, to some degree, post-apartheid, but in many ways not at all. We are living in a democracy that is at the same time violently, pathologically unequal."[29] Riffing on notions of entangled time, Naidoo continues:

> I want to argue that the comrades I have worked with in the student movement are not so much mad as they are *time-travellers*. Or rather, that their particular, beautiful madness is to have recognised and exploited the ambivalence of our historical moment to push into the future. They have been working on the project of *historical dissonance*, of clarifying the untenable status quo of the present by forcing an awareness of a time when things are not this way. They have seen things many have yet to see. They have been experimenting with hallucinating a new time.[30]

She then explicates what she understands by "hallucinating a new time," offering a framework for what has been called "decolonization":

> The first task in this hallucination has been to kill the fallacies of the present: to disavow, no to annihilate, the fantasy of the rainbow, the non-racial, the Commission (from the Truth and Reconciliation, to Marikana, and Heher ...), even of liberation. The second task is to arrest the present. To stop it. To not allow it to continue to get away with itself for one more single moment. And when the status quo of the present is shut down the third task—and these have been the moments of greatest genius in the student movement—is to open the door into another time. It is difficult to work

on the future while the present continues apace. There has to be a measure of shut down in whatever form, for the future to be called.

(Naidoo, 2016)

The echoes from Naidoo's hallucinations resound forward and backward, invoking Frantz Fanon: "Decolonization, which sets out to change the order of the world, is, obviously, a program of complete disorder."[31] Echoing Fanon, Eve Tuck and K. Wayne Yang insist that decolonization is not a metaphor: "Decolonization brings about the repatriation of Indigenous land and life; it is not a metaphor for other things we want to do to improve our societies and schools."[32]

This essay resists the use of decolonization as a metaphor, arguing that it must be located within real embodied subjects in actual decolonization struggles. It is not accidental that the term "decolonization" has a verb form, "decolonize" or "decolonizing." This discussion takes a cue from the ways in which the term "postcolonialism" has been used within biblical studies, most often as a metaphor "for other things we want to do" within the discipline.[33] For while postcolonial biblical criticism has been minimally and cautiously imported into South African biblical scholarship,[34] decolonization work is more thoroughly "African." It is no accident that Musa W. Dube's seminal book, adapted from her U.S.-based doctoral dissertation, is titled *Postcolonial Feminist Interpretation of the Bible*,[35] while an article on her Africa-based work is titled "Reading for Decolonization (John 4:1—42)."[36] Indeed, Dube's work resonates with decolonization discourse and praxis, even when she uses the term "postcolonial," echoing the distinctive features identified in this essay and advocating for a biblical interpretation praxis that collaborates "with" real African subjects in actual projects of decolonization.

Method is central to African decolonization projects. Musa Dube devotes considerable space to "method in decolonizing literature,"[37] identifying a range of "anti-imperial literary strategies of decolonizing."[38] "The struggle to regain control over their own lands" is fundamental to decolonization, a struggle which in both Botswana and South Africa "continues well after the colonized have regained their so-called independence."[39] Political independence, important as this moment is, "deceptively suggested that total autonomy was won, but postcolonial subjects have painfully learned that political independence without cultural and economic control over their lands is a mockery of power."[40] "Struggle" is the central conceptual category of decolonization, with the struggle to regain control of African land as "the goal of the colonized."[41]

Rereading and rewriting are companion decolonization strategies, for, "given the centrality of cultural texts to imperialist projects, the struggle for liberation is not limited to military, economic, and political arenas. It necessarily requires and includes a cultural battle of reader-writers who attempt to arrest the violence of imperializing texts."[42] The African anecdote introduced above is reiterated by Dube: "When the white man came to our country he had the Bible and we had the land. The white man said to us, 'let us pray.' After the prayer, the white man had the land and we had the Bible." Dube says this anecdote "highlights that the Bible is one of the imperializing texts."[43] "While the colonizing approach employed the biblical text to displace the cultures of the natives, to suppress difference, and to supplant it by some uniformity, decolonizing rereadings counteract the oppressive dualisms and hierarchies of imperialism," locating the Bible "within and equal to" indigenous culture.[44] "The Bible no longer goes against and above the culture."[45] Significantly, alongside local oral and literary literature, no longer privileging biblical stories over local ones, the biblical text "has become the language of the colonized." "However," Dube continues, "they use it not in compliance with imperialism, but to articulate their distress as well as to counteract the atrocities of imperialism."[46] The "critical twinning of biblical and indigenous religious stories is," for the women of the African Independent Churches among whom and with whom Dube does her interpretive praxis, an "anti-imperial decolonizing method,"[47] enabling these African Christian women "to articulate the struggle for liberation and resistance."[48]

African indigenous rereadings generate a hybrid biblical and indigenous language that offers resources for retelling and rewriting the Bible.[49] Spirit-led (*Semoya*) "readers," including specifically African women, "yoke the wisdom of biblical and African religions in the service of life and diversity," using "song, drama, dance, symbols, and ritual."[50] Such retellings are also forms of rewriting as ordinary African Christians participate communally in "editing, revising, and adding to the Bible" in the quest for a more "inclusive Bible."[51] *Semoya* readers rewrite an inclusive Bible, using participatory and communal genres in the African struggle for survival, healing, resistance, and empowerment.[52] "The biblical story is an unfinished story: it invites its own continuation in history."[53] In sum, says Dube, decolonization "calls for a practice of reading, imagining, and retelling biblical stories in negotiation with other religious stories in the post-colonial era."[54]

Dube is clear that decolonization goes "beyond just providing a deconstructive analysis that exposes the imperialist construction embedded in narratives. A decolonizing reading's main objective is liberation."[55] A decolonizing reading uses the Bible to get the land back.[56]

Using the Bible to Get the Land Back

The SACP does not distinguish the Bible as a significant feature in its analysis of the South African postcolony. But as discussed here, the Bible is integral, succinctly captured in the African anecdote. This anecdote has been exegeted by generations of South African black theologians, with each offering a distinctive insight.

> When the white man came to our country he had the Bible and we had the land. The white man said to us, "let us pray." After the prayer, the white man had the land and we had the Bible.

The first phase of South African black theology, represented by theologians like Desmond Tutu and Allan Boesak, used this anecdote to make the point that, despite its ambiguous lineage as a missionary-colonial brought book, the Bible had become African. Desmond Tutu has told this anecdote regularly.[57] On some of these occasions he has added, "And we got the better deal!" This humorous commentary on the anecdote indicates the hermeneutic of trust characteristic of the first phase of South African black theology during the 1970–1980s. The Bible is in substantive respects "the Word of God,"[58] and as such in much of African theology the Bible is considered to be a primary source of black theology.[59] The Bible belongs to black theology in the sense that doing theology without it is inconceivable, since the Bible is perceived to be primarily on the side of the black struggle for liberation and life and against settler colonial apartheid.[60]

While there is definitely an awareness within this first phase of South African black theology that there are different, even contending, theologies in the Bible, this is understood as evidence of the thoroughly contextual nature of the Bible. But because the pervasive theological trajectory is perceived to be one of liberation, the plurality of theologies in the Bible is assumed to be unproblematic. Those who use the Bible against black South Africans are therefore misinterpreting the Bible, because the Bible is substantively on the side of black theology's liberatory project.[61]

The second phase of South African black theology, represented by theologians like Takatso Mofokeng and biblical scholars like Itumeleng Mosala in the late 1980s, adopted and advocated a hermeneutics of struggle. The notion of "struggle" was a key analytical concept across South African liberation theologies,[62] but it was the central category for South African black theology in its second phase.[63] Rather than celebrating the anecdotal transaction (Bible-for-land), this phase of South African black theology laments the transaction and would prefer to "be rid of the obnoxious Bible."[64] However, Mofokeng acknowledges, reluctantly, that there is a long history within the church of "the weakest, neglected, poor and marginalised people" recognizing "the usefulness of the Bible as a book with a message of survival, resistance and hope," giving them "a reason for hoping for a different future and believing in their right to a decent human existence."[65] What this historical legacy offers us, continues Mofokeng, is a historical praxis that is "a new kind of struggle, . . . namely, the struggle for the Bible or, to be more precise, the struggle for control of the Bible."[66] While Mofokeng identifies this "new kind of struggle," Mosala offers the tools with which to analyze how the final form of the Bible has already come under the control of dominant and dominating ideological sectors and how to identify and recover the voices of marginalized sectors within the biblical past.[67] For Mosala, the "the texts of the Bible are sites of struggle,"[68] intrinsically and inherently. "The insistence on the Bible as the Word of God must be seen for what it is," argues Mosala, "an ideological manoeuver whereby ruling class interests evident in the Bible are converted into a faith that transcends social, political, racial, sexual, and economic divisions. In this way the Bible becomes an ahistorical, interclassist document."[69] So Mosala's contention is that most of the Bible "offers no certain starting point for a theology of liberation within itself."[70]

At the methodological level, Mosala's biblical hermeneutics offered insight and access into the ideological redactional history of the Bible. His historical materialist analysis "laid bare" "the class character and ideological commitments of [a particular redactional layer of] the text,"[71] enabling contemporary working-class black South Africans to recognize four things. First, Mosala's method offered a way of analyzing both biblical text and contemporary sociohistorical context. The method was useful for each of these terrains of struggle, whether ancient sites of struggle that produced the biblical texts or contemporary sites of struggle that generated a black working class.[72] Second, Mosala's method offered black working-class Christians a way of connecting "kin struggles,"[73] identifying and foregrounding the economic and ideological connections between biblical text and contemporary context.[74] Third, Mosala's method, by identifying the ideological and economic agenda of a particular (layer of) text, enabled black working-class Christians to recognize when they must interpret with the ideo-economic grain or against the ideo-economic grain of a particular (layer of) text.[75] And fourth, Mosala's method is meant to demonstrate that ideo-economic sectoral co-optation does take place, for it is evident in the redactional history of the Bible's formation, with dominant ideological and economic forces co-opting and displacing the ideological and economic perspective and practices of marginalized sectors. Indeed, insists Mosala, North American black theology, South African black theology, and South African contextual theology have succumbed to precisely this danger—the danger of collaborating with the Bible's dominant ruling-class ideologies. In so doing they engage in a "useless sparring with the ghost of the oppressor, whom . . . [they] have already embraced in the oppressor's most dangerous form, the [final] ideological form of the [biblical] text."[76]

Having lamented the Bible-for-land transaction reflected in the anecdote, but acknowledging the Bible's African entanglement, Mosala recites the anecdote with the following addendum: "The task now facing a black theology of liberation is to enable black people to use the Bible to get the land back and to get the land back without losing the Bible."[77] But, insists Mosala, "in order for this to happen, black theology must employ the progressive aspects of black history and culture to liberate the Bible so that the Bible may liberate black people. That is the hermeneutical dialectic."[78]

Mosala does not envisage a Bible-less African Christianity. He is clear that interpreting the Bible is part of the African struggle for land, and so the task of interpretation must be undertaken using a hermeneutic of suspicion with respect to the various compositional "source" texts that constitute the Bible. The final canonical form of the Bible is not ideologically innocent, and using it uncritically will not enable Africans to reappropriate their land, which is why Mosala's emphasis is on interpretive method. Without an appropriate method, African Christianities in general and black theology in particular are susceptible to the ideology of the final form of the biblical text and so to the ruling-class ideologies that control and co-opt "other" ideologies.

For Mosala there is a need for both an analogy of struggle (discerning potentially useful resonances between South African sites of struggle and sites of struggle within and behind the biblical text) and an analogy of method (deploying related critical interpretive tools in order to analyze both South African sites of struggle and sites of struggle in contexts of the Bible's production). While the first phase of black theology focuses on the former, the second phase of black theology, Mosala insists, must focus on both, emphasizing the latter, for it is the latter that provides the necessary structural-systemic capacity to the former.[79]

The third phase of South African black theology, represented by the work of theologians like Tinyiko Maluleke, reorients this anecdote by prompting a focus on the verbs rather than the nouns. Maluleke agrees with phase two practitioners that this anecdote "captures something of the problem as diagnosed by Black Theology. It is the paradox of a severely subjugated people who have nevertheless taken to the religion of their oppressors rather enthusiastically. Even the process of decolonization—where and when it has occurred—has not reduced the apparent Black adherence to the Christian religion."[80] "The Bible" in the anecdote is "a symbol of the entire package" of missionary-colonial Christianity, and "built into the anecdote is the suspicion that there might be a logical and coherent connection between Black poverty (material and spiritual) and Black adherence to Christianity. Equally taken for granted here is the 'foreignness' of Christianity to Black people."[81] So, for Maluleke, the key question is what it means for Africans "to have" the Bible.

Maluleke recognises that "the suspicion of possible connections between Black adherence to the Christian religion and Black 'poverty' not only in South Africa but also on the continent is not the monopoly of Black Theology." Indeed, he goes on to state that "almost all African Christian theologies have expressed the same suspicion—albeit in different ways."[82] However, what is distinctive about South African black theology, in its second and third phases, is its ideological and analytical capacity to probe the connections between black Africans and the Bible/Christianity.

The third phase of South African black theology, from the 1990s to the early 2000s, reconsiders the place of African culture and/or religion as a way of asking whether black culture might "re-place" Christianity and the Bible as the primary locus of black theology. So a distinctive feature of the third phase of black theology is the return of culture and the related recognition of African Traditional Religions (ATRs) and African Independent/Instituted/Initiated Churches (AICs) as "significant" interlocutors for black theology.[83] While race-class (as understood within the contours of apartheid racial capitalism) remains the central tenet of each of the phases of black theology, and while gender emerges within the first phase and becomes more foregrounded in the second phase, culture and religion are reevaluated in phase three. Whereas the first phase of black theology "ventured somewhat into cultural . . . issues," argues Maluleke, phase two "became more and more concerned with the struggle of black people against racist, political and economic oppression."[84] However, even within phase two, "At crucial moments connections with African culture would be made—provided that culture was understood as a site of struggle rather than a fixed set of rules and behaviours."[85] Culture remains problematized in phase three, but the envisaged rapprochement with ATRs and AICs that characterizes phase three foregrounds culture in a form not found in phase two. Because of the class dimension of black theology's analysis of race, both ATRs and AICs offer black theology in its third phase "another chance of demonstrating solidarity with the poor," for ATR is the religion of the poor and AICs are the churches of the Christian poor.[86]

The methodological consequence of this commitment to the black poor, Maluleke points out, is that by making culture and/or religion a site of struggle, black theology relativizes Christianity (and the Bible). For if, as Mosala has argued,[87] African culture and/or religion can be a primary site of a hermeneutics of struggle, supplemented only with a political class-based hermeneutics, then Christianity is not a necessary component in a black theology of liberation.[88] A key question for Maluleke, echoing Mosala, is whether black and African theologies have made "the necessary epistemological break from orthodox or classical Christian theology" required to effect the kind of critical and creative reappropriation of ATR and AICs envisaged by the third phase of black theology.[89] Put differently:

> What needs to be re-examined now . . . is the extent to which the alleged popularity of Christianity assumed in South African black theology is indeed an accurate assessment of the religious state of black people. If it were to be shown that ATRs are as popular as Christianity among black South Africans then in not having given much concerted attention to them, Black theology might have overlooked an important resource.[90]

Clearly, one of the important features of phase three black theology is the recognition, recovery, and revival of its links with ATRs and AICs, and in so doing renewing a dialogue with African theology in its many and various forms. Indeed, Maluleke could be said to be revisiting and questioning Mofokeng's assertion that "African traditional religions are too far behind most blacks."[91] Is this actually the case, asks Maluleke? Gabriel Setiloane asks the question even more starkly: "Why do we continue to seek to convert to Christianity the devotees of African traditional religion?"[92] "This," says Maluleke, "is a crucial question for all African theologies [including South African black theology] as we move into the twenty-first century."[93]

Significantly, while Maluleke can envisage forms of African liberation theology that do not draw on orthodox Christian categories, he accepts that the Bible remains an integral part of such theology. Maluleke, like Mofokeng, doubts whether "pragmatic and moral arguments can be constructed in a manner that will speak to masses without having to deal with the Bible in the process of such constructions." And as long as it is a resource, it must be confronted, agrees Maluleke with Mosala, "precisely at a hermeneutical level."[94] However, unlike Mosala, who characterizes the biblical hermeneutics of AICs as "the hermeneutics of mystification,"[95] Maluleke is more nuanced in his analysis, arguing that "on the whole, and in practice, [ordinary] African Christians are far more innovative and subversive in their appropriation of the Bible than they appear."[96] While they "may mouth the Bible-is-equal-to-the-Word-of-God formula, they are actually creatively pragmatic and selective in their use of the Bible so that the Bible may enhance rather than frustrate their life struggles."[97] The task before phase three black theology in Maluleke's analysis, then, is "not only to develop creative Biblical hermeneutic methods, but also to observe and analyse the manner in which African Christians 'read' and view the Bible,"[98] to interrogate what it means "to have" the Bible.

The most recent work on South African black theology, a fourth phase, uses the African cultural-religious (re)turn of phase three as a way of returning to and recasting the question of class. Heeding Maluleke's reminder that the phases of black theology, though historically ordered, are not discrete but overlap, we can consider the return of class as a marker of a fourth phase. For the first (1970–1980s) and second (late 1980s) phases of black theology, the focus was on the political-economic dimensions of black reality rather than the cultural-religious. This was a distinctive feature of South African black theology, a demarcation from other African theologies and Christianities. Culture and religion were significant but only if infused with political and economic analysis, especially in the South African context where apartheid was constructed on particular (white and Western) notions of culture (and religion).[99] The third phase of black theology (1990s) drew on these earlier understandings but recognized that significant numbers of the black poor had forged their own hybrid forms of various combinations of cultural, political, and economic elements in the many diverse AICs.[100] It was imperative, therefore, that black theology theorize and theologize this "cultural-religious" reality. And because the third phase of black theology emerged in the mid-1990s, along with political liberation (though not economic liberation), there was space for a return to and a reassessment of the cultural-religious domain that had not been there before.

While most postcolonial biblical criticism avoids the question of class, this is not the case with the work of Makhosazana Nzimande, who stands in the tradition of South African black theology, supplementing its resources with the work of African women's biblical hermeneutics and postcolonial biblical hermeneutics. She inaugurates a fourth phase in South African black theology (2000s).[101] Her *imbokodo* (grinding stone)[102] hermeneutics draws deeply on Mosala's work, seeking to locate the struggles of "the oppressed and exploited in the text," and taking up his challenge of what it means to use the Bible to get the land back.[103] She also draws on the South African postcolonial feminist work of Musa Dube, for whom the land is a central question,[104] and who, like Mosala, recognizes the importance of the economic domain.[105]

The imperial powers and the apartheid beneficiaries must be held to account for the land they seized and the proceeds of this plunder, insists Nzimande. But, she continues, "for black African women in post-apartheid South Africa and in related postcolonial contexts where patriarchy reigns supreme, land restitution would not be beneficial unless there is a radical change in the patriarchal family structures."[106] In other words, "neotribal" patriarchal family structures are part of the problem.

Nzimande's contribution to the post-apartheid land restitution project is to bring her South African context into dialogue with kindred struggles "over stolen lands" in the biblical text.[107] Her first interpretive move follows Mosala, using historical-critical resources to historically locate the biblical text (1 Kings 21:1–16) historically. But her next move is not a materialist sociological analysis of this period; instead, she draws on feminist literary analysis in order to provide a detailed characterization of the leading female character (Queen Jezebel). The sociological contribution comes in her next move, where she locates the text within its imperial setting (Phoenician imperialism), giving attention to both the literary imperial setting and the sociohistorical imperial setting. Her final interpretive move is to delineate the class relations within this imperial context (including Jezebel as part of a royal household).[108]

She then brings this text and her set of (*imbokodo*) interpretive resources into dialogue with the South African context, recovering the identity and roles of African queen mothers in their governance of African land. The recovery of African culture and/as religion, as envisaged by the third phase of black theology, is apparent. But, she does not conclude her work with this indigenous cultural-religion recovery. She pushes the boundaries of feminist postcolonial criticism to include matters of class, recovering the "voices" of "those at the receiving end of the Queens' and Queen Mothers' policies."[109] She uses her *imbokodo* hermeneutics "to read with sensitivity towards the marginalised and dispossessed," recognizing that "the beneficiaries" of such indigenous elites, including the queens and queen mothers, "are themselves and their sons, rather than the general grassroots populace they are expected to represent by virtue of their royal privileges."[110]

"While a postcolonial *Imbokodo* hermeneutics acknowledges black female presence and activity [including female governance of African geographical territories] in African historiography, it also notes with regret the pervasive injustice that reigned supreme in African political systems of governance."[111] Remembering these powerful African women is a postcolonial imperative, insists Nzimande; but so is de-ideologizing, for in so doing we also remember those women from the lower classes these elite women had power over.[112]

Makhosazana Nzimande laments the "absence of justice" in the story of Naboth's vineyard.[113] Following Nzimande, but taking as his starting point the Natives' Land Act of 1913 and the "slow progress on land reform" in the South African postcolony, Ndikho Mtshiselwa returns to this biblical text to see if he can find evidence of land redress that might speak to the South African context.[114] Working in the #FeesMustFall "decolonization" era, Mtshiselwa's work demonstrates the commitment on the part of African biblical scholars "to use the Bible to get the land back and to get the land back without losing the Bible."[115]

Mtshiselwa uses a sociohistorical analysis of 1 Kings 21:1–29 to ascertain whether there was any socioeconomic redress and/or land expropriation following the injustice done to Naboth. He reflects on whether Jehu's "elimination of the Omri dynasty (with its relations with the Phoenician) in 2 Kgs 10:1–17 contains an element of justice," but concludes, using South African deolonization logic, that "because the land that was forcefully acquired by the Omri dynasty was not returned to the original owners or farmers, it is doubtful that justice was obtained."[116] Coming to similar conclusions to Nzimande, Mtshiselwa argues that "after killing Ahab and his family Jehu probably did not redistribute the repossessed fertile land to Naboth's family but rather claimed it and subsequently passed it to his sons."[117] Unfortunately, he finds, a sociohistorical analysis demonstrates that expropriated land "was not returned to the original owners but retained by those in power," benefiting political elites rather than their own poor.[118] While "the portrayal of socio-economic redress and the restoration of seized land in Jehu's story could empower a marginalised

South African reader who is by and large poor and landless," the marginalized South African reader must still contend with "the black political élites and the white farmers who continue to reap the agricultural wealth of the country."[119]

A substantive part of the problem of land redistribution in the South African postcolony, argues Mtshiselwa, is based on forms of neoliberal, globalized, neocolonial capitalism: "The influential neo-liberal economic globalisation, with its emphasis on privatisation, competitive production, and economic growth, does not appear to be helpful in the pursuit of socio-economic redress in particular of land redistribution."[120] The "compromise," which the postapartheid South African state has made with globalized capitalism,[121] mitigates against contemporary decolonial land redistribution.

The presence of forms of neoliberal globalized neocolonial capitalism lurks over African postcolonies, a point that resonates with the decolonizing work of Musa Dube. This "third stage of colonialism"[122] disrupts and destabilises African postcolonial nation-states, as transnational and multinational companies use "wealth stolen from the colonised countries"[123] to construct "new" forms of colonialism, utilizig the very economies of extraction they established during colonization, co-opting and corrupting African elites in forms of what the South African postcolony refers to as "state capture."[124]

THE RETURN OF RACE AND ETHNICITY

An emphasis on economic analysis is common in South African decolonization biblical hermeneutics. But, as indicated, race, ethnicity, and culture remain significant features of the South African postcolony. Shortly after political liberation, Tinyiko Maluleke, reflecting on the third phase of South African black theology, reminded South Africans that, in a context "where race is no longer supposed to matter," racism often takes on different guises and becomes "more 'sophisticated.'"[125] Recognizing this reality of racism after apartheid, Hulisani Ramanstwana locates his recent work on decolonizing biblical hermeneutics within a contested notion of biblical studies' use of "social location":

> Social location as a hermeneutical device in our African context cannot be divorced from the dynamics of colonialism (the imperial relationship of domination and exploitation between "European-Western-White" and the Other, "African-Native-Black") and coloniality (a continuity of the colonial form of domination, exploitation, and racialisation by the dominant racial groups in the postcolonial era).[126]

"The demise of the colonial-apartheid regime in South Africa did not result in a radical shift in the production of knowledge," Ramanstwana argues, pointing to the bulk of work being done within South African biblical studies.

> The continuance of the status quo basically implies the continuity of White dominance in the production of knowledge in the field of biblical studies. It is wishful

thinking to assume that Whites will, out of their own good, voluntarily give up their privileged position. The demise of colonialism and apartheid was not voluntary; it was because of internal and external pressure that the apartheid regime entered into negotiations for a new constitutional order in South Africa. Just as the Land Reform Programme, which encouraged White landowners to voluntarily sell their land, has produced little result, we cannot expect much to change on a voluntary basis, even in the field of biblical studies. The Black Other is still underrepresented in the field of biblical studies. Biblical studies in South Africa, as a social location, is still predominantly producing "White" knowledge.[127]

Decolonizing biblical studies in the South African postcolony requires two related shifts. As Ramanstwana argues, "The South African context as a social location, given the history of colonialism and apartheid, requires us to scrutinise the body-politics of knowledge, on the one hand, and the epistemological location of the African reader, on the other."[128] With respect to body-politics, Ramanstwana makes it clear that decolonization requires

> subaltern [South African] Whites to accept that the colonial system has thrown them onto the underside of the colonial matrix of power and to understand that their liberation has to become intertwined with that of the Blacks. This position would require White [South] Africans to give up their continuing attempts to maintain their privileged position and to let their struggle become one with the Black struggle. For as long as the White [South] Africans do not embrace the Black struggle and let it envelop them, they remain linked to the colonial system of power, which will continue to work through them to maintain dominance.[129]

In my own work, reflecting on my White South Africanness, I have made a similar argument, insisting that becoming "one with the Black struggle"—doing biblical studies within a black frame—requires the betrayal of our white ancestors and the systems that sustain our privilege. I envisage "betrayal" in three movements. The initial movement is one in which we not only declare and own our social location but also demonstrate to black others how our social location works—what the "logic," mechanisms, or conceptual systems of our identity construction are and how they are materially embedded. This initial movement is followed then by a second in which, in collaboration, we allow black others to engage with and to partially reconstitute the logic of our social locations. The third movement includes a collaborative forging of strategic alliances and coalitions across our partially reconstituted social locations and their respective resources around the particular contextual issues that confront us.[130] For white (South) Africans, this threefold movement requires "a *lifetime* of unrelenting struggle against the ideology of white superiority and the materiality of white control."[131]

My use of the concept of being "partially constituted by work with others," derived from feminist poststructuralist notions of identity,[132] goes some of the way toward Ramanstwana's second shift—the shift to an African epistemology. Once again we note an articulation between the global and the local.

> Given the history of colonisation and the continuity of the structures of coloniality in Africa as a social location, African biblical scholars should have a two-fold commitment: they need to be committed to understanding the workings of the current global system in order to avoid perpetuating the structures of coloniality in, and from our social location, and they need to be committed to producing alternative knowledge on the basis of our own African knowledge systems and experiences.[133]

Ramanstwana is clear that a return to African epistemology is not a romantic "obsession" to "the long-gone, outmoded, precolonial past; rather, it is an epistemological reorientation in the present that refuses to abandon the rich heritage of the African ancestors and draws knowledge from the experiences of suffering from colonialism and coloniality."[134] Decolonization requires "relinking" "with our African ancestors through rethinking, remembering, and preserving the rich heritage left for us. Epistemic delinking from Europe without relinking with our own indigenous knowledge system is to remain trapped within the structures of coloniality."[135]

Relinking with "our" African ancestors does not, I would argue, preclude white (South) Africans from such an epistemic relocation, and it does not limit us to "engaging in White talk."[136] For some of us white (South) Africans, we are Africans, albeit "Africans of a special type," given the realities of the South African postcolony. Our most distant ancestors are African, if we would claim them, as are our most immediate ancestors if we would also claim them and allow them to partially reconstitute us.[137] More challenging is Ramanstwana's (re)turn to ethnicity,[138] for when he offers "an example of how a relinking with our African knowledge system can be applied in the reading of biblical texts,"[139] he turns to a Tshivenda proverb, deliberately "anchoring" "the Bible in indigenous discourse."[140]

The recognition that African proverbial wisdom is a significant site of indigenous knowledge has a long history in African biblical scholarship and theology.[141] But the work of Madipoane Masenya (ngwan'a Mphahlele) has added a feminist-liberation dimension to the inculturation/postcolonial orientation,[142] shifting the appropriation of African proverbial wisdom toward an overtly decolonial emphasis,[143] and in so doing has provided an emerging decolonial biblical hermeneutics. A specific contribution of Masenya has been the particularity of African ethnic identity and indigenous knowledge. Indigenous knowledge for Masenya is Northern Sotho indigenous knowledge.[144] Similarly, for Ramanstwana, relinking to African knowledge systems is relinking to Tshivenda indigenous knowledge.

Ramanstwana uses a Tshivenda proverb in reading Genesis 47, a proverb that is "a critique of those in positions of power: "*Dza musanda dzi kumba thole* (literally, 'The chief's livestock draws a heifer,' i.e., attracts a poor family's heifer to mingle with, and thus become legally part of the herd); that is, those in power tend to thrive at the expense of the poor." This proverb reflects, he continues, "a critical stance towards those in power, especially when they deprive the poor of their basic necessities."[145] Though using a specific ethnic-cultural entry point, Ramanstwana locates his reading within South African "cattle culture" more generally. The proverb highlights, in general, "the value that the African people attached to the cattle or their livestock" and, specifically, how the "ownership of a heifer implied better prospects for the future and improvement in one's social status."[146] Ramanstwana's "liberationist" orientation, "choosing" "to read the text with the interest of the poor, suffering, and exploited," becomes clear in his choice of this particular proverb, "for ordinary people, a heifer, that is, a young female cow that had the potential to produce other cattle, was a valuable asset with which they were not willing to part. To lose a heifer simply because it mingled with the chief's livestock was to be disempowered economically, and this hurt ordinary people the most."[147]

Read from the perspective of African indigenous cattle culture, "the unwillingness of the Egyptians to give up their livestock comes as no surprise to the African mind,"[148] and it generates an ironic reading of Genesis 47:25. "The Egyptians' sarcastic denouncement of Joseph should be viewed as a critical stance against oppression,"[149] precisely because

> two contrasting ideas stand side by side in this instance: the Egyptians are saved (or given life), on the one hand, but they are turned into slaves, on the other. If Genesis 47:25 is read positively as an expression of positive sentiments by the Egyptians, then it would indeed function as an apologia defending Joseph's image. However, I would say that the statement in Genesis 47:25 is more effectively viewed as sarcasm. How could Egyptians be thankful for being rendered slaves in their own land through a foreigner in the Egyptian royal court? This while the Hebrews, the family members of the foreign elite, retained their livestock, were given the best part of the land, and were now also in charge of Pharaoh's livestock (Gen. 47:3–5). The statement in Genesis 47:25 is not one of appreciation; rather, the Egyptians were ridiculing Joseph for rendering them slaves. If Genesis 47:25 is viewed as sarcasm, it may just as well be rendered: *Thank you for nothing.*[150]

In a typical African tripolar biblical hermeneutical move,[151] Ramanstwana brings the biblical text (pole one) into dialogue with the South African context (pole two), using a decolonial ideological frame (pole three). The focus of his contextual engagement is the expropriation of land neighboring then South African President Jacob Zuma's homestead. "The pinnacle of the Nkandla saga is the injustice inflicted upon the four neighbouring households of Jacob Zuma's Nkandla homestead. They were forced to give up their ancestral lands in order to create security in comfort for President Zuma and his family."[152] The Tshivenda proverb, *Dza musanda dzikumba thole*, "calls for the denouncement of oppressive tendencies among those in power, irrespective of who that power might be."[153]

In another decolonial reading of Genesis 47 (and other related Hexateuchal texts), Ramanstwana focuses on interethnic tension within the Hexateuch, arguing that "the Joseph tribe, as part of asserting its authority and claim to power, excluded the tribe of Levi from its right to land through its demand for more than one allotment,"[154] displacing the Levites, and so marginalizaing them, for "to be a Levite was to belong to the damned of society."[155] "To be a Levite was to belong in the same class as the alien, the fatherless and the widow (Deut 26:12–13)—that is, those who are susceptible to exploitation and abuse. In decolonial terms, to be a Levite was to live in the zone of non-being."[156] What is clear in this decolonial reading is how Ramanstwana relentlessly chooses as his dialogue partners the landless, whoever they might be, granting an epistemological privilege to the landless of biblical texts as well as to the landless of the South African postcolony, including *Abahlali base Mjondolo*, the urban "shack-dwellers" movement among the many millions of landless black (South) Africans "in the townships where the black masses have to share the limited space by opening up rooms for rental, building back rooms or erecting shacks in the yard as a means of survival and a means of accommodation for the landless."[157] A decolonial dialogue becomes possible, linking dispossessed Levites and black South Africans dispossessed of their land:

> The Levites' exclusion from land allotment in the Hexateuch invokes an historical memory of the colonial dispossession of the indigenous people of their land. Landlessness, which is a characteristic of blackness in the South African context, cannot be divorced from colonialism and the colonial matrix of power which continue to shape our social-spatial structures.[158]

Ramanstwana's appropriation of indigenous ethnic knowledge is a critical appropriation. Like Makhosazana Nzimande, he interrogates what she refers as an "oppositional ethnicity," evident, she argues, within the story of Naboth's vineyard "whereby the reigning Queen [Jezebel] imposes her own Phoenician identity on the whole community while in the process of deliberately and harshly silencing any other identity prevalent."[159] Black South African women, she argues, "know firsthand the negative ramifications of ethnic superiority and prejudice in their own context under the British and Afrikaner apartheid brutality."[160] The use of the story of Naboth's vineyard, like the use of the story of Joseph, in the contemporary South African postcolony "prompts readers who are interested in decolonising the bible and those in solidarity with them to seek practical ways and means of protesting and dismantling contrastive ethnicity and identity constructions while promoting unitary and aggregative paradigms."[161]

Conclusion

In the South African context, the recent Rhodes-Must-Fall Campaign, Fees-Must-Fall Campaign, and calls for decolonization of the curricula in South Africa's universities all speak to an environment in which structures of colonialism continue to survive. Furthermore, the continuing landlessness of masses of people in the South African context also speaks to the continuing structures of colonialism.[162]

Decolonization is as old as the struggle against colonialism. Both liberation and postcolonial trajectories of this struggle offer significant resources to African postcolonies (and other postcolonies). The related emerging South African discourse of decolonization also offers resources to these postcolonies. The South

African postapartheid, postliberation, and postcolony demands forge decolonizing praxiological discourses that contribute to work in respective disciplinary perspectives, including biblical studies.

The Bible remains a site of struggle, in both Itumeleng Mosala's economic-liberation sense and R. S. Sugirtharajah's postcolonial sense.[163]

However, as Ramanstwana argues, a decolonial optics, "while it recognises the imperial sponsorship on the development of some of the biblical texts, does not necessarily regard the biblical text to be an irredeemably imperial-sponsored product or as monolithic. Though certain biblical texts were composed under the sponsorship of the imperial powers, it does not follow that the only voices that can be heard from the text are the assenting and the colluding voices. Therefore, a decolonial reading also seeks to uncover the voices of those who have been marginalized and the suppressed voices of resistance within the same Bible."[164]

African and South African biblical studies in uncovering and recovering these voices by decolonizing the Bible, redeploys them in the actual work of decolonizing land in South African postcolonies.

Notes

1. R. S. Sugirtharajah, "Afterword: The Future Imperfect," in *Voices from the Margin: Interpreting the Bible in the Third World*, ed. R. S. Sugirtharajah (Maryknoll: Orbis, 2006), 495.
2. Justin S. Ukpong, "Developments in Biblical Interpretation in Africa: Historical and Hermeneutical Directions," in *The Bible in Africa: Transactions, Trajectories and Trends*, ed. Gerald O. West and Musa Dube (Leiden: E. J. Brill, 2000).
3. Eric Anum, "Comparative Readings of the Bible in Africa: Some Concerns," in *The Bible in Africa: Transactions, Trajectories and Trends*, edited by Gerald O. West and Musa Dube (Leiden: E. J. Brill, 2000), 468.
4. Knut Holter, *Old Testament Research for Africa: A Critical Analysis and Annotated Bibliography of African Old Testament Dissertations, 1967–2000* (New York: Peter Lang, 2002), 89.
5. Gerald O. West, "African Biblical Scholarship as Tri-Polar, Post-Colonial, and a Site-of-Struggle," in *Present and Future of Biblical Studies: Celebrating 25 Years of Brill's Biblical Interpretation*, edited by Benny Tat-siong Liew (Leiden: Brill, 2018), 242–247.
6. SACP, "The South African Road to Socialism: 13th Congress Political Programme of the Sacp 2012–2017: Sacp's 5 Year Plan," SACP, 2012. http://www.sacp.org.za/docs/docs/2012/draftpol2012.pdf.
7. Gerald O. West, *The Stolen Bible: From Tool of Imperialism to African Icon* (Leiden and Pietermaritzburg: Brill and Cluster Publications, 2016), 19–84.
8. Donald Moodie, *The Record; or, a Series of Official Papers Relative to the Condition and Treatment of the Native Tribes of South Africa* (Capetown: A. S. Robertson, 1838), 8.
9. Edward Lahiff, "Land Reform in South Africa 100 Years after the Natives' Land Act," *Journal of Agrarian Change* 14, no. 4 (2014): 587; see also William Beinart and Peter Delius, "The Historical Context and Legacy of the Natives Land Act of 1913," *Journal of Southern African Studies* 40, no. 4 (2014).

10. Cherryl Walker, "Critical Reflections on South Africa's 1913 Natives Land Act and Its Legacies: Introduction," *Journal of Southern African Studies* 40, no. 4 (2014).
11. Ed Stoddard, "Explainer: South Africa Aims to Expropriate Land without Compensation," *World News* (2018), https://www.reuters.com/article/us-safrica-land-explainer/explainer-south-africa-aims-to-expropriate-land-without-compensation-idUSKCN1GQ280; ANC, "Passing of Expropriation Bill Is a Victory for Millions of Dispossessed South Africans," (2016), http://www.anc.org.za/content/passing-expropriation-bill-victory-millions-dispossessed-south-africans.
12. Sampie Terreblanche, *A History of Inequality in South Africa, 1652–2002* (Pietermaritzburg: University of Natal Press, 2002), 14–15.
13. Gerhard Maré, "Race Counts in Contemporary South Africa: 'An Illusion of Ordinariness,'" in *Transformation: Critical Perspectives on Southern Africa* 47 (2001); Kevin Durrheim, Xoliswa Mtose, and Lyndsay Brown, *Race Trouble: Race, Identity and Inequality in Post-Apartheid South Africa* (Pietermaritzburg: University of KwaZulu-Natal Press, 2011); Fiona Anciano, "A Dying Ideal: Non-Racialism and Political Parties in Post-Apartheid South Africa," *Journal of Southern African Studies* 42, no. 2 (2016).
14. Johannes Petrus Claasen, *Die Sieketroosters in Suid-Afrika, 1652–1866* (Pretoria: N. G. Kerkboekhandel, 1977), 21; West, *The Stolen Bible*, 44–48, 54, 60.
15. O. M. Suberg, *The Anglican Tradition in South Africa: A Historical Overview* (Pretoria: University of South Africa, 1999), 12.
16. Suberg, *The Anglican Tradition in South Africa*, 13.
17. West, *The Stolen Bible*, 85–231.
18. Robert Moffat, *Missionary Labours and Scenes in Southern Africa* (1842; reprint, London: John Snow, 1969), 618.
19. John L. Comaroff and Jean Comaroff, *Of Revelation and Revolution: The Dialectics of Modernity on a South African Frontier*, 2 vols., vol. 2 (Chicago: University of Chicago Press, 1997), 168.
20. Takatso Mofokeng, "Black Christians, the Bible and Liberation," *Journal of Black Theology* 2 (1988): 34.
21. Tinyiko S. Maluleke, "Black Theology as Public Discourse," in *Constructing a Language of Religion in Public Life: Multi-Event 1999 Academic Workshop Papers*, edited by James R. Cochrane (Cape Town: University of Cape Town, 1998), 2; John W. de Gruchy and Steve de Gruchy, *The Church Struggle in South Africa: Twenty-Fifth Anniversary Edition*, 3rd ed. (London: SCM Press, 2004), 150; Daniel R. Magaziner, *The Law and the Prophets: Black Consciousness in South Africa, 1968–1977* (Athens and Johannesburg: Ohio University Press, 2010), 85–90.
22. The "time of African existence," argues Achille Mbembe, can be characterized as "the *time of entanglement*," for "this time of African existence is neither a linear time nor a simple sequence in which each moment effaces, annuls, and replaces those that preceded it, to the point where a single age exists within a society. This time is not a series but an interlocking of presents, pasts, and futures, each age bearing, altering, and maintaining the previous ones"; Achille Mbembe, *On the Postcolony* (Berkeley: University of California Press, 2001), 16.
23. Terreblanche, *A History of Inequality*, 14.
24. Terreblanche, *A History of Inequality*, 15.
25. Leigh-Ann Naidoo, "Hallucinations," *Mail & Guardian* (2016), https://mg.co.za/article/2016-08-17-leigh-ann-naidoo-delivers-compelling-speech-at-ruth-first-memorial-lecture; see also "The Role of Radical Pedagogy in the South African Students Organisation and the Black Consciousness Movement in South Africa, 1968–1973," *Education as Change* 19, no. 2 (2015).

26. The Deputy Vice-Chancellor of the College of Humanities at the time, Cheryl Potgieter, and her organizing committee invited me to be one of the respondents to Naidoo's lecture. I am grateful to them and to Naidoo for the opportunity to explore, from a white male academic-activist South African perspective, our collaborative task; http://ndaba-online.ukzn.ac.za/UkzndabaStory/1167/decolonising-the-curriculum-by-centring-the-black-intellectual/#sthash.7oLxNNmo.dpbs
27. Naidoo, "Hallucinations."
28. Naidoo, "Hallucinations." Emphasis in the original.
29. Naidoo, "Hallucinations." Neville Alexander, in delivering the fourth Strini Moodley Annual Memorial Lecture, held at the University of KwaZulu-Natal on May 13, 2010, speaks of the South African postcolony as an "unfinished revolution"; see Neville Alexander, "South Africa—An Unfinished Revolution?," *Links International Journal of Socialist Renewal* (2010).
30. Naidoo, "Hallucinations." Emphasis in the original.
31. Frantz Fanon, *The Wretched of the Earth* (New York: Grove Press, 1963), 36.
32. Eve Tuck and K. Wayne Yang, "Decolonization Is Not a Metaphor," *Decolonization: Indigeneity, Education & Society* 1, no. 1 (2012): 1.
33. Roland Boer, "Remembering Babylon: Postcolonialism and Australian Biblical Studies," in *The Postcolonial Bible*, edited by R. S. Sugirtharajah (Sheffield: Sheffield Academic Press, 1998); "Marx, Postcolonialism, and the Bible," in *Postcolonial Biblical Criticism: Interdisciplinary Intersections*, edited by Stephen D. Moore and Fernando F. Segovia (London and New York: T&T Clark, 2005); Gerald O. West, "What Difference Does Postcolonial Biblical Criticism Make? Reflections from a (South) African Perspective," in *Postcolonial Interventions: Essays in Honor of R. S. Sugirtharajah*, edited by Benny Tat-siong Liew (Sheffield: Sheffield Phoenix Press, 2009).
34. "Finding a Place among the Posts for Post-Colonial Criticism in Biblical Studies in South Africa," *Old Testament Essays* 10 (1997); Jeremy Punt, "Postcolonial Biblical Criticism in South Africa: Some Mind and Road Mapping," *Neotestamentica* 37, no. 1 (2003); "Why Not Postcolonial Biblical Criticism in (South) Africa: Stating the Obvious or Looking for the Impossible?," *Scriptura* 91 (2006).
35. Musa W. Dube, *Postcolonial Feminist Interpretation of the Bible* (St. Louis: Chalice Press, 2000).
36. Musa W. Dube, "Reading for Decolonization (John 4:1–42)," *Semeia* 75 (1996).
37. Dube, *Postcolonial Feminist Interpretation of the Bible*, 97.
38. Dube, *Postcolonial Feminist Interpretation of the Bible*, 101.
39. Dube, *Postcolonial Feminist Interpretation of the Bible*, 101.
40. Dube, *Postcolonial Feminist Interpretation of the Bible*, 102.
41. Dube, *Postcolonial Feminist Interpretation of the Bible*, 98.
42. Dube, "Reading for Decolonization (John 4:1–42)," 42–43.
43. Dube, "Reading for Decolonization (John 4:1–42)," 37, 43.
44. Dube, *Postcolonial Feminist Interpretation of the Bible*, 105.
45. Dube, *Postcolonial Feminist Interpretation of the Bible*, 105.
46. Dube, *Postcolonial Feminist Interpretation of the Bible*, 107.
47. Dube, *Postcolonial Feminist Interpretation of the Bible*, 108.
48. Dube, *Postcolonial Feminist Interpretation of the Bible*, 106.
49. See, e.g., the retellings and rewritings of the story of Ruth and the story of the bleeding woman in Mark 5:24–43 respectively in Musa W. Dube, "The Unpublished Letters of Orpah to Ruth," in *Ruth and Esther: A Feminist Companion to the Bible*, edited by Athalya Brenner

(Sheffield: Sheffield Academic Press, 1999); Musa W. Dube, "Fifty Years of Bleeding: A Storytelling Feminist Reading of Mark 5:24–43," in *Other Ways of Reading: African Women and the Bible*, edited by Musa W. Dube (Atlanta: Society of Biblical Literature, 2001).
50. Dube, *Postcolonial Feminist Interpretation of the Bible*, 40.
51. Dube, *Postcolonial Feminist Interpretation of the Bible*, 14. Dube is particularly committed to "the integration of post-colonial analysis into the liberationist vision of feminist biblical readers"; Dube, "Toward a Postcolonial Feminist Interpretation of the Bible," *Semeia* 78 (1997): 17.
52. Musa W. Dube, "Readings of *Semoya*: Batswana Women's Interpretations of Matt. 15:21–28," *Semeia* 73 (1996): 120, 26.
53. Dube, "Toward a Postcolonial Feminist Interpretation of the Bible," 12.
54. Dube, "Toward a Postcolonial Feminist Interpretation of the Bible," 22.
55. Dube, "Toward a Postcolonial Feminist Interpretation of the Bible," 22.
56. Itumeleng J. Mosala, *Biblical Hermeneutics and Black Theology in South Africa* (Grand Rapids: Eerdmans, 1989), 153.
57. Steven D. Gish, *Desmond Tutu: A Biography* (Westport, CT: Greenwood Press, 2004), 101.
58. J. N. J. Kritzinger, "Black Theology: Challenge to Mission" (PhD diss, University of South Africa, 1988), 93.
59. John S. Mbiti, "The Biblical Basis for Present Trends in African Theology," in *African Theology En Route: Papers from the Pan-African Conference of Third World Theologians, Accra, December 1977*, edited by Kofi Appiah-Kubi and Sergio Torres (Maryknoll, NY: Orbis, 1977).
60. Desmond Mpilo Tutu, *Hope and Suffering: Sermons and Speeches* (Johannesburg: Skotaville, 1983), 124–129.
61. See Magaziner, *The Law and the Prophets*, 56; de Gruchy and de Gruchy, *The Church Struggle in South Africa*, 151, 54–60, 63–64, 70–71, 74–75, 79.
62. Albert Nolan, *God in South Africa: The Challenge of the Gospel* (Cape Town: David Philip, 1988), 157.
63. Kritzinger, "Black Theology: Challenge to Mission," 93.
64. Takatso Mofokeng, "Black Christians, the Bible and Liberation," *Journal of Black Theology* 2 (1988): 40.
65. Mofokeng, "Black Christians, the Bible and Liberation," 38.
66. Mofokeng, "Black Christians, the Bible and Liberation," 39.
67. For a detailed account of Mosala's hermeneutical processes see Mosala, *Biblical Hermeneutics and Black Theology*; Gerald O. West, *Biblical Hermeneutics of Liberation: Modes of Reading the Bible in the South African Context*, 2nd ed. (Maryknoll, NY and Pietermaritzburg: Orbis Books and Cluster Publications, 1995), 135–146; West, *The Stolen Bible*, 328–340.
68. Mosala, *Biblical Hermeneutics and Black Theology*, 185.
69. Mosala, *Biblical Hermeneutics and Black Theology*, 18.
70. Mosala, *Biblical Hermeneutics and Black Theology*, 121.
71. Mosala, *Biblical Hermeneutics and Black Theology*, 185.
72. Mosala, *Biblical Hermeneutics and Black Theology*, 4, 192.
73. Mosala, *Biblical Hermeneutics and Black Theology*, 188.
74. Mosala, *Biblical Hermeneutics and Black Theology*, 4–5.
75. Mosala, *Biblical Hermeneutics and Black Theology*, 32, 41, 123–153, 73–89.
76. Mosala, *Biblical Hermeneutics and Black Theology*, 28.

77. Mosala, *Biblical Hermeneutics and Black Theology*, 153.
78. Mosala, *Biblical Hermeneutics and Black Theology*, 153.
79. West, *Biblical Hermeneutics of Liberation*, 75.
80. Tinyiko Sam Maluleke, "Black Theology as Public Discourse," in *The Multi-Event 1999: Constructing a Language of Religion in Public Life*, ed. James R. Cochrane (Cape Town: University of Cape Town, 1998), 1.
81. Maluleke, "Black Theology as Public Discourse," 1.
82. Maluleke, "Black Theology as Public Discourse," 1.
83. Maluleke, "Black Theology as Public Discourse," 2.
84. Tinyiko S. Maluleke, "African Traditional Religions in Christian Mission and Christian Scholarship: Re-Opening a Debate That Never Started," *Religion and Theology* 5 (1998): 133; de Gruchy and de Gruchy, *The Church Struggle in South Africa*, 146. As Alistair Kee recognizes, one of the most significant contributions of South African black theology has been in "tracing the origins of oppression back to interest and relations of power" (a contribution he attributes to Mokgethi Motlhabi) and in so doing locating "oppression in the economic base of society"; Alistair Kee, *The Rise and Demise of Black Theology* (Aldershot and Burlington: Ashgate, 2006), 87; Mokgethi Motlhabi, "Black Theology and Authority," in *Black Theology: The South African Voice*, edited by Basil Moore (London: C. Hurst & Co., 1973).
85. Maluleke, "African Traditional Religions in Christian Mission," 133.
86. Maluleke, "Black Theology as Public Discourse," 2.
87. Itumeleng J. Mosala, "The Relevance of African Traditional Religions and Their Challenge to Black Theology," in *The Unquestionable Right to Be Free: Essays in Black Theology*, edited by Itumeleng J. Mosala and Buti Tlhagale (Johannesburg: Skotaville, 1986).
88. Maluleke, "African Traditional Religions in Christian Mission," 133.
89. Maluleke, "African Traditional Religions in Christian Mission," 135.
90. Maluleke, "African Traditional Religions in Christian Mission," 134.
91. Mofokeng, "Black Christians, the Bible and Liberation," 40.
92. Gabriel Setiloane, "Where Are We in African Theology?," in *African Theology En Route: Papers from the Pan-African Conference of Third World Theologians, Accra, December 17–23, 1977*, edited by Kofi Appiah-Kubi and Sergio Torres (Maryknoll, NY: Orbis, 1977), 64.
93. Tinyiko S. Maluleke, "Half a Century of African Christian Theologies: Elements of the Emerging Agenda for the Twenty-First Century," *Journal of Theology for Southern Africa* 99 (1997): 13.
94. Tinyiko S. Maluleke, "Black and African Theologies in the New World Order: A Time to Drink from Our Own Wells," *Journal of Theology for Southern Africa* 96 (1996): 14. A central argument in my book *The Stolen Bible* is that African receptions of the Bible are hermeneutically separable from African receptions of Christianity.
95. Mosala, "The Relevance of African Traditional Religions," 57.
96. Maluleke, "Half a Century of African Christian Theologies," 14–15.
97. Maluleke, "Black and African Theologies in the New World Order," 13.
98. Maluleke, "Black and African Theologies in the New World Order," 15.
99. Frank Chikane, "The Incarnation in the Life of the People in Southern Africa," *Journal of Theology for Southern Africa* 51 (1985); Buti Tlhagale, "Culture in an Apartheid Society," *Journal of Theology for Southern Africa* 51 (1985).
100. Mosala, *Biblical Hermeneutics and Black Theology*, 191–192.

101. West, *The Stolen Bible*, 345.
102. "*Wathint' abafazi, wathint' imbokodo*" (You strike a woman, you strike a grinding stone).
103. Makhosazana K. Nzimande, "Reconfiguring Jezebel: A Postcolonial *Imbokodo* Reading of the Story of Naboth's Vineyard (1 Kings 21:1–16)," in *African and European Readers of the Bible in Dialogue: In Quest of a Shared Meaning*, edited by Hans de Wit and Gerald O. West (Leiden: Brill, 2008), 230.
104. Dube, "Toward a Postcolonial Feminist Interpretation of the Bible."
105. Nzimande, "Reconfiguring Jezebel," 233.
106. Nzimande, "Reconfiguring Jezebel," 234.
107. Nzimande, "Reconfiguring Jezebel," 234.
108. Nzimande, "Reconfiguring Jezebel," 234–237.
109. Nzimande, "Reconfiguring Jezebel," 243.
110. Nzimande, "Reconfiguring Jezebel," 243.
111. Nzimande, "Reconfiguring Jezebel," 242–243.
112. Nzimande, "Reconfiguring Jezebel," 244, 52–54.
113. Nzimande, "Reconfiguring Jezebel," 252.
114. Ndikho Mtshiselwa, "A Re-Reading of 1 Kings 21:1–29 and Jehu's Revolution in Dialogue with Farisani and Nzimande: Negotiating Socio-Economic Redress in South Africa," *Old Testament Essays* 27, no. 1 (2014): 205–206.
115. Mosala, *Biblical Hermeneutics and Black Theology*, 153.
116. Mtshiselwa, "A Re-Reading of 1 Kings 21:1–29," 219.
117. Mtshiselwa, "A Re-Reading of 1 Kings 21:1–29," 223.
118. Mtshiselwa, "A Re-Reading of 1 Kings 21:1–29," 224.
119. Mtshiselwa, "A Re-Reading of 1 Kings 21:1–29," 225.
120. Mtshiselwa, "A Re-Reading of 1 Kings 21:1–29," 212.
121. Mtshiselwa, "A Re-Reading of 1 Kings 21:1–29," 209; see also Gerald O. West, "Religion Intersecting De-Nationalization and Re-Nationalization in Post-Apartheid South Africa," in *Dynamics of Religion Past and Present, Proceedings of the XXI World Congress of the International Association for the History of Religions, Erfurt, August 23–29, 2015*, edited by C. Bochinger, J. Rüpke, and E. Begemann (Berlin: De Gruyter, 2017).
122. Musa W. Dube, "Looking Back and Forward: Postcolonialism, Globalization, God and Gender," *Scriptura* 92 (2006): 179.
123. Nzimande, "Reconfiguring Jezebel," 234.
124. Pieter Labuschagne, "Patronage, State Capture and Oligopolistic Monopoly in South Africa: The Slide from a Weak to a Dysfunctional State?," *Acta Academica* 49, no. 2 (2017); Ruth Hall, "Elite Capture and State Neglect: New Evidence on South Africas Land Reform," *Review of African Political Economy* 44, no. 151 (2017).
125. Maluleke, "Black Theology as Public Discourse," 61, 62.
126. Hulisani Ramantswana, "Decolonising Biblical Hermeneutics in the (South) African Context," *Acta Theologica* Supplement 24 (2016): 180–181.
127. Ramantswana, "Decolonising Biblical Hermeneutics in the (South) African Context," 183.
128. Ramantswana, "Decolonising Biblical Hermeneutics in the (South) African Context," 181.
129. Ramantswana, "Decolonising Biblical Hermeneutics in the (South) African Context," 186.
130. Gerald O. West, "White Theology in a Black Frame: Betraying the Logic of Social Location," in *Living on the Edge: Essays in Honour of Steve De Gruchy, Activist and Theologian*, edited by James R. Cochrane et al. (Pietermaritzburg: Cluster Publications, 2012), 72.

131. James W. Perkinson, *White Theology: Outing Supremacy in Modernity* (New York: Palgrave Macmillan, 2004), 19. Emphasis is added.
132. Sharon D. Welch, *A Feminist Ethic of Risk* (Minneapolis: Fortress, 1990), 151.
133. Ramantswana, "Decolonising Biblical Hermeneutics in the (South) African Context," 189. Emphasis in original.
134. Ramantswana, "Decolonising Biblical Hermeneutics in the (South) African Context," 190.
135. Ramantswana, "Decolonising Biblical Hermeneutics in the (South) African Context," 190.
136. Ramantswana, "Decolonising Biblical Hermeneutics in the (South) African Context," 186.
137. Gerald O. West, "The Vocation of an African Biblical Scholar on the Margins of Biblical Scholarship," in *Voyages in Uncharted Waters: Essays on the Theory and Practice of Biblical Interpretation in Honor of David Jobling*, edited by Wesley J. Bergen and Armin Siedlecki (Sheffield: Sheffield Phoenix Press, 2006).
138. I would want to problematize "white," whether "white English" or "white Afrikaner" ethnicity, in similar ways to race.
139. Ramantswana, "Decolonising Biblical Hermeneutics in the (South) African Context," 190.
140. Ramantswana, "Decolonising Biblical Hermeneutics in the (South) African Context," 191.
141. Kwesi Dickson, "African Traditional Religions and the Bible," in *The Jerusalem Congress on Black Africa and the Bible, April 1972/Le Congres De Jerusalem Sur L'afrique Noire Et La Bible: Proceedings*, ed. Engelbert Mveng and R. J. Z. Werblowsky (Jerusalem: The Israel Interfaith Committee, 1972); John Mbiti, "Christianity and Culture in Africa," in *Facing the New Challenges: The Message of Pacla (Pan African Christian Leadership Assembly): December 9–19, 1976, Nairobi*, edited by Michael Cassidy and Luc Verlinden (Kisumu, Kenya: Evangel Publishing House, 1978); "Christianity and African Religion"; "The African Proverbs Project and After," *Lexikos* 12 (2002); see also Mejai B. M. Avoseh, "Proverbs as Theoretical Frameworks for Lifelong Learning in Indigenous African Education," *Adult Education Quarterly* 63, no. 3 (2013).
142. Madipoane Masenya, "Proverbs 31:10–31 in a South African Context: A Reading for the Liberation of African (Northern Sotho) Women," *Semeia* 78 (1997); Madipoane (ngwana' Mphahlele) Masenya, "A *Bosadi* (Womanhood) Reading of Proverbs 31:10–31," in *Other Ways of Reading: African Women and the Bible*, edited by Musa W. Dube (Atlanta and Geneva: Society of Biblical Literature and WCC Publications, 2001).
143. "Is White South African Old Testament Scholarship African?," *Bulletin for Old Testament Studies in Africa* 12 (2002); Madipoane Masenya (ngwan'a Mphahlele), "Struggling with Poverty/Emptiness: Rereading the Naomi-Ruth Story in African-South Africa," *Journal of Theology for Southern Africa* 120 (2004).
144. Masenya, "Proverbs 31:10–31 in a South African Context."
145. Ramantswana, "Decolonising Biblical Hermeneutics in the (South) African Context," 191.
146. Ramantswana, "Decolonising Biblical Hermeneutics in the (South) African Context," 191.
147. Ramantswana, "Decolonising Biblical Hermeneutics in the (South) African Context," 191.
148. Ramantswana, "Decolonising Biblical Hermeneutics in the (South) African Context," 192.
149. Ramantswana, "Decolonising Biblical Hermeneutics in the (South) African Context," 192.

150. Ramantswana, "Decolonising Biblical Hermeneutics in the (South) African Context," 194. Emphasis in original.
151. West, "African Biblical Scholarship as Tri-Polar, Post-Colonial, and a Site-of-Struggle."
152. Ramantswana, "Decolonising Biblical Hermeneutics in the (South) African Context," 195–196.
153. Ramantswana, "Decolonising Biblical Hermeneutics in the (South) African Context," 197.
154. Ramantswana, Hulisani, "Decolonial Reflection on the Landlessness of the Levites," *Journal of Theology for Southern Africa* 158 (2017): 83.
155. Ramantswana, "Decolonial Reflection on the Landlessness of the Levites," 87.
156. Ramantswana, "Decolonial Reflection on the Landlessness of the Levites," 91.
157. Ramantswana, "Decolonial Reflection on the Landlessness of the Levites," 79.
158. Ramantswana, "Decolonial Reflection on the Landlessness of the Levites," 78.
159. Nzimande, "Reconfiguring Jezebel," 250.
160. Nzimande, "Reconfiguring Jezebel," 250.
161. Nzimande, "Reconfiguring Jezebel," 251. We must include here the contrastive identity constructions of hetero-patriarchy; see Jeremy Punt, "Queer Theory, Postcolonial Theory, and Biblical Interpretation," in *Bible Trouble: Queer Reading at the Boundaries of Biblical Scholarship*, edited by Teresa J. Hornsby and Ken Stone, Semeia Studies (Atlanta: Society of Biblical Literature, 2011); Naidoo, "Hallucinations."
162. Ramantswana, "Decolonial Reflection on the Landlessness of the Levites," 73.
163. Sugirtharajah, "Afterword: The Future Imperfect."
164. Ramantswana, "Decolonial Reflection on the Landlessness of the Levites," 74–75.

Bibliography

Alexander, Neville. "South Africa—an Unfinished Revolution?" *Links International Journal of Socialist Renewal* (2010). Published electronically http://links.org.au/node/1693.
ANC. "Passing of Expropriation Bill Is a Victory for Millions of Dispossessed South Africans." Published electronically May 27, 2016. http://www.anc.org.za/content/passing-expropriation-bill-victory-millions-dispossessed-south-africans.
Anciano, Fiona. "A Dying Ideal: Non-Racialism and Political Parties in Post-Apartheid South Africa." *Journal of Southern African Studies* 42, no. 2 (2016): 195–214.
Anum, Eric. "Comparative Readings of the Bible in Africa: Some Concerns." In *The Bible in Africa: Transactions, Trajectories and Trends*, edited by Gerald O. West and Musa Dube, 457–473. Leiden: E. J. Brill, 2000.
Avoseh, Mejai B. M. "Proverbs as Theoretical Frameworks for Lifelong Learning in Indigenous African Education." *Adult Education Quarterly* 63, no. 3 (2013): 236–250.
Beinart, William, and Peter Delius. "The Historical Context and Legacy of the Natives Land Act of 1913." *Journal of Southern African Studies* 40, no. 4 (2014): 667–688.
Boer, Roland. "Remembering Babylon: Postcolonialism and Australian Biblical Studies." In *The Postcolonial Bible*, edited by R. S. Sugirtharajah, 24–48. Sheffield: Sheffield Academic Press, 1998.
Boer, Roland. "Marx, Postcolonialism, and the Bible." In *Postcolonial Biblical Criticism: Interdisciplinary Intersections*, edited by Stephen D. Moore and Fernando F. Segovia, 166–183. London and New York: T&T Clark, 2005.

Chikane, Frank. "The Incarnation in the Life of the People in Southern Africa." *Journal of Theology for Southern Africa* 51 (1985): 37–50.

Claasen, Johannes Petrus. *Die Sieketroosters in Suid-Afrika, 1652–1866*. Pretoria: N. G. Kerkboekhandel, 1977.

Comaroff, John L., and Jean Comaroff. *Of Revelation and Revolution: The Dialectics of Modernity on a South African Frontier*. 2 vols. Vol. 2. Chicago: University of Chicago Press, 1997.

de Gruchy, John W., and Steve de Gruchy. *The Church Struggle in South Africa: Twenty-Fifth Anniversary Edition*. 3rd ed. London: SCM Press, 2004.

Dickson, Kwesi. "African Traditional Religions and the Bible." In *The Jerusalem Congress on Black Africa and the Bible, April 1972/Le Congres De Jerusalem Sur L'afrique Noire Et La Bible: Proceedings*, edited by Engelbert Mveng and R. J. Z. Werblowsky, 155–166. Jerusalem: The Israel Interfaith Committee, 1972.

Dube, Musa W. "Reading for Decolonization (John 4:1–42)." *Semeia* 75 (1996): 37–59.

Dube, Musa W. "Readings of *Semoya*: Batswana Women's Interpretations of Matt. 15:21–28." *Semeia* 73 (1996): 111–129.

Dube, Musa W. "Toward a Postcolonial Feminist Interpretation of the Bible." *Semeia* 78 (1997): 11–26.

Dube, Musa W. "The Unpublished Letters of Orpah to Ruth." In *Ruth and Esther: A Feminist Companion to the Bible*, edited by Athalya Brenner, 145–150. Sheffield: Sheffield Academic Press, 1999.

Dube, Musa W. *Postcolonial Feminist Interpretation of the Bible*. St. Louis: Chalice Press, 2000.

Dube, Musa W. "Fifty Years of Bleeding: A Storytelling Feminist Reading of Mark 5:24–43." In *Other Ways of Reading: African Women and the Bible*, edited by Musa W. Dube, 50–60. Atlanta: Society of Biblical Literature, 2001.

Dube, Musa W. "Looking Back and Forward: Postcolonialism, Globalization, God and Gender." *Scriptura* 92 (2006): 178–193.

Durrheim, Kevin, Xoliswa Mtose, and Lyndsay Brown. *Race Trouble: Race, Identity and Inequality in Post-Apartheid South Africa*. Pietermaritzburg: University of KwaZulu-Natal Press, 2011.

Fanon, Frantz. *The Wretched of the Earth*. New York: Grove Press, 1963.

Gish, Steven D. *Desmond Tutu: A Biography*. Westport, CT: Greenwood Press, 2004.

Hall, Ruth. "Elite Capture and State Neglect: New Evidence on South Africas Land Reform." [In English.] *Review of African Political Economy* 44, no. 151 (2017): 122–130.

Holter, Knut. *Old Testament Research for Africa: A Critical Analysis and Annotated Bibliography of African Old Testament Dissertations, 1967–2000*. New York: Peter Lang, 2002.

Kee, Alistair. *The Rise and Demise of Black Theology*. Aldershot and Burlington: Ashgate, 2006.

Kritzinger, J. N. J. "Black Theology: Challenge to Mission." PhD diss., University of South Africa, 1988.

Labuschagne, Pieter. "Patronage, State Capture and Oligopolistic Monopoly in South Africa: The Slide from a Weak to a Dysfunctional State?" *Acta Academica* 49, no. 2 (2017): 51–67.

Lahiff, Edward. "Land Reform in South Africa 100 Years after the Natives' Land Act." *Journal of Agrarian Change* 14, no. 4 (2014): 586–592.

Magaziner, Daniel R. *The Law and the Prophets: Black Consciousness in South Africa, 1968–1977*. Athens and Johannesburg: Ohio University Press, 2010.

Maluleke, Tinyiko S. "Black and African Theologies in the New World Order: A Time to Drink from Our Own Wells." *Journal of Theology for Southern Africa* 96 (1996): 3–19.

Maluleke, Tinyiko S. "Half a Century of African Christian Theologies: Elements of the Emerging Agenda for the Twenty-First Century." *Journal of Theology for Southern Africa* 99 (1997): 4–23.

Maluleke, Tinyiko S. "African Traditional Religions in Christian Mission and Christian Scholarship: Re-Opening a Debate That Never Started." *Religion and Theology* 5 (1998): 121–137.

Maluleke, Tinyiko S. "Black Theology as Public Discourse." In *Constructing a Language of Religion in Public Life: Multi-Event 1999 Academic Workshop Papers*, edited by James R. Cochrane, 60–62. Cape Town: University of Cape Town, 1998.

Maluleke, Tinyiko Sam. "Black Theology as Public Discourse." In *The Multi-Event 1999: Constructing a Language of Religion in Public Life*, edited by James R. Cochrane, 1–2. Cape Town: University of Cape Town, 1998.

Maré, Gerhard. "Race Counts in Contemporary South Africa: 'An Illusion of Ordinariness.'" *Transformation: Critical Perspectives on Southern Africa* 47 (2001): 75–93.

Masenya (ngwan'a Mphahlele), Madipoane. "Struggling with Poverty/Emptiness: Rereading the Naomi-Ruth Story in African-South Africa." *Journal of Theology for Southern Africa* 120 (2004): 46–59.

Masenya, Madipoane. "Proverbs 31:10–31 in a South African Context: A Reading for the Liberation of African (Northern Sotho) Women." *Semeia* 78 (1997): 55–68.

Masenya, Madipoane (ngwana' Mphahlele). "A *Bosadi* (Womanhood) Reading of Proverbs 31:10–31." In *Other Ways of Reading: African Women and the Bible*, edited by Musa W. Dube, 145–157. Atlanta and Geneva: Society of Biblical Literature and WCC Publications, 2001.

Masenya, Madipoane (ngwana' Mphahlele). "Is White South African Old Testament Scholarship African?" *Bulletin for Old Testament Studies in Africa* 12 (2002): 3–8.

Mbembe, Achille. *On the Postcolony*. [In English.] Berkeley: University of California Press, 2001.

Mbiti, John. "Christianity and African Religion." In *Facing the New Challenges: The Message of Pacla (Pan African Christian Leadership Assembly): December 9–19, 1976, Nairobi*, edited by Michael Cassidy and Luc Verlinden, 308–318. Kisumu, Kenya: Evangel Publishing House, 1978.

Mbiti, John. "Christianity and Culture in Africa." In *Facing the New Challenges: The Message of Pacla (Pan African Christian Leadership Assembly): December 9–19, 1976, Nairobi*, edited by Michael Cassidy and Luc Verlinden, 272–284. Kisumu, Kenya: Evangel Publishing House, 1978.

Mbiti, John. "The African Proverbs Project and After." *Lexikos* 12 (2002): 256–263.

Mbiti, John S. "The Biblical Basis for Present Trends in African Theology." In *African Theology En Route: Papers from the Pan-African Conference of Third World Theologians, Accra, December 1977*, edited by Kofi Appiah-Kubi and Sergio Torres, 83–94. Maryknoll, NY: Orbis, 1977.

Moffat, Robert. *Missionary Labours and Scenes in Southern Africa*. 1842; reprint, London: John Snow, 1842[1969].

Mofokeng, Takatso. "Black Christians, the Bible and Liberation." *Journal of Black Theology* 2 (1988): 34–42, 34.

Moodie, Donald. *The Record; or, a Series of Official Papers Relative to the Condition and Treatment of the Native Tribes of South Africa*. [In English.] Cape Town: A. S. Robertson, 1838.

Mosala, Itumeleng J. "The Relevance of African Traditional Religions and Their Challenge to Black Theology." In *The Unquestionable Right to Be Free: Essays in Black Theology*, edited by Itumeleng J. Mosala and Buti Tlhagale, 91–100. Johannesburg: Skotaville, 1986.

Mosala, Itumeleng J. *Biblical Hermeneutics and Black Theology in South Africa*. Grand Rapids: Eerdmans, 1989.

Motlhabi, Mokgethi. "Black Theology and Authority." In *Black Theology: The South African Voice*, edited by Basil Moore. London: C. Hurst & Co., 1973.

Mtshiselwa, Ndikho. "A Re-Reading of 1 Kings 21:1–29 and Jehu's Revolution in Dialogue with Farisani and Nzimande: Negotiating Socio-Economic Redress in South Africa." *Old Testament Essays* 27, no. 1 (2014): 205–230.

Naidoo, Leigh-Ann. "The Role of Radical Pedagogy in the South African Students Organisation and the Black Consciousness Movement in South Africa, 1968–1973." *Education as Change* 19, no. 2 (2015): 112–132.

Naidoo, Leigh-Ann. "Hallucinations." *Mail & Guardian* (2016). Published electronically August 17, 2016. https://mg.co.za/article/2016-08-17-leigh-ann-naidoo-delivers-compelling-speech-at-ruth-first-memorial-lecture.

Nolan, Albert. *God in South Africa: The Challenge of the Gospel*. Cape Town: David Philip, 1988.

Nzimande, Makhosazana K. "Reconfiguring Jezebel: A Postcolonial *Imbokodo* Reading of the Story of Naboth's Vineyard (1 Kings 21:1–16)." In *African and European Readers of the Bible in Dialogue: In Quest of a Shared Meaning*, edited by Hans de Wit and Gerald O. West, 223–258. Leiden: Brill, 2008.

Perkinson, James W. *White Theology: Outing Supremacy in Modernity*. New York: Palgrave Macmillan, 2004.

Punt, Jeremy. "Postcolonial Biblical Criticism in South Africa: Some Mind and Road Mapping." *Neotestamentica* 37, no. 1 (2003): 59–85.

Punt, Jeremy. "Why Not Postcolonial Biblical Criticism in (South) Africa: Stating the Obvious or Looking for the Impossible?." *Scriptura* 91 (2006): 63–82.

Punt, Jeremy. "Queer Theory, Postcolonial Theory, and Biblical Interpretation." In *Bible Trouble: Queer Reading at the Boundaries of Biblical Scholarship*, edited by Teresa J. Hornsby and Ken Stone, 321–341. Semeia Studies. Atlanta: Society of Biblical Literature, 2011.

Ramantswana, Hulisani. "Decolonising Biblical Hermeneutics in the (South) African Context." *Acta Theologica* Supplement 24 (2016): 178–203.

Ramantswana, Hulisani. "Decolonial Reflection on the Landlessness of the Levites." *Journal of Theology for Southern Africa* 158 (2017): 72–91.

SACP. "The South African Road to Socialism: 13th Congress Political Programme of the SACP 2012–2017: Sacp's 5 Year Plan." SACP, 2012. http://www.sacp.org.za/docs/docs/2012/draftpol2012.pdf.

Setiloane, Gabriel. "Where Are We in African Theology?" In *African Theology En Route: Papers from the Pan-African Conference of Third World Theologians, Accra, December 17–23, 1977*, edited by Kofi Appiah-Kubi and Sergio Torres, 59–65. Maryknoll, NY: Orbis, 1977.

Stoddard, Ed. "Explainer: South Africa Aims to Expropriate Land without Compensation." *World News* (2018). Published electronically March 15, 2018. https://www.reuters.com/article/us-safrica-land-explainer/explainer-south-africa-aims-to-expropriate-land-without-compensation-idUSKCN1GQ280.

Suberg, O. M. *The Anglican Tradition in South Africa: A Historical Overview*. Pretoria: University of South Africa, 1999.

Sugirtharajah, R. S. "Afterword: The Future Imperfect." In *Voices from the Margin: Interpreting the Bible in the Third World*, edited by R. S. Sugirtharajah, 494–497. Maryknoll, NY: Orbis, 2006.

Terreblanche, Sampie. *A History of Inequality in South Africa, 1652–2002*. Pietermaritzburg: University of Natal Press, 2002.

Tlhagale, Buti. "Culture in an Apartheid Society." *Journal of Theology for Southern Africa* 51 (1985): 27–36.

Tuck, Eve, and K. Wayne Yang. "Decolonization Is Not a Metaphor." *Decolonization: Indigeneity, Education & Society* 1, no. 1 (2012): 1–40.

Tutu, Desmond Mpilo. *Hope and Suffering: Sermons and Speeches*. Johannesburg: Skotaville, 1983.

Ukpong, Justin S. "Developments in Biblical Interpretation in Africa: Historical and Hermeneutical Directions." In *The Bible in Africa: Transactions, Trajectories and Trends*, edited by Gerald O. West and Musa Dube, 11–28. Leiden: E. J. Brill, 2000.

Walker, Cherryl. "Critical Reflections on South Africa's 1913 Natives Land Act and Its Legacies: Introduction." *Journal of Southern African Studies* 40, no. 4 (2014): 655–665.

Welch, Sharon D. *A Feminist Ethic of Risk*. Minneapolis: Fortress, 1990.

West, Gerald O. *Biblical Hermeneutics of Liberation: Modes of Reading the Bible in the South African Context*. 2nd ed. Maryknoll, NY and Pietermaritzburg: Orbis Books and Cluster Publications, 1995.

West, Gerald O. "Finding a Place among the Posts for Post-Colonial Criticism in Biblical Studies in South Africa." *Old Testament Essays* 10 (1997): 322–342.

West, Gerald O. "The Vocation of an African Biblical Scholar on the Margins of Biblical Scholarship." In *Voyages in Uncharted Waters: Essays on the Theory and Practice of Biblical Interpretation in Honor of David Jobling*, edited by Wesley J. Bergen and Armin Siedlecki, 142–171. Sheffield: Sheffield Phoenix Press, 2006.

West, Gerald O. "What Difference Does Postcolonial Biblical Criticism Make? Reflections from a (South) African Perspective." In *Postcolonial Interventions: Essays in Honor of R. S. Sugirtharajah*, edited by Benny Tat-siong Liew, 256–273. Sheffield: Sheffield Phoenix Press, 2009.

West, Gerald O. "White Theology in a Black Frame: Betraying the Logic of Social Location." In *Living on the Edge: Essays in Honour of Steve De Gruchy, Activist and Theologian*, edited by James R. Cochrane, Elias Bongmba, Isabel A. Phiri, and Desmond P. van der Water, 60–78. Pietermaritzburg: Cluster Publications, 2012.

West, Gerald O. *The Stolen Bible: From Tool of Imperialism to African Icon*. Leiden and Pietermaritzburg: Brill and Cluster Publications, 2016.

West, Gerald O. "Religion Intersecting De-Nationalization and Re-Nationalization in Post-Apartheid South Africa." In *Dynamics of Religion Past and Present, Proceedings of the XXI World Congress of the International Association for the History of Religions, Erfurt, August 23–29, 2015*, edited by C. Bochinger, J. Rüpke, and E. Begemann, 69–83. Berlin: De Gruyter, 2017.

West, Gerald O. "African Biblical Scholarship as Tri-Polar, Post-Colonial, and a Site-of-Struggle." In *Present and Future of Biblical Studies: Celebrating 25 Years of Brill's Biblical Interpretation*, edited by Benny Tat-siong Liew, 240–273. Leiden: Brill, 2018.

CHAPTER 28

MATERIALIST/MARXIST INTERPRETATIONS AND POSTCOLONIAL BIBLICAL CRITICISM

NIALL MCKAY

INTRODUCTION

> Marxist biblical criticism is clearly here to stay, if its growth in the last decade is anything to go by.
>
> Roland Boer

MARXIST critical theory constitutes a far-reaching stream of analysis. It is deep and broad and touches on almost all aspects of society.[1] Marxist criticism cannot be thought of as a singular approach to be compared and contrasted with one or more other approaches—even within the relatively focused field of biblical criticism. Thus the intention of this article is not to summarize Marxism but rather to highlight important traditions of Marxist thought that have inspired fruitful avenues in biblical criticism. This essay will pay special attention to the coherencies and incoherencies between Marxist and postcolonial critical interrogations of the Bible.

Before beginning, it is important to note that Marxist theory and criticism is significantly older than postcolonialism, at least in its self-conscious iterations. Though the term was probably first popularized by Karl Kautsky, formal Marxism can be attributed to the writings of Marx and Engels as early as the mid-1800s, with socialist antecedents stretching back centuries earlier. Postcolonialism, on the other hand, is a movement that arises most self-consciously in the twentieth century, especially in the work of Gayatri Chakravorty Spivak, Edward Said, and Homi Bhabha. As such, postcolonialism draws on a wider range of critical theory including, importantly, the literary poststructuralism of the 1960s onward. This is not to say that postcolonial reading and resistance does not draw on older historical struggles, but rather that this critical theory cannot be said to have coalesced into a coherent form until much later. Moreover, alongside a range of twentieth-century movements of resistance and liberation, postcolonialism is indebted to Marxism, however indirectly.[2]

Marxist thinking has often provided both an inspiration and a base of departure for liberative movements. Even poststructuralism, which has inspired key avenues of postcolonial thought, can be traced to the left milieu of 1960s Paris and dissatisfaction with public and totalitarian iterations of communism, especially in the shadow of Stalin's reign.[3] Marxism's long history means not only that there is significantly more Marxist writing to engage with but also that materialist and Marxist analyses were fully mature forms *before* the development of postcolonial theory. Moreover, because theory does not develop in a vacuum, postcolonialism and Marxism are not simply parallel approaches to the world. Rather, postcolonialism developed in part as a reaction to Marxist traditions—whether this reaction was made explicit or not. Early progenitors of postcolonialism, such as Frantz Fanon and W. E. B. Du Bois, were influenced by labor movements and the political developments of Eastern Europe in the first half of the twentieth century.[4] Their early contributions were written to bring these movements into the contexts of oppression in North Africa and the United States. Any investigation of postcolonialism must, therefore, ask questions about how postcolonial theory diverged from or rejected the liberative and revolutionary trajectory of Marxism and whether it is time for the two schools to find common ground once more. Within biblical criticism, the time is certainly ripe for some reconciliation.

On a more theoretical level, it is also problematic to summarize Marxism without collapsing the dialectic oppositions that shape it. Nevertheless, in the guild of biblical criticism, avowedly Marxist and materialist approaches to the Bible's text, though growing, do not seem to have gained as much traction as the growth in marginal, liberationist, or identity-focused readings that have emerged over the past few decades. In response to this, this chapter proposes a dialectic discussion of Marxist thought in biblical criticism rather than a summary of Marxist biblical criticism as such. The discussion points to some of the key characteristics of Marxist theory that are pertinent to biblical scholarship today and highlights some of the ways in which Marxist theory can productively interact with other liberative approaches for clearer analysis of, and more potent response to, systemic oppression in and around biblical communities.

The chapter avoids getting mired in debates about whether Marxist or postcolonial biblical criticism is better suited to the tasks of understanding the biblical texts in an age of renewed interest in empire.[5] Nor does it cast judgment on the tactical efficacy of each set of approaches for the sake of liberative readings of the Bible—partly because readers strongly committed to liberation often find ways to read the Bible through both materialist and postcolonialist prisms. Typically, it is a circumstance or (intellectual) relationship that has opened the door for these scholars to engage in more nuanced, countercultural readings. The presentation here tries to avoid the temptation, on both sides, to ignore or even to reject that which is of value in both perspectives simply because there are valid criticisms to be made. It is not sufficient to sideline the depth of anti-Stalinist Marxist insight because of a justified criticism of totalitarian tendencies of institutional communism. Neither is it acceptable to reject the value in identifying and resisting modern empires characteristic of biblical postcolonialism, simply because of the valid criticism that the configuration of modern and ancient empires makes them different enough to reject simple equivalencies. On both sides, it is not enough to reject biblical texts as simply the tools of empire,[6] colonial power, or the bourgeoisie—though they certainly have been that. Instead, for the sake of liberation, these texts should be regarded as products of a contested economic and political world that can be productive for contemporary analysis. The most contested of texts may yet be generative of political resistance as the voices of the subaltern and popular classes are recovered.

Marxist Criticism

Marxist criticism and practice rests on the notion that the world of ideas proceeds, in an almost doctrinal sense, from the material world. This underlying materialism reveals itself in Marx's historical appropriation and reframing of Hegel's dialectic as the primary mode of thinking in Marxism. It also constitutes a connecting thread among the diverse aspects of Marxist theory. In the most "vulgar" understandings of historical materialism,[7] there is an economic determinism that proffers a total progression from base to superstructure.[8] In this view, culture, religion, and so on are regarded purely as products of material forces. In response to this position, however, other Marxist thinkers have acknowledged, in practice if not always explicitly, the two-way interplay between the material and supramaterial in Marxist analysis. For these thinkers, historical materialism constitutes the process by which Marxist frameworks are drawn from history. With an initial focus on the industrial revolutions of Western Europe, Marxist analysis proceeds to describe the various stages of capitalism that surround particular historical contexts. At the same time, materialist economics is especially attuned to unveiling the myths of bourgeois capitalist ideologies that simply perpetuate systems of accumulation and the alienation of workers from the products of their labor (both material and cultural).

Whether or not historical materialism is an analytic or a predictive philosophy has been the subject of debate for several reasons. First, as history attests, the interpretation of Marxism as predicting an inevitable move from capitalism to (global) communism is problematic. Second, and perhaps more problematically, twentieth-century forays into communism have led to the totalitarianism of Stalin, Mao, and others. Thinkers in the Frankfurt School (among others) have offered alternative frameworks for Marxist projects, but at this stage viewing the Marxist project in terms of historical certainty or even as a historical ideal is contested—not the least by postmodernism. Writing about the last decades of the twentieth century, Terry Eagleton suggests that "what bred the culture of postmodernism, with its dismissal of so-called grand narratives and triumphal announcement of the End of History, was above all the conviction that the future would now be simply more of the present . . . What helped to discredit Marxism above all, then, was a creeping sense of political impotence."[9] Nevertheless, irrespective of its ability to predict or even to produce a certain future, Marxism continues to offer a powerful means of analysis and a set of highly specific critical tools that produce insightful evaluations and readings of history, culture, and even religious practice. Ironically, however, because Marxism is at its core a critique of capitalism, and unfettered capitalism attempts to dominate the world, Marx's key predictions and criticisms are more pertinent than ever. According to Eagleton, "In our own time, as Marx predicted, inequalities of wealth have dramatically deepened. The income of a single Mexican billionaire today is equivalent to the earnings of the poorest seventeen millions of his compatriots . . . What used to be apocalyptic fantasy is today no more than sober realism. The traditional leftist slogan 'Socialism or barbarism' was never more grimly apposite, never less of a mere rhetorical flourish."[10] Despite its marginal status in Western scholarship, Marxist criticism remains, therefore, the most coherent and devastating means of unveiling and undermining capitalism and its deep incoherencies.

Marxist Biblical Criticism

Adopting a Marxist frame of reference within the guild of biblical criticism requires a couple of hermeneutical and contextual adaptions. This is primarily because Marxism developed as a response to and critique of the emerging capitalism of European industrial revolutions, whereas the biblical contexts of production predate capitalism proper. Historians of the ancient world and biblical critics bridge this contextual distance in a couple of ways. First, they take the critical tools and categories of Marxist theory and apply them to the various historical circumstances of the ancient world. For example, while the class conflict between workers and the capitalist classes has had a particular historical meaning over the past 150 years, economic class distinctions may yet be discerned and analyzed in the ancient world. In Ste. Croix's reading of the classical and Roman worlds, for example, the proletariat and bourgeoisie are replaced by "the propertied class"[11] and the class of "unfree labour," comprising slaves, serfs, and those in debt bondage.[12] In biblical studies, Norman Gottwald adopts the terms "upper or ruling class"[13] and "lower class"[14] when investigating ancient Palestine. Because of the great span of history Gottwald covers, these terms are necessarily broad but speak to class conflict. Similarly, the key Marxist categories of labor, alienation, and access to the means of production can be used in both eras. When analyzing the ancient world, this typically means a focus on access to land and agricultural technologies.

Another way in which to apply Marxist criticism to the ancient world (championed by Roland Boer and Christina Petterson) is to look to the emergence of capitalist economic forms and their concomitant social apparatuses. With a special focus on the movement from sacred to slave economies, Petterson and Boer's work on the legal category of private property, especially in the Roman Empire,[15] is a clear forerunner to the moral categories underpinning capitalism proper. Moreover, within the broader "stages of history" conception, Marx's (sub-)Asiatic mode of production both describes the ancient world and serves as a forerunner to later modes of production. The analysis thus allows, within the Marxian philosophy of history, an interrogation of the ancient world as it gives birth to later history.

Once the interpretive distance is bridged within a theoretical framework, Marxist biblical scholars typically proceed to use the ideas and tools of Marxist scholarship to analyze the Bible in materialist terms. These analyses range from a close attention to trade, production, land use, value extraction, and other economic categories (often relying on archaeological evidence) through to higher-level readings of these texts in terms of the reinforcement and maintenance of particular relationships of production through social and cultural means. Marxist biblical critics have thus justified their application of dialectical thinking to uncover the deep contradictions in the modes of production of the ancient Near East. They have identified situations of class conflict and demonstrated the way in which this conflict generated social, political, and even economic change. Marxist inquiry has also shown how the superstructural apparatuses of a mode of production proceed from the basic material (economic) arrangements of a society in biblical contexts, allowing a rigorous critique these arrangements. Where these arrangements are appropriated ideologically into the context of late capitalism, often through Western Christianity, they form a basis for political and cultural resistance. Moreover, Marxist conceptions of alienation, fetishization, and idolatry (to name but a few) have been used productively in the interrogation and hermeneutical appropriation of biblical texts for the sake of critique and resistance.[16]

Another movement in Marxist scholarship that has some bearing on religious thinking in general, and studies of the Bible in particular, is a multifaceted and dialectic treatment of utopianism and the utopian drive expressed in artistic and other cultural productions. Though Engels used the term in its more common pejorative sense,[17] later thinkers like Ernst Bloch saw in the utopianism of Western culture traces of revolutionary possibility. Bloch's magnum opus, the three-volume *Das Prinzip Hoffnung* (The Principle of Hope),[18] forced Marxist critics to take utopianism seriously and look for revolutionary potential within art, literature, architecture, and even religious/theological thought. This potential can be discerned even when cultural productions are compromised by their bourgeois and pre-bourgeois context. Bloch's guarded interest in religious expressions challenged more ardently atheistic Marxists to move beyond simplistic or reactive rejections of scriptures and religious writings. And, as the later Marxist literary critic Fredric Jameson picks up, understanding utopianism in literature is the first step in developing a framework for revolutionary praxis.[19]

A final point to make explicit about Marxist critical theory is its deep commitment to "always historicize."[20] In practice this has meant that theory and criticism must emerge from, or be applied to, the particularities of historical circumstance, rather than emerging (ex nihilo) from the realm of pure thought. Indeed, it may be argued that Marx's dialectics can be contrasted with Hegel's on the key point that Hegel seeks to justify the material world—especially state structures—from a set of (theo)logical and philosophical first principles. In contrast, Marx prefers to develop theory *from* "real" historical circumstances which he classifies within various "modes of production." This historicizing preference has remained strong in critics influenced by Marxist thought. David Graeber, for example, is roundly critical of the capitalist myth of the origins of money. There is simply no historical evidence that an ancient village ever existed where it was decided that money would be a more convenient way to facilitate the preexisting barter system. Instead, Graeber argues that the emergence of money was tied to historical circumstances of governing oppression in order to measure and manage debt and, importantly, it became necessary for various military excursions as soldiers ventured far from home and were unable to rely on immediate access to food and shelter.[21] This view of the emergence of money is relevant to the historical context of biblical texts. Another example arises in *Idols of Nations*,[22] where Boer and Petterson unpick the use of biblical motifs in the work of the early captains of capitalist thought, especially Hugo Grotius, John Locke, and Adam Smith. Alongside a full-throated dismissal of the simplistic appropriation of the fall narratives by a number of these thinkers, Boer and Petterson demonstrate the mythic element underlying so much of the justification for capitalist economics—a kind of dehistoricized romanticism that papers over capitalism's deep contradictions. Not surprisingly, Boer and Petterson prefer the more historically locatable analysis of capitalism found in Marx.

JAMESON'S H/HISTORY

More recent Marxism also offers a sophisticated theoretical understanding of history itself. For example, in Jameson's estimation, it is "only Marxism [which] finally offers a philosophically coherent and ideologically compelling resolution to the dilemma of historicism."[23] Yet in order to construct this framework, the term "history" itself must be unpacked. Broadly speaking, in the Marxism of Jameson, at least three different working definitions of (H/h)history may be discerned. The first is History, with a capital "H," that totality of everything that is and that happens, the "untranscendable horizon [which] needs no particular theoretical justification."[24] It is, in dialectical terms, the experience of Necessity—the "inexorable form of events" that must happen because they do happen. The problem, of course, is that just as History is untranscendable, it is also unable to be captured or contained. Text, discourse, and desire are all attempts to represent and shape this History. Yet against this, Necessity sets "inexorable limits," dialectically constraining the trajectories of Freedom. The consequence is that all representations of History are incomplete. History can never be accounted for entirely by history.

Jameson's second notion of history (lowercase "h") is a more unwieldy conception and refers, in its simplest form, to limited and temporary representations of History. This history refers to nothing more (and nothing less) than the variety of ways of telling or approximating History that have been designated to be "history." It is this history that "'enters' the text... precisely as *ideology*."[25] Though history has often been misleadingly equated with History, for Jameson history is instead a collection of the productions that arise from applying the competing models or "philosophies" of representing History. And for Jameson, this "genuine philosophy" is described by Marxist dialectical materialism as it illuminates the conflict and class struggle intrinsic to History. Dialectical thinking, in Jameson's approach to H/history at least, is concerned both with the ways in which History and history shape each other and the ways in which different histories collide. In history, and I would argue in all artistic-textual representations, Freedom may, for a moment, sublate Necessity. These moments, however, do not arise randomly. They are instead part of the wider coherence of class struggle, the "engine of history" traced out by Marxist analysis.

This then brings me to Jameson's third, and less explicit, designation of history (again lowercase "h"). In this case, however, "history" refers primarily to the products of the aforementioned "genuine philosophy" of history. In fact, though Jameson's reflection on H/history is relatively brief in the body of his work, it is this final "genuine" history that seems to be intended when the term "history" is used without qualification. This genuine history is a subset of wider histories but, because it is ultimately superior, it might also be regarded as somehow outside of other historical productions for the simple reason that it, as a theory, is able to account for and critique them.

Marxist Historicism and Postcolonialism

It is the commitment to historical analysis that provides a helpful starting point for fruitful dialogue between Marxist and postcolonial thought.[26] As postcolonial thinkers attempt to unpick the damaging myths imposed by colonial invaders, careful attention to the historical circumstances of colonial times are needed—to understand and demythologize the colonial enterprise and also to claim some sense of cultural identity beyond the colonial view. And, because the form of colonialism across much of the world for at least two hundred years has been one of capitalism expansion, Marxist criticism may assist postcolonial thinkers to recognize the various ways that capitalism asserts and maintains control. Moreover, the demythologizing drive of Marxism may also assist postcolonial thinkers to avoid the trap of replacing one dehistoricized ideology of oppression with another. For example, care must be taken in rejecting imperial Christianity not to replace it with an idealized, but also oppressive, caste system.[27] Attention to the historical circumstances of all economic classes, both in precolonial and colonial times, may assist postcolonial thinkers to establish social and political models that resist class oppression. And Marxist criticism reminds us that this is a fraught enterprise if it does not adequately address the realities of global capitalism that force postcolonial nations into continuing patterns of oppressive behaviour.

On the other hand, Marxist thought does need to be reframed or extended to incorporate the context of postcoloniality. Frantz Fanon foretells an alliance of sorts between the colonized and Marxists: "In the colonies the economic infrastructure is also a superstructure. The cause is effect: You are rich because you are white, you are white because you are rich. This is why a Marxist analysis should always be slightly stretched when it comes to addressing the colonial issue."[28] Biblical criticism is, in my opinion, the poorer for overlooking this exhortation. Both Marxists and postcolonial critics have some work to do.

Key Figures in Marxist Biblical Criticism

A full list of important contributors to the body of Marxist biblical criticism would be far too lengthy to cover here. Some particular voices are, however, important to mention. Norman Gottwald's *Tribes of Yahweh* is a seminal work tracking key social, political, religious (sacerdotal), and economic structures in which the texts of the Hebrew Bible were formed.[29] Gottwald analyzes these structures in terms of overarching modes of production (sub-Asiatic) and the forces of production at work in distorting and extracting value.[30] Richard Horsley is generally less overtly Marxist in political commitment than Gottwald but regularly utilizes Marxist sociological structures and analytic tools, especially conflict theory.[31] David Jobling explores Marxist biblical criticism in relationship to other interpretive movements like feminism and postcolonialism,[32] and Neil Elliot's work brings Marxist analysis to bear on the Paul corpus.[33] Perhaps most important is Roland Boer's prodigious contribution to the fields of biblical studies, theology, and religion in relationship to Marxism. Now, often in concert with Christina Petterson, Boer pays careful attention to key Marxist thinkers and applies their thought to biblical texts and their subsequent development in theology more broadly. His exegetical work has typically been focused on Hebrew texts but more recently has begun the work of developing overarching materialist constructions of the world of the New Testament.[34] For a concise summary of Marxist criticism, especially as it pertains to biblical studies, the introduction to Boer's *Marxist Criticism of the Hebrew Bible* is an excellent place to start.[35]

Marxism and the Biblical Texts

Perhaps the first hermeneutical question of Marxist biblical criticism is how to account for texts that are contextually removed from the development of Marxism. It is methodologically unsound simply to apply nineteenth-century methods to the ancient

Near East. Instead, fundamental decisions must be made about each text and context under scrutiny. Broadly speaking, this means determining to what extent texts are products of a dominating class and where traces of resistance and the perspective of oppressed "working" classes have survived various processes of transmission, redaction, and appropriation. For some Marxists, the answer is almost axiomatic. All religious texts are tools of ideological control and are used by the bourgeoisie and other dominant classes to maintain control. Biblical texts must, therefore, be ignored or their ideology unmasked and rejected. Other Marxists adopt a more nuanced approach. For these thinkers the Bible is regarded as a product of scores of contributors (authors, storytellers, and redactors) spanning vastly different historical circumstances. If class conflict "drives" history as Marxism supposes, these texts must, therefore, contain traces of this conflict. Moreover, they can also be interrogated for the sake of recovering revolutionary politics today. Central to this approach is a kind of historical modeling, using textual and extratextual information to recreate the world in which the text originally functioned for the purpose of discerning the central points of conflict and resistance. A careful mapping between these points of conflict and the situation of the interpreter may then unmask analogous or complementary political tactics. This view is particularly helpful for interpreters writing from situations of oppression where the Bible retains social and religious status.

A final view that is, perhaps, a variation or extension of the second approach suggests that all texts, or at least all texts with narrative elements, may be read for the sake of revolutionary politics—even when they are obviously products of a dominant culture. In this view all texts may be read "against the grain," noting the dominating voices but also open to being read tangentially or even ironically—self-consciously from the perspective of the voiceless for the sake of vindicating the oppressed and fomenting revolution. This approach differs from previous approaches not because it avoids naming the conflicting historical forces represented in the text, but because it refuses to arbitrarily dissect the text. In this approach, difficult sections are not easily discarded. Instead, all texts should be read as connected narratives, even as they are read through the lens of the oppressed classes. In the English canon of literature, both Jameson and Eagleton especially exemplify this approach as they read everything from Shakespeare to pulp science fiction through a Marxist lens without excising oppressive voices. When Eagleton does turn to biblical texts, he attempts to model the same approach.[36] Apart from those (anti)readers who discard the Bible without even opening it, Marxist critics recognize the power and historical significance of the biblical texts throughout history, firstly in Europe and surrounds (North Africa, Southeast Asia, East Asia, and so on) and now across the entire globe. The Bible cannot safely be ignored, even by the most ardent Marxist. Moreover, those critics committed to an approach that stems from Marxist historiography look carefully at the circumstances of production, transmission, and interpretation to discern class conflict and the various voices speaking through the text. Finally, Marxist critics read the Bible not simply to interpret it but rather to change the world in each historical moment.

Fernando Belo and Itumeleng Mosala

Perhaps the most ardent and prodigious Marxist biblical critic and archivist of Marxist approaches to biblical, theological, and religious texts in general has been Roland Boer. Indeed, his work on the Hebrew Bible in the second edition of *Marxist Criticism of the Hebrew Bible* constitutes a concise and yet comprehensive collection of fruitful Marxist readings of texts from the Hebrew Bible. Though obviously only a smattering of biblical texts are analyzed, it feels like it is only a matter of applying the Marxist approaches and frameworks collected by Boer to other biblical texts to generate a bevy of insightful readings. Rather than regurgitating or even critiquing Boer's work, I turn instead to two earlier Marxist biblical critics whose focus includes close readings of New Testament texts. Marxist analysis of the New Testament is a slowly blossoming field, which is being supported by social and historical analysis of the ancient Near East and changing modes of production of the twenty-first century. Fernando Belo's 1974 reading of Mark's gospel[37] and Itumeleng Mosala's 1989 reading of Luke[38] provide helpful examples of the use of Marxist criticism in biblical interpretation. Moreover, as Mosala writes directly from late apartheid South Africa, a context at the edge of colonial and postcolonialism, and Belo writes from a context steeped in the experience of colonial Latin America,[39] their avowedly Marxist readings resonate with many of the issues raised by explicitly postcolonial critics.[40] Even if the heavy hand of oppressive and reactionary authors, editors, and compilers is evident in biblical texts, traces of class conflict and revolutionary utopianism can often be discerned when the text is viewed in its full historical circumstance. Mosala's reading of Micah and Luke 1–2 in *Biblical Hermeneutics and Black Theology in South Africa*, and Fernando Belo's idiosyncratic and insightful, though often ignored, *A Materialistic Reading of the Gospel Mark* are both excellent examples of this kind of analysis. In both cases the biblical texts are read in their historical context to discern the voices of the oppressors and the oppressed as a way of underlining resistant thinking and practice in the authors' own contexts. In particular, both authors are convinced that the imperialist colonial enterprise is driven by the capitalist mode of production. Thus, any postcolonial or, more properly, anticolonial analysis must be configured in terms of its relationship to capitalism. For these authors, the clearest alternative to capitalism is, of course, revolutionary communism. From this starting point, then, Belo and Mosala interrogate biblical texts as both texts of oppression, wielded by the colonizers and part of the superstructure of control, and as texts of potential resistance, to be seized and turned back toward those in power.

A Materialist Reading of the Gospel of Mark

Belo's seminal *A Materialist Reading of the Gospel of Mark* regards the biblical text of Mark's gospel as primarily a product of a class conflict in first-century Palestine. Belo reads Mark as a text that emerges from a context of class struggle between working classes and ruling classes of the Roman Empire and its vassal states. This context was exacerbated by the extrabureaucratic demands of a forced integration of the economy of Palestine with that of the wider Empire.[41] Drawing on Josephus, Belo sees in the Essenes, Pharisees, and Zealots hints of resisting classes that recover a tradition of liberative messianism as a revolutionary trope.[42] For Belo, the Gospel of Mark should, then, be read as a text within a context of conflict, and the tensions, symbolic oppositions, and delayed (proairetic) fulfillment of narrative prophecy must be understood in terms of the inherent contradictions of an oppressive mode of production,[43] which the resistant narrative makes manifest. This oppressive mode of production highlights the active conflict between the current (oppressive) regime and a new alternative. In the case of Mark, this alternative regime is an apocalyptic political formation. Belo's version of a close reading is drawn directly from the "fluid" structuralism of Roland Barthes' S/Z, an idiosyncratic though immensely powerful set of tools for narrative analysis.[44]

Belo's conclusions are primarily concerned with the constitution of a "materialist ecclesiology" and a focus on how the Gospel narrative sequences engender materialist practices.[45] These practices inspire an itinerant and hopeful community that encourages careful analysis, charity, and prophetic declaration. Most importantly, however, is the focus on embodiment that Belo sees in the Markan text. Specifically, an embodied messianism which is uniquely productive for communist projects. Ultimately, and helpfully, Belo is less interested in whether Mark is "on the whole" a text of the ruling or the "popular" classes. Instead he recognizes that the Markan narrative displays elements of class disruption, a reframed understanding of power, and clear practices for the constitution of a body that is thoroughly materialist and ecclesial—the Christian communist community. Likewise, while Belo is clear that the messianic narrative of Mark is not revolutionary, this is because "revolution was impossible or doomed to failure, as 70 shows."[46] He also explores the difference between the Jesus movement and Zealotry as a way of rejecting wanton, ill-directed, or even counterrevolutionary violence. Importantly, however, this does not rule out the possibility of a revolutionary moment for the Markan community—simply that revolution at the time of writing was tantamount to "collective suicide."[47] Belo's Marxist allegiance is tempered by his exploration of Mark, which shows how risky the use of violence can be—something relevant for the Latin American political resistance of the 1970s and 1980s. Though not explicitly stated, I expect that Belo is wary of violence because it can so easily break the solidarity of the popular and working classes. Or, as the Zealots demonstrate, violence can too easily compel retribution and extinguish the opportunity for substantive change.

The key relevance of Belo's insightful and wide-ranging reading of Mark for Marxist and postcolonial reading is twofold. First, if Belo has a clear audience at all, it is those Christian communities resisting ongoing capitalist structural injustice, starting with those in Latin America. His attempts to show how Christian texts like Mark's Gospel are inspirational and speak of class conflict within a rapidly changing mode of production in first-century Roman-occupied Palestine open the door for a more thoroughgoing materialist analysis of the situation of twentieth-century colonial capitalism. For the popular "working" classes of Latin American Christians under Pinochet, Videla, and so on, identifying with the class struggle of the ancient peasant classes of Mark's world could only be enriched by a similar identification with the class struggle of communists around the world. Eschewing the (post-)Stalinist Soviet bloc and other iterations of totalitarian state communism,[48] Belo nevertheless sees allies in the Marxist "heroic combatants" of Russia and China but also in Vietnam, Algeria, Cuba, and Chile.[49] In the late twentieth century, Belo contended that revolutionary Marxism should direct class struggle among oppressed (Christian) communities in the colonial world.

Second, Belo recognizes that in many contexts of (colonial) oppression it is impossible to develop a resistant politics without engaging the texts of the (Christian) Bible. In so doing, Belo diverges from the preponderance of classical Eurocentric Marxism.[50] Indeed he regards engaging in biblical texts to be indispensable for the projects of colonial class struggle. Here Belo's work resonates with postcolonial biblical scholars who approach biblical texts from a variety of different angles, reading from below and from outside to develop heterogenous interpretations for the sake of colonized communities. If Belo and other Marxist biblical critics recognize in biblical texts the elements of class struggle and even revolution, postcolonial biblical scholars may recognize the experience of the colonized and their struggle for identity in, around, and through the realities of colonialization. Importantly, class struggle and the struggle for identity and purpose are often thoroughly integrated projects in the colonized world.

Biblical Hermeneutics and Black Theology in South Africa

At a similar time to Belo's writing, Itumeleng Mosala was exploring Marxist readings of the Bible from the context of postcolonized apartheid South Africa. In *Biblical Hermeneutics and Black Theology in South Africa*, Mosala writes from the unique colonial history of South Africa where there was no final transition from colonial to popular "democratic" rule until 1994—far later than most other formal political transitions. Moreover, Mosala's analysis is shaped by an explicit discussion of racial categories that was necessarily brought to the fore by the divisions built into apartheid. Anti-apartheid scholars turned to North American Black Theology more regularly than is evident in Latin America and even other parts of Africa. Within this vein, then, Mosala's *Biblical Hermeneutics* deals not only with Marxist categories around class but also with the way that race and class intersect within his interpretive struggle.

Perhaps Mosala's most influential piece of work, *Biblical Hermeneutics* is written with the particular needs of the anti-apartheid movement in mind. Part of its aim is to challenge and inspire allies in the struggle with the tools and commitments of Marxism. In the circles of the anti-apartheid church and supportive biblical scholars, the attitude to Marxist thinking was ambivalent at best. Yet Mosala's commitment to Marxist analysis is regarded as indispensable for reading the Bible and for understanding the role of

Black Theology in the lives of oppressed South Africans. Though the language of colonization itself does not direct his work, there is a tendency to recover African (black) experience and cultural understanding, a characteristic of postcolonialism evident in Mosala's writing. In a sense, it is wrestling with the colonial situation that gives energy and direction to Mosala's hermeneutics, and he finds in Marxist literary criticism the tools needed to read biblical texts for the sake of understanding them in terms of oppression and liberation.

Mosala begins his work with a lengthy exploration of his historical context and the theoretical shape of a reading that will assist his primary task of finding liberation in and through Black Theology in apartheid South Africa. For Mosala, the resistant hermeneutical promise of Black Theology is brought into conversation with the emergence of the social sciences in attempting to model the contexts that produce the biblical texts. And yet he finds the dominant sociological modeling adopted in biblical criticism wanting. In particular, structuralist functionalist modeling is regarded as offering little liberative potential as it simply continues the trajectory of liberal biblical criticism.[51] Rejecting the Weberian "sociological idealism" of John C. Gager,[52] Mosala argues that this kind of modeling reinforces idealized "stable" descriptions of the ancient world and explains away difficult questions about class conflict and unequal material conditions within this world. For Mosala, the need to affirm a deeply contradicted stability in the context of biblical production is both historically implausible and insufficient for the project of resisting apartheid. A Marxist sociology is preferred because of its ability to account for and direct the conflict that is inherent in all (unjust) modes of production. Mosala sees in both the biblical texts and the context of black Africa an underground communal mode of production that is subsumed by, but also resists, the dominant tributary and capitalist modes that shape, especially, twentieth-century South Africa. If Black Theology, borrowed as it was from North America, is to be "genuinely liberating in its use of the Bible, it will have to identify for itself contemporary forms of black history and culture that will better situate it so that it can re-appropriate past struggles in a critical and hermeneutically fruitful way."[53]

Mosala goes on to read texts from the books of Micah and Luke, finding in Micah evidence of dominance and of oppression. He dissects the biblical texts and discards large sections of the narrative on the basis that they reflect oppressive class interests. Later, he turns to the texts of Luke 1–2 and regards the entire text as a product of ruling ideology, thus also to be discarded. Whether the reader agrees with Mosala's final assessment, the way he applies his Marxist criticism is clear. Citing Terry Eagleton especially,[54] Mosala looks at the productive forces at play in and around the biblical texts—an important worthwhile task—and then carefully dissects the text into sets of competing voices that represent the different interests at play.[55] It seems that for Mosala, revolutionary hermeneutics in apartheid South Africa must reclaim the Bible from the oppressor, find resistance voices within it, and then look to those voices to direct and inspire liberation. Even more important, however, is the task of rejecting texts of oppression and of the colonial and racist masters who use the Bible as a tool of coercion and control.

Mosala exemplifies a connection point between the interests and methods of materialist and postcolonial criticism of the Bible, especially with those strands of postcolonialism that see the Bible as (mostly) a tool of imperial control. Mosala's work resonates closely with Sugirtharajah's reading of Akiki K. Nyabongo's *Africa Answers Back*,[56] in which the teaching of biblical stories by the hapless missionary Hubert is carefully analyzed and then held up to ridicule by virtue of the evident historical and mythological contradictions. In Sugirtharajah's estimation, the core turning point for the protagonist Mujungu (and his people) is polygamous marriage, practiced widely in Southern Africa and in the Hebrew scriptures—but rejected by the colonial piety of "Hubert, the missionary." The ridicule of Hubert becomes acute when he is unable to adequately reconcile the polygamy of Solomon with the prohibition of polygamy in colonizing, missionary Christianity.

In many ways Hubert is a straw man for Nyabongo and also, it seems, for Sugirtharajah. While the missionary's simplistic and patronizing attitudes were no doubt common in the colonial enterprise, if Hubert represents the totality of the missionary enterprise it is difficult to see how it achieved all that much. Moreover, the status of the Bible in Southern Africa today suggests a far richer and more sophisticated interaction with the biblical narratives than is suggested in this reading. A connection may be made to Mosala and his opponents—those who are allies in the struggle, but have failed to embrace Mosala's particular Marxist dissection of the Bible—and are thus presumably unable to fully understand the biblical texts in a way adequate for liberation. For example, if the texts of Luke 1–2 are as simply and obviously texts of oppression, as Mosala maintains, then why do they remain inspirational for so many Christians battling oppression in South Africa?[57] Mosala is correct to state that the Gospel needs to be liberated from the ruling class ideology that he attributes to Luke, the author. Yet this cannot be achieved by a simple dissection of the text. A more nuanced and dialectic reclamation of its liberation potential is preferable. Such an approach may be found, somewhat ironically in Mosala's interpretive guide, Eagleton, whose sophisticated approaches to the canon of English literature are far more nuanced and liberatively productive than Mosala's.

Concluding Connections

The risks of Marxist criticism are well known and have been recounted so often in the capitalist West that they are assumed a priori by many scholars, including many in the guild of biblical studies. Does historical materialism *predict* the future? Does communist practice *always* lead to totalitarian regimes? Does Marxist theory really understand "human nature" or are we truly some contradictory hybrid of *Homo economicus* and self-absorbed individualists? Such simplistic criticisms, even if they are partly accurate, are too often simply diversions that allow otherwise rigorous historians, social critics, and cultural warriors to avoid engaging with the richness of the Marxist tradition or taking seriously Marxism's deep critiques of the capitalist mode of production. In many respects, the opposite is true for postcolonialism, at least in scholarly circles where a flowering of identity-focused readings and a genuine awareness of the historical evils of colonialism have led to an embrace of marginal perspectives. And, even though a rigorous engagement with the literary consequences of poststructuralism is not common in biblical criticism, the plurality of meanings and an aversion to "final" answers to interpretive questions have become commonplace within the guild. In this general milieu of ignorance toward or rejection of Marxism, there are important challenges that lie ahead for postcolonial biblical criticism.

First, there is a risk that postcolonial biblical criticism will become primarily a way of demythologizing and disarming the colonial project of one of its most powerful weapons—the Bible. If so, such a task will find many allies among historians, theoreticians, social scientists, and sociologists inside and outside the guild. The way that the Bible has been used to reinforce colonial enterprises and offer them a deep theological and philosophical imprimatur has been well established and is a worthy goal in itself. I would suggest, however, that there is greater potential for postcolonial biblical readings to not simply consign biblical texts to the rubbish bin but to appropriate them for projects of liberation. In this, postcolonial biblical scholarship must guard against becoming a collection of case studies in reception history. Taking a longer view and incorporating historical-critical insights about the formation of the texts, and their reception and use in *other* contexts, may afford a more effective unpicking of colonialism. In the case of *Africa Answers Back*, Sugirtharajah's focus on the way in which Mujungu's people recognize affinities between African matrimonial practices and those of Solomon may open the door to seeing in the Bible allies in anticolonial and anti-imperial projects. Yet there still remains the need to keep material liberation front and center, and drawing on the rich Marxist critical tradition may assist in this task. In the case at hand, it is helpful to recognize that the polygamy of Solomon looks like the practice of African people. It requires a further step to recognize that Solomon was an oppressive ruler who represents a system of politics and extractive economics that required resistance in the ancient world of the text. Can something similar be said for the idealized precolonial politics advocated by unmaterialist postcolonialism?

Second, postcolonialism should be clear in recognizing empire as more than a political and cultural phenomenon. There is the tendency in the work of Bhabha in particular to focus on the cultural counters of precolonial contexts in order to reclaim characteristics of a social order that have been excised or covered over by imperial conquest and colonial enterprise.[58] When this cultural reclamation affirms a sense of (communal) identity for oppressed or colonized groups, it is a helpful process. But when this cultural reclamation is divorced from a careful economic and materialist analysis of the relations of production (and power) or, even more worryingly, when older cultural arrangements are advocated without attending to matters of justice and class conflict within them, scholars risk (re)introducing another set of oppressive forces into a social mix. It is at this level that the careful materialist analysis of Marxism may assist postcolonial theory to avoid "golden age" thinking.[59] If postcolonialism is to continue to undermine systems of oppression and seek liberation, it is not enough to banish the demons of European colonial history. A better alternative must be offered—one that moves beyond the systematic oppression of colonization but also beyond the preexisting cultural orders of oppression that existed before European invasion. As Said suggests, what is needed is a new kind of humanism[60]—a competing grand narrative in an era when grand narratives remain unpopular.

Finally, and by way of conclusion, I join with Gerald West in his concern that, for all its hermeneutical value, if postcolonial biblical criticism moves away from a central commitment to liberation, it may well lose its ability to realize a deep critique of colonial history and concomitant institutions.[61] Moreover, without some reclamation of the Marxian dictum that philosophy's great failing is that it does not change the world, postcolonial cultural theory too may simply describe it. If theory and philosophy intersect, as they tend to do in biblical criticism, Marx's challenge may be historicized. The risk of interpretive theory, especially that of postcolonialism, is that it simply explains and interprets the situation of the colonized world and its peoples. Without careful materialist analysis, the appreciation of class conflict, an allegiance to a grand narrative to stand against capitalism, and a commitment to liberation hermeneutics, postcolonial theory may miss the point.

Notes

1. Roland Boer, *Marxist Criticism of the Hebrew Bible*, 2nd ed. (London and New York: T & T Clark, 2015), 1.
2. The collected essays in *Nation and Narration* are examples of postcolonialism that do touch upon Marxism. See Homi K. Bhabha, ed., *Nation and Narration* (London and New York: Routledge, 1990).
3. A fascinating discussion about the interrelatedness of and deep divisions between post-structuralism and later Marxism can be found in Jacques Derrida, *Specters of Marx*, trans. Peggy Kamuf (New York and London: Routledge Classics, 1994);' and in response, Michael Sprinkler, ed., *Ghostly Demarcations: A Symposium on Jacques Derrida's Specters of Marx* (London and New York: Verso, 2008).
4. I find Lynne St. Clair Darden's description helpful because of its simplicity and historical location: "The term *postcolonial* was first used after World War II to demarcate an historical period following the dismantling of European colonies in Africa, Asia, the Caribbean, and Latin America and the ensuing reconfiguration of the various leaderships, parties, and governments that had gained their independence from colonial rule." Lynne St. Clair Darden, *Scripturalizing Revelation: An African American Postcolonial Reading of Empire* (Atlanta: SBL, 2015), 46, italics original. Whatever postcolonial theory has explored, it must not lose its roots in the specific challenges facing the contexts of its origins.
5. I use the plural "biblical texts" in contrast to the "bible text" or "the Bible." Approaching the Bible as a unified artefact is common to many postcolonial critics. This monolithic treatment of the biblical text is justifiable by virtue of the way in which it was "brought" by the colonizers, but it is not the only way to understand the texts.

6. Space does not permit an exploration of nationalism and inter-/transnationalism as it pertains to postcolonialism and the utopian hopes of Marxism. Suffice it to say that "the nation" is a contested conception and part of a wider dialectic that involves ongoing mediation. If postcolonialism breaks the borders of nationalism from the particularities of colonized experience, Marxism tends to challenge these same borders through human solidarity across working classes.
7. A term often used by one Marxist to undercut another. See, e.g., McKenzie Wark, "Four Cheers for Vulgar Marxism!!!!," Public Seminar (Online), 2014, http://www.publicseminar.org/2014/04/four-cheers-for-vulgarity/.
8. The use of the opposing metaphors of "base" and "superstructure" are common in Marxism and generally denote the divisions between the material factors underlying a society—technology, population, (social) class—with expressions and institutions that arise from it, such as culture, ideology, political systems, and religious institutions. For a longer discussion on how these metaphors should be understood see Boer, *Marxist Criticism of the Hebrew Bible*, 7–9.
9. Terry Eagleton, *Why Marx Was Right* (New Haven and London: Yale University Press, 2011), 6.
10. Eagleton, *Why Marx Was Right*, 8.
11. G. E. M. De Ste. Croix, *The Class Struggle in the Ancient Greek World: From the Archaic Age to the Arab Conquests* (Ithaca, NY: Cornell University Press, 1981), 114ff.
12. Ste. Croix, *The Class Struggle in the Ancient Greek World*, 133–137.
13. For example, Norman Gottwald, *Tribes of Yahweh: A Sociology of the Religion of Liberated Israel, 1250–1050 BCE* (Sheffield: Sheffield Academic Press, 1999), 557.
14. For example, the Canaanites; Gottwald, 217ff.
15. Roland Boer and Christina Petterson, *Time of Troubles: Christianity in the Context of Greco-Roman Economics* (Minneapolis: Fortress, 2017), 115–118.
16. Boer is, again, the most prolific author in this area. See especially his series *On Marxism and Theology*, especially Roland Boer, *Criticism of Heaven: On Marxism and Theology* (Leiden: Brill, 2005); Roland Boer, *Criticism of Religion: On Marxism and Theology II* (Leiden: Brill, 2009); Roland Boer, *Criticism of Earth: On Marx, Engels, and Theology* (Leiden: Brill, 2012).
17. Friedrich Engels, *Socialism: Utopian and Scientific*, trans. Edward Aveling (New York: Cosimo, 2008).
18. Ernst Bloch, *The Principle of Hope*, trans. Neville Plaice, Stephen Plaice, and Paul Knight, 3 vols. (Cambridge, MA: MIT Press, 1995).
19. See Fredric Jameson, *Archaeologies of the Future: The Desire Called Utopia and Other Science Fictions* (London and New York: Verso, 2005).
20. Fredric Jameson, *The Political Unconscious: Narrative as Socially Symbolic Act* (London and New York: Routledge, 1981), 9.
21. David Graeber, *Debt: The First 5000 Years* (New York: Melville House, 2011), 21–72.
22. Roland Boer and Christina Petterson, *Idols of Nations: Biblical Myth at the Origins of Capitalism* (Minneapolis: Fortress, 2014).
23. Jameson, *The Political Unconscious: Narrative as Socially Symbolic Act*, 19.
24. Jameson, *The Political Unconscious: Narrative as Socially Symbolic Act*, 102.
25. Terry Eagleton, *Criticism and Ideology: A Study in Marxist Literary Theory* (London: NLB, 1976), 72, italics original.

26. Indeed, I feel that postcolonial theory is at its most useful when it is adopted alongside other frameworks. See, e.g., Dube on feminism and postcolonialism in *Postcolonial Feminist Interpretation of the Bible* (St. Louis, MO: Chalice, 2000). See also Lynne St. Clair on the African American context in *Scripturalizing Revelation: An African American Postcolonial Reading of Empire*, 77. What seems to be missing, for the most part, is an extended interaction between materialist and postcolonial biblical criticisms—though Horsley's empire studies might be heading in that direction. See, for example, Richard A. Horsley, *Jesus and Empire: The Kingdom of God and the New World Disorder* (Minneapolis: Fortress, 2003).

27. I try to avoid the unqualified use of the term "Christianity" and its use in contrast to other so-called world religions like Hinduism. Apart from the fact that these religious movements are hardly monolithic, reading the Bible through these categories is anachronistic for understanding the ancient world and inhibits the ability "to recognize parallels between Jewish and Christian origins and the current struggles of imperially subject peoples to renew their own traditional way of life in the face of persistent western imperial encroachment." Richard A. Horsley, "Renewal Movements and Resistance to Empire in Ancient Judea," in *The Postcolonial Biblical Reader* (Malden, MA, Oxford, UK, and Carlton, Australia: Blackwell, 2006), 76.

28. Frantz Fanon, *The Wretched of the Earth*, trans. Richard Philcox (New York: Grove Press, 2004), 5.

29. Gottwald's insights should not be understated, even for those unconvinced by or antithetical to Gottwald's Marxist leanings. As Walter Brueggemann notes: "Gottwald has made unmistakably clear that liberated and liberating theology must have careful and sustained attention to methodology, so that it does not at the outset concede the main points in question, or in turn become itself a noncritical ideology." "Review: The Tribes of Yahweh," *Journal of the American Academy of Religion* 48, no. 3 (1980): 450.

30. Gottwald, *Tribes of Yahweh: A Sociology of the Religion of Liberated Israel*.

31. See, e.g., Richard A. Horsley, *Jesus and the Spiral of Violence: Popular Jewish Resistance in Roman Palestine* (San Francisco: Harper & Row, 1987); Richard A. Horsley, *Sociology and the Jesus Movement* (New York: Continuum, 1994); Richard A. Horsley and John S. Hanson, *Bandits, Prophets, and Messiahs: Popular Movements at the Time of Jesus* (San Francisco: Harper & Row, 1985); Richard A. Horsley, *Galilee: History, Politics, People* (Harrisburg, PA: Trinity Press, 1995).

32. David Jobling, "Feminism and 'Mode of Production' in Ancient Israel: Search for a Method," in *The Bible and the Politics of Exegesis: Essays in Honor of Norman K. Gottwald on His Sixty-Fifth Birthday* (Cleveland: Pilgrim, 1991); David Jobling, "'Very Limited Ideological Options': Marxism and Biblical Studies in Postcolonial Scenes," in *Postcolonial Biblical Criticism: Interdisciplinary Intersections* (London and New York: T & T Clark, 2005), 184–201.

33. See, e.g., Neil Elliott, *Liberating Paul: The Justice of God and the Politics of the Apostle* (Minneapolis: Fortress, 1994).

34. Boer's works are too numerous to list in full but see, e.g., Boer, *Marxist Criticism of the Hebrew Bible*; Boer and Petterson, *Time of Troubles: Christianity in the Context of Greco-Roman Economics*; Boer, *Criticism of Heaven: On Marxism and Theology*; Boer, *Criticism of Religion: On Marxism and Theology II*; Roland Boer, "Resistance versus Accommodation: What to Do with Romans 13?," in *Postcolonial Interventions: Essays in Honor of R. S. Sugirtharajah*,

ed. Benny Liew Tat-Siong (Sheffield: Sheffield Phoenix Press, 2009), 109–122; Roland Boer, "Opium, Idols and Revolution: Marx and Engels on Religion," *Religion Compass* 5, no. 11 (2011): 698–707; Boer and Petterson, *Idols of Nations: Biblical Myth at the Origins of Capitalism*; Boer, *Criticism of Earth: On Marx, Engels, and Theology*; Roland Boer, "Twenty-Five Years of Marxist Biblical Criticism," *CBR* 5, no. 3 (2007): 298–321.

35. Boer, *Marxist Criticism of the Hebrew Bible*.
36. Eagleton's interest tends to be more theological than biblical. It is also clear when he does engage in biblical exegesis that his impressive command of English literature dwarfs his credentials in biblical studies.
37. Fernando Belo, *A Materialist Reading of the Gospel of Mark*, trans. Matthew J. O'Connell (Maryknoll, NY: Orbis, 1981).
38. Itumeleng J. Mosala, *Biblical Hermeneutics and Black Theology in South Africa* (Grand Rapids: Eerdmans, 1989). See also Takatso Mofokeng, "Black Christians, the Bible and Liberation," *Journal of Black Theology* 2 (1988): 34–42. This important article is brought into conversation with recent postcolonial thinking in Jobling, "'Very Limited Ideological Options.'"
39. Belo, *A Materialist Reading of the Gospel of Mark*, 1ff.
40. As they wrote in the 1970s and 1980s, neither Belo nor Mosala use the term "postcolonial" explicitly. However Belo does acknowledge the colonial situation in Belo, *A Materialist Reading of the Gospel of Mark*, 82, 280. Mosala has been used as a source by numerous biblical critics dealing with resisting colonialism and biblical interpretation in Africa see, e.g., Gerald West, "Negotiating with 'the White Man's Book': Early Foundations for Liberation Hermeneutics in Southern Africa," in *African Theology Today* (Eugene, OR: Wipf and Stock, 2002).
41. Belo, *A Materialist Reading of the Gospel of Mark*, 81–82.
42. Belo, *A Materialist Reading of the Gospel of Mark*, 84.
43. Sub-Asiatic and the slave economy are modes of production explicitly identified in Belo, *A Materialist Reading of the Gospel of Mark*, 26–30.
44. Roland Barthes, *S/Z: An Essay*, trans. Richard C. Miller (New York: Hill & Wang, 1974).
45. The practices of the "foot," "hand," "eyes," and "seed word." See Belo, *A Materialist Reading of the Gospel of Mark*, 244–250.
46. Referring to fall of the Second Temple in about 70 CE. Belo, *A Materialist Reading of the Gospel of Mark*, 283.
47. Belo, *A Materialist Reading of the Gospel of Mark*, 283.
48. In a fascinating study, David Chioni Moore argues convincingly that the Soviet and Chinese iterations of communism should be counted as examples of colonial expansion at the expense of the colonized. The antipathy to Marxism in postcolonial theory no doubt stems from a wariness of communist invasions throughout the twentieth century. David Chioni Moore, "Is the Post- in Postcolonial the Post- in Post-Soviet? Toward a Global Postcolonial Critique," *Publications of the Modern Language Association of America* 116, no. 1 (2001): 111–128.
49. Belo, *A Materialist Reading of the Gospel of Mark*, 295. Belo's view is challenged by the postcolonial criticism of Régis Debray who suggests that Marxism offered simply another panacea in Algeria, Vietnam, and even Cuba (in the 1950s and 1960s). Referenced in Timothy Brennan, "The National Longing for Form," in *Nation and Narration*, ed. Homi K. Bhabha (London and New York: Routledge, 1990), 51–52. That Marxism can

be sold (and bought) as a cure-all is a justified criticism. Nevertheless, to overlook Marxism's generative power for resistance and change because it does not solve everything seems short-sighted.

50. Or, as Thom calls it, the "Germanism" of Marx. Martin Thom, "Tribes within Nations: The Ancient Germans and the History of Modern France," in *Nation and Narration*, ed. Homi K. Bhabha (London and New York: Routledge, 1990), 40.
51. Mosala, *Biblical Hermeneutics and Black Theology in South Africa*, 55–56.
52. Mosala, *Biblical Hermeneutics and Black Theology in South Africa*, 60.
53. Mosala, *Biblical Hermeneutics and Black Theology in South Africa*, 98.
54. Mosala, *Biblical Hermeneutics and Black Theology in South Africa*, 32–33, 46, 49–55, and so on.
55. I have written elsewhere that I feel Mosala is too simplistic in his reading of Luke, especially the *Magnificat* and the *Benedictus*, which retain traces of liberation. See Niall McKay, "Apartheid Resistance and Biblical Interpretation: From Christian Confession to Materialist Analysis," *PR* 8, no. 2 (2015): 12–13. Mosala dismisses these connections by suggesting that the Maccabean songs of liberation are useless because the Maccabean revolution was simply appropriated by the Hasmonean nationalist ideology. The fact that texts *have been* or *may be* co-opted by ruling ideologies does not, however, necessarily rob them of their liberative potential.
56. R. S. Sugirtharajah, *The Bible and Empire* (Cambridge: Cambridge University Press, 2005), 202–211.
57. Another example can be found in the reading of Naboth by Robert Wafawanaka, who identifies the competing economic interests and control in the biblical text but uses this as a means of understanding and generating a response to twenty-first-century arrangements of global capital, especially around debt. Such an insightful and historically locatable study would be enriched by an explicit engagement with Marxist theory. The fact that it does not demonstrates the distance between postcolonial theory and Marxism today. See Robert Wafawanaka, "The Global Crisis of Debt in Context Biblical and Postcolonial Reflections On the Ideology of Empire," in *Reading the Bible in an Age of Crisis: Political Exegesis for a New Day* (Minneapolis: Augsburg Fortress, 2015), 163–190.
58. *Nation and Narration*, edited by Bhabha, does contain some engagements with Marxism—though more on the level of reviewing specific Marxist movements in twentieth-century history rather than theory itself. Not much of this engagement has carried through into Bhabha's disciples in biblical studies. For example, see R. S. Sugirtharajah, ed., *The Postcolonial Bible* (Sheffield: Sheffield Academic Press, 1998); Sugirtharajah, *The Bible and Empire*; Jeremy Punt, "Postcolonial Biblical Criticism in South Africa: Some Mind and Road Mapping," *Neotestamentica* 37, no. 1 (2003): 59–85.
59. I think it is critical, for example, to pay attention to Sugirtharajah's work on the way that the Bible functioned as a "marginal and minority text" in parts of Asia and Africa as a way of recovering a more nuanced and multivoiced view of the way biblical texts may function in different ways to the manner in which they were used by the colonizers. See R. S. Sugirtharajah, *The Bible and the Third World: Precolonial, Colonial and Postcolonial Encounters* (Cambridge: Cambridge University Press, 2004), 13–44.
60. Especially in Edward W. Said, *Orientalism* (London: Penguin, 2003).
61. Gerald West, "Doing Postcolonial Biblical Interpretation @Home: Ten Years of (South) African Ambivalence," *Neotestamentica* 42, no. 1 (2008): 154.

Bibliography

Barthes, Roland. *S/Z: An Essay*. Translated by Richard C. Miller. New York: Hill and Wang, 1974.
Belo, Fernando. *A Materialist Reading of the Gospel of Mark*. Translated by Matthew J. O'Connell. Maryknoll, NY: Orbis, 1981.
Bhabha, Homi K. Ed. *Nation and Narration*. London and New York: Routledge, 1990.
Bloch, Ernst. *The Principle of Hope*. Translated by Neville Plaice, Stephen Plaice, and Paul Knight. 3 vols. Vol. 1. Cambridge, MA: MIT Press, 1995.
Boer, Roland. *Criticism of Heaven: On Marxism and Theology*. Leiden: Brill, 2005.
Boer, Roland. "Twenty-Five Years of Marxist Biblical Criticism." *CBR* 5, no. 3 (2007): 298–321.
Boer, Roland. *Criticism of Religion: On Marxism and Theology II*. Leiden: Brill, 2009.
Boer, Roland. "Resistance versus Accommodation: What to Do with Romans 13?" In *Postcolonial Interventions: Essays in Honor of R. S. Sugirtharajah*, edited by Benny Liew Tat-Siong, 109–122. Sheffield: Sheffield Phoenix Press, 2009.
Boer, Roland. "Opium, Idols and Revolution: Marx and Engels on Religion." *Religion Compass* 5, no. 11 (2011): 698–707.
Boer, Roland. *Criticism of Earth: On Marx, Engels, and Theology*. Leiden: Brill, 2012.
Boer, Roland. *Marxist Criticism of the Hebrew Bible*. 2nd ed. London and New York: T & T Clark, 2015.
Boer, Roland, and Christina Petterson. *Idols of Nations: Biblical Myth at the Origins of Capitalism*. Minneapolis: Fortress, 2014.
Boer, Roland, and Christina Petterson. *Time of Troubles: Christianity in the Context of Greco-Roman Economics*. Minneapolis: Fortress, 2017.
Brennan, Timothy. "The National Longing for Form." In *Nation and Narration*, edited by Homi K. Bhabha, 44–70. London and New York: Routledge, 1990.
Brueggemann, Walter. "Review: The Tribes of Yahweh." *Journal of the American Academy of Religion* 48, no. 3 (1980): 441–451.
Derrida, Jacques. *Specters of Marx*. Translated by Peggy Kamuf. New York and London: Routledge Classics, 1994.
Dube, Musa W. *Postcolonial Feminist Interpretation of the Bible*. St. Louis: Chalice, 2000.
Eagleton, Terry. *Criticism and Ideology: A Study in Marxist Literary Theory*. London: NLB, 1976.
Eagleton, Terry. *Why Marx Was Right*. New Haven and London: Yale University Press, 2011.
Elliott, Neil. *Liberating Paul: The Justice of God and the Politics of the Apostle*. Minneapolis: Fortress, 1994.
Engels, Friedrich. *Socialism: Utopian and Scientific*. Translated by Edward Aveling. New York: Cosimo, 2008.
Fanon, Frantz. *The Wretched of the Earth*. Translated by Richard Philcox. New York: Grove Press, 2004.
Gottwald, Norman. *Tribes of Yahweh: A Sociology of the Religion of Liberated Israel, 1250–1050 BCE*. Sheffield: Sheffield Academic Press, 1999.
Graeber, David. *Debt: The First 5000 Years*. New York: Melville House, 2011.
Horsley, Richard A. *Jesus and the Spiral of Violence: Popular Jewish Resistance in Roman Palestine*. San Francisco: Harper & Row, 1987.
Horsley, Richard A. *Sociology and the Jesus Movement*. New York: Continuum, 1994.
Horsley, Richard A. *Galilee: History, Politics, People*. Harrisburg, PA: Trinity Press, 1995.

Horsley, Richard A. *Jesus and Empire: The Kingdom of God and the New World Disorder.* Minneapolis: Fortress, 2003.

Horsley, Richard A. "Renewal Movements and Resistance to Empire in Ancient Judea." In *The Postcolonial Biblical Reader*, 69–77. Malden, MA, Oxford, UK, and Carlton, Australia: Blackwell, 2006.

Horsley, Richard A., and John S. Hanson. *Bandits, Prophets, and Messiahs: Popular Movements at the Time of Jesus.* San Francisco: Harper & Row, 1985.

Jameson, Fredric. *The Political Unconscious: Narrative as Socially Symbolic Act.* London and New York: Routledge, 1981.

Jameson, Fredric. *Archaeologies of the Future: The Desire Called Utopia and Other Science Fictions.* London and New York: Verso, 2005.

Jobling, David. "Feminism and 'Mode of Production' in Ancient Israel: Search for a Method." In *The Bible and the Politics of Exegesis: Essays in Honor of Norman K. Gottwald on His Sixty-Fifth Birthday.* Cleveland: Pilgrim, 1991.

Jobling, David. "'Very Limited Ideological Options': Marxism and Biblical Studies in Postcolonial Scenes." In *Postcolonial Biblical Criticism: Interdisciplinary Intersections*, edited by Fernando F. Segovia and Stephen D. Moore, 184–201. London and New York: T & T Clark, 2005.

McKay, Niall. "Apartheid Resistance and Biblical Interpretation: From Christian Confession to Materialist Analysis." *PR* 8, no. 2 (2015): 358–378.

Mofokeng, Takatso. "Black Christians, the Bible and Liberation." *Journal of Black Theology* 2 (1988): 34–42.

Moore, David Chioni. "Is the Post- in Postcolonial the Post- in Post-Soviet? Toward a Global Postcolonial Critique." *Publications of the Modern Language Association of America* 116, no. 1 (2001): 111–128.

Mosala, Itumeleng J. *Biblical Hermeneutics and Black Theology in South Africa.* Grand Rapids: Eerdmans, 1989.

Punt, Jeremy. "Postcolonial Biblical Criticism in South Africa: Some Mind and Road Mapping." *Neot* 37, no. 1 (2003): 59–85.

Said, Edward W. *Orientalism.* London: Penguin, 2003.

Sprinkler, Michael. Ed. *Ghostly Demarcations: A Symposium on Jacques Derrida's Specters of Marx.* London and New York: Verso, 2008.

St. Clair Darden, Lynne. *Scripturalizing Revelation: An African American Postcolonial Reading of Empire.* Atlanta: SBL, 2015.

Ste. Croix, G. E. M. De. *The Class Struggle in the Ancient Greek World: From the Archaic Age to the Arab Conquests.* Ithaca, NY: Cornell University Press, 1981.

Sugirtharajah, R. S. *The Bible and the Third World: Precolonial, Colonial and Postcolonial Encounters.* Cambridge: Cambridge University Press, 2004.

Sugirtharajah, R. S. *The Bible and Empire.* Cambridge: Cambridge University Press, 2005.

Sugirtharajah, R. S. Ed. *The Postcolonial Bible.* Sheffield: Sheffield Academic Press, 1998.

Thom, Martin. "Tribes within Nations: The Ancient Germans and the History of Modern France." In *Nation and Narration*, edited by Homi K. Bhabha. London and New York: Routledge, 1990.

Wafawanaka, Robert. "The Global Crisis of Debt in Context Biblical and Postcolonial Reflections Onthe Ideology of Empire." In *Reading the Bible in an Age of Crisis: Political Exegesis for a New Day*, 163–190. Minneapolis: Augsburg Fortress, 2015.

Wark, McKenzie. "Four Cheers for Vulgar Marxism!!!!" *Public Seminar (Online)*, 2014. http://www.publicseminar.org/2014/04/four-cheers-for-vulgarity/.

West, Gerald. "Negotiating with 'the White Man's Book': Early Foundations for Liberation Hermeneutics in Southern Africa." In *African Theology Today*. Eugene, Oregon: Wipf and Stock, 2002.

West, Gerald. "Doing Postcolonial Biblical Interpretation @Home: Ten Years of (South) African Ambivalence." *Neot* 42, no. 1 (2008): 147–168.

PART VI

POSTCOLONIALISM, BIBLICAL STUDIES, AND THEORETICAL ORIENTATIONS

CHAPTER 29

THE RISE OF POSTCOLONIAL CRITICISM IN BIBLICAL STUDIES AND ITS CURRENT STATUS

RAJ NADELLA

"Everything was lost. But a voice inside me said no—not everything. I still had one thing. My Story. I had journeyed through the Land of the Indians and had witnessed many things that my companions had preferred to revise, embellish, or silence. What had been changed, perverted, or left out was the heart of our story, the part that could not be explained, but could only be told. I could tell it. I could right what had been made wrong. And so I began to write my account. For every lie I had heard about the imperial expedition that had brought me to the edge of the world, I would tell the truth."

– Estebanico, formerly Mustafa a-Zamori[1]

MUSTAFA a-Zamori was a Moroccan who was sold into slavery in 1522 and was renamed Estebanico ("Little Stephen"). He became the first Black explorer to the Americas when he was forced to participate in Panfilo de Narvaez's sixteenth-century Spanish expedition to La Florida. Estebanico is the narrator in *The Moor's Account*, Laila Lalami's 2015 historical fiction based on the expedition. Lalami wrote the novel to give voice to Estebanico, who was a cultural interpreter but was reduced to a minor footnote in the official Spanish account that celebrates his White male companions' roles in the expedition. As the narrator, he retells the story from his perspective, resuscitates silenced voices, and elevates characters, himself included, who were rendered invisible in colonial accounts of the conquest. He exposes how, in post-conquest interviews at a church, his companions justified the conquest by modifying damaging details, omitting torture and rape, and depicting Native Americans as savages.

Postcolonial criticism examines depictions of colonial subjects in European literature between the eighteenth and twentieth centuries and the role such representations played in justifying and perpetuating the colonial project. It analyzes additions, embellishments, omissions, and distortions in the colonial literature with the goal of enabling formerly colonized communities to see themselves in stories about them. The discourse offers tools for examining issues of representation and power dynamics in textbooks, novels, and histories, as well as a paradigm for more liberative engagement with the past and the present. It retells stories from the perspective of the colonized and allows the colonized to reclaim their stories for liberative purposes. As Homi Bhabha has noted, "a range of contemporary critical theories suggests that it is from those who have suffered the sentence of history—subjugation, domination, diaspora, displacement—that we learn our most enduring lessons for living and thinking."[2] Postcolonial criticism explores the political, economic, geographic, social and cultural impact of colonialism on former colonies, as well as colonial powers and the ongoing relationship between the two. Colonialism is the backdrop against which stories and histories are read and the prism for viewing geopolitical dynamics and cultural exchanges in the contemporary world.

Resistance Discourse: The Origins of Postcolonial Criticism

Western novelists like Joseph Conrad, John Buchan, E. M. Forster, Rudyard Kipling, and Alice Perrin, who wrote during the colonial era, essentialized and exoticized the former colonies of European empires. In their literary constructs, the East is rendered mysterious, uncivilized, irrational, and immoral, thus making it inferior vis-à-vis Western nations. Kipling was enamored with the beauty of India even as he depicted the people as irrational and barbaric. At one point, Kim, the protagonist in Kipling's Nobel-prize-winning novel by the same name, remarks, "A fair land—a most beautiful land is this of Hind—and the land of the Five Rivers is fairer than all."[3] Such seemingly paradoxical depictions of India were consistent with colonial ideology of seeing the natives as aberrations in their own lands. I will return to this point later in the chapter.

Writers like Chinua Achebe, Gabriel Garcia Márquez, Tayeb Salih, and Salman Rushdie challenged such colonial depictions by offering alternative narratives about their homelands and describing the colonial experience from the perspective of the colonized. Their novels feature characters who try to make sense of their colonial condition and the cultural, political, economic, and psychological impact of European colonialism on their societies on individual and collective levels. Achebe's *Things Fall Apart*, published in 1958, is a quintessential postcolonial novel that describes the trauma of the colonial condition by calling attention to the destructive effects of British colonialism on an Igbo community in Southeastern Nigeria. Tayeb Salih's *Season of Migration to the North* powerfully captures how the culture and identity of communities in rural Sudan were adversely impacted by British imperialism. Whereas European writers attempted to whitewash and glorify the colonial enterprise as being in the best interests of colonized communities, these writers from former colonies attenuated their colonial gaze and agendas and offered counternarratives. Writing at the height of colonialism, they exposed the impact of colonialism and encouraged their communities to envision a different reality and identity for themselves. Their works were influenced by independence movements and provided alternative spaces for carrying out resistance and, in some instances, served as catalysts for fostering and intensifying such movements. V. S. Naipaul, whose ancestors were forced by the British to move from India to the Caribbean islands as *girmits* (indentured laborers), wrote profoundly about displacement and metaphorical homelessness in his novels *Half a Life, A House for Mr. Biswas*, and *The Mystic Masseur*. Even as he called attention to the adverse impact of colonialism, however, he held that descendants of formerly colonized communities were ultimately responsible for their own destiny.[4]

Aimé Césaire's *Discourse on Colonialism* exposed how colonialists commodified humans and weaponized the notion of European civilization to justify their military conquests. He argued that colonialism was defined by relations of domination and submission which "turned the colonizing man into a classroom monitor, an army sergeant, a prison guard, a slave driver, and the Indigenous man into an instrument of production."[5] Frantz Fanon's critique of the colonial condition analyzed psychological effects of colonialism and provided a theoretical framework for the political and intellectual struggle for freedom. Fanon astutely observed how the colonial condition creates in the colonized communities a desire for culture, values, and power of their colonizers and called for emancipation from the past.[6] Achebe's "Education of a British-Protected Child" explicates how the British dehumanized the colonized communities in Africa to justify their occupation and exploitation. In highlighting the destructive effects of cultural imperialism, Achebe challenged orientalizing depictions of Africans in the novels of John Buchan and Joseph Conrad and critiqued how their novels had instilled in him the notion that White colonizers were superior. "I took sides with the white men against the savages. The white man was good and reasonable and smart and courageous. The savages arrayed against him were sinister and stupid, never anything higher than cunning."[7] Ngũgĩ wa Thiong'o's *Decolonising the Mind: The Politics of Language in African Literature* critiqued linguistic imperialism in former colonies of the British and French empires that undermined vernacular modes of expression. Contending that "the bullet was the means of the physical subjugation. Language was the means of the spiritual subjugation," he called for English to be replaced with local languages as the medium of instruction and writing in Africa.[8] As Robert Young has articulated, these political and intellectual traditions provided the impetus and source materials for postcolonial thought and theory that emerged starting in the late 1970s.[9]

Postcolonial versus Post-colonial: What's in the Hyphen?

There have been numerous discussions about whether the term "postcolonial" should be hyphenated. While the term "post-colonial" refers to a time period beyond colonialism, "postcolonial" refers to a discourse that challenges hegemonic modes of knowledge that lend themselves to the colonial enterprise.[10] Much of the debate about the appropriate term pertains to whether colonialism is a thing of the past or continues in the present.

Historian Robert Gildea has forcefully argued that although formal colonialism may have ended in the middle of the twentieth century in many parts of the world, former colonial powers like Britain and France and new ones such as the United States continue to maintain their economic and military power through global networks. He describes financial networks like the International Monetary Fund and the World Bank as the "global financial republic" that amounts to new imperialism.[11] To this list, one can add cultural networks such as Hollywood and Western news media as institutions that extend Western hegemony over nations in the Global South. Michael Hardt and Antonio Negri made a distinction between imperialism, which relies on fixed boundaries, and empire, which transcends them. European imperialism was "really an extension of the sovereignty of the European nation-states beyond their own boundaries . . . In contrast to imperialism, Empire establishes no territorial center of power and does not rely on fixed boundaries or barriers. It is a decentered and deterritorializing apparatus of rule that progressively incorporates the entire global realm within its open, expanding frontiers."[12] They describe a passage from imperialism to empire, a term that in their view describes the current global world order. Imperialism in the traditional understanding of the term might not exist, at least to the extent it used to, but the empire is ubiquitous in the contemporary world.

Postcolonial criticism clarifies that colonialism is still present in its various forms and offers an intellectual framework for conceptualizing and envisioning a world beyond colonialism, a post-colonial society. As Robert Young has observed, "The postcolonial . . . is concerned with colonial history only to the extent that that history has determined the configurations and power structures of the present, to the extent that much of the world still lives in the violent disruptions of its wake, and to the extent that the anticolonial liberation movements remain the source and inspiration of its politics."[13]

The Rise of Postcolonial Criticism in the Academe

Beginning in the late 1970s, postcolonial discourse made its way into the Western academe along with other critical fields of study such as race theory and feminism. English departments at several prominent universities in the West began developing courses that built upon insights from the postcolonial body of literature. The result was the development of a powerful and rapidly growing academic field of postcolonial criticism. Diasporic scholars such as Edward Said, Homi Bhabha, and Gayatri Spivak provided a theoretical framework for critiquing the discourse, strategies, and legacies of colonialism. They drew from the political and literary stages of postcolonialism, as well as from feminism, race theory, and post-structuralism.

Edward Said's seminal book *Orientalism*, published in 1978, explicated the interconnectedness of colonialism and orientalism and the ways in which the latter facilitated and accentuated the former. While the term "colonialism" refers to European imperialism between the eighteenth and twentieth centuries, "orientalism" refers to Western constructions of the orient, in this case the Middle East, as exotic, uncivilized, barbaric, sexually promiscuous, and unclean. In positing orientalism as an intellectual phenomenon that seeks to justify European military colonialism, Edward Said explicated a symbiotic relationship between knowledge and power. Those who have power produce knowledge—novels, textbooks, histories, art, and movies—in ways that justify their power and perpetuate it. The discourse of power employs its position of privilege to produce the kind of knowledge that accentuates its power.

Jean-Leon Gerome, a nineteenth-century French artist, was one of the early examples of orientalism whose paintings stereotyped and exoticized people in the Middle East. "The Snake Charmer" featured on the cover of Edward Said's 1978 book is one of Gerome's paintings from the 1860s. It depicts a naked Middle Eastern boy holding the head of a snake with the rest of its body wrapped around his body, with people around him are sitting idly watching the spectacle. Linda Nochlin has argued that while Gerome presented this image as representing something he witnessed, it was likely a product of his own construct of the orient, the other. As she put it, "The Snake Charmer" "may most profitably be considered as a visual document of colonialist ideology, an iconic distillation of the Western's notion of the Oriental couched in the language of a would-be transparent naturalism."[14] "The Slave Market," another of his paintings, depicts several men examining the teeth of a naked enslaved woman in a Middle Eastern market, exoticizes the orient and paints it—literally and metaphorically—as the inferior, uncivilized other. Said argued that Silvestre de Sacy, a French linguist, initiated a whole field of orientalism "without ever leaving France" and created a canon of textual objects that is passed on from generation to generation.[15] He described Joseph Ernst Renan, a French philologist, as a second-generation orientalist, who systematized the official discourse of orientalism by establishing institutions.[16]

Niccolao Manucci, an eighteenth-century Italian who worked for the British and French in India, perpetuated Western fantasies of India by depicting it as a land filled with snakes and irrational people.[17] He described Parsis, worshippers of fire, as irrational and destructively superstitious:

> Their religious belief is such that, if through misadventure anyone's house takes fire, on no account will he allow the fire to be interfered with or extinguished, it being,

according to them, the greatest good luck and cause of rejoicing that he could have, he believing that his gods have conferred on him an especial gift and favour, in return for the adorations he has paid to them.[18]

In a different context, he says that if a Hindu committed a great sin "against the idols, or by forsaking his religion" and wished to be cleansed, [Brahmans] "give him cow-dung dissolved in its urine, adding a little butter, some sweet and some sour milk."[19] James Mill, a nineteenth-century Scottish historian, argued in his three-volume *History of India* that the prevalence of idolatry made Indians morally and rationally incapable of ruling themselves.[20] Mill, who "made a career out of India," ironically "never set foot in India or learned any Indian languages.[21]

Orientalism exoticizes cultures from the global South, essentializes them and turns them into an inferior other by dichotomizing the West and East. The West is enlightened, civilized, morally and culturally superior, and normative. The East is its diametrical opposite: unenlightened, uncivilized, and morally and culturally inferior.[22] Orientalism had three direct effects. First, as Edward Said has noted, "The East is a career." Said made this comment about Benjamin Disraeli, but it is also true of other orientalists like Mill, who objectified Eastern cultures and commodified them in problematic ways in order to achieve professional advancement. Second, as Said argued, the process of acquiring knowledge about the orient is thoroughly political because the West's representations of the East are inconsistent with reality and were designed to justify the colonial enterprise. Since they are barbaric, uncivilized, and incapable of ruling themselves, colonialism was civilizing and liberating them from themselves. Accordingly, colonialism was no longer an oppressive force, exploiting resources from its colonies and dehumanizing people, but a benevolent enterprise. As Said put it, "Orientals were rarely seen or looked at; they were seen through, analyzed not as citizens, or even people, but as problems to be solved or confined or—as the colonial powers openly coveted their territory—taken over."[23]

Third, as already mentioned, the seemingly paradoxical depictions of India that one finds in Kipling's novels, and to a lesser degree in Perrin's, were consistent with colonial ideology. The land is beautiful and wondrous and must be rescued from the undeserving locals. Colonialists desired the land but sought to exclude local people in order to gain exclusive access to its resources. An insight from Hardt and Negri about the conquest of North America is relevant here: "Just as the land must be cleared of trees and rocks to farm it, so too the terrain must be cleared of the native inhabitants . . . they had to be excluded from the terrain in order to open its spaces and make expansion possible."[24] Ania Loomba's insightful observation that colonialism was the forceful acquisition of land and economy in order to fuel the European economy is helpful here. Drawing insights from Aimé Césaire, she argues that colonialism was ultimately a capitalist enterprise that objectified people and robbed them of their essence.[25] Seen within this framework, orientalism was the fulcrum for the political apparatus of colonialism which allowed the wheels of its capitalist juggernaut to run smoothly.[26]

Said drew his concept of "knowledge-power" symbiosis from post-structuralists such as Michel Foucault. Building upon Antonio Gramsci's notion of cultural hegemony and Denys Hay's concept of Europe, he observed that "It is hegemony, or rather the result of cultural hegemony at work, that gives orientalism the durability and the strength . . . indeed it can be argued that the major component in European culture is precisely what made that culture hegemonic both in and outside Europe: the idea of European identity as a superior one in comparison with all the non-European peoples and cultures."[27]

Said may have suggested in *Orientalism* that the East was consistently docile in its relationship with the West, but he qualified his observations in a later book, "Yet it was the case nearly everywhere in the non-European world that the coming of the white man brought forth some sort of resistance. What I left out of Orientalism was that response to Western dominance which culminated in the great movement of decolonization all across the Third World."[28] He observed that the Western discourse about the East was "premised on the silence of the native"[29] and insisted that the "interventions of non-European artists and scholars cannot be dismissed or silenced."[30] He posited postcolonialism as a disruptive reading strategy that exposes the knowledge-power symbiosis and offers a new lens and framework for engaging the orient.

Achebe, too, critiqued orientalism, although he never used that term. In his essay, "African Literature as Restoration of Celebration," he exposed how colonizers constructed "elaborate excuses" for their actions. He said, "You say, for instance, that the man you dispossessed is worthless and quite unfit to manage himself or his affairs. If the worse should come to the worst, you may even be prepared to question whether such as he can be, like you, fully human."[31] Like Said and Achebe, Gayatri Spivak was attentive to reading practices and strategies of the West. Her reading strategy entails the ethical responsibility of relating to the other on an individual level and eliciting responses on both sides, an approach she describes as "ethical singularity."[32]

Homi Bhabha complexified the colonizer-colonized binary and argued that the two should be viewed in a composite rather than a dichotomous framework. He explicated the ambivalence of colonial discourse which otherizes the colonized while simultaneously desiring to create a "reformed, recognizable other, as a subject of difference that is almost the same, but not quite."[33] Colonial discourse encourages colonial subjects to mimic colonizers in what amounts to "the sign of a double articulation; a complex strategy of reform, regulation, and discipline, which appropriates the Other as it visualizes power."[34] Colonial subjects respond to the empire ambivalently, rejecting it but at other times also being attracted to it.[35] The colonized are often repulsed by the power and ethos of the empire but at times mimic the habits and values of the colonizer in the hope of acquiring some of the power of the latter. When colonial subjects imitate their colonizers, the colonial gaze is displaced and now directed at the colonizer, but because the mimicry is partial and at times an act of mockery, it is at once resemblance and menace.[36] Bhabha describes mimicry as a hybridizing process that signifies and results in the presence of two or more perspectives or entities in a given space. Hybridity disrupts cultural, linguistic, and epistemological boundaries between the colonized and colonizer; undermines the possibility of unadulterated spaces; and creates a third location, an in-between space, that is not clearly demarcated. As Sugirtharajah notes, while "Said and Spivak treat postcolonialism as a reading strategy, Bhabha sees postcoloniality as a condition of being" that disrupts the "dominant systems of thought"[37] and is characterized by hybridity and ambivalence toward the colonizer.

Naipaul personified hybridity having embodied three worlds—Trinidad, England, and India—and, as Victor Ramraj observes, exhibited postcolonial ambivalence toward India, the land of his ancestors, and the West.[38] Naipaul's trilogy on India stereotypes Indian culture and offers a scathing critique of it but at times depicts the country in positive terms. His postcolonial ambivalence is especially evident in his frequent vacillation between repulsion and attraction toward the empire as well as his critique and defense of colonialism. Ambivalence, however, is not always a state of the mind but also, at least in part, a posture of negotiation with imperial realities and a strategy for coping with the power and structures of the empire.

Goals of Postcolonial Criticism

Postcolonial criticism seeks to contest and undermine the political, ideological, and intellectual power of the empire that continues to wreak havoc throughout the world and robs marginalized communities of their ability to flourish. Specifically, it critiques orientalism, the intellectual arm of the colonial enterprise, by exposing Eurocentric modes of knowledge production and their role in perpetuating hegemonic political and economic structures—past and present—that dehumanize communities in the global South. The discourse offers people from former colonies tools and paradigms to deconstruct colonial discourses about them, reclaim their histories by retelling them from their perspectives, and shape their own identities. For every Gerome, Conrad, and Renan, there are scholars like Said, Spivak, and Achebe offering intellectual counterweight to what was uncontested and considered normative. As Said put it, "I am an Oriental writing back at the Orientalists, who for so long have thrived upon our silence. I am also writing 'to' them, as it were, by dismantling the structure of their discipline, showing its metahistorical, institutional, anti-empirical, and ideological biases."[39] When orientals write back, they offer everyone a new paradigm for reorienting toward the orient. Robert Young notes, "postcolonial cultural critique involves reconsideration of [colonial] history, particularly from the perspective of those who suffered its effects, together with the defining of its contemporary social and cultural impact."[40] Postcolonialism is a body of knowledge that attenuates knowledge systems that facilitated the colonial enterprise and continue to perpetuate its power in modern times, albeit in subtle forms. Young describes it as tricontinentalism, a theoretical and political position that embodies an active concept of intervention within such oppressive circumstances."[41]

Biblical Texts in Service of Empire

Religion has a long and troubled history of providing justification for the empire, with biblical texts playing a key role in it. Describing his first encounter with Native Americans in 1497, Amerigo Vespucci supposedly said:

> They live together without king, without government, and each is his own master. They marry as many wives as they please; and son cohabits with mother, brother with sister, male cousin with female, and any man with the first woman he meets. They dissolve their marriages as often as they please, and observe no sort of law with respect to them. Beyond the fact that they have no church, no religion and are not idolaters, what more can I say?[42]

As Benjamin Schmidt notes, Jan Van der Straet's 1580 engraving "America" depicts Amerigo Vespucci arriving in the Americas clutching "a banner emblazoned with the stars of the freshly discovered Southern cross in his right and a mariner's astrolabe in his left."[43] He meets a naked Native American woman lying in a hammock in this virgin land. A few feet away a group of cannibals is roasting a human thigh. The caption under the figure of Vespucci says "Amerigo discovers America" as he "arouses the sleeping, virginal America."[44] Vespucci's words and Straet's engraving together suggest that the Natives were uncivilized, irreligious, and immoral and needed to be conquered so that they could be saved, liberated from themselves, and governed according to proper rules. And Vespucci's expedition was divinely sanctioned precisely to accomplish those purposes.

Many biblical scholars participated in the colonial enterprise between the eighteenth and twentieth centuries by providing facile, blatant, and at times sophisticated justification for the empire. John Winthrop, a Puritan lawyer who founded the Massachusetts Bay Colony in the seventeenth century, tried to justify violence against Native Americans by arguing that Native Americans did not subdue the land as God commanded in Genesis 1:28, but Christian colonialism was able to accomplish it.[45]

James Henley Thornwell, an influential Presbyterian minister and professor in the early nineteenth century, who was writing in the context of the American South, used the Bible to justify slavery. Thornwell argued that "The master is nowhere rebuked [in the Bible] as a monster of cruelty and tyranny, the slave nowhere exhibited as the object of peculiar compassion and sympathy."[46] He acknowledged that Blacks were created in God's image like Whites but insisted that it was more important to save their souls from eternal damnation than to ameliorate the material conditions that enslaved them. In privileging their spiritual welfare over emancipation and shifting the locus of liberation from the material to the spiritual, he sought to maintain the status quo even as he seemingly advocated for Blacks to be treated as equals to Whites.[47]

Chinua Achebe called attention to the problematic intersection of empire and religion and the ways in which Christian theologians provided excuses for the colonial enterprise in Africa. He has observed that "Churchmen at some point wondered about the soul itself. Did the black man have a soul? Popes and theologians debated that for a while."[48] R. S. Sugirtharajah has noted that during the British Empire, interpreters like William Arnot employed biblical texts to condone the empire's oppressive military and economic practices in India. Building upon allegorical readings of the parable of the tenants in Matthew 21, Arnot suggested that the East India Company was analogous to the landowner, India to the vineyard, and Indians to the tenants, "the wicked tenants." In his reading, Indians are sneaky, violent people who do not abide by the rules, but the British Empire, like the landowner, is patient and kind in dealing with Indians. By equating the landowner with the British and God, he suggested that the British were justified in using excessive violence to destroy the wicked tenants, the Indians.[49] Not coincidentally, this interpretation appeared not long after the Great Indian Rebellion of 1857, which was ruthlessly suppressed by the British. Arnot suggested that the chaos toward the end of the parable was analogous to a "paralyzed" government and added "but in those regions such anarchy was not uncommon then,—is not uncommon now."[50] By suggesting that the Indian government was paralyzed, Arnot was providing theological justification for the British Empire in India, which formally began in 1858, a year after the Great Rebellion.

These are just a few examples of how biblical texts were used to provide justification for the empire. They illustrate how the kind of symbiotic relationship between knowledge and power that Said explicated has been at work in Western biblical interpretation in the context of European imperialism. As Sugirtharajah aptly observed, "The trouble with texts, especially if they are ancient and sacred, is that they can be summoned and assigned meanings to prove or legitimize any cause, theory, or perspective. When European colonialism was at its peak, biblical texts were taken out of context to prove biblical sanction for such a venture."[51] An irony in colonial biblical readings is that much of the Bible was written in the context of and often in opposition to the empire—Neo-Assyrian, Babylonian, Persian, Hellenistic, Roman, etc-and yet scriptures were often weaponized to justify the colonial enterprise.

BIBLICAL STUDIES IN SERVICE OF STATUS QUO

For much of the twentieth century, the field of biblical studies was dominated by traditional methods of interpretation. Fernando Segovia named four paradigms of biblical criticism that have been prevalent in the last several decades: historical criticism, literary criticism, cultural criticism, cultural studies.[52]

Historical criticism, which emerged out of enlightenment, subscribed to the notion that questions such as authorship and date can be correctly answered if scholars employed the right set of methods and tools. As Segovia has observed, "historical criticism was perceived and promoted as the proper way to read and interpret biblical texts but also as the ultimate sign of progress in the discipline, the offer of the (Christian) West to the rest of the (Christian) world and the means by which the backward and ignorant could become modern and educated."[53] On some level, such an approach was an imitation of the European colonial enterprise: conquer lands by employing excessive military force and enlighten them; capture textual meanings by using sophisticated methods. Even as European nations were busy expanding their empires, proponents of traditional, historical-critical methods were largely indifferent to such life and death issues and rarely acknowledged centuries of colonialism and the extensive violence it caused in the global South. Such methods amounted to effacement of colonial contexts in which scriptures were written and the contexts in which many communities in the global South read them. Nevertheless, because of their social location and power in the guild, proponents of such methods carried unchallenged epistemological authority that allowed them to table issues, set the tone of the conversation, and adjudicate what count as acceptable, sound academic readings. In his book—*The Bible and the Third World*—Sugirtharajah has powerfully exposed how the field of biblical studies refers to Western, male interpretations as *the* interpretations, implying that they are normative hermeneutics but designates *other* readings with modifiers such as Asian, African, or Chinese accounts.[54] He observes that scholars from marginal spaces who want to be included in *the* interpretations "must conform to rules or criteria developed within the Western academic paradigm."[55] Building upon insights from Segovia and Sugirtharajah, one can suggest that the normativized hermeneutics not only deflect attention from issues of life and death but also discount readings from the margins that foreground such issues by characterizing them as unacademic, creative, or peripheral. Such twin processes of deflection and discounting have the effect of reinforcing the status quo with regard to oppressive structures in the society.

Literary criticism focuses on the world within the text but uses insights from historical criticism as the point of reference. Its premise that various literary aspects of the Bible can be determined with certainty is consistent with key assumptions of historical criticism. Moreover, in a subtle imitation of the latter, literary criticism largely failed to address issues of the empire in the Bible. Many early critics of colonialism—Achebe, Salih, Rushdie, for instance—produced works that were literary in nature, but whereas they used literature to challenge the empire, literary criticism's explication of the bible as literature often, although not always, had the effect of ignoring issues of power and politics. Cultural studies championed by Bruce Malina, Jerome Neyrey, and Joseph Fitzmyer were interested in discovering and reconstructing the social world of biblical texts. Proponents of this method—"scientific, objective, impartial and informed readers," to use Segovia's phrase—built upon historical methods, and undertook extensive, "objective" searches for the world behind the texts and the right meanings buried in them.[56] Their pursuit is akin to the obsessive and futile attempts by the Spanish and the British empires to find El Dorado, the kingdom of gold depicted in V. S. Naipaul's *The Loss of El Dorado*. The place did not exist or could never be found, as "no one was quite sure what he sought or where it was to be found."[57] The search was detrimental to people in Trinidad and directed attention and resources away from concerns that mattered to communities at the margins. Similarly, historical critical methodologies deflect attention from critical issues in biblical interpretation that remain relevant to oppressed communities.

Segovia has critiqued how generations of biblical scholars have been initiated into such historical-critical and cultural paradigms of biblical scholarship by White male scholars whose "main concern is not with the Bible as word of God but with the Bible as a cultural record of antiquity."[58] The knowledge-power symbiosis that Said described has been at work in biblical studies on three levels: (1) In many instances, biblical scholars blatantly abetted the colonial project by providing scriptural justification for it; (2) Many historical critical readings tacitly endorsed the colonial project through their preoccupation with questions such as authorship and date that deflected attention from various manifestations of empire in the Bible and in current settings.[59] While they have not facilitated the colonial project of weaponizing of scriptures, as Arnot, Winthrop, and Thornwell have done, they indirectly facilitated the status quo by failing to address issues of power and oppression. (3) In other instances, scholars enabled the colonial project by spiritualizing texts that were written in the context of empire and address issues of power and oppression. Such attempts to spiritualize texts meant that abstract issues such as the trinity, predestination, and eschatology took precedence over life and death issues faced by communities at the margins.

SHIFT IN BIBLICAL STUDIES

A shift occurred in 1991 with the publication of *Voices from the Margin: Interpreting the Bible in the Third World*, edited by Sugirtharajah. The volume featured essays from scholars across the global South and from diverse social locations. Contributors introduced a range of new interpretive strategies, concerns, and perspectives that took their marginalized social locations, as well as that of biblical texts, seriously. It was a full-fledged attempt by the margins to decenter the center by questioning its interpretive agendas, concerns, and epistemological assumptions that were largely driven by historical critical methods.

The first edition of the volume did not employ postcolonial theoretical framework as the primary focus, but akin to what Achebe, Thiong'O, and Rushdie accomplished in their works, several contributors highlighted empire as the prism through which to view biblical texts. Elsa Tamez exposed how, in the context of Spanish conquest of the Aztec in 1519, the Spaniards claimed a divine right to conquer and rule. In his letters, Herman Cortez stated, "we carried the flag of the cross and fought for our faith . . . God gave us so much victory that we killed so many people."[60] The Spanish justified their occupation of the land by depicting themselves as saviors liberating the natives. They compared the suffering of the natives to the ten plagues in Exodus. Whereas the story in Exodus signifies divine punishment of an oppressive regime, ironically the Spanish used it to justify their conquest.[61]

Along similar lines, Musa Dube's essay highlighted how the Bible became a tool in the European conquest of African lands. She narrates an African saying: "When the white man came to our country, he had the Bible and we had the land. The White man said to us, 'let us pray'. After the prayer, the white man had the land and we had the Bible."[62] The essay reveals the extent to which Africans, and other colonized nations, were victimized by their acceptance of European readings of biblical texts. The essays by Tamez, Dube, and others representing marginalized voices—aboriginal, Native American, Palestinian, African American, and Latin American—disrupted, more implicitly than explicitly, the kind of colonial readings mentioned earlier. They sought to reclaim biblical texts for liberative purposes and return the Bible to the margins where it was mostly written. *Stony the Road We Trod: African American Biblical Interpretation*, published the same year, centered race as the foci for engaging biblical texts.[63] Contributors exposed the subjective, ideological nature of Western interpretations that downplayed the role of Blacks in biblical texts at times rendering them invisible. That is, African influence and cultures that are evident in some biblical texts have been diminished and Whitewashed in Western interpretations.

The Arrival of Postcolonial Biblical Criticism

Sugirtharajah's 1996 essay in the Asia Journal of Theology "From Orientalist to Post-Colonial: Notes on Reading Practices" explicitly placed biblical interpretations in dialogue with postcolonial criticism and introduced the discourse to the field of biblical studies.[64] This essay critiqued orientalist readings which made a false assumption that understanding ancient Hindu texts—Vedas—would help them master the native culture and population. Orientalists perceived Hindu texts and people as the other, the different, that needed to be conquered and equated India with the biblical world in ways that essentialized oriental cultures. The essay also critiqued Anglicist approaches that dismissed the usefulness of native traditions for interpreting biblical texts and imposed Western interpretations as the norm. From a Western standpoint, oriental traditions should either be conquered or silenced. Sugirtharajah proposed the postcolonial approach as a paradigm that sees Hindu and Christian texts as complementary and celebrates subaltern interpretive traditions.

A formal attempt at postcolonial scriptural interpretation started with an initial session of the "Postcolonial Studies and Biblical Criticism" section at the 1999 annual meeting of the Society of Biblical Literature. Simultaneously, many academic works were being published along these lines. As Stephen Moore and Fernando Segovia have noted, the origins of postcolonial discourse go back to two key academic contributions.[65] The first was a Semeia volume called *Postcolonialism and Scriptural Reading* (1996), edited by Laura E. Donaldson. Donaldson's introductory essay that delineates the meaning and scope of "postcolonial" suggested that the discourse should dismantle apparatuses of imperialism and attend to colonial layers in biblical texts, not just in interpretations. Three aspects of the book stand out. (1) A critique of Exodus traditions that Donaldson argued were appropriated by White settlers as a theological and scriptural justification of their conquest of Native American lands. (2) Building upon her 1992 book, *Decolonizing Feminisms: Race, Gender & Empire Building*, Donaldson exposed the failure of White feminists to take the issue of colonialism seriously. (3) There are areas of intersection between postcolonialism and other resistance readings.

The second was the launching of a book series called *The Bible and Postcolonialism*, with *The Postcolonial Bible* (1998) as its first volume. In this volume, edited by Sugirtharajah, contributors explicitly employed postcolonial theory and lenses to examine how biblical exegesis aided colonialism and to read texts in light of lived experiences and concerns of diverse marginalized groups—Aboriginals, Latinx, African-Americans, Asian-Americans, women. As the editor noted in his introduction, the contributors emerged from disparate social locations but were guided by a shared commitment to follow Edward Said's exhortation to peruse the "texts for the gaps, absences and ellipses, the silences and closures" in order to recover suppressed or distorted history or narrative."[66] A key contribution of this book is an attempt to move the conversation beyond the colonizer-colonized binary and focus on subaltern groups who continue to occupy marginal spaces within former colonies partly due to internal imperialism that receives insufficient attention in the postcolonial discourse.

Vernacular Hermeneutics (1999), the second volume in the series *The Bible and Postcolonialism*, took commitment to contexts even further. Because postcolonial discourse engages the broad matrix of empire, scholars have a proclivity to engage global issues and rely on Western hermeneutical tools with insufficient attention to Indigenous traditions and concerns. This volume engaged hitherto obscure vernacular traditions and foregrounded Indigenous identities, methods, and concerns as the loci of their interpretations. As Sugirtharajah notes, the volume emerged out of a commitment to "being nearer home and getting closer to roots."[67] Laura Donaldson's essay "The Sign of Orpah," which reads the story of Ruth and Orpah from a Native American perspective, illustrates such a commitment. Ruth emerges as the "paradigmatic convert" who turns her back on her people and collaborates with occupiers, but Orpah returns to her Moabite roots.[68] In celebrating Orpah, who is mentioned just twice in the book of Ruth, Donaldson resuscitates silenced voices. David Adamo's essay "African Cultural Hermeneutics" problematizes Western scholarly preoccupations with issues such as authorship and date and highlights the ways Nigerian Indigenous churches moved past such preoccupations and recovered the life-giving power of Psalms.

While *Vernacular Hermeneutics* is about returning to one's roots, *Interpreting Beyond Borders* (Segovia 2000b) is about disrupted borders and interpreting from hybrid locations. Contributors in this volume embrace their diasporic contexts as hermeneutical loci that allow them to speak meaningfully to their homelands and to adopted homes. Francisco Garcia-Treto's essay "Hyphenating Joseph" posits diasporic location not as assimilation but as hyphenation that allows Joseph, and by extension biblical scholars, to see things clearly from both the center and the margins. Together with the *Postcolonial Bible*, the three volumes highlight the ways the discourse is undertaken in hybridized contexts and social locations by scholars who embody multiple identities and write about issues pertinent to the Western academy as well as to contexts of their origins.

Sugirtharajah's *Asian Biblical Hermeneutics and Postcolonialism: Contesting the Interpretations* (2002) took the readers back to home contexts to focus on English biblical commentaries produced in colonial India. It critiques the concerns, agendas, and ideologies that undergirded those commentaries and explicated their continued impact on the Indian Church. It exposes how traditional biblical scholarship engaged in orientalizing reading practices that posited Western Christianity as superior vis-à-vis Judaism and the non-Western Church. The books mentioned so far went back and forth between home and diasporic interpretive contexts reflecting the multiple spaces and audiences postcolonial biblical scholars engage. Each book has its own specific focus, but they all have a common goal: questioning the assumptions, concerns, and agendas of traditional biblical scholarship. They expose how Western biblical scholarship participated in the colonial project either by providing theological justification or through a posture of indifference to imperial settings of biblical texts that resulted in deflecting attention from various manifestations of the empire—past and present.

Attenuating the Empire: Reading the Bible Through Postcolonial Lens

In the last three decades, Postcolonial Biblical criticism has gained significance as a discourse that engages colonial contexts of biblical texts and their interpretations. Practitioners in the field represent disparate margins but share a commitment to the cause of liberation. The discourse is not exclusive of historical-critical methods—it engages some of the questions raised by historical-critical methods,[69] but insists on taking seriously issues of materiality and power engendered by empires. Postcolonial discourse also challenges the notion of objectivity that is central to historical-critical readings and embraces interpreters' social locations and their commitments to justice as key components of its hermeneutical project. Given the ways social locations influence readings, it subscribes to the notion that there are no neutral readers.

It would be an understatement to note that the history of biblical interpretation vis-à-vis the empire is very complex. The Bible has been used to oppose the empire in various historical contexts but also to support it. At times, the same texts have been employed toward both ends within the same contexts. Scriptures have been used by colonials to create a racialized society but also by enslaved people to envision a different reality, as

Vincent Wimbush's book *White Men's Magic: Scripturalization as Slavery* (2014) has powerfully demonstrated. Wimbush presents scripturalization as a reading strategy that is less about drawing meaning from scriptures and more about making meaning out of them. It is about how we employ the sacred texts vis-à-vis the empire and what we make them do for us. Drawing from Olaudah Equiano's autobiography and the image of him wielding the Bible, Wimbush argues that whereas the colonial masters created race-based identities using the Bible, Equiano was able to make the Bible, "the (supreme) English book," "speak" to him and through his own writing "speak" back to the oppressive structure by strategically aligning with strangers (Indians) and ex-centrics (White religious dissenters, thinkers and politicians).[70] Building upon Wimbush's motif of *scripturalization*, Jacqueline Hidalgo's book *Revelation in Aztlán: Scriptures, Utopias, and the Chicano Movement* explores how scriptures such as Revelation served as utopian homing devices that inspired displaced communities, the Chicanx movement in the Americas in this case, to contest and reimagine a different reality for themselves. An insight from Hidalgo is that since their displacement entailed a religious and scriptural dimension, the movement had to take back the notion of the sacred in order to remake the world better for the displaced.[71]

In Lynne St. Clair Darden's reading of Revelation, John's resistance strategy is a "blurred copy" of Rome's oppressive practices that serves as a cautionary tale against mimicking the practices of the American empire. Using the motif of scripturalization, Darden calls upon African American biblical scholars to sustain the tradition of counternarration to a racist ethos that is built upon biblical imagery and ensure that the community does not accommodate the values of the American empire due to its own hybrid identity and growing economic and political might in segments of the community.[72] Darden, Hidalgo, and Wimbush explicated the dynamic and fluid nature of scriptures which lend themselves to disparate uses vis-à-vis the power, ethos, and agendas of the empire. But they went beyond the motif of reclaiming the scriptures for liberative purposes and highlighted reading practices of oppressed communities that often reinvented the scriptures in order to remake their social and political spaces.

In addition, people in hybrid positions—i.e. people ambivalent about the empire because of their complex relationship with it—used the Bible at times to resist the empire but at other times to support it or remain indifferent toward it. Given such complex history of interpretation, postcolonial criticism takes seriously the various colonial contexts at work in the production and interpretation of biblical texts, especially but not solely during European colonialism.[73] It raises questions such as: who interpreted the biblical texts (historically), and how did their location vis-a-vis power influence their readings? What are the implications of their readings for communities, both then and now? Who stands (or stood) to gain from those interpretations? To build upon Said's insight, an overarching question is: "what role did power play in interpretation of biblical texts, and how did those interpretations in turn impact power relations in those contexts?" But to extend Said a bit further, the question on power applies also to postcolonial readers, who in some contexts tend to perpetuate intranational colonialism even as they challenge transnational colonialism.

It is important to look at how biblical texts were (mis)read in the past. Juxtaposition of oppressive and liberative readings allows readers to see the disparate locations of interpreters, disparities in power and the various agendas. Still, it does not do enough to undermine the hegemonic power of the empire that not only facilitates oppressive readings but also actively and creatively co-opts readers who seek to challenge it. Therefore, even as we examine readings from the past, it behooves us to consider how descendants of previously colonized communities engage oppressive readings from the past and appropriate biblical texts very differently in their current contexts. Postcolonial discourse offers theoretical frameworks and hermeneutical paradigms to analyze the implications of misuse of biblical texts, enervate such readings and reclaim texts for liberative purposes. To paraphrase Sugirtharajah, "postcolonial discourse allows us to understand the past in order to assess the present and be alert"[74] to the future. And to add, it also allows us to envision a different future.

On a macro level, the discourse examines the roles various empires played in interpreting the Bible and the hermeneutical strategies they employed to perpetuate their oppressive power. On a micro level, it analyzes the roles individuals played along similar trajectories. It disrupts hegemonic interpretations that suppressed marginal and resistant voices in texts and seeks to resuscitate silenced voices, as Donaldson has done in her reading of Orpah's story.

One cannot, however, paint the Bible with a broad brush and suggest that all biblical texts are anti-imperial. Akin to interpretations, the Bible itself responds to the empire in complex, disparate ways. Many of the biblical texts reflect various models of resistance to the power and agendas of the empire in its various manifestations. Steed Davidson's book on Jeremiah that employs postcolonial theory to address historical-critical questions about Jeremiah highlights how the book signifies and reflects social, if not physical, resistance to the empire.[75] Other biblical texts accommodate the ethos and values of the empire while yet others resist the empire on some issues even as they accommodate it on other matters. Margaret Aymer has highlighted how the book of James challenges the Roman imperial worldview on economic issues but mimics it with regard to issues of gender.[76] At times, texts respond to the empire ambivalently in ways that reflect the political realities and paradoxical social locations of authors and communities that produced them. Characters within texts negotiate and respond to realities of the empire in complex, ambivalent ways, simultaneously rejecting the empire but also participating in it, as Shanell Smith has noted in her 2014 book on Revelation.[77]

Still other texts mimic and reinscribe imperial ethos. In his book *Untold Tales from the Book of Revelation: Sex and Gender, Empire and Ecology*, Stephen Moore builds upon Homi Bhabha's concept of mimicry to call attention to the ways Revelation reinscribes the Roman imperial worldview and ethos even as it challenges them. In Moore's reading, the simultaneous processes of resistance and mimicking result from the seer's ambivalence toward Rome and signify hybridity. Along similar lines, Tat-Siong Benny Liew argued that despite Mark's opposition to Roman officials and modes of authority, the gospel mimics those modes in its depiction of Jesus and ascribes to him absolute authority, which allows him to ignore instructions he himself has given to others. In Liew's reading, the gospel creates a hierarchical community akin to Rome that reduces even his disciples to "sidekicks."[78] Along similar lines, Randall Bailey has called attention to the ways African presence and influences have been downplayed not just in Western interpretations but even from one strand of biblical texts (J) to another (P).[79] Aymer, Bailey, Davidson, Liew, Moore, and Smith have highlighted the extent to which ideology and social locations shaped not just interpretations of texts about empire but even the texts themselves in complex ways that defy easy categorizations. Their works demonstrate that just as interpretations are not monolithic, texts themselves are multifarious reflecting the social locations and worldviews of the communities that produced them as well as their negotiations with the imperial apparatuses.

Recognizing that biblical texts are not monolithic in their response to the empire, Moore and Segovia build upon insights from Ernst Bloch, a Marxist, to suggest the task of criticism is to sift between such conflicting traditions and unearth alternatives to the dominant system.[80]

Postcolonial discourse should explore if there are specific layers that are more amenable to colonial readings than others either in their original contexts or in contemporary settings. It should ask if there are texts that signify the kind of ambivalence and hybridity that Bhabha has articulated and lend themselves to competing readings, perhaps reflecting the paradoxical context of communities associated with texts. And it should resuscitate suppressed voices that offer liberative potential. However, such a task becomes challenging when one considers the fact that what might be considered liberative in one context might be viewed differently in another context.

Whether at the level of texts or at the level of interpretation, postcolonial criticism uses empire as the matrix against which texts and histories are read and the prism for viewing the contemporary world and its geopolitical dynamics. As Segovia notes, "In effect, just as feminist criticism foregrounds the question of gender, liberation criticism of class, minority criticism that of ethnicity-race, and queer criticism that of sexual orientation, so, I would argue, does postcolonial criticism highlight the question of geopolitics—the realm of the political at the translocal or global level, with specific reference to the phenomenon of imperial-colonial formations."[81]

Postcolonialism and Emphasis on Intersectionality

Segovia's observation that feminist criticism foregrounds the question of gender is only partially true. Musa Dube's landmark contribution—*Postcolonial Feminist Interpretation of the Bible* (2000)—challenged Western feminist scholars to take seriously the intersection of imperialism and patriarchy as twin systems of oppression. Building upon Chandra Mohanty's and Laura Donaldson's critique of Western feminism, Dube called attention to the ways Western feminist biblical scholars have inscribed themselves in imperialist parameters by homogenizing women all over the world and decentering issues of colonialism.[82] Their focus on issues of gender in early Christianity might have empowered Western women, but by downplaying the imperial setting of early Christianity they replicate "the violence of imperial oppression against non-Western and non-Christian biblical feminists."[83] Explicating Matthew's story of the Canaanite woman, Dube invites Western feminist biblical scholars to engage the intersection of empire and gender and build meaningful coalitions among women in different contexts across borders.

The Postcolonial Biblical Reader (Sugirtharajah 2006) too focused on the motif of intersections. It explicated how the theme of empire intersects with gender, canonicity, exegesis, and anti-Semitism. Calling attention to the intersection of global racism, sexism, and anti-Semitism in the colonial imagination, Kwok Pui-lan's essay, "Making the Connections: Postcolonial Studies and Feminist Biblical Interpretation" invites people to turn these contact zones into "places of mutual learning, and places for trying out new ideas, and strategies for the emancipation of all."[84] Along similar lines, Mitzi Smith's *Womanist Sass and Talkback: Social (In)Justice, Intersectionality and Biblical Interpretation* (2018) combines a womanist activist hermeneutic with a postcolonial critique to foreground an intersectional (race, gender, class, sexuality, and neocolonialism) analysis of social injustice. Writing as an African American woman, Smith highlights how (neo)colonialism and religious ideologies joined forces to reinforce oppressive structures that disproportionately impact poor Black women. Raising readers' consciousness about contemporary justice issues such as police brutality, sexual violence, oppressive pedagogies, and the privatization of water, she posits intersectionality as a tool for engendering activism through conscientization and a liberative hermeneutical strategy.

Intersectionality of a different nature is the leitmotif in *Postcolonial Biblical Criticism: Interdisciplinary Intersections* (2005) edited by Stephen Moore and Fernando Segovia. Rich on methodology, it delineates the origins of the field, outlines the contributions of key players, and offers an honest account of its strengths, areas of growth, and future directions. It explicates how the discourse intersects with and builds upon related methodologies—Marxism, Feminism, Ethnic/Racial Studies, Post-structuralism—but also departs from them in substantial ways.

Postcolonial Criticism and Empire Studies

Several books published between 1994 and 2008 explicitly engaged the imperial matrix of early Christianity, in addition to its religious matrix, with interpretive implications for the current world. Richard Horsley's edited volume *Paul and Empire: Religion and*

Power in Roman Imperial Society (1997) highlighted the political nature of Paul's mission and gospel and posited his *ekklesiai* as an "international anti-imperial alternative society."[85] In a similar vein, Horsley's *Jesus and Empire* (2002) called attention to the neocolonial context of the United States and to its paradoxical, competing identities: as the new Israel and as a new Rome. Even as the social gospel movement inspired by Jesus' message about the kingdom of God remained a strong force in the U.S., America became an empire mimicking Rome's political institutions, ethos, and orientalist policies toward the East. Horsley offers a scathing critique of how Jesus and his various first-century contexts have been reduced to religion, one that has been orientalized, so that he could be domesticated by the American empire. Jesus emerges as a resistance leader who promoted an alternative social order that has great relevance to the new world disorder.

Both these volumes typically fall into the category of "Empire studies" because they shifted focus from the religious to the imperial matrix of biblical texts or because of the word "empire" in their titles.[86] Neither book explicitly employed postcolonial lens to explore biblical texts but both share many concerns and commitments of the discourse. Other books in this broad category that have focused primarily on the Roman imperial context of texts include *Matthew and Empire: Initial Explorations* (Carter 2001), *In Search of Paul: How Jesus's Apostle Opposed Rome's Empire with God's Kingdom* (Crossan and Reed 2005), *The Roman Empire and the New Testament: An Essential Guide* (Carter 2006), *Christ and Empire: From Paul to Postcolonial Times* (Rieger 2007), *God and Empire: Jesus Against Rome, Then and Now* (Crossan 2008), *Unveiling Empire: Reading Revelation Then and Now* (Howard-Brook and Gwyther 1999), *Liberating Paul* (Elliott 1994), *The Message and the Kingdom: How Jesus and Paul Ignited a Revolution and Transformed the Ancient World* (Horsley and Silberman 1997) and *Paul and Politics: Ekklesia, Israel, Imperium, Interpretation* (Horsley 2000).

Sugirtharajah's *Postcolonial Criticism and Biblical Interpretation* (2002) returned to a focus on ideological assumptions behind orientalist readings of texts. Whereas many previous books focused on challenging orientalist readings, this book went further and provided a theoretical framework for alternative readings as responses to colonialism and its continued manifestations. One such alternative was Appasamy Pillai, a heritagist who read Indian sacred texts as compatible with Christian traditions and disrupted orientalist readings that sought to otherize the Vedas and conquer their meaning. A key aspect of this book that has hitherto received insufficient attention is the extent to which Bible translations participated in the colonial project. Missionaries saw the presence of multiple local languages as an impediment to growth of the gospel and sought to standardize the languages resulting in the loss of diverse linguistic expressions and worldviews. More damaging were their attempts, in countries such as India, to substitute English words for native words and create neologisms either because existing vernacular words were perceived as corrupted, having been employed to express native religious meanings, or because they were considered inadequate to sufficiently express the sophisticated theological and intellectual concepts of Western Christianity.

Sugirtharajah extended these conversations further in *Exploring Postcolonial Biblical Criticism: History, Method, Practice* (2011). The volume delineates how postcolonial theory, which originated in humanities, entered biblical studies and emancipated postcolonial scholars from the tyranny of Western biblical scholarship by allowing them to frame their own questions that were not guided by reformation or enlightenment. While many of the previous volumes justifiably focused on problematic aspects of Western scholarship, this volume suggested two distinctly Eastern interpretive methods—the contrapuntal method and Edward Said's "Late style"—as alternatives. Contrapuntal method shows how the stories of Buddha and Jesus that emerged out of different contexts can mutually critique, enhance and gain from each other while retaining their unique identities. Unlike Western methods, which problematized "contradictory" stances of Paul, "Late style" shows how an author can adopt in their later years a position very different from an earlier one. Accordingly, seemingly contradictory viewpoints signify theological and intellectual growth rather than a lack of consistency.

Postcolonial Commentary on the New Testament Writings edited by Segovia and Sugirtharajah (2009) is an ambitious volume and the first to engage the whole of the New Testament and employ a variety of theories and concepts such as hybridity, mimicry, and ambivalence. Segovia's chapter on John's Gospel helpfully explicates the significance of the prefix "post" in postcolonial and argues that it is a social-psychological term that refers to a state of the mind rather than a historical-political term connoting a period after the end of colonialism. Contributors placed biblical texts in dialogue with colonial contexts in which they were written and with the interpretive contexts in the 18th 19th and 20th centuries. While many prioritized recovering the liberative aspects of texts, others read the texts as colonial (Liew on Mark), ambiguous toward empire (Burrus on Luke-Acts), or mimicking the empire (Moore on Revelation). Its Hebrew Bible counterpart *Postcolonial Commentary and the Old Testament* that came out in 2020 is more methodological in nature and less focused on engaging the breadth of each book in the Hebrew Bible (perhaps less theoretical too). Like *Postcolonial Biblical Criticism: Interdisciplinary Criticism* (2005), this volume explores methodological intersections. Whereas the 2005 volume highlights how postcolonialism intersects with Marxism, Feminism, and ideological criticism, this commentary placed postcolonial criticism in dialogue with historical criticism to demonstrate how they can inform and enhance each other. Perhaps that is one of the key contributions of this volume—that postcolonial and historical criticism are compatible and complementary.

Colonialism and the Bible: Contemporary Reflections from the Global South (2018) edited by Liew and Segovia traces the complex and complicated relationship between the Bible and colonialism—past and present. While such a complex relationship has long been acknowledged, the book's unique contribution lies in its delineation of how that relationship played out in different geographical locations across different time periods. Contributors, all of them from the global South, call attention to a fascinating spectrum of uses of the Bible in different parts of the world and explore complex layers of such uses—resistance, accommodation, ambivalence, mimicry, and hybridity—at the level of interpretation.

A Few Current and Future Trajectories

Postcolonial biblical criticism has successfully foregrounded empire—past and present—as an essential lens for reading biblical texts and shifted the focus of textual exploration to life and death issues. With a fine combination of engagement with everyday issues, hermeneutics committed to justice and sophisticated methodologies, the discourse continues to enervate misuse of biblical texts and reclaim them for liberative purposes. The shift has been slow but significant and irreversible. The dozens of volumes that have been published on the subject matter in the last twenty-five years as well as the increasing number of sections on postcolonial criticism at the Society of Biblical Literature meetings signify the impact and growing relevance of the discourse in the guild.

Postcolonial scholars still largely occupy marginal spaces in the guild—their marginality is evident, in part, in the use of the modifier "postcolonial"—but they speak powerfully from their margins and decenter dominant interpretive paradigms in order to foreground their concerns. On some level, however, the center-margin dichotomy is both simplistic and problematic. Just as there is a center vis-à-vis the many margins in a given setting, there is a center—literal or figurative—within each marginal space. Each margin, then, is in turn potentially a center with multiple margins of its own that it continues to marginalize and render powerless. A key task of postcolonial biblical criticism is to go beyond a simple center-margin dichotomy and focus also on internal colonialism within former colonies of the empire so that fruits of liberation are accessible to all sections, especially the marginalized communities in those countries. Sugirtharajah puts it well, "Postcolonial studies are not simply about what went wrong during colonial days and what went wrong in the anticolonial struggle where gender and class went unnoticed or were subsumed under the nationalist cause, but has also to do with the non-materialization after the euphoria of freedom of greater democracy, justice for Indigenous people, and minorities like Dalits and Burakumins, gender equality and the end of poverty and hunger."[87]

Margins are sites of oppression, but they have power, especially when they join forces, as anticolonial movements have demonstrated. Along those lines, postcolonial discourse should embrace the intersectionality of social locations such as race, gender, sexuality, and class. However, even as the postcolonial discourse embraces a global hermeneutical stance of intersectionality, it should resist the urge to coopt hermeneutics arising from other marginalized spaces and social locations.[88] It should acknowledge the unique realities and lived experiences that have engendered those hermeneutics and work with them as equal partners. Here intersectionality becomes a political strategy whereby alliances are formed across various marginal spaces such as African American, Minjung, Latin American, Dalit, tribal, gay, queer, Burakumin, and Native American. Intersectionality is also a hermeneutical strategy whereby the discourse builds upon interpretive insights from these disparate yet overlapping social locations and envisions liberation that will be realized only if/when all the marginalized groups are able to occupy liberative spaces and share in their benefits.

The postcolonial commitment to the margins should also translate into a more consistent exploration of early Christian texts that have been excluded from the traditional Christian canon. On one level, engaging noncanonical books gives contemporary communities access to the rich diversity of early Christian perspectives on key issues but, on another level, to the extent the process of canonization was a manifestation of the empire, engaging those books becomes a postcolonial hermeneutical stance. It is a way of resuscitating suppressed voices and letting them retell early Christian traditions and struggles from their perspective.

Postcolonial biblical scholars should continue to engage vernacular and Indigenous languages, traditions, and interpretive paradigms and take local realities seriously in addition to global geopolitical dynamics. They must remain in conversation with concerns and hermeneutical practices of their roots, even as they engage Western reading strategies. A failure to engage vernacular traditions amounts to disconnectedness from one's roots, as the volume *Vernacular Hermeneutics* has shown. It will also result in a loss of rich traditions, stories, and worldviews that have significant liberative potential. A task of postcolonial biblical studies is to continue to build upon traditions and interpretive paradigms that have been marginalized by centuries of Western biblical scholarship.

The question of engaging vernacular and Indigenous traditions raises further questions of who gets to speak about these issues, to whom and for whom, especially if such engagement is undertaken by diasporic scholars. *Postcolonial voices from Downunder: Indigenous Matters, Confronting Readings* (2017) edited by Jione Havea raises such questions in helpful ways. It asks, "For which and whose third world do postcolonial theorists speak and advocate? From under the protection of British and American empires, do postcolonial theorists see the real struggles of the everyday third world(ed)?"[89] Along similar lines, Stephen Moore has highlighted Aijaz Ahmad's incisive and insightful observation that postcolonial theory replicates global capitalism within the Western academy.[90] In Ahmad's view, postcolonial scholars who occupy coveted academic positions in the West and are insulated from the harsh realities of the third world gather raw materials—colonial archives, Indigenous stories, missionary tracts—and turn them into fine academic products that are consumed by Western academics and graduate students.[91] A subtext of Ahmad's observation is that diasporic postcolonial scholars have been coopted by the West, their hermeneutical commitments notwithstanding.

To build upon insights from Havea and Ahmad, postcolonial scholars cannot claim to advocate or speak for anyone. They can only speak about the contexts that they have come from and, in many cases, inhabited for much of their lives. More importantly, diasporic postcolonial scholars "speak to" [the Western academy] rather than "speak for" anyone. The Western academy that is located in the heart of British and American empires and exerts significant influence over them should consistently be confronted by embodied activist voices. Such voices come from many locations—former colonies of the empire, the margins within Western metropolitan centers and every place in-between. The metropolitan-colony dichotomy is simplistic because margins can only be defined in relative rather than absolute terms. There are colonized spaces and conditions within Western metropolitan centers and metropolitan-like spaces in the former colonies or "the third world," to use Ahmad's term. Many postcolonial scholars located in the global South occupy privileged academic positions and lead vastly more comfortable lives compared to communities about which they write. At the same time, many diasporic scholars stay connected to harsh realities of the margins both within metropolitan centers and in the third world. The question is not how close to—or far from—the center of the empire does one reside, but how does one use one's location and voice to respond to the ethos and agendas of the empire. The task of postcolonial scholars is to turn their disparate locations into subversive spaces that challenge the might and agenda of the empire in the academy as well as in the world beyond it. Along those lines, diasporic scholars who are situated close to the heart of the empire should be intentional about using their voices and proximity to the empire prophetically and loudly to ensure that the empire can hear them and be held accountable.

Finally, environmental degradation has been a key aspect and legacy of colonialism, and empires have unleashed violence against nature in order to terrorize and displace native populations and to reshape the lands in line with their own imaginations and agendas. The British Empire was especially complicit in ecological destruction by exploiting the nature for raw materials and displacing Indigenous communities who have a long history of nurturing the nature.[92] In numerous countries in the global South, multinational corporations, a manifestation of neocolonialism, remain the root cause of environmental degradation, loss of biodiversity, and displacement of people. As a result, communities in the former colonies, especially Indigenous and tribal people, continue to bear the brunt of climate change more than any in the West. Despite such realities, many of their governments are largely indifferent to ecological concerns perceiving or depicting such concerns as Western preoccupation. Such an incongruity between ground realities and government policies requires that postcolonial discourse—both in the secular academy and in biblical studies—should be attentive to these issues in its intellectual articulations and embodied activism. Environmental concerns and a commitment to reversing ecological degradation have indeed become key aspects of postcolonial criticism but given the scale of past ecological damage and continued violence against nature, the discourse should intensify its focus on the issue and provide new paradigms for repairing human relationship with the earth in order to ensure human as well as environmental welfare.

Conclusion

Empire is very much a current phenomenon as are attempts to justify it. This is evident in the new manifestations of an empire that Gildea has described and in the surge of new books defending the empire.[93] Biblical interpreters continue to employ texts to justify the empire in the public square and adversely impact people's lives. Such misuse of texts suggests that as long as empire remains a reality, the Bible will continue to play a role in it and will likely be weaponized.

The Bible has been appropriated and misused by empires over the centuries, but it also has a long history of challenging and attenuating the empire in its various manifestations. Given these disparate uses of biblical texts, postcolonial biblical criticism should engage texts as well as their interpretations in all their complexity—resistance, accommodation, and ambivalence—with the goal of liberation. It should continue to expose oppressive strands in texts and interpretations, reclaim biblical texts from oppressive frameworks, and suggest liberative paradigms, methods, and insights for engaging biblical texts. One of the limitations of postcolonial biblical scholars is that their influence is largely limited to the guild, in part because of the seemingly theoretical and esoteric nature of the discourse. Scholars should resolve this conundrum by exploring creative, accessible, and praxis-oriented readings to engage the public square even as they continue to pursue theoretical sophistication in their hermeneutics. The two—theoretical sophistication and praxis-oriented readings—are not mutually exclusive but can enhance each other. The discourse grew out of anticolonial movements on the streets, and it is time to return to those roots so that it can engage the public square with integrity and authenticity. Postcolonial biblical criticism should continue to operate and thrive in tensive and seemingly paradoxical spaces: global and local; English and vernacular; and theoretical sophistication and praxis-oriented engagement. The goal is not to find a balance between any two components but to explore and exploit the power of such tensive spaces.

Notes

1. Laila Lalami, *The Moor's Account* (New York: Vintage Books, 2015), 286.
2. Homi Bhabha, *The Location of Culture* (New York: Routledge, 1994), 246.
3. Rudyard Kipling, *Kim* (Mattituck, NY: Amereon Limited, 1998), 131.
4. Patrick French, *The World Is What It Is: The Authorized Biography of V. S. Naipaul* (New York: Vintage Books, 2008).
5. Aimé Césaire, *Discourse on Colonialism* (New York: Monthly Review Press, 2001), 42.
6. Frantz Fanon, *The Wretched of the Earth* (New York: Grove Press, 1963), 169. Other prominent writers in this category include Aimé Césaire, A. Memmi, and C. L. R James.
7. Chinua Achebe, "African Literature as Celebration of Restoration" in *The Education of a British-Protected Child* (New York: Knopf, 2009), 118.
8. Ngũgĩ wa Thiong'o, *Decolonising the Mind: The Politics of Language in African Literature* (Portsmouth: Heinemann, 1981), 9.
9. Robert Young, *Postcolonialism: An Historical Introduction*. Anniversary Edition (Oxford: Blackwell Publishing, 2016), xi.
10. R. S. Sugirtharajah, *Postcolonial Criticism and Biblical Interpretation* (Oxford: Oxford University Press, 2002), 13. Such a distinction between the two terms, however, is not always maintained within the discourse.

11. Robert Gildea, *Empires of the Mind: The Colonial Past and the Politics of the Present* (Cambridge: Cambridge University Press, 2019), 117–120.
12. Michael Hardt and Antonio Negri, *Empire* (Cambridge: Harvard University Press, 2000), xii.
13. Young, *Postcolonialism*, 4.
14. Linda Nochlin, *The Politics of Vision: Essays on Nineteenth-Century Art and Society* (New York: Routledge, 1991), 50–51.
15. Edward Said, *Orientalism* (New York: Vintage Books, 1978), 127–129.
16. Said, *Orientalism*, 131.
17. Niccolao Manucci, Storia o Mogor; or, Mogul India 1653–1708 (London, Ontario: Scholar's Choice, 2015), 197, 228.
18. Manucci, 64.
19. Manucci, 155.
20. Swagato Ganguly, *Idolatry and the Colonial Idea of India: Visions of Horror, Allegories of Enlightenment* (New York: Routledge, 2019), 10.
21. Ganguly, *Idolatry and the Colonial Idea of India*, 10. Mill famously claimed that his absolute lack of familiarity with India gave him the advantage of being objective about the country, its religions and culture.
22. Orientalism is very much a current phenomenon. One has to simply watch movies such as "Indiana Jones and the Temple of Doom" and "Stargate" to witness this phenomenon.
23. Said, *Orientalism*, 207. One might recall that the United States occupied Iraq in the aftermath of 9/11 on the pretext of promoting democracy.
24. Hardt and Negri, 170.
25. Ania Loomba, *Colonialism/Postcolonialism* (New York: Routledge, 2015), 40–41.
26. Walter D. Mignolo and Catherine E. Walsh employ the phrase "colonial matrix of power" to describe the factors that facilitated European political and cultural hegemony over communities in the global South. Walter D. Mignolo and Catherine E. Walsh, *On Decoloniality: Concepts, Analytics, Praxis* (Durham: Duke University Press, 2018).
27. Said, *Orientalism, Empire*, 7.
28. Said, *Culture and Imperialism* (New York: Vintage Books, 1994), xii.
29. Said, *Culture and Imperialism*, 99.
30. Said, *Culture and imperialism*, 212.
31. Achebe, *The Education of a British-Protected Child*, 112.
32. Gayatri Spivak, *A Critique of Postcolonial Reason: Toward a History of the Vanishing Present* (Cambridge: Harvard University Press, 1999), 383–384.
33. Bhabha, *The Location of Culture*, 122.
34. Bhabha, *The Location of Culture*, 122.
35. Bill Ashcroft, Gareth Griffiths, and Helen Tiffin, *Post-Colonial Studies: The Key Concepts* (New York: Routledge, 1998), 12–13.
36. Bhabha, *The Location of Culture*, 123.
37. R. S. Sugirtharajah, ed. *The Postcolonial Bible* (Sheffield: Sheffield Academic Press, 1998), 93.
38. Victor Ramraj, "'Trapdoors into a Bottomless Past': V. S. Naipaul's Early Ambivalent Vision of the Indo-Caribbean Experience," in *Journal of Caribbean Literatures*, 5, no. 2 (Spring 2008): 33–46. Ramraj helpfully highlights the deeply problematic nature of Naipaul claiming his Indian roots while never acknowledging Trinidad, where he was born and raised, as his home.

39. Edward Said and Gauri Viswanathan, *Power, Politics. and Culture: Interviews with Edward W. Said* (New York: Vintage Books, 2002), 38.
40. Robert Young, *Postcolonialism*, 4.
41. Young, *Postcolonialism*, 57.
42. George Tyler Northup, trans., *Mundus Novus: Letter to Lorenzo Pietro di Medici* (Princeton, New Jersey: Princeton University Press, 1916), 1–13.
43. Benjamin Schmidt, *Innocence Abroad: The Dutch Imagination and the New World, 1570–1670*. Illustrated edition (Cambridge: Cambridge University Press, 2006), 130.
44. Schmidt, *Innocence Abroad*, 130.
45. Patricia O'Toole, *Money and Morals in America: A History* (New York: Clarkson Potter, 1998), 18–19.
46. James Thornwell, *Collected Writings of James Thornwell*: Vol. 4 (Carlisle: Applewood Books, 2009), 385.
47. Matthew J. Tuininga, "The 'Great Conservative Power': James Henley Thornwell and the Gospel of Southern Conservatism," *Journal of Church and State* 61, no. 1 (Winter 2019): 59–77.
48. Achebe, *The Education of a British-Protected Child*, 113.
49. William Arnot, *The Parables of Our Lord* (London: Thomas Nelson & Sons, 1884), 237–239. In his widely acclaimed 2019 book *The Anarchy: The East India Company, Corporate Violence, and the Pillage of an Empire*, William Dalrymple narrates how, in fact, it was the British East Company, which began its reign in India in 1765, that facilitated excessive violence, loot, and anarchy.
50. Arnot, *The Parables of Our Lord*, 237–239.
51. Sugirtharajah, *Postcolonial Criticism and Biblical Interpretation*, 1.
52. Fernando F. Segovia, *Decolonizing Biblical Studies: A View from the Margins* (Maryknoll: Oribis Books, 2000), 15–33.
53. Segovia, *Decolonizing Biblical Studies*, 38.
54. R. S. Sugirtharajah, *The Bible and the Third World: Precolonial, Colonial and Postcolonial Encounters* (Cambridge: Cambridge University Press, 2001), 61.
55. Sugirtharajah, *The Bible and the Third World*, 61.
56. Segovia, *Decolonizing Biblical Studies*, 37–39.
57. J. H. Elliott, "Triste Trinidad," *New York Review of Books*, May 21, 1970, https://www.nybooks.com/articles/1970/05/21/triste-trinidad/.
58. Segovia, *Decolonizing Biblical Studies*, 64–90.
59. There have, of course, been exceptions.
60. Elsa Tamez, "The Bible and the Five Hundred Years of Conquest," in *Voices from the Margin: Interpreting the Bible in the Third World* (25th Anniversary Edition), ed. R. S. Sugirtharajah (Maryknoll: Orbis Books, 2106), 4–6.
61. Tamez, "The Bible and the Five Hundred Years of Conquest," 4–6.
62. Musa Dube, *Voices from the Margin*, 353.
63. Cain Hope Felder, ed., *Stony the Road We Trod: African American Biblical Interpretation* (Minneapolis: Fortress Press, 1991).
64. Ralph Broadbent describes a "chance encounter between R. S. Sugirtharajah and Edward Said's Orientalism in a now long-defunct Birmingham bookshop called Hudson's" that birthed his 1996 essay and served as a catalyst for postcolonial biblical criticism. R. S. Sugirtharajah, *Exploring Postcolonial Biblical Criticism: History, Method, Practice* (Oxford: Wiley-Blackwell, 2011), 59.

65. Stephen D. Moore and Fernando F. Segovia, "Postcolonial Biblical Criticism: Beginnings, Trajectories, Intersections," in *Postcolonial Biblical Criticism: Interdisciplinary Intersections*, ed. Stephen D. Moore and Fernando F. Segovia (New York: T&T Clark, 2005), 2–4.
66. Sugirtharajah, *The Postcolonial Bible*, 18.
67. R. S. Sugirtharajah, *Vernacular Hermeneutics* (Sheffield: Sheffield Academic, 1999), 13.
68. Sugirtharajah, *Vernacular Hermeneutics*, 32–33.
69. Postcolonial Commentary on the Old Testament that will be discussed later highlights how the two methodologies can inform each other.
70. Vincent L. Wimbush, *White Men's Logic: Scripturalization as Slavery* (New York: Oxford University Press, 2014), 16–18.
71. Jacqueline M. Hidalgo, *Revelation in Aztlán: Scriptures, Utopias, and the Chicano Movement* (New York: Palgrave Macmillan, 2016).
72. Lynne St. Claire Darden, *Scripturalizing Revelation: An African American Postcolonial Reading of Empire* (Atlanta: SBL Press, 2015).
73. Hans Leander's 2013 book analyzes the complex ways nineteenth-century readings of Mark were at work in European imperialism and offers strategies for reclaiming texts. See Hans Leander, *Discourses of Empire: The Gospel of Mark from a Postcolonial Perspective* (Atlanta: SBL Press, 2013).
74. R. S. Sugirtharajah, *Exploring Postcolonial Biblical Criticism*, 3.
75. Steed Verynyl Davidson, *Empire and Exile: Postcolonial Readings of the Book of Jeremiah* (New York: Bloomsbury, 2013).
76. Margaret Aymer, *James: Diaspora Rhetoric of a Friend of God. Phoenix Guides to the New Testament* 17 (Sheffield: Sheffield Phoenix, 2015).
77. Shanell T., Smith, *The Woman Babylon and the Marks of Empire: Reading Revelation with a Postcolonial Womanist Hermeneutics of Ambiveilence* (Minneapolis: Fortress Press, 2014).
78. Tat-siong Benny Liew, "The Gospel of Mark" in *A Postcolonial Commentary on the New Testament Writings*, ed. Fernando F. Segovia and R. S. Sugirtharajah (New York: T&T Clark, 2009), 105–132.
79. Randall C. Bailey, "Beyond Identification: The Use of Africans in Old Testament Poetry and Narratives," in *Stony the Road We Trod*, 170–173.
80. Moore and Segovia, "Postcolonial Biblical Criticism: Beginnings, Trajectories, Intersections," 16–17.
81. Segovia, "Mapping the Postcolonial Optic in Biblical Criticism," in *Postcolonial Biblical Criticism*, 23.
82. Musa W. Dube, *Postcolonial Feminist Interpretation of the Bible* (St. Louis: Chalice Press, 2000), 23–28.
83. Dube, *Postcolonial Feminist Interpretation of the Bible*, 28.
84. Kwok Pui-lan, "Making the Connections: Postcolonial Studies and Feminist Biblical Interpretation," in *The Postcolonial Biblical Reader*. ed. R. S. Sugirtharajah (New York: Wiley-Blackwell, 2005), 60.
85. Richard Horsley, *Paul and Empire: Religion and Power in Roman Imperial Society* (Harrisburg, PA: Trinity, 1997), 3.
86. See Moore and Segovia, *Postcolonial Biblical Criticism*, 7.
87. Sugirtharajah, *Postcolonial Criticism and Biblical Interpretation*, 23.
88. Gerald O. West offers helpful discussion of uniqueness of regional hermeneutics such as African and Asian. See Gerald West, "Doing Postcolonial Biblical Interpretation @Home: Ten Years of (South) African Ambivalence," *Neotestamentica* 42, no. 1 (2008): 147–164.

89. Jione Havea, ed., *Postcolonial Voices from Downunder: Indigenous Matters, Confronting Readings* (Eugene, OR: Pickwick, 2017), 3.
90. Stephen Moore, "Questions of Biblical Ambivalence and Authority under a Tree outside Delhi; or, the Postcolonial and the Postmodern," in *Postcolonial Biblical Criticism*, 82.
91. Moore, "Questions of Biblical Ambivalence and Authority," 82–83.
92. William Beinart and Lotte Hughes document the ecological degradation caused by British imperialism in the last 500 years. William Beinart and Lotte Hughes, *Environment and Empire* (Oxford History of the British Empire Companion) (New York: Oxford University Press, 2009).
93. David Gilmour's *The British in India: A Social History of the Raj* (2018) attempts to shift the focus from political and military to social (= benign and benevolent) aspects of the British empire. In a 2006 article in *The New York Review of Books*, Gilmour complained that "most postcolonial writing has no room for altruism [of the empire]. "The Case for Colonialism," Bruce Gilley's controversial 2017 essay, which has since been withdrawn from *The Third World Quarterly*, is a blatant attempt to portray centuries of European colonialism as a civilizing mission.

BIBLIOGRAPHY

Achebe, Chinua. *Things Fall Apart*. Oxford: Heinemann, 1958.

Achebe, Chinua. "African Literature as Celebration of Restoration" in *The Education of a British-Protected Child*. New York: Knopf, 2009.

Ahmad, Aijaz. *In Theory: Classes, Nations, Literatures*. New York: Verso, 1992.

Arnot, William. *The Parables of Our Lord*. London: Thomas Nelson & Sons, 1884.

Ashcroft, Bill, Gareth Griffiths, and Helen Tiffin. *Post-Colonial Studies: The Key Concepts*. New York: Routledge, 1998.

Aymer, Margaret. *James: Diaspora Rhetoric of a Friend of God*. Phoenix Guides to the New Testament 17. Sheffield: Sheffield Phoenix, 2015.

Beinart, William, and Lotte Hughes. *Environment and Empire* (Oxford History of the British Empire Companion). New York: Oxford University Press, 2009.

Bhabha, Homi. *The Location of Culture*. New York: Routledge, 1994.

Brett, Mark G. *Political Trauma and Healing: Biblical Ethics for a Postcolonial World*. Grand Rapids: Eerdmans, 2016.

Brown, William P. *A Handbook to Old Testament Exegesis*. Louisville: Westminster John Knox, 2017.

Carter, Warren. *Matthew and the Margins: A Sociopolitical And Religious Reading* (Bible & Liberation). Maryknoll: Orbis Books, 2001.

Carter, Warren. *The Roman Empire and the New Testament: An Essential Guide*. Nashville: Abingdon Press, 2006.

Césaire, Aimé. *Discourse on Colonialism*. New York: Monthly Review Press, 2001.

Conrad, Joseph. *Heart of Darkness*. New York: Bedford/St. Martin's, 2010.

Crossan, John Dominic and Jonathan L Reed. *In Search of Paul: How Jesus' Apostle Opposed Rome's Empire with God's Kingdom*. New York: HarperOne, 2005.

Crossan, John Dominic. *God and Empire: Jesus Against Rome, Then and Now*. New York: HarperOne, 2008.

Cuellar, Gregory. *Empire, the British Museum, and the Making of the Biblical Scholar in the Nineteenth Century: Archival Criticism*. Palgrave, 2019.

Dalrymple, William. *The Anarchy: The East India Company, Corporate Violence, and the Pillage of an Empire*. London: Bloomsbury, 2019.

Darden, Lynne St. Claire. *Scripturalizing Revelation: An African American Postcolonial Reading of Empire*. Atlanta: SBL Press, 2015.

Davidson, Steed Verynyl. *Empire and Exile: Postcolonial Readings of the Book of Jeremiah*. New York: Bloomsbury, 2013.

Donaldson, Laura E. *Decolonizing Feminisms: Race, Gender and Empire Building*. Chapel Hill: The University of North Carolina Press, 1992.

Donaldson, Laura E., ed. *Semeia 75: Postcolonialism and Scriptural Reading*. Atlanta: Scholars Press, 1996.

Dube, Musa W. *Postcolonial Feminist Interpretation of the Bible*. St. Louis: Chalice Press, 2000.

Elliott, J. H. "Triste Trinidad." *New York Review of Books*, May 21, 1970. https://www.nybooks.com/articles/1970/05/21/triste-trinidad/.

Elliott, Neil. *LIBERATING PAUL: The Justice of God and the Politics of the Apostle*. Minneapolis: Fortress Press, 1994.

Fanon, Frantz. *The Wretched of the Earth*. New York: Grove Press, 1963.

Fanon, Frantz. *Black Skin, White Masks*. New York: Grove Press, 2008.

Felder, Cain Hope, ed. *Stony the Road We Trod: African American Biblical Interpretation*. Minneapolis: Fortress Press, 1991.

Forster, E. M. *A Passage to India*. Orlando: Mariner Books, 1965.

French, Patrick. *The World Is What It Is: The Authorized Biography of V. S. Naipaul*. New York: Vintage Books, 2008.

Ganguly, Swagato. *Idolatry and the Colonial Idea of India: Visions of Horror, Allegories of Enlightenment*. New York: Routledge, 2019.

Gildea, Robert. *Empires of the Mind: The Colonial Past and the Politics of the Present*. Cambridge: Cambridge University Press, 2019.

Gilmour, David. *The British in India: A Social History of the Raj*. New York: Farrar, Straus and Giroux, 2018.

Hardt, Michael, and Antonio Negri. *Empire*. Cambridge, MA: Harvard University Press, 2000.

Havea, Jione, ed. *Postcolonial Voices from Downunder: Indigenous Matters, Confronting Readings*. Eugene, OR: Pickwick, 2017.

Hidalgo, Jacqueline M. *Revelation in Aztlán: Scriptures, Utopias, and the Chicano Movement*. New York: Palgrave Macmillan, 2016.

Horsley, Richard A. *Paul and Empire: Religion and Power in Roman Imperial Society*. Harrisburg, PA: Trinity, 1997.

Horsley, Richard and Neil Asher Silberman. *The Message and the Kingdom: How Jesus and Paul Ignited a Revolution and Transformed the Ancient World*. New York: Putnam, 1997.

Horsley, Richard. *Paul and Politics: Ekklesia, Israel, Imperium, Interpretation*. Harrisburg: Trinity Press, 2000.

Horsley, Richard A. *Jesus and Empire: The Kingdom of God and the New World Disorder*. Minneapolis: Fortress, 2002.

Howard-Brook, Wes and Anthony Gwyther. *Unveiling Empire: Reading Revelation Then and Now* (Bible & Liberation). Maryknoll: Orbis Books, 1999.

Kim, Uriah Y. *Identity and Loyalty in the David Story: A Postcolonial Reading*. Sheffield: Sheffield Phoenix, 2008.

Kipling, Rudyard. *Kim*. Mattituck, NY: Amereon Limited, 1998.

Lalami, Laila. *The Moor's Account*. New York: Vintage Books, 2015.

Leander, Hans. *Discourses of Empire: The Gospel of Mark from a Postcolonial Perspective.* Atlanta: SBL Press, 2013.
Liew, Tat-Siong Benny, and Fernando Segovia, eds. *Colonialism and the Bible: Contemporary Reflections from the Global South.* Lexington, 2018.
Loomba, Ania. *Colonialism/Postcolonialism.* New York: Routledge, 2015.
Manucci, Niccolao. *Storia o Mogor; or, Mogul India 1653–1708.* London, Ontario: Scholar's Choice, 2015.
Mignolo, Walter D. and Catherine E. Walsh. *On Decoloniality: Concepts, Analytics, Praxis.* Durham: Duke University Press, 2018.
Mohanty, Chandra. "Under Western Eyes," in *Colonial Discourse and Postcolonial Theory: A Reader,* edited by Patrick Williams and Laura Chrisman. New York: Columbia University Press, 1994.
Moore, Stephen and Fernando Segovia, eds. *Postcolonial Biblical Criticism: Interdisciplinary Intersections.* New York: T&T Clark, 2005.
Naipaul, V. S. *A House for Mr. Biswas.* New York: Penguin Books, 1961.
Naipaul, V. S. *An Area of Darkness: A Discovery of India.* New York: Vintage Books, 1964.
Naipaul, V. S. *India: A Wounded Civilization.* New Delhi: Vikas Publishing, 1977.
Naipaul, V. S. *India: A Million Mutinies Now.* New York: Vintage, 1990.
Nochlin, Linda. *The Politics of Vision: Essays on Nineteenth-Century Art and Society.* New York: Routledge, 1991.
Northup, George Tyler, trans. *Mundus Novus: Letter to Lorenzo Pietro di Medici.* Princeton, New Jersey: Princeton University Press, 1916.
O'Toole, Patricia. *Money and Morals in America: A History.* New York: Clarkson Potter, 1998.
Ramraj, Victor. "'Trapdoors into a Bottomless Past:' V. S. Naipaul's Early Ambivalent Vision of the Indo-Caribbean Experience." *Journal of Caribbean Literatures* 5, no. 2 (Spring 2008): 33–46.
Rieger, Jorge. *Christ and Empire: From Paul to Postcolonial Times.* Minneapolis: Augsburg Fortress, 2007.
Said, Edward. *Orientalism.* New York: Vintage Books, 1978.
Said, Edward. *Culture and Imperialism.* New York: Vintage Books, 1994.
Said, Edward, and Gauri Viswanathan. *Power, Politics. and Culture: Interviews with Edward W. Said.* New York: Vintage Books, 2002.
Schmidt, Benjamin. *Innocence Abroad: The Dutch Imagination and the New World, 1570–1670. Illustrated edition.* Cambridge: Cambridge University Press, 2006.
Segovia, Fernando F. *Decolonizing Biblical Studies: A View from the Margins.* Maryknoll: Oribis Books, 2000a.
Segovia, Fernando F., ed. *Interpreting Beyond Borders.* Sheffield: Sheffield Academic Press, 2000b.
Segovia, Fernando F., and R.S. Sugirtharajah, eds. *A Postcolonial Commentary on the New Testament Writings.* New York: T&T Clark, 2009.
Smith, Mitzi J. *Womanist Sass and Talk Back: Social (In)Justice, Intersectionality, and Biblical Interpretation.* Eugene, OR: Cascade Books, 2018.
Smith, Shanell. *The Woman Babylon and the Marks of Empire: Reading Revelation with a Postcolonial Womanist Hermeneutics of Ambiveilence.* Minneapolis: Fortress, 2014.
Spivak, Gayatri. *A Critique of Postcolonial Reason: Toward a History of the Vanishing Present.* Cambridge: Harvard University Press, 1999.
Stanley, Christopher. *The Colonized Apostle: Paul in Postcolonial Eyes.* Minneapolis: Fortress, 2011.

Sugirtharajah, R. S. "From Orientalist to Post-colonial: Notes on Reading Practices." *Asia Journal of Theology* 10, no. 1 (1996): 20–27.

Sugirtharajah, R. S., ed. *The Postcolonial Bible* (The Bible and Postcolonialism). Sheffield: Sheffield Academic, 1998.

Sugirtharajah, R. S. *Vernacular Hermeneutics.* Sheffield: Sheffield Academic, 1999.

Sugirtharajah, R. S. *The Bible and the Third World: Precolonial, Colonial and Postcolonial Encounters.* Cambridge: Cambridge University Press, 2001.

Sugirtharajah, R. S. *Asian Biblical Hermeneutics and Postcolonialism: Contesting the Interpretations.* Maryknoll: Orbis Books, 2002a.

Sugirtharajah, R. S. *Postcolonial Criticism and Biblical Interpretation.* Oxford: Oxford University Press, 2002b.

Sugirtharajah, R. S. *Postcolonial Reconfigurations: An Alternative Way of Reading the Bible and Doing Theology.* St. Louis: Chalice Press, 2003.

Sugirtharajah, R. S. *The Bible and Empire: Postcolonial Explorations.* Cambridge: Cambridge University Press, 2005.

Sugirtharajah, R. S., ed. *The Postcolonial Biblical Reader.* Oxford: Blackwell, 2006.

Sugirtharajah, R. S. *Exploring Postcolonial Biblical Criticism; History, Method, Practice.* Oxford: Wiley-Blackwell, 2011.

Sugirtharajah, R. S. *Voices from the Margin: Interpreting the Bible in the Third World.* 25th Anniversary Edition. New York: Orbis Books, 2016.

Thiong'O, Ngũgĩ. *Decolonising the Mind: The Politics of Language in African Literature.* Portsmouth: Heinemann, 1981.

Thornwell, James. *Collected Writings of James Thornwell: Vol. 4.* Carlisle: Applewood Books, 2009.

Tuininga, Matthew. *Journal of Church and State* 61, no. 1 (Winter 2019): 59–77.

West, Gerald O. "Doing Postcolonial Biblical Interpretation @Home: Ten Years of (South) African Ambivalence." *Neotestamentica* 42, no. 1 (2008): 147–164.

Wimbush, Vincent L. *White Men's Logic: Scripturalization as Slavery.* New York: Oxford University Press, 2014.

Young, Robert J.C. *Postcolonialism: An Historical Introduction.* Anniversary Edition. Oxford: Blackwell Publishing, 2016.

CHAPTER 30

EMPIRE, POSTCOLONIAL CRITICISM, AND BIBLICAL STUDIES

SHARON JACOB

When I was approached to contribute an essay on postcolonial criticism and empire studies for the *Oxford Handbook of Postcolonial Biblical Criticism*, the picture in my head was crystal clear. I was going to map the ways in which postcolonial criticism and empire studies have played an important role in the field of biblical studies. However, just as I was beginning to write my chapter, the United States, in the grips of a deadly pandemic, witnessed the horrific murder of George Floyd that brought about worldwide condemnation and protests, forcing all of us to look hard at racism and how it affects all our lives. It was around that time that President Trump decided to do his famous photo op in front of St. John's Episcopal Church in Lafayette Square in Washington, D.C. This incident was controversial for a couple of reasons: first, a group of peaceful protestors who had gathered in Lafayette Square was dispersed with tear gas and brutal police force so that President Trump could engage in his photo op; and second, President Trump not only stood in front of the church but did so while holding up a Bible for all to see. Richard A. Horsley writes, "Americans have a special relationship with the Bible. They also have a special relationship with empire."[1] The image of the President of the United States posing with a Bible in front of a church is illustrative of the close and complicated relationship between the Bible and empire in a postcolonial world.

When it comes to the relationship between Bible and empire, we can trace its historical development along three phases of scholarship: the first is Bible and ancient empires; the second is Bible and colonial empires; and the third is Bible and postcolonial empires.[2] An important development in the relationship between Bible and empire is, of course, the presence of postcolonial studies. Historians began using the term "postcolonial" in the aftermath of World War II, along with other terms like "nation-state."[3] It is important to note that the term "postcolonial" does not refer to the end of colonialism but rather encapsulates the complex and difficult relationship between the colonizer and the colonized after the traumatic event of colonization. In his chapter, "And So We Came to Rome: Mapping Postcolonial Biblical Criticism," Stephen D. Moore writes, "It simply cannot account for the complex relations of dominant and submission, dependence and independence, resistance and collusion that typically characterize the exchanges between the colonizer and colonized not only during colonial occupation but also after official decolonizing."[4] As we shall see in the sections that follow, the relationship between Bible and empire is never developed in the abstract; postcolonial studies reveal the ways in which this connection is embodied in the world.

Bible and Ancient Empires

When it comes to the relationship between the Bible and ancient empires, the focus, for the most part, remains on the past and on the imperial contexts in which these texts were written. It must be noted that even though historical-critical scholarship has drawn our attention to historical contexts, empires continued to remain in the background in biblical studies. Adam Winn writes, "Though Christianity was birthed under the power of this empire and every page of Christian Scripture was written under its shadow, the Roman Empire has played a relatively insignificant role in the history of modern New Testament scholarship."[5] Winn observes that even though the history of religions considered the impact of Roman ideas on the development of early Christian theology, few interpreters actually sought to understand and expose the ways in which the Roman Empire and its power could lead to a deeper understanding of Christian theological expression, mission, and practice.[6] By the same token, scholars in Hebrew Bible have also illustrated that readers of the Hebrew scriptures often ignore the idea that Israel was born out of resistance to Egypt and the Canaanite Empires. In his essay, "Early Israel as an Anti-Imperial Community," Norman K. Gottwald points out that "Early Israel was born as an anti-imperial resistance movement that broke away from Egyptian and Canaanite domination to become a self-governing community of free peasants."[7] The dominant supposition in biblical studies continues to be that the texts we are reading and interpreting are apolitical, and scholars continue to read the ills in the text as "personal failings" that can be corrected by individuals via a change of heart.[8] Biblical scholars who highlight ancient imperial contexts use empire as a hermeneutical lens through which they read and interpret texts. It is important to note that biblical scholars who have focused on the ancient imperial contexts have tended to draw on the field of classics, not postcolonial studies, as their interdisciplinary interlocutors. It must be reiterated that while historical-critical scholarship referred to the imperial background sporadically, these scholars maintained a steady and unwavering gaze on ancient empire and made it an important part of their scholarly work. Some of the important voices in this section have been Richard Horsley's 1998 essay, "Submerged Biblical Histories and Imperial Biblical Studies," and, similarly, Horsley's book entitled, *Hearing the Whole Story*, published in 2001. In *Hearing the Whole Story*, Horsley focuses on the Gospel of

Mark, takes a holistic approach, and argues for an understanding of Mark's Jesus as a prophet who opposed economic exploitation by the Roman Empire and Judean elite.[9] Similar to Horsley, other scholars, such as John Dominic Crossan, also made a significant impact by cementing the ways in which the Bible, read through the lens of empire, brings about a political interpretation of these texts and introduces the prophet Jesus as a political figure who resists empire. Moore explains Horsley's aim in writing that "implicit in Horsley's reading of Mark is the notion that this Gospel, properly understood is consistently anti-imperial in thrust, and hence a solid basis for theological critique of hegemonic ideologies and institutions, whether those of ancient Rome or the United States."[10] It is important to note that Horsley's push to make connections with the contemporary context is an important development in this scholarship, one that encourages scholars to make connections between past and present.[11]

In fact, a closer look reveals a divide among these scholars. Moore illustrates this when he writes, "Whereas some of them seem solely interested in the ancient imperial contexts in which the biblical texts were generated—others are intent on keeping the ancient imperial contexts in dialogue with the contemporary contexts in which the biblical texts are appropriated."[12] Some of the important works along these lines are *Jesus and Empire, Matthew and Empire, The Gospel of Matthew in Its Roman Imperial Contexts, Paul and Roman Imperial Order,* and *Unveiling Empire: Reading Revelation Then and Now,* to mention a few.[13] It is interesting to note that, within this group, the words *empire* and *imperial* are often part of the titles and illustrative of empire as a legitimate lens for interpretation. It must be reiterated that while historical-critical scholarship referred to the imperial background sporadically, it was these scholars who maintained an unwavering gaze on ancient empire and made it an important part of their scholarly work. At the same time, scholars who often fall under this category belong to a particular social location and write from a Western perspective. Winn writes:

> [A]s a product of the modern West, modern New Testament scholarship belonged, and to a great extent still belongs, to the world's wealthy, powerful, and privileged. Because virtually all New Testament interpreters were citizens of powerful nations (empires?) and benefitted from that power, they were (and still today often remain) predisposed to see themselves and their own situations in these texts.[14]

Furthermore, it must be noted that not only did the scholars engaging in this work belong to the West and were privileged, but they also were often male scholars. Scholars such as R. S. Sugirtharajah have made similar observations. Sugirtharajah writes, "The current metropolitan interpretation, although historically distinct from the colonial project and not directly involved in it, still participates in it by organizing and reinforcing perceptions of colonialism. It exerts its colonial power by viewing the world from a single privileged point of view, namely white, male and Western."[15] The single, unified, and hegemonic reading of Bible and ancient empire is countered by another strand of scholarship that continues its gaze on the Bible but centers its relationship to colonial empires.

BIBLE AND COLONIAL EMPIRE

There are two scholars whose work has been particularly influential in this category, and they are R. S. Sugirtharajah and Musa Dube. There is also the work of the Irish Catholic Priest Michael Prior, who wrote *The Bible and Colonialism: A Moral Critique* and the essay "The Bible and the Redeeming Idea of Colonialism." Prior observes that European nations during the period of colonization distinguished themselves by their sense of superiority over other peoples around the globe. He writes, " 'Colonialism' was still a noble word, capable of being presented as the (altruistic) bestowal of civilization and good order upon inferior peoples."[16] Unlike scholars in the previous category, these scholars focused on the relationship between the Bible and colonial empires. R. S. Sugirtharajah's work is particularly important in this section because he not only demonstrates this relationship but also pushes further and uncovers the ways in which the biblical text has always been part of contexts such as Africa and Asia. Using biblical texts as evidence, Sugirtharajah notes the important presence of African and Asian characters, places, and contexts in scripture. He writes, "One often overlooks the fact that, of the twenty-seven books of the New Testament, nearly half were either written in Asia Minor or written as letters to Christian communities there. The popular perception is that Christianity arrived in Asia only a couple of centuries ago under the aegis of the European powers, when they were making political inroads into that region."[17] Noting the contextual presence of ancient Asia and Africa in the Bible is an important move in stressing precolonial roots that allow one to see the text as part of one's own heritage rather than a foreign import.[18] Thus, in making this relationship visible, Sugirtharajah deviates from the rest of the scholars whose focus remains on either the imperial or colonial past. Highlighting precolonial roots allows for the emergence of a *third way* of understanding the relationship between Bible and empire.

Paradoxically, the dissemination and distribution of the Bible throughout colonial contexts also signified resistance and provided colonized people the opportunity to speak back at the colonial empire. Sugirtharajah notes, "Anti-colonial reading is not new. It has gone on whenever a native put quill pen to paper to contest the production of knowledge by the invading power."[19] When it comes to tracing the relationship between Bible and colonial empire, it is important we also map the resistance that was displayed by native readers, for whom the British Raj was the new Rome. One of the main tools against imperial resistance is language, and when it comes to the Bible, the translation, diffusion, and dissemination of biblical texts into vernacular languages must also be read as a push against colonialism. Sugritharajah observes, "This resistance to making the Bible available in vernacular languages pointed to the Church's linguistic conservatism. Giving vernacular versions to the common people was regarded as casting pearls before swine."[20] The transmission of the Bible in vernacular languages caused church authorities to fret over the misreading and irreverent interpretation of this holy text. But, pushing this point further, translating the Bible into vernacular languages not only allows for the easy accessibility of this sacred text but also diminishes the power of Empire that attempts to divide people via a false linguistic imperialism.[21] The thread of empire in the ancient world and colonial context exposes the ways interpretations of texts continue to privilege certain voices and certain contexts. The location of the interpreter not only plays a significant role in interpretation but also reinforces imperial notions and highlights certain perspectives and contexts over and above others.

Another work that is equally important in this section is the work of Musa Dube's monograph entitled *Postcolonial Feminist Interpretation of the Bible*. Dube's work is an in-depth study of contextual hermeneutics, using her own context of Botswana. Dube reads the exodus narratives in the Hebrew Bible along with selected text from the Gospel of Matthew, where Jesus is confronted by a Canaanite woman. Dube brings into the scholarly guild the voices of non-academic readers, specifically female members of the African Independent Churches.[22] In this move, one can see how placing the biblical text into non-academic hands is an act of resistance by making this text accessible.[23] The influence of postcolonial methodology is an important factor in in the scholarship of both Dube and Sugirtharajah. Homi K. Bhabha, in his book *The Location of Culture*, one of the cornerstones of Postcolonial Studies, devises the concept of a *third space*. A third space is the in-between space between colonized and colonizer where identities are interwoven to create a new way of reading that resists essentialist interpretations. A similar concept can be detected in Dube and Sugirtharajah's work, who forge a third way of understanding the relationship between the Bible and empire. This third way, while separate from the relationship of Bible and ancient empire, still draws on the lens of empire to understand the complex relationship between the precolonial and imperial past but gazes beyond ancient Rome. The use of postcolonial methodology in this section demonstrates how postcolonial studies has been an important part of biblical studies, especially in the work of those scholars who have used empire as a hermeneutical lens.

Bible and Postcolonial Empire

When it comes to postcolonial biblical criticism, we begin mapping outside the field as we move inward. In his article, "Scripture, Scholarship, Empire: Putting the Discipline in Its Place," Sugirtharajah writes:

> if we want the Bible and biblical interpretation to be an important and integral part of the academic curriculum, then I suggest that we need to take a new programmatic commitment to study the Bible in a global framework—a commitment that recognizes not only the multi-cultural context in which the Bible emerged but in which also it will have to be appropriated and expounded.[24]

For the most part, conversations about Bible and empires are limited to their historical contexts; however, as I have already noted, there were a few exceptions in this trajectory.

Scholars engaging in postcolonial biblical criticism consecutively connect and engage with empires in the ancient, colonial, and postcolonial contexts. In other words, the ability to not only see the connections between the past and the present demonstrate a deeper understanding of the colonizer and the colonized in how the scholarly work under this category can best be explained. At the same time, it is important that if we were to talk about postcolonial studies, we must begin with the triad of scholars whose work has influenced postcolonial biblical critique. These scholars would be Edward Said, Homi K. Bhabha, and Gayatri Spivak.

The work of these three scholars is seminal in postcolonial studies. The first major contribution is *Orientalism*, published in 1978 by Edward Said.[25] The second is Gayatri Chakravarty Spivak's controversial and important 1985 essay, "Can the Subaltern Speak?"[26] Finally, the third is Homi K. Bhabha's 1994 book *Location of Culture*. Engagement with these three scholars introduced a set of new terms and propelled a much more nuanced readings of the biblical text. As Bradley L. Crowell points out, the work of these three scholars is important because they "have provided a broad collection of theoretical concepts to expose the ways in which colonial powers have constructed and controlled the identities of subjugated peoples, and how that has shaped the postcolonial experience."[27] It is important to note that up until the development of postcolonial criticism as a lens in biblical studies, the relationship between the Roman Empire and its subjects was viewed one-dimensionally, with little to no agency given to the colonized "other." Postcolonial criticism illustrates how the colonizer and the colonized are imbricated within one another, forming a relationship that is complex, hybrid, and ambivalent. In addition to the work of these scholars, there are other scholars whose work has impacted postcolonial biblical criticism in a significant way. The first among these is Frantz Fanon, a psychologist and a writer from Martinique who wrote during the time of the Algerian independence movements. Fanon's monograph *Black Skin, White Masks*, Chinua Achebe's *Things Fall Apart*, and Albert Memmi's *The Colonizer and the Colonized*, along with others, are important in that these authors, having lived in the transition period between colonialism and postcolonialism, were reflecting the complexity of colonialism. [28] In the work of Spivak, Said, and Bhabha, the importance and influence of French structuralist/poststructuralist theory cannot be underestimated. While Said reads with Michel Foucault, Spivak reads with Jacques Derrida and Bhabha reads with Jacques Lacan, Derrida, Frantz Fanon, and others.[29] Said's monograph *Orientalism*, for example, strategically uses the analytical categories of Michael Foucault and Antonio Gramsci to talk about the ways "the Orient" is constructed in the Western imagination.[30] When it comes to the work of Spivak, the primary influence in her work is Derrida. Spivak is labelled a "feminist Marxist deconstructivist" by Collin McCabe in the foreword to her book *In Other Worlds*.[31] The third scholar in this triad, Bhabha, also uses Derrida in his work, along with Jacques Lacan, and other theorists such as Foucault, Roland Barthes, Julia Kristeva, Louis Althusser, and Mikhail Bakhtin.[32] It is at this point that we notice how the field of biblical studies, and particularly New Testament studies, has drawn on and been influenced by postcolonial studies and the work of these scholars, namely Said, Spivak, and Bhabha.

Postcolonial studies came into the field of biblical studies in the mid-1990s and entered the field of theology in the early aughts.[33] There appears to be a natural way in which the field of biblical studies gravitates toward postcolonial theory. It also must be said that New Testament studies took to postcolonial studies much earlier than the scholars of the Hebrew Bible. Crowley notes this development, writing that "New Testament scholars have used postcolonial concepts since the mid-1990s, but scholars of the Hebrew Bible are only beginning to incorporate the observations and methodological approaches of postcolonialism."[34] There have been a number of critical methodological approaches that have risen to prominence in the field of biblical studies over recent years; namely, feminist criticism, ideological criticism, liberationist interpretations, empire criticism, and now postcolonial criticism.[35]

The term "postcolonial criticism," which encompasses biblical studies and postcolonial studies, focuses on the relationship between the center and margins in colonial contexts and, on a global scale, the imperial and colonial.[36] There is also the misnomer that somehow postcolonial studies is limited to the events of colonization; however, those of us who engage with this methodology often note the possibilities of postcolonial criticism for current contexts. Segovia makes this point by observing that "the 'postcolonial' period of time may never move beyond the formal political phase, since other types of domination and dependence—whether social, economic, cultural, or any combination thereof—continue unabated or even intensify."[37] The continuation of the relationship between the dominant and the submissive after colonization is an important contribution of postcolonial studies. Pushing the relationship between the colonizer and the colonized further, postcolonial biblical criticism highlights the ways that colonial identities are internalized and reproduced by the colonized in various postcolonial contexts.

One of the best examples of this kind of work is Tat-Siong Benny Liew's *Politics of Parousia*. It is interesting to note that this monograph was published in 1999, about the time of Horsley's work. Liew's monograph is important in that it takes issue with those interpreters who read the Gospel of Mark exclusively as a document of liberation. Drawing on the work of Homi K. Bhabha, Liew argues that the author of Mark, in fact, duplicates colonial ideology much more than he resists it.[38] Bhabha explains that "The effect of mimicry on the authority of colonial discourse is profound and disturbing. For in "normalizing" the colonial state or subject, the dream of post-Enlightenment civility alienates its own language of liberty and produces another knowledge of its norms."[39] Thus, drawing on this concept of "colonial mimicry," Liew argues that Mark's duplication of Roman imperial ideology must not be read as resistance but rather a reproduction of Roman imperialism. This reading demonstrates that colonized subjects in the Gospel of Mark internalized the imperial politics of Rome and mimicked its ideology. At the same time, postcolonial biblical criticism—drawing on theories such as poststructuralism, psychoanalysis, Marxism, and feminist theory—enables us to understand the internalized, intimate, and nuanced relationship between colonizer and colonized.

Similarly, other scholars engaging in postcolonial biblical criticism argue for the ways in which systems of power are often duplicated and accommodated within biblical texts.

Winn writes, "Many New Testament texts seem to be accommodated or even supportive of Rome's Empire. Perhaps most noteworthy are passages like Rom 13:1–7, in which Paul encourages submission to Roman power as it has been instituted by God, the payment of Roman taxes, and the giving of honor to political figures."[40] Looking at the work of these scholars, one begins to see the clear development of a path that slowly but surely separates itself from preceding trajectories. In other words, postcolonial biblical criticism draws our attention to the ways empire impacts the lives of the colonized. Fernando Segovia writes, "In this grand model, the reader was no longer a scientific reader—a reader above history and culture, but rather a reader fully imbricated in all the different layers of human life and fully interested at all times—a reader immersed and engaged in history and culture."[41] The emergence of the flesh-and-blood reader as a hermeneutical lens brings about a host of scholarship sharply divergent from the historical-critical method that dominated the field for around 150 years.[42] Thus, what postcolonial biblical criticism does in the field of biblical studies is to place interpretive possibility and responsibility onto the bodies of readers, enabling them to read from their social location and experience. This is another way postcolonial biblical criticism differs from the scholarship of Bible and ancient empire. The latter focuses on the historical and political context of the text and rarely considers the locations and experiences of the readers. However, as always, even this scholarship has exceptions; some in this group choose to bridge the distance between the historical past and the contemporary present in their interpretations.

As I said before, postcolonial criticism reveals the relationship between Bible and empire. One of the works that demonstrates this is Sze-kar Wan's essay, "Collection for the Saints as Anticolonial Act: Implications of Paul's Ethnic Reconstruction." Wan demonstrates hybridity by noting that, even though his reading is not strictly postcolonial, it nevertheless coincides with specific aspects of postcolonial studies. Ethnic-integrity, self-determination, and anti-colonial and anti-imperial elements are suffused throughout his work.[43] Thus, the relationship between Bible and empire is one that never develops in the abstract and takes postcolonial criticism into account either directly or indirectly. When it comes to the work of scholars in this category, what distinguishes them is their ability to be interdisciplinary and draw on fields outside biblical studies. Although scholars in the first two sections either do not engage with postcolonial studies at all or draw on it only lightly (however, as we have seen, there are exceptions), these scholars do draw heavily on postcolonial theory.[44] The first volume to appear along these lines is an edited volume by Susan VanZanten Gallagher, titled *Postcolonial Literature and the Biblical Call for Justice* and published in 1994.[45] The next edited volume, by Laura E. Donaldson, *Postcolonialism and Scriptural Reading*, had more influence than the previous volume.[46] The essays in this volume are eclectic, and while some essays are rooted in extrabiblical postcolonial studies, others are not.[47] Another book in this category is that of Portuguese scholar Fernando Belo, *A Materialist Reading of the Gospel*. Belo draws on the work of Roland Barthes and argues that Mark's Gospel is a politically subversive text that pits the poor and the oppressed against the Roman Empire and the Jewish elites of the ancient world.[48] Other biblical scholarship that is fluent in postcolonial theory and draws upon the analytical work of scholars such as Bhabha is Erin Runions's *Changing Subjects: Gender, Nation, and Future in Micah* and Roland Boer's *Last Stop before Antarctica: The Bible and Postcolonialism in Australia*.[49] Postcolonial biblical criticism also seamlessly blends with ideological criticism, the other recent development in biblical studies.[50]

This section would not be complete without mention of Stephen Moore and Fernando Segovia's edited volume, *Postcolonial Biblical Criticism: Interdisciplinary Intersection*.[51] This volume, featuring essays by Tat-Siong Benny Liew, Laura E. Donaldson, Roland Boer, David Jobling, along with Segovia and Moore, covers interdisciplinary connections with poststructuralist theory, feminist theory, Marxist theory, and critical race/ethnicity studies. This volume is also important because it takes into account the way postcolonial theory came into biblical studies.[52] The second essay in this volume, "Mapping the Postcolonial Optic in Biblical Criticism: Meaning and Scope," is its lengthiest essay, in which Segovia unpacks the definitions of postcolonial analysis and draws on the work of Leela Gandhi, Ania Loomba, and John McLeod. Their work addresses questions of scope, relevant periods, as well as field of inquiry. Moore's essay entitled, "Questions of Biblical Ambivalence and Authority under a Tree outside Delhi; or, the Postcolonial and the Postmodern" demonstrates how poststructuralist work interacts with Postcolonialism. Moore maps Homi Bhabha's work in relation to that of Jacques Derrida, Frantz Fanon, and Jacques Lacan, among others. In doing so, Moore also remaps how biblical studies have used Bhabha by highlighting the ways in which ambivalence, colonial mimicry, and hybridity are used in postcolonial biblical interpretations.[53] Other essays in this volume demonstrate the intersectionality between postcolonialism and other fields. Another important contribution by Moore, when it comes to Bible and postcolonial criticism, is his *Empire and Apocalypse: Postcolonialism and the New Testament*, published in 2006. In this monograph, Moore draws on the works of postcolonial theorists such as Bhabha and Spivak as he meticulously exegetes the Gospels and the book of Revelation and attempts to bring to light critical sensibilities that are brought to bear on literature produced in the shadow of the Roman Empire.[54] The nuanced relationship between the colonizer and the colonized is important because it gives readers a glimpse into the ways colonized subjects internalize their oppression in colonial contexts. In other words, a postcolonial reading of Mark's Gospel discloses the complexities of colonization, making these texts relatable to those of us who come from contexts that had been colonized in the recent past. Winn writes, "Even when colonization is resisted by the colonized, the colonized are inevitably affected by the realities of colonization. As a result, the colonized are in many ways hybrids of their own cultural realities and those imposed by their colonizers."[55]

At the same time, the complicated emotions that a colonized person feels toward the colonizer, including desire and disgust, resistance and cooption, are demonstrative of how the psychology of the colonized continues to duplicate its cycle of oppression and violence without really interrogating why this cycle cannot be broken. Thus, one could argue that the relationship between the Bible and postcolonial empire is one that focuses on how colonization affects the subjectivity of the colonized person. In doing so, the cluster of scholars producing scholarship under this heading differentiate their readings from the previous two sections by focusing on the ways oppression is internalized by subjects living under the shadow of empires. However, it must be noted that there remain exceptions within each of these groups of scholars as postcolonial criticism continues to illuminate the study of Bible and empire.

Conclusion

When it comes to postcolonial studies, two terms used quite often are "ambivalence" and "hybridity." Hybridity, often used by Homi Bhabha, refers to the ways colonized subjects accept certain aspects of colonial culture and yet are constantly transforming these aspects, thereby demonstrating their agency and ability to resist and subvert the powers of colonization.[56] One of the best ways to describe the development of the relationship between the Bible and empire in the ancient, precolonial, and postcolonial worlds is the notion of hybridity. In other words, the scholarship produced under each group is hybrid in the sense that the relationship between Bible and empire is constantly evolving and transforming, and through this process the practice of resistance and agency toward imperial ideology becomes clearer.

Thus, while the study of the Bible and empires in the ancient world initially focused on the historical context and rarely brought modern readers and their social locations into their interpretations, scholarship that focuses on precolonial times draws attention to the ways biblical texts were already part of the Asian and African contexts and how these texts, when translated into vernacular language, empowered ordinary readers. It is important to note that under this scholarship, the use of binaries played an important role in describing the relationship between the Bible and colonial empires. Sugirtharajah writes, "Colonialists often discursively constructed contrastive paradigms such as Christian/savage, civilized/barbaric and orderly/disorderly in order to define themselves, and also to explain the dominance and acceleration of colonial rule."[57] Thus, as we can see, it is through this group of scholarly works that the notion of binaries, and the ways in which they hold the power to differentiate the colonized from the colonizer, is introduced. The introduction of binaries is common to works focused on the Bible and precolonial and postcolonial empires. In fact, it is the ability to deconstruct these binaries that connects these two bodies of scholarship.

Another commonality between them is to give the reader's social location precedence. However, when it comes to the relationship between the Bible and postcolonial empires, postcolonial theory plays an important role in highlighting how oppression and subjugation are internalized by the colonized. At the same time, one can see the categories in which the scholarship mapping the Bible and empires is not as neat and clear cut. In other words, as Bhabha does with *hybridity*, the scholars within each of these categories display their own hybridity in their works. The complex relationships between binaries is illustrated in the ways scholars and their works are themselves hybrid, in that they can fit into more than one category at a time. Although the work of scholars such as R. S. Sugirtharajah and Musa Dube may be placed under the category of Bible and precolonial empire, it is also relevant to that of Bible and the postcolonial empire. Similarly, Richard Horsley's edited collection *Paul and Empire* and Warren Carter's *Matthew and Empire*, along with others, while typically placed under the category of ancient empires, display their hybridity by putting ancient texts into conversation with contemporary contexts. Thus, one can argue that the development of empire studies and postcolonial studies in the field of biblical studies is hybrid in that the categories overlap, draw from, and extend the work of each other. It also must be noted that the spirit of postcolonialism runs through these three categories either overtly or covertly, thus connecting them at some points and deviating at others.

Notes

1. Richard A. Horsley, "Introduction: The Bible and Empires," in *In the Shadow of Empire: Reclaiming the Bible as a History of Faithful Resistance*, ed. Richard A. Horsley (Louisville: Westminster John Knox Press, 2008), 1.
2. A similar delineation can be found in R. S. Sugirtharajah's book, *The Bible and the Third World: Precolonial. Colonial, and Postcolonial Encounters* (Cambridge: Cambridge University Press, 2001). In this book, Sugirtharajah traces the relationship between the Bible and Empire into three different phases of colonialism which he then terms as Precolonial Reception, Colonial Embrace, and Postcolonial Reclamations.
3. Bill Ashcroft, Gareth Griffiths, and Helen Tiffin, *Post-Colonial Studies: The Key Concepts* (London and New York: Routledge, 2nd ed, 2001), 186.
4. Stephen D. Moore, *Empire and Apocalypse: Postcolonialism and the New Testament* (Sheffield: Sheffield Phoenix Press, 2006), 5.
5. Adam Winn, "Striking Back at the Empire: Empire Theory and Responses to Empire in the New Testament," in *An Introduction to Empire in the New Testament*," ed. Adam Winn (Atlanta: Society of Biblical Literature Press, 2016), 1.
6. Winn, "Striking Back at the Empire, 1.
7. Norman K. Gottwald, "Early Israel as an Anti-Imperial Community," in *In the Shadow of Empire: Reclaiming the Bible as a History of Faithful Resistance*, ed. Richard A. Horsley (Louisville: Westminster John Knox Press, 2008), 9.
8. Both Gotwald and Winn make similar points in their essays. Gotwald, in "Early Israel as an Anti-Imperial Community," writes, "Bible readers often fail to consider the particular circumstances of political economies in ancient Israel, easily falling subject to mistaken reading of texts" (12). In the similar vein, Winn points out, "The prevailing assumption was that the writings of the New Testament were apolitical, that they were primarily concerned with spiritual realities rather than the worldly practices of ancient empires" ("Striking Back at the Empire," 1).
9. Richard A. Horsley, *Hearing the Whole Story: The Politics of Plot in Mark's Gospel* (Louisville: Westminster John Knox Press, 2001), 23.
10. Moore, *In the Shadow of the Empire*, 12.
11. Richard A. Horsley, *Jesus and Empire: The Kingdom of God and the New World Disorder* (Minneapolis: Augsbury Press, 2003). In this book, Horsley's introductory chapter,

"American Identity and a Depoliticized Jesus," illustrates the ways in which the US empire has domesticated the image of Jesus as political prophet. In the same book, his epilogue titled, "Christian Empire, American Empire," brings these connections of imperialism to light.

12. Stephen D. Moore, *Empire and Apocalypse: Postcolonialism and the New Testament* (Sheffield: Sheffield Phoenix Press, 2006), 18.
13. Warren Carter, *Matthew and Empire: Initial Explanations* (Harrisburg: Trinity Press International, 2001); John Riches and David Sims, eds., *The Gospel of Matthew in Its Roman Imperial Context* (Journal for the Study of the New Testament Supplement Series, 276; New York: T&T Clark International, 2005); Richard A. Horsley, *Paul and the Roman Imperial Order* (Harrisburg: Trinity Press International, 2004); Wes Howard-Brook and Anthony Gwyther, *Unveiling Empire: Reading Revelation Then and Now* (Maryknoll: Orbis Books, 1992).
14. Winn, "Striking Back at the Empire," 2.
15. R. S. Sugirtharajah, *The Bible and the Third World: Precolonial, Colonial, and Postcolonial Encounters* (Cambridge: Cambridge University Press, 2001), 61.
16. Michael Prior, CM. "The Bible and the Redeeming Idea of Colonialism," in *Studies in World Christianity* 5, no. 2 (1999): 129.
17. Sugirtharajah, *The Bible and the Third World*, 14.
18. Another important work in this trajectory is Samuel High Moffett's, *A History of Christianity in Asia*, vol. 1: *Beginnings to 1500*, revised and corrected edition (Maryknoll: Orbis Books, 1998). Moffett points out that Christianity was present in Asian contexts before it even moved into Europe. He writes, "first centers were Asian. Asia produced the first known church building, the first New Testament translation, perhaps the first Christian king, the first Christian poets, and even arguably the first Christian state," xiii.
19. R. S. Sugirtharajah, "A Brief Memorandum on Postcolonial and Biblical Studies," *Journal for the Study of the New Testament* 73 (1999), 3.
20. Sugirtharajah, "A Brief Memorandum on Postcolonial and Biblical Studies," 47.
21. Sugirtharajah, "A Brief Memorandum on Postcolonial and Biblical Studies," 59.
22. Musa W. Dube, *Postcolonial Feminist Interpretation of the Bible* (St. Louis: Chalice Press, 2000). Also cf. Stephen D. Moore, *Empire and Apocalypse: Postcolonialism and the New Testament* (Sheffield: Sheffield Phoenix Press, 2006), 16.
23. Sugirtharajah, *The Bible and the Third World*, 59. Similar to Dube, Sugirtharajah notes the power of placing the biblical texts in the hands of everyday readers: "The Bible was promoted as the only text among all the sacred writings of the world which could be made readable for men of every color and in every country."
24. R. S. Sugirtharajah, "Scripture, Scholarship, Empire: Putting the Discipline in its Place," *The Expository Times*, 117, no. 1 (Oct. 2005): 1.
25. In addition this work, Said also published the following: *Literature, Politics, and Theory* (London: Metheun, 1986) and "Orientalism and Beyond," in Bart Moore-Gilbert, Gareth Stanton, and Wiley Maley, eds., *Postcolonial Criticism* (London: Longman, 1997), 34–73.
26. In addition, Spivak has published *A Critique of Postcolonial Reason: Toward a History of Vanishing Present* (Cambridge: Harvard University Press, 1998), as well as similar works.
27. Bradley L. Crowley, "Postcolonial Studies and the Hebrew Bible," *Currents in Biblical Research* 7, no.2 (2009): 219.
28. Frantz Fanon, *Black Skins, White Masks*, trans. Charles Lam Markmann (New York: Grove Press, 1991 [French original 1952]); Chinua Achebe, *Things Fall Apart* (London: Penguin,

2001 [1958]); Albert Memmi, *The Colonizer and the Colonized*, trans. Howard Greenfield (London: Earthscan, 2003 [French original 1966]). Also cf. Stephen D. Moore, *Empire and Apocalypse: Postcolonialism and the New Testament* for a detailed analysis of these works.
29. Moore, *Empire and Apocalypse*, 6.
30. Edward W. Said, *Orientalism* (New York: Vintage Books, 1978). Also cf. Moore, *Empire and Apocalypse*, 80.
31. Gayatri Chakravorty Spivak, *In Other Worlds: Essays in Cultural Politics* (London and New York: Metheun, 1987), ix. Also cf. Moore, *Empire and Apocalypse*, 80.
32. Some works that lay out this relationship in a more detail are Robert J. C. Young, *White Mythologies: Writing History and the West* (London and New York: Routledge, 1990); Peter Childs and Patrick Williams, *An Introduction to Post-Colonial Theory* (London and New York: Prentice Hall/Harvester Wheatsheaf, 1997); R. S. Sugirtharajah, *Asian Biblical Hermeneutics and Postcolonialism: Contesting the Interpretations* (Maryknoll: Orbis Books; Sheffield: Sheffield Academic Press, 1998); Steven J. Friesen, *Imperial Cults and the Apocalypse of John: Reading Revelation in the Ruins* (Oxford: Oxford University Press, 2001).
33. Kwok Pui Lan, "Postcolonial Preaching in Intercultural Contexts," in Homiletic (Online) 40, no. 1 (2015): 9.
34. Crowley, "Postcolonial Studies and the Hebrew Bible," 218.
35. Crowley, "Postcolonial Studies and the Hebrew Bible, 218. He writes, "This new collection of critical approaches, including feminism, liberation theology, ideological criticism, identity-specific readings, and Marxist criticism, has in the past decade been joined by postcolonial criticism."
36. Fernando F. Segovia, "Postcolonial and Diasporic Criticism in Biblical Studies: Focus, Parameters, Relevance," *Studies in World Christianity* 5, no. 2 (1999): 180.
37. Segovia, "Postcolonial and Diasporic Criticism, 181.
38. Tat-Siong Benny Liew, *Politics of Parousia: Reading Mark Inter(con)textually* (Leiden: E. J. Brill, 1999), 104.
39. Homi Bhabha, "Of Mimicry and Man: The Ambivalence of Colonial Discourse." *October*, 28 (1984): 126.
40. Winn, "Striking Back at the Empire," 11.
41. Segovia, "Postcolonial and Diasporic Criticism," 179.
42. Segovia, "Postcolonial and Diasporic Criticism, 178. He writes, "For a long period of time—in fact, for approximately a hundred and fifty years, from the early 1800s through the mid-1970s—one such paradigm, historical criticism, reigned supreme, as the discipline remained firmly grounded throughout in historical studies."
43. Sze-kar Wan, "Collection for the Saints as Anticolonial Act: Implications of Paul's Ethnic Reconstruction," in *Paul and Politics*, ed. Richard A. Horsley (Harrisburg: Trinity Press International, 2000), 192.
44. Also cf. Moore, *Empire and Apocalypse*, 19. One example of scholarship that overlaps with work focused on the Bible and colonial and postcolonial empire would be Musa W. Dube and Jeffrey L. Staley, eds., *John and Postcolonialism: Travel, Space, and Power*, The Bible and Postcolonialism, Vol. 7 New York: Continuum, 2002).
45. Susan VanZanten Gallagher, *Postcolonial Literature and the Biblical Call for Justice* (Jackson: University Press of Mississippi, 1994).
46. Laura E. Donaldson, ed., *Postcolonialism and Scriptural Reading* (Atlanta: Scholars Press, 1996).

47. Donaldson, ed., *Postcolonialism and Scriptural Reading*, Also cf. Moore, *Empire and Apocalypse*, 20. He writes, "It would be misleading however, to relay the impression that all the essays in this eclectic collection—which range over topics as diverse as colonial Yehud under the Persian Empire; *El Evangelio de Lucas Gavilan*, a modern Mexican paraphrase of the Gospel of Luke; African-American spirituals."
48. Fernando Belo, *Lecture Matérialiste de l'Évangile de Marc: Récit, Pratique, Idéologie* (Paris: Cerf, 1974): Matthew J. O'Connell; Maryknoll, NY: Oribis Books, 1981). The original work was published in French. Belo draws on the work of Roland Barthes, *S/Z*, trans. Richard Miller (New York: Hill & Wang, 1974). Interestingly, Homi Bhabha also draws on the work of Roland Barthes in his volume *The Location of Culture*.
49. Erin Runions, *Changing Subjects: Gender, Nation and Future in Micah* (Sheffield: Sheffield Academic Press, 2001), and Roland Barthes, *Last Stop before Antarctica: The Bible and Postcolonialism in Australia* (Sheffield: Sheffield Academic Press, 2001).
50. The important works under this category are David Jobling and Tina Pippin, eds., *Ideological Criticism of Biblical Texts* (Atlanta: Scholars Press, 1992).
51. Stephen D. Moore and Fernando F. Segovia, eds., *Postcolonial Biblical Criticism: Interdisciplinary Intersections* (London: T&T Clark International, 2005).
52. Erin Runions, "Decentering Authority: The Postcolonial Challenge to Certainty," *Journal for the Study of the New Testament* 30 no. 4, (2008): 473–479. She writes, "*Postcolonial Biblical Criticism* (Moore and Segovia 2005) is exceptional in a number of ways: it situates and differentiates postcolonialism within and from cultural studies; it gives overviews of key issues in postcolonial theory; and it gives an account of the way in which postcolonial theory has come into biblical studies."
53. Stephen Moore, "Questions of Biblical Ambivalence and Authority under a Tree outside Delhi; or, the Postcolonial and the Postmodern," in *Postcolonial Biblical Criticism: Interdisciplinary Intersections*, ed. Fernando Segovia and Stephen D. Moore (London: T&T Clark International, 2005), 79–96.
54. Moore, *Empire and Apocalypse*, x. He writes, " I have no desire to downplay the extent to which all three exegetical investigations are informed and enabled by a sensibility that owes much to Bhabha specifically—a predisposition to construe life under colonialism as characterized less by unequivocal opposition to the colonizer than by unequal measure of loathing and admiration, resentment and envy, rejection and imitation, resistance and cooption, separation and surrender."
55. Winn, "Striking Back at the Empire," 12.
56. Winn, "Striking Back at Empire," 12. He writes, "Bhabha uses the term 'hybridity' to describe this phenomenon and the responses to colonization that it creates (154–156). Hybrid responses to colonization often involve the colonized embracing some aspect of the colonial culture that has been imposed on them but then enacting or embodying that aspect of colonial culture in some new or different way" (144–165).
57. Sugirtharajah, *The Bible and the Third World*, 62.

Bibliography

Achebe, Chinua. *Things Fall Apart*. London: Penguin, 2001 [1958].
Ashcroft, Bill, Gareth Griffiths, and Helen Tiffin. *Post-Colonial Studies: The Key Concepts*. 2nd ed. London and New York: Routledge, 2001.

Barthes, Roland. *Last Stop before Antarctica: The Bible and Postcolonialism in Australia*, Sheffield: Sheffield Academic Press, 2001.

Belo, Fernando. *A Materialist Reading of the Gospel of Mark*, edited and translated by Matthew J. O'Connell. Maryknoll, NY: Oribis Books, 1981. Originally published as *Lecture Matérialiste de l' Évangile de Marc: Récit, Pratique, Idéologie*. Paris: Cerf, 1974.

Bhabha, Homi. "Of Mimicry and Man: The Ambivalence of Colonial Discourse." Discipleship: A Special Issue on Psychoanalysis, *October*, 28 (Spring, 1984): 125–133.

Carter, Warren. *Matthew and Empire: Initial Explanations*. Harrisburg: Trinity Press International, 2001.

Childs, Peter, and Patrick Williams. *An Introduction to Post-Colonial Theory*. London and New York: Prentice Hall/Harvester Wheatsheaf, 1997.

Crowley, Bradley L. "Postcolonial Studies and the Hebrew Bible." *Currents in Biblical Research* 7, no. 2 (2009): 217–244.

Donaldson, Laura E., ed. *Postcolonialism and Scriptural Reading*. Atlanta: Scholars Press, 1996.

Dube, Musa W. *Postcolonial Feminist Interpretation of the Bible*. St. Louis: Chalice Press, 2000.

Dube, Musa W., and Jeffrey L. Staley, eds. *John and Postcolonialism: Travel, Space, and Power*. The Bible and Postcolonialism, Vol. 7. New York: Continuum, 2002.

Fanon, Frantz. *Black Skins, White Masks*. Translated by Charles Lam Markmann. New York: Grove Press, 1991 [1952].

Friesen, Steven J. *Imperial Cults and the Apocalypse of John: Reading Revelation in the Ruins*. Oxford: Oxford University Press, 2001.

Gallagher, Susan VanZanten. *Postcolonial Literature and the Biblical Call for Justice*. Jackson: University Press of Mississippi, 1994.

Gotwald, Norman K. "Early Israel as an Anti-Imperial Community." In *In the Shadow of Empire: Reclaiming the Bible as a History of Faithful Resistance*, edited by Richard A. Horsley, 9–24. Louisville: Westminster John Knox Press, 2008.

Horsley, Richard A. *Hearing the Whole Story: The Politics of Plot in Mark's Gospel*. Louisville: Westminster John Knox Press, 2001.

Horsley, Richard A. *Jesus and Empire: The Kingdom of God and the New World Disorder*. Minneapolis: Augsbury Press, 2003.

Horsley, Richard A. *Paul and the Roman Imperial Order*. Harrisburg: Trinity Press International, 2004.

Horsley, Richard A. "Introduction: The Bible and Empires." In *In the Shadow of Empire: Reclaiming the Bible as a History of Faithful Resistance*, edited by Richard A. Horsley. Louisville: Westminster John Knox Press, 2008.

Howard-Brook, Wes and Anthony Gwyther. *Unveiling Empire: Reading Revelation Then and Now*. Maryknoll: Orbis Books, 1992.

Jobling, David, and Tina Pippin, eds. *Ideological Criticism of Biblical Texts*. Atlanta: Scholars Press, 1992.

Lan, Kwok Pui. "Postcolonial Preaching in Intercultural Contexts." *Homiletic* (Online) 40, no. 1 (2015).

Liew, Tat-Siong Benny. *Politics of Parousia: Reading Mark Inter(con)textually*. Leiden: Brill, 1999.

Memmi, Albert. *The Colonizer and the Colonized*. Translated by Howard Greenfield. London: Earthscan, 2003 [1966].

Moore, Stephen D. *Empire and Apocalypse: Postcolonialism and the New Testament*. Sheffield: Sheffield Phoenix Press, 2006.

Moore, Stephen D. "Questions of Biblical Ambivalence and Authority under a Tree outside Delhi; or, the Postcolonial and the Postmodern." In *Postcolonial Biblical Criticism: Interdisciplinary Intersections*, edited by Fernando Segovia and Stephen D. Moore, 79–96. London: T&T Clark International, 2005.

Prior, Michael CM. "The Bible and the Redeeming Idea of Colonialism." *Studies in World Christianity* 5, no. 2 (October 1999): 129–155.

Riches, John, and David Sims, eds. *The Gospel of Matthew in Its Roman Imperial Context*. Journal for the Study of the New Testament Supplement Series 276. New York: T&T Clark International, 2005.

Runions, Erin. *Changing Subjects: Gender, Nation and Future in Micah*. Sheffield: Sheffield Academic Press, 2001.

Runions, Erin. "Decentering Authority: The Postcolonial Challenge to Certainty." *Journal for the Study of the New Testament*, 30, no. 4 (2008): 473–479.

Said, Edward. *Orientalism*. New York: Vintage Books, 1978.

Segovia, Fernando F. "Postcolonial and Diasporic Criticism in Biblical Studies: Focus, Parameters, Relevance." *Studies in World Christianity*, 5, no. 2 (1999): 177–195.

Spivak, Gayatri Chakravorty. *In Other Worlds: Essays in Cultural Politics*. London and New York: Metheun, 1987.

Spivak, Gayatri Chakravorty. *A Critique of Postcolonial Reason: Toward a History of Vanishing Present*. Cambridge: Harvard University Press, 1998.

Stephen D. Moore, and Fernando F. Segovia, eds. *Postcolonial Biblical Criticism: Interdisciplinary Intersections*. London: T&T Clark International, 2005.

Sugirtharajah, R. S. *Asian Biblical Hermeneutics and Postcolonialism: Contesting the Interpretations*. Maryknoll, NY: Orbis Books; Sheffield: Sheffield Academic Press, 1998.

Sugirtharajah, R. S. "A Brief Memorandum on Postcolonial and Biblical Studies." *Journal for the Study of the New Testament*, 73 (1999): 3–5.

Sugirtharajah R. S. *The Bible and the Third World: Precolonial, Colonial, and Postcolonial Encounters*. Cambridge: Cambridge University Press, 2001.

Sugirtharajah, R. S. "Scripture, Scholarship, Empire: Putting the Discipline in its Place." *The Expository Times*, 117, no. 1 (Oct. 2005): 2–11.

Wan, Sze-kar. "Collection for the Saints as Anticolonial Act: Implications of Paul's Ethnic Reconstruction." In *Paul and Politics*, edited by Richard A. Horsley, 191–215. Harrisburg: Trinity Press International, 2000.

Winn, Adam. "Striking Back at the Empire: Empire Theory and Responses to Empire in the New Testament," In *An Introduction to Empire in the New Testament*," edited by Adam Winn. Atlanta: Society of Biblical Literature Press, 2016.

Young, Robert J. C. *White Mythologies: Writing History and the West*. London and New York: Routledge, 1990.

INDEX

Figures are indicated by an italic *f* following the page number

A

Abraham, 8, 261–262, 285, 305–306, 541, 581
Achaemenid Empire, 11, 89–91, 97–98, 102, 108–109
Achebe, Chinua, 565, 567–573, 704–705, 709, 711–712
Acosta, José de, 272
Acts of Philip, 249
Acts of the Apostles, 262
Acts of Thomas, 12, 239–240, 242–253
Adamo, David, 716
Africa
    Bible in, 568–570, 652–660
    Bible translation in, 477–479, 495–506, 634–635
    Christian missionaries in, 496–498, 503–504, 606–609, 649, 690
    colonialism in, 495, 497–498, 501–502, 505, 565, 568–572, 580, 660–664, 711–712, 715
    decolonization in, 606–608, 610–611, 615–616, 650–653, 660–662, 664–665
    enslavement and, 611–612
    land and farms of, 580, 658–660
    same-sex relationships in, 543, 546, 552n36
African American biblical scholarship, 718
African Americans, 13–14, 397, 406–413
African biblical hermeneutics, 647, 654–655, 663
African biblical scholarship, 14–15, 647–648
African Christians and African Christianity, 477–479, 497–504, 584–585, 592, 607–610, 632–635, 653–658
African epistemology, 661–664
African Independent/Instituted/Initiated Churches (AICs), 656–658
African indigenous religions, 498–506
African languages, 495, 497, 500–506, 634–635, 653
African Traditional Religions (ATRs), 656–657
agrarians and neo-agrarians, 577–586, 589–592
Ahiqar, 102–105
Ahmad, Aijaz, 725–726
Ahmadinejad, Mahmoud, 89–90
AICs. *See* African Independent/Instituted/Initiated Churches
Akbar (emperor), 480–481
Akio, Dohi, 434
Albright, W. F., 34
Alexander I, 8, 11, 118–119, 122, 142
Althaus-Reid, Marcella María, 630, 632
Amadiume, Ifi, 501–502, 543
Amarna Letter 51, 38
ambivalence and ambiveilence, 174, 226–228, 535, 558, 710, 744
Amos, Book of, 592
An Ch'ang-ho, 449, 456–458
Anderson, Benedict, 483
Anderson, Emily, 14
Anderson, William J., 409, 411
Anglo-American settlers, in America, 13
anticolonialism, 4, 178, 389, 686
anti-imperial resistance, 390, 599, 611, 721–722, 738
anti-imperial texts, 239, 742
    Bible, 10, 140–141, 154–155, 169, 611, 737
Antiochus III (king), 129
Antiochus IV Epiphanes (king), 129–134
anti-Semitism, 167, 381, 721
Antonio de Montalvo, Francisco, 280
Anum, Eric, 647

Apadana, the, 107–108
Appasamy Pillai, A.S., 722
apocalypse and apocalypticism, 194–196, 199, 205, 229, 411
Apocrypha, the, 11–12, 239–253, 256n72. *See also* Acts of Thomas
Arnot, William, 712, 714
Asian Biblical Hermeneutics and Postcolonialism (Sugirtharajah), 717
Aššur, 49–54, 57–58, 63
Aššurbanipal (king), 50, 52–53, 59, 63
Aššurnaṣirpal II (king), 50–51
Assyrian Empire, 11, 32–33, 49–66, 69n60
Assyrian Royal Inscriptions, 51–53, 57–58
Aster, Shawn Zelig, 58
ATRs. *See* African Traditional Religions
Atwell, James, 37
Aune, David E., 217
Awolalu, J. O., 497–498
Ayme, Margaret, 719

B

Babylonian Empire, 11, 64, 70–85, 89, 100–102, 128, 133
Badimo, 502–503, 505–506
Bagnall, Roger, 121
Bailey, Randall C., 29, 720
Bakhtin, Mikhail, 28
Baldwin, James, 410–411
Bälz, Erwin, 389
Bantu language, 505
baptism, 304–308, 311, 481
Barclay, John, 119–120
Barkataki-Ruscheweyh, Meenaxi, 484
Barr, James, 588
Barrett, C. K., 342–343
Beal, Timothy K., 519
Beatitudes, 154
Beaulieu, Paul-Alain, 101
Becking, Bob, 102–105
Bediako, Kwame, 479
Behistun, 103–105
Belo, Fernando, 686–688, 742
Bengali language, 482, 486
Benjamin, Walter, 16
Ben Sira, 124–125
Bercovitch, Sacvan, 402

Berry, Wendell, 578, 582–583, 589
Betanzos, Domingo, 270–271
BFBS. *See* British and Foreign Bible Society
Bhabha, Homi, 27, 691, 740, 743
   on ambivalence, 227
   on hybridity, 121, 220, 535, 709–710, 744
   on mimicry, 130, 226, 362, 535, 615, 741
   on third space, 739
Bhatia, Vijay K., 244
Bible, 2–3. *See also* Gospels, NT; Hebrew Bible; New Testament; Old Testament
   in Africa, 568–570, 652–665
   African Americans on, 409–410
   ancient empires and, 736–737, 742
   as anti-imperial text, 10, 155, 611
   Babylonian Empire in, 70–83
   black theology on, 653–657
   in British Empire, 336–344, 361–364, 598–599, 614, 712
   canon, 7, 616, 655
   in colonialism, 296–297, 299, 374–376, 542, 546, 608, 623, 635–637, 653, 738–739
   Dutch Reformed colonial use of, 299, 301–303
   eco-agrarian reading of, 585–589
   empire and, 6–10, 12, 598–600, 602–606, 611, 614–616, 711–712, 717–720, 726–727, 735–744
   in German Empire and imperialism, 372–373, 377–380, 382–383, 386, 388–389
   imperialism and, 6–7, 10, 546, 652–653, 715, 737–739
   for Japanese empire, 431, 436–442
   KJV, 7–8, 504, 517, 519, 522, 611–612, 614–615
   in Korea, 452
   in Korean nationalism, 448, 455–460
   land and, 581–586, 589, 592, 653–660
   LDS on, 402–403
   in liberation theology, 609–610
   Marxism and, 684–685
   Negro spirituals on, 409–413
   NRSV, 202, 249, 504, 522
   Othering and, 533–534
   postcolonial empire and, 739–744
   in postcolonial world, 558
   race, racism and, 310, 560–561, 563–564, 602, 610–611
   Rastafari and Ethiopianism on, 611–616

RSV, 504, 522
slavery and, 301–303, 407–408, 711
South African black theology on, 653–654, 689–690
in US, 398–399, 402–403, 735
women missionaries in Singapore on, 361–362
"world religions" and, 566
Bible and Postcolonialism, The (Sugirtharajah), 716–717, 725
Bible translation, 14–15, 510, 523n5, 738–739
in Africa, 477–479, 495–506, 634–635
approaches to study of, 475–480
in Asian Christian identity, 521
in China, 514–521
by Christian missionaries, 477–480, 495–498, 511–516, 520
in colonization and colonialism, 477–479, 488, 495, 501–502, 511–514
cross-textual, 519–523
decolonization and, 495, 504
homosexuality in, 543
in India, 471–472, 475, 479–489, 523
indigenous African religions and, 498–506
in Korea, 516
missionary and colonial linguistics on, 475–477
naming God in, 499–501, 504–505, 515–517, 522
NT, 480–482, 488
queer criticism of, 542–543
biblical criticism, 471, 479, 488–489, 534–548, 632, 677–682, 712–714
biblical exegesis, 431, 433, 561–563, 623–639, 716
biblical hermeneutics, 471, 627, 647, 654–665, 684–685, 688–690, 713, 717
biblical scholarship and studies, 17, 558–563, 636–639, 660, 711–715
African, 14–15, 647–648
British Empire and, 13, 329, 336–344
collusion with colonialism, 5–6, 17–18, 638, 711, 713–714, 717
Biggar, Nigel, 332–333
Blackness, 310, 614, 664
black theology, 15, 653–661, 669n83, 688–690
Blair, Tony, 331
Bledsoe, Seth, 104

Blenkinsopp, Joseph, 96–97
Bloch, Ernst, 681, 720
Blount, Brian K., 221
Blumhardt, Christoph Friedrich, 386–389
Boer, Roland, 677, 680–682, 684, 686
Boer War, 340
Boesak, Allan, 654
Bolívar, Simón, 284–285
Book of Acts, 152, 343, 377–379, 410
Book of Judges, 590–591
Book of Mormon, 402–403, 406
Book of the Twelve, 62, 65
Borg, Marcus, 17
Bosch, David, 377
Boughton, George Henry, 398–399, 398*f*
Bousset, Wilhelm, 384–386
Bovon, Francois, 245
Boyce, Mary, 244
Bremmer, Jan, 241, 243, 247–248
Brett, Mark, 586–587
Briant, Pierre, 90, 108
British and Foreign Bible Society (BFBS), 480–482, 484–485
British Empire, 5, 9–10, 14, 246
Bible and biblical scholarship in, 13, 329, 336–344, 361–364, 598–599, 614, 712
Biggar and, 332–333
Christianity of, 354–359, 604
colonization and colonialism by, 3–4, 18, 252, 336–337, 339–342, 355, 481, 568–572, 650, 704–705, 712
Ethiopia and, 613
in Jamaica, 611–612
Japan and, 449
occupation of India, 18, 252, 331, 334, 339–340, 481, 603–604, 712, 717
occupation of Singapore, 13, 353, 355–356, 358–359, 363–364
slavery and, 339, 355, 602
in South Africa, 610, 649
in Victorian era, 329–330, 336–342
women in, 338–340, 342–343, 354–355, 360–364
British imperialism, 136n20, 299, 330, 333–334, 337, 705
Broadbent, Ralph, 13
Brooten, Bernadette J., 219

Brown, Arthur, 451–452
Brown, Gordon, 331
Brown, Raymond, 164
Browne, R. W., 604–605
Brueggemann, Walter, 83–84, 92, 582, 694n29
Buddhism, 174, 177, 428–429, 517
Burge, Gary M., 171
Burns, Anna, 19
Burns, W. C., 358
Burrus, Virginia, 154
Burton, Antoinette, 354–355
Bush, George W., 62, 226
Buss, Ernst, 379
Byrd, Jodi, 601, 605

C

Caesar Augustus (emperor), 142, 144–145, 149, 151–152, 218, 223–224
Caird, George Bradford, 342
Calancha, Augustín de, 277
Callahan, Allen Dwight, 221
Campe, Joachim Heinrich, 376
Canaan, 409, 579, 589–591
Canaanites, 262, 272, 277, 310, 590–591, 605, 632
Cañizares-Esguerra, Jorge, 12
Canons of Dordt, 305–306, 311
capitalism, 441–442, 660, 679–683, 686–689, 692, 708
  race and, 15, 599–602, 609, 649–650
  slavery and, 407, 568, 601–602
Capitein, Jacobus Eliza, 311–312
Carey, Hilary, 355
Carrillo, Martín, 278
Carter, Warren, 11, 148, 151, 164–166, 168, 177, 179, 180n15
Cassidy, Richard J., 164
catachresis, 215–216, 222
Catholicism and Catholics, 305, 310–311, 449
  Jesuit translation projects, 473–474, 481, 484–486
  missions and missionaries, 299, 450
  Roman Catholic Church, 248, 261–262, 270, 280, 281f, 282f, 297, 303
  saints of, 280, 281f, 282f
Catholic nations, 598–599
Césaire, Aimé, 335–336, 705, 708
Charles V (king), 267–269

China, 4, 13, 387, 441, 514–521, 626
  Singapore and, 356, 358–361, 363–364
Chinese Christianity, 517–520
Chitnio, 360–364
Christian in Singapore, The, 353–359
Christianity, 7, 510
  Acts of Thomas and, 242, 248–249
  African, 477–479, 497–504, 584–585, 592, 607–610, 632–635, 653–658
  of African Americans, 407
  Asian Christian identity, 521
  of British Empire, 354–359, 604
  capitalism and, 681
  Chinese, 517–520
  colonial fantasies and, 374–375
  in colonialism, 173, 335–336, 355, 387–388, 438–441, 498, 602–603, 711
  of colonized and colonizer, 299
  Constantinian, 174–175
  conversion of Indians to, 280, 281f
  democracy and, 458–461
  Dutch Calvinism, 297, 299, 304, 307–308, 311–313
  Dutch Reformed, 296, 299–312, 314
  empire and, 333, 603–605, 611, 615–616
  Hinduism and, 482–483, 517, 715, 722
  imperialism and, 3–4, 241, 603, 615, 683
  Islam and, 500
  Japanese, 427–443, 454–455, 459, 462n9
  Johannine, 172, 174, 177–178
  Judaism and, 383, 385, 438, 553n45, 717
  in Korea, 440, 448–460
  Korean nationalism and, 448, 453–460
  racialization and, 310
  racism in theology, 711–712
  Rastafari and, 611
  Roman Empire and, 241–242, 253, 379, 736
  social, 386
Christianization, 314, 379, 440, 459, 511, 514, 518, 599, 602–604
Christian missionaries, 310–312, 314
  in Africa, 496–498, 503–504, 606–609, 649, 690
  African decolonization movement and, 606–608
  Bible translations by, 477–480, 495–498, 511–516, 520

in China, 512–514, 519–521
in colonialism, 363, 375–376, 389, 498, 511, 513, 520, 602–603, 606, 608, 629, 649, 656, 690
on education, 355–356, 359–360, 364, 430, 608
in empire and imperialism, 173, 511, 520, 602–603, 606–609
German, 372, 376–381, 389
in India, 377–379, 480–481, 485
in Japan, 429–431, 436–439, 441
in Korea, 449–454, 516
missionary linguistics and, 475–477, 481–483, 489
Nevius Method of, 450–451
in New Zealand, 628–629
Protestant, 299, 450–452, 477–478, 485, 512, 519
on race, 605–606, 608–609
in Singapore, 353–364
Christians, 141
African, 477–479, 497–504, 584–585, 592, 607–610, 632–635, 653–658
the Apocrypha and, 239
Japanese, 427–443
in Roman Empire, 144, 146, 164
Thomas Christians, 12, 240, 243, 247–253
Christian slavery, 299, 301, 305, 307–308, 310–312, 409
Christology, 150–151, 163, 166, 171, 173, 176–177, 456
Churchill, Winston, 18, 334
Church of Jesus Christ of Latter-Day Saints (LDS), 402–406
Clark, William A., 399–402, 401f
class, 358–359, 656–657, 683, 686–688
Claudius (emperor), 144, 219
Clines, D. J., 96
Cocceius and Cocceians, 303, 318nn73–75
Colenso, John William, 343
Colley, Linda, 330
Collins, John J., 99, 120, 123, 128
colonial fantasies, 13, 371–381, 389–390
colonialism, 5, 66
in Africa, 495, 497–498, 501–502, 505, 565, 568–572, 580, 660–664, 711–712, 715
agrarian perspectives on, 580

baptism and, 307
Bible in, 296–297, 299, 374–376, 542, 546, 608, 623, 635–637, 653, 738–739
Bible translation and, 477–479, 488, 495, 501–502, 511–514
biblical scholarship in collusion with, 5–6, 17–18, 638, 711, 713–714, 717
British, 3–4, 18, 252, 336–337, 339–342, 355, 481, 568–572, 650, 704–705, 712
capitalism and, 442, 650, 683, 686–687, 708
Catholic, 305
Christianity in, 173, 335–336, 355, 387–388, 438–441, 498, 602–603, 711
Christian missionaries in, 363, 375–376, 389, 498, 511, 513, 520, 602–603, 606, 608, 629, 649, 656, 690
coloniality of knowledge, 229
Dutch, 297–302, 305, 307, 311, 313–314, 373
in environmental degradation, 726
gender and sex in, 538–539, 542–543, 545, 548, 624–626, 629
geoeschatology in, 296–297
German, 370–386, 389–390
Gilley on, 332–333
horizontal violence in, 121–122, 130, 167
imperialism-colonialism, 121, 168–171, 174–179, 342, 650, 720
Japanese, 431–433, 438–442, 448–449, 451, 453–454
in literature, 704–705, 708, 713
map-making and, 400–401, 401f
missionary linguistics on, 476
Nazism and, 336, 346n51
orientalism and, 707–709
postcolonialism and, 140, 564–565, 704–706, 718, 723, 735–736
race and, 601–603
racialization and, 309
racism and, 372, 546
Roman imperialism and, 140–141, 241–242
scripturalectics in, 572
scripturalization and, 565–566
settler, 399
slavery and, 296–297, 299–302, 304, 311, 313
US, 397, 399–400
Colonialism and the Bible (Liew and Segovia), 723

colonial linguistics, 476–477
colonization
    of African languages, 495, 505–506
    by British Empire, 336–337, 339–340, 355
    Christianization and, 511
    Dutch, 298
    German, 373, 376, 380, 382, 385
    by Japanese empire, 431–432, 439–440
    land and, 580–581, 648–649
    Old Testament and, 262, 272
    patriarchal domination and, 625
    racialization and, 605
    racism in, 568
    Rastafari against, 613
    Roman, 170–171, 191–192, 219
    sexual imagery of, 537–538
    Spanish, 270–273
    by US, 397
colonized and colonizer, 27, 704–705, 736
    ambivalence and, 227, 710
    Bhabha on, 709
    in Bible translation, 511–512
    catachresis and, 215–216
    Césaire on, 335
    Christianities of, 299
    gender and, 175–176
    Gospel of John and, 172
    under Hellenistic power, 119–134
    hybridity of, 121, 709–710, 743–744
    in Japanese empire, 432, 453–454
    Johannine community and, 176–177
    land and, 581
    mimicry and, 61, 68n56, 121–122, 130–132, 134–135, 168, 225, 362, 615, 741
    on NT Gospels, 141
    postcolonial criticism on, 120–122, 740
    power polluting, 548
    racialized identities of, 297
Colossians, Epistle to the, 361, 375–376
Comaroff, Jean, 602–603, 606
Comaroff, John L., 602–603
Commission on Race and Ethnic Disparities, UK, 5
Confucianism, 514–515
Constantine (emperor), 7–8
Constantinian Christianity, 174–175
Constantinian Judaism, 175, 184n81
contact zones, 28, 171–173, 177, 626–627, 630, 721
Conway, Colleen M., 166
Cooke, Sophia, 354–355, 358–360, 364
Corinthians, Epistles to the, 190–205, 208n16, 343, 378
Corps of Discovery, 399–402
Cosgrove, Charles, 243
cross-textual translation, 519–523
Crouch, Andy, 156
Crouch, Carly, 60–61
Crowell, Bradley L., 740
Ctesias, 91, 106–107
cultural imperialism, 173, 565
cultural studies, 163, 480, 712–714
Culture Protestantism, 377, 382, 385–386
Currid, John, 29
curse of Ham, slavery and, 13–14, 272, 277–278, 303, 310, 406, 408–411, 561
Cyrus (king), 80–81, 92–93, 97, 103, 106, 108
Cyrus Cylinder, 89–90, 97

D

Dale, Canon, 603, 606
Dalit theologians, 488
Dalrymple, William, 333–334
Daly, Mary, 638
Daniel, 70, 77–78, 80, 83, 94
Daniel, Book of, 70, 77, 98–103, 128, 132–134
Darden, Lynne St. Clair, 225–226, 231n10, 718
Darius I (king), 98, 100, 103, 107
Dass, Peter, 482
David (king), 30–31, 34, 126, 266–269, 273, 279
Davidson, Steed, 15, 719
Davis, David, 601
Davis, Ellen F., 15
Dead Sea Scrolls, 11
decolonization, 5, 11–13, 15, 63–66, 332, 390
    in Africa, 606–608, 610–611, 615–616, 650–653, 660–662, 664–665
    Bible translation and, 495, 504
    of biblical studies and biblical hermeneutics, 660–665
    civilization and, 312–314
    postcolonialism and, 652, 709
    postcolonial translation studies in, 472, 495
De Ethnicorum Pueris Baptizandis, 305–306
Defoe, Daniel, 565

Deissmann, Adolf, 11
De Mey, Johannes, 304
Deodatus, Giovanni, 306
De Quetteville, Harry, 89
De Raad, Georgius, 303–304
Deuteronomy
  Hellenistic power and, 122–124, 127–178
  on Jerusalem temple, 132
  just war theory and, 302
  Spanish Empire on, 262, 270–271, 274
  on tithes, 36
  VTE and, 59–61
De Vos, Willem, 312
diaspora, 85, 118, 127
  Jewish, 98–102, 122–123, 215–216, 220–221
  Korean, 452–453
Diehl, Judith A., 11
Dom Pedro V (king), 497
Donaldson, Laura E., 376, 715–716, 720–721, 742
Douglass, Frederick, 409–412, 614
Downs, Roger, 25
Dube, Musa W., 502–504, 624–626, 629–631, 634–635
  on Bible as imperializing text, 652–653, 715
  on colonial empire, 738–739
  Johannine scholarship by, 169–173, 175–176, 178
  Mosala and, 658
  Sugirtharajah and, 738, 745
  on Western feminism, 720–721
Du Bois, W. E. B., 227, 411, 678
Du Bose, Hampden, 518
Dunch, Ryan, 359
Dutch Calvinism, 297, 299, 304, 307–308, 311–313
Dutch colonialism, 297–302, 305, 307, 311, 313–314, 373
Dutch East India Company (VOC), 297–298, 300–302, 308, 311, 313–314, 648
Dutch Empire, 12–14, 296–307, 310, 312, 648–649
Dutch Reformed Christianity and Dutch Reformed Church, 296, 299–312, 314

E

Eagleton, Terry, 679–680, 685, 689
Earth Bible, The, 586

East India Company (British), 331, 712
Ebina Danjō, 434, 437–441, 443, 444n16
Ecclesiastes, 125–126
eco-agrarianism, 577–582, 585–592
ecology and ecological studies, 577, 582, 585, 589–592
Edney, Matthew, 401
Egypt, 11, 25–33, 81, 118, 580, 587–588, 663, 736
Eighty Years' War, 296, 302, 315n2
Elijah, 284
Elisha, 275, 409
Elkins, Caroline, 4
Ellicott, Andrew, 405f
Ellis, Marc H., 184n81
Ely, Geoff, 370
empire, 142
  the Apocrypha and, 239–248
  Bible and, 6–10, 12, 598–600, 602–606, 611, 614–616, 712, 717–720, 726–727, 735–744
  bodies and, 537–539
  Book of Revelations and, 214, 220–223, 228–229
  capitalism and, 600–602
  Christianity and, 333, 603–605, 611, 615–616
  Christian missionaries and, 511, 520, 602–603
  Christology as response to, 166
  in contemporary world, 18–19
  Encratism and, 244–246
  gender and sex in, 537–539, 548, 721
  imperialism *versus*, 706
  indigenous peoples and, 599
  "the Jews" and, 166–167
  Johannine literature and, 162–169, 174, 179
  logic of, 606–611, 615
  postcolonial biblical criticism on, 537, 544–545, 717–720, 724
  postcolonial criticism of John and, 169–180
  postcolonialism and, 70, 535, 537, 691
  race, racism and, 600–602, 608, 611
  Rastafari against, 600, 611–616
  religion and, 51–52, 296, 299, 354–355, 711–712
  scriptural imperialism in civilizing mission of, 511–515
  torture and, 168
empires, 2–4, 10–12, 16, 156, 726, 736–737, 742

empire studies, 154–157, 163–169, 175, 177–180, 721–723
Enciso, Martín Fernández, 261–262
Encratism, 244–247
Engels, Friedrich, 677, 681
Enoch, 123–124, 127
enslaved people, 5, 94–98, 106, 227, 296. *See also* slavery
   African Americans, 13–14, 406–412
   curse of Ham and, 13–14, 277, 310, 406
   indigenous, 277, 300, 317n45
   missionaries converting to Christianity, 311–312
   racialization of, 307–308
   in Roman Empire, 203, 221–222
Enuma Elish, 37
Ephesians, Epistle to the, 340, 375–376
Equiano, Olaudah, 718
Erdrich, Louise, 400–401
Esarhaddon (king), 50–51, 59, 63
Escalona Agüero, Gaspar de, 276
Esfandiari, Golnaz, 89
Esther, Book of, 98–99, 101–102
Etherington, Norman, 602
Ethiopianism, 612–615
ethnicity, race and, 660–664
Eucharist, 246–247
Evarts, Jeremy, 402
exile, 71–85, 94–95, 100–102, 128, 133
Exodus, 25–26, 224, 407, 587–590
   Moses in, 266
   slavery and, 301, 303
   Spanish Empire on, 272, 714–715
   Zimbabwean revolutionary struggle and, 609–610
Exploring Postcolonial Biblical Criticism (Sugirtharajah), 723
Ezekiel, 403, 411, 587–588
Ezra, 94–98, 108

F

Fabri, Friedrich, 380–381
Fanon, Frantz, 16, 335, 652, 678, 740
   on colonialism and Marxism, 684
   on colonized and colonizers, 121–122, 130, 705
   on imperial power, 124, 126–127

farms and agriculture, 578–585, 589, 591–592
femininity, 166, 537, 539, 628–629
feminism and feminists, 15, 223–224, 343, 354, 410, 483, 488
   postcolonial biblical exegesis, 624–639
   postcolonial scholarship, 175–176, 178, 624–626, 636, 639, 658
   Western, 624, 720–721
Fensham, F. Charles, 95–96
Ferdinand VII (king), 284
Ferguson, Niall, 330, 332
Fernández, Dagoberto Ramírez, 221
Fewell, Dana, 100
Figueroa, Yomaira C., 229
Flavius Josephus, 29
Floyd, George, 415n6, 735
Foster, Paul, 244
Foucault, Michel, 534, 549n4, 709, 740
Fox, Michael, 39
Francke, August Hermann, 377–378
Frankena, Rintje, 59
Fraser, Nancy, 548
Freire, Paulo, 225
French Revolution, 336, 343
Fretheim, Terence, 587–588
Fried, Lisbeth S., 93
Frilingos, Christopher A., 226–227

G

Galatians, Epistle to the, 196, 200–204, 208n16, 541
Galilee, 142–143, 152
Garcia-Treto, Francisco, 717
Garvey, Marcus, 613–614
Gates, Henry Louis, 418n42
Gehazi, 409
gender and sex, 175–176, 179, 197
   in Bible translations, 501–502, 504, 542–543
   in Book of Joshua, 632
   Book of Revelation on, 218–219, 223–228
   in Christianity and Judaism, 553n45
   in colonialism, 538–539, 542–543, 545, 548, 624–626, 629
   in empire, 537–539, 548, 721
   Genesis on, 539, 550n18
   of God, 540–541, 550n23
   heteronormativity and, 539

of Jesus Christ, 543, 552n39
  in NT, 540–541, 547
  oppression, postcolonialism and, 624–625
  Othering, 545
  in Paul's letters, 540–543, 551n31, 630–631
  political nature of, 537–539
  in postcolonial feminist biblical exegesis, 624–626, 629–634
  in postcolonial interpretation histories, 634–636
  queer and postcolonial biblical criticism on, 533–548
  sexualized social hierarchy, 536–537
  Western feminists on, 720–721
gender performativity, 534, 545, 548n1
Genesis, 37, 70, 124, 274–275
  on animals and land, 581, 584–586
  on baptism, 305
  cross-textual reading of, 522–523
  Egypt in, 25, 27, 29–30
  on gender, 539, 550n18
  Mormons on, 403–404
  Noah in, 410–411
  Rastafari on, 614
  slavery and, 310, 407–409, 663
  translation in African indigenous languages, 502
genre
  of the Apocryphal Acts, 239
  of the Christian Apocrypha, 240
  noncanonical, 243
  politics of 244, 253
Gentiles, 200, 203–205, 208nn14–15
geoeschatology, 296–297
geophysical imperialism, 15, 577
George, Annie, 485
Gerbner, Katharine, 299
German colonialism, 370–386, 389–390
German Empire, 13, 370–390
German imperialism, 370–373, 379–380, 386, 389–390
Germany, C. H., 434
Gerome, Jean-Leon, 707
Gerstenberger, Erhard S., 109
Gezer, 31, 35
Ghosh, Amitav, 14
Gildea, Robert, 706, 726–727

Gilley, Bruce, 332
Glancy, Jennifer A., 168, 183n51, 227
Glass, Zipporah G., 172–173
Gnosticism, 174, 239–240, 244
God. *See also* YHWH
  African indigenous deities and, 499–501, 504–505
  Babylon and, 71–72, 75–76, 78–79, 81–84
  Babylonian kings as "God's servant," 70, 76–81, 83
  Caesar and, 342
  gender and sex of, 540–541, 550n23
  German Empire and, 386–387
  as imperial ruler, 205
  in Israel, 357, 384
  Jesus as "Son of God," 149, 165, 203
  Kingdom of God, 9, 147–148, 154, 156–157, 163, 458–461, 722
  naming, 499–501, 504–505, 515–517, 522
  nations and, 356–357
  Paul's letters on, 202–205
  queer, 540–541
Goldingay, John, 92–93, 99
Gopal, Priyamvada, 4, 334
Gorman, Amanda, 414–415, 420n74
Gospel harmonies, 9
Gospel of John, 162–180, 387–388, 456, 723
Gospel of Luke, 151–154, 358, 384, 439–440, 442, 457
  in liberation theology, 609
  Marxist criticism of, 686, 689–690
Gospel of Mark, 379, 383, 386–387
  Jesus in, 140, 146, 148–150, 387, 736–737
  Marxist criticism of, 686–688
  on Roman Empire, 148–150, 686–687, 719–720, 741–742
Gospel of Matthew, 150–154, 302–303, 385–386, 605, 632, 712
  Jesus Christ in, 146, 148, 249, 388
  on Roman Empire, 150–151
Gospel of Thomas, 239–240
Gospels, NT
  as anti-imperial texts, 140–141, 154, 169, 737
  Beatitudes in, 154
  British biblical scholarship on, 342
  on households, 540–541
  Jesus in, 140–141, 146–156, 163–165

Gospels, NT (*cont.*)
   Paul's letters on, 191–193
   Roman Empire and, 146–156, 162
   subversion by, 147, 152, 154, 165–166
   Synoptic Gospels, 11, 148–149, 152–154, 163
Gossai, Hemchand, 11
Gott, Richard, 333
Gottwald, Norman, 680, 684, 694n29, 736
Grabbe, Lester, 98, 122
Grayson, James Huntley, 450
Greek empires, 119, 121
Greeley, Horace, 406
Gregoratti, Leonardo, 240
Greifenhagen, F. V., 25–26, 28
Griffiths, Valerie, 359–360
Grotius, Hugo, 300, 302–303
Gruen, Erich, 119–120
Guardiola-Sáenz, Leticia, 171, 175
Guevara, Doña María de, 278
Gunkel, Hermann, 17

H

Habel, Norman, 586–588
Hall, Catherine, 355
Halpern, Baruch, 71–72
Hanks, William, 473
Happer, Andrew Patton, 512
Hardt, Michael, 600, 706, 708
Harrison, Beverly W., 638
Hastings, Adrian, 519–520
Havea, Jione, 725
Hayes, Newton, 518
Headlam, Arthur, 341
Heaney, Robert, 66
Heber, Reginald, 334
Hebrew Bible, 8, 196, 383, 499, 538, 741
   agrarian writings of, 577–578, 580–581, 583, 585–586, 592
   Assyrian Empire in, 56–66, 69n60
   cross-textual translation and interpretation of, 522–523
   Egypt in, 25–33, 580, 587–588, 736
   gender of God in, 540
   Marxists on, 684, 686
   in the New World, 265
   on Nineveh, 62–63
   on Persian rule, 91–105

Hebrew language, 38–39, 504–505, 516
Hegelian dialectic, 679, 681–682
Heitmüller, Wilhelm, 383, 385–386
Hellenism, Judaism and, 119–120, 384
Hellenistic power, 118–134
Hellenistic rulers, 95, 97–98, 102, 124–125, 131, 134
Helm, Charles Daniel, 497
Henze, Matthias, 99
Hepburn, J. C., 514
Herder, Johann Gottfried von, 474
Herero Rebellion, 381
heresy, 244–248, 253
Herling, Bradley L., 474–475
Hermanson, Eric, 499
Herod (king), 145–146, 151–152
Herod Antipas, 153, 541
Herodotus, 90–91, 103, 106, 108, 252
Herrnhutter missions, 311–312, 323n155
Hertzog, O. G., 518
Heschel, Susannah, 8
heteronormativity, 227, 536, 539–540, 546–547, 552n44
heterosexism, 536, 546
Hezekiah (king), 58–59
Hidalgo, Jacqueline M., 12, 718
Hidalgo y Costilla, Miguel, 283
hidden transcripts, 147–148, 166, 181n22, 222–223
Hinduism and Hindu texts, 474, 482–483, 517, 715, 722
historical criticism, 712–714
historiography, 90–91, 94, 152, 286, 462n14
History/history, Jameson on, 682–683
Hoffmeier, James K., 30, 37–38
Holland, Tom, 89
Holm, Tawny L., 99–100
Holter, Knut, 648
Holy Piby, The (Rogers), 612–615
Holy Roman Emperor, 262, 267
Hommius, 301
homoeroticism and homosexuality, 536–537, 542–543, 549n13, 552n36
Hondius, Jacobus, 303
horizontal violence, 121–124, 130–131, 136n20, 167, 225
Horsley, Richard, 123–124, 206n1, 684, 721–722, 735–737, 740, 745

Hort, Fenton John Anthony, 338, 340–341
Hosea, Book of, 32–33
Hough, James, 252
Howard-Brook, Wes, 123
Howell, Leonard, 613–614
H. P. Müller, 101–102
Huber, Lynn R., 227
Huffard, E. W., 173
Huie-Jolly, Mary, 173
Hull, John, 514
Hulsebos, A. J., 305
Humphreys, W. L., 99–100
Hunts, William Remfry, 512–513
Hutton, Clinton, 612
Huxley, George, 250–251
hybridity, 27–28, 100, 128, 175, 223, 225
   of Asian Christian identity, 521
   Bhabha on, 121, 220, 535, 709–710, 744
   of colonized and colonizer, 121, 709–710, 743–744
   of postcolonial biblical scholars, 742, 744–745
   of Roman Empire, 220
   in use of Bible, 718
Hyksos people, in Egypt, 30
Hymn of Aten, 39

I

identity politics, 5, 544, 547
ideological criticism, 163, 511, 723, 741, 743
imperialism, 11, 414. *See also* Roman imperialism
   Babylonian, 71, 79–80, 83–84
   Bible and, 6–7, 10, 546, 652–653, 715, 737–739
   British, 136n20, 299, 330, 333–334, 337, 705
   capitalism and, 441–442, 600, 650, 686
   Christianity and, 3–4, 241, 603, 615, 683
   Christianization and, 599, 602
   Christian missionaries in, 173, 520, 603, 606–609
   cultural, 173, 565
   empire *versus*, 706
   Epistle to the Romans on, 607
   geophysical, 15, 577
   German, 370–373, 379–380, 386, 389–390
   heteronormativity and, 539
   internal, in former colonies, 716
   Japanese, 436, 439, 441, 456, 459
   language and, 705
   liberal, 604, 609
   patriarchy and, 720–721
   postcolonial feminist biblical exegesis on, 631–633
   race in, 599, 605
   scriptural, 511–515
   settler colonialism and, 399, 605
   sociology on, 658–659
   violence and, 131–132
   Western European, 3–4, 155, 213–214, 219–220
imperialism-colonialism, 121, 168–171, 174–179, 342, 650, 720
imperial power, 75–80, 82–84, 120–129, 133–134
inculturation, 479, 482–484, 495, 498–500, 514, 647–648, 662
India, 178, 376, 708, 710
   the Apocrypha on, 249–253, 256n72
   Bible translation in, 471–472, 475, 479–489, 523
   British occupation of, 18, 252, 331, 334, 339–340, 481, 603–604, 712, 717
   Christian missionaries in, 377–379, 480–481, 485
   Jesuit translation projects in, 473–474, 481
   Thomas Christians of, 12, 248–253
Indian Removal Act of 1830, 402–403
India's Women and China's Daughters, 354, 360
indigenous peoples, 129, 330, 599, 724–725. *See also* Native Americans
   African, 498–506, 662–664
   conversion to Christianity, 280, 281f
   enslavement of, 277, 300, 317n45
   land and, 400–401, 580–581, 586, 648–650, 664, 726
   Native Americans, 13, 397, 400–403, 405–406, 417n27, 605, 711
   of the New World, 262–265, 272–273, 277, 279–280, 283
Inoue Tetsujirō, 437
interfaith dialogue, 479, 482, 484, 520–521
intersectionality, 455, 460–461, 540, 543–545, 636, 743

postcolonialism on, 720–721, 724–725
intertextuality, 3, 175, 243–244, 564
Iran, modern, 89–91
Iraq War, 62
Isaiah, Book of, 33, 76, 107, 276, 592
    anointing of Cyrus in, 92–93
    on Assyrians, 57–59, 61, 64, 66
    Book of Revelation and, 225
    in Christian imperialism, 603
    Luthuli on, 607–608
Islam, 500
Israel, 12, 150, 539–540
    Assyrian Empire and, 50, 66
    Babylonian Empire and, 70–72, 75–76, 78–82, 85
    Canaan and, 590–591
    Dutch Reformed Church on, 308–309
    eco-agrarian approach to Scriptures of, 577, 580–582, 585–588, 590
    Egypt and, 11, 26–27, 29–40, 81, 580, 588, 736
    God in, 357, 384
    Judaea/Israel, 118–119, 122, 127, 129, 132–134, 136n20, 142–143, 152
    Native Americans and, 405
Israel, Hephzibah, 14
Israelites, 357
    Canaanites and, 262, 590–591, 632
    Egyptian influence on society, 33–40
    land and farms of, 580–583, 585–586
    Mormons on, 403
    Spanish Empire and conquistadors on, 262–263, 266, 271–273, 277, 285

J

Jackson, Andrew, 402
Jackson, Ashley, 330–331
Jacob, Sharon, 16
Jacobs, Harriet, 410
Jaisohn, Philip, 451, 458
Jamaica, 611–613
James, C. L. R., 346n65
James I (king), 7–8
Jameson, Fredric, 681–683
Janes, L. L., 438
Japan and Japanese Empire, 14, 427–443, 448–455, 459–461, 462n9, 463n21, 463nn24–25
Japanese imperialism, 436, 439, 441, 456, 459
Japheth, 271–272, 310
Jason, 130–131
Jefferson, Thomas, 399
Jehu, 659–660
Jeremiah, Book of, 78–83, 133, 279–280, 362, 604, 719
Jerusalem, 33, 58–59, 589
    Babylonian Empire and, 72–74, 76
    in Book of Revelation, 219, 222, 224–225, 403
    Hellenistic power and, 118, 125–132, 134
    Jesus in, 146
    Mormons on, 403–405
    Paul's collections for, 198–199, 201–202
Jerusalem temple, 127, 130, 132, 143, 193
    destruction of First Temple, 99, 216, 221
    Ezekial on, 403
    Jesus' body and, 175
    Second Temple, 75, 215
    Spanish Empire on, 266, 269
    tithes and offerings to, 145–146
Jesuit translation projects, 473–474, 481, 484–486
Jesus Christ, 537, 635
    in Acts of Thomas, 246, 249
    birth of, 152–153
    Christian missionaries in Korea on, 451–452
    crucifixion of, 153, 164, 167–168, 172, 195, 457
    double command to love, 155–156
    on eunuchs, 539, 550n26
    feminists on gender of, 175
    gender and sex of early followers, 541, 550n26
    gender of, 543, 552n39
    German scholars on, 383–388
    in Gospel of John, 163–168, 170–172, 174–177, 179–180, 387–388
    in Gospel of Luke, 152–154
    in Gospel of Mark, 140, 146, 148–150, 387, 736–737
    in Gospel of Matthew, 146, 148, 249, 388
    in Gospels, 140–141, 146–156, 163–165
    historical, 17, 149
    on households and family bonds, 540–541, 547
    as Jew, 142
    Johannine Epistles on, 173–174

Judaism and, 383–385
  on Kingdom of God, 9, 147–148, 154, 156–157, 163, 722
  Korean nationalists on, 456–458
  as Messiah, 150, 167, 383
  Mormons on, 403
  Paul's letters on, 192–196, 200–201, 203–205
  Pharisees on, 151
  Pilate and, 146, 149, 153, 164, 166–167
  queering, 541, 543, 551n27
  resurrection of, 150–151, 195, 197
  Roman Empire and, 142, 146, 149–156, 162, 166–168, 195, 736–737
  Schleiermacher on, 374–376
  as "Son of God," 149, 165, 203
  as "Son of Man," 154
Jewish identity, 120, 123, 127, 133
Jewish Roman War, 220–221
Jewish writings and texts
  Book of Revelation and, 213, 215, 221, 224–225
  Gospel of Matthew, 150–151
  Hellenistic power and, 118, 122–123, 221
  NT Gospels, 141
Jews
  in Babylonian exile, 71–85, 100–102, 128, 133
  in Court Tales, 101–102
  diaspora, 98–102, 122–123, 215–216, 220–221
  Gentiles and, 200
  in Gospel of John, 166–168, 170–172
  Hellenistic colonizers and, 121–124, 126–135
  Hellenistic culture and, 119–120, 125, 128, 130–131
  Jesus, 142, 385
  on Jesus and Messiah, 150
  Palestinians and, 591–592
  Paul's letters on, 190, 200, 204, 208nn14–15
  Persian Empire and, 95–96, 98
  Roman colonization of, 191–192
  in Roman Empire, 142, 144, 148–153, 164, 166–168, 175, 215
  Spanish Inquisition and, 264
Jezebel, 224–225, 628, 658–659, 664
Johannine Christianity, 172, 174, 177–178
Johannine community, 163, 166, 168, 171–173, 176–177, 184n69
Johannine Epistles, 173–174, 181n20
Johannine literature, 12, 162–180, 385–386. *See also* Revelation, Book of
John and Postcolonialism (Dube and Staley), 171–173
John I (king), 266
Jonah, Book of, 11, 62–65, 69n60
Jørstad, Mari, 585–586, 588
Joseph, Clara, 12
Joseph and Joseph tribe, 27, 122, 303, 663–664, 717
Josephus, 122, 129, 135, 136n20, 687
Joshua, 261–262
Joshua, Book of, 589–590, 625, 630, 632
Jowett, Benjamin, 337–339
Judaea/Israel, 118–119, 122, 127, 129, 132–134, 136n20
  in Roman Empire, 142–143, 152
Judah, 32–33, 36, 64, 581
  Assyrian Empire and, 57–59, 61
  Babylonian Empire and, 72–73, 78–79, 81–82
Judaism, 84, 94
  Christianity and, 383, 385, 438, 553n45, 717
  Constantinian, 175, 184n81
  German academy on, 382–385, 389
  Hellenism and, 119–120, 384
Judas, 460
Judeans, 11, 58, 64, 75, 103–104, 131–132
Judson, Adoniram, 517
Julius Caesar (emperor), 145, 194
just war theory, 302–303

K

Kale, Madhavi, 363
Kang, Jina, 14
Karlsson, Mattias, 53
Kashiwagi Gien, 441–443
Kass, Leon, 85
Katchadourian, Lori, 90
Katō Hiroyuki, 437–438
Kebra Nagast, 612
Keller, Catherine, 70
Kgalemang, Malebogo, 626
Kiboko, J. Kabamba, 504
Kidd, Colin, 299
Kil Chin-gyŏng, 457
Kil Sŏn-ju, 457–458
Kim, Jean K., 175

Kim Namchŏn, 459–461
King, Thomas, 400
Kingdom of God, 9, 147–148, 154, 156–157, 163, 458–461, 722
King James Version (KJV), 7–8, 504, 517, 519, 522, 611–612, 614–615
Kings, Book of, 30–31, 33–34, 36, 58, 72, 279, 409, 628, 658–659
Kinyua, Johnson Kiriaku, 479
Kipling, Rudyard, 704, 708
Kisanga language, 504
KJV. *See* King James Version
Klassen, Pamela, 400
Klauck, Hans-Josef, 243
Klijn, A. F. J., 242, 245–246, 251
Kombo, J. O., 500
Koodapuzha, Xavier, 251
Korea, 439–442, 448–461, 462n14, 463n21, 463nn24–25, 464n28, 465n49, 516
Korean nationalism, 448–449, 452–461
Koyama, Kosuke, 521
Kruger, Michael J., 243
Krüger, Thomas, 126
Kuhrt, Amelie, 90, 106
Kumar, Amitava, 19
Kumiai Kyōkai, 434, 439, 441, 454–455, 459
Kwok Pui-lan, 376, 626–627, 629, 631, 634, 638, 721

L

Ladies Bible and Tract Society, 355–356, 359, 363
Lalami, Laila, 693
Lalitha, Jayachitra, 178
Lambdin, Thomas, 39
Lamentations, 72–75
land, 400–401, 579–586, 589, 592, 648–650, 653–660, 664–665, 726
land-community, 581, 585, 589
land ethic, 579–580
land restitution, 658–659
La Peyrère, Isaac, 310
Las Casas, Bartolomé de las, 262–263, 276
Lay, G. Tradescant, 518
LDS. *See* Church of Jesus Christ of Latter-Day Saints
Le Couteur, Howard, 355

Lee, Archie, 14
Lee, Timothy S., 448, 456
L'Enfant, Pierre, 404, 405f
Leopold, Aldo, 579–581, 585
Levant, the, 29–30, 33, 35, 54–55
Levinson, Bernard, 59
Lévi-Strauss, Claude, 567
Levites, 663–664
Lewis, Meriwether, 399–401, 401f
liberalism, 599, 601, 603–604, 606, 608–611, 615–616
Liberal Protestantism, 378, 382
liberal theology, 13, 373–376, 430–431, 599
liberation theology, 154–155, 609–610, 654, 657
Liew, Tat-siong Benny, 12, 149, 170–173, 178, 719–720, 723, 740
Lightfoot, Joseph Barber, 338–339
Lim, Stephen, 13
Lincoln, Bruce, 109
Lisa Lowe, 601–602
literary criticism, 712–714
Liverani, Mario, 51–52, 54–56, 63
Llewellyn-Jones, Lloyd, 91, 106
Lobengula (king), 497
long (the dragon), in Chinese Bible, 517–519
Longkumer, Arkotong, 483
Loomba, Ania, 708
López, Gregorio, 270
López de Palacios Rubios, Juan, 262
Lozada, Francisco, Jr., 173
Lucas, Bernard, 9–10
Luthuli, Albert, 607–609

M

mabira, 503–506
Maccabees, 119, 122, 124, 129–134, 612
Macedonians, 200
Machinist, Peter, 57, 64
Mafico, Temba, 499, 580
magic, 244, 247–248
Maier, Harry O., 214
Malamat, Abraham, 31
Malayalam language, 486
Malthus, Thomas, 336, 343
Maluleke, Tinyiko, 656–658, 660
Mandair, Arvind-Pal S., 474
Mandarin language, 517

Manetho, 29
Manichaeanism, 244
Manucci, Niccolao, 707–708
maps and map-making, 399–402, 401f
Marathi language, 486, 488
Marchal, Joseph A., 630–631
Marchand, Suzanne, 371, 381, 388
March First Movement, 440, 442, 449, 452–455, 457, 461
Martin, Clarice J., 221, 343
Martyn, J. Louis, 164
Marx, Karl, 677, 681–682
Marxism and Marxist critical theory, 15, 677–685, 689–692, 740
Marxist biblical criticism, 677–678, 680–682, 684–691
Mary, cult of, 281, 283–284
Marzouk, Safwat, 11
masculinity, 166, 175, 536–540, 543, 552n44
Masenya, Madipoane, 630, 632–634, 662
Massey, James, 488
Master, Daniel, 35
Masters, Adrian, 12
Mata, Roberto, 224
Mateer, Calvin, 514
materialism, 679, 681–684, 686–688, 690–692
Mattathias, 130–132, 134
Maxey, Trent, 429
Maxwell, David, 606, 608
Mbiti, John, 499–500
Mbuwayesango, Dora R., 14
McArthur, Harvey, 9
McCarthy, Thomas, 601, 605–606
McCaskie, T. C., 90
McClatchie, Thomas Booth, 512
McKay, Niall, 15–16
McKinlay, Judith E., 627–630
Mehta, Uday Singh, 603
Menéndez-Antuña, Luis, 219–220
Mesopotamia, 26–27, 36–37, 55
Mettinger, Tryggve, 34
Mexico, 283
Micah, Book of, 579–580, 592, 686
Mignolo, Walter, 600–601
Mill, James, 708
Mills, Wallace, 609–611
Milne, William, 519

mimicry, 128
　Bhabha on, 130, 226, 362, 535, 615, 741
　in Book of Revelation, 223–228, 718–719
　Chitnio and, 362–363
　colonized and colonizer and, 61, 68n56, 121–122, 130–132, 134–135, 168, 225, 362, 615, 741
　in Gospel of Mark, 741
　in Paul's letters, 199–205
Min, Kyung-jin, 97
missionary linguistics, 475–477, 481–483, 489
Modimo, 501
Moffat, Robert, 496–497
Mofokeng, Takatso, 654, 657
Mogrovejo, Toribio de (saint), 280, 281f
Mohanty, Chandra Talpade, 624, 720–721
Mojola, Aloo Osotsi, 501, 505
Monegro, Juan Bautista, 268
Montesinos, Licenciado Fernando de, 273–274
Monzón, Francisco de, 273
Moore, Stephen, 150, 164, 174–175, 225–227, 638, 715, 720–721, 725, 736–737, 743
Mormons, 402–407, 413, 417n27
Morrison, Robert, 359, 519
Morrison, Toni, 314
Mosala, Itumeleng, 654–658, 665, 686, 688–690
Moses, 26–27, 262–264, 266–267, 272, 280, 281f, 357, 412, 590
Mtshiselwa, Ndikho, 659–660
Mugabe, Robert, 546
Mukyōkai, 434–435
Müller, Friedrich Max, 376, 566–567
Mundadan, A. Mathias, 251
Museum of the Bible, 414, 420n72
Muzorewa, Abel, 609–610
Mwari, 500–501, 505
Myers, Jacob, 94–96
Myers, Susan E., 246

N

Naaman, 409
Naboth, 659, 664
Nadella, Raj, 16
Naga languages, 483–484
Nahum, Book of, 11, 62–65
Naidoo, Leigh-Ann, 650–652
Naipaul, V. S., 705, 710, 713–714

Naranch, Bradley, 370
nationalism, 5, 175–176, 397, 483, 502
　in Africa, 502, 609
　Korean, 448–449, 452–461
Native Americans, 13, 397, 400–403, 405–406, 417n27, 605, 711
Natives Land Act of 1913, 648, 659
Natural Law, 262, 300
Naughton, John, 3
Naumann, Friedrich, 373, 386–387
Nazism and National Socialism, 336, 346n51, 370, 376, 390
Nebuchadnezzar (king), 70, 72, 76–81, 83, 99–100, 133
Nedungatt, George, 251–253
Negri, Antonio, 600, 706, 708
Negro spirituals, 410–413
Nehemiah, Book of, 94–97, 108
Neil, Stephen, 18
neocolonialism, 18, 178–179, 376, 545, 626, 637, 639, 660, 721, 726
Nero (emperor), 145, 216, 223
Nerva (emperor), 144–145
Nettleford, Rex, 613
Neusner, Jacob, 84
Newcombe, Hessie, 358
New Israel, 398–399, 404–405
Newman, Judith, 13
New Revised Standard Version (NRSV), 202, 249, 504, 522
Newsom, Carol, 100
New Testament (NT), 7–8, 11, 190–191, 741–742. *See also* Gospels, NT; Paul, epistles of; Revelation, Book of
　British biblical scholarship on, 337–338, 342–343
　empire studies and, 155–156
　gender and sex in, 540–541, 547
　Marxist analysis of, 686
　masculinity and patriarchy in, 538
　Roman Empire and, 142–143, 145, 155–156
　translations of, 480–482, 488
New World, the, 262–265, 270, 272–275, 279–281, 283, 285
New Zealand, 627–628
Ngoshi, Hazel, 609
Nickelsburg, George, 123

Niebuhr, Reinhold, 414
Niedner, Frederick, 73–74
Nightingale, Florence, 331, 338
Nineveh, 62–65, 69n60
Nkulunkulu, 500
Noah, 271–272, 275, 408–411
Noah, Mordecai Manuel, 405
Nock, Arthur Darby, 194
nonviolent resistance, 133, 181n22, 221, 248, 453, 608
NRSV. *See* New Revised Standard Version
NT. *See* New Testament
Ntloedibe-Kuswani, Gomang Seratwa, 500–501
Nyabongo, Akiki K., 690–691
Nzimande, Makhosazana, 658–659, 664

O

Obama, Barack, 559
O'Connor, Kathleen M., 82–83
Old Testament, 11
　Catholic saints and, 280, 282*f*
　on colonization and slavery, 262, 272
　the New World and, 262–265, 273–275, 279–281, 283, 285
　in Spanish Empire and imperialism, 12, 262–281, 282*f*, 283–286
　translation of, 517
Olyan, Saul M., 104
Oriel College, 332–333
orientalism, 535, 538–539, 722
　in British biblical scholarship, 342–343
　Catholic, 474
　colonialism and, 707–709
　German, 371, 374, 381–383, 388
　on Hindu texts, 715
　postcolonialism and, 584, 709–710
　of Protestant missionaries in China, 512
　in Western academies, 68n59, 335
Orientalism (Said), 334–335, 371, 582–584, 707–709, 740
Oriya language, 486
Orpah, 716, 719
Oshima, Takayoshi, 103
Ostenberg, Ida, 107
Other, the, 13, 81–84
　Christian missionaries on, 512, 520
　colonial control of, 566

demonizing, 517–519
  "the Jews" as, 166
  in orientalism, 343
  postcolonial and queer studies on, 533, 632
  self and, 53–54, 229
Othering, 200, 533–535, 538–539, 545, 547, 627–630
Oxford University, 332–334, 338, 344

P

Pagán, Melissa, 229
Paine, Thomas, 343
Palafox y Mendoza, Juan de, 276–277
Palestine, 32, 38, 145–147, 149–152, 686–688
Palestinians, Jews and, 591–592
Pals, Daniel, 9, 17
Páramo, Luis de, 264
Park, Albert L., 463n21
Parthian Empire, 240, 242, 244–245, 247, 252–253
patriarchy, 197, 201–202, 223, 263, 538, 637–638
  African Bible translations and, 501–502, 506
  imperialism and, 720–721
  land restitution and, 658
  postcolonial feminist biblical exegesis on, 625–628, 633
Paul (apostle), 12, 379, 541, 721–722
Paul, epistles of, 537. *See also* Romans, Epistle to the
  Colossians, 361, 375–376
  Corinthians, 190–205, 208n16, 343, 378
  Ephesians, 340, 375–376
  Galatians, 196, 200–204, 208n16, 541
  gender and sex in, 540–543, 551n31, 630–631
  on Jesus, 192–196, 200–201, 203–205
  on Jews, 190, 200, 204, 208nn14–15
  Philemon, 202–205, 339
  Philippians, 194–195, 200–201, 630–631
  on Roman Empire, 190–206, 630–631
  Thessalonians, 200
Paul, Shalom, 92–93
Payne, David, 92
"Penitential Prayer," 94–98
Pentateuch, 25–28, 262
Peppard, Michael, 149

Perdue, Leo, 124
Persepolis, 107–108
Persian Empire, 11, 88–109, 124
Persian language, 480–481
Peru, 273–277, 279–280, 284
Peter, Epistles of, 190, 360–362
Pettersburgh, Fitz Balintine, 612–613
Petterson, Christina, 680–682, 684
Pharisees, the, 151, 171, 176, 380, 388
Philemon, Epistle to, 202–205, 339
Philip (king), 267–268, 273
Philippians, Epistle to the, 194–195, 200–201, 630–631
philology, 475–476, 483, 489
Picardt, Johan, 310, 322n146
Pilate, Pontius, 146, 149, 153, 164, 166–167
Pippin, Tina, 223
Plummer, Alfred, 342
Polaski, Donald C., 100
Pongratz-Lesiten, Beate, 52
Porter, Andrew, 299, 520
Portier-Young, Anathea, 132–133
Postcolonial Biblical Criticism (Moore and Segovia), 743
Postcolonial Commentary on the New Testament Writings (Segovia and Sugirtharajah), 723
postcolonial criticism, 1–3, 27, 61–62
  on colonized and colonizer, 120–122, 740
  colonized voices in, 334–335
  on Court Tales, 100–102
  ecological studies and, 577
  empire studies and, 721–723
  feminist, 175–176, 178, 624–626, 636, 639, 658
  geopolitical contexts in, 169–170
  of Hellenistic power and Greek empires, 121–122
  of Japanese empire, 427–428
  of Johannine literature and empire, 162–163, 169–180
  of Paul's letters, 190, 206
  of Protestant mission, 299
  queer criticism and, 533–548
  resistance discourse in origins of, 704–705
  on Revelation's ethics, 220–228
  in Western academe, 706–710

Postcolonial Criticism and Biblical Interpretation (Sugirtharajah), 722
postcolonialism, 1–3, 178, 240
  of African biblical scholarship, 647–648
  colonialism and, 140, 564–565, 704–706, 718, 723, 735–736
  decolonization and, 652, 709
  empire and, 70, 535, 537, 691
  empire studies and, 154–157, 168–169, 177–180
  gender and sex oppression and, 624–625
  imagination of, 623
  on intersectionality, 720–721, 724–725
  in literature, 704–705
  Marxist theory and, 677–678, 683–684, 691–692
  New Testament studies and, 190–191
  orientalism and, 584, 709–710
  "post-colonialism" *versus*, 706, 723
  Sugirtharajah on, 553n50, 637–638, 665, 719, 724
  on Western colonization and Japanese empire, 432
postcolonial-liberation, 648, 650
postcolonial optic, 121, 169–171, 174
postcolonial translation studies, 472–475, 495
poststructuralism, 677–678, 707
Powery, Emerson, 409
Premnath, D. N., 11
Prior, Michael, 738
Promised Key, The (Howell), 613
prophetic ecology, 589–592
Protestantism and Protestants, 379
  on baptism, 304–305
  on Bible translations, 482, 485–487
  in biblical studies field, 559
  Culture Protestantism, 377, 382, 385–386
  exceptionalism, 304
  on German Empire, 370–371, 381–388
  Japanese, 431, 434, 438–439
  in Korea, 448, 450–451, 456, 462n14
  Liberal Protestantism, 378, 382
  mainline, 381–388
  missions and missionaries, 299, 450–452, 477–478, 485, 512, 519
  in US, 407–409
Protestant nations, 297–298, 374, 598–599
Protestant supremacy, 305–308
Proverbs, 39
Psalms, 37–38, 73–75, 276, 283, 309, 361–362, 578–580
  Ethiopianism on, 612–613
  in justifications of empire, 603–605
Ptolemaic Empire, 118–119, 121–125
Ptolemy, 118, 122–123
Punt, Jeremy, 15, 629
Puritans, 398–399, 402–403

Q

Qohelet (king), 125–127
queer biblical criticism, 534–548, 551n27, 632
queer God, 540–541
queer studies and queer theory, 15, 179, 227–228, 533–548, 548n3

R

Raboteau, Albert, 409, 411
race
  Bible and, 310, 560–561, 563–564, 602
  black theology on, 656–657
  capitalism and, 15, 599–602, 609, 649–650
  Christian missionaries on, 605–606, 608–609
  class and, 656–657
  colonialism and, 601–603
  empire and, 600–602, 608, 611
  in imperialism, 599, 605
  in Japanese colonies, 431–432
  in South Africa, 660–664
  in Western academy, 560–562
racialization, 297, 299, 307–310, 381, 407–409, 567–568, 605
racism, 18, 332, 340, 381–383, 431–432
  Bible and, 610–611
  in Christian theology, 711–712
  in colonialism and colonization, 372, 546, 568
  slavery and, 410–411, 561
Rafael, Vicente, 473, 511, 523n5
Rahab and Rahab's reading prism, 625, 632
Raheb, Mitri, 62, 591
Ramanstwana, Hulisani, 660–665
Ramraj, Victor, 710
Ramusack, Barbara, 359
Rastafari, 15, 600, 611–616

Rayan, Samuel, 342
Redford, D. B., 34
Reinhartz, Adele, 167, 172–173
Remus, Harold, 247
Reps, John, 403
requerimiento, 261–263, 274
Reveil movement, 312–313
Revelation, Book of, 12, 70, 387, 403, 411, 457, 517–519
    Roman Empire and, 213–228, 718–719
Revised Standard Version (RSV), 504, 522
Reynolds, David, 334
Rhee, Helen C., 241
Rhenish Mission, 376, 380–381
Rhodes, Cecil, 332–334, 497
Riebeeck, Jan van, 301
Rieger, Joerg, 13
Robinson, Cedric, 600–601
Robinson, Maxwell R., 342
Robinson Crusoe (Defoe), 565
Robson, James, 91, 106
Rodríguez de León, 276–277
Rogers, Robert Athlyi, 612–615
Roman colonization and colonialism, 170–171, 191–192, 217, 219
Roman emperors, 143–145, 152, 154, 192, 201, 206
    Book of Revelations and, 216–218
    on heresy, 248
    Pope and, 262
Roman Empire, 7, 71, 118, 141–148
    the Apocrypha on, 11–12, 239–242, 247–248
    as "Babylon," 216–219, 222–228
    Book of Revelation and, 213–228, 718
    Christianity and, 241–242, 253, 379, 736
    Christians in, 144, 146, 164
    Constantinian Christianity and, 174–175
    economy of, 198–199, 201–202, 217
    gender in, 218–219
    Gospel of John on, 163–171, 174–175, 178–179
    Gospel of Mark on, 148–150, 686–687, 719–720, 741–742
    Gospel of Matthew on, 150–151
    Gospels and, 146–156, 162
    hybridity of, 220
    Jesus and, 142, 146, 149–156, 162, 166–168, 195, 736–737
    Jews in, 142, 144, 148–153, 164, 166–168, 175, 215
    in Johannine literature, 162, 172
    Judaea and Galilee in, 142–143, 152
    NT and, 142–143, 145, 155–156
    Paul's assemblies *versus*, 196–198
    Paul's letters on, 190–206, 630–631
    private property in, 680–681
    slaves in, 203, 221–222
    violence and torture by, 167–168, 174, 179
Roman imperialism, 721–722
    Book of Revelation and, 215, 218–219, 222
    Gospels on, 140–141, 148, 162, 164–165, 741
    imperial cult of, 143–145, 216–218
    modern imperialism and, 213–214, 219–220, 228, 241–242
Romans, Epistle to the, 312, 341–342, 451–452
    Christian missionaries on, 607
    liberation theology and, 609
    queer reading of, 536, 542–543
    on Roman Empire, 193–194, 197, 199–200, 204–205
    on taxation, 199, 742
Root, Margaret, 107–108
Roscio to Nirgua, 284–285
Rose, John, 76
Rossing, Barbara R., 223
Royal Parchment Scroll of Black Supremacy, The (Pettersburgh), 612–613
RSV. *See* Revised Standard Version
Rubin, Benjamin B., 218
Rudolph, Wilhelm, 95–96
Ruiz, Jean-Pierre, 217
Runesson, Anna, 190–191
Runions, Erin, 85, 227–228
Russo-Japanese War, 436, 449
Ruth, Book of, 630, 632–634, 716, 719

S

Sacagewa, 400
SACP. *See* South African Communist Party
Said, Edward, 16, 388, 535, 710, 716, 718
    on humanism, 692
    on knowledge-power symbiosis, 709, 714
    Orientalism by, 334–335, 371, 582–584, 707–709, 740
    on postcolonialism, 27
Salih, Tayeb, 705

Salt Lake City, blueprint for, 403–405, 404f
Samaritans, 165, 172, 176, 178, 385
Sánchez, David A., 222–223
Sánchez Rangel de Fayas y Quiroz, Hipólito, 284
Sancisi-Weerdenburg, Heleen, 90
Sandgren, Ulla, 482
Sanneh, Lamin, 477–479, 498, 500, 502
Sanskrit, 482–483, 485–486
Sargon II, 55–56, 63
Satan, 517–519
Satia, Priya, 18
Schellong, Dieter, 381
Schereschewsky, Joseph, 517
Schipper, Bernd, 32–33
Schlegel, Friedrich, 474–475
Schleiermacher, Friedrich, 13, 372–376, 380, 383, 389, 391n25, 391n30, 434
Schmidt, Benjamin, 711
Scholz, Susanne, 15
Schott, Jeremy M., 241–242, 248
Schurhammer, Georg, 251
Scott, James, 108, 131, 181n22, 222–223
scripturalectics, 567, 572–573
scriptural imperialism, 511–515
scripturalization, 420n74, 562–572, 718
Second Temple Judaism, 94
Segal, J. B., 35
Segovia, Fernando F., 121, 169–170, 712–715, 720–721, 723, 740, 743
Seland, Eivind Heldaas, 242
Selassie, Haile, 613–614
Seleucid Empire, 118–119, 121–125, 129–130, 132, 134
Sennacherib (king), 127–128
Seow, C. L., 100
Serampore Baptist missionaries, 480
Setiloane, Gabriel, 657
Setswana people and language, 497, 500–503, 505–506
settler colonialism and settler imperialism, 399, 605
sexualized social hierarchy, 536–538
Shalmaneser III (king), 50–52
shalom, 591–592
Sherwood, Yvonne, 638
Sheshonq I (king), 31–32, 34–35

Shona people and language, 500–501, 503–506
Short, John Rennie, 399
Shottroff, Luise, 164
Shupak, Nili, 39
Sigüenza, José de, 268
Sinapia, 277–278
Singapore, 13, 353–364
Singh, Sundar, 517
Sino-Japanese War, 443n1, 449
slavery, 18, 94–95, 663
　abolition and abolitionists, 313, 339, 406, 409–410
　baptism and, 304–307
　Bible and, 301–303, 407–408, 711
　British Empire and, 339, 355, 602
　capitalism and, 407, 568, 601–602
　Christian, 299, 301, 305, 307–308, 310–312, 409
　colonialism and, 296–297, 299–302, 304, 311, 313
　curse of Ham and, 13–14, 272, 277–278, 303, 310, 406, 408–411, 561
　Douglass on, 409–412
　in Dutch Empire, 296–307, 310–312
　Ethiopianism on, 612–613
　Exodus and, 301, 303
　Genesis and, 310, 407–409, 663
　Mormons on, 406
　Negro spirituals on, 411–413
　Old Testament on, 262, 272
　racialization in, 307–308, 407–409
　racism and, 410–411, 561
　requerimiento on, 261–262
　Reveil movement against, 312–313
　Spanish Empire and, 261–262, 272, 277
　in US, 340, 711
slave trade, 298, 300–301, 306–307, 408f
Smalley, William, 477
Smelik, Klaas A. D., 79
Smith, Adam, 355
Smith, Joseph, 402–404, 406
Smith, Mitzi, 721
Smith, Shanell T., 227
Smith-Christopher, Dan, 11, 100
Smytegelt, Bernardus, 304
Soares-Prabhu, George, 523
Society of Biblical Literature, 559, 724

Solomon (king), 30–32, 34–35, 37, 126, 583, 690–691
    Spanish Empire on, 266–269, 273, 275–278
Song of Songs, 39
Sor Juana Inés de la Cruz, 278–279
South Africa, 372, 606–607, 610, 632–633, 648–665
South African black theology, 15, 653–658, 660–661, 669n83, 688–690
South African Communist Party (SACP), 648–650, 653
Southwood, Katherine, 104–105
Spanish conquistadors, 261–263
Spanish Empire, 12, 261–281, 282f, 283–286, 714–715
    Dutch Empire and, 296, 298, 300
Spanish Inquisition, 263–265
Spivak, Gayatri, 27, 121, 215–216, 533, 535, 709, 740, 743
Stainforth, F. J., 604
Staley, Jeffrey L., 171–173
Stanley, Brian, 477
Stea, David, 25
Stegeman, Janneke, 12–13
Steymans, Hans Ulrich, 59–60
Stolz, Thomas, 476
Strawn, Brent, 107
struggle, in South African black theology, 654–656, 661
Stulac, Daniel, 579–580, 592
Suárez de Peralta, Juan, 272
subversion, 61–62, 147, 152, 154, 165–166, 220–223
Sugirtharajah, R. S., 27, 68n57, 168, 221, 240, 357
    Asian Biblical Hermeneutics and Postcolonialism by, 717
    on Bhabha, 710
    The Bible and Postcolonialism edited by, 716–717, 725
    on Bible studies and colonialism, 635–637, 712
    on biblical hermeneutics, 713, 717
    on Christian missionaries, Bible and, 479
    on colonial empire, 737–739
    on colonized and colonizer, 744
    Dube and, 738, 745
    Exploring Postcolonial Biblical Criticism by, 723
    on indigenous peoples, 397
    on Jesus research in Asia, 635
    on Johannine literature, 173–174
    on liberation-postcolonial discourse, 647
    on Nyabongo, 690–691
    on Paul and empire, 607
    on postcolonial biblical studies, 623, 715, 739
    Postcolonial Commentary on the New Testament Writings edited by Segovia and, 723
    Postcolonial Criticism and Biblical Interpretation by, 722
    on postcolonialism and postcolonial studies, 553n50, 637–638, 665, 719, 724
    on translation, 551n32
    Voices from the Margin edited by, 714–715
    on white, male, Western scholars, 737
Sumner, John Bird, 336–337
Susanne Binder, 25
svikiro, 504–505
Swahili language, 505, 635
Swanson, Tod, 171
Sweeney, Marvin, 92–93
Synoptic Gospels, 11, 148–149, 152–154, 163

T

Tacitus, 131
Tamez, Elsa, 714–715
Tamihere, Donald, 88
Tamil language, 473–474, 476–477, 481–482, 485–487
Tangsa languages, 484
taxation, 36, 145–146, 154, 199, 341–342, 742
Taylor, Vincent, 341
Tcherikover, Victor, 119
Teenstra, Marten Douwe, 312
Telugu language, 487
Ten Commandments, 283, 362, 383
Terreblanche, Sampie, 650
texts and textualism, 560–561, 563–564
Tharoor, Shashi, 333
Thatcher, Tom, 166–167, 175, 183n50
Thessalonians, First Epistle to the, 200
Thien, Madeline, 19

Things Fall Apart (Achebe), 565, 567–573, 704–705
Thiong'o, Ngũgĩ wa, 5, 705, 714
Thomas Aquinas, 244
Thomas Christians, 12, 240, 243, 247–253
Thompson, Stephen, 38
Thornwell, James Henley, 711, 714
Thrall, Margaret, 342
Thürmer-Rohr, Christina, 638, 645n103
Tiberius (emperor), 151
Tiglath-Pileser III (king), 50, 54–55
Tilliander, Bror, 482
Tissot, Yves, 245
Tobit, Book of, 103, 105, 127–128
Togarasei, Lovemore, 503–505
Tokugawa Ieyasu, 428–429, 443n5
Tolbert, Mary Ann, 627
torah, 592
Torquemada, Tomás de, 264
Tower of Babel, 70, 85, 512
Trajan (emperor), 144–145, 164, 180n15
trauma, 75, 84, 704–705, 735–736
Trevelyan, C. E., 513
Trevor-Roper, Hugh, 331
Trocki, Carl, 358
Trump, Donald, 4, 18, 398, 735
Truth, Sojourner, 410
Tubal, 271–272
Tubalcain, 277
Tubman, Harriet, 412
Tuck, Eve, 652
Tutu, Desmond, 654
Two-Thirds World, 169, 176, 623, 625, 630

U

Uchimura Kanzō, 434–437
Udemans, Godefridus, 302–304, 310–311, 313
Uemura Masahisa, 438
Ukpong, Justin, 498–499, 647
Underwood, Lillias H., 516
United Nations Security Council, 89
United States (US), 340, 414, 559–561
 agriculture in ecological crisis of, 582–583
 Bible in, 398–399, 402–403, 735
 colonialism and colonization by, 397, 399–400
 empire, 227, 397, 414, 420n71, 722, 735
 Indian Removal Act of 1830, 402–403
 Japan and, 449
 Korea and, 457–458
 LDS and Mormons in, 402–407
 Native Americans, 13, 397, 400–403, 405–406, 417n27, 605, 711
 neocolonialism of, 179
 as New Israel, 398–399
 Protestants in, 407–409
 Puritans in, 398–399, 402–403
 racism in, 410–411
 Singapore and, 356–359
 slavery in, 340, 711
 Western, mapping, 399–402, 401f
utopianism, 403, 681

V

Van den Bosch, Lourens P., 250–252
Van der Straet, Jan, 711
Van der Toorn, Karel, 103
Van Geuns, Jan, 312
Van Prinsterer, Groen, 312–313
Van Wijk-Bos, Johanna W. H., 95
Vargas Machuca, Bernardo de, 276
Vassal Treaties of Esarhaddon (VTE), 59–61
Verkuyl, 313
Vespucci, Amerigo, 711
Virgin of Guadalupe, 283–284
Viterbo, Annio de, 271–272
Vitoria, Francisco de, 274
VOC. *See* Dutch East India Company
Voetius and Voetians, 303, 310, 318nn73–74
Voices from the Margin (Sugirtharajah), 714–715
VTE. *See* Vassal Treaties of Esarhaddon

W

Waddell, Hugh, 514
Wafula, R. S., 634–635
Walker, E. A., 360
Walsh, Lynda, 28
Wan, Sze-kar, 742
Warburton, David, 37
Warneck, Gustav, 377–379, 387
Warnke, Ingo H., 476
Warren, Max, 18
Watase Tsuneyoshi, 437–438, 440–441, 443

Waters, Kenneth L., 165, 181n20
Weinfeld, M., 59
Wellhausen, Julius, 382–383
Wenger, Tisa, 399
West, Gerald, 15, 692
Westcott, Brooke Foss, 338–339
Westermann, Claus, 92–93
West India Company (WIC), 297–298, 300–302, 306–308, 311, 313
Whately, Richard, 337
whiteness, 12–13, 310, 314, 409, 603
white South Africans, 661–662
white supremacists and white supremacy, 4–5, 179, 307–308, 409
white woman's burden, 354–355
white women missionaries, in Singapore, 353–364
WIC. *See* West India Company
Wiesehöfer, Josef, 89
Wigand, Ann-Firstin, 103–104
William of Orange, 297, 308–309, 315n16
Williams, George Washington, 409
Williams, Ronald, 38
Williams, Rowan, 510, 523
Williamson, H. G. M., 96–97
Willis, J. W., 331
Wilson, Woodrow, 452
Wimbush, Vincent L., 15, 639, 717–718
Winn, Adam, 736–737, 742–743
Winthrop, John, 397, 413–414, 711, 714
Wisdom of Amenemope, 39
Wollstonecraft, Mary, 343
woman's movement, 354–355
women. *See also* feminism and feminists
    African, 501–502, 504, 623–624, 658–659
    Bible translation and, 501–502, 504, 513
    in British Empire, 338–340, 342–343, 354–355, 360–364
    mysticism, 551n29

Two-Thirds World, 176, 625, 630
    white, missionaries in Singapore, 353–364
Wooley Bible translation, 502–503
Wright, G. Ernest, 6, 34
Wright, John, 107
Wright, N. T., 146
Wright, William, 242

X

Xavier, Ângela Barreto, 474
Xavier, Jerome, 480

Y

Yamazaki-Ransom, Kazuhiko, 153
Yang, K. Wayne, 652
Yee, Gale, 626
Yelle, Robert A., 485
Yeo, K. K., 190–191
YHWH, 76–77, 79–81, 83–84
    Assyrians and, 57–59, 64
    in Bible translation, 516, 522
    Cyrus and, 92–93
    eco-agrarian readings of, 578, 586–591
Yi Kwang-su, 451
Yi Man-jip, 455–457
Young, Brigham, 406
Young, Robert, 599, 705–706, 710
Young, William, 248
Young Choi, Jin, 11–12

Z

a-Zamori, Mustafa, 703
Zantop, Susanne, 371
Zapata y Sandoval, Juan, 279
Ziegenbalg, Bartholomäus, 377–378
Ziegenbalg, Bartholomeus, 481
Zimbabwe, 580, 606, 609–610
Zionism, 175
Županov, Ines G., 473–474, 485